W9-CTW-639

Contemporary
Literary Criticism
Yearbook 1992

Guide to Gale Literary Criticism Series

For criticism on	You need these Gale series
Authors now living or who died after December 31, 1959	*CONTEMPORARY LITERARY CRITICISM (CLC)*
Authors who died between 1900 and 1959	*TWENTIETH-CENTURY LITERARY CRITICISM (TCLC)*
Authors who died between 1800 and 1899	*NINETEENTH-CENTURY LITERATURE CRITICISM (NCLC)*
Authors who died between 1400 and 1799	*LITERATURE CRITICISM FROM 1400 TO 1800 (LC)* *SHAKESPEAREAN CRITICISM (SC)*
Authors who died before 1400	*CLASSICAL AND MEDIEVAL LITERATURE CRITICISM (CMLC)*
Authors of books for children and young adults	*CHILDREN'S LITERATURE REVIEW (CLR)*
Black writers of the past two hundred years	*BLACK LITERATURE CRITICISM (BLC)*
Short story writers	*SHORT STORY CRITICISM (SSC)*
Poets	*POETRY CRITICISM (PC)*
Dramatists	*DRAMA CRITICISM (DC)*
Major authors from the Renaissance to the present	*WORLD LITERATURE CRITICISM, 1500 TO THE PRESENT (WLC)*

For criticism on visual artists since 1850, see

MODERN ARTS CRITICISM (MAC)

ISSN 0091-3421

Volume 76

Contemporary Literary Criticism

Yearbook 1992

The Year in Fiction, Poetry, Drama, and
World Literature and the Year's New
Authors, Prizewinners, Obituaries, and
Outstanding Literary Events

James P. Draper
EDITOR

Christopher Giroux
Marie Lazzari
Kyung-Sun Lim
Sean René Pollock
David Segal
Janet Witalec
ASSOCIATE EDITORS

Jennifer Brostrom
Jeffery Chapman
Ian A. Goodhall
Brigham Narins
Lynn M. Spampinato
ASSISTANT EDITORS

 **Gale Research Inc.** • DETROIT • WASHINGTON, D.C. • LONDON

STAFF

James P. Draper, *Editor*

Christopher Giroux, Drew Kalasky, Marie Lazzari, Kyung-Sun Lim, Sean René Pollock, David Segal, Janet Witalec,
Associate Editors

Jennifer Brostrom, Jeffery Chapman, Ian A. Goodhall, Margaret A. Haerens, Brigham Narins, Lynn M. Spampinato,
Assistant Editors

Jeanne A. Gough, *Permissions & Production Manager*
Linda M. Pugliese, *Production Supervisor*
Donna Craft, Paul Lewon, Maureen Puhl, Camille Robinson, Jennifer VanSickle, Sheila Walencewicz, *Editorial Associates*

Sandra C. Davis, *Permissions Supervisor (Text)*
Maria L. Franklin, Josephine M. Keene, Michele Lonoconus, Denise Singleton, Kimberly F. Smilay, *Permissions
Associates*
Jennifer A. Arnold, Brandy C. Merritt, Shalice Shah, *Permissions Assistants*

Margaret A. Chamberlain, *Permissions Supervisor (Pictures)*
Pamela A. Hayes, Keith Reed, *Permissions Associates*
Arlene Johnson, Barbara Wallace, *Permissions Assistants*

Victoria B. Cariappa, *Research Manager*
Maureen Richards, *Research Supervisor*
Robert S. Lazich, Mary Beth McElmeel, Tamara C. Nott, *Editorial Associates*
Karen Farrelly, Kelly Hill, Julie Leonard, Donna Melnychenko, *Editorial Assistants*

Mary Beth Trimper, *Production Manager*
Shanna Heilveil, *Production Assistant*

Cynthia Baldwin, *Art Director*
Nicholas Jakubiak, C. J. Jonik, Yolanda Y. Latham, *Desktop Publishers/Typesetters*

Library of Congress Catalog Card Number 76-38938
ISBN 0-8103-4982-5
ISSN 0091-3421

Printed in the United States of America
Published simultaneously in the United Kingdom
by Gale Research International Limited
(An affiliated company of Gale Research Inc.)
10 9 8 7 6 5 4 3 2 1

I(T)P™

The trademark **ITP** is used under license.

Contents

Preface vii

Acknowledgments xi

IN MEMORIAM

TOPICS IN LITERATURE: 1992

Preface

A Comprehensive Information Source
on Contemporary Literature

Scope of the *Yearbook*

C *ontemporary Literary Criticism Yearbook* is a part of the ongoing *Contemporary Literary Criticism (CLC)* series. *CLC* provides a comprehensive survey of modern literature by presenting excerpted criticism on the works of novelists, poets, playwrights, short story writers, scriptwriters, and other creative writers now living or who died after December 31, 1959. A strong emphasis is placed on including criticism of works by established authors who frequently appear on syllabuses of high school and college literature courses.

To complement this broad coverage, the *Yearbook* focuses more specifically on a given year's literary activities and features a larger number of currently noteworthy authors than is possible in standard *CLC* volumes. *CLC Yearbook* provides students, teachers, librarians, researchers, and general readers with information and commentary on the outstanding literary works and events of a given year.

Format of the Book

CLC, Volume 76: *Yearbook 1992,* which includes excerpted criticism on more than twenty-five authors and comprehensive coverage of four key issues in contemporary literature, is divided into five sections—"The Year in Review," "New Authors," "Prizewinners," "In Memoriam," and "Topics in Literature: 1992."

- **The Year in Review**—This section consists of specially commissioned essays by prominent writers who survey the year's works in their respective fields. Dean Flower discusses "The Year in Fiction," Allen Hoey "The Year in Poetry," Robert Cohen "The Year in Drama," and William Riggan "The Year in World Literature." For introductions to the essayists, please see the Notes on Contributors.

- **New Authors**—This section introduces eleven writers who published their first book in the United States during 1992. Authors were selected for inclusion if their work was reviewed in several prominent literary periodicals.

- **Prizewinners**—This section begins with a list of literary prizes and honors announced in 1992, citing the award, award criteria, the recipient, and the title of the prizewinning work. Following the listing of prizewinners is a presentation of eleven entries on individual award winners, representing a mixture of genres and nationalities as well as established prizes and those more recently introduced.

- **In Memoriam**—This section consists of reminiscences, tributes, retrospective articles, and obituary notices on five authors who died in 1992. In addition, an Obituary section provides information on other recently deceased literary figures.

- **Topics in Literature**—This section focuses on literary issues and events of considerable public interest, including Feminism in the 1990s, Gay and Lesbian Literature, Native American Literature, and Rap Music.

Features

With the exception of the four essays in "The Year in Review" section, which were written specifically for this publication, the *Yearbook* consists of excerpted criticism drawn from literary reviews, general magazines, newspapers, books, and scholarly journals. *Yearbook* entries variously contain the following items:

- An **Author Heading** in the "New Authors" and "Prizewinners" sections cites the name under which the author publishes and the title of the work covered in the entry; the "In Memoriam" section includes the author's name and birth and death dates. The author's full name, pseudonyms (if any) under which the author has published, nationality, and principal genres in which the author writes are listed on the first line of the author entry.

- The **Subject Heading** defines the theme of each entry in "The Year in Review" and "Topics in Literature" sections.

- A brief **Biographical and Critical Introduction** to the author and his or her work precedes excerpted criticism in the "New Authors," "Prizewinners," and "In Memoriam" sections; the subjects, authors, and works in the "Topics in Literature" section are introduced in a similar manner.

- A listing of **Principal Works** is included for all entries in the "Prizewinners" and "In Memoriam" sections.

- A **Portrait** of the author is included in the "New Authors," "Prizewinners," and "In Memoriam" sections, and an **Excerpt from the Author's Work,** if available, provides readers with a sampling of the writer's style in the "New Authors," "Prizewinners," and "Topics in Literature" sections.

- The **Excerpted Criticism,** included in all entries except those in the "Year in Review" section, represents essays selected by editors to reflect the spectrum of opinion about a specific work or about the author's writing in general. The excerpts are arranged chronologically, adding a useful perspective to the entry. In the "Year in Review," "New Authors," "Prizewinners," and "In Memoriam" sections, all titles by the author are printed in boldface type, enabling the reader to easily identify the work being discussed.

- A complete **Bibliographical Citation,** designed to help the user find the original essay or book, follows each excerpt.

- **Cross-references** have been included in the "Prizewinners" and "In Memoriam" sections to direct readers to other useful sources published by Gale Research. Previous volumes of *CLC* in which the author has been featured are also listed.

Other Features

The *Yearbook* also includes the following features:

- An **Acknowledgments** section lists the copyright holders who have granted permission to reprint material in this volume of *CLC*. It does not, however, list every book or periodical reprinted or consulted during the preparation of this volume.

- A **Cumulative Author Index** lists all the authors who have appeared in the various literary criticism series published by Gale Research, with cross-references to Gale's biographical and autobiographical series. A full listing of series referenced in the index appears at the beginning of the index. Readers will welcome this cumulated author index as a useful tool for locating an author within the various series. The index, which lists birth and death dates when available, is particularly valuable for locating references to those authors whose careers span two periods. For example, Ernest Hemingway is found in *CLC,* yet a writer often associated with him, F. Scott Fitzgerald, is found in *Twentieth-Century Literary Criticism.*

- Beginning with *CLC,* Vol. 65, each *Yearbook* contains a **Cumulative Topic Index,** which lists all literary topics treated in *CLC Yearbook* volumes, the topic volumes of *Twentieth-Century Literary Criticism* and *Nineteenth-Century Literature Criticism,* and *Literature Criticism from 1400 to 1800.*

- A **Cumulative Nationality Index** alphabetically lists all authors featured in *CLC* by nationality, followed by numbers corresponding to the volumes in which the authors appear.

- A **Title Index** alphabetically lists all titles reviewed in the current volume of *CLC*. Listings are followed by the author's name and the corresponding page numbers where the titles are discussed. English translations of foreign titles and variations of titles are cross-referenced to the title under which a work was originally published. Titles of novels, novellas, dramas, films, record albums, and poetry, short story, and essay collections are printed in italics, while all individual poems, short stories, essays, and songs are printed in roman type within quotation marks. When published separately, the titles of long poems (e.g., T. S. Eliot's *The Waste Land*) are printed in italics.

- In response to numerous suggestions from librarians, Gale has also produced a **Special Paperbound Edition** of the *CLC* title index. This annual cumulation, which alphabetically lists all titles reviewed in the series, is available to all customers and will be published with the first volume of *CLC* issued in each calendar year. Additional copies of the index are available upon request. Librarians and patrons will welcome this separate index: it saves shelf space, is easy to use, and is recyclable upon receipt of the following year's cumulation.

Citing *Contemporary Literary Criticism*

When writing papers, students who quote directly from any volume in the Literary Criticism Series may use the following general forms to footnote reprinted criticism. The first example is for material drawn from periodicals, the second for material reprinted from books:

[1]Anne Tyler, "Maniac Monologue," *The New Republic* 200 (April 17, 1989), 44-6; excerpted and reprinted in *Contemporary Literary Criticism,* Vol. 58, ed. Roger Matuz (Detroit: Gale Research, 1990), p. 325.

[2]Patrick Reilly, *The Literature of Guilt: From 'Gulliver' to Golding* (University of Iowa Press, 1988); excerpted and reprinted in *Contemporary Literary Criticism,* Vol. 58, ed. Roger Matuz (Detroit: Gale Research, 1990), pp. 206-12.

Suggestions Are Welcome

The editor hopes that readers will find *CLC Yearbook* a useful reference tool and welcomes comments about the work. Send comments and suggestions to: Editor, *Contemporary Literary Criticism,* Gale Research Inc., Penobscot Building, Detroit, MI 48226-4094.

Acknowledgments

The editors wish to thank the copyright holders of the excerpted criticism included in this volume, the permissions managers of many book and magazine publishing companies for assisting us in securing reprint rights, and Anthony Bogucki for assistance with copyright research. We are also grateful to the staffs of the Detroit Public Library, the Library of Congress, the University of Detroit Library, Wayne State University Purdy/Kresge Library Complex, and the University of Michigan Libraries for making their resources available to us. Following is a list of the copyright holders who have granted us permission to reprint material in this volume of *CLC*. Every effort has been made to trace copyright, but if omissions have been made, please let us know.

COPYRIGHTED EXCERPTS IN *CLC*, VOLUME 76, WERE REPRINTED FROM THE FOLLOWING PERIODICALS:

American Book Review, v. 13, October-November, 1991; v. 14, December, 1992 & January, 1993. © 1991, 1993 by *The American Book Review*. All reprinted by permission of the publisher.—*The American Poetry Review,* v. 21, July-August, 1992 for "A Poetry of Daily Practice: Adrienne Rich, S. J. Marks, Dorianne Laux" by Sam Hamill. Copyright © 1992 by World Poetry, Inc. Reprinted by permission of the author.—*The American Spectator,* v. 24, August, 1991. Copyright © *The American Spectator* 1991. Reprinted by permission of the publisher.—*Astounding Science Fiction,* 1941. © 1941 by Street & Smith Publications, Inc. All rights reserved. Reprinted by permission of the publisher.—*Belles Lettres: A Review of Books by Women,* v. 7, Summer, 1992; v. 8, Fall, 1992. Both reprinted by permission of the publisher.—*Book World—The Washington Post,* April 28, 1991; May 26, 1991; October 27, 1991; February 23, 1992; March 1, 1992; June 7, 1992; June 14, 1992; June 21, 1992; July 5, 1992; August 2, 1992; August 23, 1992; September 13, 1992; September, 20, 1992. © 1991, 1992, *The Washington Post*. All reprinted with permission of the publisher.—*Books in Canada,* v. XXI, November, 1992 for "Perfect Pitch" by Gary Draper. Reprinted by permission of the author.—*Boston Review,* v. XVII, September-October, 1992 for a review of "The Sioux Dog Dance: Shunk Ah Weh" and "Home Country" by Sam Cornish; v. XVII, September-October, 1992 for a review of "The Long Night of White Chickens" by Yvonne Fraticelli. Copyright © 1992 by the Boston Critic, Inc. Both reprinted by permission of the respective authors.—*Chicago Tribune,* September 29, 1991 for "Gains and Losses" by Jane Ayres; March 3, 1992 for "A Challenging New Voice, An Auspicious Debut" by James Idema; August 16, 1992 for "When the Kids and Their Lives Turn Mysterious" by Carol Anshaw. © copyrighted 1991, 1992, Chicago Tribune Company. All rights reserved. All reprinted by permission of the respective authors./ April 8, 1992. © copyrighted 1992, Chicago Tribune Company. All rights reserved. Reprinted by permission of Tribune Media Services./ July 9, 1992; August 9, 1992. © copyrighted 1992, Chicago Tribune Company. All rights reserved. Both used with permission.—*Chicago Tribune—Books,* June 23, 1991 for "Novelists vs. Terrorists" by Jerome Klinkowitz; April 5, 1992 for "Crossing Cultural Bridges" by Hilma Wolitzer. © copyrighted 1991, 1992, Chicago Tribune Company. All rights reserved. Both reprinted by permission of the respective authors./ March 10, 1991; November 3, 1991; May 31, 1992. © copyrighted 1991, 1992, Chicago Tribune Company. All rights reserved. All used with permission.—*The Christian Science Monitor,* February 28, 1992 for "Portrait of a Black Artist" by Merle Rubin; July 24, 1992 for "A Homeland Rife with Discord" by Marjorie Agosin. © 1992 the respective authors. All rights reserved. Both reprinted by permission of the respective authors.—*Columbia Journalism Review,* v. XXX, January-February, 1992 for "Myths That Men (and the Media) Live By" by Leslie Bennetts. © 1992 Graduate School of Journalism, Columbia University. Reprinted by permission of the publisher and the author.—*Commentary,* v. 89, March, 1990 for "Rap and Racism" by Terry Teachout; v. 93, February, 1992 for "Inhuman Comedy" by Hillel Halkin; v. 93, February, 1992 for "New Wave Feminism" by Charlotte Allen. Copyright © 1990, 1992 by the American Jewish Committee. All rights reserved. All reprinted by permission of the publisher and the respective authors.—*Commonweal,* v. CXVIII, August 9, 1991; v. CXIX, February 28, 1992. Copyright © 1991, 1992 Commonweal Foundation. Both reprinted by permission of Commonweal Foundation.—*Contemporary Review,* v.

COPYRIGHTED EXCERPTS IN *CLC,* VOLUME 76, WERE REPRINTED FROM THE FOLLOWING BOOKS:

The Year in Review

The Year in Fiction

by Dean Flower

Any retrospective assessment of recent fiction might begin with a look at those works which are themselves retrospective, speaking less of 1992 when they happened to be published than of earlier decades. Such collections can remind us of more timeless or enduring standards of value, certainly, but perhaps their greater interest is perspectival: they clarify so well how recent fiction differs from its precursors. Joseph Mitchell's **Up in the Old Hotel** (Pantheon) provides a good case in point. The book constitutes all four of Mitchell's previous story collections (long out of print), from *McSorley's Wonderful Saloon* in 1943 to *Joe Gould's Secret* in 1965, plus additional previously uncollected sketches. There should no longer be any doubt that Mitchell is a great writer, a Balzac of lowlife New York with its endlessly quirky misfits and brilliant oddballs. His reportorial realism is not as wide-ranging as John O'Hara's or Dos Passos's, but he has a finer ear and a subtler gift for characterization than they did. Mitchell invented in the pages of *The New Yorker* a style of humorous sketch that melded fact and fiction seamlessly. He was often imitated, notably by John McNulty and E. B. White, but none could listen so well to ordinary people and discover—or make into a story—the profound sadness behind their comic facades. Mitchell's work exposes the manipulativeness and self-consciousness of most recent story writing. He is so free of calculated surprises or the coercions of subjectivity or crafty ironies. Reading him today is a lesson in disinterestedness. Other notable collections include Donald Barthelme's posthumous **The Teachings of Don B.** (Turtle Bay Books), which exemplifies again that uncanny ability he had to turn literary games and linguistic parodies into lyrical and poignant stories, and Thomas William's **Leah, New Hampshire** (William Morrow), a collection of stories ranging from 1957 to 1991, the year Williams died. Working in that exclusively masculine realm mapped out by Hemingway and Faulkner (nature, hunting, tests of identity and moral courage), Williams has never been adequately appreciated for his understated complexity, despite major nominations and prizes. While his subject matter seems to align him with other woodsy masculinists like Howard Frank Mosher, William Humphrey, and James Dickey, Williams in fact has more in common with writers like André Dubus, and ought to be valued for the introspectiveness and skepticism of his male concerns.

If contemporary relevance is the criterion, then the major retrospective of the year must be **The Collected Stories of William Trevor** (Viking). A previous gathering appeared ten years ago, comprised of five separate titles, but the latest book attests to significant changes in Trevor's career.

It includes *The News from Ireland* (1986) and *Family Sins* (1990), both masterful story collections which reveal Trevor's sharply increased interest in Ireland as a locus of potentially explosive moral and political issues. Trevor's strategy is always to locate such issues in the simplest, most fundamental places: in a husband's grudging recognition of his failed marriage, in the honeymoon of a woman who has married beneath her, in a daughter's sacrifice to secure the family's land. The more recent stories also reveal Trevor's increasingly complex awareness of what narration itself may be: how lies and self-deceptions jump—with ominous ease—from one story teller's head to another, how the traditional systems of communal understanding can be invaded and attacked by modern journalism's prejudices, how one person's imperious fictions can be forcibly imposed on others, how a writer himself can become, as he puts it, "a sort of predator, an invader of people." Trevor has gradually transformed himself from a wry English satirist and comedian into a Joycean ironist and moralist whose model is *Dubliners*. He has

Joseph Mitchell, author of Up in the Old Hotel.

3

even made a story about one of the *Dubliners* stories ("Two More Gallants"). Trevor shares with Joyce the capacity to refine himself out of existence in his fiction. He is in fact the most selfless of narrators, the opposite of predatory and invasive. Everything in a Trevor story expresses the characters—their speech, their syntax, their contradictions, their dreams. That represents a distinctive achievement in an age when most story writers— American ones, at least—like to rely on their own performative voices or that of a thinly-disguised persona.

Nowhere is this more evident than in the sudden burst of activity among African-American writers in 1992. The story collections of Randall Kenan, John Edgar Wideman, and Gloria Naylor are all marked, despite their differences, by a boldly improvisatory orality and a strong homing instinct, locating every story in the same well-defined community. These are story sequences rather than collections, modeled perhaps on the Faulknerian genre of interwoven Yoknapatawpha tales or on Eudora Welty's multi-voiced chronicle of Morgana, Mississippi in *The Golden Apples*. What's curious is that so little in the work of their more immediate forbears—Ralph Ellison, James Baldwin, Ishmael Reed, Toni Morrison—seems to have anticipated this development. *Let the Dead Bury Their Dead* is Randall Kenan's second book about Tims Creek, North Carolina, a remote hamlet of his invention that is peopled as much by the spirits of the dead as by the living. Kenan's purpose is a comic exploration of small-town hypocrisies, deceits, and cross-purposes. His title story consists of tall tales, anecdotes, letters, and diary entries that have been (we are to suppose) collected by a preacher, Rev. James Malachai Greene, and edited by a local folklore scholar, Reginald Kain (an obvious stand-in for the author himself). But the comedy here—and in the whole book—has its powerful darker sides, its grisly exhumations of the dead with all their unappeasable suffering, its episodes of racism and madness. Kenan's characters are mostly black and poor, but he usually does not emphasize their skin color: they are first of all mill workers or farmers, lawyers or preachers, or just cussed human beings, all of them so busy telling stories, inventing their own mythologies, that they have little time left for suffering. *The Stories of John Edgar Wideman* (Pantheon) are set in Homewood, the black neighborhood in Pittsburgh where Wideman grew up. All his autobiographical writing since 1981 has concerned that place, including his memoir *Brothers and Keepers* (1984). The latest story sequence consists of ten new Homewood stories, under the title "All Stories Are True," followed by a reprinting of Wideman's two earlier collections, *Fever* (1989) and *Damballah* (1981). His gift is for a richly colloquial style, his own remembering voice mingling with the voices of his mother or grandmother, his brother or uncle, or the voices of his street-wise friends and acquaintances: "Voices are a river you step in once and again never the same Bubba here you are dead boy dead dead dead nigger with spooky Boris Karloff powder caked on your face. . . ." So begins the brilliant one-sentence story, "Everybody Knew Bubba Riff," a jazz riff on the life and style of a boyhood friend who has just been killed. Voices are indeed the river in

which all of Wideman's stories run, a book-long elegy for the casualties of his family and his race. The river often rages, in response to endless cruelties, deprivations, hostilities, and indifference. In this he clearly takes on the mantle of the late James Baldwin. But Wideman does more than that: he keeps coming back to Homewood to understand where the resilience comes from, how the capacity to survive and sing can exist at all. It is no accident that the sequence ends with a girl bouncing on her toes, serving take-out chicken, and singing "something old like Bach with Christ's name in it . . . and it sounded so fine I hoped she'd never stop singing."

The past is not so easily traveled or shared with others in Gloria Naylor's *Baily's Café* (Harcourt Brace Jovanovich). This is her best book since *The Women of Brewster Place* (1983), but it reflects harsher perceptions of suffering. The man called Baily runs a café in Brooklyn with an ill-assorted (but all black) clientèle, including Eve who keeps a nearby brothel. Both places attract the abused and weary, some with axes to grind and others who just want to escape. Baily presides over the book, framing each person's monologue. Naylor's interest lies in the naturalistic accumulation of these grim histories. It resembles *Winesburg, Ohio;* each speaker clings to a truth that has become grotesque. The story of Sadie is a litany of losses, from her husband's death all the way down to the most degrading alcoholism and prostitution. The story of Peaches begins with the fatality of a repressive father and leads with relentless logic to her bloody self-mutilation. Even Baily himself has a story—one of exploitation and disillusionment that began when he assumed a patriotic purpose ("We're gonna kill some japs!") in World War II. Naylor is especially adept with the more aberrant figures, the transvestite Miss Maple, and the lesbian Jesse Bell, patiently letting them unfold their plain-spoken stories. The only sort of consolation Naylor suggests for her isolated figures is that they find momentary asylum from their troubles simply by telling them. But as Baily says at the end, "If life is a song, then what we've got here is just snatches of a few melodies."

Four African-American novels of distinction appeared in 1992. Two of them are so complex as to be nearly self-defeating, making the other two—both first novels—seem all the fresher and more promising. Alice Walker's *Possessing the Secret of Joy* (Harcourt Brace Jovanovich) is scarcely a novel at all, so schematically does it dramatize the rituals and taboos of black African culture as the products of white racist imperialism. Walker's story—part allegory, part polemic—takes as its central issue the ritual clitoridectomy and genital mutilation of young African women. Tashi, its protagonist, chooses to submit to the bloody ritual as a proof of Pan-African solidarity, against all the arguments of her American counterpart and soulmate, Olivia. Tashi's prolonged suffering provides Walker with a framework for discussing the sexual politics that oppress all modern women in the Western world, and all blacks as well. Walker angrily exposes the favored myth of whites, that "Black people are natural, they possess the secret of joy." Everything in her story shows the opposite—the dispossession of blacks, their deprivation of joy. Walker eventually rewrites that original formula: "*resis-*

tance is the secret of joy." But most readers were disappointed long before that conclusion, finding Tashi rather anonymous, the action too archetypal, the impassioned arguments too involuted and abstract. Admiration for Walker remains high, even though she has not yet invented the right sort of novel for her ideas.

Toni Morrison's fiction is never abstract. In fact it has grown increasingly polyphonic and palimpsestic, notably in *Song of Solomon* (1978) and *Beloved* (1988). Her latest novel, *Jazz* (Knopf), is no less complex and multilayered, but it fails to be as richly convincing. The scene is Harlem in 1926, at the height of the Jazz Age, when Joe Trace, a 50-year-old cosmetics salesman, shoots and kills his eighteen-year-old mistress. Joe's wife Violet attempts to slash the corpse in the open casket, and the rest of the novel investigates what led up to these crises and how the couple attempt to resolve their losses. Joe is not arrested "because nobody actually saw him do it, and the dead girl's aunt didn't want to throw money to helpless lawyers or laughing cops when she knew the expense wouldn't improve anything." What makes everything problematic is the voice-over narrator, an unnamed commentator who emerges as the hypothesizer, improvisor, and conjecturer of the story—not its authoritative source. The voice seems at first to be male, city-wise, ready to play verbal riffs with his material, but it soon grows nebulous, disappears alto-

gether, or reappears with self-conscious intrusiveness. Morrison seems to have wanted to unfix her story, so that Joe and Violet cannot really be known, only guessed at, so that the city itself may determine their fates. Or else it was some familial "wildness" that came out of their pasts? But that is the least convincing material. The novel works best when Morrison goes back to 1926, characterizes the dead girl, Dorcas, and her aunt, Alice Manfred, and her skeptical friend, Felice. In the end what saves the novel is the realism of such scenes and the prevailing warmth of Morrison's tone. At her melodious best she can write like an angel with the blues.

Rita Dove does not rely on such performative rhetoric. But she has defined a superb subject for her first novel, **Through the Ivory Gate** (Pantheon): the difficulty of a young black woman who does not want to be defined by the prevailing ideology of her race. The story begins when her mother thrusts a politically correct black doll into Virginia King's unwilling hands. Despite a privileged upbringing in Arizona, studying the cello, excelling in college, and pursuing a career in acting and puppet theater, Virginia finds herself back where she was born, in blue-collar Akron, Ohio, teaching in a public school. She finds it increasingly difficult to ignore either her familial roots or the claims of her racial community. The narration is unevenly realized; Dove's accomplishments as a poet have not been instantly translated into her prose. But the novel suggest a wholly new sort of voice to listen for in the next generation of African-American writers—a voice distanced from and critical of the racial obsessions of her predecessors.

Another such voice—and a much more assured one—is Darryl Pinckney's. His autobiographical first novel, **High Cotton** (Farrar Straus Giroux) is a high-style satiric monologue masquerading as a Bildungsroman. He too finds his skin color a private aggravation rather than a tragic fate. But Pinckney's narrator, unlike Dove's, treats it all as a cosmic joke. He is a shapeshifter and neurotic avoider whose inability to accept his blackness makes him all the more obsessed with it. Pinckney has studied at Columbia and Princeton, published in *Granta* and *The New York Review of Books,* and settled far from his native Indianapolis—in Berlin. So it is not surprising that the novel's protagonist admires more than anyone else in the family his grandfather, a Congregational minister "educated in the Holy Land"—meaning at Harvard and Brown. He views the members of his own race (including himself) with an amused detachment. He is for example fascinated by the "high yellow" coloration of his Aunt Clara, and by his fastidious Uncle Castor, a flamboyant dresser and world traveler down on his luck, who speaks "as primly as George Washington Carver" and resides in an upstairs bedroom. He is equally detached about himself, trying on identities like hats—civil rights demonstrator, Anglophile pedant, expatriate intellectual—as if to prove that none of them fits. In each guise he exposes not only his own foolishness but the racial hypocrisies of everyone around him. If the style is sometimes extravagant, that is because he's something of a mystery to himself, a new form Invisible Man. He can only make himself visible through verbal improvisations, a series of sardonic self-deflating asides. No wonder he keeps gravitating toward the example of his crusty old grandfather. The point of view is unique, perhaps even revolutionary. What other black writer has confessed that he used the prestige of his skin color to manipulate whites, especially white liberal politicians? What other black writer could have admitted that he was "exercising my fictitious cultural birthright to run off at the mouth"? Note the barb in "fictitious." Pinckney breaks new ground in this courageous and funny book.

Another genre that flourished in 1992 was the historical novel. Not to be confused with the ever-popular costume novel, which is scarcely historical at all, the historical novel as practiced nowadays (E. L. Doctorow, Simon Schama) tends to be a post-modernist affair: commentaries on the fictiveness of history, improvisations on its myths, parodies and deconstructions of its "truth." The year's wittiest and most elegant example was **The Death of Napoleon** (Farrar Straus Giroux) by Simon Leys. Imagine that Napoleon escaped from St. Helena by means of an elaborate conspiracy which involved substituting a look-alike and smuggling the Emperor aboard a ship bound for France. But plans go awry. First the ship is diverted to Antwerp, stranding him without benefit of the conspiracy that attests to his identity. And then his double on St. Helena dies, making his real existence even harder to prove. "From now on," he realizes, "Napoleon would have to make his way not only against Napoleon, but against a Napoleon who was larger than life—the memory of Napoleon." What that historical, larger-than-life construction is becomes the question explored by the rest of the story: Napoleon visiting Waterloo as a tourist and unable to remember the sites touted as famous, or finding himself in competition with those who have made him legendary, both charlatans and eyewitness authorities, or (in the funniest, most poignant scene of the novel) going to an insane asylum where *everyone* thinks he is Napoleon. Leys manages to suggest a range of issues—about history, identity, the sources of power, the idea of glory—that go far beyond his brief tale.

Susan Sontag ventures into the genre somewhat less successfully with **The Volcano Lover** (Farrar Straus Giroux), a recreation of the Admiral Nelson-Lady Hamilton affair in which she reverses the usual romantic readings of the past: Nelson is not the hero but a vainglorious posturer; Lady Emma is not the vulgar "Hamilton Woman" but richly sensuous, self-sacrificing, something of a feminist martyr; Sir William is not the sterile old cuckold but a civilized and affectionate husband, quite at ease in the *ménage à trois*. Sontag conceives of history as almost infinitely revisable, a vast flea market (as her prologue images it) in which one is free to amuse oneself, buying whatever seems interesting. So the novel is rich with her inventions and speculations, her observations about women, travel, liberal intellectuals, art, performance, even telling jokes and polluting the environment. History is there to be *used*, to be revamped. But that is the novel's weakness too. It gradually devolves into its interesting fragments, and concludes with some feminist special pleading that sounds distinctly modern.

Malcolm Bosse creates an equally rich eighteenth-century

Rita Dove, author of Through the Ivory Gate.

world in **The Vast Memory of Love** (Ticknor & Fields), but he goes in for a bawdy, Hogarthian realism rather than a meditation on history. Bosse's story of a country lad who quickly loses his innocence in the mean streets of 1753 London owes something to Fielding's Tom Jones and John Barth's Ebenezer Cook. The power of the novel lies in its detailed evocations of cruelty, disease, rampant sexuality, and social disorder. John Updike also tries out the role of self-conscious historian in **Memories of the Ford Administration** (Knopf), moving back and forth between modern times and the nineteenth-century of James Buchanan, our only unmarried President. But his modern narrator, a promiscuous professor busy about his infidelities, fails to be a plausible author of a manuscript defending the ineffectual Buchanan. Most readers found the novel a rhetorical display, effectively parodying the fusty language of Buchanan's era, but tedious for all that, and superficial in its representation of the President Ford era. Susan Minot's **Folly** (Seymour Lawrence/Houghton Mifflin) is a careful reconstruction of Boston society in the post-World War I era, much more convincing than Updike's scheme, but it suffers from its own restraint. Minot seems to offer a scenario reminiscent of *The Yellow Wallpaper,* but the unhappy marriage and the missing romance fail to yield any great revelations.

The most successful historical novels of the year were

Maureen Howard's *Natural History* (William Morrow) and Pat Barker's *Regeneration* (Dutton). Howard's novel is a chronicle of Bridgeport, Connecticut, the city where she was born. It begins in the 1940s by tracing the fortunes of an Irish-Catholic family—a son who ends up in Hollywood with a career in Grade B movies, a daughter who lapses into a suicidal skid in New York and ends up back in Bridgeport, isolated and withdrawn. But the novel is woven of many other lives as well, teachers and social workers, children of the rich or the indigent, each of them a strand in the fabric of a city's history. Howard's meandering narrative creates a strong sense of the purely accidental nature of what we dignify as history. Her most brilliant chapter, "Double Entry," continues the story on the right hand page while presenting on the left a collage of historical detritus about Bridgeport: newspaper clippings, old woodcuts from magazines and advertisements, old photographs of the town, its parks and statues. Mixed with this are jottings from the novelist's notebook, observations about her characters, favorite quotations, poems and *pensées* that bear on her themes. By the end of the novel Howard has managed to convey an almost archeological sense of historical strata. Bridgeport's history is ignominious, riddled with delusion and fraudulence, but it eludes any final judgments; we live somehow in the midst of history's confusions, Howard suggests, and manage to bear up remarkably well.

Pat Barker's novel has a much narrower focus. It is a painstaking reconstruction of the encounter between Siegfried Sassoon, the British poet, and Dr. W. H. R. Rivers, his therapist at an asylum in Scotland in 1917. When Sassoon, a distinguished combat officer, suddenly "disavowed" the war, it was arranged that he be declared "mentally unsound" to avoid a court martial or worse. The unrepentant Sassoon was perfectly sane; all sympathy in the novel goes to Dr. Rivers who gradually persuades Sassoon to take up again his military duties, although neither man is wholly convinced that is the right thing to do. Barker portrays Rivers with extraordinary sympathy, working partly from hospital records, partly from Rivers' actual publications in psychiatric journals, and largely from her own imagination.

Barker is especially good at conveying the doctor's outward patience—a monumental self-control—in contrast to his inner vulnerability. Those he helps do not realize how much they use and consume him. He begins to stutter, and has insomnia; old sexual insecurities begin to surface. The horrors of the war were unprecedented, and so were its psychic casualties. There were no textbooks to guide Rivers; each patient he saw presented unique problems. But Barker does not need to explain any of that: she manages simply to make each case human and immediate, and to make Rivers the most interesting case of all. The novel is a rare instance of history and fiction working perfectly together.

The year also produced an unusual number of powerful political novels: André Brink's *Act of Terror* and Ben Okri's *The Famished Road* about Africa; Norman Manea's *October, Eight O'Clock* and Imre Kertész's *Fateless* about the death camps in Nazi Germany; Joyce Carol

Oates's *Black Water,* a story based on Edward Kennedy's disaster at Chappaquidick. In the context of these works Gunter Grass's *The Call of the Toad* is a disappointingly mild satire on capitalism along the German-Polish border, and Julian Barnes's *The Porcupine* seems oddly to lament the collapse of Communism in eastern Europe. The best political novels of the year were all something more than the label can suggest.

Ian McEwan's *Black Dogs* (Nan A. Talese/Doubleday) is the investigation of a failed marriage that began just after the end of World War II when two idealistic young English intellectuals chose to become Communists. June and Bernard Tremaine hope to take part in reforming the world. Most of the novel, however, takes place in 1989 as the Berlin Wall comes down. Bernard, now a journalist and television personality, goes to Berlin with his son-in-law Jeremy, the novel's narrator, to witness the historic event. The story moves between these divergent eras as well as between June and Bernard, who separated—mysteriously—shortly after their honeymoon. Jeremy's inquiry into the Tremaines becomes McEwan's way of commenting on the unresolved conflicts and submerged violence of Western Europe in the Cold War era. The crucial event turns out to be June's terrifying encounter with a pair of vicious black dogs while she and Bernard were

touring Provence on their honeymoon in 1946. As Jeremy reconstructs these events he increasingly empathizes with June, and begins to recognize and fear his own capacity for violence. McEwan's triumph in the novel is to have suggested how deeply embedded are the sources of violence and evil in humans. A politics that fails to recognize this fundamental destructive irrationality—fails to see the black dogs—is, McEwan suggests, not only inadequate but dangerous.

Michael Ondaatje on the other hand suggests that politics is chaos. Each of his characters in *The English Patient* (Knopf) would escape the claims of ideology, patriotism, or social responsibility. The anonymous Englishman whose skin has been burned away lies dying in a bombed out villa near Florence. Determined to care for him, a young Canadian nurse, Hana, scavenges the building (once a field hospital) for medical supplies. Another Canadian isolato appears, a spy-thief named Caravaggio, the friend of Hana's dead father. Then a young Sikh soldier joins them, an expert at defusing bombs. Each of these characters listens in a different way to the stories of the North African desert (of survival, of doomed love, of death) that the English patient tells. They are all war experts, of one sort or another, all victims of the idea of British imperialism. But Ondaatje's narration resists such explanation and labelling: it offers instead fragments of story, elliptical metaphors, a dreamy interweaving of identities. Only Kirpal Singh, the bomb expert trained sedulously by Britain's finest, tells his experiences matter-of-factly. If the novel ends without a satisfactory resolution, it is nevertheless haunting: every love story in it has been contaminated by war.

Another novel distinguished by its political acumen is Isaac Bashevis Singer's *The Certificate* (Farrar Straus Giroux). Serialized in Yiddish in 1967 and now translated posthumously, the story chronicles the desperate poverty of Warsaw Jews in the winter of 1922. Yet as usual Singer can be irresistibly funny when dealing with the grimmest material. His native protagonist, David Bedinger, arrives penniless in the city and sets about the task of surviving. Luckily he is offered a certificate allowing his emigration to Palestine, on the condition that he agree to a marriage of convenience. The wealthy Minna Ahronson can travel on the certificate only if she is married. The ensuing complications entangle David, the virtuous son of a rabbi, in relationships with three women, and in a welter of Zionists, Fascists, atheists, and Communists all jostling one another in Warsaw. The certificate remains tantalizingly just out of reach; it identifies and yet traps David—just as being a Jew does. Singer teases his hero and exposes the manipulative streak in him, sending him home defeated in the end. But the novel suggests a politics of survival: there is a great deal to be won if you use your wits, Singer implies, especially when you can outwit your own suffering.

The other best novels of the year elude categories, or create their own. Beyond any doubt Cormac McCarthy's *All the Pretty Horses* (Knopf) is the most perfectly realized novel of the year, and the most surprising: perfect in the certainty of its language, in the clarity and logic of its storytelling, and surprising in its rediscovery of Ernest

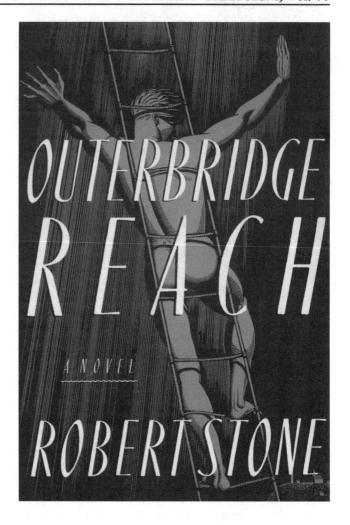

Hemingway as a meaningful source and model. McCarthy's novel is in effect a brilliant selection from and improvisation on what's best in Hemingway: the determined exteriority, the sentences that configure landscapes, the dissolves into Spanish, the paratactic accumulations, the brevities of plainest speech, the poetic factuality. The story seems at first just an archetypal American fable, updated to 1950: a youth exiled from his patrimony, a South Texas horse farm, heads out for the Territory—in this case the mountains of Coahuila in northern Mexico. But John Grady Cole is not alone; his pal Lacey Rawlins and the unwanted kid Blevins complicate, and eventually bring a disastrous end to, the Edenic life that they find as *vaqueros* at a ranch called La Purisma. McCarthy never lets the reader forget that this is an alien landscape and a foreign culture. Sometimes *all* the conversation is in Spanish, a bold and effective decision on McCarthy's part. John Grady listens to some family history from the matriarchal Duena Alfonsa, but he does not understand. He follows his own desires, falls in love, obeys his own codes of honor and responsibility, and the consequences are tragic. The novel is less about horses and the vanishing American frontier than most critics have claimed. Its more important issues concern the border and what happens when we cross it. However its theme is defined, this novel has a breadth and somber dignity that are virtually unknown in recent fiction.

Many critics found faults and flaws in Robert Stone's **Outerbridge Reach** (Ticknor & Fields), but it is at least as interesting as McCarthy's prizewinner. Owen Browne, the protagonist, is a compendium of the weaknesses Stone likes to dwell on in his other novels: a shallow idealism, a tendency toward self-doubt and depression, fits of anger and resentment, elaborate self-deception, twinges of sentimentality. A graduate of the Naval Academy and Vietnam veteran, Browne is a vaguely dissatisfied boat salesman who suddenly steps into an opportunity to sail single-handed in a round-the-world race. Recording Browne's preparations for the race in a promotional film is a thoroughly nasty filmmaker, Ron Strickland, who clearly finds Browne a fool. Both characters grow in complexity as this voyeur-victim relationship continues. Browne's family is investigated by Strickland too—the brittle facades of his wife and daughter are exposed. Gradually Browne begins to seem less of a fool, and the possibility of something meaningful in this risky exploit emerges, clouded though it may be with confused hopes and uneasy assumptions. There is something tragic in Browne; he sees his weaknesses but cannot change. He is clearly superior to the sneering Strickland, who—curiously—now begins to seem more pathetic than nasty as his victim prepares to depart. Stone is no longer writing the hard-boiled adventure story that he once was: the writing here is exact and lean, but it goes deeper into the shady areas than it ever has before. Bitter though his conclusions are, they seem pithier than anybody else's. Note how assiduously all the reviewers of **Outerbridge Reach** analyzed its plot.

Another underestimated novel is Mona Simpson's **The Lost Father** (Knopf), which must have disappointed some critics (it was not nominated for any major prizes) because it fails to be as funny as *Anywhere But Here* (1987). But Simpson is a gifted storyteller, able to make the homeliest incidents vivid and entertaining—an awkward telephone call, the broken English of a letter, a houseguest's embarrassment, it does not seem to matter what it is, Simpson makes it interesting. Having broken free of her oppressive mother, Mayan Atassi (a.k.a. Ann Stevenson in the first novel) now seeks her missing father. She is 28 and in medical school, supposedly, but she becomes obsessed with finding her father, who abandoned the family when she was ten. The notion will not let her alone. As Mayan's quest grows increasingly intense, a monstrous selfishness begins to show. Where once she was obsequious or apologetic in her investigation, she is now unconscious of presumption—just as her awful mother used to be. Paradoxically, however, Mayan's excursions back home to Wisconsin in both fact and memory serve to reaffirm where her real family is: not in her overbearing mother and inaccessible father. Simpson manages to keep her first-person narrator just buoyant enough, just vulnerable enough, so that she remains affecting even when behaving very badly—and that sustains a 500-page novel.

Rosellen Brown's **Before and After** (Farrar Straus Giroux) is a much darker, more disturbing book. It invents

an outwardly normal and happy family living in rural New Hampshire: the wife (Carolyn Reiser) is a pediatrician, the husband (Ben) a semi-successful sculptor; their son Jacob is fifteen, and Judith is twelve. When a girl in Jacob's classmate is bludgeoned horribly to death, he disappears and the Reisers discover that Jacob committed the murder. The story is told from the changing, increasingly isolated points of view of mother, father, and daughter. We come to learn of Carolyn's fateful detachment and Ben's rages, and of Judith's fear of them all—especially her father, who succeeds in covering up Jacob's guilt. The limitations of each character are shrewdly devised, so that nothing cataclysmic happens. There are two trials, but Ben refuses to testify (he goes to jail for a time), and his son is not punished. But as Judith clearly knows, it is her father's rage that allowed Jacob to kill. At the end she withdraws into a shell, fearing them both. The family stays together through this grim ordeal, even after they move to Houston and pretend to start a new life. But staying together is no virtue. Clearly, nothing has been resolved—which is why the novel is finally so disturbingly persuasive.

The final remarkable feat of 1992 is that *two* novels by Anita Brookner were published in the United States, and they are both masterful. **A Closed Eye** (Random House) takes its title from a sentence in Henry James's *Madame de Mauves:* "She has struck a truce with painful truth, and is trying awhile the experiment of living with closed eyes." That idea befits almost all of Brookner's inhibited heroines over the course of twelve published novels, which is one reason that some reviewers have sounded a little impatient with them recently. Yet each is characterized so particularly and distinctly that there need not be any disappointment. They are all individuals. Brookner is singularly adept at creating the suspense of inaction: Harriet in *A Closed Eye* ought not to let her friends use her, ought not to marry the older man her parents choose for her, ought not to permit her daughter's rudeness, ought not to let her one chance for romance slip away. But she does keep failing to act, because that is after all her prevailing instinct. But is it her fate? Thus the tension builds, sometimes unbearably. Brookner is incisively good at characterizing children in this novel—the pale Elizabeth who fends off attentions and the spoiled Imogen who knows exactly how to get what she wants.

But then Brookner is even better at portraying the elderly, such as Harriet's parents: she catches their smug childishness, their rituals and cover-ups, their magnified fears. In *Fraud* (Random House) Brookner gives us the feisty Mrs. Marsh, full of illusions about her independence, angrily impatient with everyone, fearful of any introspection, quick to excuse her own selfishness. Such portrayals as these suggest how complex and interesting the elderly can be, and how routinely they are caricatured in most modern fiction or omitted altogether. The central figure of *Fraud* is the anorexic Anna Durrant, whose life has been stultified by caring for her mother. Anna's fraudulence is to be too good at forgiveness. Pretending she has no desires of her own, or any right to anger, Anna effectively paralyzes these impulses, even after her mother dies and there's no reason to continue denying herself. Brookner also gives a wickedly detailed history of Lawrence Halliday, the doctor who sees both Anna and Mrs. Marsh. Halliday might almost have fallen in love with Anna were it not for his sexual greed and his cowardly passivity; he is clearly still another interesting fraud. Both *A Closed Eye* and *Fraud* reflect Brookner's opposite qualities as a novelist: her consistently clear-eyed understanding and the forthrightness of her language. She too is in a category by herself.

The Year in Poetry

by Allen Hoey

The process of reading most volumes of poetry published in the U.S. during an entire year provides a wider basis for drawing conclusions about "the state of American poetry" than most casual readers would willingly invite; the nineteen collections reviewed were selected from nearly 200 perused. Sadly, most books read over this year and last demonstrate minimal craft, both in terms of the poets' abilities to use aural, rhythmic, metrical, or figurative elements and their broader skills at structuring poems to reflect a complex of emotional and intellectual responses to the world. To call most books published in any given year "mediocre" states a statistical commonplace; more troubling, the quality of work produced by widely published and honored poets ranks as slight when measured against a standard that includes the best of what has been written. The institutionalization of mediocrity, ratified by committees that dispense such annual laurels as the Pulitzer Prize and National Book Award, reflects not only a nationalized indifference to the state of poetry but a frightening level of ignorance concerning it.

Two collections of essays by accomplished poets speak to this situation. Given the much-publicized bickering between new formalists and dedicated "free verse" writers, we might not expect frequent agreement between Dana Gioia and Denise Levertov, yet their essays, which address a wide variety of problems involving contemporary poetry, occupy extensive common ground.

The centerpiece of Gioia's selection is his hotly discussed 1991 essay which gives the volume its title, *Can Poetry Matter?: Essays on Poetry and American Culture* (Graywolf). Additionally, "Notes on the New Formalism" and "The Poet in an Age of Prose" provide cogent insights into the state of the art; Gioia's assessments in these essays are buttressed by the incisive analyses he displays in treatments of individual poets as diverse as Wallace Stevens, Weldon Kees, and Ted Kooser, among others. Gioia reads poems with both acuity and sensitivity; his ear rarely errs. While clearly partisan in the debate over the use of form, Gioia articulates convincing arguments for broadening our poetic base; in "The Dilemma of the Long Poem," he speculates how an intelligent eighteenth-century reader might respond to our claims for the "scope and diversity" of contemporary American poetry:

> His overall reaction, I suspect, would be a deep disappointment over the predictable sameness, the conspicuous lack of diversity in what he read. Where are the narrative poems, he would ask, the verse romances, ballads, hymns, verse dramas, didactic tracts, burlesques, satires, the songs actually meant to be sung . . . ? The panoply of available genres would seem reduced to a few hardy perennials that poets worked over and over again with dreary regularity—the short lyric, the ode, the familiar verse epistle, perhaps the epigram, and one new-fangled form called the "sequence," which often seemed to be either just a group of short lyrics stuck together or an ode in the process of falling apart.

The acerbic wit as well as the scathing judgement are typical. And while some might argue with individual points (no lesser a poet than Yeats often worked in the "sequence" to powerful effect), much of our strong reaction against Gioia's scorn results, I suspect, from defensiveness and denial.

Denise Levertov's *New & Selected Essays* (New Directions) gathers nine essays published in her two previous volumes of essays together with sixteen newer ones, grouping earlier with more recent essays in clusters concerning the work of William Carlos Williams, poetic technique, the place of the poet in the world, and her own spiritual growth as reflected in her work. Her essays on Williams' work underscore the problems of intelligent poetry criticism in this country; she undertakes in **"On Williams' Triadic Line"** to correct several generations of critics' misreadings of Williams' prosody. Her essays concerning technique also address the impoverished condition of poetic awareness and the need for greater clarity concerning such essential technical matters as the line. "Not only hapless adolescents," she writes in "On the Function of the Line," "but many gifted and justly esteemed poets writing in contemporary nonmetrical forms, have only the vaguest concept, and the most haphazard use, of the line." Yet, she stresses, the line "is a *tool,* not a style." Her essays are guided by a vision of "aesthetic ethics," a pervasive sense that "artistic quality . . . [is] bound up with artistic integrity." Shaped by this ideal, they provide a firm guide for our readings in contemporary poetry.

This year's most significant publication is Hayden Carruth's *Collected Shorter Poems* (Copper Canyon). For too long Carruth suffered the lack of a consistent publisher; as a result, much of his best work has gone unnoticed or too little noticed. Notable in a volume as diverse as this are Carruth's monologues and poems about characters delivered in lines that echo their speech; as the speaker in "John Dryden" notes, "have you noticed / I can't talk about him without talking like him?" Like Frost, Carruth captures a sense of character and place while subtly presenting a complex set of meanings, discovering the kind of "natural symbol" ordinary people grapple with to understand their lives. One of the most powerful, "Marvin McCabe," is a monologue by an inarticulate speaker whose friend "Hayden" acts as amanuensis for the poem. Marvin McCabe details his upbringing and the accident that left him incapacitated—able to think but not talk. The credible voice, by turns bitter and accepting, builds through tonal control to a powerful conclusion:

> Sometimes I sit

here in this bay window and look out
at the field, the hills, the sky, and I see the boul-
    ders
laughing, holding their sides and laughing,
and the apple trees shaking and twisting with
    laughter,
the sky booming and roaring, the whole earth
heaving like a fat man's belly, everything
laughing. It isn't because we're a joke, no,
it's because we think we aren't a joke—that's
what the whole universe is laughing at. It makes
no difference if my thoughts are spoken or not,
or if I live or die—nothing will change.
How could it? This body is wrong, a misery,
a misrepresentation, but hell, would talking
    make
any difference? The reason nobody knows me
is because I don't exist. And neither do you.

Other poems in this mode include "Johnny Spain's White Heifer," "Lady," "Marshall Washer," and "Regarding Chainsaws."

Carruth's lyrics display a range of diction and vocabulary which allows him to modulate easily from low to high style and to incorporate moments of humor in otherwise serious, even solemn poems without violating that tone. As in the following passage from "Once More," his lyrics often derive from careful observation of the natural world, not merely to see things but to consider, as he writes in "The Ravine," "relationships of things":

Once more by the brook the alder leaves
turn mauve, bronze, violet, beautiful
after the green of crude summer; galled
black stems, pithy, tangled, twist in the
flesh-colored vines of wild cyclamen.
Mist drifts below the mountaintop
in prismatic tatters. . . .

Typically, Carruth presents his observations through details objective enough to allow us to "see" the situation yet in language that renders the emotional construct of the subject.

The later poems in the volume, following Carruth's move to Syracuse, New York, in 1979, shift not only idiom and locale, as in *Asphalt Georgics,* a group of poems written in syllabic ballad stanzas employing frequently hyphenated enjambments, but open up very different poetic territory in the Whitmanesque-lined and loopingly discursive poems from *Tell Me Again How the White Heron Rises and Flies Across the Nacreous River at Twilight Toward the Distant Islands.* The first of these laments the passing of the agrarian lifestyle that provided the basis for traditional georgics while celebrating the persistence of human life amid suburban sprawl that threatens that spirit. The strategies of apparent tangent and indirection Carruth uses to build these poems evolves into structures, in the second, which accumulate like jazz riffs and motifs: they seem to diverge wildly from the "point" of the poem only to swoop around at the end to enlarge the idea of the point. Unfortunately, the newest poems are not consistent; both the selections from the late *Sonnets* and the section of new poems are less fully achieved.

Finally, a collected poems provides a perspective on a

poet's career. And this volume demonstrates what some readers have long known: Hayden Carruth possesses greater range of style, scope of subject, and diversity of formal skills than any other poet working in the United States today.

Gary Snyder's *No Nature* (Pantheon/Random House) is billed as *New and Selected Poems,* yet the generosity of selection suggests that the process was closer to that of a collected rather than a selected volume. Snyder's greatest accomplishment is his ability to hew to a chosen subject matter and style yet discover means to broaden and enlarge the approach. His style—a combination of language, line, and informing attitude—has changed little from the poems gathered in *Riprap* to the newest poems in this collection. (One complaint about the volume's apparatus: nowhere are initial publication dates of original books available; even the copyright page is of little use.) In fact, those first poems, including Snyder's versions of the poems of Han Shan, are among the strongest in the collection. Here, the influence of Chinese poetry and Kenneth Rexroth make for concise, evocative descriptions of places and people, in which commentary is kept to a minimum. "Hay for the Horses," one of the strongest, recounts a nameless worker's trip "From far down San Joaquin / Through Mariposa, up the / Dangerous mountain roads" to deliver hay, ending, as he shares lunch with a narrator whose presence is restricted to distanced presentation, with these lines in the worker's words:

"I'm sixty-eight," he said,
"I first bucked hay when I was seventeen.
I thought, that day I started,
I sure would hate to do this all my life.
And dammit, that's just what
I've gone and done."

This simplicity of presentation eludes Snyder through poems in the middle period, where the influence of Pound, with a layering of counter-cultural preachiness, becomes more dominant. The poems from his 1983 collection, *Axe Handles,* come closest to returning to this clarity of voice, particularly the title poem, which concerns Snyder's realization, as he shows his son how to make a handle for a hatchet, that the wisdom of an Oriental master, "First learned from Ezra Pound"—" 'In making the handle / Of an axe / By cutting wood with an axe / The model is indeed near at hand' "—applies precisely to the rearing of his own children. This volume contains enough of these gems to rank Snyder as an important journeyman in contemporary poetry.

While we expect a certain amount of weeding when a poet prepares a volume of collected poems (not the same as "complete," which should include all work gathered in books as well, perhaps, as previously uncollected poems and even juvenilia), a selected poems should result from a very different process of inclusion. Last year in this space I complained about the lack of both apparatus and rigor in Robert Creeley's *Selected Poems* (U. California); this year's raft of selected poems prompts another cavil regarding such volumes. A selected poems should, first and foremost, be justified by a poet's maturity (older than fifty) and stature; success over the long haul seems reasonable warrant. Beyond that, extreme rigor should be exercised: weed and prune, then go at it again, leaving the representative best, period. Galway Kinnell and Hayden Carruth have produced models of what a selected poems can be; theirs weigh in at 148 and 165 pages, respectively, and Carruth, in particular, is a prolific writer. Finally, because a selected volume garners the best, poets should resist the impulse to include new work side by side with old. The new work, however strong, has not survived the acid tests of time and critical evaluation; a selected volume, at its best, serves a specific function, and that does not include testing fresh work.

By these criteria, William Matthews' ***Selected Poems and Translations, 1969-1991*** (Houghton Mifflin) ranks highest of the volumes surveyed, failing only the test of length. The selections from newer volumes are more generous than from his earliest, which is to be expected; poets should grow. The selection confirms that Matthews possesses greater wit and intelligence than most of his contemporaries in what David Dooley calls the "Interregnum generation." This selection also suggests that Matthews' strengths are rarely well served by the way he chooses to cast his poems. From his earliest collection, *Ruining the New Road* (1970), Matthews' poems most often employ the accepted period style such as it evolved from spindly poems with an au courant politically tinged surrealism, through the prose poems and one-liners that mark his second collection, to the increasingly wider lines and stanzaic forms in his more recent volumes. The flat rhythms and throw-away enjambments that characterize academic poetry in the seventies and eighties are not the best vehicles for an epigrammatic and formal wit; sharp wit requires equally sharp articulation, the way Auden wrapped his wit in masterfully poised rhymes and meters.

Matthews' early poems, when they free themselves of cute, neo-surrealist flourishes, seek to reveal the mystery contained in the mundane, a calling that attracted him to the work of Jean Follain, a selection of whose prose poems (translated with Mary Feeney) are included. Yet even his treatment of themes involving childhood, the pleasures of company, and pervasive loneliness, find fuller treatment in later volumes. *Flood* (1982) contains the moving lyric consideration of life among the divorced, "Good Company," which begins:

> At dinner we discuss marriage.
> Three men, three women (one couple
> among us), all six of us wary.
> "I use it to frighten myself."
> Our true subject is loneliness.
> We've been divorced 1.5 times
> per heart. "The trick the last half
> of our lives is to get our work done."

The strongest work occurs in his most recent collection, *Blues If You Want* (1989), which shows Matthews testing the waters of metrical verse. Many poems use rhymes, not quite irregular enough to be accidental but not yet with applied consistency, and two extended monologues in the voice of jazz musicians approach blank verse. These poems, "Every Tub" and "Straight Life," employ extended narration in a way new to his work. We might not completely believe that we're hearing unedited commentary by

black musicians, but Matthews gets the tone and details right, and we can believe that Matthews' imagination has won over new territory.

Like Matthews, Stephen Berg has seemed a representative Interregnum voice, yet his ***New & Selected Poems*** (Copper Canyon) shows off an underappreciated talent. The selection from four previously published collections contains some poems cut from period cloth, but even his early work shows an affinity for a long line and a depth of emotional probing unusual in a generation of poets too often willing to settle for surface effects. Both "Sister Ann," with its sprawling Whitmanesque lines, and "Desnos Reading the Palms of Men on Their Way to the Gas Chambers" exceed cataloguing to inhabit worlds of suffering. Several poems from his second collection, *Grief* (1975), confront the poet's despair concerning not only his father's suffering and death but his own inadequacy—or the language's—to articulate his grief, as in the concluding lines of "What I Wanted to Say":

> The streetlamps glow with a sudden brightness,
> you feel satisfied with the cracked chimneys,
> the dull orange haze blowing across the stars,
> you could sit endlessly on the steps, smoking,
> doing nothing, and never speak again.
> But this isn't what I wanted to say.
> The birds were calling me, I think. Or someone.
> There were tears. I stumbled. My jaws ached.
> I bent over my sleeping children to say goodbye
> and each one turned to me and smiled. But this
> came back—your dead face was a blank white
> flower opening in me, which I couldn't touch.
> I stood somewhere, saying, "Nobody can say
>   this."

Notice how the end-stopped lines prevent the rhythm from building, keeping the pace steady, somber, accumulating its effect so that we pause, weighting even the final "this" of the only completely enjambed line in the passage.

The final third of this volume is a selection of newer poems, including a group of prose pieces from a work-in-progress, *Shaving*. Here, the newer work seems included after considerable weeding, and is justified if only because of the power of the final poem, "Homage to the Afterlife," published as a limited edition. This extended poem, owing more to Ginsberg's remaking of the Whitman line than to Whitman himself, gathers force through its anaphoric refrain, "Without me." Individual "lines," ranging from a few words to nearly two pages in length, drive us with their accumulation yet force us to read carefully because Berg utilizes asyntactic composition to represent the logic of associative thought, delving into anger and fear surrounding parental loss and rejection conflated with a first, defining sexual encounter. A brief passage cannot capture the poem's force, but these lines give a taste:

> Without me, the doctor answers my pleading
>   question Why did she hate
>   me so much with Because you exist
> Without me, but that is not the story it's beyond
>   not in details
>   memories feelings washed up into the present by the wounds

> struggles to understand survive walk talk
> eat work sleep and in
> between the story
> Without me, wanting to understand wanting to
> get rid of who we are
> what's happened to us and not act can't
> have accept can't accept

Details accrue slowly, through repetition; the poem attempts to unfold the ways in which we simultaneously seek to hide from and reveal the things that hurt and grace us most powerfully.

We might first ask why Tom Clark's *Sleepwalker's Fate: New and Selected Poems, 1965-1991* (Black Sparrow) was necessary. Born in 1941, Clark has 48 published volumes listed at the beginning of this new collection, and the author's note indicates that this is the fifth volume of his selected poems issued by Black Sparrow since 1978, the last most recent published in 1990. Granted that not all of the 48 books are volumes of poetry and even that being prolific is itself no single grounds for condemnation of quality, the question of need remains. Many of this book's 212 pages are scarcely filled. One section of new poems, "Diary of a Desert War," is comprised of often no more than one or two lines per page; one reads in its entirety, "Rode into brown hills—death in the air." This 44-page section could easily have been printed in ten pages, with no loss either of poetic effect or design quality—and this, like all Black Sparrow books, is beautifully designed and produced. This kind of profligate wastefulness seems an apt metaphor for Clark's talent; he has wit and intelligence but is too often satisfied with a brief, cute impression, the kind of tossed-off effort that characterizes so much Black Mountain derivative poetry. Better if inspiration were allowed time to deepen, the work granted more opportunity for revision. Overall, the older, selected work satisfies more, perhaps because time has done the difficult job of winnowing every poet should be expected to perform in assembling a book.

If at times we wish Julia Randall's *The Path to Fairview: New and Selected Poems* (LSU Press), which gathers work from her six previous collections, were a bit shorter, it is not because line by line the poems lack craft, intelligence, erudition, and even humor; rather, while her craft has developed since her first volume was issued in 1952, style and subject from the earliest poems resemble those from the sampling of new work. Randall writes about nature and the place of humans in it, whether backyard gardens or woodland, but nature imbued with something beyond the purely natural or human, suggesting something of the divine. And Randall knows more about nature underfoot than most of us, as evidenced in these lines from "The Banana Tree at Carney":

> I asked the audience what they found obscure
> about my work, and one said,
> "Words like *sycamore.*"
> I wouldn't try *paulownia* on him
> though they're so common in the Shenandoah
> I cropped some pods for Mother, coming home
> one Christmas, thinking
> how nice they'd look on the mantel, but as usual
> with what an adult daughter brings,

> my mother said, "What the hell are these
> things?"

Somewhat peculiar is her tendency to break regular meter and use, as above, occasional strict rhyme, a habit that spans her career. If the book occasionally drags, continued reading yields frequent pleasure.

Much less rewarding is Mary Oliver's *New and Selected Poems* (Beacon), winner of the 1992 National Book Award. Arranged in reverse chronology, this selection exemplifies critic Sven Birkerts' complaint regarding this practice: "If . . . the poet has declined, then the arrangement scarcely serves his or her best interests—though, admittedly, when that's the case any policy other than self-censorship is a bad one" (*The Electric Life* 197). The earliest poems in this over-long volume show a promising talent for detail and lines whose rhythms build at least minimal tension, as in this passage from "A Letter from Home":

> Here where my life seems hard and slow,
> I read of glowing melons piled
> Beside the door, and baskets filled
> With fennel, rosemary, and dill,
> While all she could not gather in
> Or hide in leaves, grows black and falls.

The tendency for line breaks over-emphasized by syntactical units could, with work, be vitalized to allow more variation, and the ability to envision these particulars could be expanded to a net to gather in more of the world. Such, however, was not the path Oliver chose.

She has developed a characteristic line that is brief and even more determined by syntax, and her eye for detail, still focused on the natural world, too often imposes a false, sentimental tint on what she imagines. Like Roethke, whose view of natural minutiae involved exploration of the self, Oliver's true subject in these poems is herself, but without Roethke's deep psychological probing; she seems satisfied with seeing something just closely and accurately enough we will likely commend her on her sensitivity, however imprecise the image. Take, for example, these lines from "Lilies": "I think I will always be lonely / in this world, where the cattle / graze like a black and white river . . . " I have watched many grazing herds of cattle, and their movement has never struck me as resembling the fluidity of water—nor does it after reading these lines. The opening stanza of this same poem (which one reviewer has singled out for praise), displays her too-typical slack lineation:

> I have been thinking
> about living
> like the lilies
> that blow in the fields.

The lines clunk predictably down at the end of the first convenient syntactical unit. This would make for dull prose, laden with prepositional phrases that bury the natural energy of the sentence. Pound demanded that poetry be at least as well written as prose; these days we need to add, "good prose."

Honoring such tepid verse seems the more perverse considering the mastery displayed by at least three of the other four nominees: Carruth's **Collected Shorter Poems,** Gary Snyder's **No Nature,** and Louise Glück's **The Wild Iris** (reviewed later), each of which takes nature as a primary subject and treats it with greater fidelity of observation, depth of feeling, and felicity of craft. Until whatever passes for a poetry establishment can recognize quality of thought, feeling, and craft as they work together to inform a body of work, American poetry will be marked by the preponderance of the trivial.

Finally, the publication of Muriel Rukeyser's poems in **Out of Silence: Selected Poems** (TriQuarterly Books) makes available work which was allowed to go out of print by her commercial publishers. Perhaps because so many of her contemporaries achieved such high levels of accomplishment and notoriety, Rukeyser's work has suffered neglect. Her work does not display the consistent mastery or polish of Lowell or Roethke, nor does it usually display the near-histrionic idiosyncrasies of Berryman or the reserved craft of Bishop, but her range and attack equal and surpass, for instance, Stanley Kunitz and Jarrell. Her work, from its earliest, seeks to merge traditional prosody with lessons learned from Modernist masters like Williams. Her poems often seek to create a mythology of the self, drawing on classical gods and heroes as well as a sense of archetypal pattern. These lines open the third section of the title poem from *Waterlily Fire* (1962):

> Many of us   Each in his own life waiting
> Waiting to move   Beginning to move   Walking
> And early on the road of the hill of the world
> Come to my landscapes emerging on the grass
>
> The stages of the theatre of the journey

Other subjects lend themselves to her radical political sentiments, often at the expense of the work; we do not appreciate enough that poetry which allows its politics to slide into propaganda, however well-intentioned, is no more savory than work which allows emotion to blur into sentimentality. This tendency is exaggerated by the editorial decision to resurrect Rukeyser as a political poet and feminist, too often overlooking the more delicate lyrics. For all that, Rukeyser's work deserves redeeming, and her editor Kate Daniels has done her justice.

Another notable restoration is Christopher MacGowan's painstakingly edited and annotated edition of William Carlos Williams' **Paterson,** apparently the final volume in New Directions' re-edited issues of Williams' complete works. By combing through every published edition and comparing them with galleys and typescripts, MacGowan has attempted to present *Paterson* in a version that best reflects Williams' intentions. The typescript versions of the preliminary drafts of a sixth book demonstrate how laborious this task was; following his strokes, even Williams' typing requires considerable interpretation. MacGowan sought not to correct every possible typographical or printing error; if an error seemed a "mistake" Williams deliberately made in composition, MacGowan chose to retain it. This volume gives us a clean, accurate version of an important poem; readers will be served by New Directions bringing out an affordable paperback edition quickly.

A book-length poem in the Williams-Pound mold, Peter Dale Scott's **Listening to the Candle: A Poem on Impulse** (New Directions) is the second volume of a projected trilogy. Like *Paterson* and *The Cantos,* it includes references to and quotations from a variety of sources: philosophical, religious, political, and poetic; unlike its precursors, it cites sources in the wide margins and appends a ten-page bibliography. Quotations from foreign languages are also marginally glossed. The quotations amplify and extend the personal references—the poem's primary subject seems the development of personality refracted through memory—to demonstrate the kind of composite "the life of the mind" is. Another theme, underscored by the telescoping references, is the difficulty of embodying understanding in language; this passage occurs toward the end:

> even the sutras say
> *Go beyond language*
>   *Bodhidharma 44*
>
> and if the excitement of childhood
>   is now elusive
>   at least to put irony behind us
>
> and so deeply inhabit
>   the night's silences . . .

At times the lines lack fluidity, but the poem's scope and intelligence propel us through the more prosaic patches.

In **Iris** (Story Line), Mark Jarman undertakes a very different kind of book-length poem, both homage to Robinson Jeffers and exploration of how his tragic vision provides a centering focus for one woman. At the outset of the poem, the eponymous heroine, a native Kentuckian who dropped out of college after she became pregnant by a fellow student she met in the course which introduced her to Jeffers, returns home with her young daughter after leaving her abusive husband. Jarman presents the rural Southern milieu credibly and handles the ensuing violence (her brothers' primary cash crop is marijuana, and they are murdered while Iris and her daughter are away from the house) with care, neither sparing detail nor wallowing in it. Following this, Iris, who has nourished a quiet passion for Jeffers since that college course—finding, if not comfort, a more expansive world view in his lines—takes her daughter and mother on a quest across the continent to Jeffers country, the rugged California coastline. The heart of this narrative is not a compelling sequence of events; after the early blood-bath, the violence is for the most part internal, deriving from frustrated passions and the apparently near-complete inability of these characters to find words to express their inner lives. Iris comes closest toward the end of the poem, in conversation with a hitchhiker. Speaking to the woman in the dark, she says,

> " . . . You'd think with
>   all the death in it, my life
> Would be a tragedy. But I've kept my real life
>   a secret—
>   reading Jeffers
> And trying to imagine him imagining someone
>   like me. . . . "

This ambitious undertaking suffers primarily from the constant comparison to Jeffers. Jarman's long-lined poem deliberately recalls Jeffers, but the diction is less elevated, the rhythm more relaxed, the syntax less fevered. While this makes for easier reading than Jeffers, this diminution signals a similarly diminished vision, the breadth of perspective deriving from the reference to Jeffers rather than any intrinsic quality of the poem itself. As the passage above suggests, Iris' life aspires to tragedy, the mainspring of the most powerful of Jeffers' poems, but the best she seems capable of—perhaps the best most of us, people and poets alike, are capable of these days—is merely melodrama flavored by the hope of something higher.

Shorter and more lyrical in its approach, Brendan Galvin's *Saints in Their Ox-Hide Boat* (LSU Press) recounts the voyage of St. Brendan the Navigator, the sixth century Irish abbot, and his small crew of Brothers who, according to conjecture, make their way to North America well ahead of Columbus. St. Brendan's voyage, a "blue martyrdom" to separate himself from worldly interruptions the better to contemplate God, was the source of considerable fancy; Galvin's poem imagines St. Brendan narrating his account to a young monastic scribe, needing constantly to curb his embroidery:

> Don't mis-hear an old man and set it down
> that we came across souls out there.
> They were as surely seals as those
> radiant blobs we sometimes plowed
> our way through in the dark were jellyfish,
> not souls. Seals, I said, not souls.

Galvin's diction seeks a middle ground between contemporary usage and a style designed to suggest an older and decidedly Irish locution. This works well for him on the whole, allowing him latitude enough to pitch toward lyric highs while not preventing the necessary and deflating humor. The breadth and depth fall short of what Jarman aims for in *Iris,* but Galvin's tauter line and greater compression of detail may sustain more consistently.

Brenda Hillman's brief *Death Tractates* (New England/Wesleyan), her fourth collection, focuses on the poet's process of grief following the loss of her closest female mentor. This sequence interrupted, a note informs us, the manuscript Hillman had been working on and finally took shape as a separate volume. Elegies are a staple of world poetry, often among the most profoundly moving poems in any language. Hillman, however, does not engage the elegiac convention directly; rather, her poems, rooted in gnostic lore, attempt to grapple transparently with the process of wrenching deep sorrow into language. The untitled central poem in the book begins:

> —So the poem is the story of the writing of itself.
> In the white tent of the psyche
> or out there in the normal fog:
>
> the mockingbird all spring:
> she looked just like a note herself,
> each bit of music slipping past her
> till it stopped—
> each time one note missing;
> it wasn't exactly failure on her part,
> she just needed something to do tomorrow.
>
> Same thing with the poem. . . .

She concludes:

> You had to be willing to let it through the sun-
>   shine
> error of your life,
> be willing not to finish it—

Many of the poems, like this one, open with a dash, and all end with one, underscoring the sense of the poems forcing themselves onto paper and the idea of the inherent incompleteness of the attempt.

Most of the poems manage a comfortable juxtaposition of commonplace imagery—supermarkets, backyard birds, libraries—with more abstract meditations on the various possibilities of the afterlife, for Hillman never doubts that the soul continues. The style, too, is an odd mix of standard syntax and punctuation that occasionally breaks down, perhaps under the pressure of expression, into less conventional forms. The voice of the poems is unabashedly personal, leaving little doubt that this is no contrived persona grappling with theoretical poetic problems. When she writes in "Split Tractate" that, even in her sorrow, she held onto "the problem / with pronouns," we see this in the shift from "I" to a "you" that is clearly the object of self-address rather than the easy avoidance of self-reference popular among too many poets. While these devices seem occasionally labored (particularly the use, almost always following an enjambment, of "What" as a catch-all term for the unknown), the poems accumulate with surprising force.

If Brenda Hillman's poems are characterized by restraint, Tess Gallagher's poems surrounding the death of her husband, the fiction writer Raymond Carver, gathered in *Moon Crossing Bridge* (Graywolf), her sixth collection, seem too often lush, orchestral arrangements heavy on the strings. The volume opens promisingly with "Yes," a poem similar in its austerity to the work of Linda Gregg:

> Now we are like that flat cone of sand
> in the garden of the Silver Pavilion in Kyoto
> designed to appear only in moonlight.
>
> Do you want me to mourn?
> Do you want me to wear black?
>
> Or like moonlight on whitest sand
> to use your dark, to gleam, to shimmer?
>
> I gleam. I mourn.

The ending is not pushed; the emotions build through restraint to the final twist: however much the darkness of death may permit love to gleam, that light cannot be a shimmer. Unfortunately, the remainder of the book does not live up to this promise. While moments in the book achieve beautiful insights into the process of mourning—like the speaker in "Paradise" rubbing oil into the feet of her deceased lover "because it is hard to imagine at first / that the dead don't enjoy those same things they did / when alive"—too often the poems descend into what seems self-congratulation; this poem continues, "And even if it happened only as a last thing, it / was the right last thing." Hillman never presumes to judge her mourning so consistently favorably. At almost twice the length of Hillman's volume, *Moon Crossing Bridge* might have served subject and reader better had greater rigor been exercised in selection.

The themes of death and grieving recur in *The Father* (Knopf), Sharon Olds' fourth collection. These poems examine the processes explicitly, clinically, seemingly motivated by the conviction, apparent in her earlier books, that truth is best approximated through sparing none of the sordid or embarrassing details. Many such details are keenly observed and register the intended emotional color. When details are recycled from poem to poem, however, vivid supporting notes become washed and finally pallid when they recur as central images. The poems also display a good ear for an effective line, but they accumulate predictably; her formal sense entertains little variety. Most distractingly, perhaps, Olds' use of metaphor deteriorates with alarming frequency, as when she writes of her father after learning that his death is imminent in "Wonder":

> When he sickened, he began to turn to us,
> when he sank down, he shined. I lowered my
> mouth to the glistening tureen of his face
> and he tilted himself toward me, a dazzling
> meteor dropping down into the crib . . .

The rapid telescoping of time, from the speaker in the present bending to kiss the father to the flash memory of him bending toward her in her crib, is nicely accomplished; but the shift in metaphor from "tureen" to "meteor" is so mixed that it startles us out of the poem to wonder how something this dreadful ever made it through the final cut. This lack of editorial rigor appears as well in her inability, as in Gallagher's volume, to prune the weaker poems, to conserve images from poem to poem rather than squandering the effect.

Whereas *The Father* renders a world-view both personal and secular in common speech, *A Gilded Lapse of Time* (Farrar Straus Giroux), Gjertrud Schnackenberg's third collection, presents a vision steeped in history, pervaded by religious intricacy, and decorated with elevated diction and syntax. The volume consists of three long poems, concerned with the web of relations among history, God, love, poetry, creation, and death, explored through the occasion of a visit to Dante's tomb; artistic renderings of scenes from the Passion; and a meditation on the life and death of Osip Mandelstam. Schnackenberg's vision rarely descends to the simply personal, though the first poem seems to derive from a feeling of loss of love and the attempt to regain it. Imagining Dante wandering the Wood of the Suicides in the fourteenth section, she writes:

> And as for me, once I had seen that seeping
> At the root of that outcry, I kept to myself,
> Afraid that if I spoke, my tongue would
> Touch those mutilated words, I was afraid
> That if I spoke, I would taste blood. . . .

Through her exchange with Dante, the speaker seems to hope to regain a sense of how poetry, informed by love, translates the world; she concludes this section noting that what she would say regarding these suicides she "heard / when [she] thought poetry was love, and [she] had / Sickened of poetry."

While not metered or rhymed with any regularity,

Schnackenberg's lines are highly wrought; the syntax is long and elaborate, though accumulation rather than subordination characterizes the build. The language itself is dense, consciously poetic and highly referential; few readers, however erudite, will make sense of these poems without frequent recourse to the appended notes. The driving motive of the poems, in fact, seems more the desire to create beautiful artifacts of language than to penetrate to the depths of any truth; she has far too much fun exploring the gilded nooks and crannies of speech and line to derail the process into a more incisive approach. She herself seems to write in that perfect time she imagines for Mandelstam,

> when poetry will be filled
> With a peripheral fleet of swans
> Glimpsed in the heavy, carved mirrors
> That bring the willow park
> With its long, statue-ringed, green ponds
> Through the windowpane
> Into the drawing room . . .
> ("A Monument in Utopia," 1)

Given such richly accomplished splendor and seriousness of purpose, we might easily lose ourselves enough not to notice—or particularly care—that the beautiful means often seem an end in themselves.

Less intoxicated by her own verbal facility, Louise Glück explores the complex relationship between God, humans, and the natural world with startling emotional depth in *The Wild Iris* (Ecco), her sixth collection. Far from the strained and occasionally awkward lines and language of her previous books, these poems strive for and usually master an elegant lyricism in the imagined voices of wildflowers; of God manifest in wind, light, and changing seasons; and of a woman who struggles to find evidence of God while laboring in a garden in a cold climate. In poems most often titled "Matins" and "Vespers," the human voice expresses fear, frustration, and love, while "checking / each clump for the symbolic / leaf" in the garden and entertaining the apprehension that God, the addressed "you" of these poems, "exist[s] / exclusively in warmer climates. . . . " Plants, most often wildflowers, counter these prayers, presenting a view more eternal for the accelerated brevity of their lives. Here is "Scilla" in its entirety:

> Not I, you idiot, not self, but we, we—waves
> of sky blue like
> a critique of heaven: why
> do you treasure your voice
> when to be one thing
> is to be next to nothing?
> Why do you look up? To hear
> an echo like the voice
> of God? You are all the same to us,
> solitary, standing above us, planning
> your silly lives: you go
> where you are sent, like all things,
> where the wind plants you,
> one or another of you forever
> looking down and seeing some image
> of water, and hearing what? Waves,
> and over waves, birds singing.

Glück's gift in these poems is a capacity for lyric eruption coupled with emotional restraint. The voices are passionate but never hysterical; plants and God chide humans, as in the poem above, for their apparently willful ignorance, but the criticism never reads as self-pity.

Perhaps most audaciously, Glück undertakes to render divine speech, the language of the "unreachable father." She succeeds by imagining the voice of God not anthropomorphically (beyond the personification implicit in imposing specifically human language on flora and the divine alike) but as natural phenomena, a pantheistic sense of divine manifestation. The poems work their magic in part by never making explicit the convention of the book; as we read, we come to understand what these different voices represent. The occasional confusions serve Gluck's purpose; we come to see how our own sense of ourselves gets imposed, repeatedly and unconsciously, on things sacred and mundane—how those very categories reflect our peculiarly human view. The centerpiece of the volume, appropriately titled "Midsummer," begins by seeming to speak for the gardener:

> How can I help you when you all want
> different things—sunlight and shadow,
> moist darkness, dry heat—
>
> Listen to yourselves, vying with one another—

And you wonder
why I despair of you,
you think something could fuse you into a
            whole—

As the poem builds, we correct our reading and understand that God regards us with the same frustrations with which we regard tomatoes that fail to blossom as we had hoped. We were not, this divine voice informs us, "intended / to be unique":

> You were
> my embodiment, all diversity
> not what you think you see
> searching the bright sky over the field,
> your incidental souls
> fixed like telescopes on some
> enlargement of yourselves—
>
> Why would I make you if I meant
> to limit myself
> to the ascendant sign,
> the star, the fire, the fury?

These poems grapple honestly and successfully with questions of ultimate reality, not sheering away from critical self-assessment nor veering into a merely postured piety. They sing and praise and renew with successive readings.

The Year in Drama

by Robert Cohen

The dramatic stunners of 1992 were, astonishingly, two different seven-hour, two-evening marathons of theatre, remarkably original, each of which originated on the West Coast and received its major national recognition after performing at the Los Angeles Mark Taper Forum Theatre. One, *The Kentucky Cycle,* won the Pulitzer Prize for Drama in 1992; the other—and the best by far of the two—would have my vote to win it in 1993. Neither play had been professionally produced in New York at the time of this writing, but the second, Tony Kushner's *Angels in America,* will have opened by the time this essay appears.

Angels in America, a relentless threnody on AIDS, dying, betrayal, guilt, racial hatred, insanity, and homophobia, is the funniest play I've ever seen. And I don't mean smiley/jokey funny either: this play is gaspingly, hyperventilatingly funny; time and time again the audience explodes in giant eruptions of hysterical giddiness, fifteen or twenty seconds at a diaphragmatic stretch, with the actors maniacally holding their places until they can go on (at full tilt) with Kushner's spastic, convulsive, rollicking text. "Nothing is funnier than unhappiness," says the dramaturge of our century (Samuel Beckett); but Kushner PROVES it.

Nobody dares to call this high-minded work a comedy, of course. Certainly Kushner doesn't: he creatively generizes it as "A Gay Fantasia on National Themes," a bill it fills to the margins (and then some): it's gay, it's fantastic, it's national and it's VERY thematic. *Angels,* indeed, is truly a momentous work: moving, appalling, surprising, central. The politics and the sex gets just about everybody where they live. And, more important, where they die, or fear to die. The great heaves of laughter emerging from this play are, in fact, violent spasms of relief: AIDS (and death, and pain) are the great holder-inners. Kushner simply pulls out the plug, and we blow it out.

The story, despite its seven hours work-up, is relatively simple: there're two couples: Prior and Louis (male and male New Yorkers, with Prior dying of AIDS), and Joe and Hannah (male and female Utah Mormans, with Joe a closet gay); parallel betrayals split each couple apart. Louis leaves Prior because he can't stand the pain of his lover's gruesome suffering; Joe walks out on Hannah when he walks out of his closet and into Louis's arms.

And then there's Mr. Cohn. That's right: Roy Cohn, the famed Jewish atheist homosexual millionaire knows-everybody divorce lawyer; protegé of McCarthy and prosecutor of the (Julius and Ethel) Rosenbergs; the oppressor of decent humanity, the wronger of inalienable rights. America's Satan, in Kushnerian terms. "I'm looking for the cloven hoof," says Cohn's (black, gay, male) hospital nurse, peering under the bedsheets of his foaming-at-the-mouth, rabidly-in-denial AIDS patient. "Butterfingers spook faggot!" Cohn screams back at him.

Cohn's relationship to the two couples is more surrealistic than real-world credible (Joe, a Utahan court clerk, somehow becomes Cohn's professional New York lackey), as is the couples' relationship to each other (Joe and Louis have an awkward two-week fling); the principals mainly appear in each other's nightmares, and in fantasies set in Heaven, Hell, and deeper Antarctica. But tight plotting and quotidian verisimilitude are not the author's goals: indeed, the play's vibrating story lines proceed more in parallel than in causal consecution; they're usually interspersed with or layered atop one another, and they radiate with angelic (see the title) fantasy. What's happening here, Kushner implies, is happening IN AMERICA (the title again) and not just in one or another('s) bedroom or boardroom. The effect takes its full seven hours to accrue its near-epic results, and it's fully worth it: *Angel*'s final and tragic punches hit with brutal force on stomachs weak from two evenings' (or a whole day's) laughter.

It's Roy Cohn that makes this play astonishing, and takes it well beyond the gay landscapes familiar to us through *Cloud Nine,* and the *Torch Song* and *Falsetto* trilogies, and even way back to *The Madness of Lady Bright* and *Boys In the Band.* Cohn is Kushner's springboard from the micro to the macrocosm, and into the darker abysses of American politics, and the coruscating social dialectics that define our country: Democrats v. Republicans, whites v. blacks, gays v. straights, Jews and Mormons v. most everybody else—and most everybody else v. them. Cohn limns, as he goes, the arts of jurisprudence (and jurisimprudence), while coloring in some great American icons: Joe McCarthy, Ethel Rosenberg ("Mrs. Reddi-kilowatt" he cheerfully calls the electric-chaired maybe-spy), Ronald Reagan ("the cowboy"), and the once-ubiquitous Marlboro Man. Cohn's no homosexual, according to him, "just a heterosexual who happens to have sex with men"; since homosexuals "have zero clout," he couldn't possibly be one. Indeed, Kushner's Cohn redefines clout, and relocates the (dead) center of the American nightmare: magnetic opportunism, manipulative megalomania, lacerating bigotry, and the ultimate powers of connectability—his calls are returned within five minutes by everyone from the President's wife on down (a sly jab, and, pre-Hillary, a prescient one). Power is Cohn's true sexuality and his religion, and lawyers are "the high priests of America," with Cohn their overarching bishop. His red-lined black smoking jacket swirls around the country's ankles, and pulls down its (our) pants. A brilliantly assaultive, sulfuric performance by Ron Liebman proves a once-in-a-lifetime opportunity not only for him, but for us as well: Liebman comes as close as we can imagine to Hell on wheels.

The Los Angeles performances, indeed, could hardly have been better. Stephen Spinella's Prior is tragically convincing as an AIDS patient, and deeply poignant as a failing drag queen, but he's breathtakingly funny as well; his performance has a wicked charisma and glittering eccentricity I can't recall since Leonard Frey's great performance—probably before Spinella was born—in *Boys in the Band*. Spinella is, by turns, heroic, pathetic, waspish, elegiacal: he's a marvel. Joe Mantello, as Louis, delivers a fully-layered complexity of a young life's uncertain accretion of love, guilt, betrayal, and wise-guy insouciance. K. Todd Freeman in peripheral roles (that, however, seem to surround the play) is a major and apt player always, as is Kathleen Chalfant as the Mormon housewife who dreams of Antarctica and other frigidities. John Conklin's set, a neo-fascist Federalist facade cracked in the middle—which parts to admit a flying angel or two—is massive, continuously amusing, scary, and effective. Direction, by Oscar Eustis (who initially commissioned the play for the Eureka Theatre) with the assistance of Tony Taccone, is first rate.

Angels is not wholly satisfying—yet. Some goofy theology and wishful sentimentalism substitutes for closure in the second half, entitled *Perestroika;* Kushner has apparently set about to rewrite it for the 1993 New York opening. His job may be as difficult as Gorbachev's and Yeltsin's (nothing is less dramatic than divinities; even the Greeks limited themselves to demigods), but with the stakes so high, and the talent so prodigious, we can afford some optimism. Even as it is, *Perestroika* is enthralling with its imagery and virtually heroic in its energy, and *Millennium Approaches* (the play's first half) is ravishing: simply as it stands, **Angels in America** (or at least **Angels** in Los Angeles) is already a masterpiece. New York will also see a new director: George C. Wolfe, who wrote and directed the current **Jelly's Last Jam** (see below), has been brought in to stage the show, and some recasting has been done (Freeman, for one, has been replaced). All of these rumored and executed changes have made for some extended bitterness and anxiety, and it's been a field day in the theatrical press. One can only hope that Kushner's great work flourishes through the process.

Portions of **The Kentucky Cycle** were originally developed at the Mark Taper Forum Theatre; subsequently the play was expanded and produced at the Seattle Repertory Theatre, receiving such acclaim that Gordon Davidson, the Taper's artistic director, turned his subscription season inside out to bring it back to Los Angeles, billing the cycle as "the theatrical event of a lifetime." The Pulitzer seems to have confirmed Seattle's adulation, and Davidson's chutzpah, but this **Cycle** is not for all waters, and leads to no lifetime revelations or epiphanies. Robert Schenkkan's unusual work—it lasts more than six hours, includes nine "plays," and spans two centuries—is a firmly revisionist history of eastern Kentucky: from the Indian rapes and deceptions of pre-Revolutionary times, to the fussin' and feudin' of the moonshinin' and Civil War eras, to the economic agonies and ecological devastations of 20th-century coal mining: bituminous filth overlorded by union goon-squads. It's a dismal, depressing tale of what Schenkkan calls a "Dark and Bloody Land," and it will earn its author no plaudits from the Kentucky Chamber of Commerce; indeed, this play might do for Kentucky's tourism what *Midnight Express* did for Turkey's.

There's no question that **The Kentucky Cycle** grabs and holds our attention: it opens with gunshots, betrayal, and murder; there's a throat cut or a shotgun fired in virtually every scene; and there's an f-ing lot of hyper-impact cussin' throughout to reminds us how high the stakes are. Nor is our attention merely begged: Schenkkan has also given us a sustained and generally compelling storyline, covering three families over several generations, plus some brilliant (and brilliantly researched) historical detail, particularly in the early scenes, together with a resolute and determined sincerity that laces through both text and performance. All of this proved, at the Los Angeles opening, mightily impressive: earning a huge shouting ovation—and even entrance applause for the actors coming out to start the cycle's second half.

I fear, however, that the **Kentucky** audience is applauding itself as much or more than it is cheering Schenkkan's play: the issues are so blatantly drawn, the themes so politically proper, the author's positions so gruesomely earnest, and the setting so unbearably drab that we are tempted to applaud the play in order to cheer the Right (which these days, of course, means the Left), and so as to put ourselves squarely on the side of those angels (in Spanish, "Los Angeles"), delighting (for once) to be in a cozy theatre in Southern California rather than a failing (and falling) coal mine in Hazard, Kentucky.

For what is there, short of ourselves, to cheer about? **Kentucky**'s Indians are as rapacious as its white men; its "Rowen" family as corrupt as its "Talbots" (the Hatfields and McCoys of Schenkkan's invention), and its unionizers—after an idyllic beginning—prove almost as greedy as their bosses. Even the women and blacks, who are rigorously abused throughout, add little light or life to the proceedings; Stephen Foster (the sun shining bright on his old Kentucky home) must have been speaking of some other Kentucky. All of this makes for a grim day (or pair of nights) at the theatre.

Kentucky's plot mechanics hinge on a series of linked trades and barters, and fully a third of the six-hour-plus action consists of prolonged negotiations: pelt by pelt between an Indian who barters skins for a white man's rifles; acre by acre (and slave by slave) between a vengeful Talbot mortgagor and a pathetic Rowen mortgagee; penny by penny between the vicious coal bosses and a grasping, riven strike committee: most of this, I'm afraid, is not dramatic action; it's simply a haggling for terms. Proud'hon said it well in three words ("Property is Theft"), and the many hours of this cycle, impassioned as they often are, mainly demonstrate and redemonstrate his famous maxim—with a steadily diminishing impact.

Kentucky's plot linkage is provided by interconnected generations (interconnected mainly through revenge—resonance here of the Aeschylean House of Atreus, as well as the Brook-Carrière *Mahabharata*), by ingenious actor-doubling, and by a totemic prop: a musical pocket watch which is handed or stolen from exploiter to exploitee, or vice versa, through the cycle's two centuries, and buried (hopefully?) at play's end. All nine plays are framed by prefatory and epilogic Titles and Encapsulating Truths, worthy enough ("Dark and Bloody") but a bit ho-hum, even though declaimed in a decidedly non-ho-hum fashion by members of the cast.

In sum, *The Kentucky Cycle* is a major (and Pulitzer-certified) work with serious limitations: it works too hard to teach us a lesson, and gives us too little as reward (or inducement) for learning it. The story-theatre staging, by Warner Shook, focuses the action sharply, and intensifies the thematic interconnections, but it also redoubles the joylessness of the author's vision, and leaves some of us wanting to go out at intermission for—let's say—a mint julep. Or, by God, an escape to *Oklahoma!*

But if Cycles and Gay Fantasias have made their marks elsewhere, it was still a wonderfully good year on Broadway. History probably will not record any world masterpieces birthed between 44th and 52nd Streets in 1992, but in no year in recent memory has the Great White Way sparkled with such confident, buoyant, and deserved enthusiasm. Maybe it was the washing-down and dolling-up of Times Square for the Democrats' Convention; maybe it was the return to the stage of a dozen or so movie stars, facing slashed salaries in recession-torn Hollywood; and just maybe it was the cocky revivals of a handful of great Broadway classics; in any case this was a year of great theatrical excitement, where old and new, innovative and conventional, stood proudly, as they should, side by side, setting a gaggle of all-time box office records. For this is what the Broadway stage is for: exuberant, polished, professional adventurism, with enough dramaturgical shocks to tweak the critics, and enough cornball entertainment to pay the (exorbitant) rents. In 1992, Broadway delivered the goodies.

It is patently perverse, I know, to head a review of the New York stage with two musical revivals, but indeed I must; somewhere in the back of their minds the creators of this year's *Two Trains Running* and *Oleanna* have got to be looking hopefully toward the fiftieth anniversary revivals of their plays—revivals that will generate the great energy of 1992's productions of *Guys and Dolls* and *Crazy for You.* Revivals, after all, give the theatre its authority, its majesty, its living indelibility. Neither nostalgia nor camp can explain the throngs hovering about the Martin Beck or Shubert Theatres at 8:00 each night, searching for unclaimed or turned-back seats; this is a theatre public craving immersion in its own history, exulting in its near-proximity to a late creative genius. Where would art be today without Picassos in the Met, Pollocks in the Modern, Kandinskys in the Guggenheim, and Frank Loesser at the Martin Beck? Suppose *Guernica* had closed in 1939? In 2040, August Wilson and David Mamet, or their descendents, will be happy that in 1992 they had to share some of the limelight with the new life given these non-hoary old masterpieces.

Guys and Dolls is, and the cliche is unavoidable, the quintessential Broadway musical: it takes place on Times Square and in never-never-land more or less at the same time. This is not the place to dwell on its multiple charms, nor on the undoubted genius of composer-lyricist Frank Loesser, nor to tell the story of a musical performed by every American high school drama group at least once in the past two generations, but it is the place to celebrate di-

rector Jerry Zaks, designers Tony Walton (sets) and William Ivey Long (costumes), plus choreographer Christopher Chadman for a revival that is, if anything, even better than the magnificent 1947 original. Certainly Nathan Lane, Peter Gallagher, and Faith Prince have equalled or excelled their earlier counterparts in the key roles (Josie de Guzman was not yet in the role of Sarah at the preview performance I saw); and the original script, "At Wanamaker's, at Saks, and Klein's" to the letter, holds up as supremely inspired Runyonana. It would be no sacrifice nor disgrace to the contemporary American theatre if this production could run till the end of time.

The deliciously corny *Crazy For You* is not at all in this league, but is ravishing all the same; the *New York Times* heralded it as up there with the second coming. This remake of George and Ira Gershwin's 1930 *Girl Crazy* (with additional songs pillaged from elsewhere in Gershwinia) has a brand new up-tempo and super-silly book (by Ken Ludwig, author of *Lend Me a Tenor*), lots of tasty scenery and costumes (by Robin Wagner and, once again, William Ivey Long), and, of course, that eminently blissful Gershwin score: "They Can't Take That Away From Me," "Bidin' My Time," "I Got Rhythm," "Nice Work if You Can Get It," and the virtually-hymnal "Someone to Watch Over Me." What is totally new here is the transformative brilliance of choreographer Susan Stroman in an absolutely breathtaking Broadway debut; Stroman's dances are filled with flying props, falling bodies, rolling scenery, and exquisite tappy metaphors; they send the audience into a frenzy: Susan Stroman, I'm crazy for you. If the show lacks a real Ethel Merman knock-out punch, or a Ray Bolger terpsichorean fantasy, Jodi Benson and Harry Groener prove bright, deft, skillful, and thoroughly engaging in the comic-romantic leads.

Revivalists beware, however; dramatic (like divine) resurrection is a dicey proposition at best, and highly touted Broadway revivals of *Most Happy Fella* (also Frank Loesser), *A Streetcar Named Desire* and *Man of La Mancha* opened and closed this year with mixed success or less. Theatre is a live art, and admits its ghosts only sparingly.

The best of Broadway's new works begins with a ghost, as a matter of fact, but since said ghost is played by the near-miraculous Gregory Hines, *Jelly's Last Jam* gets off to a vivacious start. This wonderful musical play/review surveys the life, career, downfall, and death of the famed Ferdinand Le Menthe (Jelly Roll) Morton: a Creole-born, Jazz-era songwriter-pianist-performer who found himself right in the center of America's multi-cultural diversity. "The Roll," as he royally called himself, was a ladies man, a braggart-naïf, and the self-styled "inventor of jazz"; his ups were transcendent, his lows calamitous. Two factors make *Jelly's* a success: Hines' performance illuminates the ups, and author-director George C. Wolfe's intensity penetrates the lows.

Wolfe starts his drama facing his last "jam"; he is dying broke in Los Angeles, and it is 1941. Suddenly we are in "The Jungle Inn—somewhere 'tween Heaven 'n' Hell," where Jelly is led back through his life. His guide (and ours) is the "Chimney Man"—sort of a cross between Satan, Martin Luther King, and Ralph Edwards hosting

This Is Your Life. Chimney takes us back to Jelly's genteel childhood in New Orleans, and his bitter expulsion by an operatic grandma (Gran Mimi) who finds the boy hanging out with scat musicians, whores, and other low-class types; soon we are following Jelly on his typically-rollercoasting career: writing, performing, and recording songs; loving and leaving the ladies, getting screwed and, well, getting screwed. Shades, perhaps, of dramatic models Bessie Smith and Ma Rainey, but Wolfe plays upon a different theme. "No coon in this Creole" is Jelly's thematic motif, and eventually we plunge into the world of black-on-black: Jelly, disowned by his high-toned frenchified background, disdaining the "niggers and coons" that swarm admiringly about him. This is a theme not forcefully explored in the theatre since Charles Gordone's *No Place to Be Somebody* in 1966, and it generates dramatic light, as well as heat. In one of the play's two dramatic moments (Gran Mimi's rejection being the first), Jelly hands a bright red jacket to Jack the Bear, his lifelong partner, and orders Jack to be his new Club doorman; it is an act of deliberate humiliation of the blacker black. Author Wolfe takes a brilliant revenge, however: *Jelly's'* first act ends with the ensemble all in bright red jackets, wearing minstrel faces (an even blacker black, a parody of black),

humbling Jelly with a mocking dance rendition of King Oliver's "Dr. Jazz." Wolfe's theatricality is stunning, and his sense of irony—first seen in his exciting *The Colored Museum* six years ago—is terrific; even though he pretty much runs out of play in Act II, *Jelly's* is an enormously satisfying, luminous experience. He has also elicited exalted performances from a supporting cast; particularly Savion Glover as the young Jelly, Keith David as Chimney Man, and Ann Duquesnay as Gran Mimi.

Jelly's Last Jam started at the Los Angeles Mark Taper Forum Theatre (and what a year for the Taper, too!) pretty much as a straight play; the New York production is not only a full-scale musical (nineteen numbers, about half by Morton), it features, in Gregory Hines, a name-over-the-title Broadway star who delivers the performance of his life. Hines is a good actor and a fine singer, but he is an absolutely extraordinary dancer, and his tap numbers—which he choreographed himself—leave the audience breathless. Star power in *Jelly's* case is not merely elevation; it's revelation, it's what makes the play work. Hines does what no mere author nor director can do alone: he brings Jelly's creativity and imagination, his talent and energy, his sheer performative wizardry, brilliantly to life; he makes Jelly not just interesting but great. Aristotle said that tragedy requires a great man to fall. *Oedipus'* greatness is in the writing; *Jelly's* has to be in the performing; without Hines' work, you've just got a victim here; just another ghost.

Straight plays in New York were, typically, a mixed bag this year, with no single work setting minds or hearts ablaze, other than momentarily. Still, major new works from August Wilson, David Mamet, John Guare, Richard Nelson, Herb Gardner, and even an agonized revision by Neil Simon gave the theatrical season some vivid jolts and satisfying evenings, and a new play by Wendy Wasserstein sold out so quickly in its small house that it closed down to reopen on Broadway in 1993. A year of great promise and substantial if not overwhelming accomplishment.

August Wilson is surely the premier playwright working in America today; his two Pulitzers (for *Fences* and *The Piano Lesson*), richly deserved, are in this reviewer's estimation overshadowed by his magnificent *Joe Turner's Come and Gone*, a tragedy ranking with the greatest in modern dramatic history. Wilson's latest work, **Two Trains Running**, may not reach the level of his finest accomplishments, but it is a measure of his all but inexhaustible talent that this work is immensely pleasurable, involving, surprising, and on several occasions profoundly moving. Not that much happens in the rundown, small (4 stools, 3 booths), unnamed Pittsburgh restaurant where Wilson's play is set: the play's major events, such as they are, are largely reported to us: a winning numbers ticket is brought in, so is a stolen ham, and a favorable court disposition; plus there are offstage visits to a (reputedly 322-year-old) seer, and a couple of funerals of folks who died of natural causes: these modest occurrences make up the dramatic action. A quiet day in a quiet place, but across town, we are given to understand there's a black power rally—a memorial to the just-slain Malcolm X—and revolution lies just around the corner. It is Wilson's poetic strength that the incipient politics of the next twenty years dominates the action without, however, fully raising its head: it's everywhere, yet still mostly overlookable—except, of course, in retrospect. And in the period's ironic resignation. "A nigger with a gun is bad news," says the restaurant philosopher. "You can't even use the word 'nigger' and 'gun' in the same sentence. You say the word 'gun' in the same sentence with the word 'nigger' and you in trouble. The white man panic. Unless you say, 'The policeman shot the nigger with his gun'—then that be alright. Other than that, he panic. He ain't had nothing but guns for the last five hundred years—got the atomic bomb and everything. But you say the word 'nigger' and 'gun' in the same sentence and they'll try and arrest you."

"Memphis," the play's central character (he owns the restaurant), is an outwardly gruff, inwardly accommodating black businessman, "wrestling with the world," as he says, generally oblivious (or resigned) to the fact that the "world" is stacked against him. A fact not lost on Holloway, the philosopher, nor Sterling, the youngster fresh from the penitentiary, nor Wolf, the numbers peddler ("every nigger you see done been to jail one time or another"), nor Hambone, a demented (but insistent) petitioner for his undelivered ham, nor Risa, the waitress who is so sick of passes made at her that she cuts up her legs with

a razor blade. Indeed, *Two Trains Running* (the title refers to life and death) sets up a shadow-world; a black world (a black market, actually, and even a black death) that underlies its white counterpart(s). In the black, or African-American world, numbers running replaces investing, seers replace doctors and psychologists, attempts at shaming replace negotiation, and food replaces salary (not to mention Social Security benefits). The play's most pathetic (and memorable) running plotline (it's almost a running gag, until Hambone dies) concerns this poor soul who some years ago painted a white man's fence for the fee of one ham, but was only given a chicken for his efforts. "I want my ham! He gonna give me my ham!" Hambone repeats idiotically, over and over at the man's door (and in Memphis' restaurant), until we all but drown in his obsessive (if sadly amusing) misery.

If *Two Trains Running* did not achieve fullest recognition in 1992, it may have been because of an unfortunately lackluster performance in the central role of Memphis. Surrounded by the near-spectacular performances of Roscoe Lee Browne as Holloway, Larry Fishburne as Sterling (both received Tony nominations, with the incendiary Fishburne getting the final nod), Sullivan Walker as Hambone, and Cynthia Martells as Risa, Al White's Memphis was uncharacteristically pallid. The role is not, as I first suspected, underwritten; it just seems that White was unable to get his spirit behind it. (It could very well be that White couldn't quite swallow his character's Uncle Tom-like acquiescence.) It's a shame: with a powerful performance in the central role—James Earl Jones inevitably comes to mind, but there are many others—this play would rank with Wilson's very best. Its humor, wisdom, deep-felt and correctly-based (and not just politically-correctly-based) anger, non-sanctimonious righteousness, and poetic force are all superior to anything currently appearing on the American stage.

Just when we feared David Mamet had permanently moved to Hollywood and films (*Homicide, Hoffa*) he once again overtook off-Broadway, weighing in, toward the end of the year, with the intellectually rip-roaring, amazingly tight-focused *Oleanna.* "To Oleanna you must go," says the folk song; there "the poorest man from the old country / Becomes a king in a year or so." Role reversal is Mamet's theme here, needless to say, but his characters aren't men and kings, they're men and women. Specifically male professors and female students, something Mamet (a sometime acting teacher) presumably knows a great deal about.

The plotline of Mamet's new work is immaculately simple: this is a single-issue play, almost totally devoid of texture, digression, peripheral concerns, or even human personality. (This is probably all to the good: coming on the heels of the Anita Hill/Clarence Thomas hearings, endlessly cycling political correctness debates, and the "year of the woman," the audience has no problems putting in its own texture, digressions, concerns, and personalities.) Act One: John (the professor) patronizes Carol (the student), gently chiding her for intellectual laziness, lapses in writing style, and in general for being uptight when he criticizes her work. Act Two: Carol patronizes (or matronizes)

John, accusing him of verbal intimidation, gender bigotry, intellectual oppression, and, by the end, attempted rape. Role reversal occurs in the intermission, when, presumably (see below), Carol has become politically energized by her unnamed "Group." From the somewhat dimwitted undergraduate of Act One, Carol is now a feminist, all-but-neo-Maoist warlord in Act Two. The brilliance of Mamet's conceit is that Act Two provides nothing but a complete re-interpretation of what we have seen in Act One: a second look (a close reading, academicians might say) at what we thought was simple fare. What we saw (and chuckled at) as professorially benevolent wit now appears, through Carol's interpretation, as patently coded intellectual terrorism. What was seen as whimsy and indulgence she sees (or says that she sees) as brutal assault. None of this is mere theatrical trickery or Pirandellian slight-of-hand; Mamet's play succeeds because both Carol and John's views are at least partly legitimate, and the audience is often divided. (There are two theatre program covers: half of us get one showing a bulls-eye superimposed on a seated John, the other half see the bulls-eye over Carol). Carol is surely an extremist, but John's off-hand put-downs, even of himself, devalue the very education Carol so persistently seeks; Carol's umbrage, whether it is neurotic overreaction or merely political guile, reflects a warranted alarm. *Oleanna* reaches closure through an act of violence (there is an Act Three, actually a second scene of Act Two), and there is a plot development that seems to cast an ill light on Carol's sincerity, but the impact of the play is its overall even-handedness, and its immensely skillful presentation of two sides of an issue, with surgically precise, point-by-point adumbration of its details. This is difficult theatre, because the issue is difficult, and because life is difficult. *Oleanna* generates rich post-performance discussions.

One unanswered question haunts the play, and robs it: does Carol undergo a real transformation between the acts, or is she deliberately (and deceitfully) setting John up in Act One? There is no indication that she has met with her "Group" before the first act, but that doesn't prevent the possibility that Act One is some sort of sting operation, with Carol leading John into precisely the behavior she will attack him for later. I can't say for sure that that's Mamet's notion, but the alternative is that Carol transforms herself from a plain-Jane academic dimwit to a guerrilla-styled rhetorical genius during the few weeks presumed to elapse between acts. Ideological (and, of course, sartorial) leaps are one thing, rapid IQ elevations are another. The problem is not merely technical, as it introduces confusion into the central, and otherwise precise, dialectic of the play. I'm afraid it also limits *Oleanna*'s force to have such pallid representatives of their kind as John and Carol; both are portrayed limply (and, I feel, performed limply, under the author's apparently intentional direction); neither emits the slightest radiance; neither remotely elicits sympathy, admiration, or excitement—either sexual or intellectual. The stammer-speech that Mamet has perfected—where characters speak in broken phrases marked by countless ellipses, mid-word halts, sentence trail-offs, nonword utterances, and mis-speakings—has now become merely a bad habit and a tired cliche; this together with Rebecca Pidgeon's choice

(if it is hers; she is also Mamet's wife) to read each of Carol's lines with a high-arching pitch that graphs like a McDonald's Golden, makes Act One unnecessarily tedious. *Oleanna* is great theatre, and stimulates great arguments. It is not, however, a great play.

Two years ago Richard Nelson showed us some Americans abroad (in *Some Americans Abroad*) seeing plays in England; this year he's showing us some Englishmen abroad, performing plays in the U. S. ***Two Shakespearean Actors,*** the very happy result, is the story of (English) William Macready's fateful 1849 performance of *Macbeth* at the Astor Place Theatre in New York; thirty-four persons were killed in riots sparked by enthusiasts of (American) Edwin Forrest's *Macbeth* performed a few blocks away. Unfortunately, Nelson's effort was only granted a brief run: the play's large cast, somewhat recherché theme, and woefully flat production conspired to make it a less than successful commercial venture. But what a play it is! Nelson has achieved the near-impossible: this is a play of Chekhovian depth, and near-Wildean wit, on the subject of classical tragic acting; a master's piece, if not a masterpiece, it represents a ghastly oversight on the part of the Pulitzer committee (which did not even nominate it for this year's award), and a magnificent opportunity for the repertory company (and director) that can give the play the dramatic precision and theatrical bravura it deserves.

Rarely has a Broadway production so failed to deliver the potential of its script. It is Nelson's gambit to superpose and skewer, as he did so brilliantly in *Some Americans Abroad,* co-equal American and British pretensions; this time, however, he also animates the passionate, alienated, and degenerative isolation of the stage artist. Yes, "stage artist": not just some sensitive rebel/author alter-ego, but the out-on-a-limb actor-manager-tragedian, beset with meeting payrolls, drawing houses, hiring understudies, mending costumes, outscheduling rivals, remembering lines, maintaining households, entertaining colleagues, inspiring critics, and, night after night, year after year, rising to the multiple occasions offered by both the world's greatest and worst dramatists. There are about a dozen actors in Nelson's play: both Forrest and Macready, the aging superstars, plus a goodly bunch of has-beens, almost-ares, will-never-bes, and for-this-part-I'll-sleep-with-anyones; by the end of the play, most of which takes place in a free-wheeling theatre tavern, we can know them all. Nelson's play is not plot-heavy: much of the celebrated Astor Place riot occurs off-stage, and basically provides a background for his real subjects: rivalry, egotism, aesthetics, art, patriotism, and Shakespeare.

Quite fabulously, we're given, within ***Two Shakespearean Actors,*** copious fragments of two different productions of *Macbeth,* seen both from the audience and backstage, plus a good glimpse of Forrest's *Metamora,* heretofore known only by committed theatre historians, together with brief and tantalizing appearances by Dion Boucicault and Washington Irving. Such argument as exists (whether or not one actor or the other should cancel a *Macbeth,* so as to avoid a riot) is mere but sufficient axis to longstanding aesthetic and geographico-political quarrels: this is an extended fencing match between aging pros, seconded by grasping apprenti. As noted, the wit is post-Wildean ("American people are really rather charming and decent as well as intelligent in an instinctive sort of way"), and the tone is Chekhovian:

> (*Pause. MACREADY sits, staring at nothing. MISS WEMYSS smiles. WEMYSS stands behind Macready's chair and sips his drink. RYDER doesn't know whether to leave or not. Blackout.*)

with more scenes than this dissolving, rather than ending, in solipsistic (and sometimes drunken) reverie, and with the play culminating, quite grandly, in a duologue between the two pros, tripping snippets of *Lear* and *Othello* lightly on the tongue, and engaging in a camaraderie that we sense goes back the 300 years to Gentle Will, and another two millennia to Aeschylus and Aristophanes as well.

Nothing in **Two Shakespearean Actors** is easy to pull off, and the Broadway production simply failed to make most of its points; what was deeply textured came off bland and amorphous, and an incomprehensibly inaudible performance in the crucial go-between role of John Ryder (an actor abandoned by Macready and picked up by Forrest) left great hunks of the play virtually unperformed. Brian Bedford and Victor Garber were independently strong as Macready and Forrest, but left the distinctions between these actors largely unrealized. A clearer, deeper, and more elegantly shaped production may eventually bring this play to the greater fruition it deserves.

After his great success with *Six Degrees of Separation,* and most likely because of it, John Guare has begun writing with a confidence and a generosity of creative spirit rarely seen in the American theatre today; indeed, he seems to actually *like* writing plays, and the apparent authorial enthusiasm that went into his whacky operetta-fragment, **Four Baboons Adoring the Sun,** remains absolutely salubrious in the astonishing if unfinished product.

"The strain of man's bred out into baboon and monkey" says Apemantus in Shakespeare's *Timon,* and, while I doubt those words were on Guare's mind (or anybody else's) at time of writing, this is very much a play about Darwinian and cultural evolution; of naked apes and the ancient archeology of the man/woman/child triad. It's Guare's conceit to place a married American couple, Philip and Penny McKenzie—an academic and a field archeologist, respectively—in rural Sicily, where, at their stone age dig, they have brought their nine former-marriage children (four of his, five of hers: a 1990s Brady Bunch) together for the first time. Philip and Penny are a love couple; their marriage began as an adulterous affair which hurtled them—through the magic of easy divorce and Alitalia Airlines—from their desperately humdrum "Universe A" to their romantically apocalyptic "Universe B." Delightful for them, of course, but where, Guare asks, does it leave the kids? What is the true universe of childhood? The play does not shrink from drawing mortal as well as moral complications.

Guare's Sicily is overseen by the love god Eros, who rises near-naked from the Sicilian volcano at play's start-up,

and sings the first bars of a broken aria of futility. In the course of the play, parents wrestle what to tell the kids; the kids wrestle what to tell the (step)parents; parents wrestle what to tell each other; and Eros torments everybody: driving the older of the children to emulate the love couple that their parents have become: to the final misery—if enlightenment—of all. To live like children, Guare suggests, is OK for adults, but fatal for kids.

Baboons has been treated to a spectacular production; it seems more a mini-opera than a play, with its grandiose Lincoln Center staging (by Peter Hall, on a set by Tony Walton: there are volcano eruptions, earthquakes, and whirling worlds), its fragments of arias, its Greeky chorus of nine children, and its toying with metaphysical themes. But it's also a social satire, in typical Guare fashion, of American means and manners, of child-rearing and family spats, of hypocrisy in academia and boredom in suburbia. Those baboons in the title are four ancient stone statues at the dig (we see them in the background); the baboons have been blinded by staring at the sun, their eyes are "burnt out because they've seen their God." The "strain of man" indeed. It's Eros that is our God today, and Guare's children are blinded by their parents' sheer effulgence. Bring back Universe A! Long live humdrum!

1992 was star season on Broadway (owing, in part no doubt, to the recession-caused cutback in star salaries in Hollywood), and three of the country's most celebrated film actors comprised the entire cast of Chilean author Arial Dorfman's **Death and the Maiden** last Spring. Glenn Close, Richard Dreyfuss, and Gene Hackman were the comprisers, and the play, a somewhat slack thesis melodrama about political torture in "a country that is probably Chile," was not really helped by their efforts.

Dorfman is a major novelist of broad international standing: a Chilean national of Argentine birth, he was raised in New York City and for the last ten years has been living in North Carolina, teaching Latin American studies at Duke and writing for the *New York Times* (and others); his books have been translated into 20 languages, and last year **Death and the Maiden** won numerous awards in its London premiere. In this production, however, the play pretty much stays on the page. Paulina (played by Close) is a deeply disturbed housewife: fifteen years ago she was imprisoned, gang-raped, and tortured by government thugs; the experience, quite naturally, continues to devastate her. Gerardo (Dreyfuss), her lawyer husband, is deeply sympathetic; indeed, democracy is now in the air, and Gerardo has just been appointed to a Presidential commission charged with investigating (but not prosecuting) the crimes of the past era. Suddenly, the "doctor" (Hackman)—the worst of Paulina's tormentors, whose fancy was to torture and rape to melodies of Schubert—appears at her door: it seems that Gerardo has brought him to the house after the doctor had stopped to help Gerardo fix a flat on the roadway. Paulina, who had been blindfolded during her imprisonment, immediately recognizes the Doctor by his voice; knocking him unconscious, she ties him up, and proceeds to put him on "trial," with her nervously ambivalent husband acting as sometime prosecutor, sometime defense attorney.

This is a "what if?" play, and the schema—with its gruesome real-life savagery as fuel—lends itself to multiple lines of the most powerful and fascinating arguments: here's Oresteian revenge versus democratic justice; male-bonding rituals versus feminist isolation and outrage; Christian idealism versus the luring (and lurid) aesthetics of torture. Though the author may have lived it, none of this comes alive. Events are scattered and go back and forth; revelations come piecemeal and without momentum; issues are drawn and then rescinded; and ambiguity rests merely in withheld information, not in fundamental paradox or human irony. I think that in striving for universality (Dorfman says the play is set "probably in Chile, but could be any country . . . after a long period of dictatorship"), Dorfman has lost too much specificity to make the situation dramatically perplexing, and, therefore, viable. Adding to the level of abstraction, he has cast strictly Anglo actors, of whom only Close seems to truly perspire.

Death and the Maiden is an engaging if not gripping play; it's continually involving and sturdily worthy, and there's a terrific ending, too: in an epilogue which is the play's single sublime moment, torturer and torturee are surprised, some time later, to discover each other in the audience of an orchestra concert. Schubert, of course. They gaze wanly at each other across the aisle, and then at us (for we are now fellow concertgoers). We gaze back at them, and at each other as well, and discover we're looking for terrorists beneath the gowns and tuxedos: **Death and the Maiden** concludes with a "no exit" moment that encloses us all. There are ex-torturers and ex-torturees sitting next to us, and maybe even within us, Dorfman cagily implies; it's a forgiving world we live in, and Dorfman's survival through exile is itself a quiet testimony to certain amnesties (and amnesias). Though the play is somewhat page-bound, at least the issues burn.

I loved Herb Gardner's **Conversations with My Father.** What astounds me is that anybody else loved it, but they apparently did: this is the only nonmusical Broadway play of 1992 to survive into 1993. My appreciation, though, is biased; after all, I, like Charlie, Mr. Gardner's conversationalist-protagonist, am also a middle-aged Jewish male whose father spent much of his life assimilating into Christian-American society. But what's in it for all those other folks?

Conversations, as the name makes clear, is a memory play, and Mr. Gardner's memory is of a father named Eddie Ross (né Goldberg) who, during the 40 year span of the play (1936 to '76), runs a bar on lower Manhattan's Canal Street. Eddie, to keep it short, isn't a lot of fun. Ill-tempered, intolerant, and more often than not mean-spirited, this commercially ambitious immigrant from old Europe has little time for conversations with his son—or anyone else for that matter—as he struggles up (and stumbles down) the American success ladder. Strong echoes here of Willy Loman and James Tyrone, perhaps, but with an earlier Goldberg—TV's Mollie—as well: this is a highly specific play of Jewish-American life in the (second) Roosevelt era, and of Jewish assimilation—and non-assimilation—into the lifeblood of U. S. culture. That it strikes a resonance with non-Jewish audiences—and a

year's run, even on Broadway, clearly demonstrates that it does—shows that the model has multiple applications. And dramatic longevity. Gardner's rambling and sometimes circling play is helped by a fine central (and centering) performance from Judd Hirsch, as the eponymous father, and even more by David Margulies as Zaretsky, an elderly barroom regular (and upstairs boarder), an ex-actor and continuing Jewish idealist who, having emerged from the old Yiddish theatre, now relentlessly harangues Eddie about the Nazi Holocaust that is threatening to engulf them all. Margulies carries the play's real weight, both historically and theatrically: his "performances" within the play (he gives us his Dybbuk as well as his Hamlet) show us exactly what Eddie's leaving behind, and what his son Charlie will want to recover. Zaretsky is, after all, a "regular Tomashevki," as my own grandparents would say of any great Jewish actor, and he's a reminder of the performative and exhibitionistic nature of Judaism, and perhaps of historic tribes (cultures) in general. It is precisely our performative exhibitionism that we abandon when we assimilate, whoever we are: maybe that's what's finally universal about Gardner's rough-cut but still glittering play.

Two reconfigured musicals (in addition to **Crazy for You**) made a big impact this year. One was the late 60's "rock opera" *Tommy,* and I am happy to report, to my genuine surprise, that the "see me, feel me, touch me, heal me" kid looks even better than he did back in flower-power daze/days. The La Jolla Playhouse production of Pete Townsend's seriously seminal work, initially performed by Townsend's The Who as an album in 1969, has now been substantially reconfigured—by Townsend himself, with the help of director Des McAnuff—into a rousing and mostly revelatory revival.

For those without memories, fond or otherwise, of the rapturous overindulgences of the 60s, *Tommy* tells the story—entirely through song—of a four-year-old boy who, savagely ordered into silence after witnessing his father kill his mother's lover, goes catatonic. Seemingly deaf, dumb, and blind, Tommy successively succumbs to gross indignities: parental neglect, sexual abuse, medical incompetence, and gross economic exploitation. Tommy finally re-emerges into a sensate existence at the age of ten, when he is led into the fine teenage art of pinball; by *Tommy*'s end, Tommy has (more or less) returned to the world, but the world hasn't really returned to him. This work is deeply into alienation (The Who was the first rock group to end their concerts by smashing their instruments over their amplifiers), and Tommy's "cure" is much more spiritual than medical: his therapy is basically a break with the past (a broken mirror serving as the semiotic prop), and a reconciliation with the future. What makes *Tommy* work, when it does, is a booming, thumping score that has just enough seductive lyricism to get us involved and just enough irony to keep us detached. Looking back, we see Townsend as an unheralded source for poprockers Webber and Boubil.

The La Jolla group has enhanced *Tommy*'s musical artistry with a spectacular visual production by McAnuff and his team, which includes John Arnone (scenery), Frances Aronson (lighting), Wendell Harrington (projections) and the indispensable Foys (flying): this is a show that rockets out in every physical direction, yet always moves with split-second, assured control; stage management here is particularly deft. Somersaulting falls, rocketing leaps, rollerblading setpieces, sure-handed followspotting, and wonderfully fluid photo/videography give *Tommy* both a Las Vegas volatility and a New York panache, yet the show, amazingly, still manages to wear a human face: when Tommy cries "see me, touch me," we actually reach out: this is a huge accomplishment amidst such cacophonous scenography.

The final curtain had the La Jolla audience up on its feet cheering, smelling a Broadway transfer, which is about to open as this essay is written. La Jolla to Broadway is not without precedent, of course: *Big River* made such a move from the same stage a few years ago. A White Way jackpot may elude the La Jolla production, however, without major changes. Choreography is strictly pedestrian by the big town's standards (presumably because the cast couldn't handle much more than a quick walk), and the continuous music is just a bit too relentlessly aggressive and unarticulated; even when freed (in "I'm free!"), Tommy still seems chained to his musical rock.

And there's a graver problem, too, I fear. Townsend and McAnuff's revision aims *Tommy* more at an adult audience this time around (when you see Townsend's photo in the program, you can understand why), but they go too far: the alienated sins of the first act (homicide, sexual abuse, teenage storm trooping) are wholly unaccounted for in the second; reconciliation is unaccompanied by remorse, regret, or even authorial acknowledgement. Tommy, totally oblivious to his earlier abuse, ends up begging for understanding from his once-creepy tormentors: Hell, they should be begging *him*. Reconciliation is a wonderful theme, to be sure, but it requires some recognition and peripety: I don't think I was the only one appalled to see Uncle Ernie, who had secretly "fiddled about" with Tommy in Act I, blithely accepted at play's end as the family's avuncular buffoon. Villainous deeds are done here; let's get some villains back.

The other musical reconfiguration on Broadway was *Falsettos,* by the redoubtable William Finn (music, lyrics, and, with James Lapine, the book): this is a composite of Mr. Finn's previous and shorter off-Broadway shows, *March of the Falsettos* (1981) and *Falsettoland* (1990), and it seems to demonstrate not only that the sum of Mr. Finn's two efforts is greater than its parts, but also that a musical whose organizing song is "My father is a homo" is not in the future going to be relegated to the theatre's fringe on account of its subject, but can entertain hopes of major mainstream (and Broadway) appeal. *Falsettos* may not be an artistic breakthrough, but it is clearly a commercial hit.

There have been gay-themed musicals before, of course (*La Cage Aux Folles, Kiss of the Spider Woman*), but these have generally traded on a certain outré exoticism, often playing more or less as a transvestite follies. *Falsettos* is simply a family drama, where the families happen to be gay as (or more) often as straight, Jewish as well as gentile; indeed, it prefigures many of the themes and storylines of the subsequent *Angels in America,* reviewed at the top of this essay. In Finn's work, Marvin leaves his wife Trina to head off to gay nirvana with boyfriend Whizzer (this is the part that was written in 1979); in Part Two (written ten years later) Whizzer comes down with AIDS and, remarkably, the now-extended families (which also include Marvin and Tina's son Jason, Tina's new husband—and the family's psychiatrist—Mendel, and two next-door lesbians) come lovingly together, celebrating Jason's bar mitzvah in Whizzer's hospital room. It is a synesthesia of sorts: joyous, rich, and poignant. Perhaps this isn't what Dan Quayle meant about family values, but it has a terrific appeal in this sadly elegiac time of our lives. Author/lyricist/composer Finn hits one right note after another: a devastatingly funny/sad "Trina's Song" in which Trina disintegrates into brilliantly comic hysterics before our eyes; a heart-stopping four-alarmer—"Something Bad Is Happening"—about the onset of AIDS; a gleefully rambunctious "three-part mini-opera" entitled "Marvin at the Psychiatrist"; and a rousingly thematic "March of the Falsettos," which boldly asks us "Who is man enough . . . ?" to march to a falsetto beat. Finn is clearly neo-Sondheiman, and his work is continually urbane, ironic, parodic, and cultured: this is a musical that fash-

ions witty rhymes from aesthetic, social, and theological speculations, and keeps them hopping to snappily shifting tunes and melodies. Like Sondheim, Finn employs a game motif: chess and baseball are essayed, and even the (minimalist) setting is a minimal checkerboard. But Finn's work surpasses much (if not most) of Sondheim's in developing both momentum and emotional payoff: this is a deeply felt and deeply feeling musical drama that gets to the heart of its subject as well as its audience. And with seven actors (no stars), no chorus of dancing girls (or boys), and only four musicians in the pit, William Finn has also redefined the downward cost parameter of the Broadway musical. *Falsettos* is a very successful work with legs; it, and Mr. Finn, should be entertaining and enthralling audiences for a very long time.

Since I reviewed Neil Simon's *Jake's Women* in its original San Diego production for the 1990 Yearbook, I will only note it briefly here. This sad and generally intelligent comedy concerns an author and his dead wife, who reappears in his life as a ghost, frustrating his current relationships. Several other ghostesses populate the play, along with some live ladies: collectively they are Jake's women; individually they're not as much as they could be. I was one of the few California reviewers to admire the earlier

version, though I publicly worried that Simon had "written two plays": one, a comic fantasy, sort of a 1990s *Blithe Spirit,* and the other a psychological study of grief. The two plays were not, however, integrated in San Diego, and I felt that Simon was just "going for the gag wherever he finds it, eliding fantasy and psychosis, eliminating dramatic tension, and abandoning his characters in the process." Simon's new version, though 70% rewritten, remains, unfortunately, like Jake's marriage, rocky. The beautiful (imagined) reconciliation scene between Jake's (dead) wife and (live) daughter is as powerful as before, and there are, as always, some good (and eminently worthy) jokes based on true-life observation, but Simon has little to offer, other than limp clichés, on love, marriage, survival, and the great art of moving on, and it's with these bromides that the play concludes. Alan Alda proved a superior Jake to his California predecessor, but I sure missed Stockard Channing as his second wife.

Five Guys Named Moe can wrap up this section of Broadway reviews; it's a Broadway revue, to be sure, and it's a simple-minded delight. The music is all by Louis Jordan: "Is you is or is you ain't my baby?" is his best-known tune; "Nobody here but us chickens" and "Caldonia" are two others that might still ring a bell with senior citizens or aficionados of 1940s American pop music. The highlight of the current show, however, is the quintuply eponymous African-American cast: Big Moe, Four-eyed Moe, Eat Moe, Little Moe, and No Moe. Plus "Nomax," a character inserted solely in order to dream up the other five, and to generate what passes for a plot. Or doesn't pass: the utter triviality of the authors' conceit is virtually an invitation for the audience to come up on stage and dance with the cast (which they do), and for the cast to join the audience in the theatre bar at intermission (which they do, too). This is a foot-stomping evening from start to finish, and the voltage of the cast—particularly Big Moe—could light up all of Broadway. Still, when I saw a TV clip of the original Five Guys from back in the 40s, the current Guys—and I hope the metaphor is not inappropriate—pale somewhat by comparison.

I will also mention just briefly the theatrical piece *Tubes* presented at the Astor Place Theatre by the Blue Man Group, which consists of Matt Goldman, Phil Stanton, and Chris Wink. I wouldn't recognize any of them on the street, because on stage they are covered from scalp to toe with very opaque blue paint. What they do is not drama, but it's certainly theatre, and it's very funny and scary, often at the same time. There are rolls of toilet paper over your head when you come into the Astor Place, and rubber tubes coming up between the seats; you can wrap yourself in toilet paper if you want, and carry on apparent conversations (with God knows who) through the tubes, and what's happening onstage is usually of interest too: I can tell you at least that there's a lot of drumming and a good deal of food is ingested (if not actually eaten). There's some gruesome (but voluntary) audience participation as well. I'm not sure that anything more need be said, except that much of the goings-on is absolutely inspired, and few of us have ever seen anything much like it. It's the perfect show to bring teenagers and visiting foreigners to. Performance art tends to close on Saturday night; *Tubes* is now

PLAYBILL®

ASTOR PLACE THEATRE

BLUE MAN GROUP TUBES

in its second year, and fully deserves its success. Michael Christofer won both the Pulitzer Prize and the Broadway Tony Award for *The Shadow Box,* a play about dying, in 1977; his newest work, ***Breaking Up,*** is also about dying, but of another sort: it's about the demise of a couple's "relationship." I put "relationship" in quotation marks, because it's the quotes that count here: "relationship" as word rather than as deed (or set of deeds); as definition rather than action (or set of actions). Steve and Alice (unless I missed something, their names are stated only in the program, not in the dialogue) are a not-quite-so-young couple: urbanish, demanding, compulsive, and unable to "commit"; but for recent headlines you'd naturally think Woody-Mia. As the title promises, we see Steve and Alice in the process of breaking apart, but we see them joining together as well: the play—which takes place in various bedrooms—is a virtual fugue of comings and goings. Christofer's topic is the problematic anomaly of the "couple" in a relativistic universe (it's Einstein, Marx, Freud, and Nietzsche against Dan and Marilyn Quayle), but, wisely, he moves into high comedy and ironic farce ("We were really in love; THAT didn't help. The love thing really did us in!") rather than the banal academizing we often get on this subject. Christofer has become a highly skilled dramaturge; he plays his tones deftly and with great professional skill. ***Breaking Up*** proves winsome and diverting throughout its intermission-less 90 minutes, and it might just give you a few moments' afterthought as well. The San Diego Old Globe production, which is the one I saw, is the third outing so far for the play, and one can expect more; it will be hard, though, to surpass the performances—by turns tentatively bouncy and wretchedly pained—of Jane Galloway and Jeffrey Hayenga in the two roles.

Readers might expect to read here of Wendy Wasserstein's widely acclaimed ***The Sisters Rosensweig*** at the tiny Mitzi Newhouse Theatre in Lincoln Center, but the show was completely sold out—and press tickets gobbled up—for the dates I was in New York in 1992. Fortunately, the play has re-opened on Broadway in the Spring of 1993, where it will be available for review in the next CLC edition. Add the Wasserstein play to the list, and it is clear that 1992 has been an enormously rich year for the American stage. A host of mature yet innovative playwrights (Wasserstein, Mamet, Wolfe, Wilson, Nelson, Guare, Schenkkan, Christofer, Kushner, Gardner, Finn, Simon), each represented by a major effort this year, speaks to a wonderfully fertile field. Revivals, splendid as they may be, will not soon dominate this bunch.

The Year in World Literature

by William Riggan

Several of the major European literatures enjoyed an excellent year in 1992, as did Asia and, to a somewhat lesser extent, Africa and the Near East. Particularly strong among the Europeans were the Germans and the French.

German

Leading the way among the German writers were the two towering figures of Günter Grass and the late Heinrich Böll. Despite a vow several years ago to forswear any further fiction writing, Grass issued a new novel in 1992, *Unkenrufe* (Eng. *The Call of the Toad*), again using, as in such earlier novels as *The Rat* and *The Flounder,* a grotesque but fantastically anthropomorphic creature as the central image in an imaginative narrative that decries the current state of the world in matters ecological, political, social, and moral. Set in Grass's native Danzig (or Gdańsk), like *The Rat* and *The Tin Drum,* the novel tracks the touching and amusingly old-fashioned late-life love affair between a stodgy German professor and a Polish art restorer who share a common dream of a Polish-German Cemetery Association which will bring about a certain post-Cold War reconciliation between East and West by allowing the many disenfranchised former Easterners a final resting place in native soil. Grass derives a good deal of humor from this quaintly idealistic idea, as the project mushrooms beyond all expectations and reason to incorporate time-share condominiums, golf courses, nature retreats, and even "tasteful" mass graves for those families unable to afford individualized plots. "Toad calls" in German are prophecies of doom, and the ominous presence of various kinds of toads throughout the novel—in the background, smashed on roadways, in photographs and literature, as the objects of nature outings—add an undercurrent of warning and menace to the satiric fun the author seems to be having with his elderly lovers and their romantic project, much as Grass in real life has constantly railed and warned against the ongoing attempts at German-German and European-wide unification.

From Böll came what would have been his first full-fledged novel, had he ignored the advice of older colleagues and editors and published it upon its completion in 1949. *Der Engel schwieg* (The Angel Fell Silent) paints a grim but open-ended and not wholly pessimistic picture of daily life in Cologne amid the immediate aftermath of World War II, as one family of six try to put back together the pieces of their small world and get on with their lives, loves, and careers and rediscover or refashion their various ambitions and dreams despite the recent traumas of wartime and the lingering hatred, guilt, and disillusionment engendered by National Socialism and the war. Appearing as it does seven years after Böll's death, the novel is a literary event of uncommon interest to many readers and critics, with its strong foreshadowings of themes, conflicts, characters, and techniques which were later to appear with such mastery and force in the major works on which the author's Nobel Prize-winning career was to rest.

Jurek Becker's latest novel, *Amanda herzlos* (Heartless Amanda), drew raves for its innovative and lively interweaving of three narratives by the heroine's three successive lovers over the last decade: a young newspaper editor, who spells out his story in great detail to his attorney; a blacklisted East German writer, who has written a novella about his seven-year affair with Amanda, only to have it both erased from his computer by his ten-year-old son and confiscated by the authorities as he naïvely tries to mail it to a publisher in the Federal Republic; and a reporter from the West, who marries Amanda and moves with her back to Hamburg in 1989 just before the crumbling of the Wall and the reunification of the two Germanies. Other highlights of the year included the poet-novelist Christoph Meckel's new novel, *Shalamun's Papiere* (Shalamun's Papers), the convoluted sequel to his futuristic 1990 fantasy *Die Messingstadt* (The Brass City); *Der Fuchs war damals schon der Jäger* (The Fox Was the Hunter Even Then) by Herta Müller, a darkly riveting account of life, love, fear, betrayal, and survival during the final years of the communist dictatorship in Romania; *Die Goldenen Heiligen oder Columbus entdeckt Europa* (The Golden Saints or Columbus Discovers Europe), Herbert Rosendorfer's imaginative contribution to the worldwide glut of works commemorating the quincentennial of Columbus's first voyage to the New World, here turning that now-legendary event on its head by having advanced and brutally destructive extraterrestrials "discover" the declining, used-up, AIDS-ridden, "primitive" Europe of the 1990s; and the wise and witty sketchbook of everyday "calendar stories" *Im toten Winkel* (loosely, "On Dead Ground") by the East German émigré poet and prose writer Günter Kunert.

French

The past and the world beyond France's borders figured large in several of the year's best French books. The historian Max Gallo's novel *La Fontaine des Innocents* uses the famed Renaissance fountain in Paris's Place des Halles and the New Testament-era slaughter which it commemorates as both setting and emblem for its vast, episodic study of modern society's gradual deterioration through the continuing destructive clash of milieus, classes, and values; not inappropriately, given its sweep and detail as well as its general theme and tone, the novel carries the Balzacian subtitle *Scènes de la vie parisienne fin de siècle* (Scenes of Parisian Life at the End of the Century). Madeleine Chapsal also reworks Balzac in *La femme abandonnée* (The Abandoned Woman), updating an identically titled short story by the nineteenth-century master in a manner which reflects the vast differences between the two ages not only in love relationships but also in matters of style, attitude, and sensibility; the experiment, in the judgment of most critics and readers, ultimately fails and only reinforces the greatness of the model on which the work is based. The single-named novelist Rezvani retreated yet another century into the past for his model and came up with a delightful updating of Diderot's *Rêve de D'Alembert* (D'Alembert's Dream) titled *La traversée des Monts Noirs* (Crossing the Black Mountains), an account of a modern-day ornithologists' convention in Russia which spins a wonderfully complex and entertaining story of crossed loves and intrigues mixed with profound and genuinely provocative speculations on the cosmos, the nature of birds and humans, and the question of freedom versus predestination. *La révolte à deux sous* (The Two-Penny Revolt) by Bernard Clavel recounts the tragic course of a weavers' strike and ultimately failed uprising in Lyon during the French Revolution. Emmanuel Roblès's *L'herbe des ruines* (Grass Among the Ruins) draws from both today's headlines and the annals of twentieth-century European history for its tale of love and passion and flesh versus soul, set against a backdrop of the atrocities of war and totalitarianism and written in a now-realistic, now-allegorical manner vaguely reminiscent of such classics as *The Plague* by Albert Camus.

Patrick Grainville's *Colère* (Anger) immerses its young hero Damien (and the reader) in the colorful and often beautiful but also very dangerous underworld of modern-day Rio as he pursues his elusive object of desire, the lovely and dedicated teacher and social worker Marine. The late Hervé Guibert's final novel, *Le paradis* (Paradise), uses voyages to Mali, Bora-Bora, and Martinique as the framework for a searing evocation of the ill-fated love affair between the young narrator and his now-deceased lover, Jayne, in an effort somehow both to understand her death and their brief life together and to find some sense of significance and transcendence in the entire devastating experience. Canadian-born Anne Hébert creates a mystery-laden, fantastic fairy tale in *L'enfant chargé de songes* (The Child Full of Dreams), replete with such archetypal figures as the Valkyrie-like horsewoman (and horse thief) Lydie and set largely within the primeval Canadian forest and on vast landscapes under seemingly endless skies where the natural world blends seamlessly with the supernatural. Pierre-Jean Remy's *Algérie, bords de Seine* (Algeria Along the Seine) divides its attention between the French capital and the former North African colony as it presents its account of a younger generation discovering the absurdity and horror of a war which not only could but should have been avoided by their elders. Amin Maalouf's somewhat programmatic novel about women's rights and powers, *Le premier siècle après Béatrice* (The First Century After Beatrice), looks two decades into the future to a time when a certain fertility powder has produced such a preponderance of males among all species that the resulting imbalance in nature may soon depopulate the world unless more people—like the right-thinking narrator—opt for daughters and recapture the feminine and maternal side of their humanity. And the Lebanese-Egyptian native Andrée Chedid gathered seventeen of her superb short stories of the last decade under the title *A la mort, à la vie* (To Death, to Life).

Russian

Four works of fiction and two of nonfiction highlighted the year in Russian letters. *Little Jinx* by Abram Tertz (pseudonym of Andrei Sinyavsky), originally published in 1980 in the émigré author's adopted homeland of France, made its official debuts in both his native Russia and in English translation in 1992. A bitter and darkly humorous fable about a dwarfish second-rate writer named Sinyavsky who inadvertently brings ill fortune and even death to siblings and friends alike, the work is on the one hand an internalized account of the fear and loathing heaped upon the author's own head in the sixties and seventies, when he was jailed and later exiled for "slandering" the Soviet Union and socialism, and on the other hand a hopeful philosophic treatise ultimately implying that today's pariah may well become tomorrow's savior. Victor Erofeyev's ambitiously complex postmodernist novel *Russkaia krasavitsa* (Eng. *Russian Beauty*), written a decade ago but published only in 1990 in Russian and now in translation, tracks the course of a Dostoevskian heroine, the sullied beauty Irina Tarakanova, through a series of affairs, scandals, and atonements in the unabashedly materialistic milieu of "cosmonauts, ambassadors, and underworld millionaires" of the late 1970s and early 1980s. The style is a postmodernist amalgam of the literary, the colloquial, the analytic, the digressively folksy, and the streetwise crude, and the unblinking description of the squalor of the Russian provinces recalls a string of classic writers extending back to the masterful Nikolai Gogol. These qualities, plus the book's raw and very un-Soviet indulgence in sex in a dizzying variety of combinations, easily sparked one of the biggest public outcries in years among the Russian reading public.

Tatyana Tolstaya's second collection of short stories, *Sleepwalker in a Fog,* has been garnering praise similar to that enjoyed by her earlier collection, *On the Golden Porch,* for the elegant musicality of its prose, the apparent timelessness of its themes, the mordancy of its wit, and the spontaneity and exuberance of its imaginative style, both in the new volume's two longer novellas and in its many shorter pieces. *Fear,* the successor to Anatoly Rybakov's much-discussed 1985 novel *Children of the Arbat,* continued the author's Tolstoyan investigation of the Stalinist purges of the 1930s and their aftermath, this time following the intersecting lives and careers of five young people who came of age in the late twenties and early thirties, one of them an ambitious young careerist in the NKVD (the predecessor of the KGB). Alternating with this story line is a series of historical sketches depicting the thoughts, conversations, and activities of several historical personages, including political leaders, secret-police chiefs and interrogators, and no less a figure than Stalin himself.

Andrei Bitov added the attribute of travel writer to his reputation as one of his country's leading novelists, producing in *A Captive of the Caucasus* an inspired, deeply thoughtful, and wholly engrossing account not only of his extended residence in Armenia but—as in the best travel writing, à la Bruce Chatwin or Paul Theroux—of his own personal voyage of self-discovery as well. And the ninety-year-old Nina Berberova surveyed more than six decades of Russian cultural and sociopolitical life in her memoir *The Italics Are Mine,* ranging in time and place from St. Petersburg of the early 1920s, to Paris of the late 1930s and the war years, to America of the fifties and sixties, and touching on such greats as Gorky, Pasternak, Bunin, Nabokov, and Roman Jakobson—though the portraits are often as vicious as they are revealing of both the subject and the memoirist herself.

Eastern Europe

From Eastern Europe came several notable new books in 1992. The 1980 Nobel laureate, the Polish poet and essayist Czesław Miłosz, issued two new works during the year. *Provinces,* the English edition of his 1990 collection *Dalsze okolice* (Regions Farther Away), is a remarkably vigorous and clearsighted performance for the octogenarian author as he meditates on such themes as youth and mortality, the redemptive powers of language, the solace of compassion and beauty, and the nature of "the human." In *Beginning with My Streets* Miłosz returns to the Lithuania of his childhood and youth in Vilnius and proceeds from there to discuss, through both essays and letters, a variety of topics, including time and ephemerality, nationalism and religion, a number of his friends and acquaintances over the years, and several literary figures and authors who in some way touched his own life and work. The Romanian writer Norman Manea, like Miłosz and Berberova now a resident of the U. S., made his debut in English with two recent works: *On Clowns,* subtitled "The Dictator and the Artist," comprises a series of essays relating directly to life in Romania under the Ceausescu regime; and *October, Eight O'Clock* is a single narrative loosely divided into several separate tales, all set in the labor camps of Romania and the Ukraine during World War II and altogether possessed of such distinction and linguistic richness as to evoke among European critics comparisons with the likes of Kafka, Musil, and Bruno Schulz—extraordinarily high praise indeed. *My Golden Trades* gathers a goodly number of the Czech writer Ivan Klíma's pre-1989 stories into a single volume for Western readers; all the selections recount in an autobiographical first-person voice the writer-protagonist's experiences in such "trades" as smuggler, painter, archeologist, and (in a bow to his Prague predecessor, Kafka) surveyor and generally eschew the expected heavily political concerns for a gentler and more general advocacy of such causes as environmental decay and declining spiritual values. *A Hungarian Romance* by Ágnes Hankiss reaches back four centuries in Hungary's turbulent history to a time when the country's independence has been lost to corrupt foreign powers, telling a story of love and intrigue that casts a revealing light on recent events in Hungary and challenges age-old assumptions about men and women, language, and history itself. Hankiss's countryman Imre Kertész was at long last introduced to the Western reading public through the translation of his 1975 novel *Sorstalanság* as *Fateless,* the harrowing, single-minded, and only lightly fictionalized account of the author's boyhood survival of wartime work camps as well as Auschwitz and Buchenwald. The work has been drawing favorable comparisons with kindred accounts by authors such as Italy's Primo Levi and Czechoslovakia's Arnošt Lustig. Péter Lengyel produced perhaps

the first major literary assessment of post-1989 life in the former Soviet block with *Holnapelött* (The Day Before Tomorrow), subtitled "A "Non-Novel" but in fact creating a postmodernistic novelistic unity out of some twenty-odd discrete "chapters" whose fragmented state is evidently intended to bolster the work's reflection of the continuing tumult and uncertainty that mark life in the East even today. Farther north, the superb Estonian novelist Jaan Kross made his long-overdue debut in English with *The Czar's Madman,* a carefully crafted, thoughtful, and deeply moving novel presented in the form of a diary kept by the peasant's son Jakob Mattik but focused principally on Jakob's brother-in-law, the Baron Timo von Bock, an actual historical personage who was a confidant of Czar Alexander I charged with the responsibility of always telling his ruler the whole truth in all things—a task which Timo discharged so well that he incurred official disfavor and spent nine years in prison (as the author himself did in the 1940s).

Other European and American Literatures

Three of Portugal's best fiction writers were made more widely available in the English-speaking world in 1992. António Lobo Antunes, already known to many readers outside Portugal through the 1983 appearance of the novel *South of Nowhere,* bolstered his reputation with *An Explanation of the Birds,* creating as his protagonist an introverted academic and privileged, dilettantish radical whose failed and irresolute life leads him ultimately to suicide on a deserted beach—a death that is suspended for over 200 pages by various postmodernist narrative devices until finally the poor fellow expires amid a swarm of shrieking, wing-beating birds eager to feast on his corpulent body. In *The Year of the Death of Ricardo Reis* the prizewinning novelist José Saramago takes as his hero one of the three fictitious "heteronyms" of the famed Portuguese poet Fernando Pessoa. Reis has returned on impulse to Portugal from Brazil in late 1935 upon hearing of Pessoa's death, attempts to familiarize himself with the country he has not seen in sixteen years, takes up with two women, and soon encounters the shade of Pessoa, magically freed from the grave for a period of nine months. The total effect is an odd but successful blend of magic realism and scathing satire on the fascist rhetoric prevalent in both Portugal (under Salazar) and through much of Europe in the midthirties. The masterful octogenarian storyteller Miguel Torga made his debut in English in 1992 with the collection *Tales from the Mountain,* which dates to 1941 but was suppressed for four decades by the Salazar regime. The stories are set in the author's northern Portugal homeland of Trás-os-Montes, a province "beyond the mountains" where "a timeless dimension of human interaction with the land, tradition, and custom gives shape to tales that exemplify universals of human experience and values."

The prolific Brazilian novelist Jorge Amado's 1944 novel *The Golden Harvest* made its long-delayed appearance in English in 1992; set among the cacao boom and bust of the 1930s in the province of Bahia, the work dramatizes the plantation workers' plight and the viciousness of the free-market system in its devastation of so many lives and fortunes but does so in a remarkably undidactic and vividly entertaining fashion, as is the famed writer's wont. And Chilean-born Isabel Allende, famed for *House of the Spirits* and *Eva Luna,* brought out **El plan infinito** (The Infinite Plan), a family chronicle and social history set mostly in the southwestern United States and ranging from the Depression to the eighties. As always, Allende spins a great yarn, here in fact a series of yarns, as she moves variously into the skin and voice of a part-Anglo (but barrio-raised) male and a Chicana who rises from poverty to success as a jewelry designer, evoking all the while a rich gallery of side characters, including an itinerant preacher in the 1930s and a sage, aged padre in 1980s Los Angeles.

Africa

Leading the year's harvest from Africa were three works in English and four in French. **From Zia with Love** is the latest in a long line of plays by 1986 Nobel Prize winner Wole Soyinka dealing with the discourse of politics and power in postcolonial Nigeria. In this case the triggering incident is the killing of several drug peddlers in the mid-1980s following the enactment of a harsh retroactive decree, viewed by many as a national disgrace in the absolute disregard for basic human rights shown by the series of military dictatorships which promoted it; the dire consequences of such actions are implicit in the title's evocation of the late Pakistani leader Zia al-Haq. As always in recent decades, Soyinka ably incorporates music and dance in a presentation that is as entertaining and visually and aurally rich as it is dramatically dexterous and effective in portraying the the infantility of "leaders" prattling over trivial matters and issuing outrageous decrees. **Ancestral Voices** by South Africa's Etienne van Heerden traces five generations of an Afrikaner farm family in the eastern Cape in exhaustive and revealing detail and Old Testament scope and weight. And Chenjerai Hove of Zimbabwe followed up his award-winning 1990 novel *Bones* with **Shadows,** the story of two innocent young lovers caught up in a world of poverty and harsh colonial law where people have little or no control over their own lives.

Tahar Ben Jelloun of Algeria, winner of France's coveted Goncourt Prize in 1987, brought out **L'ange aveugle** (The Blind Angel), a collection of fourteen poignant, gripping short stories set in southern Italy and Sicily and together constituting chapters of a single "novel about the mafia" (the working title of the still-uncompleted work) and its pervasive reach into every aspect of life in these regions. Six stories by the late Algerian/Berber author Mouloud Mammeri (deemed the undisputed founding father of Francophone Algerian literature) from the years 1953-81 were collectively issued for the first time in book form as **Escales** (Ports of Call); their common thread is contact, whether between two individuals or two cultures, much as in real life the author extolled his native Berber culture while simultaneously using the French language as "an absolutely indispensable instrument of expression which translates us infinitely more than it betrays us." The outstanding Senegalese writer and filmmaker Sembène Ousmane saw two of his recent novellas disseminated via English translation as **Niiwam and Taaw,** both richly evocative of the daily life of the poor in Dakar; in one an old

man transports his son's body by bus to a distant cemetery for dressing and burial, enduring all manner of humiliations and difficulties while en route; in the other a tyrannical father makes life miserable for his family, particularly his academically gifted son and his resourceful young second wife, who ultimately shames and repudiates him publicly for his years of abuse. Henri Lopes of the Congo presented in **Sur l'autre rive** (On the Other Shore) the lyric and mysterious tale of a young Caribbean woman's long "internal voyage" back to Africa, to the banks of the Congo in Gabon, where she at last begins to fathom her origins and heritage and to gain some sense of what the future holds for her.

Middle East

Sugar Street, the third and final installment of *The Cairo Trilogy* by Egypt's 1988 Nobel Prize winner Naguib Mahfouz, presents a bitter and pessimistic yet vital and wonderfully readable Dickensian account of the unraveling and decline of the aging patriarch Ahmad Abd al-Jawad's family through the 1940s, its completion coinciding with the ascent to power of Gamel Abdel Nasser in 1952. Also appearing for the first time in English was Mahfouz's 1983 novel **The Journey of Ibn Fattouma,** an allegorical and experimental work based on the *Rihlat,* the noted travel narrative of the fourteenth-century Moroccan author Ibn Battuta. Cast in a florid medieval style and language, the account takes its eponymous narrator-protagonist through a series of representative lands and cultures illustrating various political, social, and religious alternatives and also marking discrete stages of life from birth to death. It is an interesting and significant effort but is generally adjudged one of the writer's less successful works of the last twenty years. Mahfouz's countrywoman Ahdaf Soueif took the unusual route of writing her massive and extremely impressive novel **In the Eye of the Sun** directly in English, telling an extraordinary tale of sexual politics focusing on the Egyptian-born and -raised, English-educated and -resettled Asya Ulama and spanning both the traditional Arab world (Egypt) and the modern-day West (England) and the overcoming of barriers not only physical and geographic but emotional and existential as well. The Egyptian woman physician Nawal El Saadawi, most noted for her trailblazing 1983 novel *Woman at Point Zero,* brought out a potentially controversial new work, **Jannât wa-Iblîs** (Jannat and Iblis; the names, however, mean "Paradises" and "Devil" respectively), which foregrounds and questions religion in a manner that may remind some of *The Satanic Verses;* both characters are inmates in an oppressive mental asylum, and through the account of their brutal treatment and the many flashbacks to their victimized, repressive, and misogynistic past, the traditional and religious concepts of good and evil are completely subverted; in the end Jannat's memory is "cured" through the complete obliteration of her memory, and Iblis is slain by the asylum director (known as God) in an ill-advised escape attempt.

The Lebanese-born Hanan al-Shaykh, rated by many as the Arab world's finest woman writer, brought out **Women of Sand and Myrrh,** a set of four intertwined first-person narratives that together paint a poetic yet hard-edged portrait of a wealthy Arab country whose women, even among the rich and privileged, are forced to remain hidden behind veils yet nevertheless find outlets that permit them to survive psychologically. *Mr. Mani* by the Israeli novelist Avraham B. Yehoshua made its much-awaited appearance in English, ingeniously and movingly tracing a history of exile and periodic return through six generations of a single Jewish family from 1982 backward to the middle of the eighteenth century. What one reads or hears are five one-sided conversations which brilliantly invoke not only the five speakers' distinct personalities and those of their unheard interlocutors but also five distinct Mr. Manis, from Efrayim Mani, a soldier in the Israeli army in Lebanon, and his father, the Jerusalem judge Gavriel Mani, all the way back to Avraham Mani, confessing a grievous sin to his dying rabbi and mentor in 1848 Athens, and Avraham's father Yosef Mani, a successful cavalry supplier in the Turkish Empire of the late 1700s and early 1800s. In *Katerina* the Hebrew writer Aharon Appelfeld reimagines his native region of Bukovina (in what is now the border region between Hungary and Romania), telling the moving story of a runaway young gentile woman who finds first shelter and charity among the Jews she had so long loathed and feared, then later true spiritual peace following protracted and bitter trials, including pogroms, rejection by her own people, and a lengthy prison term for murder.

Asia

Two younger writers led China's literary production in 1992. Han Shaogong's *Homecoming? and Other Stories* revealed a mid-1980s shift from social realism to an experimental style heavily indebted to García Márquez and Kundera, among others, yet continued the author's obsession with Chinese history and tradition in his search for the causes of the spiritual void left in his nation by the Cultural Revolution. In the title story, for example, a young man passing through a remote mountain village is mistaken for a city youth sent down to the village during the Cultural Revolution and suspected of the murder of a local bully; the longer the protagonist lets matters go without clearing up the confusion, the more surreal the situation becomes, reaching a point where he even thinks he recalls events from the life of the other youth and grows ever more unsure of his own identity. *Brocade Valley* by Wang Anyi offered a trilogy of lyric, intimate novellas on the shocking (for China) theme of women involved in extramarital affairs, becoming a best seller and effectively ex-

ploding the sexual puritanism that has characterized official Chinese writing for decades.

Japan's preeminent novelist Kenzaburô Ôe brought out two new works in 1992. *Boku ga hontô ni wakakatta koro* (When I was Truly Young) is a seemingly autobiographical novel about a college student still only *thinking* of writing novels but also a probing into the depths of time, memory, guilt, and the unconscious, spurred by the tragic death of a college classmate some thirty-five years earlier. *Jinsei no shûkan* (The Habit of Being) gathered ten essays and lectures from the last five years, all dealing with the conflict between "central" power and "peripheral" culture and centering on such topics as the 1989 coronation of Japan's new emperor and illness and deformity as a determining cultural and literary theme, both in Ôe's own work and generally. More of the noted classic postwar Japanese writer Osamu Dazai's superbly crafted stories made their first appearance in English in *Blue Bamboo: Tales of Fantasy and Romance.* The popular Ryu Murakami (no relation to the even more famous Haruki Murakami) added to his fifteen-year stream of humorously provocative best-selling novels and stories with *69,* an alternately cynical and hilarious roman à clef about coming of age in the late 1960s, when baby-boomers felt they really could change the world before it changed them. And "Banana mania" finally made its way into English with the translation of Banana Yoshimoto's wildly successful 1988 novella *Kitchen,* a smart and knowing look at the world of the contemporary young Japanese woman; a more poignant and intense treatment of that subject is found in "Moonlight Shadow," a novella included in the same volume.

The best of the year's production on the Indian subcontinent was *Cracking India* by Bapsi Sidhwa, a brief and seemingly simple novel (it is narrated by a little girl from a well-off Parsee family in Lahore, now in Pakistan) about the 1947 India-Pakistan partition that proves astonishingly moving in conveying the horrors, the suffering, and the tragedy visited upon so many millions as a consequence of that event. And lastly, from Duong Thu Huong came *Paradise of the Blind,* a richly detailed and wholly unsentimental evocation of the author's native Vietnam in the 1980s which focuses on the very modernized young woman, Hang, and her traditionalist mother, a food peddler, but also offers fully drawn portraits of other relatives and characters both urban and rural, both young and old, to convey an enormous variety of contemporary Vietnamese life-styles.

Notes on Contributors

Robert Cohen is Professor of Drama at the University of California, Irvine, and the author of the recent *Acting in Shakespeare*. He has written several well-known theatre texts and treatises, including *Theatre, Giraudoux: Three Faces of Destiny, Acting Power, Acting One, Acting Professionally, Creative Play Direction,* and *Eight Plays for Theatre*. He contributes essays to various academic and theatre journals and has reviewed "The Year in Drama" for *Contemporary Literary Criticism* since 1986. A professional stage director as well, Cohen is co-artistic director of Theatre 40 in Los Angeles and a regular guest director at the Colorado and Utah Shakespeare Festivals. He holds his Doctorate in Fine Arts from the Yale School of Drama and has lectured widely on theatrical topics in the U.S. and abroad.

Dean Flower teaches modern fiction, American literature, and short story writing at Smith College in Northampton, Massachusetts. He has reviewed fiction for the *Hudson Review* since 1976 and currently serves as advisory editor for that journal. Flower's essays and reviews have also appeared in the *New York Times Book Review,* the *New England Quarterly,* the *Massachusetts Review, Essays in Criticism,* and *Boston Review*. The author of monographs on Henry James and nineteenth-century painting, Flower has also edited several anthologies, including *Henry David Thoreau: Essays, Journals, and Poems*.

Allen Hoey is the author of *A Fire in the Cold House of Being*, a verse collection which was chosen by Galway Kinnell for the 1985 Camden Poetry Award. An Associate Professor in the Department of Language and Literature at Bucks County Community College, Hoey has contributed poems and reviews to such publications as the *Georgia Review,* the *Hudson Review,* the *Ohio Review, Poetry, Southern Humanities Review,* and the *Southern Review*. He holds an M. A. and D. A. from the English Department of Syracuse University. *What Persists,* a collection of his poetry, was published in 1992.

William Riggan is Associate Editor of *World Literature Today* at the University of Oklahoma, with responsibilities for coverage of Third World, Slavic, Anglo-American, and smaller European literatures. He holds a doctorate in comparative literature from Indiana University, is the author of *Picaros, Madmen, Naïfs, and Clowns: The Unreliable First-Person Narrator,* has written extensively on the history and selections of both the Nobel Prize in Literature and the Neustadt International Prize in Literature, and regularly reviews new foreign fiction and poetry for several journals and newspapers.

New Authors

Cristina Garcia
Dreaming in Cuban

Garcia is a Cuban-born American journalist and novelist, born in 1959.

INTRODUCTION

Praised for its poignant depiction of women who struggle to regain a sense of personal and cultural identity in the aftermath of political upheaval, *Dreaming in Cuban* chronicles the irrevocable effects of the Cuban revolution on the del Pino family from the 1930s to the early 1980s. The novel focuses primarily on three maternally related women of Cuban heritage, each of whom perceives her history and culture differently. While Celia, the matriarch of the del Pino family, has become disillusioned as a result of an unrequited love affair and an unhappy marriage, she derives a sense of strength and hope from the Communist revolution to which she dedicates her life. The revolution, however, is also a divisive and alienating force within the family. Celia's daughter Lourdes fiercely rejects communism and moves to New York, where she embraces capitalism and achieves success as the owner of a bakery. Generational estrangement is perpetuated as Lourdes's daughter, Pilar, similarly repudiates her mother's belief in the American dream and mourns her lost Cuban identity and heritage. Garcia has garnered praise for her lyrical prose style, use of shifting time frames and narrative voices, and vivid blend of realism and dream-like hallucination. Michiko Kakutani commented: "Fierce, visionary, and at the same time oddly beguiling and funny, *Dreaming in Cuban* is a completely original novel. It announces the debut of a writer, blessed with a poet's ear for language, a historian's fascination with the past and a musician's intuitive understanding of the ebb and flow of emotion."

CRITICISM

Michiko Kakutani   (review date 25 February 1992)

[*In the following review, Kakutani commends Garcia's sensitive examination of political and spiritual exile in* Dreaming in Cuban.]

In Cristina Garcia's dazzling first novel [*Dreaming in Cuban*], three generations of women dream about Cuba.

Their birthplace haunts their memories and reveries, shapes their hopes and ambitions. For Celia del Pino, the matriarch of the clan, Cuba means both separation from her lover in Spain and the promise of revolutionary changes. She has waited for Fulgencio Batista's departure and cheered the ascension of Fidel Castro (or El Líder as she calls him) and she sees herself as "part of a great historical unfolding."

For Celia's daughter, Lourdes, who was raped by a revolutionary soldier, Cuba is a prison, a Communist pigsty. "She wants no part of Cuba, no part of its wretched carnival floats creaking with lies, no part of Cuba at all." She is happy in New York, where she cherishes the winter weather: "the cold scraping sounds on sidewalks and windshields, the ritual of scarves and gloves, hats and zip-in coat linings."

For Lourdes's daughter, Pilar, however, Cuba represents the childhood garden she's been exiled from since she was a little girl. She dreams about her grandmother, Celia, whom she left behind in Cuba, and she dreams about the country's hot paradisal sun, the green of its landscape and her grandmother's wicker swing overlooking the sea.

"Most days Cuba is kind of dead to me," says Pilar.

> But every once in a while a wave of longing will hit me and it's all I can do not to hijack a plane to Havana or something. I resent the hell out of the politicians and the generals who force events on us that structure our lives, that dictate the memories we'll have when we're old. Every day Cuba fades a little more inside me, my grandmother fades a little more inside me. And there's only my imagination where our history should be.

Shifting gears effortlessly between Pilar's angry, irreverent and often very funny reminiscences and the more lyrical, languid recollections of her grandmother, Ms. Garcia stands revealed in this novel as a magical new writer. It is remarkable that this is a first novel: it is even more remarkable that Ms. Garcia achieves in her debut what many more experienced writers never even attempt. She has tackled the large historical theme of political and spiritual exile in this book, using the much abused form of the family epic, and she has produced a work that possesses both the intimacy of a Chekhov story and the hallucinatory magic of a novel by Gabriel García Márquez. Though one is dazzled by the book's small fireworks of imagery, though one stops to marvel at some of the fantastic events that bloom on its pages, the reader is never distracted from the gripping story of its extraordinary heroines and the passions that bind and separate them from one another and the country of their birth.

The story begins back in the 1930's. Pre-Castro Cuba, in Celia's mind, is "a pathetic place, a parody of a country," but her attention is consumed by an intense love affair with a Spanish lawyer named Gustavo. Within months, Gustavo returns to his wife in Spain and Celia takes to her bed, feverish and mad with grief. Although she agrees to marry another suitor, a businessman by the name of Jorge del Pino, she will continue to write Gustavo love letters: once a month for the next 25 years.

Celia contemplates running away to Spain, but she soon finds herself pregnant with her first child, Lourdes. The pregnancy seems to heighten her despair, her sense of entrapment. Her husband sends her off to an asylum, and leaves on a series of lengthy business trips. Celia becomes pregnant again, and names her second child Felicia, after a friend in the asylum, who killed her husband by dousing him with gasoline and setting him afire. It is an ill-omened choice of names, and Felicia, in time, will uncannily fulfill her fate.

Indeed, Felicia inherits both her mother's susceptibility to emotional disorder and her taste for impossible men. She begins to practice black magic, and eventually marries a swaggering merchant sailor, who gives her syphilis and three children. One hot summer day, Felicia decides to murder him: the flaming towel soaked in hot oil that she throws at him disfigures his sensual face. Felicia's twin daughters, Luz and Milagro, drift off into a world of their

> Ms. Garcia stands revealed in [*Dreaming in Cuban*] as a magical new writer. . . . She has tackled the large historical theme of political and spiritual exile in this book, using the much-abused form of the family epic, and she has produced a work that possesses both the intimacy of a Chekhov story and the hallucinatory magic of a novel by Gabriel García Márquez.
>
> —*Michiko Kakutani*

own; her son, Ivanito, becomes a gangly, timid child who listens to the radio, dreaming of America and Wolfman Jack.

After the Communist takeover, Felicia's sister, Lourdes, leaves for America with her shy, ineffectual husband and their daughter, Pilar. Lourdes curses El Líder for taking over Cuba, and she curses her mother for supporting El Líder. She vows to reinvent herself in America, and soon becomes the successful proprietor of a chain of Yankee Doodle bakeries. From time to time, she sends her mother snapshots of her pastries. "Each glistening éclair," writes Ms. Garcia, "is a grenade aimed at Celia's political beliefs, each strawberry shortcake proof—in butter, cream and eggs—of Lourdes's success in America, and a reminder of the ongoing shortages in Cuba."

Pilar, who mocks her mother's belief that she can "fight Communism from behind her bakery counter," fumes about her parents' reactionary politics, and plots her own return to Cuba. Art school, college, punk rock, romances with a succession of young men: the pieces of her life in America will fall into place, she thinks, if only she can return home and see her grandmother again. In fact, it is through Pilar's efforts that the family will once again be reunited in Cuba, and their years of solitary dreaming will come to an end.

Fierce, visionary, and at the same time oddly beguiling and funny, *Dreaming in Cuban* is a completely original novel. It announces the debut of a writer, blessed with a poet's ear for language, a historian's fascination with the past and a musician's intuitive understanding of the ebb and flow of emotion.

> Michiko Kakutani, "The Dreams and Yearnings of a Family of Exiles," in The New York Times, *February 25, 1992, p. C17.*

Alan West (review date 1 March 1992)

[*Below, West praises Garcia's finely drawn characters, lyrical narrative style, and vivid depiction of painful aspects of Cuba's history in* Dreaming in Cuban.]

Cuba's history can be viewed in many ways, but unquestionably it is a story filled with separations, exiles, longings, dreams realized or dashed. They began long before

Castro's ascent to power in 1959: Jose Marti, Cuba's most revered figure, spent much of his adult life away from the island; Alejo Carpentier, its most distinguished novelist, likewise. But the Revolution threw many families into disarray as the political realities forced them to make choices that became irreversible, whether the choice was exile, trying to be neutral (an impossibility), or staying on to join the Western Hemisphere's first socialist experiment. Cristina Garcia's first novel, **Dreaming in Cuban,** captures the pain, the distance, the frustrations and the dreams of these family dramas with a vivid, poetic prose and considerable good humor.

The axis of the novel is the women of the del Pino family, particularly Celia, the *fidelista* matriarch who remains in Cuba, and her punk-rebellious, American-artist granddaughter, Pilar. For Pilar, her grandmother Celia is a guardian spirit, holding a missing link in her emotional jigsaw puzzle. For Celia, Pilar will be her memory and that of the family. In between the two are Lourdes (Celia's daughter and Pilar's mother), who wears a size 26, is a rabid anticommunist and whose insatiability wears out her husband, Rufino Puente; and Lourdes's sister, Felicia, who is deranged, has disastrous luck with men and is captivated by *santeria,* Cuba's blend of Catholicism and traditional Yoruba religion.

Garcia deftly shifts the narrative from third to first person, mixing in a series of Celia's letters to her long-lost Spanish lover, Gustavo. Likewise, she shifts from the past to the present, from Brooklyn to Havana, from character to character caught in the web that blood and history have set up for them, often with cruel irony. Celia is a case in point. Although she was married to Jorge del Pino, her true love was Gustavo, a Spaniard she wrote to for 25 years without response, until Pilar was born, 11 days after the triumph of the Revolution.

She never saw much of her husband, who later emigrated to the U.S., ostensibly for health reasons. Celia stays on and dedicates her life to Fidel and the Revolution. Despite her commitment to social change, her life is difficult: scorned by her in-laws, a daughter and grandchild in exile, the other daughter (Felicia) mad, suicidal and possibly homicidal, and her son gone to live in Czechoslovakia. A feeling beyond loneliness, reaching a volatile mixture of separation and death, pounds gently away at her, like the waves she looks at from her balcony in Santa Teresa del Mar.

Pilar, on the other hand, is always trying to bridge the distances (political, geographical, emotional, cultural) between her and Celia. It isn't easy, given her quarrelsome relationship with her mother, her youth and inexperience and the political realities of the Revolution and the exile community. (Exiles were not allowed to even visit Cuba until the late '70s). But even Pilar knows that her reunion with Celia in Cuba will not solve everything:

> I've started dreaming in Spanish, which has never happened before . . . I could happily stay on one of those wrought-iron balconies for days or keep my grandmother company on her porch . . . I'm afraid to lose all of this, to lose Abuela Celia again. But sooner or later I'd have

to return to New York. I know now it's where I belong—not *instead* of here, but *more* than here. How can I tell my grandmother this?

Despite the humor, the finely etched characters (only Pilar is a bit too precocious for credibility, at times), the easy, lyrical flow of the narrative, this is a bittersweet novel that leaves a reader with a tender, but clinging sadness. And that sadness is made even stronger by the deadly uncertainties that Cuba continues to live through.

> *Alan West, "So Near and Yet So Far," in* Book World—The Washington Post, *March 1, 1992, p. 9.*

Richard Eder   (review date 12 March 1992)

[*Eder is a Pulitzer Prize-winning American film, drama, and literary critic. In the following review, he comments on Garcia's interweaving of realistic and magical elements in* Dreaming in Cuban.]

Ninety miles is a distance, but there is a country where it is an identity, a syndrome that governs like a climate. Poor Cuba, the saying goes, so far from God and so close to the United States.

Those 90 turquoise miles are the subject of Cristina Garcia's poignant and perceptive first novel, **Dreaming in Cuban.** It tells of a family divided politically and geographically by the Cuban revolution.

It tells of the generational fissures that open subsequently on each side. In Cuba, between a grandmother who is a fervent Castro supporter and a daughter who retreats into an Afro-Cuban *santeria* cult; in America, between another daughter, militantly anti-Castro, and her own rebellious punk-artist daughter, who mocks her obsession.

And it tells of the ghostly ties that tug on all of them, like a guillotined body that wanders in search of its severed head.

The story of Celia del Pino, her husband, Jorge, and their three children and four grandchildren flutters back and forth from the mid-1930s to 1980. It is told in a mix of realism and dreamy hallucination.

Cuban history—its unnatural closeness to the United States until 1958, and its unnatural separation ever since—is a wound; and the wound breeds fever and delusion.

The realism is exquisite; the magical elements are more problematic. They are thematically and emotionally effective, but sometimes Garcia, a Cuban-American journalist-turned-novelist, is indulgent and awkward in her use of them.

Dreaming opens in 1972, at night. Celia is sitting in the porch swing of her house in a beachside town outside Havana. She sweeps the horizon with binoculars, "guarding the north coast of Cuba." The *Yanquis* came once, and they may come again.

She is also wearing her best housedress, drop pearl earrings and lipstick. It is a revolutionary honor to have been chosen by the neighborhood committee but, revolutionary or not, the middle class is the middle class. As much as hardships allow, Celia dresses up. It is a perfect image. The revolution, despite the three decades that have gone by and all its hardening and polarization, has never quite overcome its contradictions of class and geography.

Castro came from a well-to-do family, has well-to-do tastes and once tried out for the Washington Senators. Because he did not play baseball better, Celia reflects, "her husband will be buried in stiff, foreign earth. Because of this their children and their grandchildren are nomads."

As a young woman, Celia played the piano and had a romantic affair with a visiting Spaniard; for a quarter-century afterward she wrote him letters that she never mailed; they appear throughout the book as a kind of private journal.

The constraints of marriage in Cuba's particularly suffocating bourgeois society drove her temporarily mad; Jorge, her husband, was kind but distant.

He worked for an American company, and his passion was for everything it represented: Northern cleanliness and order. He endured the revolution bitterly and emigrated to New York when illness gave him an excuse.

Lourdes, the eldest daughter, was already there. She had married a rich Cuban and fled with him and his family. Felicia, her sister, remains in Cuba through three disastrous marriages, a growing mental instability and physical deterioration and membership in a *santeria* group.

Javier, their brother, is a scientist who went to Czechoslovakia in the glory days of Cuban internationalism; by the end of the book, he is back again, bitter and an alcoholic.

The sharpest portrait is of Lourdes. She is a woman of enormous appetites, energy and anger. Vastly overweight, she works diligently to run two bakeries in Brooklyn, supporting her husband and her daughter, Pilar.

A fierce right-winger—she joins the auxiliary police for the pleasure of the heavy boots and nightstick—she is Cuban intransigence personified.

She also has an odd, wild appeal. To taunt her "Communist" mother, she sends her a photograph of her bakery: "Each glistening eclair is a grenade aimed at Cuba's political beliefs."

Pilar, her rebellious daughter, has a deep curiosity about Celia and Cuba. After the death of Felicia, she persuades her mother to go with her on a visit.

While Lourdes trumpets her anger at everything she sees—at one point, she shouts "Asesino!" at Castro—Pilar and Celia tentatively explore the lost years between them.

No one is stable or complete on either side. The Cuban illness has deeply maimed, in fascinatingly different ways, Celia, Jorge and his children; Pilar may or may not suggest a glint of future reconciliation.

Garcia maps out the maiming, sometimes with excessive colors, but for the most part, acutely and with a rare sweetness.

Richard Eder, "Cuban Revolution Tugs on Family Ties," in Los Angeles Times, *March 12, 1992, p. E10.*

Amelia Weiss (review date 23 March 1992)

[*Below, Weiss praises* Dreaming in Cuban *for its imaginative celebration of Cuban heritage and identity.*]

In her impressive first novel, **Dreaming in Cuban,** Cristina Garcia takes back her island. A former *Time* correspondent and Miami bureau chief, Garcia left Havana with her family when she was two. Her story is about three generations of Cuban women and their separate responses to the revolution. Her special feat is to tell it in a style as warm and gentle as the "sustaining aromas of vanilla and almond," as rhythmic as the music of Beny Moré.

Dressed in her best housedress, Celia del Pino, a 63-year-old revolutionary, sits in a wicker swing "guarding the north coast of Cuba." She wears the drop pearl earrings left by her departed Spanish lover and dreams of being honored by Fidel Castro—"El Líder himself"—on a red velvet divan. Instead, before dawn, she sights her dead husband, iridescent blue and "taller than the palms, walking on water in his white summer suit and Panama hat."

Celia's children live in cold countries. Her son has immigrated to the East bloc. Her daughter Felicia is mad. And

---

An excerpt from *Dreaming in Cuban*

I wonder how different my life would have been if I'd stayed with my grandmother. I think about how I'm probably the only ex-punk on the island, how no one else has their ears pierced in three places. It's hard to imagine existing without Lou Reed. I ask Abuela if I can paint whatever I want in Cuba and she says yes, as long as I don't attack the state. Cuba is still developing, she tells me, and can't afford the luxury of dissent. Then she quotes me something El Líder said in the early years, before they started arresting poets. "Within the revolution, everything; against the revolution, nothing." I wonder what El Líder would think of my paintings. Art, I'd tell him, is the ultimate revolution. . . .

I've started dreaming in Spanish, which has never happened before. I wake up feeling different, like something inside me is changing, something chemical and irreversible. There's a magic here working its way through my veins. There's something about the vegetation, too, that I respond to instinctively—the stunning bougainvillea, the flamboyants and jacarandas, the orchids growing from the trunks of the mysterious ceiba trees. And I love Havana, its noise and decay and painted ladyness. I could happily sit on one of those wrought-iron balconies for days, or keep my grandmother company on her porch, with its ringside view of the sea. I'm afraid to lose all this, to lose Abuela Celia again. But sooner or later I'd have to return to New York. I know now it's where I belong—not *instead* of here, but *more* than here. How can I tell my grandmother this?

Cristina Garcia, in her Dreaming in Cuban, *Knopf, 1992.*

her eldest daughter Lourdes—a ferocious anti-communist who scans the newspapers for signs of leftist conspiracies—owns the Yankee Doodle Bakery in Brooklyn and sells apple pie to Americans.

Lourdes loves the cold. She relishes "the ritual of scarves and gloves, hats and zip-in coat linings. Its layers protect her." Raped by revolutionaries who afterward carved "crimson hieroglyphics" into her soft belly, she wants "no part of Cuba, no part of its wretched carnival floats creaking with lies, no part of Cuba at all." But her Americanized daughter Pilar, born in Cuba when the revolution was 11 days old, misses her *abuela*: "Every day Cuba fades a little more inside me, my grandmother fades a little more inside me. And there's only my imagination where our history should be."

Garcia's imagination is ambitious. Not only does she reunite Pilar with her grandmother; she also claims her own aesthetic identity. Like a priestess, in passages of beautiful island incantation, she conjures her Cuban heritage from a land between "death and oblivion," so that she too can fasten on Abuela Celia's drop pearl earrings, sit in a wicker swing by the sea, and watch as the radiant spirits of her forefathers "stretch out a colossal hand."

> Amelia Weiss, "Fantasy Island," in Time, New York, Vol. 139, No. 12, March 23, 1992, p. 67.

Hilma Wolitzer   (review date 5 April 1992)

[*Wolitzer is an American novelist. In the following review, she discusses Garcia's characters, structure, and style in* Dreaming in Cuban.]

Cristina Garcia's spirited and affecting first novel [**Dreaming in Cuban**] is a welcome addition to the growing literature of Latin American emigre experience. Like Judith Ortiz Cofer's *The Line of the Sun* and Julia Alvarez's *How the Garcia Girls Lost Their Accents*, **Dreaming in Cuban** deftly bridges two divergent cultures.

The book traces the fortunes, between 1972 and 1980, of a Cuban family divided by both geography and politics. The four central female characters comprise three generations of the colorful Del Pino family. Eleven years after the Bay of Pigs invasion, Celia del Pino, the aging matriarch and a resolute supporter of Fidel Castro ("El Líder"), scans the horizon in Santa Teresa Del Mar on the North coast of Cuba for signs of a yanqui-inspired counterrevolution. Instead, she sights the larger-than-life ghost of her husband, Jorge, and is thereby informed of his death that day far away in Brooklyn, N.Y. In nearby Havana, Celia's daughter, Felicia, receives the news more conventionally, by way of a telephone call from her older sister, Lourdes, who has been in attendance during their father's battle with cancer.

Separated by miles and their disparate personalities, Lourdes and Felicia share a common antipathy for their mother's hero. To poetical, delusional Felicia, who worships the arrow-studded Saint Sebastian, Castro is no better than a common tyrant, although he appears prominently in her sexual daydreams. From her bountiful

Brooklyn bakery—the Yankee Doodle—the more practical Lourdes, who has grown obese and insatiably lustful on American abundance, measures El Lider severely by the ongoing shortages in Cuba. Her idol is the rich and powerful industrialist, E. I. Du Pont.

Soon after Jorge's death, Lourdes' daughter, Pilar, an energetic young painter, begins an abortive pilgrimage back to Cuba (where Cristina Garcia, who now lives in Los Angeles, was also born). Pilar is fed up with American values and customs, particularly those of her plutocratic mother and philandering father. "Like this is it?" she muses wryly as her family sits around staring at one another with nothing to say. "We're living the American dream?"

Pilar dreams of the Cuba she left as a baby, and she longs for Celia, the grandmother who serves as a model of feminine spirituality and independence. It is Celia whose voice she conjures up before she falls asleep each night, for comfort and advice. As Pilar makes her secret way south, Celia yearns for her, too, worrying that her favored grandchild's eyes have become unused to the "compacted light of the tropics." Meanwhile Lourdes suffers her daughter's disappearance and her father's death, and Felicia continues to fight her private demons.

The novel is divided temporally, and then subdivided into chapters devoted to individual characters. Felicia, who sets fire to her first husband and periodically falls into madness, is certainly the most flamboyant of the del Pino women. But each of them is an original in her own right. Celia is notable for her fierce loyalties and her prescience, Lourdes for her determined capitalism and robust appetites, and Pilar for her witty, punky style. When they all converge near the novel's end, they are a formidable collective presence.

Occasionally, Garcia dips further back in time with unmailed letters from Celia to Gustavo Sierra de Armas, the lover she lost when he returned to Spain in the 1930s. These letters track the parallel progress of her personal life and the sociopolitical life of her country. The final one, for instance, written the day Pilar is born, also notes the onset of the revolution 11 days before. Celia's ardent commitment to Gustavo seems to be smoothly transferred to Castro, and her self-imposed obligation to be a recording witness is passed on to her granddaughter, who, she predicts, "will remember everything." Pilar obliges by keeping a diary that her mother periodically invades in their struggle for control.

In addition to the four engaging heroines, there are several lesser yet well-defined characters, including Felicia's three husbands; her twin daughters, Luz and Milagro; her son, Ivanito; Lourdes' husband, Rufino; various other relatives and friends; and, of course, Jorge's omnipresent ghost, who gives credence to one character's observation that "There's always new hope for the dead." This is a large cast for a relatively small novel, but Garcia manages to keep them all nimbly in action and clearly in focus. And although the intimate lives of its characters are at the center of the story, the Cuban revolution and its ramifications are never far from our attention.

At its lyrical best, Garcia's writing owes a debt to the magic realism of Gabriel García Márquez and Isabel Allende. As Lourdes is being raped by one of Castro's soldiers,

> She smelled the soldier's coarse soap, the salt of his perspiring back. She smelled his milky clots and the decay of his teeth and the citrus brilliantine in his hair, as if a grove of lemons lay hidden there. She smelled his face on his wedding day, his tears when his son drowned at the park. She smelled his rotting leg in Africa, where it would be blown off his body on a moonless savanna night. She smelled him when he was old and unbathed and the flies blackened his eyes.

There are a few lapses into more extravagant prose, in which similes clash and cancel one another out. In one short paragraph references are made to thoughts that "tumble together like gems in the polishing, reaching their hard conclusions" and "obscenities that hung like electric insects in the air." And sometimes Celia's letters to Gustavo seem too much like a device to further the exposition. But these are minor flaws in an otherwise delightful debut. Cristina Garcia has something vital to say about the workings of family and government and art, and she says it in this novel with considerable authority and charm.

Hilma Wolitzer, "Crossing Cultural Bridges," in Chicago Tribune—Books, April 5, 1992, p. 4.

Thulani Davis (review date 17 May 1992)

[*In the following review, Davis declares* Dreaming in Cuban *"a jewel of a first novel" and examines Garcia's treatment of the relationship between language and cultural identity.*]

Cristina Garcia's marvelous first novel, **Dreaming in Cuban,** is, as its title suggests, about the specific mysteries of place and the hidden passions people often carry into exile. The members of the del Pino family, scattered from the Cuban village of Santa Teresa del Mar to Havana, Brooklyn and Eastern Europe, live in exile from home, lovers, family. Only Celia, the family matriarch who stayed on in her seaside home and who welcomed change, has managed to understand who she is and in what language she dreams. When Celia's husband, Jorge, finally gives up on her beloved revolution and goes to New York, she replaces his bedside portrait with a picture of Fidel Castro, *El Líder,* and seems to pay it no mind. The politics of the Cuban revolution and its aftermath divide Celia's family, as it did many families, yet at the same time some other inability to keep the family together continues its deadly work.

Only the unseen communications of Celia's and Jorge's spirits bring solace and healing to their children, who, for their part, accept these telepathies as commonplace and reliable. It is perhaps this ordinary magic in Ms. Garcia's novel and her characters' sense of their own lyricism that make her work welcome as the latest sign that American literature has its own hybrid offspring of the Latin American school.

Dreaming in Cuban is grounded in specific Cuban realities—like food shortages and the grief of mothers who lost sons in Angola—or unrealities, as they may appear to exiles returning in 1980 to a surreal island of faded pastel villas, revolutionary billboards and 30-year-old Oldsmobiles. But it is foremost a novel about obsession and what Celia terms ruinous passion.

Celia's daughters, Felicia and Lourdes, are both given to extremes; each is driven, almost hurtling through time, by vengeance and painful memory. In Cuba, Felicia has her mother's lust for poetry and romance but suffers from months of syphilitic madness, finally committing acts of violence after days of dancing to the seductive voice of Beny Moré, the king of Cuban balladeers—and making oblations to the still-lively African gods in hopes of salvation. Lourdes, blindly loyal to her father, a compulsive eater and a fanatical anti-Castro convert to American patriotism, runs a bakery in Brooklyn and dreams of taking her place with the nouveau-moguls she sees getting rich in the United States. Their brother, Javier, who ran off secretly to Czechoslovakia, finds he is fragile, too, when he loses his family. Celia's grandchildren can only be described as lost and abandoned by the obsessions of the parents. Of these, Lourdes's daughter, Pilar Puente del Pino, a would-be painter and student in New York, becomes the secret sharer, a distant repository of the family's stories and some of its demons.

Dreaming in Cuban is beautifully written in language that is by turns languid and sensual, curt and surprising. Like Louise Erdrich, whose crystalline language is distilled of images new to our American literature but old to this land, Ms. Garcia has distilled a new tongue from scraps salvaged through upheaval. Her characters sometimes address us directly in first-person narrative, and Celia speaks in her own voice in love letters between herself and the lover of her youth written in 1934-59. But even the third-person sections reveal the voices of each individual: Felicia's mad solipsisms and her humorous rages over people in square sunglasses; her son Ivanito's trusting sweetness, his eventual assault by a lecherous teacher. The voices are poignant and also funny, circling around familiar incidents from different points of view, taking potshots at one another.

Some of Ms. Garcia's most daring ventures are those moments of violence or sex that are taken so seriously by the participants but that are hilarious in the telling—being sent on a revolutionary brigade as a cure for madness, heartbreak or politically dangerous art; imagining Fidel Castro as mom's sex object.

The most interesting voice is Celia's, despite the misadventures of the others and the stories they might tell, because she is like the sea she watches day after day, moving with all the forces around her, changing constantly and thus remaining constant. Her distinctive voice is desperate with passion and yet detached: "*Mi querido* Gustavo," she writes her lover in 1934, "A fish swims in my lung. Without you, what is there to celebrate?" Twenty years later she writes, "*Querido* Gustavo, Javier won the children's national science prize for a genetics experiment. His teachers tell me he's a genius. I'm very proud of him, but I'm not exactly sure for what. . . . I'm reading *Madame Bovary* in French now, grievously, very grievously." Other characters pale somewhat next to her, particularly young American Pilar, an ex-punker given to angry-at-the-world-and-mom diatribes perfectly typical of her age and inexperience, but a little tiresome to plow through.

Ms. Garcia also tracks the subtle changes in language as the del Pinos cross borders and decades. "Pilar, her first grandchild, writes to her from Brooklyn in a Spanish that is no longer hers. She speaks the hard-edged lexicon of bygone tourists itchy to throw dice on green felt or asphalt." Lourdes runs around the island asking people what their hourly wages are and telling them what they would make in the States.

While taking very seriously those ideas that have truly riven so many families in recent years, leaving many obsessed with the politics of Cuba, Ms. Garcia also portrays the costliness of such an obsession and the fading of the light between mothers and daughters, between lovers, as communication fails. The language of such love songs as once were sung must be saved, Ms. Garcia seems to say, so that we may make songs in exile. I have no complaints to make. Cristina Garcia has written a jewel of a first novel.

Thulani Davis, "Fidel Came between Them,"
in The New York Times, *May 17, 1992, p. 14.*

Merrihelen Ponce   **(review date Fall 1992)**

[*In the following review, Ponce focuses on Garcia's vivid characterizations and blend of personal and political themes in* Dreaming in Cuban.]

[**Dreaming in Cuban**] captures the loves and hungers of four women whose lives are affected by the 1959 Revolution led by Castro. Each woman pines for what was lost when the popular revolution changed their lives, and those of their compatriots, forever. Similar in theme to *Cantando Bajito/Singing Softly* by Carmen de Monteflores, the novel touches on the universal longings of expatriates to return home.

The women's voices are distinct. Celia mourns an old lover and, to a lesser degree, her dead husband. Her son has fled to Czechoslovakia; her daughter succumbs to U.S. capitalism. True to the ideology of the revolution—and *el lider*—Celia nightly patrols the seashore, looking for invading Yankees, while conversing with the spirit of Jorge, her dead husband. Disillusioned with men and love, Celia dedicates her life to Castro, labors in a sugar cane field, and shares prosperity with others.

Felicia, Celia's daughter who chooses to remain in Cuba, is suicidal, a victim of domestic violence, forced to join the Cuban Army along with reactionaries and those in opposition to Castro: an "army of discontents." Felicia hungers for a man to make her life complete; her children hunger for their long-gone father.

The strongest voice is that of Lourdes, Celia's ambitious, obese daughter now living the American Dream in Brooklyn as owner of the Yankee Doodle Bakery. Unable to satisfy her hunger for a more sexual mate and the unconditional love of Pilar, her daughter, she daily stuffs herself with *pan.*

For the bakery's celebration of "the 200th Birthday of America," Pilar, an aspiring artist, paints (unknown to her mother) a politically damaging portrait of the Statue of Liberty that is attacked by a spectator. The following ensues:

> mom swings her new handbag and clubs the guy
> cold. . . . She tumbles forward, a thrashing av-
> alanche of patriotism and motherhood. . . .
> And I, I love my mother very much.

Bread is a metaphor for a greater need: for sustenance, home, family, and, for Lourdes, a daughter who loves and appreciates her. Like bread-eaters throughout the world, for whom the Bread of Life comes in many forms, Lourdes feels an emptiness in her heart and stomach. And like the yeast in the breads she daily bakes, Lourdes rises warm and moist each day, ready to take on life.

Pilar is assimilated to Anglo culture, yet yearns to return to the Cuba she knows only through osmosis (she left at age two). Her relationship with her mother is tenuous, strafed by political overtones. An independent Pilar feels that "the family is hostile to the individual." To Lourdes, Pilar is like Celia, "disdainful of rules of religion, of everything meaningful, neither of them shows respect for anyone, least of all themselves." And yet it is Pilar who brings the family together. A hip artist more at home in Brooklyn ghettos than at an Ivy League university, Pilar feels a closeness to Celia's estranged grandmother that neither time or distance has eroded. Yet when in Cuba, she realizes her destiny lies not in Cuba but in her adopted country.

Interspersed in the narrative are a series of letters from Celia to Gustavo, her first love, that intrude in the smooth narration. Another problem is the overuse of metaphors, particularly in the first sections: "Herminia . . . is wearing a cream-yellow blouse with a collar the luster of the absent moon"; "La Madrina beckons in a voice hoarse with a vocation to the unfortunate . . . her face is an almond sheen of wheat." To be commended is the author's ability to show the contradictions inherent in a "new" social order without being didactic or biased. Rather, the reader is made aware of conditions, both economic and political, in Castro's reformed Cuba that are darkly humorous yet very real.

Merrihelen Ponce, "Hungers of the Heart," in
Belles Lettres: A Review of Books by Women,
Vol. 8, No. 1, Fall, 1992, p. 15.

Francisco Goldman
The Long Night of White Chickens

Born in 1955, Goldman is an American novelist, short story writer, and journalist.

INTRODUCTION

The Long Night of White Chickens, which was inspired by Goldman's experiences as a reporter in Central America during the 1980s, has been praised for its potent characterization and the subtlety and equanimity of its political content. In this novel Goldman chronicles the life and eventual murder of Flor de Mayo Puac, a young Guatemalan woman whose work as an orphanage director brings her into contact with her country's foremost political, financial, and military figures. The novel is narrated by Roger Graetz, the eldest son of a Boston family for whom Flor once worked as a maid. After learning that Flor was murdered in Guatemala in 1983, Roger begins an investigation into her death. Over the course of the novel—in which Goldman shifts between the past, present, and the future to create a kaleidoscopic, hallucinatory narrative—the reader learns that Flor left Boston for Guatemala City at a time when Guatemala's military regime was at its most tyrannical. Roger's search for the truth behind Flor's death becomes Goldman's means to examine the forces that controlled Guatemalan life throughout the 1980s and to reveal how the Reagan Administration's policies contributed to Central American instability. Critics note, however, that *The Long Night of White Chickens* is not a left-wing jeremiad and that Goldman's wit and humor adds human dimension and complexity to the novel. Goldman has said that "the last thing I wanted to do, read, *or* write, as a fiction writer, was an angry diatribe about Central America." He has concluded that "a novelist should not denounce the absence of freedom . . . he should exemplify freedom by using his imagination."

It's almost supernatural, Francisco Goldman tells us, "the way Guatemala infests you." Goldman's first novel [***The Long Night of White Chickens***], is like the country, then: It takes you over, leaves you feeling like occupied territory, full of new memories of people and events you obviously had forgotten somehow before you opened the book. Afterwards, his story fidgets in the mind like an old family tale that no two relatives tell quite the same way, with small questions that will never be answered but are somehow absorbing to think about.

It's a novel and a fine one, this remembrance of the Massachusetts life and the Guatemalan death of Flor de Mayo Puac, sometime maid and confidante and older sister-surrogate to the narrator, Roger Graetz, a consumptive and difficult Guatemalan-American boy. It reads, however, rather like Roger's journal entries stitched together with an anecdote here, a digression there. Some of it turns out to be crucial, other bits are irrelevant, much of it is

CRITICISM

Joanne Omang (review date 7 June 1992)

[*In the following review of* The Long Night of White Chickens, *Omang discusses the strengths and weaknesses of Goldman's narrative structure.*]

funny, and all of it by turns is jarring and floating, like memory itself.

The technique could not be more appropriate to the story, the narrator's meandering struggle to understand the mystery that is the book's ostensible focus: Flor's brutal murder. Was Flor de Mayo a baby-seller when she returned to Guatemala, as the Guatemalan security forces say, killed by her accomplices in a web of corruption? What about her links to the guerrillas, to Roger's American father, to her secret lover, a married man? What about that brutalized, beautiful, shimmering country called Guatemala—does it really exist?

These questions are all explored, but anyone expecting to read here a conventional murder mystery or political thriller will be disappointed, for as Roger Graetz probes his memory and his conscience, it becomes clear that the murder is secondary to a possible betrayal of friendship and of self that lies at the novel's heart. This is a coming-of-age story set in that fitful torment of the half-understood life, the hyphenated American's divided spirit.

Goldman, now 35, is a contributing editor to *Harper's* magazine and well-known for his short stories and journalism from Central America. Like his protagonist, he is Guatemalan-American, and the novel appears more than a little autobiographical; you can taste the snowy Massachusetts winter. The book jacket promises some magical realism on the order of Gabriel Garcia Marquez's patented recipes, but only one or two moments even seem intended to lift away completely: Flor's odd handprints, for example—one crowded with lines, the other plain and blank. The rest, like the bizarre protest of the Guatemala City garbage-dump residents which follows the death of the zoo's hippopotamus, have the solid quirkiness of real life.

Instead, like someone trying to focus in on a nagging worry, the book is filled with a confusion of flashes forward and back that seems at first to be writerly error. We begin on the Pasteleria Hemmings mezzanine in chaotic downtown Guatemala City. But is it the day the government arbitrarily reversed traffic on all the city's one-way streets, causing "a demolition derby of the damned"? Or are we in the same place five or six years later, remembering it all?

Roger's aristocratic Guatemalan mother calls him from Boston, but he seems to answer from his job tending bar in Brooklyn. And when his old Guatemalan school chum Moya turns up to talk about Flor, their mutual obsession, the conversation seems to occur partly on the mezzanine, partly in a sleazy Guatemalan hotel and partly in New York. But the story turns back to Namoset, and before that to the Guatemalan highlands, where the whole thing started.

It all sorts itself out, but first there is the eponymous long night of white chickens, when Moya and Flor talk and talk over rum in a Chinese restaurant. We wait, as mesmerized as Moya, for Flor to move toward him enough so that the ends of her long dark hair might fall into the bowl of sweet-and-sour sauce. By then, we know, Moya will be in love.

On and on they talk, right through the overnight chicken delivery, the feathery kitchen slaughter that seems as casual, as appalling and as normal as anyone's life and death in Guatemala. "It hit me this morning, just like that," Roger writes. "Our investigation [into Flor's murder] isn't meant to go anywhere. Like this is Moya's design, his original *intent.* Come and investigate a murder in Guatemala. It won't go anywhere! See? See what it's like here, America?"

But that's too simple for Moya and for the labyrinthine connections that gradually emerge, complex as history, funny as love, painful as death. The mystery of Goldman's Guatemala is the mystery of anyone's family, anyone's friendships and obsessions, and the novel's eventual understandings of self and life are as simple and tenuous as those of most of us. It is a wonderful book.

> *Joanne Omang, "No Escape from Guatemala," in* Book World—The Washington Post, *June 7, 1992, p. 9.*

Victor Perera   (review date 19 July 1992)

[*In the following review, Perera praises Goldman for the realism, insightful details, and complex characters of* The Long Night of White Chickens, *but suggests that some of the author's anecdotes and descriptions of sexual encounters are not necessary to the narrative.*]

It takes one's breath away when a new talent bursts on the scene and lives up to its billing. The advance promo for *The Long Night of White Chickens*—"best first novel I've ever published," trumpets its publisher—is matched by the author's wordless swagger: Move aside, Jay McInerney, here's GOLDMAN!

This is McInerney in Garcia Marquez country; more accurately, in Miguel Angel Asturias country, but who reads Guatemala's Nobel laureate? The setting is Guatemala City. The schizzy, sexy heroine, Flor de Mayo, is a lower-class mestiza rumored to be running a baby-selling racket. The protagonist, Roger, is himself a cocky mixed-breed of Guatemalan Catholic and Boston Jewish parents.

The drug that pervades this story isn't coke, hash or sex—although these are all in evidence—but an endemic violence so horrendous and rooted in the novel's landscape that it overshadows the richly conceived characters and becomes the protagonist. (Having grown up in Guatemala, I find this story hauntingly familiar; even the electric train I lusted after as a boy is here, hypnotically circling the window of Roger's uncle's toy store.)

Several recurrent Guatemalan themes are given a fresh lease by Goldman. Celso Batres, the handsome newspaper publisher and presidential aspirant, is modeled on the grandson of Guatemala's premier newspaperman, Clemente Marroquin Rojas, who was murdered on the dictator's orders. Roger's best friend, Moya, is recognizable as Julio Godoy, the dashing and brilliant young journalist who was forced to flee Guatemala after he exposed corruption in high places. Roger's mother, Mirabel, is the romantic daughter of an upper-class *criollo* family with an iron-willed *abuelita* (grandmother) and a grandfather who periodically goes mad, singing entire Verdi operas by heart and squandering the family fortune on his slutty mistress. On the other side of the coin is Roger's father, Ira, a Jewish retired policeman from a suburb in Boston where Roger grew up sharing his passion for Harvard football.

But above all, *The Long Night of White Chickens* is the story of Flor de Mayo, the provincial orphan girl adopted by Mirabel and Ira as a part-time maid and companion to little Roger. Dark-eyed, slender and alluring, Flor makes an indelible impact on Roger—as have generations of Guatemalan nannies on their tender masters—beguiling him with her sensuality and her secretive, worldly-wise ways.

Flor attempts bravely to bury her troubled past (her father was decapitated by a farmer when he tried to steal some chickens) by enrolling in a suburban Boston grammar school when she is past 12. By dint of sheer will, Flor completes high school and goes on to graduate from Wellesley College.

But old habits of self-destructiveness die hard; "Guatemala," she writes Roger, "is bottomless grief in a demitasse." Flor antagonizes Mirabel and disappoints Ira—who loved her as if she were his own daughter—when she threatens to marry a long-haired Cuban drifter and waste her brilliant opportunities.

Flor eventually returns to Guatemala, where she becomes head of an orphan-adoption agency patronized by wealthy Americans and Europeans. She also takes up with a succession of lovers who live on the cutting edge of Guatemala's treacherous public arena, among them Roger's old buddy Moya and—rumor has it—Moya's employer, the handsome and ambitious Celso Batres. Shortly after Flor's agency places a small Indian girl with a wealthy European couple, Flor is murdered.

The bulk of the novel—what Roger calls his "main assignment"—comprises his efforts to come to grips with Flor's contradictory nature and to make sense of her terrible end. The story of Flor de Mayo, Roger learns, is the story of Guatemala, and what a fecund metaphor this turns out to be!

Roger's own bedeviled dualities and contradictions—and those of his friend Moya—get all wound up with the search for Flor's murderer, and for a credible rationalization of her erratic behavior. A nursemaid accuses Flor of running an illicit "fattening house" for babies to be sold abroad—a lucrative contraband that has grown rampant in Guatemala. Malicious gossip, sex and the unending war between the military and the leftist insurgents fuel the mystery of Flor's years in Guatemala, of her secret liaisons and her gruesome end.

Roger becomes obsessed, not only with clearing Flor de Mayo's name but also with exonerating his friend Moya, who became Flor's lover shortly before she was killed and who might have acted as an unwitting accomplice. (The Moya/Mayo acronym plays rather cutely on the linkage.) This candescent material plumbs the lower depths of Guatemala, and Goldman pulls together the threads of the story brilliantly, moving back and forth in time like a nimble Mayan weaver creating an elaborate *huipil*.

As the story unfolds, the sections narrated by Roger and by the less-than-omniscient narrator become so interwoven that the line between protagonist and storyteller attenuates and all but disappears. ("I can be a very romantic and self-deluding person," Roger confesses, evidently speaking for both himself and the narrator.)

At one point, Goldman steps out of the narrative to confront his old schoolmate Moya/Godoy, who has heedlessly bragged of his affair with Flor. Did he know, the narrator asks repeatedly, that Celso Batres was making love to Flor? More than a friendship is at stake here; the narrator's sanity hangs in the balance. And why not? Guatemala's violence has cut down far larger and sturdier spirits than Flor's, Roger's, Moya's, or Celso Batres' for that matter. "Have I ever just come right out and said," Roger/Goldman asks near the end of the book, "that this is an unbelievably sick and evil place? But that so much of it seems to happen with a certain genius, leaving behind almost nothing but invisibility and silence?"

Because this is Guatemala, Flor's murderer will never be known, any more than we will ever discover the authors responsible for the 40,000 "disappeared" and unaccounted for over the past 30 years, not to mention the 100,000 or so Guatemalans known to have been assassinated by the military.

The best Roger can hope for is the assurance that Guatemala had not corrupted Flor altogether, as it has hundreds of other bright, educated compatriots of hers who acted with the best of intentions. Still, the novel leaves behind too many unanswered questions.

Roger is hardly an existential hero for our times. In his obsessive search for Flor's murderer, he is a harsh judge of others and yet can be stubbornly opaque about his own motivations. He belittles Moya: "His mind is not so original; more than occasionally his vanity, his highest hopes, his embarrassing certainties were overruled by his suspicions." Of course, Roger is really talking about himself, and of his macho pique that his old friend and rival Moya had taken his longed-for place in Flor's bed, if not in her affections.

This blind spot hints at what may be the novel's largest short-coming. Given the narrative's open-endedness, the real missing character here is a disciplined editor, who might have blue-penciled dozens of tangential anecdotes, superfluous sexual encounters and "magic realist" passages. Were they retained to bolster the book's claim to Marquezian stature? They are hardly necessary. Flor de Mayo is the heart and soul of this fine novel, and her story would have packed a more powerful wallop at a lean 300 pages than it does at an overinflated 450. (pp. 3, 8)

Victor Perera, "A Metaphor for Guatemala," in Los Angeles Times Book Review, *July 19, 1992, pp. 3, 8.*

Francisco Goldman with Wallace Shawn (interview date 21 July 1992)

[*Wallace Shawn is an American dramatist, screenwriter, and actor; he has appeared in many films, notably Louis Malle's* My Dinner with André *(1982), for which he co-wrote the screenplay. In the following interview, he asks Goldman about his childhood, his career as a journalist, and the political issues addressed in* The Long Night of White Chickens.]

[*Shawn*]: *What's your earliest memory?*

[Goldman]: Well, I think my earliest memory is of sitting in a window-seat in my grandparents' house in Guatemala City—my grandmother was blind, and there was a maid who used to read Zane Gray cowboy novels out loud to my grandmother and my grandmother's sister because they loved Zane Gray novels—and I think my earliest memory is of sitting in the window seat and passing a little toy truck out the window to an Indian woman who had her child in a sort of papoose or sling and watching her take the child out and put it on the sidewalk to play with the truck, and me being astonished that the child was naked . . . My grandmother's house was a great place to be a little kid. It was fascinating to watch chickens be slaughtered—and have all these little pets—and sit in that window seat all day long . . . And we have all these pictures of me at that time and I am such a spoiled little brat—you can tell. I'm dressed in these little knickers, and I have huge stuffed animals that tower over me, you know, from the store. And whenever I try to go back to whatever the beginning is, it's always images of that house. It was very sensual . . . I wonder, why would you always remember three maids standing around a big vat of oil, frying potato chips? I don't know, but I've never been able to forget it. And the store—I loved the store—the way the rainy season would make the paint on all the toy soldiers come off in your hands . . .

What do you remember most about your grade school and high school days?

Well, I think I spent my entire time in that town, Needham, Massachusetts, in a complete and utter fog, really. I basically felt very sort of . . . uneasy . . . And I was a very, very bad student. I went through high school with a D-minus average—I even got F's in Spanish—and I was a troublemaker in class. I think a lot of it was because there was nobody around to tell me how to be an American kid, because I was raised essentially by Guatemalan maids, I mean I spent all my time with Guatemalan teenage girls who were all out of convent orphanages and things. So I knew nothing—I was extremely naive—I remember being so proud of this new football shirt I had, and I remember getting off my Sting Ray bike in this shirt and all the high school girls laughing hysterically at me, because the number was 69 and I had no idea what that meant. And of course I think my town, you know, God bless them, a lot of those people were very fine people, but at that time, before the town changed to what it is today—I remember when a few black kids got shipped out to our school in one of those busing programs—some of the kids in the cafeteria used to throw food at them and

dump trays of food over their heads. So at that time it was a very, very white town and a tough town.

So you were bad in your schoolwork. But did you think that you were, somehow, smart in other ways?

No, I didn't think I was the least bit smart.

But outside of school, did you read? Did you know people who liked books?

Well, my father grew up in that Depression generation that revered writers. I had this sense that he revered writing above all other things—you know, Faulkner, Hemingway, Fitzgerald, and also the immigrant writers who wrote about their own backgrounds. And he had a friend whom I called Uncle Mattie who was an incredible storyteller. And Uncle Mattie had a dog named Moot, and he used to always tell me Moot stories. Incredibly inventive stories. You know, Moot was a lot like William Wegman's dog. That's how I always pictured Moot. And Uncle Mattie used to give me these beautiful hard-bound books—Dickens, *Oliver Twist*—which I still have. And I was always just digging into books that were around . . . I remember being over at some relative's house in some paneled basement—I was about eight, 10, I don't know, I was a little elementary-school kid, and finding *Portrait of the Artist* and sitting there immersed in it until slowly—you know how *Portrait of the Artist* begins very readable and by the end it starts to get what we think of as Joycean?—reading it until finally the confusion became overwhelming. But I always sort of knew that that's what I wanted to be. I remember being 13 years old and I had just read in *Life* magazine—I was always looking for omens—and in *Life* magazine Hemingway had said something like, "Every writer knows he's going to be a writer by the time he's 13." And I was 13 and I knew I wanted to be a writer. And I remember being in a complete trance down in this big empty field behind my house, hitting rocks with a baseball bat and just knowing it was true . . .

Did you write stories and things at school?

Yes, a lot, and I had one teacher who became utterly my savior by encouraging me, but most of the teachers didn't. I remember I once wrote a 40-page story about a Jewish lumberjack in the 19th century—he ended up committing suicide—and the teacher gave it an F because he said I should have written something set in the present. Another teacher assigned us to make up a myth—I did one on the origin of chocolate milk—and she accused me of plagiarizing it. At one point I was actually selling stories to a few of my friends, because I could dash off a story really fast. And in fact we had a literary magazine called *Even a Rag Like This,* where the teachers would select supposedly the best stories, and often they wouldn't choose mine but they would choose stories I'd written for my friends. And they were in there under those kids' names.

Gosh. But then you did go to college.

Yes. I was a good runner and jumper—good at track—and that helped me get into college.

So then after college you were writing fiction, and you spent some time in Guatemala, and eventually Esquire *asked you if you wanted to do a nonfiction article.*

Yes. I'd never thought of being a journalist. But *Esquire* said they would send me any place I wanted, so I said I wanted to go back to Guatemala. Well, what happened then was that Reagan became president and declared war on Central America basically. So I just kept on going back there. Added all together, I lived in Guatemala City for a total of five years during the '80s, although I did most of my journalism in other parts of Central America.

And what was that like?

Well, of course I felt extremely passionately about everything that was going on—it was the defining experience of my life, I'm sure, having this opportunity to work as a journalist in Central America. But I also loved the plain adventure of it all too, in an almost boyish way. I was thrilled to have the chance to go running around in the war zones and out on patrols with the Sandinista Army in Nicaragua and be shot at and all that. Although I have to admit, my overriding impression of actual combat is that all the bullets are aimed into the treetops—all these twigs and leaves fluttering down—and that nobody gets hurt. War seemed like a pretty safe place to be, which shows you how little *fighting* I actually saw. Anyway, I loved all that stuff—Panama under Noriega, the contras' Tegucigalpa. But then there were long stretches in Guatemala City—well, I mean, I used to spend months and months down there—and it still baffles me—doing nothing! Absolutely nothing. Not doing journalism. I was perfectly happy, somehow, just walking up and down Sexta Avenida.

[I] knew that ultimately the act of writing a novel was not about declaring the anger I felt at that moment. The fact is, I think you're showing an enormous disrespect for the intelligence of your readers if you think they need a novel to know that there's injustice in the world.

—*Francisco Goldman*

Really? But how can you be Jewish and not feel guilty about spending your time just walking up and down the street?

I don't know. I felt perfectly happy. And I remember a friend came down from New York, and he noticed I wasn't doing much work, and he went back and he told my agent, "Frank says that just walking up and down Sexta Avenida he feels he's done his day's work." And she phoned me up and said, "I think it's time for you to come home." And I wanted to buy a little piece of land on a river down there, and my mother said, "You'll never come back . . ."

Did you hang out at all with the other journalists there?

Yes. There's something about journalists—the good ones, anyway. They're the last bohemians, as a friend of mine says. They don't really make much money. And there's something very unegotistical about them. Of course, some wonderful journalists are complete egomaniacs! But they live without any desire to be famous, because you don't get fame as a journalist. They love stories. The simple fact of going to a place and coming back and saying, "This happened while I was there." And they love places. And they're not nearly as concerned with the propriety of places—what place is hip and what place is this or that— they just feel thrilled to be sent off to some place no one has ever heard of. And of course they love to talk about politics—I mean they understand that politics is just sort of one more aspect of life and one more thing which is every bit as perplexing and interesting as the life of movie stars. You know?

So for a while you stopped writing fiction, and then in the mid '80s you started again, and eventually you wrote **The Long Night of White Chickens,** *right?*

Well, first I wrote some terrible, terrible short stories. It was really like the first attempts to make a fly or whatever that was in *The Fly*. They came out like mangled meat. But there was a plan—I was beginning—I was beginning to find my way out of . . .

Can you define what your problem was?

Well, my sense of the world and my sense of what I wanted to write about had completely outgrown my ability to write about it. I knew enough about the writers I personally loved that the last thing I wanted to do, read, *or* write, as a fiction writer, was an angry diatribe about Central America. On the other hand, I knew I didn't have at all the inner balance or the largeness of vision or the discipline or the soul to write anything *but* a diatribe. And I essentially knew I had to shut up until I would be able to do something else. Because the history of the '80s in Central America was a traumatic, tragic, horrible piece of history, and I felt like I had had my face rubbed in it. I mean, when people talk about what has defined this century, it's been this kind of thing—powerful people slaughtering unpowerful people—and I got my taste of it. And my anger was—I mean I could not watch the news on TV without throwing things at the TV. In Guatemala, during that Holy Week when they abducted and killed the relatives-of-the-disappeared activists? We all knew those people! One of them was found with human bite-marks on her breasts and her baby's fingernails had been torn off. And the U.S. State Department issued this statement that seemed to confirm the Guatemalan Army's story that they'd died in a car accident! And then the State Department spokesman was shown on Guatemalan TV saying that! Well, for me, that was a culminating moment, the moment of watching that State Department spokesman on TV—the things I experienced as a U.S. citizen, as a Guatemalan, as a *human* . . . But I knew that ultimately the act of writing a novel was not about declaring the anger I felt at that moment. The fact is, I think you're showing an enormous disrespect for the intelligence of your readers if you think they need a novel to know that there's injustice in the world. To know that the United States State Department goes out of its way to cover up crimes. Your readers are not the least bit interested in any amount of moral superiority or smugness you might feel toward anybody, and so I was certainly not going to write a book to prove that I was politically or morally superior to anybody. Of course, when I started working on my novel, I wrote hundreds and hundreds and hundreds of pages that were exactly the kind of pages that you would expect—pages that might seem politically indignant in one way or another. Well, I hope not one of them has survived. I remember I used to spend hours and hours in the bars where the right-wing Americans hung out in Guatemala City. And I used to think, I am really going to use all this, some day I am really going to skewer these guys. Right? And when I wrote my novel, I didn't use that stuff at all. Why? Because I already know what I think about those people. I knew what I thought about them before I sat down to write. And I mean, you don't write to express what you already know. The reason you're a novelist is to find out what you don't know. And if you can find an impulse to tell a story— It's—well, it's very important to write about love! And to me, there's something impolite about a foreigner who goes down to the tropics and broods on nothing but the injustice everyone's suffering. The point is that a novelist should not denounce the absence of freedom: that isn't news! Instead, he should exemplify freedom by using his imagination.

What do you mean?

I mean that imagination is probably the thing we most lack. And for a reader, a novel should be a place where we *have* to use our imagination because we're listening to somebody else use *their* imagination. The only way to have a sense, really, of the world we're *living* in, and the society we're living in, is to be able to imagine lives that are different from ours. And feel some sympathy. And when we say, you know, we don't care what happens in this part of the world or that part of the world, or all that matters is our own little corner of the earth, that's a lack of imagination. All solidarity, if there is such a thing, is imagination. I mean, even when we end up with a choice between these political candidates we have, that is a complete lack of imagination.

I know what you mean.

In other words, why would a person like Reagan get elected? It's because people think, "Goddamnit, my neighbor Bill could run this country better than some guy who's spent his life studying how to do it." And so they go out and vote for the guy who's most like their neighbor Bill.

A recycling of what's familiar. And obviously this sort of provincialism has a lot to do with the fact that North Americans are so ignorant about what goes on in other countries. My God, I had the most unbelievable conversation about Cuba the other day—

Oh—

I mean, that's always an infuriating subject. Because the situation is infuriating.

Well, Castro is no longer a modern man in any sense of the term.

You mean, because he doesn't seem to get the idea of—I guess—pluralism?

Right. You know, the Sandinistas in Nicaragua may or may not have been nine democratic *comandantes,* but every soldier in their army believed the rhetoric that they were defending pluralism and democracy. The Sandinistas were seeding expectations of pluralism in a way that, even if they had secretly coveted a one-party state, they would never have been able to achieve it. Whereas Castro—I mean, it's *absurd* to believe that Cubans don't want a say in their own political destiny. It's *absurd* to believe that the younger generation is complacent and happy with merely—merely, I say, with appropriate irony—having grown up with university educations and health. Of *course* they take that for granted now. And they want pluralism. And of *course* he's a tyrant for not giving it to them. And if he *does* lead the country into a Romania-type chaos and anarchy, the U.S. will be thrilled to have an excuse to insert themselves into it, and the Miami Cubans will have exactly the excuse *they* need to flood the place and turn it into an island of busboys and chambermaids. Not that the people in Cuba would just submit to that—they'd have their own ideas. But at a certain point, they might not be able to prevent it.

What amazes me is how many so-called sophisticated New Yorkers know all the details about how authoritarian Cuba is, but they totally buy the line that the other countries in the region are "fledgling democracies."

Well, any place, whether they have elections or not, any place where you see 2 per cent of the population owning 80 per cent of the land can't possibly be a democracy, because only 2 per cent of the people, at most, would ever vote for that.

What about 1 per cent of the population owning 30 per cent of the wealth and 90 per cent of the population owning 32 per cent? How could we be a democracy? Anyway, 1992 seems to find you mainly in New York, so you clearly have found some way to stand living here.

I do feel at home in New York.

I envy that. For me it's all too predetermined. I mean, if I go to a New York cocktail party, I feel that my being there was actually inevitable, even before my birth. I mean, given my parents, my upbringing, what could I have done not to be there? And so I look around and I think, well, everybody at this party looks exactly like me, they talk exactly like me, and they are *exactly like me, and we are exactly the same. But, on the other hand, I hate myself, I hate them, and I've got to get out of here. It's a kind of an alienation.*

Well it's true that I don't have the anguish of the kind of alienation you're talking about, because, first of all, I don't get invited to any of those parties. And I guess nobody could have foreseen that I'd end up as I have today if you saw how I'd grown up, because I'm a completely, in some ways, self-invented person. But I had to be. I had no choice. Because what would I have done instead? I mean, some people in my family to this day cannot stand my creative writing teacher for having dissuaded me from becoming—I don't know—an accountant. But I just couldn't have done that. And I feel at home in New York because New York's the kind of city that was built for people like me. People aren't puzzled by me here the way they are in other parts of America. I mean, the Midwest terrifies me. I'm sure it's a wonderful place and there are wonderful people there, but it *terrifies* me. I just hate feeling that different from everybody else. I hate *looking* that different from everybody else. And you know, in London people look at me and they assume that I'm some Third World thing. So then they say outrageously anti-Semitic things in front of me. And so of course then I say, "Er—I'm Jewish!" And in Madrid! In Madrid, for instance, I was hanging out with these Arab guys and we'd be in a bar. And the bartender would come over and say, "Listen, there are too many Arabs here—it doesn't look good—some of you have to go." I would buzz stores, they wouldn't let me in. One day I was just a Good Samaritan—a man's car was stuck in the slush and I gave it a push. So he gave me a tip. Or once I had just bought a toy in a market to send to some friends' children back in the States. And I was standing on the corner with the toy and a man came along in a suit and snatched it out of my hands and said, "How much do you want for this?" Or I would be at a bar and suddenly I'd see people staring at me with hate-filled eyes, young guys in black leather jackets. And I'd walk by and they'd go, "*Moro de mierda . . .*" It was just incredible.

And a moro *is what?*

A Moor.

Oh.

So I'm at home in New York.

Yes. I get it. But I wanted to ask you—My question is—

Do I want to go to fancy New York literary cocktail parties? No. In fact I'd say right now people shouldn't even invite me to them.

Uh-huh.

Because I don't want to go to them.

Right. Okay. But no, you see, I wanted to ask something slightly different. I mean, I know New York can be incredibly enjoyable. But after all you've seen in the last 10 years, how can you still enjoy things?

Well, you see, I just don't forget—You have to keep yourself free inside, and that means being able to be happy. And I feel like I have an obligation to be happy. I really do. It's my nature, you know? I mean, in my next life if I could come back as anything, I'd want to be a trumpet player—just one of those obscure trumpet players who get to wear the white suit and stand in the back row in a merengue band and get to do those steps . . . and just travel around through the Latin Caribbean and just—just be a complete hedonist, you know. I would love that.

Yes. Exactly. Well, let's hope to God that does happen. (pp. 90-1, 93)

Francisco Goldman and Wallace Shawn, in an interview in The Village Voice, *Vol. XXXVII, No. 29, July 21, 1992, pp. 90-1, 93.*

An excerpt from *The Long Night of White Chickens*

[In] 1979 Flor ended up back in Guatemala City, where she was eventually hired to be director of a private orphanage and malnutrition clinic called Los Quetzalitos. On the seventeenth of February, 1983, towards the end of General Ríos Montt's highly successful counterinsurgency campaign, which according to what I've read in the papers and elsewhere added tens of thousands of new orphans to Guatemala's already huge orphan population, Flor was found murdered. She was discovered by some of her orphans lying on her bed in her room at the orphanage just before six in the morning, wearing pajamas, and dead from a single deep knife gash in her throat.

And the very next day the two major Guatemala City dailies came out saying that just two days previous the National Police had uncovered a clandestine safe house for hiding babies—also called a *casa de engordes,* or fattening house—many of them not even orphans but illegally purchased and even stolen babies, and that they were being kept there until their illegal adoptions could be arranged. That is, until they could be sold to childless couples in Europe and the United States, this apparently being a highly profitable and widespread business in Guatemala and elsewhere in Central America—"a business angle to civil war and violent repression," as one human rights publication I read phrased it. The newspapers ran photographs of a house full of crowded cribs. And close-up shots of the frightened face of a captured *niñera,* or nursemaid, who was quoted as saying that her employer, or rather one of her employers but the only one who ever came to the safe house in person, was Flor de Mayo. And the newspapers and police theorized that behind this lay the probable motive for the murder, since Flor couldn't have run that kind of business all alone: so that it must have been her partners, tipped off somehow about what the *niñera* had said, who had silenced Flor forever, before the police had been able to procure the order for her arrest. The police said they were searching for these anonymous partners and that justice would be done, not just for the crime of an internecine murder but for the defamation and disgrace that all such baby-selling rings brought upon the *patria. . . .*

The newspapers highlighted Flor's beauty, though not to any specific purpose. And they made very much of the fact that, although she was Guatemalan born, this alone could not account for her corruption as she was a United States citizen who had spent more than half her life in her adopted country and had graduated from one of its most elite colleges for women. Direct U.S. military aid to the Guatemalan military government had been cut off by Congress since 1978 because of the human rights violations, considered the most excessive in the hemisphere. . . . But the military, and many in the Guatemalan press, and many Guatemalans who considered themselves patriots, such as my relatives, liked to think of that cutoff as a kind of blanket violation of all Guatemalans' human rights and as a new and hypocritical form of imperialism, and now the newspapers posed Flor's case as another form of hypocrisy and imperialism: a highly educated U.S. citizen selling, for personal profit, the surviving victims of the *alleged* human rights atrocities that North Americans professed to be so concerned about.

It was into that scandal that my father and I flew together, to bring Flor's body home for burial.

Francisco Goldman, in his The Long Night of White Chickens, *The Atlantic Monthly Press, 1992.*

Marjorie Agosin (review date 24 July 1992)

[*In the following review of* The Long Night of White Chickens, *Agosin notes the novel's primary strengths and weaknesses.*]

The North American public envisions Guatemala as a land of striking physical beauty and of perpetual political strife, besieged by countless dictatorships and terrorized by human-rights violations.

Guatemalan writers also share in their collective literary imagination a vision of a troubled land—a nation divided between rich and poor, Indians and Mestizos, military and civilians. And the political turmoil within Guatemala has become a pervasive theme in Guatemalan literature. Miguel Angel Asturias led the way with his classic *El Señor Presidente,* and a series of Guatemalan novels that depict the violence of authoritarian regimes in the country has followed.

Francisco Goldman, a talented writer of Guatemalan-American origin, shares with Asturias and other native writers a deep love for Guatemala, their land of turbulent political history. In his brilliantly crafted first novel, ***The Long Night of White Chickens,*** Goldman captures with great skill and poetic beauty the history of Guatemala, the corruption caused by its military rule, and the terror resulting from the human-rights abuses committed there.

The novel takes place in the 1980s, during one of the country's most brutal dictatorships. The narrator, Roger Graetz, grew up in Boston with his Guatemalan mother and North American Jewish father. His mother employed a young Guatemalan orphan, Flor de Mayo Puac, as their household maid. During Roger's childhood, Flor de Mayo was a sister and a friend to him. She was later to become an obsession.

After growing up in the Graetz's household and finishing her studies at Wellesley College in Massachusetts, Flor de Mayo returns to Guatemala City to run an orphanage. Years later, she is mysteriously murdered, and Roger goes to Guatemala to search for her assassin as well as for his own complex identity.

The reader experiences a journey into Roger's life, his childhood growing up in Boston as a Guatemalan, and the indifference of his mother, Mirabel, to the social injustices of her native land.

Mirabel and his grandmother Abuelita represent the Guatemalan elite or oligarchy:

> . . . Abuelita's patriotism was as ebullient as her feeling for God and absolutely inseparable from it. There was a Guatemala that God approved of and all the other possibilities which He didn't. And the Guatemala He approved of had everything to do with Order: orderly progress that was possible through Order; . . .

During Roger's search for Flor, the reader meets a variety of characters, such as the dignified journalist Moya, who also attempts to uncover the mystery of her death, and the sympathetic and yet distant North American consul, who advises against a Guatemalan funeral for Flor.

In the novel, Flor's death becomes a metaphor for the senseless political violence and corruption that wracks Guatemala. The truth of her death is never uncovered, yet the reader is haunted by the constant presence of her disappearance and assassination. Though dead, she is powerfully alive for Roger because, through her tragedy, he goes not only to his beloved Guatemala, but to himself.

Goldman is an eloquent narrator, and his novel has the ability to captivate the reader with its powerful descriptive voice. Yet, the thriller element with an almost detective subplot diminishes the overall quality of the narration and makes it at times too repetitive. Though sections of the book are longer than the plot actually warrants, ***The Long Night of White Chickens*** is a story worth reading—a tale that sensitively depicts the very best of human dignity and love.

> *Marjorie Agosin, "A Homeland Rife with Discord," in* The Christian Science Monitor, *July 24, 1992, p. 14.*

Constance Casey (review date 16 August 1992)

[*In the following review, Casey offers a generally positive assessment of* The Long Night of White Chickens, *praising in particular Goldman's depiction of "life distorted by paranoia."*]

Francisco Goldman, the son of a Guatemalan mother and an American father, has been reporting on his mother's country for Harper's Magazine. The ungainly title of his first novel strains to suggest magical realism, but ***The Long Night of White Chickens*** is a solidly realistic and richly detailed evocation of what it's like to live in Guatemala.

The long night of the title refers to the time when two of the novel's three major characters, Flor de Mayo Puac, director of an orphanage in Guatemala, and Luis Moya Martínez, a liberal journalist, fell in love. The two lingered long enough in a Chinese restaurant to see the next day's chickens being delivered by hand, alive and struggling, dangling two by two, upside down, prompting Flor to observe, "Everything gets done here in some stupid, slow and inevitably cruel way." And that, of course, is what the novel is about—a stupid, cruel way of life in a small country.

As the story begins, Flor's body lies in the Guatemala City morgue, beside two bodies that show signs of torture. She was not tortured, but someone had gone to her bedroom at the orphanage and severed her windpipe with a kitchen knife. The novel takes the form of an unofficial murder investigation conducted by Flor's lover, Luis Moya, and his school friend Roger Graetz, a Guatemalan-American.

At 13, Flor had been plucked from a Guatemala City orphanage by Roger's extremely authoritarian upper-class

Guatemalan grandmother and sent to suburban Boston to be his family's maid. Just eight years older than Roger, Flor became part mother and part sister to him. Her name, Flor de Mayo, or May flower, suggests that she is a 20th-century pilgrim to Massachusetts.

Roger's father, the son of immigrant Russians, was not, to put it mildly, comfortable with having a maid. The family pressures that buried Roger, a sickly boy, "somehow lifted Flor up." The family sent Flor to school, pushing her to study until she won a scholarship to Wellesley College. Back in Guatemala in the summertime, attending a prestigious secondary school, Roger met Moya, another scholarship student, son of a seamstress.

Part of the mystery is why Flor, an oddity, a highly educated Indian, went back to Guatemala. Her need to reconnect, explained as being like the feeling of an amputee for a phantom limb, is particularly dangerous in its timing—the early 1980's, when the military regime was conducting a war against the highland Indians. Flor attracted additional attention by caring for the orphans created by the war.

Mr. Goldman's strength is subtlety. Sometimes, though, he's so careful to avoid overstatement that the reader is confused because the action slides forward and backward from the day of Flor's murder, and Mr. Goldman has difficulty guiding us about in time and deciding what's essential information. But he has a gift for suggesting and explaining complex feelings. Roger, for example, has mixed emotions about the Indian girl who has become his quasi sister. She was a heroic achiever in school; he was in the bottom fifth of his high school class. She has a job placing orphan babies in comfortable European and North American homes; he's working as a bartender in New York. Flor may not have been as purely heroic as she seems to outsiders. Roger learns she'd been pressured by a high bureaucrat to give him $20,000 in return for an exit visa for an Indian boy who needed a kidney transplant. She may have come to some kind of short-term arrangement for the long-term good. Secret lovers and a serious error in judgment in placing an orphan come to light, and there are suggestions that she had more than the usual powerful official enemies.

Roger's expatriate mother, with what Roger calls her "Empire of Beautiful Nostalgia" for the Guatemala of her own childhood, is a wonderful contrast to Flor. Roger despises his mother for her exquisite consciousness of social gradations, but can still love her sincerely. "For so many years," Roger observes, "my mother considered it one of the great offenses of life in the United States that even the plumber might assume she was Puerto Rican."

Speaking through Roger, Mr. Goldman has an interesting take on the Guatemalan rich, his mother's class, especially the boys Roger met in school in Guatemala in the summers. They were, he recalls, "tiny versions of the men they would grow into, fanatically fastidious in appearance, shoes always blazingly shined, shirt cuffs rolled crisply back to expose expensive, gold-banded scuba diver's and astronaut's wristwatches, boys pampered into an effemi-

nateness contradicted by their obstinately extroverted, boisterous, violent-gestured personalities."

The finest portrait is that of Luis Moya Martínez, who cultivated and obtained a Harvard fellowship and attends to his influential connections as carefully as Roger's mother does. Moya needs those connections to stay alive—Harvard professors who can phone senators who can phone generals to say, "We know you've snatched him and do not harm another hair on his head or you can kiss even your nonlethal military aid goodbye!"

Moya appreciates the attention that being a star in the corrupt little country gets him. He's catnip to European and North American women, who find him exotic—a quetzal in a jacaranda tree, decorative and endangered. He's used to being treated as a hero, and "truly, whether he fully deserved such treatment or not, he accepted it all gratefully." His courage is indisputable, but part of the truth is that he works for a low-circulation newspaper, with never more than 12 pages. He's often so preoccupied with writing columns that have just enough sting, and not too much, to attend to chores like checking his facts.

One day, should things change a lot—so much he becomes president—Moya sees himself bringing justice to the Indians. To his credit, he recognizes the irony in the fact that he's probably seen less than the average tourist has of the Indian *altiplano*. Military roadblocks are common on the empty highways through the mountains, and Moya knows he could easily be snatched and killed before the news got to Aunt Irene (his telephone code for Amnesty International).

But Moya too is tired of tales of human rights abuse, where the very phrase often translates into being "disappeared." "Every time I look at Time magazine or The New York Times," he says, "I find myself skipping over the articles on, for example, Ethiopia. Out of guilt I make myself go back and read them, imagining how uninteresting the same kinds of articles on Guatemala must seem to the average citizen of the world." How does a Guatemalan writer like Moya, or Francisco Goldman, communicate what it's like to live a life distorted by paranoia? (By completely justified paranoia.) By writing a good novel.

Constance Casey, "Paranoids with Real Enemies," in The New York Times Book Review, *August 16, 1992, p. 20.*

Yvonne Fraticelli   (review date September-October 1992)

[*In the following review of* The Long Night of White Chickens, *Fraticelli praises Goldman's characterizations and his prose style.*]

From the opening passages describing the murder of Flor de Mayo Puac, a Guatemala City orphanage director, Francisco Goldman's extraordinary first novel plunges the reader into a violent, chaotic world. After 30 years of civil war, unidentified torture victims are so common in the Guatemala of *The Long Night of White Chickens* that a newspaper takes a novel approach to the story by printing a photo of a victim's shoes. Death squads frequent a special after-hours club, the police murder street children or recruit them into criminal gangs, and the counter-insurgents relocate Indian refugees in model villages without regard for tribe or language. The disorder is spiritual as well as physical: according to the Guatemalan journalist Moya, "Even the religious landscape had for many become one of confusion and delirium, because how to speak to the soul without addressing the terror so many felt there, and how to name the devil without increasing the terror?"

Like Moya and the novel's protagonist, Roger Graetz, Flor is an exile. Through the efforts of Roger's wealthy maternal grandmother, 13-year-old Flor travels from a convent orphanage in Guatemala to the Graetzs' home in Boston, where she works as a maid for Roger's mother, Mirabel. Treated as an adoptive daughter by Roger's father Ira, if not by Mirabel, Flor becomes the center of the discontented family. Roger muddles through an isolated childhood, Mirabel endures her lowered social standing in the United States, and decent, courageous Ira vests his compromised ambitions in Flor. At 22, Flor is Ira's "Wellesley girl," paying for her assumed identity with a fundamental falseness that distorts and betrays genuine emotions.

The novel traces Roger's efforts to discover the identity of Flor's murderer. At Moya's urging, Roger returns to a country where even the late afternoon light illuminating an Indian marketplace seems false, its apparent elevation of the Indians' suffering "a trick of shadows and dust and sinking highland sun." Yet that light, and the disquieting silence accompanying it, lead Roger to an insight as close as he will come to the truth about Flor, "the unconscious truth that artificiality was essential to what we had, and lay like silence near the heart of everything. . . ."

A consummate storyteller, Mr. Goldman provides a vivid cast of supporting characters, living, dead, and legendary: cousin Catalina, whose checkered past includes a hasty marriage to a Canadian skycap; Patti Mundinger, the rich girl obsessed with her country's inequities; Flor's late father, the victim of a machete-wielding neighbor, whose ghost wanders the highlands searching for water; and her married lover, the newspaper publisher Celso Batres. In a thumbnail sketch of Batres and his world, we learn that the publisher's devout father, friend of archbishops and papal nuncios, has groomed Celso to be Guatemala's political savior, and that the powerful man has the means, in the death squad of an extreme rightist party, to protect his son. Would this Batres, Moya wonders, commit "ei-

ther the most foolish or the most redemptive act of his life" by marrying Flor?

Playing his own role—"detective, anthropologist, father confessor and seducer all at once"—with self-mockery bordering on contempt, Moya craves the attention of his influential foreign visitors but scorns them when they return to their countries with a clear conscience, happy to leave Guatemala's struggles behind them. Boasting of secrets kept even from shadow, Moya wonders what violence he would condone for the sake of the revolution, and whether he deliberately betrayed Flor by revealing their affair to Batres.

Goldman's Guatemala is rich in tradition. The confused, bitter legacy of the Conquest—bloodshed, intolerance, repression, Christian faith and "pagan" belief—permeate daily life. One Indian myth describes a goddess who blows the wind across a lake in order to clear its waters of drowned fishermen; another, eerily reflective of the widespread personal and cultural dislocation, warns that the souls of children buried far from their villages will wander forever in exile from their ancestors.

Rich prose, fully realized characters, and a plot filled with murky politics distinguish this novel; but its triumph is Flor, a heroine as complex and fragile as the society she inhabits. In the end Flor emerges as a confused and compassionate woman exhausted by the sense of her own hollowness and the limitless suffering she witnesses. And Roger, who has drifted aimlessly until then, remembers her: "Memory is like a long conversation, during which, at any moment, Flor might tell [me] something unexpected. . . ."

Yvonne Fraticelli, in a review of "The Long Night of White Chickens," in Boston Review, *Vol. XVII, No. 5, September-October, 1992, p. 38.*

FURTHER READING

Coe, Jonathan. "What Else Is New?" *London Review of Books* 15, No. 5 (11 March 1993): 18.
    Calls *The Long Night of White Chickens* a remarkable debut, although it fails "to pack the emotional punch which it constantly seems to be promising."

Siri Hustvedt
The Blindfold

Hustvedt is an American novelist, translator, and poet, born in 1955.

INTRODUCTION

A psychological novel exploring the theme of identity in the modern world, *The Blindfold* centers on Iris Vegan, a graduate student living in New York City. Through a series of bizarre encounters with other people, Iris's sense of self becomes increasingly fragmented. In the first of *The Blindfold*'s four related narratives a writer hires Iris to tape-record, in a whisper, descriptions of certain objects that once belonged to a woman who was murdered: a soiled glove, a used cotton ball smeared with makeup, and a mirror. In the second segment of the novel Iris poses for George, a photographer who takes a striking but grotesque picture of her. She begs George to destroy the portrait, but he refuses. In the third episode Iris is hospitalized for treatment of persistent migraine and, while heavily sedated, encounters Eleanor, a psychotic old woman who addresses Iris as Eleanor. Iris participates in and even encourages the woman's delusions. In the final, longest section, which many critics consider the most intriguing, a professor asks Iris to translate a German novel about a sadistic youth named Klaus Kruger. Soon Iris begins to think and behave like Klaus, cutting her hair and frequenting seedy bars dressed in a man's suit. She admits: "The brutal boy found his second incarnation in me." Iris's identity is further blurred by her friendship with Paris, an art critic who encourages her to reinvent herself by taking on different identities. Critical discussions of *The Blindfold* have focused on Hustvedt's ambiguous and complex portrayal of Iris. Hustvedt's narrative leaves uncertainty about whether Iris is a willing participant in other people's fantasies or a naive young woman manipulated by the people around her.

CRITICISM

Kirkus Reviews   (review date 1 February 1992)

[*In the following review, the critic describes* The Blindfold *as a postmodernist novel with a distinctly feminine voice.*]

Poet Hustvedt's first novel [*The Blindfold*] is unabashedly cerebral, a disturbing and disarming fiction that explores the mysteries of identity. It's a postmodernist puzzle with a queasy eroticism and hints of perversion, and owes much to the work of Beckett, DeLillo, and her husband, Paul Auster. But Hustvedt adds to their explorations in silence and unspeakability her distinctly feminine voice: innocent, intimate, victimized.

These four related narratives circle around the life of Iris Vegan, a distraught and hypersensitive graduate student in literature at Columbia. A beautiful, blue-eyed blond from the Midwest, she's continually at the mercy of others, mostly men who shroud themselves in mystery. Iris's first story finds her working as an assistant to a strange writer, a collector of women's discarded objects, who asks her to record her observations so that he may reconstruct their previous owners. After playing this bizarre Scheherazade, Iris is unalterably changed, but not as dramatically as in her second narrative, in which a photographer's portrait of her proves an invasion of her privacy. Her boyfriend at the time admits that cruelty makes him "feel more alive." As her personality begins to disintegrate, Iris (in the third piece) admits to minor hallucinations, which land her in the hospital whacked out on Thorazine and tormented by one of her roommates, a withered old woman who also desires her in some strange way. To demonstrate further that "distortion is part of desire," Iris then alters herself, taking on the role of a brutal boy, a role she has adopted from a German novella she co-translates with her professor/lover. Roaming the city in drag, she indulges her fantasies until the much older professor catches her in disguise. In playful "blindness," she loses all sense of self but also turns out to be as mysterious as all her tormentors, so that we wonder, just who is playing with whom?

Hustvedt brings her dark urban landscape to life with her camera eye and Iris's tenacious, Midwestern common sense—the perfect balance to all the existential weirdness.

> *A review of "The Blindfold," in* Kirkus Reviews, *Vol. LX, No. 3, February 1, 1992, p. 133.*

Michiko Kakutani   (essay date 28 April 1992)

[*In the following essay, Kakutani examines the structure and style of* The Blindfold.]

The New York City depicted in Siri Hustvedt's disturbing first novel is a sinister, predatory place where identities can easily be misplaced, where chance encounters with strangers can permanently alter the shape of one's life. Midtown, with its dour office buildings and its emphasis on commerce, does not exist for Ms. Hustvedt's characters; nor do the family neighborhoods of the Upper East and West Sides. Rather, Ms. Hustvedt's people commute exclusively between the hectic, grungy streets near Columbia University and the swank bars, galleries and lofts of SoHo.

In Ms. Hustvedt's portrait of New York, there are echoes of the work of her husband, Paul Auster; there is even an overt reference to his 1989 novel *Moon Palace,* in the novel's second chapter. For that matter, *The Blindfold* often feels like a veritable echo chamber of other writers' work. The air of menace that hovers over the novel brings to mind Harold Pinter's plays, while the philosophical game-playing recalls the fiction of Peter Handke. Ms. Hustvedt's characters are linked by tenuous, existential bonds of dependency not unlike those found in the work of Samuel Beckett, and they are portrayed, like so many of the people in Thomas Bernhard's novels, as manipulative, predatory creatures.

Yet if *The Blindfold* feels derivative in terms of its architecture and themes, the novel also attests to Ms. Hustvedt's thoroughly original style and her lucid contemporary voice, and it introduces an intriguingly vulnerable narrator named Iris Vegan.

Iris, we learn, is a graduate student at Columbia University. She is a tall, blond woman from the Middle West who, much like the hero of Mr. Auster's *Moon Palace,* leads a

marginal, impoverished existence. She never knows how she is going to pay the next month's rent, and she sometimes skips meals to make ends meet. Though she is intelligent and outspoken, she is also strangely impressionable and passive, and her encounters with five strangers lead to a radical reconfiguration of her life.

The first of these individuals to be introduced is an eccentric writer named Mr. Morning, whom Iris meets when she answers his ad for a research assistant. Her job, Mr. Morning tells her, is to describe several objects in minute detail. The objects—a soiled glove, a used cotton ball, a mirror—once belonged to a woman he knew. Iris is to record her descriptions of these objects on a tape recorder, and she is to speak her descriptions in a whisper.

When Iris tries to track down the identity of the owner of the objects, she learns that the woman was murdered and that Mr. Morning was a suspect in the police investigation. She confronts her mysterious employer, then flees when he asks her to give him one of her own possessions.

> The New York City depicted in Siri Hustvedt's disturbing first novel is a sinister, predatory place where identities can easily be misplaced, where chance encounters with strangers can permanently alter the shape of one's life.
>
> —*Michiko Kakutani*

The second person Iris tells us about is a photographer named George. Iris meets George through her boyfriend, Stephen; she later begins to suspect that George and Stephen have been lovers. There is something vaguely unsettling about George's request to photograph her, but Iris nonetheless complies. The finished photograph, an oddly cropped portrait full of severe shadows and angles, disturbs Iris because it seems like a picture of someone else. It's not long before the photo has provoked an argument between Iris and Stephen, effectively ending their romance.

Some eight months later, Iris finds herself in a New York hospital. For weeks now, she has been suffering from debilitating migraine headaches, and her doctor has sedated her with Thorazine. The pain and the medication leave her in a perpetual state of anxiety and dislocation, and she soon becomes obsessed with another patient in the room, a mentally unstable woman named Mrs. O. who may or may not have sinister designs on her as well.

The last two people Iris introduces seem vaguely threatening, too. Paris, a short, ugly denizen of the art world, keeps popping up in Iris's life, asking impertinent questions. Though Iris is somewhat frightened of Paris, she makes him her confidant, confessing the details of her affair with a professor named Michael Rose. Professor Rose asks Iris to help him translate a book, a creepy German novel about a boy with sadistic impulses. The book, much like George's photograph, quickly takes on a life of its own, permeating Iris's consciousness and warping her relationship with Professor Rose.

Why is Iris so susceptible to the bad vibes of Professor Rose, Paris, Mrs. O., George and Mr. Morning? Is Iris a willing victim, eager to submit to others; a blank slate for the fantasies of strangers? Or is she simply a naïve young woman, cruelly deceived and manipulated by the sadistic people around her? Is Iris's story meant to be an illustration of the tenuousness of identity in the modern world? Or is she simply a high-strung woman, suffering from delusions of persecution?

Ms. Hustvedt, of course, supplies no answers to such questions; her narrative is deliberately cool, elliptical and elusive. It is so elliptical, in fact, that the reader ends up feeling that *The Blindfold* is less an organic novel than four short stories sharing a common heroine and common theme. The last of these stories, which is flawed by an overly melodramatic climax rendered in uncharacteristically turgid prose, tries to tie the earlier chapters together, but it leaves the reader curiously unsatisfied, hungry for at least a hint of emotional catharsis.

This letdown at the end of *The Blindfold,* however, should not detract from Ms. Hustvedt's genuine achievement. All in all, this is an impressive and dexterous debut, the announcement of a talented new writer's arrival.

> *Michiko Kakutani, "How 5 Strangers Reconfigure a Narrator's Life," in* The New York Times, *April 28, 1992, p. C18.*

Emily White   (review date May 1992)

[*In the following review of* The Blindfold, *White admires Hustvedt's prose and insight.*]

The Blindfold tells four interrelated stories from the life of Iris Vegan, a wistful Columbia graduate student who's susceptible to migraines, destructive affairs, and long walks in the dark. She is a superstitious woman with a strong sense of doom; she feels there's a crack in the world waiting to swallow her soul. Sometimes she has visions: "big, ragged hole[s]" eating away the walls of her apartment, or "hundreds of bright sparks" crowding the air.

Throughout the book, strangers enter Iris's life and throw her further off balance. In the first section, she is hired as a research assistant by a man called Mr. Morning, who asks her to write descriptions of a series of objects that belonged to a dead woman: a single glove, a soiled cotton ball, a pocket mirror. As Iris stares at the glove, which smells of sweat and dust, she grows obsessed with the woman's life, but Mr. Morning won't give her story away. Iris desperately wants to attach a world to these bits of debris. She is sure the woman was killed, and dreams of her corpse, "bloodied and torn apart."

In the second section, a photographer named George traps Iris in his gaze. This encounter is another storm she can barely weather. He takes her picture, then violently crops and distorts it—to Iris the photo is a stilled nightmare, a

glimpse of her own body torn apart. The third section finds Iris in the hospital being treated for migraines. She sees herself reflected in her roommate, the mad Mrs. O., who was "a delicate woman in her late seventies, the victim of some nervous catastrophe. That event or series of events had left her incoherent. What remained was a fragmented being." Iris and Mrs. O. recognize each other across the room—both are in the process of shattering.

> **[Hustvedt] is a writer of strong, sometimes astonishing gifts; there's a spareness and ominousness about her prose that at its best recalls Rilke. There are also ways in which her voice feels undeveloped, not quite trustworthy. A persistent, nagging flaw is Iris's tendency to lapse into half-baked philosophical ruminations. . . .**
>
> **—Emily White**

The most stark and haunting section of this novel is the last, in which Iris falls for the aging Professor Rose. He asks her to help him translate a novella from the German. It's the story of Klaus, a boy tempted to commit small acts of violence: choking cats, shattering his mother's vases. Iris begins to feel the character's voice inside her, possessing her; at night she dresses up in a suit and walks the streets of New York, calling herself Klaus. Dressed as a man, she can travel far into unknown neighborhoods without being harassed. One night she runs into the professor, and they go home together. Near his house he blindfolds her, telling her to walk the rest of the way without sight. Iris remembers: "Those six blocks were an odyssey. My equilibrium was gone with my sight, and I lurched and tottered forward."

The Blindfold is Hustvedt's first work of fiction, though she's already published a collection of poetry [*Reading to You,* 1983]. She is a writer of strong, sometimes astonishing gifts; there's a spareness and ominousness about her prose that at its best recalls Rilke. There are also ways in which her voice feels undeveloped, not quite trustworthy. A persistent, nagging flaw is Iris's tendency to lapse into half-baked philosophical ruminations—in the second part, she makes the dreary observation, "The 'I' which had always designated the whole of my inner life seemed to have shifted elsewhere, and for a minute I stopped walking, overcome by my own strangeness to myself." Such bland forays into analysis slow the momentum of the book and distance us from what's most interesting: Iris's feverishness, her irrational sense of loss and losing. At other times, though, her insights are wise, illuminating. "Distortion is part of desire. We always change the things we want."

For readers seeking "positive representations" of women, Iris will be trouble. She is always surrendering herself; always, in one way or another, allowing herself to be blindfolded. Like the heroines of Jean Rhys novels, Iris is passive, confounded. Playing sex games with Professor Rose, she thinks, "I . . . felt my femininity as the game of all women, a mysterious identification in which I lost myself. He was caught too, and I wondered what he saw, whom he saw. It didn't matter. Let's drown, I thought." Iris takes pleasure in succumbing; the idea of being trapped stimulates and inspires her. She wonders, in a detached way, how long she can remain in this position, prone, with her hands tied above her head. Siri Hustvedt's prose is the prose of the drowned; she's not a writer interested in resolution or redemption. Sometimes I wanted to save Iris, but I realized she was too heavy, too far away, and after a while I sank down to the bottom of the ocean to meet her.

Emily White, in a review of "The Blindfold,"
in VLS, *No. 105, May, 1992, p. 5.*

David Foster Wallace   (review date 24 May 1992)

[*In the following essay, Wallace discusses the philosophical ideas of self-identity and objectification as portrayed in* The Blindfold.]

The point of this review is going to be that *The Blindfold* is a really good book.

The first neat thing about it is that the jacket copy and blurbs are interesting. Don DeLillo is arguably the best living fiction writer in the United States, and he rarely blurbs anybody except his good friend Paul Auster, and so DeLillo's endorsement carries weight, and on the back cover he calls this novel "completely urban and modern but working at the reader's emotions with the undistanced intimacy of a traditional tale." What's cunning about this blurb is that Siri Hustvedt's "tale," which is really four interconnected novellas, is "traditional" only in a very specific sense.

Though features of *The Blindfold* will remind readers of any number of novelistic touchstones—Beckett's *Molloy,* Sartre's *Nausea* and Camus' *The Fall,* Fowles' *The Magus* and Auster's *New York Trilogy*—Hustvedt's accomplishment is hard to appreciate fully without reference to a loopy philosophical tradition that runs from Descartes to R. D. Laing and then back to Bishop Berkeley. Because the most impressive thing about this novel is its ingenious distaff inversion of that most haunting preoccupation of modern art-fiction, the problem of philosophical skepticism.

The problem of skepticism is Cartesian and phallocentric and presumes the ontological priority of the Subject: I know I exist OK, but how can I trust my perceptions enough to be equally sure that any of the non-me Objective stuff I seem to see around me exists, etc. Since your thinking man avoids solipsism at just about any cost, this skeptical Subjective insecurity—in which the integrity of the self depends on an efferent relation between the Subject as active perceiver and world as reliable Object—sits brooding astride the whole canon of Anglo-American 20th-century lit, from Eliot and Joyce to Bellow and Larkin.

A defining characteristic of this century's important *feminist* fictions, though, has been its obversion of the skeptical

dilemma. The best feminist lit has co-opted ideas such as quantum theory's axiom that any observation affects its object, post-structuralism's revolt against the "metaphysics of presence," and existentialism's (Heidegger's, Sartre's, Laing's) idea that the really significant ontological insecurity is that of the self about itself, all to alter the skeptical angst-dynamic in their best fictions from *Subject*-ive to *Object*-ive.

Instead of a secure Subject brooding Cartesianishly over the reliability of an Exterior's appearance, most interesting feminist novels involve the ontological insecurity of a female whose sense of her own authentic existence is bound up with how she herself is perceived by other (male) Subjects. The philosophical touchstone of important novels such as Jean Rhys' *Good Morning, Midnight* or Kathy Acker's *The Childlike Life of the Black Tarantula* is not Descartes but Bishop Berkeley, whose ultra-empiricist tenet that existence consists all and only in being *perceived* is way more congenial to a gender whose sense of authenticity has for a long time been dependent on an afferent relation between the self as alluring Object and the world as a male Subject whose attention defines her sexual (the equivalent, for these feminists, of ontological) security.

The Blindfold is the best novel I've ever read in this Berkeley/Laing mode. In contrast to Rhys, whose portraits of disintegrating female selves were prescient but sort of simplistic and freighted with a passive self-pity, and Acker, who's up on all kinds of cutting-edge French theory but is crippled by easy anger and a penchant for cute, easy formal tricks like rendering her females' ontological fragmentation through sharp juxtapositions of different narratives and enraged autobiography, Hustvedt's protagonist Iris (her name both an inversion of the author's "Siri" and, literally, a perceiving eye) struggles to establish an actual self—literally to make herself up—in the face of relentless and surreal objectification by the males she's drawn to. Here the book's jacket copy is not only accurate but incisive: It describes *The Blindfold* as "a story particular to our time, when a woman no longer expects to move from parents to husband but must forge a separate identity to hold at bay that which others impose upon her."

Written in self-consciously simple English, this intricate novel's best complexity is the neurasthenic Iris' ambivalence about her objectification by Others—all of whom both attract and repel her—so that she's split not only existentially but emotionally. This seems real. And her ambivalence is justified by the hypnotic power with which Hustvedt constructs Iris' manipulative Others: the weird old hack writer who hires Iris to compose descriptions of a murdered girl's personal effects; the demented, "disintegrated" old woman who sees in an invalided Iris a reflection of her own shattered identity; the gifted photographer whose truncated portrait of Iris becomes a triangular third character and destroys her relation with a lover who prefers the photo to the real woman; the academic superstar whose translation of a fake [?] novella called *The Brutal Boy* plunges Iris into a schizoid transsexual identification with the story's sadistic protagonist.

None of these synopses does the jeweler-fine complexity of the four narratives' plots justice. It's not surprising that a couple of them won great praise and Best-Of anthologizing when they were published as short stories in literary magazines: each of the novellas ends up a moving, troubling story about metaphysical erasure: In her struggle to construct a self in a relationship with males and elders (rather than in some cruder, Ackerish opposition to them), Iris ends up dismantling others' psyches to the precise extent that she preserves the integrity of her own.

What is remarkable is the haunting effect of these novellas' combination. Hustvedt has created in Iris both a stunning synecdoche of female skepticism—a fecund, symbolic exploration of the question whether a distinctively female character is even possible—and a compelling, utterly three-dimensional fictional character, a heroine in every old and some new senses of the world.

The Blindfold both intrigues and annoys in its efforts to align itself with another tradition, too. It's not surprising that Don DeLillo's praise adorns the jacket, because *The Blindfold* is clearly a feminist reworking of some of the central themes of DeLillo and his literary compadre, Paul Auster. Lines like " 'What you've forgotten is that some things are unspeakable. . . . Words may cover it up for a while, but then it comes howling back' " and "There is no end to such discussions. They wind in on themselves" sound almost straight out of *Great Jones Street* or *White Noise*.

Hustvedt's preoccupation with silence and the untellable, inanimate objects and their spatial arrangement, the modal potency of names, the geometric expansion of images, even the urban-blighted surrealism of the novel's setting are overwhelmingly reminiscent of DeLillo and Auster. And so are her prose rhythms, developed carefully via short sentences and oblique repetitions. A problem is that *The Blindfold*'s prose lacks both DeLillo's wit and ear for speech and Auster's lapidary compression and lucidity.

Blurbers praise this novel's "brain wave-altering prose," but I think they confuse style here with tone. The narrative tone is masterly—at once flat and sharp, disassociated and intimate—but the prose itself is sometimes so clunky it seems as if it has been poorly translated from some foreign language. Besides dialogue that often sounds stilted and written, *The Blindfold* is also pocked with ponderous bits of exposition like "The connection seemed rife with meaning, and yet it spawned nothing inside me but a feeling akin to guilt" and "I didn't know what the words meant, but they seemed to identify an amorphous truth."

It seems fair to point out the ways Hustvedt is inferior to DeLillo and Auster, since she seems to try so hard to associate her work with theirs. Besides the DeLilloish meditations, *The Blindfold* is dedicated to Auster, has characters eating in restaurants named after Auster novels like *Moon Palace,* and is studded with weird throw-aways like "I heard someone shout the name Paul. I waited for an answer. None came." Since Hustvedt is Auster's spouse, I guess some of these are at least explainable. But a little of this stuff goes a long way. At certain points the reader gets the sense that *The Blindfold* is in some ways a *roman a clef,* except a cozy inter-author *roman a clef,* with inside jokes and references from which those outside a small circle are consciously excluded.

I am giving these flaws so much attention because they're just about the only ones I could find. I don't know that I'd call this novel fun to read, but it's very powerful, and awfully smart and well-crafted, a clear bright sign that the feminist and post-modern traditions in America are far from exhausted. For its sensitive, surreal illumination of the Objectified psyche, *The Blindfold* is likely to end up recognized as one of the more important first novels to appear in this decade.

An excerpt from *The Blindfold*

Klaus was born in a bar, my Klaus anyway. The brutal boy found his second incarnation in me, and as soon as I took his name, I knew that from then on, the nights belonged to Klaus. In fact, he had been around for some time. The lie was a kind of truth, a birth announcement of sorts. My answer to Mort catapulted the sleeping homunculus into the world, and he woke up, a man. It never could have happened in Webster. My hometown is too small. People talk. But in the city it was easy to change my name, to be someone else. I was just another character, and not even an outlandish one. No one challenged my name or my appearance. Nevertheless, I did have a few close calls. Once, I nearly ran headlong into a group of graduate students from Columbia on Broome Street, and another time, I fled Magoo's when I saw a neighbor from 109th Street coming through the door. I was a regular at Magoo's, had befriended Mort; Fat Eddie, who was rail thin; Elise, the waitress; and Dolly, a disheveled woman with long gray hair who drank vodka only. Dolly was the one I really liked. She beat me on the back a lot and said, "You're a mixed-up kid, Klaus, but you're a cracker." To them I had confided a fictional life in bits and pieces, and the idea of being exposed was unbearable. When I saw Frank's face in the doorway, I leapt from the barstool, made an excuse, pulled my hat down to hide my face, and, passing my neighbor, heaved myself out of the door.

In early August I cut off my hair. A barber did it for five dollars, and when I came out, my hair was no more than an inch long all over my head. The barber clicked his tongue in dismay throughout the procedure, but I didn't look back. My new small head brought me a kind of steely satisfaction. I wasn't beautiful, but it didn't matter. The day of the haircut, I came home very late. After work I had gone to Magoo's and then to a strip joint called the Babydoll Lounge, where I often went to chat with one of the girls. Ramona went to business school during the day and stripped at night. Between shifts, she would often sit with me at the bar, wearing a little blue robe and her big glasses. She told me her dream was to open a toy store, and we spent time thinking up names for it. I liked the Purple Dog, but Ramona didn't. Anyway, after I said good-bye to Ramona, I wandered for a couple of hours, and it must have been three o'clock by the time I returned to my apartment. The phone rang. I thought my father was dead. I picked up the receiver expecting to hear my mother's voice. It was Paris.

Siri Hustvedt, in her The Blindfold, *Poseidon Press, 1992.*

David Foster Wallace, "Iris' Story: An Inversion of Philosophical Skepticism," in The Philadelphia Inquirer, *May 24, 1992, p. M2.*

Jenifer Levin   (essay date 7 June 1992)

[*In the following review of* The Blindfold, *Levin praises Hustvedt's sensitive handling of psychological turmoil but finds fault with the novel's apparent lack of direction.*]

It is difficult to know quite how to discuss Siri Hustvedt's first novel, ***The Blindfold,*** which, although the product of obvious talent, is in the end less likable and successful than one hopes for. Part of the problem is summarized by Ms. Hustvedt's main character herself. Commenting on a former lover's failings, she says, "Although he cultivated ideas that embraced the perverse and forbidden, Stephen was squeamish, and his adventures were strictly of the fashionable, literary sort." One might say the same of this book. Despite its lacks, though, it also has its strengths.

The Blindfold concerns several key events and relationships in the life of Iris Vegan, a young Columbia University graduate student from the Midwest, as she struggles through course work, translations, oral exams, unsuccessful love affairs and friendships, financial hardship, nervous collapse. The banality of this plot framework—a sort of academic coming-of-age story, really—is offset somewhat by the fact that Ms. Hustvedt does, on more than one occasion, offer up some eerily memorable images, and gives voice to fascinating and complex ideas.

The novel's opening section, in which Iris accepts a job examining and tape-recording descriptions of seemingly unimportant objects that belonged to a young woman (who, we learn, was recently murdered), is the weirdest, most imaginative and in some ways the best. Her strange employer claims that he is "looking for anonymity so the purity of the object won't be blocked from coming through, from displaying itself in its nakedness." Is he the dead woman's murderer? We never find out—at least, not in words. "What you've forgotten," he insists—and the voice of the author rings through clearly here—"is that some things are unspeakable. . . . Words may cover it up for a while, but then it comes howling back. A storm. A plague. Only half remembered."

Like Don DeLillo, Siri Hustvedt seems fascinated with the potential significance of inanimate objects, numbers, names, of writing itself—also, with the propensity of intellect, when unbalanced by heart and feeling, to coldly objectify human life. This propensity opens the door to at least a possible study of the etiology of evil. It raises bold and grand ideas. But the author fails to take us through the door she toys at opening. The rest of the novel rapidly loses the bizarre and evocative sense of direction implied by the intriguing first chapter's trail of ideas, traveling off into vague intellectual explorations of notions of identity, brutality, nothingness and love, and does not hang together.

Indeed, it seems as if two separate stories begged to be told here, and the author chose to give short shrift to the more tantalizing and original one. As a result, ***The Blindfold*** as

a whole fades readily, time and again, back into the humdrum of young intellectual-academic urban life. Powerful though their feelings are to the mostly young characters involved, they are neither unique nor profound enough to truly grip us or transform our understanding of the world.

An exception is the elegant job Ms. Hustvedt does with depicting Iris's subjective experience of a nervous breakdown. "I was overcome . . . by loneliness, by a sense that I was shut inside a body that was going its own way. I've done it, I thought. I've created this huge, bad head, summoned the voice of my mother, dreamed up dead bodies and generally caused my own disintegration, but how can I undo it all? I'm a ghost." In this strong sequence, the author achieves a delicate blend of passion and irony, creating a sort of understated stylistic freneticism that matches Iris's physical, psychological dilemma.

What Ms. Hustvedt does clearly imply, thankfully, is that the kind of academic existence she describes, in which all grandeur comes from literature and only disappointment from life, can be dangerous, can function for the individual as a series of masks that, when donned, conceal raw emotions and ugly, twisted impulses. And Iris does seem to yearn to escape from it all, to uncover real tenderness and affection in both friends and lovers beneath their tiresome layers of intellectual cat-and-mousing. Regrettably, though, most of these masks are never pulled away. Iris continually plays masochist to the mildly sadistic, confused men in her life. Her own emotional quandary—a combination of sensitivity crippled by passivity, youth and its relative lack of power, and clinical depression—does not give her a chance.

One senses that, as an author, Siri Hustvedt is all dressed up without much of anywhere to go. On the other hand, she displays considerable sophistication and polish. She has a knack for intimate detail, for suggesting, with some intensity, the compulsive psychological spiral of drowning souls, for creating powerful moods with just enough words. In short, she has all the tools, but—as of yet, at any rate—nothing much to say. When she does, the result should prove worth waiting for.

Jenifer Levin, "Grad School and Other Horrors," in The New York Times Book Review, *June 7, 1992, p. 33.*

Marisa Januzzi and Priya Joshi   (review date Fall 1992)

[*In the following review, Januzzi and Joshi praise the realism and narrative style of* The Blindfold.]

This delicate, bizarre novel [***The Blindfold***] about a student in the graduate English program at Columbia University is the first book in a long time that has actually kept me company. It tells stories I never could have hoped anyone would be able to extract, this precisely and evocatively, from my own home turf. Before admitting to actually *being* a Ph.D. student in this same (far, far from fictive) program, and living two blocks from Hustvedt herself when she and husband Paul Auster were at Columbia, I should say that the turf Hustvedt manages to traverse with her mirroring heroine is social, mental, and emotional turf. This four-part rendition of Iris Vegan's encounters will be instantly accessible to anyone who has ever felt radically vulnerable within the strange negotiations of daily life, relatively uninsulated by age, gender, money, pretense, or power, in New York. I read it slowly, and was strongly reminded of the virtues of clarity in narrative.

To call this discontinuous batch of experiences a "novel" foregrounds the coherence and integrity of Iris herself, a kind of nineteenth-century heroine like the ones she studies, walking around in female noir for the nineties— and also is humorous, considering how quickly the issue of the whole and its chronology is handled in the last part. The writing feels "fast," thereby qualifying this as a "good read," yet it has at times the character of a beautiful woman, from an other point of view (Iris/Siri?). I read the pages quicker than I wanted to, and their absolute substance would often register as a slightly belated surprise.

For instance, Iris, who is from a small midwestern town called Webster, translates a German story called "The Brutal Boy," and simultaneously becomes involved with her professor, its editor. She also takes on the identity of its main character Klaus—to the extent that an initial, unrelated experiment in cross-dressing leads (after the rape of a woman in her building) to her assumption of the alias character, who in turn leads her to a solitary nightlife of bars, night friends, and wanderings. When Iris notes that Klaus "never could have happened in Webster," the simplicity and clarity of her observation come through, before the unselfconscious knowledge implicit in the pun does.

Understanding, for Iris, goes beyond the retinal: she ventures toward what she looks at, and her kaleidoscopic gaze has the character of Klaus's stripper friend in its generous, non-narcissistic dilations and extreme discoveries. At the same time, Iris is not made out to be overly elastic, and even when she becomes one of her own case studies, she remains characterized by the wisdom that we are somehow defined by what we agree and refuse to take into ourselves. Despite the payments it exacts, Iris manages radical yet non-abusive, intimate contact with subjects of her concern. Her commentary gets close to evils and ambiguities, without seeming to capitulate to them, and thus reads like an ethical gift to the barren cities of our fictions.

The only criticism I have of this novel pertains to my unsatisfied curiosity about what sustains Iris, in this odd-cropped life she leads. Then I realized that perhaps that is one of its own questions, or designs. Articulating a modernist concern about the sustaining value of language, Pound once wrote, "Any general statement is like a cheque drawn on a bank. . . . [It] is GOOD if it be ultimately found to correspond with the facts." When Mr. Morning, who has given Iris a badly needed job (to write meticulous descriptions of some possessions of a murdered woman), pays her with a check written out to the alias she has taken as a precaution, Ms. Hustvedt gives Pound's faith an updated, nearly invisible, and particularly sisterly twist. This writer, who says she believes that "story, narrative is . . . a neurological necessity," has given us compelling reasons to look for her work in the future. (pp. 189-90)

Marisa Januzzi and Priya Joshi, in a review of "The Blindfold," in Review of Contemporary Fiction, *Vol. 12, No. 3, Fall, 1992, pp. 189-90.*

David Plante   (review date October 1992)

[*In the following review, Plante commends the interesting structure and content of* The Blindfold.]

[Siri Hustvedt's ***The Blindfold***] is a novel worth considering at length.

The modernist injunction "make it new" has to a large extent become in America "make it weird." Perhaps America *is* weird, and any fiction set there must account for the weirdness. In lesser fiction, the weirdness is mere decoration; in Siri Hustvedt's fiction, set in New York, it is essential and heartbreaking, and reveals desperation at the center.

> A young woman approached me late on a Thursday night. Bleecker Street was crowded, and she came toward me. I guessed that she wanted directions, but she took my hand and said, "Do you know what she did?" "No," I said. The girl was short and wore thick glasses. I noticed a gray shadow of dirt on her neck. "The horses," she grunted. "The bitch stole the horses." I moved backward, but she grabbed my forearm and dug her nails into my skin, snarling. "Right out of the barn."

The Blindfold is an extraordinary novel, all the more so because it is a first novel. Formally, it is very interesting, consisting of four parts, each self-contained, but the first part becomes a glass through which one reads the second, and these two parts become double panes through which one reads the next, and so on; in the end, one is reading through all the parts, as if through many-layered panes. The effect of seeing through layers of glass is heightened by the clarity of the writing. Hustvedt adds just the slightest coloration here and there, just the slightest magnification caused by her sparing use of metaphors and similes.

In the first part, Iris, the narrator, a graduate student at Columbia University, gets a much-needed job that involves simply *describing* objects that once belonged to a murdered woman; these objects are now owned by a man who may or may not have killed her. They include a glove, a ball of cotton wool coated with makeup, a mirror. The intense presences of these things—which Iris, by describing them, must "purify" for the owner so that they will "display" themselves in their "nakedness"—suggests André Breton's *Nadja,* and, indeed, there is something of a surreal atmosphere in the novel, but with a difference.

In the second part, Iris finds that her boyfriend Stephen is closer than she had thought to a photographer named George. The two men may or may not be lovers, and Iris never knows where she is with them. George takes a photo of her that she hates but that the two men admire. The photo becomes known throughout New York, and this nightmarish turn of events causes in Iris such a violent identity crisis that her brutal migraines return as if to kill her.

Iris, in the third part, goes to a hospital because her migraines are unbearable. Her bed is near that of Mrs. O., an old woman who suffers from multiple personality. One night Mrs. O. gets into Iris's bed and presses herself against her and kisses her, sticking her tongue into Iris's mouth. A horror comes over Iris, who sees Mrs. O. as an alien, malign presence. Then Mrs. O., on all fours at the end of her bed, calls out to Iris, "Eleanor, Eleanor," which is her own name. She sees herself in Iris, and this so shocks Iris that she goes into a strange state of unconsciousness. By the next morning, Mrs. O. has mysteriously disappeared, along with Iris's migraines.

The final part, the longest, is a rich account of an affair Iris has with her teacher at Columbia, Professor Rose, for whom she translates a German novel called *Brutal Boy* by Johann Kruger, a "little-known" writer exterminated in a Nazi concentration camp because of his homosexuality. The main character of this novel, Klaus, is a good boy who discovers that he is tempted to do bad things, such as tripping an old woman in the street or piercing his dog's eyes with a needle, and as she gets deeper into translating the novel Iris finds herself identifying with Klaus. Professor Rose leaves New York for a year and a half, and Iris enters a sinister state. She is appalled by her desire to kick a homeless man whose hand is curled up against his chest in a fetal position.

She takes to wearing a man's suit, first as a disguise for a Halloween party in a SoHo loft, then almost all the time to go to a seedy bar, where Professor Rose accidentally meets her when he returns. He and Iris start a sexual relationship, though he, married and with children, feels greatly torn. Their relationship becomes more and more impossible to define in terms of love or sex. The last scene with the professor has Iris blindfolded with a scarf he gave her and trying to find her way, as he walks beside her, back to her apartment after dinner. And their last night of love is violent: Iris bites the professor and he hits her across the mouth. They have no idea what is happening, and though at this point I worried that the risks Hustvedt takes in the conversation between the professor and Iris about the pos-

sible meaning of what has happened to them might appear too much like commentary—the professor says, "What I mean is that I've seen you, really seen you, and what I've seen isn't simple or small. It's complex, ambivalent, mysterious, and it's driven me crazy"—the terror Hustvedt arouses in the scene carries it off.

The novel is about evil, but, more, it is about identity, or the fragmenting of identity, and to say so is to state the obvious. Hustvedt states her subject almost as if she were writing a thesis novel, thereby risking accusations of obviousness—or, worse, pretentiousness. She holds to her subject as if it contained and embodied all her intention in writing the novel, all her strict control of her story. But the novel is also a quite thrilling work of art. Yes, she tells us the book is about identity—as clearly about identity as her clear prose can make it—but the subject in all its obviousness is like a sharply cut crystal that reflects the space around it: a very deep and frightening darkness.

How does Siri Hustvedt achieve depth in a novel that is so deftly but tightly controlled it would seem there was no space in it for anything to occur she herself did not intend? I mentioned earlier that **The Blindfold** suggests the surrealist novel *Nadja,* but with a difference. Hustvedt uses similar devices—an unknowing narrator, strange occurrences that are left unexplained, sudden references to seemingly irrelevant details that seem half in and half out of context. But these devices only point to some great darkness in the book which is too *conscious,* too metaphysical, to be surreal. Perhaps the novel to compare **The Blindfold** to is Maurice Blanchot's *Death Sentence.* **The Blindfold** is filled with an awareness of the infinite darkness implied in any number of identities, or in total non-identity, and it is darkness that gives this short novel so much space. (pp. 99-102)

David Plante, in a review of "The Blindfold," in The Yale Review, *Vol. 80, No. 4, October, 1992, pp. 99-102.*

Additional coverage of Hustvedt's life and career is contained in the following source published by Gale Research: *Contemporary Authors,* **Vol. 137.**

Edward P. Jones
Lost in the City

Jones is an American short story writer, born in 1951.

INTRODUCTION

Lost in the City is a collection of fourteen short stories set in poor, working-class neighborhoods in Washington, D. C. during the 1950s. Depicting both the hardships and the dignity of African-Americans as they struggle against poverty, crime, and disillusionment, these stories chronicle a transitional time in African-American history. Many of Jones's characters have relocated to Washington from the American South for economic reasons and are confronting the ambiguity and alienation of inner-city existence. In the story "Gospel," for example, a female gospel singer is so moved by the sight of a man tipping his hat to her that she drives through a snowstorm searching for the person who made that "respectful gesture out of a country time." In "The Girl Who Raised Pigeons," Jones describes a widower's ambivalence at raising his infant daughter alone. As the man considers abandoning his baby on the street, "[it occurrs] to him perversely that if he decided to walk away forever from her and the carriage and all her stuff, to walk but a few yards and make his way up or down 1st Street for no place in particular, there was not a damn thing in the world she could do about it." Critics praise Jones for skillfully giving voice to the experiences of a group too little heard in modern American literature. Jones's ability to find the redemptive in the tragic, his avoidance of sentimentality and rancor, his ear for dialogue, and keen insights into human nature are the qualities most critics find distinctive in *Lost in the City*. Contrary to the views expressed by many commentators, Jones has said that he is not attempting to express African-American anger. "Ultimately," Jones states, "I'm trying to write literature."

CRITICISM

Christopher Lehmann-Haupt (review date 11 June 1992)

[*In the following review, Lehmann-Haupt praises Jones's ability to depict tragic events in engaging ways,*

noting that he dignifies his characters without recourse to anger or sentimentality.]

A photograph accompanies each of the 14 stories in Edward P. Jones's powerful fiction debut, *Lost in the City,* about the lives and souls of black people living in Washington. Most of these pictures depict bleakly gray cityscapes, and in doing so they seem to reflect, at least in retrospect, the frustration and despair experienced by so many of Mr. Jones's characters.

For instance, in **"The Night Rhonda Ferguson Was Killed,"** an angry high-school girl named Cassandra stakes her freedom to rebel on the knowledge that her best friend is about to sign a recording contract and lift Cassandra to fame with her. At the end of a day in which Cassandra burns several bridges of friendship behind her, she learns that her friend has been shot to death by a lover.

In **"The First Day,"** a woman finally takes her daughter to her first day of school only to discover that the building she has been pointing out to the child for so long is in the wrong district. When they arrive at the right place the mother must ask a stranger to fill out the application forms for her.

And in the volume's most powerful story, **"Marie,"** an old woman named Marie Delaveaux is continually asked to report to the Social Security offices "so we can see if you still deserve to get Supplemental Security Income payments." She is then made to sit for endless hours without an interview.

> She was 86 years old, and had learned that life was all chaos and painful uncertainty and that the only way to get through it was to expect chaos even in the most innocent of moments. Offer a crust of bread to a sick bird and you often drew back a bloody finger.

And yet the cumulative effect of these stories is by no means depressing. The people in them are proud and without self-pity. Mr. Jones consistently dignifies them and never stoops to sentiment or anger. **"The First Day,"** told from the child's point of view, ends with the sounds of the mother's footsteps going away down the hall, an effect that conveys both the child's apprehension and the mother's determined pride.

And at the height of Marie Delaveaux's frustration with the Social Security bureaucracy, a student knocks on the door of her apartment and asks her to take part in an oral-history project. The transcription of her recollections transforms her from an overlooked statistic to a significant voice in history.

True, most of Mr. Jones's characters are lost in the city. They are lost like the title story's Lydia Walsh, who tells the nurse who phones to inform her of her mother's death not to pull the sheet up over the corpse's face, and then bribes a cabbie to get lost in the streets of the city on the way to the hospital. Or like Woodrow L. Cunningham in **"A New Man,"** who drives his teen-age daughter away in a burst of rage and then spends years wandering the city looking for her.

But some of the characters are lost in other senses of the word. They are lost like the protagonist in **"The Girl Who Raised Pigeons,"** who at the end of the story watches the last of her birds fly away after their rooftop coop has been attacked by rats.

> He caught an upwind that took him nearly as high as the tops of the empty K Street houses. He flew farther into Northeast, into the colors and sounds of the city's morning. She did nothing, aside from following him, with her eyes, with her heart, as far as she could.

And they are lost like old Marie, who long ago got off a train on her way to live in Baltimore and took a streetcar ride in the Capital. "The more I rode, the more brighter things got. You ain't lived till you been on a streetcar. . . . I knowed I could never live in a place that didn't have that streetcar and them clackety-clack tracks. . . ."

It shouldn't come as a surprise—but it does as one reads these pages—that people perceived to be down and out

can live such rich and varied lives. Here are the young and the old, the rich and the poor, the enterprising and the criminal, the believing and the cynical, the highfalutin and the down to earth.

Equally impressive is the variety of dramatic effects Mr. Jones pulls off. In **"The Dark,"** the experience of a violent thunderstorm recalls a frightening rural past to a group of ancient ladies. In **"Gospel,"** the devoted leader of a gospel-singing group loses her faith in things when she discovers that her best friend has a secret lover. "In the end, it grew cold in the car, and colder still, and at first she did not notice, and then when she did, she thought it was the general condition of the whole world, owing to the snow, and that there was not very much she could do about it."

In the collection's 10th story, **"A Butterfly on F Street,"** Mildred Harper runs into "the woman her husband had lived with for the last two years of his life." Here would seem to be an occasion for anger or humor, to judge by the tempers of the stories that have preceded this one. But again, Mr. Jones goes off in an unexpected direction:

> Mildred had crossed to the island from Morton's, going to Woolworth's, her eyes fixed upon a golden-yellow butterfly that fluttered about the median. A child swatted half-heartedly at the butterfly, which rose as high as seven or so feet at moments, zigzagging back and forth over people's heads and around an advertising kiosk and around the small, lifeless trees. Then the butterfly set off into the traffic heading toward 13th Street. It astonished her to see such a thing, wild, utterly fragile, in the midst of the buildings, the noise, the cars and buses, and she figured the thing must have lost its way. Before long, the butterfly was consumed in the colors of 13th Street.

Another creature lost in Mr. Jones's city that helps to bring it to kaleidoscopic life.

> *Christopher Lehmann-Haupt, "Dignity Survives amid Grimness of an Inner City," in* The New York Times, *June 11, 1992, p. C18.*

Jonathan Yardley   (review date 21 June 1992)

[*In the following review of* Lost in the City, *Yardley maintains that the stories "Young Lions," "The Store," and "The Sunday Following Mother's Day," all of which address the theme of survival, are the best in a fine collection.*]

Edward P. Jones's first book contains 14 stories, all of which are fine and three of which—**"Young Lions," "The Store"** and **"The Sunday Following Mother's Day"**—are uncommonly so. That Jones is a writer of both promise and accomplishment is self-evident, but to readers hereabout there is far more to him than that. Jones is a native of the District of Columbia whose subject is the people who live in parts of the city—Northeast, Southeast, Anacostia—that have gone unnoticed by all but a handful of writers of fiction; thus he writes about what is, to thousands who live here, the "real Washington," and he writes about it with knowledge, candor and deep sympathy.

As has been noted in this space before, the emergence of black writers into the forefront of American fiction may well be the most significant literary development of recent years. Why this has occurred remains something of a mystery—only a few years ago, after all, publishers routinely claimed that fiction by and about blacks "doesn't sell" and declined to publish it—but the facts are beyond argument. All over the country, black writers are bringing out stories and novels in unprecedented profusion. Some of these writers, like their white counterparts, are mere writing-school clones; others, like Edward P. Jones, are original and arresting new voices.

In one of his stories an older woman tells her daughter, "God don't put no more on us than we can bear." Perhaps that is so, but in each of these stories Jones puts that proposition to the test. Though there are many themes in his work, none is more important than the daily struggle of ordinary people against terrible odds. Some of these are imposed from without: Discrimination and segregation, though only occasionally brought to the forefront, are stunting, inescapable realities. But so too are those imposed from within, by people who have ignored or forgotten a grandfather's advice: "Don't get lost in the city."

That city is a powerful presence in these stories, but it is a city scarcely acknowledged in the "Washington novel" as that genre has developed. The world of downtown, of influence, of museums and monuments, is scarcely glimpsed herein. The central character of **"Young Lions"** has "never come down to the world below Constitution Avenue, except for those times when relatives came from out of town"; the protagonist of **"The Store,"** harassed by a white cop, prays, "Just get me back to one fifteen New York Avenue safely and I'll never come to their world again . . ." Some of these people enter that world by day, mostly to work in the bureaucracy, but it is an alien place in which they are rarely at ease; those few who enter it for good, such as the successful young lawyer in the title story, do so with powerful unease and a lingering, damning sense of betrayal.

Jones is no sentimentalist. He finds much to admire in the community about which he writes—it is, after all, where his own heart is—and his sympathy for his characters is bottomless, but in these stories there is a persistent sense that "life was all chaos and uncertainty and that the only way to get through it was to expect chaos even in the most innocent of moments." How these people deal with that uncertainty—how they come to terms with "everything [they] did not yet understand"—is a recurrent and central motif in Jones's small universe.

Many of the principal characters in *Lost in the City* are young, and the lessons they learn are often harsh. Most of the stories appear to take place from the mid-'50s to the mid-'70s, so there is little sense of the drug-and-crime haunted place that the inner city has become, but danger and death are never far in the background. A promising young singer is murdered; a husband kills his wife; a young man takes his first steps into the criminal life—these are the realities with which Jones and his characters must come to grips.

In the first of the aforementioned three outstanding stories, **"Young Lions,"** the young man who becomes a criminal does so at the cost of losing the love and trust of the woman to whom he had been the center of the world; in the third, **"The Sunday Following Mother's Day,"** the husband who kills his wife loses the son and daughter, who, for the rest of their lives, are left to confront the unsolvable mystery of why he did it. Yet the second, **"The Store,"** is the story of an alienated young man who finds work and gradually—so slowly that he barely understands what is happening—grows into responsibility and an ever-expanding "sense of neighborhood"; sometimes Jones grants his people the possibility of redemption, through their own efforts and the kind attentions of others.

Jones is a lucid, appealing writer. He puts on no airs, tells his stories matter-of-factly and forthrightly, yet his prose is distinctive and carries more weight than first impressions might suggest. A story called **"Gospel"** ends with a paragraph that is characteristic of both his style and his themes:

> A few people came and went about her, but the snow now covered the windows of her car and all she could make out were shadows moving about. She could hear voices, but she could not understand any of what people said, as if all sound were being filtered by the snow and turned into garble. She could not let anyone read her watch, but she continued to tell herself that in the next minute she would start up the car and go home . . . In the end, it grew cold in the car, and colder still, and at first she did not notice, and then when she did, she thought it was the general condition of the whole world, owing to the snow, and that there was not very much she could do about it.

Any number of things can be said about that lovely paragraph, by no means least of them that it utterly transcends race. So, in the end, do all of the stories in *Lost in the City,* even those that seem most particularly fixed on black life and culture. Edward P. Jones writes about black people, to be sure, but it is more accurate to say that he writes about people who happen to be black. For that reason his stories will touch chords of empathy and recognition in all readers, which is exactly what fiction is supposed to do.

Jonathan Yardley, "On the Streets Where We Live," in Book World—The Washington Post, *June 21, 1992, p. 3.*

Michael Harris (review date 12 July 1992)

[*In the following review, Harris praises Jones's narrative style and intimate knowledge of his characters and their environment.*]

To the list of America's fine short-story writers, add the name of Edward P. Jones. This first collection [*Lost in the City*], would merit praise whenever it appeared, but especially now, in the wake of the Los Angeles riots, when whites and blacks need more than ever to believe in each other's humanity. These 14 stories of African-American life in Washington, D. C., affirm that humanity as only good literature can.

There's no secret to it, or only the final, most elusive secret: Jones has near-perfect pitch for people. A motherless girl who raises pigeons, old women stirred by a lightning storm to remember the dark rural past, a boy whose demanding lady boss at a grocery store becomes his best friend, a man who finds a new lifestyle knocking on strangers' doors in search of his runaway daughter, a woman whose father, imprisoned 25 years for killing her mother, wants to get back into her life—whoever they are, he reveals them to us from the inside out.

Technically, Jones has all the equipment he needs: a polished style, a good ear, a street-by-street knowledge of his city. He shows us a society of unsung people whose only connection with the emblematic Washington is the occasional job as a museum guard or government clerk. It's a society rich in relationships, but every relationship is tenuous, threatened by violence, drugs, divorce, accidents—all the ways people can get lost in the city.

Jones' skill rewards him—and us—with moments that transcend these stories' sturdy realism. An Ivy League-educated lawyer is so shaken by her mother's death that she climbs into a taxi and tells the driver to go anywhere, and everywhere they go she sees the humble landmarks of her childhood. A Navy veteran tells his bride: "We're never gonna believe in anything but right now. Not very much of tomorrow. Maybe a little of the tomorrow mornin' but no farther than that." A much-married gospel singer drives through a snowstorm in hopes of finding a stranger she glimpsed tipping his hat, "a respectful gesture out of a country time . . . when a little girl would watch dark young men as tall as trees stand respectfully close to young women. . . . Where had all such men gone?"

> *Michael Harris, in a review of "Lost in the City," in* Los Angeles Times Book Review, *July 12, 1992, p. 6.*

Mary Ann French   (essay date 22 July 1992)

[*In the following essay, Jones comments on what influenced him to write* Lost in the City.]

In the dream, it was always Saturday. Ordinarily, that was the day his mother, a dishwasher, left for work at noon and didn't come home until after 11 at night. But in the dream it was worse. It got to be midnight, then 1 o'clock and 2 o'clock. Finally, along about 3 o'clock or 4, he and his sister began to realize their mother wasn't coming back at all.

The dream came many times after she died, drenching him in childish doubts, tricking his grown-up self, plunging him into the past.

Yesteryear. That's where Edward P. Jones lives much of the time, in the Washington of his youth, a city full of black working-class people who labor against such odds that he considers them heroes. **Lost in the City** is the collection of critically acclaimed short stories Jones has written to give his Washingtonians their due.

He is supposed to be talking about the curious fact that most of the book's 14 stories are written from a female per-spective. That's what he has been asked about. But instead, he veers into reverie.

An excerpt from "The First Day"

"These the forms you gotta use?" my mother asks the woman, picking up a few pieces of the paper from the table. "Is this what you have to fill out?"

The woman tells her yes, but that she need fill out only one.

"I see," my mother says, looking about the room. Then: "Would you help me with this form? That is, if you don't mind."

The woman asks my mother what she means.

"This form. Would you mind helpin me fill it out?"

The woman still seems not to understand.

"I can't read it. I don't know how to read or write, and I'm askin you to help me." My mother looks at me, then looks away. I know almost all of her looks, but this one is brand new to me. "Would you help me, then?"

The woman says Why sure, and suddenly she appears happier, so much more satisfied with everything. She finishes the form for her daughter and my mother and I step aside to wait for her. We find two chairs nearby and sit. My mother is now diseased, according to the girl's eyes, and until the moment her mother takes her and the form to the front of the auditorium, the girl never stops looking at my mother. I stare back at her. "Don't stare," my mother says to me. "You know better than that."

Another woman out of the *Ebony* ads takes the woman's child away. Now, the woman says upon returning, let's see what we can do for you two.

My mother answers the questions the woman reads off the form. They start with my last name, and then on to the first and middle names. This is school, I think. This is going to school. My mother slowly enunciates each word of my name. This is my mother: As the questions go on, she takes from her pocketbook document after document, as if they will support my right to attend school, as if she has been saving them up for just this moment. Indeed, she takes out more papers than I have ever seen her do in other places: my birth certificate, my baptismal record, a doctor's letter concerning my bout with chicken pox, rent receipts, records of immunization, a letter about our public assistance payments, even her marriage license—every single paper that has anything even remotely to do with my five-year-old life. Few of the papers are needed here, but it does not matter and my mother continues to pull out the documents with the purposefulness of a magician pulling out a long string of scarves. She has learned that money is the beginning and end of everything in this world, and when the woman finishes, my mother offers her fifty cents, and the woman accepts it without hesitation. My mother and I are just about the last parent and child in the room.

> *Edward P. Jones, in his "The First Day," from* Lost in the City, *William Morrow and Co., 1992.*

"I don't even pretend to *begin* to say what my mother went through when she went out to work each morning," says Jones. "She could have gotten up one morning and gotten on the bus and never come back. But she didn't. She always came back in the evening."

Seventeen years after her death, and Jones, 41, is still memorializing her. He is still stunned by an adult understanding of her lot.

Washington used to consist of whole neighborhoods of people who had come up from the country, as she had from South Boston, Va. They would settle alongside others from their neck of the woods, creating urban compounds of kinfolk.

"It was still the country for them," says Jones, "where everybody looked out for each other, 'cause if you didn't, everybody would just go over the brink."

That's part of why Jones came to live in 18 different places in a 10-by-15-block area during his first 18 years. Third and Fourth and L streets and New Jersey Avenue NW—that was the center of his mother's adopted universe. The Yale Laundry, Bible Way Church, No. 2 Precinct, a slash of abandoned freeway—those were her landmarks.

"That was what she knew," says Jones. "All her friends were around there."

He and his sister and mother moved often because there was always something wrong that got worse in the row house rooms and apartments where they landed. Toilets overflowed, boilers busted, rats ransacked their food, landlords removed windows in the winter if they were late with the rent.

"You move into a place because that's the best you can do at the time," Jones says. "When that place gets too bad you have to move on to something else. But of course you can't move up because you can't afford to move up."

Jones's stories are snapshots of survival techniques from a time that seems quaint compared with today. Life was sometimes simpler in its segregation, and in some ways sweeter in its separation. Children still played with a certain oblivion. But the makings of the current mess were there in the background. And Jones makes no attempt to airbrush them out of the picture. For the most part, his photos are plain and realistic. He toys with the aperture a bit, but only to direct the eye to his subject.

There is an edge of anxiety to his work. And just as in life, there is conflict, but little resolution. Motives are seldom stated.

The result is both mundane and eloquent. And unpredictable. The writer doesn't pretend to know all, and the reader may come away irritated and unfulfilled.

"The writer challenges the reader," says E. Ethelbert Miller, head of a writing program at Howard University and vice president of the PEN/Faulkner Foundation. "And if you find the story ends abruptly, then you, the reader, have to bring something to the table. Like with poetry, you can't read these once."

John Casey, a writer who taught Jones at the University of Virginia, says his former student excels at two things:

> He's inhabited the main characters so completely and knows them so well that you're completely convinced that you're in the life of whoever it is. . . . The other thing is that his knowledge of these people is filled with such compassion, but it's not sentimental writing at all. . . . He has an intimacy with the material and a kind of detachment that very good writers are always seeking.

Jones himself says he seeks to do for the black working-class people of Washington what James Joyce did for his Irish contemporaries. As Joyce described it, he created "a picture of Dublin so complete that if the city one day suddenly disappeared from the Earth it could be reconstructed out of my book."

Despite his rave reviews, which are unusual for an unknown author and rarer still for a book of short stories, Jones continues to work his old job. Success in this business doesn't necessarily equal wealth, even with a bestseller, as *Lost in the City* is locally. A second book may bring more bucks. But for now, Jones says, "It's not my nature to think anything is a big deal, because one day you're up and the next day they cut your knees out."

Jones writes a column for Tax Notes, a publication aimed at tax attorneys and accountants. It's a natural fit, since Jones's first field was math, which he studied on scholarship at College of the Holy Cross in Worcester, Mass. He switched to literature after he did poorly in a calculus class. It never occurred to him that the reason he was getting numbers wrong was because he needed glasses.

"I sat in the back of the room because I was shy and because the class was full of white boys," he says.

His lip curls when he says the word. It's the only naked note during an afternoon interview that turns out to be a presentation of poverty as nobility, mastery as serendipity.

"I don't think I'd be very comfortable writing about people who have a lot of money," says Jones. "I wouldn't be able to say with any certainty what it is they are, for example, when they got up in the morning."

He's more at ease with the stark scenarios of his childhood. Yet even these he tones down for his stories, no sensationalism here. Indeed, if there is any controversy over *Lost in the City,* it will likely involve Jones's reluctance to harp on the historical and political reasons behind his fictional predicaments.

Has Jones written something that transcends race? Or has he mainly struck a tone that isn't threatening to the majority population? Has he surpassed stereotypes and taken black literature toward a new level? Or has he come up with a new palliative?

His publisher, William Morrow & Co., bills the book as a look at black life in the nation's capital that "steers clear of angry ghetto stereotypes." And reviewers are gushing over Jones's habit of writing engagingly about people who "happen to be black."

Miller, who also heads Howard's African American Resource Center, dismisses such comments as "post-L.A. talk."

Jones says he has plenty of anger, but that he wouldn't attempt to express it in his stories.

"Whatever lessons there are, somebody else has to do those," he says. "I can't do that myself. . . . Ultimately, what I'm doing, what I'm trying to do, I'm trying to write literature."

"I found it interesting that white people are marginal to all of his stories," says Miller.

Or are they integral?

"It's a book that's particularly apt for white people," says John Casey, 53, who grew up in Washington as a "little fat pink boy with a crew cut."

"Here is the other—not the other half of your city—but here is the other three-quarters, and presented in such a way that you really feel that it's a sort of lost part of yourself."

There are things about Jones's work that he wants you to notice. Or rather, there's an absence of things. The word "nigger," for example. "That's one thing I'm particularly proud of," he says.

> In all these stories, all of these dozens of black people, there's never the word "nigger." And that was conscious. . . . I figured it's been used enough times so if someone wants to read something with the word in it, they can find it in someone else's work.

Driven with dignity, Jones will take no easy shots. There are no buzzwords and few flashpoints. Situational subtlety is his challenge and his specialty.

There's a story about a mother whose 20-year-old son buys her a dream house with money that is ill-gained. She talks about catching sight of the contraband:

> A few tiny, clear packets fell out of his jacket pocket onto the floor. She picked up the packets and placed them on the coffee table. She could have counted on one hand the times she had seen the stuff, but each time she did, the cream-colored nuggets always reminded her of small chunks of white Argo starch she had eaten when she was pregnant.

The word "crack" never appears. No distractions here. "I didn't want to sit down and write another drug story," Jones says. He would rather you focus on the mother's denial, her culpability. He wants you to know that she doesn't think long about what the stuff really is. "As the story began to develop in my head," he says, "this woman was so overwhelmed with the fact that she finally had this thing that she never thought she would have, she puts off all responsibility for how it came to be that way. And I think that happens a lot."

He is annoyed by those who don't see the hope in his stories. Witness the father in **"The Girl Who Raised Pigeons."** When his wife died and left him with a newborn girl, he briefly considered abandoning her, as Jones thought his mother might have done to him.

> He was the only moving object within her sight and she watched him intently, which made him uncomfortable. She seemed the most helpless thing he had ever known. It occurred to him perversely, as he settled her in, that if he decided to walk away forever from her and the carriage and all her stuff, to walk but a few yards and make his way up or down 1st Street for no place in particular, there was not a damn thing in the world she could do about it. The carriage was facing 1st Street Northeast, and with some effort—because one of the wheels refused to turn with the others—he maneuvered it around, pointing toward North Capitol Street.

"Lo and behold, he was forced into it, and he turned out to be a fairly good father," says Jones. "Too many people write too many bad things about black men."

And yet there is also the story about the husband who kills his wife, stabbing her repeatedly in the same apartment where their two small children sleep.

"He's just a horrible, horrible guy," Jones says. "You think, 'God, am I contributing to people saying [negative things about blacks]?' But you're compelled by things, by the images and what's going on in the story. You really can't stop yourself."

There is no attempt to trace the pathology of the violence, no need to explain. "That's not what the story is about," Jones says. "The story is about the effect of the act on the kids. . . . It doesn't matter why he did it. There can be no justification."

One time Jones's mother unknowingly moved him into an apartment directly across the street from a place where his estranged father was living with another woman. The couple didn't work. Their apartment had two front windows. He would sit at one, she at the other. All day they would sit, looking out.

One day Jones's mother sought out his father to tell him that one of their children—Jones's brother—had been scalded in an accident.

"My mother felt my father should know," Jones says.

> She went across and told him, and despite all these years of neglect by my father, she was rather impressed that he told the woman to shut up while my mother explained what happened. I didn't think that was such a big deal, but my mother has a soft heart, so . . .

So all these things manage to show up in his stories. Not in fact, but in mood, empathy, appreciation.

Like the story about a single mother who rides the Metro Orange Line train to Ballston. Every day she's got to get her three children ready early enough to travel from their home near the stadium, uptown and over to 12th and L NW, where she drops her two boys at Thomson Elementary before continuing up 12th Street to her mother's house, where she leaves her daughter for the day before traveling back downtown to the telephone company's headquarters, where she works as a service representative.

One day on the train, her children make friends with a man who stands out because he wears his hair in dreadlocks. They start looking for him every morning. Before long, the mother is looking too. He touches her hand accidentally and a thought flashes through her mind: Aside from handshakes, no man has touched her in months. He fills her fantasies. And then he disappears.

"I wanted her to be more than a mother," says Jones.

> She needed to have needs beyond just—well, she was a woman. She was a healthy, young, 30, 35-year-old woman, and I wanted to put down all that entails. . . . She's trying to keep herself together despite the fact she has three kids. And it must be hell getting up, you know, getting these kids together. You know how you can see black people on the train and the girls' hair is really well combed, and the boys, the shoes are shined and everything? People don't realize they don't spring out of bed every morning like that. There's some adult who takes them through all the motions to get them there. And yet I think I saw her kind of teetering off at the end. . . . She's on the edge, kind of, because it's very, very hard.

The Washington of Edward P. Jones is no more. A warm world of families traditional and not. A section of the city just north and west of its center full of folks who took the early bus to work. People who were sometimes cloaked in despair, but most often armed with a determination to live fully and well and responsibly. Citizens of the '50s and '60s; when trouble meant stealing a brother-in-law's car and then getting lost in Southeast. When senseless deaths were few and there was time enough between to grieve. A neighborhood that was bewildered by the urban upheaval and renewal of the '60s and withered away completely in the '70s.

Jones lives across the river now, high up in one of the behemoth buildings that line Arlington's highways. In his simply furnished apartment, he can focus on the shadows of days gone by.

He writes seemingly simple stories about people and situations that were so commonly found that they won't seem at all remarkable to the average city dweller. Other readers say he creates sympathy through understanding—a sadly needed service that is too seldom performed. (pp. G1, G4)

Mary Ann French, "Edward P. Jones's Ordinary Eloquence," in The Washington Post, *July 22, 1992, pp. G1, G4.*

Jonathan Levi

A Guide for the Perplexed

Levi is an American novelist and editor.

INTRODUCTION

Bearing the same title as a work written by the twelfth-century Jewish philosopher Moses Maimonides, Levi's *A Guide for the Perplexed* is ostensibly the latest of a series of travel guides edited by Ben, a mysterious travel agent and the latest incarnation of Maimonides. The majority of the novel comprises a series of letters written to Ben by Holland and Hanni, two women who find themselves stranded in the fictional Spanish city of Mariposa on New Year's Eve 1991. Holland, an English filmmaker, is making a documentary on Sandor, a reclusive Russian violinist; Hanni, a widow from Miami and a direct descendent of Maimonides, is searching for "Esau's Letter," a document that links the expulsion of the Jews from Spain with Columbus's voyage to America. As the night progresses, the women discover that the voyage was actually part of a plan to establish a Jewish homeland in America. They also realize that their lives are interconnected with those of others they meet: Sandor, for instance, is really Zoltan, with whom Hanni had an affair as a teenager; and Ben is not only Hanni's son but the father of Holland's daughter, Isabella.

Critics have compared Levi's lyrical prose style in *A Guide for the Perplexed* to that of John Barth, and his blend of fantasy and history to the magic realism of Gabriel García Márquez. They have been particularly impressed with "Esau's Letter," a fantastic tale about travel, persecution, and survival that has prompted reviewers to describe *A Guide for the Perplexed* as a metaphor for Jewish history. While some critics have argued that Levi's characters are abstractions and that his complicated allusions and interconnections are excessive, most have praised the novel as ambitious and highly imaginative. Donna Seaman has remarked that "although Levi writes with a fabulist's magical logic, he is firmly anchored to the imagery of the senses and emotional truth."

CRITICISM

Kirkus Reviews (review date 1 May 1992)

[*In the following review, the critic assesses the strengths and weaknesses of* A Guide for the Perplexed.]

[*A Guide for the Perplexed* is a] debut novel from the American co-founder of *Granta* that, appropriating its title from the work by the great Talmudic scholar Maimonides, provides an ingenious if metaphorical twist to the events of 1492.

When a strike delays their flight out of Mariposa, Spain, two women—Holland, an English filmmaker; and Hanni, an aging American searching for her family's treasured "Letters from Esau," as well as for a son she hasn't seen since his birth in war-torn Berlin—find they have the same travel agent, Ben. Ben is the author of a travel book called *A Guide for the Perplexed,* which offers "no itineraries, no *routes touristique*" but only help for those who no longer know where or how to go. In a series of set pieces, the narrative—interspersed with letters, historical lore, excerpts from the guide—moves back and forth from the 15th century to the present, from Inca kingdoms to Berlin, as the women while away the wait for the delayed flight. They wander from a bordello bar to an adult-movie house, from the home of the mysterious violinist Sandor to the richly symbolic Cave of Esau. On these wanderings, lugging a mysterious trunk Ben has entrusted to Hanni, the two women meet a host of characters, including Holland's long-lost daughter Isabella; a Peruvian descendant of Maimonides; and a British rock band. Connections and coincidences multiply as life histories are told, and family legends of famous Jewish ancestors are recalled. In a climatic scene in the Cave of Esau, from which Esau had sailed with Columbus to found a Jewish nation in the Americas, all is made clear. Destinies are linked, and the real purpose of the centuries of wanderings by Hanni's ancestors is revealed: "Esau said it best—we are all Jews. Our survival is in our motion."

Conceptually [*A Guide for the Perplexed* is] quite brilliant—but with too many tricks, too many mirrors, and too little really at the center of it. Promising but flawed. (pp. 560-61)

> *A review of "A Guide for the Perplexed," in* Kirkus Reviews, *Vol. LX, No. 9, May 1, 1992, pp. 560-61.*

Patricia Ross (review date 15 June 1992)

[*In the review below, Ross offers a favorable assessment of* A Guide for the Perplexed.]

Brilliantly conceived, flawlessly executed, this extraordinary first novel [*A Guide for the Perplexed*], uses magic realism and travelers' tales to achieve a startlingly unique revisionist history of the discovery of America. Like a Chagall painting, Levi's novel weaves together Jewish folk tales, dreams, violins, flamenco, and even Led Zeppelin into a rich, constantly evolving tapestry. Two women—Holland, a documentary filmmaker, and Hanni, who is searching for an ancient family letter—are stranded overnight in Spain. Holland and Hanni find a connection in the same mysterious travel agent, Ben, and in young Isabella, who might be Holland's daughter and Hanni's granddaughter. As Hanni's successfully located letter is read aloud, it reveals the history of the Jewish people, ending with their expulsion from Spain and the discovery of America by Esau, Hanni's ancestor. It may all be a grand cosmic joke engineered by Ben, but Levi, a cofounder of *Granta*, has accomplished a stunning tour de force that shouldn't be missed. Highly recommended for most collections.

> *Patricia Ross, in a review of "A Guide for the Perplexed," in* Library Journal, *Vol. 117, No. 11, June 15, 1992, p. 102.*

Richard Eder (review date 28 June 1992)

[*An American critic and journalist, Eder received the*

Pulitzer Prize for criticism in 1987. In the following review, he identifies travel as the principal theme in A Guide for the Perplexed *and describes the plot as overly clever and the characters as literary abstractions.*]

Cleverness can be like a stutter. We can get distracted from what is said because of the way it is being said. Except that the stutterer's urgency to express himself will burn through the handicap, while some kinds of cleverness may strike us as a way to mask a lack of urgency.

Jonathan Levi's historical-philosophical fantasy is generally clever, always ambitious, sometimes provocative and often entertaining; yet it turns into its own mask. It winds together such things as the discovery of America, the Arab settlement in Spain, the expulsion of the Jews, an argument for linking Flamenco song, Bach's music and the Sephardic Kol Nidre, the repeatedly transformed figure of the Medieval Jewish philosopher Maimonides, and the Wandering Jew, also repeatedly transformed, as a symbol of all Jews and perhaps of all humanity.

Told through the dream-like encounters and recollections of two present-day travelers in Spain, *A Guide for the Perplexed*—the title of Maimonides' masterwork—holds our curiosity for a while. We accumulate questions, and answers are fed teasingly back. Curiosity dulls after a while, yet answers keep coming even after we are no longer asking questions. The author sits cross-legged, finishing the puzzle he has set out.

Levi's excursion begins with two women stranded by a strike in the airport of Mariposa, a fictional city in southwestern Spain not far from the port Columbus sailed from. One is Holland, an English filmmaker who has just recorded a performance of a Bach partita by Sandor, a world-renowned violinist. The other is Hanni, an old widow who has come from Miami to search for a lost manuscript demonstrating that her ancestor Esau, a Spanish Jew, sailed with Columbus and was in fact the discoverer of the American mainland.

Hanni and Holland in the airport are described with fleeting realism, but it is the realism of Alice as she is about to fall down the rabbit hole. Thereafter, their encounters, adventures and flashbacks have the comically or mysteriously arbitrary quality of Wonderland, as well as a good deal of its didacticism.

Each woman has had her trip arranged by Ben, a cosmological travel agent. He directs the odd things that happen to them in what turns out to be a voyage of philosophical and historical enlightenment. Each has a copy of his tourist guide, entitled, naturally, *Guide for the Perplexed.* Ben, it will be suggested at the end of the book's myriad twists and turns, is Hanni's son and the father of Holland's daughter. He is also the latest incarnation of Maimonides, who moved in the upheavals of his time from North Africa to Egypt, and whose writing sought to reconcile classical learning with religious belief.

Maimonides, Ben and other variations who appear in the book teach travel of all kinds, and travel is the central theme and image. "We are all Jews," one of the characters declares; "Our survival is in our motion." To Levi, Queen Isabella's expulsion of the Jews in 1492 was not their setback but their glory. Clearly no Zionist, he suggests that not only the Jews but all men fulfill their civilizing mission by wandering. Ben, the wanderers' magus, had arranged the boatloads of Vietnam refugees, the flotillas of Cubans from Mariel, the escape of Eastern Europeans through the Iron Curtain, the exodus of Ethiopian Jews to Israel, and—no Zionist either—the travels of PLO leaders between Tunis and Beirut.

A whole section is devoted to the manuscript of Esau, which turns up in the violin case of a pupil of Sandor's who, it turns out, is also Holland's daughter. The book's turnings-up, turnings-out and general turnings-into—its transformations—are successively intriguing, dizzying, wearying and static.

Esau's letter, however, approaches a straightforward narrative and an interesting one. There are digressions—one concerns some magical violin strings belonging to the daughter of a Medieval Arab noble and his Jewish wife— but mostly it is a droll and suggestive alternate history.

The purpose of [*A Guide for the Perplexed*] and its author—as of Maimonides and his avatars—is to expand, not restrict, the possibilities.

—Richard Eder

Esau, son of a Jewish map-maker, is taken from his family by Santangel, one of Queen Isabella's mightiest ministers and a reluctant convert from Judaism. Knowing the Jews will be expelled, Santangel wants to find a haven for them. Poring over maps and travelers' accounts for seven years, Esau "discovers" America for his patron. Santangel bundles him and nine other Jews—a Minyan—aboard Columbus' ships. Columbus insists he is heading for the East Indies; Esau and Santangel know better.

At the end of his account, Esau will have clambered ashore in Florida, where he settles among some baseball-playing Indians, marries a princess and fathers a line of American Jews. True, one character points out, the descendants of an Indian mother are not technically Jewish; but the purpose of the book and its author—as of Maimonides and his avatars—is to expand, not restrict, the possibilities.

The Esau section is told, with a touch of facetious archaism, as a chronicle of the time; with some of the effect of John Barth's *The Sotweed Factor*. It can be whimsical and long-winded, but it succeeds on the whole, and it is the brightest part of the book.

Hanni's and Holland's encounters and conversations, on the other hand, grow tedious and confusing. The spirit of Ben—we meet him mainly through their letters to him— hangs over them like the shadow of a Prospero at discount. There are talks with gnomic and discursive rock-singers, a barman, a taxi driver and a Peruvian travel

agent. They are themselves but, in the most portentous and discouraging possible way, they are also part of the spirit of History that Hanni and Holland are filling up on.

Their instruction, relentlessly verbal, is not merely that. There are also instructive metamorphoses. When Hanni goes to Germany at 18 with her father—they work as the Gestapo's designated Jewish travel agents, and smuggle out Jews in their clients' packing cases—she turns blond and grows Marlene Dietrich-like cheekbones. After Holland has Ben's baby, she suddenly grows tall and voluptuous.

It is all meanings, suggestions and connections but, except for some parts of the Esau story, the figures meant, suggested and connected are literary abstractions caught in a traffic jam. *Guide* is a treasure hunt held indoors, all clues and few of the countryside wanderings that are a treasure hunt's real point. Levi has written an academic game that runs down, an echo (muffled) of Eco (Umberto). (pp. 3, 11)

Richard Eder, "Pinta, Niña and Maimonides," in Los Angeles Times Book Review, June 28, 1992, pp. 3, 11.

Joseph Coates   (review date 9 July 1992)

[*In the following excerpt, Coates maintains that the overabundance of coincidences in* A Guide for the Perplexed *detracts from the novel's tone of magic realism.*]

A Guide for the Perplexed takes its title from a work by the Jewish philosopher Maimonides, exiled from Spain in the 12th Century, who makes a cameo appearance here.

The book purports to be a new edition of an anciently established vade mecum, and the "current *Guide,*" compiled by a master travel agent named Ben, "contains a series of letters from three women facing a common dilemma in the south of Spain" on New Year's Eve 1991, interspersed with correspondence from such older users as Cervantes, who defends the beauty of his Quixote's love, Dulcinea, against the editor's skepticism, probably as a means of disarming ours also.

The three women are Holland, a beautiful, 6-foot documentary filmmaker who has on tape a rare private performance by the legendary violinist Sandor; an expatriate Jew named Hanni, 65, late of Miami, hunting the Esau Letter, written in 1506 by an ancestor who sailed with Columbus from the town in which all three women are stuck by an airline; and Isabella, a wunderkind student of Sandor's.

Each digs fearfully for her "own personal time bomb," as Hanni puts it, her own being the letter lost with her violinist lover as they fled Berlin for Spain in 1944. Datelined Maiyami, it shows Hanni's ancestor to have converted enough Indians in south Florida by 1495 to "hold the first minyan on the North American continent." Furthermore, Esau had intuited the existence of that continent, plus the theory of plate tectonics, from a copulation on a beach in the Old World with a girl named Florida, and communicated both pieces of data to the man he knows as "Colon" who, of course, turns out to be Jewish too.

Unfortunately, the chutzpah of the author's conception and of his characters is not matched by the author's talent, and the stuffing leaks out after being punctured by just a few too many coincidences. Magic realism degenerates into tasteless whimsy, and even if the reader enjoys the many fine things that follow, he is haunted by the brilliance of the book that might have been.

> *Joseph Coates, "2 Ingenious Novels That Expand the Genre," in* Chicago Tribune, *July 9, 1992, p. 3.*

Diane Cole   (review date 2 August 1992)

[*Cole is an American nonfiction writer and critic. In the following review, she examines the metaphorical relationship between Levi's novel and Jewish history.*]

Jonathan Levi's *A Guide for the Perplexed* is a seriously funny, beguilingly ambitious first novel that calls to mind the fanciful storytelling flights of Cynthia Ozick and John Barth, the outrageous satire of Monty Python, and the globetrotting trendiness of *Vanity Fair* magazine, all at once.

Levi, a cofounder and now the American editor of the tony British literary quarterly *Granta,* cleverly joins together all these disparate strands in a fabulously complicated tale of travel, exile and renewal that ultimately becomes a metaphor for Jewish history.

The novel borrows its title from the famous religious and philosophical tract of the same name by the 12th-century Jewish philosopher and Talmudic scholar Moses Maimonides. In an entertaining twist, Levi also uses it as the title of a curious modern-day travel manual written by an all-knowing but always invisible travel agent who signs himself, simply, Ben. In this allusion and throughout the book, Levi is nothing if not erudite: Maimonides was also known as Moses Ben Maimon, and Benjamin of Tudela was a famous Jewish travel writer and geographer of the same period.

This guide, however, seems to be for the primary benefit of two solitary women travelers whose courses converge in Mariposa, Spain, on New Year's Eve 1991.

Holland, at 46, is a driven television documentary producer based in London who has just completed filming a long-sought interview and private concert with a reclusive octogenarian violinist named Sandor. Divorced and unattached, she finds herself haunted by memories of a failed love affair that had led her to this same region of Spain some years before.

Almost 80, Hanni at first appears deceptively sedate—the opposite of the flamboyant, outspoken Holland. But though Hanni has retired to Miami and is recently widowed, it soon becomes clear that both her personal history and her family's past have been anything but placid.

Claiming direct descent from Maimonides himself, Hanni sees her family as embodying two of the major, recurring themes of Jewish history—persecution and survival. When Spain's 12th-century Muslim rulers banned the Jewish religion, for instance, her famed ancestor Maimonides was forced to become a secret Jew, then flee Spain altogether, before ultimately settling in Egypt, where he prospered as both a scholar and a physician.

Hanni also recalls how, during World War II, she and her father masqueraded as loyal Nazis in order to conceal their real work as Resistance workers smuggling untold numbers of Jews to safety. One of them, in fact, was an exquisite violinist named Zoltan with whom the teen-aged Hanni had her first love affair as they made their secret trek together across Europe. Alas, even as they approached the safety of the Spanish border, Zoltan disappeared, leaving a pregnant Hanni to wander in search of him. Now, thrown together through the accident of a wildcat Spanish airplane strike, Holland and Hanni exchange their stories and wonder if Zoltan and Sandor are one and the same.

But it is yet another historical quest that has brought Hanni back to Spain, the site of her abandonment. It is the eve of 1992, Hanni reminds Holland—the 500th anniversary not only of Christopher Columbus's discovery of America but of the final expulsion of the Jews from Spain by Ferdinand and Isabella. And, according to Hanni, if she could but find it, a long lost manuscript written by yet another ancestor, a 15th-century Spanish mapmaker and traveler named only Esau, reveals the true story behind Columbus's voyage—a journey designed not to open new lands for Spanish conquest but to locate a new homeland for Spain's exiled Jews. Thus, Hanni has come to Spain to find the lost "Esau Letter" and, at the same time, to reclaim a part of her own lost past—one in which, it turns out, Holland and even the mysterious Ben also play large parts.

In addition to providing us with Esau's lengthy picaresque account of New World adventure, Levi sprinkles wondrous, mythic tales of Hanni's family history throughout *A Guide for the Perplexed,* at times embedding stories within stories within stories. This tangled web of interlocked tales is entertaining, but eventually the connections between the characters and the stories themselves become so convoluted that the reader pauses in confusion. For Levi ultimately piles so many fantastic events upon [one] another that in the end the whole structure risks collapsing upon itself.

Similarly, Levi's hip references to everything from *au courant* name brands to abstruse historical events speak to his eclectic sensibility, but at a certain point I longed for him to stop showing off and let his story speak for itself. For when he does, it becomes clear that Levi has so many gifts that *A Guide for the Perplexed* should be only the first of many tales to come.

> *Diane Cole, "Exile and Cunning," in* Book World—The Washington Post, *August 2, 1992, p. 11.*

An excerpt from *A Guide for the Perplexed*

Santángel scooped a handful of water from the fountain, said a few words in Latin, splashed my face. "You need a new name," he said, "a Christian name for your baptism in Christ."

"Esau," my father's father said. I turned and saw the wrath, the hatred twisting his tongue against his lips. "Esau, that's his name, his new name."

"But, grandfather," Santángel went on, "Esau is a Jewish name, Esau was a Jew."

"And Esau sold his birthright because he was hungry," my grandfather said. " 'Let me swallow, I pray thee,' Esau said to his brother Jacob, 'some of this red, red pottage, for I am faint.' And Jacob said, 'Sell me first thy birthright.' And Esau said, 'Behold, I am at the point to die, and what profit shall the birthright do to me?' And Jacob gave Esau bread and pottage of lentils, and he did eat and drink, and rose up and went on his way. Esau despised his birthright." My grandfather looked out over the congregation, over the soldiers. "No self-respecting Jew would name his son Esau. It's the perfect Catholic name. Tell that to your queen." And reaching down inside his throat, my grandfather collected the larger part of his frustration and terror and hatred into a gob of spittle as red and thick as any mess of pottage and, with a mighty effort, baptized the other side of my face.

So I became Esau. Esau Benavides. I had to wait only one week to discover why Santángel had chosen me. My parents were grateful it wasn't longer. For in that week, the Jews turned away, the New Christians turned away. All income from the shop dried up, all patronage at the tavern crossed town. My brother sang alone, the lions stood silent.

Friday evening at sundown, a royal courier knocked on the door. I was forbidden to bring anything with me, neither map nor hat. Only my brother kissed me good-bye. It was the first time I had traveled on Shabbat.

On the eve of the third day, the courier pointed to the castle of Zahara de los Membrillos, the gateway to the Muslim kingdom of Andalusia. Wheeling his horse around, he galloped back the way we had come. I turned my head back to the pass. I felt calm and clear. Though I had never seen the sea, I knew where to go.

I rode through the night, resting my horse during the day. Cloaked in a skin of invisibility, I passed easily by the Muslim sentries. At noon of my sixth day out of Córdoba, made bold by the smell of salt water, I rode into the Muslim port of Mariposa. The muezzin was calling the faithful to their midday prayers, singing a tune my mother had often played. I thought how delighted she would be by the music of the city, so open and alive after the walls of the Judería. There was no pain in the memory, only the thrill of discovery as the streets emptied before me. My horse found his way to the beach. I was thirteen. I was a man of my family. I was off to the sea.

Jonathan Levi, in his A Guide for the Perplexed, *Turtle Bay Books, 1992.*

Elizabeth Gleick   (review date 2 August 1992)

[*In the following review of* A Guide for the Perplexed, *Gleick faults Levi for allowing his scholarly concerns to overshadow his characters.*]

First, some guidance on this guide: the elements are many, and the reader must accept from the beginning that illumination will be slow in coming. This is a novel of intertwining, crisscrossing, backtracking and fast-forwarding stories—stories about Maimonides, Christopher Columbus, the Wandering Jew, travel agents, violinists, baseball, the origins of flamenco, love, loss, letter writing and two women who are a generation and worlds apart. Get the idea? ***A Guide for the Perplexed*** is a scholarly work, a first novel of monumental ambition and striving imagination. In it, Jonathan Levi, one of the founders of the literary quarterly *Granta,* uses as inspiration sources as diverse as Lewis Carroll, Dante, Gabriel García Márquez and various Jewish philosophers.

Oh, there's a plot, too, only a small bit of which will be described here. Holland, a middle-aged documentary film maker for the BBC, has come to Mariposa (an imaginary Spanish town) to make a movie about Sandor, a reclusive but legendary violinist. Hanni, in her 60's, a descendant of the 12th-century philosopher Moses Maimonides, whose most famous work was called *Guide for the Perplexed,* has come from Miami Beach to Mariposa in search of a family artifact called the Esau Letter.

The two women, it turns out, share a travel agent, the elusive and also legendary Ben, author of a most unusual travel book named ***A Guide for the Perplexed.*** (Though this image is not commensurate with the novel's intellectual aspirations, I kept being reminded of the old "Charlie's Angels" television show—these two beautiful women write to Ben, depend on him; he seems to hold the answers to the mysteries they're unraveling, and yet he never appears.) Hanni and Holland first meet at the Cristóbal Colón airport, where they are marooned by a strike; they encounter each other several times again during the course of the very long night, New Year's Eve, 1991, during which the greater part of the novel takes place.

Hanni and Holland write alternating letters to Ben, who incorporates them into his guide, with a few of his own travel tips sprinkled in; thus, at first, the reader only gets pieces of Hanni's and Holland's puzzles. Each woman, it turns out, harbors an obsession with a violinist of extraordinary virtuosity; each has lost a lover and a child; each has journeyed far, and somewhat miraculously, in her own way. Hanni, the daughter of a travel agent who arranged the escape of German Jews during World War II, adheres to a lesson that's been passed down in the family: "Our survival is in our motion." And this refrain echoes throughout, for it is not only Hanni and Holland who are wandering, searching and ultimately surviving, it is also the Jews who were expelled from Spain in the 15th century by Ferdinand and Isabella, the explorers who went in search of the New World, even Maimonides himself.

These threads come together at the center of the book in the Esau Letter, a nearly 500-year-old document passed down to Hanni through generations of her family. The letter, written by a Spanish Jew to his son at the time of the Inquisition, tells a new and gorgeously imagined story of Columbus's discovery of the New World and the arrival of the first Jew in America. It is the greatest achievement of Mr. Levi's novel—a fable of fantastical lushness, reminiscent of the best fairy tales, of *A Thousand and One Nights* and the travel logs of ships, of the Bible. The Esau Letter works so magnificently, in fact, that it shows up the shortcomings of the rest of the novel.

For although *A Guide for the Perplexed* has its compelling moments—in particular Hanni's account of her escape from Nazi Germany—and much sensual, lyrical writing, it suffers badly from a case of first-time-out overkill. One can picture all too easily the author poring over his sources—medieval manuscripts, maps, histories of Spain—in a dusty library. Hanni and Holland, sad to say, remain trapped in that library. Their stories, their dialogue, even the minor characters they encounter, are suffocated by Mr. Levi's encyclopedic interests. And his efforts at incorporating the magic realism of a García Márquez, his desire to make universal, eternal connections, result in a patchwork of, yes, perplexities.

> *Elizabeth Gleick, "What Brings You to Mariposa?" in* The New York Times Book Review, *August 2, 1992, p. 9.*

Irving Malin   (review date Spring 1993)

[*Malin is an American educator and critic. In the following review, he suggests that* A Guide for the Perplexed *has multiple levels of meaning.*]

Although Levi gives the reader a first novel, he refuses to write about the trials of youth, the thinly disguised fictional memoir—*The Catcher in the Rye* for example. He is brave and experimental; he offers a complex, postmodern novel about the possible meanings of exile, faith, history. I hasten to note that he understands serious play. The title immediately alerts me to the pattern of the novel. I think of the treatise by Maimonides, the medieval Jewish philosopher. And when I read that the same title is that of a hip "tourist" guide (published by Benjamin) for modern trav-

elers, I recognize that the novel moves on two planes. And when I read, furthermore, that the novel *itself* has the identical title, I understand that there is another level. I recognize dazzling design.

It is difficult to summarize the plot. Two women, stranded in contemporary Spain because of an airline strike, meet and search for common ground. They are, if you will, perplexed travelers. One is an elderly woman, Hanni; she has come to Spain from Florida to find "The Esau Letter," a document which she believes will explain her heritage, her association with her Spanish ancestors (the ancestors are Sephardic Jews). The other woman is a sprightly English journalist returning from filming a reclusive musician. Holland—her name suggests the country—is so far removed in taste and manners from Hanni that at first she takes her as a fanciful "White Rabbit" (there are so many references to *Alice in Wonderland* that I am tempted to view the novel as a commentary on Carroll's novel). It is important that the two women who *seem* to belong to different worlds—the Old and the New—search for an understanding of each other's *identity*. Thus we have two tourists exploring the city in which they are exiled and the truth of each other's reasons for travel. The matter is, of course, more complicated. They both write to Benjamin, the author of the travel guide, *A Guide for the Perplexed,* for advice. Although they have never seen him, they believe that he knows the land, that he is a trustworthy, necessary guide (a kind of spiritual guardian). I view these three characters in a multifaceted way. This view reflects the three possible levels of meanings. And it suggests that Levi is playing with numbers in an obscure, almost cabalistic manner.

I have not done justice to Levi's text. My text is a guide for beginners. Now it is up to other readers to fill in the gaps by reading—traveling through—*A Guide for the Perplexed.* (pp. 270-71)

> *Irving Malin, in a review of "A Guide for the Perplexed," in* The Review of Contemporary Fiction, *Vol. 13, No. 1, Spring, 1993, pp. 270-71.*

Bill Morris

Motor City

Born in 1952, Morris is an American novelist and journalist.

INTRODUCTION

Motor City, published as *Biography of a Buick* in England, is a portrait of American society and the automotive industry during the 1950s. A tale of industrial espionage, *Motor City* describes how Ted Mackey, CEO of General Motors Buick Division, attempts to determine who leaked a new bumper design to rival car company Plymouth. The themes of greed and betrayal recur throughout *Motor City*—Mackey is having an affair with his secretary, his public relations director is considering writing an exposé on Buick, and Buick's vice president of styling is on the verge of the auto industry's "greatest invention," built-in obsolescence. The novel's focus on corruption and power is underscored by references to McCarthyism, covert espionage and terrorist missions in Vietnam and Central America, and the segregation policies of the 1950s. Some critics have faulted Morris's many allusions to historical events and popular icons, claiming that the random appearances of such celebrities as Elvis Presley, Marilyn Monroe, President and Mamie Eisenhower, and Jack Kerouac interrupt and trivialize the novel's plot. Others, however, have asserted that this attempt to evoke a particular era of American history and culture is reminiscent of E. L. Doctorow's *Ragtime* and the books in John Updike's *Rabbit* tetralogy. Praising *Motor City* for its accurate depiction of the 1950s, Sylvia Steinberg observed: "Morris displays the zealous detachment of a sociologist as he exposes fissures in the decade's bland materialism."

CRITICISM

Loren D. Estleman   (review date 14 June 1992)

[*An American novelist and short story writer, Estleman is best known for his detective fiction, which is frequently set in Detroit. In the following essay, he praises Morris for his accurate portrayal of the automotive industry in the 1950s, but faults his gratuitous references to popular icons of the era.*]

Nestled between the patriotic bunting of World War II and the radical paisleys of the Vietnam era, the 1950s are often repainted in tones of sepia and beige, the predominant hues of early color television. They were originally done in the bright, scrubbed primaries of a magazine ad: simple, eyeball-snatching colors that in the flush of postwar prosperity represented an American Dream seemingly as obtainable as an easy payment plan on a new Buick.

The hero of Bill Morris's novel **Motor City** is a Buick: the 1954 Century, a long, low sweep of newborn pink and garter-belt black, dripping with chrome and upholstered like an airport diner. The turning point in automotive design from the bulbous brontos of earlier years, it symbolizes both America on the move and upward mobility for Ted Mackey, the aggressive CEO of General Motors' Buick Division. The fortunes of car and man are intertwined.

The crack in this glossy finish is industrial espionage. Someone has apparently sold the Century's bold new front-bumper design to rival Plymouth, and much of the plot details Mackey's Captain Queeg-like obsession to identify and punish the culprit.

Spinning in his orbit is a galaxy of characters unmistakably American and uniquely 1950s: Harvey Pearl, vice-president of styling and the revered inventor of Detroit's single biggest money-maker, the annual model change, now beginning to question his lifelong dedication to an industry responsible in part for the mutilation at Hiroshima of his Japanese girlfriend; Milmary Mackey, Ted's wife and a former freelance writer of promise, withering in her husband's dynamic shadow; Morey Caan, a Washington, D.C. columnist determined to burst the bubble of Eisenhower-era complacency; and Claire Hathaway, Mackey's mistress and a draftswoman in GM's styling department whose voluntary bondage bids fair to free Milmary from hers. The 500,000th Century to roll off the line represents the watershed in all these lives.

Mackey's explanation for his spy-search is a credo for his time:

> We're the second-largest division in the largest corporation in the world. When you're that big, when you've got that much to lose, you can't afford to take any chances. It may not seem like the end of the world to you if a piece of a competitor's car resembles a piece of one of ours. But if there's a reason for it other than pure coincidence, then I damn sure better find out—otherwise I won't be around for long . . .

Mackey's other twin fixations are the Wildcat, his dream sports car to rival the Corvette, and Marilyn Monroe, his dream choice for a celebrity to endorse it. The latter is an obsession he shares with author Morris, whose insistence upon walk-ons by Monroe, husband Joe DiMaggio, Dwight and Mamie Eisenhower, Vladimir Nabokov, Joe McCarthy—and yes, Elvis the Pelvis—threatens at times to destroy the book's balance. At these times it looks less like a modern Greek tragedy in the tradition of John O'Hara than a "Where's Waldo?" for the "Happy Days" set.

The character of journalist Caan is equally gratuitous, serving only to introduce some of these period icons and to bleed all over the page on the subjects of Hiroshima and Eisenhower's alleged mistreatment of Nazi POWs during his stint as commander of operations in the European war theater. As a conduit to national events Caan merely saps pressure from the Detroit boiler.

For the most part, however, *Motor City* paints a disturbingly accurate picture of an industrial leviathan rolling fat on the profits from its biggest year, oblivious to the faint rumble from the factories of the Far East and the cancerous cells feeding on its own vitals. Acetylene sparks flash, ice cubes crash, Lucky butts mash. The whole thing has the look and feel of those "Dynamic Detroit" pamphlets the Chamber of Commerce circulated by the thousands under Mayor Louis Miriani, but with an understanding of the filthy engine throbbing beneath that polished hood. It's a vivid and entertaining expedition in the literary quest for the exact moment when the Streets of Gold began to transmute into base metal.

Loren D. Estleman, "Wheels of Fortune," in Book World—The Washington Post, June 14, 1992, p. 6.

Michiko Kakutani (review date 7 July 1992)

[*In the following essay, Kakutani praises Morris's depiction of the "American Dream" in* Motor City.]

The year is 1954, and what's good for General Motors is supposed to be good for the country. There are faint rumblings, far away, in a place called Vietnam, and Joseph McCarthy is noisily looking for Communists, but it's the marriage of Marilyn Monroe and Joe DiMaggio that dominates the tabloid headlines. Elvis is on the verge of his first big break, the McDonald brothers are starting a chain of hamburger stores, and Jack Kerouac and Neal Cassady are preparing for their adventures on the road. In Detroit, automobiles are about to sprout fins and menacing bumpers as the folks at rival car companies struggle to capture the imagination of the American people.

In his energetic [*Motor City*], Bill Morris, a columnist for *The Greensboro News and Record* in North Carolina, wants to do two things. He wants to tell the story of the men and women who work at a fictionalized version of the Buick design division: the story of their private hopes, dreams and romances. He also wants to use their story to illustrate the promises and betrayals of the American Dream, and in doing so, give the reader a comprehensive portrait of American life in the 50's.

The Buick part of his story begins, simply enough, with a bumper. It seems that the front bumper of the new Buick Century—a bumper "that looked like it could scoop dead cows off the road, a silver slab punctuated by two sharply tipped, mammiferous bulbs"—has been stolen by the designers at Plymouth. At least that's what Ted Mackey and Harvey Pearl, Mr. Morris's fictional Buick executives, think. They decide to take some McCarthyite measures to find the leak.

The phones in the Buick design division are bugged, and lists of suspects are compiled. Ted also takes it upon himself to personally cultivate a spy. His choice is Claire Hathaway, a beautiful young designer who's working on the new Buick Century and who uncannily reminds him of his wife, Milmary, when she was young. Claire reluctantly agrees to try to ferret out some information, less out of company loyalty than out of a growing attraction to Ted, the company's so-called great white shark.

Will Lomax, a former reporter who has just become Buick's top public relations man, is dismayed by his bosses' behavior. Although he had prided himself on being unshockable, "this time he had underestimated the automobile industry's capacity for savagery." For years, Will has been planning to write "The Book," a scathing tell-all account of the Buick division, but now he's afraid he has too much at stake in the company himself. He has mixed feelings when his best friend, Morey Caan, a muck-raking journalist from Washington, arrives in town to do a story on the Buick division's latest design.

Writing in crisp, engaging prose, Mr. Morris does a wonderful job of introducing these characters in the early chapters of *Motor City.* He has the same gift John Updike displayed in his *Rabbit* novels, a gift for delineating his characters' inner lives while at the same time making their dilemmas emblematic of impulses in American society at large. He is a vigorous, nimble writer, and by cutting back and forth between various characters' stories, he's able to immerse us in a well-upholstered fictional world.

We get caught up in the thrill—and as described by Mr. Morris, it actually is a thrill—of readying a new automobile design for production, and we also get caught up in the personal dramas of his characters' lives. Ted's affair with Claire; his wife's determination to write fiction; Will's growing ambivalence toward his job; Morey's decision to investigate the Buick division: all are smoothly dramatized.

Unfortunately, Mr. Morris is not content to let his characters' individual stories speak for themselves. Rather, he periodically switches to a wide-angle lens that he hopes will comprehensively capture the mood and concerns of America at mid-century. Toward this end, he begins shoehorning bigger and bigger issues into the main narrative: Harvey Pearl, for instance, falls in love with a woman horribly disfigured by the atomic bomb dropped on Hiroshima. At the same time, Mr. Morris also starts introducing more and more famous people in cameo roles.

Unlike their counterparts in E. L. Doctorow's *Ragtime,* these celebrities don't really interact with the other characters, they just have annoying walk-on roles. Ted talks to Marilyn Monroe about doing a Buick promotion. Claire corresponds with Vladimir Nabokov. Morey interviews Joseph McCarthy and President Eisenhower and investigates stories involving people like Robert Oppenheimer.

Such encounters with symbolic figures of the 50's multiply toward the end of [*Motor City*], and they begin to feel increasingly preposterous and contrived. Not only do these scenes distort the shape and symmetry of the book, they also seem to have diverted Mr. Morris from the original story he set out to tell. Indeed, the fates of Ted, Harvey, Milmary, Claire, Will and Morey are hurriedly tied up, as Mr. Morris spends more and more time performing narrative contortions to introduce people like Elvis Presley and Jack Kerouac.

It's a disappointing conclusion to a book that got off to such a roaring good start. Given the abundance of Mr. Morris's talents, it seems unlikely that he will make a similar mistake in his next novel.

> *Michiko Kakutani, "Promise and Betrayal of the American Dream," in* The New York Times, *July 7, 1992, p. C15.*

Roz Kaveney   (review date 24 July 1992)

[*In the following essay, Kaveney offers a positive assessment of* Motor City, *published as* Biography of a Buick *in England.*]

There is a particular thrill in doing things for the first time.

The strength of Bill Morris' [*Biography of a Buick*], in which he stacks icons of the American 1950s in a house of cards that never quite tumbles into banality, is that he regularly manages to capture that thrill.

This is a novel in which characters watch their first colour television, hear their first Elvis Presley record, and discover for the first time that US world power is built on shabbiness, treachery and massacre. Morris does not over-rate innocence as a virtue, but he is fascinated by the process of its loss.

The elaborate plot is tied to the General Motors Buick division, and its design and publicity departments. Someone has leaked details of the new model's bumper design to a rival firm, and general manager Ted Mackey is determined to find out who. He is also determined to push through plans for a car, the Wildcat, named after the planes he flew in the Pacific, and to rise as high and as fast as he can. Mackey is not simply a villain, though he is a lecher, a hypocrite and a hirer of thugs. He is, we come to feel, the significant underside of the spirit of his age.

The men and women whom he dominates and uses are also types as well as characters: Claire, worried about being a blue-stocking, humiliated by an affair and learning self-respect; Harvey, the elegant designer obsessed with the Japanese women he loved as a boy, now a scarred survivor of Hiroshima; Will, the PR man anxious to keep faith with his talent; Morey, the reporter with a nose for a story. This is a novel full of moral absolutes—betrayal, adultery, fraud.

If Morris' humane imagination did not make these dilemmas emotionally appealing, this would be a compilation of clichés. As it is, he uses character, rather than mere brand-name detail, to build his portrayal of how a period felt when it was the present and not the nostalgic or despised past. Morris has understood the moral imperatives and idealism of the time as well as its brutality and tackiness, to the extent that, at times, this reads like a novel of, not about, the 1950s.

The biggest, though most predictable, risk that Morris has taken is his threading of major personalities into his plot. He manages this as efficiently as E. L. Doctorow, acknowledging from the outset our sense that he is playing a game.

We learn early that Claire's college instructor was that most ludic of novelists, Nabokov. Monroe, Presley and Kerouac drift in and out of the lives of the characters, key manifestations of the process of the plot as well as dramatisations of their aspirations. This comes to seem less an exploitation of dramatic irony than a reminder of frailty and mortality.

Morris also knows enough not to push his luck. Mackey's attempt to use Monroe to publicise the Bearcat never comes to anything, and Morey's interview with the young Presley has no particular effect on either career. There is a tact in much of this that stops the game becoming an indulgence; the only real exceptions, which have us tapping our feet with impatience, are the lectures in which Morey's ex-CIA friend acquaints him with the sordid de-

An excerpt from *Motor City*

Harvey Pearl and John Nickles strode into the office. As he rose to shake their hands, Will wondered how it was possible that these two men worked for the same corporation. Harvey was a dandy, a cocky little tyrant who'd had a hand in the design of more than thirty million GM cars over the past quarter-century, the visionary who had given Detroit its greatest money-maker since mass production, the annual model change. He wore his hair in a brush cut, and he favored bow ties and suspenders and suits that strayed a long way from the corporate uniform of dark blue. Will thought of him as a proletarian Napoleon. Today he was wearing a bottle-green suit, a pale blue shirt and a scarlet bow tie.

John Nickles, on the other hand, was textbook General Motors. The head of Buick styling had begun his career with the company nineteen years ago, and no one doubted that he would work there until he turned sixty-five or dropped dead, whichever came first. His claim to fame was the ventiports, the notched chrome holes in the front quarter panels that served no purpose but had become a Buick trademark over the years. Three ventiports made the car a "three-holer," the smaller Special and Century models, while the Roadmaster was a "four-holer," the big body, the biggest engine, the true status boat. John Nickles understood status better than anyone else Will had ever met. Yet he had a lumpy, bald head, and he always wore drab suits, white shirts, black shoes. Will had never seen him laugh. He thought of him as an executive serf. When they were seated, Ted stood up, clamped his hands behind his back and started pacing in front of the windows. Will expected him to say something about Joe DiMaggio and Marilyn Monroe. But he said, "I trust everyone saw our commercial during the Rose Bowl."

Will twisted in his chair. The tone of Ted's voice reminded him why he'd dreaded this moment. Suddenly he felt clammy and tired. He nodded along with Harvey and John.

"And I trust everyone saw the Plymouth commercial during the Cotton Bowl," Ted said.

Harvey and John nodded. Will said, "Umm, afraid I missed it. The baby was sick all weekend."

Ted glanced at him, then looked back down at the brushed-steel carpet, continued pacing. "Well, for your information, the fucking Plymouth's front bumper is a spittin' image of ours. That means one thing: we've got a design leak somewhere. And that means for the next four years we're going to sit around with our thumbs up our asses wondering how much Plymouth knows about our new designs. We just spent forty-two million redesigning our line this year"—he looked straight at Will—"and now we're *fucked*!"

"Now hold on one second, Ted," John Nickles said.

"I'm not finished." Ted continued pacing. "You'll recall that the company canceled a quarter of a million dollars of advertising with the *Wall Street Journal* last year when they ran pictures of the '53 Pontiacs before the official unveiling date. And I don't have to tell you that Hugh Lund is no longer g.m. at Pontiac. He's at Studebaker studying upholstery combinations or some such shit. Why? Because if you can't keep your new models a secret, you've flushed your biggest selling point straight down the toilet. Am I right, Harvey?"

Bill Morris, in his Motor City, *Alfred A. Knopf, 1992.*

tails of the Guatemala coup and the "Other Losses" scandal. We, unlike Morey, know all this already. We do not need to be confronted more than minimally with our lapse from good faith in, briefly, loving 1950s America.

Roz Kaveney, "First Loves," in New Statesman & Society, *Vol. 5, No. 212, July 24, 1992, p. 42.*

William Leith   (review date 26 July 1992)

[*In the following essay, Leith praises* Biography of a Buick *as an insightful analysis of American society in the 1950s.*]

The year is 1954. Will Lomax, a publicity man for General Motors, whose job is to dream up ideas to make people want the 1954 Buick Century, a big fat boat of a gas-guzzling car, comes back home from a business trip, goes to bed, gets up, goes back to work, comes home again.

His wife is standing at the kitchen sink, arms crossed. "Who's Cindy?" she snaps, "I found her name and number in your shirt pocket." Lomax doesn't miss a beat. "Oh, *that* Cindy," he snaps back. "That's Cindy Warhover, district manager in LA."

She's not, of course—she's an air hostess—but Lomax, pushing into middle age, is honing his skills as a middle-aged man: youthful idealism draining away, he's getting good at compromise, lying, meeting his sales targets. And that's what this perceptive, readable book [*Biography of a Buick*], is all about: it's all about how, in 1954, America was in exactly the same position as Will Lomax.

Ted Mackey, who heads the General Motors Buick division, is even better at being middle-aged than Will. A former wartime pilot, Ted spends his days barking out large numbers and examining pictures of tail fins and his evenings pumping away at his sexy mistress who looks like his wife looked 15 years ago. Ted goes around "jacket off, tie loose, shirt sleeves rolled up, drink in his fist, pure Detroit."

That's not just a description of Ted Mackey—that's a description of America in 1954: the war over, jacket off, tie loose, America is a middle-aged salesman at a party. This isn't only the era of huge fat cars; it's the era of Ike and Mamie, of Marilyn and Joe DiMaggio, of spreading suburbs, witchhunts, blunders in Vietnam.

Perhaps the most impressive thing about [*Biography of a Buick*] is the author's sense of history—this may be the story of a few people going to sales meetings and getting off with each other, but on every other page he makes you feel you're witnessing the origins of the world we know today. And he weaves in some interesting cameos—Ray Kroc, the founder of McDonald's; the young Elvis Presley; even Vladimir Nabokov gets a look-in, deflowering one of his students as he struggles with the manuscript of a weird book he's writing about a middle-aged man who can't take his eyes off nubile girls.

So all this stuff is happening—the cynical modern world is being born—and just about nobody notices. Something else, something much more important, is happening: *the front bumper of the Plymouth looks exactly like the front bumper of the Buick!* Ted Mackey can hardly believe it. Is there a spy in the GM styling division? Surely not—surely the world can't really be as rotten and horrible and lowdown as that.

The answer, of course, is yes—the world *is* that horrible, and the one man in the book to see this is Morey Caan, a journalist who decides to write an investigative piece on the Detroit car industry. When he arrives, he is staggered. He thinks: "Now we're getting in touch with the essence of American sickness." Which is something the author of this book has done admirably. Read [**Biography of a Buick**] on the beach—or, alternatively, in the social science seminar.

> *William Leith, "Dreams of Tail-Fins and Gas-Guzzling," in* Independent on Sunday, *July 26, 1992.*

Valentine Cunningham   (review date 23 August 1992)

[*In the following essay, Cunningham offers a negative assessment of* Biography of a Buick.]

Once upon a time, point of view in a novel was a mere matter of setting up your easel in some nice spot and jotting down what you saw, all unruffled and unruffling. But since tin-drummer-boy Günter Grass and the dictatorship of the South American fabulists the business has got tougher, involving increasingly extremer camera-angles, and trying to hit on ever more enticing gadgets, far-fetched gizmos, technicolor technics in order to magick the real into sharp grabbing focus.

Whatever next, so to say, after *Flaubert's Parrot*? Well, some have resorted to the vista from the automobile, and that's Bill Morris's way [in **Biography of a Buick**]. In ambitious quest of a key to all Fifties mythologies he's hit on the 1954 revival by General Motors of the Buick Century motor-car, all Cold War supremacist chrome cowcatchers, with McCarthyite ventiports (big, hollow, of no use), and thrusting Elvis-pelvis fin-jobs.

It's a wheeze to go with, if gas-guzzling heaps of prettied-up iron are your buzz. Trouble is, that however keenly this Book of the Buick gets its bobby-dazzler of meanly low-slung chromium flash all revved up, the beast goes nowhere much. Granted the chapter in which a stop-at-nothing salesman works all the old selling scams to get a crippled war vet parting with more loot than he wants to for a heavily publicised boiled-oyster pink and anthracite black V8 special, does push quite close to the classically awesome money-grabbing excitements of the bonds-trading scene in [Tom Wolfe's] *The Bonfire of the Vanities*—a novel that haunts this one.

But aside from these odd moments of business tremor, Morris's Buicks fall rather short of the central visionary,

mythic force they're evidently supposed to bear. 'Engine Charlie' Wilson, Ike Eisenhower's choice for government military boss, may have famously linked the fates of General Motors and the USA, but Bill Morris's efforts scarcely bear the great car maker out.

The efforts are brave, not to say desperate. The novel's Buick people are granted fingers in all possible historical pies. The plot's main female Buick 'stylist' just happens to have a brother flying undercover missions to help the French in Dien Bien Phu. The big shot who conceived General Motors' sales-hiking new-model-every-year idea happens to be involved with a Japanese woman who gets hideously burned at Hiroshima. There's a journalist doing a Biography of a Buick feature for *Life* magazine who makes a handy ear onto and nose into every hot political scandal of the day—H-bomb tests, the Oppenheimer framing, McCarthyism, CIA doings in Guatemala, Ike's rumoured maltreatment of German POWs.

But all these would-be connective tissues between Buickry and the US Fifties keep sounding too tricksy for conviction. Even, or especially, at their most attractively joker-in-the-pack zany—as when Professor Vladimir Nabokov turns out to have been the teacher of our female 'stylist' at Cornell and has her in the back of the old Buick on blocks that he writes *Lolita* in; or when Neal Cassady and Jack Kerouac turn up in the crew of layabout weirdoes hired in Detroit to ferry the new Buicks across the country. On the road indeed.

But how much more welcome are these daftly far-fetched schemings of Morris than his habitual resort to the corniest of plot devices and the mushiest of banal sentiments. He rivals a J. Archer or a Susan Crosland in his devotion to the belief that it's mainly adultery that makes novels—like Buicks—go round. The heart sinks at the combination of all this writerly ambition with such imaginative feebleness. Even sax-player Ornette Coleman is wheeled on to assure a wild milk-shake maker salesman that jazz-men and salesmen are all about 'heart' and doing 'what we gotta do.' Even Buick fans gotta do better than this.

> *Valentine Cunningham, "All Revved Up and Nowhere to Go," in* The Observer, *August 23, 1992, p. 47.*

Frank Rich   (essay date 7-14 September 1992)

[*Rich is an American newspaper editor and film critic. In the following excerpt, he discusses* Motor City *as a part of a literary trend that recognizes the "darker view of the 1950s."*]

[The] '50s were decried, even at the time, as sterile, conformist, and materialistic by such sociological debunkers as David Riesman, William H. Whyte, Vance Packard, C. Wright Mills, and Lewis Mumford, not to mention writers as various as Grace Metalious and John Cheever. It was the heyday of "the men in the gray flannel suits, the country-club Christians, the organization men, the frightened herd that composed the lonely crowd," as Dan Wakefield summarizes the contemporaneous anti-'50s line in his memoir of New York in those years [*New York in the 50s*].

There is now a new and voluminous literature on the '50s, and it takes a decidedly darker view, arguing that the decade not only failed to offer a prescription for America's present ills but was in fact an early symptom of them. In this reading, the air-brushed vision of the decade that America would like to believe in today, and that its politicians would like to sell to voters, was as much a Fantasyland as the one that Walt Disney opened in Anaheim in 1955, its sitcom family values a sham and its industrial cunning tarnished or gone. . . .

Morris's [*Motor City*], a skillful first novel written like non-fiction, lays out the broad, public cultural-political highways of the decade.

Set mostly in Detroit in 1954, but with side trips to the other '50s centers of power in New York, Washington, and Hollywood, *Motor City* tells of the occasionally clever and often ruthless means by which some General Motors executives, stylists, and salesmen hope to make the new Buick Century, a fiftieth-anniversary model, the best-selling Buick of all time. From the opening chapter, in which the characters gather on New Year's Day to watch the Rose Bowl Parade on a new twenty-one-inch RCA color television, Morris evokes a glossy environment dominated by the family-oriented consumer goods that greeted the growing leisure class and its baby boom. The kitchens in *Motor City* are invariably stocked with products like the Power-Chef Mixer and the Hurri-Hot Electri-Cup ("It cost $14.95 and looked like some sort of stainless steel toadstool"). The "futuristic dream machines" that the Detroiters design and drive come in color combinations like "boiled shrimp and anthracite" and are equipped with "basketball-hoop-sized" steering wheels and seats "pleated with red vinyl, like the booths in diners and bowling-alley cocktail lounges."

Motor City amply demonstrates that the '50s were the first American decade that could be caricatured by the brand names of its material goods, and Morris recaptures the clean, voluptuous pleasure of it all. At times his book suggests, not necessarily pejoratively, that America had been freshly plastered over with that home-decorating miracle known as Con-Tact paper, the vinyl, self-adhering wall covering described by Thomas Hine a few years ago in his study of '50s consumer kitsch, *Populuxe*, as "a 1954 invention which resulted in an explosion of pattern all over the house . . . [and which] sometimes proved addictive." After applying his figurative Con-Tact, however, Morris inevitably must strip it away to reveal what is hidden underneath.

In the *Ragtime* manner, he brings his fictional car people into contact with historical figures who set the true tempo (more ferocious than ragtime) of the age. The Buick division general manager Ted Mackey relentlessly pursues Marilyn Monroe to recruit her image ("a little bit dangerous, but not *too* dangerous") for the promotion of a new sports car called the Wildcat. Mackey has an extramarital affair with Claire Hathaway, a talented Buick stylist whose first lover (in the back seat of a Buick, no less) had been her favorite Cornell professor, Vladimir Nabokov. When, in a well-oiled publicity stunt for *Life* magazine, Buick sells its 500,000th car to a couple living in Levit-

town (on a highly photogenic block where all the other look-alike homes also have Buicks in their driveways), the driver delivering the vehicle is Neal Cassady, accompanied by Jack Kerouac. And on one road or another, *Motor City* contrives cameo appearances by Ray Kroc (soon to put the hamburger on the assembly line), Berry Gordy, Sonny Rollins, and Robert McNamara, along with the ineluctable Elvis.

By the novel's final chapters Morris has slammed his foot down on the gas, and the fictional-historical juxtapositions accelerate into ludicrous overkill. Before then they are often witty, but they do steer the book to a fixed polemical destination. Rather than using the real-life characters to imagine the '50s as they might have spontaneously occurred before they were calcified as The Fifties, Morris exploits the celebrities retrospectively, and on occasion mechanically, to buttress his bleak parallels with the 1990s.

It is no surprise to learn that Morris is a journalist—a columnist for the Greensboro (North Carolina) *News and Record*. And it is no wonder that his book's hero, to the extent it has one, is a fictional '50s Washington journalist named Morey Caan who works alongside Russell Baker, Drew Pearson, and Stewart Alsop. Morey is reporting the Buick story for *Life* when he is not collecting tidbits for a pet project, *Straight from the Horse's Mouth*, a book that will be "a series of direct quotations from Ike himself, verbatim gobbledygook, double-talk, and gibberish, an encyclopedia of Ike-speak."

As *Straight from the Horse's Mouth* might be considered the Ur-text of *Bushisms*, so most of the other stories Morey encounters during *Motor City* portray a '50s Republican Washington that, far from being paradise, is but an earlier incarnation of the capital of four decades later. Ike, who "had not attended church during his entire adult life," becomes a pious, regular churchgoer, lest anyone question that his family values are out of sync with Father Patrick Peyton's popular imperative that "the family who prays together stays together." But this platitudinous president's tireless pitch for the family—"Mamie and I both think they make a lovely couple," he says of the newly married DiMaggios at a press conference—proves a front for another, corrupt variety of paternalism: to him, the American public are children best kept in the dark about his big secrets. Morey stumbles on a rumor that Eisenhower "single-handedly starved a million German POWs to death during the occupation of '45" and uncovers clandestine administration and CIA schemes (some of them involving Howard Hunt) to pump up Saddam Hussein-like regimes in Guatemala, Thailand, and Vietnam.

To Morris, Detroit was no more of an industrial nirvana in its supposed golden age than it is now, but a twin image of the corruption, arrogance, and p.r. chicanery of Washington. It's no joke when Eisenhower's nominee for secretary of defense, former GM President Charles "Engine Charlie" Wilson, testifies before Congress that "what was good for the country was good for General Motors—and vice versa." When Mackey suspects his underlings of selling Buick design ideas to Plymouth, he starts a witch-hunt employing dirty tricks borrowed from Joe McCarthy. Though Buick is spewing out more cars than can possibly be sold for each instantly obsolescent model year, first-hand reports of a new, more efficient automobile industry culture in companies such as Nissan and Toyota in Japan are cavalierly ignored by Detroit magnates.

If the covert corporate and political cancers of the '50s of *Motor City* are familiar to citizens of the '90s, so are the racial divisions isolating Motor City from Motown. Except for "the first Negro ever hired as a stylist at General Motors" and a smattering of legendary musicians hovering on the fringes of show business, blacks are relegated to the unseen bowels of industry and the ghetto. (They aren't allowed to live in Levittown.) The as yet unknown Elvis, described by an onlooker as one of those "whites trying to look like the colored" and by Morris in Detroit-speak ("his hair was lovingly sculpted and watered and looked like polished metal"), is poised to make more money from black music than any black artist could imagine.

Yet the most rotten institution in the '50s, according to this book, was the most pervasive and celebrated one: the American family, that fount of Norman Rockwell tableaux and the touchstone for today's yearned-for traditional values. In Morris's account, the smiling '50s family, that alleged monument to togetherness, proves to be built largely on the subjugation and the suffering, even the incarceration, of women, who are trapped at home with their kids and appliances while their husbands race about in their new cars, often to toy with those deviant women still single.

As *Motor City* would have it, Nabokov's notion of *poshlost* (his term for "not only the obviously trashy, but also the falsely important, the falsely beautiful, the falsely clever and attractive") is synonymous with populuxe; and it is most perfectly illustrated by an advertisement in *Life* depicting "a gleeful mom and dad and their kiddies jumping for joy beside their shiny Tucker." That definition plays out in Morris's story, which reveals the *Life* family diorama as a nasty hoax. The newly affluent American men in this novel are not in love with their wives or kiddies but with their cars, which Detroit specifically designed to be "wildcats" catering to male fantasies of phallic aggression.

Sprouting buxom headlights and bumper guards up front and fins in the rear, '50s cars "looked like a chorus girl coming and a fighter plane going," wrote Hine in *Populuxe.* Women were stuck with station wagons—neutered, utilitarian extensions of the home, designed for the hauling of children and consumer goods. And the '50s home, as *Motor City* dramatizes, was often hell, a model of family values for display purposes only. Ted Mackey's wife, well-educated and long ago the author of one published story in *The New Yorker,* now languishes in an alcoholic fog in Grosse Pointe.

Claire, Ted's mistress, resembles his wife in so many ways that she might as well be a new model in the same product line. "I feel like a piece of property. Or a toy," she tells Ted after a confrontation that is reminiscent of Billy Wilder's bleak depiction of an ill-fated extramarital liaison in '50s corporate America in *The Apartment;* soon Claire will

fly to New York for an illegal abortion (secured by Professor Nabokov). Even the one ostensibly happily married housewife in *Motor City,* the spouse of a likable Buick flack, feels "a kind of sadness without end, a feeling that . . . all the striving and bloodshed, the accumulation of homes and gadgets and toys and babies, the sense that things would always keep getting better and better—all of it felt like a stupendous waste."

These fictional women's feelings are not ideological boilerplate exactly, but they do fit neatly into the mold of the grim, proliferating historical views of the '50s. In his important essay "Did Success Spoil the United States?" the late historian Warren Susman showed that Americans of the '50s were bombarded with family imagery, from "I Love Lucy" and "I Remember Mama" on television to "all the family words enveloping the new suburban lifestyle: family-sized carton, family room, family car, family film, family restaurant, family vacation." And yet, while "one can represent the new affluent society collectively in the image of the happy suburban home," the propaganda did not entirely take. Those suburban homes existed in an "age of anxiety" prompted by internal tensions as well as external fears of the cold war's nuclear arsenals. The happy family, praying together or not, was often elusive. Juvenile delinquency, once thought to be safely cordoned off in slums, was rapidly spreading "in the affluent suburbs, where everybody had a car and access to all the goods and services that money could buy."

In *Young, White, and Miserable,* Wini Breines, a feminist sociologist who grew up in the '50s, elucidates this anxiety, while making her own arguments that the "nostalgic and rosy" memory of the decade is a facade. "Innocent and white (and these descriptives are most definitely linked) teenage girls sipping Cokes at the soda shop after school evoke longing for supposedly simpler and happier times," she writes before dismantling this and other "Happy Days" clichés. Like Morris, Breines finds the decade's women trapped in a paradox: even as the expansion of higher education and the economy gave women greater social equality and more access to the job market, the "politically and culturally conservative" family values "socialized [them] to consider marriage as their only future" and barricaded them in their populuxe homes. Those values, eventually challenged in 1963 by Betty Friedan in *The Feminine Mystique,* are, of course, the same ones [Vice President Dan Quayle trumpeted] so loudly. (pp. 39-41)

Frank Rich, "The Best Years of Our Lives?" in The New Republic, *Vol. 207, Nos. 11 & 14, September 7 & 14, 1992, pp. 38-43.*

John Syme   (review date 13 September 1992)

[*In the essay below, Syme positively assesses* Motor City, *concluding that it focuses on both contemporary American culture and the automotive industry of the 1950s.*]

Nostalgic name-dropping is a major part of the game in *Motor City,* Bill Morris' first novel. The book is an engaging, Sidney Sheldonesque romp through the good old days of Chesterfields-and-three-martini, postwar Detroit.

First-hand anecdotes of Ike and Mamie and Marilyn and Kerouac and McCarthy and Nabokov and Levittown and a host of other cultural icons dress up the full-speed-ahead, sometimes cursory action like so many fins, gills and headlamps on a '54 Buick.

The '54 Buick Century, in fact, is the vehicle that carries the story. Character and content revolve around the machine's development, sometimes even retiring to the ease of back-seat driver—much Nick at Nite poetics and uncannily prescient meanderings about Vietnam, the environment and the generally unhealthy procession of politics toward 1992. The Republican convention in particular, you get the feeling.

Claire Hathaway is a young, attractive Buick designer; Ted Mackey is the general manager of the Buick division. Claire has an affair with Ted (her first was with Professor Vladimir). Harvey Pearl, the head of styling at General Motors, has hired Will Lomax, a former reporter for *The Washington Post,* as a public-relations flack. Will's best buddy, Morey Caan, also of the *Post,* joins the fray to write a "Biography of a Buick" magazine piece.

Morris, a Greensboro *News & Record* columnist who grew up in Detroit, knows his subjects: the grit and glamour of Detroit's heyday, the randy adolescence of the consumer culture seen through a cracked prism of healthy capitalism turned to greed for its own sake, and the paranoid self-helpfulness and political correctness it spawned.

The book is a curious blend, not only of cameos by familiar faces, but also of familiar subjects: illicit sex, corporate treachery, atom-bombed wartime romance, dysfunctional family life, the boozy clarity of cynical writers. . . .

The anecdotes are mostly episodic, never quite gelling, but always getting the page turned to see who's going to show up next, doing what to whom. Morris' journalistic "healthy skepticism" sometimes threatens to bring up too much of a dark side of such an innocuously entertaining story, but overall that skepticism provides some of the novel's sharpest insights.

Whether writing of journalists, flacks or car salesmen (hmm), he aptly describes the political reality that the fittest often are the most venal:

> Hayes had forgotten about Bob losing his left foot to frostbite at Chosin Reservoir. He felt like smacking his forehead. How could I forget something like that, he asked himself, when it meant the guy couldn't operate a clutch and the automatic Dynaflow transmission was already sold?

Motor City is a fun read with a dark side, familiarity with contempt. But Morris does not make the mistake of trying to build up to any grand conclusions. In fact, that seems to be his point: This Is Your Life, too.

The subplots, mostly, resolve themselves.

The characters, mostly, get theirs.

The Buick Century and the American Century roll on.

> *John Syme, "Novel's Joy Ride Has a Dark*

Side," in Winston-Salem Journal, *September 13, 1992.*

Bill Morris with *CLC Yearbook* (interview date 22 January 1993)

[*In the excerpt below, Morris discusses* Motor City, *his aims as a writer, and his literary influences.*]

[*CLC Yearbook*]: *Did you conduct background research for* **Motor City**?

[Morris]: I spent more than a year prowling the libraries at Duke University, reading anything I could find that sprang from or looked back on the 1950s—histories, newspapers, magazines, biographies, autobiographies, technical journals, congressional hearings, memoirs, fiction. I was particularly drawn to advertisements. It was an age when sports heroes touted their favorite cigarette brands, when it wasn't a crime to eat red meat and drink brown liquor. And of course there was an astonishing gush of consumer goods, ranging from kitchen appliances to toys, furniture, food, clothing, electronics and, above all, those luscious, chrome-encrusted automobiles that seemed to rocket off the page.

Are your personal experiences incorporated into **Motor City**? *If so, how?*

Since the action in the novel takes place almost exclusively during the calendar year 1954, when I was two years old, very little of my personal experience comes into play. Having said that, I would quickly add that all writing is in some sense "autobiographical." A novelist is always using personal experience, filtered through the imagination, to create characters and their predicaments in a fictional world. For instance, my father worked for Ford Motor Company while I was growing up in Detroit in the '50s and '60s, and though I've never been inside a car stylist's mind when he received a flash of inspiration, I have visited car styling studios, have seen the sketches and clay models, have talked to stylists and marveled at their creations.

Similarly, though I've never eavesdropped on a telephone conversation between Marilyn Monroe and an auto executive, though I've never watched an atomic bomb survivor unwrap a gauze mask to reveal her scarred face—moments that occur in *Motor City*—I have heard movie stars and executives talk, and I have seen people with horrible burns. So I've used what I know along with what I've been able to imagine.

Were you inspired to write this book by any specific events or people?

The inspiration for this book was very specific. It's pink and black and it weighs 3,795 pounds. It's a "three-hole" 1954 Buick Century I'd been driving for a dozen years when it began presenting me with questions. Who designed that sweeping, wraparound windshield? That basketball hoop-sized steering wheel? Those sharply tipped chrome bulbs on the front bumper? How many were made? Why did it go so fast? Was it a common car or a status symbol?

Growing up in Detroit I had heard the name Harley Earl,

the design czar at General Motors since the 1920s. So one day I walked into a library and looked him up in the 1954 Reader's Guide. There was a first-person article by Earl in the Aug. 24 *Saturday Evening Post* entitled "I Dream Automobiles."

That article led me to others, and I soon realized 1954 was a year loaded with telling moments: the wedding (and divorce) of Joe DiMaggio and Marilyn Monroe; the Army-McCarthy hearings; the fall of the French at Dien Bien Phu in Vietnam; Elvis' first recording sessions in Memphis. Suddenly I was seeing my '54 Buick against a richly textured background. I was on my way.

What are your primary aims or goals as an author?

The nicest compliment I've ever received was from a *New York Times* reviewer, who wrote that **Motor City** displays "a gift for delineating (the) characters' inner lives while at the same time making their dilemmas emblematic of impulses in American society at large."

That's precisely what I set out to do. I'm fascinated by the way the individual and the larger American society shape, corrupt and enrich each other. Historical context—the feel of an era as much as its particular players and events—is therefore very important to me. Beyond that, my only goal is to break new ground every day and never write the same thing twice.

As you write, do you have a particular audience in mind or an ideal reader?

I wish I did, but I'm afraid I don't. This may explain my love for letter writing: It's the only time you're absolutely sure of your audience.

But I always try to write as I speak, and I always read what I've written out loud. The goal is simply to talk to one person at a time. It so happens I'm the first person to hear what I've written. After that, any person will do.

Who are your primary literary influences, and why?

If I had to name a primary influence, it would be Henry Miller. This is not so much because of what he wrote, which was sometimes brilliant, frequently humdrum and occasionally downright bad. It's more because of how he *lived,* the way he endured immense hardship and rejection on the way to finding his voice as a writer, the way he forcibly drowned himself in the horrors of the modern age and managed to come up laughing. He was the first person to show me, particularly in *Tropic of Cancer,* that writing can be a form of salvation.

There are others. Flannery O'Connor showed me the humor in the most horrible human moments. I have a weakness for the stylistic pyrotechnics of such writers as Martin Amis, Tom Wolfe, Jack Kerouac, Hunter S. Thompson, H. L. Mencken, Robert Penn Warren and Louis-Ferdinand Celine. I love the sweet muscular poetry of Philip Levine; the quiet prose and rich inner worlds of Walker Percy; the sheer doggedness of Joyce Carol Oates; the unstated menace that hums through Joan Didion's fiction. And Jim Harrison, because he writes so lovingly about food, and because each new book is so wildly different from the last.

Do you currently have any other works in progress? Do you foresee a departure or continuation of the style/themes of your first work?

I'm just now putting the finishing touches on a novel about a country/western disc jockey who has lost his soul in the byzantine city of Nashville. It's a comedy, but it's meant to be serious as well as funny. It's told in the first person and set in the twilight of the recent era of Republican rule, so stylistically it's a sharp departure from **Motor City.** But I'm trying once again to capture the feel of an era—a go-go time when greed had a way of devouring dreams—and I'm using a very mixed-up individual to show how the larger American society lost its way.

Lawrence Norfolk
Lemprière's Dictionary

Norfolk is an English novelist and editor, born in 1963.

INTRODUCTION

In *Lemprière's Dictionary,* which was first published in Great Britain to critical acclaim, Norfolk combines history, fiction, and classical mythology to explore the themes of greed, revenge, and death. Based in part on a dictionary of mythology published by English scholar John Lemprière in 1788, the novel centers on Lemprière's attempt to unravel the mysterious circumstances surrounding the death of his father, who was killed by a pack of dogs in an episode that mirrors the Greek myth of Actaeon and Artemis. After arriving in London from the English island of Jersey to settle his father's estate, Lemprière learns of a document that ties his family to the British East India Company. As he simultaneously compiles his dictionary and investigates his family's history, Lemprière collects letters, receipts, and other clues that link such historical events as Cardinal Richelieu's siege of the French city of La Rochelle in the early 1600s to a fictional conspiracy during which the British East India Company tried to gain control of France's economy on the eve of the French Revolution. Incorporating shifting time frames, multiple viewpoints, and diverse characters and locales into his narrative, Norfolk creates what a *London Times* critic has called "a quest, a political thriller, and a cultural meditation."

Noting Norfolk's focus on history and scholarship, critics have compared *Lemprière's Dictionary* to the antiquarian romances of Umberto Eco and A. S. Byatt. Most commentary has centered on Norfolk's multilayered narrative, integration of fact and fiction, and use of anachronisms. While some critics have charged that the novel's plot is overly complex and the characters simplistic, others have asserted that Norfolk's rich prose deserves high praise. Describing Norfolk's style as masterful, Alfred Corn has commented that in the brilliant descriptions of Jersey and eighteenth-century London "Norfolk's 19th-century forerunners find an authentic disciple."

CRITICISM

Betty Abel   (review date October 1991)

[In the following excerpt, Abel focuses on the interaction of historical and fictional events in Lemprière's Dictionary.]

The extraordinary novel entitled **Lemprière's Dictionary** concerns a family quest occasioned by a bequest passed down through two hundred years. The present day descendant of a member of the East India Company (formed in about 1600) finds the manuscript whose contents were to govern his actions, as it had done those of his eighteenth-century ancestor. The structure of the classical dictionary of Lemprière is used as the basis of a novel which traces the mystery involving a hitherto unknown cabbala, deep within the East India Company and utilising its powerful commercial connections. Voyages of discovery, piratical thefts and plots faking the loss of ships bearing valuable cargoes are only a few of the activities of this 'inner wheel'. But they do not stop at murder; for the puzzling factor in the story is the reason for a century-long feud existing between the Lemprière family and the East India Company itself. Through the examination of the *Dictionary* published in 1788 by John Lemprière, his descendants try to discover the origin of a crime which particularly concerns them, that of a murder which he has solved and which subsequently results in tragedy for him too. He has followed his inborn passion for ancient history too far but he has at least resolved the old feud and has found out the Jersey origin of his family. The book, tortuous though many of the author's scholarly disquisitions appear to be, is rewarding in the quality of its prose and in the astonishing range of knowledge it covers. It has much in common with [Umberto] Eco's *The Name of the Rose,* although nothing in its content is similar: another clerkly 'who-dun-it', it reaches into the present and future as well as the past.

A form of historical novel in which the insignificant details as described by the author are true because fully investigated by him seems to bring [*Lemprière's Dictionary*] within the orbit of social history. Norfolk explains his method thus: although his novel is historical, there are certain conventions he has deliberately flouted in order to create dramatic effect: anachronisms, too, exist in it, partly for the same purpose but also to show the impact of 'prevalent' influences near the event in question. There are a good many 'historical groupings' of this kind, the better to demonstrate some influence on real or imagined incidents. 'Time sequences' are, he says, 'broadly correct'.

At intervals in the novel these and other divergences from the usual historical reckoning are explained. The interpenetration of fact and fiction is his stated aim but only to further the story, never to hinder its flow. Interpretation rather than literal narration has been his purpose: 'Generally my practice has been to take the thought-horizon in 1788 as the historical reality . . . If something could be imagined at the time (and I could write it credibly) then it went in whether it actually existed or not'. If language could be used as it now is, he says, then the use of modern technology and terminology is justified. Perhaps a new form of science fiction is by this token on the horizon, especially since Norfolk also invokes theory of Chaos in his description of the seige of La Rochelle in the 17th century, two hundred years before any such theory was known. Such cyclical views of history seem suspiciously like the deconstructive methods controversially used in literary criticism. It hardly seems necessary or appropriate to the work in hand and is more like destroying one thing in order to build something else with the pieces. (pp. 214-15)

> *Betty Abel, in a review of "Lemprière's Dictionary," in* Contemporary Review, *Vol. 259, No. 1509, October, 1991, pp. 214-15.*

Richard Gehr   (review date September 1992)

[*In the following excerpt, Gehr applauds* Lemprière's Dictionary *as a refreshing and ambitious blend of history, science, and mythology.*]

Lemprière's Dictionary, the dazzling first novel by *Times Literary Supplement* poetry reviewer Lawrence Norfolk, will either restore your faith or vacuum-pack your prejudices concerning the dearth of erudite writing. In the same way that Martin Amis's apocalyptic *London Fields* made Tom Wolfe's *Bonfire of the Vanities* seem a cartoon zeitgeist by comparison, 29-year-old Norfolk is challenging such obvious influences as [Thomas] Pynchon and Umberto Eco. But as Pynchon descends into increasingly dark meditations on entropy, paranoia, and the Fall, Norfolk explores new models of complexity based on chaos theory and universal metamorphosis. (Ovid's work is the book's most fully digested subtext.) And where Eco's two daunting tomes explored the narrative possibilities of academicism, *Lemprière's Dictionary* offers a much more readable take on the pleasures of scholarship, and of writing as a means to exorcise (too much) reading.

> Norfolk expertly blends his mythology, history, and science into a sprawling cultural poetics whose eddies, currents, and sandbars run interference patterns against one another.
>
> —*Richard Gehr*

At 400-plus extremely dense pages, the novel defies synopsis. It is primarily a quest, mystery, and love story that careens through 17th and 18th century England, teeming with naïfs, shady villains, and assorted oddballs. As a quest, the tale concerns gangly young scholar John Lemprière's attempt to unravel the convoluted skein of circumstances leading to the death of his father. A Jersey islander full to bursting with knowledge of classical mythology, Lemprière subsequently becomes Actaeon, Theseus, Daedalus, and Paris as he unravels the machinations of the East India Company's secret committee, a BCCI-like cabal whose ultimate goal, one year before the Revolution, is to own France lock, stock, and croissant. The Company's trouble with the Lemprière family boils down to a single document, the interpretation of which inspires not one but two dictionaries: the rigorous classical dictionary John Lemprière composes as an exorcism of his father's death, and an earlier, wilder antidictionary written by the first Lemprière involved with the Company and hidden in an "archive of monstrous proportions."

Like Pynchon, Norfolk views history as a hallucinatory scrim disguising an epic freak parade of assassins, whores, and dope-smoking "pansocratic" pirates. Upon receiving his first pair of glasses early on in the book, Lemprière decides that "it was possible to see too much." His vision leads to a sort of madness reflected by a city preoccupied with "Lottery suicides," ritual murders, a worker uprising, and an ineffable conflagration known simply as "the Dispute." There's something in the air, but

> Already the air was mutating, cross-cut with insurgent impulses and pockets of distortion, the

patrician contract was on a blocked frequency emerging in obscure and unintelligible pitches. Strange acts prevailed. The much-bruited cat-eating contest between Lord Barrymore and the Duke of Bedford had entered its third round last week. Live cats too. . . . The body politic was turning itself inside out, lewdly exposing its organs for vulgar fingers to pinch and prod.

Norfolk expertly blends his mythology, history, and science into a sprawling cultural poetics whose eddies, currents, and sandbars run interference patterns against one another. As the book surges toward its potent yet inevitable climax, Norfolk pauses for a moment, looks around, and ruminates on the ambition of his work:

Whole orders of information wafted and gusted past in secret sweet abandon rippling through the billion blades of grass, grains of sand, motes of dust, and if there was an instrument to register the effects of this system, from its merest nanospan to greatest gigascale it was a land mass nothing short of Europe.

OK, so Norfolk's is an overreaching ambition. But that makes this no less of an important and inspiring novel—a match for equally ambitious readers.

> Richard Gehr, in a review of "Lemprière's Dictionary," in VLS, No. 108, September, 1992, p. 5.

Michael Dirda (review date 20 September 1992)

[*In the following essay, Dirda praises Norfolk's narrative techniques and illustrates similarities between* Lemprière's Dictionary *and other novels in the antiquarian romance genre.*]

In 1600 the British East India Company was founded, and quickly grew into a vast global enterprise. Sailing ships plied their way patiently to India and back, bringing with them wealth beyond the dreams of avarice. That much is certain.

In 1627-1628 the French port city of Rochelle, a Huguenot stronghold, was besieged by the Catholic forces of Cardinal Richelieu and its citizens slowly starved to death. Virtually no one escaped, many people choosing to immolate themselves and their children in the town's citadel rather than surrender. Another fact.

Consider one more detail: In 1788 John Lempriere, a young classicist in his early 20s, brought out a dictionary that established itself, for well over a century, as the standard guide to classical mythology.

Three innocent-seeming bits of history: a business, a massacre, a reference book. What connection could they possibly have? Surely none.

Yet, according to *Lempriere's Dictionary,* Lawrence Norfolk's extravagantly spectacular first novel, a few troubling questions remain. Could there, for instance, be some truth to the legend that a winged being escaped from the burning tower at Rochelle? Why too have all the Lempriere men died violent deaths? And what is the veiled meaning

of three fragile pamphlets—perfervid attacks on the East India Company—composed early in the 17th century by "Asiaticus"? For that matter, who is he? And what became of the crucial fourth pamphlet? Did Capt. Alan Neagle really glimpse whales in the Eastern Mediterranean shortly before he disappeared—or had he discovered something he shouldn't have? What of the symbol, a not quite complete circle, that appears in a luxuriously illustrated edition of Ovid's *Metamorphoses,* on signet rings, even carved in the table at a tavern? One may, of course, also wonder about the automatons, the unnatural orange trees, the orgiastic Pork Club and the Indian assassins, not to mention the elusive and gorgeous Juliette, the blind Sir John Fielding, the Company's "secret committee," the butchered prostitutes. Oh yes, and the French Revolution—and the high cost of immortality.

Lempriere's Dictionary touches on all these, and much more, deftly mixing what cannot be with what might have been. Imagine [Umberto Eco's] *Foucault's Pendulum* set in the England of Samuel Johnson, with highlights from *The Woman in White,* [Victor] Hugo's *Notre Dame de Paris,* and Sax Rohmer's tales of Dr. Fu Manchu. Norfolk's book is, in short, a further addition to that diverting sub-genre that one might call the antiquarian romance.

A loose and baggy category, the antiquarian romance embraces Umberto Eco's *The Name of the Rose,* A. S. Byatt's *Possession,* John Crowley's *Aegypt,* Milorad Pavic's *Dictionary of the Khazars,* and Robertson Davies's *What's Bred in the Bone,* as well as such recent entertainments as Bruce Sterling and William Gibson's *The Difference Engine,* Katherine Neville's *The Eight,* and Charles Palliser's *The Quincunx.* As different as these novels are, they tend to juxtapose the present and the past, disclose awesome, frequently game-like conspiracies at work in history, draw heavily on some branch of arcane learning (chess, Renaissance hermeticism), provide a trail of scholarly "documents," pastiche earlier styles of speech, offer "intellectual" conversation, and emphasize a Gothicky atmosphere of mystery and foreboding. Not least, they are frequently long, leisurely and deliberately old-fashioned, or seemingly so.

What makes these up-to-date sensation novels so appealing to readers—and many have been best sellers—is that they are not simply tales of wonder, but tales specifically about the wonder of reading and the pleasures of scholarship. The main character must nearly always learn to interpret correctly a game, a document, a painting or a book, and thus discover the extraordinary behind the ordinary.

Early in *Lempriere's Dictionary* the hero's father searches for evidence of a phantom ship, and in so doing describes the defining moment of the antiquarian romance:

Somewhere in the morass of receipts, bills, bonds, affidavits and orders of acquisition which lay strewn about the room, there was a pattern. Somewhere within the pages of handwritten accounts, diaries, letters and notes ran a thread. But he could not find it. A single memorandum, a scrawl on a dog-eared endpaper might supply the link, the key to the pattern. It was here, bur-

ied here somewhere. Perhaps he had already
seen it and missed its significance.

Only the predestined hero, typically a studious sort, can
find the thread, read correctly the signs and portents of
these adult fairy tales.

Things, after all, are never as they seem. If knowledge is
power, then extensive and strange learning implies extensive and strange power. After a secret meeting in a hidden
room deep below London, the shadowy mastermind of
Lempriere's Dictionary daydreams of

> other such chambers. The sanctum of the Eleu-
> sinian mysteries, the inner temples of Orphic
> cults, . . . the other cabbalas which had direct-
> ed the course of the world's maturation. Hushed
> meetings such as these had pulled the strings of
> puppet-despots, directed the transient wills
> above. The slow rhythm of decisions taken here
> determined the worldly pulse. The catastrophes,
> the wars, the deaths of kings were nothing but
> skipped measures, brief interruptions in the
> noiseless music of subtler agendas and agree-
> ments between those whose faces remained un-
> seen.

That the world is run by magicians and grey eminences
for purposes of their own may seem fantastic, but there
lingers something Calvinistic in our souls—witness the
popularity of conspiracy theories and New Age occult-
ism—that yearns for an alternative to mere chance and absurdity as the engines of history.

Shortly after Charles Lempriere's death—he is ravaged by
hunting dogs in a scene that mirrors the destruction of Actaeon—his son John leaves the island of Jersey and goes
up to London to hear his father's will. There he falls in
with a gadabout named Septimus Praeceps who lures him
to the Pork Club where an orgy takes place reminiscent
of Circe's transformation of Odysseus's men into swine.
That evening young Lempriere meets a nobleman who
wishes to buy a document, a kind of contract, that has
been in his family's possession for well over 150 years. It
appears to grant, in perpetuity, one ninth of the profits
from the British East India Company. Mysteries surrounding this agreement, as well as the hope of meeting
again the beautiful Juliette, daughter of the imperious Viscount Casterleigh, keep Lempriere in London.

That city itself is one of dreadful night, a stygian realm of
both honeyed laughter and sudden death.

> Outside, it is the hour of suspicion. The closed
> hour when men walk the streets with the air of
> interlopers in a drama played out in silence . . .
> A cloaked figure crosses the street at a diagonal,
> his shadow lengthening as he moves away from
> the lamp. Someone loiters on a corner with stud-
> ied casualness, looking first one way then the
> other, offering no clue to explain his watchful-
> ness. The city is almost still, but the slow arc of
> the moon brings it to something like life . . .

Against this sinister backdrop, the novel slowly knots together a half dozen strands: Lempriere works feverishly

on his mythological dictionary, its major entries—for
Danae, Iphigenia—uncannily echoed in his own life; an
old sea captain learns a secret about the mysterious ship,
The Vendragon; Sir John Fielding tries to solve the ritual
murder of a woman hideously killed by a shower of molten
gold; Nazim the assassin searches relentlessly for the mysterious Nine; an impresario commissions 27 gigantic stone
tortoises as roof decorations for his failing opera house;
the elusive Farina whips up London with his calls for revolution; a crew of very old pirates kidnaps the internuncio
of the Austro-Hungarian emperor; and a plan is laid that
turns on a famous date, July 14. All these, especially Lempriere's confrontation with his own bizarre destiny, explode in a grand-guignol climax, featuring a cast of thousands. It is eminently satisfying.

Less satisfying are some of Norfolk's coloratura prose
arias and descriptive excesses; a few scenes remain so
phantasmagoric that you're not quite sure what is going
on. At times the supposedly clever Lempriere even seems
just a tad slow on the uptake. Some of the conspirators'
elaborate stratagems overlook simpler means to the same
end.

But these are mere cavils compared to one major baffle-
ment: In crossing the Atlantic *Lempriere's Dictionary* has
suffered something of a sea-change, with *an* important
character eliminated, a virtuosic epilogue dropped, and a
linchpin of the novel cast aside. As a result, a number of
small mysteries are no longer satisfactorily resolved: Who
or what frightens the Viscount when he is about to push
our hero from a high roof? Why does Lempriere slightly
resemble another character? And why is that character
afraid of fire? Who is Farina? One cannot help but feel that
the book has been simplified for American readers; the result is a leaner, faster-moving novel but not quite as magical a one.

Nevertheless, even in its trimmer format, *Lempriere's
Dictionary* remains a magnum opus of narrative gusto.
Besides allowing the reader to sup on horrors, Norfolk
dishes out some keystone comedy, including the misadventures of the Pantisocratic Pirates and an evening with
a pair of Tweedledee and Tweedledum scholars who give
Lempriere the idea for his dictionary. Characters like the
ancient Lady Alice de Vere or the vain archivist Theobald
Peppard could have walked out of Dickens. As for Juliette, what is she? By turns ingenuous, robotic and whor-
ish, to Lempriere she becomes the heroine with a thousand
faces.

As an artist, Norfolk shows a partiality for multiple perspectives and cinematic cuts: He may hint, for example at
some nefarious plan by the cabbala, later follow Lempriere
up to the moment of its climax, then abruptly shift away
to another character's point of view, going back into the
past and advancing again to the climactic moment which
is finally shown in its full and sometimes gory detail. The
technique seems almost musical, a theme that builds, then
falls away, only to return unexpectedly and rush to a final
cadence. There is a similar use of leitmotifs. Watch closely, for instance, the deadly progress of Lempriere's miniature of his mother: Stolen by the prostitute Rosalie, acci-

dentally left behind with the debarred lawyer Peppard, casually picked up by the assassin Nazim, unexpectedly cru-

cial in the battle with Le Mara, the 18th-century equivalent of the Terminator.

Myriad wonders and pleasures abound in **Lempriere's Dictionary.** Not too surprisingly, Zygia, the last entry in Lempriere's actual classical dictionary, provides just the right hint to the ending of Lawrence Norfolk's superbly entertaining novel. (pp. 1, 14)

> *Michael Dirda, "The Secret Masters of the World," in* Book World—The Washington Post, *September 20, 1992, pp. 1, 14.*

David Streitfeld (essay date 20 September 1992)

[*In the following excerpt, Streitfeld examines the differences between the British and American editions of* Lemprière's Dictionary.]

Everyone complains that book editors don't edit anymore. All sorts of books are pointed to as evidence, but the case is most often made against best-selling fiction. Novelists who get paid in seven figures for their work quite naturally take this to mean they have complete and utter command of the language, and woe betide any mere salaried employee who argues differently.

In truth, of course, there are all types of editors—from those who truly never read the material they're supposedly responsible for to those, at the other extreme, who do such substantial rewrite jobs that they might as well be listed as coauthors. In either case, the editor's role is hidden from public view. Only the putative author of the book and those inside the publishing firm know the real story.

Except sometimes. Two years ago, there was an extremely minor *cause célèbre* involving A. S. Byatt's *Possession.* For its appearance in this country, the book editor's requested some changes, including making the hero slightly more "masculine" and cutting out some of the poems. Byatt did the first but resisted the second, and the book went on to become a tremendous success here. The editor was consequently made to look foolish, as if she wanted to dumb down Shakespeare.

Another example goes back 30 years: *A Clockwork Orange.* For its appearance here, the last chapter—where the hero realizes the error of his thuggish ways—was cut, turning what is basically an optimistic book into a bleak one. Anthony Burgess complained that his vision had been truncated. (Since the movie followed the American version, his unhappiness was compounded.) Another example of an editor intruding on the work of a master? Maybe, but Burgess has now shifted his position, and says "my aesthetic judgment may have been faulty."

Now there's a case that somewhat parallels *A Clockwork Orange.* Lawrence Norfolk's **Lempriere's Dictionary** was one of the most successful first novels published in England last year, and Harmony Books is pulling out all the stops to achieve a breakthrough in this country. But in its voyage across the Atlantic, the novel changed; American readers are in for a somewhat different experience.

Here's what happened: Although **Lemprière's Dictionary**

An excerpt from *Lemprière's Dictionary*

[Juliette Casterleigh] stood as if fixed by the gazes from either side of the pool, the father and the son. As she took the cold kiss of the waterfall on her body, John Lemprière's eye was caught by a faint birthmark on her upper arm, but before he could make out what it was, she had turned.

Skin of alabaster, eyes of jet, the girl's body swung from son to father. On the other side of the pool, Charles Lemprière had seen all his son had seen. All but one detail. White flesh in the black water and the dark glitter of water drops as they skated from her skin. And when she turned, he saw those drops scatter about her like a silver noose rising out of the pool. He saw the black triangle between her legs, and her breasts, and her eyes which were blacker yet, and the breath caught in his throat. And as her body turned for him, he saw the mark, the imperfection his son had glimpsed a moment before and not recognized. But the father recognized it and he knew it as a sign he dreaded above all others, burning into him as once it would have been burnt into her. A broken circle, the signature of all he had fought against. And he knew then that his patient, faceless adversaries had bested him, that all his efforts, and his father's, and his father's before him had again come to nothing. The account against him would be settled now and his life was forfeit to it. They had found him. For a moment he knelt as if entranced by the recognition of defeat, and then he rose, the protest welling in his throat, to scream mindlessly.

"No, no! Not now! Not here!"

Then he heard the pack. He stopped dead, the words dying in his throat as he realized *he* had been their prey from the beginning, from the very first. But the time for any kind of thought was past.

The dogs broke cover forty yards downstream, moving fast and low over the ground. He turned to the naked girl who now watched him from the pool. Her black eyes glittering, sinking into him. He told himself not to run, to face whatever might come. But run he did, flailing wildly at the ferns and bushes in his way, while on the other side of the pool, under cover of the overhanging trees, a pair of legs tried to run, and could not. A pair of hands tried to claw their way out of the emerging nightmare, and could not. A voice tried to scream, and heard only the screams of his father as the dogs pulled him down.

The long, dark cloud bank moved silently overhead, shading the hills, fields, and valleys as it went. It shaded the gashed and twisted body by the pool. It shaded his son, wrapping its gray shroud about him. A gray shade touched his skin with cold fingers, like mist. He felt dry, racking sobs force their way up his throat. There were no words at first. Deep inside him, at his center, a black gland was already leeching its transfiguring thought through his body and its channels, observing its own slow seepage into the basin of his brain, offering its mouth to him in his grief, and as it coupled with him, it was accepted. In his mind's eye, the book was still open on the table in his room. Actaeon was still alive, still waiting for the dogs to reach him. Here, half lying in the pool, was his father's torn cadaver. Between both these bodies was his own, which connected them, turning one into the other.

> *Lawrence Norfolk, in his* Lemprière's Dictionary, *Harmony Books, 1991.*

is being published a year later in this country, editors on both sides of the ocean received the manuscript at about the same time. Independently, they came to different verdicts. In England, the editor made some minor changes and cut about 1 percent from the manuscript. In the U.S., Harmony's John Michel wrote the author a long letter suggesting both minor and major adjustments.

The major work involved considerable trimming of the book's fantastical element. "It didn't work for me, and I didn't think it was going to work for an American audience," Michel says now. "My worry was the book being categorized as fantasy or sci-fi, and getting taken completely out of the literary-historical genre."

This, admittedly, is a market consideration, but Michel says, "I didn't just do this because I thought I'd sell lots more copies. If I really wanted to pander, I'd have asked for more sex scenes. I thought the fantasy detracted."

Norfolk's first reaction to Michel's proposals: "Rage." Then he thought about them for a while, and decided they made sense—or were at least sensible. "I've never been to America. I don't know what American readers will or won't take."

He made the cuts, slicing about one-fifth from the book. "I wasn't looking for it to be better in any way, to be frank with you. In fact, I was half hoping I'd wreck the book and make my own case. But I was surprised." The American *Dictionary,* the author feels, "is clearer about what it says. You lose some of the depth of the argument, but what you gain is a forward momentum."

Which, however, is "the preferred text," to use the lit professors' term? Norfolk refuses to choose. "If I had my way, I'd produce a thousand different versions. At the moment, all I can do is two. That's moving in the right direction, as far as I'm concerned."

> *David Streitfeld, "Indefinite 'Dictionary'," in* Book World—The Washington Post, *September 20, 1992, p. 15.*

Alfred Corn   (review date 20 December 1992)

[*Corn is an American poet and critic. In the following review, he offers a mixed assessment of* Lemprière's Dictionary.]

Discovering a new talent always brings a sharp, pleasurable intake of breath, and, feeling that after a few pages of this novel, I hoped to join those who welcomed its appearance in Britain last year with astonishment and praise. Like Peter Ackroyd's *Chatterton,* A. S. Byatt's *Possession* and *The Quincunx,* by Charles Palliser, Lawrence Norfolk's ***Lemprière's Dictionary*** attempts a historical and literary reconstruction—in this case, a late-18th-century subject treated in a style based on Fielding, Scott, Thackeray, Dickens, Stevenson and Hardy. As with those works of his contemporaries, though, it's finally a modern work, and Mr. Norfolk has a particular debt to James Joyce and

Thomas Pynchon, perhaps as well to Peter Greenaway's films and the Gothic animations of the Quay brothers.

Reading the opening chapter, no one would think it was the work of a first novelist in his 20's. Mr. Norfolk describes the English Channel island of Jersey with a sensuous eeriness and verbal bravura that prepare us for some, though not all, of the strangeness to come. John, the son of Charles Lemprière, is a young student of Greek and Latin. His eyes are already myopic from years of reading, and we see him fitted with a first pair of spectacles; almost at the same moment hallucinated versions of classical mythology invade his experience.

Any pretense to plausible narrative is left behind in a baroque scene in which John stumbles on Viscount Casterleigh's daughter, Juliette, bathing nude in a spring while Casterleigh's hunting hounds suddenly rush up to attack John's father, by chance also present. Transfixed with horror, John recognizes that the myth of Diana and Actaeon has just been re-enacted, this time with his lady love cast in the role of avenging goddess. The father's death and John's journey to London to settle his estate initiate the plot of what develops into an enormously intricate novel, involving a power struggle among the old East India trading company, its dispossessed heirs and a henchman in the service of the Nawab of the Carnatic (Karnataka in modern India).

A number of myths recounted in Ovid's *Metamorphoses* commandeer the plot at regular intervals, always in the key of mayhem. But what looks at first like authorial contrivance eventually emerges as a machination perpetrated by secret antagonists, who devise fantastic engines of destruction and foolproof automatons disguised as people in order to control young Lemprière. Literary works of any sophistication usually include a self-critique: this is Mr. Norfolk's. For plot twists, mistaken identities, coincidences, cliffhangers and engineered disasters, his novel outstrips any I've read. And only one or two of his characters seem more complex than robots in the service of an overweight plot that is subject to spells of sluggishness.

The great virtue of novels, their portrayal of characters we'd like to know more about, Mr. Norfolk sacrifices to the minor value of suspense. Using the term "cloak-and-dagger" here is not a journalistic reflex. Characters *do* wear cloaks and wield daggers, and spill gallons of blood. But soon the reader begins to sense that it's stage blood only. Melodrama keeps the pages turning, granted, but so would the invention of vivid, believable characters, and more defensibly. Masterly style is the next best thing, and, as for writing, I can't remember seeing passages in recent fiction as brilliant as the Jersey scenes, or the baffled young hero's arrival in London, or a number of paragraphs scattered throughout the novel in which Mr. Norfolk's 19th-century forerunners find an authentic disciple.

Why would anyone with his gifts for language also use the kind of undergraduate plot manipulation that fills out the pages of this long novel? At best, the answer might involve

familiar pronouncements about post-modernism and artificiality, at worst, it suggests the beginner's efforts to woo
an audience that would really rather be engrossed in a
thriller pure and simple.

I recommend reading the book with the Oxford English
Dictionary near at hand, as well as a good reference work
to check classical allusions. After his arrival in London,
John Lemprière himself takes up, among other less serene
activities, the composition of the classical dictionary mentioned in the title. There was, to be sure, a real John Lemprière who wrote a real classical dictionary, but the history of the real man and book has little resemblance to this
novel. Why does the novel's Lemprière write the dictionary? That is impossible to explain without actually entering the labyrinth of the plot, from which no reviewer is
going to emerge in one piece. Classical learning is only
part of the book's referential tonnage. Mr. Norfolk braids
in such historical set pieces as accounts of the French Hu-
guenots under siege in 17th-century Rochelle, of Louis
XVI at Versailles, of the Turkish-Austrian conflict and of
social upheaval in late-18th-century England. There is
also a lot of curious lore having to do with sailing ships
and their navigation, a peep at Italian opera in Georgian
London, vignettes from the low life of the great city and

much, much more, all of it turned ironic by Mr. Norfolk's
droll and ferocious sensibility.

In the midst of this erudition, it's odd to bump into mistakes such as having a snatch of the Chopin Opus 35
played in 1787 or seeing the Palais Royal misspelled. But
that's inevitable in a work of these proportions and is
nothing compared with the problem already described. If
Mr. Norfolk had added a few people we could care about
to this erudite and pyrotechnic book, it would have swept
the board. True, there is a love interest, the battered lexi-
cographer does get his girl, and his all-powerful opponents
are defeated. But that's a bit hard to swallow, considering
all that happens earlier—or even considering ordinary reality, where public defenders who buck the Company
don't normally get away with it. William Dean Howells
said the American public wanted "a tragedy with a happy
ending," and this young British writer has produced a
Gothic-historical fantasy-tragedy with one. The unliterary
primitive within all of us is exposed in the pleasure we feel
when Lemprière, his Juliette and his dictionary go off
hand in hand at the novel's close.

Alfred Corn, "In the Key of Mayhem," in The
New York Times Book Review, *December 20,
1992, p. 6.*

Brian O'Doherty

The Strange Case of Mademoiselle P.

O'Doherty was born in Ireland in 1934 and currently resides in New York City. He is an art critic, novelist, and editor.

INTRODUCTION

The Strange Case of Mademoiselle P. is a fictionalized account of Doctor Franz Mesmer's attempt to restore the sight of Marie Thérèse von Paradies, a well-known, eighteenth-century Austrian pianist and composer. Blind since age three, Marie was taken by her parents to numerous Viennese physicians—none of whom could detect any physical defects in her eyes—before being brought to Mesmer when she was eighteen. Mesmer, known for his theory of "animal magnetism," believed that illnesses stemmed from imbalances in an individual's magnetic forces and recommended massage and relaxation as a means of restoring harmony between mind and body. Under his care, Marie gradually regained her sight, but her ability to play the piano declined. Her father, Josef von Paradies, feared that the deterioration of his daughter's musical skills would adversely affect his position as a court secretary to Empress Maria Thérèsa of Austria, who was very fond of his daughter's music. Consequently, the father plotted Mesmer's downfall and succeeded in banishing the doctor from Vienna on charges of malpractice and witchcraft. After Mesmer's departure, Marie reverted to complete blindness. The novel concludes with Mesmer, twenty years later, contemplating the nature of his relationship with Marie.

Critical reaction to *The Strange Case of Mademoiselle P.* has been mixed. Commentators note that while O'Doherty's use of first-person narratives allows him to explore his characters' motivations, such issues as whether Mesmer's feelings for Marie were sexual or paternal remain unclear. Others maintain that O'Doherty's close adherence to historical sources contributes to weaknesses in the novel's plot. Nonetheless, critics have praised O'Doherty's rich descriptions of eighteenth-century Vienna, his deft handling of psychological and philosophical issues relating to Mesmer's theories, his metaphorical depictions of blindness, and his ideas on visual perception. Leslie Granston has observed that "the fates of both doctor and patient [in *The Strange Case of Mademoiselle P.*] challenge our ideas of what 'vision' really means."

CRITICISM

Michael Harris (review date 14 June 1992)

[*In the following review, Harris offers a mixed assessment of* The Strange Case of Mademoiselle P.]

Before settling on "Humbert Humbert," the narrator of [Vladimir] Nabokov's *Lolita* considers adopting several other pseudonyms, including "Mesmer Mesmer"—a tribute to the Svengali-like legend surrounding the 18th-Century Austrian pioneer of medical hypnosis, whose name comes down to us as a verb: *to mesmerize.*

In Brian O'Doherty's beguiling first novel [*The Strange Case of Mademoiselle P.*], Dr. Franz Anton Mesmer is innocent of nymphet-chasing, but the father of one of his patients, 18-year-old Marie Therese Paradies, suspects him of it and contrives to ruin his career. Decades later, near death, Mesmer himself is tortured by erotic dreams of the girl and comes to doubt his previous rectitude.

For the other characters, too, reality is flickering and elusive. Marie Therese, hysterically blind since age 3, experiences her first glimmerings of renewed sight as disorientation and pain. A gifted pianist (she plays duets with Mozart), she loses her touch once she can see her hands. Her father, an official at the court of Empress Maria Theresa, is oblivious to his own responsibility for his daughter's condition and is so blinded by cynical "common sense" (and by understandable skepticism about Mesmer's theory that illness is caused by disturbances in "magnetic fluids" that flow through the universe and every creature in it) that he sabotages the treatment, plunging the girl back into darkness.

It's the old, sad story of the innovator who hooks a big fish but can't pull it out of the water to identify it, and the envy and hostility this half-discovery arouses. O'Doherty has turned a bit of history into a meditation on the perils of truth-seeking, a deft mimicry of period style, a fugue of three contrasting voices. He excels in rendering delicate psychological and visual states. The only flaw is that most of the drama comes at the beginning; if this *were* music, it would be a crashing chord followed by a lingering echo.

Michael Harris, in a review of "The Strange Case of Mademoiselle P.," in Los Angeles Times Book Review, *June 14, 1992, p. 6.*

Michiko Kakutani   (review date 19 June 1992)

[*In the following review, Kakutani praises O'Doherty's prose and use of dialogue in* The Strange Case of Mademoiselle P., *but faults the work's lack of character motivation and narrative momentum.*]

It's hard to read Brian O'Doherty's first novel, *The Strange Case of Mademoiselle P.,* without thinking of one of the most famous novels of the last decade: D. M. Thomas's *White Hotel.*

In this case, the doctor isn't a fictional Freud, but a fictional version of Franz Anton Mesmer, a Viennese doctor whose theories of "animal magnetism" enjoyed a vogue during the 1770's. The patient under his treatment is one Marie Thérèse Paradies, a young blind pianist known as Mlle. P., who, in real life, became friends with Mozart and founded an institute for music education in Vienna.

As in *The White Hotel,* the reader is asked to draw parallels between the story of one woman and her doctor, and the historical era against which her story takes place. As in *The White Hotel,* the reader is also asked to piece together this heroine's story from a series of elliptical documents: in this case, first-person reminiscences delivered by Dr. Mesmer, Mlle. P., and her father, Josef Von Paradies, the Imperial Secretary to Empress Maria Theresa of Austria.

When Mlle. P. first arrives at the office of Dr. Mesmer, she is 18 years old. She has been blind since the age of 3, but has become an accomplished pianist and a favorite of her namesake, Empress Maria Theresa. Her parents have taken her to practically every doctor in Vienna: she has had leeches applied to her head, shocks administered to her eyes, every manner of medicine and purgative pre-

scribed. But while the physicians can find nothing organically wrong with her eyes, she remains blind and ill, subject to strange fits and fainting spells.

Finally, out of desperation, Mlle. P.'s father brings her to Dr. Mesmer, a physician who had gained renown for his theories of animal magnetism, a belief that human beings, like the rest of nature, are subject to a magnetic force that may be adjusted through the judicious use of magnets and massage. His detractors whisper that he and his assistants take advantage of the young women who come into his care; his supporters boast of the miraculous cures he has effected.

Certainly, Mlle. P. seems to thrive under his care. Removed from the company of her hysterical mother and her stern, demanding father, she starts to relax. Music—played by her young friend Wolfgang Amadeus Mozart—helps soothe her ragged nerves. And the ministrations of Dr. Mesmer, who regularly gives her massages to redistribute the magnetic fluid in her body, appear to give her new vitality and health. Miraculously, her sight begins to return. At first, there is a new sensitivity to light, then, gradually, the ability to discern the shape and color of objects.

The experience is as frightening as it is marvelous. Mlle. P. is appalled and amused at the configuration of the human face, and mystified by the sight of her own reflection in a mirror. Most troubling of all is the sudden decline in her musical abilities: the gift of sight seems to have damaged her perfect ear, impaired her instinct for harmony.

As Mlle. P. and Dr. Mesmer regard it, this is a painful, but necessary step in her progress toward wholeness; with time and work and perseverance, she will regain her musical gifts, and enjoy the pleasures of sight that most people take for granted. But from the point of view of her father, Dr. Mesmer is a charlatan who has coaxed her "out of her once fruitful darkness," and left her bereft of her singular musical talents. He now says he would prefer that she were blind and innocent, untainted by the confusions of the world at large.

Is the father's antipathy toward Dr. Mesmer motivated by his desire to ingratiate himself with the Empress Maria Theresa? Are we to trust a man who slaps his wife and disparages the compositions of Mozart?

But what about Dr. Mesmer? Is he any more trustworthy a witness? Are his theories of magnetism the ravings of a crackpot, intent on seducing his patients? Does his fall from grace represent the triumph of Enlightenment reason over superstition? Or is he an earnest, if misguided man, who's simply fallen afoul of Vienna's Byzantine court politics?

And what of Mlle. P. herself? Is she the victim of a cruel, conniving father, or the victim of a lustful and manipulative doctor? Is she a symbol of the plight of women in 18th-century Europe, or is she simply another neurotic, suffering from severe psychosomatic symptoms?

By allowing Mlle. P., her father and Dr. Mesmer to speak to us directly, Mr. O'Doherty raises such questions obliquely. Each monologue he has created for these characters is vivid, evocative and beautifully detailed. He conjures up the treacherous, gilded world of Hapsburg Vienna with easy sleight of hand, while at the same time, admitting us to the inner lives of his three main characters. The prose is musical and patterned, returning, again and again, to certain images and motifs.

Throughout most of **Strange Case** this mesmerizing prose combines with the book's thrillerlike plot to compel the reader's attention. Perhaps because Mr. O'Doherty felt constrained by the actual historical facts of his characters' stories, there is a sharp falling off at the novel's end. Most of the questions he has raised in the earlier part of the story are simply sidestepped or ignored; most of our expectations are left dangling in midair.

As a result, we finish the volume, disappointed and unmoved, as though we had opened a beautiful Fabergé egg and found nothing but a cheap, windup toy inside. One hopes only that a writer as amply gifted as Mr. O'Doherty will next time produce a novel that more completely fulfills the promise and allure of its craft.

Michiko Kakutani, "Eyesight Returned, Musical Ear Lost," in The New York Times, *June 19, 1992, p. C28.*

Janet Barron   (review date 7 August 1992)

[*In the following review, Barron commends O'Doherty for his sophisticated handling of the perceptual, psychological, and philosophical issues related to Doctor Franz Mesmer's therapeutic methods.*]

The Strange Case of Mademoiselle P. is one of the summer's best offerings, by an Irish writer now living in New York. Brian O'Doherty trained as a medic and studied visual perception, which is what this novel is about. It is based on a true story, of a girl, Marie-Thérèse Paradies, who was blind from the age of three. Dr Mesmer, the mesmeriser, tried to restore her sight, but as he did so he destroyed her ways of coping with the world. Previously a brilliant pianist, she became disoriented and lost the only thing that gave her pleasure: her music.

The setting is 18th-century Vienna, and the novel is rich with a sensual perceptiveness that slides into eroticism. This is writing you can taste and smell, as evocative as Patrick Suskind's *Perfume*. It is also profoundly true psychologically, and intellectually sophisticated in its handling of philosophy. Marie-Thérèse Paradies was in the patronage of the Habsburgs, whose conflicts and jealousies form the backdrop to this story, but Brian O'Doherty does not aim for tableau effects of court life. What interests him are the intense and claustrophobic relationships of her family.

Her mother is a hopeless hysteric, and it is partly a fear of being like her that has pushed Marie-Thérèse into her state of unseeing. Her father is a courtier, machinating against his rivals and doting on his daughter with an obsessiveness the girl is unable to challenge.

At the beginning of the novel the atmosphere is weirdly gothic, as O'Doherty describes Marie's terrible condition under "orthodox" medicine, with leeches clinging to her

> O'Doherty's writing is pared down and precise, almost clinical, and his style and insight give *The Strange Case of Mademoiselle P.* its disturbing and tremendous power. It tails off towards the end, and could have done with one more twist, but it is certainly a stunning debut.
>
> —*Janet Barron*

cheeks like black tears. An alternative has to be found, but the twist in the story is that Dr Mesmer is himself hallucinating and deluded, and he brings Marie-Thérèse back to sight to a world in which she can gain no perspective and nothing will stay still.

This is a frightening, moving book by a writer of exceptional talents. Marie-Thérèse's experience is so painfully realised that it cannot fail to grip the reader, and Dr Mesmer's attraction to her involves a subconscious sexuality that terrifies him with thoughts of damnation in his waking hours. O'Doherty's writing is pared down and precise, almost clinical, and his style and insight give *The Strange Case of Mademoiselle P.* its disturbing and tremendous power. It tails off towards the end, and could have done with one more twist, but it is certainly a stunning debut.

Janet Barron, "Vision Mixer," in New Statesman & Society, *Vol. 5, No. 214, August 7, 1992, p. 38.*

Julian Duplain   (review date 7 August 1992)

[*In the following review of* The Strange Case of Mademoiselle P., *Duplain discusses Doctor Franz Mesmer's therapeutic methods and Josef von Paradies's motivation for ending his daughter's treatment.*]

For a doctor who intends to pursue his science logically, unconventional practices call for a particularly complete methodology. As a medical student at the University of Vienna in 1766, Franz Anton Mesmer reasoned that the lunar pull, which causes tides, must act as much on the human body as on the world's oceans. From this, he developed his theory of animal magnetism, which holds that forces are transmitted through an ultrafine fluid, linking all bodies in the universe. "There is", he believed, "only one disease and one cure": all ills result from an imbalance in the patient's personal magnetism. His treatment was massage or the transfer of magnetism between patients linked by iron bars submerged in dilute sulphuric acid.

Marie-Thérèse von Paradies, one of Mesmer's most celebrated cases before he was forced to leave Vienna, in 1778, accused of malpractice verging on witchcraft, provides Brian O'Doherty with material for both a medical conundrum and a period drama. Blind since the age of three, Mademoiselle P. was the daughter of a court official and the protégée of her namesake, the Empress, who admired her skill at the piano. Such was the girl's renown that Mo-

An excerpt from *The Strange Case of Mademoiselle P.*

On February 9th, I removed the bandages and presented myself to her imperfect sight—the first being she had seen (if seeing it was) since the onset of her malady at the age of three. What memories she had of sight or light I could never elicit. Any attempt to recover that lost paradise only added to her confusion, certain though I was that such memories would assist her now. Standing before her, no more than a meter away, I slowly moved my hands and arms, and fixed on my face a reassuring smile. We both stood, face to face, in the twilight. Her response was to cover her face and shrink from me as if she had seen something that aroused her disgust. Only when I spoke to her was she reassured, though it was a shock to her that my voice issued from the apparition which she now studied from between her fingers, covering and uncovering her eyes. In my concern, I moved closer to her and gazed solicitously into her eyes—so innocent of the world—speaking reassuringly all the while. To my surprise, she burst into laughter. Not knowing the source of another's laughter is, of all things, most irritating.

I joined in the laughter, witlessly. Marie Thérèse pointed at me, and since the distance between us was so small, and her estimate of distance so insecure, she poked her finger into my face. When I opened my eyes, she had fixed on my nose. Having located this feature, she redoubled her laughter, which in a lady of breeding (which she was) with no impairment of vision would be more than rude. Not only did she lay her finger on my nose, but she pushed it from side to side, to her further merriment, if not to mine. . . .

Relieved as I was to hear her laugh, and pleased as I was to be the source of such a new emotion, I was greatly puzzled. When I removed the bandages the following day, the same scene was repeated, and the following day, until my nose provoked only a mild amusement. The answer was borne home to me only after the deepest reflection. Marie Thérèse had no idea of a face. Instead she saw its most prominent feature, complete in itself and unrelated to those around it. The environs of the nose, its setting, were not part of her awareness. Thus isolated, noses can indeed be comical, as I found when I tested the idea at several subsequent gatherings. This way of seeing, infantile as it must be, was Marie Thérèse's first introduction to the visible world, which causes us few surprises but which to her was full of frights and amusements unknown to the rest of us. She saw another world from mine (ours), and I puzzled as to how I might best assist her to see several separate things as they contributed to a familiar configuration rather than seeing one detail and then another and another. Thus decomposed, the objects of her sight jostled each other as unfamiliar fragments thrown up in a chaotic sea, in which near and far reversed themselves from glance to glance. This, it seemed to me as she wandered precariously around the darkened room, her eyes unbandaged, was a dangerous affliction, and I did not wonder that her new-born sight was for her more a terror than a blessing.

> *Brian O'Doherty, in his* The Strange Case of
> Mademoiselle P., *Pantheon Books, 1992.*

and popular acclaim. But, as Marie-Thérèse struggled with the confusions of sight, "the little trained animals", her hands at the keyboard, "began to quarrel, leaving me no way to subdue their disagreement". As she struggled to piece together the elements of rooms and faces (noses caused her particular difficulty and hilarity), her father's fury with the charlatan doctor increased.

O'Doherty has Mesmer, Marie-Thérèse and the outraged Josef von Paradies speaking a series of monologues, containing a fair pastiche of eighteenth-century mannerisms. Obsessed with rank in the family as well as at court, Herr von Paradies fumes at Mesmer's usurping of his paternal responsibility and the fact that any permanent cure for his daughter seems likely to deprive her of her main accomplishment. He plots the doctor's downfall. Intrigue and manipulation reach a climax when Herr von Paradies arrives at the Mesmer establishment, swordstick in hand, to liberate and reclaim his daughter from Mesmer's therapeutic caresses. The resulting fracas brings down a permanent darkness for the rest of her life.

In a long coda, the doctor, writing in old age, is disturbed by an erotic vision of Marie-Thérèse, but remains convinced that his motives in massaging her humours were pure. None the less, he finds he's half-inclined to believe popular fictions that he knows to be untrue, for instance, that he attended a recital his former patient gave at the Concert Spirituel in Paris, a decade later, and left before she played a note, unable to bear the fact of her blindness. When he unearths his own contemporary account of her treatment, it fails to reassure him on the question of his ethics. The only thing Mesmer remained sure of was his theory; he was appalled when a Royal Commission of Inquiry in Paris in 1784 dismissed his work with hysterics as the mere play of imagination and suggestion. O'Doherty's Mesmer, seated in a darkened room, working quietly and sympathetically with a single patient, throws a long shadow forward in the direction of Charcot and Freud.

> *Julian Duplain, "Therapeutic Caresses," in*
> The Times Literary Supplement, *No. 4662,*
> *August 7, 1992, p. 18.*

Miles Hoffman   (review date 23 August 1992)

[*In the following review, Hoffman finds O'Doherty's insights into blindness and memory in* The Strange Case of Mademoiselle P. *interesting, but considers the novel lacking in plot, character development, and imagination.*]

The Strange Case of Mademoiselle P., Brian O'Doherty's first novel, is based on the true story of physician Franz Anton Mesmer's treatment of a celebrated blind Austrian pianist and composer, Marie Therese von Paradies (1759-1824). Using the therapeutic property that he described as "animal magnetism" and his techniques of "magnetization" (the precursor of modern hypnosis), Mesmer temporarily restored the 18-year-old girl's sight. Her parents grew dissatisfied with her progress, however, and withdrew her from the doctor's care, attempting in the process

zart, scorned by her father as a "gifted machine", wrote a concerto for her. In Mesmer's healing hands, the veils of her blindness were gradually unwound, to professional to discredit him and precipitating a violent confrontation in their daughter's presence that resulted in the girl's regression to permanent blindness.

The novel has five chapters, all written in the first person, in the voices of three different characters. The first two chapters belong to Mesmer, the third to Marie Therese, the fourth to the girl's father, Josef, court secretary to the Empress Maria Theresa of Austria, and the fifth to Mesmer again, many years later.

This brief book is beset by many problems. A metaphor for the gravest of these can be found early in the first chapter: "When one first hears any pianist, one's ears hold to an almost automatic schedule; first, does the player reach a level of technical competence that advances player and listener to the next phase of attention . . .?" Ubiquitous dissonances between relative pronouns and their antecedents, discords of mood and tense, dangling participles, confused generics ("you" and "one" in the same sentence), wrong words ("inferred" for "implied")—rarely have I seen such a daunting compendium of grammatical mistakes and awkward constructions. O'Doherty does demonstrate the occasional graceful turn of phrase, but he invariably precedes or follows it with an unnecessary clause or two, and his editors have obviously been of no help.

If one chooses to advance to the "next phase" anyway, one finds an author who is a sharp observer, obviously intelligent and thoughtful, but whose sensibility seems more suited to essays or criticism than to fiction. In any case, O'Doherty's book certainly does not feel like a novel. It feels in fact like what it purports to be in fiction: a collection of journal entries.

The book seems motivated less by plot or character development, in other words, than by a desire to muse and comment, to jump from one insight to the next. O'Doherty's insights themselves are often worthwhile: His metaphors of darkness are interesting, as are his perceptions of life at the imperial court and his final-chapter musings on the nature of memory. But insights must come by the by in a novel, as natural reflections occurring in the course of the unhurried unfolding of a story. And there simply isn't enough story here. Indeed, the sole plot element for an entire last third of the book is aged Mesmer's wondering whether he might ever have felt an erotic attraction towards Marie Therese. Meanwhile, there is hardly anything in the rest of the book that would even lead us to think that this is a particularly important question.

With regard to the limitations of the story, I am troubled, too, by how closely O'Doherty sticks to the versions written by the real Mesmer and Josef von Paradies. One reads the first three chapters assuming the author has imagined the scenes and situations, and it turns out he has merely taken the available accounts and dramatized and embellished them. Some of the embellishments are lovely, but this is closer to fictionalization than to fiction. Furthermore, a note at the end of the book tells us that a manuscript which makes up a significant portion of chapter five is "freely adapted" from a published translation of one of Mesmer's treatises. "Lifted verbatim" is closer to the mark, with a few additions and interjections.

The brevity of the novel ultimately seems less like admirable compactness and more like a shortness of imaginative breath. What happened during Mesmer's 20-odd years of undocumented wanderings? That's what I'd like to know. And why did he abandon his wife in Vienna? The most compelling voice in the book, in fact, is the father's, in chapter four, precisely because it is the most freely imagined and the most passionate. Facts, in fiction, are less important than truth.

Miles Hoffman, "Dr. Mesmer's Magic Touch," in Book World—The Washington Post, *August 23, 1992, p. 4.*

Additional coverage of O'Doherty's life and career is contained in the following source published by Gale Research: *Contemporary Authors,* Vol. 105.

Darryl Pinckney
High Cotton

Pinckney is an American critic, essayist, and novelist, born in 1953.

INTRODUCTION

High Cotton chronicles a young man's struggle to achieve a sense of personal identity and an understanding of his black heritage. Generally considered an autobiographical work, *High Cotton* is narrated by an unnamed protagonist who is the descendant of several generations of educated blacks. These ancestors, referred to by Pinckney as "The Also Chosen," were among the first African-Americans to break racial barriers in white-dominated colleges and professions. Growing up in a comfortable suburb of Indianapolis during the 1950s, the narrator feels no personal affiliation with his black heritage. However, the contrast between his background and the social reality of racial segregation and discrimination becomes a source of confusion as he matures. Competing with whites at Columbia University, on Wall Street, and in the publishing world of New York City, the narrator is haunted by the legacy of a racial history he alternately embraces and repudiates. Many critics praised Pinckney's sensitive and insightful examination of racial themes, his vivid characterizations, and humorously ironic narrative tone. Much commentary, however, has focused on the novel's sketchy, disconnected structure and detached narrative voice. While some reviewers have faulted these qualities, others have found them representative of Pinckney's themes of confusion and alienation. Richard Eder commented: "The result is a book that is allusive and elusive, cloudy and gleaming by turns, that skips many narrative connections and can seem indifferent to being grasped, that plays tag with its readers, in short. Yet when it lets itself be caught, it can be astonishing."

CRITICISM

Pearl K. Bell   (review date 1992)

[*In the following review, Bell examines* High Cotton's *structure, style, and characters and emphasizes the work's theme of personal and racial identity.*]

Darryl Pinckney is the most astute and independent-minded critic of black literature in America today. In trenchant essays about such revered figures as Alice Walker and Countee Cullen, he has raised hackles by refusing to be intimidated by orthodox pieties about race and gender. Pinckney has now published his first novel, ***High Cotton,*** which reads less like imaginative fiction than a thinly disguised autobiography of an exceptionally precocious and high-spirited young man, born in 1953 into a black family in Indianapolis. More *Bildung* than *roman,* the book takes its title from the folk saying "If you're chopping in high cotton, you've got it easier." In other words, the higher the social class, the better the life: *High Cotton* portrays a world very different from the more familiar accounts, fictional or otherwise, about the black experience in America.

Pinckney comes from what W. E. B. DuBois called "the talented tenth"—the educated and socially mobile segment of black society. His world is not the Spike Lee inner-city ghetto of poverty and despair, but an eminently respectable upper-middle-class black family in which four generations have earned college degrees. As the narrator tells us at the start, "No one sat me down and told me I was a Negro. That was something I figured out on the sly." But as he learns soon enough, being part of "the talented tenth" does not absolve him from wrestling with the problems of blackness, even if he cannot share the older generations' anxious vigilance about the slings and arrows of outrageous bigotry.

What the young hero of *High Cotton* struggles to convey is the confusion and uncertainty about his race and status that someone born into the black elite in the early fifties had to try and sort out. When the family moves to the suburbs, the nameless narrator describes himself as one of the Also Chosen—the small number of black students in a predominantly white school. His immediate tactic is to deny there's anything special about his situation, with a wry proviso: "There was nothing to be afraid of as long as we were polite and made good grades. . . . You were just as good as anyone else out there, but they—whoever 'they' were—had rigged things so that you had to be close to perfect just to break even."

The tension between his nonchalant affectation of indifference and the intractable reality of race is put to the test when, in adolescence, he visits relatives in the South, which he calls "The Old Country." There the lines demarcating black and white are not as conveniently blurred as they seemed to be in Indiana:

> The Old South became a sort of generalized stuffy room. . . . It wasn't safe to explore the South. The old-timers themselves discouraged too much curiosity about what lay beyond the gate. It was a place of secrets, of what black people knew and what white people didn't. . . . Meanwhile, television passed on its pictures, the connecting tissue. The representations survived the subject and eventually overtook my own images, which were less durable than waxwork figures in an exhibition of Black Life at the Smithsonian.

Since *High Cotton* is constructed, in the manner of autobiography, of self-enclosed episodes that represent the stages of a developing life, it is sometimes hard to discern the thread—other than the wry tone of the narrator—that connects these events. Whatever tenuous unity exists comes from the fascinating figure of the young man's Grandfather Eustace. He, not the mercurial and nameless narrator, is the most fully realized character in the book, the one who represents a view of his race and identity that the narrator thinks he can neither share nor entirely reject with impunity. "I spent much of my life running from him, centripetal fashion, because he was, to me, just a poor old darky" who came from the Old Country—Georgia. What "old darky" means in this context is not some shuffling stereotype from *Gone With the Wind* but a man whose view of blackness his grandson thinks obsolete, intransigently resistant to the changing times. A graduate of Harvard and Brown, Grandfather Eustace became a Congregationalist minister, always eloquently spoken and elegantly dressed, an awful snob who rarely visited his grand-

son's family because they lived on the wrong side of Indianapolis, "right there with the hoi polloi." What his race meant to Grandfather was elementary: he was black at a time when everyone was white and it was his duty "to pass on the record of alienated majesty" to his descendants.

As his grandson moves into the revolutions of the sixties, assaulted in equal parts by condescension, celebration, and hostility, he finds Grandfather's notions more and more unacceptable. With his highly developed sense of comic irony, he often offends his solemn black classmates, but he is also eager to have "the social satisfaction of being a Black Power advocate in a suburban high school." Yet he can't let go of the feeling "that everything all-Negro, separate, and tribal was a corral, and anything white a great opening-up to the general dance." Torn by what he calls his "Popular Front mentality" he seesaws between pride in his blackness and chronic resistance to being part of a Movement that is inimical to ironic detachment.

Neither irony nor ellipitcal detachment provided much comfort when he entered Columbia in the early seventies, years after "the golden days of '68." He searches out the Harlem scene yet can't feel himself to be part of it. But he discovers soon enough that being black in New York is not the same as being black in Indiana. Staying on in the city after graduation, he finally gets a dose of the racism he had more or less escaped back home and, characteristically, finds some comedy in the ugliness:

> Taxi drivers would not stop for me after dark, white girls jogged to keep ahead of my shadow thrown at their heels by the amber streetlamps. Part of me didn't blame them, but most of me was hurt. I carried props into the subway—the latest *Semiotext(e)*, a hefty volume of the Frankfurt School—so that the employed would not get the wrong idea or, more to the point, the usual idea about me. . . . That Bicentennial summer I got over it.

But it was not so easy to get over the racism of the aged Djuna Barnes, the legendary relic of the avant-garde twenties who hired him one summer to run errands and be generally useful. One day she orders him to wash out a blouse, and he refuses. "She started to say that she didn't understand why blacks had become so touchy, caught herself. . . . but I knew what she meant." He walks out and decides to write a caustic attack on every writer who ever wrote a disparaging word about blacks.

When that proves impossible, he finds another menial job, and then goes on to some predictable adventures in London and Paris. But Pinckney regains his stride toward the end of the book, when the young man in search of authenticity but distrustful of enthusiasm and wary of commitment returns to the Old Country on a visit which induces very different thoughts and feelings than those he had as a child. The mournful reverie of the closing pages, as he walks over the bridge from Georgia into South Carolina, reveals a soul no less divided than in his earlier years, but fiercely honest about the understanding he has reached, not without difficulty, about his blackness and himself as an individual in relation to his race. In a beautifully unsentimental passage toward the end of the novel, Pinckney writes: "I minded the strict rules of conduct and the tribal code that said that I, as a black, had a responsibility to my people, to honor the race. Now I am sorry that I went to such lengths not to be of much use to myself just so no one would be able to ask anything of me. To have nothing to offer was not, after all, the best way to have nothing to lose." No longer teetering on the ambiguous knife-edge of irony, our young hero is now free to grow up. (pp. 288-91)

Pearl K. Bell, in a review of "High Cotton," in Partisan Review, *Vol. LIX, No. 2, 1992, pp. 288-91.*

Janet Byrne   (review date 5 February 1992)

[*In the following review, Byrne discusses* High Cotton's *narrative style and plot, noting that the book "seems more like a memoir than a novel."*]

"No one sat me down and told me I was a Negro," says the unnamed narrator of Darryl Pinckney's first book [*High Cotton*]. Probably no one had to. The "high yellow" (light-skinned) family elders he was forced to visit every summer in the broiling South were vain, obsessive and algebraic about how faintly black they were. His grandfather Eustace was very dark but had a beige second wife. An iconoclast, snob and preacher, educated at Brown and Harvard, Eustace liked to talk over his congregation's heads. After losing an oratorical shootout from the pulpit one Sunday with an organist who cut his sermon short, he was fired.

Excerpts from Eustace's last ecclesiastical stand take up a 10-page sequence about a third of the way through *High Cotton.* Otherwise there isn't much talking in this *Bildungsroman,* which is a beautifully written book with an identity problem: Self-consciously ironic, it seems more like a memoir than a novel. And—strangely for a coming-of-age story—the narrator isn't Mr. Pinckney's most interesting, endearing, or even most fully realized character; Eustace is.

World-weary from the start, brainy, pampered, the narrator is raised mostly in a 1950s Indianapolis suburb. But, like the book itself—and perhaps as his missing name is meant to suggest—he suffers from an invisibility that goes beyond his being an anomalous black in suburban white America. Nothing can, or does, seem to touch this narrator, at least throughout the book's first half. Arrested in what seems to be a permanent state of moral lassitude, he speaks in a passive, elliptical, poetic shorthand that—ignoring Pound's oft-ignored dictum that poetry should be at least as clear as prose—occasionally sacrifices meaning for cadence:

"The future was put away for us." Mr. Pinckney writes. ". . . the way meatloaf was wrapped up for the next nervous quiz meal and answers to our stormy looks were stored up for that tremendous tomorrow."

In school, the narrator mingles impassively with the white kids in Weejuns, wraparound denim skirts, crew-neck sweaters and loafers. He's invulnerable to everyone but Eustace, who periodically shows up to remind him that, though he goes to school with crackers, he is still a Negro.

At a meeting of the junior-high journalism club, Eustace, "like an impeccable waiter of the old school," serves shrimp to a cool ninth-grader. "Never touch the stuff," the young man says. "I'm kosher."

Maybe you find that funny, maybe you don't. Mr. Pinckney's punch lines are usually fairly cryptic, abbreviated and stylized. When the stories are put into the narrator's disingenuous words—a kind of stream-of-childhood—they often become even harder to follow, though Eustace is never far away with his private reality principle. In high school in the '70s, for example, the narrator flirts with Anglophilia and other bookish pastimes like so many phases his character must pass through: "It is easy to live with the idea of life," Eustace tells him, "and when you lose it, you will think of the time when you had it, green and gold."

The narrator goes to London, then on to Columbia University, still getting money from Daddy (a somewhat disembodied character, as are the narrator's mother and two older sisters). He has several Lost Weekends and at least one whole lost summer in New York before taking a succession of vaguely literary jobs. Among these is one that Mr. Pinckney, a journalist and book critic, actually had (and has elsewhere written about)—assistant to Djuna Barnes, the author of the 1937 novel *Nightwood* and a famous recluse.

The narrator—and narrative—come into their own when, in some nice plot confluences, the narrator's relationship with his grandfather develops in the Northeast. (Both have left home and become solitary wanderers, but their paths converge every once in a while.) When Eustace dies, the narrator journeys briefly to his grandfather's old farm in Georgia for some bucolic nostalgia, but finds a South of malls.

The narrator's passage from precocious upper-middle-class child to cerebral world searcher begins to take hold in the final chapters, in a rush of regretful, chastened understanding. "I had taken a utilitarian view of Grandfather. What else were old blacks for, except to be repositories of racial lore? Beautiful, maligned, obsolete Negroes, discussing themselves . . . and feeling like philosophers. . . ."

High Cotton ends in a burst of self-doubtful and mildly self-contemptuous philosophizing by the narrator. He thinks, soon "I may be someone's old darky . . . telling someone who may insist on being called a Senufo-American how in my day so many . . . were afraid of black teenagers in big sneakers with the laces untied. . . ." Something of a baby boomer's *Black Boy*, Mr. Pinckney's novel and laconic hero seem to have sprung reluctantly, and with some amused disgust from the absurd racial and economic contradictions of the past four decades.

Janet Byrne, "A Black Baby Boomer Comes of Age," in The Wall Street Journal, *February 5, 1992, p. A9.*

Henry Louis Gates, Jr. (review date 23 February 1992)

[*Gates is an American scholar, essayist, and critic who has received numerous awards for his writings on literary theory and African-American literature. Below, he presents a positive assessment of* High Cotton, *praising Pinckney's understated tone and insight into the significance of black history in relation to community, family, and personal identity.*]

Black writers may wax nostalgic over such heydays of creativity as the Harlem Renaissance of the '20s or the Black Arts movements of the '60s, but the truth is that more of them have published more books to more acclaim in the past decade than at any other period in America's literary history. And while the '80s can clearly be characterized as an era of black women's writing—dominated by Toni Morrison's sublime artistry, which many of us expect to be duly recognized with a Nobel Prize—it has also provided a nourishing environment for a new generation of black male writers who have left the macho rats-and-roaches naturalism of an earlier era far behind.

True, less talented black men have sometimes grumbled that black women's writing has succeeded at their expense, and depicted themselves as victims of a conspiracy to hold them back. But don't you believe it. Our literary portfolio now contains the names of Rita Dove, Gloria Naylor, Terry McMillan, Marita Golden, Jamaica Kincaid and Thulani Davis—but it also includes such promising black male writers as Trey Ellis, Jake Lamar, Steve Corbin, Melvin Dixon and Randall Kenan. To their number, we can now add Darryl Pinckney, with his uncompromising first novel, *High Cotton.*

Pinckney's relation to black America's literary past is distinguished by an intense, and self-conscious, ambivalence—and he has turned that ambivalence into an advantage both intellectual and literary. Through much of the '80s, Darryl Pinckney established himself as a judicious critic of African-American literature, displaying an exquisite sensitivity to language and an impressively broad grasp of the canon of European and American literature. In long, reflective essays published largely in *The New York Review of Books,* Pinckney has engaged in a sustained meditation on both the canonical authors of the tradition (Jean Toomer, Sterling Brown, Zora Neale Hurston, Langston Hughes, Countee Cullen, Richard Wright, and James Baldwin) and the works of his older contemporaries (Alice Walker, Paule Marshall and Ishmael Reed, among others). Resisting the urge toward ethnic cheerleading, Pinckney has served as one of our most important critical consciences (and I say this even though I sometimes strenuously disagree with his judgments): His carefully considered assessments are never swayed or softened by considerations of politics or politesse. His criticism is accordingly revered and reviled.

High Cotton captures the experiences of a third generation of college-educated middle-class African Americans, those Pinckney terms the "Also Chosen," Ivy League "trained" survivors of Jack and Jill (a club for the children of the black bourgeoisie), all-too-eager pioneers in the

> In many ways *High Cotton* is an ironic riff on the old saying that what the fathers forget, the grandsons remember. The nameless protagonist is alternately attracted to and repelled by the African-American past.
>
> *—Henry Louis Gates, Jr.*

great drama of integration. The grandchildren of W. E. B. Du Bois's "talented tenth," the members of this Third Generation presented themselves as carefully scrubbed, evenly greased, stocking-capped emissaries to the court of a foreign potentate located somewhere across "the glossy edge of the New Frontier." They integrated suburban white high schools and Ivy League colleges in the late '60s and early '70s as if the life of "the race" depended on it. And in so many ways, it did.

Using the accommodating form of the picaresque, Pinckney maps in the first person the progress of his nameless pilgrim from the self-contained world of that "old darky," his grandfather, a world—sheltered but stifling—where subtle distinctions of color and kink loom large. From here, the protagonist moves across the color line into white neighborhoods, white summer camps and white schools. In flight from his own skeptical temper, he is absorbed by the black nationalist fervor of the late '60s and the discovery of "Blackness." What follows is a classic series of fly-in-the-buttermilk encounters as he moves on to college, Wall Street, the world of New York publishing, and then on to Europe and back. Pinckney brilliantly combines empathy and acid as he details the attractions of black nationalism and its rhetoricians—revealed to be every bit as bourgeois and status-obsessed as an earlier generation of would-be assimilationists.

In many ways *High Cotton* is an ironic riff on the old saying that what the fathers forget, the grandsons remember. The nameless protagonist is alternately attracted to and repelled by the African-American past. Indeed, the mooring of the novel and of its narrator is the complexly ambiguous figure of Grandfather Eustace, "the emperor of out-of-it," and yet a man who "tried, in his way, to answer all the questions." Educated at the "Holy Land," Brown and Harvard, the old man "had a finely developed idea of his own worth and enjoyed, like ill health, the suspicion that no one else shared it."

"Even before I was old enough to listen he was in the prompter's box," the narrator tells us,

> anxious to pass on that record of *alienated majesty.* I spent much of my life running from him, centripetal fashion, because he was, to me, just a poor old darky. I did not return his phone calls, I cashed in his train tickets, I went to the movies when he came to visit, but he was forever rising through the waves of my denial, sustained by the knowledge that he, his father and mother

before him, his brothers and sisters, his sons and daughters, were a sort of dusky peerage with their degrees, professions, and good marriages among their own kind.

Echoing the shadowy and enigmatic figure of the grandfather figures in Jean Toomer's *Cane* and Ralph Ellison's *Invisible Man,* Pinckney has fashioned a compelling, if ironic metaphor of the African-American past devoid of sentiment or saccharine. Grandfather Eustace is a figure both admired and despised, determining his grandson's actions precisely to the degree that he seeks to flee the pattern of his grandfather's life, to outwit his logic, to escape the net of the fate that closes in upon him. Rarely has history found a more suggestive embodiment. This rendering of the past-in-the-present is a major achievement.

But so is Pinckney's chilly lyricism, his unflagging gift for apercus, and the book bristles with well-turned phrases and alum-sharp insights. He writes of "the paralysis of someone both too afraid and too superior to compete"; explains why "I couldn't allow myself to look back, having presented myself to myself as one who had never been anywhere but where I was." "Like taking a vow," he confides, "going to visit Aunt Clara in Opelika, Alabama, demanded that a part of the self must die."

There is also a mother lode of racial lore here that rings true to the experience of our generation of the desperate-to-be-integrated, an experience that was often denied during the heady days of black nationalism: "Aunt Odetta made my sisters walk with their books on their heads or took a ruler between our spines and the backs of her dining room chairs," the narrator tells us. "She used to say that thought began in the mouth, that we should practice comporting our lips so that the lower one did not protrude too much, because eversion was fine for the masks of the Dan people but it made American Negroes look 'deficient'." With an almost Jamesian eye for the large significance of small niceties, Pinckney has given us the kind of "black history" not celebrated in Black History Month: the coming of age of the Also Chosen and the passing of the old Negro.

This is not a novel that wears its heart on its sleeve. Pinckney never ingratiates; he writes with a pitiless and unsparing vision that amounts, almost, to an ordinance of self-denial. But that's finally what gives the book a formidable kind of moral solidity, the sense that his mordant attack on the myths of community and the comforts of family is simultaneously an act of self-wounding. "This hurts me more than it hurts you," the scourge always promises; but in this case, we believe it.

With *High Cotton,* Pinckney joins the first ranks of American writers, and he does so without thunderous crescendos, showy effects or bids for easy emotional appeal. The preference is for quiet, colloquial understatement. And yet its rhythm of recollection proves hypnotic. Pinckney writes with deceptive simplicity, and he never raises his voice. But then, he doesn't have to. (pp. 1, 9)

> *Henry Louis Gates, Jr., "The Great Black Hope," in* Book World—The Washington Post, *February 23, 1992, pp. 1, 9.*

An excerpt from *High Cotton*

To know where you were going, you had to know where you'd come from, though the claims that the past had on you were like cold hands in the dark. Those elderly relatives, old-timers in charcoal-gray suits and spinsters in musty fox tails, who went out of their way to come to Indianapolis to have a look at you, those wizards licking gold fillings and widows coughing on their bifocals whom you didn't want to travel miles and miles or eat ice cream with—they were among the many pearly reasons you had to hold your Vaselined head high, though you were never to mention in company your father's Uncle Ralph Waldo, who had lived the blues so well that he wound up in a nuthouse without the sense he was born with because of a disease. Grandfather Eustace spelled its name so fast not even your sisters were able to catch the letters.

Above all, you had to remember that no one not family was ever going to love you really. The Also Chosen were one big happy family, though the elderly relatives who hung over holidays like giant helium balloons couldn't stand the sight of one another, which gave fuel to the blue flame of confidences and bitter fine points that burned until the stars folded up. Sometimes the old-timers seemed to be all there was. They far outnumbered their younger relatives. The family tapered off, depopulated itself from shelf to shelf, but the ranks of the old-timers promised never to thin. They enlisted the departed in their number, on their side, which added to their collective power to dominate those of you who would never know what they knew.

> *Darryl Pinkney, in his* High Cotton, *Farrar, Straus and Giroux, 1992.*

Richard Eder (review date 23 February 1992)

[*Eder is an American critic who in 1987 received both a citation for excellence from the National Book Critics Circle and a Pulitzer Prize for criticism. Below, he associates Pinckney's elusive, disjointed narrative style in* High Cotton *with the novel's theme of estrangement from African-American history.*]

The narrator is a graduate of Columbia University and, from all indications, a writer. His father's profession is not mentioned but he lives in Indianapolis and belongs to the fairly-well-off middle class. His grandfather was a Congregationalist minister. His great-grandfather was a Baptist minister. His great-great-grandfather was a slave.

So where does that leave Darryl Pinckney? That is the point of *High Cotton*—Who am I? Or, more exactly, how do I think of myself?—except for a quibble. Pinckney calls his book a novel, not an autobiography, so although the narrator is Pinckney's alter ego, the thinnest of veils floats around him. Not to get tangled in it, and since the narrator is given no other name, I shall call him Pinckney. If you can have a fictional autobiography, why not a fictional review?

But the veil is also the point. Pinckney is a literary intellectual for whom to discriminate is more important than to declare. Postmodernist irony and ambiguity are as much a part of his identity as forthright affirmation has been for contemporaries and predecessors in the Black Power and civil-rights movements; or as a contradictory yet resilient discourse of pride and patience once was to his ancestors in the South, or what he calls "the Old Country."

Pinckney (his creator of the same name not only went to Columbia but also won a Guggenheim, a Whiting Award and a Princeton fellowship) is trying to place himself in black history. Not to do so would betray his forebears, and particularly the grandfather around whom many of his musings revolve. But to do it in slogans or simplifications, or anything but his own intellectual terms, would betray not only himself but those same forebears and that grandfather who thought for himself to the point of eccentricity and isolation.

The result is a book that is allusive and elusive, cloudy and gleaming by turns, that skips many narrative connections and can seem indifferent to being grasped, that plays tag with its readers, in short. Yet when it lets itself be caught, it can be astonishing. And the reader suspects that the elusiveness is not arbitrary, or not *only* arbitrary. Pinckney is on what may be an impossible search, and on such a search you don't want followers who keep asking where they are. It is a search for a language to speak of himself in.

A child of the '50s, and attending Indianapolis' best public schools, young Pinckney saw no great need to identify himself as black. He tended to think of himself as English, in fact. He daydreamed of being crowned king of England, and explained London's subway system to family freinds going abroad. In high school, he dabbled in black radicalism and attended a few meetings of a tiny offshoot of the Black Panthers. He had no car, though; a white friend had to drive him. At college, he was regarded skeptically by his activist friends who refered to him as "Dr. Thomas" (Uncle Tom with a degree).

It was not so much a gap of sympathy as of speech. The affirmations used by activism were alien to him. Yet he considers, bemusedly, the tortured language of denial that he heard in his family as a child. It had evolved through generations of proud and educated black people who made a life and found dignity for themselves under segregation. The advantage of Jim Crow, an Alabama aunt declared, was that it kept you from contact with uneducated whites. Separate but superior.

In Pinckney's comfortable home in Indianapolis, the word was: "All men are created equal." Even so, Pinckney writes, "lots of mixed messages with sharp teeth waited under my Roy Rogers pillow." They read, in part: "You were just as good as anyone else. . . . But you had to be close to perfect just to break even. You had nothing to fear, though every time you left the house for a spelling bee or a Music Memory contest, the future of the future hung in the balance." It was a three-beat contradiction, e.g.: "Forgiveness was divine." But the person who short-changed them in the shop, or wouldn't serve them at the airport restaurant, "would get what was coming to them, though they acted that way because they didn't know any better."

Most of **High Cotton** is made up of selected episodes and reflections that are Pinckney's experiments in ways of feeling black. Some are told with an awkward, chilly reluctance. A time spent in London as a would-be down-and-out radical is inert; so is his time as a Paris expatriate in the company of a Holly Golightly-like black woman who is only able to love white men. One absence in the book is any mention of contemporary personal relationships. In view of the full portraits of other relatives and forebears, it is interesting that only the most cursory mention is made of the narrator's parents.

On the other hand, there is a beautifully written account of working as a part-time companion to avant-garde novelist Djuna Barnes. All but bedridden, she lived in a tiny house and of slumming in a raunchy room cluttered with mementos from her Paris days. Pinckney was careful not to exploit her and he tried to avoid asking about her recollections. Snippets would emerge here and there. Colette was "that silly blue-haired woman." Of *Nightwood,* her most celebrated work, she exclaimed: "Did I write this? How did I do it? Do it while you're young. Put all your passion into it."

The richest and most suggestive parts of the book are Pinckney's encounters with his grandfather. He knew him as a troublesome, itinerant old man, whose Harvard education and argumentiveness had lost him his church position. He wanders in and out of Pinckney's life, nosy and officious, imperious and forlorn. The narrator tries to keep his distance; he senses a profound demand on his conscience.

It is only when the old man dies in a nursing home that Pinckney lets himself sense the bond. In his day, his grandfather shocked his congregation by reading them the indubitably white and indubitably literary Robert Browning. He mocked the segregated pieties of his own time; later he would criticize the civil-rights movement as bad-mannered. He once recounted to Pinckney the legend of Luther and Erasmus walking among the dead in a battlefield. "They died in a just cause," Luther proclaimed. "They were men and had something better to do today," Erasmus replied.

It is Erasmus that Pinckney hears, finally, in his grandfather. And in the book's conclusion—choked, elliptical, puzzling and suddenly beautiful—Pinckney seems to find Erasmus in himself. Unable to throw himself into his countrymen's battles and glories, he is unable to separate himself from them. He attends with his oblique voice; he participates through estrangement. (pp. 3, 8)

> *Richard Eder, "A Place in Black History," in*
> Los Angeles Times Book Review, *February
> 23, 1992, pp. 3, 8.*

Merle Rubin   (review date 28 February 1992)

[*In the following review, Rubin argues that* High Cotton *lacks unity and meaning and that its disjointed structure and elliptical style dissipates the reader's interest.*]

The name Darryl Pinckney may well be familiar to readers of *Harper's, Vanity Fair, The New Republic, Granta,*

The New York Review of Books, The Village Voice, and other prominent journals that have featured his reviews and personal reflections on the topics of race, gender, and cultural identity. **High Cotton** is his first book. It is billed as a novel, but seems more like a collection of autobiographical essays.

Calling a book a novel may be a way of allowing the author freedom to modify the autobiographical material he is using, but, unfortunately, it does not automatically transform a disjunctive series of hasty, impressionistic reminiscences into an organic and shapely whole.

The 12 chapters tracing the boyhood and youth of the unnamed narrator (there seems no reason not to refer to him as Pinckney) can be taken as a sort of "portrait of the artist" and also as an implicit discussion of the meaning of being black.

But, despite the intelligence and (one suspects) the originality of thought at work, the result is something of a missed opportunity, providing neither a cohesive discussion of blackness nor a clear picture of an individual sensibility.

It's a promising subject: the story of growing up amid a plethora of mixed signals and coming of age in an era fraught with changes and conflicting messages.

The narrator (like Pinckney) hails from Indianapolis. He's raised in the family tradition of "Negro Firsterism"—which is not the black equivalent of American isolationism, but rather the pride taken in being the first Negro to achieve a new distinction or penetrate a new barrier, whether it's being the first to graduate from Harvard or the first to move into a previously whites-only neighborhood.

Around the narrator, barriers are falling. The promise of the New Frontier is that his generation will finally have the opportunities previous generations were denied.

"There was nothing to be afraid of as long as we were polite and made good grades. After all, the future, back then, assembled as we were on the glossy edge of the New Frontier, belonged to us, the Also Chosen."

To this child of the future, the South of his grandparents was the "Old Country."

Although "You were not an immigrant" and "there were no foreign accents, weird holidays, or funny foods to live down . . . still you did not belong to the great beyond out there; yet though you did not belong it was your duty as the Also Chosen to get up and act as though you belonged, especially when no one wanted you to."

The tension between the brave new world of the future and the legacy of past generations who prayed and fought for that future is encapsulated in the young narrator's offish relationship with his grandfather Eustace.

A highly educated minister whose lot in life has been to preach recondite sermons over the uneasy heads of congregations who would have preferred a more fervent, emotional pulpit style, Eustace is a man who never really fits in.

He is such a fixture of his grandson's life that the younger man takes him for granted. When Eustace's disgruntled second wife (known as the "beige stepgrandmother") tells Darryl he'd be surprised to hear what his grandfather really thinks of him, Darryl is shocked: "It had never occurred to me that he didn't dote on me or that, if he did, his feelings could change. An old man's loyalties were, I assumed, like a fixed income: barely enough for necessities . . . but something to count on."

Outside the family, acceptance is even harder to find. The young narrator knows he's not like the "bad boys" who hang out on street corners bound for trouble, but he's also uncomfortable amid the "right" sort of black students who congregate at their own table during lunch period.

As a high school student regularly accused of being an Uncle Tom, he decides to "cop an attitude" and does a brief stint as an errand boy for a local cell of revolutionary black nationalists. Going to New York City to attend Columbia University, he tries to steep himself in the black culture of nearby Harlem but only succeeds in nearly falling victim to a con game.

The tone in which these adventures are narrated is so disaffected, and the author's elliptical, offhand style is so difficult to follow, that whatever interest the reader may have had in these events is likely to have evaporated in the course of attempting to read about them.

It's not that Pinckney lacks talent. He is quite capable of crisp and amusing passages, like his account of his teenage Anglophilia:

> My bicycle became a motorcycle and anyone whose feet dragged from the back seat was Rita Tushingham.
>
> I was a bloke, like those who dangled cigarettes at the proper angle in grainy black-and-white films, though I wasn't sure what a quid was.

Some of his "characters" are memorable, like Eustace, or the offbeat young black woman called Bargetta who mixes her own perfumes and gives them names like Maginot: " 'Wear Maginot and get invaded,' " she quips.

On a more profound note, this same young woman reflects,

> The farther you are from something, the more wonderful it seems. You're walking down a street in a foreign country and spot one light in a dark house and wish you could have that life. But if the window were yours you'd be plotting to break out of it.

But most of the book is simply not this good.

A lot more of the writing reads like this clumsily overwritten passage about a southern aunt:

> Aunt Clara talked like someone who had made up her mind not to leave any footprints. The lotus hum of her intermittent conversation, like the current from the electric fans in opposite corners of the sun porch, subdued hours. Her odd singsong pursued the smell of butane from my mother's lighter.

The characters float by like ships in the night, nothing much happens, the verbal fireworks fizzle, and the reader is left with the feeling of having spent time with someone who was trying harder to seem clever than to write a meaningful book.

Merle Rubin, "Portrait of a Black Artist," in The Christian Science Monitor, *February 28, 1992, p. 13.*

James Idema (review date 3 March 1992)

[*Below, Idema provides a positive review of* High Cotton, *focusing on Pinckney's humorously ironic tone, vivid characterizations, and thoughtful examination of racial themes.*]

The persistent presence of his Grandfather Eustace, above all others, in the life of the unnamed young narrator is what gives this remarkable first novel [*High Cotton*] about coming of age its special intonation. By turns rueful and contented, scornful and affectionate, caustic and tender, it is especially humorous and ironical. Irony is the narrator's best defense against Grandfather.

"I spend much of my life running from him, centripetal fashion, because he was, to me, just a poor old darky."

Grandfather is a lot more than that, of course. Ever the stern preacher, even as he fades throughout the course of the story to become "another broken Brahmin," he seems at times the narrator's very conscience. He is "forever rising through the waves of my denial, sustained by the knowledge that he, his brothers and sisters, his sons and daughters, were a sort of dusky peerage with their degrees, professions, and good marriages among their own kind."

"Their own kind" has a special connotation. This unusual four-generation family of scholars, preachers and teachers—Grandfather had been educated at Brown and Harvard—represents a black class that W. E. B. Du Bois called "the talented tenth" and the writer sometimes refers to as the "Also Chosen." Middle class, yes, but achievers who, as they strove to assimilate, were often ambivalent about their blackness. In early instances they prized lighter skin, noting Caucasian strains in the lucky one's ancestry.

The novel, which poses as autobiography, deals with questions of color in a way far removed from the apocalypse of James Baldwin and the anger of Richard Wright. Skeptical and cool, with an eye for the odd and incongruous, Darryl Pinckney's narrator goes it alone after leaving his childhood home in Indiana, trying out different attitudes as a student (Columbia University), office worker, book salesman, handyman, expatriate (Paris) and plain loafer.

The story frequently returns, however, to the "Old Country," as the author refers to South Carolina and Georgia, inhabited by the old-timers who are his elders and who haunt his spirit no matter how far from them he wanders.

Patriarchal Grandfather, despite his dominating place in the novel's scheme, is only one in an album of vivid family portraits. The majority of them are women, eloquent, sharply individual, wise even in their frequently outrageous commentary.

The narrator's Aunt Clara, educated as a teacher, presides over a household of female sisters and cousins. She liked to "go places," as she says, and traveled rather extensively before settling down to the indoor life, where "the lotus hum of her intermittent conversation, like the current from the electric fans in opposite corners of the sunporch, subdued hours."

News from the neighborhood and the black world beyond is regularly purveyed to Aunt Clara by Nida Lee, though her sister Arnez is a close rival in the gossip-mongering department. Their talk, as they try to one-up each other, makes for some of the book's most amusing dialogue. They accuse a younger sister, Muriel, of stealing. Muriel takes food from the kitchen to the men working on the other side of the creek, apparently more to hear them talk than to give charity.

The style of *High Cotton* is tight and elliptical, packed with metaphor and allusion. One is richly rewarded, however, for taking one's time. This writer's debut as a novelist is an auspicious one.

James Idema, "A Challenging New Voice, an Auspicious Debut," in Chicago Tribune, *March 3, 1992, p. 3.*

Christopher Lehmann-Haupt (reivew date 5 March 1992)

[*In the following review, Lehmann-Haupt praises Pinckney's characterizations, themes, and comic tone in* High Cotton.]

"No one sat me down and told me I was a Negro," reads the opening sentence of Darryl Pinckney's eloquent first novel, *High Cotton.*

> That was something I figured out on the sly, late in my childhood career as a snoop, like discovering that babies didn't come from an exchange of spinach during a kiss. The great thing about finding out I was a Negro was that I could look forward to going places in the by and by that I would not have been asked to as a white boy.

One of the places he would go was into the high cotton of his title, among whose several meanings must surely be where a runaway hides. For as the nameless narrator makes self-mockingly clear, he was no ordinary black but instead a member of the upper bourgeoisie, otherwise known as "upper shadies," or "the Talented Tenth" or even "the Also Chosen." So although he came to consciousness during the civil rights revolution of the 1960's, he spent a good part of his growing-up years hiding from himself.

He hid in many places, as we learn from this novel in the form of a memoir. (Or is it a memoir in the form of a novel?) He spent much of his childhood in Indianapolis lost in Anglophilic dreams of glory, which of course would not be fulfilled when he eventually spent an Orwellian interlude down and out in London. He attended Columbia

College and stayed on in New York City to explore Harlem, to become a handyman who ran errands briefly for the writer Djuna Barnes and eventually to get his "first real job" as a reader in a publishing house that his boss knew "was in trouble because the employees didn't steal its books."

But the masks with which he disguised himself from himself wore thin. As he puts it:

> The ledger of how to be simultaneously yourself and everyone else who might observe you, the captain's log of travel in the dual consciousness, the white world as the deceptive sea and the black world as the armed galley, gave me the comic feeling that I was living alongside myself, that there was a me and a ventriloquist's replica of me on my lap, and that both of us awaited the intervention of a third me, the disembodied me, before we could begin the charade of dialogue.

High Cotton realizes that dialogue, becoming at its best a richly complex mockery of the author's disdainful outlook on his forebears, although sometimes, particularly later in the book, it grows so convoluted and elliptical that it retards the pace of the narrative.

At one point he reports of his youth: "The pleasure of my circumstance depended . . . on superstition, on a Lot-like contract of deliverance. I couldn't allow myself to look back, having presented myself to myself as one who had never been anywhere but where I was."

Yet, luckily for the reader, he does look back. He draws warmly comic portraits of the older members of his family: of Aunt Clara, of Opelika, Ala., who used her light skin to get what she wanted, and who liked to plan her funeral but couldn't be interred with her dead husband because "he was buried on the wrong side of town." Of Uncle Castor, a talented musician who once played first piano for Noble Sissie and His International Orchestra at Les Ambassadeurs in Paris, but who had fallen on hard times in the narrator's youth and showed him "what the paralysis of being both too afraid and too superior to compete looked like."

And of Uncle Ulysses, who kept "two intensely cherished" German pike helmets in a fragile glass cabinet and who "was suspicious of Negro magazines, Model Cities programs, quotas, Harlem, James Brown." The author adds, "He never 'bought black' in his life."

But the ghost who all but materializes in these pages is the narrator's grandfather Eustace, a minister educated at Brown and Harvard. "He was a terrible snob," the author writes,

> his pride somehow outrageous and shaky at the same time. He had a finely developed idea of his own worth and enjoyed, like ill health, the suspicion that no one else shared it. He took the high road, but because he made the journey in a black body he lived with the chronic dread that maybe he wasn't good enough.

Wherever the narrator tries to hide, Eustace circles and chivvies him, trying to raise him to the family standard. He pays the old man back by making him the subject of the best scenes in the book, especially one in which he preaches before a congregation to which he so obviously feels superior that it ends up dismissing him.

Of course he fled this grandfather, at least until the old man seemed to lose interest, whereupon the narrator would circle back to lay down a new scent. "I had taken a utilitarian view of Grandfather. What else were old blacks for, except to be repositories of racial lore? . . . I used to sit back and wonder how they managed to be all-inclusive. It never occurred to me that they might be making it up as they went along . . ."

And of course there was regret after Grandfather Eustace finally died. "Now I miss those whom injury made gracious and also those who simply uglied up and died," the author writes " . . . Now I am sorry that I went to such lengths not to be of much use to myself just so no one would be able to ask anything of me. To have nothing to offer was not, after all, the best way to have nothing to lose."

But this book makes amends. It tells what life was like in the high cotton, and also provides the author a way to come out of hiding.

> *Christopher Lehmann-Haupt, "Growing Up Disdaining the 'Terrible Tenth',"* in The New York Times, *March 5, 1992, p. C21.*

Michael Wood   (review date 26 March 1992)

[*Wood is an English-born American critic. In the following review, he considers the structure and style of* High Cotton *and interprets the work as an introspective examination of the psychological significance of being black in America.*]

Summertime, the song says, is when the living is easy. Fish are jumping, and the cotton is high. Ease is a relative notion, of course, and in the world of *Porgy and Bess* it means only a modest letup in a very hard life. Similarly the high cotton of Darryl Pinckney's title [*High Cotton*] signals a realm of relative comfort and privilege which is nevertheless haunted by a sense of barriers and denials and difficulties, and is only (at the most) four generations away from slavery.

The narrator's grandfather was "educated in the Holy Land," we learn, but *his* grandfather was a slave. The Holy Land is not Palestine, but Brown and Harvard. The biblical joke glances at grandfather's later career as a Congregational minister, but also at the curious mingling of class, culture, and religion in the mythology of American blacks. The narrator wryly describes his own family as picturing themselves as the Also Chosen, a shifting category which may include all or most black people or only those who behave themselves. "Also" means as well as (upper-class) whites, a kindly cultural afterthought on God's part; or it hints at a special destiny of election and oppression, a second Jewry. The immediate members of the Also Chosen, the narrator's father and mother, are respectable and college-educated. They don't let the children play with the rough kids on the block, and when the living gets easy enough, they move from central Indianapolis to a white suburb.

Visits to the South are excursions into a spiky and complicated past, a rigid, alien country: Grandfather's stern church in Louisville, Kentucky, and Aunt Clara's crowded house in Opelika, Alabama. The aunt's house is "a zoo of things," and she herself seems "like an exhibit, part of the uncontrolled decor, a specimen in the menagerie of ceramic dog figurines." She is genteel ("Aunt Clara talked like someone who had made up her mind not to leave any footprints") and fairly well-off (driver, Cadillac, Steinway), and her mother has taught her that segregation serves chiefly to keep "nice Negroes" away from white trash. But just down the hill and across the creek are the cabins with broken windows, the apparently eternal Bottom of the social order ("Every town had a Bottom, every Negro had a story with a Bottom in it").

The dust jacket (but not the title page) describes *High Cotton* as a novel, and the book's characters and events just might be fictional. But its setting in time and place is thoroughly historical—we hear of Selma, the death of Marilyn Monroe, early civil rights demonstrations, the fall of Saigon, we are in Harlem, in Paris, at a vividly detailed Columbia, there are graphically described New York killings and beatings—and it doesn't read like a novel at all. Calling it one seems to be not so much an assertion of genre as a means of allowing imaginative leeway to a quirky and brilliant memoir. Certain figures or moments must have been shifted or shaped for satire or discretion, and toward the end the book does begin to feel like fiction: scenes seem to be arranged to dramatize plights and questions rather than to reconstruct experiences. For the rest, the effect is of a writer delicately, intelligently tracing pieces of an uninvented life. The art is in the selection of the traces and in the angle of vision.

> **High Cotton is the story not of a development but of a preoccupation; its episodes, although chronologically ordered, highlight important patches of memory and consciousness rather than any steady sequence or growth.**
>
> —*Michael Wood*

There is plenty of art, and at times the book seems cramped by its will to elegance, as if it were a high-gloss, New York version of Aunt Clara's drawing room. Sentences, ambushed by irony, turn into epigrams before they have a chance to draw any sort of declarative breath. "I would have gone on a retreat but my check to the religious order bounced"; "All men were created equal, but even so, lots of mixed messages with sharp teeth waited under my Roy Rogers pillow"; "I wasn't heartless, but I was the next best thing: almost heartless."

These are good sentences, but taken together—there are

dozens, maybe hundreds of similar sentences—they tend to turn the style into a form of anxiety, a bid for control, the expression of a desire to be nobody's fool but your own. Metaphors and similes crackle like new banknotes. "To look at this woman for the first time was to feel yourself about to get run over at an intersection." Aunt Clara's pearls lie "like a pet against the folds of her neck"; dawn enters an old man's room "like a nurse"; heat falls "like an edict." Black demonstrators accumulate "like pennies," roll away "like beads of mercury." The family house looks "like a wrecked boat tossed on a hill," and the old-timers who keep appearing are "like arguments for the spontaneous regeneration of barnacles." Some of these images are remarkable and some of them—the wire mesh of a porch "as black as Ray Charles's sunglasses," the Christmas punch "that put us in mind of English pond life"—have a splendid self-parodying kick. But many suggest the writer hiding among his phrases, disappearing into glitter the way the child he portrays keeps disappearing into Anglophile fantasy.

Fortunately, this very disappearance—and its alternatives—are a major subject of the book, and the writing, while remaining stylish, does escape its obsession with style. It can't let go, but it learns to relax, and at its best Pinckney's prose—funny, observant, lyrical, self-deprecating—is as good as any now being written in English. "The choir warped a few more hymns of adoration . . .": "warped" hints at a biased warble, or a warble that got lost, or maybe just an inability to stay in time or tune, and "a few" suggests the narrator wasn't counting but knew there were too many for his liking. "I wish I could say I was thinking about him," the narrator says of a boy killed outside a New York bar, and now wrapped in a sheet on the bar floor, "stopped, subtracted, about his parents asleep, unprepared for the anniversary that had entered their lives." "Stopped" and "subtracted" make us see this death as both simple and unimaginable, and it is characteristic of the moral complication and richness of Pinckney's story that his narrator should not be thinking of the boy or his parents—should think of them now, that is, in the writing and remember that he did not think of them then.

High Cotton has two dubious but memorable heroes: the narrator's grandfather and the narrator himself. The narrator's own parents are oddly vague figures, kindly but unvisualized sources of shelter, prohibitions, comments, and the occasional check. He has a theory about this—"Every generation is an enemy of its father's and a friend of its grandfather's"—but he doesn't show any enmity between child and parent, only an eagerness to keep the parents out of the picture. The theory in any case is perhaps rather wishful, and suggests more choice in matters of ancestry and formation than most of us may think we have. The theory has us writing our own ticket by skipping a generation; skipping, that is, all the clearest writing already on the ticket: home, and the daily, clock-marked influences of our childhood. The narrator does find it "chastising to speculate about your parents as people who had another life . . . and had been through more than a few texts," but this is not the book where he chastises himself much on this topic.

Still, he knows exactly what he is doing, and the very wish-fulness of the theory reminds us of something important about the work. If it is not fiction, it is not autobiography either. If the parents are vague, the narrator's affective life and adventures are not even that, they are absent. The book is full, so to speak, of things that are not there. **High Cotton** is the story not of a development but of a preoccupation; its episodes, although chronologically ordered, highlight important patches of memory and consciousness rather than any steady sequence or growth. It is not about being black but about thinking and behaving black even (especially) when you imagine you're beyond that kind of stuff. Of Pinckney's twelve chapter titles only two do not refer, explicitly or implicitly, to color, and one of those two, "Summertime," involves a reference to Gershwin's black opera.

Grandfather is Eustace, who was born on a farm near Dublin, Georgia, in 1898, and died in a retirement home in Indianapolis in 1985. He is "the emperor of out-of-it," the narrator says, "yet he was also a distinguished man who tried, in his way, to answer all the questions . . . anxious to pass on that record of alienated majesty." Grandfather insists not on the sufferings but on the triumphs of blacks who know how to get on in the world, but he also remarks that "the poor die differently from everyone else," and is said to have "loved sinners," although he was himself a good, even an incorruptible man. "He found being himself a protection of sorts," the narrator rather obscurely says—the phrase makes more sense if we think of the admiring, ambivalent narrator as lacking both protection and self. The narrator as a boy fears and patronzies his grandfather, a dim old darky from that other world. As a young man he patronizes and yearns for the old boy, as if he were a script with a secret, the one message the past couldn't fail to give.

On the last page of the book the narrator is picturing himself as becoming his grandfather, "someone's old darky, exercising my fictitious cultural birthright to run off at the mouth," but then the irony fades and sheer mournful eloquence takes over. Grandfather and grandson are now a single voice, the voice of anyone who remembers what others have forgotten, yet cannot say what it is they remember, and only pass on to us their passionate belief in the act of remembrance itself. These are the last words of the book:

> I may elect myself a witness and undertake to remember when something more important than black, white, and other was lost. Even now I grieve for what has been betrayed. I see the splendor of the mornings and hear how glad the songs were, back in the days when the Supreme Court was my Lourdes, beyond consolation. The spirit didn't lie down and die, but it's been here and gone, been here and gone.

It is a spirit we are to remember, not a circumscribed self or a set of problems. Eustace and Aunt Clara have names, as do Uncle Castor and Uncle Ulysses, and the militant Sister Egba, the doorman Jesse, the singer Jeannette, the college friend Bargetta. But the narrator's parents and sisters don't, and he doesn't. The family name is that of a "Carolinian . . . English planter family," and amuses

Djuna Barnes—she makes a striking guest appearance when the narrator does odd jobs for her—with its "antebellum echo." The narrator's first name also amuses Miss Barnes because of its "contemporary Dixie-cup quality," and she calls him Mr. D. "Darryl Pinckney" would fit the bill here, but our narrator is determined on a Proustian indirection, and we are not to learn any more except that he admits to a certain "goofiness" in his name. Delmore Schwartz is reported as saying, "Delmore Schwartz, what a beautiful name!" as if he had just found it, or as if someone had just made it up.

This silence is not trivial, since the case, I take it, is exemplary as well as individual. Our narrator, perhaps like many others, is not entirely a person. To be a person he would have to see himself, not only the dazzling masks he employs; and the self he would see would be, among other things, undeniably black. He has a dream in which he joins the Vienna Boys Choir, but in the dream he sees only the uniform because he can't put a black face and hands into that angelic and sanitized vision. It's not that he denies his blackness or is ashamed of it—although there are moments when he comes close to that—it's that he cannot accept the drastic simplifications the acknowledgment of blackness seems to imply. He sees his color as an unmanageable and unrefusable legacy, not who you are but something you can't not have. The same goes for any color, we might say, but the rewards are better for whites, and the chance of complacency infinitely greater. The narrator much admires his friend Bargetta because without in any way denying her color she takes "the black experience" as "just so much light opera." But that too is a way of being marked by what you wish to reject; an entangled sort of freedom.

What our narrator wants is an exemption from the human connection which will nevertheless allow him to be a nice guy, and to do his bit (now and again) for the right cause. The most courageous thing in this book is his recognition of this desire as a long, debilitating fallacy. There is wit and grace in the recognition too. "I would rather have lived with the Murdstones," the narrator says in his David Copperfield phrase, "than be needed by anyone." And later: "Now I am sorry I went to such lengths not to be of much use to myself just so no one would be able to ask anything of me. To have nothing to offer was not, after all, the best way to have nothing to lose." This is a more than chastising thought; it is also the point at which style drops all disguise and turns to limpid understanding. "I didn't like the togetherness that expressed itself as suspicion," the narrator comments, and there are all kinds of togetherness which many of us would be very keen to refuse. But then terrible beauties might be born without us, and we could find ourselves regretfully saying, with Pinckney's narrator, "Now I miss those whom injury made gracious and also those who simply uglied up and died." (pp. 13-14)

Michael Wood, "Easy Living," in The New York Review of Books, *Vol. XXXIX, No. 6, March 26, 1992, pp. 13-14.*

Esther B. Fein   (essay date 9 April 1992)

[*In the following essay, based on a conversation with Pinckney, Pinckney discusses the process of writing his first novel and his resistance to being categorized exclusively as a spokesman for middle-class African-Americans.*]

The narrator of Darryl Pinckney's debut novel *High Cotton* is clearly a refraction, if not a reflection, of the author. The anonymous narrator is a young black man, like Mr. Pinckney, raised in Indianapolis by educated parents who were the children of educated parents. His grandfather, like Mr. Pinckney's own, was a graduate of Brown and Harvard who became a minister. He wears thick glasses, is a bit of an Anglophile and graduated from Columbia, like Mr. Pinckney.

And the narrator, like the author, is in search of what being black means to him, both practically and in a way so integral it is almost genetic, but neither is looking for what being black means to anyone else.

"I never wanted this book to be identified as this statement about the black middle class," Mr. Pinckney said in a recent interview at his publisher's office in New York.

> I think too often people have read novels by black authors looking to see who has the true interpretation and who is defining the black experience. And if someone wrote about the black middle class it was seen as being at the expense of blacks in another class. I don't want to come off like a black neo-con in the book, but at the same time I'm not a cultural militant. I don't believe in black agreement. I don't think I have to.

It seems an unavoidable and mixed blessing that certain authors by dint of their backgrounds become, without effort or intent, symbols, voices of their generations or their people. They may be hailed as brilliant writers, but whether they are gay, black, young or Hispanic, they are also read as windows onto other worlds.

David Leavitt's books, for example, have been praised for their writing, but he is not thought of as just a writer: he is a gay writer. Sandra Cisneros's stories reveal the lives of Mexican-Americans and in the process have turned her into a Hispanic literary spokeswoman. Jay McInerney and Bret Easton Ellis wrote about the young and the hip and quickly came to represent the people they portrayed.

The mantle is at once sought after and unwanted. It can draw attention to authors, but it can also burden them with a perceived social responsibility they may not want.

Mr. Pinckney is a likely candidate for such symbolism, but he rejects it. He may be young, black and educated, and he may explore all of those parts of himself in his autobiographical novel, but his book derives as much from Dostoyevsky and Colette, he said, as it does from James Baldwin and Zora Neale Hurston.

It's not that Mr. Pinckney denies the influence black writers have had on him or that he backs away from the subject of race and racism. He credits Baldwin as being "a big part of my growing up" and speaks reverently about Hurston. *High Cotton* begins with the narrator saying, "No one

sat me down and told me I was a Negro," leaving no question that blackness is the very territory Mr. Pinckney intends to explore.

But Mr. Pinckney, at 38 years old, is also a literary critic of considerable regard, and he contributes regularly to *The New York Review of Books*. He wants his book to be testimony not only of his race but of his devotion to literature as well.

"The book you try to write is really in some funny way a love letter to the books you've loved," Mr. Pinckney said.

> You want in your book to honor literature as an idea. You want to write for literature, for other books. It's not that you can be these other books or that you have an ambition to be them, but they find their way into your writing consciousness. I don't really think you write for an ideal reader or audience you can describe according to a code. I don't think that's the way to do it, because someone's always going to be ticked off, including yourself.

Critics have praised *High Cotton* as witty, ironic and intelligent. If the narrator is Mr. Pinckney, then he has described himself well. He is shy and observant, "free and complex," as he writes in the book. Speaking about his Grandfather Eustace and family stories from the "Old Country," meaning the South, the narrator is neither sentimental nor confessional, and neither is Mr. Pinckney when he speaks of his family history.

He said the book was not born of some family tradition of stories passed on from father to son but from stories "that happened to be in the air" in his family, some apocryphal, he is sure, others real.

"I don't really know what people mean when they talk about oral culture," he said. "I don't really recognize that thing of sitting on the porch and someone is telling stories. I didn't have it as a child because adults didn't talk to children."

In an overly polite home, he took in the world around him and filed away amusing and insightful details that give the book its humor and candor, from a description of Uncle Castor, a jazz musician who "drank coffee with a cube between his teeth, wiped his hands with a soft handkerchief that he tucked up his left sleeve," to his recollections of a civil rights march he went to as a boy where there were "sunburnt men with toothpicks and milkshake straws rotating like cranks in front of their thin lips."

Despite the wealth of material he had collected and absorbed since his childhood, Mr. Pinckney struggled for 10 years in the terrifying terrain between conceiving the idea for his book and creating it. In that time, he worked for a publishing firm, began writing reviews, received several grants and moved to Berlin.

"I learned that the hardest thing about fiction is starting," he said.

> You have to have some idea and some idea of where you are going. In nonfiction the occasion is there. In fiction, it's for you to find. And actu-

ally once you think you've figured it all out, the process changes everything. I mean, the idea you have in your head when you start is always layered over, things get lost. Maybe good things.

It's never entirely what you had in mind or you're worried that its not as good as you would have liked for it to have been. Just line by line things. Word changes. They always say a book is not finished, it's just abandoned, and part of that is letting other people make of it what they do, seeing in it what they see. You can't control how people interpret what you've done and maybe you shouldn't try. Or maybe it's a good thing that people can feel very differently about it.

(pp. C17, C26)

Esther B. Fein, "A Writer, but Not a Black Everyman," in The New York Times, *April 9, 1992, pp. C17, C26.*

Hilton Als   (review date 18 May 1992)

[*In the following review, Als discusses* High Cotton's *themes of personal identity and race and praises the novel's humorous and detached style.*]

For years before the appearance of his first novel, **High Cotton,** I read, over and over again, [Pinckney's] essays, the majority of which appeared in *The New York Review of Books.* These essays were models of reasonableness on the "hot" subject of difference. Discussing, in the main, African-American writers prominent in the historical field (Jean Toomer, Zora Neale Hurston, Claude McKay, Langston Hughes, Countee Cullen, James Baldwin, Ishmael Reed), Pinckney addressed his collective subject with intelligence and grace. Here was a critic enthralled by words, intent on discovering the writer's meaning. Toomer, Hurston, Baldwin, Reed—they were writers first, Pinckney argued, whose blackness, politics and flesh and blood made history through their language. With his fine critical intelligence, Pinckney furrowed the historical field. Writing of everyone from Hughes to Baraka, he created a "geographic." What lessons as a writer of fiction would he be able to take from what he had charted?

In his elegiac essay on Baldwin written shortly after the writer's death, Pinckney connected me to the specialness of his reading of Baldwin's work by widening the parameters of my own:

> I do not think I am alone when I say that for young blacks Baldwin's candor about self-hatred was both shocking and liberating. A message slid under the cell door. . . . If there was no acceptable version of himself as a black man, he would have to invent one.

Pinckney's **High Cotton** is a message slid under the cell door. In this case, the cell is blackness as defined by the family, replete with the burden of history and his own personal privilege.

"No one sat me down and told me I was a Negro," begins the nameless narrator in the aptly titled first chapter, "The New Negro." "There was nothing to be afraid of as long as we were polite and made good grades. After all, the future, back then, assembled as we were on the glossy edge of the New Frontier, belonged to us, the Also Chosen." The Also Chosen to whom the narrator refers are a family of college-educated blacks. And, as critic Michael Wood has pointed out, "also . . . hints at a special destiny of election and oppression, a second Jewry." This "election" is what Pinckney describes with mastery. He begins doing so where the brown page of ancestry curls, and on that page, embossed in gold, is Grandfather Eustace's name.

Grandfather Eustace—a graduate of Harvard, clergyman, member of W. E. B. Du Bois's Talented Tenth (i.e., black elite)—represents the burden of race and class consciousness the narrator would like not so much to disavow as disaffect. The narrator prefers to observe rather than submit to feelings Grandfather Eustace's experience as the penultimate race man provokes. The narrator would like to be a New Negro (a phrase devised during the Harlem Renaissance by philosopher and Talented Tenth disciple Alain Locke) but a contemporary one, which is to say unlike Grandfather, whose taking of the high road through life, knowing he made the journey in a black body, culled "the chronic dread that maybe he wasn't good enough."

For what? To withstand "people who moved away from you at the movies, tried to short-change you at the new shopping mall" on one side of the wall and, on the other, those elderly relatives for whom one learned to hold one's "Vaselined head high." The image of the "correct" Negro who achieves "just like white boys" in the dead groves of academe, in his career—what can his image mean in a world that does not see him, a world that is implacable to the fact of his existence, cruel regardless of his caste? In a political world in flux, as the narrator's Indianapolis of the late fifties and early sixties is, when **High Cotton** begins, white people, seemingly, may even have power over the Lord (Grandfather's field; Grandfather's terrain). Could they stop His truth from marching on? Perhaps. Because "until His truth made it as far as restricted Broadripple Park, you did not go swimming." No baptism for the willing.

Of course, the narrator's continual questioning of Grandfather, his lore, his name, his image, as the children say, an attempt to deal with how the black man speaks, is a theme not particularly well-mined in Afro-American literature. (Perhaps the most notable example of it as a specific issue to be explored is playwright Suzan-Lori Parks's *The Death of the Last Black Man in the Whole Entire World.*)

In much of Afro-American literature, the patriarch is generally absent (Bigger's father in Wright's *Native Son*), a lout (Mister in *The Color Purple*) or a source of degradation and abuse (anything by Gayl Jones). The historical field rarely contained a presence that I recognized as being, potentially, myself. Not so for Pinckney, who looks to those elders less for validation than for background relief: He is fascinated by the sheen of questions such as, How does a son speak his father's name? Is it his own? Or something different? Baldwin has written around this subject, of course: "The [Negro man] has never . . . owned anything, not his wife, not his house, not his child, which could not, at an instant, be taken from him . . . by the power of white people. This is what paternalism means."

High Cotton's narrator does not even want to own himself: His existence can be viewed as a commodity; his future has already been bought. "The future was something my parents were either earning or keeping for my two sisters and me, like the token checks that came on birthdays from grandparents, great-uncles, great-aunts." Launched into *his* era of the New Negro, when his family moves to a white suburb in 1966, the narrator devises or believes he has devised a protective screen between himself, blackness and the burden of history. "No one knew who I was, and what I was I set aside every morning at 7:45." He may disavow race but not his privilege. He is constantly compiling lists of black Also Chosen achievement—"six guys in the House of Representatives, one man in the Cabinet"—an activity it would be impossible not to note, given the assumption he will achieve some kind of distinction, too. But as what? "Free and complex," he drifts to Columbia University, far away from the hissing of suburbia's summer lawns, to the eventual sense that, not unlike Grandfather Eustace, "I did not want people to have the usual idea about me." But these ideas of others about one—do they not in part comprise a self? And what of one's own sense of authenticity? "I wasn't real but everyone else was, a comfortable resignation of the self that was also useful as a sort of certificate of exemption. But one thing about the real world, if you aren't careful it will tell you what you are and just how low you stand." Pinckney makes his narrator's language drift, circularly, always back to the question of the self, against a backdrop of events that are sometimes sad, always lyrical, generally amusing.

As a black militant with little regard or capacity for terror, what with his ever-present thick glasses and Anglophilia, the narrator joins the Heirs of Malcolm, a wonderfully imagined portrait of a slightly less militant, more inert version of the Black Panthers, where he researches "real" blackness. And to what end? His joining the Heirs was not unlike his parents' and grandparents' trucking on over to the N.A.A.C.P. to register *their* blackness. The narrator would never admit this because "I simply refused to see myself through his eyes," he says, referring to Grandfather Eustace, the model of the correct. "He had not a clue as to how free and complex I thought I was about to become . . . and how much a prisoner of the predetermined forces in black history I considered him to be."

Since ***High Cotton***'s narrator was born into a position of relative privilege, he must speak of oppression from the fringes. But this distance allows him to see how oppressive history can be as well. Throughout the book, he is pulled between inclusion in one faction of his society (the Also Chosen) and exclusion from most others because of it. By not naming the narrator, Pinckney asks, via Ralph Ellison, Can one be enslaved by history, be "different" from that monolith, The Negro? And how does one begin? With Grandfather:

> The old-timers boasted of their ability to bug you from the grave, saying one day you'd want to talk to them and they wouldn't be there anymore. . . . Your dearest reminded you of the

problem you would never, never get away from. However, escape I did, the burden of consciousness was lifted from my round little shoulders, and for a while there I was gorgeously out of it. . . . Grandfather Eustace was the Emperor of out-of-it, yet he was also a distinguished man who tried, in his way, to answer all the questions. . . . I spent much of my life running away from him, centripetal fashion, because he was, to me, just a poor old darky.

This portrait of Grandfather as darky is not revolting but necessary. Children begin to define themselves by reacting to what family members decree their lot to be: Negro or not, Also Chosen or not. The form of the reaction depends on the child. For one as grotesquely well-bred as the narrator of ***High Cotton,*** bookish and alone, taught to hold his Vaselined head high, refuge and even revenge can be found in wit, a mute rejoinder sounding in the head as Dad or Grandfather lectures on and on about responsibility-as-identity.

Pinckney's wit—distanced, learned—saves him, time and again, from first-novel sentimentality and self-absorption. Such nonwriting supported by nonthinking never appears in ***High Cotton.*** Pinckney elevates despair to the lyrical. From his earliest days in Indianapolis to eventually visiting Grandfather's home, "the Old Country" of the South, Pinckney's narrator will not escape from knowing his name in the end:

> One day—if it comes—I may be someone's old darky, exercising my fictitious cultural birthright to run off at the mouth, telling someone who may insist on being called a Senufo-American how in my day so many—black, white and other—were afraid of black teenagers in big sneakers. . . . I will be on my feet and the Senufo-American will be suicidal to get away from me, as I sometimes felt in the presence of Grandfather. . . . I may elect myself a witness and undertake to remember when something more important than black, white and other was lost.

That loss may be inevitable, but writing one's name beautifully anyway is what ***High Cotton*** is about. The novel is a *bildungsroman* that moves, albeit in "centripetal fashion," within a strict narrative line. Each of its twelve chapters begins a set of entirely new technical problems that Pinckney presents as questions about tone, mood, the representation of the narrator's truth or lack thereof. While these units are seemingly independent of one another, this is deceptive. One must rely on the author's absolute but unobtrusive control over his material, and his depiction of the narrator's sensibility, to realize just how much of a whole ***High Cotton*** is.

From the book's beginning, when we are introduced to Aunt Clara, a "high yellow" who is "as obsessed as Thomas Jefferson with the 'algebraical notation' of blood mixture," and Uncle Castor, a jazz musician who is Grandfather Eustace's brother and who "sailed on the Ile de France" and made "the Dolly Sisters laugh," ***High Cotton*** is, if anything, about the examination of character and the manner in which character is observed: What can one learn? Does this observation help to create a new self or avoid old mistakes?

As the narrator moves on to New York, where he meets Bargetta, "my only black friend at school [Columbia]," and especially later, working briefly for Djuna Barnes, language itself becomes a character in **High Cotton.** The people he prefers to observe are enthralled by the transformative power of words as well. And it is in language—avoided, created, experienced—that history can be spoken. Pinckney's author strains to avoid that history, but finds his voice in its bedrock on a return visit to the Old Country of Grandfather Eustace's youth. In the end is his beginning. An elegy will always speak the truth. What Pinckney has given him is the voice needed to write his name in the field of existence. (pp. 667-70)

> Hilton Als, "Word!" in The Nation, *New York, Vol. 254, No. 19, May 18, 1992, pp. 667-70.*

Adam Mars-Jones   (review date 14 August 1992)

[*Below, Mars-Jones faults Pinckney's language in* High Cotton *and the undefined, detached nature of the novel's protagonist.*]

On page 48 of Darryl Pinckney's novel [**High Cotton**], which has been highly acclaimed in America, the young narrator is told by a playmate that his grandmother is a witch. He replies, "So what, you're a black nigger and you don't have a television." On the next page, the narrator is hardly any older, but television is discussed in rather different terms: "Television passed on its pictures, the connecting tissue. The representations survived the subject and eventually overtook my own images, which were less durable than waxwork images of Black Life at the Smithsonian." A little bit of experience, remembered or invented, and a lot of analysis, overlaid on it, as if the registers didn't clash; that is the dismaying pattern of **High Cotton.** A vivid spark every few pages, smothered before it can catch by a fire-blanket of nervous, insistent literary effect.

Pinckney's hero refuses an identity based on his skin colour. He goes against the grain of his time by choosing white culture over black, literature over politics. He lives by *The Way of All Flesh* rather than *Soul on Ice.* People think he's a black separatist when he's really only shy.

This is a brave starting-point, no question about that. It is also where Pinckney sticks for 300-odd pages, though his narrative leaps selectively forward through the 1960s, 70s and 80s. His narrator must be one of the least self-revealing in literature. Of his grandfather and great-aunts he tells us much, of his parents little, of himself virtually nothing. He may be in rebellion against identity politics, but the result seems to be not freedom from politics, only loss of identity.

When he is employed by a publisher, he gives elaborate accounts of office life that don't directly involve him. If he has friends, he passes on their stories about someone he doesn't himself know (one Dee Dee Beane in particular), in preference to anything more immediate. Borrowing other people's ancestors, as it is described at one point,

sounds an attractively liberating notion, but it can also be a euphemism for rejecting yourself and your own.

The narrator's inauthenticity shows up, as it must, in the language he chooses. In passing on family stories, he can't help but denature them: "Great-grandmother sucked her dental bridge and said that Grandfather's revelation, his maiden sermon ventilated before the sinners of Yamacraw, had about it, like everything else he did in those mongrel years, a touch of the psychotic." This sentence of reported speech defies any attempt to reconstitute the original, from which the words "psychotic", "ventilated" and "mongrel", in descending order of certainty, were presumably absent. But what are you doing when you pass on someone's utterances while denying the voice in which they were made? You sacrifice the authenticity of experience to an illusory authority of register.

Aunt Clara has a less muffled access to the reader:

> She was proud that Mattiwilda Dobbs had sung at my mother's wedding, that a Washington cousin's collection of poems had been reviewed in the *New York Evening Post* before the Depression silenced him, proud even of his parting remark that Jefferson must have had her in mind when he said he had yet to find a black who uttered a thought above the level of plain narration.

The last part of this sentence is kept a characteristic number of removes from the narrator—it's only a quotation from Jefferson with which, way back when, a Washington cousin teased Aunt Clara—but it is likely to haunt a reader toiling through a book which has so morbid a fear of direct statement, and is so convinced that unadorned language amounts to a relapse into the primitive.

A typical sentence will fall starkly into two halves, one plain and one fancy, of which the fancy half will serve no purpose beyond the not being plain: "She hated it that Grandfather had a family, connections she couldn't do anything about, those extraneous mouths round the soup of the evening, beautiful soup". Literary language here is not so much a vehicle for perception as a certificate of exemption—as if black life, uncertificated, could have no dignity or interest.

The narrator places whole areas of his life in a prose oubliette where they can only be guessed at. We don't learn he has been in trouble with the law until Grandfather alludes to it, as if this narrator suffered from a neurological deficit that prevented him from remembering things unless reminded by another:

> He didn't have to spell out which crimes he was referring to. The true bill I returned against myself included grand theft auto, reckless endangerment and perjury. I went soggy inside at the memory of the tears and the smashed metal and squad-car lights, the two trucks and the lettering on the lawyer's door. Luckily, my two joy rides and destruction of three automobiles had not ended in jail or in terrible injury either to myself or others.

This is downright confessional by the narrator's standards, but the moment passes and these dramatic incidents aren't referred to again. Nor can he bring himself to tell us who cried those strangely abstract "tears".

Perhaps joyriding seems too ethnic to be acknowledged more fully, too much of a rite of passage to be dwelt on by someone who denies belonging to the peer group which claims him. But sexuality, which can hardly be described in those terms, is repressed even more thoroughly than joyriding. When the narrator moves into a Manhattan apartment in 1976, he mentions in passing: " . . . the nights of the wide bed, of the mattress large enough to hold the combat of two, were definitely over". His first reference to such nights is the announcement that they are over. This is as close as he comes to acknowledging the existence of desire.

The narrator's best black friends, at one stage of his life, are Bargetta, a sexy woman, and Gilles, a campy gay man, but he goes to great lengths to establish that neither of them would choose to sleep with someone black. Fine, that makes it clear that neither would desire him, but does he desire either of them? Is it too hideously crass to want, in a first-person novel, some tentative twinge of connection with a body—that is, the narrator's own.

Another question that is likely to occur to the reader is: what's the narrator's name? We know, indirectly, some of its characteristics. When the narrator does odd jobs for Djuna Barnes, his employer meditates on its elements: "Miss Barnes thought my given name, with its contemporary Dixie-cup quality, ridiculous, and my surname, with its antebellum echo, only barely acceptable. I had to admit that it had the goofiness of a made-up name." The reader is here forced to conjure up a name and is offered no alternative to the one on the book's dust-jacket and spine: Darryl Pinckney.

A similar game has been played earlier in the book: "that giant silkscreen of the once-fugitive professor of philosophy, the then-captive gap-toothed beauty with an Afro like the lunar corona". If that phrase doesn't summon up the name "Angela Davis", then it has failed. But what would be lost, exactly, by writing "my poster of Angela Davis"? Identity in **High Cotton** is always a matter of default, something you lack the strength to go on denying rather than anything less hangdog.

To invent is to lie—true enough. To testify is to make yourself vulnerable—also true. Yet anyone who writes in the first person must take one of those risks, usually both of them.

In two passages in particular, **High Cotton** gives something like an explicit account of itself. The first is characteristically tortuous:

> The ledger of how to be simultaneously yourself and everyone else who might observe you, the captain's log of travel in the dual consciousness, the white world as the deceptive sea and the black world as the armed galley, gave me the comic feeling that I was living alongside myself, that there was a me and a ventriloquist's replica of me on my lap, and that both of us awaited the intervention of a third time, the disembodied me, before we could begin the charade of dialogue.

Why would Pinckney or his narrator be expecting to find identity in a state alienated beyond alienation? Why would personal truth lie outside the body?

The other passage, which occurs just before the end of the book, is more direct:

> I minded the strict rules of conduct and the tribal code that said that I, as a black, had a responsibility to help my people, to honor the race. Now I am sorry that I went to such lengths not be of much use to myself just so no-one would be able to ask anything of me. To have nothing to offer was not, after all, the best way to have nothing to lose.

This voice is less furiously abstract than the norm for **High Cotton,** disembodied mainly in the sense that it comes from nowhere. Nothing up to this point has prepared for this note of regret, a virtual retraction of the novel's premisses.

Adam Mars-Jones, "Other People's Identities," in The Times Literary Supplement, *No. 4663, August 14, 1992, p. 17.*

Jane Shapiro
After Moondog

Shapiro is an American novelist.

INTRODUCTION

After Moondog traces the tempestuous relationship of Joanne and Willie over a span of twenty-five years. After meeting on a New York City street in 1965, the two marry and begin a family. Throughout their marriage, they grapple with such matters as infidelity, aging grandparents, and their teenagers' experiments with sex and drugs. Although they divorce, neither Joanne nor Willie are able to disentangle themselves from each other's lives and they eventually reconcile. "We feel things will work out," Joanne states at the end of the novel. "We'll try, and we can probably do it: raise the kids, grow up ourselves, and stay together—be a family. People do this all the time; it can't be beyond Willie and me." *After Moondog* is considered a domestic drama that accurately and movingly portrays such problems associated with relationships and family life as lack of communication, restlessness, and jealousy. While *After Moondog* has been occasionally faulted for its weak plot, most reviewers have praised the work's irony, imagery, and realistic dialogue.

CRITICISM

Kirkus Reviews   (review date 15 April 1992)

[*In the following review of* After Moondog, *the critic praises Shapiro for her realistic portrayal of marriage and divorce.*]

Just when you thought you never wanted to read one more suburban divorce saga, Shapiro's wry and affectionate first novel, [*After Moondog*], comes along, bringing new life to an old story.

It all begins in 1965, when Joanne Green, age 20, stands on a New York City street corner talking to a local character named Moondog and a law student, William, whom she's just met. After their chat with Moondog, William and Joanne go out for coffee. The rest, as they say, is history. It's a 25-year history that, superficially, could belong to many people: marriage, two children, a move to New Jersey, extramarital affairs, divorce, troubles with adoles-

cent children and aging grandparents. But it's Joanne's version of this history—wise, darkly funny, never self-pitying—that makes it all her own. Without missing a beat, she can juxtapose the early days after William has moved out and she drifts from room to room looking for him "as if he were something I'd mislaid" with the experience of watching her cat get neutered by a veterinarian who's whistling "Moon River." She can appreciate her children's beauty as they grow into teenagers who live secret, dangerous lives, involving fast cars, dark nights, and not infrequent throwing up. She can forge a bond with her tiny, chic, pink-haired mother, Lolly, who does her best to keep everyone at arm's length. And finally, inevitably, there is William. The man she cannot stop fighting with. The man who is always there in times of family crisis. The man who used to tap dance around the kitchen. What Shapiro makes clear is that a marriage has no statute of limitations, and, if we're honest, no divorce is ever really final.

Scenes from a marriage, snapshot sharp—not even divorce can blur the focus.

> *A review of "After Moondog," in* Kirkus Reviews, *Vol. LX, No. 8, April 15, 1992, p. 496.*

Andrea Caron Kempf   (review date 1 May 1992)

[*In the review below, Kempf offers a favorable assessment of* After Moondog.]

Although [*After Moondog*'s] gutsy heroine must grapple with such tough issues as infidelity, divorce, aging parents, and teenage experimentation with sex, drugs, and alcohol, this outstanding first novel is never depressing. Resilient Joanne Green, picking her way throughout the minefield of modern existence, tries and generally succeeds in maintaining a sense of perspective. Shapiro's writing has a luminescent quality that imbues each episode—whether it's Joanne's trip with her former husband to visit his parents in Florida, an agonizing night when neither of her teenagers comes home until dawn, or a vigil at her mother's bedside after cancer surgery—with a clarity of vision that makes the protagonist's experiences our own. *After Moondog* is a tragicomedy for our times.

> *Andrea Caron Kempf, in a review of "After Moondog," in* Library Journal, *Vol. 117, No. 8, May 1, 1992, p. 120.*

Sybil Steinberg   (review date 4 May 1992)

[*In the review below, Steinberg praises Shapiro's sympathetic characters and sensitive depiction of relationships.*]

A first novel of uncommon grace and substance, this story about a marriage and its consequences marks the debut of an assured writer and chronicler of the contemporary scene. The knowing and ironic narrative [of *After Moondog*] spans 25 years, opening with a prologue in which narrator Joanne Green meets William, the man she will marry. It is 1965; they are both talking to Moondog, the New York street character who wore a Viking helmet and stood on the corner of 54th Street and the Avenue of the Americas for many years. Recalling the moment, Joanne says, "I was 20 . . . still easily, routinely stunned by the beauty of the known world."

The 17 chapters that follow work as connected but discrete stories that take Joanne and William from the chaos and concentrated anger of the Vietnam era to the cynicism and emptiness of the Reagan years. Out of a marriage built on "supervening inordinate love" come two appealing children and a suburban life supported by William's law practice. But infidelities poison the air, and a divorce becomes sadly inevitable.

Shapiro captures the essence of nuanced family communications as well as that of life with teenage children, and her dialogue is frequently sidesplitting as well as deftly on the money. The particularly complicated resonance that can fill the relationships between married partners and their parents-in-law is hilariously done here, with Joanne's mother and William's father playing central roles in the family drama. But most important, Shapiro has created in Joanne Green a sympathetic narrator who offers appealing and unpretentious wisdom that is genuine and immediate; her nostalgia for what has been lost is the universal mourning for times past, for lives lived.

> *Sybil Steinberg, in a review of "After Moondog," in* Publishers Weekly, *Vol. 239, No. 21, May 4, 1992, p. 43.*

Amanda Vaill   (review date 5 July 1992)

[*In the following review of* After Moondog, *Vaill praises the work's imagery and dialogue.*]

In the 18th century William Hogarth painted a series of six pictures under the title "Marriage-a-la-Mode," depicting the stages of a fashionable marriage from love to its "Disastrous Consequences." In her funny, graceful, preternaturally assured first novel, *After Moondog,* Jane Shapiro also traces the course of a modern marriage; but instead of scenes entitled "In the Countess's Dressing Room," she treats us to "Not Telling the Children About the Divorce" or "Visiting the Ex-in-Laws in Florida."

Shapiro's narrator, Joanne Green, first meets her husband-to-be, William, on a Manhattan summer evening in 1965 when both are chatting with Moondog, the blind musician-composer who was one of the first celebrity street people. Soon William and Joanne have gone on to dinner, and their relationship assumes its inevitable shape: "On the way out of the coffee shop, passing the register, he held my forearm, too tight; I tugged it away and he looked injured: already we were a couple, with problems."

Joanne and William marry, move to a tidy suburban town, and have two precocious children, Zack and Nora. William opens a law practice, Joanne teaches "bad boys who couldn't read" at a training school for juvenile offenders. Although they still share moments of intimate hilarity, constructing imaginary scenarios in which their friends or families do wildly improbable things (a favorite involves William's father advising President Ford on foreign policy and cold cuts), something has gone subtly wrong between them. Suddenly there are pointless quarrels, resentful silences and sly insults, rebuffs and evasions.

Joanne has an affair with a married professor of economics with whom she has virtually nothing in common. When it ends, she and William try counseling with two therapists called Bonnie and Earl. It's a futile attempt: All Bonnie and Earl can provide is material for William and Joanne's impersonations of them. Soon Joanne inadvertently traps William into an admission of infidelity, and the marriage is officially over—although they can't bring themselves to break the news to the children until after William has already paid a month's rent on the apartment he still hasn't moved into.

Joanne moves on, or tries to. There's a bleak, lonely period in which she sleeps all day and suffers her first New Year's Eve alone. But she pulls herself together; visits her mother (who has a punk hairdo and Ungaro suits and a townhouse in Boston); teaches at the training school; takes

Zack and Nora to stay with William's parents in Florida. Perversely, although they are divorced, she finds it impossible to become unmarried from William. After he moves out they sleep together, furtively, when they think no one will know. Later they stay with William's father when his mother is in the hospital; still later they will share a motel room when they go to Zack's college graduation.

Time passes. The children grow into "tall, slender, competent people" who spend hours "blow-drying their marvelous hair" when they're not out all night with their friends or speaking to their mother in tones of amused tolerance. Joanne's mother's husband dies, William's mother dies, John Lennon dies. Joanne starts writing a book about families, and she acquires a new lover, Ewing, a Southern psychiatrist who has a problem making commitments. They spend their first date in an emergency room, and it's all downhill from there.

After Moondog has a haunting permanence: Images, bits of dialogue, stay with us long afterwards; characters seem to have a reality beyond the pages where they appeared. To have achieved this at all is rare enough. For a novelist to manage it first time out is a real distinction, and proof that Jane Shapiro is a writer of unmistakable talent.

—*Amanda Vaill*

It's commonplace to say someone "writes like a dream"— but that's literally true of Jane Shapiro. Her eye for detail and her uncanny ear for dialogue give her prose the startling immediacy of dream narratives. Here are William and Joanne on the day he moves out: " 'What are you doing?' I cried. 'My mother gave me that desk! You can't take my desk!' 'I'm taking it.' 'You can't!' I cried, and pulled at his sweater sleeve—it was surprisingly soft, cashmere." The cashmere is a wonderful touch. Then there's the description of Joanne's friend Deenie Roseman, who "always greeted you as if you had been held hostage for months then debriefed in Germany and she was meeting you at Kennedy on the tarmac."

If there's a criticism to be made of this fine novel, it's that it has a dreamlike inconclusiveness: Things happen, but they don't seem to come to a point. Motivations are not always clear: Although we can see William and Joanne's marriage unraveling, we're never certain of what the cause is. Historical events unroll like screen credits superimposed on the novel's narrative. Although Vietnam and presidents Ford and Reagan and Patty Hearst and Amy Carter are alluded to, they're not connected to the reality the characters inhabit, and the references to them have the arbitrariness of dreams.

Still—again like a dream—*After Moondog* has a haunting permanence: Images, bits of dialogue, stay with us long af-

terwards; characters seem to have a reality beyond the pages where they appeared. To have achieved this at all is rare enough. For a novelist to manage it first time out is a real distinction, and proof that Jane Shapiro is a writer of unmistakable talent.

Amanda Vaill, *"Scenes from a Marriage,"* in Book World—The Washington Post, *July 5, 1992, p. 11.*

Elaine Kendall   (review date 24 July 1992)

[*In the following review, Kendall applauds Shapiro's accurate portrayal of American life during the 1970s and 1980s.*]

All through the 1960s, Moondog stood on the corner of 54th Street and Avenue of the Americas in his battered silver Viking helmet, wearing an assortment of blankets and assailing passers-by with a torrent of words.

Although there were other street people even then, none was as theatrical, none as exuberant. The characters in [*After Moondog*], like everyone else in that age of innocence, assumed that Moondog stood there because he enjoyed the ambiance. *Homeless* was still only an adjective, not a noun. New Yorkers seemed oddly proud of him; a shining symbol of the city's diversity. One day he simply vanished, leaving the streets to the lost, the mad and the menacing.

Joanne Green, the narrator of this wry and worldly novel, met her husband on Moondog's corner. William was a law student with a passionate interest in jazz; Joanne was wondering what she'd do after graduation. All that was quickly settled. They married; William became a lawyer, and the Greens moved to the suburbs and had two children.

Their story is a social history of the succeeding two decades, told in separate chapters that lock together in a tight, mortarless bond. Spare and terse, *After Moondog* speaks so directly to general experience that it seems almost interactive. Reading the story of Joanne and William, we supply the connections and the details, participating in spite of ourselves.

The opening chapter is followed by a fast forward to a time when the Greens' daughter, Nora, is 6; her brother, Zack, 7. The Vietnam War is finally over, but people aren't quite as relieved as they expected to be.

When major problems disappear, minor ones loom large. Joanne and William have become estranged "while we were looking the other way." Joanne is teaching remedial English at a school for juvenile delinquents, an occupation that offers a wonderful opportunity for her to display both wit and compassion.

Once in a while, they still amuse each other doing impersonations, but these occasions are separated by increasingly long stretches of tension. No explanation is necessary when Joanne acquires a lover.

Aside from his interest in dance, Dan is every bit as tedious as William, but in a different, more endearing way. He's a international economist, specializing in the theory of rational expectations, which Joanne interprets to mean "if you decide to do it, it's already done," a perfect precis of their affair. During this period, William is also having a fling, and the rift widens.

A divorce is embarked upon, divorce being the central metaphor of our time, perhaps even the central experience of our century. While no more or less excruciating than most, this one is more fascinating to read about, because the author has kept the acrimony to a minimum while emphasizing the ambivalence.

The children, Nora and Zack, have grown into delightfully sage and winsome adolescents, offering some geniunely astonishing glimpses of teen culture in a New Jersey university town during the early 1980s. We're reintroduced to Joanne's mother and William's father, who supply a generous measure of both pathos and humor to what otherwise might be a somewhat hermetic story line.

And that is essentially where *After Moondog* excels. The focus is kept firmly upon the particular, against an increasingly encroaching background of the general. Although Jane Shapiro's narrator modestly describes the book as "a story about us when we were young, more plausible than most," the "us" is an entire generation; maybe two, observed by a woman who manages to keep the subjective and objective in exquisite balance.

> *Elaine Kendall, " 'After Moondog': A Wry, Worldly Novel," in* Los Angeles Times, *July 24, 1992, p. E2.*

William Ferguson   (review date 2 August 1992)

[*In the following review, Ferguson, a novelist, discusses themes, narrative structure, and dialogue in* After Moondog.]

Jane Shapiro's first novel, *After Moondog,* is about a savvy, well-to-do young New Jersey couple who end their marriage but can't seem to disentangle their lives. Joanne and Willie Green's divorce seems like a pointless exercise, since they have a clear affection for each other and show themselves to be utterly compatible, even in their style of choosing lovers.

According to Joanne, who narrates throughout, the reason she and Willie married and had babies was to "deepen our sense of stability and own a small green lawn." This remark is not necessarily ironic. By the middle of the novel, miserable without her husband, Joanne comes to the startling conclusion that "married life is the only life there is"; during a happier time, she announces that "Willie and I have a project together: growing into our life."

On this emotional arbor, a family's history blooms. Joanne's quiet, self-deprecating, keenly observant intelligence leads us through the adolescence and young adulthood of Nora and Zack, the couple's agreeable children; various sea changes in the lives of parents, in-laws and friends; and Joanne's more intimate experiences as an unhappy lover, as a teacher at a school for troubled teen-agers and finally as a researcher—not insignificantly—into the anthropological implications of the traditional family dinner hour.

The novel's chapters and episodes (some of which have already appeared in *The New Yorker*) are often finely drawn and charming in themselves, yet they have no obvious thematic relationship to one another—except that they all in some way concern the Greens. But this seems to be precisely the point. In Ms. Shapiro's fictional world, nothing can finally cohere unless the family unit can be shown to be intact.

In what is presented as an environment of high sophistication and cultural advantage, it is curious that Joanne's male contemporaries should be so extremely awkward in their speech. Her brother-in-law, Tom, for example, attempts to cheer her up with the observation that "the maudlin is not your proper refuge"; Joanne's lover, an economist named Dan, is comically unable to express himself except in the sort of language he uses on the job ("to hope is to imagine the mean is sort of better than it is"). Willie, a lawyer, is by far the worst offender in this regard. "If I exit," he remarks to Joanne in a motel room, "that'd enhance your ability to settle in." Since the dialogue of Ms. Shapiro's other characters is at once beautifully crafted and utterly convincing, these other means of expression must be a parody—perhaps of individual conversational styles, more likely of an entire male generation's addiction to professional jargon.

For her part, Joanne does not seem to mind that her husband sounds like a book. We are told that she and Willie have the habit of telling stories together (indeed, the title of the novel refers to a street person they knew when they first met in New York, for whom they imagined a private life). Perhaps if Willie had had the floor, he would have made his own voice more credible. The notion of life as a narrative, in any case, and most especially of marriage as two people's attempt to tell a coherent story, is the dominant metaphor of *After Moondog.*

An excerpt from *After Moondog*

Willie started coming over. Two or three nights a week, after the kids went to bed I'd listen and wait, sitting on the couch like somebody in a waiting room, with Bonky in my lap. When they slept, I'd phone him. I'd walk out onto the front lawn and watch for his headlights. Standing on the frozen grass in the dark, I was an addict about to binge—queasy and eager and compelled, alone with my secret craving. By day we continued to complain about each other, exhaustively and sincerely, to our friends. We didn't tell any of them about our nighttime life: they couldn't take it. Our illicit congress was making us very lonely.

The car would wheel in and brake as if hitting a wall. He would drop his arm around my shoulders, then walk like a man in a hurry into his former home.

We didn't talk. We lay there and made love for long hours, elaborately and hopelessly. We woke at five and he tiptoed out. In four months I never saw his face in daylight.

When summer came, we were still married.

Jane Shapiro, in her After Moondog, Harcourt, 1992.

Sometimes, to be sure, the vehicle is far from grand. At a crucial point in the novel, Joanne is filling in a crossword puzzle; she is doing this, she says, so that when she finishes she will have "a whole completed thing that will not change." Beyond its stylish facades, *After Moondog* appears to be that most enduring of items: a love song to traditional marriage.

William Ferguson, "Married Life Is the Only Life There Is," in The New York Times Book Review, *August 2, 1992, p. 11.*

Carol Anshaw   (review date 16 August 1992)

[*In the following review of* After Moondog, *Anshaw praises Shapiro's use of language and imagery.*]

The book reviewer is always at the rail holding a longshot bet, hoping to be astonished by the unexpectedly wonderful book, the writer of uncommon grace. *After Moondog* provides just this sort of payoff. In its unassuming way, this novel-in-stories manages to be stylish and resonant and fiercely funny, even while staying on that most well-worn of fictional turf—the domestic drama.

The book's plot is negligible, barely locomotive enough to pull its protagonist, Joanne Green, through a predictable sequence of life events: she falls in love, marries, has children. The marriage falters, the children become unknowable adolescents, her mother contracts cancer, her latest lover leaves. In Shapiro's hands, though, this threadbare material becomes a complex narrative weave of modern female life, a fictive world reminiscent of Grace Paley's great, tricky stories of relationships that fail even as they succeed, of the subtle, terrible, sadly hilarious ways we short-circuit our relationships with everyone important to us.

Shapiro's greatest strength is her ability to capture in a phrase or two the essence of any moment, the net worth of any character. She can put this gift to significant use, drawing a portrait of parenthood in this harrowing end of the century or battle diagrams of marriage as equal parts ardor and will. Or she can employ a single brushstroke to catch a minor player in mid-air, as with this description of Joanne and her husband Willie arriving at a party, being welcomed by their hostess: "Deenie always greeted you as if you had been held hostage for months then debriefed in Germany and she was meeting you at Kennedy on the tarmac."

Much of the first part of the book documents the ways Joanne and Willie help their marriage along in its disintegration. She has an affair with an international economist; he has an affair with a former Miss Florida, which Joanne finds out about. "It occurred to me that I loved William and I wanted to stay with him. Or perhaps I wanted to stand up and slam this tall, doleful man against the side of the gazebo. His head would bounce, he would look amazed."

When they do eventually split up and he moves out, Joanne, of course, misses him terribly.

At night, after he'd been gone a day, I went out to the car and looked in, to see if he were lying in the back seat. It was dark. I pressed my face against the window. His suitcases would be hidden in the trunk or squashed down behind the steering wheel. He would be lying flat, breathing quietly, watching the perforations on the ceiling; patiently, pliantly waiting for me.

Willie's absence leaves Joanne alone in the wind tunnel of Nora and Zack's adolescence—a period of several years when her children become virtual Martians.

On the face of it, the kids had only grown, into tall, slender, competent people. But they were mysterious . . . . After school, at the health food cafe, Zack made sandwiches invented during the sixties; Nora helped run a theater program for tiny children, walking the kids to the bathroom, tying their masks onto their little faces, restraining the biter . . . doing the well-known, complex adolescent impersonation of people fully engaged with the daytime things. But what was becoming clear was: Everything happened at night.

This "everything" consists of costuming ("calculated shabby black") and attendance at concerts, then at parties featuring beer drunk from shoes (Shooting the Boot) and poured through funnels directly down the throat, along with "the usual seductive killer drugs, and a fluid called Liquid Lady. Nora and Zack told me about these events. Did their friends drink and take drugs? I asked. Zack said amiably, 'The bottles to be wary of are the ones that look like cologne.'"

For Joanne, the long nights become darkened waiting rooms, where she is held in suspension, imagining the worst—which her kids and their friends escape miraculously. "On a back road at the end of Halloween night, driving home from a party, at about ninety miles an hour, two kids rolled a car. They climbed out, stood up, vomited on their ghost costumes, and walked away in the moonlight."

Waiting for Nora and Zack's return is always a solitary state, an ex-husband not being readily at hand. "I dialed Willie, let it ring. He was out. I saw him in an expensive Parisian hotel, moist limbs entwined with those of a young woman in complex lingerie, while teenagers continued to terrorize me and grind up what remained of my hapless life."

Through every phase of living this hapless life, Joanne narrates her story with a mix of irony and jaunty despair. In her, Shapiro has created a protagonist for the VH1 generation, for everyone over 40 who has come through it with at least a few oldies lyrics and a sense of humor intact.

Carol Anshaw, "When the Kids and Their Lives Turn Mysterious," in Chicago Tribune, *August 16, 1992, p. 5.*

Donna Tartt
The Secret History

(Full name Donna Louise Tartt) Tartt is an American novelist, born in 1964(?).

INTRODUCTION

Variously characterized as a suspenseful mystery, a treatise on morality, and a comparative examination of classical and modern art and philosophy, *The Secret History* focuses on a close-knit group of affluent college students engaged in the study of ancient Greek with Julian Morrow, an eccentric scholar. Intrigued by the clique's aura of mystery and sophistication, the student narrator, Richard Papen, convinces Julian to accept him into the group and fabricates a wealthy upbringing to win the approval of his new friends. Richard gradually discovers that four of the group's five members have committed an unpremeditated murder during a midnight Dionysian ritual through which they attempted to achieve a violent and euphoric abandonment of the self. When the innocent member of the group discovers their secret, he is also murdered, and the remainder of the book focuses on Richard's involvement in the killing. Although some critics have faulted *The Secret History* for hollow characterizations and cumbersome literary references, most reviewers have deemed the work an outstanding achievement for a first novelist. Tartt has generally received praise for her elegant writing style, effective use of suspense, and erudite application of classical themes to a modern story.

CRITICISM

Martha Duffy (review date 31 August 1992)

[*Below, Duffy provides a generally positive assessment of* The Secret History.]

> What are you doing up here? said Bunny, surprised, when he found the four of us waiting for him.
>
> Why, looking for new ferns, said Henry.

Then, with Henry leading the ambush, Bunny's buddies push him down to his death in a ravine. A quick look

round for dropped keys or glasses. "Everybody got everything?"

This little shocker is just the beginning of [*The Secret History*], a long, ambitious first novel by a young Mississippian. The publisher has ordered up a 75,000-copy first printing. Director Alan Pakula (*Klute, All the President's Men*) has bought it for the movies. What Donna Tartt has attempted—and largely brought off—is a challenging combination of a mystery (will they get caught or won't they?), an exploration of evil, both banal and bizarre, and a generous slice of the world as seen by the author, a brainy graduate of Bennington who has mastered Greek and English literature and doesn't care who knows it. It all adds up to confidence verging on bravura.

The little band of murderous fern seekers are students at Hampden, a small, very liberal arts college in Vermont. Acute, cerebral and tasteful to a fault, the group have become acolytes of an eccentric Greek scholar who demands that what few pupils he takes study only his curriculum.

There is Henry, rich, seductive, depraved; Francis, a homosexual with a very convenient house in the nearby hills; Athena-like Camilla and her twin Charles. Charles drinks too much, but then they all do, including Bunny, the feckless, unreliable odd man out.

This cabal is crashed by the narrator, Richard Papen, a penniless transfer student who had taken some Greek. He is as close as the book comes to an objective center, but the device gets shaky because Richard is a facile, silly liar, boasting about an imaginary family oil well. He will do anything to be accepted by these sophisticates. Anything.

What he gradually learns is that four of the five, excluding Bunny, have already killed, in the course of what they are pleased to call a Greek bacchanal. A luckless farmer strayed into the path of their late-night revels, and, chitons aflap, fueled by booze and drugs, they butchered him. For Charles it was a doomed awakening of conscience. For Henry it was a revelation of quite another sort. Before, he explains to the perpetually horrified Richard, he "lived too much in the mind." After, "I know that I can do anything that I want."

Well, there is one necessity on Henry's agenda. Bunny—the unserious one, the blabbermouth, the buffoon—begins to suspect the quartet of the killing in the field. In general Tartt shows a superior sense of pace, playing off her red herrings and foreshadowings like an old hand at the suspense game. The book's only lag occurs in her needlessly elaborate effort to turn Bunny from a likable pest into someone obnoxious enough for Richard to want to kill (for the others, fear of detection is enough). The cause of Bunny's mounting hysteria, of course, is simple: he is going from suspicion to terror.

The Secret History offers the zest of the author's energy and the pleasure of seeing a young mind tackle classic forms. Is Vermont, or a microcollege, a stand-in for the author's native South? No, the shaggy, druggy ways of small schools around the country are sharply, and often humorously, captured here. But in its large-scale concept and its shell-game view of plotting, *The Secret History* distinctly evokes the Southern tradition.

> Martha Duffy, "Murder Midst the Ferns," in
> Time, New York, Vol. 140, No. 9, August 31,
> 1992, p. 69.

James Kaplan   (essay date September 1992)

[*In the following article, based on several interviews which Kaplan conducted, Tartt discusses various experiences from her childhood and college years that influenced the development of her writing career. Kaplan also briefly interviews several of Tartt's former college classmates, including Bret Easton Ellis, and praises* The Secret History *as "a book whose very essence is the survival of formality in a formality-starved era."*]

Donna Tartt, who is going to be very famous very soon—conceivably the moment you read this—also happens to be exceedingly small. Teeny, even. "I'm the exact same size as Lolita," she says. "Do you remember that poem from the novel?" She recites,

> Wanted, wanted: Dolores Haze
> Her dream-gray gaze never flinches.
> Ninety pounds is all she weighs
> With a height of sixty inches.

We're sitting over a country breakfast in Smitty's, a homey café in Oxford, Mississippi—site of the university, Ole Miss, and hometown of another Mississippi writer, name of Faulkner. Who may have won a Nobel, but whose books never, in his lifetime, made anything like the commercial splash Donna Tartt has already made with her first novel, *The Secret History,* published this month by Knopf.

Tartt taps her Marlboro Gold on the ashtray. She is a kind of girl-boy-woman in her lineaments, with lunar-pale skin, spooky light-green eyes, a good-size triangular nose, a high, pixieish voice. With her Norma Desmond sunglasses propped on her dark bobbed hair, her striped boy's shirt and shorts from Gap Kids (the only store whose ready-to-wear fits her), and her ever-present cigarette, she is, somehow, a character of her own fictive creation: a precocious sprite from a Cunard Line cruise ship, circa 1920-something. A Wise Child out of Salinger.

"I know a *ton* of poetry by heart," Tartt says, when I comment on her recital of the Nabokov rhyme. It's true. She has an alarming ability to simply break into passages, short or long, from her favorite writing. She quotes, freely and naturally, from Thomas Aquinas, Cardinal Newman, Buddha, and Plato—as well as David Byrne of Talking Heads and Jonathan Richman of the Modern Lovers. And many others.

"When I was a little kid, first thing I memorized were really long poems by A. A. Milne," she says. "Then I went through a Kipling phase. I could say 'Gunga Din' for you. Then I went into sort of a Shakespeare phase, when I was about in sixth grade. In high school, I loved loved *loved* Edgar Allan Poe. Still love him. I could say 'Annabel Lee' for you now. I used to know even some of the shorter *stories* by heart. 'The Tell-Tale Heart'—I used to be able to *say* that.

"I *still* memorize poems," she says. "I know 'The Waste Land' by heart. 'Prufrock.' Yeats is good. I know a lot of poems in French by heart. A lot of Dante. That's just something that has always come easily to me. I also know all these things that I was *made* to learn. I'm sort of this *horrible repository* of doggerel verse."

Donna Tartt seems, in many ways, a figure from another decade: a small, hard-drinking, southern writer, a Catholic convert, witheringly smart, with an occluded past, sadness among the magnolias. Wasn't that Flannery? Or Carson? Or Truman, or Tennessee? Surely not a figure from the post-MTV generation. Yet here she is, not yet thirty, coming out of obscurity in Greenwich Village—where she lives with a cockatiel, Horace, and a pug, Pongo (and no television)—into supernova-hood, weighing in among the serious contenders. For *The Secret History* is, amid its vast entertainingness, an extremely serious book: a book whose very essence is the survival of formality in a formality-starved era.

It's commercially serious, too. In early 1989, Tartt's Bennington classmate and friend Bret Easton Ellis introduced her and her project (it was three-quarters done; she had an outline for the rest) to his agent, ICM honcho Amanda Urban. This was more than a favor: Ellis had been reading the novel, as it progressed, for six years, since he and Tartt were in their second year at college. He thought she had the goods. So did Urban. "She said, 'My God, it's incredibly well written—I can't stop turning the pages,'" Ellis recalls.

Urban accepted Tartt as an unsigned client; two years later, with the completed (866-page) manuscript in hand, Urban was able to whip up a bidding frenzy among several publishing houses. The winner, Knopf, paid $450,000 for the book (which it made back almost immediately, and then again, in foreign sales). Shortly thereafter, Alan Pakula's Pakula Productions paid another large sum for the privilege of attempting to turn the book into a motion picture. This is a book that was on boil long before it even hit the stores: so great was the demand for five-hundred-page advance reader's editions of *The Secret History* that Knopf had to print an unprecedented second run.

What's all the fuss? This: *The Secret History* is about a small, singular cadre of classics students at Vermont's Hampden College (a tiny ultra-liberal, ultra-artistic school not unlike Bennington) who, for the strangest of possible reasons, slay a stranger, and then one of their own. It is a huge, mesmerizing, galloping read, pleasurably devoured in a few evenings: a book which, unlike the vast preponderance of page-turners—or, for that matter, the vast preponderance of first novels—is gorgeously written, relentlessly erudite, and persistently (and quite anachronistically) high-minded. It is (the strangeness compounds) a murder mystery in which the two killings (and all sex scenes) take place offstage, and in which the only mystery is *why*—the who, what, when, where, and how all being known virtually from the word go.

> The snow in the mountains was melting and Bunny had been dead for several weeks before we came to understand the gravity of our situation.

Thus—deadpan, chockablock with beauty and portent—one of the classic first sentences of our vehemently anti-classical time.

But then, Donna Tartt is more than mildly fixated on things classical. As good a place to begin as any is the fact that she has a largish obsession, bordering on the cultic, with T. S. Eliot. The ringleader and chief malefactor in *The Secret History,* an eerily grave polymath called Henry Winter, comes from Eliot's hometown, St. Louis, has the same first name as Old Tom's brother, wears tiny, old-fashioned steel-rimmed glasses and "dark English suits and carrie[s] an umbrella (a bizarre sight in Hampden) and . . . walk[s] stiffly through the throngs of hippies and beatniks and preppies and punks with the self-conscious formality of an old ballerina."

Tartt's answering-machine message is the Man Himself, reading, solemnly, from "The Waste Land": "I see crowds of people, walking round in a ring. / Thank you. If you

> [*The Secret History*] is a huge, mesmerizing, galloping read, pleasurably devoured in a few evenings: a book which, unlike the vast preponderance of page-turners—or, for that matter, the vast preponderance of first novels—is gorgeously written, relentlessly erudite, and persistently (and quite anachronistically) high-minded.
>
> —*James Kaplan*

see dear Mrs. Equitone, / Tell her I bring the horoscope myself: / One must be so careful these days."

Indeed. Like Eliot, and like another idol, J. D. Salinger, Tartt is not at all averse to interest in her work. Period. When it comes to the perky, personal, prying tone of our time, her reservations are grave. The title of her book is not without autobiographical meaning. Her skittishness about being interviewed is formidable. But as Bret Easton Ellis (the co-dedicatee of *The Secret History*) will later tell me, with the rueful tone of One Who Knows, "You can't be Salinger and be represented by ICM."

One can do one's best, however.

Grenada, Mississippi, sits astride the Yalobusha River at the eastern fringe of the Delta, a sleepy, sunstruck southern town like many other southern towns, with a dead railroad depot (Illinois Central), a moribund square (where the Confederate monument still stands), and, outside of what used to be the center of things, two miles of new strip lined with bright prefab despair. Off the strip, time moves like molasses: children play in the dirt, big rusting Fords sit under carports, the kudzu creeps. In June, the air is like a hot sponge; the radio plays seventies rock and commercials for boll-weevil poison. Grenada is a town of small distinction, Mississippi-generic. It has produced a Miss Teen U.S.A. Mr. Borden, of Borden's milk, used to keep his polo ponies here. There was a yellow-fever epidemic in the nineteenth century. The Old Families die out or move on, or stay and gather moss. One of them, the Boushés, produced Donna Tartt's mother; her father's people were newer blood.

Don Tartt was an upwardly mobile small-town operator who went from working in a grocery store to owning a freeway service station to becoming a successful local politician. At one point he was president of the Grenada County Board of Supervisors. He and his wife, Taylor, a secretary for much of the time they were married, stayed together for two decades—on the evidence, not happy ones. They produced two daughters; the elder showed unsettling signs of precocity.

At an age when most girls her age were reading *Misty of Chincoteague,* Donna Tartt idolized Heinrich Schliemann, genius linguist and excavator of Troy. "When I was little," she says, "my grandmother gave me this book about archaeology, which was my favorite thing in the world. It was *not* a child's book. When I graduated from high school, one of the girls I had been in kindergarten with had a tape—her mother had brought a tape recorder to our kindergarten graduation. At Miss Doty's Kindergarten for Girls. They made us all stand and say what we wanted to be when we grew up. And when it was my turn, it was exactly my voice, except it was much higher-pitched. And I said, 'My name is Donna Louise Tartt, and when *I* grow up, *I* should like to be an ar-chae-ologist.' I was the only child that said *should*—all the other children said *would.* It was starting even then. Child is father to the man."

Memphis, a hundred miles north, may have been the big city, but Oxford, only half that distance away, was her beacon, especially during her adolescent years, when her insatiable hunger for learning had exhausted the resources of the Elizabeth Jones Library. Oxford had a good bookstore, and after shopping for shoes with her mother at Neilson's, she would pursue her self-education. She read and read, and listened.

"Something I think you're very conscious of growing up in the South is people who speak correctly and people who don't," she says. "George Orwell said, 'Englishmen are all branded on the tongue.' It's the same for southerners. I grew up around people who had wonderful, mellifluous voices; there's also that twangy cracker accent. And then you were also aware of black English. And the fourth thing that I was sort of *hyper*-aware of was—my mother read to me a lot when I was a little girl. The first book she ever read to me was *The Wind in the Willows,* which I still like. I read a lot of English children's books. And I was very conscious of the fact that Rat and Mole didn't talk the way that my mother talked, or that our housekeeper talked, or that my friends at school talked. I thought literature was English. Books seemed to speak to me in English accents."

She wrote her first poem at age five, lying on her stomach in front of the TV; she had to wait eight more years to be published, with a sonnet in a Mississippi literary review. By the time she was in high school, she was churning out the words in a promiscuous frenzy, winning prizes for her essays on patriotism and the dangers of alcohol, writing short stories about death. Then came college.

"Fall of '81 I came here, seventeen years old, looked like I was about twelve," she says. "And acted like I was about twelve. Went through rush my first week, and pledged. It was what you did, and I did it."

We're driving slowly among the neo-Colonial brick piles and live oaks and wide lawns of Ole Miss, where, surrealistically enough, hundreds upon hundreds of identically T-shirted nymphets twirl, march, and chant in sweetly hortatory voices: Mid-South Cheerleading Camp is in session. Which, surrealistically enough, Donna Tartt seems to have once attended.

We have decided to trespass in the sacred precincts, the plush powder-blue fastness of the Delta Rho chapter of the Kappa Kappa Gamma sorority at Ole Miss: Kappa House, stronghold of Southern Womanhood, inviolable

and pristine. This being summer, the place is cleared out. We tiptoe and whisper nevertheless, surrounded by the rustling presences of the Debbies and Tammies and Vonda Sues, the big blonde sunny girls born to marry Rhetts and Trents and live by the golf course and raise flocks of blond children and forever hold dear the Kappa ideal ("The Kappa is not an intruder upon life, / But rather an inner presence who seems to softly and naturally emerge . . . "). This is where Donna Tartt once stuffed the Sunshine Box—which her fellow Kappas would fill with sayings on scraps of paper, epigrams dear to their hopeful hearts, apothegms of uplift, treasured mots about life and lemons and lemonade—with vile sayings by Nietzsche and Sartre. "God is dead. . . . And we have killed him." "Hell is other people."

"Everybody knew it was me," Tartt says as we sneak up from the Kappa basement. "There was this dire meeting—they told me I had to confess, 'on your honor as a woman.' " (Did she? "Of course not," she replies indignantly.)

She laughs. "Here I was, this small, dark, thoughtful person among all these towering happy blondes. I mean, if you didn't dress up like Scarlett O'Hara to go to biology class, you were a total oddball. And I was. They were embarrassed by me. Their boyfriends would see me sitting around reading Ezra Pound cantos in the rain, and ask who this person was. And they'd have to grit their teeth and say, *'Oh, she's a pledge.'*

"I remember my first couple of weeks, eating in the Union by myself, reading Nietzsche. I was so happy. Not lonely. There were forty people in my graduating class in high school, and I had known them since kindergarten. You never saw anybody that you hadn't known your whole life—didn't know their whole family history. So it was very exhilarating to come here—you'd see people you didn't know, and they didn't know you.

"It seemed like it would be a good thing to work on *The Daily Mississippian.* I didn't really have very much in the way of newspaper articles to submit, so I gave in some short stories. And the fellow called me back into his office and said, 'These are great! These are wonderful!' And 'How old are you? Did you write these by yourself?' It was raining. And I reached in my pocket and got out this pack of Lucky Strikes. It was like, 'Oh my God—where did you *come* from?' "

"They said, 'We can't hire you to be on the paper, but this is still really good.' So I said thank you, and went off to sit in the Union by myself, and I was happy again. But without my knowing it, the guy at the paper had given a copy of one of my stories to Willie Morris. And I was in a bar at the Holiday Inn, and Willie came up to me and gave me his hand and said, 'Are you Donna Tartt?' And I said yes. And he said, 'My name is Willie Morris, and I think you're a genius.' "

Morris—former editor of *Harper's* and New York literary darling, author of *North Toward Home* and several other autobiographical books—is part of the third wave of Mississippi writers, Faulkner and Eudora Welty representing the first and second. If the state has always been desperately poor economically, it has been loaded literarily. And Donna Tartt is a new wave all by herself.

"On the one hand she was immensely grown-up; on the other hand she was a child," says Morris, then writer-in-residence at Ole Miss. "It was a very attractive combination. She was very elfin. Kind of a sufferer—I had the impression she wasn't very happy back at home in Grenada. And just *riven* with sensibility. An amazing writer. I was always so impressed by her powerful and evocative use of language—it got to me right off."

"Willie told me she was very good, and, man, she sure was," says fellow third-waver Barry Hannah, who admitted Tartt, as a freshman, to his graduate short story course. "She was *way* out ahead of all those graduate students." Hannah and I are sitting in the courtyard of an Oxford bar, a college hangout. Drink in one hand, Marlboro in the other, Tartt is at the other end of the table, being talked to by an intense man in a yellow suit and yellow golf hat. If she looked twelve then, she looks perhaps sixteen now. At the same time, she seems infinitely older than the college kids around us.

Inside the bar, the band crashes and booms; out here, the big frat boys and blonde coeds, their shining faces as uncomplex as the music, pack the terrace, smiling. Overhead, the purple-brown sky erupts periodically with the most amazing heat lightning I've ever seen: gigantic, reticulate, like something out of a particularly unsubtle horror movie. Mississippi summer. "People call me a star-maker," the handsome gray-haired Hannah says, sipping his tonic. "Shit, Donna made herself."

Later on, Tartt and I inch our way out of the packed bar, shouldering through the crush as the amplifiers, louder than loud, imperil our eardrums. We find ourselves outdoors. Suddenly she grabs my arm and breaks into a run, pulling me along, sprinting down the sidewalk as if her life depended on it. At first I don't understand, but then I see: this is, pure and simple, escape. The silent lightning carpets the sky.

The Secret History's narrator, Richard Papen, hails from the fictional and deadly Plano, California—"drive-ins, tract homes, waves of heat rising from the blacktop"—where his father runs a gas station and his mother is a secretary. Tartt is highly guarded (to say the least) about any relationship between the novel and her own life, but there is surely common ground between her own vision of an ornately southern girlhood amid colorful elderly aunts and wisteria-twined old houses, and Richard's accounts of staring at TV and being bored in flat Plano. One can only speculate on how it felt to arrive from Mississippi in Bennington, circa 1982, as Tartt did, after having transferred from Ole Miss at the urging of Willie Morris and others. "Hampden College, Hampden, Vermont," her book's protagonist intones. "Even the name had an austere Anglican cadence, to my ear at least, which yearned hopelessly for England and was dead to the sweet dark rhythms of little mission towns."

Richard wants to continue his studies in ancient Greek, but is told that the one man who teaches the subject—Julian Morrow, a brilliant aesthete with a possibly check-ered past, once an intimate of Eliot and Pound and Orwell and Sara Murphy—is a haughty eccentric who has only five students and will accept no more. And in fact he turns Papen down for his Greek class. But then, with a Horatio Alger–esque feat of intellectual pluck, Richard impresses some of Morrow's students with his knowledge of the subject, and is accepted into the fold.

And what a fold it is! Morrow's one demand is simple: that the new student take every course with him. This is not so much a class as a cult. But who, exactly, is the leader?

> His students—if they were any mark of his tutelage—were imposing enough, and different as they all were they shared a certain coolness, a cruel, mannered charm which was not modern in the least but had a strange cold breath of the ancient world: they were magnificent creatures, such eyes, such hands, such looks—*sic oculos, sic ille manus, sic ora ferebat.* I envied them, and found them attractive; moreover this strange quality, far from being natural, gave every indication of having been intensely cultivated. . . . Studied or not, I wanted to be like them. It was heady to think that these qualities were acquired ones and that, perhaps, this was the way I might learn them.

There is the aforementioned Henry Winter; the beautiful (and very close) southern twins Charles and Camilla Macaulay; the rich, thin, elegant neurasthenic Francis Abernathy. And then there is the doomed Bunny, Edmund Corcoran, a big "sloppy blond boy, rosy-cheeked and gum-chewing, with a relentlessly cheery demeanor" and a loud, honking voice with a Locust Valley–lockjaw upper-crust accent. Bunny is the sole nonintellectual in the bunch—in the end, in a way, this is why he is singled out and dispensed with—but otherwise he fits right in. They are all of them, Julian included, fabulous monsters: a very catalogue of Waspocratic quirk, with their pressed white shirts and dark suits and tea drinking and euchre playing and constant smoking and drinking, their insistence on using fountain pens and tossing off conversational sallies in classical Greek. They're something, this crowd—something out of Edward Gorey. There is about them more than a smack of the between-wars, oh-so-U, Fascist-friendly British elite, Sir Oswald Mosley and the lost Mitford sisters and their like. Not to mention Leopold and Loeb, and the bloody-toothed English schoolboys of *Lord of the Flies.* And Richard, the outlander, is their mascot and greatest admirer.

But these people do more than drink tea. Richard's admiration turns to worried awe when he learns that some members of the group, obsessed with divine madness and the losing of self, have had a bacchanal. Not just an orgy, mind you, in the sloppy post-Roman sense, but an actual mystic rite, complete with hymns, holy objects, and, at last, a sacred trance: "Torches, dizziness, singing. Wolves howling around us and a bull bellowing in the dark. The river ran white . . . the moon waxing and waning, clouds rushing across the sky. Vines grew from the ground so fast they twined up the trees like snakes." God, in the form of Dionysus, appeared to the celebrants. Certain sexual acts took place. And then, the *pièce de résistance,* a murder.

The group, finally, has become as close as close can be: united in blood.

[Tartt's characters in *The Secret History* are] **fabulous monsters: a very catalogue of Waspocratic quirk, with their pressed white shirts and dark suits and tea drinking and euchre playing and constant smoking and drinking, their insistence on using fountain pens and tossing off conversational sallies in classical Greek.**

—*James Kaplan*

It is Donna Tartt's ability to make us believe, utterly, in all this—at the moment of sacred insanity, we are at one with the celebrants. We would follow her tumbling, mellifluous prose anywhere. The best writers are necromancers, levitation their specialty. But it is human nature to think of mirrors and wires even at the moment of enchantment: where did these people come from?

"Hampden is *not* Bennington," Donna Tartt tells me, and it's tempting to believe her. We're walking around the Bennington campus on a cool gray day between terms, and even though there is about the place a certain flat creepiness consonant with the atmosphere of *The Secret History,* it's hard to reconcile it with the rapturous New England richness Richard Papen drinks in with all his senses. Bennington is tatty around the edges. First opened during the Depression, the school has never gotten out from behind the fiscal eight ball, despite the highest tuition costs in the country.

But it has never lacked for vitality—or decadence. Bennington in the early to mid-1980s was a pinnacle of something, a kind of omphalos of refined depravity, money and drugs and hormones and scholarship (formal and very much otherwise) all mingling in a supersophisticated soup. Bret Ellis, who published *Less than Zero* after his third year at Bennington, becoming world-famous even as he flunked his courses, memorializes the milieu in his second novel, *The Rules of Attraction.* The school color is, of course, black. And who else but Eric Fischl would be right for designing the school pamphlet: " 'Some of the chic jet-setting nihilistic Eurotrash who live off-campus, nude, standing around with dogs and fish. Welcome to Camden College—You'll Never Be Bored.' "

This isn't Hampden College. But even in the tiny real-life society of Bennington (five hundred students) there were sets and cliques and worlds apart, worlds through which the elfin, brilliant transfer student from Mississippi moved with ease. "I had lots of friends here," Tartt says. "I was one of the few people that kind of traversed boundaries."

"She was very headstrong, and very together," Bret Ellis recalls. "There was a lot of opportunity at Bennington for almost *Sybil*-like self-transformation. You'd see some girl from Darien, with her Ralph Lauren blouse and her hair in a blond bob—by midterm she'd have shaved her head and be shooting up. Donna was one of the few people there who was *really* exotic, in that she pretty much stayed the same. I remember seeing her at a Fling into Spring party, where everybody else was in black, in her seersucker suit, with a cigarette and a gin and tonic.

"Her room was a little bit of a salon. She and I, Jill Eisenstadt. Two writers named Mark Shaw and Orianne Smith. Donna gave what were supposed to be teas, but she had this little cabinet with liquor in it. We'd get totally shitfaced. Donna is the only person I know who can drink me under the table. I mean, she's this tiny person, and I'm really big, but at the end of an evening I'll be tap-dancing in the street and yodeling, and she'll be exactly the way she was at the beginning, not even slurring her words."

"Of all the people I knew well at Bennington, I knew least about her," another former classmate recalls. "She was very put-together, very controlled. One year at the end of term, a bunch of us had been up all night for days; I remember she calmed us all down by reading aloud from P. G. Wodehouse. And Donna was always *dressed.* She wore what was appropriate for the hour of the day. She dressed for dinner. She liked well-tailored boys' suits. If you went to her room at four A.M.—she was an insomniac—you'd find her sitting at her desk, smoking a cigarette, wearing a perfectly pressed white shirt buttoned to the top, collar studs, trousers with a knife crease."

"She was sort of a star early on—she was a big influence on me," says the novelist Jill Eisenstadt. "There was a lot of awful writing at Bennington, but Donna's stories were very sophisticated, very mysterious, very structurally sound. She was the only person I knew who'd studied Greek and Latin, who'd read all of Proust."

"When her stories came in, nobody could say anything," Bret Ellis says. "They were flawless. People would check out literary magazines to see if she'd cribbed them from someplace. It was this very decorative hothouse prose—frilly, piss-elegant, but even if you didn't like it, very impressive. The stories always ended in death. There was one about a rich southern couple arguing as they were getting dressed for a party. There was this great one called 'The Goldfish,' about a little boy who ran away from home and drowned in a lake."

Tartt began writing the novel that would become *The Secret History* in her second year at Bennington. She began showing it to Ellis almost at once. "I don't know if any of this would've happened without Bret," she says now. "I started seeing it around 1983," Ellis says. "It wasn't much different at all from the way it is today."

Then, as now, the story centered on a small group of over-refined classics students; only then no one had any doubts about the book's sources. Early on at Bennington, Tartt had fallen in with a small clique of literature students that clustered around Claude Fredericks, a brilliant but odd teacher who admitted few people to his classes. "I wanted to take Greek from him, but he turned me down," Jill Eisenstadt says, raising an eerie echo of *The Secret History.* "I always thought if you *wanted* to take Greek, why should anyone turn you down? I don't think he liked women."

Like Fredericks, the group was exceedingly well-tailored—a startling eccentricity at Bennington, where even the children of the super-rich wore the rattiest jeans and T-shirts. Tartt was the only female in the group. Soon her friends noticed she'd exchanged skirts and dresses for trousers, and begun getting her hair cut boy-style. She also developed an intense friendship with Paul McGloin—a tall, thin, pale upperclassman with a dry, sarcastic wit, a dazzling facility for languages, and a partiality for dark suits, who reminded one classmate of a quieter William S. Burroughs.

The group kept very much to themselves. An encyclopedia entry about Bennington notes, "A close relationship between students and faculty is encouraged." Some would say this understates the case. The school has always had a hothouse atmosphere, and tutorials are the rule. "Cliques grow up around certain teachers, and the mentor relationships get very intense," an alumnus says. "*Very* intense. There was definitely an air of Svengali about Fredericks—it seemed to go beyond even what was normal for Bennington."

No one is suggesting human sacrifices took place. But friends noticed the changes in Tartt—who was a wonderful storyteller, but famously closemouthed when it came to her own life—and wondered whether the novel was somehow a key.

"The only really tense moment she and I ever had was in this writing tutorial where she'd brought the novel," Bret Ellis says. "It was just me and Donna and one other girl. At that point I'd read the first eighty to ninety pages of *The Secret History.* I thought it was beautifully written; I only had one criticism. I said, 'Here's this guy, the narrator, a freshman at college, and he has no sort of sexual feeling, no desire at all. It just doesn't seem realistic.' She gave me the stoniest look I ever got. I almost wilted into my chair.

"And you couldn't say anything about Claude Fredericks in front of her," Ellis adds. "It'd be the end of the evening."

Ellis, who took one course with Fredericks and failed, paid an esoteric tribute both to the strange coterie and Tartt's nascent novel in *The Rules of Attraction,* referring, en passant, to "that weird group of Classics majors stand[ing] by [at a party], looking like undertakers," and "that weird Classics group . . . probably roaming the countryside sacrificing farmers and performing pagan rituals." How far was his tongue in cheek? It's always hard to tell with Ellis.

As for Tartt's relationship with McGloin, "I never did get a handle on it—it didn't seem right to ask," says a friend. "They were very, very private people. The kind of people who would invite you into the drawing room, but never upstairs."

Donna Tartt has her own secret history. Her childhood in Grenada should not, must not, be talked about. Bennington places, but no Bennington people, may be associated

with her book. McGloin may not be spoken to. The novel itself is a thicket of literary references and inside jokes: the narrator's surname is the same as that of the Weimar Republic chancellor who knuckled under to the Nazis; Bunny, whose real name is Edmund, has the same nickname as literary critic Edmund Wilson. The hotel where Henry and Camilla go off together, the Albemarle, has the same name as the English Channel hotel where T. S. Eliot, recuperating from a nervous breakdown, revised "The Waste Land." What does this mean? Perhaps we shouldn't overinterpret—but then, maybe we shouldn't underinterpret, either. When, pleased with my discovery, I point out the Albemarle correspondence to Tartt, she grows chilly. "I have nothing to say about that," she says.

The Secret History is co-dedicated to Bret Ellis and to Paul McGloin, "muse and Maecenas . . . the dearest friend I can ever hope to have in this world." Some say that Tartt and McGloin shared lodgings, in Boston and New York, after her graduation from Bennington, and that he supported her while she finished her book. "After I graduated from college, I lived with a friend who didn't make me pay rent" is all she will say. "My mother was helpful. I was in Boston, then I was in New York. I worked at a bookstore called the Avenue Victor Hugo for three months, in Boston. Then in New York I worked as an assistant to a painting teacher at Parsons. I was the monitor, and I helped him in his classes."

Was the accommodating friend McGloin, who went to Harvard Law School after graduating from Bennington, and who is now a member of a Manhattan law firm? She won't tell. The one thing she allows is "Paul was very good on sloughs of despond." Of which there appear to have been several. Even though Tartt's preternaturally graceful writing style seems to have been with her almost from the beginning, there were times when the structural challenges—not to mention the demands on her energy—of constructing such a huge novel almost defeated her. "There were nights I thought, I've just wasted my life," she says.

The reward of her travail is a wonderment of a book, anachronistically rich with both intellectual and narrative wallop. As Bret Ellis puts it, mildly, "Bennington is so tolerant of any type of behavior, it seems odd that anyone who went there could write *The Secret History.* It's a much more traditional view of the novel than you'd think would come from there." Certainly more traditional than *Less than Zero.* Yet apparently Ellis's early criticism of asexuality in Tartt's book took hold, however it may have stung, for in subsequent drafts the absence magically became a subterranean presence. "I mean, this is basically a novel about repressed sexuality," she says. "There's sex all in the book, but it's really pressed down. And that's basically the plot—it's like a water pipe with weak spots, and it'll kind of *explode* in different places. But it's very *controlled.*

"It's a way of giving events back their power that have been cheapened by overuse," she says. "Because these are the most powerful things we have—there's nothing more powerful. And we sap their power every day. You know, it's better to kind of keep them in reserve for when you really need them. Well, not necessarily *better.* But it's a way of looking at things."

No one looks at things the way she does. To make an actual bacchanal come to life, with real force, in this day and age—and at a place like Bennington, which seems to have been one continuous bacchanal—is no small achievement. And Henry Winter is one of the most chilling characters in recent memory. Does it matter whom he's based on, and what that person is to the author? And why, Donna Tartt seems to be asking—most anachronistically—should her private life be brought into it at all?

We're driving down a dark back road in Bennington, and I suddenly wonder how fame and wealth will take her. "I'm like Huck Finn," she says. "I can be perfectly happy on no money at all. Now that I have money, my life has changed not a bit. Everybody's expecting me to buy a condo, make investments. I don't care about any of that. I like ephemera—books, clothes. Food. That's all." I ask, musingly, if she ever intends to settle down and have a family. She shakes her head firmly. *"Je ne vais jamais me marier,"* she says.

Suddenly she spots, with delight, a whirling flock of goldfinches. "Look at these goldfinches—do you see?" she cries. "Goldfinches are the *greatest* little birds, because they build their nests in the spring, a long time after all the other birds do. They're the last to settle down—they just fly around and they're happy for a long time, and just sing and play. And only when it's *insanely* late in the year, they kind of break down and build their nests. I love goldfinches," she sighs, huddling tinily in the big car seat. "They're my favorite bird." (pp. 248, 250-51, 276-78)

James Kaplan, "Smart Tartt," in Vanity Fair, *Vol. 55, No. 9, September, 1992, pp. 248, 250-51, 276-78.*

An excerpt from *The Secret History*

"Why does that obstinate little voice in our heads torment us so?" he said, looking round the table. "Could it be because it reminds us that we are alive, of our mortality, of our individual souls—which, after all, we are too afraid to surrender but yet make feel more miserable than any other thing? But isn't it also pain that often makes us most aware of self? It is a terrible thing to learn as a child that one is a being separate from all the world, that no one and no *thing* hurts along with one's burned tongues and skinned knees, that one's aches and pains are all one's own. Even more terrible, as we grow older, to learn that no person, no matter how beloved, can ever truly understand us. Our own selves make us most unhappy, and that's why we're so anxious to lose them, don't you think? Remember the Erinyes?"

"The Furies," said Bunny, his eyes dazzled and lost beneath the bang of hair.

"Exactly. And how did they drive people mad? They turned up the volume of the inner monologue, magnified qualities already present to great excess, made people so much *themselves* that they couldn't stand it."

"And how can we lose this maddening self, lose it entirely? Love? Yes, but as old Cephalus once heard Sophocles say, the least of us know that love is a cruel and terrible master. One loses oneself for the sake of the other, but in doing so becomes enslaved and miserable to the most capricious of all the gods. *War?* One can lose oneself in the joy of battle, in fighting for a glorious cause, but there are not a great many glorious causes for which to fight these days." He laughed. "Though after all your Xenophon and Thucydides I dare say there are not many young people better versed in military tactics. I'm sure, if you wanted to, you'd be quite capable of marching on Hampden town and taking it over by yourselves."

Donna Tartt, in her The Secret History, *Knopf, 1992.*

Nisid Hajari (review date September 1992)

[*Below, Hajari praises Tartt's dark view of college life and rituals in* The Secret History.]

College life breeds melodrama. Every slight, every conflict looms as an issue of life and death. Yet at the same time, lulled by some unfortunate confluence of youth and privilege, the undergraduate embraces the certainty of living forever. Rendering that obsession with mortality literal, Donna Tartt's much-hyped debut novel, ***The Secret History,*** presents "College" both as setting for a Gatsbyesque morality play and, viewed from a distance, as the tale itself.

Begun eight years ago while Tartt attended Bennington (with Bret Easton Ellis, to whom *History* is co-dedicated), this ivied, neo-Gothic tragedy weaves the academy into an accomplished psychological thriller. The plot follows the unraveling of a tight-knit clique of classics majors and their eccentric and devilishly charismatic professor, Julian Morrow. In his first seminar, Morrow explains how the Furies drove people mad: "They turned up the volume of the inner monologue, magnified qualities already present to great excess, made people so much *themselves* that they couldn't stand it." Tartt submits her characters to a similarly horrifying treatment.

Through the eyes of the 20-year-old narrator, Richard Papen, the five young classicists appear an unremarkably rich and bright, if somewhat curious, bunch. But, like an inert tissue sample that squirms alive under the microscope, they gradually unveil traces of a darker influence: "they shared a certain coolness, a cruel, mannered charm which was not modern in the least but had a strange cold breath of the ancient world."

After Papen's initial acceptance into this circle, events tumble quickly upon one another. Four of the students engage in a midnight bacchanalia that leads to accidental death (they crush a Vermont farmer's skull), a murder, and the slow, excruciating disintegration of friendships. Tellingly, the idea of recreating a Dionysian ecstasy grew out of a classroom lecture:

> [W]hat could be more terrifying and beautiful . . . than to lose control com-

pletely? . . . To sing, to scream, to dance barefoot in the woods in the dead of night . . . If we are strong enough in our souls we can rip away the veil and look that naked, terrible beauty right in the face; let God consume us, devour us, unstring our bones. Then spit us out reborn.

For a first novelist, Tartt has a stunning command of the lyrical. But her impressionable undergraduate characters are too easily swayed by such beautiful rhetoric. Their felonious actions are more humorous than gruesome, if only because the entire affair fits so neatly into English-major paradigms: creatures of thought and rationality vs. creatures of action and passion; beauty vs. terror; immortality vs. murder; modern anomie vs. ancient clarity. Or perhaps their misdeeds caution that when uptight people lose it, they *really* lose it.

Yet what's absolutely chilling, as well as truly though unintentionally funny, about Tartt's bacchanalian device is its perverse kinship with that other, archetypal college ritual—the frat party. Both "Greek" ceremonies incite the un-selfing of drunken youths, and if one carries the weight of Literature, the other brings decadence to its fullest fruition. In each, moments of heedless frenzy briefly allow the delusion of immortality. Tartt simply reattaches a collegiate tradition to its fecund roots—a gesture at once alluring and disturbing.

Of course, whether a hangover or an FBI investigation, these ceremonies have consequences. The book spins centrifugally off its second murder, the dispatch of Edmund "Bunny" Corcoran. His incriminating knowledge of the others' nighttime spree, folded upon the hurt of having been *left out,* transforms Bunny-the-chum into a merciless threat. Embarrassing revelations are deadly on a small campus, where a friend's betrayal can feel like the greatest and most tragic of sins. So the decidedly unsymbolic execution Bunny receives seems—in the warped moral universe Tartt has constructed—quite deserved.

With that act the author wickedly fulfills the undergrad's fondest wish, the dream "of no one marrying or going home or getting a job in a town a thousand miles away or doing any of the traitorous things friends do after college." Unfortunately, as Bunny's murder occurs halfway through the novel, the reader must endure the lengthy decline of the remaining students. While the first half of the book drags the reader along at an amphetamine clip, the second cautions against the tediousness of having the same friends for the rest of your life.

Nevertheless Tartt manages throughout to impart a creepy sense of familiarity, as if these crazy people and their crazy deeds were manifestations of the hyperreal dreams endemic to dorm rooms everywhere. **The Secret History** succeeds as college noir by carrying an unmistakable plausibility: after reading it, grad school seems at best an uneasy prospect.

Nisid Hajari, in a review of "The Secret History," in VLS, *No. 108, September, 1992, p. 7.*

Lacey Fosburgh   (review date September 1992)

[*Fosburgh is an American novelist and journalist. In the following review, she praises technical and stylistic aspects of* The Secret History *but faults the novel's characters as lacking plausibility and substance.*]

The Secret History, an impressive first novel by twenty-eight-year-old Bennington College graduate Donna Tartt, is a puzzler. Set on a rural college campus, the book covers Dionysian rituals and academic mayhem, with the Greek language as a serious subtext, but its focus is murder and the students who commit it. The book is beautifully written, suspenseful from start to finish. I couldn't put it down, but it hung about me in an unsettled way.

In a potential best-seller like this with spectacular good luck written all over it—Book-of-the-Month Club selection, a hot agent, famous Hollywood director holding an option, hints of a major magazine profile—how often is the writing anything more than an encumbrance to wade through? What to compare it to: *Damage? Vox?* Let's be serious. Donna Tartt has class. She's one of the best young writers to come out of Bennington. Her next book may well be better, but the elegance of her writing alone kept me in my chair. This ought to be enough.

There's a lot to her talent. Her knowledge alone is interesting, no matter how pretentious or self-conscious it might be as the book follows these students, five male and one female, through a series of events at college that lead to not one but two murders—and their subsequent efforts to avoid being caught. In somewhat unlikely fashion, they quote Van Gogh's letters, Cyril Connolly's scribblings, and Ethel Merman's songs. One even speaks familiarly of the Sitwells and T. S. Eliot but can't remember Marilyn Monroe's name.

As a result, fast as one turns the pages, rushing through wonderful scenes and rich language, one can't help but notice that a lot is left unexplained about these unlikely young people who rarely play sports, go to the movies, or spend Christmas with their families. I might not expect my questions to be answered in an ordinary murder book, but this one is so intelligent, it's vulnerable to the matter of rising expectations.

So even as the reader is caught up in the atmosphere of dank Vermont weather and an alcohol-sloshed campus, it is difficult to accept Tartt's characterizations of Bunny (who is killed), Richard, Henry, Charles, Camilla, and Francis. Why does their moral code, if there is one, permit them to go this far? What are they really like? Why have they consternation but no guilt, remorse, or even sadness over what they've done? You want to know what Tartt intended, if anything, from the core emptiness of these five friends, who routinely lie to each other and plow through trust funds as if there's no tomorrow.

Except for Richard Papen himself, the androgynous, passive first-person narrator, they are more a collective than individuals. Are they just overly spoiled, if gifted, and discarded, youths? Or is there true character and the potential for tragedy here?

The promotion for the book makes much of "golden

youth" gone astray, but mere wealth and a talent for Greek does not make for golden. There must be true talent, more than a hint of potential, some sense of its realistic actualization. But for these lost souls, the only explanation ultimately given for their astonishing criminal behavior is that they're just weird.

One is not at all certain that they might ever have done more with their lives than eventually meet the sorry ends described, had not murder come their way. Their arrogance and condescension toward virtually everyone, including most of all the adults they encounter, might ultimately have limited their transactional skills in the outside world equally as much as murder.

Lacey Fosburgh, "Forbidden and Gothic," in
Vogue, *Vol. 182, September, 1992, p. 380.*

Laura Shapiro and Ray Sawhill (review date 7 September 1992)

[*In the following review, Shapiro and Sawhill discuss the extensive publicity surrounding* The Secret History *and question whether Tartt's future success as a novelist will be impeded by the critical scrutiny that inevitably accompanies fame.*]

Who is Donna Tartt and why is everyone talking about her new book? OK, maybe not everyone ("One thing I can tell you is, everybody's not talking about it in Iowa City."—Paul Ingram, bookseller, Iowa City), but Tartt, 28, is featured in the latest issues of *Vanity Fair, M, Esquire, Vogue, Elle* and *Mirabella*. In September she embarks on a 20-city publicity tour (including Iowa City). Her book is called ***The Secret History*** and Knopf paid $450,000 for it—an astonishing amount for a first novel, especially one that isn't just glitzy trash or about cave dwellers. Foreign rights have been sold to 11 countries for more than $500,000, paperback rights went for another half million, it's a Book of the Month Club selection, and Alan J. Pakula (*All the President's Men*) has bought the movie rights. Most first novels get a first printing of about 10,000 copies; Tartt's is getting 75,000. "I can't remember a first literary commercial novel with this much push from the publisher behind it," says Ingram.

All this for a book that shows a great deal of talent and ambition but remains every inch a first novel. A murder mystery without the mystery, ***The Secret History*** is about a coterie of college students fanatically devoted to the study of ancient Greek. Halfway through the novel the group murders one of its own, and from then on the book is concerned with the ramifications of their deed, especially the psychological consequences. This could have been a successful page-turner if only the characters were compelling, but they are the weakest element. It's impossible to distinguish one student from another without continually flipping back to the page where Tartt introduces them. She adorns them with quirks, but none has a personality; and her amateur's device of keeping them constantly drunk or on drugs gets tedious fast. Unlike the truly startling debuts of recent years, such as Mona Simpson's *Anywhere But Here,* or Jonathan Franzen's *The Twenty-Seventh City*—highly sophisticated achievements both

technically and emotionally—***The Secret History*** feels strained and pretentious, as if Tartt were determined to Write a Novel, rather than eager to tell a story.

But it's nice and fat, it's set on a college campus, the characters scatter classical Greek quotations across their conversation like parsley and Knopf is betting that the same readers who made best sellers out of *Presumed Innocent* and *The Firm* will stick ***The Secret History*** into their briefcases and backpacks. "This is an audience that looks for quality and reading pleasure at the same time," says Knopf president Sonny Mehta. "I think this book has got a kind of classic status available to it, or at the very least some kind of cult status."

Mehta is famous for his ability to catapult writers to stardom; what's unusual about Tartt's case is that stardom has been scheduled to begin right at the outset of her career. Tartt began writing ***The Secret History*** while she was a student at Bennington College. One of her classmates was Bret Easton Ellis, whose own first novel was the best-selling *Less Than Zero.* (The two are very different writers, though their characters—vacant-eyed Yuppies with designer wardrobes—are kin). Ellis introduced her to his agent, and then Tartt got lucky. Her book went up for sale in the spring of 1991, just before the convention of the American Booksellers Association, the publishing industry's giant annual confab. The big-bucks auction, the sale to Knopf, the foreign publishers rushing to obtain rights and the fact that by chance no other major book was being touted at the time all resulted in what one editor calls "a huge buzz" at the ABA. "The book might not have caused such a fuss if it had been bought at another time of year," says an editor at another house. Knopf kept the buzz going all year by sending galleys to booksellers, whipping up the sales force to pitch the book and using the 1992 ABA to hawk the novel and introduce Tartt to booksellers and reviewers.

"People say we're great at hyping, which I don't think is the case," says Tartt's editor, Gary Fisketjon, Knopf's curator of hip fiction. Many would disagree with him. "Sonny has done a pretty amazing job," says bookseller Paul Yamazaki of San Francisco's City Lights bookstore. "With all the publicity, I'm sure it will do well at first. The real question is whether we'll still be selling it in two months."

Another real question is whether—money aside—such a gigantic fuss is in the best interest of a first-time author. "The landscape is littered with the corpses of overpraised young writers," says a New York editor. "You need space to make mistakes." Anthony Brandt, author of a forthcoming history called *In the Mouth of Fame: The Making of Literary Reputations,* says the big publishing houses can't afford to give young writers that kind of space. "They have so much overhead and so much in the way of profit expectations that it's tough for them to justify letting a writer grow, maybe losing money on three or four books before they make money," he says. "It's produce or die."

Whether Tartt will be a star for more than an instant is unknown; her novel has just hit bookstores, and the early reviews are mixed. Right now she is still in something of a daze over her good fortune. "A piece of cataclysmic luck like this is a force of nature," she says. "There are plenty of extraordinary people who write books far better than this that don't get half this attention. It's like the lottery. I'm expecting a car to hit me to offset this." Tartt's response to all the hype has been miraculously sensible: she went straight to work on a second book and is trying to make it better than the first. "There really are no child prodigies in writing," she says. "You have to have been around the track. My best work is ahead of me. I'm young!" And rich! Which she also likes. "I wrote this for fun, not for money," she says. "I'll never write a book for money, and with this I'll never have to. That's a wonderful feeling." (pp. 54-5)

Laura Shapiro with Ray Sawhill, "Anatomy of a Hype," in Newsweek, *Vol. CXX, No. 10, September 7, 1992, pp. 54-5.*

Lee Lescaze   (review date 9 September 1992)

[*In the following review, Lescaze faults* The Secret History *as a pretentious work that is unworthy of the extensive publicity and critical attention it has received.*]

Like the coming of a comet, Donna Tartt's first novel was heralded for months, arousing considerable anticipation as it drew near.

Book pages bubbled with news of the $450,000 advance Ms. Tartt received. Alan Pakula rocketed past, picking up the film rights. Foreign sales and paperback bidding zoomed higher and higher.

Alas, like many comet arrivals, Ms. Tartt's ***The Secret History*** is a big letdown. You plan to stay up all night for the event, but there's not much to it, so pretty quickly you're yawning and heading for bed.

As with much else these days, the hype causes the disappointment. ***The Secret History*** isn't presented as just another piece of candy for the eyes to keep you going until you're in the right mood to do justice to *Moby Dick.*

If it were, it would hold its own perfectly well on the racks with other novels full of cardboard characters, awkward dialogue and tricky but unconvincing plot development. Instead, *Vanity Fair* brings us the daunting news [in "Smart Tartt," September 1992] that Ms. Tartt has written "a book whose very essence is the survival of formality in a formality-starved era." "It's possible for a book to be literary and still keep you up all night," Ms. Tartt says in a Knopf press release.

The Secret History is the story of six loathsome students at a small, elite New England college (Ms. Tartt went to Bennington) who pursue a drunken, drug-using, childish course through an exotic curriculum of Greek and Latin taught by a strange and cultic professor. Along the way they become murderers.

In pursuit of a fuller understanding of the classical world, several of these self-absorbed sapheads stage their low-rent version of a Dionysian frenzy by dressing in bed sheets, fasting, drinking and dancing through the chilly Vermont woods—with sad consequences for a farmer who stumbles upon the bacchanal.

Like many their age, these sodden youths habitually sneer at adults, ridicule most emotions and twist themselves in ever-tighter circles of egomania. But Ms. Tartt fails utterly to convince that they have interesting minds, let alone the gifts in classics she attributes to them all, but particularly to their leader, Henry Winter. This is a young man who translates *Paradise Lost* into Latin in his spare time as someone else might do a crossword puzzle. Henry reportedly picks up languages as easily as others catch colds. His spoken Greek impresses our narrator as more eloquent than his English. Of course, his English isn't anything special.

Neither is anyone's in ***The Secret History.*** Referring to the group's mesmerizing teacher, Ms. Tartt has her narrator confess: "He was a marvelous talker, a magical talker, and I wish I were able to give a better idea of what he said, but it is impossible for a mediocre intellect to render the speech of a superior one . . . without losing a good deal in the translation." It shouldn't be necessary to note that good writers don't let the magic disappear.

"It was glorious," Henry declares of the bacchanal. But, killing the farmer leads to much peevishness among the students, the most oafish of whom cannot resist blackmailing his guiltier and richer pals into providing free meals, booze and other goodies. They turn upon him with bloody and grievous consequences all around.

The Secret History may prove a best seller and keep people with sleep disorders busy at night. But it is not literary. Its only literary touches come from its habit of dropping the names of English, Latin and Greek writers where another pop novelist would be concentrating on brand names of clothing.

Ms. Tartt does herself no favor by inviting readers to compare her novel with *Crime and Punishment.* She does her editor no favor by praising him in her acknowledgments with the same phrase from Dante that T. S. Eliot used in dedicating *The Waste Land* to that poem's editor, Ezra Pound. ***The Secret History*** belongs more properly in a class with the works of Ms. Tartt's Bennington friend and the book's co-dedicatee, Bret Easton Ellis.

Here's a sampler of Ms. Tartt's prose:

> She was breathing hard and deep circles of red burned high on her bright cheeks; in all my life I had never seen anyone so maddeningly beautiful as she was at that moment. I stood blinking at her, the blood pounding in my veins, and my carefully rehearsed plans for a goodbye kiss forgotten, when unexpectedly she flew up and threw her arms around me.
>
> . . .
>
> "Henry," I said. I wanted to say something profound, that Julian was only human, that he was old, that flesh and blood are frail and weak and that there comes a time when we have to transcend our teachers. But I found myself unable to say anything at all.

Fortunately, many good novelists who are both accessible and serious do exist. Unfortunately, publishers are more inclined to put their marketing dollars behind fiction like *The Secret History,* a work that amply demonstrates that a little learning is a tiresome thing.

> Lee Lescaze, "Groves of Academe Shed Gold and Yawns," in The Wall Street Journal, September 9, 1992, p. A12.

Amanda Vaill   (review date 13 September 1992)

[*In the following review, Vaill asserts that the numerous literary references in* The Secret History *contribute to a tone of artifice in the novel.*]

Donna Tartt's mellifluous, ambitious first novel, *The Secret History,* arrives trailing clouds of glorious associations: its dedication is to her "muse and Maecenas" (the latter was the patron of Horace and Virgil); its acknowledgements thank among others the author's editor, *"il miglior fabbro"*—which any English major can tell you is how T. S. Eliot dedicated *The Waste Land* to Ezra Pound, "the better craftsman." This is pretty heady stuff, and it doesn't stop there.

Among the collegiate heroes of *The Secret History* is a young man named Edmund Corcoran, whose nickname, Bunny, inevitably recalls that celebrated man of letters, Edmund "Bunny" Wilson; Wilson's *Axel's Castle* contains one of the definitive critical appraisals of Eliot. Also in the cast is a French professor named Laforgue; Jules Laforgue, the French Symbolist poet, was one of the most important influences on the early work of (here he is again) T. S. Eliot. And Eliot himself even turns up in the form of a lengthy quotation from *The Waste Land.*

These allusions are not only meant to signal Tartt's own seriousness of purpose, her sense of writing in a tradition that extends from classical to modern literature; they are also a way of indicating the bonds of a civilization from which her young heroes try to break free, with disastrous results. As one of her characters, the magus-like Greek professor, Julian Morrow (a friend of—predictably—Pound and Eliot, as well as Orwell and Harold Acton), puts it, "The more cultivated a person is, the more intelligent, the more repressed, then the more he needs some method of channeling the primitive impulses he's worked so hard to kill." And that, simply put, is the thesis of *The Secret History.*

Tartt's narrator, Richard Papen, is a working class boy from California—not the California of orange groves and swimming pools but a flat, dusty anyplace of tract houses and shopping malls—who manages to procure a scholarship at a progressive Vermont college with more than a passing resemblance to Bennington, the author's alma mater. Here he falls under the spell of the charismatic Julian Morrow and his tiny coterie of exquisite upper-class epigones: Henry Winter, a T. S. Eliot look-alike from St. Louis; Francis Abernathy, an "angular and elegant" exotic from Boston; Charles and Camilla Macaulay, orphaned twins "from somewhere down south" with the faces of "Flemish angels"; and Edmund, or Bunny, Corcoran, a

snub-nosed Connecticut country-club WASP who is the least cerebral of the bunch. They spend their class time in philosophical discussions of the sublime, trade Homeric epithets instead of lines from *Wayne's World,* smoke and drink a lot, buy beautiful clothes, and drive around to great little restaurants where they order multi-course meals.

Desperate to be accepted by them, Richard conceals his blue-collar background (and his scholarship status); and he also ignores some vaguely troubling signals that something is going on between the other members of the group that he's not privy to. But finally he discovers that—during an attempt to recreate a Dionysian mystical experience—they have actually killed someone, a blameless Vermont farmer who crossed their path while they were out of their minds with ecstatic abandon. And Bunny, the only one of the original group not to have been involved in the killing, has found out about it and is alternately blackmailing them and threatening to blow the whistle on the lot.

From there to killing Bunny is a shockingly easy step for these effete and privileged children (although it takes nearly 100 pages): He's pushed over a cliff to make it look like a hiking accident. And Richard, whether through inertia or desire to belong—or a combination of the two—goes along with it. After an extensive manhunt, a police investigation, and a funeral, the conspirators appear poised to get off scot free—but then, just as the strain of concealment has begun to break at least one of them, a potentially lethal piece of evidence turns up in a most unexpected place, precipitating a denouement that leaves almost as many dead and injured bodies as the last act of a Jacobean tragedy.

Donna Tartt has invested this simple and—in the last hundred or so pages—suspenseful plot with a considerable amount of atmosphere and philosophical significance. I'm not sure she needed to do this—in fact, the least successful parts of this novel are those where one feels her left hand heavy on the bass notes, and her foot on the pedal. Take this supposed quotation from Richard's journal, written just after Julian has given his students his little homily on repression and ecstatic sublimity: "Trees are schizophrenic now and beginning to lose control, enraged with the shock of their fiery new colors. Someone—was it Van Gogh?—said that orange is the color of insanity. Beauty is terror. We want to be devoured by it, to hide ourselves in that fire which refines us." Maybe Tartt is trying to show us Richard's undergraduate preciosity, but I don't think so.

She is at her considerable best when she lets her characters and situations speak for themselves. Oddly—for all the care with which she burnishes the portraits of her elite band of classicists—the one who rises most forcefully from the page is the unfortunate Bunny. A hidebound, homophobic preppie and chronic sponger, he nonetheless exhibits a kind of reflexive courtesy: He inquires about the absent maitre d' at a favored restaurant, and when the waiter says, "I'll tell him you asked for him," he replies, "*Do* that, wouldja?" Dyslexic, with "an attention span . . . as short as a child's," he's capable of lunatic leaps of the imagination, as shown by a paper he writes about John Donne that provides one of *The Secret Histo-*

ry's few moments of authentic laughter. By comparison his comrades often seem rather bloodless.

Perhaps it's not surprising that some of the book's most effective scenes involve Bunny's funeral, a horrific, almost Cheeveresque affair at which Bunny's father yaws sickeningly between buoyant WASP glad-handing ("Well, well, well . . . If it's not the old Carrot Top. How are you, boy?") and sobbing, gut-wrenching grief. By the side of the grave, after reciting Housman's "With Rue My Heart Is Laden" (one of Bunny's favorite poems), Henry throws a handful of dirt onto the coffin of the lightfoot lad he put there, and then "with terrible composure, he stepped back and absently dragged the hand across his chest, smearing mud upon his lapel, his tie, the starched immaculate white of his shirt." At moments like this one senses Donna Tartt's real talent as a writer.

One also wonders why she felt she had to burden her story and her characters with the thematic machinery invoked by all her literary references. Was she seduced by the very artifice she was trying to chronicle? At the novel's end Richard tells us he has become a scholar of Elizabethan and Jacobean drama, with a particular fondness for Christopher Marlowe—an instructive detail. For all his poetic brilliance, Marlowe was something of a mechanist: His great classical erotic narrative "Hero and Leander" derives its imagery almost entirely from the art of jewellers and metallurgists. The late Elizabethan scholar Herschel Baker used to enjoy pointing out the contrast between that poem and Shakespeare's "Venus and Adonis," which draws its images from the barnyard and the hunting field. It's the warmth and vitality of his works—their life—that make Shakespeare a great writer, and the lack of those qualities that makes Marlowe merely a very interesting one. Without wishing to draw impossible comparisons, it's fair to say that when Donna Tartt forgets about trying to write literature and simply lets it rip, she's a very good writer indeed; and when she doesn't, she's just an interesting one. (pp. 3, 9)

Amanda Vaill, "Beyond Good and Evil," in Book World—The Washington Post, *September 13, 1992—pp. 3, 9.*

Joanne Kaufman   (review date 14 September 1992)

[*In the following review, Kaufman asserts that the characters in* The Secret History *lack definition and context.*]

It's a complicated tale that Richard Papen, the narrator of this ambitious and highly touted first novel, [***The Secret History***], has to tell. It is grim; it is grisly; it is compelling—and ultimately unrewarding.

Chafing against the barrenness of life in a Northern California town and determined to study ancient Greek, Richard snares a scholarship to a small Vermont college. Initially rebuffed by the only professor in classics, Richard perseveres and is soon studying Plato with the five other students in the program. They are an odd, arrogant, callous lot: the ringleader and intellectual, Henry; the homosexual, Francis; the blond twins, Charles and Camilla; and

the boob of the group, Edmund (Bunny). Inspired by one of the professor's lectures, all except Richard and Bunny attempt to replicate a bacchanal, in the process inadvertently killing a passerby. When it looks as though the unstable Bunny might squeal, the others, Richard included, calmly plot his murder.

The Secret History is full of references to Pliny, Milton, Constable and poems like Eliot's "The Waste Land." But while Tartt, something of a show-off, has done her homework as a scholar, she hasn't quite passed as a novelist. She fashions some intriguing relationships, like the peculiar tie between Henry and the professor, but fails to give them shape or context. Incidents that appear to be leading somewhere prove dead ends. Worse, Tartt never quite makes palpable her characters' supposed charisma or makes comprehensible their hold on Richard.

Meant to be a tale of golden youth tarnished, of privilege and intellect run amok, ***Secret*** is instead 544 pages of low-wattage *Crime and Punishment.* Sadly, it's the reader who does time.

Joanne Kaufman, in a review of "The Secret History," in People Weekly, *Vol. 38, No. 11, September 14, 1992, p. 28.*

Brooke Allen   (review date October 1992)

[*In the following review, Allen asserts that Tartt's writing, although highly accomplished, is limited by a juvenile and overly romantic tone.*]

For those who follow promotional hype in the literary world, Donna Tartt is the newest young star around. In the middle of a time of severe belt-tightening among publishing houses, she received a $450,000 advance (for a first novel) from Knopf, and Knopf's bold move was almost immediately justified by large foreign and film rights sales for the book, ***The Secret History.*** Touted by literary lights as diverse as Willie Morris and Bret Easton Ellis, Tartt has been hailed as a major talent, a classical, formal, "serious" novelist in an MTV world.

After having read *Vanity Fair's* fulsome puff-piece ("Smart Tartt," September 1992), in which Tartt reveals herself as an accomplished, if not very subtle, self-promoter, I was eager to get my hands on the book itself. For it is true that erudition and formality have become increasingly rare and valuable attributes in the novel, and if Tartt were all that she and Knopf's publicists crack her up to be then we should be grateful for the advent of this new talent. Suspicions of pretentiousness, however, are inevitable (Tartt chats at length about her youthful precocity, classical scholarship, and wide learning), and they begin to be confirmed as early as the acknowledgments, for what is one to make of thanks "to Gary Fisketjon, *il miglior fabbro*"? It would be nice to give Tartt the benefit of the doubt and believe that she is simply making a joke, albeit an arcane one. But the identification with Eliot is no joke. References to him are inserted so conspicuously into the book that it's hard not to trip over them, and two of her characters—the narrator, Richard Papen, and another protagonist, Henry Winter—are Eliotic in conception.

Tartt's self-identification with Eliot becomes, over the course of the book, obvious. She sees herself as an intellectual and a polymath, born, changeling-like, in a culturally benighted American wasteland (in Tartt's case Mississippi, where in a former life she was *outré* enough to pledge Kappa Kappa Gamma at Ole Miss); an Anglophile; a religious convert (Catholic to his Anglo-Catholic); a classical writer working in close accordance with a broad Western tradition. She even picks up Eliot's technique of inserting quotations into her work whole—an eye-catching trick, though somewhat less original than it was in Eliot's day.

The difference from Eliot, of course, is one of depth. While he worked his quotations and references fully into the fabric of his poetry, Tartt dots them around like cake decorations. It's the Woody Allen method of self-salesmanship: if you do enough assiduous intellectual name-dropping, people will finally believe you to be genuinely erudite. Not that Tartt hasn't read deeply and extensively; it's just that her love of learning seems that of an intellectual groupie, a young woman star-struck by writers and professors rather than by rock or movie stars. For in spite of the glitter and the fine (often genuinely fine) writing, *The Secret History* is an adolescent's book, with an adolescent's values and perceptions. And of course even an obsession with Eliot is an adolescent's obsession.

The Secret History takes place in Vermont, at an artistic, liberal, expensive institution called Hampden College (Tartt herself attended Bennington). The narrator, Richard Papen, arrives at Hampden as a transfer student. He is from Plano, California, a small silicon town in the desert that plainly symbolizes the spiritual and intellectual wasteland that typifies the contemporary world. Being neither rich nor preppie, he is an anomaly at Hampden, and does all he can to hide his ignominious middle-American roots and invent a Beverly Hills-style background for himself.

He would like to study ancient Greek. But Greek is taught by Julian Morrow, a Svengali figure only loosely connected with the rest of the college, and Julian insists that his students virtually withdraw from all other classes and study only with him. Richard is turned down by Morrow and languishes in isolation, observing the Classics students—the lucky few—from a distance. He becomes enamored of this bizarre group, and Tartt tries hard to convey their glamour.

> His students—if they were any mark of his tutelage—were imposing enough, and different as they all were they shared a certain coolness, a cruel, mannered charm which was not modern in the least but had a strange cold breath of the ancient world: they were magnificent creatures, such eyes, such hands, such looks—*sic oculos, sic ille manus, sic ora ferebat.*

Eventually, by a tricky demonstration of his knowledge of Greek syntax, Richard infiltrates the group and gets accepted to Julian's classes. The Greek students become his friends: Henry Winter, the leader of the group, tall, imposing, ascetic, learned in any number of Near Eastern languages; Francis Abernathy, hypochondriac, neurotic, homosexual; Edmund (Bunny) Corcoran, a none-too-bright,

noisy, obnoxious preppie, hideously brought up by Connecticut parents verging on the lunatic; the twins, Charles and Camilla Macaulay—Charles, a golden youth headed swiftly toward dipsomania, and Camilla, Richard's ostensible love-interest, a beautiful but rather characterless creature. The group as a whole forms a rogue's gallery of stereotypical East Coast WASPs; Richard is hypnotized by their patina and by their affected demeanor.

> "We could play bezique, or euchre if you'd rather," [Henry] said, the blue and gold [of playing cards] dissolving from his hands in a blur. "I like poker myself—of course, it's rather a vulgar game, and no fun at all with two—but still, there's a certain random element in it which appeals to me."

This kind of talk bedazzles the provincial, twenty-year-old Richard, but the reader is less likely to be charmed by these self-conscious examples of *jeunesse dorée*. Large portions of the book thus become tedious at best, since these, for better or worse, make up our cast of characters.

As Richard gets more and more involved with his new friends, he realizes that they seem to be hiding something from him: there is much to-ing and fro-ing during the night, muddy sheets in the laundry, and other tell-tale signs of secret activity. It is not until he catches them all (with the exception of Bunny) in a foiled attempt at flight to South America that he discovers the truth. Henry, Francis, and the twins, encouraged by Julian, have for some months been trying to conduct a Bacchanal—a real one, involving consciousness-altering, hallucinations, and unspecified sexual acts. They finally succeed; but when they come to their senses they find that they have inadvertently killed a farmer who happened onto their ceremony. An elaborate cover-up follows, involving, eventually, a second murder, that of the hapless Bunny. The rest of the book involves the ramifications of the crimes, the group's remorse, and its ultimate break-up.

[Tartt's] love of learning seems that of an intellectual groupie, a young woman starstruck by writers and professors rather than by rock or movie stars.

—Brooke Allen

Tartt is lavish with intricate, well-observed detail, especially when treating the core group of characters, Julian Morrow and his *crème de la crème*. In spite of this, these characters remain as dead as mutton. Julian, for example, the cosmopolitan sophisticate, intimate of George Orwell and Harold Acton, is repeatedly described as witty, elegant, utterly charming; Tartt never succeeds, however, in making him sound anything but ridiculously fruity.

> "Poor Charles," he said. "It's not *serious,* is it? . . . Is he allowed any visitors? I shall, regardless, telephone him this afternoon. Can you

think of anything he might like? Food is so dreadful in the hospital. I remember years ago, in New York, when a dear friend of mine was in Columbia Presbyterian—in the bloody Harkness Pavilion, for goodness' sake—the chef at the old Le Chasseur used to send her dinner to her every single day. . . . "

The entire group speaks in the phony accents of characters from a Hollywood "society" film of the Thirties. This jars with the narrator's flowery, heavily elegiac tone and with the rather more realistic and better-realized subsidiary characters. While Tartt would clearly like the doomed group to take center stage, the lesser, comical sidekicks often usurp that position.

For Tartt has an unexpected, underutilized gift for comedy, and the only parts of *The Secret History* that come to life are those in which she lets herself roll on the minor characters: Judy Poovey, Richard's scorned neighbor in the dorm; Cloke Rayburn, the college drug dealer; Bunny's terrible parents. The longish section on Bunny's funeral is the best in the book. Here, for example, the parents check out Bunny's "floral tributes":

> Mrs. Corcoran began to inspect the ferns, lifting up the fronds to check for dead foliage, making notes on the back of the envelopes with a tiny silver screw-point pencil. To her husband she said: "Did you see that wreath the Bartles sent?"
>
> "Wasn't that nice of them."
>
> "No, in fact I don't think it appropriate for an employee to send something like that. I wonder, is Bob thinking about asking you for a raise?"
>
> "Now, hon."
>
> "I can't believe these plants, either," she said, jabbing a forefinger into the soil. "This African violet is almost dead. Louise would be humiliated if she knew."
>
> "It's the thought that counts."
>
> "I know, but still, if I've learned one thing from this it is never to order flowers from Sunset Florists again. All the things from Tina's Flowerland are so much nicer. . . . "

The Corcorans in their dreadfulness are far more alive than any of the central characters into whom so much of the author's emotions have been invested, and scenes like this are of great value within the lengthy, diffuse narrative. Compared with the superbly observed Corcoran scenes, the more emotional ones fall horribly flat. This problem is evident in the attempted descriptions of Camilla's beauty, in which Tartt has always to resort to hokey clichés: " . . . she seemed not at all her bright unattainable self but rather a hazy and ineffably tender apparition, all slender wrists and shadows and disordered hair, the Camilla who resided, dim and lovely, in the gloomy boudoir of my dreams."

The scenes of astringent comedy, it will be evident, come as a welcome relief. But like so many only half-good writers, Tartt's sense of comedic nuance is inextricably connected to her sense of scorn. Her best characters are her funny ones, but she can only be funny about people who are beyond the pale in some sense.

And the sense tends to be a social rather than a moral one. For *The Secret History*'s claim to be a morally centered novel is in fact spurious; the author's exhaustive exploration of guilt, the narrator's wallowing in remorse, ring false throughout. "It's a terrible thing, what we did," states Francis after the Vermont farmer's death; "I mean, this man was not *Voltaire* we killed. But still. It's a shame. I feel bad about it." Now is the reader supposed to feel bad for these selfish, affected children? Yes, apparently: more so than for the farmer, since the students are golden youths who should have had great futures before them, the farmer only a farmer—"not Voltaire." Francis's statement is the more repellent in that the author does not really intend it to be so; the reader is supposed tacitly to share Francis's assumptions, and the group's scorn for *hoi polloi* is subtly approved by Tartt. This is a snobbish book above all, and though its heroes sin gravely they are beautiful and brilliant and therefore not damned; the damned are those who sin socially, whose veneer is grossly flawed—the idiotic Bunny; his crude parents; the other Hampden students, beer-swilling and coke-snorting their way through college.

In spite of everything that is wrong with this book, I do not want to give the impression that Tartt is without talent as a writer. Her faults are those of youth (though at almost thirty she should be old enough to have outgrown them): romanticism, snobbishness, overwriting. She is also too ambitious, frequently writing beyond what her skills will allow. She has overreached herself, for example, in choosing to employ a male narrator; as a result, and in spite of obvious efforts from the author, Richard is curiously sexless, and his conversations with other men ring false—for Tartt, unlike Jane Austen, dares to portray men talking outside the company of women. The tired device of using a narrator who is essentially an outsider, an observer, deprives the story of much of its immediacy. Tartt's heavily descriptive, ornamental style reflects the worst rather than the best of the Southern literary tradition; her themes and attitudes are juvenile. Yet, in spurts and odd moments, she displays a genuine gift for observation and for sly humor. It is to be hoped that she continues to develop this, rather than the more baroque vein so much in evidence in *The Secret History*. (pp. 65-8)

> *Brooke Allen, "Panpipes & Preppies," in* The New Criterion, *Vol. XI, No. 2, October, 1992, pp. 65-8.*

Alexander Star   (review date 19 October 1992)

[*In the following review, Star argues that Tartt's artistically ambitious exploration of morality and human nature is limited by artificiality.*]

Although the university is one of America's last competitive assets, most of our campus fiction arrives from abroad. Still, readers must reckon with such homemade goods as the "Bennington novel"—a casually interlinked corpus of work produced by Bret Easton Ellis and Jill Eisenstadt in the mid-'80s. Matching a minimal prose style to an even more minimal human understanding, Ellis and Eisenstadt retailed myths of collegiate decadence to readers hungry for news of a purportedly lost generation. Where campus satires once picked on the faculty, their up-to-date reports focused on the students, or at least on the heavily aerobicized and anesthetized student body. The predictable result was instant notoriety, and Hollywood.

But the Bennington novel may be entering a new phase, or at least Donna Tartt, whose first book is dedicated to her classmate Ellis, has written something different. *The Secret History* is an elaborately conceived and artistically ambitious thriller that turns not on the quest for tenure or pills, but on such matters as "sin unpunished, innocence destroyed, and evil passing itself as good." The narrator, Richard Papen, is a modest young man from a modest Californian home who is burdened with a "marked longing for the picturesque" and a compulsion to "make interesting people good." Arriving at Hampden College in Vermont, he dreams of "cellos; bleak windowpanes; snow." Before long he is moved by an even more picturesque sight: the school's classics students, with their foppish dress and forbidding ways, stand out from "the throngs of hippies and beatniks and preppies and punks" like Evelyn Waugh characters lost in a Fox sitcom. Led by the tall, umbrella-toting Henry Winter, they worship their professor Julian Morrow, a famed classicist devoted to educating the "smooth-cheeked, soft-skinned, well-educated, and rich." It is not long before Richard joins them.

Tartt succeeds in coaxing plausible anxieties out of implausible circumstances. Inspired by their tutor to purge the "burden of self," Richard's companions practice Bacchic rites in the woods. Hampden's motto is "Learn by Doing," and while Morrow's austere paternalism hardly matches the school ethos, he unwittingly impels his students to carry out the maxim with his talk of divine madness and the beauty of terror. In the midst of one of these rituals, a local farmer is inexplicably murdered and mutilated. Richard becomes aware of the deed, as does Bunny Corcoran, an amiable shambles of a boy with little aptitude for Greek but a genius for teasing his friends and spending their trust funds. When Bunny's hectoring ways become an intolerable burden to the group, they resolve to kill him.

> The psychic toll of their unknown crime is a descent into despondency and madness. It is the accumulation of these troubles, narrated with detached foreboding, that gives the book its slow, creeping force.
>
> —*Alexander Star*

None of the cast is a very credible mystagogue, and the accounts of their chiton-clad evenings are not especially convincing: "You saw Dionysus, I suppose?" But Tartt rapidly proceeds to more promising topics—crime and conceal-

ment, the waning of moral restraints, the escalation of dread. Friendly and fidgety, exasperating but not bad, Bunny is an unlikely sacrificial victim, and the cover-up of his murder becomes a bruising business for the group. The psychic toll of their unknown crime is a descent into despondency and madness. It is the accumulation of these troubles, narrated with detached foreboding, that gives the book its slow, creeping force.

Tartt handles suspense with care. In one well-paced episode, Richard waits interminably for Morrow to flip over a piece of stationery and discover a vital clue. This scene not only slyly parodies its own page-turning momentum but also adequately summarizes Tartt's method: the brisk pace of dialogue and description clashes with delayed gratification of the reader's desire. Richard's understated disclosures hold the melodrama in check throughout, although the reader does catch an occasional whiff of scented undergraduate ink—"the gloomy boudoir of my dreams."

Tartt's larger ambition, only partly realized, is to contrast the "narrow, relentless" force of classical literature with the "whimsical, discursive" surfaces of modern writing. Richard is fascinated with ancient Greek, a "language obsessed with action, and with the joy of seeing action multiply from action." He wonders again and again if his fate was foreordained; if anything could have reversed the "rapid progression of events." But he also inhabits a fantasy world of blurred colors and forgotten deeds in which murder is merely "a dropped stone falling to the lake bed with scarcely a ripple." "Any action, in the fullness of time," he hopes, "sinks to nothingness." He broods over whether the murder was "selfish" and "evil" or merely "wild" and "picturesque," over whether he was someone's "alarm bell" or simply a "bystander." Divided against himself, he rambles back and forth between two worlds—Hampden's tedious partygoers with their "diabolical rap" and his own haunted and high-minded friends.

Contrasting the solid and the shadowy, the consequential and the ephemeral, Tartt scatters objective correlatives to Richard's confusion throughout her book. The fall landscape, crisply etched, is set against the "glorious blur" of landmarks suddenly associated with the murder, spots where the world has gone out of focus. For the most part these competing languages are placed side by side, but they abruptly join in a description of Bunny, around whose corpse all of these words grow: "Viewed from a distance his character projected an impression of solidity and wholeness which was in fact as insubstantial as a hologram; up close, he was all motes and light, you could pass your hand right through him. . . ."

Richard's double vision creates a more graceful patterning of image and idea than one expects to see on such a high-speed trip. But Tartt does not really do justice to either of the literary modes that she employs. She is too busy managing her narrative economy, rationing secrets and suspense according to the thriller's laws of supply and demand. Some of her vignettes of oddball professors and ordinary nihilists are musty (Professor Laforgue, forever on the watch for "enemies" in his department); others are more amusing ("Oh you know Flipper. . . . Everybody called her Flipper because she flipped over her dad's Volvo, like, four times freshman year"). But they are all a little like music piped in to cover a change in scenery; they are designed to distract, not to reveal. And her open-ended conclusion notwithstanding, Tartt relies on a tired moral—the categorical imperative, Bennington style. Henry's error is not to crave divine madness, but to regard others only as obstacles in his way. He hoists himself cooly above the law: Bunny's death was, after all, simply a "redistribution of matter." "Never once," Richard writes, "did it occur to me that any of this was anything but a game."

Tartt presumably wants to expose this stance, to communicate the peril of judging others and oneself by intellectual and aesthetic standards alone. Dividing her characters into the frivolous and the cunning, she takes aim at both the shallow narcissists and the icy egoists among them. But the chilling arrogance of young Nietzscheans—or, in this case, Dionysians—is an overworked theme, especially after Hitchcock's *Rope*. Most of her creations are stand-up targets, heavily painted with the colors of New England autumn. A hint of self-conscious play-acting clings to their actions. The evil in the woods seems merely the pretense of evil; Richard's anguish, the pretense of guilt.

Tartt records the aftereffects of unpunished crime with great skill. But her efforts to transform a chronicle of suspense into a study in sensibility are less successful. Dostoyevskian turmoil does not relocate easily to contemporary Vermont, and the stage-props of ancient Greece don't make the trip any smoother. Even the refusal of moral resolution can become a smug gesture (as recent films by Woody Allen and Robert Altman have inadvertently demonstrated). Like her Bennington peers, Tartt offers the aroma of decadence, not its anatomy; stylish intimations of misbehavior, not visions of hell. She leaves her hero hanging out at the abyss, admiring his new sneakers. (pp. 47-9)

> Alexander Star, "Less Than Hero," in The New Republic, *Vol. 207, No. 17, October 19, 1992, pp. 47-9.*

James Saynor   (review date 25 October 1992)

[*Below, Saynor praises the technical competence of Tartt's prose but characterizes* The Secret History *as a fundamentally undistinguished suspense novel.*]

The young American author, Donna Tartt, has a name like a smoking bimbo, but her much-hyped début novel contains not much kissing and an awful lot of telling. The opening paragraphs refer to a story related 'simply and well', which is a fair description of the 520-page narrative that follows, chronicling in inordinate detail the guilt trip experienced by a clique of homicidal New England students.

The saga has a curiously amoral American feel to it: it's not so much about crime and punishment in the self-lacerating, Christian-psychological way we'd approach these things in a European context, but more about career-ism and self-absorption in an America bent on survival at any cost.

Such issues seem hugely pertinent during the cover-up circus of a US presidential election, though Tartt lacks the novelistic machinery to make any such links with the wider culture. Her story-telling is entirely functional, not metaphorical. *The Secret History* is one of those opportunistic projects—like, say, *Fatal Attraction*—that touches important chords in the contemporary psyche, but without seeming conscious of them; the book is ethically airless, with little sense of circumspection or irony.

The narrator, Richard Papen, an impoverished Californian, takes us almost hour-by-hour through the history of his college career—salad days with a goodly number of slugs in them. He's holed up in the chill, fastidious climate of a minor Vermont campus, studying Ancient Greek at the feet of an oddball pedagogue, amid other mixed-up white kids. The rivals for peer-chief are the feckless, dandyish Bunny, and the austerely charismatic Henry.

Funnily enough, it's classical European culture that's the source of the evil (though 'evil' isn't really a notion that comes into this novel: we probably need to say 'the bad stuff'). Enthused by their tutor's relish for Dionysian ritual, some of the chums go on a Bacchic 'wilding' spree, during which they borrow a farmer's entrails without his permission. Then, to kick over their hoof marks, Henry decides they have to rub out the dangerously talkative Bunny, sending him over a cliff minus the aid of a hang-glider.

These two incidents of murderous horror are presented sketchily and indirectly, and most of the book occupies itself with the endless surface details of the cover-up. By the denouement, we don't really care whether the 'studes' get sent to the chair or awarded Congressional Medals, though the outcome is fairly well signalled by the title of the novel.

There's no questioning the technical sheen of Tartt's prose, and she describes well the privations of an American college education plus the Clinton-ish manoeuvres you need to get through the system. The rest of it, though, with its matter-of-fact style and neither-here-nor-there generic quality, is Ruth Rendell without the ruthlessness. The most enthusiastic thing you can say about *The Secret History* is that it's a rattlingly competent yarn.

> James Saynor, "The Wrong Stuff," in The Observer, *October 25, 1992, p. 65.*

James Wood   (review date 19 December 1992)

[*In the following review, Wood asserts that Tartt's prejudiced portrayal of a class-conscious, glamorous world in* The Secret History *suggests her own ambivalent fascination with elitism.*]

Though a mystery story, Donna Tartt's first novel *The Secret History* holds few secrets. It is as open as a child: its revelations are too frequent to be significant, and its secrets too helpless to be revealing. It is a fairy-tale about a poor Californian who arrives at a rich New England college and quickly falls in with glamour and murder. Apparently about the nature of evil, it is full of wonder and romance—the romance of money, class, intelligence and beauty. It is swoonily compulsive, like listening to your own heartbeat: its sequence flatters you with what you want to hear. As the book's narrator, Richard Papen, discovers the golden campus and its gang of five mysterious Classics students, so his yearning to find out more about this cosy world becomes identical with the reader's, and a childish pact is joined (as in the best romances).

Tartt's writing has the self-delighted explicitness and wonderment that we know so well from children's fiction, or from adult versions like Swift and Dickens. This is not to be despised, for this wonderment returns fiction to its first principles, its primal scene. But it is startling to find it so openly done in a contemporary American novel. The wonderment begins where it must, at the beginning of the *real* story. What has happened to Richard Papen in California before his arrival at Hampden College, Vermont is lightly sketched in a few opening pages, because it is strictly unimportant: this story, not life, must confer enchantment. So only a few pages into the book Richard gets off the bus in Hampden, and is duly enchanted. 'The sun was rising over mountains, and birches, and impossibly green meadows . . . it was like a country from a dream.' Richard wants to major in Classics, but he is told that the subject is in the hands of one professor, Julian Morrow, who has only five students. He decides to seek out Morrow, and the writing excitedly complies:

> Once at the top I found myself in a long, deserted hallway. Enjoying the noise of my shoes on the linoleum, I walked along briskly, looking at the closed doors for numbers or names until I came to one that had a brass card holder and, within it, an engraved card that read JULIAN MORROW. I stood there for a moment and then I knocked, three short raps. A minute or so passed, and another, and then the white door opened just a crack. A face looked out at me.

Thus the narrator becomes the reader, and we share an ecstasy of wide-eyedness. Repeatedly, the novel returns to this function:

> as I was climbing out of the car, the moon came out from behind a cloud and I saw the house. It was tremendous. I saw, in sharp, ink-black silhouette against the sky, turrets and pikes, a widow's walk. 'Geez,' I said.

This novel is a prolonged and happy 'Geez'.

Richard first encounters the five Classics students in the library. ('My interest in Julian Morrow and his Greek pupils, though still keen, was starting to wane when a curious coincidence happened. It happened the Wednesday morning of my second week, when I was in the library.') The five are working together and discussing aloud the merits of the dative. ('Ablative's the ticket, old man,' suggests Bunny.) Richard speaks a password—'I'm sorry, but would the locative case do?'—and is given membership of the group. Its leader is Henry Winter, who 'wore dark English suits' and apparently published a translation of Anacreon, with commentary, when still 18. Later in the

novel he expresses surprise to learn that man has walked on the Moon. The oaf of the gang is Bunny Corcoran, Bunny 'being somehow short for Edmund' (presumably a little allusion of Tartt's: Bunny was Edmund Wilson's nickname); Francis Abernathy is the wimp; and the twins, Charles and Camilla Macaulay, are the beauties.

The members of the gang have no life outside their poses. There is nothing here unmotivated, no detail that is not telling ('he carried an umbrella, a bizarre sight in Hampden'), no revelation that is not a disclosure. Too zealously mapped, the novel cannot go its own way. The story compels, but it doesn't involve. We do not really care when Richard learns that the gang (minus Bunny) have murdered a farmer while dancing in the woods in a bacchanalian frenzy. Nor when the gang (plus Richard) kill Bunny, who figures out, too late, that his friends are murderers.

This is the sealed chamber of the fantastic, where everything fits. It is strange that Donna Tartt should have gone this way, for there are moments in the book when she proves herself a decent realist with a hospitable ear. Outside the ludicrousness of the gang, for instance, she provides a very sharp portrait of an expensive liberal arts college (she herself went to Bennington). Consider the names of some of the other students: Judy Poovey (a Californian who turns out to be the novel's true hero), Cloke Rayburn (the campus coke-dealer), Laura Stora, Jack Teitelbaum, Sophie Dearbold, Flipper Leach. Here is Judy Poovey's conversation:

> You know, I think Laura has an eating disorder, not anorexia, but that Karen Carpenter thing where you make yourself puke. Last night I went with her and Trace to the Brasserie, and I'm totally serious, she stuffed herself until she could not breathe. Then she went into the men's room to barf and Tracy and I were looking at each other, like, is this *normal?*

Now consider the feeble inaccuracy of the naming of the gang, and the implausibility of their speech, and it is difficult not to see the failure as instructive. With cold brilliance, Tartt sees accurately a world (of drugs and MTV and mindlessness) she clearly despises; but she is unable to do the same with a world (of pretension, class-consciousness and difficult learning) about which she is rather lovingly ambivalent. Is it unfair to suggest that the author's ambivalence—more in love with the glamour than she can admit—clouds her depiction of this world? That just as the novel too happily satisfies the reader's wants, so, perhaps, these unlikely Classics students satisfy her own wants? Their implausibility, after all, protects them from the censure of realism; they are murderers, but they are not *real* murderers; above all, they remain glamorous ('ablative's the ticket old man'). The novel is not really about the glamour of evil, but the glamour of glamour. This is the novel's childishness: it offers mysteries and polished revelations on every page, but its true secrets are too deep, too unintended to be menacing or profound.

This kind of moral vagueness is hardly new in American fiction of course. What separates Tartt's first novel from Fitzgerald's, for example, is its slyness and strange maturity. *This Side of Paradise* is hopelessly in love with glamour, and never seeks to hide it: Tartt's book has none of that uncalculated rapture and hapless sublimity. Tartt's novel is clever, mature and utterly calculated, down to its references to *Gatsby* and to Philip Roth's first novel *Goodbye, Columbus.* Her ambivalence is less easily fathomed than Fitzgerald's and less likeable. (p. 17)

> *James Wood, "The Glamour of Glamour," in* London Review of Books, *Vol. 14, No. 22, December 19, 1992, pp. 17-18.*

Prizewinners

Literary Prizes and Honors

Announced in 1992

•Academy of American Poets Awards•

Fellowship of the Academy of American Poets

Awarded annually to recognize distinguished achievement by an American poet.

J. D. McClatchy

* * *

The Lamont Poetry Selection

Established in 1952 to reward and encourage promising writers by supporting the publication of an American poet's second book.

Cater Stripling Byer
Wildwood Flowers

* * *

Peter I. B. Lavan Younger Poets Award

Established in 1983 to annually recognize three accomplished American poets under the age of forty.

Cyrus Cassells
Richard Lyons
Rosanna Warren

* * *

Walt Whitman Award

Secures the publication of the first book of a living American poet.

Stephen Yenser
The Fire in All Things

•American Academy and Institute of Arts and Letters Awards•

Academy-Institute Awards

Given annually to encourage creative achievement in art, music, and literature.

Alice Adams, John Crowley,
Richard Foreman, Vicki
Hearne, Ruth Prawer
Jhabvala, Tim O'Brien,
Simon Schama, August Wilson
(Awards in Literature)

* * *

Witter Bynner Foundation Prize for Poetry

Established in 1979 and awarded annually to recognize an outstanding younger poet.

George Bradley

Sue Kaufman Prize for First Fiction

Awarded annually to the author of the best first fiction published during the preceding year.

Alex Ullmann
Afghanistan

* * *

Richard and Hilda Rosenthal Foundation Award

Awards given annually for accomplishment in art and literature. The literature award recognizes a work of fiction published in the preceding year which, while not a "commercial success," is considered a literary achievement.

Douglas Hobbie
Boomfell

* * *

Morton Dauwen Zabel Award

Presented in alternating years to poets, fiction writers, and critics, to encourage progressive, original, and experimental tendencies in American literature.

Jorie Graham

•James Tait Black Memorial Book Prize•

Sponsored by the University of Edinburgh and awarded annually for the best work of fiction published during the previous year.

Iain Sinclair
Downriver
(fiction)
(see entry below)

•Booker Prize for Fiction•

Britain's major literary prize is awarded annually in recognition of a full-length novel.

Michael Ondaatje
The English Patient
(see entry below)

Barry Unsworth
Sacred Hunger
(see entry below)

•Booker Russian Novel Prize•

Awarded annually to recognize best new Russian novel. This award was established in 1992.

Mark Kharitonov
Lines of Fate, or Milashevich's Trunk
(novel)

•Cervantes Prize•

Awarded annually to an accomplished Spanish-speaking author.

Dulce María Loynaz

142

•Commonwealth Writers Prize•

Awarded annually to promote new Commonwealth fiction of merit outside the author's country of origin.

Rohinton Mistry
Such a Long Journey
(novel)
(see *CLC,* Vol. 71)

Robert Antoni
D
(first novel)

•Goncourt Prize•

Awarded annually in France by the *Academie Goncourt* to recognize a prose work published during the preceding year.

Patrick Chamoiseau
Texaco
(novel)

•Governor General's Literary Awards•

To honor writing that achieves literary excellence without sacrificing popular appeal. Awards are given annually for works written in both English and French in the categories of prose fiction, prose nonfiction, poetry, and drama. Officially known as the Canadian Authors Association (CAA) Literary Awards.

Michael Ondaatje
The English Patient
(fiction)
(see entry below)

Lorna Crozier
Inventing the Hawk
(poetry)

John Mighton
*Possible
Worlds*
and
*A Short History
of Night*
(drama)

Anne Hébert
L'enfant chargé de songes
(fiction)

Gilles Cyr
Androméde attendra
(poetry)

No award given
in 1992
(drama)

•Guggenheim Fellowships•

Awarded annually to recognize unusually distinguished literary achievement in the past and exceptional promise for future accomplishment.

Gish Jen, Brian Alan Kitely,
Norman Manea, E. Annie
Proulx, Matthew Philip
Stadler, Christopher Tilghman
(fiction)

T. R. Hummer, Jane
Kenyon, Susan Mitchell,
Donald Revell, Elizabeth
Spires, Adam Zagajewski
(poetry)

•Hugo Awards•

Established in 1953 to recognize notable science fiction works in several categories.

Lois McMaster Bujold
Barrayar
(novel)

Nancy Kress
Beggers in Spain
(novella)

Issac Asimov
"Gold"
(novellette)

Geoffrey A. Landis
"A Walk in the Sun"
(short story)

•Ruth Lilly Poetry Prize•

Awarded annually to an outstanding American poet.

John Ashbery

•Los Angeles Times Book Awards•

Awards are given to authors in various categories to honor outstanding technique and vision.

Adrienne Rich
An Atlas of the Difficult World: Poems, 1988-1991
(poetry)
(see entry below)

Art Spiegelman
Maus: A Survivor's Tale II: And Here My Troubles Began
(fiction)
(see entry below)

•Lenore Marshall/*Nation* Poetry Prize•

Established in 1974 to honor the author of the year's outstanding collection of poems published in the United States.

Adrienne Rich
An Atlas of the Difficult World: Poems, 1988-1991
(see entry below)

•National Book Awards•

Established in 1950 to honor and promote American books of literary distinction in various categories.

Cormac McCarthy
All the Pretty Horses
(fiction)

Paul Monette
Becoming a Man: Half a Life Story
(nonfiction)

Mary Oliver
New and Selected Poems
(poetry)

James Laughlin
(Distinguished Contribution to American Letters)

•National Book Critics Circle Awards•

Founded in 1974, this American award recognizes superior literary quality in several categories.

Jane Smiley
A Thousand Acres
(fiction)
(see entry below)

Albert Goldbarth
Heaven and Earth: A Cosmology
(poetry)

•Nebula Awards•

Established in 1965 to honor significant works in several categories of science fiction published in the United States.

Michael Swanwick
Stations of the Tide
(novel)

Alan Brennert
"Ma Qui"
(short story)

•New York Drama Critics Circle Award•

Awards are presented annually in several categories to encourage excellence in playwriting.

Brian Friel
Dancing at Lughnasa
(best new play)

August Wilson
Two Trains Running
(best new American play)
(see *CLC,* Vol. 63)

•Nobel Prize in Literature•

Awarded annually to recognize the most distinguished body of literary work of an idealistic nature.

Derek Walcott
(see entry below)

•Obie Award•

Awards in various categories are given annually to recognize excellence in off-Broadway and off-off-Broadway theater productions.

Donald Margulies
Sight Unseen
(see entry below)

Robbie McCauley
Sally's Rape

Paula Vogel
The Baltimore Waltz
(see entry below)

•PEN American Center Awards•

Faulkner Award for Fiction

Annually recognizes the most distinguished book-length work of fiction by an American writer published during the calendar year.

Don DeLillo
Mao II
(novel)
(see entry below)

•Edgar Allan Poe Awards•

Mystery Writers of America awards these prizes annually in recognition of outstanding contributions in mystery, crime, and suspense writing.

Elmore Leonard
(grand master)

Lawrence Block
A Dance at the Slaughterhouse
(best mystery novel)

Peter Blauner
Slow Motion Riot
(first mystery novel)

•Pulitzer Prizes•

Awarded in recognition of outstanding accomplishments by American authors in various categories within the fields of journalism, literature, music, and drama. Literary awards usually recognize excellence in works that concern American life.

Jane Smiley
A Thousand Acres
(fiction)
(see entry below)

James Tate
Selected Poems
(poetry)

Robert Schenkkan
The Kentucky Cycle
(drama)

Art Spiegelman
*Maus: A Survivor's Tale II:
And Here My Troubles Began*
(special award)
(see entry below)

•Rea Award•

Presented annually to recognize outstanding achievement in the short story genre.

Eudora Welty

•Tony Awards•

Officially titled the American Theatre Wing's Antoinette Perry Awards, this prize is presented in recognition of outstanding achievement in the Broadway theater.

Brian Friel
Dancing at Lughnasa
(best play)

•United States Poet Laureate•

Created in 1986 by an act of Congress to honor the career achievement of an American poet.

Mona Van Duyn
(see *CLC,* Vol. 63)

•Whitbread Literary Awards•

Awarded annually in several categories to encourage and promote English literature.

Alasdair Gray
Poor Things
(novel)

Tony Harrison
The Gaze of the Gorgon
(poetry)

João Cabral de Melo Neto
Neustadt International Prize for Literature

Born in 1920, Cabral is a Brazilian poet.

INTRODUCTION

Cabral has earned international acclaim as one of Brazil's most original and influential poets of the post-World War II era. In his poetry, which is often described as objective and formalistic, Cabral uses rigid poetic structures and multiple perspectives to examine the metalinguistic aspects of language. Unlike many Brazilian poets, he considers poetry a written rather than an oral art form, and his consequent emphasis on syntax rather than phonetics and lyricism renders his work distinct from most Brazilian verse. Djelal Kadir, in awarding Cabral the Neustadt International Prize for Literature, stated: "[Cabral] is an artfully subtractive poet engaged in the labors of winnowing, culling, paring down. A poet who opts for the economy of the minimal with maximum effect. He practices a laconic art of deference in a poetry that curtails its own voice, as well as the ego of its author, yielding to the human context that links poetic vocation with daily life and worldly experience."

Cabral spent the first ten years of his life on his family's sugar plantation in Pernambuco, a state in northeastern Brazil. The region's geography and culture deeply influenced Cabral, and he often incorporates images of Pernambuco into his work. His family moved to Recife, the capital city of Pernambuco, when Cabral was ten. After publishing two verse collections, *Pedra do sono* and *O engenheiro,* Cabral joined Brazil's diplomatic service in 1945. During a career that spanned four decades, Cabral served in Spain, Great Britain, Switzerland, and Paraguay and was appointed Ambassador to Senegal and later Ambassador to Honduras. The author of more than twenty-five books of poetry, Cabral was elected to the Brazilian Academy of Letters in 1968 and awarded the São Paulo Literary Prize in 1992. Since retiring from diplomatic service in 1987, Cabral has resided in Rio de Janeiro.

Cabral is known for his repetition of images and his tightly structured syntax. For example, images of life in northeastern Brazil recur throughout much of his poetry. In such poems as "Morte e vida severina" Cabral describes the misery of an impoverished peasant fleeing drought, while "A cana dos outros" depicts the relationship between the owner of a sugar plantation and the peasant who performs the labor. Cabral also uses images of such objects as knives, razors, and scalpels to describe anything with a piercing or aggressive quality. In "As facas Pernambu-

canas," for example, Cabral describes different types of knives to symbolize the disaffection between the people of Pernambuco's interior and those of its coastal areas. Critics also note Cabral's distinctive use of syntax and what some have called visual onomatopoeia to achieve movement in his poetry. In "Jogos frutais" Cabral uses a form of extended anadiplosis to achieve sinuous movement of an idea from one stanza to another, while in "Tecendo a manhã" he suggests the back and forth movement of a shuttle in a loom solely through repetition of words and enjambment of lines.

Believing that poetry should communicate the interrelationships between the organic and inorganic, Cabral often uses multiple comparisons to capture the true essence of a subject or object. In "Estudos para uma bailadora andaluza," for example, Cabral compares an Andalusian dancer to fire, a mare, a telegraph operator, a tree, a statue, and a maize plant. Through such comparisons Cabral emphasizes the interconnectedness of all things and promotes his belief in the primacy of collective humanity over the individual. Cabral also advocates objectivity and understatement in many of his works. For example, in the collection *A psicologia da composição com a fábula de Anfion e antiode,* he attacks what he considers the principal weaknesses of modern verse—excessive lyricism and romanticism. Throughout his career, Cabral has compared poets to engineers and poems to machines. Upon ·being awarded the Neustadt Prize, he further explicated his thoughts on the nature of poetry: "[Poetry] is the exploration of the materiality of words and of the possibilities of organization of verbal structures, things that have nothing to do with what is romantically called inspiration, or even intuition. In this respect, I believe that lyricism, upon finding in popular music the element that fulfills it and gives it its prestige, has liberated written . . . poetry and has allowed it to return to operate in territory that once belonged to it. It has made possible too the exercise of poetry as emotive exploration of the world of things and as rigorous construction of lucid formal structures, lucid objects of language."

PRINCIPAL WORKS

Pedra do sono (poetry) 1942
Os três mal-amados (poetry) 1943
O engenheiro (poetry) 1945
A psicologia da composição com a fábula de Anfion e anti-ode (poetry) 1947
O cão sem plumas (poetry) 1950
Joan Miró (criticism) 1950
O rio ou relação da viagem que faz o Capibaribe di sua nascente à cidade do Recife (poetry) 1954
Pregão turístico (poetry) 1955
Duas águas (poetry) 1956
Uma faca só lâmina (poetry) 1956; published in *Duas águas*
Morte e vida severina (poetry) 1956; published in *Duas águas*
Paisagens com figuras (poetry) 1956; published in *Duas águas*
Aniki Bobó (poetry) 1958
Quaderna (poetry) 1960
Dois parlamentos (poetry) 1961
Serial (poetry) 1961; published in *Terceira feira*
Terceira feira (poetry) 1961
Poemas escolhidos (poetry) 1963
Antologia poética (poetry) 1965
A educação pela pedra (poetry) 1966
Morte e vida severina e outraos poemas em voz alta (poetry) 1966
Funeral de um Lavrador (poetry) 1967
Poesias completas (poetry) 1968
Museu de tudo (poetry) 1975
A escola das facas (poetry) 1980
Auto do frade (poetry) 1984
Agrestes (poetry) 1985
Os melhores poemas de João Cabral (poetry) 1985
Crime na Calle Relator (poetry) 1987

Museu de tudo e depois (poetry) 1988
Poemas pernambucanos (poetry) 1988
Sevilha andando (poetry) 1989
Primeiros poemas (poetry) 1990

CRITICISM

Richard Zenith   (essay date July-December 1987)

[*In the following excerpt, Zenith identifies objectivity as the principal thematic and stylistic concern in Cabral's poetry.*]

Contemporary Brazilian poetry, virtually unknown in the United States with the possible exception of Carlos Drummond de Andrade, is one of the most critical and self-conscious poetries in the Americas—"self-conscious" not for being concerned with the *poet's* self, but with *poetry's* self or identity. Brazilian poets are acutely aware of where their poetry stands in relation to the poetic continuum in their own country and other countries as well. The Brazilian Concrete poets [who, Zenith states in a footnote, "abandon[ed] traditional verse in favor of a poetry that exploits the sonoric and graphic as well as semantic possibilities of words"] have made some of the most daring assaults on verse in recent decades, but they are intimately acquainted with their precursors, inside and outside Brazil, and have spent at least as much time critiquing and translating the poetry of [Ezra] Pound, [Stephen] Mallarmé, [Vladimir] Mayakovsky and [e. e.] cummings as they have spent writing their own.

While the Concrete experiments have yielded some highly provocative and no doubt enduring poetry, the movement has lost the momentum it carried in the 1960's, and in fact the leaders themselves, having once sworn off verse, are now writing poetry which, albeit innovative, employs what must be called verses. Such a move does not invalidate the earlier attempts to achieve a "verbi-voco-visual" poetry made of words outside their usual semantic setting, i.e. the sentence or phrase, but it does suggest that verse, which has been synonymous with poetry for most of its history, is liable to be the dominant variety for some years to come. If the Concrete poets put too much faith in the aesthetic possibilities of the *"palavra-coisa"* ["word-thing"], one might charge that poets from other countries have gone too far the other way, using words for their semantic value only. Contemporary American poetry reveals and expresses, but it seems to do little *creating.*

The subject of this article, João Cabral de Melo Neto, is remarkable for having held one of the foremost positions in his country's literary vanguard for some 40 years without ever departing from traditional verse form. His works trace an ever-advancing course in his poetics, which have insisted on poetry as construction rather than as revelation, while retaining an *antropofágica* compulsion that has searched farther than the Modernists, incorporating and reworking everything from the *cordel* [handbill] poetic forms of Northeastern Brazil to the *cuaderna vía* of the Spanish clerical poets. As with all of Brazil's better poets, Melo Neto has devoted considerable energies to the study and criticism of other poets and plastic artists as well, and he freely acknowledges the importance of Drummond de Andrade, Mendes and other Brazilians, [Paul] Valéry, [Francis] Ponge and Marianne Moore for his own development. Far from making his poetry tend toward imitation (as is liable to happen in mediocre poets), these influences have spurred Melo Neto to a pure and strict verse which uses language to create landscapes rather than to announce them.

Melo Neto has been extensively translated into every major European language except English. Brazilian scholars in the U.S., however, have not been slow to recognize the importance of this poet. While Carlos Drummond de Andrade is generally considered Brazil's greatest living poet, Melo Neto is often cited as the most influential among younger writers. [In his *The Modernist Movement in Brazil*] John Nist calls him the "undisputed leader of the Generation of 1945 in Brazil," thereby demonstrating a correct estimation of the poet's stature, though he has mislocated Melo Neto, who might be better described as one who stood apart from the group and influenced other poets to follow his lead. While sharing the 45 Generation's criticism of Modernism for having fallen into petty nationalism and formal sloppiness (Oswald and Mário de Andrade would have to be exempted from both these charges), Melo Neto faulted the new movement for its use of cheap devices, such as puns and gratuitous emotion, in lieu of disciplined composition. The 45 Generation was, at its worst, a nostalgic return to the highly refined "poetic" language of pre-Modernist or even pre-Symbolist days, and Melo Neto took pains to disassociate himself from this "idealistic preference" which would celebrate the "sublime against the prosaic." [In **"A Geração de 45,"** *Diário Carioca* (1952)] Melo Neto's criticism of this position was sharp:

> This is a poetry of super-realities, made with exclusive parts of man, in order to communicate highly subtle information which can only be found in the most ethereal and abstract part of the dictionary. The prosaic word is heavy with reality, dirty with common realities that come from the common world, and in such angelic atmospheres it can only serve as a neutralizer.

These words were written in 1952, at which point the foundation of Melo Neto's own poetic program was already well established, though over the past three decades he has consistently confounded those critics who would categorize him and disappointed the literary schools that have claimed him. His evolution is no passive maturing process, nor has it come by spontaneous shifts in the poet's psyche, but rather by uncompromising adherence to the rigor and logic of his basic proposal: to forge a vigorous poetry that needs no superfluous niceties of diction or personal interferences to prop it up. Images and other poetic elements are reduced to their essential structural lines, which are then tightly organized into a kind of "poem-

machine" that functions on its own with as little intrusion from the poet as possible.

Joao Cabral de Melo Neto was 22 years old when he published his first book of poems, **Pedra do Sono (Stone of Sleep)**. Here the poet is still searching for his way, oscillating between a surrealistic preoccupation with the poetry latent in sleeping states (*sono*) and his desire for hard clarity (*pedra*). In these short poems Melo Neto makes free and even playful associations of words, but the sometimes ethereal quality of these verses is brought down to earth by the plastic relief of their images. Significant are his poem addressed to André Masson, who was initially influenced by Surrealism but later adopted the Cubist technique, and a quotation from Mallarmé ("Solitude, récif, étoile . . . ") as the book's epigraph. Melo Neto's critical/intellectual orientation and concern with the poetic process are further confirmed in his verses:

> The poem's liquid voices
> urge crime
> a revolver
>
> They speak to me of islands
> which even dreams
> cannot reach.
> **"O Poema e a Agua" ("Water and the Poem")**

O Engenheiro (**The Engineer**) has none of the intuitive technique and emotional suggestion of Melo Neto's first collection. No longer concerned with the expression of subjective states, here the poet makes verses with the logic and objectivity of a builder. His epigraph, ". . . machine à émouvoir . . . ", is from LeCorbusier, whose books Melo Neto once cited as the essential and definitive influence on his work. Never had a Brazilian poet been so audacious (or humble?) as to propound in the plainest terms this "poetry of construction," from which the Concrete and succeeding vanguard figures would take their cues:

> Light, sun and the open air
> surround the dream of the engineer.
> The engineer dreams clear things:
> surfaces, tennis-courts, a glass of water.
>
> A pencil, a T-square, paper,
> designs, projects, numbers.
> The engineer imagines the world correct,
> a world which no veil covers.
>
> (Sometimes we went up
> the building. The daily city,
> like a newspaper for all to read,
> gained a lung of cement and glass.)
>
> The water, the wind, the brightness,
> the river on one side and the clouds on high
> made a place in nature for the building,
> growing by its own simple strength.

This title poem not only tells, but shows by its very form, the aspiration and technique of the poet-engineer. His "dream" is not wishful, nor does it proceed from the imprecise world of the subconscious. The engineer's dream is thought itself, the projecting of definite ideas onto paper or into concrete. It is as if the engineer would by his labors show us a Platonic world of pure ideas ("a world which no veil covers") existing not in the individual psyche, but in the natural order of which man is only a part. The engineer works on behalf of the human community rather than for single members of it, and separations are not admitted. The city, and the building within the city, have their places in nature right alongside the clouds and the river. If man the individual is somewhat slighted, mankind (the city) is exalted as its most original component (not, however, as its conqueror). The poet-engineer's building-poem gives a lung to the city and a perspective (third stanza) from which we can see the city as plainly as we read a newspaper; finally the engineer stands back, allowing his construction to take its place in the world, growing by its own force and logic (last lines). True to these words, Melo Neto succeeds in announcing a new and radical poetic program without resorting to personal appeals or oratory. He applies his techniques—analogy, assonance and the four-line stanza, all of which will become mainstays in his poetry—in such a way that the poem seems to carry itself forward.

Melo Neto does not dismiss the subconscious, as if it did not exist (in fact he has undertaken extensive self-analysis), but his poetry reifies intuition and feelings, subsequently organizing them into rigorously logical verses. This objectifying process (which is the creative process) can only be partially realized. **"A Bailarina" ("The Dancer")** describes the poet's frustration in trying to capture the subconscious in verses:

> The dancer made
> of rubber and bird
> dances on the porch
> in front of the dream.
>
> In the third sleeping hour,
> beyond all dreams,
> in the secret chambers
> which death reveals.
>
> Among monsters made
> with writing ink,
> the dancer made
> of rubber and bird.
>
> Of the slow and daily
> eraser I chew.
> Of the insect or bird
> I cannot catch.

Notice that we pass in front of the dream and beyond the dream, but we never enter into it. This is the "insect or bird" which he cannot lay hold of; it is the vital stuff of his poetry, the dancer, without which a writer can only produce monsters. The work of the poet (symbolized by the eraser—Melo Neto affirms that he has rewritten certain poems dozens of times) combines with the supersensible, and the resulting tension is true poetry. What matters for the poet is not to understand the dream but *to make something of it*. He turns his visions into things, while at the same time viewing these and all things with a visionary's enthusiasm. The concrete of his images is vivid and even phosphorescent, as in **"A Mesa" ("The Table")**:

> The newspaper folded
> on top the small table;
> the tablecloth clean,
> the dishes white

> and fresh like bread.
>
> The green orange:
> your landscape always,
> your open air, sun
> of your beaches bright
>
> and fresh like bread.
>
> The knife that sharpened
> your dull pencil
> your first book
> whose cover is white
>
> and fresh like bread.
>
> And the verse born
> of your vivid morning,
> of your dream just ended,
> still warm, light
>
> and fresh like bread.

The poem, created out of the poet's last dream of the night, is presented as one more of the various objects on the table, but this leveling in no wise diminishes the worth or role of poetry. Rather, Melo Neto wishes to raise everything to the poetic level. The things on the table radiate cleanliness and clarity, and (most explicitly in the case of the orange) they stand for larger realities, not as symbols but as microcosmic versions. While his images are often didactic, pointing to more general concepts, they never *merely* represent. The immediate semantic value of Melo Neto's lines is sufficient to justify them as poetry, and he is careful to keep his words and images close to earth. Even the fleeting imagination is placed on firm ground, as in this odd little still life:

"A Woman Sitting" ("A Mulher Sentada")

> Woman. Woman and doves.
> Woman among dreams.
> Clouds in her eyes?
> Clouds over her hair.
>
> (The visitor waits in the hall;
> the news, on the telephone;
> death is growing even now,
> and spring outside the window.)
>
> Woman sitting. Calm
> in the hall, as if flying.

The woman is wholly immersed in her own mind's world, but the reader is not allowed to forget physical reality. The first sentence reveals only the generic existence of the woman, and as we gradually discover that her mind is wrapped up in her own thoughts—"woman and doves," "woman among dreams"—we are always reminded of her physicality: *woman*. "Clouds in her eyes?" Is her eyesight dominated by the clouds of this dream state? Are they an essential aspect of her vision? The poet denies it vigorously. The clouds hover above the woman, but her identity does not depend on them. She coexists, indeed may for a time be lost in reverie, but it does not constitute a part of her person. Despite the fanciful or perhaps fantastic notions that cross her mind, the third stanza informs us that the woman is seated and tranquil, and the last line should be understood as meaning that she would be just as tranquil if she were literally flying. No matter how far or fast a person's mind or body wanders, there is an essential tranquility in his/her organic substantiality. This expresses an interesting philosophical view that might be neatly juxtaposed with Eastern philosophy as formulated in the Vedas. There the physical world is illusion, real only to our unenlightened eyes, while our true self, the *atman,* is ineffable, beyond both the physical and psychical aspects of the human being. Melo Neto, on the other hand, finds the essential thingness of an object in its face value, and reality is that which is most visible. The outside world is unreal to the seated woman, who does not perceive the phenomena listed in the second stanza (hence the parentheses), but they are listed to remind the reader what is real. Interestingly enough, both Melo Neto's "materialist" persuasion and the Vedantic pursuit of a spiritual idea lead to a not dissimilar universal vision in which humanity matters more than the individual human.

[João Cabral de Melo Neto] finds the essential thingness of an object in its face value, and reality is that which is most visible.

—*Richard Zenith*

Perhaps it is inappropriate to talk about philosophy in a poet who eschews metaphysical speculation in favor of tangible production. Melo Neto's investigations in *The Engineer* are at the level of poetry, and the mechanics of poetic creation become the nearly exclusive theme of the trilogy published in 1947: *A Psicologia da Composiçao (Psychology of Composition)*, *Fábula de Anfion (The Fable of Amphion)*, and *Antiode*. Taking the "white struggle on paper" ([a] phrase from **"A Lição de Poesia" ("The Lesson of Poetry")**), in *The Engineer* to its furthest limit, Melo Neto's project becomes, as Haroldo de Campos notes, "decidedly Mallarméesque: creation considered as the struggle against chance" ["O Geômetra Engajado," in his *Metalinguagem*].

In Melo Neto's *Fable,* the first section, "O Deserto" ("The Desert"), describes the "white land" of the desert with its "lucid sun," where Amphion finds himself among unrealized words ("stones like forgotten fruits that refused to ripen"), with a flute that is drying under the desert sun. The second section, "O Acaso" ("Chance"), tells of Amphion's struggle with chance, which finally causes his flute to sound, and Thebes is born. In the final section, "Anfion em Tebas" ("Amphion in Thebes"), Amphion (the poet) regrets having made the city (the poem):

> I longingly desired
> a smooth wall, and white
> pure sun in itself . . .
>
> Where is the airborne
> city, the civil
> cloud I dreamed of ?

Then he asks:

> A flute: how
> can it be governed,
> free and headstrong horse?

And he throws his flute into the sea, seeking anew the lost desert.

Psicologia discusses in direct fashion the difficulties and frustration of poetic creation presented in *Anfion,* whereas *Antiode* denounces (or renounces?) lyrical poetry with an evangelical fervor. The subtitle—"against so-called profound poetry"—stands as a fundamental tenet of Melo Neto's program, and he wastes no time in removing poetry from its sacred standing:

> Poetry, I spelled you
> flower! knowing
> you are feces. Feces
> like any other . . .

Later the poet would discover that he could again call poetry "flower," but with this difference:

> Flower is the word
> flower, verse
> inscribed in verse, as
> mornings in time.

"Flower" is no longer a metaphor but is what it is: the word *flower,* with no more right to inclusion in the poem than *feces* or any other word.

Having refined his principles and sharpened his tools, Melo Neto takes up the task of converting into poetry the world around him, i.e. the objective world shared by us all. He has harsh words for the "poema moderno" which tends to be preoccupied with individualistic themes without the least concern for the reader:

> This type of individualistic poet only gives of himself. The reader's mission of contributing indirectly to the creation goes unrecognized or is denied. This poet refuses to receive, and he doesn't understand that anything of value must have its origin in reality
> **["Poesia e Composição—A Inspiração e o Trabalho de Arte,"** in *Vanguarda Européia e Modernismo Brasileiro*].

The most pressing realities for Melo Neto come from the dry and economically depressed landscape of Northeastern Brazil, where he was born (Recife, 1920) and raised. Having purified his verse of the sublime and decorative language often considered "poetic" (traces of which were still present in *Pedra do Sono*), Melo Neto is well prepared to write about austere subjects with uncompromising diction. The poetic tension that characterized *The Engineer* and *Psicologia* is somewhat relaxed to accomodate the narrative style of *O Cão sem Plumas (The Featherless Dog)*, which tells of the Capibaribe River and the poverty-stricken people whose lives it traverses. It is a common, unsophisticated man rather than a sociologist who speaks, and his unpretty, unpolished language reinforces the message of frank misery. The featherless dog is a semantic parallel to the river, and the poem contains many other such equivalences. Metaphors are introduced in the most commonplace manner, by *como* and *quando,* for here even poetry must yield to the urgency of the discourse. This is no sloppy art or poetic laziness; on the contrary, every prosaic element and even clichés have been deliberately placed. This is in keeping with Melo Neto's ambition: to achieve a poetry whose architecture perfectly and *purposefully* fits its thematic content, so that the two become indistinguishable.

The communicative emphasis is increased and poetic tension further reduced in *O Rio* (*The River*), a poem divided into 29 segments bearing marginal captions to indicate where the Capibaribe River (which is the first-person narrator) passes on its way to Recife. The epigraph, "Quiero que compongamos io e tú una prosa," is from the Spanish poet Gonzalo de Berceo (1195-1264), who used colloquial language to address the comon people, an example followed in *The River,* although stylistically it more nearly resembles the *cantigas de cordel* of Northeastern Brazil, where the popular verse-makers can be found distributing and declaiming their works in the streets. Repetition of speech patterns characterize the tone of *The River,* which is the least dense of Melo Neto's poems, but its monotony and the slowly winding ways of its form make it a successful homology of the Capibaribe River as it dispassionately flows past great beauties and great tragedies.

Melo Neto's communicative success reaches its highest point in *Morte e Vida Severina* (*Death and Life of a Severino*), the most widely read and translated of all his works. A staged version of the dramatic poem (subtitled *A Pernambucan Nativity Play*) won prizes in Brazil and France, and brought international stature to Melo Neto. "We are many Severinos, equal in everything in life," says the protagonist, a prototype of the Northeastern migrant who journeys hopefully to Recife. He encounters exploitation and misery in the "rosary of small towns" along the way, and at the end of his travels reports:

> And arriving, I discover
> that in this trip I took
> I followed unknowingly, since
> the Sertao, my own funeral.
> But I must have arrived
> a few days ahead of time;
> the funeral waits at the door:
> the dead man still has life.

The "life" promised in the title is not the divine incarnation of the traditional Nativity plays but is human life itself which, no matter how oppressed, still offers some hope for change. Confronted by life and its possibilities, Severino decides not to hurry his death.

Death and Life of Severino which has gone through many editions and continues to be popular as a book, a play and a film, is not especially interesting from the point of view of artistic technique, but it accords perfectly with Melo Neto's desire to take poetry out of the literary salon and place it instead "at the door of modern man." And yet Melo Neto has been attacked as cerebral and inhuman, too much of a technician, and certain of his collections by their very titles—*The Engineer, Educação pela Pedra* (*Education by Stone*), *A Escola das Facas* (*The School of Knives*)—suggest the severity of the poet's undertaking.

The insistent dialectic of his creation might take Melo Neto's poetry into an ideal atmosphere all its own if it were not for his other concern: to make of poetry an instrument by which to see the world, and especially the grim conditions of his homeland, in stark clarity. Melo Neto already recognized and accepted the duality of his agendum in 1956 with the publication of his collected works under the title *Duas Aguas* (*Two Waters*), described in the flyleaf as "poetry of reflective concentration and poetry for larger audiences." The first *água,* elsewhere called "critical poetry" by the poet, makes no concessions in its pursuit of a pure poetic construction built on images that will withstand the most trenchant analysis. The second *água* is deliberately more prosaic, written in the language of the migrant "Severinos" of whom and for whom it speaks. The second *água* includes *The Featherless Dog, The River,* and *Death and Life of a Severino* (published for the first time in *Two Waters*), while the first would include *The Engineer, Psychology of Composition* and two new works: *Uma Faca Só Lâmina* (*A Knife All Blade*), subtitled *or servitude to fixed ideas* and again concerned with the problem of language's inability to represent reality, and *Paisagens com Figuras* (*Landscapes with Figures*), whose landscapes alternate between the poet's native Pernambuco and Spain, where he had been living since 1947.

The opening poem of *Landscapes* achieves a startling unity between the linguistic and sociological considerations that constantly (though in varying measure) inform Melo Neto's work. Here is revealed his vision, not of what should be but of what is, and what the role of poetry is:

"Tourist Pitch for Recife" ("Pregão Turístico do Recife")

> Here the sea is a mountain
> fair and blue and round,
> taller than the coral reefs
> and the shallow swamps to the south.
>
> From the sea you can extract
> (from the sea that laps our coast)
> a thread of mathematical
> precise light or metal.
>
> In the city itself old
> lanky tenements crowd
> together their limy shoulders
> on both sides of a river.
>
> With the tenements you can learn
> a lesson of long experience:
> from the architecture, a light
> sense of balance in writing.
>
> And from this wretched river,
> this blood-mud flowing between
> sclerosis and cement
> at such a sluggish rate,
>
> and from the people who stagnate
> in the river's membrane linings,
> entire lives on a thread
> slowly rotting to death,
>
> you can learn that man
> is always the best measure,
> and that the measure of man

is not death but life.

Melo Neto may be considered the first of the Concrete poets insofar as he fills his poetic universe with tactile images. In the first two stanzas of **"Tourist Pitch"** he turns liquid into rock, and light becomes objective to the point of changing into metal. The material reality of the "tourist" scene is thus firmly established, and the process of reification takes an interesting turn in the poem's most beautiful image: old lanky *sobrados* ("multi-story houses," translated here as "tenements" but not to be understood necessarily as "slums") squeezing their limy shoulders against one another on both sides of a river. What was already concrete takes on physiologically human aspects as well, and this unity of mineral with human is extended to the "indigent" Capibaribe River, endowed with "blood-mud" (*sangue-lama*) and mucuous membranes (*mucosas*). Close examination smashes the illusion presented in travel brochures, and as the architecture of the *sobrados* and all concrete images reveal something of the human condition, so does poetry. The "lesson of experience" is to use language to decipher reality in the way that images discover it via the relation mineral-human, but it does not necessarily occur spontaneously. While founded in nature, the image is a poetic device whose force is made effective by the skillful use of language. The homologue between the tourist promoter's attitude toward the image and the poet's toward language makes the final stanza doubly optimistic. Melo Neto's obsession with objectivity does not make his poetry a mere potpourri of pretty things, for they interrelate and lead finally to a statement about man's condition, which in **"Tourist Pitch"** might seem hopeless until the last lines, where we are told in effect that man can determine both how he will build/change the world and, if we apply the "lesson of experience," how he will speak/poetize his "pitch" to make it true and effectual.

> **Melo Neto's obsession with objectivity does not make his poetry a mere potpourri of pretty things, for they interrelate and lead finally to a statement about man's condition. . . .**
>
> —*Richard Zenith*

Quaderna (*Four Spot*) intensifies the identification [with] Sertao-Spain; Melo Neto's contact with the unyielding *meseta* and its discouraged inhabitants (still under Franco) seemed to sharpen his recollection of the flatness and poverty of Northeastern Brazil. "Quaderna" refers to the four spot on a die but also to the *cuaderna vía* poetic form used by the Spanish clerical poets from the 13th to the 15th centuries. Modern poets such as Antonio Machado had revived the *cuaderna vía,* and for Melo Neto it served as a constant, an invariable structure that would accentuate the thematic diversity of his poems while at the same time suggesting underlying connections between them. Here are poems about women, rare in Melo Neto's work,

poems about poetry itself (most importantly, **"A Palo Seco,"** a Spanish expression signifying "pure, unadorned"), and poems about cemeteries. Common to all of them is the poet's ever starker diction, which seeks to communicate subjects in their most essential aspects. In **"Cemitério Pernambucano (Floresta do Navio)" ("Cemetery in Pernambuco")** the poet ironizes political orators of Northeastern Brazil, whose florid rhetoric contrasts sharply with the

> . . . flat sheet
> of the backlands, where naked
> life does not make speeches
> but talks with sharp words.

It is this language of the Sertão (the arid backland of Northeast Brazil) which Melo Neto takes as his model, and the Sertão, more than a geographical area, represents honest perception, "naked life." The *cuaderna vía* acts as a check on poetic excesses, since all its themes must be expressed within the general framework of the quatrain. Even beyond structural considerations, Melo Neto's varying themes may be seen as superpositions: the Sertao, the Spanish plateau, woman and poetry, all of them frankly exposed—part of the engineer-poet's "clear vision" (as expressed in the title poem of *The Engineer*).

The quatrain continues to serve as building block in *Serial,* while the poet steps further into the background. The 16 "series" are not the anonymous production of an assembly line, but neither are they presented as the objects of a sublime art. *Serial* is the work of an artisan without pretensions beyond the skillful handling of his craft. His finished products are like common household goods, all of them highly useful and expertly fashioned. Rather than invoking hidden meanings, the poet strives for an equivalence between word and image, whereby the poem would read like an objective document. In "O Sim Contra o Sim" ("Yes Against Yes"), Melo Neto praises Mondrian, Miró and other artists for endeavoring to free their art from individualism. Speaking of Mondrian's right (painting) hand, Melo Neto says:

> He grafted in rulers, T-squares
> and other tools,
> making his hand give up
> all improvisation.

For Melo Neto poetry is more work than inspiration, and he is known to be a severe critic of his own texts, taking them through successive revisions before arriving at a "symmetrical" and therefore "artistic" result. Melo Neto's penchant for symmetry, which he understands as the rigorous and precise organization of thematic material, has prompted some to call him an "antipoet," a title which he has never sought to repudiate.

This criticism (or tribute, depending on one's viewpoint) was exacerbated in 1966, with the publication of *Education by Stone,* self-styled as an *antilyric* in the dedication to Manuel Bandeira. This collection of 48 two-part poems, divided into two sections and subdivided into two more, looks almost like an exercise book, but this is not mere didactic effort, any more than Bach's 48 Preludes and Fugues. It is worth taking the comparison further, for

Melo Neto achieves a masterful counterpoint by the ingenious facing off of key words and images within the fanatically symmetrical structure. Even banal subjects (there are poems about aspirin and chewing gum) are handled with an artistry that makes some of our modern "I" poets seem capable of little more than indulgent self-description. Melo Neto's purpose in writing about chewing gum is not to reduce poetry to a technical virtuosity independent of its subject matter; rather, he seeks to demystify poetry, to show that the world is not divided into poetic and unpoetic categories but that everything is poetry if correctly viewed. And his anti-individualism derives from the conviction that poetry is collective, residing in the texture that binds together things and persons. This interrelation, transcending even the boundaries between human and inorganic, is beautifully drawn in **"Tecendo a Manha"** **("Weaving the Morning"):**

By himself a cock can't weave a morning.
Always he'll need other cocks:
one to take up the cry he makes
and shout it to another, another cock
to take up the cry of the cock before
and shout it to another, and other cocks
joining with many other cocks to cross
the threads of sunlight with their cries
so that the moring, from a tenuous tissue,
will grow by the weaving of all the cocks.

2.

And enlarging into a fabric involving all,
erecting itself a tent where all may enter,
extending itself for all, in the awning
(the morning) that hovers free of any frame:
the morning, awning made of a weave so airy
that, once woven, it rises by itself: a balloon of
    light.

The strict weave of the poem's structure corresponds to the criss-crossing of the "threads of sunlight with their cries" which in turn points to the collective nature of human actions. The first three verses of the second stanza are a *tour de force* of interlinear assonance and alliteration, thereby heightening the sense of solidarity.

This poem, as with any good poem, succeeds not because of what it affirms but because its own construction *demonstrates* what it affirms. The whole business of poetry, then, depends on an ever increasing proficiency with one's tools. The impressive evolution of Melo Neto's poetic (or antipoetic?) skill proves his contention that poetry is process: "an education by stone, says the title poem, "in lessons; to learn from the stone, . . . to capture its unemphatic, impersonal voice (it begins its classes with one on diction). Only by exact and systematic operations can one's poetry attain the consistency and resilience of a stone.

Museu de Tudo (*Museum of Everything*) will be left aside in this discussion of the author's evolution since, as the title hints, it gathers together previously unpublished work written throughout the poet's career since 1946.

The poems of **The School of Knives** return thematically speaking to Northeast Brazil, but they represent yet a further advance in Melo Neto's style. These poems are as tightly constructed as ever, without gratuitous elements;

in addition, they are imbued with a lyric quality which, though never wholly absent (despite the poet's own claims to the contrary), is now more accessible. The geography of Pernambuco is as barren as ever, the knives (and the poet's words) just as sharp, but the poetry seems to sing nevertheless—a consolation among so much misery. But if some beauty can be had in the descriptions of desolate lives, it is also clear that the effects of human suffering reach farther than man's flesh, as in **"A Voz do Canavial"** **("The Voice of the Canefield"),** where even the wind is not immune:

Spitless voice of the cicada,
of dry crumpling paper,

of the newspaper when it folds:
so is the singing of the canefield

to the wind which through its leaves
from razor to razor breathes,

wind which all night and day
leafs through and is left grazed.

Melo Neto's . . . **Auto do Frade (The Friar),** is another sort of return, this time to the dramatic narrative style of **Death and Life of a Severino.** It would be more accurate to regard both works as plays written in poetic style, and this most recent *auto* will no doubt find its way to the stage in short order. **The Friar** tells the last day in the life of Frei Caneca, sentenced to death by the Court in 1825 for republican ideas and for his leadership in the "Confederação do Equador." The supplications of Joaquim do Amor Divino (Frei Caneca) speak for the Northeastern people he led and inspired, and if the *auto's* very format prevents it from sustaining the poetic rigor of his "critical poetry," this merely confirms the poet's detachment from his art. He willingly adapts his instrument for the sake of his commitment to social justice. Thus **The Friar** takes its place in the second of Melo Neto's two (*waters*), and is made

> **João Alexandre Barbosa on the metalinguistic aspects of Cabral's poetry:**
>
> [Cabral's poetry is] an eminently metalinguistic poetry: not a poetry about poetry, but a poetry that borrows the language of its objects in order to construct the poem with it. One should not think of an empty formalism: precisely because of its high educational tenor—from one who teaches by learning—João Cabral's work does not depart, for a single moment, from its intense historicity. To read reality through a poem is always to remake the history of previous readings of poetry. Therefore, metalanguage and history in his work are richly interpenetrating: the historicity of this poetry is always directed toward two fundamental spaces: namely, that of social and historical circumstance and that of the history of the very language with which he names the former. His poetry is historical exactly to the extent that he always goes further to put the meaning of his language in check.
>
> *João Alexandre Barbosa, in his "A Study of João Cabral de Melo Neto,"* World Literature Today, *Autumn, 1992.*

more effective by the ever increasing force and clarity of the first *água,* his critical poetry.

Following the slow "education by stone" which couples patience with passion, Melo Neto has achieved a poetry that on the one hand is veritable and verifiable art, and on the other hand participates meaningfully (precisely for its artistic rigor) at the sociological level. The poet himself has stayed in the background, like the engineer who from a distance regards his constructions, "growing by their own simple strength." (pp. 26-41)

Richard Zenith, "Joao Cabral De Melo Neto: An Engineer of Poetry," in Latin American Literary Review, *Vol. XV, No. 30, July-December, 1987, pp. 26-42.*

John M. Parker   (essay date Autumn 1992)

[In the following excerpt, Parker presents an overview of Cabral's career.]

The award of the latest edition of the Neustadt Prize to the Brazilian poet João Cabral de Melo Neto confirms what poetry lovers in that country and foreign specialists in Latin American literature have known for a long time: namely, that the author of works such as *O Cão sem Plumas, Morte e Vida Severina, Uma Faca só Lâmina, A Educação pela Pedra,* and *Auto do Frade*—to name but a few of his nineteenth individual titles in verse—is one of the major poets of this second half-century. I myself concluded the second of two articles on João Cabral, published in the Portuguese journal *Colóquio/Letras* in 1976, with the certainty that he was *the* major Latin American poet since World War II.

When those articles were written, *A Educação pela Pedra* (*Education by Stone*), published in 1966, was still Cabral's most recent volume of verse, and it was not yet clear what direction his poetry might take during the next ten years or so. The publication of his *Poesias Completas,* dated 1968, added no further material, and the poet, who on an earlier occasion had been close to giving up writing poetry, had confessed himself sucked dry by what was then his thirteenth individual title. And indeed, after his earlier struggle to eliminate the fortuitous, the sentimental, and the influence of lyric fantasy from his verse, João Cabral had reached such a peak of discipline, both in self-control and in the control of his creative "machine," and so great a power of formal compression, that one might be forgiven for wondering what he could add to his achievement. In the event, by the time my articles appeared, a further volume of verse, with the engaging title *Museu de Tudo (Museum of Everything),* bringing together compositions written in the intervening years (1966-74), offered some sort of answer to one's query. Any doubts that João Cabral might have abandoned—or been abandoned by—poetry have been further set to rest by the regular appearance of subsequent titles throughout the 1980s. But before asking if the last quarter-century's production has seen changes in the poet's attitudes, toward poetry and toward the world about him, and in his technical discipline, some considerations on the first twenty-five years are in order.

[In an interview recorded in 1968 and later published in *Diário de Pernambuco* (1979)] Cabral has recounted how, in his late teens, he was introduced to the poetry of [Guillaume] Apollinaire and the French surrealists, so that when he began to write poetry himself, theirs were the footsteps he attempted to follow. On an earlier occasion, however, he had declared that the starting point for the poems of his first book, *Pedra do Sono (Stone of Sleep),* published when he was twenty-two years old, was the influence of Murilo Mendes, often regarded as close to the surrealists in the oneiric nature of his visual landscape and the fortuitous manner in which persons and objects appear and interact. Certainly the poems of *Pedra do Sono* invoke a world more akin to the substance of dreams than to the ordered expectations of everyday reality, a world in which women swim back and forth in invisible rivers and flowers grow out of photographs or are the heads of saints. Still, as the poet recognized, although the imagery of these poems might be termed surrealist, the type of poem associated with that movement, with its recourse to automatic writing and lack of formal discipline, was quite alien to Cabral's temperament. He added the book was a hybrid, remarking on the discernment of the critic Antônio Cândido, whose contemporary review had classed it rather as cubist: in fact, though one of the poems is entitled **"A André Masson"** and is thereby dedicated to the French surrealist painter, another rather more pointedly addresses a **"Homenagem a Picasso."**

Cabral referred to *Pedra do Sono* as a "false book," rejecting a number of the poems for his *Poesias Completas,* and critics tended to accept the poet's statement at face value. A subsequent consensus, however, may be summed up in the closing sentence of a useful reappraisal of the collection's status: *"Pedra do Sono* is not prehistory: it is the first stage of [an] unending process" [J. Gledson, "Sleep, Poetry, and João Cabral's 'False Book': A Revaluation of *Pedra do Sono,"* *Bulletin of Hispanic Studies* (1978)]. Or rather part of the first stage, for we find ourselves in somewhat similar territory in parts, at least, of *Os Três Mal-Amados (The Three Ill-Loved Ones)* and *O Engenheiro (The Engineer),* which do nevertheless mark the beginnings of a critical attitude toward the matter and nature of poetry. In the first the "interwoven monologues" [Stephen Reckert, "João Cabral: From *Pedra* to *Pedra," Portuguese Studies* (1986)] of the three speakers, or the monologue-plus-*diálogo implícito* equation preferred by another scholar [Antônio Carlos Secchin, *João Cabral: A Poesia do Menos*], present different attitudes toward poetry. One of these, devoured by passion, constitutes a political dead end; the other two offer a dialectic between imagination, over which the poet has little control, and discipline, in which poetry becomes a pre-established system, a "lucidity alone capable of allowing us a complete new way of seeing a flower, of reading a line of poetry" [João Cabral Melo de Neto, *Poesias Completas*].

The poems of *O Engenheiro,* as the dates show, were to some extent contemporaneous with those of *Os Três Mal-Amados* and share similar concerns. As Stephen Reckert comments, "*O Engenheiro* does not immediately cast off the lexical and imagistic legacy of its predecessors, with their *nuvens, sonhos, fantasmas,* and general vague air of menace." The title poem, however, though it uses the word *dream* as noun and verb, in its first verse surrounds it with light, sun, open air, and what the poet calls "bright things" (*coisas claras*); and by the second verse the engineer—Cabral's metaphor for the poet—is thinking, thinking about "a world not masked by any veil," where everything is in its appointed place and the building (i.e., the poem) grows organically, of itself ("out of nothing but its own strength"), as if it were part of the natural scene. If this means what it seems to, **"A Lição de Poesia"** presents a less optimistic view, urging the need for vigilance, which was to be so important for Cabral's future creative work, and introducing for the first time the idea of extreme concision ("twenty words, always the same"), while emphasizing the constructive process in the metaphor of the "useful machine" (*máquina útil*).

Still, the dialectic between inspiration, with its unpredictability, and purposeful control was far from decided. The opposing forces were lined up once more in the seminally important *Psicologia da Composição* (*Psychology of Composition*), which, together with **"Fábula de Anfion"** and **"Antiode,"** first appeared in a version hand-printed by the poet himself. The order of the title page is not obeyed by the texts, which open with the **"Fabula de Anfion"** in a version clearly intended to counteract the *poésie pure* connotations of Valéry's "Amphion." A glance at the three poems immediately reveals an important innovation, in that each of them is organized in sections, but following a different pattern in each case: **"Fábula"** is in three parts, indicated by Arabic numerals, with further subdivisions shown by asterisks; **"Psicologia da Composição"** is arranged in eight numbered parts, this time using Roman numerals; the five sections of **"Antiode"** are marked A to E. The title poem of *O Engenheiro* already refers to "the design, the project, the number," and this virtual obsession with order was to mark all Cabral's subsequent poetry in one way or another. In the interview referred to earlier, the poet explained that being a constructivist, he follows in his poems a rigid, mathematically preordained scheme, which starts as an empty framework, to be filled slowly and methodically. The three long poems which make up *Psicologia da Composição* constitute, in essence, an attack on lyric excess, on romantic inspiration, and on poetic diction, in the name of constraint, understatement, and rigor.

By this time João Cabral had entered his country's diplomatic service and soon left Brazil on his first posting, as vice-consul in Barcelona (1947-50). There began a relationship with Spain and Spanish culture the influence of which cannot be excluded from any reading of his poetry. At the same time, his absence from the Brazilian literary scene preserved him from involvement in the literary "politics" enjoyed by various of his contemporaries, the young lions who had begun to call themselves the "Generation of '45" and to engage in skirmishes with the established poets ([Carlos] Drummond de Andrade, Manuel Bandeira, Augusto Frederico Schmidt, et alii), from whose influence they dearly wished to free themselves. Cabral did in fact intervene, publishing a series of articles under the title **"A Geração de '45"** in the Rio daily *Diário Carioca* in late 1952, upon his return to Brazil. With a de-

gree of objectivity, he criticized both sides, his main argument being that the young poets had not found an established poetic vision, a definition of poetry valid for their time, but rather a number of individual poets, each with his personal manner, which the younger writers had tended to follow in an initial phase. It was his judgment that this stage had been passed and that the "Generation of '45" poets had extended the repertoires of their immediate predecessors while largely reconciling the differences between them in a way Cabral felt could produce what he called a "modern Brazilian expression."

Part of what Cabral wrote in these articles can be found, more fully developed but shorn of specific allusions to the Brazilian literary scene, in a lecture he delivered to the São Paulo Poetry Club (Clube de Poesia) in November of the same year. The lecture was entitled **"Poesia e Composição: A Inspiração e Trabalho de Arte"** and clearly reflected the problems which had afflicted his own poetry. He also introduced a further problem, remarking on the absence of communication in contemporary poetry, whether this was created under the aegis of inspiration or was the result of disciplined artisanship. He spoke of the hermeticism of contemporary verse, and it must be admitted that most of his own poetry up to that time is not of easy access, certainly not to the general reading public.

This is true even of *O Cão sem Plumas,* a tightly woven narrative poem almost as long as the three poems of *Psicologia da Composição,* in which Cabral turns to the physical and social reality of his native state, Pernambuco, and its capital city, Recife. The "featherless dog" of the title is in fact a metaphor for the Capibaribe River, whose course becomes the poem's discourse, transferring its nakedness to the poverty-stricken inhabitants of the *mangues* or mud flats on the city's outskirts.

> Like the river
> those men
> are like featherless dogs
> (a featherless dog
> is more
> than a plundered dog;
> is more
> than a murdered dog. . . .)

The poem's final section concentrates its discourse around the words *live* (verb and adjective) and *dense*—the Portuguese word is *espesso,* meaning "thick," as in thick soup or when we say that blood runs thicker than water, so that *espesso* is used here for the solid density of real things: a man's blood is "much thicker . . . than a man's dream," and an apple is "much thicker / if a man eats it / than if a man sees it." In the final instance the notion of *thickness,* having hammered the claims of reality, sordid social reality, to poetic treatment of a wholly unsentimental nature, is installed, so it seems, as a precept for the poet himself to follow: "the day that is gained / each day / (like a bird / second by second / achieving its flight)."

The period of some five or six years beginning with the composition of *O Cão sem Plumas* was a particularly productive one for João Cabral, as well as being important for his reputation. His feeling that contemporary poetry had given priority to expression over communication, in the process abandoning such publicly more accessible forms as the fable and narrative poetry, led him to compose two works intended for general consumption: another narrative poem, *O Rio* (*The River*), more descriptive in nature, and the reverse drama *Morte e Vida Severina* (*Death and Life of a Severino*), cast in a popular dramatic mold. In the already-quoted interview he admitted wryly that his plan to produce "poetry for the people" did not work out quite as he had intended, since he wrote both works with the idea that they would be read aloud in Recife's São José market. Ironically, *Morte e Vida Severina* has found its way to a wider public than any other of Cabral's works and provides an interesting example of the way different sociopolitical contexts can impose new readings on texts. Written during an open phase of Brazil's recent political history, it was later performed by the São Paulo University drama group, with music by Chico Buarque de Holanda, at the University Theater Festival in Nancy (France), where it was awarded first prize. This was in 1966, two years after the military coup in Brazil introduced an oppressive political regime, severely restricting the democratic rights achieved after the fall of Getúlio Vargas. In such a climate the play's central character, Severino, a symbol of the poor peasant fleeing the drought of his native *sertão* (badlands), could acquire the much wider connotation of a whole oppressed populace, and its final message of optimism could be seen to offer more hope than in the original circumstances. The play was also performed in the poor districts of São Paulo as well as in towns in the interior.

At the same time as he was engaged in the play's composition, Cabral continued to write verse intended for the individual reader, poems, as he himself put it, "to be read in silence . . . requiring more than one reading." Such are the poems of the short collection *Paisagens com Figuras* (*Landscapes with Figures*), eighteen texts on topics evenly divided between the poet's native Northeast and that Spain which was to occupy an increasingly large place in his poetry, cast for the most part in the traditional Portuguese quatrain form (heptasyllables rhyming *a b c b*). To class these as descriptive vignettes would do the poems little justice, for what Cabral does is rather to define, metaphorically, the real places or people he takes as his starting point, seeking a lesson in the appropriateness of the chosen analogy. In the long poem *Uma Faca só Lâmina* (*A Knife All Blade*), which he wrote almost simultaneously, he was to conclude that reality is too violent to be grasped by any image. Here, however, he had started not from real referents but from the semantic features of linguistic signs, three in number—bullet, clock, and knife—in accordance with the poem's subtitle, "The Usefulness of Fixed Ideas."

The two books thus seem to complement each other, as if the discourse of *Uma Faca só Lâmina* had germinated from the argumentative **"Diálogo"** of *Paisagens com Figuras,* in which two speakers, A and B, seek to define the nature of the Andalusian *cante hondo* (deep song). The method is oddly reminiscent of the *desafios* and *repentes* still popular in Brazil's Northeast and which have much to do with the choice of words and images, suggested by one participant and put in doubt or corrected by the other, continuing back and forth until one of the participants

fails to respond—all intoned in a droning chant which Cabral's quatrain seems to simulate. So here speaker A, who suggests the first comparison, also completes the dispute, picking up the knife image proposed by B and limiting it first to the blade, then to "the purpose which completes a knife," which is, however, to be found "on the reverse side of nothing."

Uma Faca só Lâmina is clearly a work of great importance in Cabral's poetic production. He had already rejected the "poetic word" and experienced the need to strip words of all prior associations. He had, as we saw earlier, begun to do things by numbers, creating a rigid framework, mathematically designed, within which to compose his text. Theme as such is of less importance, perhaps because "the medium is the message," which is to say that the process of composition is, in a sense, its own theme, for Cabral's poetry henceforth is essentially metapoetic and metalinguistic. Recent studies have stressed the concrete nature of his poetic language or his constant struggle to excise what Antônio Carlos Secchin calls the "*overflow* of the signified." The poet himself, to quote once more from the 1968 interview, considered that, for him, creation was not "the spilling of an excess of being, but a lack of being," which seems similar to his image of "the reverse side of nothing."

In a poem entitled **"Autocrítica,"** from the later volume *Escola das Facas* (*School of Knives*), Cabral considered that two things alone had forced him into poetry, and both were Pernambuco; but one was the real Pernambuco, his home state, whereas the other was Andalusia. The former vaccinated him against "rich speech"; the other made him a "mad challenge," which was to show the *sertão* and Seville in verse. After *Uma Faca só Lâmina* João Cabral's poetry does indeed center almost obsessively on topics related to Pernambuco and Seville. Over the next ten years he composed the texts which make up the four titles published between 1960 and 1966: *Quaderna, Dois Parlamentos, Serial,* and *A Educação pela Pedra.* The first three appeared together in 1961 under the title *Terceira Feira* (*Third Fair*), the fourth in 1966; in 1968 came the first edition of his complete poems, and in 1969 he was elected to Brazil's Academy of Letters.

The title *Quaderna,* referring to the four-spot on a die or, alternatively, to each of the quarters on a coat of arms, seems to be justified by the constant use of the quatrain form and the organization of the texts in multiples of four, not forgetting their total, which numbers twenty. Cabral, by his own account, was always fond of the number four, which seemed to him "the rational number par excellence"; and *Serial,* with its sixteen poems, is even more rigorously based on it, whereas the forty-eight poems of *A Educação pela Pedra* (*Education by Stone*) all have sixteen or twenty-four lines, always divided into two parts, suited to the argumentative binarism which is a mark of his poetry. The division into parts or sections, already observed in the longer poems, is carried over into *Quaderna* and *Serial,* each of which contains a number of poem sequences in which Cabral explores different aspects of a topic, testing the semantic capacity of the linguistic sign to equate to the features he discerns in the object in question (the flamenco dancer, the *cante hondo,* the city of Re-cife, a goat, et cetera) or to define the creative processes of writers and artists with whom he identifies (Graciliano Ramos, Marianne Moore, Francis Ponge, Joan Miró, Mondrian). Now in his forties, João Cabral had reached great maturity as a poet, and these volumes are so full of magnificent poetry that one hesitates to single out individual poems; the choice is almost inevitably one of personal favorites.

Among the best known of the poem sequences in **Quaderna** are the "Estudos para uma Bailadora Andaluza" ("Studies for an Andalusian Dancer"), forty-eight quatrains divided into six equal sections which test six images for their appropriateness as analogies for the dancer, who is compared in turn to fire, a mare, a telegraph operator, a tree, a statue, and the spike of a maize plant. At the same time, the *bailadora* and her dance must be understood as offering analogies with the poet and his text, or the creative process, at least as Cabral would have them. So the image of the mare immediately includes that of the rider and the impossibility of distinguishing between the two or separating them, which invites comparison either with the poet engaged in creating or with the content and form of the text. The telegraphist analogy, suggested by the foot tapping, deals more overtly with messages and the emitter-receiver relationship, while the final comparison introduces what was to be a productive image for Cabral, with decided erotic overtones, as he sees the unfolding of the dance as the "undressing" of the maturing maize spike. The importance of the image is emphasized by the repetition, in the poem's closing verse, of the word *espiga* and the participial adjective *espigada:* analogous to the image which the dancer's final movements will engrave on the mind's eye, we may infer, should be the reader's sense of revelation as the poem's final lines release its total communicative thrust.

João Cabral started out with a stone, though it was merely part of the name of a backwater town somewhere in Pernambuco (Pedra do Sono), and the **"Pequena Ode Mineral"** of *O Engenheiro* already warned him to "Seek the order / you see in a stone"; but we have to wait until *A Educação pela Pedra* for the stone to, as it were, bear fruit. Over the years the poet has shown a marked tendency to favor things that are dry and spare, sun and fire, naked or clear-cut shapes, metal objects, sharp instruments, which somehow equate to his rational manner and his need to rationalize his poetic process. The stone which was destined to appear in the title of the collection published in 1966 is such a thing. A thing: simultaneously object and instrument, challenge and example, metaphor and metonym. Although the poet was from the humid, fertile coastal area of Pernambuco, born and educated in Recife, accustomed to life on the family sugar estates, he identified strongly with the dry, barren *sertão,* more akin to the "lack of being" he saw in himself. He similarly identified, poetically, with the way of speech of the inhabitants of the *sertão,* which he called their "idioma pedra," as if there were a language called "Stonish," since he refers to the "native speaker of this tongue" in the poem **"O Sertanejo Falando"** (**"The Way a *Sertanejo* Speaks"**). In "stone language" the words are so hard, "stony almonds," that they

form ulcers in the mouth, so that the speaker, "that stony tree," must articulate them slowly and with the utmost care, which explains why he is anything but loquacious. The analogy is clear but is given a more obviously social dimension in the title poem, **"A Educação pela Pedra,"** for if the first part of the text extols the virtues of the stone—its "unemphatic, impersonal voice," its "cold resistance . . . to being shaped," its "concrete flesh"—the shorter second part transports us to the *sertão,* where the stone has nothing to teach, because the inhabitants are born with it in their very souls.

> **For all the discipline and rigor and the extremely rational cast of his verse, there is nothing classical in Cabral's choice of metaphor and comparison. . . .**
>
> —*John M. Parker*

The writing of poetry has clearly been a serious business for João Cabral de Melo Neto, but this does not mean that his verse is ponderous or plodding. In fact, one of the words I would use when speaking or writing about it is *wit,* not with that term's more recent connotations of facetiousness, but in its older sense as we relate it, for instance, to the intellectual ingenuity of so-called metaphysical poetry. For all the discipline and rigor and the extremely rational cast of his verse, there is nothing classical in Cabral's choice of metaphor and comparison, as the example of the Andalusian dancer will have shown. In a Penguin anthology of Latin American writing published all of twenty-five years back, the notes on João Cabral advised the English reader that he would "see some resemblances to the wittily fantastic poetry of Marianne Moore" [J. M. Cohen, ed., *Latin American Poetry Today*]. Cabral may have come into contact with Moore's poetry during his spell of diplomatic duty in Great Britain, between 1950 and 1952, since her *Collected Poems* appeared in 1951 under the Faber imprint. However, the first reference to her in Cabral's verse occurs in **Serial,** a collection of poems written between 1959 and 1961, and more specifically in the poem sequence "O Sim Contra o Sim" ("Yes Against Yes"), four texts of eight verses each, invoking alternately two poets, then two painters, and the same again, so that in all the poet focuses on creative processes in eight artists (Moore, Ponge, Miró, Mondrian, Cesário Verde, Augusto dos Anjos, Gris, Dubuffet). The poem's title indicates Cabral's approval of his "models," despite the differences among them, but it is hardly necessary; for although there is no direct linguistic (i.e., grammatical) evidence of the poet's presence, the impersonal affirmations betray his systematic preferences in the choice of words like *scalpel, clean, economical, learn anew, discipline, clear water, firmness, geometry, simple, cohesive, magnifying glass, microscope, stethoscope, ausculation.*

The scalpel is obviously another form of the knife, or rather the naked blade, which Cabral used to such effect in

Uma Faca só Lâmina, the "angry blade" as he called it then; but in the case of Marianne Moore the blade becomes the writing implement, substituting for the pencil, and the poet a surgeon. Although the Brazilian poet clearly admires Moore, one infers that her skill is wholly dependent on the choice of instrument, viewed not so much as an object but rather as a metaphor for a process. Cabral's admiration was by no means a momentary homage, but we must wait until *A Escola das Facas* for the next direct reference. Not only is the poem **"A Imaginação do Pouco" ("Imagination on a Small Scale")** prefaced by an epigraph from one of Moore's poems ("imaginary gardens with real toads in them"), but she herself is mentioned by name, giving Cabral the opportunity to stress his own limited capacity in relation to things of the imagination. *Agrestes* opens with a Moore epigraph ("Where there is personal liking we go. / Where the ground is sour") and contains no fewer than three poems which take Moore and her poetry as their subject. **"Ouvindo Marianne Moore em Disco" ("On Hearing a Recording of Marianne Moore")** praises Moore's undeclamatory reading of her own poetry as being very much in tune with the poetry itself; **"Homenagem Renovada a Marianne Moore" ("Renewed Homage to Marianne Moore")** is more metapoetic in pointing up the formal, constructive nature of poetry as practiced by Moore and Cabral. There is also a hint here of poetry as an aid to self-construction, "a crutch for a gammy leg," but the personal identification is to be found in the aptly entitled **"Dúvidas Apócrifas de Marianne Moore" ("Apocryphal Doubts of Marianne Moore")**. Spoken in the first person, as though by Moore herself, the voice can be identified with Cabral, who uses this device to express his awareness that "talking about things" in poetry can be just another way of talking about oneself.

The choice of what Cabral elsewhere calls "a luva sósia" (a glove's double) tells us more about ourselves, but any choice—as when one compiles an anthology—is meaningful; and although the Brazilian poet has generally preferred to write about those in whom he detects similarities, his more recent volumes have been less rigorous in this respect. After *A Educação pela Pedra* there is a noticeable lessening of the tension which reached its high-water mark in the metaphorical dialectic of that work. Marta Peixoto sees a different sort of dialectic in the long-awaited *Museu de Tudo,* between "discouraging effort and spiritual renewal" [Marto Peixoto, *Poesia com coisas*]. It seems to me that the poet himself puts his finger on the problem in the opening text, where he more or less explains the title. As he tells us, a museum can be a "garbage can or an archive," and his book "is the warehouse of what's inside," lacking a presiding design. Cabral ranges wide in subject matter in this collection of what often seem little more than comments but which on closer perusal bear the epigrammatic stamp that is a frequent mark of his art. People, places, books, works of art, and even soccer all find their way into this collection of eighty texts—perhaps not all that surprising in a poet who had elevated chewing gum and aspirin to poetic respectability in his previous book. Pride of place, however, goes to artists: no fewer than thirty-five texts bring the manner of other poets or, quite as often, painters, sculptors, and architects under the microscope.

A Escola das Facas covers a much shorter period, and although it contains little more than half the total of poems found in *Museu de Tudo,* the texts occupy approximately the same amount of printed space. There are few of the eight-liners so frequent in the previous collection, but poems arranged in sequences are again in evidence, such as the ten-part "Descrição de Pernambuco como um Trampolim" ("Description of Pernambuco as a Trampoline"), the eight-part "Prosas da Maré na Jaqueira" ("Chatting with the Tide at Jaqueira"), or the six-part "Tio e Sobrinho" ("Uncle and Nephew"). The nephew in this last sequence is certainly the poet himself, for the first time explicitly and systematically present in his own verse. Often, it is true, this is done through the oblique third person; but significantly, the opening poem, **"Menino de Engenho" ("Plantation Boy")**, makes no bones about using the first person and, at the same time, with its intertextual nod to Lins do Rego's famous novel, points to the other systematic bases of *A Escola das Facas,* which might almost have been entitled "Memories of Pernambuco." Moreover, the book's title includes allusions to the titles of two earlier collections, *Uma Faca só Lâmina* and *A Educação pela Pedra,* as if to remind us that a possible *recherche du temps perdu* will not mean giving in to mere sentiment. Still, the poet himself suggests that this retrospective view is less critical (**"De Volta ao Cabo de Santo Agostinho" ["Going Back to Cape Santo Agostinho"]**), because he now appears to doubt the usefulness of his earlier critical vision, of the debates and the protests for which it was in some way responsible.

João Cabral prefaced *A Escola das Facas* with a poem addressed to his publisher in which he hinted that this might be his last book. In the event, it was, to date, the last but four, and the next showed that the vein of poetry was far from exhausted. Furthermore, the doubts implied at the end of the previous collection are well and truly silenced, as the poet comes back in the full force of a dramatic poem, a "poem for voices" as he calls it, but certainly intended as a public poem, establishing an irresistible link with *Morte e Vida Severina* almost thirty years on. *Auto do Frade (The Friar's Way)*—the word *auto* doubling for "play" and "auto da fé"—narrates, dramatically, the martyrdom of Frei Caneca, the liberal Carmelite friar condemned to death for sedition due to his activities in the Pernambucan revolution of 1824. This is a text one imagines Cabral would have wanted to publish during the dark days of military oppression in Brazil, for despite its historical context one cannot misinterpret the allusion to an authoritarian power which transforms the armed forces into an instrument of oppression against the country they were intended to defend. Caneca is shown as a luminous figure, in stark contrast with the darkness of his prison, an obvious reference to the obscurantism of his surroundings. He has to suffer ecclesiastical degradation before he can be led to the scaffold, to be executed as a common criminal, but the authorities are unable to make anyone perform the execution and are obliged to recognize Caneca as a military opponent, worthy of a military death by firing squad. *Auto do Frade* is an exhilarating performance, a text of enormous dignity in which we recognize the qualities of luminosity, precision, and compression which we have come to associate with João Cabral de Melo Neto's poetry.

In the same period as one assumes he was working on *Auto do Frade* the poet continued to write the shorter poems which he published in 1985 as *Agrestes,* a title with two meanings: the adjective means "wild" or merely "rustic," whereas the noun refers to the area of rocky land with low vegetation situated between the fertile *mata* and the arid *sertão* in northeastern Brazil. Not that the poetry describes this landscape, suggesting that the word, used in the plural, is essentially metonymous, reminding us of Cabral's penchant for the dry, the stony, and the unemphatic. There is, admittedly, a section of the book entitled "Do Outro Lado da Rua," made up of poems associated with the poet's years in West Africa, which include desert conditions; but when the epigraph from Marianne Moore, mentioned earlier, talks of "Where the ground is sour," such is a chosen territory, for it corresponds to a "personal liking." However, one cannot expect all the poems in a total of some ninety texts to be directly related to an introductory epigraph, the more so since the book's final section consists of poems on death.

Poems on Spain, more specifically on Andalusia and Seville, began to appear in Cabral's works as far back as 1956, and any consideration of his verse needs to take this into account. The poet was fascinated by bullfighters, by Andalusian Gypsies, particularly the flamenco dancers, and by the city of Seville itself. The bullfighters, Manolete in particular, impressed him with their technique, in which he sought those qualities he admired in poets and painters. Manolete is remembered in a text in *Agrestes,* **"Lembrando Manolete" ("Recalling Manolete"),** in which Cabral stresses bullfighting as running the most terrible risks "with the coolness of one whose life is not on a knife's edge." In other words, the bullfighter (i.e., the poet) constantly exposes himself to danger while being in control of the situation—not the sort of social control referred to in **"Conversa de Sevilhana,"** whose talkative female speaker sends all policemen, doorkeeper, and petty bureaucrats to hell. Flamenco dancing is also a form of risk: in **"Uma Bailadora Sevilhana"** the speaker criticizes another dancer because she "dances without taking chances, without danger" and defines the style of dancing as "always a doing, never a done." Exactly as poetry should be, for, as Cabral puts it in a closing poem, **"Postigo" ("Back Gate"),** "writing is always from scratch / and the old hoe is no use this time." The flamenco singer similarly exposes himself in the *cante hondo,* for his voice, as it were, carried him to the top of a mast and the slightest miscue will bring him crashing down. Poems like these should, of course, be read intertextually with those of earlier books, particularly, in the present cases, the justly famous **"Estudos para uma Bailadora Andaluza"** and **"A Palo Seco,"** both from *Quaderna.*

Cabral was also fascinated by the women of Seville, whose mixture of provocative elegance and imaginative verve he used as a figure of comparison for others, as in the hyperbolic opening of **"Portrait of a Lady"** (*Agrestes*)—"I've never seen even an Andalusian woman / use her legs as you do"—or the riposte to a would-be compliment: says he, "Sleeping with you would be great," to which she replies, "Is that all you would do? / Sleep? Do I perhaps have a face like a sleeping pill?" He was also attracted by

the Andalusian habit of the *infundio,* the white lie or tall story, exemplified in the poem **"As Infundiosas"** in his next collection of verse, *Crime na Calle Relator* (*Crime on Relator Street*). Interestingly, he vouches for the truth of what he recounts when he parenthetically states that the three speakers were known to him personally, being friends of his: thus, imagination can run wild without the poet's running the risk of being accused of wild fantasy. The poems of this collection are mainly narrative, stories with a point to them, though the point may be left to the reader, as in the slightly macabre **"Funeral na Inglaterra,"** where a lady diplomat apologizes to her hosts for having stepped unintentionally on what she took to be a flowerbed covered over with fertilizer, only to be told that the "fertilizer" was the ashes of the deceased, who had wished to be among friends. Cabral can be humorous, as this book reveals, but never hilarious!

By this time (1987) the poet had been widowed and had remarried, wedding another poet, Marly de Oliveira, for whom he wrote the poem **"A Sevilhana que Não se Sabia"** (**"The Seville Woman Unknown to Herself"**)—which appears in his last two books of verse—and whose qualities as muse are attested by her undoubted presence in other poems in his most recent book. Retired from the diplomatic service after a final stint in Portugal, Cabral has settled with his wife in Rio de Janeiro. After *Crime na Calle Relator,* with its mixture of poems once more devoted to Pernambuco and Andalusia, in 1989 he gave us *Sevilha Andando,* with its fifty-two poems all about aspects of Seville or anything that reminds him of Seville, as in **"Na Cidade do Porto,"** with its chance view of "uma mulher de andar sevilha" (a woman with a Seville walk), with her determined elegant step, head held high like the maize spike at its spikiest—an allusion which takes us back again to the metaphor used in the **"Estudos para uma Bailadora Andaluza."** Here we find Cabral being, as it were, forced by the very circumstances of his discovery into a most unexpected oxymoron: the simile of the "chama negra" (black flame) for the woman's hair, which fuses with the "sol negro" (black sun) in which he discovers a "farol às avessas" (inside-out lighthouse) to light his way with each new waking day.

Seville, then, has become a composite metaphor for many qualities which the poet admires, and which he otherwise found in isolated objects, places, or people. On the evidence of this most recent volume, it is more than that, particularly in the first of the two unequal parts into which the poet divides the collection, "Sevilha Andando"; for if the book as a whole is dedicated simply "Para Marly," it is this first part that is most marked by her presence, the poet's "novo álcool," the woman whose presence "like Sevilha / is within-without, is nightday." However, the book's longer second part, "Andando Sevilha" ("Around Seville"), is no less alive, for there is no hint of its being in the past, no suggestion of nostalgic recollection. Instead, these latest poems by João Cabral are almost all in the present tense, as if the poet were present at the instant of penning the diverse moments of his travelogue.

One is tempted to ask what Brazilian readers who have never visited Seville might make of these poems about places unknown to them and whether they would gain by prior knowledge. The poet's answer might be that the places only begin to exist in his verse, since description is not his purpose, and despite the "literariness of his imagination," the vision is a very personal one. Certainly, it is not the chance construction effected more than forty years before, in the **"Fábula de Anfíon,"** when Anfíon's flute raised the walls of Thebes, because João Cabral never forgot that lesson. It would require, however, a much more detailed and specialized study of his poetry to illustrate his unremitting labor to build those walls with his own hands, brick by brick, and to discover where, if at all, his vigilance may have flagged. When Vinicius de Moraes classed him as a diamond, João Cabral preferred to define himself, or his poetry, in terms of an industrial diamond, lacking the rarity value of the precious stone but having qualities similar to a cactus (**"Resposta a Vinicius de Moraes,"** *Museu de Tudo*). The poet has undoubtedly mellowed since then; the diamond may have lost its abrasiveness but not its cutting edge. (pp. 609-16)

> John M. Parker, "João Cabral de Melo Neto: 'Literalist of the Imagination'," in World Literature Today, *Vol. 66, No. 4, Autumn, 1992, pp. 609-16.*

Cabral on lyricism and poetry:

[It] is not because of simple aversion that I refuse to inscribe myself into that exclusive club of "lyrics" that today constitutes almost entirely the poetry written in our world. Nor is there any disdain on my part for that lyricism manifested in popular music—I think, on the contrary, that those new techniques have given lyricism a possibility of expression and communication never known before. I am merely offering a possible topic of meditation to the theoreticians of literature, and appealing to them not to seek in not-sung (or unsingable) poetry written today a quality, that of lyricism, that was never the intention of the authors to achieve or even to explore.

Poetry seems to me something much broader: it is the exploration of the materiality of words and of the possibilities of organization of verbal structures, things that have nothing to do with what is romantically called inspiration, or even intuition. In this respect, I believe that lyricism, upon finding in popular music the element that fulfills it and gives it its prestige, has liberated written and not-sung poetry and has allowed it to return to operate in territory that once belonged to it. It has made possible too the exercise of poetry as emotive exploration of the world of things and as rigorous construction of lucid formal structures, lucid objects of language.

João Cabral de Melo Neto, in his "Laureate's Acceptance Speech," World Literature Today, Autumn, 1992.

Flora Süssekind (essay date Autumn 1992)

[*In the following excerpt, Süssekind remarks on Cabral's disdain for lyricism and examines the influence*

that poet Marianne Moore and painter Joan Miró have had on Cabral's poetry.]

Whenever there is an attempt to classify the poetry of João Cabral de Melo Neto within Brazilian literature, the process usually tends toward exclusion. Although secluded, a place of honor is usually reserved for Cabral on the basis of the precision of his poetry's construction. This isolated position is further bolstered by the fact that the poet, as a diplomat, has spent a large portion of his life abroad. There is no doubt, on the other hand, that the density reached by Cabral's poetic expression is a result, at least in part, of his discriminating reconstruction of the fundamental components of colonial narrative poetry and of modern Brazilian literature. In the colonial period those elements are the cultivation of historical themes (accomplished by Cabral in his *Auto do Frade*), as found, for example, in *Prosopopéia* by Bento Teixeira, or the descriptive-geographic concerns of such texts as "A Ilha de Maré" by Botelho de Oliveira (in Cabral's case one recalls *O Rio*). In the realm of modern poetry those elements are found in the unpretentious articulation of Manuel Bandeira, in the allusions to prose in Carlos Drummond de Andrade's verses, in the perspective of poetry as a rational construct as created by Joaquim Cardozo, and in Murilo Mendes's flexible images. Those aspects were reviewed and synthesized, in a very personal way, by João Cabral. This essay, encompassing a discerning dialogue with other texts, seeks to examine this specific trait of his poetry and what seems to distinguish Cabral's poetic method.

Because it is a regular topic in interviews granted by João Cabral de Melo Neto, his lack of interest in music is well known. Within a field such as Brazilian literature, which is strongly imbued with a quality of orality through a connection between poetry and voice and—mostly after the second romantic generation—by a musicality in the verse, this fact is of considerable significance. It seems that the poet takes particular pleasure in stressing his indifference toward music. With the exception of *frevo*, for its noise, and flamenco, for its blasting potential, he associates music in general with a kind of distant and halfhearted reception which opposes what should be, from his viewpoint, a characteristic of poetic communication: "I hate everything that makes me sleepy: music, for example." In 1989 Cabral observed:

> My life's struggle is to awaken myself. What I look for in a medicine or in any author I may be reading is not something that makes my consciousness sleep, like a romantic author or this kind of 'lullaby' poetry. I don't want to be rocked; I want to be awakened. Therefore, I look for things that enhance my consciousness of reality, my self-recognition, and an awareness of what I am doing. I look for poetry as if it were caffeine.

Cabral's poems on the subject of the Andalusian *cante hondo* (deep song) are geared in this direction. In **"Ainda El Cante Flamenco"** ("Again *El Cante Flamenco*") from *Museu de Tudo (Museum of Everything)* he defines the *cante* as "the desired music / that does not put one to sleep / the opposite of the swaying / and the soothing song," like a "sleepless song" (*canto insonífero*), exposed backward. His verses on the *cante hondo* define it as the opposite of a "smooth flowing of melody." One example is found in **"O Poeta Thomas Hardy Fala" ("So Speaks the Poet T. H.")** from *Agrestes:* a verse like a "knotty wooden plank," "hard on the teeth," stumbling into the ear like a "metallic sound."

In Hardy's situation, however, the "musician's ear" of someone who was a flutist as a young man is introduced in the poem's very first verse. Cabral, on the other hand, always strives to call attention to his own lack of a "musical ear" ("I don't have a musical ear in the sense that I don't have an ear for melody. I'm unable to distinguish one song from another") and to his incapacity for auditory concentration ("I really need my sight, and I am only able to concentrate through reading or seeing; I can't concentrate by listening").

On this subject, a minor typographical correction Cabral once made in a letter to Manuel Bandeira should be recalled. The incident occurred at the time Bandeira's *Mafuá do Malungo,* a book of poetic vignettes, appeared from the small printing shop founded by Cabral while he was serving in the Brazilian consulate in Barcelona. In the letter Bandeira thanks Cabral and praises the edition, but advises Cabral on a small mistake perceived in the sonnet **"A Maneira de Olegário Mariano" ("Like O.M.")**: instead of "passaro sem dono" (bird without an owner) in the fourth verse of the first stanza, "pássaro cansado" (tired bird) was printed, due to Bandeira's own absentmindedness. Cabral, however, added another interpretation to the emendation, in a letter he wrote to Bandeira, dated 20 July 1948: "As regards that mistake, I must tell you that 'pássaro cansado' is in the manuscript you sent to me. I am sure of this, although I don't have it handy, because this image seemed to me to be excellent. [I found it] so wonderful that only after I read your letter did it occur to me that 'cansado' did not rhyme with the first verse. This reminds me again of my total ineptitude with the phonetic aspect of poetry."

It is enough, however, for one merely to think of Cabral's difficult options for rhyme, for assonance, of his intended changes to the decasyllabic and heptasyllabic verses common in Brazil, of his work with octosyllabic verses, in order to understand his repeated references to his antimusicality and to the phonetic ineptitude he usually extends to oral communication in general: "A poem is to be read in a soft voice. If you want to torture me, invite me to attend a lecture. The spoken language does not enter my head." These words are rather ways to enhance his distance from the "oratorical" edge of Brazilian literature and to stress, on the contrary, the superiority of visualization over melody and his understanding of poetry as characterized by "an exposition through words" rather than to explain a "deafness" in his poetic method. "Is language only to be listened to?" Such a question, in a letter from Cabral to Clarice Lispector, was leveled during a fit of temper against someone who wanted him to change the title **"The Vein in the Pulse"** only because the noun *a veia* (the vein) could be read as *aveia* (oats). This acquires a larger dimension in the context of Cabral's reflections on

sonority. It can be understood not only as a comment on the possibility of cacophony or ambiguity in a title, but also as an indication of the neglect, on Cabral's part, of poetry's explicit requirement of musicality and melodic, flowing rhythm. In his case these elements are replaced by a different sensibility of rhythm, a kind of visual, syntactic rhythm.

The distance Cabral kept from musicality and the auditory aspect of poetry is accompanied, somehow paradoxically, by a prolific number of references in his work to accent, speech, rhythm, diction, sound, stress, and voice. Accent is found, for example, in poems such as **"A Carlos Pena Filho" ("For C. P. F.")** and **"A Pereira da Costa" ("For P. da C.")** and in "a certain accent in being, / bitter but not hostile," as in **"O Pernambucano Manuel Bandeira" ("The Pernambucan M. B.")** Diction, in sentences suggestive of a row of stones, another characteristic of Cabral's poetic language, is found in **"Paráfrase de Reverdy" ("Free Translation of Reverdy"),** in the peculiar "diction of coughing and stuttering" in the introduction to *A Escola das Facas,* and in the observation about diction as an apprenticeship of a "mineral" neutrality, as in *A Educação pela Pedra.* References to sound are found in "the voice's cutting edge" in **"A Palo Seco"** and in "the song of Andalusia" (from the poem of that title, **"O Canto da Andaluzia")** that the poet "lights in his own soul" as he "searches in the Nothingness, / as a search for nothing / is the senseless fight / between the bullfighter and the bull." By the same token, in **"Estudos para uma Bailadora Andaluza" ("Studies for an Andalusian Dancer")** the woman's dance is associated with specific sounds, a singular telegraphy, for the dancer, "while stepping, / inclines her attentive head, / as if trying to listen / to a vague voice."

One finds Murilo Mendes's "muffled voice" in **"Murilo Mendes e os Rios" ("M. M. and the Rivers"),** and the "stony metered voice" of Miguel Hernández, made of "a suffering and beaten / land," "roughed up by war," "straight," in **"Encontro com um Poeta" ("Encounter with a Poet").** One uncovers "a vivid conversation" in an uncle's "educated voice" in **"Tio e Sobrinho" ("Uncle and Nephew")** and "the smell of lavender" in the voice of someone who attempts an impossible return to the homeland in **"The Return of the Native."** The voice of Clarice Lispector requests that they talk again about death, after having chatted about soccer, in **"Contam de Clarice Lispector" ("What They Say about C.L.").**

In *Serial,* a poem composed around a speech attributed to Graciliano Ramos, Cabral incorporates the qualities of the fictionist's discourse in a poem, itself dry, terse, and succinct. The poet also contrasts and reflects upon the varieties of vocal development between the poetic diction of Pedro Salinas and Jorge Guillén in **"Dois Castelhanos em Sevilha" ("Two Castilians in Seville")** from *Sevilha Andando* (*Walking Through Seville*). In this poem the point of departure is the same space at different moments, and the two poets demonstrate their diverse ways of expressing themselves: Guillén speaking in a low voice, Salinas lecturing to his classes "by shouting at them." As for the range of their voices, Salinas could be heard by students standing across the street, whereas Guillén missed those "auditing" students. This difference between the two poets is portrayed in the poem's first three stanzas and redefined in its last two, when range and duration are separated.

> I imagine him whispering his classes,
> as he always whispered the poems
> he composed, with a ruler and a square.
> Does the less lively voice live less?
> Anyway, although it would not reach
> even the sidewalks across from him,
> the extension of his voice went much farther.
> It infiltrated beyond the border police.

"Does the less lively voice live less?" This question seems to run through much of Cabral's work, indicating an interest in "the language of the other," as in **Agrestes.** The non-uttering voices of Marianne Moore, Thomas Hardy, Jorge Guillén; the discipline of speech, the apprenticeship of "anonymity," according to "Berceo's Catechism"—it is in these developments of voices "less lively" that Cabral's specific diction emerges, by avoiding it. It is characterized by a form of voice intentionally impeded, a sort of a "speechless écriture."

Beyond the literary field, the poet alludes to another kind of problematic speech, "painful," "forced," registered through the mask of "a smooth intonation" on a "stony language," as is explained in **"O Sertanejo Falando"** **("The Speech of a Man from the Backlands")** from *A Educação pela Pedra.*

> The speech of the backlands man is misleading:
> his words are uttered, as if sugar-coated
> (pastried word, pill), under the icing of
> a smooth intonation, sweetened.
> Indeed, under it, hard and hardening
> the stony seed, the petrified almond,
> of this rocky tree (the backlands man)
> unable to express himself other than through
>   stones.

"Speech devoid of voice" is opposed, on the other hand, to "a boisterous speech" in **"Uma Enorme Rês Deitada"** **("A Huge Cow Lying Down"),** opposed to the "oral, tropical flowering / salivated by our nation" in **"Sujam o Suicídio" ("They Dirty the Suicide")**; and to the "unique national style: the reading of a speech as if it were a sonnet; / the inability of writing without a voice; / and of uttering words exempt of ostentation," as conveyed, with accurate irony on the local cultural life, in **"Um Piolho de Rui Barbosa" ("A Parasite of Rui Barbosa").**

Brazilian literature is characterized by an orality connected to the fact that it is irrevocably geared toward "a society that comprises people who are illiterate, uneducated, or little inclined to reading." Therefore Brazil's many lecturers, speakers, and elocutionists, as well as their public, established as listeners—as observed by Antônio Cândido de Melo e Sousa in "O Escritor e o Público" ("The Author and the Public")—all get used to demanding from the writer "some characteristics of easiness and emphasis and a certain oral rhythm that become the sign of good literature." From this results a discourse to be recited along an extremely rooted verbosity and sentimentalism. As Cândido put it: "The great majority of our authors, in prose and

in verse, *speak* while writing, and imagine a reader who listens to the sound of their voices as if it were emerging between the lines."

Therefore, opposed to these forms of loquaciousness and erudite verbosity, Cabral makes an effort in presenting a voice devoid of sound, a kind of rhyme that "muffles" the verse, and a language "without a discourse." Because of this, even when he describes the literature "hanging from a string" (*folhetos de cordel*), the blind men and the singers in the open markets, and even when he talks about the contacts he had during his childhood with the "novels on a string" and, in this context, opposes the wordiness of closed spaces—he embraces all this with the same empathy felt for the "stony expression" of the backlands man. He points out the inadequacy of the connection between the author and the person who reads aloud his story, between an educated reader wearing a distant air and the field peasants who listen attentively around him. The poem **"Descoberta da Literatura" ("Discovering Literature")** conveys the Sunday routine when the plantation boy used to read popular novels to the laborers on the farms.

> the tension was so dense,
> it was increasing so alarmingly,
> that the reader who read it
> like a living loudspeaker,
> without realizing it, had magnetized
> everybody standing there,
> afraid that they confused
> what was close with what was far away,
> the real with the magic,
> his small frame with that of the giant,
> and that they would take him
> for the creative author
> or that he had to face
> the anger of someone picking a fight.

At the outset, the poet builds a contrast between the "unintentional" purpose of someone who, while reading without any special emphasis, was able to provoke tension and the garish atmosphere experienced by the listeners. Because of this, he, a mere interpreter, was afraid of being confused with the "creative author" of such adventures. The distance between voice and discourse, emotional reception and cool diction, typical of a "living loudspeaker," is the pretext, on the one hand, for João Cabral's search to undermine the idea that "the author is everything," separating author from text. On the other hand, he emphasizes the materialization on the part of listeners to the fictional object, led by a voice that, detached from any possible personal experience related to the things that are told, is able to make vivid and believable a "magic space" among them.

It is precisely around such a potentiality that the voice is able to extend beyond itself and at the same time expand along another imaginary dimension, which is visible in the poem **"A Antonio Mairena, Cantador de Flamenco" ("To A. M., a Flamenco Singer")** from *Agrestes.*

> Living as someone who runs some risks
> as in this *cante* in which he dives:
> the *singer* at the top of the pole
> lifted there by his own voice,

is in possession of himself for his tense voice,
along its perennial growth;
for him flaws are forbidden
lest he fall from the pole,
from the pole created by his voice,
that can only be at the highest point,
because any sudden oversight
would make him fall from his *cante*.

It is not difficult to discern in this poem a significant exercise on dexterity. At the same time that it describes the delicate steadiness of the voice self-hoisted to an almost unbearable height, the poem itself seems to be constructed among demands defying the purpose of balance: blank pages and the uninterrupted sequence of double-line rhymes creating an enjambment, from the first to the last verse, along a tense movement between those limits.

Cabral's poetry is manifest mostly through voices devoid of sound, coarse, cold, half-mute. Sometimes these are apparently distant, as if coming from a "loudspeaker," at other times on the border line, as if in a *cante hondo*. It seems that the purpose is to call attention, along a vocal track, to precisely the opposing direction, marked by anti-sonority. Perhaps herein lies the reason for the excessive details on diction in Cabral's poems, on matters truly devoid of voices, such as things and elements of nature. There are the "liquid voices of the poem" that "suggest crime, / gun" in **"O Poema e a Água" ("The Poem and the Water";** *Pedra do Sono*)**; there are "colors in a loud voice" in a Mondrian painting; and there is a possibility, according to Raimundo in *Os Três Mal-Amados (The Three Ill-Loved Ones)*, of one's coming to "understand the voice of a chair, of a dresser." There is the search for the stone's "voice of silence," which "speaks motionless" in **"Pequena Ode Mineral" ("Short Mineral Ode";** *O Engenheiro*)**; there is the "voice of a coarse bird" in **"O Relógio" ("The Clock")**. On the other hand, there is the description of the Capibaribe River, a "dog without feathers" like a "tree without a voice," in *O Cão sem Plumas;* the "round voice" of the coconut grove; the "cicada's voice without saliva, / like dry paper that is crumpled / when a newspaper is folded"; the "canefield's voice" in **"Voz do Canavial";** the "land's grave voice" and that of rivers, in **"O Mercado a que os Rios" ("The Market Where the Rivers [Go]"** from *A Escola das Facas (The School of Knives)*; and the "screaming voices, angry" of the wind and sea during the northeastern winter, in **"Cenas da Vida de Joaquim Cardozo" ("Scenes of J. C.'s Life";** *Crime na Calle Relator* [*Crime on Relator Street*]).

The qualities and the situations exercised in Cabral's poetry to describe the human voice indicate, in general, its range as short, its expression as impeded by several obstacles (coarseness, stuttering, dryness), its support as precarious (as measured by the "pole's height" in the poem about Antonio Mairena). Still, the audibility of things and landscape is presented as less problematic, due to the absence of a real voice in these elements as well as to the fact that these images constitute a basic displacement between a virtually nonexistent speaker and a voice that is nevertheless caught. For Cabral, voice is poetically conceptualized in the tension between its intensity and duration, distant speech and emotional reception, the possibility of ma-

terialization and hesitancy in self-support, the inanimate utterance and its significant speech, and between a vocal abstraction and its plastic configuration (round, black-and-white, in color). This conceptualization is accompanied by a movement of deliberate instability and by an effort in the direction of muffling and depersonalizing vocal manifestations. Such an act seems to be present in Cabral's selection of Marianne Moore as an imagined interlocutor for matters related to diction and as an emblematic—though distant—presence for the kind of voice that is projected in his poems.

Cabral makes an effort in presenting a voice devoid of sound, a kind of rhyme that "muffles" the verse, and a language "without a discourse."

—Flora Süssekind

There are five poems by João Cabral de Melo Neto composed as direct dialogues with the poetry of Marianne Moore. The first part of "O Sim contra o Sim" ("Yes Against Yes"; *Serial*) takes up Moore's precise, surgical form of writing, extracting from the last two verses of "Those Various Scalpels" its meditating tone: "But why dissect destiny with instruments / more highly specialized than components of destiny itself?" This is converted in "Yes Against Yes" into a series of approaches between a pencil and a scalpel: verse and wound, writing and dissection. These images are particularly dear to Cabral's poetry itself. One need only recall the most elaborate image in *Uma Faca só Lâmina,* in constant tension with other images (watch, bullet, memory, reality), or of the images of cutting edges—knives, *peixeiras,* sickles, daggers—portraying the landscape and the people from Pernambuco in poems such as **"A Escola das Facas" ("School of Knives"), "As Facas Pernambucanas" ("Knives of Pernambuco"),** and **"Duelo à Pernambucana" ("Duel in a Pernambucan Fashion")**. By the same token, a description of personal reminiscences is portrayed in **"Menino de Engenho" ("Plantation Boy";** *A Escola das Facas*), of someone who still preserves from childhood the scar of a gash made by the sugarcane's sharp edge.

In **"A Imaginacção do Pouco" ("Imagination on a Small Scale"),** from the same book, there reappears a reference to Marianne Moore, starting with its title, which is extracted from the most extensive version of the poem "Poetry." In the same way as in Moore's poem—and as in an essay by W. B. Yeats about the drawings by William Blake for *The Divine Comedy*—there is a commentary on the need of a poem to start building objects that are simultaneously imagined and legitimate. In **"Imagination on a Small Scale"**—this time with Moore intervening—there is a blending of parts of the graceful tales of Siá Floripes with an infusion of reality among the inhabitants created in her "animals' heaven."

Some animals were known,
and she described those that weren't:
of those that she invented
(connecting a "paca" to a "jia")

she gave a precise description,
not only of its strange anatomy
but also of its speech, religion,
and of its habits.

Fictionality and literalness appear constantly as a duo, according to the classification of Blake as "a too literal realist of imagination [by W. B. Yeats, "William Blake and His Illustrations to the *Divine Comedy*," in his *Essays and Introductions*], which was endorsed by Marianne Moore. It constitutes a precise description of invention, perceived in the Siá Floripes of the poet's childhood, about whom Cabral said in the poem's last stanza, "Marianne Moore would have admired her." This observation should be added to the previous comment on Moore's writing, begun by Cabral in "O Sim contra o Sim." On the one hand, his characteristic preciseness is stressed once more through Floripes. On the other, it enhances "realism" (as in "the real frogs" in the "imaginary gardens" in "Poetry," mentioned by Cabral), except that this realism is linked to a decisive poetic confirmation of the imaginary and [as Marianne Moore writes in *The Dial*] to a "conjunction of fantasy and determination": "What is more precise than precision? Illusion," as in "Armor's Undermining Modesty."

In the three poems about Marianne Moore included in *Agrestes*—which start with a title derived from "The Hero"—one goes from the perception of its surgical precision and the discussion about the literalness of imagination to an attempt to define diction, the "voice tonality" of the poems. In **"Homenagem Renovada a Marianne Moore" ("Renewed Homage to M. M.")** the movement of objectivity is observed as a characteristic of its texts—by someone who knows that "poetry is not inside, / for it is like a house, that is outside"—and therefore linked directly to her inclination toward "verse, in prose." This inclination is clear in poems such as "When I Buy Pictures" or in the somehow ironic invitation to listen to a narrative, "Have you time for a story / (depicted in tapestry)?," with which "Charity Overcoming Envy" begins. It is further thematized by Moore in "The Past Is the Present," which mingles a call to Habakkuk and an observation about Hebrew poetry, defined as "prose / with a sort of heightened consciousness."

In **"Dúvidas Apócrifas de Marianne Moore" ("Apocryphal Doubts of M. M.")**, an imaginary Marianne Moore is transformed into the subject of a poem about the continual effort at depersonalizing the discourse. It is accompanied by a reflection on the possibility of an involuntary exposition of the person through such a self-effacing effort: "I always avoided talking about myself, / talking to myself. I wanted to talk about things. / But on the selection of these things / there will not be a word about me?" This speech seems to be a clear echo of such passages by Moore as the question that opens "Tell Me, Tell Me": "where might there be a refuge for me / from egocentricity / and its propensity to bisect, / misstate, misunderstand / and obliterate continuity?"

There is an emphasis on a prose cadence and a calculated impersonal tonality found in **"Ouvindo em Disco Marianne Moore" ("Listening to M. M. on a Record"),** from *Agrestes*, accompanied by comments on her voice in the recorded readings of her poems.

She undressed poetry,
as one takes off clothes,
of its verticality, of its loudness,
less than by a preacher, it proclaims,
as someone who forgets that a microphone
stands at two spans of his mouth
because while shouting, one imagines
that overexposing an emotion is best.
On a record, the unknown voice,
that never shrieks nor sings,
does not get out of the cold voice's tune
of the printed poem.

This low tone of voice, devoid of emotion, closer to the discourse, nearer rather to the printed word than to speech, which one hears in Moore's recording, is perfectly consistent with Cabral's idea of an "objective poem," in which "the author's personal exposure is not allowed." In the case of Moore, the measured voice is a contrary clue, which, instead of leading to the dramatically personal voice of the originator, guides us toward the "voice in the discourse."

If, nevertheless, a cold and unimpressive voice seems perfectly adequate to Cabral's poetic project, it is not for this alone that attention has been paid to the vocal aspect of Moore's poetry. There is, for example, the observation by T. S. Eliot in his 1923 book review of *Poems*" [reprinted in Helen Vendler, "Marianne Moore," in her *Part of Nature, Part of Us]*: "Rhythm, of course, is a very personal matter. . . . What is certain is that Miss Moore's poems are very good when read aloud." Jean Garrigue, in *Observations*, called it "a voice from beginning to end." We think too of Grace Schulman's classification of Moore's poetry as "spoken art" [*Marianne Moore: The Poetry of Engagement*]. We also recall Moore's own observations about this subject. In a 1916 article titled "The Accented Syllable," wherein she reflects on what would mark a difference between "the written tonality of voice" and a text, or an author—either thinking of him as unequivocal author ("If an author's written tone of voice is distinctive, a reader's speaking tone of voice will not obliterate it") or depersonalizing him ("It is true that written tones of voice may resemble each other and that a distinctive tone of voice employed by one author may resemble that same tone of voice as employed by another author"). She points indirectly to what Cabral himself explicitly indicated in 1952 as "a sharp consciousness of what in him is an echo" as a characteristic of the modern author.

At the same time, "Poetry" indicates a compelled neglect of eloquence: "These things are important not because a / high-sounding interpretation can be put upon them." Another manifestation of the same theme is found in the article "Feeling and Precision," a sort of defense of natural hesitation and of the transfer of colloquialism to the written discourse, as if it were a matter of diction—impact and exactness—the understanding of Moore's precision, which is of fundamental significance in her poetic and descriptive-reflective method. She associates precision with a naturalness of tone, which, according to a confession in 1967, forced her, after a certain level of discomfort in listening to her own recorded poems in the 1930s, to change her methods of composition in order to bridge the gap between the printed and spoken languages. In *Poetry of Engagement* Grace Schulman calls attention to such changes as having occurred in poems like "When I Buy Pictures," "Peter," "England," "Picking and Choosing," and "The Student," and she also points to Moore's statement, "Do you think it sounds natural, as in real life? As though I am talking to you? That's what I think it ought."

This does not exactly indicate a process of turning poetic writing into oral expression, but rather a continual experiment with resources typical of the discourse, "in lieu of the lyre" (as Moore says in one of her poems), in the establishment of a poetry within an original rhythmic pattern. Though offering a natural tone for quotes and other people's speeches, for instance, she uses a privileged way of reinforcing a certain deemotionalization and a withdrawal of the voice from her poetry. This effect is supported by a characteristic attitude of description and reasoning, explicit in Moore's poems by the definition she adopted for them: observations. This is perceived in descriptive texts such as "The Fish," "A Jelly-Fish," and "The Steeple-Jack" and in argumentative ones, anchored in details, such as "Critics and Connoisseurs" and "No Swan So Fine," the latter a wonderful memento mori inscribed in antique ceramic figurines representing swans.

It is no wonder that Marianne Moore represented for João Cabral a sort of an antisound voice and the kind of exposed diction he incorporates into his own poetry. As with Moore, Cabral also tends to merge the most diversified argumentation and abstractions into a powerful process of visualization, an expository objectivism that enables him to dress up Africa's voice with "rags, white cotton cloth, or silks," to change time into "a cancer of cancer" or into a river, to transform writing into an act of "picking beans" or of "defecating," to change a question about body and soul into an observation on "the latrines of the religious school in Recife," to convert death by car accident into a matter of smell and punctuation.

Cabral favored a movement toward the materialization of voice along with a certain bashfulness enhanced by a reliable method of describing things. This method unfolded into a sequence of geographic poems such as **"O Rio"** (**"The River"**), and **"Pregão Turístico do Recife"** (**"Tourist Proclamation of Recife"**); into essays on urban landscape such as **"Imagens em Castela"** (**"Images in Castile"**), **"Paisagens com Cupim"** (**"Landscapes with Termites"**), **"O Regaco Urbanizado"** (**"The Urbanization of a Shelter"**), and **"Calle Sierpes"** (**"Sierpes Street"**); into descriptions of plants (**"Um Baobá no Recife"** [**"A Baobab Tree in Recife"**]) and animals (e.g., the ones in the poem about the Andalusian dancer) and a variety of things (a knife, a hammock, aspirin, a watch). The same descriptive process can be perceived in a variety of ways: as a reference in the poem **"Alto do Trapuá"** (**"The Heights of Trapuá"**); in the distant perspective from an airplane, as in **"De um avião"** (**"From an Airplane"**); in

an exposition "on the borders of denotation," as in **"O Ovo da Galinha"** (**"The Chicken's Egg"**), as observed by João Alexandre Barbosa [in "Linguagem and Metalinguagem em João Cabral," in his *A Metáfora Crítica*]; in the "geographic overlapping of two regions," as in **"Poema(s) da Cabra"** (**"Poem[s] of the Goat"**), **"Na Guine"** (**"In Guinea"**), and **"Volta a Pernambuco"** (**"Return to Pernambuco"**), already examined by Benedito Nunes [in *João Cabral de Melo Neto*], in the sequence of images in reciprocal juxtaposition (**Uma Faca só Lâmina** [**A Knife All Blade**]), a procedure examined by Luiz Costa Lima in *Lira e Antilira;* and in the process of continual enumeration and listing of things (as can be seen in **O Rio**), a basic procedure for Cabral's exercises in description.

In the face of such exposition, it is no wonder that so many of Cabral's poems take on the traits of travel chronicles. The basic procedures in this genre—the transmutation of the visible into a discourse—are his unique way of describing things directly, the visual information imparted about places visited, and specific details related to them. However, instead of the adventurers and scientists who are usually the spokespersons, Cabral selects as mouthpieces for his chronicles the elements themselves, which are already included in the poems as the objects described: the river-narrator of **"Account of the Journey by the Capibaribe River from Its Source to the City of Recife,"** in **O Rio;**

or a local character such as the migrant Severino, who narrates his own migration, following the same Capibaribe River from the backlands to Recife in *Morte e Vida Severina* (*Death and Life of a Severino*). There is also the to-and-fro motion along the Caxangá road in **"O Motorneiro de Caxangá"** (**"The Caxangá Driver"**), from *Quaderna;* there is the description of the journey by car through Provence, England, and La Mancha in **"O Automobilista Infundioso"** (**"The *Infundioso* Driver"**); we have the outside view of the Capibaribe River in *O Cão sem Plumas* and in **"Pregão Turístico do Recife,"** the interior view, as in *O Rio*, of a fluvial route, described by the Ebro River itself, in **"Outro Rio: O Ebro"** (**"Another River: The Ebro"**), from *Paisagens com Figuras;* and there is the walk on foot from the prison to the church and from the church to the fortress, in the course of which the execution of Friar Caneca is told in *Auto do Frade* (*The Friar's Way*). If, on the one hand, these accounts seem to enhance the aspect of Cabral's poetry that emphasizes exposition and description, on the other hand they tend to create an instability in the accounts due to their narrative qualities and sometimes for their extension or effusion.

An ambiguity of purposes exists which sustains a certain instability between description and account, almost to the point of halting the movement of displacement that characterizes the chronicle (e.g., the river's "almost nullified march" in **"Pregão Turístico do Recife"**) or to the excess of erasing landscapes (as in **"Fábula de Anfion"** [**"The Fable of Anfion"**]), scenes, and people (as in **"Vale do Capibaribe"** [**"The Capibaribe Valley"**]). Nevertheless, this ambiguity suggests what seems to distinguish Cabral's method: the convergence, in continual tension, of an expository tone and a narrative pace in the poem's composition.

The convergence between the pursuit of configuration, typical of descriptive prose, and the property of displacement, characteristic of the narrative, being particularly magnified in the poems' descriptions of travels, is, however, in general terms, fundamental to João Cabral's process of writing. This is the case in those of his texts which are virtually nonnarrative. One example of the process of convergence is the poem **"Agulhas"** (**"Needles"**), from *A Educação pela Pedra,* a two-part poem-landscape about the beaches of northeastern Brazil. It begins with a concentration on a unique image—that of a needle—through which are defined the acid light, the metallic air, and the citric sea. The image of the needle contrasts with another that defines the wind as of "cotton," "blowing a breeze." As a matter of fact, the landscape does not incorporate history; there is nothing in it that recalls the time sequence typical of narratives. On a second reading, however, the poem's composition in distich form, with continuous run-on lines, indicates a sense of narrative that is less explicit yet still related to a descriptive mood. The poet creates, in this way, a dialectic sequence between the verses: "However, on the northeastern beaches / not everything comes with needles or like razors," and "On the northeastern beaches everything suffers / from the tip of very thin needles." Such images contrast with others which until then were predominant in the landscape. Because of these sequential links among verses, there is an internal dynam-

ic factor, a moving form, from the viewpoint of the poem's syntactic organization, within the expected languidness typical of a beach landscape.

This sequence indicates an adjustment of the syntactic-expository description, similar to descriptions in many of Cabral's diptiches: **"O Mar e o Canavial"** (**"The Sea and the Canefield"**) and **"O Canavial e o Mar,"** **"Coisas de Cabeceira, Recife"** (**"Reveries on a Pillow, Recife"**) and **"Coisas de Cabeceira, Sevilha"** (**"Reveries on a pillow, Seville"**), **"Habitar o Tempo"** (**"To Dwell in Time"**) and **"Bifurcation of 'To Dwell in Time,'"** plus a series of poems such as **"Cemitério Alagoano"** (**"Cemetery in Alagoas"**), **"Cemitério Paraibano"** (**"Cemetery in Paraíba"**), and **"Cemitério Pernambucano"** (**"Cemetery in Pernambuco"**) from *Quaderna,* along with poems about death gathered under the title **"A 'Indeseiada das Gentes'"** (**"The Undesirables"**) in *Agrestes.* In a general way, the sequence of expository description and its inherent ambiguities exist in Cabral's poetry even when they are not obvious.

Cabral's interest in Joan Miró, to whom he dedicated a book-length essay in 1950, is not surprising. His attention was drawn to the painter by the dynamic element he found in Miró's art, its internal drive, and by Miró's treatment of time applied to a texture usually seen as static and spatial. This fact, Cabral observes [in *Joan Miró*] is due basically to the selection of an element that is mobile—the line, particularly the loose line—as its basic pictorial element:

> In this composition the line is not a dangerous element, as happens with traditional composition, where it is an element of dissociation when not tamed. In [Miró's] composition the line is the main support. It is not only what one can contemplate, but also the sign, the guide, the rule for contemplation. The line takes one by the hand so strongly that it transforms into circulation what was fixed, and into time what was instantaneous.

Therefore the idea of balance is replaced by an idea of rhythm, the foundation of the creative process. Cabral faced this redefinition as a sort of "sharp and continual struggle" by the Catalan painter against the Renaissance pattern of composition, the usual "viewed harmonies" and the "demands of what is static." "His painting," Cabral states, "is the expression of a making within a struggle, amid a struggle." Miró did not work toward a harmonic art, but rather toward a "dynamic" form of painting, using a method through which "the painter himself eroded his vocabulary." He did so by submitting his figures and other pictorial elements to a sequence of ironic amendments. Cabral works in the same way with the intimate images of his poems and with those that present a sequence of parts.

One example of self-erosion in Cabral's work is *O Cão sem Plumas,* written at the same time as the book on Miró. The unfolding of the image of the Capibaribe River into images of a dog and a sword, which were associated with other images as well, before returning to the source of them all, the river, "is in my memory / like a living dog / in a room." Self-erosion is present also in the exposition and even selection of these images (dog, river) that display a double orientation (configurative and dynamic) in Cabral's poetry. In **"Agulhas,"** as well as in other poetic series by Cabral, one sees, as a matter of fact, a process of mediation in the inclusion of movement into what seems to be static; sometimes, in the process of poetic composition, this procedure is inverted as well. The poet tends to convert it into spatial terms, as the only appropriate image of a feeling, as he does with a past love story represented by the image of the city of Seville in **"O Profissional da Memória" ("A Professional of Remembrances").** He also uses a process of transforming images of fluidity and movement, such as the river and the ocean, into dense emblems, such as "bulls of a different character," in **"As Águas do Recife" ("The Waters of Recife"),** to mention but two of the poems from *Museu de Tudo.*

This does not mean that one sees now an effort to create a configuration, then a compromise, although sometimes one process seems to intervene with the other. This can be observed in a simple view from a window in **"The Girl and the Train"** from *O Engenheiro* (*The Engineer*), a brief holding of a moment; the figure becomes unstable and dispersed under an unexpected acceleration of time: "the girl at the window / sees the plant growing up / feels the earth rotate: / for the time is plentiful / that it allows to be seen." As with a dynamic street capable of concentrating all attention on itself, as in **"Num Bar da Calle Sierpes, Sevilha,"** one can see the sudden dissolving of any consciousness of time: "Seeing so many things going by / I do not see the time. / In the street's twisting corridor / it is less dense." One can observe the same treatment of a landscape that is barren and altogether different from the previous one in **"Viagem ao Sahel" ("Journey to the Sahel"),** in which time resists any attempt to materialize and "the wind is vacuous / its flesh is nothing, nihil, / it is not aggressive toward the landscape: / it works from the inside."

Cabral's method of composing demands a simultaneous exchange of giving configuration to what is sequential and making what is static move. Sometimes this double direction coincides on the same theme, as in **"O Alpendre no Canavial" ("A Veranda on the Canefield"),** a description of a view that is transformed in the passing of a river, in the passing of time, of a time that seems to acquire a physical substance, and then, out of its slowness, returns to its point of departure, to things, to the view. The same occurs in **"Prosas da Maré no Jaqueira,"** where, through a dialogue once more with the Capibaribe River, the subject in the poem reports on the geographic apprenticeship of time: "River with which I lived / unaware that such a familiarity, / almost a drug, gave me / the most ambiguous of vices: / whenever from the debris of the docks / I followed your dense course, / I acquired the vices of listening / and feeling the time overcoming me." Paradoxically, it is in the spatiality, in the fixed vision of a fluvial image such as this that movement and a commitment to time are stressed. This double situation receives an extra unfolding from Cabral, who usually employs the river as one of his typical configurations for the passing of time, as in **"Rio e/ou Poço" ("River and/or Well")** from *Quaderna.* In

this poem there is either a vertical configuration of the water (as a well) or a horizontal one (as a flow of water), a sort of a woman-river, an aquatic configuration that is concurrently one and double. This method points to the inside of a poem, enhancing its time frame (momentary and in sequence) and its spatial support (loose and in movement), simultaneous and double, both present in Cabral's poetry.

This, as a matter of fact, seems to designate another duality: that of a writing which aspires simultaneously to spatial and temporal frames, as Cabral himself pointed out in an interview granted in 1990:

> A painting is able to simulate movement as a potential, whereas cinema is able to simulate movement as a fact. Literature, like cinematography, is simultaneously space and time. Great fictionists tell stories that are developed in time and space. Great poets are the ones who are able to work with the two dimensions.

Therefore he makes the observation in **"A Literatura como Turismo" ("Literature as Tourism")** that "space-time, like the woods" can feasibly be created through literature. Furthermore, he also emphasizes bidimensional situations carrying an expressive tension (between verse and prose, voice and writing, description and narrative, figure and movement) which, sometimes, he literally dramatizes in his work; see, for example, *Os Três Mal-Amados, Dois Parlamentos* (*Two Voices*), *Morte e Vida Severina,* and *Auto do Frade.* On the other hand, see also the semi-ironic alternation of the meaning of double movement in **"Vale do Capibaribe."**

Thus, the landscape is virtually chiseled into monumental compromises with time, with "touches of a *geste,*" as in the poem on the valley, and is preserved as pure topography "where nothing / ever took place." The continual search for an epic dimension, of "history and ruins," begets a dimension of spatiality devoid of a larger nobility, as in **"Fotografia do Engenho Timbó" ("Photo of the Timbó Plantation"),** with its "urinals and cuspidors." This might indirectly indicate that "space-time" and its movement of convergence and conflict seem to be fundamental in the poetic methodology of Cabral, that space and time, as in **"Prosas da Maré na Jaqueira" ("Conversations of the Tide in Jaqueira"),** are "two and nobody." (pp. 648-55)

Flora Süssekind, "Stepping into Prose," translated by Regina Igel, in World Literature Today, *Vol. 66, No. 4, Autumn, 1992, pp. 648-56.*

FURTHER READING

Reckert, Stephen. "João Cabral: From *Pedra* to *Pedra.*" *Portugese Studies* 2 (1986): 166-84.

Examines the ways in which Cabral manipulates syntax to create metaphors, depict movement, and achieve perspectivistic and onomatopoeic effects in his poetry.

Don DeLillo

Mao II

Prize: PEN/Faulkner Award for Fiction

(Has also written under the pseudonym Cleo Birdwell) Born in 1936, DeLillo is an American novelist, playwright, and short story writer.

For further information on DeLillo's life and work, see *CLC*, Volumes 8, 10, 13, 27, 39, and 54.

INTRODUCTION

DeLillo's *Mao II* is considered an explication on the loss of faith in modern society. Addressing such themes as terrorism, politics, history, and religion, DeLillo examines the social ills of the late twentieth century as well as the writer's role in the world. Bill Gray, the protagonist, is a reclusive writer who has not published a book in twenty years and who lives in virtual isolation except for interactions with his two assistants. After spending two decades struggling to complete a novel, Gray has become disillusioned and cynical. To alleviate the drudgery of his routine, he uncharacteristically allows a Swedish photographer, Brita, to take his picture—the first of him to appear in print in more than thirty years. Gray's acquaintance with Brita leads to contact with others and he inadvertently becomes involved in international politics. At the urging of a negotiator and his publisher, Gray agrees to appear at a London press conference, where he is supposed to read the poems of a Swiss poet to help obtain his release from a terrorist group in Beirut. Gray learns, however, that the terrorists actually want to take him hostage in exchange for the Swiss poet. The novel ends with Gray traveling to Lebanon.

Throughout the novel, DeLillo incorporates images from such incidents as the student massacre in China's Tiananmen Square, Ayatollah Khomeini's funeral in Iran, and the wedding of 13,000 Moonies at Yankee Stadium. Critics note that these scenes underscore DeLillo's belief that the increasing influence of mass movements, terrorist activities, and graphic albeit disassociated media images contribute to feelings of isolation and nihilism among individuals. In the novel Gray laments: "Years ago I used to think that it was possible for a novelist to alter the inner life of the culture. Now bomb-makers and gunmen have taken that territory. They make raids on human consciousness." While some critics have faulted *Mao II* for what they consider a convoluted plot, flat characters, and bleak prose, others have praised the novel's realistic dialogue, evocative descriptions of diverse locales and situations, and powerful depiction of fear and paranoia.

PRINCIPAL WORKS

Americana (novel) 1971
End Zone (novel) 1972
Great Jones Street (novel) 1973
Ratner's Star (novel) 1976
Players (novel) 1977
Running Dog (novel) 1978
The Names (novel) 1982
White Noise (novel) 1985
Libra (novel) 1988
Mao II (novel) 1991

CRITICISM

Sven Birkerts (review date 26 May 1991)

[*In the following review, Birkerts assesses the strengths and weaknesses of* Mao II.]

If Don DeLillo has not yet been canonized as the leading

American novelist, then he is just a few quibbles short. It will happen. The man is brilliant and daring, tense with intuition. No one else can do the police in so many different voices. "It's just a feeling of there's something wrong," says a character, and it's dead-on. Never mind that his people are flat, or that his plots at times dissolve into vague patches of shimmer, DeLillo has something we cannot do without. Nerve. He stalks our atomic landscape like a human geiger-counter, and his books come at us clicking.

Mao II is DeLillo's 10th novel and it is one of his best. The basic features will be familiar to his readers immediately: the terrorists and conspiracies, the obsession with media images, the off-kilter characters who act like survivors of a future that hasn't yet arrived and the relentless one-sentence snapshots that tell us what we really think about our times. *Mao II* is also DeLillo's strongest statement yet about the crisis of crises. Namely: that we are living in the last violet twilight of the individual, and that "the future belongs to crowds."

"All plots tend to move deathward," quipped the author in his 1985 novel, *White Noise.* This plot is no exception. But death here carries a different weight. For Bill Gray, the protagonist, a writer of Pynchonesque reclusiveness, has already removed himself from the world out there. He lives in his circuit of words, writing and revising, and refusing to publish. A young man named Scott, an admirer of his two early books, takes care of Gray's earthly needs. The master is free to drink, smoke, and brood.

As the novel begins, however, Gray has granted permission to a photographer named Brita to visit him in his seclusion to do a "shoot." His explanation? "Well it's a weariness really, to know that people make so much of this. When a writer doesn't show his face, he becomes a local symptom of God's famous reluctance to appear." Brita is herself a strange creature. Convinced that writers are an imperiled species, she jets from place to place gathering their images.

This one contact precipitates others, and before long Gray has agreed to his editor's request that he take part in a hush-hush hostage-release ploy. The writer is to appear at a press-conference in London; at the same moment, in Beirut, a terrorist sect will release a Swiss U.N. worker who has been taken hostage. Publicity is the aim, but—as always in DeLillo—aims contort into disasters. Gray learns that Abu Rashid, the terrorist leader, wants Bill Gray. And, with predictable unpredictability, he starts traveling eastward to his fate.

The plot is, of course, nowhere near so linear. Indeed, if there is a problem with this novel, it's formal. The tension that gathers around Gray dissipates towards the end and the final pages feel unfocused. Still, DeLillo keeps busy with his secondary characters. He shuffles in scenes and subplots featuring Brita, Scott and Scott's girlfriend, Karen. There is always a new angle, a new window onto a world in its paroxysms of transformation. Karen, for instance, is a former Moonie with a preternatural empathy for human suffering. She stares at the TV with the volume

off. "She was thin-boundaried. She took it all in, she believed it all, pain, ecstasy, dog food, all the seraphic matter . . . She carried the virus of the future."

And the future, we have learned, belongs to crowds. The crowd motif is threaded through the work in a hundred ingenious ways. We see the gathering masses in China, at soccer games, at a collective Moonie wedding, at Khomeini's funeral . . . The images flow at us through TV screens, via photographs, in endless reproductions of faces by Warhol (the title refers to the artist's silkscreen of Chairman Mao). The novel fills up with eerie intimations of masses in formation.

Gray himself emerges as the apotheosis of a dying breed—the writer pledged to individuality. He and his kind are becoming superfluous, and his perceptions of the truth ring with bitter irony. "What terrorists gain," says Gray at one point, "novelists lose. The degree to which they influence mass consciousness is the extent of our decline as shapers of sensibility and thought. The danger they represent equals our own failure to be dangerous." The making of sentences has given way to the handing down of sentences; as individuality expires, morality becomes a chimera. This is not a happy book, but since when do we read DeLillo to feel good about things? The one consolation is that a statement about our irrevocable decline, if made with sufficient penetration and grace, can itself become a momentary stay against that decline, if not an agent of reversal. (pp. 1-2)

> *Sven Birkerts, "The Future Belongs to Crowds," in* Book World—The Washington Post, *May 26, 1991, pp. 1-2.*

Michiko Kakutani   (review date 28 May 1991)

[*In the review below, Kakutani discusses the characters and themes in* Mao II.]

Don DeLillo's characters are obsessives and compulsive organizers, marginal individuals in search of some system of belief that might provide them with the illusion of order against the terror of chaos and death. In his last nine books, these people have sought refuge in a startling array of obsessions that run the gamut from the mundane to the bizarre, from the harmless to the apocalyptic: football and technological warfare (*End Zone*), mathematical equations and scientific formulas (*Ratner's Star*), the Central Intelligence Agency and murderous cults (*The Names*), terrorism (*Players*) and conspiracy theories (*Libra*).

The characters in his latest novel (*Mao II*) share this desperate need to find a way of ordering their lives. Karen, a young woman cut off from family and purpose, becomes a Moonie; the cult temporarily provides her with the soothing sense that she belongs to something larger than herself, that she need only carry out a series of prescribed rituals to bring about "new life, peace eternal."

Karen's boyfriend, Scott, finds comfort, if not meaning in the worship of a famous writer named Bill Gray: as Gray's assistant, he spends his days filing, collating, retyping and indexing his employer's words, reducing an overwhelming torrent of prose into neatly typed stacks and cartons of paper.

As for Bill Gray himself, he has long sought a sense of control in the creation of narratives: stories, for him, have been a means of subduing reality and altering "the inner life of the culture." Now, however, Gray is beginning to have his doubts. He has been having problems with his latest novel—he has spent years in seclusion, rewriting the same sentences over and over again—and his assistant, Scott, is trying to persuade him to shelve the entire project. By publishing, Scott argues, the myth of the elusive, reclusive author will be destroyed; only by not publishing will his celebrity metastasize and grow.

To make matters worse, Bill has become obsessed with the writer's diminished role in the world. As he sees it, society—or American society, at any rate—has become so distracted, so overstimulated and benumbed by the noise of television and advertisements, by news, gossip and fear, that it has become virtually deaf to the pronouncements of artists and wise men. The new "shapers of sensibility and thought" have become the bomb makers and gunmen, the terrorists who claim the media's attention and insinuate themselves in the consciousness of the world.

These themes, of course, have frequently been sounded in Mr. DeLillo's more recent work: in *Players,* a disaffected yuppie gets involved with terrorists who want to bomb the New York Stock Exchange; in *The Names,* a risk expert finds himself caught between the machinations of the C.I.A. and the plans of a murderous cult; and in *Libra,* Lee Harvey Oswald plots to make his mark on history. Bill Gray, too, will find himself venturing into the dangerous world "out there," beyond his book-lined study. Asked by his editor to speak out in behalf of a poet who has been taken hostage by terrorists, Bill will agree to use his celebrity as an author to help win the poet's release; and he will find himself drawn, by events and by his own fascination with violence, into the terrorists' shadowy world.

Disturbing, provocative and darkly comic, *Mao II* reads, at once, as a sociological meditation on the perils of contemporary society, and as a kind of new-wave thriller. Imagine a script written by David Mamet and Sam Shepard (with a little additional dialogue by Joyce), directed by Godard or Antonioni. While it's not as fluent (or as funny) a performance as *White Noise*—there are patches of authorial pontification in the dialogue, and an overly schematic plot—the book succeeds in re-orchestrating all of Mr. DeLillo's favorite themes with new authority and precision. The writing, as usual, is dazzling; the book's images, so radioactive that they glow afterward in our minds.

The media's role in turning authors and terrorists alike into celebrities; the power of images (created by television, photography or words) to mediate reality; the dissolution of individuality in crowds and mass movements, all these themes in the novel are summed up, for Mr. DeLillo, by Andy Warhol's repetitive and manipulative paintings of famous people and objects. Indeed the novel's title comes from Warhol's famous series of Mao prints, brilliantly reproduced on the book's stylish dust jacket.

With his nihilistic repudiation of originality, his fascination with the bright shiny surfaces of contemporary consumer culture and his determined pursuit of publicity, Warhol himself seems like the embodiment of Mr. DeLillo's bleak vision of an America, perched on the brink of apocalypse and self-destruction, a vision defined and redefined in all 10 of his novels.

Because they were grounded in no vision of his own, Warhol's efforts to appropriate the effluvia of American culture tended to fall short of the mark. Although Mr. DeLillo's novels have also been criticized for their willful topicality—everything from chemical accidents to terrorist raids to the assassination of President John F. Kennedy seems to leap from the headlines into his books—he does not, like Warhol, simply exploit such events. Rather, he implants these sordid bits of news in his novels, much the way Jasper Johns and Robert Rauschenberg insert pieces of reality into their work, provoking his audience into a reappraisal of a chaotic and mysterious world.

> *Michiko Kakutani, "Fighting against Envelopment by the Mass Mind," in* The New York Times, *May 28, 1991, p. C15.*

Richard Eder   (review date 9 June 1991)

[*In the following review, Eder discusses DeLillo's exploration of political extremism and crowd mentality in* Mao II.]

In Yankee Stadium, 13,000 followers of the Rev. Sun Moon are being married by their master. The most personal of rites is turned into an avalanche of polyester suits, cheap bridal gowns and tired young faces; into a mass ceremony with a militant collective purpose.

Outside the stadium stretch hundreds of acres of tenements, burnt out, ruled by drug gangs and squatted in by fragmented families—a sample of the world's collective despair wedged into upper Manhattan. It is a second mass phenomenon, this one chaotic and purposeless, but in some obscure way the reciprocal of the fanatically organized energies inside the stadium walls.

Mass purpose, mass dereliction; each is a threat to and in some way a consequence of a third Manhattan. The one where people go to work, go shopping, juggle with debt, personal safety and a suppressed fear of disintegration, all the while, struggling to think of themselves as Western individuals with private choices. As Don De Lillo writes in [*Mao II*], his new pre-Doomsday novel:

> . . . people ride escalators going up and sneak secret glances at the faces coming down. People dangle tea bags over hot water in white cups. Cars run silently on the autobahns, streaks of painted light. People sit at desks and stare at office walls. They smell their shirts and drop them in the hamper. People bind themselves into numbered seats and fly across time zones and

high cirrus and deep night, knowing there is something they've forgotten to do.

The future belongs to crowds.

The mass wedding is a prologue to *Mao II*, a novel about the crowds of our times, their manipulators and various individuals who struggle among them. They struggle, that is, like fish in an industrially polluted stream, with convulsive movements and a clouding eye.

There are the Moonies and Karen, a young upper-middle-class woman who joins them, leaves them and never is free of them. There is an Arab terrorist organization of hooded youngsters who unquestioningly follow a middle-aged Mao-like "father," and the Swiss poet who is their hostage. There is a different kind of crowd, with a different kind of manipulator: our own society, with financial and publicity mechanisms, whose purposes are as bottom-line as Mao's; and an admired, embittered and would-be-solitary novelist, whose solitude and art are made into a commodity and poisoned.

Bill Gray, variously suggestive of J. D. Salinger, Thomas Pynchon and Harold Brodkey, has written two brilliant novels that have achieved cult status. He has secluded himself, shunning all interviews and outside contacts. A formidable expectation has built up around this seclusion, especially since it has been years since he has published anything.

Brita Nilsson, a famous photographer of great events and calamities, penetrates the seclusion. Weary of the great-event game—everything has become publicity—she seeks the authentic. Perhaps she will find it by photographing nothing but writers; if these aren't private and authentic, who is? Nobody is more private and, presumably, authentic, than Gray.

She is contacted by Scott, Gray's assistant and acolyte, and spirited in secrecy to a backwoods home. There she finds not the Wizard of Oz, but a lonely, talkative, sad-faced man with a bad stomach, smoker's lungs and no magic in him. Every scrap he had ever written or received is archived around him in a kind of bunker—Scott, assisted by the ex-Moonie Karen, who sleeps alternatively with him and his employer, is sedulous and methodical. Gray has finished a novel but he knows it's heavy, static and self-conscious. He keeps working away, not in hopes of improving it but because he is trapped.

He had isolated himself as a simple artistic reflex, looking for peace and the opportunity to work. But the media have seized on this isolation, made it into a myth, given it the most devastating celebrity, and set up a disabling public expectation. He wants to deflate the pressure; perhaps Brita's photographs, released bit by bit, will do it. Perhaps he can come out of seclusion, eat at restaurants, recover some of the naturalness. "Remember literature, Charlie?" he asks an old associate later, when he comes to New York. "It involved getting drunk and getting laid."

Gray's paralysis goes beyond isolation, adulation and beleaguerment. There is a feeling of uselessness. The novelist has become irrelevant and no longer possesses the power "to alter the inner life of a culture," he declares. The world

is organized and manipulated in crowds; the novelist's transforming influence has been taken over by terrorists: "The danger they represent equals our own failure to be dangerous."

Charlie, now a hotshot publisher for a big international conglomerate—"It's all about limousines," he explains—has just the thing for him. A new Arab terrorist group has sprung up and kidnaped a Swiss writer. A new publishers' group also has sprung up. Both need publicity. The publishers will issue a public appeal, the Arabs will make a public gesture, and everyone will benefit. And if Gray appears at the press conference—"Recluse Speaks Out for Prisoner"—it will be a smash hit and, incidentally, drive up the sales of Gray's book, which Charlie is determined to acquire. There will be no problem, of course, in breaking "the crumbling remnants of a contract" with Gray's "old, dusty, lovable skinflint house."

Escaping his obsolete calling, Gray tries to deal with his activist successors, the terrorists. After a series of cloudy encounters, a bombing and a trip to Greece, the negotiations collapse. Far from being "novelists," the terrorists are one more group of corporate maneuverers. Gray, increasingly unhinged and ill with cancer, makes a valiant but ignominious ending.

De Lillo writes with characteristic corrosiveness and wit. Like his previous sorties against the dismay of our times, *Mao II* is winged and agile, flying us to odd and seemingly unreachable vantage points for a view that would be purely chilling if we didn't feel so exhilarated at getting there to see it.

The description of Karen's life among the Moonies—"Prethink your total day," a supervisor tells the pencil-selling initiates. "Then jump it. Jump it. Jump it"—is baleful and arresting. So are the marks of servitude that remain after she escapes. "I think we ought to have our intercourse now," she tells Gray, after putting him to bed.

De Lillo's satirical portrait of a modern publisher is wickedly satisfying, and his talent for moral suspense, reminiscent of Graham Greene's, makes a splendid portrait of the ambiguous Arab intermediary between Gray and the terrorists. And nobody, of course, is better placed to write about the poisonous exposure and solitary agony of the contemporary writer.

Perhaps, in fact, De Lillo is too close. The scenes with Gray, particularly in his retreat, bog down in their very intensity; besides the portrait of a writer immured inside himself and going dry, they suggest a confessional. There are times when we wonder whether Gray, lamenting the inertness of his book, is not De Lillo foreshadowing what we shall find in parts of his. For much of the time, it is as if the author's corrosive voice had begun to eat at itself; as if darkness had swollen to blot out the contrasts—De Lillo's talent for a fugitive tenderness, the slapstick shuffle in his funeral marches—by which darkness can be made out.

Richard Eder, "Hermetically Seared," in Los Angeles Times Book Review, *June 9, 1991, p. 3.*

DeLillo on writing:

Every sentence has a truth waiting at the end of it and the writer learns how to know it when he finally gets there. On one level this truth is the swing of the sentence, the beat and poise, but down deeper it's the integrity of the writer as he matches with the language. I've always seen myself in sentences. I begin to recognize myself, word by word, as I work through a sentence. The language of my books has shaped me as a man. There's a moral force in a sentence when it comes out right. It speaks the writer's will to live.

Don DeLillo, in The New York Times, *19 May 1991.*

Lorrie Moore   (review date 9 June 1991)

[*Moore is an American short story writer, novelist, and essayist whose works include* Self-Help *(1985) and* Like Life *(1990). In the following review, she praises the narrative and thematic complexity of* Mao II.]

If terrorists have seized control of the world narrative, if they have captured the historical imagination, have they become, in effect, the world's new novelists? For sheer influence over the human mind, have they displaced a precariously placed literature? Are writers—lacking some greater if lethal faith—the new hostages? "Is history possible? Is anyone serious?" These are some of the questions posed by *Mao II,* the latest novel by Don DeLillo, who has already proved with such books as *Players, White Noise* and *Libra* that no one can match his ability to let America, the bad dream of it, speak through his pen.

Mao II, takes its title from one of Andy Warhol's famous portraits of Mao Zedong. For Mr. DeLillo, the Warhols are more than mock chinoiserie: they anticipate the televised image of the official state portrait of Mao, defaced with red paint in Tiananmen Square. In *Mao II,* the Warhol pictures marry the ideas of totalitarianism and image-making, prompting speculation about how fame is transformed into a death mask, how a portrait can freeze the mind behind the face. Fittingly enough, the novel begins and ends with a wedding, that most stereotypically photographed occasion. And yet, while this bookending creates a palindromic comedy, these are anti-comedic, apocalyptic nuptials.

Not that *Mao II* doesn't now and then attempt a joke. As with so much of Mr. DeLillo's work, the novel has a discursive sweep, and its narrative movement from serious idea to serious idea is rigorously un-neat, like the gathering and associative movement of the brain itself. But as a story about a reclusive writer, written by a reclusive writer, it has a sense of humor. Early on in the novel, a mad street person, "great-maned and filthy, rimed saliva in his beard, old bruises across the forehead gone soft and crumbly," bursts into a bookstore; "I'm here to sign my books," he tells the security guard. Later, when the protagonist, a novelist named Bill Gray, falls into the company of a Maoist terrorist sympathizer, their tense conversation takes an unexpected turn: "There's something I wanted to

ask the other evening at dinner," says the other man. "Do you use a word processor?"

But over all, as one might expect from Mr. DeLillo, this is a dark tale, one that is focused on the writer Bill Gray and the various characters circling his life at a time when Gray is particularly weary of his well-guarded seclusion. Indeed, that seclusion has become a kind of captivity; in a way, he is looking for a changing of the guards. Thus Gray escapes the confines of his country home to visit a friend at a New York publishing house, then finds himself agreeing to go to London to give a reading on behalf of a poet held captive in Beirut. When he arrives in London, however, the reading is postponed because of a bomb threat. But Gray moves ineluctably toward the Middle East (via Athens and Cyprus) and toward the fate of the poet-hostage, which, in an act of professional brotherhood but also of spiritual mystery, Gray insists on trying to prevent or share—or appropriate. In that contest between art and life, this is a scenario that both mirrors and *is* the "master collapse" that is Gray's final book.

The people in Gray's life at this critical time include Scott, a compulsive and maniacal fan who has tracked Gray down and volunteered himself as an assistant, enforcing Gray's solitude, managing Gray's career, commanding Gray's life. There is also Scott's lover, the waiflike Karen (who is sometimes Gray's lover as well), a former follower of the Rev. Sun Myung Moon with a visionary streak that allows her to see what others can't and to speak, in eerie mimicry, what others speak. And there is Brita, the literary photographer whose portraits of Gray, she and he both briefly believe, will help usher him out into the world of the living, though it is not long before she gives up photographing writers and turns to those who make the real news—the terrorists.

Mr. DeLillo has written about terrorists before, in the 1977 novel *Players,* but *Mao II* has something else haunting it: the ordeal of Salman Rushdie. Mr. DeLillo shares a publisher with Mr. Rushdie, and in *Mao II* the New York publishing house that Gray visits is one at which there are visitor searches and guards. The idea of a writer held hostage is so understandably traumatizing to Mr. DeLillo that he has used his narrative to work variations on this theme: the blindfolded poet in a basement in Beirut; the hermitic and professionally hamstrung novelist in a study in upstate New York. And, lest the pairing seem merely a melodramatic metaphor, Mr. DeLillo, with a kind of insistence, makes these lives intersect. This can really happen, he seems to be saying. Look for a writer, and you will find a terrorist. And a hostage. This is the new literary dialectic. It is also the evening news.

No one's prose is better than Mr. DeLillo's. "I'm a sentence-maker, like a donut-maker only slower," says Bill Gray. Mr. DeLillo's description of a writer's face through the viewfinder of a camera becomes a poem complete unto itself: "She watched him surrender his crisp gaze to a softening, a bright-eyed fear that seemed to tunnel out of childhood. It had the starkness of a last prayer. She worked to get at it. His face was drained and slack, coming into flatness, into black and white, cracked lips and flaring brows, age lines that hinge the chin, old bafflements and regrets."

The novel is also filled with set pieces that show off the author's great skill with a scene and with multiple points of view. There is, for example, the Orwellian opening, a mass wedding of 13,000 at Yankee Stadium. "It's as though they designed this to the maximum degree of let the relatives squirm," says one of the "flesh parents," futilely scanning the bridal veils for her daughter. "How they hate our willingness to work and struggle," thinks Karen, the daughter she is looking for. "They want to snatch us back to the land of lawns."

When, toward the end of the novel, Mr. DeLillo has Bill Gray (who is suffering internal injuries from a hit-and-run accident in Athens) sit down in a Cyprus restaurant to make witty if coded chitchat with some British tourists, ıı is a portrait of the artist as the dying Mercutio, and it provides the book some of its best dialogue—speech that sounds like speech rather than writing. Often in the complex orchestration of his ideas, Mr. DeLillo makes his characters name and sing all his tunes for him, speaking in dazzling chunks of authorial essay that read as if they had been created by someone who no longer cared—or perhaps no longer knew—how people really spoke. Here, though, in this careful, bitter dinner scene, everything— the tension, the tone, the dialogue—is exactly right.

Among the myriad other things to admire in *Mao II* are Mr. DeLillo's way of capturing a representative slice of a city, his ability to reproduce ineffable urban rhythms, his startling evocations of sights and smells. He has a discerning and satirical eye, which notes unexpected details like Gray's "sepia toenails" or the "cancer coloring book" in the pocket of a car door.

Indeed, it is to the larger idea of the image—its use as a bridge between public and private, its doubtful integrity, its sanctimonious politics—that *Mao II* keeps returning. A mass wedding, a photo session with a writer, an international revolution—all attempt an elimination of the self through the imagistic replication of the self. Seen this way, imagery is a kind of cemetery, a repository for the proliferating residue of life. ("The room drained the longings out of him," Mr. DeLillo writes of his hostage poet in that basement cell. "He was left with images.") In Mr. DeLillo's metaphorical system, the self figured and multiplied is death: an army is the opposite of a person. Likeness is the canvas of farewell. Only anarchic Beirut seems to have "consumed all its own depictions"; Gray has trouble even finding a map of the place.

If one remains less moved by *Mao II* than engaged and impressed, that is the contract a reader must often make with a book by Mr. DeLillo; he is seldom an emotional writer. Nonetheless, one may find oneself hoping just a little for something approximating the feeling and power of, say, Marguerite Oswald's monologue in the closing chapter of *Libra,* or even the chill gallows humor of *White Noise,* which accomplished so much sustained and mournful queasiness.

Still, within its own defined parameters, within the boundaries of its own paradoxical discourse, Mr. DeLillo's new book succeeds as brilliantly as any of his others. One thinks of the novel's own refrains: Bill Gray's memory of a family joke, repeating the instructions in the hat section of Sears catalogue, "Measure your head before ordering"; and the prayerful chant of an unheeded street beggar, "Still love you. Spare a little change. . . . Still love you." (pp. 7, 49)

> Lorrie Moore, "Look for a Writer and Find a Terrorist," in The New York Times Book Review, *June 9, 1991, pp. 7, 49.*

Lee Lescaze   (review date 13 June 1991)

[*In the following review, Lescaze asserts that* Mao II *lacks credibility and narrative momentum.*]

[*Mao II*] begins in sunlight at Yankee Stadium and ends in the darkness of ruined Beirut. But images in Don DeLillo's hands are tricky things.

His first scene is a Moonie-style mass wedding—6,500 couples, strangers to their mates, matched by the Master—parading across the bright baseball diamond while unhappy parents squint in vain from the stands hoping to catch a glimpse of their own child.

The last scene is also a wedding. At night, the bride and groom stroll with friends through Beirut—following a tank rented for the occasion. Yet here, in the shell-cratered streets is the joy, the triumph of the individual spirit so absent from the sad Yankee Stadium ceremony.

Individual spirit, the power of crowds and the madness that can infect both are at the center of *Mao II.* Mr. DeLillo is the preeminent novelist of the political nightmare and, in his 10 novels, political terror has been a frequent preoccupation. He builds stories around the temper—or more accurately, distemper—of the times. *Mao II* is crowded with ideas, mixing terrorism, cults, the romance of news and the failing power of words.

W. H. Auden and Christopher Isherwood intuited more than 50 years ago that a deluge of horrors on the horizon was ushering in an age of news heros. In their *Journey to a War* they wrote: "A disillusioned journalist is the Byron, the romantic Hamlet of our modern world." Even without imagining television they understood that the world was plunging dizzyingly into a turbulence that would make the ironic journalist—not the novelist—seem the central figure.

Mao II updates this clash between news and literature. "News of disaster is the only narrative people need. The darker the news, the grander the narrative. News is the last addiction before—what?" says Bill Gray, the protagonist of *Mao II.*

Gray has become a cult figure in part because of two wildly popular novels and in part because he has gone into hiding, making a mystery of himself like J. D. Salinger or Thomas Pynchon. . . . In his self-imposed isolation Gray fears that history is passing into the hands of the crowd— the Moonie crowd, the Ayatollah-worshipping crowd, the unreasoning mob that waved Mao Tse-tung's red book of thoughts.

But if Gray fears for the public fate of words and truth at the hands of crowds, he is privately tortured by the fate of his words. For 23 years he has been working on a novel he is now terrified to publish. Gray's talent is gone. He is sitting on a dead book and the moment it appears, the world's fanatic admiration will end.

So, Gray is powerless inside his hide-away life.

Gray's personal failure mingles with his despair that words and specifically novels are less and less heeded. "There's a curious knot that binds novelists and terrorists," Gray says. "In the West we become famous effigies as our books lose the power to shape and influence . . . Years ago I used to think it was possible for a novelist to alter the inner life of the culture. Now bomb-makers and gunmen have taken over that territory."

Mr. DeLillo can be a spellbinding writer, but the story of *Mao II* never gathers much momentum or wins much credibility. Timing is one problem. The madness of Chairman Mao's Cultural Revolution is over; mass marriages are less frequent. Even terrorism has declined from its heyday. News addiction still keeps millions from pushing the "off" button on their remote controls, but the delusion of crowds seems in remission.

Of course, such mad phenomena can rage again, but *Mao II* has a deeper problem. Mr. DeLillo has crammed it fuller than a 22-minute evening news show on the first night of a war. Image quick-cuts to new image. People fill the screen and then flicker away. Ideas pile upon ideas. The clutter makes for confusion. Inside this short novel is a longer novel seeking to burst out.

Gray is a rich character, but his final quest to sacrifice himself in exchange for a little-known Swiss poet held by Beirut terrorists seems an overly quixotic means of self-destruction rather than the meaningful quest it is intended to be.

Yet, the best scenes of *Mao II,* like the stadium wedding and Gray's doomed days in Cyprus seeking passage to Beirut, stick vividly in the memory. The Beirut ending is beautifully written. In just a few pages, Mr. DeLillo creates one of fiction's memorable terrorists and brings the cursed city alive.

"Terror makes the new future possible," says the pompous terrorist Abu Rashid. "History is not the book of human memory. We do history in the morning and change it after lunch." He adds: "There is a longing for Mao that will sweep the world."

That, of course, is nonsense—as a character is quick to point out. Yet, in the context of a novel so alive to the evils of terrorism, it is disappointing to find such a flim-flam artist working the bellows that fan those fears. It's a bit like the old story of climbing a remote mountain to find the guru with life's secret, only to hear him offer: "Life is a fountain."

Lee Lescaze, "The Distemper of the Times," in The Wall Street Journal, *June 13, 1991, p. A14.*

Jerome Klinkowitz   (review date 23 June 1991)

[*In the review below, Klinkowitz examines DeLillo's treatment of such themes as faith and meaning in* Mao II.]

The arts have always considered social politics a valid subject, but only in our own day does the very act of treating such a subject come off like comedy or camp. Jacques Louis David painted the coronation of Napoleon, producing an artwork as serious and monumental as the event itself. But when Andy Warhol rendered Mao Tse-Tung in art, the result was a silk-screen extravagance that served as Warhol's excuse for scribbling over, defacing and eventually transforming Mao's famous visage into something riotously amusing and disconcertingly alive.

There's the same difference between Walt Whitman's image of Abraham Lincoln and Robert Coover's of Richard Nixon—think of all those pratfalls the president is made to suffer in Coover's *The Public Burning.* Even when the writer's purpose is deadly serious, as Don DeLillo's was with Lee Harvey Oswald in *Libra,* readers find it hard to read along with either the solemnity accorded to history or the suspended disbelief reserved for fiction. And now, in *Mao II,* DeLillo takes that very ambivalence between history and fiction, politics and art, and uses it to propel his narrative through several highlights of our shared social life in the American 1990s.

Like our decentered times, *Mao II* has no protagonist, just a set of individuals who are linked by their pursuit of meaning. There's Karen Janney, a young former Moonie who has been sufficiently deprogrammed to wander passively into a similar situation with Scott Martineau, who has found his own Reverend Moon in the person of writer Bill Gray, a J. D. Salinger-like recluse.

Scott and Karen have become Gray's personal keepers, making sure that he will continue to revise, but never publish, his endlessly revised novel—for if Gray and his new work were to take their rightful places in the world, Scott and Karen would lose theirs. But their motives are not entirely selfish, because no finished novel could live up to the long-awaited masterpiece Gray is expected to produce. And were he to emerge from seclusion, he would prove to be no more interesting than his bland, colorless name.

The catalyst that moves Gray, Scott and Karen out of this suspended state is Brita Nilsson, who is dedicated to photographing all the world's authors and creating an archive as a memorial to their cultural role. Scott comes to New York to meet her, and Karen follows her back, a device that lets DeLillo effectively undertake one of the novelist's old-fashioned tasks: addressing the social conditions of the age. Some of the book's best writing is reserved for the plight of the homeless and the psychology of living in crowds.

For Bill Gray, Brita brings a message from his old editor. He wants my new book, Gray presumes, but actually it is the book's nonexistence and Gray's notorious absence that the editor wishes to exploit.

There's a hostage in Beirut, Gray learns, whose freedom can be won if Gray appears at a news conference and reads from the detainee's poetry. It is here that the irony kicks in, and DeLillo makes his most serious points about the new world in which we live.

The hostage is a relief worker, not a writer; the dozen or so poems he's published are incidental. But styling the hostage as a writer makes him more interesting to the media, while the writer whose media appearance supposedly will free the hostage is famous for not writing and for not having been seen in public for decades—as hermetically sealed off from the world as the poor hostage has been.

What this says about the fate of writers and their writing is chilling: Absence is more effective than presence, and silence speaks a more compelling language than articulation. The most famous writers are those who don't write at all, and the most compelling books remain those that are never written.

DeLillo's point is not just to bewail the state of writing in a world that has abandoned reality in favor of image and political effect. Long before his involvement with the hostage situation, Gray remarks on the "curious knot that binds novelists and terrorists." True, the writers have become "famous effigies as our books lose the power to shape and influence," power that now belongs to "bomb-makers and gunmen." Yet in hard-nosed terms, the terrorists are just as fatuous as the writers, for their attacks are not on military objectives but "on human consciousness."

The struggle for the future, then—the struggle over who will define reality—is between novelists and terrorists. Each group uniquely understands the other, as a terrorist spokesman later tells Gray: "Through history it's the novelist who has felt affinity for the violent man who lives in the dark. Where are your sympathies? With the colonial police, the occupier, the rich landlord, the corrupt government, the militaristic state? Or with the terrorist?"

However, terrorists and writers come at the problem from opposite directions. By punishing an innocent hostage, Gray comes to learn more about what happens when "you begin to empty the world of meaning and erect a separate mental state, the mind consuming what's outside itself, replacing real things with plots and fictions."

The terrorist's fiction "takes the world narrowly into itself," while the writer's art is better at "pushing out toward the social order, trying to unfold into it." It is the writer and not the terrorist who creates in order to reveal, increasing meaning rather than restricting it. Detaining the poet, as limited as his writing has been, only "drains the world of one more thimble of meaning."

Terrorists, Moonies, eccentric artists and reclusive writers—*Mao II* gathers them all in a world that is full of crowds but promises little more than the isolation of the homeless. DeLillo's genius, however, is to question rather than to condemn—to ask, as does the father of Karen, his wanly pliable ex-Moonie, "When the Old God leaves the world, what happens to all the expended faith?"

Because there is still a struggle over such faith—a struggle between novelists and terrorists, between messiahs and message-makers—*Mao II* suggests our current style of life may not be meaningless after all. Rather, it is a life-or-

death contest among those who would define meaning. (pp. 1, 4)

Jerome Klinkowitz, "Novelists vs. Terrorists," in Chicago Tribune—Books, *June 23, 1991, pp. 1, 4.*

DeLillo on what inspired him to write *Mao II*:

I saw a photograph of a wedding conducted by Reverend Moon of the Unification Church . . . and it was just lying around for months . . . a wedding in Seoul in a soft-drink warehouse, about 13,000 people. And when I looked at it again, I realized I wanted to understand this event, and the only way to understand it was to write about it. For me, writing is a concentrated form of thinking.

And I had another photograph—it was a picture that appeared on the front page of *The New York Post,* in the summer, I think, of 1988, and it was a photograph of J. D. Salinger. They sent two photographers to New Hampshire, to stalk him. It took them six days, but they found him. And they took his picture. He saw them and they saw him. When they took his picture he came at them. His face is an emblem of shock and rage. It's a frightening photograph. I didn't know it at the time, but these two pictures would represent the polar extremes of *Mao II,* the arch individualist and the mass mind, from the mind of the terrorist to the mind of the mass organization. In both cases, it's the death of the individual that has to be accomplished before their aims can be realized.

Don DeLillo, in The New York Times, *19 May 1991.*

Robert Towers (review date 27 June 1991)

[*In the following review, Towers states that while the narrative of* Mao II *is weak, the work contains impressive imagery and powerful themes.*]

Don DeLillo's reputation had been advancing stealthily for more than a decade before the publication of **White Noise** (1985) and **Libra** (1989) secured his current position as one of the most original, intelligent, and visionary novelists now writing in America. He had by this time created a distinctive fictional world, a technologically sophisticated place riddled with conspiracy and coded messages, subject at times to bursts of terrorist fire. The "paranoia" of DeLillo's vision—especially notable in **Running Dog** and **The Names**—has something in common with Pynchon's and Burroughs's, but it is less wild, less surreal, far more deeply grounded in the reality made known to us by journalists and intelligence agents testifying at congressional hearings.

In **White Noise** DeLillo widened his scope to include a sendup—at once hilarious and ominous—of the shopping-mall culture, written in exuberant prose combining up-to-date technological jargon with the soothing hum of television commercials; and he revealed an unexpected gift for domestic comedy that was wonderfully compatible with the latent horrors of "the airborne toxic event" and his narrator's obsessive fear of death at the center of the novel. In *Libra* DeLillo brought the Oswald-Kennedy-Jack Ruby story to vivid fictional life, endowing it with his own "theory" of rogue CIA agents, Cuban connections, and the Mafia, and managing—despite everything already known—to create an almost unbearable suspense: Would the President indeed be shot, or would the complex scheme at the last moment fail?

Mao II is a more somber work, less concentrated as a narrative; and it is shorter than either of its predecessors. The cast of characters is relatively small, and the characters themselves, while sharply delineated, are perhaps less interesting in the long run than the images and themes that cluster around them. The novel opens with a scene at Yankee Stadium, where a pair of anguished parents watch helplessly as their daughter Karen is married by the Reverend Moon in a mass ceremony involving more than six thousand chanting couples in identical blue suits and white bridal gowns. Karen and her husband, a young Korean whom she met only two days before, have been matched by the Master and will lead an entirely communal life devoted to accomplishing the divine mission of their leader. The scene ends with the statement of one of the novel's major themes, "The future belongs to crowds."

Karen, however, is not an important character in her own right. She is essentially a blank stare, a malleable young woman with a minimum of ego, who is among the satellites revolving around the novel's dominant figure: a famous and famously reclusive writer named Bill Gray. Following the Yankee Stadium scene, the story immediately jumps forward several years to a meeting between a young man, Scott Martineau, and a Swedish photographer, Brita Nilsson. After a successful career of shooting sordid urban scenes, Brita has decided that her work was unsatisfactory ("No matter what I shot, how much horror, reality, misery, ruined bodies, bloody faces, it was all so fucking pretty in the end"), and she now photographs only writers. She wants to make a complete photographic record of writers—"a species count," as if the breed were threatened with extinction.

Scott has come to New York to escort her to the secret upstate house of his employer, the writer Bill Gray, who has unexpectedly decided to have his picture taken for the first time in thirty years. As Scott and Brita follow a complicated route of concealment, traveling by night through a network of dirt roads, gravel roads, and old logging trails, Brita says, "I feel as if I'm being taken to see some terrorist chief at his secret retreat in the mountains," to which Scott replies, "Tell Bill. He'll love that."

The household, Brita discovers, consists of Bill Gray, who has managed to disappear even more successfully than Salinger or Pynchon; Scott, who has attached himself to Bill as his assistant, secretary, archivist, and de facto keeper; and Karen, the ex-Moonie, never fully "deprogrammed," who has attached herself to Scott but also from time to time slips into Bill's bed. When Brita at last meets Bill, he promptly makes the connection between novelists and terrorists. "Years ago," he tells Brita during their first photo session, "I used to think it was possible for a novelist to alter the inner life of the culture. Now bomb-makers

and gunmen have taken that territory. They make raids on human consciousness. What writers used to do before we were all incorporated." And a little later, "News of disaster is the only narrative people need. The darker the news, the grander the narrative."

Bill is a defeated man, a writer of stubborn integrity, a semi-alcoholic, addicted to the medicines he is taking. He has not published a book in twenty years. Obsessed by the mystique of the perfect sentence—in a way reminiscent of the sentence-turning Lonoff in Philip Roth's *The Ghost Writer*—Bill has been been endlessly revising the sentences of a finished novel, though he knows that the revisions are worthless. "Every sentence," he tells Brita,

> has a truth waiting at the end of it and the writer learns how to know it when he finally gets there. . . . The deeper I become entangled in the process of getting a sentence right in its syllables and rhythms, the more I learn about myself. I've worked the sentences of this book long and hard but not long and hard enough because I no longer see myself in the language. . . . I've lacked courage and perseverance. Exhausted. Sick of struggling. I've let good enough be good enough. This is someone else's book. It feels all forced and wrong.

Brita urges Bill to publish the novel, but the insanely possessive Scott is opposed to the idea. Bill, he says, is at the height of his fame simply because he has not published for so long.

> We could make a king's whatever, multimillions, with the new book. But it would be the end of Bill as a myth, a force. Bill gets bigger as his distance from the scene deepens.

Bill, however, is restless, tired of his isolation. His book has become horrible to him—"a neutered near-human dragging through the house, hump-backed, hydrocephalic, with puckered lips and soft skin, dribbling brain fluid from its mouth." He longs to re-enter the world, and when Brita delivers a cryptic message from his editor, he goes to New York, gives Scott the slip, and accepts his editor's proposal to go to London in an effort to win the release of a young Swiss poet held prisoner by terrorists in Beirut.

What follows in the novel's second half is a series of events as Bill pursues his improbable mission; these include a terrorist bombing in London, an interview with a Lebanese emissary of the terrorists in Athens, a street accident that leaves Bill with a lacerated liver, a ferry trip from Cyprus to Lebanon that ends with Bill lying dead in his bunk. Interspersed with these, and serving as an elaborate counterpoint to Bill's story, are scenes in which Brita, Karen, Scott, the emissary, the wretched Swiss poet, and the head terrorist himself, the Mao-inspired Abu Rashid, all figure.

Written with the nervous terseness and descriptive immediacy that DeLillo has perfected, these episodes all, in one way or another, reinforce the novel's presiding themes. *Mao II* is a book in which many of the motifs recurrent in DeLillo's fiction, at least since *Running Dog,* are given their baldest, most explicit statement.

Bill's point concerning the impotence of fictional narration when compared with the news of violence and disaster is underscored when, early in the novel, Karen turns off the sound on the TV set and watches as hundreds of English soccer fans are crushed against a wire fence:

> She sees people caught in strangle-holds of no intent, arms upflung, faces popping out at her, hands trying to reach, the fence but only floating in the air. . . . In people's faces she sees the hopelessness of knowing. They show men calmly looking on. They show the fence from a distance, bodies piling up behind it, smothered, sometimes only fingers moving, and it is like a fresco in an old dark church, a crowded twisted vision of a rush to death as only a master of the age could paint it.

This preoccupation with the mesmeric power of disaster is reminiscent of the course in car crashes given by the witty professor of popular culture in **White Noise;** here, however, the treatment is deadpan, untouched by the comedy of the earlier novel.

"The future belongs to crowds." Scenes of crowd behavior recur again and again, from the orderly marching of the Moonie couples in the prologue to the mob of countless frenzied mourners snatching at the body of the Ayatollah Khomeini during his funeral. We are taken by Karen to Tompkins Square in New York, which has been occupied by the wretched of the earth, and then, as Karen again watches television with the sound off, to another famous square, in which a million people are gathered, a square with a portrait of Mao Zedong in the distance into which troops of jogging soldiers come, leaving behind dead bodies entangled in their fallen bicycles. Over the crowds loom the figures of the Masters—the Reverend Moon, the Ayatollah, Mao Zedong.

It is the image of Mao that figuratively dominates the novel just as it dominates the square in Beijing. It is Mao who inspires the little band of terrorists in Beirut and whose writings provide them with their ideology, their rationale; and it is Mao with whom Bill Gray—the isolated novelist, the voice of the stubborn, unprogrammed, palpably dying free spirit—finds himself locked in symbolic conflict. DeLillo provides a paradoxical twist to the image of Mao. In the novel we see him not through official photographs or portraits, but through a pencil sketch called "Mao II" which Scott has given to Karen.

> It was by a famous painter whose name she could never remember but he was famous, he was dead, he had a white mask of a face and glowing white hair. Or maybe he was just supposed to be dead. Scott said he didn't seem dead because he never seemed real. Andy. That was it.

Andy Warhol's art of course epitomizes the deadpan, passive fascination with disaster (car crashes), the personal tragedy of celebrities (Marilyn, Jackie), the impersonal cruelty (the electric chair) and power (Mao) that pervade a consumerist, television-addicted society like ours, which, as a character in **White Noise** puts it, suffers periodic "brain-fade." By the multiplication of his images Warhol creates his own crowd effect, while he is himself

subject to almost infinite reproduction and multiplication. Brita's photograph of him is hung in a gallery show devoted to Warholiana: "Andy's image on canvas, Masonite, velvet, paper-and-acetate, Andy in metallic paint, silkscreen ink, pencil, polymer, gold leaf. . . ." Warhol, like Mao, is the spiritual enemy of everything that Bill Gray has stood for in his life of "gas pains and skipped heartbeats, grinding teeth and dizzy spells and smothered breath."

There is much to admire in **Mao II.** DeLillo's impassioned determination to write a work charged with contemporary ideas and issues is fully matched by his ability to find arrestingly contemporary images to embody them. I have in mind particularly the final scene, in ravaged, explosion-wracked Beirut, where Brita, standing on a balcony at four o'clock in the morning, witnesses a joyous wedding party proceeding down the cratered street with a ruinous, grafitti-covered old Soviet tank leading the way:

> She wants to dance or laugh or jump off the balcony. It seems completely possible that she will land softly among them and walk along in her pajama shirt and panties all the way to heaven. The tank is passing right below her, turret covered in crude drawings, and she hurries inside and pours another glass of melon liqueur and comes out to toast the newlyweds, calling down, "Bonne chance" and "Bonheur" and "Good luck" and "Salám" and "Skäl," and the gun turret begins to rotate and the cannon eases slowly around like a smutty honeymoon joke and everyone is laughing. The bridegroom raises his glass to the half-dressed foreigner on the top-floor balcony and then they pass into the night, followed by a jeep with a recoilless rifle mounted at the rear.

DeLillo's prose has never been more vigorous, more graphic, yet I found the novel less engrossing than either **White Noise** or **Libra,** and less suggestive than the mysterious and haunting **The Names.** For all the brilliance of its parts, **Mao II** is not entirely satisfying as a whole. The narrative does not gain in momentum and excitement as it advances. The main conflicts are ideological rather than personal. Bill Gray is movingly and convincingly described, but in action he is much less persuasive. His leap from festering isolation to committed involvement in behalf of a stranger thousands of miles away is too swift—and too symbolically "right"—to be believable even as an act of impulse.

Similarly, Scott's attachment to Bill, and Karen's to Scott, are presented more as fixed points in a quasi-allegorical scheme than as either the choices or compulsions that emerge from an ongoing action; only Brita seems to be a relatively free agent, capable of spontaneity and real surprise. None of them is given a voice as lively and original and engaging as those DeLillo contrived for his "real" characters, Marguerite Oswald and Jack Ruby, in **Libra.** The short cuts in motivation and the sometimes excessively stylized dialogue (Brita and Scott sound exactly alike) would not matter if the texture of the book were less realistic, were more frankly arbitrary and surreal. What we have is an over-schematized work of realist fiction, theme-ridden to the degree that the novel's articulation becomes somewhat creaky.

These considerations should not count too heavily. *Mao II* is the work of a major novelist writing almost, though not quite, at the top of his powers. What will remain with me is a series of extraordinary images presented with a complex intensity that no photograph or Warhol silkscreen, or even a film sequence, could achieve. (pp. 17-18)

Robert Towers, "History Novel," in The New York Review of Books, *Vol. XXXVIII, No. 12, June 27, 1991, pp. 17-18.*

Mark Feeney   (review date 9 August 1991)

[*In the following review, Feeney offers a mixed assessment of* Mao II.]

In Don DeLillo's previous novel, *Libra,* a CIA operative assigned to write the secret history of the Kennedy assassination comes to realize that "his subject is not politics or violent crime but men in small rooms." Those last four words accurately reflect DeLillo's tenth novel, *Mao II.*

Of course, men in small rooms have figured throughout DeLillo's fiction. He has crowded his books with solitaries: the math-prodigy hero of *Ratner's Star,* the reclusive rock-star hero of *Great Jones Street,* Lee Harvey Oswald in *Libra,* even (briefly) Adolf Hitler immured in his Berlin bunker in *Running Dog.* Yet in no other DeLillo novel have so many of them filled so many rooms. *Mao II* is a book about writers, terrorists, and hostages—men *professionally* located in small rooms—chained to a typewriter, chained to a conspiracy, or chained literally. As against these singled-out individuals, there is the equally disturbing spectacle of identityless crowds (the book opens with the famous Moonie mass wedding in Yankee Stadium; later a character involved in the wedding finds herself obsessed with the throngs of homeless in the East Village). Hyperconsciousness or the loss of self—these are the alternatives *Mao II* offers.

Narrative has never particularly engaged DeLillo, and the plot here is straightforward enough. The book's protagonist, Bill Gray, is an acclaimed novelist who takes intricate pains to preserve his anonymity. His old editor, a man named Charlie Everson, heads a human-rights group. Everson's organization has reached a tentative agreement with a terrorist group for the release of a young poet being held hostage in Beirut. The agreement is to be announced at a London news conference, and Everson has hit upon the media-pleasing idea of having Gray appear at the press event to read a selection of the hostage's poems. Hands across the water, the pen is mightier than the sword—and generous publicity for all concerned.

Gray surprises both men and agrees to Charlie's proposal. He's sixty-three, alternately dismissive of the novel he's been working on for twenty-three years, and terrified at the prospect of publishing it. Involving himself in Everson's project is a way of escape. It also feeds into his own growing misgivings with the writer's enterprise. "There's a curious knot that binds novelists and terrorists," he muses. "In the West we become famous effigies as our

books lose the power to shape and influence. . . . Years ago I used to think it was possible for a novelist to alter the inner life of the culture. Now bomb-makers and gunmen have taken that territory. They make raids on human consciousness. What writers used to do before we were all incorporated."

That last sentence has an ironic cast. DeLillo himself is very much *un*incorporated. He doesn't teach, he doesn't tour. He just keeps adding to what is as impressive a body of fiction as any American novelist has produced over the past twenty years. Only Thomas Pynchon surpasses him as a master of what one might call the paranoid style in American fiction. (DeLillo, who greatly esteems Pynchon's work, has clearly drawn upon him for Bill Gray. Pynchon, in turn, has contributed one of his rare blurbs to *Mao II.* Even paranoids, it would seem, have mutual-admiration societies.)

DeLillo's fictional world is one charged with menace and meaning. In it, "everything" is "a shape, a fate, information flowing." For DeLillo, facts have auras, and Bill Gray is only half kidding when he complains, "Nothing happens until it's consumed. . . . Nature has given way to aura. A man cuts himself shaving and someone is signed up to write the biography of the cut. All the material in every life is channeled into the glow." In all DeLillo's books an almost medieval sense of immanence collides with a clinical delight in the amassing of data. The results have been memorable, unsettling, and occasionally hilarious.

Some DeLillo novels have been very funny indeed (*End Zone, Great Jones Street, White Noise*), while in others laughter would have been very much an alien presence (*The Names, Libra*). *Mao II* belongs to the latter group. It's apocalyptic in a way none of his previous novels has been. Black humor enlivened *White Noise*'s "airborne toxic event"; and *Libra,* which took for its subject the one event America has come to regard as its own twentieth-century apocalypse, managed to conclude with a graveside epiphany from Marguerite Oswald. Yet from the packing-case shanties of Tompkins Square to the "millennial image mill" of Beirut, a desperate unease pervades *Mao II;* nothing mediates it. Even something as bright and familiar as Broadway feels "as if blocks of time and space had come loose and drifted. The misplaced heartland hotel. The signs for Mita, Midori, Kirin, Magno, Suntory—words that were part of some synthetic mass language, the esperanto of jet lag."

"Esperanto of jet lag" is the sort of brilliant phrase only Don DeLillo might come up with. *Mao II* has many such bravura observations. Ultimately, though, there's something hollow about the novel. One reads it with constant interest and excitement—excepting Pynchon, no other author sees the way we live now quite so compellingly as De-Lillo does—but one also reads it with a growing sense of disappointment. The connection between terrorists and novelists never exists on other than a purely intellectual level; and even there, it remains little more than a powerful conceit. Endings have always been a problem for De-Lillo, and *Mao II* concludes without ever really resolving—Bill's own fate becomes almost incidental. This is

DeLillo's most personal novel; one detects an intimate feeling in the writing about Bill Gray and his vocation that is absent from DeLillo's other books. But that kinship carries with it a patness that trades more on our assumptions about novelists—or, rather, Great Novelists—than on what such a strange and terrible individual must actually be like. It takes a great novelist to render a Great Novelist. In *Mao II,* we get only the first half of the equation. (pp. 490-91)

> Mark Feeney, "Pictures of Bill Gray," in Commonweal, *Vol. CXVIII, No. 14, August 9, 1991, pp. 490-91.*

An excerpt from *Mao II*

[People] ride escalators going up and sneak secret glances at the faces coming down. People dangle teabags over hot water in white cups. Cars run silently on the autobahns, streaks of painted light. People sit at desks and stare at office walls. They smell their shirts and drop them in the hamper. People bind themselves into numbered seats and fly across time zones and high cirrus and deep night, knowing there is something they've forgotten to do.

The future belongs to crowds.

> Don DeLillo, in his Mao II, *Viking, 1991.*

Dennis Kucherawy   (review date 12 August 1991)

[*In the following review of* Mao II, *Kucherawy discusses DeLillo's treatment of such subjects as terrorism, religious cults, and international politics.*]

During the past 20 years, American author Don DeLillo has received critical praise for his intelligent political novels about the paranoia, corruption and dislocation at the heart of contemporary life. He won a 1985 National Book Award for his eighth novel, **White Noise,** and made the best-seller lists in 1988 with **Libra,** his ninth, a fictional speculation that Lee Harvey Oswald's assassination of John F. Kennedy was a Cuban plot that got out of hand. DeLillo's provocative new novel, **Mao II,** explores such themes as terrorism and religious cults. **Mao II** begins with a startling image: a mass marriage of thousands of couples by cult leader Rev. Sun Myung Moon at New York City's Yankee Stadium. Moon in fact did stage such an event involving thousands of his Unification Church followers—known as Moonies—but it was in New York's Madison Square Garden in 1982. With the mass-marriage prologue, DeLillo establishes the novel's central conflict—the struggle between the individual and mass conformity.

DeLillo tersely describes a modern world of people living in isolation as they work in offices, fly across the ocean and ride escalators. "The future," he concludes, "belongs to crowds." Tying in with the prologue in unexpected ways, the novel that follows raises the intriguing idea that terrorists have replaced novelists as the shapers of contempo-

rary thought. "Years ago," says Bill Gray, the reclusive 63-year-old writer who is *Mao II*'s central character, "I used to think it was possible for a novelist to alter the inner life of the culture. Now bomb makers and gunmen have taken that territory. They make raids on human consciousness."

Famous for two books that were published decades ago, Gray has been compulsively revising a third that he completed two years ago but fears to publish. Convinced that it is grossly inferior to his first two books, he believes that the work, if printed, would destroy the mythic stature that he has acquired during his long years of hiding from the public. As his assistant Scott remarks, "Bill gets bigger as his distance from the scene deepens."

However, Gray has grown weary of the effort required to maintain his concealment. He agrees to let a photographer named Brita become the first person to take his picture for publication in 30 years. She arrives at his rural hideaway where he lives with Scott and Karen, one of the Moonies married at Yankee Stadium, who has since been deprogrammed. Brita brings Gray a message from a former publishing colleague who wants him to participate in a scheme to free a Swiss poet who is being held hostage in Beirut. When Gray agrees to try, it becomes a case of one missing writer helping another. The story takes Gray to London, Athens and Beirut as he attempts to use his fame to counter the terrorists' actions.

Mao II's title comes from the name of a series of Andy Warhol silk screens—Scott gives a copy of one of them to Karen—and references to former Chinese Communist leader Mao Zedong crop up throughout the book. One character points out that leaders like Mao have amassed power by appealing to society's "yearning for order." But clearly that yearning can lead to catastrophe. In one scene, Karen watches images of the 1989 Tiananmen Square massacre on TV with the sound off. In that Beijing footage, she sees "the portrait of Mao in that daylit square with paint spattered on his head," and, moments later, "dead bodies attached to fallen bicycles, flames shooting in the dark."

Mao II is a cerebral book, a novel that depends more on ideas than it does on plot, character and action. DeLillo's contemporary world is an overheated engine running out of control. He depicts the numbing helplessness and dissociation that people feel when inundated with news that informs but does not elucidate. He ponders how faith, morality and ethics have almost disappeared in the expedient world of international politics. DeLillo, who tells his disturbing story with sparse and precise prose, deftly creates a psychological drama of foreboding and paranoia.

> Dennis Kucherawy, "Reign of Terrorism," in MacLean's Magazine, *Vol. 104, No. 32, August 12, 1991, p. 43.*

Julian Loose   (review date 30 August 1991)

[*In the following review of* Mao II, *Loose praises DeLillo's realistic depiction of consumerism and terrorism.*]

At once familiar and unsettling, the world of Don DeLillo's fiction is (to borrow a phrase from an early novel) "as American as a slice of apple pie with a fly defecating on it". His characters take comfort in the sight of televised calamity, find motel rooms oddly liberating, conjure Tibetan monasteries out of gleaming supermarkets and hear the music of a dead universe in the phone's dialling tone. No writer better captures modernity's disquieting excess, our sense of "too much everything, more things and messages and meanings than we can use in ten thousand lifetimes". In *Mao II,* his tenth novel, DeLillo reaches beyond America to address the most pervasive of present anxieties: the city homeless, international terror, Beirut and its hostages.

DeLillo published his first book, *Americana,* in 1971 at the relatively late age of thirty-five. The story of a self-regarding television executive who goes off to make avant-garde films in a small Kansas town, it marked out DeLillo's fictional territory: quests of obscure significance, tersely described action and hedged, elliptical conversations which develop into monologues of runaway speculation as speakers become "blinded by the neon of an idea". What sustains and carries this rambling "literary venture" is DeLillo's extraordinarily assured voice, both hard-edged and lyrical, spinning a hilarious, gnomic commentary on his characters' unequal encounters with "tremendous contemporary forces".

Giving up what must surely have been a promising career crafting the "synthetic mass language" of advertising copy, DeLillo proceeded to write novels ranging over an astonishing variety of subjects. In *End Zone* (1972), a college football player studying modes of disaster technology is guiltily entranced at the prospect of nuclear megadeath; *Great Jones Street* (1972) tells the story of a famous rock star, hiding from his fans and in possession of a stolen military drug sought by sinister subversives. Then came the long and formally complex *Ratner's Star* (1976), which relates the distracted attempts of a child mathematics prodigy to decipher a message from another planet; *Players* (1977) features a bored yuppie trader on the New York stock exchange who becomes involved with Queens-based terrorists; and in *Running Dog* (1978), a radical journalist and a renegade section of the United States military go in improbable pursuit of a pornographic film shot in Hitler's bunker during the final days of the war.

From the beginning, DeLillo won significant critical acclaim, John Updike for one praising his ability to read the "sinister ambiguities, the floating ugliness of America's recent history". Commercial recognition was slower in coming, but then DeLillo's own reticence could not have helped: describing himself as "not a public man", as one who knows "what it is like to be an outsider in this society", he has given few interviews and refrains from teaching and lecturing. He has also on occasion obeyed the mock self-injunction issued in *Ratner's Star,* to "make absolutely sure your work leaves readers strewn along the margins". *The Names* (1982), his seventh book, starts straightforwardly enough: set in 1979 ("the period after the shah left Iran, before the hostages were taken"), it depicts a circle of American business men in Athens, transients all too aware of themselves as terrorist targets. Yet

DeLillo's narrative becomes unexpectedly embroiled with a bizarre cult whose central precept is murder according to alphabetical principles, leading at least one reviewer to accuse him of taking refuge in mumbo-jumbo.

DeLillo finally reached a wider audience with the two superb and highly accessible novels that followed. He won the National Book Award for *White Noise* (1984), a devastatingly comic evocation of late-century American suburbia, bombarded by media information and preoccupied with death. Then in the bestselling *Libra* (1988) he brought artistic shape to the darkly clouded history of J. F. Kennedy's assassination. As we learn from *Introducing Don DeLillo,* a patchily useful first collection of essays on DeLillo's work, the American right was provoked by *Libra*'s assumption that Oswald was not a lone gunman, but rather a dupe for covert US operatives wanting to force another invasion of Cuba. The *New Criterion* protested at this insidious vision of events, and columnists for the *Washington Post* attacked the book's "ostentatiously gloomy view of American life and culture", branding it "an act of literary vandalism and bad citizenship".

Such responses may sound absurd. Yet what is exhilarating about DeLillo's novels is that they do seem dangerous, liable (quoting again) to "detonate in the gut of America like a fiery bacterial bombshell". His starting-point is a deep unease at the state of things—as a character laconically remarks in *Mao II.* "Think of the future and see how depressed you get. All the news is bad." DeLillo persists in identifying a complicity between the "blur and glut" culture of consumerism and the violence we see all around us. Indeed, it is a tenet of his spies and misfits that the true "underground", the secret system of terror and control, resides with the corporations and the banks, the military and the government. His originality, though, lies less in levelling accusations than in probing why we should find multiple plots and "connections, links, secret relationships" so beguiling and so necessary.

Mao II's central figure is the novelist Bill Gray, an ageing cultural icon: special issues of literary quarterlies are devoted to his work, people talk of "a Bill Gray place", he receives significant quantities of cranky fan mail. Avoiding his public with the elaborate caution of a Thomas Pynchon or a J. D. Salinger, Bill has gone unseen for thirty years and unpublished for twenty, and rumours circulate about his disappearance, his change of identity, his suicide, his return to work. Bill is an example of DeLillo's enduring interest in the power which accrues to those in retreat, whose withdrawal becomes "a local symptom of God's famous reluctance to appear". Like the rock star in *Great Jones Street* whose only possible next career move is suicide, and who discovers that hiding in "a small crooked room" only adds to his fame, Bill lives the end-game irony that "the less you say, the more you are".

Bill's only companions are Scott who, having hunted down his favorite author, now serves him with absolute devotion; and Karen, an ex-Moonie who has escaped both the Unification Church and her own family's attempts to kidnap and deprogramme her. Both devote their existence to easing Bill's eternal labour of revision, but this is clearly not enough: Bill's latest novel, although effectively finished, is a "master collapse", a failure so profound it makes even his great early work look suspect. Burnt out, alcoholic and hypochondriac, Bill pictures his work-in-progress as a monster, "a neutered near-human dragging through the house, humpbacked, hydrocephalic, with puckered lips and soft skin, dribbling brain fluid from its mouth".

Under mounting pressure to produce, if not the awaited novel, then at least some sign of his presence, Bill decides to pose for a series of photographs. He selects Brita, an accomplished New York photographer and one of DeLillo's more quixotic characters, whose self-imposed task is to make a photographic species count of writers "hunched in chairs from here to China". She tells Bill that Charlie Everson, his former publisher, needs to talk. Everson is a typical DeLillo middleman. As chairman of a new committee on free expression, he has a proposal: a Swiss poet working for the United Nations in Beirut has been taken hostage by an obscure Maoist group, certain negotiations have been made behind the scenes and, if Bill agrees, he's to give a public reading of the poet's work before the world's press in London, Bill's presence alone ensuring the maximum publicity for both terrorists and committee.

Bill is curiously attracted to the idea, so much so that he continues with the plan even when a bomb destroys the venue where he was due to read. If anything he seems encouraged by these sinister developments, allowing himself to be lured on to Athens; and, when a promised meeting with the terrorist leader fails to materialize, opts to go in search of the group in the slums of Beirut. DeLillo's protagonists are frequently asked to become "players" in such deadly games, accepting offers they should, but don't, refuse. Bill, for instance, knows that if he does get to Beirut the terrorists will almost certainly kidnap him, and yet faced with the "shitpile of hopeless prose" that is his novel, he finds the brutal isolation of the hostage compelling; it will be "unsparing, stony, true, the root thing he'd been rehearsing all these years".

Philip Roth, in his celebrated essay "Writing American Fiction" (1961), pointed out that novelists face a reality which, to an almost embarrassing degree, exceeds their own imagination. For Bill the problem has become both more specific and more acute:

> Years ago I used to think it was possible for a novelist to alter the inner life of the culture. Now bomb-makers and gunmen have taken that territory. They make raids on human consciousness. What writers used to do before we were all incorporated. . . . We're giving way to terror, to news of terror, to tape recorders and cameras, to radios, to bombs stashed in radios. News of disaster is the only narrative people need. The darker the news, the grander the narrative. News is the last addiction.

Bill's notion that writers were ever in a position to "shape and influence" society may seem naive, yet it would be wrong to *suppose he has merely* mistaken his artistic failure for a wider cultural malaise. DeLillo has gone further than any of his "paranoid" literary contemporaries in fathoming the illicit lure of media disasters and revolu-

tionary violence, the elemental pull of crowds and sects. But in *Mao II,* for the first time, he discovers in this sinister attraction a problem for the novel. Novelists and terrorists are indeed engaged in a zero-sum game: Bill's predicament dramatizes the difficulty facing any writer who, like DeLillo, is ambitious enough to want to make an impact beyond the literary.

The plots you seek, however, are not necessarily the plots you enter. Bill's attempts to abandon his own plots and live by someone else's are frustrated simply because it is 1989, and Beirut is in turmoil: coffins are stacked outside already full cemeteries, the Syrians are sweeping through the southern suburbs, thousands are fleeing the city. Forgotten, Bill has a "helpless sense that he was fading into thinness and distance"; in the end it is a meaningless street accident, rather than an assassin's bullet, which leaves him fatally injured. Scott and Karen live on in Bill's house: they will release a selection of the photographs but withold the novel, allowing it to collect "aura and force, deepening old Bill's legend, undyingly".

Every line of *Mao II* impresses by its poise and economy. Yet while characteristically attentive to "the uninventable poetry, inside the pain, of what people say", this novel subordinates places and individuals to DeLillo's main subject: history or, as he might put it, the crowd. As *Libra* was an imaginative reply to the moment of Kennedy's assassination, so *Mao II* is an extraordinary response to certain events of 1989. We remember this as the *annus mirabilis* which saw the end of the Cold War, and tend to forget the unnerving television images of random disasters and political convulsions which preceded the dismantling of the Berlin Wall. Recorded in the hesitant, spiralling prose with which he conveys Karen's "thin boundaried" gaze, it is these scenes that evoke DeLillo's most powerful writing:

> She sees the fence up close and they stop the film and it is like a religious painting, the scene could be a fresco in a tourist church, it is composed and balanced and filled with people suffering. . . . In people's faces she sees the hopelessness of knowing. They show men calmly looking on. They show the fence from a distance, bodies piling up behind it, smothered, sometimes only fingers moving, and it is like a fresco in an old dark church, a crowded twisted vision of a rush to death as only a master of the age could paint it.

This is Hillsborough, although it could be other disasters recalled and witnessed in *Mao II:* the massacre of students at Tiananmen Square, the mass frenzy only three days later at Ayatollah Khomeini's funeral. Like the successive assassinations of Kennedy and Oswald, caught on film and then shown repeatedly on television, this flurry of events seems "an aberration in the heartland of the real". DeLillo further stresses television's chilling accidental artistry by dropping these scenes into the narrative without warning, as though we ourselves have just flicked on the set to experience the "cold stilled excitement that prepares you for something vast".

Mao II is full of such insistent echoes and fearful symmetries. The novel opens with a bravura passage describing the joint wedding of some 6,000 Moonies in Yankee Stadium, concluding with the millennial prophecy, "The future belongs to crowds". Such apocalyptic language is recalled when Karen discovers Tompkins Square, the public park which became a tent city or "refugee camp" for New York's homeless. The accelerating atrocity on the streets makes all cities seem one, inducing in the reader a "vertigo of intermingled places": New York, its crowded pavements torn apart by steam-pipe explosions and gas-main ruptures is, as people keep remarking, "just like Beirut".

Bill's decline is shadowed by the unlikely counter-example of Mao Zedong—who staged dramatic returns after periods of retreat, and who collapsed the distinction between books and political terror by himself becoming "the history of China written on the masses". Yet, as the title suggests, it is actually in Andy Warhol's faux-naive appropriation of Mao's image that the novel finds its emblem. "Mao II" is a pencil-drawing in a series of portraits by Warhol which, hung on pink-faced Chairman wallpaper, create a pulsing visual field—"Photocopy Mao, silk-screen Mao, wallpaper Mao, synthetic-polymer Mao". As in many of Warhol's pictures of the famous dead, drastically altered context and delirious repetition make for an oddly cogent comment on an already ubiquitous image. Scott, at MoMA's Warhol retrospective, wonders if he had ever before realized "the deeper meaning of Mao", and *Mao II* leaves us asking ourselves the same question of the "grand narratives" that unfold on our television screens. Prompting us to recognize that it is our familiarity with these images of terror which is truly strange, De-Lillo demonstrates with compelling artistry his conviction that the novel can accommodate and shape our catastrophic present. (pp. 20-1)

Julian Loose, "Shaping Up to Catastrophe," in The Times Literary Supplement, *No. 4613, August 30, 1991, pp. 20-1.*

John Whitworth   (review date 7 September 1991)

[In the following review, Whitworth faults Mao II *for its weak plot and unconvincing characters.]*

[*Mao II*] is a smart book written in short sentences. Often without verbs. Like advertising. Brita is a photographer who does writers. Nothing else. She makes a living at it, God knows how.

She photographs a writer named Bill who is *very famous.*

The book goes in for short paragraphs too. Like Hemingway brought up to date. People say things like, 'Fear has its own ego, hasn't it?' and 'To withhold a work of art is the only eloquence left.'

Bill is oldish (63) and hasn't published anything for ages, though he has a book ready. There is an acolyte named Scott who doesn't think he should publish this because of the withholding business. Brita photographs Bill, who hasn't been photographed for ages, like the famous American novelist Thomas Pynchon, who recommends this book strongly on the back cover. But then you know what Mandy Rice-Davies said.

Brita and Bill talk a lot about Art. Well, everybody in this book tends to. Brita likes watching television with the sound off (an American habit perhaps?). She watches the young fans at Hillsborough being crushed to death and admires the composition. There's the photograph to show us what she means. Now, if I were Mr DeLillo I would have baulked at the photograph, but then to him the whole thing happened a long way away, which is how everything in the book seems to be treated anyhow.

This is the stuff about how television processes events into soap opera, though I must say it didn't seem like that when fat Boris climbed onto a tank recently to make a speech that might well have been his last on earth, but then I kept the sound on.

There is a girl called Karen loosely attached to Scott. She is an ex-Moonie, a beautiful idiot terrific in bed and very trying on the page.

All these people, though American, could certainly bore for England, and things don't really improve by a scene-shift to the Middle East, bullets and bombs punctuating the portentous remarks. The book is called *Mao II* after a picture by Warhol which decorates the dust cover. It is full of images of terrorism, with the wily oriental gentleman in the middle. Karen, incidentally, has never heard of Warhol. Good grief!

I am afraid that what we have here is a poetic novel. It is put together, rather like the Warhol artwork, from significant cut-out ingredients: the great writer who can't write any more; his acolyte; the photographer who thinks only in visual images and lacks a moral centre; the Dostoevskian Idiot (these last two are the eternal feminine—sexist crap surely?); the hostage and his teenage captor in Beirut. There are actual photographs: the Hillsborough one, mourning millions round the body of Khomeini, two Arab children in a trench, smiling and giving victory signs. The photographs are certainly better than the ostentatious prose that surrounds them and the elliptical conversations where I keep forgetting who says what.

There is the ghost of a plot involving Bill, the writer-shaman who understands the terrorist rage as all novelists do (Kingsley Amis?). The people are empty, no more than their encapsulated descriptions, and this is presumably part of the point, but I don't buy it. The writing is meretricious narcissism, the whole weary windbaggery and I should never have made it to the end but for the call of duty and curiosity to see if anything actually *happened*. It doesn't. After all this poeticism, let me end with an anonymous verse:

> As I was laying on the green
> A small volume it chanced I seen.
> Carlyle's *Essay on Burns* was the edition—
> I left it laying in the same position.

DeLillo is the modern Carlyle and I can't say fairer than that. (pp. 34-5)

John Whitworth, "The Modern Carlyle," in The Spectator, *Vol. 267, No. 8513, September 7, 1991, pp. 34-5.*

Cornel Bonca   (review date October-November 1991)

[*In the following review, Bonca discusses* Mao II *as an explication on the loss of faith and spirituality in contemporary society.*]

When Nietzsche's madman announced God's death back in 1882, he also realized that he had come too early, that the "tremendous event" was really "still on its way." If Don DeLillo's tenth novel, *Mao II,* is any indication, His death throes are now well into their second century, and they show no signs of quieting down. If anything, DeLillo is saying, God is being resurrected—in ever more mysterious forms—by a "longing deep in time, running in the earthly blood." And *Mao II* is a meditation on a question posed early in the text: "When the Old God leaves the world, what happens to all the unexpended faith?"

These days, that's not a very sexy question. The hipper postmodernists either give the whole idea of faith the big yawn or else get murderously indignant at the mincing herd mentality of the religiously inclined. Coover and Gass started their careers with hateful diatribes against the niggardliness of church-thinking and have never looked back; Kathy Acker and many of the second generation boho postmodernists are just freaked at the thought: people who believe—even people who don't but are filled with an "unexpended faith"—are, like, *aliens.* But for some years, at least since *The Names,* DeLillo has been exploring the postmodern—the "aura" created by postindustrial capitalism and the mass media—as a manifestation of spiritual yearning. When he calls the supermarket in *White Noise* the "modern cathedral," he's being less ironic than we think. Supermarkets really do seem like the presagement of heaven: with their abundant white light, the stacked gleaming fruit a testament to nature's bounty, the hum of voices speaking need and want, the tabloids trumpeting the eternality of Elvis, the supermarkets provide the lineaments of gratified desire. And that's what cathedrals have always done. Just ask Dostoevsky's Grand Inquisitor. The white noise and consumer madness of contemporary life aren't just cultural detritus, DeLillo is saying, but the result of a yearning that grips us with the force of a terror. And that yearning can't be simply dismissed as archaic, unhip, or weak.

There is plenty of unexpended faith in *Mao II,* and most of it finds some outlet: the novel begins with a breathtaking description of a mass Moonie wedding at Yankee stadium presided over by The Master himself:

> There is stark awareness in their faces, a near pain of rapt adoration. He is Lord of the Second Advent, the unriddling of many ills. His voice leads them out past love and joy, past the beauty of their mission, out past miracles and surrendered self. There is something in the chant, the fact of chanting, the being-one, that transports them with its power. Their voices grow in intensity. They are carried on the sound, the soar and fall. The chant becomes the boundaries of the world.

Here spiritual longing finds refuge in a mass hallucination created by the power of crowds roused to a single purpose. It would be easy to dismiss all this, as one character does,

as "millennial hysteria," but practically everyone else in the novel yearns just as hysterically. An aging writer turns the ritual of taking his pills into a "sacrament"; a young man and woman try to deify the writer by exploiting his cult status; Palestinian terrorists elevate Mao into a god, claiming that "there is a longing for Mao that will sweep the world." In this novel, as Dylan once said, "everybody's gotta serve somebody."

It's a formidable theme that DeLillo explores by focusing primarily on Bill Gray, a sixty-three-year-old writer who has published two acclaimed novels and has spent the past twenty-three years in seclusion writing a third, which presently sits, all but completed, in six manuscript boxes waiting for Bill to decide to stop tinkering. The characterization, rich, thoroughly credible, always surprising, can't help but spark associations: of Salinger writing (we hope) in his New Hampshire shack; of Pynchon's seventeen-year silence; of Gass and Brodkey holding onto their big novels as if "the withheld work of art," as one character puts it here, "is the only eloquence left." But DeLillo's not just being topical. The man in self-imposed exile, trying to shape a self in a near void, is an obsession of DeLillo's, one that virtually swallows up his earlier *Great Jones Street.* Except in that novel, the exile was Bucky Wunderlick, a Rock 'n' Roll God who has been nearly consumed by fame. Here, Bill Gray is working in the inveterately uncharismatic mode of the printed word, which gives DeLillo the chance to ask the novel's other major question: has the novel become totally irrelevant in the age of mass media? Scott Martineau, Bill's obsessed amanuensis scheming to immortalize his hero, puts it this way:

> The novel used to feed our search for meaning. Quoting Bill. It was the great secular transcendence. The Latin mass of language, character, occasional new truth. But our desperation has led us toward some thing larger and darker. So we turn to the news, which provides an unremitting mood of catastrophe. This is where we find emotional experience not available elsewhere. We don't need the novel. Quoting Bill. We don't even need catastrophes, necessarily. We only need the reports and predictions and warnings.

Bill's sense that the pain of his enforced solitude may be in the service of nothing but an exquisitely wrought irrelevancy is what sets the novel's (pretty slack) plot in motion. (DeLillo has never been strong on plot. His strength has always been detailing the febrile and mysterious atmosphere of a culture constantly remaking itself through images.) He brings a photographer named Brita to his retreat for a photo shoot, then invites her to stay for dinner with Scott, himself, and a young woman of "thin ego boundaries" named Karen, who, it turns out, was married at the Moonie extravaganza in the novel's prologue and has since redirected her passion from Reverend Moon to Bill Gray. The first third of the novel is filled with amazingly assured writing and some patented DeLillo touches: a dinner scene where five or six strands of conversation weave together like an atonal fugue; eruptive speeches that have the eloquence and lucidity of revelation. The care DeLillo takes in his craft, particularly in dialogue, is an absolute joy to witness. He captures, as Bill says a novelist should, "the uninventable poetry of what people say."

The dinner conversation throws Bill into a turbulent state. His work suddenly seeming puny and futile, he abandons his retreat and takes up his editor's offer to participate in a staged media event in London designed to gain release of a poet now held hostage in Beirut. The sight of this reclusive literary celebrity, a bumbler in the real world, making his way to London—and then to Athens to confront the terrorists when the media event falls through—becomes the occasion for subdued comedy and more of DeLillo's relentless cultural dissection. At the same time, the novel's two themes—"unexpended faith" and the fate of the novel—dovetail. For Bill realizes it is terrorism, not the novel, that has become the great secular transcendence; it is terrorists—whose maniacal faith and eagerness for violence make them the purest vehicles of TV fascination—who have the power to satisfy our longings for event, furor, apocalyptic transformation. So it's with great anticipation that we await Bill's encounter with some eloquent terrorist who'll engage him in a dialogue about the power of terrorism and the power of the word. And of course we want to know whether a writer can get a hostage set free.

Well, we get the eloquent terrorist—Abu Rashid is his name—but we never get the encounter. I'm not sure whether DeLillo deliberately avoided the kind of head-on confrontation that would force the novel into some kind of closure (DeLillo prefers the glancing blow), or whether there may have been a loss of nerve, but DeLillo concocts a situation (which I won't divulge) that effectively prevents the meeting from ever taking place. Instead, in an epilogue, Brita the photographer meets Rashid, and he tells her things (e.g., "terror is what we use to give our people their place in the world") that we would love to have heard Bill respond to. Brita simply takes pictures, her one visceral response to Rashid's terrorist apologia ("eloquent macho bullshit") coming too little too late, and something she doesn't utter aloud anyway.

DeLillo, too, is a kind of photographer, a supremely artful framer of elements of the contemporary real, and he makes no more moral pronouncements than Brita does. Still, he is miles away from the sensibility of Warhol's silkscreens of Mao that inspired the book's title. At a Warhol exhibition, Scott is struck by the fact that "he had never seen work that was so indifferent to the effect it had on those who came to see it." DeLillo's work is distanced and impeccably cool, but never indifferent. He sees as clearly as anyone alive the dilemma of the artist facing mass culture with nothing but words strung out end to end. He suspects that the "more clearly we see terror" on our TV screens, "the less impact we feel from art." But he also knows that "stories have no point if they don't absorb our terror."

Mao II certainly has a point. While mass media reflect postmodern terror, *Mao II* absorbs it, transforms it into terms we can assimilate and contemplate. We see terrorism, Islamic fanaticism, American charismatic fundamentalism, even art itself, as aspects of the same "longing deep in time," the same manifestation of unexpended faith. The

novel may lack *Libra*'s narrative power or the manic effervescence of *White Noise,* but its uncanny knowingness, its ability to penetrate and illuminate contemporary culture in commanding terms, makes it almost possible to use the word Zeitgeist again. Because if anybody is on to it, DeLillo is.

Cornel Bonca, "Longing for Furor," in The American Book Review, *Vol. 13, No. 4, October-November, 1991, p. 18.*

Marvin J. LaHood   (review date Winter 1992)

[*In the review below, LaHood praises the thematic complexity of* Mao II.]

Don DeLillo is one of the best American novelists writing today. He received the National Book Award for *White Noise* (1985), his eighth novel. His writing is clean and sharp, more Hemingway than Faulkner. It is intelligent and pungent, observant and clever. His tenth novel, *Mao II,* is perhaps his best.

Mao II is not about Mao Zedong, at least not exactly, although many of Andy Warhol's Maos grace the jacket. It is about a famous but spiritually arid author, Bill Gray, a recluse in upstate New York, whose two famous novels have been followed by twenty-three years of work on a novel that his companion Scott does not think publishable. Add to this household an ex-Moonie, Karen, married with 6,500 other couples at Yankee Stadium by the Reverend Sun Myung Moon in the novel's opening scene, and Brita, a Swedish photographer whose session with Gray brings him back to the world.

Gray's return to the world comes about because his former editor and friend convinces him that he can help free a minor Swiss poet from his captors in Beirut by giving a press conference in London. That is the beginning of the end, in a way, and the novel moves to a brilliant and surprising conclusion amid the chaos of Beirut. Along the way DeLillo raises some startling images and questions about individuality and crowds, writers and terrorists, peace and war. Besides the compelling image of the mass wedding at the beginning, other symbols and symptoms of our time include frenzied mourners at the funeral of the Ayatollah Khomeini completely out of control and a mob stampeding other spectators to death at a soccer match. The effect of such scenes is unnerving and compelling. DeLillo's prose makes them real again, so real in fact that for a moment they seem the only reality.

Can Bill Gray, the writer, carry the torch of individuality and sensitivity through the debacle of our time, or will mobs win out? Will 90s humans be buried under an avalanche of events that they cannot understand or control? Are terrorists the last individuals in our society? (There is even a scene showing Arafat performing before cameras in Athens.) Obviously DeLillo has attempted something here that demands our attention. He asks some huge questions. He gives no answers. His picture on the book jacket shows a man who looks as if he's had a vision of the future too terrifying to contemplate, too disastrous to confront, yet this is precisely what he does in *Mao II.*

Marvin J. LaHood, in a review of "Mao II," in World Literature Today, *Vol. 66, No. 1, Winter, 1992, p. 132.*

FURTHER READING

Bell, Pearl K. "DeLillo's World." *Partisan Review* LIX, No. 1 (Winter 1992): 138-46.
> Provides an overview of DeLillo's canon, including a brief summary of *Mao II*.

Lanchester, John. "Oh My Oh My Oh My." *London Review of Books* 13, No. 17 (12 September 1991): 13-14.
> Compares the themes and characters in *Mao II* to those in DeLillo's earlier works.

Lemon, Lee. Review of *Mao II*, by Don DeLillo. *Prairie Schooner* 66, No. 1 (Spring 1992): 123-27.
> Discusses isolation of the individual as the main theme in *Mao II*.

Mason, David. Review of *Mao II*, by Don DeLillo. *The Hudson Review* XLIV, No. 4 (Winter 1992): 691-97.
> Examines the themes, characters, and dialogue in *Mao II*, stating: "*Mao II* is literary pulp fiction, and taken as such it is very rewarding."

Menand, Louis. Review of *Mao II*, by Don DeLillo. *New Yorker* LXVII, No. 18 (24 June 1991): 81-4.
> Relates *Mao II* to DeLillo's other works.

Passaro, Vince. "Dangerous Don DeLillo." *The New York Times* (19 May 1991): 34-6, 76-7.
> Feature article in which DeLillo provides biographical information, discusses his writing techniques, and explains how he came to write *Mao II*.

Streitfeld, David. "Don DeLillo's Gloomy Muse." *The Washington Post* (14 May 1992): C1, C4.
> Introduces *Mao II* as the winner of the 1992 PEN/Faulkner Award and provides an overview of DeLillo's career.

Tabbi, Joseph. Review of *Mao II*, by Don DeLillo. *Review of Contemporary Fiction* XI, No. 3 (Fall 1991): 269-70.
> Discusses DeLillo's use of language and depiction of current events in *Mao II*.

Wolcott, James. "The Sunshine Boys." *Vanity Fair* 54, No. 6 (June 1991): 34, 38.
> Compares DeLillo's *Mao II* and Gordon Lish's *My Romance*.

Additional coverage of DeLillo's life and career is contained in the following sources published by Gale Research: *Contemporary Authors*, Vols. 81-84; *Contemporary Authors New Revision Series*, Vol. 21; *Contemporary Literary Criticism*, Vols. 8, 10, 13, 27, 39, 54; *Dictionary of Literary Biography*, Vol. 6; and *Major 20th-Century Writers*.

Donald Margulies
Sight Unseen

Prize: Obie Award

Margulies is an American playwright.

INTRODUCTION

Sight Unseen centers on Jonathan Waxman, a Jewish-American painter who is suffering an identity crisis and questioning the integrity of his work. Receiving commissions for works "sight unseen," Jonathan has succumbed to commercialism and is suffering from lack of inspiration. The protagonist's doubts about his personal integrity are further intensified when he is interviewed by an abrasive German journalist. Troubled by the reporter's queries, which he views as anti-Semitic and which suggest that he has divorced himself from his religious heritage, Jonathan continues to question his values, the motivations for his actions, and the validity of his work. Critical discussion of the play has emphasized its provocative examination of the problems of assimilation and aesthetic originality. Critics have also noted that the Margulies's surrealistic and nonlinear narrative structures and absurdist techniques rival much of the work of dramatist Harold Pinter. John Simon observed: "[Margulies's] play fascinates. The dialogue is abrasive and unsettling; the situation fraught with potential mayhem; the predicament human. Margulies manages to write a Pinter play better than Pinter."

PRINCIPAL WORKS

Pals (drama) 1979
Gifted Children (drama) 1982
Found a Peanut (drama) 1984
The Model Apartment (drama) 1988
What's Wrong with This Picture? (drama) 1988
The Loman Family Picnic (drama) 1989
Sight Unseen (drama) 1991

CRITICISM

Sylvie Drake **(review date 23 September 1991)**

[*In the following excerpt, Drake favorably appraises* Sight Unseen *as a "form of dramatic impressionism."*]

There is a stealthy design to Donald Margulies' *Sight Unseen,* a rich and personal new play. . . .

It has the earmarks of a jigsaw puzzle. It leaps back and forth through time, with characters who say one thing to mean another, and has meaningful looks and pregnant, if-not-quite-Pinteresque pauses. And it knows how to bide its time.

This latest piece by the author of *The Model Apartment, Found a Peanut,* and *What's Wrong With This Picture?* is a form of dramatic impressionism.

It pits a super-successful American painter, Jonathan Waxman, against his future and his past.

Jonathan, who, at the ripe old age of 37 is having a retrospective in London, takes the opportunity to look up a former lover living in the English countryside. Patricia is an American archeologist now married to a British archeologist, the taciturn Nick, and the two seem something less than thrilled by Jonathan's visit.

The play turns into a fascinating deconstruction of time and events in which the past returns to haunt the present and all that went wrong between Jonathan, who is Jewish, and Patricia, who is not, is re-examined in the context of that cultural difference.

We can't call it a religious difference, because it's clear that neither of them is religiously inclined. But at the heart of the break-up was Jonathan's inability to either sign on as a Jew, or to become assimilated. And in the course of this struggle with identity, he loses not only the girl (whom he hurts badly) but a good part of himself.

Jonathan's meteoric rise to the megabuck stratosphere of artistic success confuses him even more. And this visit to his old flame, now locked in a loveless marriage, does nothing to clear things up. It merely stirs up the mud in the waters between Patricia and Nick (who would have lived happily ever after if he had never laid eyes on Jonathan), and stirs the knife in Patricia's unhealed wounds.

The theme is that thoroughly modern one of cultural dispossession: Unable to be in one culture what we were told we were in another, we become less and less sure of what we have become or will become. As a successful artist, Jonathan has lost his compass, the impulse that made him paint; he hopes that seeing Patricia will help him find it. That it doesn't should come as no surprise.

[But with the play's] carefully measured direction, getting from there to here is always an absorbing journey. Margulies mines thoughts like artifacts in an archeological dig of the soul. He pumps up the personal scenes with fragmentary ones of an overintellectual interview with a German named Grete whose latent anti-Semitism sets off all kinds of reactions in Jonathan. The juxtaposition works beautifully, with one aspect of the play subtly informing the other.

Margulies has said of *Sight Unseen* that it deals with his familiar obsessions in a new, more mature way. One can only agree. This is easily his most interesting—and mature—piece of writing to date, the more rewarding since it is also a commissioned play [by the South Coast Repertory of California] and those can be dicey as art.

No need to worry. The title ambiguously refers both to Waxman's yet-unpainted paintings, that, in the skyrocketing art market of the '80s, already carried a price tag—and to the elusive heritage that shapes his present through his past, but leaves his future in doubt. It's a nice image, which slips through our consciousness like water through a sieve.

Production values are simple but efficient and [the director's] staging sees to it that body language is largely what's spoken here. . . .

Nick is often funnier for what he fails to tell us than for

the words Margulies puts in his mouth. [Bottled up] Jonathan walks around in a quasi-permanent state of tormented embarrassment, apologizing for his emotional failures, his new-found affluence, his life. But it is [the] supervulnerable Patricia who is hardest to forget. She presents a forthright, unsentimental, often heartbreaking portrait of a once-joyous and expansive woman, beaten down by rejections that have inflicted irreversible damage.

The issue of a painting of a black man and a white woman making love in a Jewish cemetery that has been defaced is the focus of much discussion. It is a bit of symbolism about innocence and corruption that often gilds the lily. But despite such occasional obfuscations, *Sight Unseen* has 20/20 vision.

Sylvie Drake, " 'Sight Unseen' a Rich, Personal Jigsaw Puzzle," in Los Angeles Times, *September 23, 1991, p. F9.*

Frank Rich   (review date 21 January 1992)

[*Rich is an American editor and performing arts critic. In the following excerpt, he praises* Sight Unseen *for its insightful examination of the themes of emotional fulfillment, self-delusion, and personal identity.*]

[*Sight Unseen* is] a smart and sad new comedy by Donald Margulies that has all sorts of unpleasant things to say about the 1980's art scene, the loss of love and the price of assimilation, both ethnic and intellectual, in an America where authenticity often has little to do with an artist's—or anyone else's—rise to the top.

The scene that reduces the house to a dead hush is an Act II encounter set in a sleek London art gallery where a provocative American painter named Jonathan Waxman is being honored with a retrospective. Jonathan, an intense, fashionably dressed young man who wears a pony tail and may or may not resemble Eric Fischl or Julian Schnabel, has been the subject of adulatory profiles in *Vanity Fair* and *The New York Times.* He has a long waiting list of patrons who have commissioned his future pictures, sight unseen, at outrageous prices. But to maintain his marketability, he must suffer through tedious interviews, like the one he is now giving to Grete, a leggy blonde German woman who is a ferocious student of his work and tends to ask long, multi-clause questions in impeccable, if strongly accented, English.

For all her flirtatious obsequiousness, Grete is a hostile interviewer. She demands that Jonathan reconcile his material success with his bleak paintings about the "emptiness and spiritual deadness of middle-class life." She asks why he employs a press agent. She traps him into spewing contempt for his own audience and for what she calls "the very system that made you what you are today." Worse, she attacks the content of his paintings from the politically correct left, reading sexual brutality and racism into a notorious canvas Jonathan regards as a celebration of physical love and a statement against bigotry.

Unsurprisingly, Jonathan squirms and grows defensive. But what holds the audience rapt is the double-edged drama Mr. Margulies has written into Grete's cross-examination. The more she closes in on Jonathan, the more Jonathan begins (and not without reason) to suspect her of anti-Semitism. But is she in fact anti-Semitic? Or is Jonathan, who has strayed far from his Brooklyn Jewish roots, just exploiting the charge of anti-Semitism to deflect this German journalist's legitimate attacks on his work and integrity? The brilliance of the scene, aside from its stiletto language, is that Mr. Margulies answers yes to both questions, refusing to let anyone, least of all the audience, off the hook. Both Jonathan and Grete are right even as they are wrong, and the rest of us, left with no one to root for, must confront Mr. Margulies's own vision of a spiritual deadness he finds in middle-class intellectual life of the present day.

Not all of *Sight Unseen* is as bracing as this one confrontation, but the evening is almost always absorbing. . . . As Mr. Margulies's daring last play, **The Loman Family Picnic,** toyed a bit with [Arthur Miller's] *Death of a Salesman,* so this one takes a leaf from *After the Fall,* its fractured time structure included. The narrative thread of *Sight Unseen,* told simultaneously in the present and in flashbacks, is the tale of Jonathan's mid-life crisis: spurred by his empty pre-eminence, his father's recent death and the impending birth of his first child, the artist takes a journey into his past to find out how he lost his way. The quest leads him both to his bohemian student days and to a reunion with his first muse and lover, a self-described "sacrificial shiksa" named Patricia who expatriated herself and married a British archeologist, Nick, after Jonathan abandoned her 15 years earlier.

While the overall arc of Jonathan's path to self-discovery is predictable, Mr. Margulies makes the individual scenes crackle with biting dialogue, fully observed characterizations and unexpected psychological complexities. In *Sight Unseen,* the metaphor of the title extends beyond a hollow painter's distant relationship to his art to a collection of long intertwined and emotionally dishonest personal relationships. The scenes in which Jonathan invites himself to Patricia and Nick's cottage in the English countryside have the lethal undercurrents of Harold Pinter's love-triangle plays, for the archeologist, a fount of malicious facetiousness . . ., becomes almost unhinged in his esthetic and personal loathing for his unwelcome house guest. As the two men battle over the history of art (and obliquely over Patricia), the question is not who will be the victor but who is the unhappier man, the bigger self-deceiver and moral sham.

> *Frank Rich, "Looking Inward and Finding Emptiness," in* The New York Times, *January 21, 1992, p. C13.*

John Simon   (review date 3 February 1992)

[*An American essayist and critic, Simon has served as a drama critic for* New York *magazine as well as a film critic for* Esquire *and the* New Leader. *In the following excerpt, he offers a positive review of* Sight Unseen *but faults Margulies for trying to incorporate too many themes into the work.*]

You should certainly catch, for all its imperfections, the exciting *Sight Unseen.* This is by far the best play Donald Margulies has yet written, and its flaws are tactful enough never to interfere with what, indisputably, is there.

Jonathan Waxman, once a devout Jew and promising painter, has become a huge, affluent success, though as fishy as any Fischl or Schnabel. He was always drawn to shiksas, but eventually jilted his first and best one, Patricia. Fifteen years later, she is lovelessly married to Nick, an odd, able, semi-impoverished British archaeologist, but finding life in archaeology and chilly England Spartanly bracing.

Jonathan, married to another shiksa too pregnant to travel, comes to London for his first European retrospective. His father has just died; he no longer wears either the yarmulke of his youth or the red bandanna of his art-school enthusiasm, when he and Patricia shared bed and ideals. Cocky on the outside but lost beneath, he calls Patricia from London and goes up-country for an overnight reconnoitering of her and Nick's and his own embattled lives. The visit turns nightmarish as Nick displays sardonic hostility, sneering both at Waxman's and all modern art, while Patricia, still secretly in love with Jonathan, proves bitter and vengeful.

Margulies ingeniously flashes forward to scenes in London with Grete, a smart young German art critic interviewing Jonathan and asking sincere but wrenching questions about his commercialism, his betrayed roots, his compromised art; questions he construes as anti-Semitic, which they may even be, and yet. . . . Finally, the play flashes back to when Jonathan and Patricia were lovers and she posed for the nude that now hangs over her and Nick's fireplace, obsessing her with nostalgia and Nick with jealousy. This nude is one of the key symbols; the other is a later Waxman painting hung in the show, which is socially, politically, and artistically incorrect.

The problem with *Sight Unseen* (a reference to the way rich collectors buy as-yet-unpainted Waxmans, and to the commercialization of art and life) is that it tries to deal with too many big themes hard to make cover one another neatly like those triangles in geometry. There is the loopy love triangle, the renegade Jew in the shadow of the Holocaust, the artist as victim or con man—runaway horses in a troika that end up upsetting the apple cart.

Bit by bit, however, the play fascinates. The dialogue is abrasive and unsettling; the situation fraught with potential mayhem; the predicament human. Margulies manages to write a Pinter play better than Pinter. (pp. 53-4)

But what a play—I haven't even mentioned how funny much of it is. Seriously. (p. 54)

> *John Simon, "Visits or Visitations?" in* New York *Magazine, Vol. 25, No. 5, February 3, 1992, pp. 53-4.*

Gerald Weales   (review date 28 February 1992)

[*Weales is an American novelist, critic, educator, editor, and author of children's books. In the following excerpt, he offers a mixed review of* Sight Unseen.]

It is easy to be unfair to Donald Margulies as a play-wright—to say, as did the friend who accompanied me to *Sight Unseen* at the Manhattan Theatre Club, that the production was excellent but that he had doubts about the play. . . .

Not that Margulies's themes are trivial. A writer-in-residence at the Jewish Repertory Theatre, Margulies has taken up the problem of assimilation for the Jewish artist in *Sight Unseen,* which was commissioned by the South Coast Repertory in California, where it played last fall. Jonathan Waxman, when we meet him, is the latest celebrity artist, a media-labeled "visionary," whose very large and presumably shocking canvases are so in demand that the art patrons are lined up for still unpainted works. Although he is seen as a critic of contemporary society, he is unwilling to explain his works to Nick ("I'm not gonna *tell* you what to see"), who would not listen in any case, or to the German journalist who interviews him in two of the play's best sequences. He is in London for his first European retrospective, which should be a moment of great triumph, but the recent death of his father, who never understood what he was up to, has made Waxman question his work and his life. His fame has brought him wealth, a gentile wife, pregnant with a son, and a farm near New Paltz, but something has been lost along the way. His Jewishness presumably.

"I'm an American painter. *American* is the adjective, not *Jewish, American,*" he tells the intereviewer, whose questions he hears as "sneaky little Jew-baiting comments." Those questions, her very slick elegance, and the abrupt way she begins to rewind the tape after he stalks out, as though she had what she wanted, seem to confirm his reaction. . . . More important than the retrospective, for the play's sake, his English visit gives him a chance to see again the love of his youth ("the pioneer. . . . The sacrificial shiksa who made your world safe for shiksas"). Patricia seduced him from his Jewish reluctance and was rejected by him two years later on the day he sat shiva at the death of his disapproving mother. Now married to Nick and to her archaeological work, Patricia pretends to have buried the past, but she will not give Jonathan the forgiveness he wants, presumably to validate his success. What he does get—at Nick's insistence—is the portrait he did of her when they first met, a work in which he sees the beginning of the artist (not the celebrity) that he became.

With so much going for *Sight Unseen,* I still understand my friend's doubt about the play. One of the problems is that Margulies has chosen to present the events out of sequence, playing with chronology in the present as well as the past. The final scene is the first meeting of Patricia and Jonathan, and perhaps it is intended to work like the final scene of Harold Pinter's *Betrayal* in which, thanks to reverse chronology, the playfulness is darkly undercut by what is to come, which we have already seen. Is the scene in Margulies's play to be read ironically as promise unfulfilled for both characters, or is it the first seduction of Jonathan from his Jewishness, a loss that so distresses him in the present although it is no greater loss than the one that Patricia suffered when he rejected her? There is not enough gained by the juxtaposition of the out-of-sequence

scenes. One comes away from the theater wondering if the dramatist used this device to disguise a fairly conventional self-doubt play. (p. 20)

Gerald Weales, "Identity Crisis," in Commonweal, *Vol. CXIX, No. 4, February 28, 1992, pp. 20-1.*

Thomas M. Disch   (review date 2 March 1992)

[*Disch is an American novelist, short story writer, editor, and poet. In the following excerpt, he provides a positive assessment of* Sight Unseen.]

Sight Unseen, by Donald Margulies, is a work of modest size but considerable impact. . . . [Its] subject is that most suspect of concerns, Art. Canny playwrights focus on the family and mother-love as being the one area of experience most certain to provide a common ground. . . . The problems faced by Margulies's hero, Jonathan Waxman, are those that for most of us are entirely hypothetical, those attendant on artistic celebrity and sudden wealth. Not only does the author manage to create a hero who is plausible as a painter of considerable talent (albeit part of that talent may be for self-promotion) but he hinges the plot on as finely balanced an ethical dilemma as one might find in the best tales of Henry James.

The story unfolds in a single day in rural England, where the artist is visiting an old flame and former model, Patricia, who is now the wife and assistant of a down-at-the-heels archeologist engaged in excavating a medieval garbage pit. Waxman is deeply shaken not so much by his reunion with Patricia, who has become a resentful slattern, but by the sight of his long-forgotten portrait of her, which seems somehow central to all his later work and which he covets for the Waxman Retrospective that has brought him to England. There are flashbacks to the moments of their meeting and of their splitting up. (pp. 282-83)

For all its emotional power, the play is no less admirable for its aesthetic shapeliness. Describing his own paintings, Waxman insists that they are fashioned in such a way that the viewer becomes an essential participant, creating their "meaning" by interpreting ambiguous imagery. Margulies's play works in much the same way. Waxman's youthful parting from Patricia may have been his first step on the road to narcissistic ruin or a prudent escape from the clutches of a manipulative woman. This is but one of the play's many interpretive cruxes, each of which leads to its own "moment of dubiety" (as against "moment of truth"). These carefully crafted irresolutions are puzzles that continue to baffle long after one leaves the theater. (p. 283)

Thomas M. Disch, in a review of "Sight Unseen," in The Nation, *New York, Vol. 254, No. 8, March 2, 1992, pp. 282-83.*

Stephen J. Dubner   (essay date 9 March 1992)

[*In the excerpt below, Dubner examines critical reaction to* Sight Unseen. *He also includes Margulies's observations concerning the play and its protagonist.*]

Sight Unseen, Margulies's eighth full-length play, is an

What I most appreciate about the critical reception for *Sight Unseen* is that it does seem to view me as someone who has been around, that I didn't just spring whole. It's probably sweeter now because of so much hard work and disappointment. And a lot of joy that, unfortunately, didn't last very long.

—*Donald Margulies, in Stephen J. Dubner's "In the Paint," in* New York, *9 March 1992.*

---

edgy and fascinating character study. Jonathan Waxman, an American Jewish painter whose controversial works are bought—sight unseen—for bundles of money, is visiting England for his first retrospective outside North America. But Waxman is a desperate man, unsettled by his volatile fame, the recent death of his father, the approaching birth of his first child, and, most of all, his loss of inspiration.

In response to the last, Jonathan ventures into the countryside to visit his long-ago lover and muse, Patricia. . . . Patricia is now married to Nick, an oafishly shy yet belligerent archaeologist who considers Jonathan's paintings—which the audience never sees—ugly and utterly artless.

Through flashbacks to Jonathan and Patricia's courtship and breakup, and flash-forwards to Jonathan's hypertensive interview with an aggressive German journalist at the London retrospective, Margulies assembles a forceful collage. There are subtle character revelations complemented by forays into modern art, anti-Semitism, and the phenomenon of celebrity. *Sight Unseen* also manages, somehow, to be very funny.

"It's a real, pure inner rage that Donald is grappling with, and thank God he has a sense of humor," says Tanya Berezin, artistic director of Circle Repertory Company and a longtime admirer of Margulies's work. "If not, I don't think we'd want to listen, would we?" (p. 50)

Sight Unseen began life about three years ago as a play called *Heartbreaker*—which Margulies now laughingly calls *The Donald Chronicles*—a rambling, autobiographical, picaresque work that had nothing to do with the big business of modern art. Although the character was already named Jonathan Waxman, he was more like Margulies himself, who studied art and still does collage.

"Once I decided that Waxman was not just an artist but a superstar artist, it galvanized the play," says Margulies. "Even if the origins of a character are autobiographical, I always raise the stakes to create situations more fraught than reality."

The play's unorthodox structure—the final scene recounts the day Jonathan met Patricia—also heightens its impact. "I think it's very moving to see the genesis of something that has gone so—not necessarily awry, but so momen-

tously, in small ways," says Margulies. "To look at pictures of your parents' courtship, let's say. It was a way to pull things together without tying a bow."

In taking Waxman away from himself, Margulies also took *Sight Unseen* out of Brooklyn, where he often locates his plays. An English setting opened up dramatic opportunities. Waxman the celebrity clashes with his expatriate former lover; Waxman the modern American artist clashes with a British-workingman academic whose appreciation of art ends with Rembrandt; and Waxman the Jew clashes with the German journalist.

"Jonathan Waxman is a very complex character," says Margulies. "And I think he's a very human character. That doesn't mean he's necessarily noble or likable or sympathetic, but I think he is *recognizable*. And that, I think, is what's exciting.

"I didn't want him to be a laughing-stock; he's very much a product of his times. I certainly don't mean to condemn him as an artist. Waxman's paintings are probably closest to Eric Fischl's, whom I admire a great deal and much of whose work thrills me."

Fischl, in fact, saw the play. And thought the work sounded much like his. And was less than flattered.

"I wasn't prepped to see it," says Fischl, "so you can imagine my being shocked. The artist came off looking like a charlatan, a character who can't defend himself. And I certainly don't know any artist whose sole purpose is to become famous and make a lot of money."

"Any serious examination of anything is going to upset somebody," says *New York* theater critic John Simon. "Margulies is remarkable because he's not simplistic. The trend now is to couch a very simplistic point of view in a sort of symbolic, absurdist, fantastical garb. Margulies cloaks things in nothing. He gives them to you as he sees them, but as he sees them very carefully and conscientiously and thoughtfully observed, from all sides." (pp. 50-1)

Stephen J. Dubner, "In the Paint," in New York *Magazine, Vol. 25, No. 10, March 9, 1992, pp. 48-52.*

Donald Margulies   (essay date 21 June 1992)

[*In the essay below, Margulies examines how his childhood, his father, and the works of other authors have influenced his writing.*]

Sometime in the early 60's, when I was around 9 years old, my parents told me and my older brother that instead of spending my father's one-week summer vacation on a bus tour of the Berkshires or Pennsylvania Dutch country (as we had done before), this time we would be spending it in The City. To Brooklynites like us, The City meant Manhattan and, until my parents announced our vacation plans, I thought of it as a special place that existed solely for school trips to the Planetarium or the occasional family outing to Radio City.

"What are we gonna do in The City?" I asked. It was not,

as far as I could tell, a place where people from Brooklyn spent the night, let alone a whole week.

"We're gonna see shows!" my parents told me, which meant, of course, Broadway. (We were cultural Jews; the only fervor that existed in our household wasn't centered on religion but on show business.)

So my mother and father and brother and I put on our nice clothes and, suitcases in tow, got on the Brighton local (we didn't own a car) and took the hourlong ride from Sheepshead Bay to Rockefeller Center. We checked into a cheap hotel in the West 50's and for the next six days saw every hit in town, shows like *Funny Girl, Fiddler on the Roof, Hello, Dolly!* As the house lights dimmed each night, plus matinees on Wednesday, Saturday and Sunday, I remember feeling almost unbearably excited by what lay ahead.

When I recently recalled my family's theatergoing vacations, they took on the mythic proportions of something we used to do all the time—until I realized that we probably did it only twice. Those two weeks, spent during two different theatrical seasons in the same funky midtown hotel, have blurred in my memory but their impact was powerful.

Herb Gardner's *Thousand Clowns* was the first nonmusical play I ever saw, and I remember how the muscles in my face hurt from grinning in pleasure for two hours. I felt privileged being in a grand Broadway theater packed with well-dressed adults and being let in on jokes they so obviously enjoyed; I was thrilled to add my small sound to all that laughter. For a boy like me, whose father worked all the time, it must have been invigorating to see a play about a man who preferred being home to toiling at a demoralizing job. In retrospect, it seems fitting that my first exposure to theater was a play about a complex father figure and his surrogate son, for the theme of fathers and sons has long figured in my plays and in my life.

The central character of my first full-length play, **Pals** (1979), had a lot in common with my father. I see now that I was trying to concretize my father's speech and thought processes as a way of understanding him. The grief-stricken father in **What Wrong With This Picture?** was a further exploration of my own father, but it wasn't until after his death in 1987 (my mother had died nine years earlier) that I was able to truly uncover him.

My black comedy, **The Loman Family Picnic** (1989), is about a middle-class Jewish family in extremis over the oldest son's bar mitzvah. The cultural, economic and social pretensions surrounding that event lead to the beleaguered father's terrifying explosion. Giving voice to that inarticulate rage helped me find my father.

In my current play, **Sight Unseen,** the father is offstage, a shadowy figure whose recent death jolts the protagonist, the painter Jonathan Waxman, into examining his loss of cultural identity and artistic purpose. His journey leads him to Patricia, the woman with whom he long ago had a relationship, which symbolized the themes of his life and which remains unresolved. "I'm nobody's son anymore, Patty," he tells her. "They're all gone now, all the disappointable people."

My parents, Charlene and Bob Margulies, were of the generation of lower-middle-class Jews who were raised during the Depression and came of age during World War II. Like many married couples of that generation, my mother was the baleboosteh, the powerhouse who embodied the cockeyed optimism and practicality of that time, while my father was the eternally haunted one who lived in fear of losing his job (even though he worked for the same people for 40 years) and who was disturbed by change of any kind.

My father was a taciturn man, physically affectionate but prone to mysterious silences, who worked six, sometimes seven, days a week selling wallpaper in a store on Flatbush Avenue. His days routinely began at 6 in the morning and didn't end until 11 at night, but his rare days off were often devoted to playing records on the living-room hi-fi. The great composers whose music wafted through our tiny apartment weren't Beethoven and Mozart but Loesser and Styne and Rodgers and Hammerstein. That was my father at his most content: playing his Broadway musical soundtracks, dozens of them, on Sunday mornings throughout my childhood. I was the only kid in the sixth grade who knew by heart the entire score of *Happy Hunting,* an obscure Ethel Merman musical I heard countless times.

When I was small, my father and I would watch old movies on television together, the beloved movies of his youth, and he'd grill me on the character actors. "Donnie, who's that?" he'd ask, pointing to the wizened old woman on the TV screen. "Maria Ouspenskaya." I'd tell him, having learned my lessons well. But as my brother and I grew more intellectually and creatively curious, he began to distance himself. We were, no doubt, challenging sons for a stolid, unanalytical father; he responded by abdicating, by leaving our education entirely up to my mother. We were fortunate that she loved to read and instilled that love of books in her children.

As a youngster, I was troubled that my father showed no interest in reading anything but *The Daily News.* How could someone not read books? I took it as a personal affront, a form of rejection. Unconsciously, I began to search for spiritual fathers, creative men with whom I could commune intellectually, older men who could help me make sense of the world. My father's silence created in me a hunger for words that drew me to surrogate fathers, men I knew only through what they wrote. Herb Gardner may have been my earliest spiritual father, but Arthur Miller came into my life not long after.

I was 11 years old when I read *Death of a Salesman,* and I remember the guilt and shame I felt for recognizing in the Lomans truths about my own family: that my mother shared Linda's chauvinism and, most frightening of all, that my father, then barely 40, might turn out to be a Willy himself. But the play's uncanny reflection of my life and worst fears also exhilarated me and made me feel less alone. I studied it with great fascination, as if it were a key to understanding what was happening to the people I loved, so that I might somehow alter my family's fate. As a boy growing up in Trump Village (the Coney Island housing project built by Donald Trump's father), I imagined that our high-rise was one of the buildings that over-shadowed the Lomans' modest house. Years later, in *The Loman Family Picnic,* I took that notion and made a play out of it.

After Miller, and as adolescence approached, I discovered in J. D. Salinger a spiritual father so empathic that he seemed to know how I felt about everything. Once I'd read *The Catcher in the Rye,* I devoured all of Salinger (just three slim paperbacks) and made a mission of tracking down the uncollected stories in old volumes of *The New Yorker.* I wanted more, but Salinger, who still writes but refuses to publish, proved to be the ultimate withholding father.

Philip Roth was not withholding. He was brainy, naughty and bursting with words: the cool daddy with whom one could talk about sex. I was 15 when I first read *Portnoy's Complaint* and for all the wrong reasons. I was scanning for tales of sexy shiksas, but what I found were stunning insights into what it meant to be a Jew and a man. Even though he was nearly a generation older, Roth and I seemed to have grown up together, surrounded by many of the same relatives, sharing many similar experiences. He opened a window for me and let fresh air into a stuffy Brooklyn apartment and gave me (and still gives me) the courage to write what I know.

Because as a child I drew well, I was encouraged by my parents and teachers to pursue the visual arts. Art dominated my public school education and when it came time to go to college, I was offered a scholarship to Pratt Institute. I lasted at Pratt for a year and a half. I was already itching to write (what, I had no idea), but I found no one there to guide me. I transferred to the State University of New York at Purchase, then the upstart liberal arts college in the SUNY system, where I made mentors of literate and wise art professors like Abe Ajay and Antonio

The confrontation scene between German journalist Grete (Laura Linney) and artist Jonathan Waxman (Dennis Boutsikaris) from a 1992 production of Sight Unseen.

Frasconi. I found inspiration in Giacometti drawings, Schwitters collages and Diebenkorn paintings.

I was a disgruntled art major with literary aspirations when I walked into the office of Julius Novick, the theater critic, who taught dramatic literature at Purchase. I boldly asked if he would be willing to sponsor me in a playwriting tutorial. He said yes and could not have imagined the impact that his decision was to have on my life: I was given permission to write. It was about this time that I discovered *The Homecoming* and *The Sound and the Fury.* On the face of it, Pinter's stark, nightmarish black comedy and Faulkner's gorgeously poetic family saga had little in common and yet, in my mind, they coexisted, thrillingly. If I was to be a writer, why couldn't I be an offspring of *all* these spiritual fathers, a son of Pinter and Faulkner—and Miller and Salinger and Roth and Giacometti and Schwitters?

After I graduated, I supported myself as a graphic designer while I wrote plays. My entry into the real world of New York theater in the early 80's eventually brought me into contact with the man who was the surrogate father to an entire generation of theater people: Joseph Papp. Stories of his enormous heart (and of his capriciousness) are now legend, and they're all probably true. When Joe loved you, he loved you extravagantly; when he loved you less, you could feel the drop in temperature.

At the peak of his affection, I'd run into him in the lobby of the Public Theater and he'd ask. "How's my Jewish playwright?" and I'd stand there and kibbitz with Joe Papp as I would with any one of my relatives, and have the exciting feeling that there, in Joe's nurturing hands, under Joe's approving eye, at the age of 29, I had somehow arrived.

My father lived to see **Found a Peanut,** my Off Broadway debut, at the Public in 1984. The opening night party was pure Joe Papp, a bar mitzvah boy's dream come true, complete with brisket, potato pancakes, hot dogs, egg creams and loud rock-and-roll. I brought my father across the crowded room to introduce him to Joe. There was something exquisite in the meeting of these two men; my father, the working-class lover of theater, the lifelong fan, meeting the self-made impresario. A crossing of the bridge at last, from Brooklyn to The City. Father of my childhood, meet father of my professional life. "Bob Margulies, meet Joe Papp."

"You've got quite a son here," Joe said as he shook my father's hand.

"Thanks to you."

"What do you *mean,* thanks to *me,*" Joe Papp yelled at my father, "Thanks to *you!*" as if to say, *"I'm not his father, you are! Take responsibility for what's yours once and for all and be proud!"*

Not until I was an adult did I understand that, in his lonely abdication, my father sought refuge from his demons, from the terrible fear that, not having had a relationship with his own father, he wouldn't know how to be a father himself; rather than try and fail, he simply retreated into silence. Years after I became a playwright, I realized that playwriting—the craft of dramatizing the unspoken—provided me with the tools I needed to get inside my father's head and figure out what he was thinking. Through the echoes of my father that occur in my plays, I have been able to give him a voice he only rarely used in life.

> *Donald Margulies, "A Playwright's Search for the Spiritual Father," in* The New York Times, *Section 2, June 21, 1992, p. 5.*

Stefan Kanfer   (review date 13 July 1992)

[*Kanfer is an American novelist, playwright, short story writer, essayist, scriptwriter, and critic. In the following excerpt, he provides a positive assessment of* Sight Unseen.]

[In Donald Margulies's *Sight Unseen*] a trendy American painter, Jonathan Waxman, takes temporary leave of his pregnant wife and comes to London for a one-man exhibition. One night he impulsively journeys north to visit his ex-lover Patricia and her husband Nick, a rural archeologist. Long ago Jonathan painted Patricia in the nude; the art work now hangs in the married couple's loveless bedroom. Jonathan wants it for his retrospective; Patricia is unwilling to give it up. It represents the life and affection she left in America.

Predictably, Jonathan's presence sets off a series of explosions, sexual from Patricia who still wants him, esthetic from Nick who believes that anything painted after the Renaissance is junk. The detonations continue at Jonathan's London gallery. In a flash forward he squirms as a German reporter, Grete, asks incisive and embarrassing questions. Jonathan claims that his profession and his religion make him an outsider, but as an artist hasn't he been thoroughly co-opted by his corporate patrons? And as a Jew hasn't he been thoroughly assimilated by American society and his *shiksa* wife?

Jonathan protests: Such inquiries are intolerable from a *Fräulein.* Yet if Grete's interrogation is tinged with anti-Semitism, it is also tinctured with truth. In a series of flashbacks the painter's integrity, and his Jewish identity,

are gradually eroded by insatiable ambition. Every now and then, though, they come to the surface, assailing Jonathan with guilt, reminding him of what he was and what he still might be.

This is hardly the first play to move time around like sand in an hourglass. In the '30s George Kaufman and Moss Hart told a story backwards in *Merrily We Roll Along* (Hal Prince turned it into a musical with equal unsuccess). Harold Pinter's *Betrayal* did the same thing a couple of generations later. So did David Hare's *Plenty.* But those works seemed gimmicky to me; the element of time had very little to do with the point of the play. Here, the structure pertains to the art itself: half objective, half abstract, with points that may—or may not—be fashionable, and may—or may not—have to do with Jewish memory. It is all in the *oy* of the beholder. (p. 23)

> *Stefan Kanfer, "Artists and Models," in* The New Leader, *Vol. LXXV, No. 9, July 13, 1992, pp. 22-3.*

FURTHER READING

Kirkpatrick, Melanie. "An Artist's Inspiration Lost." *The Wall Street Journal* (14 February 1992): A9.
> Praises Margulies's examination of "embittered love, artistic inspiration and the corruption that success can bring" in *Sight Unseen.*

Kramer, Mimi. "Reverse Angle." *The New Yorker* LXVII, No. 50 (3 February 1992): 70-1.
> Offers a mixed assessment of *Sight Unseen* and likens the play to many modern British dramas.

Torrens, James S. "A Trio from the Theater Club." *America* 166, No. 18 (23 May 1992): 463-64.
> Examines Margulies's characterizations in *Sight Unseen.*

Michael Ondaatje

The English Patient

Awards: Booker Prize for Fiction and Governor General's Award for Fiction in English

(Full name Philip Michael Ondaatje) Born in 1943, Ondaatje is a Ceylonese-born Canadian poet, novelist, editor, critic, and filmmaker.

For further information about Ondaatje's life and career, see *CLC,* Volumes 14, 29, and 51.

INTRODUCTION

The English Patient delineates the relationships that develop between four individuals during the last months of World War II. Set in the ruins of a convent in Italy, Ondaatje's novel begins with Hana, a Canadian nurse, caring for a severely burned and unidentified English soldier after whom the novel is named. Early in the work, David Caravaggio, a Canadian spy and thief whom Hana knew when she was growing up, stumbles across the make-shift hospital. While being treated for wounds he received after being caught by the Germans, Caravaggio protects Hana and aids her in her duties. The fourth character, Kirpal "Kip" Singh, is an Indian Sikh who has been recruited by the English army to defuse the bombs German troops left in the area. As the novel progresses, the relationships between the characters are shaped by the secrets that are divulged and the stress of their situation. Critics note that some of the most powerful passages in the novel are those in which the characters' histories are revealed: the English patient recounts memories of his lover and her death, Kip relates his experiences as a third-world citizen and his exploits as a demolitions expert in London during the blitzkrieg, and Caravaggio discovers that the burn victim is really a Hungarian count and German spy. Incorporating figurative language and poetic imagery into *The English Patient,* Ondaatje has been praised for dramatizing the characters' ability to find love in the midst of tragedy, the dangers of deception, and the strength of the human spirit.

PRINCIPAL WORKS

The Dainty Monsters (poetry) 1967
The Man with Seven Toes (poetry) 1969
The Collected Works of Billy the Kid: Left Handed Poems
 (poetry and prose) 1970

Leonard Cohen (nonfiction) 1970
Rat Jelly (poetry) 1973; also published as *Rat Jelly, and Other Poems, 1963-78,* 1980
Coming through Slaughter (novel) 1976
There's a Trick with a Knife I'm Learning To Do: Poems, 1963-1978 (poetry) 1979
Running in the Family (memoir) 1982
Secular Love (poetry) 1984
In the Skin of a Lion (novel) 1987
The Cinnamon Peeler: Selected Poems (poetry) 1991
The English Patient (novel) 1992

CRITICISM

Cressida Connolly   (review date 5 September 1992)

[*In the following essay, Connolly offers high praise for* The English Patient.]

If there is anyone out there who can write as well as Michael Ondaatje, then I'd like to hear about them. Until discovering his books ([*The English Patient*] is his fifth novel) only a few weeks ago, I'd limped through contemporary fiction like an obedient dog on a very short leash. I'd wagged my tail at Ian McEwan and Martin Amis; had scratched at bookshop doors when a Jeanette Winterson was in the offing. When Marquez or Ivan Klima published new novels, I'd panted with enthusiasm. But this book is like literary pedigree chum. If it were advertised on television, the commercial would show an eager pack of fiction reviewers, leaping and bounding through the long grass for joy; with the slogan—'Top Readers Recommend It.'

[*The English Patient*] is set in northern Italy at the end of the second world war. It tells the story of a young nurse, Hana, who is living in a crumbling villa which has been requisitioned by the allies and turned into a hospital. In an upstairs room, burned beyond recognition, lies the English patient. He can speak, but he cannot move. The house has been evacuated, but Hana refuses to leave. Caring for this one man is her way of coming to terms with her own war-wounds; the wounds of bereavement and loss, and the constant memory of the death and suffering she has witnessed in field hospitals. Into this sad and rarefied house come two others. One is a former allied agent who knew Hana as a child in Canada, and the other is a young Sikh, a sapper called Kip, who has come to clear the area of enemy mines.

The developing relationships between these four people form the dynamic of the book, and the stories of their various past exploits are interwoven as its plot. And what stories these are. They are the stuff of boy's own adventure: feats of daring espionage; aeroplanes mysteriously buried beneath desert sand; archaeological exploration in the Sahara; and nail-biting accounts of bomb-disposal, against a nervous clock.

This is not all. Michael Ondaatje is a poet as well as a novelist, and the discipline and cadence of poetry informs all his writing. Prose-poetry has come to be associated with mawkish romances and purple passages, but this is the real thing: muscular, resonant, alive with simile.

The writing is so heady that you have to keep putting the book down between passages so as not to reel from the sheer force and beauty of it. Colour and landscape are evoked with such vividness that whole chunks of description become assimilated into the readers mind—when I finished the book I felt as dazed as if I'd just awoken from a powerful dream.

The English patient was burned when his plane crashed in the desert, where he had been working as a spy. Before the war he had been one of a party of explorers, charting the wilderness of the Libyan desert. The descriptions of this place are some of the best parts of the book, conjuring up a magical, ever-changing topography. Two anthologies of writing about the sea have come out this year but there is not, so far as I know, a collection yet devoted to the dry oceans of sand. When such a book is compiled, Ondaatje's account must be there, with Doughty, Philby, Lawrence and Thesiger; among the greats of desert literature.

Ondaatje was born in Sri Lanka, educated in England and now lives in Toronto. Perhaps his own journey has allowed him to cross national boundaries with such ease and grace in his fiction. Writing about the divides of race and culture also enables him to depict the common ground which unites people. His characters all share fear, loneliness and the secrets of their past. And they all long for intimacy: this is a love story, too.

[*The English Patient*] ends with the bombing of Hiroshima, and the end of the war. The little group at the villa is fragmented. The horror of the atom bomb lends poignance to the preceding time at the empty house and garden in Tuscany. Obliquely, this is a way of showing the dawn of the nuclear age as the Fall; the events of the novel those of a small and faded Eden. This is a wonderful and surprising novel. If it doesn't win the Booker prize, I'll eat my hat.

> Cressida Connolly, "A Time to Love and a Time to Die," in The Spectator, Vol. 269, No. 8565, September 5, 1992, p. 32.

Hana's alone in a male world, that's the central tension in [*The English Patient*]. She's surrounded by male history, the war, Hiroshima. . . .

—*Michael Ondaatje, in an interview in* The Observer, *18 October 1992.*

Lorna Sage   (review date 11 September 1992)

[*In the following essay, Sage provides a positive assessment of* The English Patient, *praising it as as a "bricolage" about intimacy, community, and vulnerability.*]

Michael Ondaatje's special gift as a novelist is to keep all the elements of a story in suspension, up in the air, seeming still yet buzzing with life, like a juggler's dinner-service. You can see space round the edge of each episode, too, which is doubtless an effect he borrows from his other self, the poet. His materials are realistic—or rather, real, in the documentary sense—but he picks and chooses them for their eccentricity and brittleness and the suggestive butterfly sheen that comes off them.

In other words, he's very much a *bricoleur,* and so likes to operate in worlds that are either not yet assembled, or in ruins. *The English Patient* is set in a battered villa on a Tuscan hillside in 1945, in a war-torn country where even the cypresses creak with shrapnel and the orchards are full of booby-trapped bombs. The building itself has served briefly as a hospital, but is now officially deserted, and is turning porous, and so available to the imagination—"Doors opened onto landscape. Some rooms had become an open aviary." Everything is wounded, but somehow, for that reason full of potential. And the quartet of characters who come together in this decaying house have the same quality of crazy openness. Hana, the Canadian nurse, is traumatized by tending the invasion's casualties, and by the news of the death of her father in another part of the war; her patient, a carbonized aviator picked up in the North African desert and dropped here to die gently, is nameless, "skin . . . tarred black, a bogman from history"; her father's Italian-Canadian friend, Caravaggio, come to find her, is himself a lost soul, mutilated and tortured in the war's last days; and "Kip", the brisk young Sikh sapper from the British army who billets himself on them, and who couldn't seem more whole, is (as it turns out) simply waiting for his mental world to be blown apart.

There's something else they have in common besides their vulnerability, however. Each of them is a kind of *mechanic*—this is Ondaatje the *bricoleur* picking up on *bricoleurs*—and, in their developing relationships and the stories from their pasts they tell each other, this skill is what guides them. Caravaggio was a thief, recruited by the secret services, the "English" patient a mapmaker, the sapper a brilliant bomb-disposal man, able to "read" the latest trick-detonators with the genius born of a third-world culture where everything is recycled. And Hana is their go-between and focus, her ear to their pulses. Isolated together, they invent for a brief while an improbable and delightful and fearful civilization of their own, a zone of fragile intimacy and understanding that can't—of course—survive, but which is offered to us, none the less, as a possible reality. A world without nations, for instance, one where skin colour doesn't divide people.

It's a dazzling performance, reminiscent of Ondaatje's extraordinary story of the building of Toronto in *In the Skin of a Lion* (1987), where dynamiting and destroying was built into the foundation-myth. Ondaatje is expert at turning the old, synthesizing formulae inside out. In the kinds of novels that were about empire-building there were rich receding perspectives, and the past tense and the third person were the order of the day. (Scott is still the archetype, with all those Celts, Scots, Angles, Jutes, Finns, Normans, Saxons, melded together at leisure in the Waverley novels.) Here, you get the present tense breaking in all over the place—"the fountain gurgling in the background, the hawks"—like rain through a leaky roof, and third persons reverting all the time to first persons, to tell their own tales, which whisk us off to the ends of the earth, into a world of difference. With Ondaatje, togetherness is a momentary, present-tense phenomenon: as soon as people start developing pasts and futures, everything becomes fissile and flies apart.

So you could say that the theme of *The English Patient* is the terminal sickness of Englishness/Europeanness, the death of the patriarchal scarecrow. The World War only truly becomes that with the dropping of the atomic bombs, which—for Kip (named a bit, I suspect, for Kipling)—

abolishes for ever the notion that civilization is white. This, however, isn't allowed to upset the fragile family of meanings the novel has put together, which survive precisely because they're hardly there at all. The reader—or this reader, anyway—emerges with the feeling of having been imprisoned in a cricket-cage: you're in collusion with the author, you don't want to know how utopian it all is. Now you see it, now you don't, as with so much in contemporary fiction.

Lorna Sage, "A Fragile Family," in The Times Literary Supplement, *No. 4667, September 11, 1992, p. 23.*

D. J. Taylor   (review date 18 September 1992)

[*Taylor is an English novelist, journalist, and critic. Here, he offers a negative review of* The English Patient.]

According to the latest critical intelligence from America, the English historical novel—a category in which Michael Ondaatje's new book seems to repose, despite its Sri Lankan author and international cast—is a devious and subversive genre, largely concerned with wounded empire, subject races and that time-honoured English hypocrisy. Happily *The English Patient* avoids these prescriptions almost entirely, and a previously loyal Indian sapper's anguish over Hiroshima provides the only tug on the anti-imperial thread.

For all that, this is a war novel of an increasingly common type, in that its action takes place not at the front line or by the parapet, but on the margins, deep within the compost of exhausted and bewildered memory. The Italian campaign of 1943 has, two years later, pushed upward into central Europe. Among the flotsam left in its wake is a damaged villa near Florence inhabited by a Canadian nurse, Hana, traumatised by the death of her father a few months ago on a French battlefield, and her mysterious patient, a laconic, badly burned "Englishman", brought to Italy after a plane crash in the North African desert.

Subsequently, two further visitors arrive at the villa: Caravaggio, a superannuated allied double agent who knew Hana's family in pre-war Toronto, and Kirpal Singh ("Kip"), a Sikh engaged in the complex task of clearing the area of mines. Although much of what follows is set in the present, in particular the sapper's relationship with Hana, the novel's focus moves effortlessly back to consider the effect of war on four individual lives: Kip's memories of defusing bombs in the Blitz; the patient's morphine-induced recollections of an epic love affair; Hana's nightmare existence in the allied military hospitals; Caravaggio's hazardous progress as a spy (he has emerged from the war without his thumbs).

These are oblique revelations, however. As you might imagine, there are secrets lurking behind the mildewed books in the library and the Englishman's informed yet curiously defensive conversation. It is Caravaggio who, by increasing the morphine dose and mixing it with alcohol, reveals what his knowledge of the North African campaign had long caused him to suspect: that the "English

An excerpt from *The English Patient*

He gazed onto the landscape under the eclipse. They had taught him by now to raise his arms and drag strength into his body from the universe, the way the desert pulled down planes. He was carried in a palanquin of felt and branch. He saw the moving veins of flamingos across his sight in the half darkness of the covered sun.

Always there were ointments, or darkness, against his skin. One night he heard what seemed to be wind chimes high in the air, and after a while it stopped and he fell asleep with a hunger for it, that noise like the slowed-down sound from the throat of a bird, perhaps flamingo, or a desert fox, which one of the men kept in a sewn-half-closed pocket in his burnoose.

The next day he heard snatches of the glassy sound as he lay once more covered in felt. A noise out of the darkness. At twilight the felt was unwrapped and he saw a man's head on a table moving towards him, then realized the man wore a giant yoke from which hung hundreds of small bottles on different lengths of string and wire. Moving as if part of a glass curtain, his body enveloped within that sphere.

The figure resembled most of all those drawings of seraphim he had tried to copy as a schoolboy, never solving how one body could have space for the muscles of such wings. The man moved with a long, slow gait, so smoothly there was hardly a tilt in the bottles. A wave of glass, a seraph, all the ointments within the bottles warmed from the sun, so when they were rubbed onto skin they seemed to have been heated especially for a wound. Behind him was translated light—blues and other colours shivering in the haze and sand. The faint glass noise and the diverse colours and the regal walk and his face like a lean dark gun.

Up close the glass was rough and sandblasted, glass that had lost its civilization. Each bottle had a minute cork the man plucked out with his teeth and kept in his lips while mixing one bottle's contents with another's, a second cork also in his teeth. He stood over the supine burned body with his wings, sank two sticks deep into the sand and then moved away free of the six-foot yoke, which balanced now within the crutches of the two sticks. He stepped out from under his shop. He sank to his knees and came towards the burned pilot and put his cold hands on his neck and held them there.

He was known to everyone along the camel route from the Sudan north to Giza, the Forty Days Road. He met the caravans, traded spice and liquid, and moved between oases and water camps. He walked through sandstorms with this coat of bottles, his ears plugged with two other small corks so he seemed a vessel to himself, this merchant doctor, this king of oils and perfumes and panaceas, this baptist. He would enter a camp and set up the curtain of bottles in front of whoever was sick.

He crouched by the burned man. He made a skin cup with the soles of his feet and leaned back to pluck, without even looking, certain bottles. With the uncorking of each tiny bottle the perfumes fell out. There was an odour of the sea. The smell of rust. Indigo. Ink. River-mud arrow-wood formaldehyde paraffin ether. The tide of airs chaotic. There were screams of camels in the distance as they picked up the scents. He began to rub green-black paste onto the rib cage. It was ground peacock bone, bartered for in a medina to the west or the south—the most potent healer of skin.

Michael Ondaatje, in his The English Patient, *Alfred A. Knopf, 1992.*

patient" is actually a former desert explorer and notorious German spy, a Hungarian count named Almásy previously employed by Rommel. Abruptly, the war ends, Kip takes umbrage over the bomb and disappears on his motorbike, and the cast is left to face an uncertain future.

Looking down the jacket copy, I had a pretty good idea of what I might find and, sure enough, there was the word "poetic". Nobody minds a lush, arboreal style, of course, but the drawbacks of densely figurative language are quite as marked as its lapel-grabbing quality. In Cairo with his mistress, for example, Almásy hears prayers from the minarets "enter the air like arrows", considers his lover's openness to be "like a wound", discerns a joint "foreignness" which is "intimate like two pages of a closed book".

For some reason, this type of writing seems simultaneously vague and overblown. The human choice is not like an arrow. In what way does openness resemble a wound? For all Ondaatje's delicacy of touch, the reader longs for a comparison that is really distinct and specific, for solidity rather than poetry.

The novel's broader structure, too, seems slightly unsatisfactory. Brilliant writing—the highpoint probably Singh's wrestling with the bombs amid the London rubble—alternates with lax connections and queer patches of inertia. What remains is a series of bright but unrelated images: Singh asleep in a Naples church suddenly awash with artificial light, Hana singing *La Marseillaise* from a Toronto table-top, Almásy stumbling upon a bound Arab girl in a French explorer's tent out along the Bedouin trail.

D. J. Taylor, "Scar Tissue," in New Statesman & Society, *Vol. 5, No. 220, September 18, 1992, p. 39.*

Nicholas Spice   **(review date 24 September 1992)**

[*In the following review, Spice examines the themes, style, and structure of* The English Patient.]

Can a penis sleep like a sea horse? The question arrests us on the first page of *The English Patient:*

> Every four days she washes his black body, beginning at the destroyed feet . . .

> She has nursed him for months and she knows the body well, the penis sleeping like a sea horse, the thin tight hips. Hipbones of Christ, she thinks. He is her despairing saint. He lies flat on his back, no pillow, looking up at the foliage painted onto the ceiling, its canopy of branches, and above that, blue sky.

Though it is possible to think of a penis as asleep and as having in sleep the shape of a sea horse, a penis is not well said to sleep *like* a sea horse, for sea horses are beady-eyed little creatures, characteristically alert and erect. Michael Ondaatje's prose is inventively figurative, but his figures do not always quite add up. A man sets off across the desert on foot, seventy miles to the next oasis: 'water in a skin bag he had filled from the *ain* hung from his shoulder and sloshed like a placenta.' As sea horses do not typically sleep, so a placenta does not slosh, at any rate not when it is functional in the womb, as here, by analogy, it is imagined to be. For figurative language to succeed it must work at the level of ordinary meaning as well as at the level of allusion. Ondaatje's images fail sometimes to achieve this balanced ambiguity. His imagery has about it something of the 17th-century Metaphysical conceit ('There was that small indentation at her throat we called the Bosphorus. I would dive from her shoulder into the Bosphorus. Rest my eye there') and it lays itself open to Johnson's criticism of that kind of poetry: its wit though 'new' is not 'natural' and it is prone to produce 'combinations of confused magnificence.' Some of Ondaatje's combinations are more confused than magnificent. There is a cloudy quality to the sea horse and placenta images, but we can still see where we are going. At other moments in *The English Patient* a fog descends: 'Cold nights in the desert. He plucked a thread from the horde of nights and put it into his mouth like food.'

One man's overwriting is another man's poetry, but in my view Ondaatje allows himself too much latitude in the direction of high-sounding prose. In its poetic vein his writing tends to self-parody, to be portentous, and to create an air of solemnity which tempts irreverence. Ondaatje spent eight years writing *The English Patient,* a fact which his publisher reports as though it somehow guaranteed the novel's quality, making Ondaatje into a kind of modern Flaubert. But it may be that Ondaatje has spent too long considering what he has written, listened to himself so often that he has occasionally lost a sense of what he is sounding like. Would Flaubert, at any rate, have written the phrase 'turn eternal in a prayer' or 'there was a thread, a breath of death in her'? For want of a sensitive editor, Ondaatje might do well to take up Voltaire's practice of reading everything that he writes out loud to his cook, or his cat.

Ondaatje's high stylistic and—as we shall see—moral seriousness asks to be taken down a peg or two. This done, *The English Patient* remains pegged near the top of the board. It is an exceptional book, and perhaps it could only have acquired its special character through the self-involvement of its author. The good here is part and parcel of the bad. A humbler spirit would have taken fewer risks and achieved less. Consider that sea horse. Only a writer who took himself very seriously would dare such an image. A man has been charred black by burns sustained when his plane went down in the desert. To the nurse who attends him, his penis (which we shall later discover has been the cause of his downfall) takes the form of a creature from the deep, cool ocean. By deft synecdoche the man himself becomes the sea horse, *hippocampus hippocampus,* that small exotic fish with the 'thin tight hips.' At the same time, he is transformed into a surreal composite of sea animals, a painting by Arcimboldi such as we could imagine

hanging in the Italian Renaissance villa where, cradled by its painted elegance, the burnt man lies dying.

Ondaatje's impulse to think figuratively is not just expressed in particular images. Figurative thinking generates this novel at every level, and if in some instances Ondaatje's figures of speech fail quite to cohere, his figures of fiction—his characters, stories and settings—work naturally, making literal as well as figurative sense. This unforced interplay, on the large scale, between primary and secondary meanings is the book's chief pleasure. Any passing irritation one may feel at the surface mannerisms of *The English Patient* is overtaken by admiration for its imaginative scope and its success as a fictional unity.

The proportions of the novel are pleasingly balanced. There's a lot going on in it, but we never lose a sense of its structure. Looking back on it, we can take it in at a glance, like a Classical building. This is more than an analogy, because the unity of the book is secured by an architectural setting: the Villa San Girolamo, twenty miles north of Florence. Here the foreground action of the novel takes place.

It is spring 1945, in Italy, 'the war moving North, the war almost over.' Behind the lines of the Allied advance a villa stands, half-boarded-up, half-destroyed. It has been a nunnery, a German stronghold (focus of a fierce battle) and an Allied field hospital. The armies have moved on. The patients and nurses that remained have now departed for safety in the South. Two stay on: a Canadian nurse—Hana—and a dying man, disfigured by terrible burns, the man they call 'the English patient.'

Hana tends the English patient with supererogatory devotion, washing him, dressing his burns, giving him shots of morphine, listening to his stories, reading to him from the English books she finds in the villa library. It is as though in soothing him Hana finds balm for her own interior wounds, for the skin of a soul which has been seared by exposure to death: the death of her father, the death of her child, the death of the father of her child, the death of countless fathers of countless children. By day, Hana looks after her patient or works in the garden, growing the vegetables which are their food. At night, heedless of the danger of unexploded mines, she wanders through the ruined rooms of the villa like a nomad, looking for somewhere to sleep: 'Some nights she opened doors and slept in rooms that had walls missing. She lay on the pallet on the very edge of the room, facing the drifting landscape of stars, moving clouds, wakened by the growl of thunder and lightning.'

Into this ghostly idyll come two men: first, David Caravaggio, a friend of Hana's father from before the war in Toronto; and later, a young sapper, Kirpal Singh, nicknamed Kip—a Sikh from the Punjab, who has been detailed to clear the area around the villa of mines. Caravaggio and Kip materialise like figures in a dream. Both are masters of stealth and delicacy: Caravaggio as a professional robber, and Kip as a dismantler of bombs. But Caravaggio can no longer steal: his hands have been maimed and his spirit broken. At the outbreak of war he was enlisted as a spy ('they had just made my skills official'). In Italy he gets caught and they cut his thumbs off.

Of the four main characters of **The English Patient** we learn least about Hana—that is to say, least about her past. The structure of the novel does not require that we should be told much. The world of the villa belongs to her more than to the men. She is its tutelary spirit, the presiding genius of a temple of stories to which the men bring their offerings: Caravaggio's nightmare vision of an incident in wartime spying and torture; the gripping accounts of Kip's dance of death with unexploded bombs in London and Naples; the English patient's tales of adventure, intrigue and romance in the North African desert.

In the archaeology of Ondaatje's novel the English patient's story is surely the oldest narrative material, the core around which the rest of the book accumulates. Given the imaginative structure of the novel, it is impossible to think of its creative genesis differently. The English patient's story lies at the centre of the book as the English patient lies at the centre of the Villa San Girolamo, like an embalmed figure in a mausoleum, Hana his votary, Caravaggio and Kip attendant knights. In this sculptured immobility, suspended between life and death, the English patient has passed beyond the condition of character—without a skin he has no attributes, he has become all story. Incapable of action and without a future, he is just a voice in a box, a door into past worlds.

At the opening of the novel the burnt man has no identity. Everything about him appears to be English—the way he speaks, his memories of English life, his dilettante polymathy. But as he talks and the fragments of his story form into a pattern, a new interpretation emerges. Caravaggio, who has worked for British Intelligence in North Africa, recognises that the English patient is not English at all but a Hungarian, the map-maker and explorer, Count Ladislaus de Almasy, a shadowy figure who helped the Germans in the first years of the war, guiding their spies across the desert into Cairo. Hana and Kip are sceptical of Caravaggio's theory and continue to think of the burnt man as English, but the novel makes it clear that Caravaggio is right.

Almasy's story begins in 1930 on the Gilf Kebir Plateau in the remote desert on the Egyptian-Libyan border. He is one of a group of explorers mapping the Gilf Kebir in search of the lost oasis of Zerzura. In 1936, Almasy starts a passionate affair with Katharine, the young wife of an English colleague, Geoffrey Clifton. Long after the affair has ended, in the last days before the war, Almasy returns to the Gilf Kebir 'to clear out the base camp.' Clifton is meant to fly in and pick him up. Instead he flies his plane at Almasy in an attempt to kill him. The plane crashes, killing Clifton and injuring Katharine. Almasy takes Katharine to a desert cave and sets out on foot to find help at the next oasis, El Taj. But in El Taj no one believes his story, and the British arrest him as a spy. It takes Almasy three years to get back to the cave. Disinterring an old plane from the sand, he flies out of the Gilf Kebir for the last time, with Katharine's body at his side. The plane catches fire. Katharine catches fire. Almasy catches fire.

He parachutes into the desert, where the Bedouin deliver him to the British. He has become the English patient.

Almasy and his story are based on fact. Using source material from the Royal Geographical Society in London, Ondaatje has imagined himself deep into the world of desert exploration in the Twenties and Thirties. Almasy's story is a gripping adventure story which is also imaginatively strange and shimmering with figurative meaning. And the same is true of Kip's story. Here, once again, Ondaatje has worked his way deep into his material, becoming an expert on bomb disposal so as to be able to bring it alive as a the stuff of adventure, and to activate it as a source of allegorical and symbolic meaning. But Ondaatje's greatest insight was to see how Almasy's story could be woven in and out of Kip's, how a story of survival in the North African desert could be set off against a story of survival in European bomb craters.

Beneath the intricate particular detail of **The English Patient** there lies the simple enough general insight that reality is a treacherous web of appearances—a minefield, a desert. The world is dangerous, a place of mirages and mirrors and trompe-l'oeil effects, a place where we are easily disorientated and innocent-seeming things prove deadly: where to move at the wrong time is to go 90 degrees off-course, where a piano or grandfather clock may blow off fragile limbs. To survive in this unsafe place, to remain intact, we must be canny as spies, artful as thieves. Almasy and Kip (Caravaggio too) are masters in this mortal game: Almasy through knowledge ('I have always had information like a sea in me') and an art of anonymity, Kip through self-containment, watchfulness, precise attention, an intuitive grace by which what he is and what he does move in perfect congruence.

The average life-span of a wartime sapper was ten days. Kip survives for years. Almasy's trips across the desert are legendary feats. But neither Almasy nor Kip can outwit Englishness, which in **The English Patient** is the ultimate symbol of life's treacherousness. By his adultery with Katherine, Almasy joins life in its game of appearances and deception. This in itself is risky, but his greater mistake is to have an affair with the wife of a member of the British Establishment, a force for dissimulation for which he is no match. Kip is cheated by Englishness in a very different way. He is taken in by its values, its false romance. While his brother sees the British for what they are and prefers to sit out the war in a Punjabi jail, Kip obeys the call of Empire and risks his life to defend Englishness. He is woken from this trance by the news of Hiroshima.

As a mechanism for ending the novel, Kip's peripeteia, his moment of truth, is extremely effective. It brings everything back to reality. Ondaatje's success in conjuring up the world of the Villa San Girolamo leaves him with a problem. His characters are caught there in a dream at the end of time, like the figures in a painting by Giorgione. Hiroshima shatters this dream, starts the clock ticking and allows the novel to end. But the sudden intrusion of polemic into this precisely constructed book seems false and hysterical. When Kip screams, 'American, French, I don't care. When you start bombing the brown races of the world, you're an Englishman,' it is not his voice which we hear but Ondaatje's, the voice of a Sri Lankan-born author living in Canada, possessed of a just outrage against the history of the British Empire.

The English Patient is a very male book, a book about different ways of being a man, different ways of being Ondaatje. Looked at this way, it becomes understandable that the bluff, earthy, blunt-spoken Caravaggio should be the character that Ondaatje has most difficulty filling out: for I guess that this is how Ondaatje sees himself. Meanwhile, the mercurial Kip can be seen as the man Ondaatje would have liked to have been, and he is created with all the love and detail with which a man creates his ideal self. As for Almasy, the man of no or any identity, the brilliant foreigner who sponges up English values and English literariness, I see him as the writer in Ondaatje, his creative intelligence. So Ondaatje's deep ambivalence about Almasy is scarcely surprising. For Ondaatje's voice is Almasy's, Almasy's style Ondaatje's, a style which at best generates things of real beauty, at worst creates effects of trompe-l'oeil which make us suspect that there is less to what we read than meets the eye. (pp. 3, 5)

> Nicholas Spice, "Ways of Being a Man," in London Review of Books, *Vol. 14, No. 18, September 24, 1992, pp. 3, 5.*

Richard Eder   (review date 11 October 1992)

[*Eder is a well-known American journalist and art critic. Here, he examines* The English Patient *as a series of intersecting narratives.*]

His face disfigured and his limbs burned black in an air crash, the English patient lies dying but lucid in a Tuscan villa. It is toward the end of World War II. The Allies, who used the villa as a hospital, have moved north, and the other patients have been evacuated. Only the burned man remains, in the care of a young Canadian nurse who has resigned from war and its attendant machineries and withdrawn her patient with her.

The Villa Girolamo, in Michael Ondaatje's magically told [*The English Patient*], is a wayside haven, a place of silence where the cacophony of world conflagration is filtered down into individual voices. Four people, each damaged, find a refuge where the rupture between their stories and their lives can begin to mend. Besides Hana, the nurse, and her patient, there are two arrivals: Caravaggio, a professional burglar who works for Allied intelligence and has been horribly tortured by the Gestapo, and Kip, a young Sikh officer who faces death each day in his lethal job of disarming unexploded mines and bombs.

Ondaatje, a Sri Lankan who became a Canadian citizen, is a poet who has written some extraordinary fiction, including *In the Skin of a Lion* and a fantasy-memoir, *Running in the Family.* In these works, and in *The English Patient,* the motivating power comes in part from story and character, but even more from white flashes of phrase or image. It is a night journey; we move from one star-shell burst to the next, and the countryside shows suddenly familiar and strange.

In part, *The English Patient* consists of the stories of its

four pilgrims, told by themselves or by the author. Two are developed: the ravishing story of Kip and his life-saving mission, and the many-layered secrets of the patient, who proves not to be English and whose discovery is the central thread. The stories of Hana and Caravaggio are told more cursorily.

None of the stories stand alone, however. Their counterpoint and the tensely shifting relationships of the characters provide the book's texture. It is a complex and delicate web whose shimmer and sway is set off by the four lives that alight and are caught in it.

Hana, the youngest, is burned out from ministering to hundreds of dying soldiers and standing as their failing last comfort. Word of her father's death had brought her to near breakdown; seclusion in the villa and the care of her single patient are a private peace. The patient is beyond hope or self-pity. Out of his blackened mouth comes a serene flow of images and stories; he has been, among other things, a scholar and a desert explorer. She finds in him something of an oracle, something of a father, and something of an old man whom she can warm by chastely sharing his bed at night.

The arrival of Caravaggio brings a bitter tension. He was caught stealing documents from the German high command, and his thumbs were sliced off during interrogation. Crippled in the exercise of his filching profession, he is jealous of the patient's hold on Hana. He knew her family in Canada; as a girl, she had a crush on him, and his feelings for her are something more than protective. But there is another element in his hostility. His work in intelligence goads him into finding out who the patient really is; he administers morphine to question him.

We hear the patient's story. He is a Hungarian named Almasy, a member of a British expedition that mapped the Libyan desert in the 1930s. He had a violent affair with the young wife of one of the parties. Later, the husband killed himself and mortally injured his wife by deliberately crashing a plane at Almasy's desert campsite, apparently in an effort to kill him. Passion aside, there was a cloudy political manipulation at work. Almasy at some point had become a German agent. His own injuries came while flying an arms mission to the Bedouins.

To the embittered Caravaggio, Almasy is a quarry. To Hana, still open to life, he is a compound of learning, mystery and grace. Ondaatje gives his musings and memories an Apollo-like quality. Hana reads Kipling to him; he tells her that Kipling wrote with a pen, pausing to look out the window and think. She should use the same rhythms when she reads him aloud.

Hana is far more than a devoted attendant. In her silence, she waits for her own healing. After Almasy falls asleep each evening, she continues reading for herself. "His books had gaps of plot like sections of a road washed out by rain." At the piano in the villa's salon, she picks out a few chords. "She paused after each set of notes as if bringing her hands out of the water to see what she had caught."

What she catches is Kip. He has been clearing the area of

mines; hearing the piano, he breaks in. The retreating Germans, it seems, made a point of booby-trapping pianos, and metronomes as well.

Kip stays on, living in a tent in the garden, going out to mortal danger each day, spending evenings in the villa. He and Almasy discuss detonators and Virgil. He and Hana become lovers. For her it is finding life again; Ondaatje suggests it in one of the associative images he uses so startlingly and naturally. Hana prepares to bathe in one of the villa's outdoor fountains. There is water only a few minutes each day; she crouches in the dry fountain waiting for it to gush out. As for Kip, his love is as absolute but divided; he is perpetually honed to his peculiar mission.

Kip's story is the book's centerpiece. A science student in India and a tinkerer and inventor by instinct, he came to England at the start of the war and volunteered for the country's pioneer bomb-disposal unit. Everything was experiment, and life expectancy was six weeks.

The leader, Lord Suffolk, is a peculiarly English type of gentleman genius. With his secretary, Miss Morden, he takes his small band of hero-tinkerers around England, feeding them cream teas, staying up late at night to theorize and speculate, treating them in the double fellowship of science and peril. In Kip, he inspires a pure devotion and unflagging sense of mission.

When Lord Suffolk, Miss Morden and four of the team are blown up by a new kind of bomb, Kip takes over. His agonizing effort to puzzle out the new bombs is brilliantly described: down in the craters with them, freezing them with liquid oxygen, reasoning desperately and playing blind hunches. But Ondaatje infuses the detail with a sense of knightly quest. Lord Suffolk had conveyed to Kip the image of Western learning at its daring and generous best. Kip made it his own. And so, when the news of Hiroshima and Nagasaki comes over the radio—Western learning indifferently applied to exterminating his people of the East—he breaks down. He flees the villa in a wild motorcycle run.

Ondaatje puts no particular dramatic emphasis on the break-up of the sanctuary at the Villa Girolamo. We hear of Hana, years later, in Canada, and of Kip, years later, in India. Nothing much is said of Caravaggio. We assume that Almasy is dead. The author's four stories are not a story that gathers momentum from start to finish. They are the widening and fading circles on a pond into which history has plunged like a cast stone.

> *Richard Eder, "Circles on a Pond," in* Los Angeles Times Book Review, *October 11, 1992, pp. 3, 12.*

Christopher Lehmann-Haupt (review date 29 October 1992)

[*In the following review of* The English Patient, *Lehmann-Haupt, an American book reviewer and critic, faults Ondaatje's labored prose style and convoluted plots.*]

"A novel is a mirror walking down a road," muses one of the characters, recalling Stendhal in Michael Ondaatje's new book, *The English Patient,* a co-winner in England (with Barry Unsworth's novel *Sacred Hunger*) of the 1992 Booker Prize. In the mirror of *The English Patient* we see bombs exploding and burning airplanes falling out of the sky. We see a woman playing hopscotch in the hall of an Italian villa and a statue of the Virgin Mary rising out of the sea. Sometimes these images coalesce to form astonishingly vivid pictures in the reader's mind. At other times, they seem laboredly poetic.

The English Patient gets off to a powerful start. The time is near the end of World War II. A nameless man burned beyond recognition lies dying in a room in a bombed-out villa north of Florence. He is tended by Hana Lewis, a young nurse from Toronto who feeds him, reads to him and keeps him dosed with morphine. They are shortly joined by two other men. David Caravaggio, a professional thief who is a friend of Hana's father, and Kirpal (Kip) Singh, a sapper in the British Army whose task it is to defuse all the bombs and mines that have been left behind by the Germans in the villa and its environs.

As these four characters begin to reveal themselves to one another, we are given a vivid picture of what the Allied invasion in Italy must have been like. "The last medieval war was fought in Italy in 1943 and 1944," one chapter begins. "Field Marshal Kesselring of the retreating German Army seriously considered the pouring of hot oil from battlements. Medieval scholars were pulled out of Oxford colleges and flown into Umbria. Their average age was 60." In one comically surrealistic scene, Kip the sapper attaches a sling and a flare to an old professor and with block and tackle hauls him high in a church in Arezzo to get a closer look at a fresco called *The Flight of Emperor Maxentius.*

The activity in the foreground of the novel's mirror is furious. Caravaggio's hands are bandaged because as a thief enlisted by the Allies he has been caught by the Germans and punished by having his thumbs cut off. Kip keeps finding hidden bombs, and in mesmerizing descriptive passages, exercises his genius at disarming them.

> He was by nature conservative but able also to imagine the worst devices, the capacity for accident in a room—a plum on a table, a child approaching and eating the pit of poison, a man walking into a dark room and before joining his wife in bed brushing loose a paraffin lamp from its bracket.

Hana, the nurse, falls in love with Kip.

Meanwhile, the burned man, under the influence of morphine, tells his story. His plane crashed in the Libyan desert. Bedouins saved him, exploited his vast knowledge of weapons, then somehow got him to a hospital in Pisa. As his narrative keeps doubling back, we learn of his familiarity with the desert and of the violent and illicit love affair that led him into that burning airplane. Caravaggio begins to suspect that he is not really English.

Yet despite all its plot, the novel also conveys a sense of time having ground to a stop. The resulting vacuum increases the force of the imagery and heightens our anticipation of some calamity bearing down. Curious details stick out. "The great pickpockets are born with the second and third fingers almost the same length," Caravaggio explains. "They do not need to go as deep into a pocket. The great distance of half an inch."

Unfortunately, you can't always trust the plot. For instance, it is hard to imagine the drug-addicted Caravaggio, minus his two thumbs, in Hana's quarters "rifling through her medicine chest, breaking the glass tab, tightening a bootlace round his arm and injecting the morphine quickly into himself, in the time it took for him to turn around." Nor can you invariably trust the language. "Kirpal Singh stood where the horse's saddle would have lain across its back," reads one ungrammatical sentence.

Increasingly as the plot winds down and the vacuum of timelessness intensifies, Mr. Ondaatje relies on precious language to convey the novel's feeling. "She sings and hums," we are told of Hana.

> She thinks him, in his tent's darkness, to be half bird—a quality of feather within him, the cold iron at his wrist. He moves sleepily whenever he is in such darkness with her, not quite quick as the world, whereas in daylight he glides through all that is random around him, the way color glides against color.

And when the dam of anticipation finally breaks, the point of the crisis is impossibly willed and tendentious and relates only superficially to the powerful imagery earlier established.

The English Patient surpasses in power Mr. Ondaatje's previous novels, *In the Skin of the Lion, Coming Through Slaughter,* and *The Collected Works of Billy the Kid.* Which, incidentally, you have to have read to understand several minor unexplained developments in *The English Patient.* Born in Sri Lanka when it was Ceylon and educated in England and Canada, Mr. Ondaatje has said he believes that familiarity with the tropics heightens a writer's sense of surrealism. Yet here his storytelling is more conventional, at least for a while, and the novel's narrative drive benefits.

Pico Iyer on *The English Patient*:

The heart of the book is the slow unraveling of the faceless patient's life, educed by morphine and haunted by scenes from Cairo nights when it was necessary "to *proceed* into the plot of the evening, while the human constellations whirled and skidded around you." That is very much how Ondaatje proceeds. One by one he introduces his characters, and slowly he unlocks their secrets, leading us through their lives as through the darkened corridors of a huge and secret house. Loves flicker, footsteps echo, lines of poetry recur. All four feel their way through darkness, by hand and memory, and with all the phantom sensuousness that darkness brings.

Pico Iyer, in his "Magic Carpet Ride," in Time, *2 November 1992.*

Mr. Ondaatje also believes, if one can trust the narrator of *The English Patient,* that "novels commenced with hesitation or chaos." The text continues: "Readers were never fully in balance. A door, a lock, a weir opened and they rushed through, one hand holding a gunnel, the other a hat."

Reading *The English Patient* you hold on to the gunnel and your hat at the start. But by the end you find yourself resting on the bottom of the boat, with your hat over your face to keep off Mr. Ondaatje's too brilliant prose.

> *Christopher Lehmann-Haupt, "Love and Death as the War Goes on All Around," in* The New York Times, *October 29, 1992, p. C22.*

Gary Draper   (review date November 1992)

[*In the following essay, Draper praises* The English Patient *as a ground-breaking novel written by "an exceptionally gifted writer at the peak of his powers."*]

Reviewers like to hedge their bets. After all, you might be wrong, in which case it's better to err on the side of being too critical rather than too generous in your estimate, or at least covering your assessments with a caveat or two. Otherwise you can wind up looking like a sap with no standards. Michael Ondaatje's latest novel, *The English Patient,* is worth the risk. There are books that change the shape of a literature. Each new book does in a way, of course, but with some you can feel the ground shift. Think of *The Stone Angel* or *The Temptations of Big Bear* or *Lives of Girls and Women.* *The English Patient,* I want to say, is such a book. It represents the work of an exceptionally gifted writer at the peak of his powers.

In the closing weeks of the Second World War, the lives of four people converge in what remains of the Villa San Girolamo in the hills north of Florence. One of these people is the English patient of the title, a man who fell burning from the sky, whose identity is lost, and who now lies "eternally dying" in this Tuscan villa. Another is Hana, a young woman from Toronto, who stayed behind to nurse the burned man when her medical colleagues departed. The third is Caravaggio, a friend of Hana's father who has sought her out. Caravaggio, an utterly charming thief and intriguer, has lost both his thumbs on account of one of his exploits. Finally there is Kirpal Singh, called Kip, a young Indian sapper who is one of those assigned to clearing Florence and its environs of mines and unexploded bombs.

It might be simplest to describe this as a love story, or perhaps a network of stories of different kinds of love, ranging from friendship through various degrees of passion. The overall structure of the book is circular and allusive, advancing, rounding back on itself, coming to endings that are not necessarily resolutions, and which may be connected to other starting points. The conclusion of the novel is fully realized and satisfying, without being "conclusive."

Within the swirls of this narrative, of course, more than love is circling. There are mysteries here, and suspense. The big mystery: who is the English patient? What is his story? But in fact the very shaping of the narrative provides a myriad of smaller mysteries. Ondaatje is a crafty writer; he often creates some acutely strange scene or image, the full meaning of which will be revealed only much later. Or he may "solve" the mystery as soon as it's been introduced. Take, for example, the opening lines of the book's eighth section, "The Holy Forest":

> Kip walks out of the field where he has been digging, his left hand raised in front of him as if he has sprained it.
>
> He passes the scarecrow for Hana's garden, the crucifix with its hanging sardine cans, and moves uphill towards the villa. He cups the hand held in front of him with the other as if protecting the flame of a candle. Hana meets him on the terrace, and he takes her hand and holds it against his. The ladybird circling the nail on his small finger quickly crosses over onto her wrist.

Kip has just carried a ladybug to Hana. But because Ondaatje imbues this act with the magic of an unexplained ritual, because he makes the actors mime the scene, and finally because of the simple beauty of his prose, the reader cannot look away before the mystery is revealed. And Ondaatje can hook the reader as much with simplicity and clarity as with mystery. The book's penultimate section begins, irresistibly, "I promised to tell you how one falls in love."

Suspense? In some ways the central informing metaphor of the novel is that of the unexploded bomb. On the literal level, Ondaatje achieves incredible tension and suspense by taking the reader through the steps of bomb defusing. Sometimes the bombs go off, sometimes they don't. The effect is that the reader is always holding his breath, waiting for the next explosion. The lives of the characters, too, are mined. There are pieces of their pasts and their futures waiting to blow up in their hands. And finally, the narrative itself is mined. The reader never knows which incident is going to be defused, which is going to explode. And because the narrative structure is circular and allusive, there are hints and foreshadowings of blasts to come. Sometimes it is only in retrospect that the reader learns that a particular bomb has—or hasn't—gone off.

As always in Ondaatje's writings, there are images and scenes here that are as intensely vivid as they are unlikely, and at the same time wholly credible. While Caravaggio, naked, is searching for an incriminating camera in a darkened bedroom in which a German general and his mistress are engaged in sex, all three are suddenly illuminated in the gleam of passing headlamps like figures in a *tableau vivant*. In an earlier scene, the English patient, burned and blindfolded, is carried from gun to recovered gun by his Bedouin rescuers and made to name each by a kind of armoury Braille. On a larger scale, there is the spectre of a deserted Naples, scoured by Kip and his fellow sappers, waiting for a switch to be thrown to find out whether or not the city will explode.

Ondaatje writes like a man in love with the sounds of language. Consider the beginning of this list of winds of the desert:

> There is a whirlwind in southern Morocco, the

aajej, against which the fellahin defend themselves with knives. There is the *africo*, which has at times reached into the city of Rome. The *alm*, a fall wind out of Yugoslavia. The *arifi*, also christened *aref* or *rifi*, which scorches with numerous tongues. These are permanent winds that live in the present tense.

This is also, then, a book about the intersection of language and memory, about the overlapping of document and art. There are many references here to painters (it is no accident that one of the central characters should bear a painter's name) and to particular paintings and their survival in the ruins of post-war Italy. There are also many instances of the interweaving of real life with books. Both Hana and her patient write their own thoughts and diaries in the margins of books. This is apt precisely because one of Ondaatje's great skills is the interweaving of documentary—including in this case his research into unexploded bombs—and invention.

Ondaatje knows the secrets of the heart as well as he knows the secrets of his craft. Hana, Caravaggio, the English patient, and—perhaps above all—Kip are strong, vivid characters. Their longings and failures and loves and sorrows are deeply felt and credibly portrayed. Early in the book Caravaggio stands over Hana, who sits at the kitchen table, weeping: "The deepest sorrow, he thought. Where the only way to survive is to excavate everything." Ondaatje takes the reader to that place. It is a harrowing, beautiful journey. (pp. 39-40)

> *Gary Draper, "Perfect Pitch," in* Books in Canada, *Vol. XXI, No. 8, November, 1992, pp. 39-40.*

Judith Grossman   (review date 1 November 1992)

[*Grossman is a novelist and educator. In the following essay, she offers a positive assessment of* The English Patient.]

One of the uncalculated effects of World War II was the way it turned a generation of young people, conscripts and volunteers, into global explorers without a guidebook. Military orders might with equal unconcern drop a London clerk into the presence of Mount Everest, or an American farm boy into Piccadilly. Or, as vividly described in Michael Ondaatje's novel of the war in Europe, *The English Patient,* a young Sikh from the Punjab into Michelangelo's Sistine Chapel, on a bomb-disposal mission at night:

> And the sergeant released the catch of the flare and held it up in his outstretched arm, the niagara of its light pouring off his fist, and stood there for the length of its burn like that. . . . But the young sapper was already on his back, the rifle aimed, his eye almost brushing the beards of Noah and Abraham and the variety of demons until he reached the great face and was stilled by it, the face like a spear, wise, unforgiving.

Mr. Ondaatje, a Canadian novelist and poet with a distinctive, eloquent voice, is especially well placed to interpret such remarkable encounters as this between Lieutenant

Singh and Michelangelo's prophet Isiah. As his memoir *Running in the Family* (1982) has revealed, he is himself a world traveler, from mingled European and Sri Lankan origins, who grew up in colonial Ceylon. He also has a genuine affinity for the romantic temperament of the 1940's. Inside his theater of war the drama that plays is one of glorious but impossible loves, evoking at times the nostalgic appeal of *Casablanca* or *South Pacific.*

The English Patient begins in 1945, in a bomb-damaged Italian villa near Florence, recently used as a war hospital. Abandoned as the Allied front moved north, it now shelters one last casualty, an Englishman slowly dying of burns received in an air crash over Libya. "A man with no face. An ebony pool. All identification consumed in a fire. Parts of his burned body and face had been sprayed with tannic acid that hardened into a protective shell over his raw skin." Hana, a young Canadian nurse, stays on devotedly, supplying him with morphine and foraged food. They are joined by David Caravaggio, a friend of Hana's family from Toronto who is a professional thief turned military spy, and by Kirpal Singh, a Sikh soldier, charged with defusing bombs and mines in the area. For this quartet of characters, the villa becomes a sanctuary in which identities damaged or erased by the war can be remade.

The Englishman, though he apparently can't recall his name, tells vivid stories of his former life as an explorer of the lost oases in the African desert. Hana is awed by his range of learning and moved by his stoic endurance; she calls him her "despairing saint." But as more of his story comes out—his great love for the wife of a young colleague, which led to a fatal confrontation at the onset of the war—new questions arise and the puzzle turns darker: is he a hero or a German collaborator in disguise? A victim or a murderer? To Caravaggio, who has barely survived torture and mutilation by Axis forces, the answers are crucial.

There's the suggestion of a classic espionage thriller in this angle of the plot, but Mr Ondaatje is after something else—a narrative reflection, perhaps, on the alternate exhilarations and terrors of life in wartime. Through interlaced scenes, each saturated with emotion, he uncovers the inner passions of his characters: Hana's grief over her father's death earlier in the war, Caravaggio's mourning for his lost vocation, Singh's terrifying exploits with the bomb squad, the nameless patient's pride in his memories of love. Their stories take us to extraordinary times and places, from muddy craters where giant "Satan" bombs are delicately disarmed by hand under unsteady flashlights to hidden rock paintings in desert caves.

Mr. Ondaatje's acknowledgments testify to his meticulous research, and the kinesthetic vitality of his descriptions bears it out. He makes the technical maze of delayed fuses and disguised wiring about as compelling as can be imagined outside of the professional situation itself.

In contrast to the brilliant short takes of explorers, spies, and army sappers probing minefields, the drama of emotions among the main characters seems much less dynamic. Certainly they come well garlanded with attributes—Hana's reticent tenderness, her patient's iron self-discipline, his lover's arrogant beauty—but the effect produced is of figures fixed in a mosaic, icons representing in turn innocence, passion, loss and endurance. When they talk together, they have a tendency toward melodramatic statements in very formal language (but then one thinks, was there once a time when people finished all their sentences in good order?)

This portentiousness is less a burden on the Canadian characters, Caravaggio especially. They have more spontaneous fluency in their scenes together, and an individual resonance deriving perhaps from the fact that they appeared in Mr. Ondaatje's earlier novel *In the Skin of a Lion,* a powerful account of men caught up in the work and politics of the building of Toronto. The hero of that book, Patrick, is the father whose death by fire during this war is mourned by Hana, the young nurse of the English patient, to whom she transfers her filial caring.

Hana's love idyll in the villa gardens with the Indian soldier, however, sometimes appears over-weighted with verbal ornament, as in the following "At night, when she lets her hair free, he is once more another constellation, the arms of a thousand equators against his pillow, waves of it between them in their embraces and in their turns of sleep. She holds an Indian goddess in her arms, she holds wheat and ribbons."

Granted, of course, that a Sikh man would by religious custom have long hair tied up in his turban—still, the unexamined feminization here of Asian man by Western woman makes me uneasy. Or is it the absence of a more balanced sense of how he experiences *her?* It troubles me also that the ending of this interracial romance, though in itself historically plausible, is effected by means of the news of Hiroshima's bombing, and an immediately ensuing breakdown on the part of Kirpal Singh. The fit between devastating public event and the fiction of private life here seems just too neatly made.

Nonetheless, *The English Patient,* which was named a cowinner of the 1992 Booker Prize last month, is a tale of many pleasures—an intensely theatrical tour de force, but grounded in Michael Ondaatje's strong feeling for distant times and places.

Judith Grossman, "Glorious but Impossible Loves," in The New York Times Book Review, *November 1, 1992, p. 7.*

FURTHER READING

Bush, Catherine. Interview with Michael Ondaatje. *Conjunctions* 15 (1990): 87-98.

   Interview in which Ondaatje discusses his experiences in Sri Lanka and England, the relationship between writer and reader, and the writing process.

Garvie, Maureen. "Listening to Michael Ondaatje." *Queen's Quarterly* 99, No. 4 (Winter 1992): 928-34.

Includes biographical information on Ondaatje and a brief interview in which Ondaatje talks about *The English Patient,* growing up bilingual, and his two documentaries.

Hower, Edward. "All is Not Quiet on the Southern Front." *The Wall Street Journal* 220 (16 October 1992): A12.
    Praises Ondaatje's use of poetic language and nonlinear narrative structures in *The English Patient.*

Laird, Sally. "Man of Magic Tongue." *The Observer,* (London), No. 10,488 (18 October 1992): 59.
    Feature article about *The English Patient* in which Ondaatje discusses history, his childhood, and poetic imagination.

Seligman, Craig. "Sentimental Wounds." *The New Republic* 208, No. 11 (15 March 1993): 38-41.
    Offers a mixed assessment of *The English Patient.* Seligman states: "Ondaatje hasn't written a novel at all, he has written a storybook, and his characters are storybook characters. That is the beauty of *The English Patient,* and that is where it fails."

Slopen, Beverly. Interview with Michael Ondaatje. *Publishers Weekly* 239, No. 44 (5 October 1992): 48-9.
    Interview in which Ondaatje talks about his use of interior monologues and his depiction of history in *The English Patient.*

Smith, Stephen. Interview with Michael Ondaatje. *Quill and Quire* 58, No. 9 (September 1992): 69.
    Interview in which Ondaatje discusses how he came to write *The English Patient.*

Additional coverage of Ondaatje's life and career is contained in the following sources published by Gale Research: *Contemporary Authors,* **Vols. 77-80;** *Contemporary Literary Criticism,* **Vols. 14, 29, 51; and** *Dictionary of Literary Biography,* **Vol. 60.**

Adrienne Rich

An Atlas of the Difficult World: Poems, 1988-1991

Awards: The Lenore Marshall/*Nation* Poetry Prize and the Los Angeles Times Book Award

(Full name Adrienne Cecile Rich) Born in 1929, Rich is an American poet, essayist, and critic.

For further information on Rich's life and career, see *CLC,* Volumes 3, 6, 7, 11, 18, 36, and 73.

INTRODUCTION

An Atlas of the Difficult World: Poems, 1988-1991 has been praised for its insightful exploration of oppression, violence, and injustice in the twentieth century. Focusing on such issues as poverty, the Persian Gulf war, and the exploitation of minorities and women, Rich creates a moral and spiritual montage of the United States. In the thirteen-poem sequence "An Atlas of the Difficult World," which comprises the first half of the collection, Rich examines the complexity of modern existence through vignettes in which people confront personal problems and widespread hardship. Rich writes: "Here is a map of our country: / here is the Sea of Indifference, glazed with salt / This is the haunted river flowing from brow to groin / we dare not taste its water / This is the desert where missiles are planted like corms / This is the breadbasket of foreclosed farms / . . . I promised to show you a map you say but this is a mural / then yes let it be these are small distinctions / where do we see it from is the question." In another section of this sequence, she comments on the American people's need for introspection and reform: "A patriot is not a weapon. A patriot is one who wrestles for the soul of her country. . . . / A patriot is a citizen trying to wake." Poems in the second half of *An Atlas of the Difficult World* deal with similar themes, but are generally considered more autobiographical and allude to Rich's commitment to feminism, her Jewish heritage, and the suicide of her children's father. Rich's use of personal experience, first-person narratives, and dogmatic language has prompted critics to compare *An Atlas of the Difficult World* to the works of Emily Dickinson and Walt Whitman. Dick Allen has observed: "Rich's book is truly a small atlas; but it is also the mature poetry of a writer who knows her own power, who speaks in the passionate, ambitious blending of the personal and the universal forever present in major work. She will be read and studied for centuries to come."

PRINCIPAL WORKS

A Change of Worlds   (poetry)   1951

The Diamond Cutters, and Other Poems   (poetry)   1955

Snapshots of a Daughter-in-Law: Poems, 1954-1962   (poetry)   1963; also published as *Snapshots of a Daughter-in-Law: Poems, 1954-1962* [revised edition], 1983

Necessities of Life: Poems, 1962-1965   (poetry)   1966

Selected Poems   (poetry)   1967

Leaflets: Poems, 1965-1968   (poetry)   1969

The Will to Change: Poems, 1968-1970   (poetry)   1971

Diving into the Wreck: Poems, 1971-1972   (poetry)   1973

Poems: Selected and New, 1950-1974   (poetry)   1975

Of Woman Born: Motherhood as Experience and Institution   (essays)   1976

*The Dream of a Common Language: Poems, 1974-1977   (poetry)   1978

On Lies, Secrets, and Silence: Selected Prose, 1966-1978   (essays)   1979

A Wild Patience Has Taken Me This Far: Poems, 1978-1981 (poetry) 1981

The Fact of a Doorframe: Poems Selected and New, 1950-1984 (poetry) 1984

Blood, Bread, and Poetry: Selected Prose, 1979-1985 (essays) 1986

†*Your Native Land, Your Life* (poetry) 1986

Time's Power: Poems, 1985-1988 (poetry) 1989

An Atlas of the Difficult World: Poems, 1988-1991 (poetry) 1991

*This work includes *Twenty-One Love Poems,* which was published separately in 1976.

†This work includes the chapbook *Sources,* which was published separately in 1983.

CRITICISM

Gertrude Reif Hughes (review date December 1991)

[*In the following essay, Hughes favorably assesses* An Atlas of the Difficult World *and views it as an extension of Rich's earlier works.*]

"No one has imagined us," declares a well-known line in Adrienne Rich's *Twenty-One Love Poems* (1976). But Rich herself has been doing just that for decades, whether you take "us" as the lesbians the line refers to, or as women more generally. At least a generation of women—mostly white, relatively privileged, both heterosexual and homosexual, and mostly now thirtysomething and up—have been finding their pleasures, hardships and quandaries spoken in Adrienne Rich's work. Her new book of poems, *An Atlas of the Difficult World,* continues the tradition. A marvelous achievement in its own right and a worthy addition to her *oeuvre,* it will inspire new readers and fulfill the expectations of long-time admirers.

The book has two parts. The first consists of the long, brilliant title work, a thirteen-poem "atlas" which identifies specific hardships of the "difficult world" and, most significantly, explores their interconnectedness. Vigilance is Rich's theme and posture in the first half of the collection, memory in the second. The book as a whole continues the witnessing that has been her project at least since 1963, when she published *Snapshots of a Daughter-in-Law,* and arguably since 1951, when she began her distinguished career. She announces as much:

> These are not the roads
> you knew me by. But the woman . . .
> watching
> for life and death, is the same.

Because Rich's work is so openly autobiographical, many of her readers greet each new book like a letter bringing the latest news of her. Before the eyes of her public, she evolved from woman of privilege, living in traditional domesticity with promising young husband and three small children, to radicalized activist who redefined both her sexual and political identities. With each new book, she lets her readers see her grieve losses, learn hard lessons, experience physical pain, as she develops new ways to maintain her vigilance.

West Coast locales now replace the East Coast settings familiar from earlier work, but the woman who speaks these new poems still stands watch over the interplay of privilege, oppression and endurance. The opening poem tells about a California fruit picker with "strawberry blood on the wrist / Malathion in the throat," who labors in a field where crop dusters spray the crops while, in a nearby hospital, premature babies are "slipping from unsafe wombs." Repeatedly in this volume, Rich registers such insidious connections: between poverty and exploitation; between battered wives and swaggering boys; how military conventions and the institutionalized violence of civilian life cooperate; and how heedless entitlement of class or gender permits the starving of schoolchildren.

Both old readers and new ones will find Rich's characteristic themes and gestures here: the long, evocative lists; the insistence on the urgency of the present tense; the lesbian love poetry, erotic and sober at the same time; the audacious mix and original range of her topics.

Though they are rare, familiar lapses reappear too. Rich's effort not to deny pain sometimes sounds martyred in a self-congratulatory way. In [the short sequence] "Two Arts," for example, a sculptor has had to redo her night's work to make it acceptable "to the arts administrator / and the council of patrons / who could never take [the statue's] measure." One is supposed to share the sculptor's anger at having to please philistine bureaucrats, but to me she sounds self-righteous. Occasionally, too, a scene intended as an epitome will come off as a stereotype. In a section of the long [sequence] "Eastern War Time," which collects various horrors undergone by Jews and Palestinians of the twentieth century, an Anne Frank surrogate whose menses have been arrested by concentration camp life remembers her aborted youth as she faces death on the operating table of a "famous doctor" given to playing "string quartets with his staff in the laboratory." Such worn scraps so quickly assembled baffle horror; they become a sort of grotesque atrocity quilt.

Other moments in the poem, however, succeed precisely because of their familiarity. For example, the double bind of Jewish parents in anti-Semitic surroundings who will wound their child equally whether they tell the truth or deny it, for "how do you say *unfold my flower, shine, my star / and we are hated, being what we are?*"

Rich's readers can recall whole room-fulls of women she made familiar. Some were already famous, like Marie Curie. Most were nameless and waiting to be named: lesbian lovers, fuming daughters-in-law, terrorized wives, estranged sisters, mourning widows, experimental poets. In this volume crazed old Marghanita, still capable of kindness, helps a dying neighbor whom everyone else has abandoned; and Olivia, a white South African student activist, learns too late that she cannot evade involvement by trying to remain "above / loyalty, love and all that trash / higher than power and its field of force."

Readers can also recall a gallery of emblematic figures who could be seen as portraits of the poet, like the "thinking woman [who] sleeps with monsters" from **"Snapshots of a Daughter-in-Law"** (1958-60) or the deep-sea diver from **"Diving Into the Wreck"** (1972). From among several possibilities in *An Atlas of the Difficult World,* I would choose the "woman of sixty" from "Eastern War Time" as the latest addition to the gallery. Like the others, she wants not only to know but to challenge. With "a century slipping from her shoulders" (like a shawl? a yoke?), the woman has devoted her life to knowing; and when she dies, her skeleton will show that knowledge has actually "entered her connective tissue" and "dissolved her cartilage." But perhaps, the poem continues, it was not knowledge; maybe it was "a dangerous questioning."

Exactly. Rich asks dangerous questions. Like her 60-year-old woman, Rich, who was born in 1929, searches "armed streets / for the end of degradation," particularly where psychological and social degradation intersect. She understood early the politics of loneliness—for example, how isolation can prevent the disempowered from finding one another and can rationalize behaviors of the empowered that are destructive both to others and to themselves. In a poem from the "Atlas" sequence, she tells a lonely white man, "You grieve in loneliness, and if I understand you fuck in loneliness." She considers the possibility that this may be "a white man's madness" and then, resisting the temptation to be distracted by compassion, decides to pursue the implications of her insight: "I honor your truth and refuse to leave it at that."

In the volume's more autobiographical second half, Rich directs her dangerous questions at herself, asking, "What does it mean to say *I have survived* / until you take the mirrors and turn them outward / and read your own face in their outraged light?" Since **Sources** (1983), Rich has increasingly explored the implications of her situation as an assimilated half-Jew who grew up amid privilege in safe, if anti-Semitic, America while in another country Jews by the millions were being corralled and slaughtered. A number of poems in the collection work with this material. In **"1948: Jews"** Rich recalls being away at college and eagerly tearing open a letter from her non-Jewish mother only to read the admonition not to *"get taken up by any clique / trying to claim you."* Sickened by the veiled anti-Semitism of her mother's warning, the daughter knows its unstated corollary: *"Marry out, like your father."*

Memory plays an important role in this collection, but it does not have power to absolve. In the final section of the "Eastern War Time" sequence, Memory explicitly disclaims redemptive power. "Want to do right? Don't count on me," she says. "I am standing here in your poem unsatisfied / lifting my smoky mirror." By imagining Memory this way, Rich denies herself the consolations of exorcism. She chooses to remain disturbed.

Though memory won't absolve her of the deaths she didn't suffer by growing up in safety, it does let her memorialize the father of her children in a **"Tattered Kaddish,"**

composed in 1989, just before the twentieth anniversary of his suicide. In another poem she affectionately recalls the sound of his speech:

> that voice overcast like klezmer with
> echoes, uneven, edged,
> torn, Brooklyn street crowding
> Harvard Yard
> —I'd have known any syllable
> anywhere.

Rich won't settle for peace and she won't settle for bitterness either.

Her new book shows us the poet as "Atlas" shouldering a burdensome world, and provides a guide to the difficulties it describes. I predict that we will be consulting this "Atlas" for years, learning how "the difficult world" is not so much harsh as unsimple. Rich wants to awaken us to the world's complexities, not just its pain. Reading her, we can keep asking the questions she poses in the title poem: "Where are we moored? / What are the bindings? / What behooves us?"

Gertrude Reif Hughes, "Eternal Vigilance," in The Women's Review of Books, *Vol. IX, No. 3, December, 1991, p. 11.*

An excerpt from "Through Corralitos under Rolls of Cloud"

> If you know who died in that bed, do you know
> who has survived? If you say, *she was weaker,*
> *held life less dear, expected others*
> *to fight for her* if pride lets you name her
> *victim* and the one who got up and threw
> the windows open, stripped the bed, *survivor*
> —what have you said, what do you know
> of the survivor when you know her only in oppo-
>   sition to the lost?
> What does it mean to say *I have survived*
> until you take the mirrors and turn them out-
>   ward
> and read your own face in their outraged light?

Adrienne Rich, in her An Atlas of the Difficult World: Poems, 1988-1991, *W. W. Norton & Co., 1991.*

Michèle Roberts   (review date 14 February 1992)

[*Roberts is an English novelist, poet, critic, and short story writer who is best known for fiction featuring strong-willed female protagonists who rebel against society's male-imposed values. In the following excerpt, she offers a negative review of* An Atlas of the Difficult World.]

Displaced Martians might write snappy imagistic postcards home; [in *An Atlas of the Difficult World: Poems, 1988-1991*] Adrienne Rich, moving from Vermont to California, despatches a long-winded dirge. The poem opens with Rich "listening for something / —a woman's voice, a man's voice or / voice of the freeway, night after night, metal streaming downcoast / past eucalyptus, cypress, ag-ribusiness empires."

The narrator of this elegy for a corrupt America dares take pleasure neither in landscape nor in language, diving straight into familiar Rich territory of doom and gloom: "gurr of small planes / dusting the strawberries . . . / Malathion in the throat, communion, / the hospital at the edge of the fields, / prematures slipping from unsafe wombs, / the labor and delivery nurse on her break watching / planes dusting rows of pickers." I'd listen to Rich's breast-beating and tub-thumping more easily if she occasionally wrote with passion or joy, but the best she can offer is squirm-inducing sentimentality: "In the writing workshop a young man's tears / wet the frugal beard he's grown to go with his poems / . . . In the classroom / eight-year-old faces are grey / the teacher knows which children / have not broken fast that day, / remembers the Black Panthers spooning cereal."

She hammers it all home with lists: "this is the desert where missiles are planted like corms / This is the bread-basket of foreclosed farms / This is the birthplace of the rockabilly boy / This is the cemetery of the poor / who died for democracy . . . / This is the capital of money and dolor."

So it goes on: self-righteous, pompous, humourless, controlling, dull. Rich's fans claim her work evinces a Whit-manesque kinship with all beings. I read it as imperialist: she's always speaking for the silent masses, a tourist of oppression, as she flits from India to Haworth to Wounded Knee. She's seen it all! Here she is discovering Ireland:

> Poetry
> in the workhouse, laying of the rails, a potato
>   splattering oven walls
> poetry of cursing and silence, bitter and deep,
>   shallow and drunken
> poetry of priest-talk, of IRA-talk, kitchen talk,
>   dream-talk, tongues despised
> in cities where in a mere fifty years language has
>   rotted to jargon, *lingua franca* of inclusion
> from turns of speech ancient as the potato.

Rich-talk isn't jargon? Certainly it's not poetry.

Michèle Roberts, "Dirges and Dreams," in New Statesman & Society, *Vol. 5, No. 189, February 14, 1992, p. 41.*

Lawrence Joseph (review date 20 April 1992)

[*In the following excerpt, Lawrence discusses* An Atlas of the Difficult World *as a statement of Rich's aesthetic and political beliefs and as a modernist's examination of social realities.*]

Adrienne Rich's contemporaneity is more overt. Acutely aware of moral and social effects, blessed with an extremely fine critical intelligence, Rich since the early 1960s has continually asserted her decision to write poetry that runs counter to the poetic language of a certain Romantic tradition that is self-centered and noncritical—an outmoded poetic language she sees mirrored in a patriarchal and imperial United States. From her earliest work, Rich has

been aware of poetry as a form of thought (for example, the title poem of her second book, *The Diamond Cutters,* is about the act of creating a work of art). In the 1960s, Rich's poetry became aware of its critical powers: Poetry becomes the means through which forms of inhuman power can be exposed. Needless to say, Rich's aesthetic is tied into her political sensibility. She defines herself as a socialist and a feminist, and these identities provide her with a strong, doctrinal language. Yet Rich remains unique in the ways in which she applies her political insights to the practice of Modernist poetry. "Socially aware" poets sometimes settle for a poetry of worked-over diction and a sloppiness of sentiment indistinguishable from the second-rate nineteenth-century versifiers. But Rich's work never reflects a primary concern with herself, nor is it ever sentimental. Although she pulls from her own experience, she's not interested in writing autobiography; though her language sometimes loses its edge and lapses into what appears to be dogma, its critical impulse persists. Rich looks at herself and her subject matter hard, pushing out the complexities of human behavior through an "I" who is essentially functional, although at the same time personal and social. For Rich, the poet inside a wrecked society must will an imagined common language to get to human love, which is for her the central subject of any personal or social order. A poetry of ideological commitment must enter the heart and mind, become as real as one's body, as vital as life itself—that's what makes it poetry. In Stevens's terms, Rich's subject is above all the poetry of contemporary political economy and morality. Her emphasis on the autonomy of art engenders an irony akin to Bertolt Brecht's. Her poetry's passionate turning back into language itself—within a society that overwhelms it with its terrors—gives Rich's work undeniable power.

> **Rich's subject is above all the poetry of contemporary political economy and morality. Her emphasis on the autonomy of art engenders an irony akin to Bertolt Brecht's. Her poetry's passionate turning back into language itself—within a society that overwhelms it with its terrors—gives Rich's work undeniable power.**
>
> **—Lawrence Joseph**

An Atlas of the Difficult World possesses this power throughout. The book's title picks up a recurrent motif in Rich's work ("The words are maps," she wrote in her famous 1972 poem **"Diving Into the Wreck"**): the creation of a cartography as a metaphor for poetic language. The mapping-out is, in the first instance, an aesthetic statement. Then, Rich projects—as she always does—her territory. Whereas her last two books, *Your Native Land, Your Life* and *Time's Power: Poems 1985-1988,* took on, respectively, the relationship between poetry and the body, and poetry and time, *An Atlas* chooses as its focal point "the *difficult* world"—as opposed to other "worlds" the poet may have chosen.

The breadth of the undertaking allows Rich to be especially expansive. The book has two parts. Part one is the title poem, comprising thirteen sections. To paraphrase what Rich has said of Elizabeth Bishop's poetry, the poem critically and consciously explores marginality, power, and powerlessness, with great beauty and sensuousness and characteristic clarity as well. "I am stuck to earth," the poet says, as she reveals worlds of hatred, suffering and violence that try our senses of light and darkness, beauty and love. The writing is graceful and gorgeous:

> Within two miles of the Pacific
>   rounding
> this long bay, sheening the light for miles
> inland, floating its fog through red-
>   wood rifts and over strawberry and artichoke
>   fields, its
>   bottomless mind
> returning always to the same rocks, the
>   same cliffs, with
> ever-changing words, always the same
>   language
>   —this is where I live now.

It is also generous—in the spirit of Walt Whitman and one of his most important legatees, Muriel Rukeyser. Through to the final section, the poem embodies its fundamental issue—"What homage will be paid to beauty / that insists on speaking truth, knows the two are not always the same, / beauty that won't deny, is itself an eye, will not rest under contemplation?"

The difficult relationship between beauty and truth in a world that necessitates resistance continues into the book's second part. Children and adults oppressed by war, poverty, deprivation, racism and moral failures are formed by language that skillfully moves emotional tones. One of the book's most heart-rending poems, **"Tattered Kaddish,"** is spoken on behalf of "all suicides":

> Praise to life though ones we knew and
>   loved
> loved it badly, too well, and not enough
>
>   Praise to life though it tightened
> like a knot
>   on the hearts of ones we thought
> we knew loved us

Each poem presents "the great question" asked by the "philosopher of oppression, theorist / of the victories of force," Simone Weil, *What are you going through?"*—purposely speaking "from the marrow of our bones." The last poem, **"Final Notations,"** a kind of epilogue, could also be the book's prologue. The poem's two pronouns, "it" and "you," overlap, explode and include the multitude of ideas, thoughts and realities that people the book. But you have to read both pronouns, first of all, as representing the act of poetry itself, that which most forcefully opens up for us the depths of the difficult world: "it will not be simple, it will not be long"; "It will take all your flesh, it will not be simple"; "you are taking parts of us into places never planned / you are going far away with pieces of our lives"; "it will be short, it will take all your breath / it will not be simple, it will become your will." (pp. 532-33)

Lawrence Joseph, "The Real Thing," in The Nation, *New York, Vol. 254, No. 15, April 20, 1992, pp. 531-33.*

Matthew Rothschild   (review date May 1992)

[*Rothschild is the publisher of* The Progressive. *In the following essay, he provides a laudatory review of* An Atlas of the Difficult World, *finding it a provocative examination of the political and social injustices of twentieth-century America.*]

Adrienne Rich is one of the great pioneers of contemporary poetry, and her power, skill, and vision reach an apotheosis in her latest work, **An Atlas of the Difficult World.**

Rich here becomes a sort of late Twentieth Century Walt Whitman or W. H. Auden, surveying the country and its condition. What she finds, especially in the extraordinary title poem which spans thirteen parts, is a country in collapse.

"Here is a map of our country," she writes, describing "the desert where missiles are planted like corms," "the breadbasket of foreclosed farms," and other incongruous landmarks.

Written in 1990 and 1991, this poem captures the dilemma of being a true patriot in George Bush's interventionist America. "Flags are blossoming now where little is blossoming," she says, "and I am bent on fathoming what it means to love my country."

In a clear reference to the Persian Gulf war, Rich declares that "a patriot is not a weapon. A patriot is one who wrestles for the soul of her country. . . . A patriot is a citizen trying to wake from the burnt-out dream of innocence."

She recognizes that the jingoism of Americans supporting the Persian Gulf war reflects widespread hurt across the countryside. "Every flag that flies today is a cry of pain," she writes.

Rich has no illusions about America's past. "Catch if you can your country's moment," she advises, mentioning "Appomattox, Wounded Knee, Los Alamos, Selma, the last airlift from Saigon," and adding subsequent references to San Quentin, Soledad, and Alcatraz.

Violence against women is one of the landmarks Rich points out. "I don't want to hear how he beat her after the earthquake," she writes, painting a horrifying yet quotidian scene of domestic abuse. "I don't want to know wreckage, dreck, and waste, but these are the materials," Rich says, refusing to avert her eyes.

She returns to this theme later in the poem when she recounts how a man shot two lesbians camping along the Appalachian Trail in 1988. "I don't want to know how he tracked them. . . . I don't want to know but this is not a bad dream of mine these are the materials."

Part of the waste Rich rails against is pollution. In the opening stanza of the poem, a plane sprays Malathion on a field of strawberry pickers. Driving across country from Vermont to her new home in California, she sees waste that "darkens the states to their strict borders, flushes down borderless streams, leaches from lakes to the curdled foam down by the riverside."

At times Rich seems to fall fully into despair, as when she writes: "The watcher's eye put out, hands of the builder severed, brain of the maker starved / those who could bind, join, reweave, cohere, replenish / now at risk in this segregate republic."

For redemption, Rich turns to nature. Right after she describes the destruction around her, she observes the natural world rescuing it: "the slow lift of the moon's belly / over wreckage, dreck, and waste, wild treefrogs calling in / another season, light and music still pouring over / our fissured cracked terrain." Rich also extols work, beauty, truth, resistance, mercy, and love, paying homage to her companion for her "woman's hands turning the wheel or working with shears."

The "Atlas" poem, panoramic yet personal, political yet intimate, is one of the most compelling works of recent years.

Rich's dozen other poems tend to be quieter but finely rendered, of a kind with her previously published work. In **"Tattered Kaddish,"** Rich gives a moving eulogy for a nineteen-year-old who committed suicide. In **"Olivia,"** she denounces a South African who infiltrated the anti-apartheid movement. Throughout, Rich returns to some of her traditional themes: being Jewish after the Holocaust and during the *intifada,* the strength of women, the importance of memory, the imminence of death. In [the sequence] "Eastern War Time," itself ten parts, Rich builds to the kind of power that characterizes her "Atlas" poem.

Adrienne Rich is our nation's true poet laureate, and her latest work rewards and rewards. (pp. 40-2)

> *Matthew Rothschild, "A Patriot Wrestling," in* The Progressive, *Vol. 56, No. 5, May, 1992, pp. 40-2.*

Rita Signorelli-Pappas   (review date Summer 1992)

[*In the following excerpt, poet Signorelli-Pappas offers a favorable review of* An Atlas of the Difficult World.]

"I have the odd feeling she is speaking for me," says Doris Grumbach of Adrienne Rich's poetry. Instantly, most of us would agree. In book after book since the 1960s, Rich has given us an abundance of elegantly crafted poems that articulate with candor, precision, and a rare visionary beauty what it is to be women, both personally and politically. She is still speaking to us in her thirteenth book of poems, *An Atlas of the Difficult World,* which offers some of the most brilliant work of her distinguished poetic career.

Like a traveler sent ahead on an exploratory journey, Rich leaves us her watchful, hard won poems as markings along the way. Throughout her work, there has always been a strong sense of vigilance figured in images that lead, orient, or direct—a map, a compass, or an atlas. In the long,

moving title poem that composes the book's first part, Rich announces her intention of defining and refiguring "the soul" of our country. Acting as guide, she confidently traces the contours of both our national landscape and ethos: "Here is a map of our country: / here is the Sea of Indifference. . . . This is the cemetery of the poor / who died for democracy." The sense of intimate camaraderie that informs this remarkable poem rises from Rich's decision to address the reader directly, which creates the illusion of personal contact with the speaker in a conversation by turns casual and urgent, individualistic and cosmic. Slowly, the map that she has unrolled vivifies before our eyes to become a mural:

> I promised to show you a map you say but this
> is a mural
> then yes let it be these are small distinctions
> where do we see it from is the question.

Rich's artistic range is nothing short of magnificent. Equally deft with either long or short poems, she delicately paces a lengthy work like "Atlas" with an exquisite sensitivity to reader response. Images like the haunting spider that unify the third section first pulse, then are elaborated with greater particularity until finally they burst in full

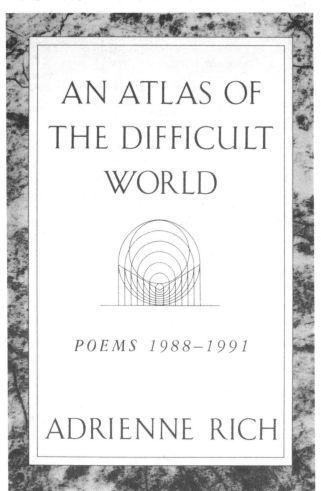

metaphoric radiance. The final lines of this section display the resonant culmination of this technique:

> she will use everything,
> nothing comes without
> labor, she is working so
> hard and I know
> nothing all winter can
> enter this house or this
> web, not all labor
> ends in sweetness
> But how do I know what
> she needs? Maybe simply
> to spin herself a house
> within a house, on her own
> terms
> in cold, in silence.

Fast-moving sections that have a more crowded, panoramic sweep are subtly alternated with ones like this to create sanctuaries of reflective solitude or elegiac pause.

The book's second part also presents shapely, often autobiographical work, introducing subjects that include the perils of artistic compromise; solace for a suffering friend ("we write from the marrow of our bones"); portraits of women in political or self-imposed exiles; and the Holocaust. As in Part I, memory's "smoky mirror" prevails. Two particularly powerful poems are the incantatory elegy for the suicide, **"Tattered Kaddish,"** and the hypnotic endpiece, **"Final Notations,"** which gives unforgettable instructions in the art of achieving a dignified end:

> it will not be simple, it will not be long
> it will take little time, it will take all your
> thought
> it will take all your heart, it will take all your
> breath
> it will be short, it will not be simple

Rich is ever her own most difficult taskmaster as she wrestles with and imagines strategies for surviving a life that only deepens in complexity with the passing years. Her readership will widen with the publication of this stunning collection. Here are verses that can be admired, trusted, and passed like bread between both men and women for generations to come. (pp. 62-3)

Rita Signorelli-Pappas, "Poets Practiced and Premiering," in Belles Lettres: A Review of Books by Women, *Vol. 7, No. 4, Summer, 1992, pp. 62-5.*

Dick Allen   (review date Summer 1992)

[*Allen is an American poet, editor, critic, and educator. In the following excerpt, he provides a positive assessment of* An Atlas of the Difficult World, *comparing Rich's style to that of poet Walt Whitman.*]

Adrienne Rich's ambitious new book [*An Atlas of the Difficult World: Poems, 1988-1991*] is flat out magnificent, its long title sequence an equal companion to Whitman's "Song of Myself." I would never have dreamed such an absorption of Whitman's style could have been made and even if made, I would not have expected it to be so deeply moving, so individualized, that its style acts more as a ful-

fillment, a complement we didn't know we had missed, than a reflection or imitation. In the thirteen-part title sequence, Rich takes us, as did Whitman, confidently through our world, blending thoughts, observations, vignettes, despairs and identifications with the men and women of the troubled planet, our troubled times. Here are "prematures slipping from unsafe wombs," "the young who are counted out," the countless lonely, "cities where in a mere fifty years language has rotted to jargon," "Waste. Waste," "the rural working poor," and

> some busy constructing enclosures, bunkers, to
>   escape the common fate
> some trying to revive dead statues to lead us,
>   breathing their breath against marble
>   lips
> some who try to teach the moment, some who
>   preach the moment
> some who aggrandize, some who diminish them-
>   selves in the face of half-grasped events
> —power and powerlessness run amuck, a tape
>   reeling backward in jeering, screeching
>   syllables—
> some for whom war is new, others for whom it
>   merely continues the old paroxysms of
>   time
> some marching for peace who for twenty years
>   did not march for justice . . .

There are touches of "Howl" and Eliot's "The Wasteland" and "Four Quartets" added to the Whitmanesque base; there are mournings of lost promises, especially those of the sixties; there is a love of the land, "old ranches, leaning seaward, lowroofed spreads between rocks / small canyons running through pitched hillsides / liveoaks twisted on steepness." Throughout, Rich drives inland, coming to terms with her own mortality, identifies, meditates on history, evil, Nature, and the poet's task. She has composed a love poem to men and women and to her nation.

The title poem is nearly equaled in quality by the poems in the book's second section, including sensual poems like **"That Mouth,"** the very moving sequence of "Eastern War Time" ("searching armed streets / for the end of degradation"), the "Praise to life" of **"Tattered Kaddish,"** meditations on victims and survivors, and on art, and at last the lovely perfection of **"Final Notations."** Rich's book is truly a small atlas; but it is also the mature poetry of a writer who knows her own power, who speaks in the passionate, ambitious blending of the personal and the universal forever present in major work. She will be read and studied for centuries to come. (pp. 329-30)

Dick Allen, "Bad, Better, Best," in The Hudson Review, *Vol. XLV, No. 2, Summer, 1992, pp. 319-30.*

Sam Hamill   (essay date July-August 1992)

[*Hamill is a poet, translator, editor, and educator. In the following excerpt, he examines how Rich uses imagery and metaphor to convey the psychological and spiritual significance of everyday experiences.*]

Re-vision—the act of looking back, of seeing

with fresh eyes, of entering an old text from a new critical direction—is for us more than a chapter in cultural history: it is an act of survival. Until we can understand the assumptions in which we are drenched we cannot know ourselves. . . . I feel in the work of the men whose poetry I read today a deep pessimism and fatalistic grief; and I wonder if it isn't the masculine side of what women have experienced, the price of masculine dominance.

I first read Adrienne Rich's comments in a fragment from the essay **"When We Dead Awaken"** more than fifteen years ago in a standard college anthology containing twenty-three male and three female poets. With the growth of publishers like Alicejames, Beacon, Seal Press, and other independents, and with the influence of feminist studies within the academy and without, poetry and criticism written by women has flourished over the last two decades as never before.

In the complete essay (in *On Lies, Secrets and Silence*), Rich also says,

> Now, to be maternally with small children all day in the old way, to be with a man in the old way of marriage, requires a holding-back, a putting-aside of that imaginative activity, and demands instead a kind of conservatism. I want to make it clear that I am *not* saying that in order to write well, or think well, it is necessary to become unavailable to others, or to become a devouring ego. This has been the myth of the masculine artist and thinker; and I do not accept it. But to be a female human being trying to fulfill traditional female functions in a traditional way *is* in direct conflict with the subversive function of the imagination. The word traditional is important here. There must be ways, and we will be finding out more and more about them, in which the energy of creation and the energy of relation can be united. . . .

Rich was calling for, searching for—and in fact had already established within her own poetry—a poetics of the mundane, a poetics of daily political, social, moral, and imaginative life in which Woman is depicted neither as abstract mystery personified nor as tragic victimized heroine, neither as temptress nor as redemptress, but as fully human, in short, a poetry of "real life." In a subsequent collection of essays (*Blood, Bread, and Poetry*), she says, "The critique of language needs to come not just from women who define themselves as writers but from women who will test the work against their experience—who, like Woolf's 'common reader,' are interested in literature as a key to life, not an escape from it." Critics who test work against personal experience and who turn to poetry—to paraphrase Robert Duncan—for evidence of the real are rare in either gender.

If the traditional roles of mother and father, wife and husband, become intolerable, destructive constraints, what happens to marriage as an institution, what happens to "the traditional family" as most of us imagine it? First of all, the "traditional family" is largely a product of a nostalgic imagination. The first shelter for battered women opened its doors in 1974. Domestic violence is undoubted-

ly less of a problem now than in the past simply because it is out of the closet and there are places for people to turn for help for the first time. In the traditional family, violence was power. And if the traditional American family of, say, the fifties, held to such high moral values, how do we account for our political behavior over the past forty years of almost continuous murder abroad and social stratification within? Traditional family values kept the homosexual community in the closet, society segregated, the world supplied with arms, and the same wealthy white males in power.

When I turn back to the poetry of the sixties, seventies, and eighties, I suddenly realize that most of the male poets who wrote those anthology poems of domestic life and love are no longer with the same partners—they are divorced, separated, exiled in some way or another, often removed even to the margins of their own emotions, and I begin to see in poetry written by men a deep pessimism, a mounting sense of grief amplified, compounded in part, by the failure of institutions like traditional marriage.

Much of the poetry of the last quarter-century has explored through personal detail the very questions Rich raises. It has done so with varying degrees of success, but there is almost nothing else like it in the annals of verse, this sudden opening into a polyphony—cultural, ethnic, philosophic—of voices, nearly each of which is dominated by the personal mode, a poetry of confession and self-revelation in almost relentless pursuit of personal redemption. Adrienne Rich—along with Robin Morgan, Carolyn Kizer, Susan Griffin, Olga Broumas, Judy Grahn, and others—brings urgent daily practice to the forefront. Over the past three decades, her stubborn truthfulness, her private politics and public passions, and her unwavering quest for a poetry of authentic experience have made her one of the essential poets of our time. I have returned to her poems over those years as one turns to a revered but critical teacher: as a constant source of personal transformation.

Rich's new book, *An Atlas of the Difficult World,* is yet another departure, a major accomplishment by any reasonable standard. The title poem is "a map of our country" that extends her already impressive sweep of understanding, providing a glimpse into her own self-transformations:

> A dark woman, head bent, listening for something
> —a woman's voice, a man's voice or
> voice of the freeway, night after night, . . .
> . . . If you had known me
> once, you'd still know me now though in a different
> light and life. This is no place you ever knew me.
> But it would not surprise you
> to find me here, walking fog, the sweep of the great ocean
> eluding me, even the curve of the bay, because as always
> I fix on the land. I am stuck to earth. What I love here
> is old ranches, leaning seaward, lowroofed spreads between rocks

small canyons running through pitched
    hillsides . . .
        These are not the roads
you knew me by. But the woman driving, walk-
    ing, watching
for life and death, is the same.

This first of thirteen movements sets the stage. The tone
is conversational, almost casual, meditative. The scene itself could have been lifted from Steinbeck. Neither poet
nor landscape is unfamiliar territory, yet Rich brings a
fresh perspective. She moves quickly to a "Sea of Indifference, glazed with salt" and

    . . . the desert where missiles are planted like
        corms . . .
        suburbs of acquiescence . . .
    whose children are drifting blind alleys pent
    between coiled rolls of razor wire
    I promised to show you a map you say but this
        is a mural
    then yes let it be these are small distinctions
    where do we see it from is the question

Her canvas is large, her initial gestures sweeping. I love
her use of corm—a *corm* being the bulb of a plant like a
crocus, an image presenting a nearly perfect counterbal-
ance to the severity of its subject, the corm so graciously
optimistic in its utter contrast with the deep pessimism of
nuclear weapons.

Aristotle says metaphor represents the poet's greatest attributes and is the one thing that cannot be learned from
others, and here as so often elsewhere Rich demonstrates
her genius for what Aristotle called "intuitive perspective." She sees within the "breadbasket of foreclosed
farms" many ghosts, she hears the reverberations of many
public lies. Continuing her meditation on a night porch in
New England, she notes,

    . . . That wind has changed, though still from
        the south
    it's blowing up hard now, no longer close to
        earth but driving high
    into the crowns of the maples, into my face
    almost slamming the stormdoor into me. But it's
        warm,
    pneumonia wind, death of innocence wind, un-
        winding wind,
    time-hurtling wind. And it has a voice in the
        house. I hear
    conversations that can't be happening, over-
        heard in the bedrooms
    and I'm not talking about ghosts. The ghosts are
        here of course but they
            speak plainly
    —haven't I offered food and wine, listened well
        for them all these years,
    not only those known in life but those before our
        time
    of self-deception, our intricate losing game of in-
        nocence long overdue?

She notes a spider spinning its web beside her, and responds:

    . . . she will use everything,
            nothing comes without labor, she is
        working so

    hard and I know
nothing all winter can enter this house or this
    web, not all labor
        ends in sweetness.
But how do I know what she needs? Maybe sim-
    ply
to spin herself a house within a house, on her
    own terms
in cold, in silence.

Like the spider, Rich weaves a world within a world, but
unlike the spider, must overcome the silence, must speak
clearly to define her struggle. She must define her own
terms. She surveys a continental terrain composed of
junked cars, truckstops, chain-link fences, and a poisoned
watershed:

    Waste. Waste. The watcher's eye put out, hands
        of the
            builder severed, brain of the maker
        starved
    those who could bind, join, reweave, cohere, re-
        plenish
    now at risk in this segregate republic
    locked away out of sight and hearing, out of
        mind, shunted aside
    those needed to teach, advise, persuade, weigh
        arguments
    those urgently needed for the work of perception
    work of the poet, the astronomer, the historian,
        the architect of new streets
    work of the speaker who also listens
    meticulous delicate work of reaching the heart
        of the desperate woman, the

Adrienne Rich

*Caricature drawing of Rich, by David Levine. Reprinted with per-
mission from* The New York Review of Books. *Copyright (c) 1991
Nyrev, Inc.*

desperate man
—never-to-be-finished, still unbegun work of re-
    pair—it cannot be done
            without them
and where are they now?

The tone and imagery are reminiscent of Ezra Pound's
early poem of exile, "The Rest." This poem also brings to
mind the pedagogy of Pound on the nature and function
of metaphor: the use of concrete imagery to convey the
meaning of immaterial relations—his famous misunderstanding of Aristotle's *Poetics*.

Rich juxtaposes image with image, often building lists like
Whitman's—carried by the phrasing, the incantatory
music of her speaking voice. Her deep sense of responsibility and encompassing vision are Whitmanesque in scope.
She is, she says, "bent on fathoming what it means to love
my country." In contrast with the poets, teachers, and
weavers exiled and silenced in the above passage, she presents an indelible image of an archetypal contemporary
male, a man struck dumb, numbed by the circumstances
of his life.

On this earth, in this life, as I read your story,
    you're lonely.
Lonely in the bar, on the shore of the coastal
    river
with your best friend, his wife, and your wife,
    fishing
lonely in the prairie classroom with all the stu-
    dents who love you. You know
        some ghosts
come everywhere with you yet leave them unad-
    dressed
for years. You spend weeks in a house
with a drunk, you sober, whom you love, feeling
    lonely.
You grieve in loneliness, and if I understand you
    fuck in loneliness.

I wonder if this is a white man's madness. / . . .

Rich extends her meditation to include the word *soledad*,
loneliness or solitary retreat, bringing into play a small
chapel, *La Nuestra Senora de la Soledad* and the California prison made infamous during Black Power movement
days. She achieves a compassionate tone toward troubled
men that is very refreshing and deeply moving:

                From eighteen to twenty-eight of his
    years
a young man schools himself, argues,
debates, trains, lectures to himself,
teaches himself Swahili, Spanish, learns
five new words of English every day,
chainsmokes, reads, writes letters.
In this college of force he wrestles bitterness,
self-hatred, sexual anger, cures his own nature.
Seven of these years in solitary. Soledad.
                . . .
where the kindred spirit touches this wall it
    crumbles—
no one responds to kindness, no one is more sen-
    sitive to it
than the desperate man.

This is an excruciatingly accurate portrait of a man I have
been. And in the years I taught in prisons, I met this man

over and over again. Her poem underscores the truth of
slogans many of us uttered twenty-five years ago as we
marched in the streets to demand social change and an end
to the Vietnam war. It is a poem of great compassion and
love and controlled anger closing, fittingly, on a generous
note of dedication to her readers. (pp. 35-6)

*Sam Hamill, "A Poetry of Daily Practice: Ad-
rienne Rich, S. J. Marks, Dorianne Laux," in*
The American Poetry Review, *Vol. 21, No. 4,
July-August, 1992, pp. 35-8.*

An excerpt from "Dedications"

I know you are reading this poem which is not in your language
guessing at some words while others keep you reading
and I want to know which words they are.
I know you are reading this poem listening for something,
torn
            between bitterness and hope
turning back once again to the task you cannot refuse.
I know you are reading this poem because there is nothing
else
            left to read
there where you have landed, stripped as you are.

Adrienne Rich, in her An Atlas of the Difficult World:
Poems, 1988-1991, *W. W. Norton & Co., 1991.*

Sandra M. Gilbert   (review date August 1992)

[*Gilbert is an American critic, editor, educator, and poet
who is best known for* The Mad Woman in the Attic:
The Woman Writer and the Nineteenth-Century Literary Imagination *(1979) and other feminist writings. In
the following excerpt, she praises* An Atlas of the Difficult World *as a collection that is distinctly American in
its themes and compares it to the work of Emily Dickinson, Walt Whitman, and Allen Ginsberg.*]

The swarmings of the visible and the invisible have always
been central in Adrienne Rich's poetry, especially the mo-
tions of the visible world in which we move and those of
the invisible history that gnaws at the edges of our minds.
In particular, from **The Will to Change** (1971), **Diving into
the Wreck** (1973), and **The Dream of a Common Language** (1978) onward, she has functioned as a sort of unofficial poet laureate of feminism's "second wave" as she
traced the interactions between past and present, between
men and women, in (to use her own words) "a succession
of brief, amazing movements // each one making possible
the next." But the movement that has made possible her
new (and thirteenth) collection, **An Atlas of the Difficult
World,** is perhaps her most amazing so far. Quite simply,
Rich has transformed herself into *the* bard of our country,
a woman who speaks *as* a woman but *for* us all with the
prophetic sureness and intensity that could only come
from a union between Dickinson and Whitman.

Both these precursors have, of course, long been important to Rich's career. Her early, taut verse-homage to

Dickinson, **"I Am in Danger—Sir—,"** along with the incisive essay **"Vesuvius at Home,"** openly proclaimed her affinities with the "Myth of Amherst." And her indebtedness to Whitman, too, was early evident in, for example, **"From an Old House in America"** (1974), a poem that I think has been too little studied. The title piece of *An Atlas,* however, seems to me to accept with eloquence and generosity a public, virtually ceremonial burden—a burden of prophecy!—that few poets in our own time have undertaken since, say, Ginsberg's now-classic "Howl."

Specifically, the thirteen-part sequence that constitutes Rich's "Atlas of the Difficult World" is a geography of America which, with passion, clarity, and uncanny detail, extends and expands those explorations of our country that were begun not just in "Howl" but also, more importantly, in "Song of Myself." Here and there, like Ginsberg's, Rich's polemics may strike some readers as needlessly extravagant ("here is the Sea of Indifference, glazed with salt")—but as one reads on, often overcome by the charity and tenderness that marks this *chef d'œuvre* completed in the shadow of the Gulf War, even that savage indignation comes to appear essential to the tormented love that drives this poet who here deeply defines herself as a patriot:

> A patriot is not a weapon. A patriot is one who
>   wrestles for the soul of her country
> as she wrestles for her own being, for the soul of
>   his country
> (gazing through the great circle at Window
>   Rock into the sheen of the Viet Nam Wall)
> as he wrestles for his own being.

As for the eerily echoing Whitmanesque cadences, to me at least, they bespeak not belatedness but a simultaneously proud and humble acquiescence in the task of personal as well as communal self-definition that ultimately brought Whitman to Gettysburg and Washington as well as to "When Lilacs Last in the Dooryard Bloom'd." "I am bent on fathoming what it means to love my country," Rich confesses, then persists in the intrepid stocktaking that empowers the great catalogs of *Leaves of Grass:*

> The history of this earth and the bones within it?
> Soils and cities, promises made and mocked,
>   plowed contours of shame and of hope?
> Loyalties, symbols, murmurs extinguished and
>   echoing?
> Grids of states, stretching westward, under-
>   ground waters?
> Minerals, traces, rumors I am made from, mor-
>   sel, minuscule fibre, one woman
> like and unlike so many, fooled as to her destiny,
>   the scope of her task?

And like Whitman, Rich has an evangelical need to tell us, and herself, that she is not just speaking *for* us but *to* us. Part XIII (**"Dedications"**) of "Atlas" offers some of the work's most poignant passages, superbly reminiscent of Whitman's confident and confidential "I stop somewhere waiting for you":

> I know you are reading this poem
> late, before leaving your office
> of the one intense yellow lamp-spot and the
> ～ darkening window

in the lassitude of a building faded to quiet
long after rush-hour. I know you are reading this
    poem
standing up in a bookstore far from the ocean
on a grey day of early spring, faint flakes driven
across the plains' enormous spaces around you.
I know you are reading this poem
in a room where too much has happened for you
    to bear
where the bedclothes lie in stagnant coils on the
    bed
and the open valise speaks of flight
but you cannot leave yet. I know you are reading
    this poem
as the underground train loses momentum and
    before running up the stairs
toward a new kind of love
your life has never allowed. . . .
I know you are reading this poem which is not
    in your language
guessing at some words while others keep you
    reading
and I want to know which words they are.
I know you are reading this poem listening for
    something, torn between bitterness and hope
turning back once again to the task you cannot
    refuse.

"The task you cannot refuse": this is the task to which *An Atlas of the Difficult World* calls us as we seek, women and men alike, to reimagine "the long ride of America." As Rich writes in **"Two Arts,"** the aesthetic statement by which I believe she herself defines her project, when you "Raise it up there"—raise up the task that is your vision or re-vision of our time and place—it "will / loom, the gaunt original thing / gristle and membrane of your life. . . . but you have to raise it up there, you / have a brutal thing to do." Worse, she adds in **"Final Notations,"** her book's brilliant concluding poem (which is as much a meditation on death as it is on art and politics) "it will not be simple, it will not be long / it will take little time, it will take all your thought." Yet *it*—the work, the living and the dying—must be done, must "become your will."

At this point, it would seem to me somewhat presumptuous to call Adrienne Rich the foremost of, the prophetess of, our "homegirls"—yet in the terms of my metaphor that is what she has become. I exult in her achievement, and so, I'm sure, would the other "homegirls" whose writings I've considered here. Emily Dickinson has boarded the Greyhound out of Amherst. Her eyes widen as she is borne across the ribs of America. Walt Whitman, with whom she just had a last cup of coffee, waits in the terminal, scribbling, weeping, wishing her luck. (pp. 301-04)

Sandra M. Gilbert, "How These New Homegirls Sing," in Poetry, *Vol. CLX, No. 5, August, 1992, pp. 284-304.*

Mona Van Duyn   (essay date 30 November 1992)

[*An American poet, editor, educator, and critic, Van Duyn was one of the judges responsible for awarding the 1992 Lenore Marshall/Nation Poetry Prize. In the following essay, in which she explains why Rich was chosen,*

Van Duyn lauds An Atlas of the Difficult World *for its powerful depiction of the human condition.*]

> . . . If you had known me
> once, you'd still know me now though
> in a different
> light and life. This is no place you ever
> knew me.
>
> . . .
>
> . . . I drive inland over roads
> closed in wet weather, past shacks
> hunched in the canyons
> roads that crawl down into darkness
> and wind into light
> where trucks have crashed and riders of
> horses tangled
> to death with lowstruck boughs. These
> are not the roads
> you knew me by. But the woman driv-
> ing, walking, watching
> for life and death, is the same

writes Adrienne Rich in her powerful long title [se-quence], "An Atlas of the Difficult World." And a diffi-cult world it still is for her, but in [*An Atlas of the Diffi-cult World: Poems, 1988-1991*] more than in any of her others, difficult for us *all,* all its struggling human cargo. More mural than map, as she says, the thirteen-section poem is packed with vignettes of people wrestling with their private and public problems, the anguish of their hearts or their nations, and is interwoven with unan-swered questions about both private and national view-points and destinations.

Adrienne Rich was born in Baltimore in 1929 and was ed-ucated at Radcliffe. She has written thirteen books of poems, her first having won the Yale Younger Poets Award when she was 21. She has also written, late in her career as a poet, three prose books: *Of Woman Born: Motherhood as Experience and Institution* (1976), *On Lies, Secrets, and Silence* (1979) and *Blood, Bread and Poetry* (1986). Her prizes and honors (Guggenheims, the Bollingen prize, a National Institute of Arts and Letters prize, N.E.A. grant, National Book Award) came to her in rapid succession through the 1960s and early '70s. The 1986 Ruth Lilly Prize recognized Rich's long, distin-guished career and the later poetry, as, in 1992, the three judges of the Lenore Marshall/*Nation* prize wish to do by honoring the fineness of her latest book.

My own review of her fifth book, *Leaflets,* in *Poetry* (March 1970), noted that it

> comes to us so garlanded with honors that one
> tends to expect each poem to be a masterpiece.
> This is, of course, unfair. Yet she does manage,
> in the book as an entirety, to display complete
> mastery, absolute assurance of movement and
> tone. . . . Most, though not all, of the poems
> seem to be written *to* someone, friend or loved
> one, and the reader has a sense of overhearing
> an extraordinarily genuine communication.
> This, it is amply clear, is achieved with unfalter-
> ing art, not artlessness. The poems are nearly al-
> ways focused on personal relationships; few are
> comments on a wider world. Even the five adap-
> tations from Dutch, Yiddish, and Russian poets

seem entirely Miss Rich's poems, in subject and sensibility.

In *An Atlas of the Difficult World,* though it is a radical departure from the purely personal, focusing primarily as it does on "others," "the woman . . . is the same" in at least one of the aspects I mention. In many of the "others" her own subject (loneliness-oppression-injustice) and her sensibility shine through to the reader even from lines quoted from other writers. Her section on **"Soledad.—f. solitude, loneliness, homesickness; lonely retreat,"** con-taining quotations from *Soledad Brother: The Prison Let-ters of George Jackson,* may serve as example:

> If my instructor tells me that the world
> and its affairs
> are run as well as they possibly can be,
> that I am governed
> by wise and judicious men, that I am
> free and should be happy,
> and if when I leave the instructor's
> presence and encounter
> the exact opposite, if I actually sense or
> see confusion, war,
> recession, depression, death and decay,
> is it not reasonable
> that I should become perplexed?
> From eighteen to twenty-eight
> of his years
>
> A young man schools himself,
> argues, . . .
> In this college of force he wrestles
> bitterness,
> self-hatred, sexual anger, cures his
> own nature.
> Seven of these years in solitary. Soledad.

There is no need for me to describe or analyze Rich's poet-ry here; every serious poetry reader knows and values it. It will only note that under the weight of the growing per-sonal anguish and bitterness in her sense of the conflict be-tween men and women, her more and more militant femi-nism, the poetry seemed for a time to straggle, stagger, strangle. She turned then to prose, searching outside her-self in history and biology for the sources of this pain. The prose books brought her a larger and larger femi-nist/lesbian constituency, into which she more or less withdrew for a while, feeling, evidently, too great a dis-comfort with the male-dominated men-and-women mix of the professional poetry world, its readings, audiences, panels, parties, its jealousies and backslaps. Although dur-ing this period some readers were estranged, one can hard-ly admire too much the courage, the resilience, the integri-ty this poet has always shown in her work.

In his 1977 critical study, *Five Temperaments,* the late David Kalstone commented about the Rich poems written between 1968 and 1974, "It is striking how many of these poems are about fresh starts, as if that position had to be re-imagined constantly to keep up the intensity of the verse, bypass disappointments, overcome the pain of bro-ken connections." Considering the later poems, he men-tioned "the tireless demand Rich's poetry has always made for reconciliation, for individual and social change. . . . [Her] poems are bound to be restless, bound to be looking constantly for new beginnings because they will never resign themselves to solitude."

What would happen to the poems, Kalstone wondered, after the prose books relieved the pressure on them of her troubled version of the bitterness between men and women? Here, in this current "new beginning," is his answer. I do not wish to condescend to the poetry with the all-too-common critical psychologizing I feel is unworthy of it, but obviously some kind of healing has taken place, a freeing of the self that enables her to aim her anger, her war against loneliness and suffering, her love and tenderness at a greater target: the human condition on this astonishing, fragile and beautiful planet. (pp. 673-74)

> *Mona Van Duyn, "The Lenore Marshall/'Nation' Poetry Prize—1992," in* The Nation, *New York, Vol. 255, No. 18, November 30, 1992, pp. 673-74.*

Iain Sinclair

Downriver; or, The Vessels of Wrath

Award: James Tait Black Memorial Book Prize

(Full name Iain MacGregor Sinclair) Born in 1943, Sinclair is a Welsh novelist, poet, and nonfiction writer.

INTRODUCTION

Downriver; or, The Vessels of Wrath is a novel comprised of twelve interconnected tales in which Sinclair explores such issues as murder, suicide, corruption, and urban blight. Containing elements of surrealism and postmodernism, including fragmented narration, shifting timeframes, and complex symbolism, *Downriver* has been compared to the works of Williams-Burroughs and Jack Kerouac. Set in a place reminiscent of the East End of London, an area also known as the Docklands, the episodes in *Downriver* are loosely linked by both setting and theme. Sinclair also uses historical events, including the sinking of the British pleasure boat *Princess Alice* in the 1880s and the murders committed by Jack the Ripper, to create an aura of fear and desperation throughout the novel. Described by Michael Moorcock as a manifesto for London's working-class, *Downriver* examines the monotony and hopelessness in the lives of such characters as Cec Whitenettle, a man who drives a train used to transfer nuclear waste. While some critics fault *Downriver* for its dense prose and superfluous literary allusions, others praise the work's apocalyptic vision of London and portrayal of the alienation, crime, and environmental degradation associated with modern urban life. Moorcock has stated: "[*Downriver*] celebrates London's vanishing uniqueness and seeks . . . to record and recreate the threatened myths and legends of an evicted, unfranchised people forced to learn a simplified and shameful version of their own history."

PRINCIPAL WORKS

Back Garden Poems (poetry) 1970
The Kodak Mantra Diaries: Allen Ginsberg in London
    (nonfiction) 1971
Muscat's Wuerm (poetry) 1972
The Birth Rug (poetry) 1973
Lud Heat (poetry) 1975
Brown Clouds (poetry) 1977
The Penances (poetry) 1977

Suicide Bridge (poetry) 1979
Flesh Eggs and Scalp Metal (poetry) 1983
Fluxions (poetry) 1983
Autistic Poses (poetry) 1985
White Chappell, Scarlet Tracings (novel) 1987
Significant Wreckage (poetry) 1988
Flesh Eggs and Scalp Metal: Selected Poems, 1970-1987
    (poetry) 1989
Downriver; or, The Vessels of Wrath (novel) 1991

CRITICISM

James Saynor (review date 3 March 1991)

[*In the following review, Saynor states that although*

Downriver *lacks narrative unity, the work is unique and imaginative.*]

Iain Sinclair knows East London like the back of his hand, and his hare-brained, sometimes intractable, yet frequently exhilarating new novel *Downriver* is a follicle-level survey of the authorial mit. In place of any conventional 'story-telling' is a jostle of 12 narratives—inchoate ruminations and phantasmagoric tall tales that surge and eddy about the metropolitan boondocks like the turbid and mysterious Thames itself. One character 'haunts the dead zones of the city looking for connections only he could activate', a description that fits Sinclair's overall project, too.

> [*Downriver*] **is not an easy book to "get into", but neither is it an easy one to get out of; something keeps the reader's eye picking its way restlessly on through the chaotic attic of the author's imagination.**
>
> —*James Saynor*

His vocabulary is a gonzo gallimaufry of trash and high-art allusions, and his writing is driven by manic, modernist reflexes; it contrives to be searingly vivid and analytically haywire at the same time. This is not an easy book to 'get into', but neither is it an easy one to get out of; something keeps the reader's eye picking its way restlessly on through the chaotic attic of the author's imagination.

The novel is peopled with sub-Bohemian riff-raff, all preoccupied with tracing their marbles—mystic hobos, stone-crazy antiquarians, narcotising boatmen, one-legged Conrad-exhumers, arm-waving media morons. Each is a *reductio ad absurdum* of someone Sinclair has known. They scurry among the wharfs, synagogues, doss-houses, and sundry deadfalls from Shoreditch to Sheerness, tracking the wraiths of Ripper victims and Aboriginal cricketers, while embarking on hilarious, Hunter S. Thompson-style safaris into the heart of lunacy and formlessness.

Nowhere in the book is more formless than the Isle of Dogs, now taken over by the Vatican and turned into a totalitarian necropolis of sorcery and depravity, explored in the funniest and most lucid of the 'narratives'. And nowhere is Sinclair more at his multi-layered, brain-boggling best than in the concluding passage as he imagines himself inside the mind of an acquaintance setting out to write a personal memoir in the style of (I think) himself (that is, Sinclair). *Downriver* is a must for all connoisseurs of heavy-duty wordsmithery; other readers may feel a little mugged by the book's cussed ironies and vengeful tirades. But there can be no doubting the power and singularity of Sinclair's vision.

James Saynor, *"Palm-Reading Pandemonium," in* The Observer, *March 3, 1991, p. 58.*

Angela Carter (review date 7 March 1991)

[*Carter was an English novelist, short story writer, and nonfiction writer. Her works include* The Passion of New Eve *(1977) and* Nights at the Circus *(1984). In the following excerpt, she examines the themes, imagery, and prose in* Downriver.]

Iain Sinclair, in the profane spirit of Surrealism, has chosen to decorate the endpapers of [*Downriver*], his new work of fiction, with a dozen unutterably strange picture-postcards. They show scenes such as that of six men, heavily veiled, veils held down by brimmed hats, posed with long-barrelled rifles. And two men in grass skirts, with feathers in their hair, intent on a game of billiards. They are Africans. And here are twenty-odd white men, in straw boaters, surrounding a prone crocodile. Joblard, Sinclair's friend, arranges the cards so that they tell a story. At once they become scrutable: they are images of imperialism. Joblard titles this picture story, what else, 'Heart of Darkness'. But the 12 interconnected stories in *Downriver* don't match up with the numbered postcards, unless in such an arcane fashion it must necessarily remain mysterious to me. *Downriver* is really a sort of peripatetic biography: Iain Sinclair's adventures at the end of time, at the end of his tether, in a city of the near future with a hallucinatory resemblance to London. The decisive influence on this grisly dystopia is surely the grand master of all dystopias, William Burroughs. Jack Kerouac, asked for a quote for the jacket of *The Naked Lunch,* said it was an endless novel that would drive everybody mad. High praise. *Downriver* is like that, too.

It is mostly about the East End. This reviewer is a South Londoner, herself. When I cross the river, the sword that divides me from pleasure and money, I go North. That is, I take the Northern Line 'up West', as we say: that is, to the West End. My London consists of all the stations on the Northern Line, but don't think I scare easily: I have known the free and easy slap-and-tickle of Soho since toddlerhood, and shouldered aside throngs of harlots in order to buy my trousseau casseroles from Mme Cadec's long-defunct emporium, undeterred by rumoured crucifixions in nearby garages. Nothing between Morden and Camden Town holds terror for me.

But I never went to Whitechapel until I was 30, when I needed to go to the Freedom Bookshop (it was closed). The moment I came up out of the tube at Aldgate East, everything was different to what I was accustomed to. Sharp, hard-nosed, far more urban than what I was used to. I felt quite the country bumpkin, slow-moving, slow-witted, come in from the pastoral world of Clapham Common, Brockwell Park, Tooting Bec. People spoke differently, an accent with clatter and spikes to it. They focused their sharp, bright eyes directly on you: none of that colonialised, transpontine, slithering regard. The streets were different—wide, handsome boulevards, juxtaposed against bleak, mean, treacherous lanes and alleys. Cobblestones. It was an older London, by far, than I was used to. I smelled danger. I bristled like one of Iain Sinclair's inimitable dogs. Born in Wandsworth, raised in Lambeth—Lambeth, 'the Bride, the Lamb's Wife', according to William Blake—nevertheless, I was scared shitless the first time I went to the East End.

Patrick White says somewhere that there is an intangible difference in the air of places where there has been intense suffering, that you can never get rid of the memory that pain imprints on the atmosphere. London's river runs through *Downriver* like a great, wet wound. Almost all the stories are affected in some way by the swell and surge occasioned when the pleasure boat *Princess Alice* sank after it collided with the *Byewell Castle,* a collier—a high-Victorian tragedy recalling the recent loss of the *Marchioness,* although Sinclair does nothing with the analogy, just lets it lie there in the water. An estimated six hundred and forty people went down with the *Princess Alice,* including the husband and two children of Elizabeth Stride. Her family gone, she took to drink, went on the streets. She became one of the victims of Jack the Ripper—the kind of ominous coincidence that fiction needs to avoid if it is to be plausible. Life itself can afford to be more extrovert.

So can Sinclair, who has no truck with plausibility but allows or persuades his densely textured narrative to follow a logic based on the principle of allusion, engaging in a sort of continuous free collective bargaining with his own imagination. For example: there is a sardonic, virtuoso description of the *Princess Alice* disaster:

> The victims chose an unlucky hour to enter the water. They were discharging the sewage from both the north and south banks into Barking Creek. Outflow. Mouths open, screaming, locked in a rictus. Rage of the reading classes. Public demand for the immediate provision of swimming-pools for the deserving poor. Let them learn breast-stroke.

Then the narrative moves like this:

> Something happens with the draw of time. With names. The *Alice.* Fleeing from the extreme interest of Lewis Carroll (weaving a labyrinth of mirrors for his English nymphet) into the tide-flow of Thames. *Can you row, the sheep asked, handing her a pair of knitting-needles.* Dodgsons. Dodgeson. Out on the river with another man's daughters: Lorina, Alice, Edith.

And thence to the enigmatic Canadian performance artist, Edith Cadiz, whose story we already know. By day, she worked as a nurse, nightly subsidising herself—for that income would never keep her—as a prostitute of the least exalted type. Edith Cadiz haunts the text, with her disinterested love for the mad children in her care, her unnerving stripper's act involving a dog and a set of street maps. One day, after copulating with a dog at the request of a Member of Parliament—this text is rich in dogs, some of them memorably unnerving—she disappears.

She is no less haunting a character because Sinclair makes plain she is not his own invention but the invention of another of the characters he has also invented. But many of the other characters, including Sinclair himself in a memorable walk-on ('a flannelled Lord Longford: on sulphate'), are drawn, kicking and screaming, one assumes, from real life. Some of them I recognise. One or two of them I know. That is Sinclair's autobiographical bit.

Think of *Downriver* as if Alice had wept a river of tears, rather than a pool; this river, like memory, full of people, places, ideas, things, all with an ambiguous reality status.

King Kole, the Aboriginal cricketer, standing at the rail of the *Paramatta,* watching a pilot-boat butt its way across Gravesend Reach, knew he had arrived at the Land of Death. Gravesend did for Pocahontas, the Indian princess, too: she died there, on her way back to Virginia. Sacrificial victims of imperialism. But less fatal presences include a writer, Fredrik Hanbury, a name transparently concealing one familiar to readers of this journal. There are painters, vagrants, Jack the Ripper, Sir William Gull, ritual murder, cricket, Homerton, Silvertown, 'The Isle of Doges' (VAT City plc).

Alice herself features at considerable length, in an extended meditation on Tenniel's illustration to *Through the Looking-Glass,* the one that shows Alice in the train. Alice 'allies herself with the order of birds; a feather grows from her severe black torque'. That feather might be a clue to the solution of the murders. What murders? Why, didn't you know? Spring-heeled Jack has returned. 'VAMPIRE AND BRIDE-TO-BE IN DOCKLANDS HORROR'. Edith Cadiz might have been a victim of this man.

But that is to suggest too much interconnectedness, to imply that a plot might be about to happen. *Downriver* is jam-packed with teasing little hints at possible plots, but these coy insinuations of resolution, climax, denouement are marsh-lights designed to delude the unwary reader into imagining that some regular kind of story might be in the offing. Fat chance. These stories, flowing all together, form a river without banks in which you sink or swim, like the victims of the *Princess Alice,* clutching at associations, quotations, references to other writers, if you can pick them up.

I picked up one or two. The American horror writer H. P. Lovecraft is economically invoked with the single phrase, 'a gibbous moon'. T. S. Eliot is constantly quoted by Edith Cadiz both before and after her disappearance; she passes round a hat that once belonged to him after she does her strip. The scarlet-haired opium addict, Mary Butts, makes a brief guest appearance and Sinclair borrows a minatory quotation from her autobiography: 'I heard the first wraths of the guns at the Thames's mouth below Tilbury.'

With this mass of literary references, the sex magic, the degradations, the torture, the rich patina of black humour, this is a book that triumphantly rejects any possibility of the Booker short-list in advance. It wears its contempt for all that on its sleeve. It is, besides, a work of conspicuous and glorious ill-humour. Sinclair doesn't seem driven, like Burroughs, by an all-consuming misanthropy: he's too romantic for that. But whenever Sinclair writes about the media, he goes pink and sputters. There is a section titled 'Living in Restaurants', about trying to make a television movie about Spitalfields. 'The *consiglieri* liked the sound of it, the authentic whiff of heritage, drifting like cordite from the razed ghetto.' The media lunches, four months of heroic eating. He hates them all. He constructs stiff, epigrammatic insults, more insult than epigram. The producer 'has that combatant attitude so prevalent among people who spend their lives bluffing genuine enthusiasts into believing they know nothing about their own subject.'

There is an *unhandiness* about Sinclair's prose, here. It creaks. His satire is splenetic but also heavy-handed. 'The Widow was a praise-fed avatar of the robot-Maria from *Metropolis;* she looked like herself, but too much so.' No prizes for guessing who *that* is. However, *Downriver* is set just a significant little bit further forward in the future, after the privatisation of the railways. And the Widow is *still* in charge. Who could have guessed, when *Downriver* went to press, that Margaret Thatcher would have resigned by publication date? Not Sinclair. When he appears in the third person in the final story, he babbles 'some bravado sub-text about considering his book a failure if the Widow clung on to power one year after its publication'. Unless he wants to claim a pre-emptive strike, he'll have to concede that, like Blake, to whose prophetic books his own bears some relation, he had, as prophet, zero success rate.

At one point, the Fredrik Hanbury character opines: 'Obsession matures into spiritual paralysis.' *Downriver* is far more than the sum of its obsessions, compelling as these are. Who can ever forget that dog of dogs, the one with *no eyes,* not a dog whose eyes have been put out but one who *never had any,* grey fur there, instead. This is an image so horrifying I don't want to understand it. What is the opposite of a dog? This question begins and ends the book, this manic travelogue of a city about to burn, and I can't even begin to answer: I will have to read *Downriver* again, to find out.

Yet, in spite of, or perhaps in order to spite that central, dominating motif of the river, none of these 12 stories flows easily. There are swirls, eddies and undercurrents but precious few stretches of clear water. When these occur, as they do, for example, two separate times in the section called 'Prima Donna (the Cleansing of Angels)', the limpid narrative achieves genuine supernatural horror; the bristling begins. One is the anecdote about Cec Whitenettle, driver of the hell-train bearing nuclear waste through Hackney. The other is the story of the Ripper's only personable victim, the 'Prima Donna' herself, that begins impeccably, better than Lovecraft, almost as good as Poe: 'I had not, I think, been dead beyond two or three months when I dreamed of the perfect murder.'

But Sinclair obviously isn't interested in plain sailing. His everyday prose is dense, static, each sentence weighed down with a vicious charge of imagery. Fighting the current, this reader was forced to ponder the ultimate function of fiction. This was very good for me. Is it to pass the time pleasantly, I asked myself. If so, they put some quite good things on television these days. But something is happening in this text that makes it necessary to go on, something to do with time itself, even if, in order to go on, you must—to mix metaphors—crack open each sentence carefully, to inspect the meat inside.

All writers of fiction are doing something strange with time—are *working* in time. Not their own time, but the time of the reader. One of Sinclair's milder obsessions is

with ritual: the project of ritual is to make time stand still, as it has apparently stood still in David Rodinsky's room in the Princelet Street Synagogue since the day, twenty-odd years ago, when he disappeared. . . . If time could be persuaded to stand still for even one minute, then the thin skin that divides Victorian London, Pocahontas's London, Blake's accursed London, Gog and Magog's London, The City of Dreadful Night, Jack London's London (*The People of the Abyss*), *Downriver*'s London of the near future, might dissolve altogether. The partitions of time dissolve in the memory, after all. They dissolve in the unconscious. At one point, Joblard and Sinclair watch Pocahontas being carried ashore to die, but that is altogether different, a purely literary trick with time. It is an easier one because the reader watches it being done on the page rather than experiences it in the act of reading. The thing is, you can't skip bits of *Downriver.* You have to move with currents as violent and mysterious as those of the Thames.

Its vision of London is pure hell. Madmen, derelicts, visionaries, 'wet-brains' live in the towers of abandoned mental hospitals. Academics voluptuously drown themselves in chains. Bohemians of a dedicated ferocity that make the behaviour of Jean Rhys and her companions, so deplored by John Bayley recently in these pages, look like the Teddy Bears' Picnic. Oh! That Imar O'Hagan, with his trained snails and his 'fridge full of blocks of frozen vampire bats "like an airline breakfast of compressed gloves" '.

It describes a city in the grip of a psychotic crisis. One image makes this concrete—a room in Well Street ('Grade 2 listed husk'), former home of a mad, addicted girl, now a suicide. The walls are covered with shrieking graffiti, protests, denunciations, phone-numbers, pyramids, quotations, lingams, crucified sparrows, horned gods, walking fish. 'The floor was clogged with mounds of damp sawdust—as if the furniture had been eaten, and, conically, excreted. Bas-relief torcs of blood were plashed over the skirting-boards. "Dogfights," Davy explained.' This, even more than the voodoo ritual later to be enacted on the Isle of Doges (*sic*), is the true heart of darkness within the city.

On the whole, the English, except for Dr Johnson, never have liked London. Cockney Blake saw, within a crystal cabinet, a refreshed, regenerate, a garden city.

> Another England there I saw,
> Another London with its tower,
> Another Thames and other hills.

Sinclair and two companions precipitate themselves out of that nightmare voodoo ceremony by an act of will and find themselves transported to just such an earthly paradise, freshly designed for the 'Nineties by a snappy Post-Modernist, a 'morning-fresh Medieval city', a 'transported Siena. Beneath us, along the riverside, a parade of windmills'. Windmills, the green sign of harmless energy. Benign, harmless windmills, the herbivores of the energy world. But when they look closer, they see the windmills are not windmills after all, but the sites of crucifixions.

Downriver is an unapologetically apocalyptic book that has, alas, found its moment, even if the Widow is now reduced to soundbites. Mother London, says Sinclair, is splitting into segments: a queasy glamour extinguishes the mad, bad past in Whitechapel, the rest of the places go hang . . . and yet these stories show how impossible it is to pull down an imaginary city. As Sinclair walks round London, he reinvents it, and remembered pain will always dance like heat in the air above the spot in Whitechapel where the Ripper struck down poor Lizzie Stride. The singing that turned to screaming continues to impress itself on the water where the *Princess Alice* went down. Listen, you can hear it on the slapping tide. (pp. 17-18)

> Angela Carter, *"Adventures at the End of Time,"* in London Review of Books, *Vol. 13, No. 5, March 7, 1991, pp. 17-18.*

Michael Moorcock   (review date 8 March 1991)

[*In the following review, Moorcock examines the complex prose and narrative structures in* Downriver *and asserts that the work is reminiscent of nineteenth-century radicalism.*]

Iain Sinclair is an original. Any comparisons I make are intended to give only a notion of the kind of pleasure he offers in his extraordinary development of a form favoured by the best Gothic writers, who in turn took their methods from the picaresque tale, the *schelmenroman,* to produce a series of fugues, or perhaps arabesques, revitalising the narrative devices that came to flower in Baghdad with the increasingly sophisticated cycle of the *Thousand and One Nights.*

A form that attracts the talents of a certain kind of British visionary, [*Downriver*'s] narrative devices are almost entirely metaphysical, proceeding through argument, symbol and exemplary metaphor rather than events, moving from complex tableau to complex tableau. Poetic and epic, it provides a massively effective antidote to those little, over-examined dishes of disease-cultures that are all that remain of what the publishing business and its academic stooges have labelled Modern English Literature.

> *Downriver*'s intensity recalls the best and most humane tradition of a 19th-century radicalism, inevitably echoing the angry passion of Blake or Shelley. It speaks for the alienated, the underdog, the dispossessed, the eccentric, the bewildered idealist.
>
> —*Michael Moorcock*

What's more, if you had despaired of finding a Welshman with a Scottish name who's not tone-deaf and incapable of patching one clunking clause on to another without giving a fair impression of Helen Keller in the earlier scenes of *The Miracle Worker,* Sinclair provides sure proof that every vacuum has, as it were, its cornucopia. He uses English with all the brave, confident relish we have come to

expect of the best Celts. There's a roll of oratory to it, a dense poetic fluency of reference. Metaphors constantly break like baroque, unclassifiable monsters through the reflecting surfaces of Sinclair's Thames and its ruined East End.

A vision of London compiled by Doré, Dali and Escher, in which a ride on the garish novelty of the Docklands Light Railway is transformed into an authentic recapitulation of De Quincey's dream journey through the Abyss, *Downriver* requires a level of interpretation no more difficult than that demanded by T S Eliot. With its delight in the miraculous and the unusual, reminiscent of Charles Fort and Fort's greatest stylistic disciple, William Burroughs, the novel celebrates London's vanishing uniqueness and seeks—like the wampum of some desperate Sioux—to record and recreate the threatened myths and legends of an evicted, unfranchised people forced to learn a simplified and shameful version of their own history.

Sinclair provides an elegy and a manifesto for a working-class and lower middle-class London colonised by a foreign power—her temples desecrated, her monuments pulled down, her experience sentimentalised, her heroes mocked, her institutions belittled by the new settlers, Thatcher's gulls, who now make our riverbanks so noisy.

Downriver is above all a defiant reclamation of the capital in the name of her indigenous, traditionally cosmopolitan population. The soul of Sinclair's London is threatened by the outrages of a *petit bourgeois* Satan, which, unconfronted, must eventually consume everything, including itself. This is a visionary novel worthy of John Cowper Powys or J G Ballard; a moral novel, but not prescriptive in any Wellsian sense.

Downriver's intensity recalls the best and most humane tradition of a 19th-century radicalism, inevitably echoing the angry passion of Blake or Shelley. It speaks for the alienated, the underdog, the dispossessed, the eccentric, the bewildered idealist. Sinclair's familiarity with the book trade, already brilliantly displayed in his first novel, **White Chappell, Scarlet Tracings,** again provides characters worthy of Mervyn Peake.

Concentrated but never exaggerated, **Downriver,** like Andrea Dworkin's *Mercy* or David Britton's *Lord Horror,* is an authentic record, psychic and physical, of what is happening in our world. This record is rather more valuable than the anaemic, phallocentric self-advertisements of Notting Hill *colons* or East Anglian clones.

Finally, it's worth mentioning what good value this book is. You get 12 tales, each witty and enjoyable and containing at least ten times the substance of, say, any latest Amis, for just £1.25 the tale. The 12 resolve into far more than the sum of their parts. If, in these hard times, you are going to buy one novel, **Downriver** looks likes being the most rewarding work you'll find this year.

> Michael Moorcock, *"London Pride,"* in New Statesman & Society, *Vol. 4, No. 41, March 8, 1991, p. 36.*

Peter Vansittart   (review date 16 March 1991)

[*In the following review, Vansittart offers a favorable assessment of* Downriver.]

Billed as 'social surrealism', here is a Stygian metropolis within reach but, for most, never reached.

> If you want to sample the worst London can offer, follow me down that slow incline. The tunnel drips with warnings. DO NOT STOP. Seal your windows. Hold your breath. This is not reassuring to the pedestrian who wobbles along a thin strip of paving, fearing to let go of the tiled wall: working the grime into his hand. Your heart fills your mouth, like a shelled and pulsing crab. Why are there no other walkers? Traffic scrapes so narrowly past. The drivers are mean-faced and locked into sadistic fantasies. White abattoir walls solicit vivid splashes of blood. You feel the brain-stem ineluctably dying, releasing, at its margins, dim and flaccid hallucinations.

As lighter contributions, the narrator lists fall-out, mouth cancer, plague, famine, bereavement, premature burial, in such settings as, ostensibly, Gravesend, Woolwich, Frog Island, Isle of Dogs, Mucking Flats, Dead Man's Point, Lower Horse, Stepney. Turner and Canaletto have been pole-axed by Doré, Albert Speer commands demolished dockland. *Downriver* evokes the old UFA films; the slanted shadows, menacing cemeteries, crooked houses, twilit streets empty yet stricken with presences. London itself, a vast post-imperial dosshouse, is not Flower of Cities All, but the City of Dreadful Night. Perhaps, as in Richard Jeffries's *After London,* it will vanish entirely, beneath the polluted waters.

Downriver offers 12 tales, each scattering bits of itself through the others. They are journeys of discovery, through nuances of grey periodically drooping into black comedy, black horror, black river depths. They differ in tone, but alike find London's heart of darkness. We see a lurid river journey under a junkie skipper, *Three Men in a Boat* becoming sinister farce. On an islet swept by voodoo apocalypse, Stephen Hawking lectures Jesuits: 'There was no Moment of Creation. The boundary condition of the Universe is that there is no boundary.' In a terrible psychic warp, a girl relives a Ripper murder. A doomed BBC project struggles to get moving and watching one producer at work resembles watching hairs grow from a wart. One poignant tale concerns Nicholas Moore, son of the influential Cambridge philosopher, G. E. [Moore]. Nicholas was poet, editor, a founder of the *New Apocalypse,* prolific for a decade, then unpublished for 40 years. Why? We are told.

The tales are fragmented into the grotesque, dotty, comic, with scraps of urban folklore, distorted memories, bizarre encounters. One glimpses Pocahontas, Wapping Riots, Thames crime, the first Australian touring cricketers, 1868, black-fellows including Dick-a-Dick, Red Cap, and King Cole who spat blood, was buried in a pauper's grave in Victoria Park, and here resurrected to confront Clive Lloyd's XI. Avatars and echoes drift throughout. Jack the Ripper, Magwitch, Wilde, Spring-heeled Jack, Carroll's Alice, a wrecked steamship, the *Alice.* A dancer steps from

her photograph to enact various identities, Ucello's 'Hunt' springs wild from a hoarding, an eccentric 'married late, and too wisely, a much younger woman who hoped, one day, to inherit most of Caithness. She satisfied his lack of desire. They ate out.'

This heightened world is sustained by multiple transformations. The Thames thickens to the Congo, Elizabeth I and Victoria fuse into Mrs Thatcher. A cracked pavement may emit a Victorian ghoul, a scrap of newspaper create fantasies never far from the real. The dead haunt tunnels, an 18th-century Polynesian sees his own death nailed to a warship's prow. It is as though Sherlock's dangerous glass magnifies the clues to a phantasmagoric capital, troll country of dreadful lazar-houses, six-in-a-bed drug dens, every labyrinthine alley a theatre of risk, an arsonist's delight, with derelicts, con-men, dotty evangelists, monsters, lying in wait, struggling for survival. Also, the more sophisticated, worrying whether a tattoo will signify bourgeois narcissism, proletarian solidarity, brotherhood with the Third World. Perhaps more important, will it attract the chicks?

A running hilarity underscores these crepuscular atmospherics, together with rare but telling intermissions of light, as when the narrator chances upon a hidden space, in desolate Whitechapel, of old courts and out-houses tethered by convolvulus, protected by thorn and nettle. For those with stamina, the verbal gusto is infectious. The blurb mentions Swift, critics mouth about Dickens and Conrad: quotes emerge from Eliot, Joyce, David Jones; also from Richmal Crompton. Sinclair, however, is his own man: 'A grin like an elephant's graveyard.' 'A Christian version of the Vatican.' His snarling compendium of obscure lives and dubious livelihoods, rotting neighbourhoods and neighbours, hypocrisy, dream, endurance, is recommended to complacent politicians and all whose London is blocked by gentility. It will repel devotees of Margaret Thatcher and Somerset Maugham, and those who expect a novel, unlike other arts, to reveal all at a single examination. It should attract not only Dracula's dentist and ageing friends of Nicholas Moore, but those delighting less in plot than the plottings of a mind obsessed by language, myth, the shadowy cities within a city. Also, perhaps, some cricketers.

> He rested and fed all his doubts into a giant oak. The tree was a metaphor for the innings he would play. The roots were laid in a vision of the city, seen from the hill. The trunk was the slow build-up of confidence: 'seeing' the ball before it left the bowler's hand. And then the branching out, the flowering. The strokes all round the wicket, sketching the tree's shape into the ground for ever.

Peter Vansittart, "River of No Return," in The Spectator, *Vol. 266, No. 8488, March 16, 1991, p. 37.*

Eric Korn   (review date 5 April 1991)

[*In the following excerpt, Korn evaluates the strengths and weaknesses of* Downriver.]

There's a footpath on the south bank of the Thames, downstream from Greenwich, just over the water from the

An excerpt from *Downriver*

If you want to sample the worst London can offer, follow me down that slow incline. The tunnel drips with warnings. DO NOT STOP. Seal your windows. Hold your breath. This is not reassuring to the pedestrian who wobbles along a thin strip of paving, fearing to let go of the tiled wall: working the grime into his hand. Your heart fills your mouth, like a shelled and pulsing crab. Why are there no other walkers? Traffic scrapes so narrowly past. The drivers are mean-faced and locked into sadistic fantasies. White abattoir walls solicit vivid splashes of blood. You feel the brain-stem ineluctably dying, releasing, at its margins, dim and flaccid hallucinations.

Iain Sinclair, in his Downriver, *Paladin, 1991.*

City Airport. According to the map it turns from River Way, becomes Mudlarks Way and then Horoshima Walk. ***Downriver,*** likewise, runs from rollicking rheology to apocalypse. I started with some prejudices. I don't see a rich lode of louche romance in the world of the bookdealer, or rather the world of bookrunners and bookscouts: not the sharks, but the pilotfish, weavers and lampreys of biblioMarineland. More seriously, I don't find Jack the Ripper an ideal topic for pranks, and I get mouth ulcers at the merest mention of the occult, while Iain Sinclair (who put the Ley in Leytonstone and the witch in Greenwich) finds omens and portents everywhere: in the baroque geometry of Docklands architecture he sees signs where I only see cosines. Finally, his locale is the dark side of the moon to an NWer like myself: I grow alienated as I head towards the sunrise and die just east of the Kingsland Road.

In spite of which, I was caught in this travelogue of the country between Docklands and Doom. Mostly by the language, but also by the nightmare landscape, the population of freaks and holy fools, the Gothic-to-Baroque terrors and gags. *Downriver* is a sort of sequel to the remarkable (and maddening) ***White Chappell, Scarlet Tracings*** which compared bookmen on the prowl with Jack the Ripper likewise, the latter being more lovely and more temperate. This one is notionally set in a not wholly improbable hyperbolic near-future (now pluperfect subjunctive), "a couple of years into her fifth term in what was now effectively a one-party state and a one-woman party". This fictional Prime Minister has made herself unassailable by disposing of her Consort, re-establishing Victorian values at a stroke. One enjoyably frantic episode describes the deliberations of the Committee considering a suitably grandiose memorial (far enough downstream to shift the centre of the State away from the Palaces of Buckingham and Westminster). The scene permits Sinclair to claw, scratch and boot an assortment of art mandarins, all, of course, imaginary.

Through a variety of real and fantasticated riverscapes Sinclair wanders, notebook in hand and dreaming standing up, a wildly unreliable guide who gets his most outlandish effects by telling the truth. (Who'd have thought that surreal sixwheeler was really rotting on Rotterdam Grove?) His prose style is endlessly inventive: by turns intimidating, dazzling, exhilarating and exhausting. His tropes and neologisms fizz like fireworks, but who can take a six-hour firework display? He Peakes too soon; and too often.

Sinclair tells an emblematic tale of marmosets and other escaped exotica that haunt a churchyard off the Ratcliffe Highway. Some fall into the hands of neurologists who excise their brains bit by bit in a vain search for the memory-store, the engram: almost decerebrate, they still retain memory, which is located nowhere, but stored everywhere. Similarly he charts the region, but not topographically. The endless to-ing and fro-ing between Shoreditch and Sheerness also traces out, I don't doubt, some occult network, as in ***Lud Heat*** (1975): the reader who cares to may trace it.

There are a dozen episodes of murder, suicide, ritual and mystery. Divers persons are "trapped in the pursuit of inexplicable icons": the complete works and world of Conrad, the identity of the Ripper, or of the narrator, the spurious photograph of the lost dancer, the story behind the twelve postcards of colonial life which are displayed on the endpapers. A map of real sublunary Thames would be more helpful, but reader-friendliness is not Sinclair's intent. There are baroque dreams of megacities, the Isle of Dogs as the malignant megalopolis or a new satanic Vatican. Sinclair and mates travel by train, boat, car, submarine and Docklands Light Railway around the landscape of a dream, or literature's longest pubcrawl.

Various kinds of corruption are displayed. Various persons come to bad ends. Dr Adam Tenbrucke drowns himself at Execution Dock, Edith Cadiz performs a cartographic strip in Brick Lane, Lee Boo dies of the flu, as does a member of the original and aboriginal Australian test team; Roland Bowman changes sex in a synagogue in Princelet Steet. . ., the driver of the nuclear waste train has a damaging encounter with a ghost, and the Ripper's victims and his fans meet again and again.

Every media modality is knocked; every newspaper and journal (even *Granta,* even this one) is mocked. Sinclair, who passes for the Outsider, is a dab at insiderpeak. ***Downriver,*** may do for Docklands what *The Serial* did for Marin County; tease its pretensions without damaging property values.

The twelve episodes (or tales or chapters or stations of the Cross or of the Docklands Light Railway) are linked by endless thematic recurrances, many obscure. Albert Speer, and various other spears including the pub called the Spear of Destiny. The Tarot. Cricket (frequently with a spectral twelfth man). The twelve photographs found in Tilbury. A more or less emblematic dog lollops significantly through each episode except one, where the keen reader may observe a cat ("the opposite of dog", perhaps, in a recurrent and strangely familiar phrase.)

All is grist to Sinclair's watermill. *Four Quartets* and *Krazy Kat*, W. H. Hodgson and Monty Python. Richmal

Crompton and reviews of **White Chappel.** The resulting loaf is tasty if unwholesome, a blend of Quatermass and Childermass, drowned in gollops of H. P. Lovesauce. As the pace quickens, the book begins to recycle itself. Later episodes concern projected or fantasized television films based on the early scenes. Names that appear on the dust-wrapper, praising the contents, reappear as part of the content. The book draws on itself so vigorously that the faint-hearted reader may stand back for fear of catching his fingers in it when it implodes. But the faint-hearted reader has long ago given up. And is the poorer for it.

Eric Korn, "Around the Landscape of a Dream," in The Times Literary Supplement, *No. 4592, April 5, 1991, p. 26.*

Additional coverage of Sinclair's life and work is contained in the following source published by Gale Research: *Contemporary Authors,* Vol. 132.

Jane Smiley

A Thousand Acres

Awards: National Book Critics Circle Award and Pulitzer Prize

(Full name Jane Graves Smiley) Born in 1949, Smiley is an American novelist, short story and novella writer, and nonfiction writer.

For further information about Smiley's life and career, see *CLC,* Volume 53.

INTRODUCTION

In *A Thousand Acres,* Smiley uses shifting viewpoints, flashbacks, and vivid imagery to explore the ways in which greed, revenge, and jealousy can lead to a family's downfall. Set in Iowa in 1979, the novel details what happens when Larry Cook, the proud owner of a thriving farm, unexpectedly decides to retire and divide his land equally between his three daughters: Ginny, Rose, and Caroline. While Ginny and Rose accept their father's proposal, Caroline, the youngest, disapproves and is immediately disinherited. After relinquishing the rights to his farm, Larry's behavior becomes erratic; he drinks excessively, takes aimless drives around the countryside, and stares at his fields for hours. Believing their father is going mad, Ginny and Rose argue about how to manage the land and eventually become embroiled in a lawsuit, initiated by Caroline, over property rights. Although a judge grants Ginny and Rose ownership, the farm ultimately falls victim to the massive farm foreclosures of the 1980s and, consequently, the family disintegrates. Like Shakespeare's *King Lear,* from which Smiley drew inspiration, *A Thousand Acres* depicts the complex relationship between a father and his three daughters. Smiley, however, also addresses feminist and environmental issues and explores the ramifications of breast cancer, miscarriage, and incest. Critical reaction to *A Thousand Acres* has generally been positive, with reviewers praising the novel's intricate narrative, potent characterization, and realistic depiction of rural life. Ron Carlson observed: "[*A Thousand Acres*] is a book about farming in America, the loss of family farms, the force of the family itself. It is intimate and involving. What, Ms. Smiley asks, is it to be a true daughter? And what is the price to be paid for trying one's whole life to please a proud father who slenderly knows himself—who coveted his land the way he loved his daughters, not wisely but too well?"

PRINCIPAL WORKS

Barn Blind (novel) 1980
At Paradise Gate (novel) 1981
Duplicate Keys (novel) 1984
The Age of Grief (short stories) 1987
Catskill Crafts: Artisans of the Catskill Mountains (nonfiction) 1987
The Greenlanders (novel) 1988
Ordinary Love and Good Will (novellas) 1989
A Thousand Acres (novel) 1991

CRITICISM

Donna Rifkind   (review date 27 October 1991)

[*In the following review of* A Thousand Acres, *Rifkind praises Smiley's characterizations and her realistic portrayal of family tragedy.*]

A tyrannical patriarch resolves to divide his kingdom among his three daughters, then shows signs of madness, cursing his offspring and venturing out alone into a fearsome storm. In the meantime, his daughters rush to take over the land before their father reclaims it. This family crisis results, as it must, in chaos: The kingdom is dissolved, the land and its occupants made barren, with bitterness the only harvest.

This may sound like *King Lear,* but it is also the premise of Jane Smiley's new novel, [*A Thousand Acres*], in which she has, with near-miraculous success, transplanted Shakespeare's harshest tragedy from prehistoric Britain to the rural Midwest in 1979. The novel's patriarch is Larry Cook, a proud, laconic man who, through hard work, shrewd calculation, and out-and-out pilfering has established a thousand-acre, multi-million-dollar farming enterprise, the pride and envy of all Zebulon County, Iowa.

Two daughters, Ginny and Rose, still live on the farm, cooking and cleaning for their father—their mother died of cancer years ago—while their husbands work the land. Their younger sister Caroline, whom they were responsible for raising, has left to become a lawyer in Des Moines. Narrator Ginny has suffered five miscarriages and can't help wishing Rose's two teenage daughters were her own. Yet otherwise she seems satisfied enough with the round of life on the farm, day by day, season by season.

Larry's announcement at a local pig roast of his retirement and his plan to form a corporation, with each daughter controlling a third part, seems innocent enough. So does the homecoming of a neighbor's son, Jess Clark, who disappeared 13 years ago to escape the draft. That these two events will shatter the rock-solid serenity of the Cook family becomes increasingly inevitable, as the novel slides, like the Lear saga, into one long ruinous denouement.

Behind the many surprises in Smiley's plot looms the certainty that the Cooks's boundless prosperity is doomed to end: the widespread farm foreclosures of the 1980s are not far in the future, heralding the strangulation of traditional American farm life. And just as this seemingly permanent institution can be destroyed, the author shows, the sure perceptions about one's family history can be demolished, as Ginny learns when some nasty family secrets become public knowledge.

This is a novel whose characters overshadow the plot: Their shifting points of view are often more breathtaking than the action itself. Where Ginny, for instance, had always counted on Rose as an ally, after the incorporation of the farm she begins to see the manipulative selfishness under her sister's friendly exterior. Rose, who calls the breast she recently lost to cancer her "pound of flesh," changes more every day into a vengeful, bullying parody of the father she despises. Ginny's new view of Rose

causes her to change also, from passive optimist to grim aggressor.

Jess Clark, who seems a mild-mannered pacifist, is in fact plotting to overthrow his own father while destroying the marriages of both Ginny and Rose. Caroline, the novel's Cordelia, is the most ambivalent character: She sues her own sisters to reclaim the land for Larry, who is showing increasing signs of dementia, yet her facade of filial devotion hides a stonily unsympathetic nature.

Even the land, itself a main character, shifts and changes without warning. When Larry's grandparents bought the original acreage in 1890, half of it lay under two feet of water. A sophisticated drainage system corrects the problem, but Ginny still imagines an ocean under the veneer of soil, "ready at any time to rise and cover the earth again."

This "eternal drip and trickle of the sea beneath the soil" becomes a metaphor for the danger Ginny sees engulfing her life. When Rose forces her to remember a devastating time in their adolescence, Ginny reflects: "What was transformed now was the past, not the future. The future seemed to clamp down upon me like an iron lid, but the past dissolved beneath my feet into something writhing and fluid. . . ."

Smiley's novel is about the power and the entrapment of the land, "where every rainstorm is thick with odor and color, and usefulness and timing, where omens of prosperity or ruin to come are sought in every change . . ." It is also about the power and the entrapment of love, which, along with bitterness and hatred, keeps the Cook family writhing poisonously, desperately together to the end.

A Thousand Acres is not a perfect book: its dialogue can be stiff, and it gains momentum a bit too slowly at the beginning. In the face of Smiley's accomplishment, however, these are small complaints, for the book has all the stark brutality, if not the poetic grandeur, of a Shakespearean tragedy. While she has written beautifully about families in all of her seven preceding books—most notably in *The Age of Grief* and *Ordinary Love & Good Will*—her latest effort is her best: a family portrait that is also a near-epic investigation into the broad landscape, the thousand dark acres, of the human heart. (pp. 1, 13)

> Donna Rifkind, "A Man Had Three Daughters. . .," in Book World—The Washington Post, *October 27, 1991, pp. 1, 13.*

Jack Fuller   (review date 3 November 1991)

[*In the following review, Fuller compares* A Thousand Acres *to Shakespeare's* King Lear.]

It has been a long time since a novel so surprised me with its power to haunt the idle moment and insinuate itself amid the practical concerns that press upon the mind of the reader who is away from the book. Jane Smiley's *A Thousand Acres,* which time and again courts literary failure, speaks with such growing authority that it overcomes all the dangers it creates for itself and triumphs even as its characters fall.

This is the deepest way in which it resembles *King Lear,* from which it freely and explicitly borrows. *A Thousand Acres* is a true American tragedy, like Theodore Dreiser's novel, even more like Arthur Miller's *Death of a Salesman.* Its despair is wholly genuine, and it is fully redeemed through the art of its telling.

Smiley places the story of Lear in the farmlands of Iowa and tells it, in effect, from the point of view of Goneril. An aging father decides to divide his large and prosperous farm—built through hard work and relentless acquisitiveness—among his three daughters. One, who has moved to the city and become a lawyer, resists, and he cuts her out of the arrangement, like Shakespeare's Cordelia, the good daughter who refuses to flatter her father to get ahold of his estate. The other two go along, but almost immediately the arrangement begins to sour.

The father, no longer in control of the decision-making about the farm, begins acting erratically. There is, of course, a scene in which he goes out to wander lost in a terrible storm. The relationship frays between the inheriting sisters, each of whom bears a deep scar. Rose (the Regan figure), has undergone treatment for breast cancer, and Ginny (Goneril), has been unable to carry a baby to term. Caroline (Cordelia) becomes outright hostile to her sisters and takes her father's side. Then things go from tense to horrifying.

It is tricky to explain how this happens without doing damage to the effectiveness of the book. Suffice it to say that because the story is told from Goneril's point of view, things are revealed about the father that explain the daughters' motivations quite starkly. So starkly, in fact, that at the moment the truth was revealed, about midway through, I had the sinking feeling that this remarkably subtle and closely observed book was going to destroy itself in polemicism.

But Smiley knows exactly what she is doing at every point, and her purpose is art rather than sexual politics. The ugliness of the truth about the father is important, but it is not what makes the book work. Its awful power comes from the way in which it examines the consequences of the truth it reveals. Its genius grows from its ruthless acceptance of the divided nature of every character, including its narrator.

This gives *A Thousand Acres* the prismatic quality of the greatest art. Its colors change with the angles of the light cast upon it. It is not one thing, it is many things. And all its contradictions are true.

At first, the reader may think that the book is going to be about the way the people have been shaped by the land. This would be quite a natural theme for a book about rural America, and Smiley is eloquent in her descriptions of the earth and the way it has divided and been divided by the people it has nurtured. Here, for example, is a passage from early in the book about the land on which the family lives, whose swamps had to be drained through buried lines of tile before it could be turned to use:

> I was always aware, I think, of the water in the soil, the way it travels from particle to particle, molecules adhering, clustering, evaporating,

heating, cooling, freezing, rising upward to the surface and fogging the cool air or sinking downward, dissolving this nutrient and that, quick in everything it does, endlessly working and flowing, a river sometimes, a lake sometimes. When I was very young, I imagined it ready at any time to rise and cover the earth again, except for the tile lines. Prairie settlers always saw a sea or an ocean of grass, could never think of any other metaphor, since most of them had lately seen the Atlantic. The Davises did find a shimmering sheet punctuated by cattails and sweet flag. The grass is gone, now, and the marshes, "the big wet prairie," but the sea is still beneath our feet, and we walk on it.

First, there is the dazzling quality of Smiley's sentences. Then the precision of observation. But only when the book has concluded and you see what people have taken from the water, from the swamps, from the land and what they have done with it, only then does the image of return to the primal unforgiving sea reach its terrible culmination.

Smiley's purpose is larger than the land. It is to examine all of nature, beginning with the nature of the troubled human soul.

The story she tells defeats all attempts to reduce it to classification. At various points there seems to be a suggestion that the chemicals used in agriculture have leached into the water supply and caused Ginny to miscarry.

In another book, this would be the point, and it would be glib. But Smiley puts the suggestion in the mouth of a man whose holistic ideas lead to nothing but pain; and another character who worries about what he eats and drinks is not of the land at all, has no natural relationship to it, and is played mostly for laughs.

The idea of treating the Lear figure as a character who to some measure deserves what he gets courts another risk. This novel depicts men with as cold an eye as any I have ever read. It might have been nothing more than an addition to the lengthening shelf of arguments against the human male.

But it is much too cunning for that. It does not excuse the women. Its purpose is not to decide between the sexes but to examine the flaws in human nature that know no gender, from which the meanness and evil of men and women alike both spring.

The largest risk Smiley runs, of course, is using the Lear story so explicitly. It could have turned this book into a kind of a precious exercise or a literary curiosity. But Smiley avoids this by the mounting brilliance of her close observations and delicate rendering of human behavior.

If it weren't for the crushing universality of its ultimate truth, *A Thousand Acres* might have been a wonderful miniature, depicting with stunning accuracy the way ordinary people live their lives. But this was not Akira Kurosawa's approach when he used Lear to create a freestanding piece of art in his brilliant epic film *Ran.* Nor was it exactly James Joyce's method in *Ulysses,* his eccentric masterpiece on the Homeric text.

It is not too much to say that what Jane Smiley has made

out of Shakespeare is strong enough to stand comparison with those magnificent, derivative works of art. This book very well may last. (pp. 1, 4)

> Jack Fuller, "King Lear in the Middle West," in Chicago Tribune—Books, November 3, 1991, pp. 1, 4.

What I wanted to do [in *A Thousand Acres*] was to bring together five things that were related in my mind, but not necessarily in the thinking of others. One was *King Lear*. Another was farming as practiced on big industrial farms in America today. Another was relationships, including incest, within a dysfunctional family and, finally, some feminist theory.

—*Jane Smiley, in the* Chicago Tribune, *24 November 1991.*

Ron Carlson (review date 3 November 1991)

[*In the review below, Carlson discusses Smiley's narration and her depiction of rural life in* A Thousand Acres.]

It is hard to resist comparing Jane Smiley's big new novel, *A Thousand Acres,* to *King Lear,* but I'm going to try. Does an imperious and domineering father divide his domain and leave the youngest of his three daughters out? Does this lead beyond mayhem to tragedy? Is someone blinded? Is there a storm? Well, yes, and a dozen other yeses, but this powerful and poignant book doesn't lean against Lear for support. Jane Smiley takes the truths therein and lights them up her way, making the perils of family and property and being a daughter real and personal and new and honest and hurtful all over again. And where? In Iowa.

A farm of a thousand acres is a magnificient thing. Certainly Larry Cook's place stands as one of the largest landholdings in Zebulon County. Amassed in deals that arose from his neighbors' failures, the farm is a tribute to Larry Cook's single-minded shrewdness.

It is May of 1979, and when a neighbor, Harold Clark, holds a community pig roast to announce the return of his prodigal son, Jess, Larry Cook uses the occasion to announce—surprisingly—that he is giving his farm to his daughters: Ginny, Rose and Caroline. At the last minute, angered by her seeming hesitance, he cuts Caroline, the youngest, out of the grant. Those rich and fertile thousand acres will do more damage to a family than any real estate since the cherry orchard.

Ginny Cook narrates the book from her position as the oldest daughter, 36 that year; but in so many ways she is the youngest, the most callow, the slowest to judge. This is one of Ms. Smiley's finest strokes, the selection of her

storyteller. For Ginny is neutral, without agenda, at times as stolid as a farm animal—almost reluctantly drawn into the events of the summer, events that will force her into discovering the true nature of her family and her past.

It's Ginny's strange innocence that accompanies us through the novel and lends the story a marvelous and personal tension so credible it is chilling. She's the kind of person who, despite lingering sadness at being childless after several miscarriages, is still perked up by the sight of the colors of a Monopoly board. She is married to Ty Smith, a good farmer, an orderly and blameless man. She is also the caretaker of the group; at the time the novel opens, she's cooking breakfast in three houses—hers, her father's and her sister Rose's. Rose, at 34, is recovering from a mastectomy.

Ginny's sisters are already more worldly wise than she. Rose has always been a realist, holding her emotions at arm's length. She says of her grandfather and father on the farm: "First their wives collapse under the strain, then they take it out on their children for as long as they can." She has kept score and lives for retribution. When her husband, Pete, broke her arm four years before, she made a sleeve for the cast that said, "PETE DID THIS." Rose and Pete live with their two daughters across the road from her father.

Only Caroline, 28, has escaped her father's world; she has become, along with her husband, Frank, a lawyer in Des Moines. The youngest, the prettiest, the most successful, Caroline was raised by her sisters after her mother's death. It is her "I don't know" when the question of returning to the farm first arises that labels her a thankless child. Larry Cook has never been a tolerant man.

He has also never been a man for whom anything but the land really mattered, and giving up the farm that was his life unmoors him. In what was supposed to be his retirement, he becomes a quarrelsome wanderer, setting off a series of events that leads to a tempestuous denouement. Typically, one of the first of these events is seemingly unimportant: buying new kitchen cabinets that sit where the delivery men left them, out in his yard unprotected from the weather, like a beacon to the community—something is wrong. His sullen idleness, his drinking, his smoldering anger lead him down a path of accident and rancor, from Ginny to Rose to his best friend, Harold Clark, to Caroline and finally to court. He can't talk, but he can curse.

As the Cooks' problems intensify, a stranger comes to town. Jess Clark, who went to Canada during the Vietnam War, has returned after several years. For Ginny and Rose, he's a welcome addition to the community, and in a wonderful early scene a marathon game of Monopoly becomes a way of exchanging news, about everything from Jess's views on organic farming to what is being said in town about Larry Cook's daughters. Jess's involvement with Ginny and Rose becomes the key to Ginny's awakening to herself, to her full understanding of Rose.

Jane Smiley knows that the forces at play in any rural society are powerful and not unsophisticated. There is nature to contend with. There's the housewives' constant struggle to keep the farm out of the house. And there is the rivalry of farmer against farmer, the competition for success with the crops, with machinery and with the bank—which ends sometimes in vying for one another's farms. Ginny remembers her father looking across the road at the Ericsons' place. "We might as well have had a catechism," she says. "What is a farmer's first duty? To grow more food. What is a farmer's second duty? To buy more land." Larry Cook closed the Ericson deal on the day of his wife's funeral.

Ms. Smiley's portrait of the American farm is so vivid and immediate—the way farmers walk, what the corn looks like, the buzz of conversation at the community dinners—that it causes a kind of stunning nostalgia. It reminds us that the passing on of farms is always difficult—and that the farmer's inherent character makes it even more so. The distance from the main house to the son's or daughter's across the road is one of the most tangible embodiments of the generation gap.

And all these struggles are played out under the gaze of the community. The flat farmland is a fishbowl. For miles one can see whose crops are thriving, whose barn is painted, whose car is headed for town or returning and at what hour. Jane Smiley's townsfolk—the bankers, neighbors and family friends—are the Greek chorus here. In fact, there is something fundamentally Midwestern about a chorus, about all that caution. The community is slow to change, hardly warm to Larry Cook's decision.

There are surprises in this book, things to be uncovered, events that turn in ways more radical and permanent than we would have supposed. When sister talks to sister in the kitchen or on the phone or in the courtroom, Ms. Smiley brings us in so close that it's almost too much to bear. She's good in those small spaces, with nothing but the family, pulling tighter and tighter until someone has to leave the table, leave the room, leave town. And she's good in the big spaces—this region is hers now, intuited and understood, and delivered with generous exactitude. Ms. Smiley's earlier work—including the novellas *Ordinary Love & Good Will* and the story collection *The Age of Grief*—has been praised by the literary world. But *A Thousand Acres* is the big book that will finally earn her the wider audience she deserves.

I was reluctant, in writing about the novel, to invoke *King Lear* (and it will be invoked, believe me) because I didn't want this story to sound like an exercise like some clever, layered construct. What *A Thousand Acres* does is to remind us again of why *King Lear* has lasted.

This is a book about farming in America, the loss of family farms, the force of the family itself. It is intimate and involving. What, Ms. Smiley asks, is to be a true daughter? And what is the price to be paid for trying one's whole life to please a proud father who only slenderly knows himself—who coveted his land the way he loved his daughters, not wisely but too well?

Ron Carlson, "King Lear in Zebulon County," in The New York Times Book Review, *November 3, 1991, p. 12.*

Richard Eder (review date 10 November 1991)

[*In the review below, Eder identifies what he considers the narrative and thematic weaknesses of* A Thousand Acres.]

A problem novel is a problem. If it is a detective story, say, or an exposure of conditions in the Chicago stockyards, we take it on its own single-minded level—solving the mystery or learning about the conditions. It needs to be lucidly and enthrallingly expounded; apart from that, we are simply grateful for whatever adornments of style or character may be thrown in.

When it is a full-fledged work of fiction, though, we feel two currents tug against each other. There is the whirlpool vortex—find the problem, explore it, elucidate it—and the freer, more complex, less foreseen tides that fiction sets going in its interplay of character, story, setting and the writer's voice.

Paradoxically, if Jane Smiley were a narrower and less gifted writer, her new novel might have worked better. The "problem" in *A Thousand Acres* is current and troubling: the disabling consequences of parental sexual abuse, and of the family denial that turns a knife thrust into a deadly infection. She sets it in a sprawling hybrid framework that is partly a rigorous psychological study, partly a deliberately lurid melodrama, and partly the subtle and affecting evocation of a family and a place. It cannot hold together.

The melodrama, employed with a touch of satire and to make a point, is a detailed reworking of *King Lear*. It is a reversal, in fact, *Lear* told from the point of view of Goneril and Regan, with Lear the terrible old man they accused him of being, and they themselves terribly damaged, and fighting to survive.

Lawrence Cook, a hard, tempestuous farmer, is a petty monarch. He works 1,000 acres of prime Iowa land, having built his holdings partly by inheritance, partly by driving energy, and partly by taking advantage of neighbors forced to sell out. His two oldest daughters, Ginny—the narrator—and Rose, and their husbands Pete and Ty, work and keep house on the Cook lands under their father's increasingly paranoid eye. Caroline, the youngest, has gone off to be a lawyer in Des Moines.

Suddenly, Lawrence announces he will retire and divide his property among his daughters. Rose and Ginny accept—Lawrence is cranky and failing, and their husbands are capable and deserve their chance—but Caroline demurs. In a rage, Lawrence casts her out.

Land and power gone, the old man turns erratic. He goes on foolish shopping sprees, he drinks heavily and smashes up his car. When Ginny and Rose insist he give up driving and get some exercise, he curses them and runs out, as it happens, into a fearful rainstorm. Before long, having sheltered with an old, equally paranoid neighbor and buddy, he is suing Ginny and Rose. He is joined in the suit by Caroline, who now returns to back up a father she never had much to do with, and whom she chooses to regard as wronged by greedy sisters.

Lear then, or rather, anti-Lear, down to having Lawrence's neighbor-buddy (Gloucester) blinded in an accident; making Ginny's easygoing husband, Ty (Albany), feel that she has been unnecessarily confrontational; and even having Ginny and Rose quarrel over a lover.

All this sits ludicrously upon the Iowa countryside, and Smiley is in no way a ludicrous writer. She is sending a signal, she is parodying her melodrama even as she uses it for a purpose. Ginny—a conscientious housekeeper—carefully grinds up river hemlock in her home-canned sausage and deposits it in Rose's larder. "I waited for Rose to die," she tells us, "but the weather was warm for sauerkraut and sausage; that was a winter dish."

The serious purpose behind this comic grisliness, of course, is to convey the wild dysfunction of abuse and concealment. Ginny has lived all her life placating, holding things together, denying her pain. For a long time, she can't even remember it. Rose, remembering every one of the 200 times that Lawrence came to her bed when she was a teen-ager, keeps silent, but she grows up to be irascible and disruptive.

What if, Smiley is asking; what if Lear were the abuser and what if his two oldest daughters were simply asserting themselves and trying to break free? The victim is blamed; the victim blames herself.

It is timely, ingenious, devastating, as a problem rigorously ventilated and as a parodic theatrical reversal used to dramatize it. But these machineries get out of control; they chew each other up. Particularly do they weaken the broader novel of character and place to which they are attached.

Smiley makes a living, breathing portrait of the Iowa landscape, so peaceable and orderly but maintained in brutal tension. In a few introductory pages, we get a bucolic picture of three neighboring farms as Ginny recalls them from her childhood. There was her family's, the Ericson place, where she and her sisters would go play, and the farm belonging to Harold Clark, Lawrence's buddy. Then she gives figures, and the peace turns baleful: Cook, 640 acres, no mortgage; Clark, 500 acres, no mortgage; Ericson, 370 acres, mortgage.

"Harold Clark and my father used to argue at our kitchen table about who should get the Ericson land when they finally lost their mortgage," she writes. It is the secret behind the picture postcard; when she resumes the narrative, now grown up and married, her father has won the argument and the land. Of that rich landscape, drained from marsh and floating on its water table, she tells us: "The stationary fields are always flowing towards one farmer and away from another."

It is Ginny's voice that relates the seemingly golden family life that the marsh will rise to flood. It is a devoted, troubled voice; a voice that clings to the positive, that resists confrontation for as long as it can. It is supple and witty, and it evokes the lives around her in all their tensions, troubles and pleasures. It is the voice, of course, of denial; yet it has created a complex fictional life. When it is turned to spinning the anti-Lear melodrama, to relating and taking part in the self-investigation and its violent consequences, it goes flat. It becomes more truthful—nothing is hidden—but less alive.

It is, again, the problem with problem fiction. In life, we may try to confront our pasts, to overcome our denials, to remove the shadows that impede us. But fiction is not therapy. It is partly the shadows that bring characters up into relief. Lighting them without flattening the characters is a complex process. Ginny is more interesting and individual when she is denying. Before the Cook family secrets are vented and their disastrous consequences endured, she is a person; afterwards, she is mainly a solution, though Smiley never suggests that it is a happy one. (pp. 3, 13)

Richard Eder, "Sharper than a Serpent's Tooth," in Los Angeles Times Book Review, *November 10, 1991, pp. 3, 13.*

[Writing *A Thousand Acres* was] laborious and exhausting. Two pages and I was wiped out. I could hardly drag myself back to the typewriter, and normally there's nowhere else I'd rather be. Despite all the success the novel has had, I still feel alienated from it. My monster child.

—*Jane Smiley, in the* Observer, *25 October 1992.*

Martha Duffy   (review date 11 November 1991)

[In the following excerpt, Duffy identifies the feminist and environmental concerns in A Thousand Acres.*]*

Larry Cook owns 1,000 acres of rich soil in Iowa. He is a tough, autocratic man, well suited to his unforgiving job, "a man willing to work all the time who's trained his children to work the same way." The Cook place is a model modern establishment with all the signs of a good farm: "clean fields, neatly painted buildings, breakfast at six, no debts, no standing water." Life is a round of chores—the endless regimen of meals, the canning frenzies, the tireless pursuit of new and fancier equipment.

One day, without warning, Larry decides to turn the property over to his daughters—Ginny, Rose and Caroline—and their husbands. If any of this reminds you of *King Lear,* read on. At the beginning the Cooks seem invulnerable. Only Caroline's defection to Des Moines and marriage to a non-farmer slightly disturb their cohesiveness. But by the end, the father has gone mad, the farm has been lost, the family splintered.

It is a tribute to Jane Smiley's absorbing, well-plotted novel that it never reads like a gloss on Shakespeare. For one thing, *A Thousand Acres* has an exact and exhilarating sense of place, a sheer Americanness that gives it its own soul and roots. More important, Ginny and Rose are not villains. Smiley had had *Lear* at the back of her mind since she first read the play. "I never bought the conventional interpretation that Goneril and Regan were completely evil," she says. "Unconsciously at first, I had reservations: this is not the whole story."

Seeing Akira Kurosawa's *Ran,* also based on *Lear,* provided the missing link. In the film the daughters are sons, and one of them tells the old man that his children are what he made them. Smiley began reading commentaries about the play, especially by feminists, and was miffed to find that even the most radical rejected Shakespeare's terrible twosome: "A remark condemning Goneril and Regan was de rigueur."

Ginny and Rose, in their 30s, make a wonderful double portrait of sisters who love and understand each other. A reader could sit around their kitchen table for hours. They are not plotters but increasingly angry victims, and their rage makes them blind. Ginny has had five miscarriages, with no surviving children. Rose has had a mastectomy. Both fall in love with Jess Clark, a local boy who arrives back in town after 13 years well informed about environmental woes. Not only the sisters but also the father and his friend Harold fall victim to the poisoned land. Blinded by anhydrous ammonia, Harold and his fate "got in everywhere, into the solidest relationships, the firmest beliefs, the strongest loyalties, the most deeply held convictions you had about the people you had known most of your life."

Though she has never lived on a working farm, Smiley, 42, has roots in rural country. She once asked her grandmother what it was like on the family's Idaho ranch; the old woman replied, "I don't remember—I was too busy cooking." Smiley, who teaches at Iowa State University, is a believer in the radical agriculture movement. But she sees an inescapable link between the exploitation of land and that of women, and here she parts company with farm reformers like Wendell Berry as well as nostalgia buffs who yearn for the smaller-scaled, prechemical days.

"Women, just like nature or the land, have been seen as something to be used," says Smiley. "Feminists insist that women have intrinsic value, just as environmentalists believe that nature has its own worth, independent of its use to man." In *A Thousand Acres,* men's dominance of women takes a violent turn, and incest becomes an undercurrent in the novel. The implication is that the impulse to incest concerns not so much sex as a will to power, an expression of yet another way the woman serves the man. (pp. 92-3)

When a novel comes even close to being a tract, its beauty and entertainment value are shrunken. The magic of *A Thousand Acres* is that it deals so effectively with both the author's scholarship and her dead-serious social concerns in an engrossing piece of fiction. We are accustomed to learning the political concerns of 19th century novelists through their books. Smiley represents a hopeful sign that feminists and environmentalists are finding imaginative ways to express their convictions. (p. 94)

Martha Duffy, "The Case for Goneril and Regan," in Time, *New York, Vol. 138, No. 19, November 11, 1991, pp. 92-4.*

Julia Just   (review date 13 November 1991)

[*In the following review of* A Thousand Acres, *Just discusses Smiley's depiction of familial relationships and her exploration of human behavior.*]

Jane Smiley's latest novel, **A Thousand Acres** is set in Zebulon County, Iowa, where the farmland is "thicker, richer, more alive with a past and future than any soil anywhere." The land is also layered with long-festering intrigues among jealous neighbors, and poisons blamed for miscarriages and cancer. This is the novel's overriding metaphor—a rich but deceptive topsoil yielding up secrets of the buried past.

Initially, the story's calm, inviting surface recalls Joan Chase's lyrical portrait of a family farm in *During the Reign of the Queen of Persia,* as well as Ms. Smiley's own previous works of fiction, with their almost uncannily precise depictions of daily life. In her widely praised books **The Age of Grief** and **The Greenlanders.** Ms. Smiley made the very ordinariness of things the most compelling substance of her narratives. But **A Thousand Acres** turns out to be closer in spirit to her ambitious recent novella, ***Good Will,*** in which seemingly innocent beginnings lead to dark revelations and unexpected violence.

The novel, set in the late 1970s, is narrated by Ginny, whose father, Larry Cook, owns the biggest and most profitable farm around—a thousand acres. Ginny is an accommodating, even malleable, sort, although at 36 she has been bitterly disappointed by a series of miscarriages with her husband, Ty. She's appealingly levelheaded, but not immune to deeper impulses; she confesses to harboring vague desires, "secret, passionate wishes."

While the youngest sister, Caroline, went to college and became a tough-talking lawyer in Des Moines, Ginny and her sister Rose stayed behind on the farm. It is soon apparent why. After their mother died, when they were teenagers, their father became an abusive tyrant who kept the entire family under his thumb. Later, Rose will force Ginny to remember just how abusive "Daddy" was; as time goes on, that word comes to have chilling, Sylvia Plath-like overtones.

When the father suddenly decides to cede the farm to his three daughters, it brings the hidden past to the surface and winds up setting each family member against the other, irrevocably. Another catalyst is Jess Clark, a neighbor's prodigal son, back from Canada, where he had been since Vietnam. For a while, he's the answer to Ginny's "passionate wishes"—and he convinces her that the farm's runoff in the groundwater is to blame for her miscarriages.

Ms. Smiley can describe compounding strains in a marriage better than anybody, and the confrontations between Ginny and Ty—quiet but devastating—are among the best scenes in the book. She's superb at depicting the surface effects of feelings "too complicated . . . to name," the way trust can "disappear into formality," and she plays off this life of the emotions beautifully against the daily necessities of the farm.

Wonderfully evoked, too, are the pressures of keeping up

appearances in a small town. Ultimately, Ginny concludes, putting the best face on things in front of the neighbors is the "broken plank you are left with after the ship has gone down." Still, as the sisters confront their old father and his tainted bequest, the unending string of disasters that follows seems more than strictly necessary, while the characters' motivations sometimes hover on the outer edges of plausibility.

It's pretty clear early on to the reader, for example, that the erratic old farmer is in the initial stages of Alzheimer's disease, but Caroline never seems to figure it out. This is overly convenient, since it's essential to the story that she blame the rest of the family for everything that happens. As for Ginny, our sympathetic companion, the ever-present litany of her household chores ("I spent the morning shampooing the carpet . . .") will eventually include preparing a jar of poisoned sausage. We've come a long way from the stewed pork chops and kitchen-table confidences that open this book.

Still, the novel's center holds firm. Its narrative momentum is undeniable, as is the psychological truth (with its deliberate nod to *Lear*) underlying the mortal combat between Larry Cook and his daughters, and among the newly estranged sisters. Indeed, if the grim patriarch dominates the first half of the book, Rose—grabby and manip-

ulative and iron-willed—dominates the second. Of all the other illusions of past and future, Ginny's adoring love for Rose, her conviction that they were a team "united" against their father, proves the most traumatic to give up. It is a point of no return, but also exhilarating:

"The strongest feeling was that now I knew them all," Ginny says of her divided family. "Rather than feeling 'not myself,' I felt intensely, newly, more myself than ever before." It is the beginning of a new life, far from the old "ordered, hard-working world."

As for the thousand-acre farm in Zebulon County, one notices right away that Ms. Smiley's novel begins in 1979—on the brink of the Midwestern farm crisis, with its falling land values and rising suicide rates. The timing is an apt and melancholy touch—as though Larry Cook foresaw it all, and wanted no part of it.

Julia Just, "Lear in Iowa: Family Farm, Family Trouble," in The Wall Street Journal, *November 13, 1991, p. A14.*

Jane Smiley with Suzanne Berne (interview date Summer 1992)

[*In the interview below, Smiley discusses her writing technique, how Shakespeare's* King Lear *influenced* A Thousand Acres, *and her interest in writing about familial relationships.*]

[*Berne*]: *Because people are always interested in beginnings, let's start there: When you begin writing a novel, what do you have to know to get going?*

[Smiley]: It all swirls around in my head until I know the *place* and then it gels. Sometimes I've been there, or passed it, or sometimes it's just a place that attracts me. When I wrote the novella **Good Will,** I set it in State College, Pennsylvania. I've driven through there.

So it's a place that's intriguing enough for you to want to live there for the duration of the novel?

Exactly.

Do you begin your short stories differently? Are they less place-oriented?

Probably. For me, a lot of short stories have to do with a couple of separate ideas coming into juxtaposition with one another. In the past I've said it's akin to having three or four interesting objects on your desk and you move them around until you can see some relationship among them.

Which also seems to be the way you write novels. With **A Thousand Acres,** *you said you consciously brought together* King Lear, *farming, and a dysfunctional family that had experienced incest. Which element came first?*

In this case what came first was a longstanding dissatisfaction with an interpretation of *King Lear* that privileged the father's needs over the daughters'. Right before I started the novel, I felt a growing sense of a link between a habit of mind that perceives daughters and children as owned things. I felt, viscerally, that a habit of mind exists in our

---

An excerpt from *A Thousand Acres*

Most issues on a farm return to the issue of keeping up appearances. Farmers extrapolate quickly from the farm to the farmer. A farmer looks like himself, when he goes to the café, but he also looks like his farm, which everyone has passed on the way into town. What his farm looks like boils down to questions of character. Farmers are quick to cite the weather, their luck, the turning tides of prices and government regulations, but among themselves these excuses fall away. A good farmer (a savvy manager, someone with talent for animals and machines, a man willing to work all the time who's raised his children to work the same way) will have a good farm. A poor-looking farm diagrams the farmer's personal failures. Most farmers see farming as an unforgiving way of life, and they are themselves less than indulgent about weedy fields, dirty equipment, delinquent children, badly cared for animals, a farmhouse that looks like the barn. It may be different elsewhere in the country, but in Zebulon County, which was settled mostly by English, Germans, and Scandinavians, a good appearance was the source and the sign of all other good things.

It was imperative that the growing discord in our family be made to appear minor. The indication that my father truly was beside himself was the way he had carried his argument with us to others. But we couldn't give in to that—we were well trained. We knew our roles and our strategies without hesitation and without consultation. The paramount value of looking right is not something you walk away from after a single night. After such a night as we had, in fact, it is something you embrace, the broken plank you are left with after the ship has gone down.

Jane Smiley, in her A Thousand Acres, *Knopf, 1991.*

---

culture of seeing nature and women in much the same way. In fact, they represent one another in a lot of writing. That's a strong element of *King Lear*. Lear's always talking about nature and his daughters, conflating the two. Thinking along those lines, I went back to the play and reconsidered my dissatisfaction with the order of the universe the play proposes, which is that the daughters have a certain relation to the father that the two older daughters betray but that Cordelia lives up to.

Because she's the good daughter.

Right. And the play also proposes that Lear changes—that he becomes more human and less proud, less self-centered and arrogant. He goes from being a king who has little self-knowledge to being a man who has gained self-knowledge over the course of his suffering. I think that's the mainstream interpretation of the play, and I disagree with it. I don't know if it's Shakespeare's interpretation, but he seems to plead for Lear. And I think that's a pleading that can only be made by a man. In fact, Lear *doesn't* change. He changes, let's say, in relation to the male world; he no longer is proud and arrogant. He becomes dependent on Kent, Edgar, and Gloucester. They become a group of equals through suffering—in the male world. But he doesn't change in his relationship to the female world. He never changes his attitude toward his older daughters, but continues to believe that they are unnatural, vicious, and brutal. And he also never changes his attitude toward Cordelia. He goes from expecting her total attention and love at the beginning, and being angry when she doesn't give it to him, to expecting it at the end and being pleased when she does. He gets his way. Cordelia is the one, finally, who's defeated.

How did you come to choose Ginny as the narrator? Why not Caroline, who is the Cordelia figure, or Rose, who is more tragic in some ways?

That was a craft decision. In my experience of pairs of daughters, the older one is often more anxious and tends to wring her hands. The younger one is often more certain of everything. From a narrative point of view, it is much more interesting to have a narrator who is uncertain of what she thinks or what should be done or what the future will hold. Otherwise, the plot predictably revolves around pride going before a fall. Also, the oldest child is often the one who, in any conflict, is torn between sympathizing with the parents and with the other siblings. Now if Rose were narrating the book, it would be continuously angry in tone. In my experience, that becomes very tedious because there's no modulation of the voice.

Because you were working with Lear, *did you know what the ending would be?*

Oh sure. I was determined to stick with the plot as far as I could all the way to the end.

You said once about your novel The Greenlanders *that what drove you to write it was your belief in apocalyptic endings. Do you still believe in them? I found the ending of* A Thousand Acres *to be quite apocalyptic.*

Actually, I feel this book is a step away from the abyss. I had a philosophical knot to contemplate. I won't say that

I solved it, but I noticed a number of things from my research into the lives of women who had been sexually abused by their fathers—one of them being that the path into the future is a very tortured and dark one. In some ways, the woman has to find a way for her life *not* to end, to not be destroyed by what her father has done to her. I felt that it was important for Ginny and Rose to thrash out that very question of surviving incest. The fact that Ginny and Rose can talk about it, and Ginny and her nieces can talk about it, and they can go into the future making lives for themselves is a movement away from the apocalypse, even in the face of the end of their life on the farm.

I was struck by the depth of knowledge you must have acquired about farming to write A Thousand Acres. *How did you come to choose farming as an element of this book?*

Farming was something I'd always been interested in. So it wasn't as though I had the thought about using *King Lear* and found a place to put it. These two paths converged as a result of realizing that nature and women were so closely connected as exploitable objects in the mind of our culture. The steps that I took in terms of feminist theory were very small and not radical at all. I had always known about the conflation of women and nature. But it was only three or four years ago that all of that clicked together and became a mode of perception that I could use to conceive of and execute a novel. The hardest part about writing the novel was working through this new way of looking at things against previous interpretations of *King Lear*. One interesting thing that I noted when I was researching the novel was that there were no feminist critics up until that point who did not distance themselves from Goneril and Regan. Shakespeare and the interpretive establishment since him have painted them so bleakly that in almost every article it was *de rigeur* for the writer to set herself apart from Goneril and Regan, to characterize them as evil or label them somehow.

Which is what happens to Ginny and Rose in their community.

That's right. In some ways, the novel is a very somber game, but it's still a game. One of the parts of the game for me was presenting, through gossip and through what Ginny perceives, the normal interpretation of *King Lear* as a counterpoint to what we know is actually happening.

How long did the book take to write?

I worked on it for about three years. It was pretty much a struggle all the way through. It was very grim for one thing. Then there was the aspect of having to think through all the details, all of the perceptions, and make sure that they weren't self-contradictory. And that felt like physical labor. I'd get up from writing and I would feel as if I'd been carrying rocks.

So having the plot of King Lear *as an existing structure didn't make the novel any easier to write?*

It made it easier in some ways and harder in others. I knew where I was going, but it was always a labor to get there. I felt that I was following someone's mind but that that mind was very hidden from me. I was teasing out the unspoken links, and the unspoken thoughts in that mind, while at the same time I was disagreeing with them and presenting my own interpretation of those events. The weight of the patriarchy is always a heavy one.

Does that have something to do with your interest in writing from a male perspective in some of your stories and novellas? Is it a way to try to understand what the view of the patriarchy really is?

Let's say I have differing allegiances with any given piece of work. A lot of my allegiances are to the dynamic and aesthetic storytelling elements. Often I will make a decision I think is good for the story, and then I'll work out the philosophical and thematic issues in relation to that decision. In *Good Will,* for example, I wanted to write about trying to be God. Bob creates his world, and I wanted to write about what the creator learns from the rebellion of the created. His son's problem is that he can't find a niche in his father's world. Everything is either something his father has made or done or something his father knows all about. I wanted that story to be about someone who very laboriously learns that the world he has created is not what he thinks it is. And I could only do that, I thought, from a man's point of view.

New York Times *critic Michiko Kakutani has referred to much of your work as "domestic fiction." What draws you so strongly to family situations? What is especially dramatic about domestic life?*

Well, she hadn't read *The Greenlanders* when she wrote that. I think she meant that remark pejoratively, because she's on a campaign to prove that American writers are too much in the house. Supposedly, European writers are more ambitious. I think what has happened in the twentieth century is that all the forms of systematic thought about society and culture have failed. They have proved themselves to be brutal or ineffective. Right now writers are trying to come up with some other system for thinking about individuals as social beings and society as formed of individuals. Clearly the intermediate form between the individual and the society is the family. Writers feel that they will figure something out if they explore the cruelties of the family as a microcosm that will lead to some understanding of the individual on one side and the society on the other side. That's certainly the way I feel.

I think it was Ward Just who said that every family is its own country, with its own customs, language, and laws.

I think that's true. And the family is the pivot between the individual and the society. Families are so different, though, that it's possible to get hung up exploring the idio-syncrasies of a given family without asking any larger questions.

You've been called one of your generation's "most eloquent chroniclers of ordinary familial love." What is ordinary familial love, do you think, especially if you view the family as a "pivot" into the larger world?

Maybe it's a discipline. A discipline that keeps you paying attention to your children and getting up with them and getting them off to school. My husband and I were just watching the movie *Mr. and Mrs. Bridge.* There's one moment in the movie that directly addresses what I'm trying to say: Mr. Bridge comes down the stairs in his robe to check the house. He comes out to the son and asks if he's closed the house up. He locks the door, closes the window, and checks something else. For people in our culture to see Paul Newman, who has played so many romantic heroes and renegades, lock a window or make sure a door is closed is a revelation.

So ordinary familial love rests in the routines that keep the family going?

Yes. It's discipline. A way of maintaining order for the sake of others, for the future. (pp. 36-8)

Jane Smiley and Suzanne Berne, in an interview in Belles Lettres: A Review of Books by Women, *Vol. 7, No. 4, Summer, 1992, pp. 36-8.*

FURTHER READING

Anderson, Jon. "Author Finds Ample Fodder in Rural Midwest." *Chicago Tribune* (24 November 1991): 1, 3.
    Interview in which Smiley discusses living in Iowa, growing up during the 1950s, and her decision to incorporate feminist revisionism into *A Thousand Acres.*

Christiansen, Rupert. "Sharper than the Serpent's Tooth." *Observer,* No. 10489 (25 October 1992): 63.
    Provides biographical information about Smiley and discusses the similarities between *A Thousand Acres* and Shakespeare's *King Lear.*

Wood, James. "The Glamour of Glamour." *London Review of Books* 14, No. 22 (19 December 1992): 17-18.
    Compares Smiley's *A Thousand Acres* with Donna Tartt's *The Secret History.*

Additional coverage of Smiley's life and career is contained in the following sources published by Gale Research: *Contemporary Authors,* **Vol. 104;** *Contemporary Authors New Revision Series,* **Vol. 30; and** *Contemporary Literary Criticism,* **Vol. 53.**

Art Spiegelman

Maus: A Survivor's Tale II: And Here My Troubles Began

Prizes: Los Angeles Times Book Award and special Pulitzer Prize

(Also wrote under the pseudonyms Joe Cutrate, Al Flooglebuckle, and Skeeter Grant) Born in 1948, Spiegelman is a Swedish-born American cartoonist.

INTRODUCTION

In *Maus: A Survivor's Tale II: And Here My Troubles Began,* Spiegelman chronicles his father's experiences in German concentration camps during World War II. Like the earlier *Maus: A Survivor's Tale: My Father Bleeds History* (1986), *Maus: A Survivor's Tale II* is written in comic-book form. In both works, Spiegelman depicts Jews as mice and Nazis as cats, a technique which most critics have praised for advancing a unique, nonstereotypical, and accessible treatment of the Holocaust. The *Maus* saga is based on a series of conversations Spiegelman had with his father, Vladek, before the latter's death in 1982. The first volume recounts Vladek's early years in Poland with his wife Anja, the couple's attempted escape to Hungary in 1944, and Anja's eventual suicide in 1968; the second volume details the horror Vladek experienced as a prisoner at Auschwitz and then at Dachau. Critical reaction to *Maus: A Survivor's Tale II* has been positive, with reviewers praising Spiegelman's use of dialect and imagery and his parallel exploration of the Holocaust and his relationship with his father. Lawrence L. Langer has stated: "Perhaps no Holocaust narrative will ever contain the whole experience. But Art Spiegelman has found an original and authentic form to draw us closer to its bleak heart."

PRINCIPAL WORKS

The Complete Mr. Infinity (comics) 1970
The Viper Vicar of Vice, Villainy, and Vickedness (comics) 1972
Zip-a-Tune and More Melodies (comics) 1972
Ace Hole, Midge Detective (comics) 1974
Language of Comics (comics) 1974
Breakdowns: From Maus to Now: An Anthology of Strips (comics) 1977
Every Day Has Its Dog (comics) 1979
Word and Turn (comics) 1979
Two-Fisted Painters Action Adventure (comics) 1980

Maus: A Survivor's Tale: My Father Bleeds History (comics) 1986
Read Yourself Raw: Comix Anthology for Damned Intellectuals [with Françoise Mouly] (comics) 1987
Maus: A Survivor's Tale II: And Here My Troubles Began (comics) 1991
Raw 3: High Culture for Lowbrows (comics) 1991

CRITICISM

Lawrence L. Langer (review date 3 November 1991)

[*In the following review, Langer praises Spiegelman's depiction of the Holocaust in* Maus: A Survivor's Tale II.]

Art Spiegelman doesn't draw comics. It might be clever to say he draws tragics, but that would be inaccurate too. Like its predecessor, *Maus: A Survivor's Tale II: And Here My Troubles Began* is a serious form of pictorial literature, sustaining and even intensifying the power of the first volume. It resists defining labels.

The author and artist Art Spiegelman continues the story of the character Artie Spiegelman, who is trying to reconstruct in cartoon form the lives of his father, Vladek, and his mother, Anja, both survivors of Auschwitz. In 1968 Anja committed suicide, and the first part of *Maus* ends with the young Artie calling his father a "murderer" for having destroyed Anja's wartime memoirs without even having read them. Early in the sequel, Artie confesses to his wife, Françoise, "When I was a kid I used to think about which of my parents I'd let the Nazis take to the ovens if I could only save one of them. Usually I saved my mother. Do you think that's normal?" His wife dryly replies, "*Nobody's* normal," leaving the reader wondering how to redefine "normal" for a family whose Holocaust legacy still exerts its influence over father and son.

With a distinctly post-modern flourish, Mr. Spiegelman reminds us throughout his text that *Maus II* is a narrative about incidents that, in many of their details, may be incommunicable. Artie admits to his wife, "I can't even make any sense out of my relationship with my father. How am I supposed to make any sense out of Auschwitz?" One might conclude that a "comic strip" portraying the Jews as mice, the Germans as cats, the Poles as pigs, the French as frogs, the Americans as dogs and the Swedes as reindeer would divert the reader from a meaningful pursuit of Artie's troubled questions—but this is not at all the case.

The "meaning" is in the effort, not the results, and the animal characters create a distancing effect that allows us to follow the fable without being drowned in its grim, inhuman horrors. Tensions abound; Vladek has forgotten little of his ordeal, but he doesn't like to think about it and he only speaks of it at Artie's prodding. Some need beyond mere curiosity or professional interest drives Artie to record and draw his parents' Holocaust experience, while at the same time, as he confesses to his psychiatrist, "Some part of me doesn't want to draw or think about Auschwitz." And whatever he does accomplish, he concedes, doesn't seem like much compared to surviving the death camp.

The struggle to transform history and testimony into art is thus a central part of the drama of the text, and the reader is constantly sucked into the maelstrom of the conflict. Who can fail to sympathize with Vladek, an Auschwitz survivor reunited with his wife after the war, only to face her suicide nearly a quarter of a century later in Rego Park, Queens? But who can fail to chide him for being so stingy that he leaves the gas burner lit all day at his summer bungalow because the cost of the gas is included in the rental and he can light his cigarettes without wasting a match? (And who can fail to conjecture about that ominous conjunction of gas with flame, over which Vladek today exerts complete control?) Artie despises his father's frugality, and with some justice, but Mr. Spiegelman con-

Vladek Spiegelman, Art Spiegelman's father.

stantly reminds us that Vladek's behavior in the present cannot be separated from his anguish in the past. The reader thus develops insights that Mr. Spiegelman's persona, Artie, can't always achieve, and this is one of the many striking examples of the author's expert handling of narrative.

If *Maus II* chronicles Vladek Spiegelman's journey from Auschwitz to Dachau and beyond, it also recounts the impact of that voyage on his son. The story alternates between past and present, but so does the inner life of its characters, reflecting the confused sense of time so many former Holocaust victims and their families have today. In the first part of *Maus* we learned that Artie's parents had a previous son, Richieu, who at the age of 3 was poisoned by Anja's sister together with her own children, to prevent the Gestapo from taking them away. Artie has lived beneath the shadow of this lost brother, whose framed picture hangs prominently in his parents' bedroom, a periodic source of remorse, shame, grief, guilt and despair. Indeed, the presence of Richieu frames the narrative, since that picture also appears on the dedication page of *Maus II*. There the words "For Richieu" seem to be meant to ease the burden of memory for the brother born after the war.

But if Richieu has the first word, who has the last? As if to confirm his doubts about making any sense out of

Auschwitz, Mr. Spiegelman ends his tale with the same melancholy answer that nearly every Holocaust testimony, written or oral, provides: the dead, those who did not return, have the last word. How could it be otherwise? Once Vladek has finished his testimony with an account of how he was reunited with Anja after the war, he asks Artie to turn off the tape recorder—he wants to sleep. The old man's last utterance, in the final panel of the text, is "I'm *tired* from talking, Richieu, and it's *enough* stories for now." So the past has conquered the present, and in Vladek's mind, the living Artie has been replaced by the dead Richieu. This panel is followed by an image of a gravestone, informing us that the real Vladek Spiegelman died in 1982. *Maus II* is his testament.

But this book is not his transfiguration, and it is to Art Spiegelman's credit that he scrupulously avoids sentimentalizing or melodramatizing his tale. He writes with restraint and a relentless honesty, sparing neither his father nor himself. Given his brother's death and his mother's suicide, to say nothing of the other extensive family losses, there is little to celebrate. We are offered a whisper of hope for the future, since the book is also dedicated to his daughter, Nadja (born in 1987), but we are left wondering what kind of shadow her father's narrative will cast over her life, when she grows old enough to read it. Like the other questions raised in *Maus II,* the answer remains shrouded in uncertainty. Perhaps no Holocaust narrative will ever contain the whole experience. But Art Spiegelman has found an original and authentic form to draw us closer to its bleak heart. (pp. 1, 35-6)

> Lawrence L. Langer, "A Fable of the Holocaust," in The New York Times Book Review, *November 3, 1991, pp. 1, 35-6.*

VLS   (review date December 1991)

[*In the review below, the critic praises the comic-book form of* Maus: A Survivor's Tale II *for being personal and accessible.*]

The two volumes of Art Spiegelman's brilliant Holocaust-memorial-in-a-comic-book should really be read as one. [*Maus: A Survivor's Tale: My Father Bleeds History*] told the story of Spiegelman's parents, Vladek and Anja, from their first meeting in 1935 to their arrival at Auschwitz in 1944. [*Maus: A Survivor's Tale II: And, Here My Troubles Began*] picks up the tale without dropping a stitch, following the Spiegelmans to the end of the war. The books also reach into the present, where we see a character called Artie Spiegelman interviewing his father about the past and agonizing over his ability to portray it. In a year that has seen several young writers deploy elaborate metaphors in attempting to describe the Holocaust, Spiegelman has created the perfect structure: *Maus*'s horror is intimate yet tolerable, its presentation gimmicky but expressive.

The crucial part of the book's comic-strip form is not the drawings but the freedom it gives Spiegelman to present Vladek directly to the reader; he puts his father's words right in his father's mouth, or at least in a balloon over his head. Vladek's Yiddish-inflected English gives him a pow-

erful presence, as when he recounts being herded into a shower at Auschwitz: "Here it was the live showers, not the dead gas showers what we heard sometimes rumors." All the characters speak for themselves, unmediated by a narrative voice. Though we know Spiegelman is organizing and editing the material, his father's tale comes to us more forcefully than it could have had "Artie" been a conventional narrator. The form also allows Spiegelman to move smoothly from the past to the present, showing his father's youthful resourcefulness and elderly irritability as two sides of a coin. Spiegelman makes no attempt to pretty things up; this isn't *Mickey Maus*. His father grew into a cranky old miser, and Artie was no perfect son. But they're both survivors, and *Maus* is a testament to their love for each other in the shadow of history.

> [*Laurie Muchnick*], in a review of "Maus," in VLS, *No. 101, December, 1991, p. 16.*

I feel so inadequate trying to reconstruct a reality that was worse than my darkest dreams. And trying to do it as a *comic strip*!

—*Art Spiegelman, in his* Maus: A Survivor's Tale II: And Here My Troubles Began, *Pantheon, 1991.*

Craig Seligman   (review date 3 December 1991)

[*In the following review, Seligman evaluates the strengths and weaknesses of* Maus: A Survivor's Tale II.]

It must have taken heroic resourcefulness and doggedness and stamina for a Jew to make it out of Auschwitz alive; and Vladek Spiegelman, the survivor-protagonist of [Art Spiegelman's *Maus* saga], is definitely a hero. He is also, three decades after the liberation, querulous, demanding, insensitive, stingy, and fatuous. The question, the mystery, is: to what extent are his opposite sides really one? And beyond that, how much of his character is innate, how much of it formed in the camps? In a world this incoherent, how do you judge character, anyway?

Maus II, the conclusion to Art Spiegelman's comic-book memoir of his father, isn't properly a sequel; it extends the story but doesn't stand alone. *Maus I,* which appeared five years ago, stops in mid-crescendo; *Maus II* continues the crescendo, building the horror to the climax of Auschwitz. The books actually follow two plots and two protagonists, Vladek and Auschwitz at the core of one, and Art, the son, prying out the old man's story, at the heart of the other.

Spiegelman gazes at his father with the resigned resentment of a put-upon child and the pitilessness of an artist. His father drives him crazy, but he doesn't try to burnish the old man's image, even though he worries, "he's just like the racist caricature of the miserly old Jew." He doesn't burnish any of his Jews; the horror of Auschwitz isn't that it was visited on innocents but that it was visited on anybody. While *Maus* may be a stab at coherence, the only coherence it achieves, or can achieve, is formal. When you finish, you're no closer to understanding what happened than you were when you began because, as Vladek sighs, "about Auschwitz, *nobody* can understand."

Most of this second volume was composed after the brilliant success of *Maus I,* and it contains some painfully self-conscious passages. ("I feel so inadequate trying to reconstruct a reality that was worse than my darkest dreams. And trying to do it as a *comic strip*!") Spiegelman plays deftly with chronology, jumping about in time, although he robs himself of a denouement by depicting the events that followed Vladek's postwar reunion with his first wife, Anja, before we get the event itself—which ends the book, splat, all of a sudden. We need more information about some characters, particularly Vladek's second wife, Mala, whose constant bickering with him spreads across the surface of the story like a rash. Vladek accuses her of revolting greed ("She screamed, 'I want the money! The money! *The money!*'"); should we take the old crank's word for it, or dismiss it as raving?

These aren't minor flaws, and yet this cartoon novel with Jewish mice and German cats (and Polish pigs and American dogs) achieves a richness and solemnity and sorrow that's as startling now as it was five years ago. Spiegelman's whimsicality (Part II adds Swedish reindeer, Gypsy moths) suggests a sweetness behind the unforgiving eye, but it also has an organizing function. The animal faces strip away the characters' individuality (you have to identify them by what they wear) and group them nationally. The bestiary ties Art and present-day Jews to the older generation in a way that words alone never could; it gives a hard, subverbal image to racial hatred. There's nothing abstract about cats and mice.

The events and personalities are too specific for the book to read like a parable, though, and we should be wary about granting too much significance to what is, at bottom, a gimmick. You accept the conventions and absorb them swiftly. The illustrations scan quickly and go straight to the point; they don't ask you to linger, they impel you. *Maus* is not a duet for words and pictures—it's closer than it looks to a conventional novel. The books' real power is language, specifically Vladek's language, a fractured Yinglish that might have been supplied by Leo Rosten. This dialect sounds as automatically funny to us as Eliza Doolittle's cockney or Amos 'n' Andy's jive, and in using it to deliver news of the century's grisliest hour, Spiegelman makes it cut like a cleaver. Most of us know about the power of Yiddish only by reputation. Think of *"oy gevalt"* as something you say when the toilet backs up or you hear that a friend is going out with a jerk. And so when the missing Vladek shows up at his parents' door and they shout, in their emotion, *"Oy gevalt!"* something lost is recovered, something true is redeemed, and the scales fall from our ears. (pp. 65-6)

Craig Seligman, " 'Maus' Redux," in The Village Voice, *Vol. XXXVI, No. 49, December 3, 1991, pp. 65-6.*

Laurie Stone   (review date 6 January 1992)

[*In the following review, Stone discusses the effectiveness of depicting the Holocaust in comic-book form.*]

It has taken Art Spiegelman thirteen years to complete [his *Maus* saga], a memoir of his parents' survival of the Holocaust and his own journey from a barbarous childhood—years spent pinned beneath the hairy paw of his tyrannical father. With the publication of *Maus II,* the author/cartoonist has achieved a wondrously spare, fanciful and profound work of art, one that takes as accurate a measure of private anguish as of global nightmare. Imaginatively, delicately, Spiegelman meditates on the saving grace of perspective—knowing what is big and what is little as contexts shift. In the face of pain and defeat, his books attest, a sense of irony is the surest consolation, the steadiest provision for sanity.

Spiegelman's ruling conceit—drawing Jews as mice, Germans cats, Poles pigs, Americans dogs, etc.—is an ample field for playing with perspective, for it immediately points up the variable sizes and shapes characters can assume. The bestiary reflects the dual perspectives of the larger world and family trauma. From the perspective of children, all adults are potential cats: large, inscrutable, capricious and autocratic. From the perspective of Jews, Nazism brutally infantilizes: denying movement, self-will, privacy.

The *Maus* books are structured around conversations, Art winnowing out facts from his father, Vladek. Since Art's mother, Anja, committed suicide in 1968, Art has only his father's version of the past and, crimping him further, Vladek has burned Anja's diaries before the start of the project. Art and Vladek are in Queens and the Catskills, and then, as Vladek narrates, we shift to Poland, Germany, the camps. Past and present counterpoint each other, showing what in human hearts remains fixed and what can alter.

Art's tactic is to worry out loud about the tangles that his work then goes on to prove he's smoothed. Near the end of *Maus I,* he fears he's reduced his father not merely to a mouse but to a rat: a "racist caricature of the miserly old Jew." There are grounds for these alarms. He shows us a Vladek who is wealthy but steals paper towels from restrooms, a man who reuses tea bags, hoards wooden matches, pleads with a store manager to take back half-eaten packages of food.

Summering in the Catskills, Vladek is shrunken and mewling—a creature with no sense of the relative size of events. Everything ushers in panic. To insure that Art returns a phone call, he pretends to have a heart attack. When Art and his wife, Françoise, visit, he pressures them to stay, all the while arranging their clothes, cajoling them to eat his preferred foods, sputtering a racist slur in Yiddish when Françoise picks up a black hitchhiker. He rants about his second wife, Mala, who has left him after years of abuse and who he claims has robbed him. Like most bullies, he portrays himself as a victim, never as tormentor.

Still, even at his puniest, Vladek comes off so extreme and

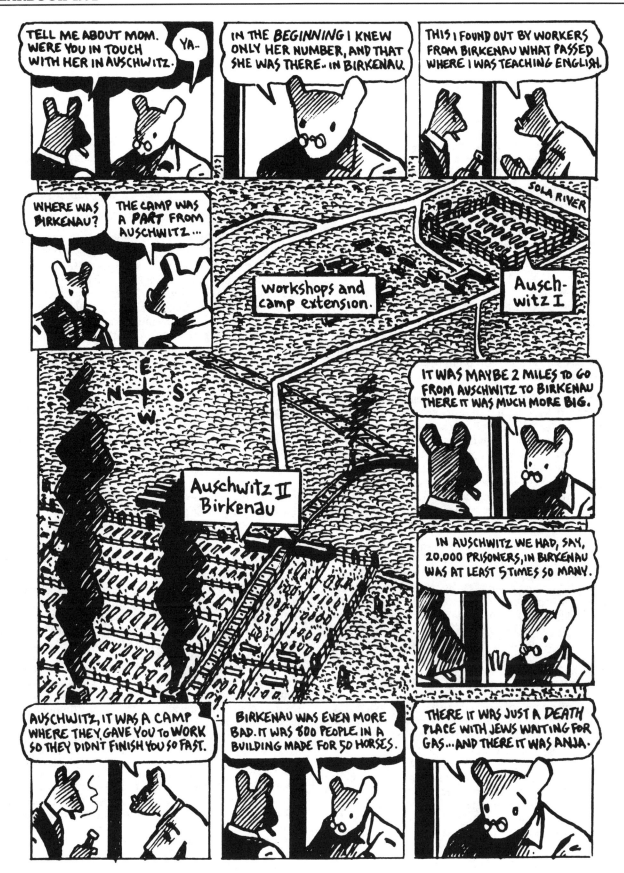

pumped, he bursts through stereotypes. He grabs readers by the lapels, lifts them off the ground and holds them in midair. Art has moved beyond the Oedipal contest to include compassion for Vladek even while shunning him. He's amused by the irony that his father is at his best when the world is at its worst, and in his books he generously restores Vladek to a stage where he can shine.

After Germany invades Poland and Vladek is tracked, he becomes resourceful and bold, all his genes coded with the imperative: Survive. He does, not in a skittering, mousy way but with a genius nose for danger and false reassurances. He escapes capture for years, distrusting phrases such as, "They're just checking papers." He hides himself and Anja in freezing barns and brashly walks the streets in search of food. Only one error has dire consequences: Believing that Jews are safer in Hungary, he arranges train passage with smugglers, who betray him and Anja to the Gestapo.

The two withstand ten months in concentration camps, Vladek in Auschwitz, where prisoners work and gradually starve to death, and Anja in adjacent Birkenau, most of whose inhabitants are quickly gassed. Vladek explains how, even amid the staggering cruelty of camp existence, culture persists in channels of communication and protection, acts of heroism and sacrifice.

For Vladek, though, survival mostly depends on luck and shrewdness. He knows English (also Polish, German and Yiddish), and the Polish kapo in charge of his barracks happens to want tutoring. When others are sent out to labor and freeze, Vladek is outfitted in sturdy garments and hidden in a back room. Prisoners are fed a daily ration of watery soup and bread made of flour and sawdust. "If you ate how they gave you, it was just enough to die more slowly," Vladek explains. His kapo gives him sausages and chocolate.

Even when forced to work, Vladek wrangles opportunity and relative safety, summoning skills he's learned or watched others apply. He mends boots for officers, labors as a tinsmith—at one point, as Russian troops advance, dismantling gas chambers and crematoria to destroy evidence of the atrocities. Still, Vladek is stalked by starvation and illness. He's savagely beaten when, working in Birkenau, he's caught talking with Anja. Twice he's examined by Mengele; during another inspection, having grown very thin and fearing he'll be sent to the gas chambers, he hides in a bathroom. In Dachau, he nearly dies of typhus.

He retrieves his past to please his son; it's a way of holding on to him. But as he goes back in time, Vladek expands. His language grows distilled, his sense of proportion reliable. He describes horror without exaggeration, so we apprehend it directly. And we see the mental adjustments required to ward off despair and madness—an ability to bear the ambivalence intrinsic to experience. Vladek tolerates the coexistence of mundane details and terror; the crematoria, he notes, resemble a bakery. In his view, fiendishness isn't divided off as inhuman and unreal but rather contained in his perceptions as all *too* human.

His failure, the **Maus** books show, is never observing the relationship between his Holocaust experience and his own impulse to dominate. He fails to see how he has played dictator in the family. Long before the war—we're shown through Vladek's own descriptions—he strong-arms routinely, pressing some pigeons with righteousness, guilt-mongering others with his pitiableness. He can be charming, caressing, but his aim is always closing deals. As he gets older, he gets worse.

Art worries that, in showing up his father's smallness, he's venting sadism. He *is* exacting revenge, exposing Vladek's pettiness, indulging gleefully in his analytic powers. Art worries that he's a know-it-all, exploitive and manipulative, just like his father, *the transgression from hell*. And indeed, Art does pursue agendas, enduring his father's hectoring and complaining to get his story on tape.

Vladek is condemned to skip back to the scarred grooves in his psyche, but Art doesn't duplicate his father's stagnation. He examines his role, his motives. He portrays himself cowed and shamed and chronicles former mental breakdowns. We see him retreat to a mousehole of silent rage, but when he exits, he exchanges self-pity for irony. He tells Françoise, "I wasn't obsessed with this [Holocaust] stuff . . . it's just that sometimes I'd fantasize Zyklon B coming out of our shower instead of water." His books reflect mastery over the damage of his childhood and of Vladek's past because he does perceive the relative size of suffering—understands that his own is less grave than his father's. Inside this man who must control is a mind swept by tides of memory.

Art anguishes that he trivializes history by comparing the Holocaust and domestic horror, but his concern isn't founded. In his work, history and psychological struggle shape each other; we see how destinies are marked by world events and how the drives of the inner life determine the way masses of people behave.

Art fears that the largeness of Nazism will be nibbled away by the simple, comic-strip means he uses to portray it. But the shifting reality of what is big and what is little is captured with special brilliance in his use of beasts, for it takes mice, with their animal appetites and vulnerability, to set the Holocaust on a human scale—not some hyper-real landscape of devils and martyrs. With these creatures so accessible, we're continually prodded to wonder: What would I do in their place?

Similarly, Spiegelman shifts our concepts of big and little art, investing the modest form of the comic strip with grandeur. Most artists who try harnessing high-art complexity to simple entertainments—the postmodern clown Bill Irwin comes to mind—succeed only in draining pleasure from the form they loved as children. But Spiegelman's drawing makes history immediate, at the same time uncovering a new capaciousness in comics.

His figures are minimal: kabuki masks for faces, signifying how each race looks alike to the others. The smallest variation—a pair of eyeglasses perched on a snout, eyebrows slanted in worry—particularizes. The strips are fluid, like movies, moving back and forth in time, halting for commentary and asides. Points of view continually change. Some frames depict a bird's-eye perspective, others look up, from the vantage point of a mouse, to the openmouthed suffering of the tortured. In any one frame, doo-dled fantasy coexists with factual horror, each box a min-iature of grab-bag reality—Breughel on a loop.

The *Maus* books should be read as a single work, and pub-lished under one cover as soon as possible. Why, they wonder, are some people frozen in place, unable to alter their perspectives? Why are some people able to imagine how others feel, picture themselves as they are perceived? Mala, who also survived the camps, tells Art that many people shared Vladek's fate and didn't turn out as rigid. Vladek recalls his father, and we glimpse another obses-sive; to avoid draft into the Russian Army, he extracted fourteen of his own teeth and demanded that his sons starve themselves for months. It's a hint to why, even be-fore Nazism, Vladek experienced life as a chase, with him-self as potential prey. Finally, though, the *Maus* books provide no certain explanations for change. All wounds don't heal in time, we see, but in the space of time the paw print of earlier life can fade—and we can make a run for it. (pp. 28-9)

> *Laurie Stone, "Chasing History," in* The Na-tion, *New York, Vol. 254, No. 1, January 6, 1992, pp. 28-9.*

David Gates   (review date 27 January 1992)

[*In the review below, Gates praises Spiegelman's uncon-ventional treatment of the Holocaust in* Maus: A Survi-vor's Tale II.]

[Art Spiegelman is as important a character in *Maus: A Survivor's Tale II*] as his father, a prisoner in both Auschwitz and Dachau. The subtitle, in fact, is ambigu-ous: Vladek Spiegelman somehow survived the camps to become an endearing yet maddeningly manipulative fa-ther; his son somehow survived *him.*

When the first volume of *Maus* appeared in 1986 nobody had ever seen anything quite like it: a comic-strip Holo-caust in which the Nazis were cats and the Jews were mice. The comforting artificiality of an animal cartoon worked both as savage irony and as a nearly transparent surface through which human horror could be imagined. It won Spiegelman a modest degree of celebrity, which oc-casioned the predictable crisis of confidence—which Spie-gelman duly makes part of the story in *Maus II.* "My time is being sucked up by interviews," the mouse-masked Spiegelman tells his mouse-masked psychiatrist. "But even when I'm left alone I'm totally BLOCKED. Instead of working on my book I just lie on my couch for hours . . . Auschwitz just seems too scary to think about . . ."

But Spiegelman does get his father's story on tape (though Vladek would rather complain about his second wife) and into his book: the beatings, the gas chambers, the mass graves. "And those what finished in the gas chambers be-fore they got pushed in these graves, it was the lucky ones," his father says, over cartoon panels showing heaps of mouse-corpses and still-living mice shrieking among flames. "Prisoners what worked there poured gasoline over the live ones and the dead ones. And the fat from the

burning bodies they scooped and poured again so every-one could burn better." All the layers of irony—the comic-strip format, the animal faces, the self-referential frame-story—can't soften that.

Nor, of course, does Spiegelman intend to. The attempt to exterminate an entire race using the techniques of mass production is so far off the scale of normal human experi-ence that conventional narrative seems inappropriate. In-deed, it's a truism among academic Holocaust scholars that the "final solution" can't be adequately described or comprehended. Which hasn't silenced survivors—or scholars. In *Maus II,* when Spiegelman is working through his cartoonist's block, the shrink himself suggests there's already a glut of Holocaust books. Spiegelman readily agrees, quoting Samuel Beckett's statement that "Every word is like an unnecessary stain on silence and nothingness." But after thinking a bit, he adds, "On the other hand, he SAID it." "He was right," says the shrink. "Maybe you can include it in your book."

> *David Gates, "Stories Out of the Silence," in* Newsweek, *Vol. CXIX, No. 4, January 27, 1992, p. 59.*

Hillel Halkin   (review date February 1992)

[*In the following review, Halkin discusses imagery and dialogue in* Maus: A Survivor's Tale II.]

Whether or not Art Spiegelman was aware of it when he chose to portray Jews as mice in his much-lauded comic-strip series about the Holocaust, he was preceded by Franz Kafka, whose "Josephine the Singer, Or the Mouse Folk" tells of a rodent people that lead "a precarious existence amid the tumult of a hostile world" and are "inured . . . to suffering, not sparing of themselves, swift in decision, well acquainted with death, timorous only to the eye in the atmosphere of reckless daring which they constantly breathe." Whom Kafka had in mind when creating Jose-phine is a good question (most likely himself as a writer, although I once met an old woman in Jerusalem who had tutored him in Hebrew when she was young and claimed that Josephine was a portrait of her), but his "Mouse Folk" was clearly modeled on the Jews.

Nor, for that matter, was this an entirely original image of Kafka's. If by no one or nothing else, it was given him by the German language, in which the noun *Mauschel* means a "kike," and the verb *mauscheln,* to speak (and why not to sing?) with a Jewish accent. These two words, to be sure, derive from the Hebrew name Moshe, which in the German-Jewish pronunciation sounds like "Maushe," but German-speakers can hardly avoid associ-ating them with *Maus* and its diminutive *Mäuschen.* Theodor Herzl actually wrote a short essay called *Maus-chel* in which, far from denying that the anti-Semitic ste-reotype of the Jew had a basis in reality, he identified it with Jewish opponents of Zionism and railed against them: "Where the *Jew* feels pain or pride, *Mauschel's* face shows only miserable fright or a mocking grin. In hard times, the Jew stands tall, but *Mauschel* cringes even more ignominiously," and so on. Kafka was fourteen at the time and may even have seen or heard of the piece.

AND EVERYBODY CROWDED INSIDE INTO THE SHOWER ROOM, THE DOOR CLOSED HERMETIC, AND THE LIGHTS TURNED DARK.

ZYKLON B, A PESTICIDE, DROPPED INTO HOLLOW COLUMNS.

IT WAS BETWEEN 3 AND 30 MINUTES— IT DEPENDED HOW MUCH GAS THEY PUT—BUT SOON WAS NOBODY ANYMORE ALIVE.

THE BIGGEST PILE OF BODIES LAY RIGHT NEXT TO THE DOOR WHERE THEY TRIED TO GET OUT.

THIS GUY WHO WORKED THERE, HE TOLD ME...

WE PULLED THE BODIES APART WITH HOOKS. BIG PILES, WITH THE STRONGEST ON TOP, OLDER ONES AND BABIES CRUSHED BELOW... OFTEN THE SKULLS WERE SMASHED...

THEIR FINGERS WERE BROKEN FROM TRYING TO CLIMB UP THE WALLS,... AND SOMETIMES THEIR ARMS WERE AS LONG AS THEIR BODIES, PULLED FROM THE SOCKETS.

ENOUGH!

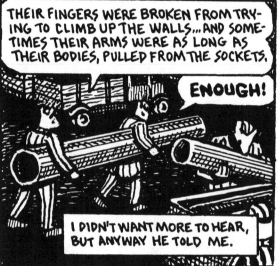

I DIDN'T WANT MORE TO HEAR, BUT ANYWAY HE TOLD ME.

THEY PULLED THE BODIES WITH AN ELEVATOR UP TO THE OVENS—MANY OVENS—AND TO EACH ONE THEY BURNED 2 OR 3 AT A TIME.

TO SUCH A PLACE FINISHED MY FATHER, MY SISTERS, MY BROTHERS, SO MANY

It can be argued, no doubt, that in choosing to make his Jews mice (his Germans are cats, his Poles pigs, and his Americans dogs) Spiegelman, no less than Kafka, was seeking to invest certain qualities that have been blamed in part for the fate of European Jewry—passivity, timidity, a sense of resigned fatalism, etc.—with a quiet and life-accepting heroism. Perhaps. Bravely resourceful mice, after all, predate him even in the cartoon world, as in the old Tom-and-Jerry movie shorts. Certainly, one can share Herzl's feelings about *Mauschels,* who are by no means an extinct species, while taking in stride Spielgelman's choice of the mouse as a Jewish totem. I would be more offended by his imagery if I were a Pole.

But what is the point of such imagery? Is there really much to be gained in our understanding of how human beings behaved in the Holocaust by imagining them as various kinds of mammals? I rather think there is more to be lost. True, if I were a high-school teacher faced with the horrendous task of teaching the Holocaust to a class of indifferent American teenagers, I might at first glance consider *Maus* to be a godsend. It is easy to get through. It is intelligently written and drawn, and the dialogue between its two main characters, the cartoonist Art Spiegelman and his elderly father Vladek, who reminisces about his experiences in Poland and Auschwitz during World War II, is credibly done with a fine ear for Vladek's immigrant English. It is historically accurate in its facts while managing, through its focus on Vladek and his family, to tell the story of the Holocaust in a coherently compact manner. (*Maus I* takes the reader from the start of World War II to Vladek's and his wife's arrest by the Nazis; *Maus II* follows them through Auschwitz to their liberation by the American army at the end of the war.) It encourages, by shuttling back and forth between Vladek's memories and his troubled relationship with his American-born son, who loves, pities, and rages against him, an identification with the author that can involve teenagers with the subject and make them care about it. And finally, it makes sense. Why did the Germans murder the Jews, who did not fight back, while third parties like the Poles let it happen? For the same reason that cats kill mice, who do not attack cats, while pigs do not care about either: *because that's the way it is,* boys and girls, and next week we will be studying the Marshall Plan and the beginning of the cold war.

But that is not the way it is and not the way it was, and it is here that our history teacher, if at all conscientious, might have second thoughts. The Holocaust was a crime committed by humans against humans, not—as Nazi theory held—by one biological species against another. And while the German campaign of annihilation against the Jews and the reactions of the various peoples caught up in it had to do with many factors, historical, political, sociological, and ideological, instinctual behavior, except insofar as we all have instincts of aggression and survival, was not one of them. Because it implicitly invokes such behavior as *the* explanation for what happened to the exclusion of any other, *Maus* is a textbook that must be used with care and only in conjunction with supplementary material.

"But wait a minute! Who ever said that Art Spiegelman produced *Maus* as a juvenile textbook?" No one. But it will be used as one, particularly for children whose reading skills are undeveloped, and if it has any particular value, this is where it lies. As literature, even as Holocaust literature, it would simply be lost in the crowd: there are hundreds, probably thousands, of fictional works and autobiographical documents that deal with stories like Vladek's far more powerfully and profoundly, and one is doing *Maus* no favors by comparing it with them.

"But that's precisely the point! *Maus* is not a novel or a story, nor is it to be compared with one. It is a comic strip, possibly the first to have attained the level of a genuine art form!" Permit me my doubts. In fact, the curious thing about *Maus* is that, although its illustrations supposedly release it from the exclusive domination of language and fuse the verbal with the visual, the book's text is far more suggestive than its drawings, and does the yeoman's share of the work.

This is not because Art Spiegelman cannot draw well, but rather because, as seen through human eyes, animal faces are extremely hard to individuate, so that Spiegelman's mouse-Jews, pig-Poles, etc. all tend to look as alike as Donald Duck's nephews Huey, Dewey, and Louie, and have an extremely limited range of facial expression. Significantly, the most movingly illustrated pages in *Maus* occur in a scene in the first volume—a flashback in which the author recalls his psychiatric hospitalization and the suicide of his mother in New York—where the animal faces are dropped in favor of human ones. To draw people as animals, *Maus* makes one realize, is doubly dehumanizing, once by virtue of the symbolism and once by virtue of graphic limitations.

And yet even this flashback fails to convince me that comics, no matter how sophisticated, have the slightest potential to vie with either literature or art as a serious medium of expression. Language may indeed be tyrannically word-bound, but the visual arts are no less tyrannically space-bound, and yoking two tyrannies together in such a way that there is a minimum of room for maneuver within either is a poor strategy for overcoming them. All that happens in the comic strip is that one ends up more bound and chained than ever. The division into small boxes limits all utterances to the shortest and pithiest statements, ruling out nearly all verbal subtlety or complexity, while the need to fill each box with a drawing has a similar effect on the illustrations. Those who like to remind us that a picture is worth a thousand words tend to forget that a thousand words can be said in less time than it takes to draw most pictures, and that an artist who has to turn out a spatially cramped and crudely reproduced graphic accompaniment to every ten or twenty words of a story can hardly produce high-level work.

Lav achbara ganav ela chora ganav, "it is not the mouse who is the thief but the mousehole," says an old talmudic maxim, and it would be unfair to blame this particular mouse for the slumming pop-culture critics who have made more of it than it is or pretends to be. "A serious form of pictorial literature . . . an original and authentic form to draw us closer to [the Holocaust's] bleak heart," declares Lawrence L. Langer, for example, in a front-page review of **Maus** in the *New York Times Book Review*. Such talk should not be held against Spiegelman, though. He has not gotten to the heart of anything, nor can he with the tools of his trade, but it is his trade and he deserves respect for taking it as seriously as he does. (pp. 55-6)

> *Hillel Halkin, "Inhuman Comedy," in* Commentary, *Vol. 93, No. 2, February, 1992, pp. 55-6.*

Spiegelman on his *Maus* saga:

I told myself it was time to take on something serious. I wanted to tell a story, but I wanted it to be a story worth telling. [My *Maus* saga is] the point where my work starts.

> *Art Spiegelman, in* New York Daily News, *14 December 1986.*

Bryan Cheyette   (review date 3 April 1992)

[In the following review, Cheyette praises the honesty and accessibility of Maus: A Survivor's Tale II.*]*

Art Spiegelman, with his wife, Françoise Mouly, is the co-founder and editor of *Raw*, a widely acclaimed underground comic and graphic journal which once declared itself to be the "Graphix Magazine of Abstract Depressionism". His father, Vladek Spiegelman, survived Auschwitz and Dachau, as did his mother, Anja, who committed suicide in 1968. In 1973, Art Spiegelman drew "Prisoner on the Hell Planet", an account of his mother's death and, a year before this, published a three-page version of **Maus** in an anthology entitled *Funny Animals* (*sic*). For the past two decades, in other words, Spiegelman has used the language of cartooning to deal with his private pain and fraught relations with his parents. *Funny Animals* was taken up again in 1978 and culminated in [**Maus: A Survivor's Tale: My Father Bleeds History**] (1986), which should be read alongside this second volume. Spiegelman rightly conceives of his work as a whole. The initial volume delineates his father's early years in Poland, his marriage to Anja, and their attempted escape to Hungary before being deported in 1944 to Auschwitz. [**Maus: A Survivor's Tale II: And Here My Troubles Began**] continues his father's account of the war years and depicts, in particular, his parents' survival in the death camps.

Although **Maus** was at first rejected by many publishers, it has subsequently become something of a phenomenon. It is now taught in many American Universities, has sold 180,000 copies, and New York's Museum of Modern Art recently had an exhibition entitled "The Making of **Maus**". Spiegelman is well aware of the dangers of turning his "graphic novel" (as it is now called) into a mere spectacle. By the second chapter of [**Maus II**] his masked persona, "Artie", tries to make sense of the critical and commercial success that threatens to engulf him ("you've read the book, now buy the vest"). He is no longer an anthropo-

morphic mouse, and his metaphorical "Mauschwitz" is turned back into historical Auschwitz: "Between May 16, 1944 and May 24, 1944, 100,000 Hungarian Jews were gassed."

It is surprising to learn in this volume that Spiegelman's father died of heart failure in 1982, and that **Maus** has been, in effect, a decade-long imaginative reconstruction of Vladek, based on twenty hours of taped personal testimony. The microphone that Artie continually thrusts in front of his father both distances him from Vladek and, simultaneously, makes it possible for them to communicate with each other for the first time. Much the same can be said about Spiegelman's stark bestiary made up of anthropomorphized mice, cats, pigs, dogs, reindeer and frogs. Once familiar with these cartoon images and self-confessed approximations, the reader is better able to absorb the details of an unspeakable history.

Maus is at once uncategorizable and totally persuasive as it reveals throughout that Artie's relationship to Vladek is intimately connected with a past that continues to overwhelm them. Spiegelman's subtitle, "A Survivor's Tale", refers as much to Artie as to his father and is also acknowledged as something of a misnomer. In what way can Vladek be described as a "survivor" when he acts as if he hasn't "survived" anything? Much to his son's embarrassment, the father's parsimony remains obsessive almost beyond belief. As a backdrop to his Holocaust story, Vladek picks up "useful" pieces of wire from the street or takes back half-eaten food to the supermarket or saves on matches. At the same time, Artie's relentless tape-recorder exhausts his increasingly weak father in a determined effort to get down every last detail of his war-story. Spiegelman's cold eye means that his work avoids the pitfalls of sentimentality while also conceding the arbitrariness of the images used to represent the past. But this, after all, exemplifies the desperate honesty in **Maus,** which is why the comic-book, in Spiegelman's hands, has finally come of age.

> *Bryan Cheyette, "Vladek's Story," in* The Times Literary Supplement, *No. 4644, April 3, 1992, p. 8.*

James Walton   (review date 4 April 1992)

[In the review below, Walton offers a mixed assessment of Maus: A Survivor's Tale II.*]*

There's no avoiding the phrase 'long-awaited sequel', I'm afraid. In 1986, [**Maus: A Survivor's Tale: My Father Bleeds History**] was published to enormous critical acclaim and with great commercial success. An unflinching account of the author's troubled relationship with his father in contemporary New York and of his father's experiences as a Polish Jew in hiding during the War, it was rightly hailed both as a fine piece of storytelling and a breakthrough for its form, the cartoon. (In interviews, Spiegelman who famously depicts his Jews as mice and his Germans as cats, replied to the obvious question, 'Why a cartoon?' with the obvious answer, 'I'm a cartoonist. What do you want I should do—a ballet?')

[*Maus: A Survivor's Tale II: And Here My Troubles Begin*], which takes up the story with the captured Spiegelman senior arriving at the gates of Auschwitz, has many of the strengths of its predecessor: the neat intercutting of the father's story with the son's astonishment as he records it for the book, together with his exasperation with his father's behaviour now; the miraculously miniaturist power of the drawing; the arresting speech patterns of the characters; Spiegelman's ability, in the great Jewish-American tradition, to confront intense emotions directly but without sentimentality or embarrassment. It also gets through an impressive amount of material, tackling not just life and death in Auschwitz, but also the absence of God from the camps, fathers and sons, Jewish guilt, Gentile guilt, the validity of Holocaust literature and much more besides. And it still has room for the self-doubting, writing-about-writing-the-book episodes (and the author-visits-his-therapist scenes) also familiar from other Jewish-American literature.

But the book's ambition, passion and undoubted power to move should not blind us to its shortcomings. The central of these is that once in Auschwitz, Spiegelman finally reaches the limits of his form. That this is acknowledged as a possibility elsewhere in *Maus II* does not mean that it is avoided. So, while the scenes of what passes for daily life in the camp are as convincing as anything in Volume

I, the most horrifying set pieces, the living and dead being burned together in mass graves, Spiegelman senior slithering over corpses to get to the toilet, simply don't work as cartoons. They seem both melodramatic and bathetic, inadequate images of his father's words. The cartoon sound effects also grate in this context. 'Sob', says one prisoner on learning he is to be gassed the following day.

Another problem is Spiegelman's wish (perhaps it's his therapist's fault) to 'make sense' of everything. This leads to some rather glib psychology about his feelings for his father, and when applied to Auschwitz itself is 'so presumptuous', as he puts it in one of his self-doubt sections, as to be doomed.

In short, Spiegelman never solves the possibly insoluble problem of saying something new about the Holocaust. Saying the usual things in a new form is not enough, though saying them to a new audience through a cartoon book may be some compensation.

Maus II's flaws are not dishonourable ones, nor are they fatal. The intensity of the dialogue, of most of the images and certainly of Spiegelman's courageous and obsessive honesty do win through in the end. But it's a close fight at times. And the fact that the most unequivocally successful passages are those set in America means that the book

always works better as the cartoon equivalent of Philip Roth rather than of Primo Levi.

James Walton, "Nothing Comic About the Holocaust," in The Spectator, *Vol. 268, No. 8543, April 4, 1992, p. 33.*

FURTHER READING

Buhle, Paul. "Of Mice and Menschen: Jewish Comics Come of Age." *Tikkun* 7, No. 2 (March-April 1992): 9-16.
> Overview of Jewish comic art in which Buhle discusses Harvey Pekar's *The New American Splendor Anthology* and Spiegelman's *Maus I, Maus II,* and *Raw 3: High Culture for Lowbrows.*

Mordden, Ethan. "Kat and Maus." *The New Yorker* LXVII, No. 7 (6 April 1992): 90-6.
> Explains how *Maus II* differs from other comic art produced during the last fifty years.

Barry Unsworth
Sacred Hunger

Award: Booker Prize for Fiction

(Full name Barry Forster Unsworth) Born in 1930, Unsworth is an English novelist.

INTRODUCTION

A novel about England's slave trade during the eighteenth century, *Sacred Hunger* dramatizes the demoralizing effects of slavery on individuals and society. Incorporating into the narrative accounts of actual historical events, including an incident during which a sea captain drowned sick slaves in order to claim insurance monies, Unsworth examines the nature of evil, the human condition, and the prevailing attitudes and economic structure of English society that enabled the slave trade to prosper. Much of the narrative focuses on Matthew Paris, the doctor aboard the *Liverpool Merchant,* a slave ship owned by his uncle William Kemp, and Paris's attempts to come to terms with his involvement in the slave trade. The first half of the book recounts the building of the ship, the journey to Africa, the purchase of slaves, and the traumatic journey to the New World. Paris's disgust for the way in which the Africans are treated eventually prompts a mutiny, and the ship's captain is killed. The remaining passengers set up a colony in Florida where blacks and whites ostensibly live as equals. The second half of the book—which critics have found less compelling than the first—centers on Erasmus Kemp, the son of William Kemp, and his reconciliation with Paris, whom he considers responsible for the demise of his family's shipping business.

Critics of *Sacred Hunger* have praised its mixture of fact and fiction and its vivid and realistic characters. The thematic concerns depicted in the novel have also prompted positive comparisons with Joseph Conrad's *Heart of Darkness (1899)* and William Golding's *Lord of the Flies (1954).* Unsworth argues that although *Sacred Hunger* is set in a specific historical epoch, the book is a timely discourse on greed and materialism. He notes: "[In the eighteenth century, money] talked in a way it probably never had before. I was very aware of certain kinds of parallels with today. It struck me that the inevitable acquisitiveness and material ambition of people was endorsed by an ideology during the last decade that gave it moral respectability. . . . I thought the slave trade was a perfect example and representative of that because it was regarded as lawful. Lawful was a great word in the eighteenth century—not legitimate but lawful. Everything was condoned be-

cause it was profitable and lawful. If you look at aspects of trade today, you find that same condoning."

PRINCIPAL WORKS

The Partnership (novel) 1966
The Greeks Have a Word for It (novel) 1967
The Hide (novel) 1970
Mooncranker's Gift (novel) 1973
The Big Day (novel) 1976
Pascali's Island (novel) 1980; also published as *The Idol Hunter,* 1980
The Rage of the Vulture (novel) 1982
Stone Virgin (novel) 1985
Sugar and Rum (novel) 1988
Sacred Hunger (novel) 1992

CRITICISM

Janet Barron   (review date 28 February 1992)

[*In the following essay, Barron, a scriptwriter, offers a positive review of* Sacred Hunger.]

"Somewhere under the skies there was, there must be, a place where a man of the cloth could play Caliban." Barry Unsworth's **Sacred Hunger** is a novel of scarred idealism. It is an immense and impressive work, philosophical in its conception, teeming with the scents and sounds of 18th-century life.

Unsworth has none of the preciosity that turns history into escapism. His imaginative world is as palpable as that of Patrick Süskind's *Perfume.* This is a novel about cruelty and greed, a dubious legacy of empire, and an indictment of the capitalist ethic. It reads history backwards, informing events with a knowledge of what they led to.

Matthew Paris, a doctor, is a proto-Darwinian, put into the stocks for his foolish courage in telling the truth. His shame leads to the death of his wife in childbirth, and, seeking a new beginning, he takes a passage as ship's surgeon on the slave ship, the *Liverpool Merchant.*

This is very much a reading of history from the E. P. Thompson perspective. Thurso, the ship's captain, is "an incarnation of the profit motive," a phrase which is singularly apt for the character Unsworth has created. He regards his cargo of black Africans as so much ballast to be ditched. There is real anger against humanity in Unsworth's treatment of exploitation, and the result is both compulsive and horrifying. "Might it be true," Paris asks, "that men would live together in peace and harmony if only the coercion of authority were lifted from them? When I look into the faces of my fellows, I find it hard to credit."

Unsworth's white liberals try to believe in perfectibility, quoting Locke while carrying on the slave-trade. This is a dark satire against England and the British Empire, as bitter and bleakly comic as the writings of Evelyn Waugh. There is a mutiny, and the captain is executed in revenge for the horrors he has inflicted. There is blood on his hands, and the narrative has great tragic stature. "Memories are grafted together in ways beyond our choosing," Unsworth reflects on the nature of the torture he has unleashed. It is part of the power of the novel that everything connects.

Paris' cousin, Erasmus Kemp, is acting in an amateur production of Davenant's *Enchanted Isle,* the sanitised version of *The Tempest.* The production becomes a metaphor for the state of England, and is not that far from A. S. Byatt's *Virgin in the Garden* sequence. **Sacred Hunger** is an intensely literary novel, drawing allusions into itself, highly intelligent but never ponderous. Echoes of William Golding's *Lord of the Flies* and *Close Quarters* are inevitably present, but Unsworth succeeds in creating something that is at once comprehensive and unique. For more than 600 pages, he keeps the reader transfixed.

This is compelling fiction, a classic on a grand scale. There is only one point at which history lets Unsworth down: a character strolls through the Albert Gate—in 1752. Perhaps that is a glance at post-modernism, or a slip of the memory. In the context of this striking work, it does not matter much.

> *Janet Barron, "Slave States," in* New Statesman & Society, *Vol. 121, No. 4073, February 28, 1992, p. 45.*

Mark Sanderson   (review date 28 February 1992)

[*In the essay below, Sanderson praises* Sacred Hunger *as Unsworth's best work and argues that its thematic concern with the fall of humankind is characteristic of Unsworth's earlier novels.*]

Sugar and Rum, Barry Unsworth's last novel, got off to a flying start: blocked author Clive Benson is strolling through the mean streets of Toxteth when a black man jumps to his death from the top of a tower-block. Benson is supposed to be at work on a "complex and ambitious new novel set against the background of the Liverpool slave trade", but the suicide—"the leap, the cry, that carpet-like sidling, the gathering fall, the peculiar crash of impact"—haunts him and he cannot stop talking about it. The "crude act of self-extinction became in his stammering mouth a paradigm of human life".

Sacred Hunger may be seen as the realization of Benson's ambition. It spans the years 1752–65, the heyday of the "Triangular Trade", when sea-borne slaves take every opportunity to jump overboard even though, with their hands and feet in chains, this means certain death. Others have no choice. There is no market for sick slaves and so they are dumped—without their expensive fetters—over the side. This enables the slavers to save precious stores and claim compensation of 30 per cent a head. The turning-point of this hulking novel occurs when Matthew Paris, surgeon of the *Liverpool Merchant,* realizes that Captain Thurso—"a simple man, being an incarnation, really, of the profit motive"—is jettisoning part of his human cargo: " 'No! he shouted. 'No'. . . . With all the strength of his lungs, aiming his voice at the sky, he shouted again: 'No!' "

But it is not just the black characters in Unsworth's novels who do the falling: white ones come a cropper too. In **Mooncranker's Gift** (1973), the priapic James Farnaby confesses that when "all the different persons I have been merge into an awful perception of what I am I fall backwards, flat on my back, in a dead faint . . . ". In **The Rage of The Vulture** (1982) Henry Markham literally falls for a young singer, his comic collapse anticipating his father's near-fatal descent into the dungeons of the Ottoman Empire. Basil Pascali, in **Pascali's Island** (1980), is shattered when the Greek statue with which he has become obsessed falls to the ground at the climax of the novel; and, as thirty-three-year-old Simon Raikes in **Stone Virgin** (1985) struggles to bring the 540-year-old Madonna back to her former glory, he is in perpetual danger of swooning and tumbling from the scaffolding. Raikes is also faced with the problem of whether the defunct Litsov fell or was pushed into the Venetian waters. Unsworth is concerned with nothing less than the fall of man.

This is made explicit in **Sacred Hunger.** During the construction of the *Liverpool Merchant,* a man falls to his death and another is badly injured, but Thurso's "small eyes contained a look of satisfaction, as at some promise fulfilled". The sadistic captain, in the same way that Benson sees "clues everywhere", believes "a reason there must always be", and yet he fails to read the signs. Paris's intervention provokes the mutiny that has long been festering and Thurso is killed. The mutineers and liberated slaves succeed in establishing a community in the backwoods of the new colony of Florida. It eventually enters folklore as "a place of eternal sunshine . . . where white and black lived together in perfect accord". But this paradise is lost because the desire for money and the appetite for power—the "sacred hunger" that caused them to be wrenched from their homes in the beginning—reasserts itself.

The downfall of Paris is precipitated by Erasmus Kemp, his cousin. Following the disappearance of the *Liverpool Merchant,* Kemp, "farouche" and "intractable", blames Paris for his father's death and the bankruptcy of the family business. He swears revenge. His enmity stems from a childhood incident in which Paris, ten years older than his young cousin, picked him up as he strove to strengthen a dam that he had made against the rising tide. It takes twelve years and an expedition half-way round the world before they can reach a kind of understanding.

Unsworth intertwines the histories of these two polarized men as each struggles to come to terms with a terrible loss. Kemp, fatherless and penniless, is forced to break off his engagement to Sarah Wolpert, the daughter of a wealthy merchant. Paris, a proto-Darwinian imprisoned for sedition, blames himself for the death of his pregnant wife. The scene in which he is pilloried alongside a sodomite—who attracts most of the public's vicious attention—is just one of the many vivid set-pieces in which one's distress at the sheer cruelty of human beings is mixed with admiration at Unsworth's skill in depicting it. Slaves are branded, seamen are flogged. The novel contains dozens of characters—landlubbers, sailors, colonists and African tribesmen—that are differentiated with economy and wit. It is not just the slaves who are prisoners. All of them, from Sir William Templeton, His Majesty's Principal Secretary to the West India Office, to Calley, the simple-minded porter press-ganged along with Deakin the deserter, are seen to be trapped—shackled to a money-spinning treadmill from which the only escape is death.

Erasmus woos Sarah by agreeing to take part in an amateur production of *The Tempest,* a bastardized version with a happy ending, courtesy of William Davenant and Dryden. Unsworth exploits many correspondences with the play and explores such age-old Shakespearian antitheses as Nature versus Nurture—as his name suggests, the mooncalf Calley is cast as Caliban—but the writer who exerts the greatest influence on the narrative is undoubtedly Conrad.

Like his mentor and William Golding before him, Unsworth uses the vehicle of the traditional sea-story to steer a course through deep waters. The concepts of justice, liberty and duty are debated through the medium of a genuinely exciting historical adventure. Paris, staggering under the white man's burden, penetrates the heart of darkness; Kemp has his own secret-sharer; the visionary Delblanc's "sacred hunger" has the same force as Mrs Gould's utterance at the end of Chapter Eleven of *Nostromo:* "Material interest". Although set much earlier than Conrad's stories, Unsworth's is without flummery or fustian. The sea-speak is convincing but not intrusive. His descriptions of the multifarious states of ocean and sky are worthy of the master. Unsworth shifts with ease from the abstract to the concrete, from the cosmic to the comic. His tenth novel is his best.

Mark Sanderson, "After the Fall," in The Times Literary Supplement, No. 4639, February 28, 1992, p. 23.

D. J. Taylor   (review date 1 March 1992)

[*Taylor is an English novelist and critic. In the following essay, he lauds Unsworth's ability to create vivid characters within the context of the historical novel.*]

At first glance, **Sacred Hunger** awakens the gravest forebodings: more than 600 pages long, with the dimensions of an offensive weapon and purporting to articulate "current concerns of corruption and distress", it reeks of Booker-inspired significance. Happily, nearly all these prejudices can be discounted. Barry Unsworth turns out to have written that very rare thing, a top-notch historical novel.

His achievement is all the more remarkable when set against the recent competition and the prevailing style. Broadly speaking, there are two types of current historical novel: on the one hand the pantomime epic in which everybody wears metaphorical coloured tights; on the other, a past refined through 20th-century consciousness, in which everything is carefully analysed with the benefit of hindsight by a superior modern eye.

Unsworth's theme is human rivalry; his subject is the slave trade of the mid-18th century. William Kemp, a declining Liverpool merchant, flings resources he can ill afford into the construction of a slave ship, and the planning of an expedition to the West Indies by way of the Guinea coast. Out of family loyalty, he appoints as ship's surgeon, his nephew, Matthew Paris, a saturnine gentleman of the Enlightenment, follower of Maupertuis, and previously imprisoned for blasphemy by the Bishop of Norwich. Paris, whose wife has suffered a fatal miscarriage after the sacking of their house by a church-directed mob, welcomes the voyage as a means to "cauterise the nerves that held him to the past".

The seeds of animosity between Paris and Kemp's son, Erasmus, turn out to have been sown by the latter's childhood. Their slow flowering occupies the rest of the book. This proceeds in parallel. Part one ends with Kemp senior a ruined suicide, the ship vanished and Erasmus, his long-cherished marriage plans now destroyed, vowing vengeance on the man he thinks responsible. The *Liverpool Merchant,* meanwhile, is becalmed east of Jamaica with the slave cargo dying of dysentery and mutinous stirrings from beneath the quarter deck. Part two, 12 years on, follows Erasmus's route (he is now a figure of power in the West Africa trade) to Florida, in search of a legendary settlement where black and white are reputed to live on equal terms, and a final showdown.

A long and complex novel, *Sacred Hunger* defies easy summary. The sea-going passages are faintly reminiscent of George Macdonald Fraser's immortal Flash for Freedom: at any rate, there is the same mad captain, the same concentration on the inhuman rituals of slavery, the same intriguing details of maritime disease.

Unsworth's strength lies in his ability to summon individuals out of the mass of perspiring seamen—Calley the half-wit, Sullivan the mournful fiddler, disputatious Billy Blair—and follow their characteristics through into the new life of the settlement. If the novel falters, it is here in the Florida colony, run on exemplary free-thinking principles by Paris and his chum Delblanc, a wealthy radical picked up in West Africa. It is not simply that the egalitarianism is too good to be true, but that the schematics start to show through. This tendency is especially marked at the point where the community's integrity is compromised by go-getters who propose to introduce their own sanitised version of enslavement. Certainly, the justification of the chief culprit ("Strong man get rich, him slave get rich. Strong man make everybody rich. Everybody dis place happy an' rich come from trade") reads suspiciously—and, presumably, intentionally—like a tutorial in free-market economics.

Part two is the weaker half. For all the mitigating circumstances, the eventual quasi-reconciliation seems forced, especially given Erasmus's 12 years of single-mindedness. His pursuit, too, has a worrying facility. But these are minor imperfections.

Full of neat descriptive writing and sharply drawn minor characters—a fastidious West Africa governor, avid to

---

Liz Heron on *Sacred Hunger*:

Unsworth is a gifted yarn-spinner who prompts absorption in the tale while urging the reader to step back and reflect on its components. In the elegant drawing-rooms and landscaped parks of the Liverpool trade barons, among the slavers of West Africa, or at the land-greedy manipulations of Florida's Creek indians, the "sacred hunger" for profit has unspoken parallels with the present. It is not only the immeasurable sufferings of the slave trade that are indicted, but the mercantile impulse which makes human beings commodities and buys human freedom with trash. While *Sacred Hunger* sees no simple remedies, it has confidence in the unquenchable power of utopian hopes.

Liz Heron, in a review of Sacred Hunger, *in* The Times Educational Supplement, *13 April 1992.*

---

hear Paris's opinion of his diet, Owen the slave factor wasting away from drink and loneliness—*Sacred Hunger* is a tremendous performance. Not the least of its achievements is the sense of blood, guts and hurricanes existing side by side with an imaginatively realised interior life.

D. J. Taylor, "The Leaving of Liverpool," in The Sunday Times, *London, March 1, 1992, p. 4.*

Adam Bradbury (review date 11 June 1992)

[*In the following excerpt, Bradbury praises the historical accuracy, prose style, and thematic concerns of* Sacred Hunger.]

Barry Unsworth spent some time in *Sugar and Rum* having a laugh at the dash and romance turned out by his protagonist's creative writing students and examining the writer's propensity to make 'meanings'. Early in that novel Benson was rebuked for trying to see signs in a man's suicide jump. He thought it may have been 'a kind of paradigm, leap of birth', but was told: 'No stages there man. When he jump off, that the end of the story'. There was a sense of desperation about the writer's position. 'Wretched spouter' he was called, 'weary of his own fluency. Not really engaged with anything'. The ennui and self-doubt which afflicted the writer-hero in that book have been well and truly jettisoned in favour of a return to classic lines of storytelling in *Sacred Hunger.* And a renewed sense of 'engagement' is evident in the minutely-detailed recreation of his chosen period and in the weight of knowledge which informs this richly researched book. The shocking pivotal crime (ditching slaves overboard to claim the insurance) accurately reflects the enduring importance gained by 18th-century marine insurance in the scheme of British commerce.

There is, however, a lot more than research to praise here. Unsworth's seamless prose is elegant and economical (perhaps surprisingly in a book this thick), his many characters for the most part fully fleshed out and his narrative pace faultless. But in one sense *Sacred Hunger* feels like a retreat from the darker corners of *Sugar and Rum.* Doubt, after all, is held to be of redeeming value in the new book, but the smooth assurance of the prose, the very clarity of the structure and the transparency of the narrative almost undermine this theme.

Sacred Hunger pushes out the boat, which, for Benson, was stuck in dry dock. As Unsworth puts it in his account of the ship's construction, 'she began to look like herself again, as is the gradual way of art'. Such self-consciousness doesn't intrude too often, although the thorny old problem of how to render 'significance' without trying too hard rears its head in the book's worst line, where Unsworth slips into a curious sarcasm, describing 'the triangular trade' as the 'greatest commercial venture the world had ever seen'. 'That the ship was a mere corpuscle in this nourishing bloodstream', he goes on, 'was not easy to imagine for the men aboard her'. I should think not. This may be meant as a joke, but seems odd from a writer whose delicacy of touch is abundantly clear in the light mockery of the courtship of Erasmus Kemp and Sarah Wolpert, wherein feverish emotions 'spring' from 'agitated' and scarcely controlled breathing amid the 'musky secretions of May'.

The triangular trade in which the vessel, the *Liverpool Merchant,* is employed—British goods and arms for Africans who were then sold on to the West Indian sugar plantations—reached its peak in the late 18th century, when, it is thought, the export of slaves from West Africa averaged 66,000 per year. It was the mother of all trades, involving the transfer of maybe twelve million Africans and the death of many more. Amid this monstrous commerce, Unsworth sets Matthew Paris, nephew of the ship's owner and free-thinking precursor to Charles Darwin. Paris 'liberates' the *Liverpool Merchant*'s cargo and establishes a kind of Rousseauesque commune in Florida. In London, meanwhile, his cousin Erasmus Kemp foresakes romance for cash and becomes a smooth operator in the sugar trade. His rise in this burgeoning market, and up through the mercantile classes, far removed from the clanking of leg-irons and the lash of the whip, gives rein to some pointed satire. Outstanding is the splendidly corrupt Dr Sugar, veteran of the sugar trade, who claims a thousand uses for the commodity, including eye and skin lotions and of course a dental paste; and there are dark bacchanalian rites at the sugar traders' club where a dancer simulates sex with a phallus made of sugar. But the satire is panoramic:

> 'Sir,' Partridge said, 'this is an expanding age, the nation is prospering, our voice is heard in the councils of Europe. As a result of this the cost of everything goes up daily and that must also include gifts, rewards and all manner of pecuniary inducements. Numbers of men are getting richer and greater numbers are getting poorer. Alas, both classes have higher expectations these days.' The attorney permitted a lean smile to move his jaws. 'In short, sir,' he said with a burst, 'there has been a leap in bribes.'

It is hard to escape the impression that Unsworth is talking about the economic miracle with which we are supposed to have been blessed in the Eighties. But he is going further, chipping away at the fundamentals of capital trade, with the question gradually emerging: would man, free and happy in a state of nature, still seek to accumulate wealth by enslaving others? Don't know, is the resounding reply. While a firmer response is not forthcoming, the fault—the dynamic which justifies injustices—is seen to lie in the very structures of Western thought. 'If we cannot proceed from particular truths to general ones our thoughts will get nowhere', says Paris, to which a 'freed' slave replies: 'Better for us you get nowhere. Partikklar to gen'ral is story of the slave trade'. The sacred hunger, commerce, is seen to enslave the masters as much as the ostensible victims, but other than in the childish head of Sarah Wolpert and a failed production of *The Enchanted Island,* Unsworth offers, in any case, little sense of a paradise lost. Even Matthew Paris's 'enlightened' theories are in danger of herding men together under some supposedly common law of human nature. Another freed slave who makes good scotches the noble savage alternative, ex-

pounding the (currently familiar) theory that the rich will drag the poor up with them: 'Strong man get rich, him slave get rich. Strong man make everybody rich. Everybody dis place happy an' rich come from trade. Some man not free, nevermind, buggerit, trade free'.

Almost exactly half-way through **Sacred Hunger** Paris comes across Delblanc, portrait-painter to the company officials, agents and merchants up and down the coast of Africa. Delblanc shows him a portrait described as 'the face of plunder, the face of Europe in Africa'. A less skilled writer might have made a hash of the hammy old technique whereby a thing (such as a portrait) is crowbarred into the narrative for the sake of a running theme. It is characteristic of Barry Unsworth's mastery throughout the book that he gets away with it. (pp. 27-8)

> Adam Bradbury, *"Guts Benedict," in* London Review of Books, *Vol. 14, No. 11, June 11, 1992, pp. 27-8.*

Thomas Flanagan   (review date 19 July 1992)

[*An American novelist, short story writer, critic, and educator, Flanagan is the author of the historical novels* The Year of the French *(1979) and* The Tenants of Time *(1988). In the following essay, he offers a positive assessment of* Sacred Hunger.]

In **Sacred Hunger** Barry Unsworth's wonderful and heartbreaking novel of the 18th-century slave trade, the captain and the doctor of the *Liverpool Merchant,* a newly built slave ship, visit the effete, languid governor of a British fortress on the Guinea coast and are then taken to the cavernous cells in which captured Africans are held for sale:

> A final turn brought them to the slave-dungeons, set side by side like cells, with barred fronts and stone walls and high barred windows, through which the afternoon sun was falling now in straight rays; he had been right, they were at the rear of the fort, against the outside walls. Three of the dungeons were occupied now, two with men handcuffed together in pairs and one with unshackled girls and women. Sunlight for this hour was caged there with them. Motes of dust moved with gauzy flies through the bright air. The bodies of the slaves were flecked and stippled and the straw that covered the earth floors was luminous gold. The smells of excrement and trodden straw seemed like a release of this flooding warmth of sunshine.

The passage seems at first reading unpleasantly mannered given its subject, that luminous sunlight stippling the naked bodies of chained and wretched captives a gauze of esthetic glitter. But the passage is carefully and precisely controlled by the word *gold,* weighty and unanswerable, the image at the novel's heart. Mr. Unsworth's book dramatizes the European and African experiences of slave trading, the greeds and hungers that allowed the traders, European and African alike, to regard slaves as mere commodities.

The perceiving eye in the passage is that of Matthew Paris, the ship's doctor and the nephew of its owner, William

Kemp. The year is 1752, and the end of the Royal African Company's monopoly has allowed investors like Kemp to turn from cotton to slaves, exploiting the infamous Triangle—with trading goods sent to Africa, slaves brought from Africa to the West Indies, rum and sugar and tobacco shipped back to England. But this particular venture, so Kemp's son, Erasmus, comes to feel, has been doomed from the start. Remembering his father clambering about the shipyard to sniff at the sections of mast, pale yellow fir from the Baltic, he wonders if the ebullient trader was not, unknowingly, sniffing at his own death.

The *Liverpool Merchant* carries away from the African coast a cargo of slaves, but also a fatal disease, a plague that makes possible a slave rebellion and a mutiny of the crew. Kemp, ruined financially, hangs himself, and Erasmus, now penniless, must abandon his shallow, middle-class life of sentimental romance and amateur theatricals. He repairs the family fortune by marrying a wealthy, plain-featured woman, consoling himself with imaginative and acrobatic whores. And he grows wealthy in the West Indies sugar trade—which also, of course, is based on human slavery.

But the *Liverpool Merchant,* believed in England to have been lost at sea, has, in fact, been sailed to Florida, where the mutineers and the surviving slaves have run her aground, far upriver. There they have established a sweet-tempered society that is polyandrous and egalitarian, and that shuns motives of gain. It is polyandrous because of the scarcity of women to avoid disaster and bloodshed, men have had to transform jealousy into some different passion. It is egalitarian because that is the instinct of Matthew Paris, who has emerged with three or four others, African and European, as a guide. But it is organized against gain by a young Frenchman named Delblanc, who is the novel's most remarkable character. A painter by training, he had joined the ship in Guinea and had quickly become Paris's friend.

This is not surprising: they are both bookish and intellectually curious. But Paris's bent is scientific. His speculations as to the vast antiquity of the earth, and the evolution of species from common ancestors, have put him afoul of the Church of England and earned him the pillory and a term in prison. Delblanc, like Rousseau (whose name is not mentioned), is a believer in human perfectibility and a hater of that "sacred hunger," as he calls it with bleak sarcasm, by which a man "becomes a flesh-and-blood form of money, a walking investment. You can do what you like with him, you can work him to death or you can sell him. This cannot be called cruelty or greed because we are seeking only to recover our investment and that is a sacred duty."

The joinings in **Sacred Hunger,** of plot, image, allegory, are cunning and strategic. Thus, at the outset, Erasmus Kemp is involved in an amateur production of *The Tempest,* or, as it was then called, *The Enchanted Island.* There is a discussion as to the humanity of Caliban, the "abhorred slave," of whom a clergyman says that "when he has to *argue* his case, he has no words, he is lost." And a few chapters later, we encounter a brute laborer named Daniel Calley, a hauler of sheep carcasses, who does not

know how to argue, who lacks the language of logic. Calley, a new Caliban, is lured away to new lands by the mate of the *Liverpool Merchant.* Strange things befall him in the swamps of Florida.

Delblanc, looking at his portrait of the English governor on the Guinea coast, tells Paris: "And so we spread death everywhere. But that sacred hunger we spoke of justifies all. The trade is lawful, they say, and that is enough. Well, it is not enough for me. That face on the easel is the face of plunder and death, sir, it is the face of Europe in Africa."

But in the enchanted groves of the New World, Delblanc, like many a Rousseauian idealist since, discovers that the ideal must be enforced with the ruthlessness of a Robespierre or a Lenin. Marauding slavers from the north must be hunted down and killed.

A sailor named Wilson, who will not share his woman, must be publicly done to death; "Wilson had been killed by everybody, it was this that made his death special, the children had been told. It was justice, it was all the people showing how much they hated this crime. Killing was justice when everybody joined in."

After 12 years, the little colony is confronted with pressures from the outside, with the avenging appearance of Erasmus Kemp—in the end, perhaps, with the emergence, even in paradise, of the sacred hunger, for gain. The novel's resolution is somber and cool. As it approaches, Matthew Paris thinks:

> Delblanc had known how to use these deaths, as he had known how to use everything. Not least of the mysteries that touched Paris's mind as he finally drifted towards sleep was how . . . an itinerant portrait painter of good birth and easy manners had been able to forge men of such metal into instruments of a higher purpose. But of course it was not a higher purpose at all, he thought, despite the rhetoric of the time. It was our purpose, Delblanc's and mine; his based on doctrines of liberty, mine on some inveterate hope. Men living free and equal in a state of nature. . . . What gave us the confidence to suppose that a state of nature could only mean what it meant to us, a notion of Eden, a nostalgia of educated, privileged men?

Beyond its major assertion of theme, this passage may hint at Mr. Unsworth's recognition of an almost inevitable imbalance in his novel. The Africans are presented without condescension, but from the outside, for the most part without sentimentality but from a considerable psychic distance. For Mr. Unsworth (the author of nine previous novels, including **Pascali's Island,** and a fellow of the Royal Society of Literature), as for many of his readers, and for Delblanc, this Floridian world is a notion of Eden, a nostalgia of the educated, privileged—and *white.* He differs from Delblanc, of course, in his ability to recognize the nostalgia, and to judge it.

It would be a pity should this imbalance run him afoul of the thought police of cross-cultural correctness. *Heart of Darkness,* which had always seemed Conrad's terrifying representation of the sacred hunger, of the face of Europe

An excerpt from *Sacred Hunger*

Paris ceased after a while to follow the bargaining, which was extremely complicated. To establish the value of the slave in bars, which he had thought at first to be the whole purpose of the proceedings, was in fact only the beginning. This bar, it seemed, was merely a value given to a certain quantity of goods. It could be half a gallon of brandy or a bag of shot or two dozen flints or a length of printed cotton. It was in order to obtain small concessions and adjustments in these values that Thurso and Yellow Henry, facing each other in their respective hats, wheedled and blustered and simulated mirth or astonishment or disgust.

The tall negro whom Paris had examined first was purchased finally for six brass kettles, two cabers of cowries, four silver-laced cocked hats, twenty-five looking-glasses and an anker of brandy, with a bonus of six folding knives and a plumed hat offered by Thurso for the goodwill of the king's trade. As soon as the deal was struck and the goods brought up, the man was dragged forward into the waist of the ship, where the branding irons had been heating all this while in the brazier.

Some fixity of the will kept Paris gazing after them. The slave was concealed from view by the men holding him down. But Paris saw the equable second mate, Simmonds, take out the bar, saw him hold it up and spit on the red-hot device at the tip, caught for a moment, against the white hull of the yawl beyond, the glowing, angular design of the brandmark—it was the letter K. Simmonds's face wore a look of concentration, a recognition of the need for accuracy, which suddenly recalled to Paris his student days, assisting at dissections. Almost, for a moment, even now, it seemed that he might find some retreat in the memory of those days, the intent circle of students clustered round the table in the lamplight, the precise and somehow stealthy approach of the knife to the cadaver. Faces too, there were, in this present circle, which showed signs of distress, like those novice anatomists of long ago. He saw Blair's face, marked still from his fighting, staring down with jaws rigidly set. The tall, dishevelled fiddler had a similar fixity of expression.

These men briefly aided Paris, abetted the illusion. But from a living man, not a drained simulacrum, the sound that came now, the single cry from below, throat-formed and pure. He saw the brief tension in the group of men holding the negro down. Barber, with the boy Charlie to help him, moved forward with the shackles for the legs. A smell of burned flesh hung in the air. My uncle has acquired his first slave, Paris thought. Through what seemed still the ripples of the cry he heard Yellow Henry's voice raised in a tone more plaintive than angry: 'For why you no got green baftees? For why you tankids no got handuls?' Bargaining had commenced over the second negro. . . .

It was death of course that made the difference, Paris told himself carefully, as if reciting a lesson. You can work your will on a dead body. Those laid out for dissection had been men and women dying destitute, stolen from paupers' graves, or criminals cut down from the gallows, with no rights whatsoever over the disposal of themselves in death. And in life? As he stood there the distinction grew blurred in his mind. Was there really so much difference?

Barry Unsworth, in his Sacred Hunger, *Nan. A. Talese, 1992.*

in Africa, has recently been rejected by some critics as thoroughly racist. I hope and trust that *Sacred Hunger* will resist that kind of ideological judgment. It is a book of grace and meditative elegance, and of great moral seriousness. (pp. 3, 23)

> *Thomas Flanagan, "And So We Spread Death Everywhere," in* The New York Times Book Review, *July 19, 1992, pp. 3, 23.*

Roland Merullo   (review date 2 August 1992)

[*In the following essay, Merullo, an American novelist, argues that* Sacred Hunger *is both a historical novel and a moral treatise on the origins and effects of evil.*]

"Money is sacred, as everyone knows," a character in Barry Unsworth's rich and beautifully written [*Sacred Hunger*] says with great irony. "So, then, must be the hunger for it and the means we use to obtain it."

Sacred Hunger is set in the mid-18th Century, though the above remark, like many of the book's moral lessons and debates, might also be applied to modern times. The plot, too—centering as it does on the purchase of slaves and their shipment from Africa to America—has important contemporary echoes. To Unsworth's credit, though, he has not merely created a cardboard past and painted it with 20th-Century political correctness; he has given us a real, sweating, breathing, bleeding, complex world, a world in which blacks sell other blacks into slavery and whites flog and cheat each other to turn a profit, and a few heroic men and women of both races struggle toward justice against the prevailing social values and their own fears and doubts.

Unsworth's pace is leisurely. The novel begins with a wealthy but debt-ridden Liverpool businessman named Kemp, who decides that the slave trade is the route out of his financial difficulties. Kemp commissions a ship to be built for this purpose, the *Liverpool Merchant,* and personally supervises the sail-making and woodworking, while his grown son Erasmus looks on.

From these very first pages, Unsworth displays his grasp of historical detail, and a talent for stitching one fine scene smoothly into the next. The proper sewing of sails, the fitting of oak planks tightly together to form the ship's main deck, the notes of reluctant subservience in a workman's voice—every thread is of the correct length, width and color. To man this slave ship, Unsworth mobilizes a cast of characters rivaling that of *Moby Dick:* a cruel, experienced captain named Thurso; a sensitive ship's surgeon, Matthew Paris, who happens to be Kemp's nephew, and a finely drawn group of seamen—fiddlers, drunks, sadists and simpletons.

As the *Liverpool Merchant* sets sail for Africa to take on its human cargo, Erasmus Kemp, home in England, sets a course he hopes will lead to marriage with a neighboring beauty named Sarah Wolpert. Though Unsworth shifts between these two story lines throughout the book, in the first half of the novel he wisely dwells on the scenes aboard ship. He has created such a convincing and intricate world there that the reader feels a small disappointment at each return to the more common domestic drama.

At sea, it does not take long for tension to develop between the pragmatic and merciless Captain Thurso and Kemp's sensitive nephew, Matthew Paris. Thurso, like the Kemps, finds nothing objectionable in the buying and selling of human beings. His morality is the morality of the herd, a commercial religion based on a kind of despicable trickle-down theory. In one of his many ironic jabs at modern economics and mores, Unsworth describes the slave-trading era in England as "a time when the individual pursuit of wealth was regarded as inherently virtuous, on the grounds that it increased the wealth and well-being of the community. Indeed, this process of enrichment was generally referred to as 'wealth-creation' by the theorists of the day."

A tyrant in a tyrannical time, Thurso mistreats not only the slaves, but his own seamen as well. The story is dotted with accounts of floggings, the application of thumb-screws, and other cruel punishments that serve to set some of the men against their captain. By the time the *Liverpool Merchant* is ready to leave the African coast with its valuable human cargo, the crew is stewing with resentment, sick with fever, hungry and thirsty. The ship reeks of excrement, is infested with rats; slaves and crew alike sicken and die, and, appropriately, the ship wallows for days in the hot African doldrums.

Meanwhile, back in England, the elder Kemp's debts have multiplied, bringing him to his own appropriate punishment. His son Erasmus, whose narcissism Unsworth goes to somewhat excessive lengths to establish, sinks into temporary disgrace, losing, in the process, his beloved Sarah. At this point, roughly 400 pages into the novel, Unsworth leaves us to imagine the climax of the building tensions aboard the *Liverpool Merchant,* and leaps forward 12 years into Erasmus' future and that of the ship's crew.

This jump wounds **Sacred Hunger,** and though Unsworth's talents are sufficient to retain our interest over the last 200 pages, the book never quite recovers its earlier pitch of dramatic intensity. The characters we cared so much about at sea return to work out a complicated morality play in another exquisitely drawn setting, but some readers may feel they have been pulled out of the theater moments before the film's climax. Details of the moral battle between Thurso and Paris are provided in deft. A very occasional but intrusive didactic voice also interrupts the smooth narrative flow: "It is when we make plans for an absence that we learn the extent to which we are needed at home." "There are no stronger fetters than those we forge for ourselves."

But this is a large and multifaceted work, almost Tolstoyan in moral and literary scope, and its beauties and strengths far outweigh these blemishes. Unsworth takes hold of the most central moral question—the causes of and responses to evil—and builds around it an entirely realistic world peopled by men and women—white, black and red—whom we care about until the last word.

In the course of this 600-page voyage, we are treated to numerous finely wrought scenes, any one of which is worth the tribulations of rough weather. We see sailors being shanghaied in English taverns, a ribald party in a private club, dinner in a sweltering colonial fortress, carpenters fitting the ship's great timbers into place; there is a bit of humor and sex, intricate psychological portraits, philosophical debates on the nature of money and goodness and the proper role of government, historical asides, sea stories, antiquated healing procedures, and beautiful descriptions of jungle, sea and sky.

Most remarkably, perhaps, the author's careful and striking accumulation of detail provides the feeling of complete realism, though the story takes place more than 200 years ago and the settings vary widely.

It requires a writer of consummate skill to pack all of the above into a serious novel while at the same time doing justice to the horrors of the slave trade. In **Sacred Hunger.** Unsworth has gone beyond that. He has shone a light into the swamps of human nature; exposed the muck of our materialism and the danger in confusing morality with marketplace values. The preeminence of those values— persisting in diluted form to this day—is what once allowed us to rationalize the selling of men and women. (pp. 3, 11)

> *Roland Merullo, "Ships, Slaves and Sadists,"*
> *in* Los Angeles Times Book Review, *August*
> *2, 1992, pp. 3, 11.*

Joseph Coates (review date 9 August 1992)

[*In the following essay, Coates praises Unsworth's depiction of the dehumanizing aspects of slavery in* Sacred Hunger.]

Even in the most honest attempts to confront racism, everybody talks about slavery but nobody does anything about it, to paraphrase an author (Mark Twain) particularly apt in this context.

If all we can do is admit slavery's unmitigated evil in Western history, we at once step back from its reality into the abstractions of "evil" and particularly "history," a word that in plain demotic American means something dead, negligible and too stupid to discuss. Meanwhile racism continues to spread, especially among blacks who've learned the hang of it from whites and now write songs about the recreational killing of white cops.

What can effectively be done about racism is the only thing left that one can do about slavery, which is to imagine it, as this reviewer did back in the 1950s by reading the following brief exchange in *The Adventures of Huckleberry Finn.*

Young Huck has just been mistaken for his friend Tom Sawyer by the latter's Aunt Sally on his arrival at the Phelps farm. He (or rather, Tom) is late for this long-planned visit to his distant relatives, and Huck invents a steamboat explosion to account for the delay.

"Good gracious!" she says. "Anybody hurt?" "No'm. Killed a nigger." And good, kind Aunt Sally, baker of such wonderful pies, says in relief: "Well, it's lucky; because sometimes people do get hurt."

The point everybody misses about both slavery and racism, one that accounts as much for Aunt Sally as for Simon Legree, is that the oppressor enslaves and dehumanizes himself when he puts another in chains. And illuminating that point is what novelist Barry Unsworth has done so brilliantly in **Sacred Hunger,** which is as much about white slavery as black, showing the stinking reality of its slave ship, the *Liverpool Merchant,* afflicting crew as much as "cargo."

This compellingly plotted novel has as a resonant subtext an amateur production of *The Enchanted Island,* the 1667 adaptation of Shakespeare's *Tempest* by Sir William D'Avenant and John Dryden. The action begins in 1752, when a successful Liverpool parvenu named Kemp, secretly brought close to bankruptcy by losses in cotton, begins building the *Liverpool Merchant* to recoup his fortune via the immense profits in the infamous "Triangular Trade"—cheap manufactured junk shipped to Africa in return for blacks enslaved in tribal wars; slaves, in shiploads of 200 or more, sold in the American colonies and especially the West Indies in return for rum and sugar.

The first part covers the ship's outfitting and its first and only foray to the Guinea coast of West Africa and the love affair between Kemp's insolent and emotionally retarded son Erasmus and the spirited Sarah Wolpert, daughter of another rich merchant, whom Erasmus woos via reluctant participation in her rehearsals of *The Enchanted Island.*

Unsworth's deftness at quirky psychological portrayal, seen earlier in such novels as **Pascali's Island** and **The Rage of the Vulture,** here shows us Erasmus, preparing to offer Sarah what he calls love, while in fact he has cut his last lifeline to human feeling by confusing it with the lust for profit that enslaves him.

The escalating sacred hungers of unbridled trade, or "lawful commerce," as the elder Kemp calls it in self-justification, is a Faustian sale of soul that sweeps all into its net, from the amiably drunken sailors shanghaied in waterfront taverns to the gifted and the high-minded, like the ship's physician Matthew Paris, a hated and disgraced cousin of Erasmus.

It is through the eyes and journal of Paris that we experience one of the great harrowing sea stories, enlivened by a hurricane and a mutiny but centering on the interplay among the vividly characterized crewmen in thrall to the terrifying psychopath Capt. Saul Thurso, whom we see scourging the flesh off a seaman's back with a cat o' nine tails to conjure wind from the sky.

Unsworth manages to find a trace of perverse humanity even in this ogre, whom at one point he calls "a simple man, being an incarnation, really, of the profit motive, than which there can be few things simpler." A seaman named Sullivan, an Ariel assigned to play the fiddle during the morning "dancing of the slaves" that Thurso considers essential to a healthy cargo, nervously interrupts the captain's dinner with a request to remove the chains during

this exercise because "the noise they make with their clankin' is swampin' me notes."

"By God, that's rich," Thurso replies, and turning to Paris says, "Here is another fellow of the same kidney as yourself. He doesn't know what is the real world either." Paris' reply is a high point of the book, a prime example of the subtlety of Unsworth's morally tangled, brutally outrageous and riveting epic. "I don't disdain the connection," says Paris, "if he doesn't."

That simple declaration of humanity is one reason the crew follows Paris to rebel against Thurso's final provocation: With the ship storm-tattered and becalmed for weeks, and having lost 67 slaves to the "bloody flux," Thurso decides to jettison those sick with the disease before they die, on the grounds that "cargo dying aboard ship of so-called natural causes was quite worthless, whereas cargo cast overboard for good and sufficient reason could be classed as lawful jetsam cargo and thirty per cent of the market value could then be claimed from the insurers."

Having translated monstrosity into human terms, Unsworth makes the unthinkable understandable even as he turns the screw of plot to the breaking point. Erasmus, rich and influential after a dozen years in London, hears that the *Merchant* has been found beached deep in the Everglades and sets off in 1765 to recover his "cargo," now reportedly much increased after half a generation of interbreeding with the mutineers.

The scene then shifts to the colony itself on the eve of its destruction, detailing the polyandrous folkways of this "natural" society of the kind Enlightenment thinkers like the painter Delbanc, a passenger on the *Merchant,* were so eager to establish. But even before the obsessed Erasmus finally confronts Paris, we learn that his withered, relentless spirit has already begun to poison utopia, for reasons the reader should discover himself.

Unsworth ends his richly detailed moral and historical panorama with the fate in 1832 of an ancient New Orleans waterfront character whose story began in a teasingly ironic prologue, a tale supposedly resurrected by Unsworth from an old book, since lost, called *Sketches of Old Louisiana* by Charles Townsend Mather.

The book's posthumous and bowdlerized editions no longer contain the tale of the Paradise Nigger, "an old plantation slave from Carolina, freed when he was past work and turned off the land," who talked "of a Liverpool ship, of a white father who had been doctor aboard her and had never died" and of "a childhood of wonders in a place of eternal sunshine." He also, "and Mather vouches for this . . . quoted snatches from the poetry of Alexander Pope."

We last see this man, some 600 pages later, dying and almost blind in a waterfront bar, where "sometimes one of the customers will set him off, winking round at the others," by saying, " 'Come on . . . what's the news from Paradise?' " One wonders what his harassers would have thought if the former slave had responded with one of his "snatches" from Pope—say, the passage from "Essay on

Man" about "the man of times to come / . . . Who, foe to nature, hears the general groan, / Murders their species, and betrays his own. . . . " (pp. 1, 6)

Joseph Coates, "The Price of Denying Humanity," in Chicago Tribune, *August 9, 1992, pp. 1, 6.*

Unsworth on greed, the slave trade, and the setting of *Sacred Hunger:*

[In the eighteenth century money] talked in a way it probably never had before. I was very aware of certain kinds of parallels with today. It struck me that the inevitable acquisitiveness and material ambition of people was endorsed by an ideology during the last decade that gave it moral respectability. It's a significant step to applaud that sort of selfishness and greed and to underplay or downgrade qualities which normally should be brought into place to balance it, like fellow feeling and compassion as a counterweight.

I thought the slave trade was a perfect example and representative of that because it was regarded as lawful. Lawful was a great word in the 18th Century—not legitimate but lawful. Everything was condoned because it was profitable and lawful. If you look at aspects of trade today, you find that same condoning. But "lawful" is very much a man-made and expedient fabrication.

Barry Unsworth, in an interview with Maris Ross, in Books, *March-April 1992.*

Gary Jennings   (review date 13 September 1992)

[*An American writer, Jennings is best known for his historical novels* Aztec *(1980),* The Journeyer *(1984), and* Spangle *(1987). In the following essay, he offers a laudatory review of* Sacred Hunger.]

The works of English author Barry Unsworth have gone rather unappreciated on this side of the water, but his newest novel should change that. I hope it does, although I think its title is unappealing, even misleading. That comes from a line of dialogue midway through the book: "Money is sacred, as everyone knows . . . So then must be the hunger for it and the means we use to obtain it." Well, the novel centers on the English-African slave trade in the 1750s, and that was of course driven by the profit motive. But *Sacred Hunger* deals with a lot more than that—with the whole human condition—so ignore the title, but read the book. It is superb.

It commences in Liverpool with the building and crewing of a ship designed solely for the transport of slaves from Africa to the West Indies. Eventually there is such a variety of seamen aboard that the reader may have trouble distinguishing among them, but some are unforgettable. There is the mad Capt. Saul Thurso, alongside whom captains Ahab and Bligh would have to rank as pussycats. There is the First Mate James Barton, whose survival depends on sycophancy. There is the ship's surgeon, Matthew Paris, who is reluctantly on board only because his

published ideas about evolution (anticipating Darwin by a century) have him fleeing a prison sentence imposed by an outraged Anglican bishop.

The bestiality of the slave trade is well-known, but Unsworth makes us aware also of the almost equal brutality common in those days even to "civilized" places like Liverpool. The scenes in which press gangs go about shanghaiing crewmen for the ship are among the best in the book. (And further along, I must warn, are scenes of gore and grue that are not for the squeamish.)

Unsworth's blending of historical fact and his own imagination is well-nigh seamless, his research impeccable. He seems to know every detail of life in the mid-18th century: shipbuilding, ocean navigation, medicine, even wig-wearing and women's dress—and every landscape and seascape from England to West Africa to the South Atlantic to the then-wilderness interior of Florida. His command of the English and other languages of the time is perfect, unflawed by modernisms (except just once, when he anachronistically employs the term "launching pad").

When the ship reaches Africa and crams its pathetic black cargo into its fetid holds, everything that can go wrong does go wrong. Some of the valuable slaves starve themselves to death; others die merely of the squalor below decks. Then both the cargo and the crew begin to get decimated by malaria, scurvy, blackwater fever and "the bloody flux." The ship is alternately becalmed in the doldrums and beset by storms. The salt beef goes putrid, the fresh water runs out. The crewmen have to suffer vicious floggings for the least offenses.

When Thurso decides to start jettisoning even the still-living slaves, to save feeding them—and because, back in England, he can collect insurance on the "loss"— Matthew Paris and a couple of other decent men on board incite a mutiny.

Meanwhile, in Liverpool, the shipowner's son, Erasmus Kemp, is having a sort of *Pride and Prejudice* romance with the daughter of a country squire. I would say that this impedes the narrative, but it does establish Erasmus as the most unlovable lover imaginable. And, being the lifelong enemy of Matthew, it is he who will bring the story to its terrible climax and conclusion.

A hurricane hurls the ship far off course and beaches it on the coast of southern Florida. The surviving white crewmen and black slaves determine to start life anew in this balmy, hospitable land. They set up a colony, whites and blacks living in communal harmony: farming, fishing, hunting, cheerfully interbreeding, being very happy indeed. And they get away with this for 12 years, because England has long presumed the ship to have been sunk at sea.

But then some other passing seamen, ashore for fresh water, stumble upon the colony. They eventually report to London, and the vindictive Erasmus comes looking for his "property." I will not give away the story's ending, except to say that Erasmus need hardly have bothered. The colony has already been fraying, with one faction trying again to make slaves of another.

Sacred Hunger is not without a few imperfections. One episode is practically lifted entire from *The Treasure of the Sierra Madre.* The dissolution of the Edenic colony is uncomfortably reminiscent of *Lord of the Flies.* And sometimes Unsworth's meticulous research gets obtrusive; his disquisitions on England's parliamentary and commercial finaglings can be tiresome. But these are matters excusable in a novel that is otherwise utterly magnificent.

By its last page, you will be close to weeping—not just for the wretched slaves and seamen, and for the many others maltreated, and for the brave, doomed colony—but for the whole of what Mark Twain once called "the damned human race."

> *Gary Jennings, "Voyage of the Doomed," in* Book World—The Washington Post, *September 13, 1992, p. 2.*

FURTHER READING

Heron, Liz. Review of *Sacred Hunger,* by Barry Unsworth. *The Times Educational Supplement,* No. 3953 (13 April 1992): 32.

> Positive assessment of *Sacred Hunger.*

Hogan, Phil. "Standing Outside England and Looking In." *The Observer,* No. 10,488 (18 October 1992): 59.

> Feature article in which Unsworth discusses his life, *Sacred Hunger,* and receiving the Booker Prize.

Ross, Maris. "Profit at Any Cost." *Books* 6, No. 2 (March-April 1992): 5.

> Interview in which Unsworth discusses the slave trade, the similarities between the economic systems and attitudes of the eighteenth century and the 1980s, and the research he conducted for *Sacred Hunger.*

Additional coverage of Unsworth's life and career is contained in the following sources published by Gale Research: *Contemporary Authors,* Vols. 25-28, rev. ed. and *Contemporary Authors New Revision Series,* Vol. 30.

Paula Vogel
The Baltimore Waltz

Prize: Obie Award

(Full name Paula Anne Vogel)   Born in 1951, Vogel is an American playwright.

INTRODUCTION

The Baltimore Waltz is Vogel's surreal tribute to her brother, who died of AIDS in 1988. Described as a second-generation AIDS play because of its metaphorical treatment of the disease, *The Baltimore Waltz* centers on Anna, a young teacher who has been diagnosed with the fatal Acquired Toilet Disease (ATD), and Carl, her homosexual brother who always appears in pajamas carrying a stuffed rabbit. The siblings travel to Europe where Anna, in a desperate attempt to live out her fantasies, engages in numerous sexual encounters, while Carl seeks comfort in men who also share an obsession for stuffed toys as he searches for a cure for ATD. Anna and Carl meet black marketeers and medical charlatans who claim to have found a remedy. As the play progresses, however, it is revealed that the action is really set in a Baltimore hospital room where Carl is dying of AIDS and that the characters' experiences in Europe are actually products of Anna's imagination.

Critical reaction to *The Baltimore Waltz* has been mixed. Many critics asserted that by writing a comedy about AIDS and using ATD to discuss the disease, Vogel diminished the seriousness of the AIDS epidemic and compromised the drama's emotional impact. Reviewers additionally faulted much of the play's symbolism, noting that Carl's stuffed animal is an inappropriate symbol for his sexual orientation and that if ATD is a metaphor for AIDS, Anna's promiscuity is deplorable. Others, however, have praised the comic aspects and "seize-the-day" mentality of *The Baltimore Waltz*, the understated poignancy with which Vogel relates Anna's grief and Carl's death, and her incorporation of psychiatrist Elisabeth Kübler-Ross's theories on death and dying. Lauding Vogel's ability to render her own grief through Anna's experiences and thereby to dramatize AIDS as a universal affliction, Robert Brustein wrote: "[*The Baltimore Waltz*] is a touching rite of loving exorcism, personal yet transcendent."

PRINCIPAL WORKS

Meg (drama) 1977
Apple-Brown Betty (drama) 1979
Desdemona (drama) 1980
Bertha in Blue (drama) 1981
The Oldest Profession (drama) 1981
The Last Pat Epstein Show before the Reruns (drama) 1982
And Baby Makes Seven (drama) 1986
The Baltimore Waltz (drama) 1989

CRITICISM

Frank Rich   (review date 12 February 1992)

[Rich is an American editor and performing arts critic. In the following excerpt, he praises Vogel's use of dreams and fantasy in The Baltimore Waltz.*]*

"To the memory of Carl—because I cannot sew," reads the *Playbill* dedication of Paula Vogel's new play, *The Baltimore Waltz* . . . . Who Carl is we can only imagine, but can there be much doubt about what kind of memorial Ms. Vogel would like to sew for him? Her play is about an elementary-school teacher named Anna who learns that her brother, a young San Francisco librarian named Carl, is terminally ill. Anna's response is to sweep her brother and herself into a fantasy world—a crazy-quilt patchwork of hyperventilating language, erotic jokes, movie kitsch and medical nightmare—that spins before the audience in Viennese waltz time, replete with a dying fall.

The result is a dizzying evening at several levels . . . . [*The Baltimore Waltz*] is not only a rare AIDS play written by a woman but also a rare AIDS play that rides completely off the rails of documentary reality, trying to rise above and even remake the world in which the disease exists.

Though ostensibly set in a Baltimore hospital, the actual landscape of Ms. Vogel's play is Anna's mind, which knows few imaginative bounds. Anna's powers of empathy are such that it is she, not her brother, who becomes the dying swan in her elaborate fantasies; she sees herself as the victim of a deadly malady that counts single teachers among its high-risk groups. Anna's dreams take her and Carl on a whirlwind tour through Europe that culminates in a macabre replay of the Carol Reed-Graham Greene thriller *The Third Man,* with its zither music, Ferris wheel and a mad doctor who usurps Orson Welles in the role of the mysterious Harry Lime.

"In art as in life, some things need no translation," says Carl. Some of *The Baltimore Waltz* too flagrantly defies translation, lacking the internal logic that can make some dream plays, including the pre-eminent Circle Rep dream play of recent vintage, Craig Lucas's *Reckless,* add up on their own idiosyncratic terms. Yet I respect what Ms. Vogel is up to and was steadily fascinated by it, even when her play seems too clever by half or less funny than it wants to be.

The fever pitch of *The Baltimore Waltz,* almost an oxygen rush at times, is always enlivened by the playwright's antic literacy and always justified by the tragedy at hand. "It's the language that terrifies me," says Anna when she first encounters the medical world, and it's language with which Ms. Vogel creates her heroine's strange wonderland. As the dialogue rifles several Berlitz phrase books or veers off into linguistic riffs (an extended declension of the sentence "There is nothing I can do," for instance), the play's words seem to splinter and finally metastasize in sync with the young bodies racked by an incurable epidemic. . . .

[It] is one of the intriguing aspects of *The Baltimore Waltz* that [Carl] is not an active character in his own drama: the play really is intended as a living memorial to him, a sister's loving, uninhibitedly sensuous, even lusty valentine to a brother whose private life away from her is represented only by a vague symbol, a child's stuffed toy rabbit, that floats benignly through the reveries. That Ms. Vogel has succeeded in creating that memorial is most apparent when she finally must burst the balloon, turning her enchanted accidental tourist back into a grieving schoolteacher, the rabbit back into a dying man's bedside totem, the mysteries of Vienna back into the cold, clammy realities of a hospital ward in Baltimore. Having turned up the volume and body heat of life so high with her dreamy theatrics, the author makes us feel the loss all the more deeply when another young corpse is carted off the stage.

> Frank Rich, "Play about AIDS Uses Fantasy to Try to Remake the World," in The New York Times, *February 12, 1992, pp. C15, C19.*

Jan Stuart   (review date 12 February 1992)

[In the following excerpt, Stuart offers a mixed assessment of The Baltimore Waltz.*]*

If we go by Elizabeth Kübler-Ross' theory on the six stages of confronting terminal illness, then contemporary theater must be somewhere between the anger and acceptance phases. In one season, *Marvin's Room* and now *The Baltimore Waltz* are drawing a bittersweet smile on the face of dying. Death is a cabaret, old chum.

Paula Vogel's new comedy falls into that burgeoning category of Allegorical Plays That Are Not About AIDS But Really Are About AIDS. Vogel establishes her little camouflage with an intriguing bait and switch. A San Francisco librarian named Carl announces to his children's reading group that he is taking a sick leave. He's oddly flip about the whole thing. What's more, he's dressed in a blazer, a pink triangle button, and a pair of pajamas. Ah *ha*, we see, he's *that* kind of sick, the damn-the-Lord-and-pass-the-AZT kind of sick.

Suddenly, we are plunged into a Hippocratic circus vaguely reminiscent of the early *Marvin's Room* scenes: chillingly pristine offices and daffy doctors who alternate between numbing medicalese and baby talk. The switch is this—the comic nightmare is happening not to Carl but to Carl's sister Anna. Anna, an elementary school teacher with a cheery naivete, has been diagnosed with ATD—Acquired Toilet Disease—a fatal new malady with a high risk factor for elementary school teachers.

Whose death is it, anyway? For the greater part of *The Baltimore Waltz,* it's Anna's, or rather it's her empathic fantasy of exchanging roles with her brother. Without a moment to lose, Carl hauls his sinking sister off on a last-stand tour of Europe's byways and bedrooms. Unlike AIDS, ATD is not sexually communicable, and Anna fully intends to fornicate herself into a stupor before she goes out "like Merle Oberon in *Wuthering Heights,* with a somewhat becoming flush and a transcendental gaze."

That line is so sumptuous I wish I could love the play

around it. But Vogel's prankster spirit is sophomorically madcap and more than a little bit dull. The main thrust, as it were, of Anna's travels are a series of sexual encounters with European men—a French waiter, a Dutch boy, a surly Berliner—all played with vaudevillian gusto by [the same actor], doing a male reversal on the international everywoman in *Stop the World, I Want to Get Off.* But the joke digs about as deep as the costume changes, unless you're inclined to double over hearing the French slang variants for penis.

While Anna is dallying, Carl is slinking around in a trenchcoat ferreting out illicit drugs for his sister. It's a wannabe takeoff on *The Third Man*—does anyone need another parody of *The Third Man?*—and a tiresome one at that. Vogel is lampooning the pathetic absurdity of black-market drug trade, but it's satire laid on with a trowel. "People will pay for these things," says Vogel's surrogate-Harry Lime about his fake elixirs. "When they're desperate, people will eat peach pits or aloe or egg protein—they'll even drink their own piss. It gives them hope." Yes. Right. Thank you, Harry.

[The characters in *The Baltimore Waltz*] carry on with such unyielding high spirits that they camouflage the thinness of the joke one moment and point it up at another. The paradox of the bland cartoon gestures is that they are embedded within a richly articulate format. Vogel emphasizes the isolating nature of the vocabulary of illness by framing her scenes as a series of foreign-language lessons; the deeper Anna moves into Europe's myriad of tongues, the larger her outside-ness as a dying person looms.

Languages, geography, Elisabeth Kübler-Ross, me oh my. You take in *The Baltimore Waltz* terribly impressed by the playwright's education, but after a time you may begin to feel slightly hoodwinked. It's the kind of play that wears its smarts on its sleeve, but is finally not saying as much as it wants you to think it's saying. If there were more than one or two really good laughs, somehow I don't think I'd mind all that much.

Jan Stuart, "Sex, Drugs, Siblings Reversing
Roles," in Newsday, February 12, 1992.

Clive Barnes   (review date 13 February 1992)

[*Barnes is an English-born American performing arts critic and editor. In the following review of* The Baltimore Waltz, *he faults Vogel for employing absurdism and for displaying private grief that lacks public relevance.*]

The difference between theater of the absurd and absurd theater is more than mere semantics, more than a play on words. The first is an attempt to show man grotesquely out of harmony with the contemporary world; it has a rationale and an agenda. Absurd theater, on the other hand, is just plain nuts.

Paula Vogel's *The Baltimore Waltz* . . . is not just plain nuts, it's even fancy nuts as well, adding a precious soupcon of pretentiousness to its overall nuttiness.

The playwright and its director describe this *Baltimore Waltz* as "a second-generation AIDS play." A what? Second generation? This is meant to be not "ho-ho, another AIDS play," but "heigh-ho, here is a play about AIDS and how to live and laugh with it," a play to put a little gaiety in gayness.

I tend to be rather suspicious of comedies about terminal illness—all those riotous jokes in the cancer ward, or the banana-skin and fatal heart-attack ploy.

Presumably, this play represents a thin-skin membrane covering a profound and private grief—I say this as it is dedicated "To the memory of Carl—because I cannot sew," and the principal character, whose death this fantasy whirligig celebrates, is also named Carl. In such a case my humble compassion, but some griefs are better kept private.

I called the play a fantasy, and so it is. It apparently takes place at the bedside of Carl and in the mind or minds of either Carl, or his sister, Anna, or both.

The fantasy is for the two siblings, after Anna has been declared terminally ill of "acquired toilet seat deficiency syndrome," to embark on the grand European tour they have always promised themselves. Anna, a schoolteacher, picked up the virus using, without proper protection, a toilet in the schoolyard. Her mother had warned her about strange toilet seats, but she was young and rash.

Now Anna and Carl, carrying his magic white stuffed rabbit, sail away on their magic mystery tour intended to end in Vienna, where a quack cure may be available. As they pass through Paris and Amsterdam (where Anna meets a boy who saved the city by putting his finger in the dike) on their way to Vienna, they have strange adventures.

Carl's are largely concerned with his quest for Harry Lime (complete with zither accompaniment), while Anna, who is making up for time lost in the schoolroom, concentrates on sex.

Through all these tediously tricksy twists and turns there appears a character called the Third Man, a polymorphic actor of all work, who is a pompous physician one moment, an amorous bellhop the next, to say nothing of Dr. Strangelove or even Harry Lime himself.

Of course, even bad things have to come to an end. Eventually we realize that there is no such thing as "acquired toilet seat deficiency syndrome," and no such place as Europe (not for them at least), and when the waltz finally comes to an end, it will not be Anna looking in vain for her musical chair, but Carl.

There are moments of real humor in this farrago of annoying nonsense, largely because of the acting which, surprisingly perhaps in the circumstances, is as engaging as it is brilliant.

But acting can't write a play—only a playwright can write a play, and here the playwright has been content to work out a muddled concept of conceivably more therapeutic use to her than value to her audience.

Clive Barnes, "'Waltz' Trips on Intentions,"
in New York Post, February 13, 1992.

David Richards (review date 16 February 1992)

[*In the following excerpt, Richards offers a mixed assessment of* The Baltimore Waltz.]

In *The Baltimore Waltz,* a discombobulating new play . . . , a brother and sister take a grand tour of Europe, while the playwright Paula Vogel goes on a guilt trip.

A few hard facts may be helpful here. In 1986, Ms. Vogel's brother Carl, then HIV-positive, proposed that she visit Europe with him. Unaware of his condition and caught up in other projects, she declined the offer. Early in 1988, Carl died of AIDS in Maryland. The trip never got taken.

Written a year and a half later, Ms. Vogel's play is the journey they might have experienced—part dream, part movie pastiche, part wish fulfillment. Carl is still Carl, a San Francisco librarian, fired for wearing a pink triangle on the job. Anna, an elementary-school teacher, is the stand-in for the playwright. An additional character, billed only as Third Man, crops up as everybody along the way, including Harry Lime, the black marketeer, whom Orson Welles played in the movie classic *The Third Man.*

The playwright's greatest deviation from reality, however, is to make Anna the sick one, not Carl. Early in the play, the doctor informs her she has ATD, "Acquired Toilet Disease," a terminal illness contracted by sitting on public toilet seats. Single schoolteachers between the ages of 24 and 40 seem to be the chief victims. Medical science is baffled. Safe toilet practices offer the only protection. "Do squat, don't sit," advises the Department of Health and Human Services.

While the European voyage will be in the nature of a last goodbye for the siblings, they entertain the tiniest of hopes that Dr. Todesrochein, an 80-year-old Viennese urologist, will be able to save Anna. Off they go—Anna, dressed in a trench coat and black slip, and determined to have one last fling in each country they visit; Carl, wearing a suit coat over his striped pajamas and clutching a stuffed rabbit, ready to explore higher, more cultural pursuits. The Third Man, for his part (or parts), is kept busy playing clichéd versions of the amorous Frenchman, the stalwart Dutchman who put his finger in the dike, the abusive Berliner in black leather and Dr. Todesrocheln, a Dr. Strangelove knockoff in a fright wig and blood-spattered laboratory coat.

Reluctant to write yet another AIDS play, Ms. Vogel has brought a bizarre sense of fantasy to bear on a situation that, unfortunately, has become all too common. But even as she's letting her imagination run riot, a terrible remorse seems to have her in its grip. One impulse wars against the other. *The Baltimore Waltz* is too tortured to be whimsical, too wigged-out to be moving and just hermetic enough so that you may not care.

The action takes place in a sterile hospital room that could also be an airport waiting lounge. (The lush travelogue music tells you when it is Paris or Vienna.) The director Anne Bogart—never one to clear up a mystery—has chosen to accent the play's eccentricities at the expense of any internal logic. The symbolism of Carl's stuffed rabbit

alone is enough to keep you in a state of befuddlement. Depending on the scene, it would seem to represent contraband, a phallus, a badge of initiation, the innocence of childhood or a stuffed rabbit.

At one point, Carl enthusiastically suggests showing the audience slides of the Rhineland. The lights are dimmed and the pictures turn out to be depressing views of Baltimore. No problem there. When shots of Disneyland creep into the mix, though, Carl is furious.

As who wouldn't be?

[*The Baltimore Waltz* will] be most meaningful to those most directly involved. Isn't therapy?

> *David Richards, in a review of "The Baltimore Waltz," in* The New York Times, *Section 2, February 16, 1992, p. 17.*

Robert Brustein on *The Baltimore Waltz:*

Never actually leaving Baltimore, [Anna] travels through a variety of countries, clutching Carl and her Berlitz guide, practicing French, German, and Dutch, seeking the Third Man (Harry Lime now traffics in illegal curative drugs), encountering various species of Eurotrash, until, at the end, finding her brother dead, she dances the Baltimore Waltz with his corpse, a stuffed rabbit clenched under his arm. [*The Baltimore Waltz*] is a touching rite of loving exorcism, personal yet transcendent, tenderly written.

> *Robert Brustein, in his "What Do Women Playwrights Want?"* The New Republic, *13 April 1992.*

John Simon (review date 2 March 1992)

[*An American essayist and critic, Simon has served as a drama critic for* New York *magazine as well as a film critic for* Esquire *and the* New Leader. *In the following excerpt, he provides a negative assessment of* The Baltimore Waltz.]

There are plays that are merely bad, and others that are downright repellent. Paula Vogel's *The Baltimore Waltz* establishes itself firmly in the latter category. The author, who teaches drama at Brown and has garnered more grants and awards than a black sofa gathers lint, informs us that her brother Carl, after being fired from his elementary-school teaching job for flaunting his homosexuality, wanted her to take a trip to Europe with him. Not knowing that he had tested HIV-positive, she declined for reasons she now rues, and Carl, without getting his trip, died of AIDS in their native Baltimore. The dedication of the play reads, "To the memory of Carl—because I cannot sew." The reference, of course, is to the AIDS quilt. Miss Vogel is being unduly modest: I am sure she sews at least as well as she writes plays.

The piece is a fantasy trip to Europe. In this fantasy, the author calls herself Anna, a first-grade teacher dying of ATD (acquired toilet disease), something that attacks young, unmarried female grade-school teachers who, as her comic physician explains, use "the johnny in the class-room to make wawa." Carl, Anna's brother and colleague, cashiered for teaching lewd homosexual songs to his tiny wards, is taking Sis to Vienna for treatment by the celebrated Dr. Todesröcheln (German for "death rattle"), "a specialist in uritosia." "He writes poems about urine?" Anna inquires. "No," Carl explains, "he drinks it." He also, as we see later, lets the patients indulge.

So off to a fantasy Europe they go, Carl making arrangements with an old school friend now living in Vienna, Harry Lime, whose former address was *The Third Man.* "There is something up," he tells Harry over the phone; "no, *that* hasn't been up for ages." It is Harry who recommended Dr. Todesröcheln, and who, in a blond fright wig, proves to be Dr. T. But let's not anticipate.

As they set off, Anna announces, "In whatever time is left, this teacher means to f--- her brains out," and so she does, with any waiter, bellhop, or other comer. Typical scene: a bed, presented vertically (this is avant-garde theater!), with Anna and a Parisian waiter under the sheets. Anna's voice, in a crescendo, repeats, "Oh, yes!" The *garçon's* voice, likewise crescendo, repeats, "Ah, *oui!*" Carl and Anna picked him up in a bistro (stuffing herself is her other indulgence) "where Hemingway threw up all over Fitzgerald's suede shoes, which really *was* a moveable feast."

While Anna's heterosexual escapades are shown bluntly enough, Carl's homosexual ones are rendered metaphorically. Wherever he goes, Carl carries his floppy toy bunny. Fishy-looking men emerge periodically from odd places; each carries the identical floppy bunny, to be furtively exchanged for Carl's in dark nooks or crannies. Why are homosexual encounters treated in this oblique fashion? The bunny trope, moreover, does not work. Whenever the siblings go through Customs, Anna must hold Carl's rabbit, lest the Customs officers, suspecting it of harboring contraband, tear it apart. First, women carrying bunnies can be just as suspected of smuggling as men. Second, there are X-ray machines expressly designed to protect bunnies from needless disembowelment. Third, how do you hand over your homosexuality to your sister during inspections? The floppy metaphor flops.

Other devices similarly misfire, e.g., the slide show of their trip Carl puts on for Anna, where the slides turn out to be seedy locations around Baltimore. Throughout, the relationship between brother and sister gets closer and stickier; then Vogel pulls her dramatic flip-flop and reveals that it is really Carl who is dying—but not until Dr. T. and Anna, as it were, toast each other with urine. Carl dies, and Anna performs a pas de deux with his corpse, which adds incestuous necrophilia to the repertoire of tastelessness. In the final scene, the dead Carl reappears in full Austrian guardsman's dress uniform, and waltzes the swooning Anna around to the music of Strauss—something out of *The Chocolate Soldier* coated with bittersweet incest.

I would not dwell on *The Baltimore Waltz* at such length if it had not earned widespread critical praise and a major grant from AT&T (which does not stand for acquired toi-let & trough disease), ensuring it productions at four reputable theaters across the country. I daresay AIDS plays nowadays command Pavlovian adulation, especially if by espousing absurdist technique they awe both sponsors and spectators. But some subjects, such as AIDS and the Holocaust, are not laughing matters, and should be protected from the likes of Paula Vogel.

John Simon, "Old Wine in New Bottles," in New York *Magazine, Vol. 25, No. 9, March 2, 1992.*

Thomas M. Disch (review date 23 March 1992)

[*Disch is an American novelist, short story writer, and poet. In the following excerpt, he praises* The Baltimore Waltz *for depicting the problems of AIDS victims and their loved ones, but questions the implications posed by Vogel's subtexts on medical ethics and sexual promiscuity.*]

Sufferings inflicted by Fate, or by Jehovah, don't make for good theater. "Why me?" Job wants to know, and the only answer he can get is "Consider the chief of the beasts, the crocodile." At least Prometheus got a straight answer, though his story, too, poses problems for the dramatist. The contest is too unequal. Human heroes are best matched against human villains.

And that has been the problem with plays about AIDS, or plays about fatal diseases in general. If it *is* a fatal disease, it will have the last word, barring the preemptive strategy of Brian Clark's *Whose Life Is It, Anyway?* Accordingly, plays about AIDS have tended to look for someone human to blame: In *Beirut* it was the Authorities, who turned the Lower East Side into a lazaret; in *The Normal Heart* it was the Medical Establishment and others complicit in minimizing the dangers of the plague and thereby assisting its wider dissemination. For reasons of both compassion and prudence, there has not yet been a play after the manner of Ibsen's *Ghosts,* in which the plague's proximate cause, the plague bearer, figures as the heavy; but in another respect Ibsen's dramatic strategy has been widely adapted, particularly when TV has ventured treatment of AIDS. Time and again, the TV characters with AIDS are portrayed not as members of those groups most devastated by the illness—gays and needle-sharers—but as women and children who acquired AIDS, as Mrs. Alving and her son got syphilis, by no action of their own.

In the theater, however, the principal characters with AIDS have been gay, usually in plays taking the form of case histories or dramas about those who are left to mourn. In any case, the disease or the death is the focus of the action, not (as in *The Lady of the Camellias*) merely incidental to a more "complex" story. [In *The Baltimore Waltz*], playwright Paula Vogel has found a way to have it both ways. Her character Carl, a gay white male who sports an activist's pink triangle, has AIDS, as does his sister, Anna, a heterosexual female schoolteacher who caught the disease (in a fantastical variant form) by using the same toilet as one of her first-grade pupils. The schoolteacher accompanies her brother on a tour of Europe and comes to terms with the disease as she has a rollicking sex holiday with representative French, Dutch and German pickups. Her brother, in the course of this trip, relates erotically only to his stuffed toy rabbit and to other men with the same improbable fetish. The odyssey ends with a visit to a Dr. Strangelove clone whose crank cure for ATD (Acquired Toilet Disease) is drinking one's own urine. In the denouement Carl is discovered dead, and we realize that all of Anna's travails have been a fantasy inspired by the spectacle of his dying in a Baltimore hospital: partly death envy, partly a sacrificial daydream.

This is a concept from which Vogel and her director get a lot of mileage, though some stretches of the trip have the *longuers* of a long-distance train ride. Vogel's talent for comedy is hit-or-miss, with a 50 percent ratio of success by my estimate . . . . There is a long *hommage* to the film *The Third Man* that tries to be both cute and sinister, yet is neither.

More problematic—as well as the play's particular virtue, I'm sure, for its most ardent admirers—are the meanings to be unraveled from its cagily elusive subtext. Anna's and Carl's search for a miracle cure leads them first to Harry Lime, the purveyor of tainted and ineffective medicine in *The Third Man,* and then to a mad scientist modeled on Peter Seller's twitchy Dr. Strangelove, who is then elided into the ordinary real-world doctor who announces Carl's death. I can't help but think that these figures reflect the tendency common to many AIDS activists to blame medical science for offering no better alleviation for the disease than AZT, which many of them, indeed, regard as wicked. There have been, of course, a variety of frauds perpetrated on AIDS victims, and these may be Vogel's intended satiric target; but as staged, her play evinces an equal horror for AIDS and for medicine *tout court.* This is an understandable feeling in one who has witnessed a brother's prolonged hospitalization and eventual death. I only wish it were more ably expressed, since, for the unconverted, these passages are the least compelling in the play.

Vogel succeeds best in the successive vignettes of Anna's sexual adventuring across Europe. Here the author's am-

bivalences are more resonant. On the surface these encounters range from pleasantly bawdy (a lesson with a bellhop on the French words for parts of the body) to silly (a Dutch boy in wooden shoes who tells a long shaggy-dog story about having his finger in a dike) to satiric (a marvelously boorish German pop anarchist). Below the surface, these encounters represent a feminist fantasy of the varieties of gay promiscuity; below that (and rather uneasy-making) there is the suggestion, never overt, that the discovery of being HIV-positive promotes a last-fling, seize-the-day mentality. The author's hypothetical ATD is not sexually transmitted, so Anna's adventures are "innocent," per the TV paradigm, but translate her story back to the real world and her plot becomes quite unsettling. In sum, while I don't think *The Baltimore Waltz* is an unqualified success, it bears pondering. (pp. 389-90)

> *Thomas M. Disch, in a review of "The Baltimore Waltz," in* The Nation, *New York, Vol. 254, No. 11, March 23, 1992, pp. 389-90.*

FURTHER READING

Evans, Greg. Review of *The Baltimore Waltz,* by Paula Vogel. *Variety* 346, No. 5 (17 February 1992): 77.

> Favorable assessment of *The Baltimore Waltz.*

Kirkpatrick, Melanie. Review of *The Baltimore Waltz,* by Paula Vogel. *The Wall Street Journal* (14 February 1992): A9.

> Negative review of *The Baltimore Waltz* in which Kirkpatrick faults Vogel's use of humor and choice of narrative focus.

Weales, Gerald. "Final Acts." *Commonweal* CXIX, No. 8 (24 April 1992): 18-19.

> Mixed review of *The Baltimore Waltz.*

> **Additional coverage of Vogel's life and career is contained in the following source published by Gale Research:** *Contemporary Authors,* **Vol. 108.**

Derek Walcott
Nobel Prize in Literature

(Full name Derek Alton Walcott) Born in 1930, Walcott is a West Indian poet, playwright, critic, and journalist.

For further information about Walcott's life and work, see *CLC*, Volumes 2, 4, 9, 14, 25, 42, and 67.

INTRODUCTION

Walcott is a highly respected author whose poetry and plays often emphasize the opposing African and European influences that characterize his West Indian heritage. Walcott's work reflects this cultural division, incorporating both the formal structure of English verse and the colorful dialect of his native island, St. Lucia. While embracing the literary tradition of England, Walcott additionally denounces the exploitation and suppression of Caribbean culture resulting from British colonization. His acclaimed poem "A Far Cry from Africa" delineates the theme of uncertain identity that has dominated his poetic career: "I who am poisoned with the blood of both, / Where shall I turn, divided to the vein? / I who have cursed / The drunken officer of British rule, how choose / Between this African and the English tongue I love?"

Walcott was born on St. Lucia, a small island in the West Indies. He has characterized his childhood as "schizophrenic," referring to the divided loyalties associated with his African and English ancestry and the fact that he grew up in a middle-class, Protestant family in a society that was predominantly Catholic and poor. His mother, a teacher actively involved in local theater, and his father, a painter, strongly influenced his artistic development. Although his father died when Walcott was an infant, Walcott drew inspiration from the numerous watercolor paintings his father left behind. Walcott has observed: "[My father's paintings] gave me a kind of impetus and a strong sense of continuity. I felt that what had been cut off in him somehow was an extension that I was continuing." Walcott's childhood ambition was to be a painter, and in his autobiographical poem *Another Life,* he and his friend, the painter Dustin St. Omer, vow to record the unique atmosphere of the Caribbean through their art: "we would never leave the island / until we had put down, in paint, in words . . . / all its sunken, leaf-choked ravines, / every neglected, self-pitying inlet. . . ."

Walcott began writing poetry at an early age, often imitating such English-language writers as W. H. Auden, T. S. Eliot, and Dylan Thomas. At the age of eighteen, he financed the publication of *25 Poems,* his first poetry col-

lection. While studying literature at St. Mary's College in St. Lucia and at the University of the West Indies in Jamaica, he completed two more volumes of poetry and produced *Henri Christophe: A Chronicle in Seven Scenes,* a historical play written in verse. *Drums and Colours: An Epic Drama,* first produced in 1958, earned Walcott a Rockefeller Fellowship to study theater in the United States. Upon his return to the Caribbean, he became intensely involved in Trinidad's artistic community, writing reviews and organizing the Trinidad Theatre Workshop, which produced several of his plays during the 1950s and 1960s. Since the 1970s, Walcott has divided his time between the West Indies and the United States, where he has taught at Yale, Columbia, and other universities.

Many of Walcott's plays, often called "folk-dramas," are firmly rooted in the common life and language of the West Indies and frequently incorporate Caribbean dialects and legends. The importance of preserving West Indian culture is related in Walcott's *Dream on Monkey Mountain,* often considered his most successful play. Many critics have interpreted the play as a metaphorical work in which the oppressed consciousness of a colonized society is symbolized through the hallucinations of Makak, an aging charcoal maker and vendor. Describing this character, Walcott observed: "Makak comes from my own childhood. I can see him for what he is now, a brawling, ruddy drunk who would come down the street on a Saturday when he got paid and let out an immense roar that would terrify all the children. . . . This was a degraded man, but he had some elemental force in him that is still terrifying; in another society he would have been a warrior."

Anger and resentment associated with the injustice of colonized history is another common motif in Walcott's work. While Walcott's poems celebrate the artistic opportunity presented by a diverse culture, they also reveal his fear that island culture will become overwhelmed by British dominance and expanding tourism. In *The Star-Apple Kingdom* he declares: "One morning the Caribbean was cut up / by seven prime ministers who bought the sea in bolts— / one thousand miles of aquamarine with lace trimmings, / one million yards of lime-coloured silk. . . ." His poem "St. Lucie" laments the loss of French patois to the national language of English: "Come back to me / my language / Come back, / cacao, / grigri, / solitaire, / oiseau." Many of Walcott's later poems also depict the artist as an outcast from the West Indian community—estranged from both African and European heritage. In "The Light of the World" from *The Arkansas Testament,* he expresses his sense of alienation and futility as a poet: "There was nothing they wanted, nothing I could give them / but this thing I have called 'The Light of the World'." Discussing the role of colonization in determining Caribbean identity, Walcott has stated: "At great cost and a lot of criticism, what I used to try to point out was that there is a great danger in historical sentimentality. . . . The whole situation in the Caribbean is an illegitimate situation. If we admit that from the beginning that there is no shame in that historical bastardy, then we can be men. But if we continue to sulk and say, 'Look what the slave-owner did,' and so forth, we will never mature."

Omeros, Walcott's acclaimed epic poem, which was cited by the Swedish Academy when he was awarded the Nobel Prize, has been interpreted as a historical and literary pilgrimage into West Indian history. Updating Homer's *Odyssey* by casting West Indian fishermen, prostitutes, and landlords in such classical roles as Achilles, Helen, and Hector, Walcott explores various cultures of the world, tracing their influence on the present identity of the Caribbean people. Oliver Taplin observed: "Throughout the poem, as in the mind, there are persistent reflections on the historical events that have directly and indirectly shaped the characters' lives: the brutal attacks of the slaves on Achille's African forebears, of Europeans on native Americans, of French warships against British when the Windward Islands were first colonized. . . . But Mr. Walcott recalls these scenes of death and suffering with the objective sympathy of a Homer, who tells what happened to Trojans as well as Greeks."

PRINCIPAL WORKS

25 Poems (poetry) 1948
Epitaph for the Young: A Poem in XII Cantos (poetry) 1949
Henri Christophe: A Chronicle in Seven Scenes (drama) 1950
Poems (poetry) 1951
Harry Dernier: A Play for Radio Production (drama) 1952
*The Charlatan (drama) 1954
The Sea at Dauphin: A Play in One Act (drama) 1954
Ione: A Play with Music (drama) 1957
Ti-Jean and His Brothers (drama) 1957
Drums and Colours: An Epic Drama (drama) 1958
†Malcauchon; or, Six in the Rain (drama) 1959
In a Green Night: Poems, 1948-1960 (poetry) 1962
Selected Poems (poetry) 1964
The Castaway, and Other Poems (poetry) 1965
Dream on Monkey Mountain (drama) 1967
The Gulf, and Other Poems (poetry) 1969; also published as *The Gulf, Poems,* 1970
Dream on Monkey Mountain, and Other Plays (dramas) 1970
In a Fine Castle (drama) 1970
Another Life (poetry) 1973
The Joker of Seville (drama) 1974
O Babylon! (drama) 1976
Sea Grapes (poetry) 1976
Selected Verse (poetry) 1976
Remembrance (drama) 1977
The Joker of Seville & O Babylon! (dramas) 1978
Pantomime (drama) 1978
The Star-Apple Kingdom (poetry) 1979
Remembrance and Pantomime (dramas) 1980
The Fortunate Traveller (poetry) 1981
Selected Poetry (poetry) 1981
Midsummer (poetry) 1984
A Branch of the Blue Nile (drama) 1986
Collected Poems, 1948-1984 (poetry) 1986
Three Plays (dramas) 1986
The Arkansas Testament (poetry) 1987
Omeros (poetry) 1990
Viva Detroit (drama) 1990
Steel (drama) 1991
The Odyssey (drama) 1992

*This work was revised into a two-act play for productions in 1973 and 1977.

†This work is frequently transliterated as *Malcochon, or, The Six in the Rain.*

OVERVIEWS

Joseph Brodsky   (essay date 10 November 1983)

[*A Russian-born American poet, essayist, and translator, Brodsky is a personal friend of Walcott and the winner of the 1987 Nobel Prize in Literature. In the following excerpt, he argues that Walcott should be considered a great poet of the English language and not just a regional artist.*]

[For the thirty years that Walcott has been writing, critics have] kept calling him "a West Indian poet" or "a black poet from the Caribbean." These definitions are as myopic and misleading as it would be to call the Saviour a Galilean. The comparison may seem extreme but is appropriate if only because each reductive impulse stems from the terror of the infinite; and when it comes to an appetite for the infinite, poetry often dwarfs creeds. The mental as well as spiritual cowardice, obvious in the attempts to render this man a regional writer, can be further explained by the unwillingness of the critical profession to admit that the great poet of the English language is a black man. It can also be attributed to degenerated helixes, or, as the Italians say, to retinas lined with ham. Still, its most benevolent explanation, surely, is a poor knowledge of geography.

For the West Indies are an archipelago about five times as large as the Greek one. If poetry is to be defined by physical reality, Walcott would end up with five times more material than that of the bard who also wrote in a dialect, the Ionian one at that, and who also loved the sea. When language encounters the absence of a heroic past a situation may emerge whereby the crest of a wave arrests the mind as fully as the siege of Troy. Indeed, the poet who seems to have a lot in common with Walcott is not English but rather the author of the *Iliad* and the *Odyssey,* or the author of "On the Nature of Things." The need to itemize the universe in which he found himself gives Walcott's descriptive powers a truly epic character; what saves his lines from the genre's frequent tedium, though, is the sparseness of his realm's actual history and the quality of his ear for the English language, whose sensibility in itself is a history.

Quite apart from the matter of his own unique gifts, Walcott's lines are so resonant and stereoscopic precisely because this "history" is eventful enough, because language itself is an epic device. Everything this poet touches reverberates like magnetic waves whose acoustics are psychological and whose implications echo. Of course, in that realm of his, in the West Indies, there is plenty to touch—the natural kingdom alone provides an abundance of fresh material; but here is an example of how this poet deals with that most *de rigueur* of all poetic subjects—the moon—which he makes speak for itself:

> Slowly my body grows a single sound,
> slowly I become
> a bell,
> an oval, disembodied vowel,
> I grow, an owl,
> an aureole, white fire.
>   (from **"Metamorphoses, I/Moon"**)

And here is how he himself speaks *about* this most poetic subject—or rather, here is what makes him speak about it:

> . . . a moon ballooned from the Wireless Station. O
> mirror, where a generation yearned
> for whiteness, for candour, unreturned.
>   (from ***Another Life***)
>   (p. 39)

To put it simply, instead of indulging in racial self-assertion, which no doubt would have endeared him to both his potential foes and his champions, Walcott identifies himself with that "disembodied vowel" of the language which both parts of his equation share. The wisdom of this choice is, again, not so much his own as the wisdom of his language—better still, the wisdom of its letter: of black on white. He is like a pen that is aware of its movement, and it is this self-awareness that forces his lines into their graphic eloquence:

> Virgin and ape, maid and malevolent Moor,
> their immortal coupling still halves the world,
> He is your sacrificed beast, bellowing, goaded,
> a black bull snarled in ribbons of its blood.
> And yet, whatever fury girded
> on that saffron-sunset turban, moon-shaped sword
> was not his racial, panther-black revenge
> pulsing her chamber with raw musk, its sweat,
> but horror of the moon's change,
> of the corruption of an absolute,
> like white fruit,
> pulped ripe by fondling but doubly sweet.
>   (from **"Goats and Monkeys"**)

This is what a "sound colonial education" amounts to; this is what having "English in me" is all about. With equal right, Walcott could have said that he has in him Greek, Latin, Italian, German, Spanish, Russian, French: because of Homer, Lucretius, Ovid, Dante, Rilke, Machado, Lorca, Neruda, Akhmatova, Mandelstam, Pasternak, Baudelaire, Valéry, Apollinaire. These are not influences—they are the cells of his bloodstream. And if culture feels more palpable among urine-stunted trees through which "a mud path wriggles like a snake in flight," hail the mud path.

And so the lyrical hero of Walcott's poetry does. Sole guardian of the civilization grown hollow at the center, he stands on this mud path watching how "a fish plops, making rings / that marry the wide harbour" with "clouds curled like burnt-out papers at their edges" above it, with "telephone wires singing from pole to pole / parodying perspective." In his keen-sightedness this poet resembles Joseph Banks, except that by setting his eyes on a plant "chained in its own dew" or on an object, he accomplishes something no naturalist is capable of—he animates them. To be sure, the realm needs it, not any less than he does himself in order to survive there. In any case, the realm pays him back, and hence lines like:

> Slowly the water rat takes up its reed pen
> and scribbles leisurely, the egret
> on the mud tablet stamps its hieroglyph . . .

270

This is more than naming things in the garden—it is a bit later. Walcott's poetry is Adamic in the sense that both he and his world have departed from Paradise—he, by tasting the fruit of knowledge; his world, by its political history.

"Ah brave third world!" he exclaims elsewhere, and a lot more has gone into this exclamation than simple anguish or exasperation. This is a comment of language upon a more than purely local failure of nerve and imagination; a reply of semantics to the meaningless and abundant reality, epic in its shabbiness. Abandoned, overgrown airstrips, dilapidated mansions of retired civil servants, shacks covered with corrugated iron, single-stack coastal vessels coughing like "relics out of Conrad," four-wheeled corpses escaped from their junkyard cemeteries and rattling their bones past condominium pyramids, helpless or corrupt politicos and young ignoramuses ready to replace them while talking revolutionary garbage, "sharks with well-pressed fins / ripping we small fry off with razor grins"; a realm where "you bust your brain before you find a book," where, if you turn on the radio, you may hear the captain of a white cruise boat insisting that a hurricane-stricken island reopen its duty-free shop no matter what, where "the poor still poor, whatever arse they catch," where one sums up the deal the realm got by saying, "we was in chains, but chains made us unite, / now who have, good for them, and who blight, blight," and where "beyond them the firelit mangrove swamps / ibises practicing for postage stamps."

Whether accepted or rejected, the colonial heritage remains a mesmerizing presence in the West Indies. Walcott seeks to break its spell neither by plunging "into incoherence of nostalgia" for a nonexistent past nor by finding for himself a niche in the culture of departed masters (into which he wouldn't fit in the first place, because of the scope of his talent). He acts out of the belief that language is greater than it masters or its servants, that poetry, being its supreme version, is therefore an instrument of self-betterment for both; i.e., that it is a way to gain an identity superior to the confines of class, race, and ego. This is just plain common sense; this is also the most sound program of social change there is. But then, poetry is the most democratic art—it always starts from scratch. In a sense, a poet is indeed like a bird that chirps no matter what twig it alights on, hoping there is an audience, even if it's only the leaves.

About these "leaves"—lives—mute or sibilant, faded or immobile, about their impotence and surrender, Walcott knows enough to make you look sideways from the page containing:

> Sad is the felon's love for the scratched wall,
> beautiful the exhaustion of old towels,
> and the patience of dented saucepans
> seems mortally comic.

And you resume the reading only to find:

> . . . I know how profound is the folding of a
>   napkin
> by a woman whose hair will go white. . . .

For all its disheartening precision, this knowledge is free

of modernist despair (which often disguises one's shaky sense of superiority) and is conveyed in tones as level as its source. What saves Walcott's lines from sounding hysterical is his belief that:

> . . . time that makes us objects, multiplies
> our natural loneliness . . .

which results in the following "heresy"

> . . . God's loneliness moves in His smallest
>   creatures.

No leaf, either up here or in the tropics, would like to hear this sort of thing, and that's why they seldom clap to this bird's song. Even a greater stillness is bound to follow after:

> All of the epics are blown away with leaves,
> blown with careful calculations on brown paper,
> these were the only epics: the leaves. . . .

The absence of response has done in many a poet, and in so many ways, the net result of which is that infamous equilibrium—or tautology—between cause and effect: silence. What prevents Walcott from striking a more than appropriate, in his case, tragic pose is not his ambition but his humility, which binds him and these "leaves" into one tight book: " . . . yet who am I . . . under the heels of the thousand / racing towards the exclamation of their single name, / Sauteurs! . . ."

Walcott is neither a traditionalist nor a modernist. None of the available -isms and the subsequent -ists will do for him. He belongs to no "school"; there are not many of them in the Caribbean, save those of fish. (One would be tempted to call him a metaphysical realist, but then realism is metaphysical by definition, as well as the other way around. Besides, that would smack of prose.) He can be naturalistic, expressionistic, surrealistic, imagistic, hermetic, confessional—you name it. He simply has absorbed, the way whales do the plankton or a paintbrush the palette, all the stylistic idioms the north could offer; now he is on his own, and in a big way.

His versatility in different meters and genres is enviable. In general, however, he gravitates to a lyrical monologue and to a narrative. That and his verse plays, as well as his tendency to write in cycles, again suggest an epic streak in this poet, and perhaps it's time to take him up on that. For thirty years his throbbing and relentless lines have kept arriving on the English language like tidal waves, coagulating into an archipelago of poems without which the map of contemporary literature would be like wallpaper. He gives us more than himself or "a world"; he gives us a sense of infinity embodied in the language as well as in the ocean, which is always present in his poems: as their background or foreground, as their subject, or as their meter.

To put it differently, these poems represent a fusion of two versions of infinity: language and ocean. The common parent of the two elements is, it must be remembered, time. If the theory of evolution, especially the part of it that suggests we all came from the sea, holds any water, then both thematically and stylistically Derek Walcott's poetry is the case of the highest and most logical evolution of the species. He was surely lucky to be born at this outskirt, at this crossroads of English and the Atlantic where both arrive in waves only to recoil. The same pattern of motion—ashore, and back to the horizon—is sustained in Walcott's lines, thoughts, life.

Open a book by Walcott, and see " . . . the grey, iron harbour / open on a sea-gull's rusty hinge," hear how " . . . the sky's window rattles / at gears raked in reverse," be warned that "At the end of the sentence, rain will begin. / At the rain's edge, a sail. . . ." This is the West Indies, this is that realm which once, in its innocence of history, mistook for "a light at the end of a tunnel / the lantern of a caravel" and paid for that dearly: it was a light at the tunnel's entrance. This sort of thing happens often, to archipelagos as well as to individuals: in this sense, every man is an island. If, nevertheless, we must register this experience as West Indian and call this realm the West Indies, let's do so, but let's also clarify that we have in mind the place discovered by Columbus, colonized by the British, and immortalized by Walcott. We may add, too, that giving a place a status of lyrical reality is more imaginative as well as a more generous act than discovering or exploiting something that was created already. (pp. 40-1)

> *Joseph Brodsky, "On Derek Walcott," in* The New York Review of Books, *Vol. 30, No. 17, November 10, 1983, pp. 39-41.*

Mark A. McWatt (essay date October 1988)

[*In the following excerpt, McWatt examines Walcott's development of a distinctly Caribbean form of literature that emphasizes the theme of artistic isolation.*]

The work of Derek Walcott must be seen in terms of his relationship to the islands and sea of the Caribbean; to the sense of people and place that awakened and forged his talent, and to the social and educational environment in which it matured. Some of the most famous voices that sing the poet's praises abroad seem (deliberately?) oblivious to his Caribbean context, and can therefore sound somewhat hollow and distorted. Joseph Brodsky, the Nobel prize-winning poet and friend of Walcott, quarrels with those who speak of him as a 'West Indian poet' or as a 'black poet from the Caribbean', and he himself prefers to think of Walcott simply as 'the great poet of the English language'.

Yet, for West Indian readers and critics there is much more to be considered than what Seamus Heaney refers to as Walcott's 'deep and sonorous possession' of the English language, or how he ranks with other English-language poets world-wide. In the first place, for the West Indian audience and critic, Walcott is not only—or even primarily—a poet, but also a man of the theatre, a playwright and the founder of important theatre movements in the region. It is probable that many more West Indians have seen his plays than have read the poems. This perception of a double Walcott—poet and playwright—is itself important, as it suggests the several aspects of 'doubleness' associated with the West Indian identity. Part of our response to Walcott involves a complex dynamic of self-recognition whereby we reciprocate his own sense of writing for his people by seeing ourselves in his personae and characters as well as in the 'schizophrenic' author behind them.

In the opening sections of the poem **"The Schooner Flight"** we find the red-nigger persona, Shabine, stealing away at dawn from his home, his sleeping mistress and his island; as he gets into the taxi that is taking him to his departing ship, the driver recognises him:

> 'This time, Shabine, like you really gone!'
> I ain't answer the ass, I simply pile in
> the back seat and watch the sky burn
> above Laventille pine as the gown
> in which the woman I left was sleeping,
> and I look in the rearview and see a man
> exactly like me, and the man was weeping
> for the houses, the streets, that whole fucking is-
>   land.

These lines of Shabine can be seen as expressing Walcott's own feelings about the islands of the Caribbean: there is the fierce, almost corrosive love for the physical beauty, for the familiar streets and houses; the domestic attachment to home and woman and yet the movement away, and the tears of frustration and betrayal caused by this wrenching. The paradox of the moment's emotions is also conveyed in the split between observing self and image in the mirror, and the sense of doubleness proliferates in the simultaneity of tears and bravado, the fineness of sensibility and the coarseness of language—the expletive and the breaking heart. All of these dualities powerfully embody the familiar (but eternally real) problems of West Indian identity as well as the particular relationship between the writer and his island home.

On 23 January 1930 Derek Alton Walcott was born in Castries, St. Lucia. As a mulatto he was aware from very early of his double heritage, of black and white ancestors; this split was reinforced by other factors such as his methodist, middle-class upbringing on an island that was largely Catholic and poor, and in particular by the colonial education which emphasised the formal language at the expense of dialect, and which taught the tradition of English literature from the classics to the moderns. This is not to say that Walcott was particularly troubled by this heritage; his was a fairly common West Indian position, in which it was easy to accept the paradoxes. Walcott himself says: 'In that simple, schizophrenic boyhood one could lead two lives: the interior life of poetry, the outward life of action and dialect.'

Walcott's great sensitivity to the literature he read at school—which included a sense of its power and the significance it bestowed on people and place—filled him with the urge to recreate his island home; as a painter he tried to capture it on canvas, as a poet he longed to summon it to the kind of life and power he discerned in the poetry he read. In **Another Life,** his long autobiographical poem, he tells how he and his friend Gregorias (the artist, Dunstan St Omer) swore

> that we would never leave the island
> until we had put down, in paint, in words,
> as palmists learn the network of a hand.
> all of its sunken, leaf-choked ravines,

> every neglected, self-pitying inlet
> muttering in brackish dialect . . .

This exuberant love for the island and the need to sanctify it in song—along with the significant experiences of his youth—comes across clearly in his earliest poetry. Walcott published privately, and within the region, his first three collections of poems; these were *25 Poems* (1948); *Epitaph for the Young: XII cantos* (1949); and *Poems* (1951).

It was, however, over a decade later that Walcott began to be known internationally, with the publication in 1962 of *In a Green Night: Poems 1948-1960.* Among the earlier poems in this collection is **'A City's Death by Fire'**, about the fire that destroyed Castries in 1948:

> After that hot gospeller had levelled all but the
>   churched sky
> I wrote the tale by tallow of a city's death by
>   fire . . .

Here one can see the deliberate assumption of the role of poet and, as Walcott carries out his self-set task, the diction and imagery echo the English poets he had been reading—particularly Dylan Thomas: the 'churched sky' becomes 'the bird-rocked sky' in a later line and the poet walks 'among the rubbled tales'. Later poems in the collection suggest the poetry of seventeenth-century England, with references to John Donne and Thomas Traherne. The title-poem echoes a line from Andrew Marvell's 'Bermudas', and that echo is reinforced throughout, with the diction and the measured formality of seventeenth-century verse, by the image of the orange tree which dominates the poem and becomes, by the end, a metaphysical conceit.

In this volume the young poet is obviously experimenting with styles, learning his craft; and yet the voice remains true to the Caribbean setting, and authentic in terms of the West Indian experience. In **'A Sea-Chantey'**, Odysseus and 'Cyclopic volcanoes'—summoned easily from the poet's familiarity with the classics—are balanced with the names of Caribbean islands and island schooners. The poem goes on to unite all in a litany that movingly evokes the calm of the island sabbath, ending with the thrice-repeated line: 'the amen of calm waters'. In other poems he is concerned as much with Caribbean man and society as with the landscape; **'Tales of the Islands'** is a virtuoso performance by the young poet, a sequence of ten sonnets which depict not only various examples of the physical landscape of the Caribbean, but also aspects of the psychological landscape as well, while the human characters such as Cosimo de Chrétien and Miss Rossignol struggle with the bewildering or sinister legacies of West Indian history. But perhaps the most important poems in the collection, in terms of the divided nature of the West Indian personality, are **'Ruins of a Great House'** and **'A Far Cry From Africa'**. In the former, Walcott juxtaposes the artistic spirit and achievements of seventeenth-century England with its appetite for bloody conquest and slaves in the Caribbean. Through a careful meditation on the transience of life and power, he arrives, almost in spite of himself ('so differently from what the heart arranged'), at a curious hollowness and vulnerability at the heart of imperial conquest, and

therefore at a sense of compassion for all. In **'A Far Cry From Africa'** he uses the Mau Mau struggle in Kenya as an occasion for reflecting on his dual ancestry; he declares himself 'divided to the vein', unable to choose between 'this Africa and the English tongue I love'. This is an important theme to which Walcott returns in later poems such as **'Verandah'** and in some of the plays.

Walcott's sense of the theatre grew out of his perception of the theatrical all around him as a boy: in the street-corner revivalist meetings at night, lit by gas-lamp and complete with song and music and dramatic conversions; in the lives of the poor whose freedom he envied; and in the derelict characters of the city whose flamboyant physical and mental defects suggested the magic of the theatre. So, apart from beginning 'marathon poems on Greek heroes', Walcott would play at theatre with his brother Roderick (also a noted dramatist): 'little men made from twigs, enacting melodramas of hunting and escape.' Walcott's first play was *Henri Christophe,* produced in 1950 by the St Lucia Arts Guild, which Walcott himself had helped to found. The play is important because of its perception of West Indian history and of the West Indian hero; Christophe afforded the young playwright the opportunity of writing about a West Indian king in the manner of Shakespearean and Jacobean drama. As with the early poetry, the style and language of this first play are derivative and experimental; the characters (including illiterates) speak in the still and remote language of Jacobean drama: all this serves, nevertheless, to portray again that split between white mind and black body which Walcott reads as part of the West Indian condition. His handling of the events of the play as 'one race's quarrel with another's God' reinforces this theme and remains true to the vision of a divided West Indian psyche.

In 1950 Walcott left St Lucia on a scholarship to the University College of the West Indies, in Jamaica, where he received a BA in English, French and Latin. In Jamaica Walcott directed a student production of *Henri Christophe* and published *Poems,* the aforementioned early volume of poetry. After leaving university he worked for a few years in teaching and journalism in Grenada, Trinidad and Jamaica, before settling in Trinidad in 1959. The move to Trinidad was an important one for several reasons: The Trinidadian population was large enough and the society sufficiently varied and sophisticated to allow a creative writer the freedom to function; Trinidad's traditions of carnival and calypso were important in the development of Walcott's later drama, and it was in Trinidad that he founded the most important theatrical group, the Little Carib Theatre Workshop, which he honed into a fine company of actors and the perfect vehicle for his own plays. The name of the group was later changed to the Trinidad Theater Workshop.

After a few shorter plays which suggested various influences, including classical Greek drama and J M Synge, Walcott completed his apprenticeship as a playwright and found his own authentic dramatic idiom in two superb plays, *Ti-Jean and his Brothers* and *Dream on Monkey Mountain.* Unlike Christophe, the protagonists in these plays have no royal pretensions, but are heroes in the folk tradition. Ti-Jean is the third son of the folk tale who succeeds where his elder brothers fail, but he is also the true revolutionary who overthrows white colonial rule, for Walcott's devil is also the old man of the forest and the white planter, both of whom are tricked by Ti-Jean's cunning and resourcefulness. Yet it is a folk cunning, and the resourcefulness of the peasant, making use of the powers of the forest creatures and the wisdom of his mother. Similarly, Makak, the ugly charcoal burner of *Dream on Monkey Mountain,* using his own resources of imagination and the richness of experience, undertakes the purifying dream of his people, wherein he undergoes suffering but emerges with a clear sense of self and identity, and rid of his fear and hatred of whiteness. It is a revolutionary dream, like Ti-Jean's actions, and these folk heroes suggest strategies for survival and success in the Caribbean context. The plays also represent Walcott's concern for, and involvement with, the community. Through an involvement with the folk and the community the hero arrives at a true sense of self, whereas in the poems the movement seems to be in the opposite direction—through a contemplation of self towards a vision of community.

In *The Castaway and Other Poems* (1965) and *The Gulf* (1970), we see concern with the self as isolated, separated from the outside world and having to forge links with that world. This balances the folk themes of the drama and it seems that, at this stage of Walcott's career, the duality or schizophrenia is reflected in the split between poetry and drama. The figure of the castaway alone on his beach suggests the loneliness of the artist, trying to make sense, not only of his world, but of himself in relation to it, whether it be the fertile horrors of a swamp, in the poem of that name, or the squalor of a teeming slum, as in 'Laventille', where the poet is isolated by his sense of history and the peculiar depth of his feeling. In 'Crusoe's Island' there are images of the castaway, the hermit and the artist, all suggesting the same condition, all emphasising separation and the failure of community. At the end of the poem the community is present in the children of Tobago, on the beach or returning for vespers, but the poet cannot reach or change them:

> . . . nothing I can learn
> From art or loneliness
> Can bless them as the bell's
> transfiguring tongue can bless.

The poet has killed God, his competitor, and cannot join their simple community of faith, he can only write about them—art becomes the substitute for community, or the consolation for its loss. In *The Gulf* the poet remains isolated; he cannot dance to the carnival music in 'Mass Man', the 'coruscating, mincing fantasies' of the themes and costumes of the bands are no match for the historical ghosts that dance in the poet's memory and he plays instead the whipped slave hanging from a gibbet, his mind already on Ash-Wednesday. The poet's art becomes one of atonement, not so much for history as for the forgetfulness and waste of the carnival culture. The separation between poet and society is further emphasised in 'Blues', where he is beaten when he approaches a gang of black youths in the American south, and in the title-poem, where he meditates on the USA and its history from be-

hind the window of a plane flying over the Gulf of Mexico. In the collection, the gulf becomes a metaphor for all kinds of separation and for the gap between the poet and the people and places he loves.

Another Life (1973), Walcott's autobiographical poem, is an important landmark in his work because it supplies details of his artistic development and early career in St Lucia, while developing some of the themes and concerns of his poetry in *The Gulf,* speculating on the nature of art and memory. All is expressed in a tough, flexible medium that proves as suitable for the sparkling flights of lyricism as it is for the narrative or meditative sections and the passages of pure invective. Apart from tracing important relationships which the young writer enjoyed (notably with the painters, Harry Simmons and Dunstan St Omer), the poem shows his love for the island and its people. He tells of an incident, an epiphany, that occurred 'in the August of my fourteenth year': wandering in the hills above the town he succumbs to a sudden wave of pity for the island and its people:

> . . . I felt compelled to kneel,
> I wept for nothing and for everything,
> I wept for the earth of the hill under my knees,
> for the grass, the pebbles, for the cooking smoke
> above the labourer's houses like a cry . . .
> . . . For their lights that shine through the hovels like litmus.

These are the love and the tears that Shabine experiences as he leaves Trinidad in 'The Schooner *Flight*'. Such intimate revelations of feeling are balanced in the poem by Walcott's more public voice, the voice he uses to castigate the philistinism of Caribbean society which allows its artists to die in poverty and neglect. The whole of the poem's chapter 19, entitled 'Frescoes of the New World II', is a scathing indictment of governments and other institutions in the regions which betray their people in order to feather their own nests or to play games of power. The chapter is probably the finest piece of poetic invective in West Indian literature. The poet consigns to the sulphurous hell of Soufrière:

> all o' dem big boys, so, dem ministers,
> ministers of culture, ministers of development,
> the green blacks, and their old toms,
> and all the syntactical apologists of the Third
>   World
> explaining why their artists die
> by their own hands, magicians of the New Vision
> Screaming the same shit.

Living in Trinidad in the late 1960s, with the growing Black Power movement which culminated in the uprising of 1970, Walcott's concern with questions of politics and ideology—and the prominence of these themes within his work—inevitably grew. These topics are treated in poems such as 'Junta', in *The Gulf,* and 'Parades Parades', in *Sea Grapes* (1976); but it is perhaps in the collection *The Star-Apple Kingdom* (1980) that this theme really comes to the fore. Shabine in 'The Schooner *Flight*' is seen to be the victim of a corrupt minister for whom he smuggled scotch—and was made the scapegoat after the minister's investigation of himself. In the title-poem of the collection, which

Walcott wrote after reading *The Autumn of the Patriarch* (1975) by Gabriel García Márquez, there is a wonderful portrait of the regional prime ministers cutting up the Caribbean sea like bolts of blue and green cloth and selling it 'at a mark-up to the conglomerates', much as Garcia Márquez's dictator had sold the sea and was forced as a result to live on the edge of a vast bowl of dust. The mood of Walcott's poem echoes the troubled mood of Jamaica under the Manley government. The sinister female figure in the poem, who calls herself the revolution and whose lineage is Latin and Catholic, suggests nevertheless the curious strength of Jamaican women and embodies both the hope and the menace of that time.

The political themes also figure in Walcott's plays of this later period. One of Walcott's ambitions of this time seems to have been to write a successful Broadway musical: in collaboration with Galt MacDermot (who was responsible for the music of the Broadway hit, *Hair*), he wrote **The Joker of Seville** (1974) and **O Babylon** (1976). Neither play found its way to Broadway, but **O Babylon** is important for its portrayal of the Rastafarians of Jamaica and their struggle against the Babylon of exploitative big business, the police and the narrow attitudes of middle-class society towards them. These two plays are also significant in that they were the last two plays performed by the Trinidad Theater Workshop under Walcott's direction; he broke with the Workshop in 1976. Two later plays, **Remembrance** (1977) and **Pantomime** (1978) also engage with political themes. The main protagonist of the former, Albert Perez Jordan, has lost his elder son in the 1970 Black Power uprising and remains bewildered and scornful of a political conviction he cannot understand. In this play Walcott explores, with satirical insight but also with compassion, the gap between the mental attitudes and the political awareness of Perez Jordan and his children; between his 'real' foreign war and their playing at revolution; between the dedication and sense of purpose he felt as a teacher, and the aimlessness of the younger generation (his younger son is an artist who paints an American flag on the roof). The other play, **Pantomime,** is a kind of black/white fable where Walcott explores the humour and irony in the two characters' reversal of the roles of Robinson Crusoe and Friday. It is a reprise of several themes—that of the castaway, of racial division (black body/white mind) and West Indian identity, and the larger theme of illusion and reality. Like Ti-Jean or Makak, the characters struggle through to an understanding not only of themselves and their relationship to each other, but also of the forces and attitudes historically responsible for the social divisions of the Caribbean; the humour in the play balances a serious message concerning the encounter of slave and colonial master and all the consequent problems of that relationship.

After his break with the Theatre Workshop in Trinidad Walcott turned his attention increasingly to the USA, where he took up sessional teaching assignments at US universities. Since 1981 he has been teaching creative writing at Boston University and returning to the Caribbean as often as he can. His most recent poetry reflects this new 'doubleness' as he is now a poet of **'North'** and **'South'** (the titles of the structural divisions in **The Fortunate Travel-**ler, 1981) and of **'Here and Elsewhere'** (**The Arkansas Testament,** 1987). In **The Fortunate Traveller** the poem, **'The Spoiler's Return'**, is important not only for its masterful depiction of Trinidadian Calypso culture or for its political and social satire, but also because it represents perhaps the high point of Walcott's handling of dialect in his poetry. He began experimenting with this tentatively in a few lines of poems such as the sonnet in **'Tales of the Islands'**, which begins: 'Poopa da' was a fete!' It developed slowly in the poetry (although the dialogue in many of the plays was largely dialect), to the point where it has become a natural, flexible and sophisticated poetic medium in **'The Schooner *Flight*'**, which Seamus Heaney describes as 'epoch-making' precisely for this reason; he says that Walcott has discovered 'a language woven out of dialect and literature, neither folksy nor condescending . . . evolved out of one man's inherited divisions and obsessions'. **'The Spoiler's Return'** duplicates this achievement. Here is Spoiler explaining how the devil (a fan of his kaiso) has let him return to Port of Spain:

> I beg him two weeks leave and he send me
> back up, not as no bedbug or nor flea,
> but in this limeskin hat and floccy suit,
> to sing what I did always sing: the truth.
> Tell Desperadoes when you reach the hill,
> I decompose, but I composing still . . .

A feature of the latest poetry is Walcott's increasing concern with the figure of the poet, and the business of writing poetry itself. From his earliest poems his work was sprinkled with metaphors about writing poetry, or about the kind of poetry he sought to write, but the tendency towards a portrait of the poet writing, towards a bleak self-contemplation or self-questioning, has become marked in the latest collections. This can be seen in a poem such as **'Hotel Normandie Pool'** from **The Fortunate Traveller,** but by the time we come to the collection entitled **Midsummer,** this is the mode that predominates:

> At the Queen's Park Hotel, with its white, high-
> ceilinged rooms
> I reenter my first local mirror. A skidding roach
> In the porcelain basin slides from its path to Par-
> nassus.
> Every word I have written took the wrong ap-
> proach.
> I cannot connect these lines with the lines in my
> face.

The same seems to hold true for the latest drama, as in the play **A Branch of the Blue Nile** (1986), which involves characters who are playwrights and actors, and a play within a play. Perhaps this is another aspect of the autobiographical urge evident in **Another Life,** or part of the proliferating complexity of character or of the ambiguities at the heart of the creative urge, that Walcott himself sees so clearly in chapter 9 of the autobiographical poem.

One poem in Walcott's very latest volume, **The Arkansas Testament,** takes us back to the poet's undying love for islands and people that has been a constant throughout his career. It takes us back to the August epiphany in his fourteenth year, to Shabine weeping for his island, to Spoiler, coming back from Hell to try to save his beloved Trinidad. The poem is **'The Light of the World'**, in which the poet takes a trip with the peasants of his native St Lucia in a mini-bus. He looks around and loves them all—one woman he considers the light of the world; he is in tune with the features and rhythms of their lives, but still remains unable to participate fully, distanced by vocation, by a habit of perception. When the poet gets off at his stop the following final scene occurs:

> Then, a few yards ahead, the van stopped. A man
> shouted my name from the transport window.
> I walked up towards him. He held out something.
> A pack of cigarettes had dropped from my pocket.
> He gave it to me. I turned, hiding my tears.
> There was nothing they wanted, nothing I could give them
> but this thing I have called 'The Light of the World.'

But the gift is indeed valuable, and the giver worthy. With his accumulated fame and honours, living as ever between two worlds, Walcott remains the poet of the Caribbean people, of islands and of sea. (pp. 1607-15)

Mark A. McWatt, "Derek Walcott: An Island Poet and His Sea," in Third World Quarterly, *Vol. 10, No. 4, October, 1988, pp. 1607-15.*

Walcott on America, colonialism, and identity:

The whole idea of America, and the whole idea of everything on this side of the world, barring the Native American Indian, is imported; we're all imported, black, Spanish. When one says one is American, that's the experience of being American—that transference of whatever color, or name, or place. The difficult part is the realization that one is part of the whole idea of colonization. Because the easiest thing to do about colonialism is to refer to history in terms of guilt or punishment or revenge, or whatever. Whereas the rare thing is the resolution of being where one is and doing something positive about that reality.

Derek Walcott, in the interview "The Man Who Keeps the English Language Alive," in New Letters, *1992.*

James Wieland (essay date 1988)

[*In the following essay, Wieland examines Walcott's use of myth to evoke the history and culture of the West Indies.*]

On the dust jacket of **Another Life,** George Lamming is quoted as having said:

> This is not the first time that Walcott has given a hint that his first passion is art as the indispensable language for interpreting reality. He is a colonial who has spent a life trying to dismantle and re-define the cultural apparatus of his imperialist tutelage.

This redefining of which Lamming speaks draws attention to Walcott's relationship with his world and to his concern to make a comprehensive and creative word-picture of the Caribbean. The history he seeks is not that which may be celebrated in monuments or honored through ruins; indeed, he faces a history of loss in which monuments are reminders of subjugation and ruins evoke memories of decay. If history is to be celebrated, Walcott says [in his **"Caribbean: Culture or Mimicry?"**], it is to be viewed "as fiction or as religion, then our use of it will be idiosyncratic, personal, and therefore, creative." As he builds fictions around his people and his place, naming and repeating actions, images, metaphors, and symbols, there evolves a coherence and a pattern to his society which moves toward the sense of myth. And while this mythic quality stands in opposition to the vacuum of history, his fictions attempt to give the annihilation significance in the contemporary world. Curnow wrote an "anti-myth" in an endeavor to provide a more inclusive view of New Zealand history and to resist any simplistic stereotypes, and Walcott's mythopoeia functions to negate the exclusive "myth of the uncreative parasitic, malarial nigger, the marsh-numbed imagination that is happiest in mud." While his experience is expressed through allusions to Adam, Odysseus, Crusoe, and Friday, the true "stars of [his] mythology" are the islanders—artists, lovers, fishermen, foresters, *charbonnières*—"These dead, these derelicts / that alphabet of the emaciated." Into the lives of these people Walcott builds the eternal struggle of being, until they are, if not epic, at least "pseudo-epic." Out of their struggle emerges the essense of what it is to be West Indian and Man. His mythology is rooted in the reality of his islands; in their history, their landscape, their folk. And the various *figurae* he uses reflect aspects of the Caribbean experience, but they reach beyond the narrow confines of time and place: his Adam's Eden is a New World Paradise, rich in ambiguity and contradiction; his Odysseus hops Caribbean islands seeking an order and pattern, and Crusoe and Friday ultimately become metamorphosed into one figure as Crusoe's experience becomes emblematic of the West Indian, cast away into a world he did not choose but with which he must come to terms.

We have suggested that the ultimate fiction leads the reader back to the essential insights of myth. This is appropriate to Walcott who sees his search as "elemental." It leads, he says, toward a

> darkness [which] must be total, and the cave should not contain a single man-made, mnemonic object. Its noises should be elemental, the roar of rain, ocean, wind, and fire. Their first sound should be like their last, the cry. The voice must grovel in search of itself until gestures and sound fuse and the blaze of their flesh astonishes them. The children of slaves must sear their memory with a torch. The actor must break up his body and feed it as ruminatively as ancestral storytellers fed twigs to the fire. Those who look from their darkness into the tribal fire must be bold enough to cross it. (**Dream on Monkey Mountain**)

And of the energy of a poem he is reported to have said that "it moves off the page and goes into the memory. It goes into the collective memory of the entire race." He sees poetry as an embodiment of the collective memory, and his ideal movement, then, is from the private and fictive, toward the communal and mythic. As he says in **Dream on Monkey Mountain:**

> For imagination and body to move with original instinct, we must begin again from the bush. That return journey, with all its horror of rediscovery, means the annihilation of what is known. Some of our poets have pretended that journey, but with an itinerary whose resting points are predetermined. On such journeys the mind will discover what it chooses, and what these writers seek, like refugees raking debris, are heirlooms to dignify an old destitution. Even this destitution, carefully invoked, is pastoral. But if the body could be reduced once more to learning, to a rendering of things through groping mnemonic fingers, a new theatre [and a new poetry] could be made, with a delight that comes in roundly naming its object.

In an interview [with Robert D. Hamner] he suggests that he is seeking that metaphor called Caribbean or West Indian, for "one had a metaphor called Ireland and a metaphor called America. . . . They were on solid ground with no broken islands," but in the West Indies, the

> . . . only historical legends that one individual writer would have are ethnic legends of sorts. Each of them is separate because the Indian would have India, the African would have Africa. But the point of this is that all of these have been erased from the memory or experience of the writer. So, what has not yet been created or is actually being created by its absence, by the chaos, by the necessity for it to be created—is a West Indies, a West Indian literature. Now that is being made out of the very knowledge that there is not one.

Just as we have seen Walcott's protagonists experience the necessary progression through exile and alienation to indifference and, then, to a sense of belonging, so the naming of the "nothing" of history is a necessary preamble to celebrating what is there: this entails going beyond the fact of history to emotion, and writing a comprehensive fiction of his people. At this early stage of naming their existence, he suggests that they

> may not even need literature, not that [they] are beyond it, but in the archipelago particularly, nature, the elements if you want, are so new, so overpowering in their presence that awe is deeper than articulation of awe. To name is to contradict. The awe of God or of the universe is the unnameable, and this has nothing to do with literacy. It is better for us to be a race of illiterates who retain this awe than to be godless, without mystery. (**"Culture or Mimicry?"**)

To consider the possibility that his people "may not even need literature" is to look for the communal and essential which may be intuited rather than learned or logically acquired. Nowhere in Walcott's work is there a denial of reason, but we sense him always reaching toward the mystery at the center of being which ultimately is beyond reason. In **Dream on Monkey Mountain** he says, "we begin again,

with the vigour of a curiosity that gave the old names life, that charged an old language, from the depth of suffering, with awe." The negation of history has been a rape of body and mind:

> When they conquer you, you have to read their books.
> Then violently, false folklorique follows;
> Maidenheads or otherwise, arrowheads,
> Their two archaeological pursuits.
>
> **("Roots")**

And before "our Homer with truer perception erect it," every memory must be stripped bare, and the poet "make without pomp, with stone acanthus, / In our time, in the time of this phrase, a 'flowering of islands.' " To so remake the islands, which is the function of his fictions, "All else will go down," all old "ambitions," "divisions," other mythologies—Helen is shorn of her eternal beauty to become "old Helen, lying alone in bed"—and all ruins save one, "Our Sirmio" at Vigie, which is transformed by the elements from a thing of sorrow to an object of beauty.

The need to name the losses before he can remake his world is a continual energizing force behind the poetry. In doing so Walcott crosses personal and national boundaries, for his own integrity and faith are under focus in addition to the identity of his people and their relationship to other countries. As we read **In A Green Night** we sense Walcott working deeper into his own being and into his heritage, groping for what he seems to glimpse at times, a kind of elemental memory or consciousness. As he studies his "historylessness"—that "stigmata of the void," as [Wilson] Harris calls it—he brings back reminders of the "fruitful" interaction "between man and man, man and nature—a salvage which seeks never to block its own agencies of vision by idolatrous fixations." He translates the reality of absences into the reality of presences, salvaging a history of emotion from the amnesia.

Walcott's probing of reality gravitates to opposite poles: to man's finiteness and his potential for infinity. The finite being is defined by such things as color, language, religion, vocation; but a concept of infinity is grasped by locating what is elemental in being. The epitome of this groping toward infinity in Walcott's poetry is the sense we have of a mind trying to grasp, through image and metaphor, what is both external and instinctive to its consciousness. It is through the release of faith, of myth, of literature, through searching for the basic rhythm of life, that one makes contact with the unknown. And while we become progressively aware that Walcott's quest is an ongoing thing, his approach to the search is fundamentally mythopoeic. Like Curnow he bathes man, landscape, and event in his imagination, giving all that constitutes his people a continuing life in time. Out of the anguish of naming the losses, out of the powerful credibility of the natural world, out of the ambivalences and contradictions of the past and present, an inchoate myth of the Caribbean begins to form. Any such myth must be inclusive, and, like the painter in **"To A Painter in England,"** Walcott wishes to define "the several postures of this virginal island." He wants to "put down . . . in words"

> all of its sunken, leaf-choked ravines,

every neglected, self-pitying inlet
muttering in brackish dialect . . .

As the epigraph to Section Two of **Another Life** suggests, the poet had assumed "Adam's task of giving things their names," and this entails naming the ruins of history, the broken men, and the natural world.

And yet this naming will be tinged with silence and humility, for the poet is concerned that "to name is to contradict"; so that, while naming may give a meaning to the presences and breathe life into the losses, it must also submit to the "awe of God or of the universe [which] is unnameable." The need to name will continue, and the names will change as the sense of the world changes and as the namers succeed to more wisdom, beginning again in the world.

In **"The Royal Palms"** he says, "Here there are no heroic palaces," and if "art is where the greatest ruins are, / Our art is in those ruins we became": which is the initial position of **"Ruins of a Great House,"** for the sense of history is conveyed through the *disjecta membra,* the decadence of the "moth-like girls," through the neglect, decay, and stench of death. But the ruins are more than a reminder of the subjugation of slaves and of a people; they become a reminder of the decline of Empire, and thus seem to take their place in a larger scheme of rise and fall. For, in compassion, the poet emerges from his "rage" into the awareness "That Albion too, was once, / A colony like ours." **"Ruins of a Great House"** brings out the ambiguities of Walcott's world and points to many of the tensions which lie behind the poetry of **In A Green Night.** It has an open-ended quality by virtue of its allusions and the multi-leveled meanings of much of the language, and it draws the reader into active contemplation with the poem, with its place in the canon, and with the various allusions. Written below an epigraph taken from Browne's *Urne Burial,* and with further allusions to it in the body of the poem, there is a complex emotional tone created out of the connotations of the **"Great House"** as an emblem of Britain's imperial power, its contrast with the present day, and the humility called for in the passage from *Urne Burial.* There is the additional irony that the age which produced Browne and Donne gave rise also to such exploitations as the slave trade to feed the energy of the age. In the very mention of "men like Hawkins, Walter Raleigh, Drake / Ancestral murderers and poets," Walcott catches the ambiguity of history, for, depending upon the perspective, the allusions open the way to a simultaneous naming of losses and gains, of heroism and cruelty. The essence of such contradictions is summed up in the implied contrast between Marvell's use of "green" and Walcott's, in the line: "The world's green age then was a rotting lime." The poem is suffused with the ambience of the seventeenth century; but the glory is tainted with horror, the richness with decay. And the allusions to Blake's "Night" and to "Faulkner's south" invoke worlds of exploitation and loss of innocence. Furthermore, behind the second verse paragraph, which draws on the thought of the epigraph, stands an allusion to the Book of Job and to Satan's words to God: "And touch his flesh, / And he will renounce thee to thy voice," which points to the despair of the downtrodden and the conviction to endure. And Walcott picks up

the ambivalence of some of Kipling's observations of Empire, for, despite his songs of Empire, Kipling also understood something of its excesses.

We attend to puns on "spade" and "rakes"—the antagonists—to the ambiguity of the fall from "evil times," and to the faith which can conceive of death as the precursor to life. The allusions and the puns expose levels of reality that must be located and discerned, and Walcott develops a richly ambiguous world which, while it focuses on the central symbol, radiates out through the allusions to a comprehensive picture of an age and its effect on the present. Whether we pick up a direct allusion, or sense the ambience, we must bring these externals to the poem. The effect is not to diffuse the energy of the poem but to deepen its implications. The poem as a consequence is never static, it has no one meaning—we attend to the open-endedness of the final allusion to John Donne—and even as the poem reaches toward certain essential truths, by its very movement and vitality and its interaction with much else that he has written, these "truths" are continually to be re-opened and studied. Further, out of the ashes rises a rich and complex fiction that captures the compassion lying at the root of Walcott's poetry, while exposing the complexities of his world.

Walcott names numerous other losses and ruins: the lonely, lost and exiled, who stand in contrast to his essential men; the failure of the West Indian Federation and the American Dream; and the need to find a faith which can give reason and order to living.

In **"Roots," "Pays Natal,"** and **"The Harbour,"** the fishermen have an innate reciprocity with their home and the poet can wish that he "might have gathered those senses in [his] arms, / As weary fishermen their honest seines." In **"The Harbour"** they stand contrasted to the "secure from thinking [who] . . . climb safe to liners," escaping the adventures and risks of being. For the fishermen the harbor is a point of departure, not a haven, and they move through a world of mystery, terror, and beauty. But there is no attempt to make of these fundamental men, gods; they need "the Virgin" and "cast their hopes with care" **("Choc Bay").** They are

The Blackhanded
Hate-bridled
Fishermen with their haul of sprats,

but they endure and, like Hemingway's "old man," the sea is their element, they respect it, and they know it. They stand for a world, primal, vital, and enduring, transforming the outward signs of isolation, exile, negation, and the veneer "Found only / In tourist booklets" **("Prelude")** into a world of meaning which the poet celebrates for its reality; its ambiguities; its ugliness and beauty; and its absences and presences.

Walcott's West Indies is defined in terms of a struggle between the dualities of heaven and hell: "The uncouth features of this my prone island" **("Prelude")** are transformed into a "heaven" in the next poem **("As John to Patmos"),** and in the beautiful lyric **"Choc Bay,"** the poet flees "from [the] paradise" he has painted in the opening stanzas into a portrayal of the "dead and the derelict" of the sonnet sequence, **"Tales of the Islands."** Personally and collectively the West Indian seems confounded by dualities and there is no certainty that they can be synthesized:

> . . . to find the true self is still arduous
> And for us, especially, the elation can be useless
>   and empty
> As this pale blue, ewer of the sky,
> Loveliest in drought.
>   **("Allegre")**

And in **"Sea Grapes,"** the title poem of a volume to which the sense of balance is central, Walcott isolates the dualities into what he contends is an immemorial struggle "between obsession and responsibility / [which] will never finish." And yet this position is a considerable advance over that of **"Allegre,"** for it accepts man's capacity to endure while realizing that there may be no one "true self" to be defined.

The classical world enters the poetry in **"Choc Bay"**: "Mary, the sea-lost, Venus, the sea-born." Both are the heritage of islanders:

> . . . the waves
> Bearing Time's bitter legends gave [them]
> To those whose lives are circled by the sea.

The "Hate-bridled Fishermen," with a prayer, give their allegiance to Mary, for "Venus lives with aristocrats," but the speaker can give allegiance to neither. He feels caught between the white goddesses and what they stand for: Christian and pagan, spirit and beauty, moral and aesthetic values, containment and release, a love which leads toward charity and selflessness and that which projects an aristocratic power and self-confidence. His "mind rides anchor" in "the rare / Width of blue air"; he feels with the hawk, prays "for the wheeling spokes / Of gulls," kneels "to the shell's mass," and pays respect to "the crab in hiding in salt grass." He flies "above time's reach," basking in the heady realm of the imagination, but "dead Venus" and the Virgin "showed / It was all a wise / Hoax" to his Daedalian dream. For all he wants "are words" to name the nothingness, and, as he says in **"Lampfall,"** invoking Penelope—the faithful wife of Ulysses, waiting and weaving—he will sing of his island. But he will catch not only the "windy leaves" and the wave's wash, for he would troll deep to the essences of his island existence to capture a sense of its enduring presence.

In a number of poems the poet gives himself to his environment, naming its presences: the amethyst sea, "the pale, blue ewer of the sky," the "wing'd sound of trees," the beaches, fish flashing, and birds diving. But in naming his environment, Walcott aims at an inclusive picture also, and a poem such as **"Return to D'Ennery, Rain"** should be read in the context of the exquisite celebration of the incantatory **"A Sea Chantey."**

> Anguilla, Adina,
> Antigua, Cannelles,
> Andreuille, all the l's,
> Voyelles, of the liquid Antilles,
> The names tremble like needles
> Of anchored frigates . . .

The poem is suffused with a profound sense of beauty and love and it evokes the emotional quotient which Walcott suggests was missing from the plans for federation in **"Map of the Antilles."** By way of contrast, through the extended metaphor of a cripple, **"Return to D'Ennery, Rain"** projects a vision of the Caribbean as a physical and spiritual dependent.

> Imprisoned in these wires of rain, I watch
> This village stricken with a single street,
> Each weathered shack leans on a wooden
>   crutch,
> Contented as a cripple in defeat.

Both visions must be held; it is crucial that the West Indian make a virtue of his losses, for love is born of pain:

> . . . greater than death is death's gift, that can,
> Behind the bright dust that was the skeleton,
> (Who drank the wine and believed the blessed
>   bread)
> Can make us see the forgotten price of man
> Shine from the perverse beauty of the dead.
>   **("Elegy")**

But such a compassion cannot be won through until we "leave the mind's dark cave," stop "praising death in life" **("Pocomania")**, and reach that mystery which is at the center of being, and to which, echoing Baudelaire, he alludes in **"A Sea Chantey"**: "Repos donnez a cils . . ." It is a peace beyond understanding, an immaculate balance: "The omen of calm waters" **("A Sea Chantey")**.

By the last poem of ***In A Green Night,*** having expressed his admiration of "those mottled marbles" of Europe, the "Aphrodite," "Venus," "Dianas," and "Ledas," he can celebrate his race:

> Not one of those in such fierce sex was fired
> Or holds its cunning secret as this one
> Of lasting bronze, art of a savage race,
> Marble, bronze, ebonwood, white, creole, black.
>   **("Bronze")**

The bronze mask stands as a synthesis, both qualitative and quantitative, for the West Indian people. Similarly La Guaira, gateway to El Dorado (with its dual connotations of physical and mental quest) and entrance to the West Indies, is "nothing": "it means nothing" **("Nearing La Guaira")**, grinned the sailor. But as the next stanza establishes, this nothing is everything: it is the "green water," the "sun . . . like a starfish," "the moon," "a cornet in the plaza," "the Morro, / Where the garbage drifts," the roaring fans at a bullfight, and the empty cathedral; it is the "soldiers drilling in the square, / And the green fountain with its sacrament." In this nadir of despair, as the vein of sexual imagery suggests, it stands also for the personal gulf felt between lovers. In the ambiguity of the last line, it is essential that two readings be held: "Nothing *is* bitter and *is* very deep" (my italics), but also, in the colloquial sense of "it doesn't matter," nothing is so deep or so bitter that it cannot be weathered. We are not, however, left with the same feeling of utter resignation and isolation that A. D. Hope offers at the end of **"The Wandering Islands"**:

> Around him he hears the monotonous voices
> Of wave and wind:

"The rescue will not take place."

Introduced in the opening poem of *In A Green Night,* the journey motif is central to the poetry. In the allusion to Dante in **"Prelude"** the dimensions of the journey are suggested: it is at once a spiritual and physical quest in which he experiences, names, and places the hell, purgatory, and paradise of his own existence and of that of his people. The Odysseus archetype is directed toward uncovering the mystery which lies at the center of Caribbean existence. In **"Map of the Antilles,"** Walcott's odyssey is explicitly compared to that of Odysseus, in which the objective is "that sense of cultural unity and purpose which could replace petty insularity." And in **"A Sea Chantey,"** although the passage through the islands may evoke Odysseus, the Caribbean archipelago has its own "Refracted embroidery," its "own histories / [and] . . . peace of green harbourage." In their association with new beginnings the Odysseus, Adam, and Crusoe-Friday figures are drawn together, throwing a complex of perspectives on the Caribbean situation.

Adam as lover and *poet,* Odysseus as sea-farer and fisherman-hero, Crusoe as castaway and namer, and Friday as adaptor, exemplify the primary nature of Walcott's mythic figures who face the isolations of love and culture but who, like the old sailor, can grin at "nothing." And in doing so this consciousness appears to fuse with the poet's as this nothing is transformed into a beautiful and vibrant world (**"Nearing La Guaira"**). But the world through which his Adam-Odysseus-Crusoe figure moves is stricken with "the old original curse" (**"A Careful Passion"**), and they are continually reminded that it is their destiny to wander isolated and alone.

Walcott's local figures are important, but what they stand for must not be seen as exclusive. To the poet, the simple "washing faiths" (**"Elegy"**) of his father could not be held, nor could he share the divine Mary with the fishermen. But while he does not deny faith, it is a part of his concept of life and art; his access to the infinite must be through his art and, in *Another Life,* his faith is at once more intellectual and elemental than any he gives us in the earlier poetry. In the long poem there is a profound sense of relationship between the poet and his universe; it is explored through his psychic and physical interactions with his place. His growth is seen both in terms of his search for love and beauty, and his understanding of the light that illuminates Gregorias "within that moment where he died," or that expansiveness of mind which can image Harry Simmons in terms of what is elemental in life. His delight is to "have shared":

> I was struck like rock, and I opened to His gift!
> I laughed at my death-grasp in the rattle of the
>   sea-shoal.
> You want to see my medals? Ask the stars.
> You want to hear my history? Ask the sea.
> And you, master and friend,
>   forgive me!
>
> (*Another Life*)

Hence, while isolation may lead to the abject futility of Hope's castaway masturbating on the beach, it may lead also to the rich

> Pleasures of an old man:
> Morning: contemplative evacuation, considering
> The dried leaf, nature's plan.
>
> (**"The Castaway"**)

In his solitude he reaches to the mystery of "nature's plan," confronts his own humanity—"We end in earth, from earth began. / In our own entrails genesis"—and comprehends, in humility and joy, his place in the order of things.

> If I listen I can hear the polyp build,
> The silence thwanged by two waves of the sea.
> Cracking a sea-louse, I make thunder split.
> Godlike, annihilating godhead, art
> And self, I abandon
> Dead metaphors

to celebrate, as Curnow has it, "birth smell, death smell."

In moving from the Old to the New World, Walcott's Crusoe undergoes a sea-change; he becomes West Indian man, and a type for all castaways. And into this figure are to be read the poets, artists, lovers, fishermen, and all those isolated souls who populate Walcott's world but who share one common characteristic: their isolation offers the possibility, if never the certainty, of access into vision. As we suggested in speaking of Hope's sense of isolation, built into it is the possibility of union for those who can extend themselves in love and joy. Such a union may be with the external world, the self, or other individuals. But, conversely, as Klein suggests by means of his "poet," the insight which develops out of being isolated may further isolate the artist from society. At the conclusion of **"Crusoe's Island,"** the poet cannot share in "the bell's / Transfiguring tongue" like "Friday's progeny"; rooted to man and his environment, he says, "I have lost sight of hell, / of heaven," and, as "second Adam" having built "His Eden" upon his island, he must make his poetry of his time and place. Like Curnow he wants his fictions to extend his vision of reality, hoping that any access to the truths of myth will reclaim vestiges of memory that will restore life to his islands and make sense of his time. His prayer is that this world, which is nothing and everything, will make

> . . . the mind
> Catch fire till it cleaves
> Its mould of clay at last.

The thought here looks back to **"The Harbour,"** where the fishermen resist the easy rescue from thought, and forward, through sense and verbal echo, to **"At Last,"** where Walcott's world "flashes with living / silver." The source of the imagery derives, however, from the Bible.

As is the case with the other poets in this study Walcott's New World is rich in ambiguity: its "green" may be "a rotting lime" or it may be "a green breath / Rebuilding . . . love" (**"A City's Death by Fire"**), just as for the West Indian the promise which the Old World saw in the new is negated by the horrors of the Middle Passage. And yet, out of being cast away, the New World Crusoe-Adam

> . . . appraises
> objects surely, even the bare necessities
>   of style are turned to use,

like those plain iron tools he salvages
    from shipwreck, hewing a prose
as odorous as raw wood to the adze,
    out of such timbers
came our first book, our profane Genesis
    whose Adam speaks that prose
which, blessing some sea-rock, startles itself
    with poetry's surprise,
in a green world, one without metaphors.
                           ("Crusoe's Journal")

The "good Fridays," picking up Crusoe's tools, at first "parrot" his "style and voice," but then they "make his language [theirs]," and out of isolation, having gone through that "longing" for companionship, they can cry

        at last, "O happy desert!"
and learn[-] again the self-creating peace
    of islands.

The affirmation of these lines stands in explicit juxtaposition to the poem's epigraph and suggests a further stage in fitting the self to the landscape. The compassion of this sentiment is in contrast to that blinkered vision of the island mentality which can conceive of no world outside.

The islanders transform Crusoe's language and his traditions to their own ends. It is a new and confident Friday, facing the sea and making a virtue of necessity, who now says:

        . . . so from this house
that faces nothing but the sea, his journals
    assume a household use,
We learn to shape from them, where nothing
    was,
    the language of a race . . .
                           ("Crusoe's Journal")

With this new language they will name and place their world; and the gift of language, like the rare whale or the now invisible God of **"The Whale, His Bulwark,"** may offer access to the great design, to the mysterious and unfathomable. Of a rumor that a whale once foundered "up the Grenadines," the poet says

    . . . when I was small
God and a foundered whale were possible.
Whales are rarer, God is invisible.
Yet through His gift, I praise the unfathomable,
Though the boy may be dead, the praise unfashionable,
The tale apocryphal.

These fictions are to be contrasted with the "lies" of the politicians in **"The Lost Federation,"** and their unimaginative mimicry of "Whitehall" in **"Parades, Parades."** For, whereas the former attempt to make sense of reality and lead toward an expansion of consciousness, the latter, he suggests, falsify the reality, and extinguish vision. In *Dream on Monkey Mountain,* Walcott contends that what would deliver the New World Negro

    from servitude was the forging of a language that
    went beyond mimicry, a dialect which had the
    force of revelation as it invented names for
    things, one which finally settled on its own mode
    of inflection, and which began to create an oral
    culture of chants, jokes, folk songs and fables;

this, not merely the debt of history was his proper claim to the New World.

And in **"Names,"** Walcott celebrates the adaptation; for gradually "the names held" and began to acquire their "natural inflections."

    These palms are greater than Versailles,
    for no man made them,
    their fallen columns greater than Castille,
    no man unmade them
    except the worm, who has no helmet,
    but was always the emperor,
    and children, look at those stars
    over Valencia's forest!

It is in *The Castaway* and *The Gulf* that Walcott most consciously picks up the New World myth and turns it over in his mind. As we have suggested he looks at it *per medium* of the American Dream, and, like Allen Curnow, he executes a defoliation of the myth. What he is seeking is a more comprehensive reading of the myth than that contained in the "Dream" and, by drawing on past and contemporary history of the United States, he outlines some of the ambiguities and contradictions which should be included in any analysis of the New World. The ideals of freedom, innocence, and equality are linked with the alienation betrayal, and guilt of his "American" poems: the cry at the opening of **"Elegy"** is: "we miss you, Liberty." No less than the Caribbean, Walcott suggests in **"Elegy"** the American Dream has been fraught with ambiguity and contradiction from the outset, and the consequences of these ambiguities carry forward into the present.

    . . . Che's
    bullet-riddled body falls,
    and those who cried the Republic must first die
    to be reborn are dead,
    the freeborn citizen's ballot in the head. . . .
    Some splintered arrowhead lodged in her brain
    sets the black singer howling in his bear
       trap . . .
    and the cherry orchard's surf
    blinds Washington and whispers
    to the assassin in his furnished room
    of an ideal America, whose flickering screens
    show, in slow herds, the ghost of the Cheyennes
    scuffling across the staked and wired plains
    with whispering, rag-bound feet,
    while the farm couple framed in their Gothic
      door
    like Calvin's saints, waspish, pragmatic, poor,
    gripping the devil's pitchfork
    stare rigidly toward the immortal wheat.

As the allusions to Eliot, Chekhov, and Traherne in the long third verse paragraph suggest, out of death or corruption may come rebirth or a new innocence, and this elegy to the United States is thematically linked to **"Veranda"** and **"Ruins of a Great House"** by this recognition. Walcott will not deny the past but, as he says in **"Culture or Mimicry?"** as a poet he is "afflicted with the superior stupidity which believes that societies can be renewed," and out of the corruption of the New World ideal may flower new promise. Any vision of a renewed world, for Walcott, must come out of the ruins of the old. This is a densely packed poem, words carrying multiple meanings and pointing to the paradox and irony which underlies it, as, in the ambience of the poem, it gains in resonance by virtue of its richness of language, its allusions, and its thematic relationship to the entire *oeuvre.* "Elegy" is, then, one further view of a broad cultural and spiritual decay of which Walcott, because of the accidents of history, is inextricably a part, and yet which acts as a catalyst to his quest for the meaning of the New World experience. In his moral indignation, like Eliot and Chekhov in theirs, he senses the loneliness of his search for value.

Balancing this malaise are Walcott's folk of integrity, his "lovely inheritors" of a "fallen" world **("Veranda")**, who endure and

> . . . stretch a darkening hand to greet those
>   friends
> who share . . . the last inheritance
> of earth . . .

Around them Walcott weaves his fictions, and the insights which flow through them are rooted in the realities of the physical world. Walcott's vision is built on differences, evil, and negation, but as his celebrations of integrity, of the complexity of being, and of the richness of his environment suggest, out of the contradictions of existence vision is born.

Walcott draws on Greek and Christian myths and the Western literary tradition, while the rhythms of his language—its music and its beat—reach back into his folk heritage that derives ultimately from Africa. As he says of his "schizophrenia": "I have one tradition inside me going in one way, and another going another. The mimetic, the narrative, and dance element is strong on one side, and the literary, the classic tradition is strong on the other" **("Meanings")**. In another essay, speaking of his duality and a general West Indian psyche, he says "our bodies think in one language and move in another" *(Dream on Monkey Mountain)*, while, earlier in the same essay, he explains that in his "simple schizophrenic boyhood one could lead two lives. The interior life of poetry, the outward life of action and dialect." Both heritages put him into contact with what Harris calls "dark energies," beyond consciousness; it is "a fusion of formalism with exuberance, a delight in both the precision and power of language, . . . [and] a panache about life that is particularly ours." Out of this synthesis evolve fictions which often aspire toward the surface clarity of prose while retaining the compactness and fused energy of poetry that seems more readily to lead toward the incandescence of myth.

In this poetry we rarely lose sight of the physical being, since it is through his experience of the external world that we see the mind in action: now studying the minute, now dilating to infinity, seeking always to hold, as the metaphysical did, a simultaneity of vision in one image, in one idea. That he can do this, is due perhaps to his breadth of soul, to "the comprehending heart" **("In A Green Night")**, which knows the need to "make us see the forgotten price of man" **("Elegy")**. Walcott's poetry, then, as Owen Barfield says of all poetry, "exists . . . not by affirming but by actually experiencing, however slightly, the ultimate

homogeneity of world and mind." We sense that the poet, like the actor, must go through "the anguish of self-creation." To do so, the imagination must glimpse once again what is most essential to being, naming its universe by inclusion and not by exclusion; by embracing the dualities and attempting to ensphere all. And it is through imagery and metaphor that this interaction is recorded.

Metaphor provides Walcott with a means of incorporating both inner and outer reality in vision; as we have noted it functions as a means of embodying relationship. Near the end of *Another Life,* he writes:

> I lolled in the shallows like an ageing hammer-
>   head
> afraid of my own shadow, hungering there.
> When my foot struck sand, the sky rang,
> as I inhaled, a million leaves drew inward.
> I bent towards what I remembered,
> all was inevitable shrunken,
> it was I who first extended my hand
> to nameless arthritic twigs,
> and a bush would turn in the wind
> with a toothless giggle, and
> certain roots refused English.
> But I was the one in awe.

As they do for Curnow, imagery and metaphor contribute to the immediacy of Walcott's poetry, and, as Baugh says, to its "concentratedness," giving cohesion to individual works and a unity to the canon. Metaphor leads always toward myth and in this poetry we sense it organically coalescing and fusing, and shaping our vision. The repetitive pattern of image and metaphor in *Another Life* works toward the unity of mind and matter; it suggests that life is rooted in primordial nature, having memory-links with the mythic and the essential. This primal world becomes Walcott's *locus,* that [which Northrop Frye has called the] "buried original form of society, now concealed under the historical layers of civilisation," out of which he draws, through his creative imagination, what is eternal and essential to mankind. It is this "vision of consciousness," expanding through time and space, which in the end informs *Another Life,* and that underlies the explorations of the previous volumes.

The resonances of this search into a collective unconscious stand as a bulwark to the ever-present fear of fragmentation and alienation that is a central concern of the poetry. The search hinges on two factors elemental to man: faith and art. Both of these are dependent upon the creative imagination and both are rooted in the world of actualities while offering access to a world of the pure essences of love, truth and beauty. To deny, however, the place of hatred, evil, and ugliness, is to exclude a vital aspect of any such inward search, and the tension between these essences is the stuff of Walcott's poetry. It is, further, a journey of exploration which is ever a beginning; as another West Indian poet [Samuel Selven] says of their search for identity: "To conclude with / There is no conclusion." This is an eternal quest by the mind, for we feel that in the paradoxes and ambiguities which are central to Walcott's whole mode of procedure, to arrive at a solution is to face dissolution.

Although we are drawn to details of time and place from

the opening lines of **Another Life,** there is an almost simultaneous contraction and dilation of the temporal and the spatial spheres of the poem. The achieved effect of this is to make of one time, all time, and of one place an archetype for all places. It is as if the seeming temporal and spatial life of the poem is unlimited; that the life being dealt with is a mask for all life; that any place is one with infinite space; and that Walcott's recognized concern for history is being transformed into an ongoing and inclusive fiction, and that through the repeated naming of his place and people his fictions are reaching toward the mythic, making them, as Browning has it, "eternity's concern." The medium for this expansion in time and space is language, and the source of this language is, of course, the creative imagination.

Another Life opens at a specific moment in the life of the poet, that moment of the poem's inception—"I begin here." It is twilight. And the twilight becomes a metaphor not only for the end of the day, but for the decline of the British Empire. This moment in personal and social history is further seen in terms of the timeless dimension of the eternal setting of suns and the motion of the ocean: it becomes a timeless moment. Attention is drawn to the eternal context by the rhetorical pattern: "I begin . . . begin . . . Begin" (in lines 4, 5, and 8), and by the placement and rhyming of "again." He will begin until "the moon's filaments wane." The figure in the landscape, gazing out at the sea from his prospect, becomes subsumed into the cosmic dimensions of the scene, as sky joins sea, and the moon and sea become the measures of time. Spatially we follow the poet's eye from the vantage point to the sea, to the horizon, to the vast sky filling with an amber light. The sea has both a material presence, and is "a book left open by an absent master." By a fusion of connotations—sea/book/imagination/poet—the poet becomes as one with the sea just as he becomes absorbed into the light: he is simultaneously both a speck in, and center of, the universe. Despite the vast space by which he is enveloped there is no loss of his own sense of being which he endeavors to integrate with the external world into, what Harris calls [in *Tradition the Writer and Society*], "a vision of Consciousness." The heaven seemed the "glaze of another life," and the twilight, almost physically, "drew a girl's figure to the open door . . . with a single stroke."

We move repeatedly from the figure, or from the village, out into boundless time and space and back again; now embracing a part, now spanning a whole. In the silhouette of twilight, the poet sketches the girl's figure at the open door and as he lifts his head he glimpses details of the Hotel, Government House, the shacks on the mountain side, and, gazing until the "vision died," the "black hills simplified / to humps of coal." This spatial extension then brings the focus back to the girl whose hair becomes a vehicle for a reference to time. It is as though she too has become subsumed into the whole meaning of twilight. In the next verse-paragraph there is a similar opening out of scene—hill/sea/moon—but by the use of "burned," "foil," and "ballooned," the vastness of the scene is contained, until the moon whitewashes all below her and the entire landscape is shrunken to a miniature. At the same time, however, through a careful attention to detail, the

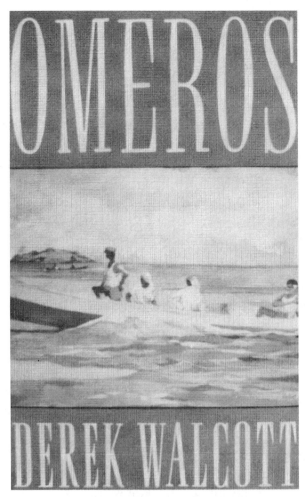

Cover of Omeros *(1991).*

integrity of each object is retained (even to the "ear-ringed portrait: Albertina"), giving a sense of order and relation between place and the vast cosmos.

Walcott's natural impulse is similar to that which Coleridge pleaded for the transcendental philosopher:

> Grant me a nature having two contrary forces, the one which tends to expand infinitely, while the other strives to apprehend or find itself in this infinity, and I will cause the world of intelligences with the whole system of their representatives to rise up before you.

Out of sheer necessity to hold the many dualities of his own personal and communal, aesthetic, religious, and historic genesis in balance, Walcott struggles to retain the essence of the components which constitute these dualities. At the same time, in the Coleridgean sense, he seeks to "dissolve, diffuse, dissipate" the boundaries in order to recreate, or to "idealize and to unify." The necessity to discover imaginatively himself and his people becomes the virtue which can liberate them all "to walk calm, renewed, [if] exhausted." Out of this comes Walcott's balance, his poise and compassion. The renewal which the poet envisages is, like that expressed by Wallace Stevens, "a renewal of earth," not a "surrender to heaven."

Edward Baugh suggests that **Another Life** is similar "in kind" to Wordsworth's *The Prelude* and Joyce's *Portrait:* it traces the growth of an artist's mind and it conveys a picture of man " 'pledged to life,' " encountering reality and bent on forging in his soul " 'the uncreated conscience of [a] race.' " It deals with various "spots of time" in the growth of the poet's mind from early childhood to the virtual "now" of the poem's completion in April 1972. And while there is a high degree of verifiable fact and detail in the poem (more so than *The Prelude,* as Baugh points out), through reverberations and repetitions of image, metaphor, event, and character it overlaps fixed time and place to touch what is elemental. Comparing **Another Life** with his earlier poems, **"Epitaph for the Young"**—a "sort of Urtext"—Walcott says he has "re-essentialised it, given it more of an essence in fact, made it more focal": a statement which points to the realistic and the mythic quality of the later work. Both concerns are united in Walcott's integrity for "the rightness of placed things," which links a concern with the placing and naming of things to the senses and to language, and thus to the larger reality which they hold in potential. His attention to detail blended with rich metaphorical invention enables him to strike to deep layers of reality while retaining both the kind of immediacy Curnow sought and the intensity of the poetry.

Through the imagination Walcott senses his unity with people and places. Of the ancient Carib Indians leaping to folly/heroism, he says [in **Another Life**]:

> I leapt for the pride of that race
> at Sauteurs! An urge more than mine,
> so, see them as heroes or as the Gadarene swine.

He projects the kind of holistic and religious mind which can find "a hermitage" in what is essential to life. The quality, he tells us, which pervades his mother, is silence: she sits "folded in silence," and in this silence "the revered, silent objects ring like glass." She exudes a serenity, a rightness, a solitude; her presence has the same quality of endurance which he attributes to his Caribbean heroes. The silence of solitude is the ultimate union between the self and some other; it is an absence which holds all presences. Something of this same sense of order suffuses Anna, Harry, Gregorias, and Margaret ("For I have married one whose / darkness is a tree,"), and it rubs off on the poet, who "emerges" out of a world of explosive rhetoric, corruption, and self-aggrandizement as "out of [a] . . . mist . . . and staggers towards his lineaments." And in his inclusive vision of his world—one which is growing with each volume we sense—he reiterates, what earlier was implicit, the need to name his losses and despair as well as his presences and affirmations: "Pour la derniere fois, nommez! Nommez!" He names the evil, "Manoir . . . that dog"; the great; and the holy:

> holy is Rampanalgas and its high-circling
>   hawks,
> holy are the rusted, tortured, rust-caked, blind
>   almond trees,

> your great-grandfather's, and your father's tor-
>   turing limbs,
> holy the small, the almond-leaf-shadowed
>   bridge
> by the small red shop, where everything smells
>   of salt,
> and holiest the break of the blue sea below the
>   trees,
> and the rock that takes blows on its back
> and is more rock,
> and the tireless hoarse anger of the waters
> by which I can walk calm, a renewed, exhausted
>   man,
> balanced at its edge by the weight of two dear
>   daughters.
> Holy were you, Margaret,
> and holy our calm.
>
>   *(Another Life)*

Out of the absences and presences, like a creative wind blowing off the sea—element of islanders, emblem of the creative mind and local reminder of the Middle Passage—grows a wisdom and a visionary hope of renewal which wants to "begin again": begin

> from what we have always known, nothing,
> from that carnal slime of the garden,
> from the incarnate subtlety of the snake,
> from the Egyptian moment of the heron's foot
> on the mud's entablature,
> by this augury of ibises
> flying at evening from the melting trees,
> while the silver-hammered charger of the marsh
>   light
> brings towards us, again and again, in beaten
>   scrolls,
> nothing, then nothing,
> and then nothing.

Out of the "amnesia" of history, out of

> . . . the untroubled ocean, the moon
> . . . swing[ing] its lantern
> and evening fold[ing] the pages of the sea

float "the lost names / of Caribs, slaves and fishermen." An essential life evolves, which reaches toward a mythic core, while trying, also, to make sense of the present.

As we read **Another Life** and turn to **Sea Grapes,** there is a deepening concern with change and with fictions that can make sense of it; but this is no new presence in the poetry. As we have suggested, central to the Adam/ Odysseus/Crusoe motif is the notion of new beginnings, of transforming Old World systems into the New, and behind Walcott's preoccupation with history is the recognition that it is in continual process. It is this sense of process which characterizes Walcott's understanding of the relationship of the Caribbean to the outside world: to England, Asia, Africa, the United States. Similarly, those poems which focus on, say, England, Africa, or the United States highlight aspects of their evolution; his history is one of change, of process. To give oneself to change and transition is, however, to risk fragmentation—and we sense Curnow's precarious grasp of a language which can describe his world—and Walcott's fictions, like Hope's, are directed toward a rightness, toward the "toil that is balance" (**"To Return to the Trees"**). This is toward a serenity in solitude which recognizes the permanence of change and can celebrate man's achievement in merely surviving; for Walcott speaks of this survival with a profound "awe"—to use his word. In **"At Last,"** he sings of those of his people who have no need of fictions; who, like

> . . . the pelican beat[-]
> to the rock of the Soledad
> to a beat which is neither
> poetry nor prose.

And employing an image cluster, used also by Hope, Curnow, and Ezekiel, drawn from the visionary books of the Old Testament, he looks forward to the flowering of his generations "from the bitterest root / and the earth that soured."

As visions blossomed out of the harsh ground of an Old Testament world, so vision may find its source in this "heartbreaking past." As Walcott says, "it is not a question for us, of returning to an Eden or of creating Utopia" **("Culture or Mimicry?")**; however, Edens are available to those who can "enter the silence" **("Volcano")**, for they retain that primal "awe" which gives them contact with the fundamental rhythms of existence; this

> . . . has been lost to our time;
> so many people have seen everything,
> so many people can predict,
> so many refuse to enter the silence
> of victory, the indolence
> that burns at the core,
> so many are no more than
> erect ash, like the cigar,
> so many take thunder for granted.
> How common is the lightning,
> how lost the leviathans
> we no longer look for!

These folk stand in contrast to the unthinking and the scheming, and Walcott makes no effort to simplify his New World. He returns to the Eden archetype, but, as he says in **"For the Altarpiece of the Roseau Valley Church, Saint Lucia,"** having worked toward a vision of Eden,

> . . . okay,
> okay, not absolute Adamic silence,
> the valley of Roseau is not the Garden of Eden,
> and those who inhabit it are not in heaven.

And his description of Dunstan St. Omar's altarpiece (which admits ambiguity into a vision of Eden) transmutes the contradictory joy and pain, beauty and ugliness, into a vibrant fiction of "the folk" of St. Lucia. The "massive altarpiece, / like a dull mirror" catches the "rich valley," the "cursed valley," the natural beauty and the broken animals and people. But it is also in Eden, he suggests in **"The Brother,"** where the "serpent . . . sleeps happiest," and Adam and "the snake"—colonizer and entrepreneur—

> . . . share
> the loss of Eden for a profit.
> So both made the New World. And it looked
>   good.
>   **("New World")**

The opening poems of **Sea Grapes**—"The Virgins,"

"Fredericksted Nights," "Fredericksted, Dusk," "Sunday Lemons," and the "Eden" poems—constitute a powerful lament for those of his people who are "lost to the American Dream" **("The Virgins")**. Instead of finding the essential truth at the bottom of the myth, the fictions they follow are false, and the poet, like Joshua, cries for his tribe following a formula of "Economics and Exodus" that will lead to a spiritual imprisonment bearing the burden of "no vision, no flame, / no deepness, no danger . . ."

But in spite of his harangue, or perhaps because of it, he believes that the American archipelago can be renewed **("Culture or Mimicry?")**. And throughout **Sea Grapes** there is a deep sense of awe and a humble affirmation of his people who have survived. So that in **"Natural History II,"** he writes, picking up the moon as image of change,

> . . . History
> is natural—famine, genocide,
> as natural as moonlight—
> and man is great who rises at this cost.

We witness an understanding and acceptance of placed things, of the larger design, of "balance," but this is not easily won, and when it is attained it is a matter of "Hold hard then heart. This way at least you live" **("The Fist")**. But the pain of loving self, some other, or country, leads to a sense of living. What emerges is a kind of primitive affinity between the mind of the poet and the essential rhythms of the universe: it amounts to an acceptance but not a submission to life's process, and "out of what is lost grows something stronger / that has the rational radiance of stone" **("Sea Canes")**.

It is as though, as he probes the mystery of being, he would move to the other side of language, to where "the silence is all." Such a silence "is deeper than the readiness"; the readiness may be articulated and suggests a choice, a logical awareness of preparedness, while the other is a felt awareness unconsciously learned, but ultimately beyond reason. It stems from a felt communion between the self and his world. With this knowledge, in which man becomes one with the world, where his sense of "home" is a mental and emotional awareness, man "can never be dispossessed."

Out of the stasis and negation which he sees around him grows a sense of movement and creative change, and he traces his odyssey through hatred, indifference, to affirmation, making of the fiction that he weaves around this journey and around his society a vision which occasionally rises to the clarity of the mythic. The temporal and particular are transformed into a seemingly eternal world:

> That child who puts the shell's bowl to his ear,
> hears nothing, hears everything
> that the historian cannot hear, the howls
> of all the races that crossed the water,
> the howls of grandfathers drowned
> in the intricately swivelled Babel,
> hears the fellaheen, the Madrasi, the Mandingo,
>   the Ashanti.
>   *(Another Life)*

If the sea is "a book left open," it is to be read, and the

story which evolves from Walcott's vast ocean is a comprehensive and continuing fiction of the place of his people in some larger order. Personal and national history, then, becomes an emotive fiction of process, and Walcott draws a line from Homer's Odysseus to Joyce's Ulysses and Hemingway's "old man," through Virgil, Dante, Marvell, Cowper, Chekhov, Conrad, and Eliot, who seek to make sense of the larger reality through a dedication to language.

"Sea Grapes" opens with the Odysseus-figure "beating up the Caribbean," thus linking this volume with all that has gone before, but the fictional use of Odysseus is made explicit. This "could be Odysseus," but equally it could be any other wanderer caught in the "ancient war / between obsession and responsibility," the solution to which is irresolvable—"will never finish and has been the same . . . since Troy sighed its last flame"—but it must continually be faced. And the poet says: "The classics can console. But not enough." As the allusions to both **"Prelude"** and **"The Banyan Tree, Old Year's Night"** (both from his first major volume) suggest, it is up to the individual to find a way in this eternal quest, making and discarding fictions, seeking what will suffice. Man must make his own fictions of consolation, or find new relevance in the old. This is not a repudiation of the "classics," for, as he insists in **"Volcano,"** man must be open to the "masterpieces," not expecting to find solutions in them but a continuing relevance and wonder: as Klein has it, they are to point directions; they do not pose destinations.

The theme of change unifies the three poems which make up the short sequence "Natural History." The walking fish adapts from one medium to another as, in an impressionistic synthesis of history, fish turn to vertebrate, mastodon's atrophy, and the pterodactyl shrinks to a bat, and, suggesting an erosion of imagination, "Dragons no longer fly." But as the fish endures through time, waiting his "geological epoch" and changing and adapting to his continually new world, it becomes associated with the poet who, likewise, can at last

> . . . name
> this foothold, with a grateful croak
> earth. I can arch my back.

He "can squat . . . Lurch up. . . . Up . . . walk," aware that

> everything has changed
>
> or has changed us.
> Or, as I
> paddle this air, breathe this new sun, am I
> still swimming through one gigantic eye?

As is the case with **"Force,"** even as the poet tries to understand what he intuits or reasons, the fiction leads ultimately toward the poet's awe at the mystery of evolution.

In **"Names,"** Walcott suggests that change is a component of his people; it is part of being a transplanted people who began "with a different fix on the stars." All they had to shape their lives, as the sky, sea, and history "foreclosed / with nothing in [their] hands," was

> . . . this stick

> to trace [their] names on the sand
> which the sea erased again, to [their] indifference.

And, as he suggests in the "Crusoe" poems, they named their worlds. Was it out of "nostalgia or irony?" he asks in **"Names."** However, in time, "the names held" and the developing consciousness transformed language to their own needs.

The more Walcott struggles to make sense of his world, the more he ponders it; and the better his tools, the more, it seems, he is conscious of "something always being missed / between the floating shadow and the pelican" **("The Village").** Reality seems continually to be shifting, but by exerting his imagination on his village, objects, and people, he strives to find more precise ways of expressing it and of drawing out its essential quality. He arrives at a position where belief is possible, but never certain:

> so that, from time to time, on Sundays
>
> between adorations, one might see,
> if one were there, and not there,
> looking in at the windows
>
> the real faces of angels.
> **("For the Altarpiece of the Roseau Valley**
> **Church, St. Lucia")**

Nevertheless, the poet's relationship to his world is always in process: "we shed freight," he says, "but not our need / for encumbrances," and feeling and poetry must be unlearned so that "true feeling" and truer poetry can endure. Such a survival may be beyond language,

> beyond joy,
> beyond lyrical utterance
> this obdurate almond
>
> going under the sand
> with this language, slowly,
> by sand grains, by centuries.

Walcott's fictions lead ultimately toward this kind of elemental understanding of reality; it is an annihilation—the journey back to the ape—in which "the voice must grovel in search of itself until gestures and sound fuse and the blaze of their flesh astonishes them" (*Dream on Monkey Mountain*). But the journey he enacts, the journey into silence, into solitude, is in the end into the reality of myth, and out of it grows the wisdom and compassion which is humanity's right.

When we look at the major volumes we sense that history, or its absence, has been transformed into a body of knowledge open to the emotional intuition of value, as well as to reason. We apprehend the present and the past as simultaneous realities and absorb the public and private worlds which have expanded to epic proportions without losing sight of the immediate realities of poverty, hardship, and pain. He has peopled the future with heroes; made of his "folk," "heraldic men"; and in remaking a place and a people, drawing on their ambiguities and contradictions, he has created the image of a civilization. His art grows toward myth, transcending the limits of its creator and reaching toward the limits of being.

Caribbean man is New World man, but with affinities to Adam, to Odysseus, to the vanished Caribs, to Africa, to Crusoe, to the whole imperial ethos of Britain from the seventeenth to twentieth centuries, and to the New World ethos of the Americas generally. Like Curnow, Walcott is conscious of being "not in *narrow* seas." The gulf between people has a tangible reality for islanders, for the sea defines human loneliness, and yet, while the sea may sunder, it also links, and in his loneliness man may come to terms with his humanity. For, like Hope, Walcott makes the journey into his own being and into the collective mind of his people, and the catalysts for such explorations are the accidents of history. And . . . Walcott's world finds parallels with the harsh environment of the Old Testament, the facing of which may lead to vision. His God is a harsh God who is largely absent, looking on with the indifference which Klein, in his despair, felt characterized his God. But, for both men, he was an "absent master," and like the ruins left behind by that other "absent master," the Imperium, mementos remain. Both leave some positive legacies, a sense of love, a language, and vestiges of ritual which may give order and coherence to life. And Walcott draws on them.

Walcott's world, like Hope's Australia and Curnow's New Zealand, is both a paradise and a hell, and the contradictions which have accrued to Australia, to a lesser extent New Zealand and Canada, accrue to the West Indies and have transacted a powerful shaping force upon the people. With a direct affinity to Klein's Adam, naming and praising his New World, and to Ezekiel's search for a sense of "season," Walcott traces the steps which lie behind the shifts in consciousness which are prior to the attainment of that "balance" which can name the complexity and praise the hardship without a longing for a pastoral simplicity or without giving oneself to hatred. Walcott's celebrations, both of the elemental sublimity of land, sky, and water, and of the stifling sense of decay and nothingness which may lead toward a capitulation to the spiritual atrophy of *nada,* assume to the proportions of myth, and his castaway is like original man cast out of Eden and facing a hostile world with imperfect tools.

But Walcott's Adam-Crusoe, who brought a language and a style to the Caribbean and to the good Fridays, like some Promethean fire, now serves as a paradigm for universal man facing his destiny. The fragmentation of the Caribbean islands, its sense of history-in-transition, its continual process of growth and decay through time, stands as a type for an ever fragmenting world, as the great monolithic societies of the past, from whom Australia, Canada, New Zealand, and the Caribbean were spawned, break up; and individual man faces the isolation and cosmic loneliness of Walcott's figures on the beach. But out of this loneliness, the poets of this study suggest, may come wisdom and faith, and a stay against a submission to a seemingly hostile and chaotic world. For, by making fictions which strive to make sense of reality out of their very act of naming the presences and absences of society, and out of their variations on particular themes, the poet rises toward the mythic and he gives to the mundane and the ordinary an illumination: and "where that moment is made radiant, epiphany happens."

In a world which is confronted with the permanence of change, in which social, cultural, and religious values have withered, Walcott asserts that history must be taught as either morality, in which case it "is religion," or as action, in which case it "is art" (**"Culture or Mimicry?"**). And to treat their respective histories, the poets in this study have sought a style and a language which can make sense of this reality; to each of them it is idiosyncratic, personal, and creative, like their reading of their people and place in time, but in each case, as Walcott says, it is "beyond mimicry."

> The stripped and naked man, however abused, however disabused of old beliefs, instinctively, even desperately begins again as craftsman. In the indication of the slightest necessary gesture of ordering the world around him, of losing his old name and rechristening himself, in the arduous enunciation of a dimmed alphabet, in the shaping of tools, pen or spade, is the whole, profound sigh of human optimism, of what we in the archipelago still believe in: work and hope. It is out of this that the New World, or the Third World, should begin. (**"Culture or Mimicry?"**)

(pp. 165-88)

James Wieland, "Adam's Task . . . : Myth and Fictions in the Poetry of Derek Walcott," in his The Ensphering Mind: History, Myth, and Fictions in the Poetry of Allen Curnow, Nissim Ezekiel, A. D. Hope, A. M. Klein, Christopher Okigbo, and Derek Walcott, *Three Continents Press, 1988, pp. 165-88.*

Derek Walcott on being a Caribbean artist:

I come from a place that likes grandeur; it likes large gestures; it is not inhibited by flourish; it is a rhetorical society; it is a society of physical performance; it is a society of style. The highest achievement of style is rhetoric, as it is in speech and performance. It isn't a modest society. A performer in the Caribbean has to perform with the right flourish. A Calypsonian performer is equivalent to a bullfighter in the ring. He has to come over. He can write the wittiest Calypso, but if he's going to deliver it, he has to deliver it well, and he has to hit the audience with whatever technique he has. Modesty is not possible in performance in the Caribbean, and that's wonderful. It's better to be large and to make huge gestures than to be modest and do tiptoeing types of presentations of oneself. Even if it's a private platform, it is a platform. The voice does go up in a poem. It is an address, even if it is to oneself. And the greatest address is in the rhetoric. I grew up in a place in which if you learned poetry, you shouted it out. Boys would scream it out and perform it and do it and flourish it. If you wanted to approximate that thunder or that power of speech, it couldn't be done by a little modest voice in which you muttered something to someone else. I came out of that society of the huge gesture. And literature is like that, I mean *theatrical* literature is like that, whether it's Greek or whatever. The recitation element in poetry is one I hope I never lose because it's an essential part of the voice being asked to perform.

Derek Walcott, in an interview with Edward Hirsch, in The Paris Review, *Winter, 1986.*

Stewart Brown (essay date 1991)

[Brown is an English critic, educator, and poet. In the following excerpt, he discusses the need to find a context in which to assess Walcott's work.]

How does one approach a body of work like the poetry of Derek Walcott? Is it enough to say that these are poems written in English in the second half of the twentieth century and assume that the trans-Atlantic critical orthodoxy which might allow a reading of, say, Ted Hughes or Gregory Corso, both his contemporaries, would be adequate to deal with Walcott's work? To an extent the answer is obviously yes, for just as we might amend our 'standard' methodology to accomodate Hughes' muscular mythologies or Corso's urban demotic we might adjust the tolerances to allow of Walcott's exotic landscape and his obsession with a 'marginal' history. What those distinctive voices share, in terms of the language and culture-of-the-poem, is more significant than their many differences. But such a position reads poetry as hamburger, as supra-cultural glop. As Geoffrey Hill remarked about Marvell—a not irrelevant comparison—"in order to empathise with a poet we need to understand him *in* his world . . . otherwise the meaning of the words on the page may elude us." The particular and peculiar circumstances of Walcott's work—and although his reputation in the U. K. and the U. S. is primarily as a poet, he is perhaps better known in the Caribbean for his plays . . .—demand careful contextualisation if its achievement is seriously to be assessed and understood.

But which contexts? Walcott's work *is,* now, part of that International Hyperculture; he takes jets between continents as easily as he once took the row-boat ferry across Castries harbour. So to understand the poems in *The Arkansas Testament* and *Omeros,* his most recent collections of poems, it is crucial to have some sense of where the poet has come from, and how; not just biographically but in terms of the Caribbean's social and cultural history. In particular, we must understand where he stands in terms of the fundamental shifts in attitudes towards personal and national/regional identity that the people of the Caribbean have experienced during Walcott's lifetime. Such a context informs our reading of the poems; it becomes apparent that the acerbic middle aged voice mocking, through the weary wit of the *Spoiler* persona, those West Indian politicians who:

> . . . promise free and just debate
> then blow up radicals to save the state,
> who allow, in democracy's defence,
> a parliament of spiked heads on a fence

has its genesis in the idealistic, optimistic, verse of a schoolboy patriot punning his critique of St. Lucia's bastard Colonial "aristocracy":

> The inheritors of manners and manors,
> the lords of cane and acre

in **'Letter to a Sailor'** from *25 Poems,* his first pamphlet collection, privately published in 1948.

The problem of establishing an adequate context for a discussion of his work is compounded by the fact that Walcott has always cultivated his ambiguities, his complexities—refusing to simplify himself or his art. He has appropriated Senghor's cunning self-assessment as "the mulatto of style" and developed his own theory of influence, of assimilation, which sanctions his (or any New World poet's) drawing succour from whatever cultural sources he feels are relevant to the task in hand. In his essay on Walcott's prose . . . Fred D'Aguiar draws attention to a lecture Walcott gave at the University of the West Indies in the early '60's—when he was working through the Crusoe metaphor—in which he writes of making a bonfire of the influences that have washed up on his castaway's shore. It is, he implies, part of the Caribbean condition that he should be at once so isolated, so distinctive, and yet so wholeheartedly open to influence. Walcott's own experience bears that out—on the one hand the St. Lucia he was born into in 1930 was just a speck on a map of the British empire, a colonial backwater, a place cut off from the main currents of world events. On the other hand history had conspired to make that island a kind of hinge between cultural worlds; French and English, North and South, Latin and Anglo-Saxon, Amerindian and Afro-American. St. Lucia was both virginal New World and the site of some of the worst atrocities of slavery days. In his own time Walcott was aware of both isolation—he was not black enough, not poor enough, a Methodist in a Catholic community, a precocious intellectual, an artist—and a communality, a shared colonial angst, a sense of being called to 'speak for' a generation, for a whole experience that was not heard in their (the metropolitan world's) books. In the several accounts, both in poetry and prose, of his boyhood, what stands out is Walcott's sense of himself as someone 'chosen', singled out by his 'gift' to address those apparent contradictions, to make something new, whole, distinctive from—to appropriate the term he applies to his inheritance of the English language—"the spoils of history". So, while not denying the importance of his personal experience and vision, the explanation of Walcott's work as the extraordinary achievement of an extraordinary man doesn't take adequate account of the complexities of his situation as a West Indian poet and the extent to which his 'individual voice' has been an expression of that cultural/regional experience. Even his poems of 'exile' in the more recent collections speak to a fundamental Caribbean concern: at one level indeed as the *defining* experience of Caribbean sensibility—just about all the people of the region are migrants in that sense—but perhaps growing out of that is a deep seated sense of rootlessness, of a willingness to dare to try to make 'another life' 'elsewhere'. Even if he's become a 'fortunate traveller' the literary celebrity jetting first-class across the globe can never escape that sense of a responsibility—albeit self-appointed and arguably self-serving—to, in some sense, represent the 'Mass Man'.

So despite his gradual accomodation, and 'domestication' as an American poet, those cultural complexities that *produced* Walcott continue to be both source and subject of his work. To read his work chronologically . . . is to follow, not so much the 'development', but the ways in which his attitudes towards those central issues of Caribbean identity modify and change over the almost half a century of his writing career. Those changes are not always a matter of the overt subjects of his work but reveal themselves in the cast of his language, and in the formal and stylistic variety of his art.

For all that Walcott's status as a poet and playwright of international stature is undoubted—certainly his work speaks to all sorts of people in all sorts of circumstances—[there is] an understanding of Walcott's commitment to the idea of his 'place' in the West Indian cultural landscape, and a belief that the context, finally, which enables us to approach "the meaning of the words on the page" is one which sees Walcott emerging from, engaging with and returning to

> The midsummer sea, the hot pitch road, this
>   grass, these shacks that made me,
> jungle and razor grass shimmering by the road-
>   side, the edge of art;
> wood lice are humming in the sacred wood,
> nothing can burn them out, they are in the
>   blood.

(pp. 7-10)

Stewart Brown, in an introduction to The Art of Derek Walcott, *edited by Stewart Brown, Seren Books, 1991, pp. 7-10.*

INTERVIEW

Derek Walcott with Richard E. Smith   (interview date 1991)

[In the following interview, Walcott discusses the impact critics have had on his work as well as the role and development of Caribbean critics.]

[*Smith*]: *What do you find most relevant in criticism in respect to your work? Have critics been able to contribute to an understanding of your work, and if yes, how or what kind of theoretical presuppositions did they have? Did they have any kind of approaches that seem to you most interesting, most relevant for an understanding of your work?*

[Walcott]: I think as a writer gets older, in a way, a writer tends to forget his debt to critics. As I try to remember what books clearly excited me that were books of criticism, the ones that come to mind are Edmund Wilson's *Axel's Castle* (1948), and (I can't put them in chronological sequence) all of Eliot's essays, particularly on the Elizabethans, and, I think, later, probably Pound's *ABC of Reading* (1934). There was also another book that was more or less a kind of report, bringing up to date what was going on in English poetry, by Francis Scarfe called *Auden and After: The Liberation of Poetry, 1930–1941* (published 1942). I'm trying to remember as accurately as I can the excitement of coming across these books, and the situation in which I came across them. I was living on an island called St. Lucia, which is a very small island, but which

had a couple, or one particularly good library. Later it got another library with more contemporary books. I think I read the Wilson in the Carnegie library in St. Lucia, and I think the Eliot essays must have come later. Now, I have to try and be precise about this, because perhaps the excitement of Wilson's book was not only the excitement of someone's enjoyment of Joyce, of Eliot. I remember being particularly excited about Joyce and the excerpts from the end of *Finnegans Wake*. Perhaps one of the excitements was the fact that I don't think I had access to *Ulysses* when I read Wilson. I certainly hadn't read any of the Jacobean or Elizabethan poets that Eliot spoke about, nor had I read a lot of Pound's very tight and strict anthology at the end of the *ABC of Reading*. So it's hard for me to say that the criticism alone was responsible for the excitement. In other words, I think that a critic is much more than an anthologist; but part of the excitement, I would imagine, would be my coming upon the very quiet but genuine excitement, which is what I think the tone of a critic is: one of very precise elation in terms of his appreciation of a work and a wish to convey the delight that he feels. But parallel to the text, there is always another text which is perhaps an echo of the frame of the text that is being described. Wilson's language never caught or imitated the language of the work he was describing, but there are some critics, particularly Eliot, who, in describing a text, take on, like a chameleon, the language of the text they are describing, and I think that this is exciting, because that is almost like having a parallel text written close to the one that is being examined. It was of no consequence to me what the prose quality of Wilson was, but the selections that he made, the examples he presented to me, I found, as a young poet, extremely exciting, and that process of making the right selection, the right quotation, can do an enormous amount of good, can have an enormous amount of influence on a young writer, in maybe two or three lines. I remember his comparison of Eliot with, probably, Laforgue, and thinking, well, those temptations, those little prickles of seduction that are there in those selections, make me want to read the whole work. Sometimes, and it's what Pound did, sometimes it's almost better not to read the whole work, because you can be disappointed; you expect the entire work to be as brilliant as the quotations. But still, those selections, I think, stylistically, were exciting to a young poet as craft, and the person who guided and conducted one to those discoveries was, of course, the person functioning as critic. Pound and Eliot, the poets, and Francis Scarfe may have written poetry; certainly Edmund Wilson practiced the craft of poetry and did one or two critical satires like "The Omelet of Archibald MacLeish." So he had an innate idea of rhythm. That's about all I'd like to kick off with, in saying that I do remember some emblematic and touchstone books that were very very exciting for me to read, probably around the age of maybe seventeen or eighteen or something.

How about the more recent critics? Have any of them influenced your work?

I think writers are very opinionated people. Most artists dismiss whole epochs or a man's lifetime work by one or two remarks, such as Gauguin paints a lot of naked women, or Van Gogh likes a lot of sunflowers, and that's it. So sometimes a whole career can be dismissed by another writer; Robert Frost once told Wallace Stevens that he wrote bric-a-brac; in a way, there's truth in that. So when I make these sort of pseudo-epigrams at age fifty-eight, I just feel I'm old enough and tired enough to make them. They're not the brashness of a young punk coming up and saying, well, here I am. It is a kind of privilege of middle age to dismiss whole epochs. I think that the French, when they run out of poets, invent a literary theory. When there's no real art going on in France, they get very desperate and something has to happen, and they think that the thing that has to happen is a lot of thinking. When people attempt to try to explain to me what the theory of deconstruction is, I just simply turn away. I just think of it as having a lot to do with Europe and my attitude to Europe. The concentric egotism of Europe is something I'm very bored with: it's the only place where the light exists, it's the only place that carries a torch, but it's the same place that destroyed so many million Jews. I can't relate the aestheticism of Europe to the barbarism of Europe. It's very hard for me to reconcile the two things. When I was very young, I remember my colonial experience consisted of thinking (and it's very hard for me to stop thinking, even at my age) of the Japanese as little yellow men with buck teeth running around trying to kill John Wayne; that's what I remember of Japanese culture. I remember that we had the portraits of four leaders on our school wall in St. Lucia: one of Stalin, who was supposed to be a benign, pipe-smoking, avuncular person, and who was a butcher of no mean merit, obviously; one of Churchill who, really, could just as well have been a Tartar as he was an Englishman, and had a tyrannical temperament, a dictatorial temperament—ask the Irish about Churchill, and they'll tell you; one of Chiang Kai-shek, who was a crook. The only person up there worth anything was Roosevelt, really; but here we were, admiring these four figures who were defending freedom. Well, when you get past that, there's a kind of cynicism that happens about a lot of aspects of history, which includes cycles of aesthetic history, and also, quite apart from some sort of distance that one tries to preserve from all the fashions and cycles of thought, I just think that when criticism gets extremely hyperactive, it is a signal of the barrenness of the culture, in a way. Whenever there is an age of reason, we get very poor poetry, usually, or indifferent poetry. You get a poetry of reason that, to me, isn't very exciting. This is a glib, opinionated statement, and I'm not saying it to provoke. I'm just saying that's how I really feel. I do not know what deconstruction means. I have absolutely no interest in what it means. The only thing it seems to mean to me is a very dirty joke about a bird which disappears up its own anus.

I can see why, when you talked about criticism, you talked about critics talking about older poets. I think it must be very different when they're talking about you personally. How do you feel about critics talking about you, about deconstructing you?

I'm really afraid of how I sound, because I've never been in a situation like this, among so many minds, being, not examined, but being here and making these very portentous statements, which I mean; and I don't make them out

of anger, nor do I mean to give myself the lineaments of some isolated traumatic figure who doesn't give a damn about things; I don't mean to do that. Nor would I say simply to another young poet, just avoid criticism, because as I've said, I've had a terrific excitement from the enjoyment of criticism, principally by poets. I teach, therefore I criticize, so it's not that I'm doing this thing which led Hemingway finally to say that critics were lice who crawl over literature. When these statements are made, generally, they're made out of a deep sense of wounding on the part of a writer who may be misunderstood, he thinks, by the critic, so that the revulsion that sometimes comes from one writer when somebody else says something about his work, is asinine, silly, and arrogant. So if you ask me about how I feel if I'm reviewed, I think that I've had a parallel equivalent, politically, to the Caribbean; in other words, I have been through, in my life, an identical series of phases which would be that of being a colonial, being someone given adult suffrage, being someone given self-government, and being someone who becomes very public so that the decades of my life may be the equivalent of the political decades of the Caribbean. Now, on the other hand, those decades or those definitions have sometimes been bestowed by the empire; in other words, the empire has said, okay, you are no longer a colonial, you can now have adult suffrage; you no longer have adult suffrage, you can now be independent; you are no longer independent, you can now be a republic. But I may have been a republic at age eighteen, do you see what I'm saying? But when I was reviewed, and when West Indian writers or African writers in the Commonwealth were reviewed by people in London, by the journals in London, they conferred the same status of colonial; in a little while you may have self-government, and then, following that, you can become a republic, and then, after that, you can join the club. But these definitions were imposed by the empire itself; in literary terms, you can say an emerging literature; an emerging literature would be the equivalent of a third world condition; so, it's like saying, they're now talking. Listen, they can talk. Second phase, they're talking very well. Third phase, it's astonishing that they can talk like that. Fourth phase, well, they're pretty good, let them in. It's the same thing with criticism of my work; but I felt more freedom and more assurance, I think, when I was writing at sixteen or seventeen; certainly less anger and irritation than I do now. So constantly one's image is manipulated very carefully by whoever is writing the criticism. For example, if I may give two examples: I have a poem that begins with an imitation of Langland's *Piers Plowman* which is, "In a summer season when soft was the sun," and I began a poem, "In idle August while the sea soft," deliberately modeling itself on *Piers Plowman*. I think, out of politeness, a lot of critics didn't see the reference; well Seamus Heaney said, look at how this is modeled directly on *Piers Plowman*, and I said, hooray, that's what I wanted somebody to say, I'm glad you said that, because that is what I was doing. That's another poet writing about it. I suffered a lot, mentally, because of what I did when I was young; I used to copy poems, in variant styles, modeled, sometimes, down, not to the rhyme, but to the exact meter of various poems. It would be Hopkins one morning; next morning it might be Spender; the next morning it might be Dylan Thomas; the next morning Eliot; the next morning Auden, and so on, and so on, or the Song of Solomon; anything that I wanted to write, and so I was making my own anthology, trying to learn the craft from exact models of the thing. Well, pretty soon, when I got published, everybody said, oh look, he is influenced by the following people, but of course I was influenced by the following people. It is obvious that I was modeling my craftmanship on these models. I don't know why you should, in the twentieth century, be reprimanded. Can you imagine a critic in the fifteenth or sixteenth century saying, look, he's trying to paint like Giotto; look, he's trying to paint like Da Vinci, and somebody saying, oh my God, I'm sorry, I apologize for trying to paint like Giotto; I'm very sorry if it looks like Leonardo. But this individuality which is part of the whole idea of democracy and the idea of individual liberty and making your own style, is another example, I think, of the decay of the idea of the guild of craftsmen, a strong medieval, and tribal, very African thing too; the idea of the guild, of the craftsman, the artist, not as an individual but as a member of a guild. So that when finally the critics got very exhausted by seeing all the influences, they started to say, well, he has a great original voice, which I don't. It's everybody's voice that makes that one song.

The apprenticeship which you have just described clearly shows the influence of a Western literary and cultural tradition. There are critics today who have questioned the validity of the idea of a cultural tradition and have suggested that the idea of a canon is inherently sexist and racist. Could you talk about what might be called a collision of cultures in your work?

What is very amusing about a lot of aspects of culture, what is almost farcical finally, is its bleached out quality. It's like stealing the Elgin marbles, which, if they were painted as they were painted, would be rejected by contemporary taste as being vulgar, because they would be painted statues; they would not be those bleached out, time-weathered looking objects; they would be like mannequins. The Greeks painted their statues. Nobody likes to remember that, because it makes the Greeks Asians; it doesn't make the Greeks Victorian, Arnold-type people. The culture is preserved when it is bleached out. The image of our historians and critics of ancient Greece is that of a lot of people walking around town speaking like Sophocles; but everybody knows it was like a mall in Puerto Rico; that's what it was like. It was bright, it was loud, it was crass, it was vulgar, and so on, but we have these bleached-out, distant images of classicism. Now when the Western cultures, who would have been slaves and barbarians in the time of the Greeks, when the barbarians become civilized, they claim the thing that civilized them as being something they invented; the English idea of Greece is something that really started in 1800 and something. It's not Greece. When somebody asks about my work, for instance, what are all these classical references about, you can't escape them, because the easiest thing to say about the work that I do is that I don't have an American scale or an American attitude. Now look at my condition: I live in an archipelago; that means I have islands, that means that there are boats going between the islands, that means

there are fishermen, that means there are people relating to the sea, that means there are storms; now, I can't apologize for the fact that I was born in an archipelago that has ships and has weather and has had battles and has had a past; the easy reference is to say he's trying to be Homer, or the derivation is from Homer. The island that I come from does not apologize to a Greek island for being what it is, so why do I have to justify these things? To me, the immediacy of Homer is not a quotation; the immediacy of the sea is not a quotation; if I walk into the sea and I nearly drown, I don't drown literally, I drown. . . . Nobody really says that about Joyce or another writer, because what is really silly is, how does the Anglo-Saxon temperament appropriate the Greek temperament? Who gives it the right to claim that that is its temperament? It's not its temperament. As West Indians, we are closer in temperament to the Greeks than they are, just as the Latin Americans are closer in temperament. Greeks are Asians; that means they're barbarians. . . . So by classic one only means the modern. If I think of the classic in the Caribbean, I think of modern. I think of the freshness of Homer. I don't think of the antiquity of Homer. I think of the immediacy of Homer. So if I feel this, yes; I understand islands, I understand sails, I understand wind, and I understand the weather. I understand that. I understand what he felt. It's not that I'm trying to be Homeric. I am on an island in an inland ocean, so the correspondence leaps centuries, whereas I can't really feel close to John Donne. I don't have that elemental relationship, that simultaneity of experience. So when these things appear to be dropped, to prop up, or fortify the poetry, as if it were part of the whole experience, it's not that; it's just as new to me as if Homer were writing here. . . . In terms of the right to quote, all I'm saying is, I have much more of a right, I feel more at home in *The Odyssey* than some boy who lives in Devon somewhere on a rainy afternoon; the weather is different, the light is different, but history teaches you a kind of genealogy or hierarchy of possession, that the barbarian takes over from the civilized and makes his or her own. As far as the idea of an African presence existing in my work at all, what I've had to say sometimes is I don't have to explain it because it's here. I don't explain the motherness of my mother; I don't say what is the motherness of my mother; birth is the motherness of my mother, pain and screaming; so if the history is there, and if Africa is there, I don't have to explain it. And those people, including black writers, who keep saying, well, where are all the black people, what's happening, where's the culture, I'm not interested in these people because they are asking me white questions.

The parallels you have drawn between the critical reception of your work and the political evolution of the Caribbean as well as the tendency of critics to overlook similarities between Greek and Caribbean islands in favor of simple notions of influence seem to suggest that it would be very difficult for a non-West Indian critic to write criticism of West Indian literature.

Well, I don't think so, no, not entirely; I think I'm talking about approach. Obviously you look at the Caribbean, and it seems all exotica; it doesn't matter if it's bitter exotica, or comic exotica; it is looked at as exotica: the vegetation, the people, all treated as if they are from the *National Geographic* or whatever. So there is the *National Geographic* attitude, or the notion of the central thing and the outskirts, the Caribbean being on the outskirts. I'm saying that American literature had the same problem at the beginning; that the English critic, when American literature was beginning, could not have any idea of space, of the immensity of America. American literature for them was, you know, the literature of a little colony on the edge of Massachusetts, whether they were writing of Emerson or Thoreau. You get some idea of space from Whitman, but you can't really understand it. You don't have to make the trip, but you can limit your boundaries mentally, and say, well, Whitman is writing about the breadth of America, and you can write that Whitman is writing about the breadth of America without being willing to undertake an understanding of the breadth of America. I think that people write about Caribbean literature in the same way that

---

An excerpt from *Omeros*

"O-meros," she laughed. "That's what we call
     him in Greek,"

stroking the small bust with its boxer's broken
     nose,
and I thought of Seven Seas sitting near the reek

of drying fishnets, listening to the shallows'
     noise.
I said: "Homer and Virg are New England farm-
     ers,

and the winged horse guards their gas-station,
     you're right."

I felt the foam head watching as I stroked an
     arm, as
cold as its marble, then the shoulders in winter
     light
in the studio attic. I said, "Omeros,"

and *O* was the conch-shell's invocation, *mer* was
both mother and sea in our Antillean patois,
os, a grey bone, and the white surf as it crashes

and spreads its sibilant collar on a lace shore.
Omeros was the crunch of dry leaves, and the
     washes
that echoed from a cave-mouth when the tide
     has ebbed.

The name stayed in my mouth. I saw how light
     was webbed
on her Asian cheeks, defined her eyes with a
     black
almond's outline, as Antigone turned and said:

"I'm tired of America, it's time for me to go back
to Greece. I miss my islands." I write, it re-
     turns—
the way she turned and shook out the black gust
     of hair.

Derek Walcott, in his Omeros, *Farrar, Straus, Giroux,
1991.*

---

they write about Latin American literature. Yes, there's a place called Brazil; yes, there's a place called Argentina; and there's a man named Borges, right, but to surrender— you see, I think it is a matter of surrendering—the critic in Europe or the critic even in America, compared to Latin America, is not really surrendering to the idea of Argentina. He's surrendering to the idea of the presence of a person called Borges, or a person called Neruda, but to widen your mind, to take in the idea, they don't do this in the way they say they're taking in Greece and Homer, or Shakespeare in England. It still is a little portal into something that they are not yet prepared to open up their minds to, because the scope becomes frightening.

Is that because there is an absence of an encompassing idea of the Caribbean or of Latin America?

No; I think it is a fear of being swamped. I think it is a fear of inundation, of a thing cascading into a little gate called English criticism, a fear that if it weren't bulwarked by a sort of defensive idea of a thing called literature belonging to England, or a literature belonging even to America, or the novel belonging to the country that writes about it critically, then things would be swept away. You'd have to say that maybe the dike is going to be broken, and maybe what will happen is that the Latin American novel now will burst through the dam, and there will just be this thing called the Latin American imagination, right, which the Anglo-Saxon imagination is not prepared to allow to invade its consciousness, because then it might fear its own extinction. That's why people don't like Marquez. That's why they call him exotic, and why they call him fanciful, or why they claim that he comes from Faulkner or whatever, because if they allow themselves to really open up their minds to Marquez, a lot of things would just be washed away. It would be like sand and the tide coming in, so, even if it is subconscious, you put up little dikes or barriers or breakwaters against the idea of this inundation.

Who are some of the Caribbean writers coming in on that tide lapping against the barriers set up by criticism?

Naipaul is a great writer, a terrific writer, but he is still within a parenthesis, and I'm saying that if that parenthesis is broken, then you'd have to admit not only that there is a Naipaul, but you would also have to take Trinidad seriously; that if you let that happen, then there's a threat of territory being swept away by the imagination into a thing called the English novel. They're immigrants. Fear the barbarians; it's always there, it's historically there. Wilson Harris's books don't take here; it's tough on him, maybe, for royalties, but in a way it's natural that they wouldn't take here because they are so organic to where they come from; unless you are prepared to understand Guyana, which nobody is prepared to do, then you are not going to understand Wilson Harris. If he just blends into a sort of superficial travelogue thing, a sociological thing about Guyana, then of course he'd become what would appear to be a major twentieth-century writer, and his name would appear more in concepts of the novel. Because he abhors format, right, then criticism which believes in format ignores him. These writers are not writers of small themes. Naipaul is a writer with immense themes; in his travels alone, he takes on India, he takes on Africa;

these are ambitious mental projects. Wilson Harris takes on Guyana's savannah, the vastness of that. The Caribbean writer of any quality is not a writer who is narrow-minded. Thematically Caribbean literature is not small and insular in terms of what it undertakes, not in the best writers. Edgar Mittelholzer's life is very varied: the places he's been, the novels he's written about what he's seen and recorded, just as a mental traveller to different places. Edward Braithwaite's poems take on an aspect of part of the African coast; they are not just literarily epic in terms of the width of what they are undertaking. And the lovely thing about Aimé Césaire is that *Notebook of a Return to the Native Land* appears to be a very small poem about Martinique, and then it widens, it dilates, in the same way that an island creates its own rings around it. That's what happens, I think. And I think the responsibility of that, the undertaking of that on the part of criticism is immense. It's an immense labor. I think Caribbean critics tend to pick a writer early, and say, well I'm going to work on Brathwaite or on Wilson Harris, and so on, and you just feel this little pigeonhole industry happening, probably because of the universities and because of teaching, that can narrow things down, to where they're not even doing the other writers. When I see a Caribbean critic just sort of padding behind that kind of safari, you know, it's distressing, because I feel that it's not laziness; there is a lot of work done; but it's just an attitude, I think, which does not follow the direction of adding Caribbean literature to something called English literature, seaming it together and saying politically it's advantageous to write like that about any place, because it's really the same province, and politically we are not in the province, though imaginatively we are.

Which Caribbean critics would you say are not padding behind the metaphoric safari that you have just alluded to?

I think that the criticism of writers like Kenneth Ramchand and Gordon Rohlehr is still close to the subject. Caribbean critics (how many there are I don't know, because they aren't published that widely, or one doesn't see them, or I have not been seeing them) are still close to the writer. I think the Caribbean critic is, in a way, as exploratory and as pioneering as this generation of Caribbean writers. So that I think there is a very close understanding of the intent of the Caribbean writer on the part of the Caribbean critic. The divisions that may happen in terms of opinion or assessment of, say, this writer's qualities or another writer's, is still based on a kind of a patriotism and a kind of an optimism about West Indian literature that is very good. Criticism, obviously, is always a generation or two behind literature, so that the enthusiasm that is there in Caribbean criticism is still fresh. It isn't that it's immature; I just think that there is a common goal between the Caribbean critic and the Caribbean writer, because they're of the same generation, almost. The goals are obvious. The societies are small. The burdens and the challenges that had to be overcome in the establishment of Caribbean literature are those that are shared by the critic, perhaps even more so, because a critic expresses opinion, repeatedly and volubly apart from university classes. West Indian literature is still young, and I think that the criticism of West Indian literature is young, not in an immature sense,

but in a very clear, clean, optimistic sense. It isn't jaded, and it's not divided into schisms and schools and so on. Where I've seen indications on the part of Caribbean critics to seem to adopt or to worry about schools of criticism that may emanate from France or may emanate from America or from Germany or wherever, it's a little distressing because you think of a university as if the world were one university with several lecture rooms in which there may be a German and a Spaniard and someone else talking about one subject, and the Caribbean critic is admitted into one of those rooms, whereas, without being belligerently nationalistic or separate, I don't think that one should let that happen, that the Caribbean critic should let himself be drawn into a sort of a global village or a university in which he is simply in another room talking in the same diction and using the same formulae or principles as, say, a German critic or a European critic, because the big temptation in the Caribbean always is to be afraid of not keeping up with things.

You're asking that the Caribbean critic shed one of the resilient metropolitan critics' stereotypes of Caribbean people, that is the stereotype of being mimics, treated with such brutal irony in Naipaul's The Mimic Men.

Yes. I think there can be a creative Caribbean criticism, which I think Gordon Rohlehr and Ken Ramchand are trying to do. I don't think they get tempted; of course, as scholars, they would know what's being bruited about. But all literature is really very provincial. In other words, it's really the language of the tribe, in a sense, so criticism is of the tribe as well. To universalize criticism is very dangerous. . . . But then you say to yourself, yes, but what is that judgment then that is outside the tribe, the interests of the tribe? Are there universals out there? Is there a sort of tidal opinion that touches the Caribbean like a big wave coming over from the Atlantic that finally washes up on the Caribbean intellect somewhere? I think that's the dangerous thing, as if you expect the wave to come from outside the horizon, approaching you. It's a temptation of every Caribbean artist, because that has an element of industry in it which involves the media, if you can think of university publications as an example of media, a communication tool. There's always that threat in the Caribbean, a feeling that one is outside of things. I think that one can know what is going on without being sucked into fashion or into what is supposed to be the ultimate judgment of whatever school of criticism exists. I've never read a single word about deconstruction. I'm not interested in it. I do not know what it means, and not because I feel isolated from it. I'm not interested in critical theories that after a while tend to become so absolute that writers begin to write in imitation of the critical theory, because it looks like the right thing to do. I think of the critic today, in the position that he or she has in the academic institution, and a lot in the media too, because in a way these journals that come out, whether *The New York Review of Books* or *The New Yorker,* these are media too, and these are places of opinion that may be very strong and very influential; I think certainly the young American writer can be influenced by the question whether his work is acceptable on the terms laid down by whatever critical power is in.

Isn't there in the Caribbean just as powerful an impulse to impose on the writer a set of expectations which may be political or cultural or even linguistic?

There was a time, particularly at the peak of the black power movement, when the division between Edward Brathwaite and myself became almost political and had nothing to do with either of our work. But I don't mind too much if that did happen. What I see happening, that I sound middle-aged about, I imagine, is I get very frightened of the narrowing down of everything to a kind of an idea called heritage, and heritage, being particularly black, emphatically black in the Caribbean, which I consider to be very narrow-minded since, obviously, the presence in the Caribbean of the Indian and the Chinese makes that idea of heritage one not always shared by people writing about Caribbean literature. They tend to write as if it's completely black, totally ignoring, for instance, or they divide it, the Indian experience from the African experience, or, say, the Chinese from the Lebanese, or whatever. Understand, I'm not talking about unanimity and homogeneity and so on; I'm just talking about the fact that very often critics in the Caribbean tend to write as if it's all a black experience, and that the diversity that is there is not really observed by the common experience of everyone in the Caribbean, of encountering, every minute of your life, people of various races. The Caribbean critic, ideally, would have to have even a larger universality than someone in Paris or London, because that's not a common experience of the person writing critically in the university in Paris or London, the experience of encountering, daily, on a very ordinary level, those various races and backgrounds and histories that one sees daily. So even in terms of either political struggle or whatever one wants to call it, or the literary struggle, it becomes narrow in the sense that it becomes, in a way, only African, only about the diaspora; what about other people's diasporas? . . . I'm not saying that Naipaul, for instance, is looked at as only an Indian writer in the Caribbean, but I'm saying that a critic must broaden his view of the Caribbean; it's very easy to be tempted to make certain kinds of slots, and allot certain niches to a certain kind of writer, and not to have a wider, deeper imagination in terms of what the experience is trying to portray, because I don't think that any of my generation could possibly realize multilingually and multiculturally, the depth of experience of each particular kind of racial origin that is there in the Caribbean. Now the racial origin may appear to be common, whether that of Cromwellian convicts or Indian people coming over after slavery or Africans, or a group like the Syrians, who are fascinating people, or the Lebanese and the Chinese. That person has to have a multifaceted critique as much as a poet has to have a multifaceted mind.

Aren't you talking about an imaginative sensitivity which places on the critic or lecturer the responsibilty of including, however passingly, the different groups in the Caribbean? For isn't it true that these groups have, in one way or another, become creolized?

If anybody has any responsibility to scholarship, it is a critic; the poet need not necessarily have such a responsibility to scholarship, although it is better to be widely read and intelligent and to be a good thinker as a poet than just to be someone working on the basis of emotion and nationalism. An ideal Caribbean critic, really, if you isolate the kind of people he is meeting in a daily encounter—the Chinese cashier behind the bank cage, the Indian cook, the African professional, the Lebanese merchant and so on; I mean, I don't think we understand the fantastic variety, the subdued and hidden, subterranean or subliminal power of the variety of experience that lies under a place like Georgetown or Port-of-Spain, particularly Port-of-Spain. So if a critic or a lecturer or someone writing has in his class a Chinese girl or an Indian boy or an African boy, or a mix of those, that should be a person confronting all the literatures of the world. That critic should be able to say, or a lecturer should be able to say to the Chinese girl, the only names one knows—Lao-Tze or Confucius—and therefore West Indian criticism, just by its very nature, by its very organic description, is immediately more varied than French criticism. What is provincial is London or Paris; what's not provincial is Port-of-Spain. You get to a point in your life when you have a sense of waste, of not doing what you might have done . . . but I would like to believe with proof what I'm saying, in the sense that it doesn't matter how people arrive in new places. It's all pioneering, whether it's the slave or the Indian, the guy coming from wherever he came from and has to go to work in the cane fields; he may be Mittelholzer's ancestor, or Naipaul's ancestor, or Jean Rhys's ancestor; it doesn't matter. The point is that what was forced to happen was some kind of definition had to be forced on the presence of these people in a very contained space. The layers of that, I think, are epical; one may say, but who are these people, these people are nothing, these are guys who came and they are now selling swordfish in a Chinese shop. But if you say that about any representative of any race, you may say about an Englishman who is driving a taxi in London that he is Shakespeare's relative; and therefore a Chinese guy selling swordfish to a black guy in some place, in some suburb of somewhere, is also the descendant of Confucius; I mean, it's all part of the tribe. And what you have is representatives of the tribes being there, with their own language, their own history; it doesn't matter whether they were the detritus of civilization or whatever you want to call them; the strength of survival that is there, and the fact that these people have come from across the world, makes for a strength underneath a place like Port-of-Spain that, at my age, is just frighteningly exciting. You can look at it historically and say, who are these people; they're just rubbish. But they are not rubbish; they are not the detritus; they are not junk; and they are more than survivors. You cannot repress the energy of any place. You can't repress natural energy, and people are natural energy. I would not like to be a West Indian critic, just because if I were honest, I couldn't handle the volume of work that would be involved. What would I know about Indian literature, and the Indian presence in the Caribbean is so ignored by Caribbean critics. The emphasis is always on the African—the old boring thing about crossing over, the middle passage. . . . It gets as boring sometimes as the Jewish diaspora. To look at other aspects of migration and settlement, that's still there for the critic to explore, because a critic talking to this Chinese girl in his class, he may be a black lecturer, really is an African talking to a Chinese. . . . I think what I'm trying to say is that it's very easy and very lazy in Caribbean criticism to do what I'm doing superficially, to talk about the amalgam and variety and so on, only on that level, and not to go down deeper, if you go from Jean Rhys, and radiate back into what is an English writer; who is Jean Rhys? Who is Jean Rhys next to Virginia Woolf? All the work that has to be done is quite staggering. . . . I think that's where Caribbean criticism can be invaluable and less narrowminded; in fact, it's actually the same thing I'm always bitching about, which is to follow the patterns dictated by what is supposed to be called history, so that to be trapped into an idea of the history of criticism, to be sucked into that is to ask, well, what's happening to Paris? What is deconstruction? What is some other kind of name or something, and then become part of that? That's still treating criticism in a historical manner, but the sort of hybrids that are presented to one now in the Caribbean novel is to say, well, that plant is not really a hybrid. It's its own plant, you know, and one has to keep tracking, to keep tracing as one tends to do historically or botanically, as if this plant were really a mixture of a rose and a mango, do you know what I mean?

It's looking at the wrong thing. It's looking at the plant rather than at its roots.

Exactly. It's beginning from the same habit of history, of thinking that is not going to produce a major Caribbean critic unless that critic is really steeped . . . I mean look at Edmund Wilson in his old age trying to learn Hebrew and realizing that, I can't understand America unless I understand Judaism, in a sense. That's not entirely why he did it; he was fascinated with the Hebrew texts, and it was not to avoid anti-Semitism, or to understand the Jewish novel, but as an American critic, even in his old age, he realized, I'd better learn something about the Indian nations, the Iroquois; I'd better understand something about the Jews. When I was there, the university I was in was nothing more than a very second-rate kind of provincial university that you may find in England, and nothing was exciting. . . . I never felt excited about being at the University of the West Indies. I didn't feel that anything was being created. I felt it was like a continuation, both in architectural design and in the teaching of, something, not alien, but just monotonous.

You seem to be speaking in terms of a critic's moral responsibility not merely to communicate the elation he or she feels about a text, but a moral responsibility to reflect the diversity of the culture the creative artist treats.

I think that the Caribbean critic has to invent a language in the same way that a poet has to invent a language. He may have his own codex; he may say, well, this is what I believe in, but at this point in a country's literature, it is a creative act to write about a parallel text, much more than it is in London or Paris or New York or wherever, because we don't have the historical weight of immediately placing a writer by alphabetical order and with the brackets for the dates in a whole system and a code of identity. That is terrific; it means that every Caribbean novelist is a different person. Just as each island is separat-

ed by the sea, each writer, in a way, is separated by that other element outside of him, which makes for a terrific stylistic variety and even conceptual variety. I'm not talking about knowing the difference between Barbados and Guyana. I'm talking about having an approach that is equal to that of the novelist or the writer, and saying, well, the only way I can understand Caribbean literature is if I can make my mind as faceted and as different as the writer himself knows if he is writing about Guyana, and that the large things that are there have to have a certain width. I think that Caribbean literature, even by Caribbean critics, is treated as if it were by nature small; rather, the scope enhances imagination; the scope of Naipaul's achievement is still measured in terms of the size of the place he came from, so that, in a way, criticism becomes very apologetic. It says, my God, look at the writers we have produced, in spite of . . . It should be taken as a natural thing that these writers would have come out of the kind of society that made them, from so many hundred years of Caribbean history, and the fact that utterance had to come from these writers. It was inevitable that there would be utterance, and the critics should begin, I think, not from that ancient reference of seeing them in an alphabetical line, and identifying them as something that came out of the Caribbean, which can now be added to the idea of English literature.

To what extent do you think the Caribbean critic may be affected by the absence of a reading public in the Caribbean, so that he writes for those outside the Caribbean who can pass judgment on his work?

I don't think the Caribbean critic should underestimate his audience, because the trap is always social responsibility. It's there for the writer, too, right? But what the Caribbean writer has to remember is that if he thinks his imagination worthwhile, then that imagination came from the guy next to him. It's part of the racial imagination. He's part of that. You can't separate the creativity of one, for example the comedy of a calypso, from the comedy of early Naipaul. You can't separate the tragedy of a Caribbean hymn from a tragic Caribbean short story. So that once a thing becomes literate and articulated, there is sort of a dropping, sometimes, into a kind of social responsibility, or into a sort of patriotic optimism, or a kind of pride, and all these things are flattened; they may blur or blunt acute perceptions, because the Caribbean critic has to be idiosyncratic. He has to be as idiosyncratic as a Caribbean novelist or poet. I miss that idiosyncracy, if you see what I'm saying.

How about your own criticism? How would you assess it in relationship to what you have just said?

Well, these were very fast jobs, sometimes, that I had to turn out.

But it's still very important, because you were really cutting new ground.

They were like reviewing. They were more like trying to do a job. I don't consider them to be really profound. I've very rarely written any criticism of poetry, for instance, because I find it tremendously frightening, even to undertake the reviewing of one book by any one poet; it is such a labor, that I've never really ever done it seriously. I don't know how I think really, you know; I don't know if I can think properly, because as soon as I write a sentence, by the time I've finished it, a contradiction is coming in, and then I have to surrender to a formula, and say you better finish saying what you set out to say; but I find that any sentence I make can almost have its negative as being valid; I think it's a poetic process that has an inherent contradiction, in the creation of a poem, which is not permissible in the creation of prose criticism. But yet great prose criticism can come out with these contradictions. Eliot was like that, Coleridge was like that, that the contradiction, that the opposite direction is much more fascinating than the one you're taking. . . . Eliot is wonderful like that. He'll say something, and you'll say, but you just said the opposite, and he'll say, well, I realize that I just said

the opposite, but I'm trying to go through with this point here, and that process is a creative process of trying to see how he's thinking before he gets to what he says. I miss that a lot, I think, in the process of the Caribbean critic as a writer. (pp. 178-95)

> *Derek Walcott and Richard E. Smith, in an interview in* Our Other Voices: Nine Poets Speaking, *edited by John Wheatcroft, Bucknell University Press, 1991, pp. 178-95.*

AWARD ANNOUNCEMENTS

James Atlas   (essay date 9 October 1992)

[*In the following excerpt, Atlas, an American editor and critic, places Walcott in the tradition of English poets and praises him as "a nation polyglot."*]

In a time when poetry has reveled in its freedom, deploying unmetered, unrhymed lines across the page, the formal properties of Derek Walcott's work are instantly visible to the eye. To open his **Collected Poems** is to find oneself in the presence of a writer for whom English poetry is no oppressive burden, to be cast off like the colonial past of Mr. Walcott's native St. Lucia, but a vibrant tradition, to be plundered and recast in his own contemporary idiom. Couplets and quatrains unfurl with a stately regularity, suffused with echoes of Shakespeare and Keats, T. S. Eliot and W. H. Auden. "Art is History's nostalgia," Walcott writes in **Omeros,** an epic-length modern *Odyssey* composed in terza rima. In his work, the voice of his English precursors resonates, animated by his own people's voice, a rich Creole patois mimed in **"The Schooner *Flight*":** "I go draw and knot every line as tight / as ropes in this rigging, in simple speech . . . "

The son of a schoolteacher who died when Mr. Walcott was a year old, the poet was raised in a bookish atmosphere. "Our house had a wire-meshed library of great books," he recalled in a memoir of his youth, "principally a uniform edition of Dickens and Walter Scott and Sabatini." His teachers recited Swinburne by heart, inculcating in him the notion that poetry was "living speech." A quatrain spoken by one of his characters could serve as an ironic autobiography:

> I'm just a red nigger who love the sea,
> I had a sound colonial education,
> I have Dutch, nigger, and English in me,
> And either I'm nobody, or I'm a nation

Clearly, Mr. Walcott is the latter—a nation polyglot in the extreme. "With equal right," as Joseph Brodsky, his friend and fellow Nobel laureate, has noted, "Walcott could have said that he has in him Greek, Latin, Italian, German, Spanish, Russian, French: because of Homer, Lucretius, Ovid, Dante, Rilke, Machado, Lorca, Neruda, Akhmatova, Mandelstam, Pasternak, Baudelaire, Valéry, Apollinaire." In part, his genius is his versatility—his re-

---

An excerpt from *Another Life*

> For no one had yet written of this landscape
> that it was possible, though there were sounds
> given to its varieties of wood;
>
> the *bois-canot* responded to its echo,
> when the axe spoke, weeds ran up to the knee
> like bastard children, hiding in their names,
>
> whole generations died, unchristened,
> growths hidden in green darkness, forests
> of history thickening with amnesia,
>
> so that a man's branched, naked trunk,
> its roots crusted with dirt,
> swayed where it stopped, remembering another
>   name;
>
> breaking a lime leaf,
> cracking an acrid ginger-root,
> a smell of tribal medicine stained the mind,
>
> stronger than ocean's rags,
> than the reek of the maingot forbidden pregnant
>   women,
> than the smell of the horizon's rusting rim,
>
> here was a life older than geography,
> as the leaves of edible roots opened their pages
> at the child's last lesson, Africa, heart-shaped,
>
> and the lost Arawak hieroglyphs and signs
> were razed from slates by sponges of the rain,
> their symbols mixed with lichen,
>
> the archipelago like a broken root,
> divided among tribes, while trees and men
> laboured assiduously, silently to become
>
> whatever their given sounds resembled,
> ironwood, logwood-heart, golden apples, cedars,
> and were nearly
>
> ironwood, logwood-heart, golden apples, cedars,
> men . . .

> *Derek Walcott, in his* Another Life, *Farrar, Straus and Giroux, 1972.*

course to what Brodsky calls "a genetic Babel." Yet however international Mr. Walcott's style, his language is quintessentially English. More than any poet of his generation, he has absorbed our poetic canon—absorbed and internalized it. Mr. Walcott, says the Irish poet Seamus Heaney, "possesses English more deeply and sonorously than most of the English themselves."

At times, he can sound derivative "We swore to make drink / and art our finishing school," he writes in the cadence of Yeats; "A white church spire whistles into space / like a swordfish" borrows shamelessly from Robert Lowell. In his earlier work, especially, Mr. Walcott's apprenticeship to his English masters has a slavish feel to it; the elaborate, knotted rhetoric is too high-pitched, inflated for rhetoric effect, as in these willed and ponderous lines from **"The Fortunate Traveler"**:

> The heart of darkness is not Africa
> The heart of darkness is the core of fire
> In the white center of the holocaust

But at his best—and there is little dross in Mr. Walcott's oeuvre—he achieves a sustained eloquence, an exhilarating amplitude; he's "a man immersed in words," the poet James Dickey has written, "not afraid of them, but excited and confirmed by what he can cause them to do."

In awarding Derek Walcott the Nobel Prize, the Swedish academy singled out his "historical vision, the outcome of a multicultural commitment." Multicultural in the demographic and political sense: Mr. Walcott is black, his homeland a Caribbean island remote from the dominant "white" culture, he is a poet for whom exile—both geographic and personal—has been the informing fact of his life. But his work vindicates T. S. Eliot's account of the way in which a poetic tradition evolves through the modification of works of art "by the new (the really new) work of art among them." In Derek Walcott, we can discern the history of what is most enduring in our tradition, invigorated, as it has always been, by the voice of our most recent immigrants. Invigorated and made new.

> *James Atlas, "Constructing Modern Idiom on*
> *a Base of Tradition," in* The New York Times,
> *October 9, 1992, p. C30.*

Walcott on the Caribbean:

I feel grateful for the kind of life that's down there. It's simple. The rhythm of life there, the beauty and simplicity of the people. All of it sounds patronizing and sort of wrong, but those values are there. Certainly the values are there in the beauty of the islands.

Derek Walcott, in the interview "The Man Who Keeps the
English Language Alive," in New Letters, *1992.*

The Observer (essay date 11 October 1992)

[*In the following excerpt, the critic provides an overview of Walcott's career.*]

Derek Walcott is a wanderer—his poetry encircles the world but begins and ends at home, in St Lucia, in the West Indies. Hard to place as a poet, he proved, on Thursday, appropriately hard to find. Hours after it had been announced that he had won the 1992 Nobel Prize for Literature, Walcott's friends could not raise him. Last seen in Trinidad at his younger daughter's wedding, he might be anywhere.

There was a frenzy of jubilant telegram-sending and frustrated telephoning; at the Royal Shakespeare Company matinée production of Walcott's play **The Odyssey,** the cast were opening champagne. All over the world, his many friends were celebrating without him.

Walcott showed up in Boston 'shocked', 'rich' (the prize is worth £670,000) and smiling. It is the first time the Nobel Prize has been awarded to anyone from the English-speaking Caribbean. At first, with characteristic self-mockery, Walcott claimed to feel like a 'phoney, third-rate Congressman' but then, on second thoughts, admitted that he felt like a Nobel Prize-winner.

Walcott is an old hand at winning awards. He won in 1988 the ridiculously named MacArthur Foundation 'Genius Award' and in the same year received the Queen's Gold Medal for poetry (recommended by Ted Hughes).

His writing has a hybrid brilliance, grafting different influences—Caribbean, European, American, classical and contemporary, and making them his own. It was his most recent work **Omeros,** written two years ago when he was 60, that most moved the Nobel judges. It is a Caribbean reworking of Homer which, like Walcott himself, marvellously combines lyrical stature with underhand vitality. Walcott dedicates the work to 'shipmates in this craft' (unable to resist the pun).

This epic poem, like much of his work, is filled with a sense of the sea—but a sea that is never formless, always held in check by metre. There is gravity and beauty about the way in which everything seems governed by water. Even Helen herself becomes a boat: 'A yellow dress whipped / like a sail in the wind when the wind comes about.'

It is a poem in which adjectives are few and innocently simple when they appear, but each verse carries a complex freight of nouns. Colours—milk white, dark pewter, curled brass, silvery green—shine through the poem, contributing to the 'luminosity' praised by the judges.

Walcott has wanted to write since he was eight. He published his first book at 18. As poet, playwright and amateur painter, he is (according to one friend) regarded by fellow-islanders as a 'saint'. Fishermen, meeting him in St Lucia, slap his hand and say: 'You do great for us, Mr Walcott.'

Many West Indian writers would agree, the novelist Caryl Phillips and the poet Merle Collins among them. But this is not the only message. Phillips explains that there is, among some West Indians, 'astonishingly hostile' feeling towards Walcott. Many say he has 'sold out'; his writing is not strictly indigenous, not written in patois, nor based on reggae rhythms.

It is lucky from their point of view that V. S. Naipaul, also a contender, did not win the prize. Negative feelings about Walcott are mild in comparison to the antipathetic rage felt towards Naipaul. It is said that the judges were almost evenly split between the two.

The irony is that Walcott is passionately focused on St Lucia—nothing he does is intended to discredit it. He loathes cultural exclusivity and insularity of all kinds. He is fascinated by the tensions between patois and English; but his net is wide and no prejudice will narrow it.

It is no accident that among his best friends are the poets Joseph Brodsky (American/Russian), Seamus Heaney (Irish) and Czeslaw Milosz (Polish). When they all meet for dinner (the dining table presumably groaning under their collective literary weight) Walcott is in his element. He is gregarious and dominating, clown and ringmaster, cracking the whip—a little theatrical.

Walcott is as much a man of the theatre as a poet. For 25 years he ran a theatre in Trinidad. Many of his plays, notably **Remembrance,** are about the legacies of colonialism. **Odyssey** at the RSC is a theatrical second-cousin to **Omeros.** It is marvellously funny, sad and digressive (like West Indian talk). On Thursday, Greg Doran, the director, told the audience before the show that Walcott had won the Nobel Prize. They applauded but, according to the cast, it had a deadly effect—they felt far too reverent to risk laughing.

He is a natural performer: it is marvellous to hear him reading his work aloud. . . . He speaks with an incantatory authority perfectly suited to the ebb of the verse. And he looks like a West Indian Odysseus, a seafarer whose face has been exposed to all weathers; his moustache is grey, lines carve his face into folds, but there is mutinous mirth in his eyes.

Although Walcott has a wonderful sense of humour and a crackling laugh, his friends volunteer that his jokes (off the page) are no good. Verdicts range from 'appalling' to 'absolutely rotten' and back. (Walcott has been known to crack up at the idea of 'Where the bee sucks, there suck I' printed in the old type where f replaces s.)

As a teacher, Walcott can be intimidating. He teaches creative writing at Boston University, where he also lives for half of each year (the other half he spends in Trinidad). Glyn Maxwell, a young English poet and a devoted pupil of Walcott's, will never forget his devastating first lesson. He began by attacking his class of 15 would-be poets.

What made them think that *anyone* would want to read their poetry? After flattening them, he then asked each student to write out a poem—any poem—that they knew off by heart. Not one student was able to do this.

It was Walcott's intention to shame them, to teach them the lesson he had learnt so well himself: to place themselves within literature, to know Shakespeare, Milton, Homer, Pope, to understand about form and history, to see that there's nothing free about 'free verse' if you don't know how to write anything else.

As a teacher, Walcott was not swift to praise. Maxwell re-

members showing him poems he'd had published in English magazines. Walcott would screw them up and chuck them in the bin. As with all people who praise infrequently, when approval came it was nectar.

Walcott was born in 1930, to a Methodist couple. His father was a schoolteacher. It was an exceptionally bookish household. His mother, whom he loved and feared, used to quote Marlowe and Shakespeare (particularly Portia's speeches from *The Merchant of Venice*). Walcott described his mother to a friend as being very tough. Meeting her in her last years, the friend found it hard to believe that the gentle woman eating the fish Walcott had caught for her birthday was the tough matriarch he had so often described. She died a year and a half ago. In the most moving scene of **Odyssey,** Odysseus wishes himself dead in order to be able to embrace his mother again.

Walcott's passion for St Lucia is sharpened by a sense of loss. He seeks to defend its beauties, imperilled by tourism. Between two volcanic spines, the trade-mark of St Lucia, lie some ancient petroglyphs. When the land was bought by a prospective hotelier, Walcott was vitriolic. He feels appalled by the idea of the Caribbean as the playground of America. No surprise, then, that in **Omeros** tourists appear unsympathetically right from the start, brandishing their soul-destroying cameras.

Walcott went to the University of the West Indies, narrowly missed going to Oxford or Cambridge (his maths wasn't up to scratch). He must be the only well-known English-speaking, West Indian writer never to have lived in England. He once said this was the making of him.

His personal life has not been easy. In 1976 he left his first wife Margaret and two daughters in Trinidad in order to teach in the US. He married again and had a son by his second marriage. But this marriage also broke up and for the last few years the central relationship in his life has been with his Norwegian girlfriend.

When he heard he had won the Nobel Prize he said one of the great joys of his life was food. He could not say drink—for drink has been a curse. Now on the wagon, he should at least be intoxicated by success when St Lucia holds a day of celebration in his honour—or when he re-reads the pages of **Omeros,** where salt waters are laced with rum.

"Homer of the Caribbean," in The Observer, *October 11, 1992, p. 21.*

Paul Gray   (essay date 11 October 1992)

[*In the following essay, Gray examines the thematic concerns of Walcott's work.*]

In handing out Nobel Prizes in Literature, the Swedish Academy is sometimes accused of political correctness, of paying undue attention to geopolitical and ethnic considerations. So in one respect, last week's award to poet Derek Walcott was unsurprising. Of mixed ancestry (African, Dutch, English), Walcott was born 62 years ago on the tiny Windward Island of St. Lucia in what was then the British West Indies. A native Caribbean writer had never before won a Nobel Prize.

But nobody suggested after the announcement was made that Walcott had won the laurel, worth $1.2 million, on charity. He has long been regarded as one of the finest living poets in English, an accolade made even more impressive by the struggles Walcott underwent to earn it.

Both of his parents were schoolteachers, although his father died when Walcott was only one, and the house in St. Lucia that he, his twin brother and older sister grew up in was filled with books. But the allure of the English language, and of the English poetry recited aloud in his classrooms, came tempered with a sense of exclusion from white British culture, the resentment felt by a subject of an alien, occupying power. In one of his early poems, he pondered his far-away African heritage and asked,

> Where shall I turn, divided to the vein?
> I who have cursed
> The drunken officer of British rule, how choose
> Between this Africa and the English tongue I
>   love?

The tension between these divided loyalties animates nearly all of Walcott's poetry. Rather than seeing his position as impossible—a poet on the margins of two mutually exclusive cultures—Walcott adopted this dilemma as one of his principal subjects. In this respect, much of his work is self-conscious; the point of contact between language and experience is, of necessity, the presiding poet, and the more difficult this contact is, the more visible the poet's struggle becomes.

But Walcott never whines or indulges in unseemly confessions; he is, in fact, inordinately harsh with himself. Sometimes he claims his material is beyond or beneath the power of his art. In **"Gros-Ilet"** he describes a small, desolate island village and concludes, "This is not the grape-purple Aegean. / There is no wine here, no cheese, the almonds are green, / the sea grapes bitter, the language is that of slaves." At other times, he is worried that his devotion to the English language has severed him from the people of his childhood. **"The Light of the World"** portrays the visiting poet on a bus filled with village inhabitants:

> And I had abandoned them, I knew that there
> sitting in the transport, in the sea-quiet dusk,
> with men hunched in canoes, and the orange
>   lights
> from the Vigie headland, black boats on the
>   water;
> I, who could never solidify my shadow
> to be one of their shadows, had left them their
>   earth,
> their white rum quarrels, and their coal bags,
> their hatred of corporals, of all authority.

Such moments revivify nostalgia in the original, classical Greek sense: *nostos* (return) plus *algos* (pain). For years Walcott has divided his calendar equally between Boston, where he teaches literature and creative writing at Boston University, and a residence in Trinidad, a base for his frequent travels elsewhere in the Caribbean. This regular shuttling between two worlds has kept his poetry balanced between heartless skill and artless passion. The speakers of Walcott's poems are half strangers wherever they find themselves, not because they want to be but because they have no choice. In **"The Lighthouse,"** an island vendor approaches the poet and smiles: "Fifty? Then / you love home harder than youth!"

This is a specific statement about a concrete emotion—Walcott rarely generalizes or resorts to abstractions—and yet it echoes well beyond its given point of utterance. At their most intense, Walcott's 10 volumes of poetry convey all the strangeness and exotica of island life—of poor, forgotten people surrounded by water on a margin of the earth—and make the whole spectacle as familiar as the view across the street.

It is misguided to praise poets for their subjects. Many of them, like Walcott, had little choice in the matter. What poets do with their inheritances means everything. And Walcott's language has evolved from his early, rather stilted imitations of English poets into an instrument of marvelous flexibility: capable of grand, sweeping imagery but also of harsh interruptions and interjections, slang, pidgin and Creole patois and subtle Caribbean syncopations. The combined effect is a verbal radiance, of scenes illuminated by "a moon so bright / you can read palms by it."

> *Paul Gray, "Bard of the Island Life," in* Time,
> *New York, Vol. 140, No. 16, October 11, 1992,*
> *p. 65.*

Paula Burnett   (essay date 16 October 1992)

[*Burnett, an English educator and critic, is the editor of* The Penguin Book of Caribbean Verse in English *(1986). In the following essay, she discusses the political aims and implications of Walcott's work.*]

If the world has begun to wake up to the works of St Lucia's Derek Walcott, it is not before time. The international spotlight of the Nobel prize could not turn on a worthier figure, particularly in this year of the Columbus quincentenary. Walcott is a great poet, and a profound and humane articulator of the post-colonial condition.

But while his recognition as a literary colossus by the Swedish Academy is to its credit, the award also serves to highlight the ambivalence in much of the Caribbean and in Britain over a *magnum opus*—an extraordinarily rich and diverse body of work that can help us to a deeper understanding of one another.

Paradoxically, Walcott has now reached a "popular" audience of a kind in Britain. He has even been on *Desert Island Discs* and makes more regular appearances here. . . . But there is still very little evidence that the creaking vessel of the British lit-crit establishment has taken him on board.

It is rather the poets—of the British Isles and elsewhere—who have led the way in recognising how exceptional he is. When his first collection of poetry by a metropolitan publisher, Jonathan Cape, came out in 1962, no less a person than Robert Graves said that Walcott "handles English with a closer understanding of its inner magic" than his English contemporaries.

Recently, Joseph Brodsky and Seamus Heaney have done their bit by publishing warm critiques in widely read essays. For Heaney, "Walcott possesses English more deeply and sonorously than most of the English themselves". Brodsky braved the unmentionable, regarding Walcott as marginalised into "West Indian" or "black" categories, and speaking of "the unwillingness of the critical profession to admit that the great poet of the English language is a black man".

It is all too obvious why the literary establishment in Britain has lagged well behind the US in taking up Walcott's works, which give a perception of the British empire that demolishes some illusions still cherished in high places. But it is sadly ironic that his reputation among Caribbean people suffers a reciprocal problem of alienation. There, he is often resented as one who has sold out by writing, from a US university (he teaches creative writing at Boston University), "elitist" works in standard English that draw on the European tradition.

While giving awesome weight to the tragedy of the [Caribbean] region's history, [Walcott] has managed to salvage its heroism: the endurance of ordinary people, victims of the abuse of power, who never gave up hope. At bleak times, it is good to read Walcott to restore one's faith in the world's possibilities.

—Paula Burnett

From an outsider's viewpoint this seems conspicuously unfair. Walcott's commitment to his Caribbean identity is rock-solid. Unlike many West Indian writers of his generation he stayed to work in the region until he was nearing 50. As well as writing poetry (which some may regard as an elitist activity), he has lived a life in the theatre, founding the Trinidad Theatre Workshop.

He is a poet of the theatre, with some 30 plays to his credit, the majority written for a socially mixed Caribbean audience. Those who criticise might see that their great epic *Omeros* begins in Caribbean English and has God speak its unique poetry.

The range of language on which he regularly draws in his poetry, as much as in his drama, includes his St Lucian patois as well as his brilliantly inventive use of Caribbean English. His poetry continually celebrates the people and culture of the region, including the African and native American heritage.

More than anyone, he has brought the Caribbean experience to the consciousness of the world; his epic intention was to "give those feet a voice". While giving awesome weight to the tragedy of the region's history, he has managed to salvage its heroism: the endurance of ordinary people, victims of the abuse of power, who never gave up

hope. At bleak times, it is good to read Walcott to restore one's faith in the world's possibilities.

Is he the Homer for the millennium? As the poet of our age who, in a time of small literary ambitions, has dared the epic on behalf of his people and achieved it, the parallel is apt, and his rhetorical use of Homeric allusion is justified. We should, however, guard against allowing Walcott's political cutting edge to be sheathed in the Homer myth that is gathering around him.

There is a risk that the centres of northern culture may use the idea of Walcott as a modern Homer to distance his work, to define it as outside their own immediate concerns and to resist its challenging implications. Something will be lost if the undoubted beauty of his poetry comes to be stressed at the expense of its dialect.

For cheek by jowl with his numinous, lyrical side is the revolutionary Walcott—a compassionate revolutionary, shaping works into a tool of resistance against all tyranny and exploitation, using the past to disclose the present. His *madre dolorosa* of revolution speaks as "the darker, the older America".

His is the voice of the third world addressed urgently to the first—through the persona of the Fortunate Traveller, for instance: "In a square coffin manacled to my wrist: small countries pleaded through the mesh of graphs, in treble-spaced, Xeroxed forms to the World Bank on which I had scrawled the word, MERCY".

A vitriolic satirist of the abuse of power, he targets western hypocrites as "sharks with well-pressed fins, / ripping we small-fry off with razor grins". In his dramatisation of Homer's *Odyssey,* which is playing to packed houses at Stratford and is due to transfer to the Barbican next year, his portrayal of the one-eyed giant Polyphemus is inspired by the totalitarianism of the modern Greek colonels but is applicable to many regimes.

He exposes the racism of supposedly civilised institutions; the "Boer cattle under Tory whips that drag every wagon / nearer to apartheid" bring to a close, for him, "the child's fairy tale of an antic England" (**Midsummer**). As he points out wryly, "black still poor, though black is beautiful".

His literary revolution is to have remodelled the citadel of the dominant culture. In Rushdie's phrase, the "empire writes back". Walcott's strategy has been to aim for the holy of holies, in order to call attention to the possibility of plural gods. Genetically and culturally, his is a multiple heritage, whose richness he celebrates, using words of comfort—even to bless. Like Joyce's Molly, his lasting word is always the affirmative.

Paula Burnett, "The Empire Writes Back," in New Statesman & Society, *Vol. 5, No. 224, October 16, 1992, p. 35.*

THE NOBEL LECTURE

Derek Walcott   (lecture date 7 December 1992)

[*In the following address, which Walcott gave on 7 December 1992 when he accepted the Nobel Prize, the poet examines the nature of history, identity, and the arts in Caribbean society.*]

Felicity is a village in Trinidad on the edge of the Caroni plain, the wide central plain that still grows sugar and to which indentured cane cutters were brought after emancipation, so the small population of Felicity is East Indian, and on the afternoon that I visited it with friends from America, all the faces along its road were Indian, which, as I hope to show, was a moving, beautiful thing, because this Saturday afternoon *Ramleela,* the epic dramatization of the Hindu epic the *Ramayana,* was going to be performed, and the costumed actors from the village were assembling on a field strung with different-colored flags, like a new gas station, and beautiful Indian boys in red and black were aiming arrows haphazardly into the afternoon light. Low blue mountains on the horizon, bright grass, clouds that would gather color before the light went. Felicity! What a gentle Anglo-Saxon name for an epical memory.

Under an open shed on the edge of the field, there were two huge armatures of bamboo that looked like immense cages. They were parts of the body of a god, his calves or thighs, which, fitted and reared, would make a gigantic effigy. This effigy would be burned as a conclusion to the epic. The cane structures flashed a predictable parallel: Shelley's sonnet on the fallen statue of Ozymandias and his empire, that "colossal wreck" in its empty desert.

Drummers had lit a fire in the shed and they eased the skins of their tablas nearer the flames to tighten them. The saffron flames, the bright grass, and the hand-woven armatures of the fragmented god who would be burned were not in any desert where imperial power had finally toppled, but were part of a ritual, evergreen season that, like the cane-burning harvest, is annually repeated, the point of such sacrifice being its repetition, the point of the destruction being renewal through fire.

Deities were entering the field. What we generally call "Indian music" was blaring from the open platformed shed from which the epic would be narrated. Costumed actors were arriving. Princes and gods, I supposed. What an unfortunate confession! "Gods, I suppose" is the shrug that embodies our African and Asian diasporas. I had often thought of but never seen *Ramleela,* and had never seen this theater, an open field, with village children as warriors, princes, and gods. I had no idea what the epic story was, who its hero was, what enemies he fought, yet I had recently adapted the *Odyssey* for a theater in England, presuming that the audience knew the trials of Odysseus, hero of another Asia Minor epic, while nobody in Trinidad knew any more than I did about Rama, Kali, Shiva, Vishnu, apart from the Indians, a phrase I use pervertedly because that is the kind of remark you can still hear in Trinidad: "apart from the Indians."

It was as if, on the edge of the Central Plain, there was another plateau, a raft on which the *Ramayana* would be poorly performed in this ocean of cane, but that was my writer's view of things, and it is wrong. I was seeing the *Ramleela* at Felicity as theater when it was faith.

Multiply that moment of self-conviction when an actor, made-up and costumed, nods to his mirror before stepping onstage in the belief that he is a reality entering an illusion, and you would have what I presumed was happening to the actors of this epic. But they were not actors. They had been chosen; or they themselves had chosen their role in this sacred story that would go on for nine afternoons over a two-hour period till the sun set. They were not amateurs but believers. There was no theatrical term to define them. They did not have to charge their psyches to perform their roles. Their acting would probably be as buoyant and as natural as those bamboo arrows crisscrossing the afternoon pasture. They believed in what they were playing, in the sacredness of the text, in the validity of India, while I, out of the writer's habit, searched for some sense of elegy, of loss, even of degenerative mimicry in the happy faces of the boy-warriors or the heraldic profiles of the village princes. I was polluting the afternoon with skeptical admiration. I misread an event through a visual echo of History—the cane fields, indenture, the evocation of vanished armies, temples, and trumpeting elephants—when all around me there was quite the opposite: elation, delight in the boys screams, in the sweets-stalls, in more and more costumed characters appearing; a delight of conviction, not loss. The name Felicity made sense.

Consider the scale of Asia reduced to these fragments: the small white exclamations of minarets or the stone balls of temples in the cane fields, and one can understand the self-mockery and embarrassment of those who see these rites as parodic, even degenerate. These purists look on such ceremonies as grammarians look on a dialect, as cities look on provinces and empires on their colonies. Memory that yearns to join the center, a limb remembering the body from which it has been severed, like those bamboo thighs of the god. In other words, the way that the Caribbean is still looked at, illegitimate, rootless, mongrelized. "No people there," to quote Froude, "in the true sense of the word." No people. Fragments and echoes of real people, unoriginal and broken.

The performance was like a dialect, a branch of its original language, an abridgement of it, but not a distortion or even a reduction of its epic scale. Here in Trinidad I had discovered that one of the greatest epics of the world was seasonally performed, not with that desperate resignation of preserving a culture, but with an openness of belief that was as steady as the wind bending the cane lances of the Caroni plain. We had to leave before the play began to go through the creeks of the Caroni Swamp, to catch the scarlet ibises coming home at dusk. In a performance as natural as those of the actors of the *Ramleela,* we watched the flocks come in as bright as the scarlet of the boy archers, as the red flags, and cover an islet until it turned into a flowering tree, an anchored immortelle. The sigh of History meant nothing here. These two visions, the *Ramleela* and the arrowing flocks of scarlet ibises, blended into a single gasp of gratitude. Visual surprise is natural in the Caribbean; it comes with the landscape, and faced with its beauty, the sigh of History dissolves.

We make too much of that long groan that underlines the past. I felt privileged to discover the ibises as well as the scarlet archers of Felicity.

The sigh of History rises over ruins not over landscapes, and in the Antilles there are few ruins to sigh over, apart from the ruins of sugar estates and abandoned forts. Looking around slowly, as a camera would, taking in the low blue hills over Port of Spain, the village road and houses, the warrior-archers, the god-actors and their handlers, and music already on the sound track, I wanted to make a film that would be a long-drawn sigh over Felicity. I was filtering the afternoon with evocations of a lost India, but why "evocations"? Why not "celebrations of a real presence"? Why should India be "lost" when none of these villagers ever really knew it, and why not "continuing," why not the perpetuation of joy in Felicity and in all the other nouns of the Central Plain: Couva, Chaguanas, Charley Village? Why was I not letting my pleasure open its windows wide? I was entitled, like any Trinidadian, to the ecstasies of their claim, because ecstasy was the pitch of the sinuous drumming in the loudspeakers. I was entitled to the feast of Husein, to the mirrors and crepe-paper temples of the Muslim epic, to the Chinese Dragon Dance, to the rites of that Sephardic Jewish synagogue that was once on Something Street. I am only one-eighth the writer I might have been had I contained all the fragmented languages of Trinidad.

Break a vase, and the love that reassembles the fragments is stronger than that love that took its symmetry for granted when it was whole. The glue that fits the pieces is the sealing of its original shape. It is such a love that reassembles our African and Asiatic fragments, the cracked heirlooms whose restoration shows its white scars. This gathering of broken pieces is the care and pain of the Antilles, and if the pieces are disparate, ill-fitting, they contain more pain of the Antilles, and if the pieces are disparate, ill-fitting, they contain more pain than their original sculpture, those icons and sacred vessels taken for granted in their ancestral places. Antillean art is this restoration of our shattered histories, our shards of vocabulary, our archipelago becoming a synonym for pieces broken off from the original continent.

And this is the exact process of the making of poetry, or what should be called not its making but its remaking, the fragmented memory, the armature that frames the god, even the rite that surrenders it to a final pyre; the god assembled cane by cane, reed by weaving reed, line by plaited line, as the artisans of Felicity would erect his holy echo.

Poetry, which is perfection's sweat but which must seem as fresh as the raindrops on a statue's brow, combines the natural and the marmoreal. It conjugates both tenses simultaneously: the past and the present, if the past is the sculpture and the present the beads of dew or rain on the forehead of the past. There is the buried language and there is the individual vocabulary, and the process of poet-

ry is one of excavation and self-discovery. Tonally the individual voice is a dialect; it shapes its own accent, its own vocabulary and melody in defiance of an imperial concept of language, the language of Ozymandias, libraries and dictionaries, law courts and critics, churches, universities, and political dogma, the diction of institutions. Poetry is an island that breaks away from the main. The dialects of my archipelago seem as fresh to me as those raindrops on the statue's forehead, not the sweat made from the classic exertion of frowning marble, but the contradictions of a refreshing element, rain and salt.

Deprived of their original language, the captured and indentured tribes create their own, accreting and secreting fragments of an old, epic vocabulary from Asia and from Africa, but to an ancestral and ecstatic rhythm in the blood that cannot be subdued by slavery or indenture, while nouns are renamed and the given names of places accepted like Felicity or Choiseul. The original language dissolves from the exhaustion of distance like fog trying to cross an ocean, but this process of renaming, of finding new metaphors, is the same process that the poet faces every morning of his working day, making his own tools like Crusoe, assembling nouns from necessity, from Felicity, even renaming himself. The stripped man is driven back to that self-astonishing elemental force, his mind. That is the basis of the Antillean experience, this shipwreck of fragments, these echoes, these shards of a huge tribal vocabulary, these partially remembered customs, and they are not decayed but strong. They survived the Middle Passage and the *Fatel Rozack,* the ship that carried the first indentured Indians from the port of Madras to the cane fields of Felicity, that carried the chained Cromwellian convict and the Sephardic Jew, the Chinese grocer and the Lebanese merchant selling cloth samples on his bicycle.

And here they are, all in a single Caribbean city, Port of Spain, the sum of history, Froude's "non-people." A downtown babel of shop signs and streets, mongrelized, polyglot, a ferment without a history, like heaven. Because that is what such a city is, in the New World, a writer's heaven.

Antillean art is this restoration of our shattered histories, our shards of vocabulary, our archipelago becoming a synonym for pieces broken off from the original continent.

—Derek Walcott

A culture, we all know, is made by its cities.

Another first morning home, impatient for the sunrise—a broken sleep. Darkness at five, and the drapes not worth opening; then, in the sudden light, a cream-walled, brown-roofed police station bordered with short royal palms, in the colonial style, back of it frothing trees and taller palms, a pigeon fluttering into the cover of an eave, a rain-stained block of once-modern apartments, the morning side road into the station without traffic. All part of a surprising peace. This quiet happens with every visit to a city that has deepened itself in me. The flowers and the hills are easy, affection for them predictable; it is the architecture that, for the first morning, disorients. A return from American seductions used to make the traveler feel that something was missing, something was trying to complete itself, like the stained concrete apartments. Pan left along the window and the excrescenes rear—a city trying to soar, trying to be brutal, like an American city in silhouette, stamped from the same mold as Columbus or Des Moines. An assertion of power, its decor bland, its air conditioning pitched to the point where its secretarial and executive staff sport competing cardigans; the colder the offices the more important, an imitation of another climate. A longing, even an envy of feeling cold.

In serious cities, in gray, militant winter with its short afternoons, the days seem to pass by in buttoned overcoats, every building appears as a barracks with lights on in its windows, and when snow comes, one has the illusion of living in a Russian novel, in the nineteenth century, because of the literature of winter. So visitors to the Caribbean must feel that they are inhabiting a succession of postcards. Both climates are shaped by what we have read of them. For tourists, the sunshine cannot be serious. Winter adds depth and darkness to life as well as to literature, and in the unending summer of the tropics not even poverty or poetry (in the Antilles poverty is poetry with a V, *une vie*, a condition of life as well as of imagination) seems capable of being profound, because the nature around it is so exultant, so resolutely ecstatic, like its music. A culture based on joy is bound to be shallow. Sadly, to sell itself, the Caribbean encourages the delights of mindlessness, or brilliant vacuity, as a place to flee not only winter but the seriousness that comes only out of culture with four seasons. So how can there be a people there, in the true sense of the word?

They know nothing about seasons in which leaves let go of the year, in which spires fade in blizzards and streets whiten, of the erasures of whole cities by fog, of reflection in fireplaces. Instead, they inhabit a geography whose rhythm, like their music, is limited to two stresses: hot and wet, sun and rain, light and shadow, day and night, the limitations of an incomplete meter, and are therefore a people incapable of the subtleties of contradiction, of imaginative complexity. So be it. We cannot change contempt.

Ours are not cities in the accepted sense, but no one wants them to be. They dictate their own proportions, their own definitions in particular places and in a prose equal to that of their detractors, so that now it is not just St. James, but the streets and yards that Naipaul commemorates, its lanes as short and brilliant as his sentences; not just the noise and jostle of Tunapuna, but the origins of C. L. R. James's *Beyond a Boundary;* not just Felicity village on the Caroni plain, but Selvon Country, and that is the way it goes up the islands now: the old Dominica of Jean Rhys still very much the way she wrote of it; the

Martinique of the early Césaire; Perse's Guadeloupe, even without the pith helmets and the mules; and what delight and privilege there was in watching a literature—one literature in several imperial languages, French, English, Spanish—bud and open island after island in the early morning of a culture, not timid, not derivative, any more than the hard white petals of the frangipani are derivative and timid. This is not a belligerent boast, but a simple celebration of inevitability: that this flowering had to come.

On a heat-stoned afternoon in Port of Spain, some alley white with glare, with love vine spilling over a fence, palms and a hazed mountain appear around a corner to the evocation of Vaughn or Herbert's "that shady city of palm-trees," or to the memory of a Hammond organ from a wooden chapel in Castries, where the congregation sang "Jerusalem the Golden." It is hard for me to see such emptiness as desolation. It is this patience that is the width of Antillean life, and the secret is not to ask the wrong thing of it, not to demand of it an ambition it has no interest in. The traveler reads this as lethargy, as torpor.

Here there are not enough books, one says, no theaters, no museums, simply not enough to do. Yet deprived of books, a man must fall back on thought, and out of thought, if he can learn to order it, will come the urge to record, and in extremity, if he has not means of recording, recitation, the ordering of memory that leads to meter, to commemoration. There can be virtues in deprivation, and certainly one virtue is salvation from a cascade of high mediocrity, since books are now not so much created as remade.

Cities create a culture, and all we have are these magnified market towns, so what are the proportions of the ideal Caribbean city? A surrounding, accessible countryside with leafy suburbs, and if the city is lucky, behind it, spacious plains. Behind it, fine mountains; before it, an indigo sea. Spires would pin its center and around them would be leafy, shadowy parks. Pigeons would cross its sky in alphabetic patterns, carrying with them memories of a belief in augury, and at the heart of the city there would be horses, yes, horses, those animals last seen at the end of the nineteenth century drawing broughams and carriages with top-hatted citizens, horses that live in the present tense without elegiac echoes from their hooves, emerging from paddocks at the Queen's Park Savannah at sunrise, when mist is unthreading from the cool mountains above the roofs, and at the center of the city seasonally there would be races, so that citizens could roar at the speed and grace of these nineteenth-century animals. Its docks would not be obscured by smoke or deafened by too much machinery, and above all, it would be so racially various that the cultures of the world—the Asiatic, the Mediterranean, the European, the African—would be represented in it, its humane variety more exciting than Joyce's Dublin. Its citizens would intermarry as they chose, from instinct, not tradition, until their children find it increasingly futile to trace their genealogy. It would not have too many avenues difficult or dangerous for pedestrians, its mercantile area would be a cacophony of accents, fragments of the old language that would be silenced immediately at 5 o'clock, its docks resolutely vacant on Sundays.

This is Port of Spain to me, a city ideal in its commercial and human proportions, where a citizen is a walker and not a pedestrian, and this is how Athens may have been before it became a cultural echo.

The finest silhouettes of Port of Spain are idealizations of the craftsman's handiwork, not of concrete and glass, but of baroque woodwork, each fantasy looking more like an involved drawing of itself than the actual building. Behind the city is the Caroni plain, with its villages, Indian prayer flags, and fruit vendors' stalls along the highway over which ibises come like floating flags. Photogenic poverty! Postcard sadnesses! I am not re-creating Eden; I mean, by "the Antilles," the reality of light, of work, of survival. I mean a house on the side of a country road, I mean the Caribbean Sea, whose smell is the smell of refreshing possibility as well as survival. Survival is the triumph of stubbornness, and spiritual stubbornness, a sublime stupidity, is what makes the occupation of poetry endure, when there are so many things that should make it futile. Those things added together can go under one collective noun: "the world."

This is the visible poetry of the Antilles, then. Survival.

If you wish to understand that consoling pity with which the islands were regarded, look at the tinted engravings of Antillean forests, with their proper palm trees, ferns, and waterfalls. They have a civilizing decency, like Botanical Gardens, as if the sky were a glass ceiling under which a colonized vegetation is arranged for quiet walks and carriage rides. Those views are incised with a pathos that guides the engraver's tool and the topographer's pencil, and it is this pathos that, tenderly ironic, gave villages names like Felicity. A century looked at a landscape furious with vegetation in the wrong light and with the wrong eye. It is such pictures that are saddening, rather than the tropics themselves. These delicate engravings of sugar mills and harbors, of native women in costume, are seen as a part of History, that History which looked over the shoulder of the engraver and, later, the photographer. History can alter the eye and the moving hand to conform a view of itself; it can rename places for the nostalgia in an echo; it can temper the glare of tropical light to elegiac monotony in prose, the tone of judgment in Conrad, in the travel journals of Froude.

These travelers carried with them the infection of their own malaise, and their prose reduced even the landscape to melancholia and self-contempt. Every endeavor is belittled as imitation, from architecture to music. There was this conviction in Froude that since History is based on achievement, and since the history of the Antilles was so genetically corrupt, so depressing in its cycles of massacres, slavery, and indenture, a culture was inconceivable, and nothing could ever be created in those ramshackle ports, those monotonously feudal sugar estates. Not only the light and salt of Antillean mountains defied this, but the demotic vigor and variety of their inhabitants. Stand close to a waterfall and you will stop hearing its roar. To be still in the nineteenth century, like horses, as Brodsky has written, may not be such a bad deal, and much of our life in the Antilles still seems to be in the rhythm of the last century, like the West Indian novel.

By writers even as refreshing as Graham Greene, the Caribbean is looked at with elegiac pathos, as prolonged sadness to which Lévi-Strauss supplied an epigraph: *Tristes Tropiques.* Their *tristesse* derives from an attitude to the Caribbean dusk, to rain, to uncontrollable vegetation, to the provincial ambition of Caribbean cities where brutal replicas of modern architecture dwarf the small houses and streets. The mood is understandable, the melancholy as contagious as the fever of a sunset, like the gold fronds of diseased coconut palms, but there is something alien and ultimately wrong in the way such a sadness, even a morbidity, is described by English, French, or some of our exiled writers. It relates to a misunderstanding of the light and the people on whom the light falls.

These writers describe the ambitions of our unfinished cities, their unrealized, homiletic conclusion, but the Caribbean city may conclude just at that point where it is satisfied with its own scale, just as Caribbean culture is not evolving but already shaped. Its proportions are not to be measured by the traveler or the exile, but by its own citizenry and architecture. To be told that you are not yet a city or a culture requires this response: I am not your city or your culture. There might be less *tristes tropiques* after that.

Here, on the raft of this dais, there is the sound of the applauding surf: our landscape, our history recognized, "at last." *At Last* is one of the first Caribbean books. It was written by the Victorian traveler Charles Kingsley. It is one of the earliest books to admit the Antillean landscape and its figures into English literature. I have never read it, but I gather that its tone is benign. The Antillean archipelago was there to be written about, not to write itself, by Froude, by Patrick Leigh-Fermor, in the very tone in which I almost wrote about the village spectacle at Felicity, as a compassionate and beguiled outsider, distancing myself from Felicity village even while I was enjoying it.

What is hidden cannot be loved. The traveler cannot love, since love is stasis and travel is motion. If he returns to what he loved in a landscape and stays there, he is no longer a traveler but in stasis and concentration, a lover of that particular part of earth, a native. So many people say that they "love the Caribbean," meaning that someday they plan to return for a visit but could never live there, the usual benign insult of the traveler, the tourist. These travelers, at their kindest, were devoted to the same patronage, the islands passing in profile, their vegetal luxury, their backwardness and poverty. Victorian prose dignified them. They passed by in beautiful profiles and were forgotten, like a vacation.

Alexis Saint-Léger Léger, whose writer's name is St.-John Perse, was the first Antillean to win this prize for poetry. He was born in Guadeloupe and wrote in French, but before him there was nothing as fresh and clear in feeling as those poems of his childhood, that of a privileged white child on an Antillean plantation, *Pour fêter une enfance, Éloges,* and later *Images à Crusoe.* At last, the first breeze on the page, salt-edged and self-renewing as the trade winds, the sound of pages and palm trees turning as "the odour of coffee ascends the stairs."

Caribbean genius is condemned to contradict itself. To celebrate Perse, we might be told, is to celebrate the old plantation system, to celebrate the *bequé,* or plantation rider, verandas and mulatto servants, a white French language in a white pith helmet, to celebrate a rhetoric of patronage and hauteur; and even if Perse denied his origins, great writers often have this folly of trying to smother their source, we cannot deny him any more than we can deny the African Aimé Césaire. This is not accommodation, this is the ironic republic that is poetry, since, when I see cabbage palms moving their fronds at sunrise, I think they are reciting Perse.

The fragrant and privileged poetry that Perse composed to celebrate his white childhood and the recorded Indian music behind the brown young archers of Felicity, with the same cabbage palms against the same Antillean sky, pierce me equally. I feel the same poignancy of pride in the poems as in the faces. Why, given the history of the Antilles, should this be remarkable? The history of the world, by which of course we mean Europe, is a record of intertribal lacerations, of ethnic cleansings. At last, islands not written about but writing themselves! The palms and the Muslim minarets are our Antillean exclamations. At last! The royal palms of Guadeloupe recite *Éloges* by heart.

Later, in *Anabase,* Perse assembled fragments of an imaginary epic, with the clicking teeth of frontier gates, barren wadis with the froth of poisonous lakes, horsemen burnoosed in sandstorms, the opposite of cool Caribbean mornings, yet not necessarily a contrast any more than some young brown archer at Felicity, hearing the sacred text blared across the flagged field, with its battles and elephants and monkey-gods, is a contrast to the white child in Guadeloupe assembling fragments of his own epic from the lances of the cane fields, the estate carts and oxen, and the calligraphy of bamboo leaves from the ancient languages, Hindi, Chinese, and Arabic, on the Antillean sky. From the *Ramayana* to Anabasis, from Guadeloupe to Trinidad, all that archaeology of fragments lying around, from the broken African kingdoms, from the crevasses of Canton, from Syria and Lebanon, vibrating not under the earth but in our raucous, demotic streets.

A boy with weak eyes skims a flat stone across the flat water of an Aegean inlet, and that ordinary action with the scything elbow contains the skipping lines of the *Iliad* and the *Odyssey,* and another child aims a bamboo arrow at a village festival, another hears the rustling march of cabbage palms in a Caribbean sunrise, and from that sound, with its fragments of tribal myth, the compact expedition of Perse's epic is launched, centuries and archipelagos apart. For every poet it is always morning in the world, and History a forgotten insomniac night. History and elemental awe are always our early beginning, because the fate of poetry is to fall in love with the world in spite of History.

There is a force of exultation, a celebration of luck, when a writer finds himself a witness to the early morning of a culture that is defining itself, branch by branch, leaf by leaf, in that self-defining dawn, which is why, especially at the edge of the sea, it is good to make a ritual of the sunrise. Then the noun "Antilles" ripples like brightening water, and the sounds of leaves, palm fronds, and birds are the sounds of a fresh dialect, the native tongue. The personal vocabulary, the individual melody whose meter is one's biography, joins in that sound, with any luck, and the body moves like a walking, a waking island.

This is the benediction that is celebrated, a fresh language and a fresh people, and this is the frightening duty owned.

I stand here in their name, if not their image—but also in the name of the dialect they exchange like the leaves of the trees whose names are suppler, greener, more morning-stirred than English—*laurier canelles, bois-flot, bois-canot*—or the valleys the trees mention—Fond St. Jacques, Mabonya, Forestière, Roseau, Mahaut—or the empty beaches—L'Anse Ivrogne, Case en Bas, Paradis—all songs and histories in themselves, pronounced not in French but in patois.

One rose hearing two languages, one of the trees, one of schoolchildren reciting in English:

> I am monarch of all I survey,
> My right there is none to dispute;
> From the center all round to the sea
> I am lord of the fowl and the brute.
> Oh, solitude! Where are the charms
> That sages have seen in thy face?
> Better dwell in the midst of alarms,
> Than reign in this horrible place . . .

While in the country, to the same meter but to organic instruments, handmade violin, chac-chac, and goatskin drum, a girl named Sesenne singing:

> *Si mwen di 'ous ça fait mwen la peine*
> *Ous kai dire ça vrai.*
> (If I told you that caused me pain
> You'll say, "It's true.")
> *Si mwen di 'ous ça penetrait mwen*
> *'Ous peut dire ça vrai.*
> (If I told you you pierced my heart
> You'd say, "It's true.")
> *Ces mamailles actuellement*
> *Pas ka faire l'amour z'autres pour un rien.*
> (Children nowadays
> Don't make love for nothing.)

It is not that History is obliterated by this sunrise. It is there in Antillean geography, in the vegetation itself. The sea sighs with the drowned from the Middle Passage, the butchery of its aborigines, Carib and Aruac and Taino, bleeds in the scarlet of the immortelle, and even the actions of surf on sand cannot erase the African memory, or the lances of cane as a green prison where indentured Asians, the ancestors of Felicity, are still serving time.

That is what I have read around me from boyhood, from the beginnings of poetry, the grace of effort. In the hard mahogany of woodcutters' faces, resinous men, charcoal burners; in a man with a cutlass cradled across his forearm, who stands on the verge with the usual anonymous khaki dog; in the extra clothes he put on this morning, when it was cold when he rose in the thinning dark to go and make his garden in the heights—the heights, the garden, being miles away from his house, but that is where he has his land—not to mention the fishermen, the footmen on trucks, groaning up mornes, all fragments of Africa originally but shaped and hardened and rooted now in the island's life, illiterate in the way leaves are illiterate; they do not read, they are there to be read, and if they are properly read, they create their own literature.

But in our tourist brochures the Caribbean is a blue pool into which the republic dangles the extended foot of Florida as inflated rubber islands bob and drinks with umbrellas float toward her on a raft. This is how the islands, from the shame of necessity, sell themselves; this is the seasonal erosion of their identity, that high-pitched repetition of the same images of service that cannot distinguish one island from the other, with a future of polluted marinas, land deals negotiated by ministers, and all of this conducted to music of Happy Hour and the rictus of a smile. What is the earthly paradise for our visitors? Two weeks without rain and a mahogany tan, and at sunset local troubadours in straw hats and floral shirts beating "Yellow Bird" and "Banana Boat Song" to death.

There is a territory wider than this—wider than the limits made by the map of an island—which is the illimitable sea and what it remembers. All of the Antilles, every island, is an effort of memory; every mind, every racial biography culminating in amnesia and fog. Pieces of sunlight through the fog and sudden rainbows, *arcs-en-ciel*. That is the effort, the labor of the Antillean imagination, rebuilding its gods from bamboo frames, phrase by phrase.

Decimation from the Aruac downward is the blasted root of Antillean history, and the benign blight that is tourism can infect all of those island nations, not gradually but with imperceptible speed, until each rock is whitened by the guano of white-winged hotels, the arc and descent of progress.

Before it is all gone, before only a few valleys are left, pockets of an older life, before development turns every artist into an anthropologist or a folklorist, there are still cherishable places, little valleys that do not echo with ideas, a simplicity of rebeginnings, not yet corrupted by the dangers of change. Not nostalgic sites but occluded sanctities as common and simple as their sunlight. Places as threatened by this prose as a headland is by the bulldozer or a sea-almond grove by the surveyor's string, or from blight, the mountain laurel.

One last epiphany: a basic stone church in a thick valley outside Soufrière, the hills almost shoving the houses around into a brown river, a sunlight that looks oily on the leaves, a backward place, unimportant, and one now being corrupted into significance by this prose. The idea is not to hallow or invest the place with anything, not even memory. African children in Sunday frocks come down the ordinary concrete steps into the church, banana leaves hang and glisten, a truck is parked in a yard, and old women totter toward the entrance. Here is where a real fresco should be painted, one without importance, but one with real faith, mapless, Historyless.

How quickly it could all disappear! And how it is beginning to drive us further into where we hope are impenetrable places, green secrets at the end of bad roads, headlands where the next view is not of a hotel but of some long

beach without a figure and the hanging question of some fisherman's smoke at its far end. The Caribbean is not an idyll, not to its natives. They draw their working strength from it organically, like trees, like the sea almond or the spice laurel of the heights. Its peasantry and its fishermen are not there to be loved or even photographed; they are trees who sweat, and whose bark is filmed with salt. But every day on some island, rootless trees in suits are signing favorable tax breaks with entrepreneurs, poisoning the sea almond and the spice laurel of the mountains to their roots. A morning could come in which governments might ask what happened not merely to the forests and the bays, but to a whole people.

They are here again, they recur, the faces, corruptible angels, smooth black skins and white eyes huge with an alarming joy, like those of the Asian children of Felicity at *Ramleela;* two different religions, two different continents, both filling the heart with the pain that is joy.

But what is joy without fear? The fear of selfishness that, here on this podium with the world paying attention not to them but to me, I should like to keep these simple joys inviolate, not because they are innocent, but because they are true. They are as true as when, in the grace of this gift, Perse heard the fragments of his own epic of Asia Minor in the rustling of cabbage palms, that inner Asia of the soul through which imagination wanders, if there is such a thing as imagination as opposed to the collective memory of our entire race, as true as the delight of that warrior-child who flew a bamboo arrow over the flags in the field at Felicity; and now as grateful a joy and a blessed fear as when a boy opened an exercise book and, within the discipline of its margins, framed stanzas that might contain the light of the hills on an island blessed by obscurity, cherishing our insignificance. (pp. 26, 28-32)

Derek Walcott, "The Antilles: Fragments of Epic Memory," in The New Republic, *Vol. 207, No. 27, December 28, 1992, pp. 26, 28-32.*

FURTHER READING

Gamerman, Amy. "West Indian Poet Derek Walcott Wins Nobel." *The Wall Street Journal* (9 October 1992): A10.
    Examines Walcott's attempts to delineate cultural gaps between the "new world" and the "old world" in his poetry.

Hamner, Robert D. *Derek Walcott.* Boston: Twayne, 1981, 175 p.
    Biographical and critical study of Walcott.

Kroll, Jack. "The Man Who Loves English." *Newsweek* CXX, No. 16 (19 October 1992): 73.
    Praises Walcott as the poet "laureate of multiculturalism."

Rule, Sheila. "Walcott, Poet of Caribbean, Is Awarded the

Nobel Prize." *The New York Times* CXLII, No. 49,114 (9
October 1992): A1, C30.

> Provides biographical information on Walcott and criti-
> cal response to his work by his contemporaries.

Terada, Rei. *Derek Walcott's Poetry: American Mimicry.* Boston: Northeastern University Press, 1992, 260 p.

> Analyzes how Walcott's works reflect his "provocative
> hypothesis—most explicitly set forth in his 1974 essay,
> 'The Caribbean: Culture or Mimicry?'—that there is
> such a thing as a collective America, and that it has a
> characteristic art of mimicry." Also included is an essay
> attempting to place Walcott's works within the post-
> modernist tradition.

Additional coverage of Walcott's life and career is contained in the following sources
published by Gale Research: *Black Literature Criticism,* Vol. 3; *Black Writers;*
Contemporary Authors, Vols. 89-92; *Contemporary Authors New Revision Series,* Vol. 26;
Contemporary Literary Criticism, Vols. 2, 4, 9, 14, 25, 42, 67; *Dictionary of Literary
Biography,* Vol. 117; *Dictionary of Literary Biography Yearbook 1981;* and *Major 20th-
Century Writers.*

In Memoriam

Isaac Asimov

January 2, 1920—April 6, 1992

(Also wrote under the pseudonyms Paul French, George E. Dale, and Dr. A.) Russian-born American novelist, short story writer, nonfiction writer, essayist, editor, historian, poet, author of children's books, and autobiographer.

For further information on Asimov's life and works, see *CLC*, Volumes 1, 3, 9, 19, and 26.

INTRODUCTION

The author of nearly five hundred books, Asimov is esteemed as one of the finest writers of science fiction and scientific fact in the twentieth century. As a fiction writer he received his greatest popular and critical acclaim for *The Foundation Trilogy: Three Classics of Science Fiction* and his robot series. Comprised of *Foundation, Foundation and Empire,* and *Second Foundation, The Foundation Trilogy* describes the "future history" of a vast galactic empire. His books about robots—most notably *I, Robot; The Caves of Steel;* and *The Naked Sun*—did much to legitimize science fiction by augmenting the genre's traditional material with the narrative structures of such established genres as mystery and detective stories, while displaying a thematic concern for technological progress and its implications for humanity. Many critics, scientists, and educators, however, believe Asimov's greatest talent was for popularizing or, as he called it, "translating" science for the lay reader. His many books on atomic theory, chemistry, astronomy, and physics have been recognized for their extraordinary clarity, and Asimov has been praised for his ability to synthesize complex data into readable, unthreatening prose. When asked about his prodigious output in such a wide range of fields, Asimov responded self-deprecatingly by saying he never had a thought that he didn't put down on paper. An editorial in *The Washington Post* concluded that he redefined the rule "as to how many things a person is allowed to be an expert on" and that his "extraordinary capabilities aside, [his] breadth of interest deserves more admiration than it gets."

PRINCIPAL WORKS

I, Robot (short stories) 1950
Pebble in the Sky (novel) 1950
*Foundation (novel) 1951
Biochemistry and Human Metabolism (nonfiction) 1952

*Foundation and Empire (novel) 1952
*Second Foundation (novel) 1953
The Caves of Steel (novel) 1954
The End of Eternity (novel) 1955
The Martian Way, and Other Stories (short stories) 1955
Races and People (nonfiction) 1955
Inside the Atom (nonfiction) 1956
The Naked Sun (novel) 1957
The World of Carbon (nonfiction) 1958
Words of Science and the History behind Them (nonfiction) 1959
The Double Planet (nonfiction) 1960
Realm of Algebra (nonfiction) 1961
The Genetic Code (nonfiction) 1963
The Human Body: Its Structure and Operation (nonfiction) 1963
A Short History of Biology (nonfiction) 1964
Of Time and Space and Other Things (essays) 1965
The Genetic Effects of Radiation (nonfiction) 1966

The Roman Republic (nonfiction) 1966
The Egyptians (nonfiction) 1967
Is Anyone There? (essays) 1967
Asimov's Guide to the Bible, Volume I: The Old Testament (nonfiction) 1968
Words from History (nonfiction) 1968
Asimov's Guide to the Bible, Volume II: The New Testament (nonfiction) 1969
The Shaping of England (nonfiction) 1969
Asimov's Guide to Shakespeare (nonfiction) 1970
The Gods Themselves (novel) 1972
Asimov's Annotated "Paradise Lost" (nonfiction) 1974
Lecherous Limericks (poetry) 1975
Murder at the ABA: A Puzzle in Four Days and Sixty Scenes (novel) 1976
Animals of the Bible (nonfiction) 1978
In Memory Yet Green: The Autobiography of Isaac Asimov, 1920-1954 (autobiography) 1979
In Joy Still Felt: The Autobiography of Isaac Asimov, 1954-1978 (autobiography) 1980
Foundation's Edge (novel) 1982
The Robots of Dawn (novel) 1983
The History of Physics (nonfiction) 1984
Asimov's Guide to Halley's Comet (nonfiction) 1985
Robots and Empire (novel) 1985
The Dangers of Intelligence, and Other Science Essays (essays) 1986
Foundation and Earth (novel) 1986
Asimov's Annotated Gilbert and Sullivan (nonfiction) 1988
Nemesis (novel) 1988
Prelude to Foundation (novel) 1988
Isaac Asimov Laughs Again (autobiography) 1991

*These works were collectively published as *The Foundation Trilogy: Three Classics of Science Fiction* in 1963.

OBITUARIES AND TRIBUTES

Mervyn Rothstein (essay date 7 April 1992)

[*In the following obituary, Rothstein reviews Asimov's life and career.*]

Isaac Asimov, the pre-eminent popular-science writer of the day and for more than 40 years one of the best and best-known writers of science fiction, died yesterday at New York University Hospital. He was 72 years old and lived in Manhattan.

He died of heart and kidney failure, said his brother, Stanley.

Mr. Asimov was amazingly prolific, writing nearly 500 books on a wide range of subjects, from works for preschoolers to college textbooks. He was perhaps best known for his science fiction and was a pioneer in elevating the genre from pulp-magazine adventure to a more in-

tellectual level that dealt with sociology, history, mathematics and science. But he also wrote mysteries, as well as critically acclaimed books about the Bible, physics, chemistry, biology, astronomy, limericks, humor, Shakespeare, Gilbert and Sullivan, ancient and modern history, and many other subjects.

Mr. Asimov's first book, **Pebble in the Sky,** a science-fiction novel, was published in 1950. His first 100 books took him 237 months, or almost 20 years, until October 1969, to write. His second 100, a milestone he reached in March 1979, took 113 months, or about 9½ years—a rate of more than 10 books a year. His third 100 took only 69 months, until December 1984, or less than 6 years.

"Writing is more fun than ever," he said in a 1984 interview. "The longer I write, the easier it gets."

> His first 100 books took him 237 months, or almost 20 years, until October 1969, to write. His second 100, a milestone he reached in March 1979, took 113 months, or about 9½ years—a rate of more than 10 books a year. His third 100 took only 69 months, until December 1984, or less than 6 years.
>
> —*Mervyn Rothstein*

He once explained how he came to write **Asimov's Guide to Shakespeare.** It began, he said, with a book called **Words of Science.**

"**Science** led to **Words on the Map,**" he remarked,

> which took me to **The Greeks,** which led me to **The Roman Republic, The Roman Empire, The Egyptians, The Near East, The Dark Ages, The Shaping of England** and then **Words From History.** It was an easy jump to **Words in Genesis,** which brought on **Words From the Exodus.** That led me to **Asimov's Guide to the Old Testament,** and then **The New Testament.** So what was left except Shakespeare?

His usual routine was to awake at 6 A.M., sit down at the typewriter by 7:30 and work until 10 P.M.

In **In Memory Yet Green,** the first volume of his autobiography, published in 1979, he explained how he became a compulsive writer. His Russian-born father owned a succession of candy stores in Brooklyn that were open from 6 A.M. to 1 A.M. seven days a week. Young Isaac got up at 6 o'clock every morning to deliver papers and rushed home from school to help out in the store every afternoon. If he was even a few minutes late, his father yelled at him for being a folyack. Yiddish for sluggard. Even more than 50 years later, he wrote: "It is a point of pride with me that though I have an alarm clock, I never set it, but get up at 6 A.M. anyway. I am still showing my father I'm not a folyack."

Isaac Asimov was born Jan. 2, 1920, in the Soviet Union, near Smolensk, the son of Judah and Anna Rachel Berman Asimov. He was brought to the United States in 1923 and was naturalized in 1928.

He taught himself to read before he was 5 years old, using the signs on his Brooklyn street. A couple of years later, with a little help from his father, he taught himself to read Yiddish. When he was 7, he taught his younger sister to read. He skipped several grades and received a high-school diploma when he was 15. After discovering science fiction on the magazine rack in his father's store—and overcoming his father's objections to fanciful subject matter—he tried writing science fiction himself and sold his first story when he was 18. The story, **"Marooned Off Vesta,"** ran in the October 1938 issue of *Amazing Stories*.

Three years later, in 1941, he sold a story called **"Nightfall"** to *Astounding Science Fiction,* then the top magazine in the field. It was edited by John W. Campbell Jr., whose ability to find talented writers was largely responsible for what is considered the Golden Age of science fiction in the 1930's and 40's. Almost 30 years after **"Nightfall"** was published, the Science Fiction Writers of America voted it the best science-fiction short story ever written.

Astounding Science paid a cent a word, Mr. Asimov once recalled. "So for a 12,000-word story I expected $120. I got a check for $150 and thought Mr. Campbell had made a mistake." But when Mr. Asimov called to tell him, "he said the story had seemed so good to him he gave me a bonus of one-quarter cent a word."

Mr. Asimov graduated from Columbia University in 1939 with a bachelor of science degree, and earned an M.A. in 1941 and a Ph.D. in chemistry there in 1948. The next year, he accepted an offer from Boston University's School of Medicine to teach biochemistry.

"I didn't feel impelled to tell them that I'd never had any biochemistry," he recalled in a 1969 interview. "By 1951 I was writing a textbook on biochemistry, and I finally realized the only thing I really wanted to be was a writer."

He was made an associate professor of biochemistry in 1955 and a professor in 1979, although he stopped teaching in 1958 and only occasionally went back to the university to lecture.

Mr. Asimov's science-fiction novels and stories won many awards: five Hugos, given by the fans, and three Nebula Awards, given by his fellow writers. His **Foundation Trilogy**—which takes place in a future galactic empire and consists of **Foundation** (1951), **Foundation and Empire** (1952) and **Second Foundation** (1953)—was given a Hugo in 1966 as Best All-Time Science-Fiction Series. Among his non-fiction works, **Asimov's New Guide to Science** is considered one of the best books about science for the layman.

Reviewing **Foundation's Edge,** a sequel to the trilogy and the first of Mr. Asimov's books to make the *New York Times* best-seller list, the critic Gerald Jonas said in *The New York Times Book Review* in 1982: "He writes much better than he did 33 years ago—yet he has lost none of the verve he brought to this series when he and the galaxy were much younger. What more could one ask?" **Founda-**

tion's Edge won a Hugo in 1983 as the best science-fiction novel of the year.

In recent years, Mr. Asimov wrote **Foundation and Earth** (1986) and **Prelude to Foundation** (1988). A final novel, **Forward the Foundation,** is to be published by Bantam Books later this year.

Mr. Asimov himself made no great claims for his work. "I make no effort to write poetically or in a high literary style," he said in 1984. "I try only to write clearly and I have the very good fortune to think clearly so that the writing comes out as I think, in satisfactory shape."

"I never read Hemingway or Fitzgerald or Joyce or Kafka," he once wrote. "To this day I am a stranger to 20th-century fiction and poetry, and I have no doubt that it shows in my writing."

He wrote his first drafts on his typewriter, and short articles and final drafts on a word processor, and he rewrote everything only once. "It's not out of conceit," he said. "But I have lots of stuff I'm committed to write and if I linger lovingly I won't be able to write at all."

Not everything, however, fell into place easily. He once did a children's book in a day, but the Shakespeare book took two years. The book he considered his favorite, **Murder at the A.B.A.** (1976), a mystery novel in which he himself was a character, took seven weeks; **The Gods Themselves** (1972), a science-fiction novel that won both the Hugo and the Nebula awards, took seven months.

"I do all my own typing, my own research, answer my own mail," Mr. Asimov once said. "I don't even have a literary agent. This way there are no arguments, no instructions, no misunderstandings. I work every day. Sunday is my best day: no mail, no telephones. Writing is my only interest. Even speaking is an interruption."

Although he wrote about space travel through countless universes and light years, Mr. Asimov himself refused to fly. "Isaac says that he loves to fly into space and span the galaxies," the editor Ben Bova once remarked. "But only in his imagination."

Among Mr. Asimov's other well-known science-fiction works were **I, Robot** (1950), in which he invented his famous Three Laws of Robotics, which govern the relation of robots to their human masters: robots may not injure a human or, by inaction, allow a human to be harmed; robots must obey humans' orders unless doing so conflicts with the first law; robots must protect their own existence unless doing so conflicts with the first two laws. Robot and galactic empire themes eventually expanded and intertwined in 14 novels.

He also wrote many nonfiction works and magazine articles on a wide range of subjects and was the editorial director of a magazine named after him—*Isaac Asimov's Science Fiction Magazine*—for which he wrote the editorials in each issue.

He received the James T. Grady Award of the American Chemical Society in 1965 and the American Association for the Advancement of Science-Westinghouse Science Writing Award in 1967.

Recently Mr. Asimov said he had had a prostate operation and was cutting back on his writing. He suspended his monthly column in *Fantasy and Science Fiction* magazine, to which he had contributed some 400 columns and articles over 33 years.

Writing 10 or more books a year was standard procedure for Mr. Asimov, and he continued his busy pace after a heart attack in 1977 and triple bypass surgery in 1983.

"I have been fortunate to be born with a restless and efficient brain, with a capacity for clear thought and an ability to put that thought into words," he once remarked. "None of this is to my credit. I am the beneficiary of a lucky break in the genetic sweepstakes."

Mr. Asimov once told an interviewer about sadly contemplating death and the end of conscious thought. But, he said, he cheered himself with the thought that "I don't have to worry about that, because there isn't an idea I've ever had that I haven't put down on paper."

Mr. Asimov married Gertrude Blugerman in 1942; they were divorced in 1973.

In addition to his brother, of Roslyn Heights, L.I., he is survived by his wife, Janet Jeppson, whom he married in 1973; a son, David, of California; a daughter, Robyn, of Manhattan, and a sister, Marcia Repanes of Queens.

> *Mervyn Rothstein, in an obituary in* The New York Times, *April 7, 1992, p. B7.*

Bart Barnes   (essay date 7 April 1992)

[*In the following obituary, Barnes provides an overview of Asimov's life and discusses his major works.*]

Isaac Asimov, 72, an imaginative and gifted storyteller and one of this century's most versatile, prolific and celebrated writers of science fiction and fact, died of heart and kidney ailments April 6 at New York University Hospital.

Mr. Asimov was author of more than 320 books, plus scores of short stories and nonfiction articles published in journals and magazines, and his total literary output is said to have been more than 20 million words in print.

A biochemist by training, he was a master at translating complicated scientific facts and principles into simple everyday prose. His work included not only science fiction stories of mystery and adventure, but also medical texts; science books for the general public on topics ranging from the nature of carbon to the genetic code; astronomy; mathematics; humor and satire; literary studies; and books about Greek, Roman and biblical history.

He could type 90 words a minute, and he revised his writing only once. "If after two typings the result proves unsatisfactory, it has always seemed to me it is better abandoned," he wrote in his autobiography. "There is less trouble and trauma involved in writing a new piece than in trying to salvage an unsatisfactory one." He once said that for him writing was a pleasure, and he generally wrote for about 12 hours a day, stopping only for meals and an occasional coffee break. He rarely took vacations

and said he never experienced the writer's block that plagues so many authors.

By his own estimate, Mr. Asimov was best known as the formulator of the "Three Laws of Robotics," which he said became the basis of more than two dozen short stories and several novels. He coined the term "robotics," he said, and its three basic laws were:

> A robot may not injure a human being or, through inaction, allow a human being to come to harm.
>
> A robot must obey the orders given it by a human being except where such orders would conflict with the First Law.
>
> A robot must protect its own existence as long as such protection does not conflict with the First or Second Laws.

Mr. Asimov's robot books included the novels *I, Robot,* published in 1950, *The Caves of Steel* (1954) and *The Naked Sun* (1957). The first of these was set in the year 2058, and it was a science fiction thriller told from the perspective of a robot psychologist, Susan Calvin. The latter two were science fiction detective stories featuring the law enforcement team of Elijah Baley, a human, and R. Dancel Olivaw, a robot. Baley and Olivaw reappeared in later stories.

In 1966, Mr. Asimov won science fiction's highest prize, the Hugo Award, for his *Foundation* series, a collection of short stories published in magazine form in the 1940s, then combined into a trilogy, *Foundation, Second Foundation* and *Foundation and Empire,* in the early 1950s. These novels were said to have been inspired by Edward Gibbon's *Decline and Fall of the Roman Empire,* and they were written as a "future history" about a society in the distant future in which the planet Earth has been forgotten and men and women are governed by an empire that has lasted 12,000 years. As his career progressed, Mr. Asimov returned time and again to his works of future history, and the series came to include themes from robot stories. A final novel, *Forward the Foundation,* was finished only months ago and will be published this year.

Mr. Asimov also was widely known for the short story **"Nightfall,"** which is the single most popular piece he ever wrote. Published in 1941, the story finished first in a poll of all-time science fiction favorites 30 years later by the Science Fiction Writers of America. It was based on a quotation from Ralph Waldo Emerson, "If the stars should appear one night in a thousand years, how would men believe and adore; and preserve for many generations the remembrance of the city of God." John W. Campbell, one of Mr. Asimov's editors early in his career, suggested to the author that he write a story about how men would react to the stars if they were visible only once every thousand years. **"Nightfall"** is the story of a civilization on a planet visited by darkness only once every 2,000 years. When nightfall occurs, the social system collapses. Campbell paid Mr. Asimov $150 for the story.

Mr. Asimov was born in the Russian village of Petrovichi, about 250 miles southwest of Moscow. The family immigrated to the United States in 1923 and settled in Brooklyn, where Mr. Asimov's parents opened a candy store. It was there that the future author first became interested in science fiction, reading stories from publications in the store's magazine rack.

He started writing science fiction while a student at Columbia University, from which he graduated and received master's and doctoral degrees in chemistry. During World War II, he worked as a chemist at the Naval Air Experimental Station in Philadelphia, then served in the Army.

After the war, he did postgraduate study on nucleic acids at Columbia, then in 1949 accepted an invitation to join the medical school faculty at Boston University. In 1950, while teaching at Boston University, he wrote his first science fiction novel, **Pebble in the Sky,** a story about a man who is transported by a nuclear accident from the 20th century to the Galactic Era 827.

With two colleagues at the medical school, Mr. Asimov wrote a medical textbook, **Biochemistry and Human Metabolism,** which was published in 1952. "That introduced me to the delights of nonfiction," he said later. "I went on to discover the even greater ecstasies of writing science for the general public."

During his years at Boston University, Mr. Asimov's classroom and laboratory duties forced him to restrict his writing to weekends. In 1958, he left teaching to write full time. His 100th book was published in 1969 and his 200th a decade later.

In 1966, he wrote **Fantastic Voyage,** a popular story about a miniaturized medical team's being injected into the bloodstream of a defecting Soviet scientist. The book later became a movie starring Raquel Welch.

He also wrote a series of juvenile science fiction novels about an astronaut named Lucky Starr, and he wrote a collection of humor and satire pieces under the name of Dr. A. These, including **The Sensuous Dirty Old Man** (1971) **Lecherous Limericks** (1976) and **Limericks: Too Gross** (1978).

Asked once by ABC Television's Barbara Walters what he'd do if he had only six months to live, Mr. Asimov answered, "I'd type faster."

His marriage to the former Gertrude Blugerman ended in divorce.

Survivors include his wife, retired psychiatrist Janet Jeppson, of New York; two children from his first marriage, David and Robyn; a sister, Marcia Rapanes; and a brother, Stanley Asimov.

> *Bart Barnes, in an obituary in* The Washington Post, *April 7, 1992, p. B6.*

Bob Greene (essay date 8 April 1992)

[*Greene is an American essayist and journalist. In the following essay, he marvels at Asimov's prolific output.*]

Even those of us in the writing business who never read a word of Isaac Asimov's work—and I must confess to being one of those who somehow missed out on his stuff—have got to salute the guy.

Asimov, who died this week at the age of 72, was famous for a lot of things—highly regarded science fiction novels, works of serious non-fiction, humorous volumes, groundbreaking books about robots—but the most impressive fact about Asimov is this:

He wrote almost 500 books.

Five hundred. Think about it. There are a lot of people who don't write 500 thank-you notes in their lives, never mind 500 books.

Actually, no one is absolutely sure about the precise number of books that Asimov wrote. According to *Who's Who,* the number of Asimov-authored books was 467, 249 of which were listed by title in his *Who's Who* entry. But the fact is, the only person who most likely was absolutely sure about how many books Asimov wrote was Asimov himself, and even he could be excused if he was off by five or six.

There were many years during which Asimov published 10 separate books. This was in addition to writing a monthly column for *Fantasy and Science Fiction* magazine (he contributed more than 400 columns and articles to that publication alone over a span of 33 years).

This is not simply a case of some eccentric guy who liked to write a lot. This was not some fellow who, say, enjoyed collecting giant rolls of twine—not some fellow to be grinned at and patronized. Writing books is hard—once you concede that it's not grueling in the same way that physical labor is, you have to circle around and say that even though you're not as likely to get a slipped disc or a hernia from writing a book as you are from lifting bricks, it's a difficult trade. There are people who spend their entire lives trying to complete a single book; more commonly, there are famous writers who routinely spend five or six years working on a book.

So here was Asimov—500 of the suckers, 500 books with his byline on the covers. Asimov could write an entire book in less time than it takes some authors to proofread galleys looking for misplaced commas.

And it's not as if the books were bad. He was the recipient of critical acclaim and of numerous awards, including, in 1966, a special Hugo Award for the best science fiction book series ever written. And if anyone could have an excuse for writing an occasional clunker. . . . Listen: If every word in today's column so far was a book instead of a word, Asimov wrote that many books. More, actually. Count for yourself.

So how did he manage to do it—and why?

"I write as a result of some inner compulsion," he told one interviewer, "and I'm not always in control of it." Asimov typed at a rate of 90 words per minute, and liked to write 2,000 to 4,000 words on an average day. He said that he genuinely had fun doing it—writing wasn't some kind of torture for him, it was an activity he enjoyed. One of his most famous quotes came when an interviewer asked him what he would do if a doctor told him he had only six months to live. "I'd type faster," Asimov said.

He was cheery about his book-writing habit. "A lot of people *can* write," he told one interviewer. "I *have* to." On the day Asimov died, I spoke with an editor who had known him slightly. "The way I understand it, the guy was an insomniac," the editor said. "He'd wake up and be unable to sleep, so he'd write away."

There are so many writers who moan and groan about the terrors of the creative process; legendary literary stories exist about talented men and women who struggle over books for a decade or more, never quite able to get the manuscript moving along. And their pain is undoubtedly real; as the eminent literary historian Dan Jenkins has pointed out, anyone who denigrates the authorial process who has never written a book "doesn't know how hard a job it is to *type* a book, never mind write one."

Which makes the accomplishments of Asimov all the more impressive. He told interviewers that every time he went three or four days without writing anything, he felt guilty or restless; he made fun of himself by saying that there was never an idea he'd had that he didn't put down on paper.

And now I'm feeling guilty that I've never read him. I think I'll get one of his books—a guy spends that much time writing, you sort of feel like you owe it to him. Reading one of Asimov's books is bound to make a person feel a little unworthy, though. You figure that in the time it takes you to read the book, Asimov would have been able to write a new one.

> *Bob Greene, in an obituary in* Chicago Tribune, *Section 5, April 8, 1992, p. 1.*

Sheldon Teitelbaum   (essay date 8 April 1992)

[*Teitelbaum frequently writes on science-fiction films for* Cinéfantastique. *In the following essay, he discusses Asimov's influence on some of America's most esteemed scientists.*]

If you ask him what he does, artificial intelligence expert Marvin Minsky will tell you that he is a robot psychologist. Or maybe a roboticist. The MIT computer scientist is quite serious about these designations and proud of his relationship with the man who invented them, Isaac Asimov.

Minsky says these professions didn't exist until they appeared in the works of Asimov, the science and science fiction author who died Monday in New York.

Minsky, who says Asimov was his childhood inspiration and later a friend, has been described as the closest living approximation to one of the author's most enduring fictional characters, robot shrink Susan Calvin, whose job was to deal with the behavioral problems of robots. Indeed, had Minsky not encountered the robot stories in the pages of John Campbell's *Astounding Science Fiction* magazine during the early '40s, the struggling field of artificial intelligence might well have been deprived of one of its leading lights.

"I remember reading the first robot stories and deciding I was going to build them," recalls Minsky, 62. "His stories asked how you could possibly impart common sense to a machine, which is something I have spent my life at."

Minsky was not alone in being thus inspired. Stanley Schmidt, a physicist who now edits *Astounding*'s daughter magazine, *Analog,* says Asimov once told him that at least half of the creative scientists he had ever encountered attributed their careers to an early exposure to science fiction.

"I haven't seen anyone do the hard research," he says,

> but I've known quite a few scientists myself, and I think I would agree with that estimate. People like Asimov and Robert Heinlein and Arthur C. Clarke and Ray Bradbury wrote about things that sounded fantastic but somehow convinced kids like me that they were possible. The existence of the space program goes back to the fact that they were planting the idea in the heads of a bunch of bright kids that, hey, we could be doing this.

Jet Propulsion Laboratory engineer George Carlysle, 39, was one of those kids. And of the titans of the genre, Asimov appealed to him most.

"As an 11-year-old reading books like the *Foundation trilogy*," he says,

> I was just agog at the possibilities. I was particularly attracted to Asimov's belief that a rational techno-culture would arise to give the world direction and save us from chaos and irrationality. It was very compelling to a mere youth not entirely familiar with how irrationality might be as much a part of human nature as the desire to learn more about science.

He was a biochemist by training, but it was as a science fiction writer that Asimov was most widely revered, and as he preferred to think of himself. Asimov's rationalist spin on robot behavior and his transfer of Edward Gibbon's *The History of the Decline and Fall of the Roman Empire* to the pan-galactic arena of *Foundation* (replete with the predictive pseudo-science of "psychohistory" which, according to Schmidt, now appears to be actually emerging as a real science) virtually revolutionized early pulp science fiction. "No one can write SF today without having been touched by his *Foundation* series," says novelist Greg Bear.

With about 500 books published, Asimov was a remarkably effective explainer of science in nonfiction as well as in his stories. Peter Nicholls, Australian-based editor of *The Encyclopedia of Science Fiction* and *The Science in Science Fiction,* believes Asimov was "a greater science journalist than he was an SF writer—possibly the best of the lot."

New York-based novelist Ben Bova concurs, who believes that Asimov "has done more to educate Americans about science than our entire school system from coast to coast."

According to Bova, Asimov's true genius was his ability to "take any subject under the sun and write about it so clearly and so simply that anybody who could read could understand it."

"His role as an explainer was colossal," says MIT's Minsky.

> His explanations were always right and to the point. He talked to everyone at every age, and he was unpretentious. If you look at other science popularizers like [Harvard paleontologist] Steven Jay Gould or even [Cornell astronomer] Carl Sagan, you get a lesson in English. It's wonderful to read or hear them talk because you're always learning new words and styles. But when you listened to Asimov . . . he'd just be telling you something.

Despite his profound effect on generations of American scientists, Asimov was oddly reluctant to stand face to face with the fruits of his imagination. Minsky recalls his own unsuccessful efforts to introduce Asimov to some actual robots he had constructed during the early '60s. Asimov demurred for close to a decade, arguing that to encounter robots at so formative a stage in their evolution would be depressing.

"He said, 'Well, if I came and looked at them I'd be stuck in the past.' I thought it was very wise of him to recognize that if you look at something in its early stages, it's going to pull you down rather than up," Minsky says.

Robert Cesarone, the assistant program manager of JPL's Deep Space Network strategy and development team, says that he'll be busy catching up on Asimov's prolific output. Cesarone, 39, has been reading SF for many years, but for some reason never got around to Asimov.

"About three or four years ago, I decided that I really ought to read the **Foundation** series if I wanted to call myself a fan," he says.

> I embarked on this, thinking this probably wouldn't be that good. Boy was I wrong. It was perhaps the best SF I had ever read, and it boasted one of the greatest characters ever invented in literature—a total despot whom you feel sympathy for.

"I can't think of anyone else who could be as inspirational," says JPL's Carlysle.

> Maybe it's something unique about the time, the postwar era, when even in the shadow of the nuclear mushroom cloud, people were convinced somehow that science and technology would lead us out of the wilderness.
>
> Asimov could appeal to a faith in the rational structure of things that can't be appealed to so readily today. . . . We've grown more jaded and cynical, and for good reason. There's a feeling a lot of this promise has also come at great cost. I think he represents an era that was a little more naive. But I hate the thought that in the process of becoming more worldly and wise about the limitations of our technology and sci-

ence, that we have exchanged it for complete cynicism about the future.

(pp. E1, E4)

Sheldon Teitelbaum, "Scientists Say Asimov Put the Stars in Their Eyes," in Los Angeles Times, *April 8, 1992, pp. E1, E4.*

The Washington Post (editorial date 10 April 1992)

[*In the following editorial, the commentator applauds Asimov's wide range of interests and the clarity with which he "translated" complex topics into readable, everyday prose.*]

Anyone lucky enough to stumble on one of Isaac Asimov's Hugo Award anthologies in the 1960s or 1970s has a pretty good idea what it must have been like to talk to the irrepressible writer of science fiction—and of science fact, mystery, criticism, essays and much else—who died Monday at age 72. Back then, Mr. Asimov was already the undisputed dean of science fiction and of a couple of other specialties, though he had not yet reached the dizzying output of later years. (At his death nearly 500 titles had appeared, and about 150 are still available through major book chains.) But the witty anthologies, in which he collected prize-winning stories and introduced their authors like guests at a banquet, made it pretty obvious that he already knew practically everything about practically everything. The impression was backed up, in due time, by books on Shakespeare, the Bible, popular culture, neurology, atomic physics and, of course, robots and space travel.

Intellectually speaking, this kind of range isn't too fashionable these days, and one charm of Mr. Asimov was that, aside from the inherent modernity of much of his subject matter, he comes across as a man from another more wide-ranging intellectual era. His outflow of prose was Victorian, almost Dickensian. His prodigious page count reflected a mind that, as he said himself, was "orderly" and blessed with the ability to assimilate large amounts of knowledge and describe them with complete clarity. His longtime editor, Truman Talley, thinks he benefited from a "film of memory" that made nearly everything he experienced or learned instantly available—and from his timing in being born on the lip of an explosion of new knowledge that put straight-forward explanations highly in demand.

The word "popularizer" sometimes dismisses that kind of talent, but Mr. Asimov himself had a more graceful word for what he did—he called himself a translator. That modesty is reflected in the writing's mild, unthreatening tone. One of his last books, **Atom,** ends its history of astonishing subatomic discoveries on a note of simple appreciation: "It shows what asking the right questions can bring about." Somehow, he must also have come by his own view, different from the conventional wisdom, as to how many things a person is allowed to be an expert on. His extraordinary capabilities aside, that breadth of interest deserves more admiration than it gets.

"Isaac Asimov," in The Washington Post, *April 10, 1992, p. A26.*

John Markoff and others (essay date 12 April 1992)

[*In the following essay, Markoff and five noted scientists—including Nobel physicist Leon M. Lederman—discuss Asimov's impact on the development of their interests and outlooks.*]

I reached the point where I could not bear to read another science fiction novel one spring day during my freshman year of college. It was the height of the Vietnam War and science fiction suddenly seemed irrelevant. I remember that moment now because I had just reread Isaac Asimov's **Foundation Trilogy** for the third time. In fact, in the preceding eight years, I had read little else besides science fiction.

There were countless trips to the library and an untold number of Ace doubles, two science fiction novels bound as one, purchased at the local junk store for 10 cents and sold back for 5. There were books by Robert Heinlein, Arthur C. Clarke and André Norton, but above all there was Asimov. His endless stream of stories about space adventures and robots were far more compelling than anything television could offer.

Like many others who grew up in the 1950's and 1960's, I came away from his books with very clear ideas about the potential of science and technology for solving the world's problems. Asimov left his readers with a sense of the adventure in technology and inspired many of them to embark on careers as scientists and engineers. The Asimov subtext was that machines were good and progress was inevitable. It was comforting reading for the generations that grew up on the brink of nuclear war.

I began with the Lucky Starr series, then read everything I could get my hands on. The **Foundation** experience encompassed the epic trilogy describing the rise and fall of a galactic civilization 10,000 years in the future.

For a teen-ager, it was compelling reading, but by the late 1960's, the Kennedy brothers had been assassinated, the civil rights marches had taken place and despite having the world's best technology, America was trapped in Vietnam. Asimov seemed increasingly disconnected from a world that was falling apart.

Ultimately, in the 80's, I returned to science fiction, intrigued by a new generation of writers with a much darker vision. Called Cyberpunk, this science fiction describes the intersection of technology and outlaw culture: modern dystopias ruled by multinational corporations where each new technology falls into the hands of opportunists and where there is no clear right and wrong.

Cyberpunk's nihilism may match the real world today more closely than Asimov's utopian vision. And last week, Asimov died. But I'm sure that in the hearts of us all—scientists, engineers, writers and others—who were deeply influenced by his work, there dwells an abiding hope that the Asimov vision will prove to be the correct one.

In any event, Cyberpunk cannot counter the influence that Asimov had on scientists like Leon Lederman or engineers like Joseph Engelberger. Their testimony is proof of the power of his ideas.

> In the early 60's, we had a few industrial robots, and some professors sought to form a learned society, to be called Robotology. I was aghast. The appellation for our discipline had been coined by Asimov in the 40's: Robotics. I am happy to say Asimov prevailed.
>
> —*Joseph F. Engelberger*

[Joseph F. Engelberger, a pioneer in industrial Robotics and chairman of a company called Transitions Research, writes:]

Some years behind Isaac Asimov at Columbia University, I followed his **I, Robot** series avidly. The impact was subliminal at the outset, but became intensely conscious by 1956, when technology made it possible to build real robots.

In the early 60's, we had a few industrial robots, and some professors sought to form a learned society, to be called Robotology. I was aghast. The appellation for our discipline had been coined by Asimov in the 40's: Robotics. I am happy to say Asimov prevailed.

Over the years we kept in occasional contact. Isaac would not come to evaluate the industrial robots we were developing nor visit universities involved in research. He felt that might contaminate the purity of his vision. But in 1989 he visited our facility, which was developing robots for personal service to humans, not just factory automatons. He saw we were working on robots to do menial service chores like commercial cleaning and running errands. He relished our dream of servants for the aged and infirm.

[Leon M. Lederman, winner of the Nobel Prize in Physics and professor at the University of Chicago, writes:]

For all of us, he was a monument. Many American scientists were drawn to science via science fiction, and Asimov's writings were read by an entire generation of scientists who grew up in the 50's and 60's.

More recently I have looked to Asimov as a popularizer of science. There is a crying need for the popular understanding of modern science. Asimov was remarkable for his ability to popularize and entertain.

He was a national resource, and there ought to be a national day of mourning for him. He had a fantastic influence on society.

There was a generation of scientists who are now between 40 and 60 who were tremendously influenced by his writing. It had adventure and it had science even though he sometimes did not understand what he was writing about. In a technical or scientific sense, it was well written and it had a sense of optimism. Intrinsic to his writing was the notion that there isn't anything that we can't master. His world view was that we can solve all the problems of the world.

[Marvin Minsky, an artificial-intelligence pioneer and computer science professor at the Massachusetts Institute of Technology, writes:]

> I first encountered Asimov's ideas some 50 years ago. I was just beginning my teens and he was only in his early 30's, yet he seemed centuries ahead. I was entranced by his stories about space and time, but the ideas about robots affected me most.
>
> After "**Runaround**" appeared in the March 1942 issue of *Astounding*, I never stopped thinking about how minds might work. Surely we'd someday build robots that think. But how would they think and about what? Surely logic might work for some purposes, but not for others. And how to build robots with common sense, intuition, consciousness and emotion? How, for that matter, do brains do those things?
>
> Isaac Asimov always encouraged his readers to try to see the world as comprehensible, to despise superstition and moral cowardice, and to think and speak clearly and simply. He was not falsely modest, but was always honest, unpretentious and humorous. To me he was among the finest of modern philosophers.

[Vladimir P. Kartsev, the director of United Nations Publishing and former head of Mir Publishers in Moscow, writes:]

> When Isaac Asimov passed away, the world lost an unbridled dreamer and at the same time a sober scientist and analyst. Asimov merged a formidable literary talent with a deep understanding of science and its meaning. He did this not only in terms of technological progress, but also in terms of the development of our own personalities, penetrating a sometimes puzzling and horrifying world of contemporary science.
>
> I remember coaxing him out to the balcony of his apartment on a high floor of a skyscraper. I was surprised by his reluctance to look down. This poet of the skies filled with unknown high-tech galaxies was afraid of heights and avoided planes. "Perhaps I am too tightly attached to the earth," he said.
>
> He was extremely influential in Russia. Almost everyone in the country has read him. *I, Robot* was his first book published in Russia. It was a small book, but hundreds of thousands of copies were printed, and it had a tremendous influence on our scientists and our intelligentsia.

[Gerard Piel, former president and publisher of *Scientific American* magazine, writes:]

> What H. G. Wells did for public appreciation and understanding of science in the first half of the 20th century, Isaac Asimov did in the second half.
>
> The wonder of his generous—torrential—response to the public's increasingly anxious in-

terest in science was his clarity and integrity. He leveled with his readers, never condescended and never overheated the story.

> He was really beginning to blossom just as we were launching *Scientific American*. Science and technology had made a breathtaking contribution to fighting World War II. Asimov and Wells both saw science and the abundance of the Industrial Revolution as having a lot to do with how the world was going to move in political and cultural terms.
>
> People were enthralled with the notion of lifting want and toil from human existence. Isaac Asimov was squarely in that tradition. Moreover, in the 1940's, science fiction was a respectable intellectual enterprise. Later it went over into fantasy and became less tied to reality as it is known in the sciences.

> *John Markoff and others, in an obituary in*
> The New York Times, *April 12, 1992, p. 8.*

David E. Jones   (review date 31 May 1992)

[*In the following review, Jones discusses* Isaac Asimov, The Complete Stories, Volume 2.]

If the measure of a man's life is, in fact, the good works that live on after him, Isaac Asimov should be remembered as a talent of galactic proportions. His recent death leaves a monumental void in the lives of those of us who vicariously, and voraciously, rode along on his fantastic literary journeys, longing for his next even as we lamentably neared the end of his last.

And although the wondrous flow of words sadly has been stemmed, the chances are still less than even that we will ever catch up to him, will cast a hungry eye on every sentence he has forged.

As the man himself wrote in the introduction to his latest publication, *Isaac Asimov, The Complete Stories, Volume 2*:

> In the first two volumes of my collected stories (this is the second), I have well over fifty stories printed, and there are still plenty more for future volumes.
>
> I must admit that it fills even me with a kind of awe. I say to myself, "Where did I find the time to write all these stories?"—considering that I have also written hundreds of books [incredibly, more than 470] and thousands of nonfiction essays. The answer is that I've been at it for fifty-two years without pausing, so all these stories mean is that I've now gotten to be a rather elderly person.

Of course, what it really means is that his was a mind that encased a thought process that never failed, an imagination that never flagged.

In explaining that his formulation of ideas was "automatic and, indeed, unstoppable," Asimov went on to write in delightful self-deprecation:

> A fellow writer died young in 1958 and got a

An excerpt from *I, Robot*

THE THREE LAWS OF ROBOTICS

1—A robot may not injure a human being, or, through inaction, allow a human being to come to harm.

2—A robot must obey the orders given it by human beings except where such orders would conflict with the First Law.

3—A robot must protect its own existence as long as such protection does not conflict with the First or Second Law.

HANDBOOK OF ROBOTICS,

56TH EDITION 2058 A.D.

. . . . .

Gregory Powell spaced his words for emphasis, "One week ago, Donovan and I put you together." His brows furrowed doubtfully and he pulled the end of his brown mustache.

It was quiet in the officer's room on Solar Station #5—except for the soft purring of the mighty Beam Director somewhere far below.

Robot QT-1 sat immovable. The burnished plates of his body gleamed in the Luxites and the glowing red of the photoelectric cells that were his eyes, were fixed steadily upon the Earthman at the other side of the table.

Powell repressed a sudden attack of nerves. These robots possessed peculiar brains. Oh, the three Laws of Robotics held. They had to. All of U. S. Robots, from Robertson himself to the new floor-sweeper, would insist on that. So QT-1 was *safe!* And yet—the QT models were the first of their kind, and this was the first of the QT's. Mathematical squiggles on paper were not always the most comforting protection against robotic fact.

Finally, the robot spoke. His voice carried the cold timbre inseparable from a metallic diaphragm, "Do you realize the seriousness of such a statement, Powell?"

"*Something* made you, Cutie," pointed out Powell. "You admit yourself that your memory seems to spring full-grown from an absolute blankness of a week ago. I'm giving you the explanation. Donovan and I put you together from the parts shipped us."

Cutie gazed upon his long, supple fingers in an oddly human attitude of mystification, "It strikes me that there should be a more satisfactory explanation than that. For *you* to make *me* seems improbable."

The Earthman laughed quite suddenly, "In Earth's name, why?"

"Call it intuition. That's all it is so far. But I intend to reason it out, though. A chain of valid reasoning can end only with the determination of truth, and I'll stick till I get there."

Isaac Asimov, in his I, Robot, *Fawcett Publications, 1950.*

---

nice obituary in the *New York Times*. Those were early years and no one expected anyone to pay attention to science fiction writers in those days. I took to brooding. When I passed on to the great typewriter in the sky, would the *New York Times* make mention of that fact, too? Nowadays I know they will but in those days I didn't. So, after I had brooded sufficiently over the matter, I wrote **"Obituary"**. . . .

"Obituary" is an intriguing tug of war between a man's pursuit of pure science and his all-too-human yearning for personal recognition. The scientist in question has discovered elementary time travel. He is able to bring back animals from the near future. However, they arrive dead. But when the point in time they have come from arrives, the corpse disappears and the live animal continues life as usual.

The scientist decides he can become known world wide by transporting himself and then miraculously coming back from the dead. But he fails to figure his much-maligned wife into the equation. He does, indeed, get to read his own obituary, but his last laugh has a hollow echo.

The tendency here is to gush over story after Asimov story. . . . [Just] be sure not to skip over **"Galley Slave,"** the story of a robot designed to perfectly proofread manuscripts, and **"The Queen's Red Race,"** about an attempt to change history and do away with the threat of nuclear war by transporting scientific knowledge back through the ages. . . .

[Also treat] yourself to one more Asimov gem, **"The Tercentenary Incident."** The father of modern robot stories explores some intriguing possibilities in a July 4, 2076 assassination tale. (Was it the president who was blown up or a robot replica programmed to represent him in public?) (pp. 6-7)

> *David E. Jones, "In Praise of Isaac Asimov's Good Works, Which Live On," in* Chicago Tribune—Books, *May 31, 1992, pp. 6-7.*

Keith Ferrell   (essay date June 1992)

[In the following essay, Ferrell provides an overview of Asimov's life and career, calling him "the Dickens of our electronic, scientific, information-oriented age."]

Isaac Asimov loved clarity above all else, save his wife and family. He shared this love of clear thinking and clear writing with his readers and audiences for more than half a century. That, on the occasion of his death, is cause as much for thanks as for sorrow. The great science communicator of our century, which is to say the greatest science communicator of all time, Isaac Asimov did more to serve the cause of rational humanism than any dozen writers or thinkers one could name.

There is a temptation in eulogizing Isaac simply to list his accomplishments. Close to 500 books, awards and honors beyond number, fame and wealth, a delightful home and social life. Along with John W. Campbell, Robert A.

Heinlein, and Arthur C. Clarke, he created modern science fiction, and a case can be made that Asimov's influence loomed largest of all. Certainly Asimov saw concepts from his fiction become paradigms in the practical world. The Three Laws of Robotics—Asimov's Laws—are the prime example of this, having made their way from the pages of his fiction into debates over the nature of the robotic and other artificial intelligences we are in the process of building. Asimov's Laws may last as long as his books.

In his nonfiction, Asimov's ambition was without boundary. He tackled every aspect of the sciences and made his way through most of the humanities as well. Shakespeare, the Bible, quantum mechanics, overpopulation, biography, sex, the nature of science fiction, physiology, exploration, the quirks and conundrums of his own personality—Isaac was not only willing to try it all, he *did* try it all, and succeeded far more often than he failed. Outside of science fiction, his novels and stories have not received the literary attention they deserve, although his lifelong detestation of critics may have prompted Isaac to view critical neglect as a blessing. Nevertheless, there is more of literary substance to his fiction than one might guess from book jackets or reviews. His prose carried readers along effortlessly. His dialogue, in some ways stilted, bore a great deal of the stories' weight. When Isaac's characters spoke, they spoke about *something*. Ideas flowed among them, propelling the stories along even as they prompted reflection and consideration on the part of the reader. One became a participant in the grand debates that raged among Isaac's creations.

And his characters! Not for Isaac to be known for self-indulgent plumbing of the neurotic soul. His people often displayed neuroses, sure, but they also displayed their ability to reach accommodation with their foibles, even to turn those foibles into assets. Much as, one might suppose, their creator had. Isaac's characters displayed feelings, goals, and dreams. Only occasionally can you feel Asimov tugging at their strings. More often than not, they tug at yours. Again, one is tempted toward the catalog: Susan Calvin and her robots, Hari Seldon and psycho-history, Lije Baley and R. Daneel Oliwaw probing mysteries in a scientific age, Andrew the artificial man who longed to be human. There are more, and they will live forever in the stories that house them.

Asimov stories are often called relentlessly logical, and up to a certain point that's true. But more is present than logic. One story, **"The Ugly Little Boy,"** is undoubtedly as logical and pitiless in its understanding of history and the forces of nature as any fiction ever written. At the same time, the story is filled with emotion, real emotion, not the histrionics and melodrama that too often pass for emotion in fiction. Read it and weep, the cliché goes; read **"The Ugly Little Boy"** and try not to.

Of course, the greatest of all of Asimov's characters was Isaac himself. As comfortable on the speaker's dais as behind the writer's keyboard, he constantly shared himself with fans and audiences. Over the last two decades, he shared a growing wisdom about our species, colored by a certain weariness over what we do to ourselves and our world. He was too much the storyteller to sermonize too often, yet the sermons—the *teachings*—are there in his work, worth your time and everyone's.

Isaac Asimov was, finally, a great writer and important—in many ways the Dickens of our electronic, scientific, information-oriented age. His work will long outlast his body, or yours, or mine, or even those of the immortal machines he envisioned. The universe of whose multifold wonders he wrote in so many forms and modes seems a dimmer place with Isaac Asimov gone. That's neither logical nor rational, but it's true.

Keith Ferrell, in an obituary in Omni, *Vol. 14, No. 9, June, 1992, p. 22.*

Additional coverage of Asimov's life and career is contained in the following sources published by Gale Research: *Children's Literature Review,* **Vol. 12;** *Contemporary Authors,* **Vols. 1-4 rev. ed., 137 [obituary];** *Contemporary Authors New Revision Series,* **Vols. 2, 19, 36;** *Contemporary Literary Criticism,* **Vols. 1, 3, 9, 19, 26;** *Dictionary of Literary Biography,* **Vol. 8;** *Major 20th-Century Writers;* **and** *Something about the Author,* **Vols. 1, 26.**

Angela Carter

May 7, 1940—February 16, 1992

(Full name Angela Olive Carter) English novelist, short story writer, poet, nonfiction writer, scriptwriter, and author of children's books.

For further information on Carter's life and works, see *CLC*, Volumes 5 and 41.

INTRODUCTION

Carter is best known for innovatively using myth, fairy tale, and eroticism to examine feminist concerns and other social and political issues related to gender roles. Many critics have praised her exploration of sexuality in such works as *The Bloody Chamber, and Other Stories,* in which traditional fairy tales are retold from the perspective of female characters to emphasize macabre and violent aspects of passionate relationships. Carter is also recognized for combining modern settings and images of popular culture with erudite literary themes. In her last novel, *Wise Children,* for example, the experiences of twin vaudevillian actresses satirically parallel those of characters from Shakespeare's plays. Lauded for her vividly imaginative prose, Carter received the Somerset Maugham Award for her novel *Several Perceptions* and the James Tait Black Memorial Prize for *Nights at the Circus.*

PRINCIPAL WORKS

Shadow Dance (novel) 1966; also published as *Honey-buzzard,* 1967
Unicorn (poetry) 1966
The Magic Toyshop (novel) 1967
Several Perceptions (novel) 1968
Heroes and Villains (novel) 1969
Love (novel) 1971
The Infernal Desire Machines of Dr. Hoffman (novel) 1972; also published as *The War of Dreams,* 1974
Fireworks: Nine Profane Pieces (short stories) 1974; also published as *Fireworks: Nine Stories in Various Disguises,* 1981
The Passion of New Eve (novel) 1977
The Bloody Chamber, and Other Stories (short stories) 1979
The Sadeian Woman and the Ideology of Pornography (nonfiction) 1979; also published as *The Sadeian Woman: An Exercise in Cultural History,* 1979

Nights at the Circus (novel) 1984
Black Venus (short stories) 1985
Wise Children (novel) 1991

OBITUARIES AND TRIBUTES

The Times, London (essay date 17 February 1992)

[*In the following obituary, the critic surveys Carter's career and major works and discusses the dark view of sexuality presented in much of her fiction.*]

There was a time when Angela Carter's evident enjoyment of the pornographic element in the literature of sexuality and her apparent relish for the macabre and the excessive in the way men orchestrate their sexual relations was perceived to be at odds with what she manifestly was—a progressive, socialistic, feminist, university-educated sort of woman, and latterly a contented wife and mother.

From the very first her writing burst the bonds of that arch restraint that had characterised the exploration of sexual situations in the novels of her contemporary (though, for the most part, somewhat older) women novelists. The world in which she operated as a writer was a far cry from their nice observation of social nuances and well-bred adulteries.

Angela Carter was an unashamed fantasist, a fabulist of daemonic energy. She dwelt naturally in the world of myth, dream and fairy tale. Above all, in writing about sex she confronted the question of whether a woman can realistically cross the barrier between her natural masochism to inhabit the sadistic terrain of the male, with a seriousness which is wholly absent from the novels of her contemporaries. She squarely faced the possibility that sex is ultimately a violent business and that women can acquiesce in that.

This sometimes led her into vulgarity. She, too evidently and too often, leaned for information on reading which ranged from the scholarly to the crudest pulp fantasy. Sometimes even her admirers might pause to wonder whether she cared about the answers to the questions she set herself. So wholeheartedly did she engage herself with sexual themes which have so long been the preserve of male novelists that a truly independent standpoint by women is very difficult to formulate without becoming strident and therefore ceasing to be literature. But she remained true to herself and emerged from this process of immersion with an uncorrupted imagination. As time went on she was accepted as being among the most original and serious women writers of her generation. This carried with it the danger of cult status. But that was not something she ever wanted for herself. Indisputably, with her, the macabre came as naturally as the leaves on a tree and was not manufactured or affected as it was in the works of so many of her fellows.

Angela Carter was born in Eastbourne and might well have been brought up on the Sussex *costa geriatrica.* But it was not to be. Grandma, a Yorkshire woman of iron resolve (Angela Carter was later to ascribe her own determination to this source), had come south to supervise the birth and felt that the south coast in the aftermath of Dunkirk was no place to bring up young children. She removed the family to the comparative safety of the Yorkshire coalfield where one of her granddaughter's earliest memories was of her standing on a slagheap and imprecating at Hitler's aircraft as they flew in to bomb Leeds and Manchester (Angela Carter's actual age at such a time suggests that myth was an early substitute for a factual memory in her dealings with the world of reality, but this was literature's gain).

Later the family moved to south London where she was educated at a girls' grammar school in Streatham. She hated the formal part of her education. More interesting were the films (sometimes ones not strictly suitable for young ladies) which her father, the second powerful influence on her life, took her to at the local cinema. Her reaction against school took a drastic form. As a subconscious objection, so she was later to claim, to the possessiveness of her mother, who had threatened to take a flat to be near her daughter should she pass into Oxford, Angela Carter developed spectacular anorexia nervosa and determined to flunk her A-levels. Her father, a man of sense and a journalist who had worked for the Press Association, saw all this was doing her no good and got her a job on the *Croydon Advertiser.* She was no journalist by nature. Her early disregard of the sanctity of fact made her an improbable member of any newsdesk which hopes to stay clear of litigation. Nevertheless, she found a niche writing record reviews and features and coexisted not unhappily with her job.

In 1960 she married Paul Carter, an industrial chemist. When, in the following year, he got a job teaching chemistry at Bristol Technical College, she went with him. For a short period she found herself being "just a wife" and spent the time between seething discontentment at the tedium, as she found it, of domestic life (this was not her husband's fault: he took her on peace marches and introduced her to jazz) and a fascination with the student and cafe life of Bristol, which she frequented in her wanderings about the streets. Then an uncle suggested she go to Bristol University, where she read English literature, immersing herself, in particular, in those areas of the middle ages which had escaped the attentions of the fanatical followers of F. R. Leavis.

She started writing as an undergraduate and made her debut with ***Shadow Dance*** (1966) which she wrote in the summer vacation of her second year. Though set in the recognisably undergraduate world of pubs, junk shop dealers and large-eyed young girls, it showed the influence of her voluminous reading with its tale of a bizarre murder carried out by a young girl who is all innocent sweetness on the surface and pure Webster's *White Devil* beneath. This work (which later embarrassed her with its Grand Guignol excesses) was followed by ***The Magic Toyshop*** in 1967 which dealt intriguingly with family relationships.

Another story strong on the mysterious and the bizarre, as well as being good on the penumbras of human nature, this nevertheless impressed critics for the control with which Angela Carter handled her material. Her third book, ***Several Perceptions,*** won her a Somerset Maugham prize in 1969 and gave her the sense of liberty which, subconsciously, she had been wanting. She and her husband agreed to part and she used her prize money to get as far away from Christian western Europe as she could. Her bolthole was Japan where she worked for a spell in the English language branch of the NHK broadcasting company and wrote ***Love*** as well as beginning ***The Infernal Desire Machines of Doctor Hoffman.*** The first, which appeared in 1971, confirmed her as someone who could deal authoritatively with the dark side of love, particularly of sibling affection, and who entwined the surreal and the macabre with the possible and the concrete in an effortless manner.

The second, which was published in the following year,

did nothing for her reputation among those who were by now really hoping to see the emergence of a major talent. Indeed, though its educated bizarreries delighted those who love anything modish, she herself was inclined to see it as something of a setback for her: "It was the novel which marked the beginning of my obscurity," she once remarked in an interview. "I went from being a very promising young writer to being ignored. . . ." This was something of an exaggeration. She kept her following and in 1984 a film version of her short story *The Company of Wolves* (originally published in *Bananas*) in 1984 brought her to a wider audience through its box office success. But as time went by there were fears that, at 40, her best work was already behind her. Later work such as *The Passion of New Eve* (1977) showed signs of succumbing to the polemicism which she had, until that point, avoided. The publication of her non-fiction *The Sadeian Woman: An Exercise in Cultural History* (1979) was provoking and perceptive but it did not get her further than her fiction does into the question which is at the heart of everything she wrote (the problem posed by Pauline Réage's *Histoire d'O*)—namely: do women subconsciously enjoy, if not actually invite, the sadistic treatment they so often get from men?

From 1976 to 1978 Angela Carter was a fellow in creative writing at Sheffield University and she later spent a year as visiting professor in the writing programme at Brown University, Rhode Island. She had scripted (with Neil Jordan) the film *The Company of Wolves* and did the same for *The Magic Toyshop,* which was made into a film in 1986.

She married, secondly, Mark Pearce, and at the age of 43 she had a son. They both survive her.

> *An obituary in* The Times, *London, February 17, 1992, p. 15.*

Salman Rushdie   (essay date 8 March 1992)

[*Rushdie is an English novelist and critic whose best-known work,* The Satanic Verses *(1988), sparked international controversy when Moslem fundamentalists denounced the book as blasphemous and called for Rushdie's punishment by death. In the following tribute, he laments Carter's death and praises her as a brilliant writer who did not receive the recognition she deserved during her lifetime.*]

I first met Angela Carter at a dinner in honor of the Chilean writer José Donoso at the home of Liz Calder, who then published all of us. My first novel was soon to be published; it was the time of Angela's darkest novel, *The Passion of New Eve.* And I was a great fan. Mr. Donoso arrived looking like a Hispanic Buffalo Bill, complete with silver goatee, fringed jacket and cowboy boots, and proceeded, as I saw it, to patronize Angela terribly. His apparent ignorance of her work provoked me into a long expostulation in which I informed him that the woman he was talking to was the most brilliant writer in England. Angela liked that. By the end of the evening, we liked each other, too. That was almost 18 years ago. She was the first great writer I ever met, and she was one of the best, most loyal, most truth-telling, most inspiring friends anyone could ever have. I cannot bear it that she is dead.

After we heard about the cancer, I rang her up and we talked about it. I said, "Angela, there's only one thing for it. You've just got to beat it, that's all." "Yeah," she said in a long, black drawl, "but what about my strong streak of Oriental fatalism?" I said: "No, listen. I'm the Oriental in this family. Would you please leave the fatalism to me, and just bloody well *win*?" "Oh," she said, as if somebody had just surprised her with a good suggestion, "O.K." And then she fought like the very devil, fought death with all her strength and all her courage, but also with her wit, her humor, her sense of its ridiculousness, her anger. Death snarled at her and she gave it the finger. Death tore at her and she stuck out her tongue. And in the end she lost. But she also won, because in her furious laughter, in her blazing satirizing of her own dying, her deflation of what Henry James so pompously entitled the "Distinguished Thing," she cut death down to size: no distinguished thing, but a grubby little murderous clown. After showing us how to write, after helping us to see how to live, she showed us how to die.

I repeat: Angela Carter was a great writer. I repeat this because in spite of her worldwide reputation, here in Britain she somehow never quite had her due. Of course, many writers knew that she was that rare thing, a real one-off, nothing like her on the planet; and so did many bewitched, inspired readers. But for some reason she was not placed where she belonged—at the center of the literature of her time, at the heart. Now that she's dead, I have no doubt that the size of her achievement will rapidly become plain. How sad that writers must die before we grant them their place in the pantheon. Of course, Angela Carter knew who she was. But we could have told her, more loudly and more often than we did, that we knew too.

Too many of the world's finest writers have been dying young lately. Italo Calvino, Bruce Chatwin, Raymond Carver and now Angela have been silenced when their voices were in the middle of their songs.

Angela's last novel, *Wise Children,* was also her finest. In it, we hear the full range of her off-the-page, real-life voice. The novel is written with her unique brand of deadly cheeriness. It cackles gaily as it impales the century upon its jokes. Like all her works, it is a celebration of sensuality, of life. More particularly, it celebrates wrong-side-of-the-tracksness, and wrong-side-of-the-blanketness too. It is a raspberry blown by South London across the Thames, a paean to bastardy (and the novel is a bastard form, never forget, so novelists must always stand up for bastards). Angela Carter was a thumber of noses, a defiler of sacred cows. She loved nothing so much as cussed—but also blithe—nonconformity. Her books unshackle us, toppling the statues of the pompous, demolishing the temples and commissariats of righteousness. They draw their strength, their vitality, from all that is unrighteous, illegitimate, low. They are without equal, and without rival.

With Angela Carter's death English literature has lost its high sorceress, its benevolent witch-queen, a burlesque artist of genius and antic grace. Those of us who have lost a friend can scarcely believe that there will be no more two-hour telephone chats with that voice that could soar to heights of scatological passion or swoop, at her most lethal moments, down into a sort of little-girl coo. Deprived of the Fairy Queen, we cannot find the magic that would heal us. Nor do we wish to be healed, just yet. We sit gazing into the huge hole her death has left, and, as we gaze into the crater of our loss, we remember.

She died on Feb. 16. Three weeks before that I gave Angela a long essay I'd written about one of her favorite films, *The Wizard of Oz,* and asked her if I might dedicate it to her. She agreed. I never found out if she was ever able to read it, which is sad. But at least in that dedication I was able to say a little of what I felt. When Dorothy asks the Good Witch Glinda if the Wizard of Oz is good or bad, Glinda replies that he is "a very good Wizard . . . but very mysterious." The Wizard of Oz turns out to be a fraud. But Angela Carter was, indeed, a very good Wizard, perhaps even the First Wizard Deluxe. A very good Wizard, and a very dear friend.

> *Salman Rushdie, "Angela Carter, 1940-92: A Very Good Wizard, a Very Dear Friend," in* The New York Times, *March 8, 1992, p. 5.*

Ann Snitow   (review date 20 April 1992)

[*In the following review, Snitow discusses Carter's unconventional treatment of family relationships and use of satirical allusions to Shakespeare's plays in her last novel,* Wise Children.]

Angela Carter died of lung cancer on February 16, age 51. For her committed readers, the loss is unbelievable. How can someone who was just in the middle of saying something so fascinating, rare and deliciously funny, all at once be dead? Almost certainly—though we can't finally measure these things—her new book, **Wise Children,** was written before she knew she was sick. On first reading, I thought it a light farrago, a repeat of old turns under the circus top, familiar to her loyal fans.

But, though we've been with Carter to strings of occasions like this before—eccentric household dinners, carnivals, magic shows, birthday parties that careen out of control—that first reading was way off. After consideration, and still quite sure that Angela had no intention of writing herself an ending here, I've come to see **Wise Children** as a complex philosophical work on the ambiguity of biological ties, on the family romance, on the theater generally (Shakespeare in particular) and, above all, on pleasure.

To some degree, this second take is no surprise: Carter has always been a demanding writer, abstract in her own rollicking way, allusive, a profoundly literary novelist of ideas. The ideas here arise out of the ever-surprising medium of one Dora Chance's raffish, also serious, attempt at writing her memoirs. She hopes for a best seller, for isn't her book about the theater, including behind-the-scenes glimpses of three generations of the gifted, beautiful and famous, also fabulous clothes, five sets of theatrical twins, jokes that are funny and magical endings like Shakespeare's romances? Even better, Dora herself, and her

twin, Nora, are "illegitimate in every way." Hers is a by-blow's story, written from the backstairs, the backstage, the dying music-hall tradition, the wrong side of the Thames, in Brixton. Like Shakespeare, gazing at everything from the Globe (which was also on the south side of the river, and appears at the end of the novel in the form of a big birthday cake), Dora sees the high and the low, takes on their different voices, mixes them in one script. And she does Shakespeare one better, making not a mosaic of difference like his but a more promiscuous melting together; her people don't sort themselves out at the end but remain scrambled in a wild democracy—to the Bard unthinkable.

Like the novel in toto, Dora is without shame, but—always the reflective twin—the *question* of her and Nora's illegitimacy haunts her. She is obsessed ("Whence came we?") and keeps trying to make sense of their origins: "Chance by name, Chance by nature. We were not planned." As far as they can gather, Dora and Nora are the unacknowledged daughters of the great Shakespearean actor Melchior Hazard (yes, dear reader, French for Chance). As the book opens, it is Dora and Nora's 75th birthday, and on this very day, which happens also to be Shakespeare's birthday, hence a day in spring, their famous father turns 100. Dora is sitting at her word processor, spinning out the family romance that has brought them all to this moment, the day of Melchior's big party, where everyone in the story will meet, change identity, reshuffle life's deck of cards and set forth again, accompanied by a song from the music halls ("Strange how potent cheap music is," Melchior told the twins one of the few times in their lives he deigned to see them):

> While teeing off a game of golf
> I may make a play for the caddy . . .
> . . . but my heart belongs to daddy.

But who is Daddy, that one's heart might belong to him? When Dora and Nora were kids, their Uncle Peregrine (or was he their father, or whose father was he?) took them to a music hall in Brighton where one Gorgeous George told the master joke, a ruling metaphor of the novel, the story of a young boy whose "thoughts turned lightly to" . . .

> So he says to his dad, "I want to get married to the girl next door, Dad."
>
> "Ho, hum," says his dad.
>
> "I've got news for you, son. When I was your age, I used to get me leg over . . . the garden wall . . . and, cut a long story short, you can't marry the girl next door, son, on account of she's your sister."
>
> The air turned blue. Mothers forced reluctant children outside, bribing with ice-cream. . . .

But the pubescent Chance sisters, soon to be in vaudeville themselves, stayed on with their Uncle Perry.

> So this boy buys a bike and . . . pedals off to Hove. . . . He comes back, he says to his father: "I've met this nayce girl from Hove, Dad."
>
> "Hove?" says Dad. "Sorry to say, son, I fre-

quently hove to in Hove when I was your age and—" . . . Say no more. . . .

This poor boy takes a train next, but up pops his father:

"We had trains in my young day, son. . . ."

The boy goes into the kitchen for a cup of tea. . . . "Looks like I'll never get married, Mum."

"Why's that, son?"

He told her all about it, she says: "You just go ahead and marry who you like, son—"

Split-second timing. That pause. Perfect.

"*E*'s not your father."

This kind of biology matters to everyone in the novel, but as in the joke, nobody seems able to get it right. They think they know who Daddy is, but they don't. More shocking, they get it wrong about Mommy, too. At first Dora thinks, "a mother is always a mother, since a mother is a biological fact, whilst a father is a movable feast." Many another feminist novelist would have left the matter right there, but not Carter. For her, the trouble is just beginning. Fathers are biology, too, in their way: "You can't fool a sperm." Then Uncle Perry suggests to Nora that she has no more idea of who their biological mother was than "whose emission sparked off our being." Was their mother, as they've been told, a Cinderella, their Grandma Chance's chambermaid? Or maybe Grandma Chance was herself the true? mother? In any case, Grandma "invented" them a family "out of whatever came to hand."

In a witty turn, Carter redefines "family romance" to mean a fiction in which a random set of people collude to love one another, to be one another's permanent destiny. "Family" becomes an idea, "love" an act of self-creation. (Carter allows herself a hilarious riff here on the troubles biological authenticity can cause one, considering how nice it would have been for Cordelia and Hamlet if someone could have danced on stage at the right moment with that punch line, "*E*'s not your father.") It's not that Carter throws biology *out*, exactly. But she keeps edging the concept of family toward the fictional—and hilarity.

At the end of the novel, Dora and Nora take on newborn twins, the next crop of Hazard bastards, and in their ecstasy at finally being parents they sing and dance in the street—

We can't give you anything but love, babies,
That's the only thing we've plenty of, babies

and "the Hazard theme song," now revealed as an anthem for the illegitimate—

"Is you is or is you ain't my baby?"

As she cavorts and pushes the double baby carriage along, Nora glimpses her new, narrative power: "We can tell these little darlings here whatever we like about their mum and dad. . . ." Finally, biology is hearsay, a tale accepted on faith, based on the protestations of other people. (At the 1990 DIA Art Foundation forum on "critical fictions"—now a book edited by Philomena Mariani, from

Bay Press—Carter lamented the new genetic tests that pretend to put an end to this complexity.) Family is a drama that unfolds. Freud holds up one side of the curtain—the family romance—and the Bard the other—the romance of the discovery scene.

Angela Carter sought a language for pleasure, a quest she took on very self-consciously as a feminist project.

—*Ann Snitow*

It was always Carter's work to retell these master accounts, the great tales, worm away at their plots, twist around their sentiments. Her Little Red Riding Hood enjoys sleeping with the wolf; the mother of the bride shoots her new son-in-law, Bluebeard, between the eyes. (For these and other radiant stories, see *The Bloody Chamber*.) Dora Chance dreams of destroying "the terms of every contract" and of setting "the old books on fire." In *Lear*, the bastard is the villain. But in *Wise Children*, God stands up for bastards at last. For the late Shakespeare, an unspoiled identity lay in lawful paternity, sealed in the final embrace between true fathers and true daughters. For Carter, that line of true descent is forever branching, a family tree gone wild. In her version, the illegitimate get to inherit, too, and they are allowed Shakespeare's special gift in the comedies, happiness.

Melchior Hazard, that pompous ass, believed of his Bard that "the whole of human life was there." Carter disagreed, and laughed at a culture that hypes Shakespeare, uses knowledge of him as a class marker and commodifies him as a National Treasure. (In one great bit, a cat keeps pissing in a sacred urn of dirt from Stratford that is meant to be sprinkled as a benediction over a haywire Hollywood production of *A Midsummer Night's Dream*.)

Carter rewrites Shakespeare, parodies him, makes fun of his icons (the Chance sisters live on Bard Road), but she has no intention of giving up her romantic duet with plays she clearly knows in her very bones. The allusions come in cascades, with an incredibly agile range of effect. A bit of rosemary caught in Dora's teeth reminds her of Ophelia's rosemary for remembrance, opening the way to precious recollection. Elsewhere that same scene from *Hamlet* replays itself as farce, as the twins' goddaughter runs mad on television and exits calling, "Hey! Somebody call me a cab, right? A cab! Right away! . . . Goodnight, everybody! . . . Sleep tight. . . . Goodnight." Dora and Nora play bellhops in the Shakespearean musical *What You Will* (variously rendered in the text: *What? You Will?, What! You Will!*, etc.). They're not sure where to deliver a package, "2b or not 2b?" Perishable as this is, it is not so very far away from their film production of *A Midsummer Night's Dream*, a magic that endures. Neither the clunky set smeared with fake fairy dust nor the grinding routine can detract from the dazzling final illusion.

Singing and dancing away, the Chance sisters faithfully give the audience their "helping of dark."

The novel's mixture of satire and silliness with homage to Shakespeare's power to enchant is very lovely. Carter dares what Shakespeare dares, his stunning reversals of fortune: Dora says it's too late for children, but it isn't. She says Uncle Perry is full fathom five, but he isn't. She says sex is over for her but, in the finale, she sleeps with Perry, even though, just like her father, he's 100. "It ain't no sin"; rather, it's magic, the late plays. The novel begins with a spring tempest and ends with the finding of the lost and with lovers meeting. This Shakespeare may be fractured, but it's beautiful.

In an interview in 1988 (some of which was published in the *Voice Literary Supplement* of June 1989), Angela Carter told me how she wished she could escape this elaborate writing of hers, the "beautiful." She envied the Australian novelist Christina Stead, who began with beauty ("exquisite rococo stories") but then "learned how to write badly." We talked this question round and round and Angela regretted that, unlike her admired mentor, she couldn't stop piling up the luminous, conspicuously clever words. She concluded that the only thing she'd been able to do to undermine her own style, this painting-an-inch-thick, was to learn how to be funny.

In *Wise Children* we can see how far Angela got with this project of using comedy to carry her work beyond the aesthetic solipsism she feared in herself. At a PEN Women's Committee meeting in 1988, she told a rapt audience she was reading theatrical memoirs but was too superstitious to say more about her current project, except that it was something "serious." Always the ironist, but still she meant it: *Wise Children* is serious. Its comedy is structural; this laughter is the pleasure that was always part of Angela's point.

Ambivalence about pleasure always interested her. On her frequent visits here, she complained about American culture's smarmy quest for "permission," a word she detested, and she wrote very funny essays about Gay Talese and Linda Lovelace on this theme (all to be found with other treasures in her collection of essays, aptly titled **Nothing Sacred**). Her original study of the Marquis de Sade, **The Sadeian Woman,** turned on the same idea: She was with Sade in his mad search for the limits, but was then disappointed when his limit turned out to be MOTHER.

Angela Carter sought a language for pleasure, a quest she took on very self-consciously as a feminist project. Pleasure was also to be for girls. Feminist critics call for this kind of writing, but the texts that actually deliver it are few. Carter's desires—ideological and literary, private and social—led her across current theoretical boundaries. Neither her polyglot word choices nor her deconstruction of myths precluded an indulgence, too, in old-fashioned closure—when she wanted that pleasure. She loved the old stories, partly because she could manipulate our nostalgia for them, but also because they delivered the goods—fantasy, distance, satisfaction, resolution. Pleasure with her was not always just a little further on, forever out of reach. She wanted it now; in contemporary parlance

(which fascinated her, always the theorist), her writing celebrated the pre-Oedipal, certainly the polymorphous and the perverse.

Wise Children offers aesthetic pleasure like a gift to the reader—elegant plot patterns, coincidences, thematic doublings, verbal leitmotifs, multiple twinning, ha, ha. Like Shakespeare, Carter is a crowd pleaser. The richness and shifting rhythms of the prose here are awesome, with now and then the dazzling, show-stopping image: When Grandma dies going to get more beer at the off-license during the blitz, the twins come home to find her empty glass, "with the lacy remnants of the foam gone hard inside it." This was a fitting goodbye from their grand, if mysterious, parent, "an old lady who looked like St. Pancras Station, monumental, grimy, full of Gothic detail."

The footman is at the door with an invitation to a party, though on another day rather like this one, he will come with a black-edged message. Angela Carter knew, better than most, that sorrow and death are always in the wings. Dora's story skips over the war that killed Grandma because, alas, "it was no carnival." Let others speak of the immovable sorrows we all face. Carter brought deep feeling to her knowledge that joy is important, fragile, more easily lost than anything. Hence entertainers have strange but precious work. The novel ends on Dora's thought, "Oh, what a joy it is to dance and sing!" She is happy, but as she knows, a happy ending depends on knowing just when to stop.

I've indulged myself by using the present tense for much of this essay, but there's no hiding from it: This loved writer is slipping away. Her thoughts, always so sensitive to the moment, will begin now to be a record of the past. Not only was she a great novelist, but also one of the very few who had any new ideas at all about sex, about men and women's desires and about the pleasures of the text. Our amazement at her is the measure of our loss; nor is there any way to comfort ourselves by pretending she'd already had her say.

Angela would have been great at old age, irritable about the loss of her senses (sans teeth, etc.) and bent on enjoying herself with whatever she had left. What should have happened, if the story went right, would have been for her to grow old like her funny, brilliant, stagy characters. At that final party, Nora Chance asks her ancient father to dance: "Give us the pleasure." (pp. 526-29)

Ann Snitow, "A Footman at the Door," in The Nation, *New York, Vol. 254, No. 15, April 20, 1992, pp. 526-29.*

John Bayley   (essay date 23 April 1992)

[*Bayley is an English critic. In the following essay, he places Carter's works in the tradition of postmodernism.*]

Postmodernism in the arts notoriously starts from the premise that "anything goes," but this is no great help if we are trying to find out what sort of fiction today is actually thought and spoken of as postmodernist. The expression has often been used about the books of Angela Carter, and so has the rather more easily definable term "magic realism." Indeed when she first started to publish in the Sixties her novels were hailed in England as an enterprising native version of the kind of thing that was being done in North America by Thomas Pynchon and in South America by Gabriel García Márquez.

The link between magic realism and the more evasive concept of postmodernism in the novel probably was that everything goes: that the hitherto separable conventions of fantasy and realism, satire and social comment, could be fused together in a single permissive whole. The process was a very self-conscious one; the novelist knew exactly how new and up-to-date he or she was being, while at the same time being careful in an egalitarian way to avoid the more exclusive and old-fashioned label of "experimental": the rigors of formalism were definitely out. But if this was postmodernism it could still be said to have been around for a long time, for critics were beginning to detect just the same brew of ingredients, even if less deliberately mingled, way back in the history of the novel. Looked at under modern eyes even *The Mayor of Casterbridge,* say, Hardy's sturdy down-to-earth survey of the rise and fall in a country town of a man of character, begins to assume a fantastic aspect, with the author's dreams and fears of failure and success clothing a fairy tale in the sober hues of business and property.

Fantasy, in short, can be seen as the basis of every novel: what matters today is the individual and original use made of it. Angela Carter scored high marks at that, from her first, *Shadow Dance* (1965), to her last, *Wise Children.* Although she is an enterprising and versatile writer, always exploring fresh themes, there is about all her novels a strong element of continuity, even communality, which may remind the reader of the claim often made for postmodernist art as "a single ongoing subcultural event" that does not distinguish between intimacy and togetherness, any more than between high art and pop art. Like other very capable modern authors Angela Carter is good at having it both ways, dressing up pop art in academic gear and presenting crude aspects of modern living in a satirically elegant style. In *Love,* her most effective and memorable novel of the Sixties, she cunningly drew a pair of youthful student hippies as a version of many traditional fraternal prototypes, including Ivan and Alyosha Karamazov. The brief novel is Dostoevskian in other ways, dramatizing a triangle of unbalanced passion and possessiveness and placing it in a squalid urban setting among students of the post-Lucky Jim type. Lee and Buzz are brothers, with an incestuous closeness between them, and Lee is pressured by her parents into marrying Annabel, who is trying to paint, and who already has episodes of madness.

The subsequent explosions leading to Annabel's suicide as she lies in bed watched over by Buzz, who has fulfilled one of her desires by shrinkingly raping her, are done with a vigor and understanding that remain impressive today, even after such Gothic goings-on in the novel have become commonplace. Carter controls the Gothic element, as well as her other literary devices, with characteristic brio, driving it firmly to a polemical end, and not indulging it for its own sake. Among other things *Love* is a vaudeville version of the Sixties, and of the young people seduced by the heady climate of the revolution seemingly so near at hand, and licensing in a communal setting whatever private violence was haunting them. A thoroughly professional artist, Carter obviously took what the fashions and emphases of an epoch sent her way. In her afterword to the revised edition of *Love* she imagines with rapid and sardonic precision the later lives of her youthful cast, who were

> not quite the children of Marx and Coca-Cola, more the children of Nescafé and the Welfare State . . . the pure perfect products of those days of social mobility and sexual license.

In the epilogue we learn that Buzz has now come out of the closet and plays in New York punk bands, meanwhile dabbling in real estate "with some success." Lee stays in dull old England, where he has found a bossy woman to patch him up after the trauma of his wife's suicide; he teaches school and becomes responsible and respectable on sound socialist lines. He is devoted to his children and severe with them, his wife having little time for them, engrossed as she is with feminist concerns:

> They row fiercely. The adolescent daughters in their attic room turn up the volume of the record player to drown the noise. Upstairs, the baby cries. The telephone rings. Rosie springs off to answer. It is the Women's Refuge. She begins an animated conversation about wife-beating, raising two fingers to her husband in an obscene gesture. . . .
>
> Suddenly the whimpering baby yawns hugely, quiets and sleeps, looking all at once like a blessed infant.
>
> The father kisses her moist meagre hair and lays her down upon her side. The older girls, trained in deference to her tyrannic sleeps, snap off their loud music but, cold-eyed strangers that they have become, continue to discuss in muted whispers their parents' deficiencies as human beings.
>
> Oh, the pain of it, thought Lee, thinking about his children, oh! the exquisite pain of unrequited love.

Note that the children of the flower children are all girls, preparing in their unillusioned and disenchanged way to lead their own styles of life. In its vigorous way the novel celebrates the Sixties but also moves on from them, questioning for new directions. It is also very funny at moments about sex, briskly aware that many happy solutions in this sphere have led to so many yet darker complications. Poor near-psychotic Buzz is excluded from what seem to the young its newly liberated joys.

> "Open your legs," he said. "Let me look."
>
> . . . Buzz crouched between her feet, and scrutinised as much as he could see of her perilous interior to find out if all was in order and there were no concealed fangs or guillotines inside her to ruin him. Although he found no visual evidence, he remained too suspicious of her body to wish to meet her eyes.

The notion of the "perilous interior," with its medieval and literary antecedents in perilous chapels and seas, affords Carter and her readers some subliminal amusement; but although she is sorry for Buzz she sticks even here to the party line: instructing us that female bodies must not be treated as objects. Still less of course as mechanical traps. Indeed if there is a common factor in the elusive category of the postmodern novel it is political correctness: whatever spirited arabesques and feats of descriptive imagination Carter may perform she always comes to rest in the right ideological position.

This was the case with her other dazzling performances in the Sixties' milieu: *The Magic Toyshop,* which was made into a film, *The Passion of New Eve, Heroes and Villains.* She shows great brilliance in updating literary and social stereotypes, and up-ending them as well. She herself invoked Benjamin Constant's *Adolphe* as the model for the doomed relationship described in *Love.* (*Adolphe,* as it happens, was also made very conscious use of in one of Anita Brookner's quietly perceptive fictions. Constant would recognize his hero and heroine in her fictional milieu but hardly in that of Carter.) And another bygone French author, Charles Perrault, would be surprised at the use Carter has made of the fairy tales he collected and popularized in his own elegant tongue. The stereotypes of Red Riding Hood and Bluebeard's wife have had their roles very much reversed in Carter's lively storybook *The Bloody Chamber* (1979). Perrault's tales, like their venerable originals, reveal the cheerful but often chilling matter-of-factness of the implicit horror, the time-honored suspense and relief: "Sister Anne, sister Anne, do you see anyone coming?" and "All the better to eat you with!"

Carter not only switches her narrative into the wholly explicit but turns the passive predicament of the heroine into one in which the convention of female role-playing seems to have no part, only brisk and derisive common sense, the best feminine tactic in a tight corner. Her Red Riding Hood is a slyly confident adolescent, removing her clothes with a sneer to enter the wolf's bed. When he speaks the hallowed formula, "All the better to eat you with!" "the girl burst out laughing: she knew she was nobody's meat." The wolf is not discomfited, but being a politically correct animal at heart he enfolds her in an egalitarian embrace, and they go blissfully to sleep in the eaten-up granny's bed.

Bluebeard's latest wife is equally cool-headed in her sexual collusion with the demon lover who is both father and husband. Interestingly, Carter's new-style heroines have one point in common with many of their prototypes in fairy tales: they could come from any country and belong to any class. Carter's brand of magic realism is also a democratic magic. In her introduction and arrangement of the stories collected in her anthology, *The Old Wives' Fairy Tale Book,* she distinguished between the different traditional feminine categories: natural witches; bad, because resourceful, girls; "good girls and where it gets them." The same enlightening categorization is to be found in her essays and theoretical writings, *Nothing Sacred* and *The Sadeian Woman: An Exercise in Cultural History.* The latter is a sardonic study of the two types who have supplied the mainstay of pornographic literature: the virtuous and therefore helpless girl, and the wicked lady. They are the Justine and Juliette of de Sade's fiction; and Carter's arguments emphasize that de Sade performed an important service in drawing attention by pornographic means to the tyranny that such man-made stereotypes imposed on women of the time, and for centuries before and since. As Voltaire satirized in *Candide* the fate of innocence and optimism in a wicked world, so de Sade revealed the fate of all women, who in a man's world had no choice but to be what men required. Justine was the stereotype of the abused wife, and Juliette the seductively wicked prostitute mistress.

Carter's essays are as vigorous as her fiction, but necessarily dated now that such insights have become received wisdom and thus commonplace. However "correct" Carter's novels may be they all demonstrate the brio and originality of true personal talent, as she showed by excursions into her own style of science fiction—*Heroes and Villains* and *The Infernal Desire Machines of Dr. Hoffman.* Although written with all her ebullience these books seem to me less memorable than earlier novels like *Love* and to be more purely "performance" novels, designed to appeal to a diverse audience.

Another of postmodernism's purely negative qualifications is that it is not "elitist": that is to say does not possess the kinds of private and individual distinction which recommend themselves to a small audience. *Heroes and Villains* is a romp allegory appealing to everyone suspicious of such minority tastes, for the heroine is a professor's daughter who has to live down that stigma by being captured by a beautiful barbarian and carried away to a paradise of primitivism, sex, and greenery. Carter uses a scenario similar to those of Swift or Orwell but without any apparent irony (irony is necessarily elitist because some may not see the point) although—to be fair—irony comes into her work of science fiction, *The Infernal Desire Machines of Dr. Hoffman,* in which a war is fought against the diabolic doctor who wants to destroy the "reality principle." A grotesque embodiment of the male principle, Dr. Hoffman is a mad scientific deconstructionist, part Mary Shelley's Frankenstein, part Dostoevsky's Grand Inquisitor.

In 1985 Carter's first experiment in radio drama produced *Come Unto These Yellow Sands,* based on the unnervingly beautiful fairy paintings of Richard Dadd, the Victorian artist who went mad and killed his father. She even spoke of "re-inventing" the paintings of Jackson Pollock with the same kind of drama performance, remarking in her cheerful way, "*That* would be a challenge." Meanwhile she exploited her talent for colorful and rollicking vaudeville plots in *Nights at the Circus* and in her latest—and, alas, last—novel, *Wise Children.* Carter's imagination has always been inspired by a stage ambiance, and the kinds of living that go with it, but *Wise Children* also associates itself with a new sort of fashion in fiction, one very effectively exemplified by two short and modest English novels recently reviewed by me in [*The New York Review of Books,* April 9, 1992]: David Lodge's *Paradise News* and Penelope Fitzgerald's *The Gate of Angels.* It is well-known that in the novel a good man is hard to find: one of the most convincing appeared a long time back in Saul Bellow's *Mr. Sammler's Planet.* With the two other English novels *Wise Children* sets out on the same journey, to explore the quality and desirability of virtue, the nature of the *honnête homme* or the *honnête femme.*

Carter's honest narrator in *Wise Children* is one of a pair of twins who have spent their lives in show business: the London music halls when young, and Hollywood in their later years. Inspired no doubt by the Dolly Sisters, a charming photo of whom decorates the cover, these heroines were conceived and born in unprepossessing circumstances, their mother being a waif of the stage door known as Pretty Kitty. Throughout an eventful lifetime the pair have remained innocents at heart, and virtuous as well, although not, of course, in what used to be the technical sense. Carter sets herself to demonstrate that the jungle law of the casting couch and the tawdry world of stage and screen can nonetheless be pure at heart, peopled not by tigers but by does and fauns, creatures who may be grotesque but are also endearing. It says much for Carter's literary charm and drive that she makes this seem perfectly possible. Her own brand of magic seems to infect her cast, and to make them believe in the magical reality of the tinsel and trappings in their hard-worked lives.

Literary models lurk as usual in the background. Dickens would at once have seen the point of *Wise Children,* and might have suggested calling the pub where its characters meet, "The Twelve Jolly Thespians," after his own Thames-side pub in *Our Mutual Friend.* Carter has also skillfully taken a leaf out of J. B. Priestley's best seller of the Twenties, *The Good Companions,* stripping its romance of sentimentality and giving its hearty fellowship the proper party line. She is also well aware that bewitching foundlings are a sure hit with any audience. Dora and Nora Chance—it is the first named who writes the record—have been on the boards from their tenderest years up to the moment when Nora begins to throw her heart away "as if it were a used bus ticket."

> She had it off first with the pantomime goose, when we were Mother Goose's goslings that year in Newcastle upon Tyne. The goose was old enough to be her father and Grandma would have plucked him, stuck an apple up his bum and roasted him if she had found out, and so would the goose's wife, who happened to be principal boy. . . .
>
> The goose had Nora up against the wall in the alley outside the stage door one foggy night, couldn't see your hand in front of your face, happily for them. You don't get fogs like that, these days. . . .
>
> Don't be sad for her. Don't run away with the idea that it was a squalid, furtive, miserable thing, to make love for the first time on a cold night in a back alley with a married man with strong drink on his breath. He was the one she wanted, warts and all, she *would* have him . . . while I stood shivering on the edge like the poor cat in the adage.
>
> But we never found out she was pregnant until

she lost it in Nottingham, the Royalty, when she haemorrhaged during a *fouetté,* we were a pair of spinning tops. Nothing like real blood in the middle of the song-and-dance act. It was long past pantomime, the goose gone off to Glasgow to do a *Chu Chin Chow,* he never wrote. Nora cried her eyes out but not because she'd lost the goose. . . . No. She wept the loss of the baby.

Oh, my poor Nora! She was a martyr to fertility.

"Nothing like real blood in the middle of the song-and-dance-act." Carter has always been keen on blood as a symbol of sexual emancipation. The wolf-girl from her updated fairy stories in *The Bloody Chamber* is inducted via menstruation into a correct and liberated social and sexual awareness. The title *Wise Children* is reminiscent of that controversial 1970s study of the subject called *The Wise Wound,* which equated the feminine cycle with all the female virtues opposing male violence and aggressiveness. But it is only fair to say that in *Wise Children* the men are as warm-hearted and as essentially humane as the women. Nora and Dora Chance turn out to be the illegitimate children of—who else?—Sir Melchior Hazard, the greatest Shakespearean actor of the day, whose hundredth birthday celebrations lead to the novel's inevitably hilarious climax. The reader more or less immune to stage charms may have experienced a certain amount of tedium by then, but it has been a gallant show, the cast supported by a producer nicknamed Genghiz Khan, and an elfin Irish alcoholic and scriptwriter who becomes Dora's boyfriend, possibly even the love of her life.

As she grows older Dora's mellowing mimetic arts let slip the occasional Wildean epigram such as "Every woman's tragedy is that after a certain age she looks like a female impersonator." One of Carter's chief talents has been to help create a new kind of persona for real women to copy. The Carter girl of the Eighties, with her sound principles, earthy humor, and warm heart, has become a recognizable type: in a sense all too recognizable, for if you are not like that by nature you have to work hard at maintaining the pose. In Carter's latest writing the show is the thing, and as every pantomime-goer knows, putting on a prodigious warmth of heart for the benefit of the kiddies can look like and even be the real thing. Dora's solid eighteen-carat whimsy rejoices in "laughter, forgiveness, generosity, reconciliation," and also in the well-timed wink with which she tells us such things will be "hard to swallow, huh?" Not necessarily. *Wise Children* is very readable, though it may not appeal to admirers of Carter who prefer her in a more wild and provocative mood.

The stage is the beginning of sincerity, as Oscar Wilde might have said. Carter's questing intelligence and the theatrical virtuosity of her language have greatly assisted her championing of new ideas and causes. But would her fictions invite a second reading, or does the vitality die in the performance? Would she continue to move us? *Love* may have the edge there, for its forlorn trio lingers in the mind with the pathos of those abandoned in a former lifestyle, although she sought in her afterword to bring them up to date. The impact of her plots and her prose can nonetheless seem to coincide too exactly with what enthusiasts and publicists say about them. No one who reads the glittering superlatives on a novel's jacket expects to find them precisely mirrored by the writing inside, and it is a trifle disconcerting to find in a Carter novel just those "stylish, erotic, nightmarish jewels of prose," and "a colourful embroidery of religion and magic," which reviews and blurb had promised. A process of inflation seems unavoidable.

In one of her *Common Reader* essays Virginia Woolf remarked of Jane Austen's juvenilia that they contained phrases and sentences clearly intended to outlast the Christmas festivities for which they had been written. However effective and well done they may be, few novels today seem aware of the old canonical notion of "good writing": they can even seem programmed for auto-destruction and replacement by more of the same. In postmodernist terms that is not necessarily a bad thing. It indicates that the job has been done, the point made. Archetypal narrative is founded on what is written but unspoken; modern narrative on what is said and claimed, and therefore can be superseded. Even when transmitted through the warm-hearted wisdom of Dora Chance, Carter's own message is unmistakable; the same could be said of her rewritten fantasies and fairy stories. Told by Grimm or Perrault, or even by Andrew Lang in his "Fairy Books," blue, green, and red, those old tales remain free and enigmatic. Retold by Angela Carter, with all her supple and intoxicating bravura, they become committed to the preoccupations and to the fashions of our moment. When Beauty is in the power of the Beast, in his baroque sinister palace, she cannot help letting out "a raucous guffaw: no young lady laughs like that! my old nurse used to remonstrate." In Carter's pages all young ladies do.

A room of one's own, or a bloody chamber? The new role model for women may seem to deny them the literary gift of privacy. But it is sad that so gifted a writer as Angela Carter, who died of cancer in February at the early age of fifty-one, will not be continuing to explore and define her new worlds in fiction. Her great talents would certainly have come up with new surprises. They say that wise children know their own fathers, and she certainly knew hers, while rejecting any concept of patriarchy. Jane Austen

and the Virginia Woolf of *Orlando* and *The Waves* would have recognized her as one of themselves and been greatly interested by her books, although they might have missed in them the privacy and individuality, the more secret style of independence, which they valued as much as good writing, and which is the supreme gift to us of their novels. Carter's achievement shows how a certain style of good writing has politicized itself today, constituting itself as the literary wing of militant orthodoxy.

This was of course not true of an earlier generation of "magical" writers like Nabokov, Borges, or Calvino, who assumed that male experience was central. Margaret Atwood, author of *The Handmaid's Tale*, has written movingly of Carter as the fairy godmother who herself so wonderfully looked the part, seeming to offer a talisman which would guide her friends and readers through enchanted forests and charmed doors. For Atwood, Carter was the supreme subversive; but the magic talisman of female subversion, though it could turn even de Sade's victims into early feminists, was also an ambiguous gift, making imagination itself the obedient handmaid of ideology. That would not worry many in the latest generation of critics, who read literature past and present by the light of political correctness. But Carter's new woman combines correctness with being a sort of jolly feminine Tom Jones, what Carmen Callil in a loving obituary has called "the vulgarian as heroine." "**Wise Children,**" she continued, "is a novel of Thatcher's Britain, a Britain split in two." This of course may not be of great interest to Europe or America, but Mrs. Thatcher as the national anti-heroine certainly looms in the background of Carter's work. She and Angela Carter could be seen as making a new heraldic opposition on the royal crest: the lion and the unicorn still fighting for the crown. (pp. 9-11)

John Bayley, "Fighting for the Crown," in The New York Review of Books, *Vol. XXXIX, No. 8, April 23, 1992, pp. 9-11.*

Additional coverage of Carter's life and career is contained in the following sources published by Gale Research: *Contemporary Authors*, Vols. 53-56, Vol. 136 [obituary]; *Contemporary Authors New Revision Series*, Vol. 12; *Contemporary Literary Criticism*, Vols. 5, 41; *Dictionary of Literary Biography*, Vol. 14; and *Major 20th-Century Writers*.

M. F. K. Fisher

July 3, 1908—June 22, 1992

(Full name Mary Frances Kennedy Fisher; also wrote under the names Victoria Bern and Mary Frances Parrish) American essayist, short story writer, memoirist, novelist, translator, journalist, and author of children's books.

INTRODUCTION

Fisher is best known for essays and reminiscences in which she used food as a metaphor for life and culture. Many of her works are considered classics on gastronomy, including *Serve It Forth, Consider the Oyster, How to Cook a Wolf, The Gastronomical Me,* and *An Alphabet for Gourmets,* which were later collected as *The Art of Eating: Five Gastronomical Works.* Fisher frequently incorporated into her writings vivid memories of her travels and experiences in Europe, some of which are collected in her memoir *Long Ago in France: The Years in Dijon,* which has been lauded for its sensual and engaging prose style. Although early critics frequently overlooked Fisher's works because of their domestic subject matter, later reviewers considered Fisher one of America's most accomplished essayists, and she was elected to the American Academy of Arts and Letters in 1991. Raymond Sokolov asserted: "In a properly run culture, Mary Frances Kennedy Fisher would be recognized as one of the great writers this country has produced in this century."

PRINCIPAL WORKS

*Serve It Forth [as Mary Frances Parrish] (essays) 1937
*Consider the Oyster [as Mary Frances Parrish] (essays) 1941
*How to Cook a Wolf (essays) 1942
*The Gastronomical Me (essays) 1943
Here Let Us Feast: A Book of Banquets (nonfiction) 1946
Not Now But Now (novel) 1947
*An Alphabet for Gourmets (essays) 1949
The Physiology of Taste [translator and editor] (nonfiction) 1949
A Cordiall Water: A Garland of Odd & Old Recipes to Assuage the Ills of Man or Beast (nonfiction) 1961
The Story of Wine in California (nonfiction) 1962

Maps of Another Town: A Memoir of Provence (memoir) 1964
The Cooking of Provincial France (nonfiction) 1968
With Bold Knife and Fork (nonfiction) 1969
Among Friends (memoir) 1970
The Boss Dog (novel) 1991
Long Ago in France: The Years in Dijon (memoir) 1991

*These works were published as *The Art of Eating: The Collected Gastronomical Works of M. F. K. Fisher* in 1954 and reprinted as *The Art of Eating: Five Gastronomical Works* in 1976.

OVERVIEWS AND CRITICISM

Joseph Coates (review date 10 March 1991)

[*In the following review, Coates praises Fisher's* The Boss Dog *and* Long Ago in France: The Years in Dijon *as vibrant and charming depictions of life in France.*]

"I know at least a couple of tricks which some people consider shoddy, especially newspaper people," begins M. F. K. Fisher's afterword to her novel ***The Boss Dog***—and one of them is the gift for writing leads like that one. With a brief sentence or paragraph she hooks the reader and doesn't let go until the last word of whatever unclassifiable but captivating piece of writing she's working on at the moment, each of which seems to be a ratatouille of food column, travel piece, personal confession and novel.

Of the Fisher books under review, ***Long Ago in France: The Years in Dijon*** is a memoir and the other, ***The Boss Dog,*** is fiction. But though the events in them occur a quarter-century apart, they have a linked, luminous theme: the initiation into the apex of civilized living in two provincial French cities at a charmed time in the life of, first, the author when she was a newlywed of 19 and, later, of her two daughters, aged 9 and 13, when the author was over 40 and trying to choose between France and California as a permanent place for the three of them to live.

"I wanted them to learn French while they were young, almost as much as I wanted and needed to speak it again myself," Fisher says in ***The Boss Dog,*** and this crisp and whimsical novel is like a distillation of the reasons for her homesickness for a place that was not her home but of which she became, and remains, a lifelong "ghost"—a constant spiritual inhabitant whether she happens physically to be there or not.

The unique thing about her essentially autobiographical writing is that it takes us deep inside as intricate a sensibility as America has produced since that of another Francophile, Henry James, and candidly describes all the things that formed it with Gallic lucidity and precision while remaining essentially mysterious—for Fisher is a person of deep reticences and startling contradictions, despite her casually candid references to the most personal things.

Through her we experience, with wit, clarity and gusto, a richly sensuous life that seems to have properly begun only in Dijon, where she and her husband went after their marriage in 1929 to study and write. There is sometimes an icy chill when she describes the astonishing and disagreeable people she often came to love in spite of themselves, but her exquisite perception seems also to co-exist comfortably with a Rabelaisian coarseness. She can handle anything.

Aside from her, only Rabelais or Balzac could have brought so pungently to the page Madame Ollangnier, the lusty landlady of an almost insane peasant frugality and shrewdness from whom she hesitantly rented a pension for herself and her husband. In physical terms, it's an awful place with 17th Century plumbing, but Fisher, loving it in all its Frenchness, "said haltingly that we would arrive the next noon."

" 'We?' she said with a sharp mocking voice that I was to know very well, and grow fond of."

" 'Yes . . . my husband . . . I am married.' "

"She laughed loudly. 'All right, all right, bring your friend along," she said, "dismissing her new tenant "with a mixture of affection and innate scorn, which I soon learned she felt for all creatures, but mostly humans."

One evening at dinner, which "probably . . . had been scraped up from the pavement somewhere, but . . . beautifully cooked," she discusses the great gastronome Brillat-Savarin with her landlord and admits that this was the first time in her life "I ever *talked* about food." But soon she is describing with the relish of a Colette a meal of a dozen oysters, "then a dozen snails, then some ripe cheese from the Cistercian abbey. . . . I drank a glass of dry white vermouth first, nothing with the almost violently alive sea-tasting oysters. . . . Nobody paid any attention to my introspective and alcoved sensuality."

Later she and her husband are consuming 5- and 6-hour meals with the ancient and honorable Club Alpin, a hiking and gustatory society, and find themselves daunted, if fascinated—"two thin little American shadows convinced for a time . . . that they were cousins of Gargantua."

After three years the Fishers find they have to flee or lose their livers to the rich Burgundian cuisine, described by a disgusted non-Dijonnaise French friend as "ancient meats mummified with spices, exhumed and made to walk again like zombies . . . dead birds rotting from their bones, and hiding under a crust five men have spent their lives learning how to put together so my guts will fall apart!" But before they leave, we have met a vividly dramatized gallery of pensionnaires, harlots high and low, foreign students and provincial French people of every metier and of nearly unbelievable idiosyncrasy.

Compared with this rich casserole, ***The Boss Dog*** is a souffle so light and crisp that it shouldn't be poked too hard with either synopsis or even praise. Some readers may find it unbearably fey because it's essentially a children's story along the lines of E. B. White's *Charlotte's Web,* but it's better, I think.

Set in Aix-en-Provence in the early '50s, ***The Boss Dog*** is about an authoritative and knowledgeable mutt who takes under his paw three Americans—a mother and her two daughters—who instantly recognize him as a *personnage formidable.* "That's King Arthur!" exclaims Mary, the youngest.

It's the kind of novel that adults who savor good writing will read to their children at bedtime while wondering how long it'll be before the kids will understand how rich and fine it really is. Or conversely, these same grownups will wish someone had been able to read it to them when they were 7 or 10. Let one risky, funny sentence about the family's first sight of Boss Dog show how Fisher constructs an instant magical world out of broken syntactical rules:

> They all looked toward the door [of the cafe] onto the great square circle, where the buses went whirling by and where the fountain

splashed and spat, and where there seemed to be a gentle endless tide of old and middle-aged and young women and baby carriages, all full of children either about to be born or eight months old, the latter smiling and cackling and waving.

Writing like this will make ghosts out of people who've never set foot in Europe and set aglow in their minds a small cheerful hearth at every mention of the words Burgundy and Provence.

Joseph Coates, "A Fervent Francophile," in Chicago Tribune—Books, *March 10, 1991, p. 6.*

Jane Giffen   (review date April 1991)

[*Giffen is an American critic and editor. Below, she praises Fisher's poignant use of realism in* Long Ago in France: The Years in Dijon.]

M. F. K. Fisher has long been admired for her gastronomic writing, but the accolades for her past work do little to prepare the reader for the sweet experience of reading her latest book, a memoir entitled *Long Ago in France: The Years in Dijon.* Few books have filled me with such an exquisite longing, not only for the France that I love, but for the one that Fisher knew and loved; the feeling is all the more poignant because the two are not so very different.

Fisher arrived in France just two weeks after her first marriage in 1929, to spend three years in Dijon studying at the *Ecole des Beaux Arts* while her husband, Al, wrote his dissertation. Looking back at her younger self with the wisdom of her 82 years, Fisher tells the story of a young woman learning to live, her marriage, disappointments, opportunities lost, and even some foreshadowing of her eventual divorce, years later.

The book is also, of course, a primer on the pleasures of the table as Fisher came to know them in these years. Here, as elsewhere, Fisher's genius lies not so much in her subject matter as in the way she conveys it. Brasseries, cafés, and meals, characters, apartments, and markets: all are described with a realism that is completely absorbing. She writes at length about the families she and Al boarded with and poignantly reports her youthful reactions to their pettinesses and their strengths.

Fisher can relate a culinary experience in a way that makes it linger in the reader's mind long after. For example, an aging grandfather plans a springtime meal of snails for weeks. Bringing branches into the house and rubbing the leaves between his fingers, he predicts when the snails will be at their peak. Once harvested, purged, and blanched, their shells cleaned with tiny brushes made in Paris, the snails are cooked in herbs and butter and served. The memory is so superbly rendered, I will never eat snails again without thinking of those tiny brushes.

In North America, where too often meals are plates of food served up in haste, this book is a homage to true gastronomic pleasure.

Jane Giffen, in a review of "Long Ago in

France: The Years in Dijon," in Quill and Quire, *Vol. 57, No. 4, April, 1991, p. 30.*

Anne Tyler   (review date 28 April 1991)

[*The winner of the 1989 Pulitzer Prize, Tyler is a widely respected American novelist, short story writer, critic, nonfiction writer, and editor. In the following review, she praises Fisher's evocation of memories through vivid descriptions of food in* Long Ago in France: The Years in Dijon, *while faulting* The Boss Dog *as a less successful work. She also questions the negative view of Fisher's personality presented in Jeannette Ferrary's biography* Between Friends: M. F. K. Fisher and Me *(1991).*]

Mention M. F. K. Fisher and almost everybody thinks of food—or more accurately, of food *literature,* of the fine art of describing a long-vanished meal so vividly that the reader can almost taste it. It's a natural assumption. Who else's autobiography would include a chapter called "The First Oyster," occurring at about the same point where another writer might have discussed her first love affair?

In fact, though, food often functions merely as Fisher's particular form of shorthand—an economical means of summing up a memory entire. In *Serve It Forth* (1937), she recalled a favorite dish from a period she and her first husband spent in Strasbourg early in their marriage. Her recipe required sitting in a window, watching soldiers pass while peeling several tangerines. The separated sections lay toasting on the radiator all morning, and then after a leisurely lunch with her husband she chilled them in the snow outside on the windowsill. In a few minutes they were ready to eat.

But her instructions didn't stop there. She went on to say *how* to eat them: how to sit observing the scene in the street below as you slowly consume your tangerines. Why are they so magical? She wonders. "Perhaps it is that little shell, thin as one layer of enamel on a Chinese bowl, that cracks so tinily, so ultimately under your teeth. Or the rush of cold pulp just after it. Or the perfume. I cannot tell."

Mouth-watering though this passage is, I doubt that many of her readers have rushed off to heap their own radiators with tangerines. Instinctively we know that to make that recipe work we'd also need the city of Strasbourg, the soldiers marching past, and not least, the brand new husband.

And we'd need M. F. K. Fisher's marvelous capacity for enjoyment. For isn't that what sets her apart? She can be crotchety, opinionated and prone to exaggeration—all these traits emerge, at one time or another, from her 20 or so books—but she has a rare and great talent for giving herself over to the experience of the moment. Generally her account of a meal is like a suspensefully plotted story in which good fairies (the disheveled chef in the kitchen, the stony dignified waiter) bestow upon the unsuspecting Mary Frances Kennedy Fisher a gift of love; and if she is lucky in her benefactors, they are no less lucky in their recipient.

It was in Dijon, she says, that she "learned it is blessed to receive." Dijon was where she and her first husband spent the first three years of their marriage, from 1929 to 1932. Admirers of *The Gastronomical Me* (1943) already know how, as a young American reared largely on white sauce and boiled dressing, she underwent a kind of epiphany while celebrating her three-week anniversary at a superb Dijon restaurant. Now, in *Long Ago in France,* she has pulled together some of those previously published reminiscences and enlarged upon them to give us a fuller sense of her whole sojourn.

[Food] often functions merely as Fisher's particular form of shorthand—an economical means of summing up a memory entire.

—Anne Tyler

The book is quintessential Fisher—crisply written, colorful, blunt. (One landlady "was a stupid woman, and an aggravating one"; she "was bedraggled and shiny and often smelled," but Fisher liked her anyway. Dijon itself "was ugly, as a matter of fact. The walls were always damp, and it was a gray, dim, dark town, very provincial.") Not surprisingly, the food descriptions are wonderful—the "terrines of pate ten years old under their tight crusts of mildewed fat," the "almost violently alive sea-tasting oysters"—and as always, they *mean* something; they reveal the very soul of a particular place and time.

Less successful is *The Boss Dog,* a knee-high view, so to speak, of Aix-en-Provence. Its hero is a raffish mongrel whose mysterious activities fascinate a visiting American woman and her two little girls. A book so slender and fanciful might be taken for juvenile fiction, except that the tongue-in-cheek tone would sail right over any self-respecting child's head. (After a waiter has recited the dessert list, "the mother savored the subtleties and the comprehension of this announcement, in a language still too subtle and all-comprehensive for her children.") For a deeper sense of Aix-en-Provence, you're better off with *Map of Another Town,* her 1964 memoir of that same visit.

Finally, we have M. F. K. Fisher as seen from outside. Jeannette Ferrary (a food writer herself, co-author of *California American Cookbook* and *Season to Taste*) wrote her a fan letter in 1977 and after a brief correspondence was invited to lunch. *Between Friends* is Ferrary's account of subsequent visits back and forth, meals shared and letters exchanged.

It's a peculiar book, because despite its worshipful attitude it paints a portrait of a decidedly difficult woman. Fisher's fierce judgmentalism, which always before seemed a valuable part of her professional equipment, here bears an uncomfortable resemblance to plain old spleenishness. At her first meeting with Ferrary, when she attacks all the foods that Ferrary had considered bringing as hostess gifts

(but fortunately did not), the reader starts wondering if there's any food she *does* approve of. Later we're told, "Her criticism of any ostentation or injustice was merciless; her analyses of people she didn't care for left them not a shred of vestigial goodness." And "she did have these unpleasant tendencies: she hated it when people made a fuss, but she was insulted if they didn't."

Well, heaven knows, M. F. K. Fisher never has come across to her readers as easygoing. But unpleasant? One has only to think of that young girl in Strasbourg, delicately sinking her teeth into a tangerine. She was certainly pleasable there. If she's not the same in real life (for Jeannette Ferrary's book does ring disconcertingly true), I don't want to hear about it. I'll just go back to her own works, thank you, and lose myself once more in some of the freshest, richest and most *enjoying* prose ever written. (pp. 4-5)

Anne Tyler, "Recipe for Living," in Book World—The Washington Post, *April 28, 1991, pp. 4-5.*

Ruth Reichl   (essay date 6 June 1991)

[*In the following essay, based on an interview, Fisher discusses her views on writing and significant events in her life and career.*]

Mary Frances Kennedy Fisher lies in her bed, propped up on pillows, eating oysters.

At 84, it is one of the few sensual pleasures left to the woman whose impeccable prose introduced two generations of Americans to what she called the "Art of Eating." Her genius has been her absolute insistence that life's small moments are the important ones. "People ask me," she wrote, in the most-quoted passage from her 30 books, "why do you write about food, and eating and drinking?" The answer: "There is a communion of more than our bodies when bread is broken and wine drunk."

Fisher's own body has, at this moment, betrayed her. Her voice has been reduced to an almost inaudible whisper, her hands cannot write much more than a signature, and her eyes no longer permit her to read. Movement is difficult. If any of this bothers her, she would not deign to show it; she is as imposing now as she was when I interviewed her for the first time 15 years ago.

"But how will you talk to her?" people have asked with alarm. These days her many visitors (Cyra McFadden was here yesterday; Alice Waters will be here the day after tomorrow) tend to come in packs and, in entertaining one another, entertain their hostess. What I found is that conversation is no problem: M. F. K. Fisher is still so intense that she virtually wills you to understand her whispers.

"Please don't whisper" is almost the first thing she says. Visitors unconsciously lower their own voices until they are no louder than hers. But Fisher will not suffer condescension. The sounds are soft on her Sonoma ranch: Occasionally a beeper gives out a peremptory honk, and there is the swish of cars moving on the road below, but the loudest noises are the quiet murmur of the television in the nurse's bedroom next door, the radio's gay, if slightly incongruous, tinkle in the living room and the thunk of the cats as they land on Fisher's bed. Into this silence her whispered command has the effect of a shout.

Things are awkward at first. She begins by putting down the oyster, sipping on a mysterious pink drink and talking—if these all-but-inaudible mouthings can be called talk—about the two new books she has just published. These are **The Boss Dog,** stories about life in Aix-en-Provence in the '50s with her two young daughters that make you wish, with all your heart, that you could have been there with her, and **Long Ago in France,** a compilation of stories from the '30s when Fisher was young, in love and living in Dijon.

She accepts congratulations for her election—just announced—to the American Academy of Arts and Letters. She says—as she always does to people who ask—that she does not consider herself a writer. (Asked which of her own books is her favorite, she has always taken the most modest route and chosen *The Physiology of Taste:* "I didn't write that, you know. Brillat-Savarin did. I just translated it," she says for what must be the hundredth time.)

Fisher goes on to say that she is working on three new books, dictating every morning when her voice is strongest. "Writing is just like dope," she says. "I have to get my fix every day." She gestures off toward the corner of the room, where there are stacks of boxes, overflowing with papers. "There are thousands of pages. It's impossible to put into order," she says with a little sniff of disdain, as if this were something of which she were vaguely ashamed.

"I've always written naturally," she says now, as if that minimized her accomplishment. "It was just something I did." She insists that writing is so much a part of her that even her children Anne and Kennedy, to whom she refers as "nice girls," never thought of her as a writer.

Can this be true? I wonder, leaving Fisher's bedroom to allow her to rest for a while. I wander around the living room/kitchen—looking at the art. On the door is a 1953 poster of Aix-en-Provence and on the wall by the refrigerator some canvases done by Fisher's second husband, unframed. There are lots of books—art books, a life of Isabella d'Este, *Little Women,* some Sylvia Plath, a copy of *Mrs. Bridge.* There are a few cookbooks, too—signed from James and Julia and Craig. The only copies of her own books I can find are the ones in fancy bindings that publishers bestow upon their authors at Christmas. I find a copy of **The Gastronomical Me,** and as I sit down to read it, the smaller of the two calicos jumps onto my lap.

Fisher's prose is so good, so strong, that in seconds I am with her in France—just married and falling in love with food. Later I will ask, "Why did you marry so young?" and she will reply, "To get the hell away from home."

Fisher's books are mostly autobiographical; her millions of readers know that she was brought up in Whittier, and that her father, Rex Kennedy, ran a newspaper. They know that she married a man named Al Fisher (who later

became the dean of English at Smith College) and went with him to study in France. And that from 1929 to 1939 she seemed to bounce back and forth between France and California and cook and eat and drink a lot of really wonderful food and wine and somehow get divorced and married again. But let her tell it.

"Paris was everything that I had dreamed, the late September when we first went there. It should always be seen, the first time, with the eyes of childhood, or of love. I was almost 21, but much younger than girls are now, I think. And I was wrapped in a passionate mist."

And in **The Gastronomical Me** this is how she described her first serious meal in France:

"We ate the biggest as well as the most exciting meal that either of us had ever had. As I remember, it was not difficult to keep on, to feel a steady avid curiosity. Everything that was brought to the table was so new, so wonderfully cooked, that what might have been with sated palates a gluttonous orgy was, for our fresh ignorance, a constant refreshment. I know that never since have I eaten so much. But that night the kind ghosts of Lucullus and Brillat-Savarin as well as Rabelais and a hundred others stepped in to ease our adventurous bellies, and soothe our tongues. We were immune, safe in a charmed gastronomical circle."

Back in the bedroom, inadvertently whispering again, I show Fisher the book. She looks at the photo on the jacket—a head shot with eyes almost closed and long hair thrown back—and says, "That's rare, you know. They pulled that jacket after the first edition. The picture was considered too sexy."

No wonder, I say, and read her the passage underneath: "He had hung all my favorite pictures, and there was a present for me on the low table, the prettiest Easter present I have ever seen. It was a big tin of Beluga caviar, in the center of a huge pale-yellow plate, the kind sold in the market on saints' days in Vevey, and all around the tin and then the edge of the plate were apple blossoms. I think apple blossoms are perhaps the loveliest flowers in the world, because of their clarity and the mysterious way they spring so delicately from the sturdy darkness of the carved stems, with the tender little green leaves close around them. At least they were the loveliest that night, in the candlelight, in the odd-shaped room so full of things important to me."

"Oh pooh," she snorts, "that's not sexy." She says it as if there must be some unfathomable generational divide between us, if I could find sexiness in a passage such as this. "They put another picture by George Hurell on the cover after that," she muses. "He was a friend. He's been taking pictures of me all my life. He used to come to Laguna Beach and eat with us and take pictures of us because he didn't have any money to pay models. He was a darling little Jewish boy. He lives quite near here now; he came two or three years ago and took a lot more pictures of me."

Fisher stares at the photo for a while, then says, "That wasn't my first book, you know."

Her first book was **Serve It Forth** ("a book about eating, and about what to eat and about people who eat"). Fisher wrote it in one of those times when she was between jaunts to France. "After Al got his doctorate," she reminisces now, "we came back from Dijon and lived in my family's beach shack at Laguna Beach. Today we would have been called far-out hippies, I think, but then we were just victims of the Depression. I was always writing, but I never sold anything. Al was writing the Great American Novel. Then Al got a job in Occidental College. He was earning $650 a year. I got a job in a postcard shop in the afternoon, but every morning I went to the library and worked on the book."

Afterwards, she says, she'd come home and show what she'd written to her husband. "I have to write towards somebody I love. Express myself as that person I love would want me to be. I've never written just for myself. That's like kissing yourself, don't you think?"

Her husband, in turn, showed it to author/painter Dillwyn Parrish, who lived next door. "He picked up little pieces and sent them to his sister Anne, who was a famous writer. She was the one who sent it to a publisher. I didn't even know it had been published until Mother and Father came to Europe in '37 and told me."

This is, of course, more of Fisher's slightly unbelievable modesty. She must, after all, have signed a contract for the book before it was published? "I guess I did," she says dismissively, "I don't remember."

What she does remember is that by the time the book was published she was living with Dillwyn Parrish, who became her second husband. Parrish was the great love of her life, and her most wonderful stories are about being with him in Europe. Fisher unhesitatingly says that of all the times in her life, "I liked being with Timmie [Parrish] the most."

Fisher wrote her third book, **Consider the Oyster,** "to amuse Timmie." She pauses. "He died just before I finished it," she whispers. And then asks me to leave so she can rest again.

This time I poke into her cookbooks. ("Food still tastes good, but I don't get much of it," she has just said. "I eat to live now. It doesn't matter much.")

The books are all well used and carefully annotated in her small, precise handwriting. Actually, the meals I remember sharing with Fisher have all been simple ones. Once she made me split pea soup and served it with sourdough bread with sweet butter and fruit compote and two kinds of shortbread cookies. A couple of times there have been salads. Once I brought her some caviar, and I could tell from her comments about liking to eat it best with a spoon that there wasn't enough to please her. Always there has been wine.

Fisher is as unpretentious about wine as she is about food. "Nobody with any humility would consider himself a connoisseur," she once told me. "I know red from white and I think I know good from bad and I know the phonies from the real, and that's about it."

But wine has always been one of her real pleasures. Now

Fisher sends the nurse out to press some wine on me. "Mary Frances wants you to know that it's in the refrigerator," she says. And indeed it is—four different kinds of white wine, all local.

"I have almost always lived near vineyards," says Fisher when I go back into the bedroom, wine glass in hand. "That's where I have been happiest."

Where she has been unhappiest is in Los Angeles. "I was horrified when I discovered that you were moving down there," she whispers. "I myself had to get out."

Fisher's Hollywood period was in the mid-'40s, during her third marriage (to publisher Donald Friede). "It was a short, dumb but good marriage," she begins. "We were living in Hollywood mostly, and commuting to the house in Hemet 120 miles away. We had two kids, two houses and a very social life. Life was too hectic." Before long Fisher is painting a picture of herself frantically trying to keep up—and not doing a very good job.

"Then Donald got me into the translation of *Physiology of Taste*. I did it," she says firmly, "under duress."

Fisher admits—has always admitted—that she is pleased with the translation. Even before she did it she wrote, "There are two kinds of books about eating: those that try to imitate Brillat-Savarin's and those that try not to." But although the book was immediately acclaimed, Friede was not satisfied; what he really wanted his wife to do was write a novel.

"He thought every writer had one novel in him, but God, no, I'm not a novelist." She grimaces a little. "I wrote my first novel when I was 9. I wrote a chapter a day, and I would tell it to my family after lunch. It was about love, with a nurse, a sailor—all things I didn't know about. They laughed. Finally I realized that they were really laughing at me—and that I was not a novelist."

Pressed into fiction once again, Fisher "tried to choose a woman who was the opposite of me—to be everything I wasn't. It really is just short stories nailed together."

The book, **Not Now But Now,** was published in 1947. It didn't sell. The same year, Fisher divorced Friede. "I didn't contest anything. I just wanted the kids. He was delighted."

The two remained friends, and it was Friede ("finally accepting that I could never be a novelist") who came up with the idea of reprinting five of Fisher's books as one volume: **The Art of Eating.** "In 1954," says Fisher, with just an edge of bitterness, "he decided that I was through. He wanted me to be a bestseller and I wasn't. So he issued the book. He's very pleased; it's never been out of print."

It's hard now to imagine how Fisher, a single mother with two children and not much money, managed to live on what a free-lance writer makes. She wrote for dozens of publications—*Vanity Fair, House Beautiful, Gourmet*—articles for which she was never particularly well paid, and for which she never once received an expense check. "They just didn't do it in those days," she says. She wrote for the *New Yorker,* too—their vaunted generosity amounted to a retainer of $50 a year.

For a while Fisher worked for her father at the newspaper. "When Rex died, he left us some money, and then Donald's mother died and left the kids $200 a month and in 1958 we went to Europe for four years. The money went far in Europe—and I wanted my girls to learn other ways and other languages."

Lots of wonderful books have subsequently come out of those years. But during the '50s themselves, Fisher was so busy writing for magazines that she published no new books. Even in 1961, when she wrote *A Cordiall Water,* a book about folk medicine, it was just to fill a pressing financial need: "Anne wanted to go to a party and she needed a dress, so I sent the book off to Little, Brown."

The next year Fisher came back to California, to a big house in St. Helena. But her children were ready to move away—and Fisher soon embarked on the one period of her life that she has never written about.

"Tell me about Mississippi," I plead.

"Let me rest awhile," she replies.

I wander onto the sun porch, a comfortably shabby sort of room filled with weathered furniture and books with curling covers. The cat nuzzles at my ankles, demanding that I sit down and make a lap. She looks sleek and well fed; no wonder. "I wouldn't feed them anything I wouldn't eat myself," Fisher had said earlier.

I grab the copy of *The Gastronomical Me* and begin to read my favorite of her stories. It is the one called **"Define This Word,"** about wandering into a restaurant in a remote French village and falling into the clutches of a waitress so passionate about her work that Fisher fears she is never going to be allowed to leave the restaurant. I reach the part where the chef sends out the dessert: "With a stuffed careful smile on my face and a clear nightmare in my head of trussed wanderers prepared for the altar by this hermit-priest of gastronomy, I listened to the girl's passionate plea for fresh dough. 'You cannot serve old pastry!' the waitress is crying"—when the nurse comes to call me back into the room.

"Mississippi?" I ask. Fisher sighs. "In 1964 the kids were all gone and I thought I'd find out if the South was as bad as I thought. So I went to teach at the Piney Woods School."

Piney Woods was a school for black students; the faculty, says Fisher, was half black and half white. She taught English. "The South was worse than I expected. I didn't go to town at all while I was there."

But why did she go in the first place? Did she plan to write a book, to fight a fight? She looks slightly horrified. "God, no, I wasn't planning on writing anything about it. And I didn't go there to fight anything. I just went."

Fisher smiles a little, remembering. "I found it took six months before the kids would eyeball me. But after six months I was without color, and so were they." She smiles. "I was not invited back," she adds with a certain amount of pride, "because I was a trouble maker." She seems pleased by this, and then abruptly stops talking;

"Did you write anything?" I prod. She nods towards the boxes. Of course, she wrote something; she has written all her life. "It's in there," she says. "Marsha Moran [the woman to whom she dictates her work every day] has all that stuff—she can do what she wants with it. I don't like to talk about it." Clearly the subject is closed.

The nurse walks in just then, she is carrying more oysters. They have been baked with a spinach topping, a sort of Rockefeller preparation. "Eating is difficult for her," she told me earlier, "but anything with oysters, she has no trouble at all."

The nurse puts down the tray. Mary Frances Fisher looks at the oysters with both longing and distaste; they are very large. She smiles up at me and whispers, knowing that the nurse can't hear her: "You know, it's a shame. Most people can't cook very well."

I look at Fisher. I look at the oysters. Suddenly a line from one of Fisher's books flashes through my head. "Oysters," I find myself thinking, "are very unsatisfactory food for labouring men, but will do for the sedentary, and for a supper to sleep on." (pp. H1, H9)

Ruth Reichl, "M. F. K. Fisher," in Los Angeles Times Book Review, *June 6, 1991, pp. H1, H9.*

Victoria Glendinning (review date 9 June 1991)

[*Glendinning is an English author, journalist, and educator who is known primarily for her critically acclaimed literary biographies. In the following review, Glendinning discusses Jeannette Ferrary's biography* Between Friends: M. F. K. Fisher and Me *(1991) and Fisher's* The Boss Dog, *emphasizing the autobiographical, sensual, and nostalgic qualities of Fisher's writing.*]

The lack of response shown by Jeannette Ferrary's California mailman in 1977, when she excitedly announced that he had brought a reply to her fan letter, taught her "that some people had not heard of M. F. K. Fisher." While not quite in that category, this reviewer was not until now an aficionado, and so came to this legendary American food writer, and to Ms. Ferrary's account of her, with a clean palate. Ms. Ferrary has not written a formal biography but what she calls "a collection of appreciations," and the record of a friendship that began after that first fan letter.

The point about her, as Ms. Ferrary notes in *Between Friends: M. F. K. Fisher and Me,* is that Mrs. Fisher is not just a food writer. If she writes better than anyone about tangerines, it's because "underneath it all, she's not writing about tangerines." The tangential nature of the tangerines is confirmed over and over in Mrs. Fisher's writing. Witness this parenthesis to an assertion about the crisp flesh of oysters, for example, in one of her early books, *Consider the Oyster* (1941): "*Crisp* is not quite right, and *flesh* is not right, but in the same way you might say that *oyster* is not right for what I mean."

So what is M. F. K. Fisher writing about? Desire, neediness, solace, comfort, satisfaction. Ms. Ferrary finds her sensual rather than sexual. Coming to the writing for the first time, I would dare to disagree. Lots of it seems to me to be about sex. But you cannot be sure. When most obviously sexual, she is at her silliest—as when she wrote, in *How to Cook a Wolf* (1942), that describing past luxuries should be "like waking from a dream of your loved one, and finding perfume on your lips."

Between recipes Mrs. Fisher writes about places, people and above all about herself. Her food writing is a continuous reminiscence, which makes it hard for Ms. Ferrary, who has written two cookbooks. Anything Mrs. Fisher, who is now 82 and bedridden, wants known about her family, her upbringing in Whittier, Calif., her three marriages, her two daughters, her travels, she has already divulged. Ms. Ferrary fills in some gaps—but, as she concedes, some odd mysteries remain. Writing in her subject's lifetime, she naturally cannot speculate. Good food books, Mrs. Fisher herself has written, not irrelevantly, belong not to the literature of knowledge but to the literature of power.

The title and subtitle of Ms. Ferrary's memoir are as apposite as were those of two of Mrs. Fisher's most autobiographical books, *Among Friends* (1970), a word play on the Quaker population of her hometown, and *The Gastronomical Me* (1943). Ms. Ferrary's enthralled, nervous, ingenuous response to her subject is in itself a topic. If you want to know about Mrs. Fisher, but don't need to know about Ms. Ferrary, this may prove an irritant. She agonized, for example, about what to contribute to a lunch at Glen Ellen, Calif., where Mrs. Fisher has lived since 1970, fretting: "It had to be absolutely correct: intellectually, culturally, personally." Ms. Ferrary dreaded discussions of what she ate when alone, "because I would have had to confess a bunch of things that were not in my image of her image of me." Such a desire to please and appease implies a craven self-effacement, and even bad faith.

Yet anyone who has been befriended by a celebrated, formidable old author will sympathize with her feelings of inadequacy, especially as Mrs. Fisher, having said, "I wish you were writing my life," did not afterward make things easy.

Ms. Ferrary refers to Mrs. Fisher's voice, "soothing and gentle, as if she were saying only nice things." But how Mrs. Fisher speaks bears no relation to what she says. Ms. Ferrary refers to the "almost lethal beauty" of Mrs. Fisher's backhanded compliments; and to a set of 60 petits-fours tins in five different patterns that she gave Mrs. Fisher as a present, and which Mrs. Fisher gave back to her for her birthday. "I don't think she knew. But maybe she did."

The rewards of thrilling friendships of this kind are not only one way. Old and famous people are sometimes lonely. Their friends may be dead, their children alienated or far away. Their powers are waning, they may, like M. F. K. Fisher, be confined to their homes. Ms. Ferrary perceives how M. F. K. Fisher uses visitors such as herself as a "means of getting around," living to some extent vicariously. Admirers who write are also, as in this case, guarantees of continuing notice and perhaps immortality.

The transaction, insofar as a friendship is a transaction, is fair. This memoir, insofar as it is a memoir, is fair too.

There are two other books of Mrs. Fisher's own just out as well. *The Boss Dog* is a short novel, previously unpublished but printed last year in a limited edition by the Yolla Bolly Press. It is the sort of book that a publicist might describe, in desperation, as suitable for the young at heart of all ages. The story is about the period Mrs. Fisher spent in Aix-en-Provence in the early 1950's with her two young daughters, and the special friendship they formed with an appealing mongrel who wandered around the town, attaching himself to certain cafes, as they did themselves. There is plenty of evocative description, and plenty of comfort eating. Even the fountain on the square, "built in layers of lions-dolphins-turtles-swans-cherubs," sounds like a dessert. The sub-text, beneath the playfulness and the charm, is Mrs. Fisher and her two daughters' sense of rootlessness and not belonging. New readers should not start here. *The Boss Dog* is strictly for the faithful, who read, as Ms. Ferrary puts it in her memoir, "every last tingling word they can find."

Long Ago in France is presented not as a food book but as a travel book, a strategy that will introduce Mrs. Fisher to a different category of readers. It is the first in Prentice Hall's "Destinations" series edited by Jan Morris, and is a *réchauffé*, a period piece put together by unnamed hands, from the accounts of Mrs. Fisher's young married life (and her culinary awakening) when she and Al Fisher were living in Dijon between 1929 and 1932; it is lifted and stitched from *The Gastronomical Me* and other books. As she wrote in a note to *How to Cook a Wolf*, "a hash can be very fine indeed." But there is more solid nourishment in *The Art of Eating* (1954), a generous compilation of five of her classic early books, which gives the hitherto uninitiated—Ms. Ferrary's mailman and me—the full flavor of the extraordinary M. F. K. Fisher in all her original freshness. At a time when only the very rich or the very bohemian knew the fleshpots of Europe in depth, she shared with American readers her pleasure in French gastronomic voluptuousness. To read her today, in an age of mass travel and sophisticated international food culture, is to recapture the essential taste of France as it was—and as it sometimes can be.

Victoria Glendinning, "The Gastronomical Her," in The New York Times Book Review, *June 9, 1991, p. 15.*

OBITUARIES

Molly O'Neill   (obituary date 24 June 1992)

[*In the following obituary, O'Neill discusses Fisher's life and career, highlighting her major works.*]

M. F. K. Fisher, the writer whose artful personal essays about food created a genre, died on Monday at her home on the Bouverie Ranch in Glen Ellen, Calif. She was 83 years old.

She died after a long battle with Parkinson's disease, her daughter Kennedy Wright said.

In a career spanning more than 60 years, Mrs. Fisher wrote hundreds of stories for *The New Yorker,* as well as 15 books of essays and reminiscences. She produced the enduring English translation of Brillat-Savarin's book *The Physiology of Taste,* as well as a novel, a screenplay, a book for children and dozens of travelogues. While other food writers limited their writing to the particulars of individual dishes or expositions of the details of cuisine, Mrs. Fisher used food as a cultural metaphor.

Her subject matter, she said in an interview in 1990, "caused serious writers and critics to dismiss me for many, many years. It was woman's stuff, a trifle." But she was not deterred. In 1943 she wrote in her book *The Gastronomical Me:*

> People ask me: Why do you write about food, and eating and drinking? Why don't you write about the struggle for power and security, and about love, the way others do. They ask it accusingly, as if I were somehow gross, unfaithful to the honor of my craft.
>
> The easiest answer is to say that, like most humans, I am hungry. But there is more than that. It seems to me that our three basic needs, for food and security and love are so mixed and mingled and entwined that we cannot straightly think of one without the others. So it happens that when I write of hunger, I am really writing about love and the hunger for it, and warmth and the love of it and the hunger for it.

In 1963, W. H. Auden called her "America's greatest writer." In a review of *As They Were,* for *The New York Times Book Review,* Raymond Sokolov wrote, "In a properly run culture, Mary Frances Kennedy Fisher would be recognized as one of the great writers this country has produced in this century."

Mrs. Fisher's work has been steadily re-collected and re-released and her books sell briskly. *M. F. K.,* an hour-long documentary by a California film maker, Barbara Wornum, released in 1992, is a comprehensive view of Mrs. Fisher. Ms. Wornum followed Mrs. Fisher for four years, she said, because the single mother and writer "is the most poetic voice of the working woman in the 20th century."

Mrs. Fisher was the first child of Rex Kennedy, a small-town newspaper owner, and his wife, Edith. Mrs. Fisher wrote of her entrance into the world: "I began in Albion, Mich., and was born there on July 3, 1908, in a heat wave. I leapt forth only a few minutes before midnight, in a supreme effort from my mother, whose husband had assured her that I would be named Independencia if I arrived on the Fourth."

She had two younger sisters, Anne, who died in 1965, and Norah, and a brother, David, who died in 1942. Before she entered kindergarten, Mrs. Fisher's father purchased *The Whittier News,* a newspaper in Whittier, a predominantly Quaker town near Los Angeles, where the Kennedy clan grew up "on the outside looking in," she said. She was an Episcopalian, and, she said was never invited to the home of a Quaker.

"Episcopalians were the third world in Whittier," she said in a recent interview. "I wrote a book about my childhood, and I wanted to call it 'Child of an Inner Ghetto.' "

Instead, the book, which was published in 1970, was called **Among Friends.** On its cover, a sepia-toned family photograph shows Edith Kennedy, tall, hatted and veiled, looking into the distance, her arm protecting a pouting Anne. Mary Frances stood alone, biting her full, lower lip, staring at the camera. "I was a haughty child," she told an interviewer.

She was removed enough to become a keen observer, and her sharp blue eyes remained pinned on significant moments of communion. She described herself, a well-loved little girl, by depicting a meal that her mother once served: "deep rich, floating puddles of hot cocoa for supper, with buttered toast sogging deliciously in them."

Her tastes and her eye for nuance continued to sharpen through adolescence. Apprenticing with the family cook, she became accomplished in the kitchen.

She also became, she said, "an insatiable reader and scribbler." After brief sojourns at Illinois College, Whittier College, Occidental College and the University of California at Los Angeles, she married a doctoral student, Alfred Fisher, in 1929 and moved to Dijon, France, where he would complete his doctorate in literature.

A beauty and an enchantress, Mrs. Fisher was photographed by Man Ray, but by her own lights, she said. "I wasn't so pretty that I didn't have to do something else." She said she "spent hours in my kitchen cooking for people, trying to blast their safe, tidy little lives with a tureen of hot borscht and some garlic toast and salad, instead of the fruit cocktail, fish, meat, vegetable, salad, dessert and coffee they tuck daintily away seven times a week."

Her writing had the same ornery passion, the same impetuous urge to soothe her readers while shaking their souls. Her first book, **Serve it Forth,** published in 1937, took America by the shoulders and said, "Look, if you have to eat to live, you may as well enjoy it." The theme was repeated in **Consider the Oyster,** which was published in 1941:

> An oyster leads a dreadful but exciting life. Indeed, his chance to live at all is slim, and if he should survive the arrows of his own outrageous fortune and in the two weeks of his carefree youth find a clean smooth place to fix on, the years afterwards are full of stress, passion and danger. . . .
>
> Men have enjoyed eating oysters since they were not much more than monkeys, according to the kitchen middens they have left behind them. And thus, in their own one-minded way, they have spent time and thought and money on the problems of how to protect oysters from the suckers and the borers and the starvers, until now it is comparatively easy to eat this two-

valved mollusk anywhere, without thought of the dangers it has run in its few years. Its chilly delicate gray body slips into a stew-pan or under a broiler or alive down a red throat, and it is done. Its life has been thoughtless but no less full of danger, and now that it is over we are perhaps the better for it.

Her ebullient embrace of the slow, sensual pleasures of the table was matched by her cool acceptance of sudden violence and evil. In a 1942 review of *How to Cook a Wolf,* in *The New York Herald Tribune,* Lewis Gannett wrote that anyone familiar with the writer's earlier work "will recall the family Gothic perversity that makes Mrs. Fisher's literature unique."

Mrs. Fisher, on the other hand, saw herself as practical. In *How to Cook a Wolf,* for instance, she suggested that when the wolf is at the door one should invite him and have him for dinner.

She saw little room at the table for caution. In *An Alphabet for Gourmets,* she wrote:

> A complete lack of caution is perhaps one of the true signs of a real gourmet; he has no need for it, being filled as he is with a God-given and intelligently self-cultivated sense of gastronomical freedom. He not only knows from everything admirable he has read that he will not like Irish whisky with pineapple chilled in honey and vermouth, or a vintage Chambertin with poached lake perch; but every taste bud on both his actual and his spiritual palate wilts in revulsion at such thoughts. He does not serve these or similar combinations, not because he has been *told,* but because he *knows.*

M. F. K. Fisher on writing:

People ask me: why do you write about food, and eating and drinking? Why don't you write about the struggle for power and security, and about love, the way others do. They ask it accusingly, as if I were somehow gross, unfaithful to the honor of my craft.

The easiest answer is to say that, like most humans, I am hungry. But there is more than that. It seems to me that our three basic needs, for food and security and love are so mixed and mingled and entwined that we cannot straightly think of one without the others. So it happens that when I write of hunger, I am really writing about love and the hunger for it, and warmth and the love of it and the hunger for it.

> *M. F. K. Fisher, in her 1943* The Gastronomical Me, *later reprinted in* The New York Times, *24 June 1992.*

Throughout the 1940's, 50's and 60's, the peripatetic writer and cook lived in California, Switzerland and France, weathered three marriages and reared two daughters. Her marriage to Mr. Fisher ended in divorce in 1937 and that same year she married the painter Dilwyn Parrish, who died after a lingering illness in 1941. Her daughter, Anna,

was born in 1943 and in 1945, she married Donald Friede, a literary agent. Her second daughter, Kennedy, was born in 1946, and she divorced Mr. Friede two years later.

In 1952, Mrs. Fisher and her sister, Norah, rented houses on neighboring vineyards in St. Helena, Calif., an area that, with the exceptions of stays in the South of France, would remain home.

In 1971, she moved to Bouverie Ranch in Glen Ellen, where her house of two sprawling rooms became a salon for visiting writers and food worshipers. She made her final trip to Europe in 1978, writing about Marseilles in *A Considerable Town,* published that year. . . .

Since then, Mrs. Fisher has worked and entertained at Bouverie Ranch. "My life is simple," she said in an interview several years ago. "When I can't write, I read. When I can't read I cook."

Bedridden in recent years, she cooked less and less. But she continued to write, *Sister Age,* was published in 1983 . . . *Dubious Honors,* [is] a collection of introductions that Mrs. Fisher wrote for others' books. *The Boss Dog,* a book for children, was published . . . in 1991.

In an interview in 1991 she said: "I've lost my appetite. But my mind and heart have never been clearer."

Plagued by diminishing sight and crippling arthritis, her voice reduced to a whisper by Parkinson's disease, she spoke of waking up before 4 A.M. and writing stories in her mind for the hours before her secretary came in to take dictation. According to her agent, Robert Lescher, the writer "has been working on a number of manuscripts which will be published posthumously."

"The purpose of living is to get old enough to have something to say," she said last year. "But by that time, your voice doesn't work and your hands won't obey you so it's tough as hell to find a way to say it all."

Mrs. Fisher is survived by her sister, Norah Barr; two daughters, Anna Parrish, of Portland, Ore., and Ms. Wright of Alameda, Calif., and four grandchildren.

> *Molly O'Neill, in an obituary in* The New York Times, *June 24, 1992, p. A18.*

The Times, London   (obituary date 29 June 1992)

[*The following obituary provides an overview of Fisher's works and career, acknowledging her significant contributions to the fields of writing and gastronomy.*]

M. F. K. Fisher, as she was always known, wrote with humour and sensuous elegance. Her fresh and personal approach to gastronomy transformed the genre from mere information to high art. Indeed, she won the much quoted praise of W. H. Auden, who wrote a substantial introduction to her collection *The Art of Eating* and considered her prose to be unsurpassed by that of any other American writer.

She had a knack for titles. Beginning with her first book, *Serve it Forth,* published in 1947, she rattled off *Consider the Oyster, How to Cook a Wolf, The Gastronomical Me* and *An Alphabet for Gourmets* over the next 12 years. The five volumes, considered to be classics of their kind, were assembled as *The Art of Eating,* in 1954.

James A. Beard, reviewing that collection, wrote:

> Mrs Fisher is a woman who has had many gifts bestowed on her—beauty, intelligence, heart, a capacity for the pleasures of the flesh, of which the art of eating is no small part, and the art of language as well. She is a rarity in American gastronomy; one of the few writers in the great European tradition of Brillat-Savarin, Maurice des Ombiaux or George Saintsbury.

Of Scottish and Irish descent, M. F. K. Fisher was born into a family with five generations of journalists on each side. Her father was the owner of a small newspaper. It never occurred to her that she would be anything other than a writer, and her interest in food as "something beautiful to be shared with people instead of as a thrice-daily necessity" also began at an early age.

In 1929, while studying at the University of California, she met and married Alfred Young Fisher, and the couple spent the first years of their marriage in Europe, mainly at the University of Dijon. It was there that her love of European cooking was born, and she later described her time in Dijon as "two shaking and making years in my life".

On their return to California, while her husband joined the faculty of Occidental College, Fisher worked in a picture-framing shop that sold pornographic postcards. In her spare time she read books on cooking in the Los Angeles public library, and it was her discovery of an Elizabethan cookbook that inspired her to begin writing on the subject herself. In *Serve it Forth* her style and attitudes were so different from those of other women writers on food, most of them trained in home economics, that several reviewers immediately assumed that "M. F. K. Fisher" was a man.

She always retained those initials for her published work to encourage the assumption.

Fisher divorced her first husband in 1938 and married Dillwyn Parrish, with whom she moved to Switzerland, cultivated a vineyard, and jointly wrote a light-hearted novel entitled *Touch and Go* under the pseudonym of Victoria Berne. Parrish died in 1941, and Fisher returned to California where she produced her most famous cookbooks over the next decade. They were spiced with historical information and literary quotations about cooking and eating, and displayed considerable narrative skill. Raymond Sokolov wrote in *The New York Times* in 1982: "She had learned everything Hemingway and Colette had to teach her about literary control and about the importance of what is left out."

Not all of Fisher's literary work was successful. A novel entitled *Not Now But NOW,* written at the urging of her third husband, Donald Friede, whom she married in 1945 and divorced in 1951, was well reviewed but turned out to be, in her own words, "a commercial turnip". She did better with *A Cordiall Water: A Garland of Odd & Old Recipes to Assuage the Ills of Man or Beast,* in 1961, and *The Cooking of Provincial France* and *With Bold Knife and Fork,* published in 1968 and 1969.

In later years Fisher's writing turned from cooking to collections of essays and short stories, many of them creating evocative portraits of Marseilles, Aix-en-Provence, and other parts of Europe where she had lived and travelled and which she loved so much. She made her final home in California's Napa Valley. "I just like to be in wine country," she said.

She leaves two daughters from her last marriage.

An obituary in The Times, *London, June 29, 1992, p. 17.*

Additional coverage of Fisher's life and career is contained in the following sources published by Gale Research: *Contemporary Authors,* Vols. 77-80, Vol. 138 [obituary].

Alex Haley

August 11, 1921—February 10, 1992

(Full name Alex Murray Palmer Haley) American journalist, essayist, and historical novelist.

For further information on Haley's life and works, see *CLC,* Volumes 8 and 12.

INTRODUCTION

Haley is best known for *Roots: The Saga of an American Family,* a fictionalized account of seven generations of his own family based on twelve years of genealogical research in Africa, Europe, and the United States. Described by critics as a blend of history and entertainment, *Roots* has been lauded as an affirmation of African-American heritage and as a universal story of humankind's search for identity. With the success of the novel and the television miniseries on which it is based, Haley became a national celebrity and a popular lecturer. However, some commentators questioned the accuracy of Haley's claims about his family background, and in 1977 Margaret Walker and Harold Courlander alleged separately that Haley had plagiarized their work in *Roots.* Charges brought by Walker were later dropped, but Haley admitted that he unknowingly lifted three paragraphs from Courlander's *The African* (1968). Despite the controversy, *Roots* remains an essential part of history and literature programs at many colleges and universities. Haley also co-wrote *The Autobiography of Malcolm X,* a work widely acclaimed upon its publication for its sensitive depiction of Malcolm X's volatile life.

PRINCIPAL WORKS

The Autobiography of Malcolm X [with Malcolm X] (autobiography) 1965
"In Search of the African" (essay) 1974; published in periodical *American History Illustrated*
"My Search for Roots" (essay) 1974; published in periodical *Reader's Digest*
*Roots: The Saga of an American Family (historical novel) 1976
"What Roots Mean to Me" (essay) 1977; published in periodical *Reader's Digest*
"Sea Islanders, Strong-Willed Survivors Face Their Uncertain Future Together" (essay) 1982; published in periodical *Smithsonian*

*This work was televised as a miniseries in January 1977. Sequels include: *Roots: The Next Generation* (1979) and *Queen* (1993).

OBITUARIES AND TRIBUTES

Rick DuBrow   (essay date 11 February 1992)

[*In the following essay, DuBrow remarks on the significance of the miniseries* Roots *in the history of television.*]

Alex Haley's 1977 miniseries, ***Roots,*** not only gave America a lasting emotional experience about black history, it also revolutionized prime-time television storytelling with its book-like novelization of a gigantic story.

Haley, who died Monday, knew—like others connected

with the 12-hour production—that even the huge success of *Roots* did not open future doors for black performers on TV as much as many hoped it would.

Nonetheless, the blossoming of the miniseries form as a result of *Roots* has continued for many years with memorable productions ranging from *The Winds of War* to *Shogun* to *Lonesome Dove.*

Before *Roots* the novel-like, 1976 series *Rich Man, Poor Man* had also been a great success. *Roots,* however, was the turning point for miniseries.

But those who worked with Haley on *Roots* and knew him over the years spoke more on Monday of his qualities as a human being and dedicated writer.

"What made him a great man was that he was such a gentle man," said David Wolper, executive producer of *Roots,* which earned nine Emmy Awards, more than any other miniseries. "From the day I met him in 1974 to the day of his death, he never changed. He treated the most famous people in the world the same as he treated anyone else."

Roots was based on Haley's remarkable, persistent search for his African ancestors.

"When I first met him," said Stan Margulies, producer of the miniseries,

> he was still so broke that he would occasionally interrupt writing *Roots* to go out and lecture. Something drove him, and it was more than just telling a story.

> One of the things that Alex referred to often was what Malcolm X told him before his death—that "we'll never know where we're going until we know where we came from."

After *Roots* had its huge impact, said Margulies, "Alex and I talked about the fact that no one set out to change the face of television, just to tell a story."

But as a story form, *Roots* did indeed change the face of the home medium, said Brandon Stoddard, now president of ABC Productions but, at the time of the miniseries, the network's vice president for motion pictures and novels for television.

"Alex Haley and *Roots* were a tremendously important part of American television history in general and ABC television history in particular, and both made massive cultural impact," Stoddard said in a statement Monday. "Alex was a gentleman and a really strong creative force. He will be greatly missed."

The lasting impact of *Roots* was proved again last month when cable TV's Family Channel reran the entire show. It was the first national broadcast of the miniseries since ABC repeated it in 1978, and it increased the Family Channel's audience by about 400%.

A Family Channel spokesman confirmed Monday that the cable network would rerun *Roots* yet again on March 29 and April 5—two Sundays—in six-hour blocks. Then, starting April 6 and continuing through April 11, the Family Channel will rerun the 1979 sequel to the minise-

ries, *Roots: The Next Generation,* said spokesman Earl Weirich.

In addition, CBS said Monday that it is proceeding with a new, six-hour miniseries offshoot of *Roots* that reunited Haley and Wolper. With the working title of "Queen," it centers, said CBS, on Haley's "half-white, half-black paternal grandmother, the product of a plantation affair who was forced to seek her destiny in the post-Civil War South."

Norman Lear, who, with Haley, co-produced the 1980-81 drama series. *Palmerstown, U.S.A.,* about two youths—one black, the other white—growing up in a Southern town, said he and the author had discussed creating a weekly black family drama for television.

CBS spokeswoman Susan Tick said that the network is "absolutely going ahead" with "Queen" and that it is expected to begin production within two months.

"Haley was the source and inspiration for the story and the consultant," said Tick. "He didn't write the script. We think the show will serve as a particularly poignant legacy because [Haley's grandmother] had a singular determination to see that her children were educated, and that included Haley's father."

Said Wolper: " *'Roots'* was his mother's side of the family. 'Queen' is about his father's side." (pp. F1, F9)

> *Rick DuBrow, "Haley Made History, Never Forgot His Roots," in* Los Angeles Times, *February 11, 1992, pp. F1, F9.*

Eric Pace (essay date 11 February 1992)

[*Pace is an American journalist and nonfiction writer. In the following excerpt, he provides an overview of Haley's life and career.*]

Alex Haley, the Pulitzer Prize-winning author of *Roots: The Saga of an American Family,* which chronicled his ancestors' origins in Africa and their passage from slavery to freedom in America, died [February 10] at Swedish Hospital Medical Center in Seattle. He was 70 years old and had homes in Knoxville, Tenn., Norris, Tenn., and Seattle.

He died of cardiac arrest, said a spokeswoman for the hospital, Jane Ann Wilder. Mr. Haley's son, William Alexander Haley, said at a news conference in Seattle . . . that his father had apparently suffered a heart attack and been taken to the hospital by ambulance. He was scheduled to speak today at the Bangor Naval Submarine Base at Bremerton, Wash., 15 miles from Seattle.

Roots, which was published in 1976, spurred an interest in genealogy among Americans of many ethnic heritages. The ABC television mini-series fashioned from the book attracted millions of viewers early in 1977.

The work, based in part on research in Africa, began with Mr. Haley's creative depiction of the birth of one of his ancestors, Kunta Kinte:

> Early in the spring of 1750, in the village of Juf-

fure, four days upriver from the coast of The Gambia, West Africa, a manchild was born to Omoro and Binta Kinte. Forcing forth from Binta's strong young body, he was black as she was, and he was bawling.

The book ended with an account of the burial of Mr. Haley's father, and the author's affirming "the hope that this story of our people can help to alleviate the legacies of the fact that preponderantly the histories have been written by the winners."

Marly Rusoff, the executive director of publicity for Doubleday, which originally published the book, said yesterday that more than 1.5 million copies of *Roots* had been published in hard cover, including book club editions, and that more than 4 million copies of the Dell paperback edition had been sold.

In addition, the book has been published in more than two dozen foreign countries, said John Hawkins, who heads the literary agency representing Mr. Haley.

The ABC mini-series of *Roots*, first broadcast in January 1977, still ranks among the 100 highest-rated programs. According to Nielsen Media Research, its eight episodes reached average audiences that ranged from 28.8 million households to 36.3 million households. The sequel, *Roots: The Next Generation* was broadcast in February 1979 and also drew large audiences.

The cast of the 1977 mini-series, produced by David L. Wolper Productions, included LeVar Burton, Ben Vereen, John Amos, Leslie Uggams, Maya Angelou, Cicely Tyson, Edward Asner, Harry Rhodes and Robert Reed. The writer and television historian Les Brown wrote that the mini-series "emptied theaters, filled bars, caused social events to be canceled and was the talk of the nation during the eight consecutive nights it played on ABC."

Speaking of his writing's impact, Mr. Haley said in a radio interview last month, "To this day, people, particularly African-American people but white people as well, will just totally, unexpectedly walk up and not say a word, just walk up and hug you and then say 'Thank you.'"

But the history of *Roots* was not untroubled. Lisa Drew, the book's editor at Doubleday, said . . . that two copyright infringement suits had been filed against Mr. Haley. One was dismissed, she said, and one led to a settlement between Mr. Haley and Harold Courtlander, who had contended that a brief passage in *Roots* was taken from a novel that Mr. Courtlander had written. Mr. Haley contended that the words came from "something somebody had given me."

Roots drew widespread praise but also criticism from reviewers, many of whom expressed uncertainty about how to approach the book, which [one critic] called a combination of fact and fiction.

James Baldwin, writing in *The New York Times,* said the work was a powerful affirmation of what he called continuities and consequences in black history. But Jason Berry wrote in *The New York Times Book Review* that while "no other novelist or historian has provided such a shattering, human view of slavery," nonetheless it would be a great loss if Mr. Haley "didn't assemble his factual data into some sort of formal statement."

And R. Z. Sheppard, writing in *Time* magazine, praised *Roots* but said it had "considerable structural and stylistic flaws." He added, "In general, the more verified facts that Haley has to work with, the more wooden and cluttered his narrative."

Mr. Haley's other writings included *The Autobiography of Malcolm X,* published in 1965. He also wrote for periodicals including *Atlantic, Harper's, Reader's Digest* and *The New York Times Magazine.*

More than six million copies of *The Autobiography of Malcolm X,* on which he collaborated with the black nationalist who was assassinated in Harlem in 1965, were reported to have been sold by 1977 in the United States and other countries.

Reviewing the work in *The Nation,* Truman Nelson said it was "a great book" and added, "You can hear and feel Malcolm in this book; it is a superb job of transcription." I. F. Stone said in *The New York Review of Books* that it was written with "sensitivity and devotion" but that Mr. Haley was "politically conventional" and had blunted part of Malcolm's views.

Mr. Haley was born on Aug. 11, 1921, in Ithaca, N.Y., the son of Simon Alexander Haley and the former Bertha George Palmer. He went on to study at Elizabeth City Teachers College in North Carolina from 1937 to 1939 and enlisted in the Coast Guard later in 1939, advancing to the rank of chief journalist before retiring in 1959. He then became a freelance writer.

Mr. Haley honed his writing skill during his years in the Coast Guard, working in his spare time. In 1952 the Coast Guard created for him the rank of chief journalist—a far cry from his first Coast Guard job as mess boy.

Musing on his career, he once said, "I was a sailor, I was a cook and this, and that, and it might be said I was bootstrapped up to being a writer." But he said "the real bootstrapping" had been done earlier by his father, who rose from humble beginnings to earn a graduate degree in agriculture and went on to teach in Southern colleges.

In later years, after *Roots* brought him fame, Mr. Haley continued to do much writing at sea, this time as a passenger on cargo vessels, which gave him surcease from the harried life of a celebrity.

His 1941 marriage to Nannie Branch ended in divorce in 1964. His 1964 marriage to Juliette Collins ended in divorce in 1972.

In addition to his son, who lives in Jefferson City, Mo., Mr. Haley is survived by his third wife, the former Myra Lewis of Los Angeles, from whom he was separated; two daughters, Lydia Ann Haley of Augusta, Ga., and Cynthia Gertrude Haley of New York City, and four grandchildren.

Eric Pace, in an obituary in The New York Times, *February 11, 1992, p. B8.*

The Times, London   (essay date 11 February 1992)

[*In the following excerpt, the commentator surveys Haley's career, focusing on the evolution of* Roots *and public and critical reaction to the work.*]

Fame came late to Alex Haley. He was 55 years old when **Roots: The Saga of an American Family** was published in 1976 and he became, overnight, the literary champion of his race. No other African-American had ever attempted to trace back his family history from its tribal origins, through the horrors of the slave trade, and on to achieving something approaching equality in the world of the white man. Though some contemporary critics condemned it as a mere novel, and Haley himself admitted that many episodes were fictionalised for dramatic effect, the impact of **Roots** was tremendous. It won the 1977 Pulitzer prize and an estimated 130 million people saw the initial showing of the 12-hour television version in 1977. Many millions more have seen it since.

The origins of the book were almost accidental. Haley, who left school at the age of 15, had begun writing while serving as a cook in the US Coast Guard during the second world war. At first his literary efforts were confined to writing love letters on behalf of his illiterate mess-mates but he soon turned to whiling away the months at sea by writing short stories. It took eight years and several hundred rejection slips before his first story was published. The coast guard, seemingly impressed, created a new post especially for him: Haley became the service's chief (and only) journalist.

In 1959 Haley retired from the coast guard to become a full-time writer. It was a skimpy existence until, in 1962, he recorded a conversation with the jazz trumpeter Miles Davis and turned it into the first of the *Playboy* interviews. Regular commissions followed and an interview with Malcolm X, radical spokesman of "the Nation of Islam", so impressed a publisher that Haley was asked to turn it into a book. As a literary "ghost" Haley was an instant success. The **Autobiography of Malcolm X,** published in 1965, sold six million copies in eight languages. Wrote one critic:

> You can hear and feel Malcolm in this book: it is a superb job of transcription. Its dead-level honesty, its passion, its exalted purpose, even its manifold unsolved ambiguities, make it stand as a monument to the most painful of truths: that this country, this people, this Western world, has practised unspeakable cruelty against a race, an individual, who might have made its fraudulent humanism a reality.

The purported author never lived to read it. Malcolm X was assassinated two weeks after the manuscript was finished.

But Haley was on his way. He signed a contract with Doubleday & Co to write a book about the American South before the 1954 supreme court decision declaring school segregation unconstitutional. It was never written, because while in London on another writing assignment Haley visited the British Museum and saw the Rosetta Stone. It was the beginning of his long journey to **Roots.** As a child Haley had heard strange words of an African

language passed down through his family from their slave forebears. Now he mused that if, like the strange hieroglyphics on the Rosetta Stone, those sounds could be properly deciphered, they, too, might unlock a buried past. On impulse, when he returned to the US he went to the National Archives in Washington and asked to see the census records of Alamance County, North Carolina, for the years following the Civil War. In these he found the names of several ancestors and the hunt was on.

For twelve years, supported by piecemeal advances from his long-suffering publishers and *Readers Digest* Haley became obsessed with tracing his maternal bloodline back through seven generations in the United States and several more in a village on the banks of the Gambia River in West Africa.

With the help of a linguist at the University of Wisconsin Haley succeeded in identifying the African words he had heard used by his family as being in the Manding dialect of Gambia. He spent $80,000 and travelled half a million miles in his quest, eventually tracking down the key figure of "Kunta Kinte", who had been kidnapped in Gambia and sold into slavery in 1767.

Haley had been lucky. In the Gambian village of Juffure he found a tribal historian who chanted for him the history of the Kinte tribe from its earliest origins in old Mali, and told of the kidnapping "when the King's soldiers came." Kunta Kinte, Haley was convinced, was the same man as his ancestor, known as "Kin-tay," who was brought as a slave to Annapolis, Maryland.

Through Lloyds of London he set out to identify the actual event, and discovered that the slave ship *Lord Ligonier,* captained by Thomas E. Davies, had sailed with captives from The Gambia on July 5, 1767. Documents in the Library of Congress confirmed that the *Lord Ligonier* had discharged her cargo of slaves in Annapolis on September 29 of that year. On September 29, 1967, exactly 200 years later, Alex Haley stood on an Annapolis pier and wept. It took another seven years to put the book together. Haley was nothing if not scrupulous in his research. He visited more than 50 libraries and archives on three continents before settling down to the formidable task of converting his vast trove of material into a readable narrative. At one point, to gain authenticity, he booked passage on a freighter sailing from West Africa to the US and spent each night down in the hold. There, stripped to his underwear on a rough board between bales of raw rubber, he tried to imagine what it was like "to lie there in chains, in filth, hearing the cries of 139 other men screaming, babbling, praying and dying around you."

Some critics were dismissive of the "factional" style of **Roots** and others disputed its factual accuracy. After an article in *The Sunday Times* questioned the work's fundamental findings, Haley came to London to defend what he described as his "symbolic history." He admitted that when dealing with oral evidence lacking any written records as in Gambia, he could not be positive about every detail. But, he said, he had spent years researching the book and everything in it stood up to scrutiny. **Roots,** he said, should be contrasted with the "Tarzan and Jane" image of Africa that he claimed had been the American cultural approach for generations.

Roots proved to be Haley's last work of significance. After it he wrote a novella, *A Different Kind of Christmas,* which told the story of Fletcher Randall, a wealthy Southern plantation owner who undergoes a moral conversion and joins the underground railroad network that helped free slaves. This work made little impact, however, and with 500 American colleges building courses around the *Roots* book, Haley discovered a talent as a public speaker and found himself in huge demand on campuses across the country.

He became a familiar figure on the US speaking circuit, and was fulfilling a engagement on the West Coast when he was suddenly taken to hospital on Sunday night.

An obituary in The Times, *London, February 11, 1992, p. 15.*

Jacqueline Trescott   (essay date 11 February 1992)

[*In the following essay, Trescott praises Haley for his talents as a storyteller and contributions to American culture.*]

One morning last week Alex Haley stood at a government-issue lectern in an ordinary hearing room in downtown Washington and once again made you feel like you were right on the front porch in Henning, Tenn.

In a deep, velvety voice Haley told the story of Queen Haley, his paternal grandmother, and described her in such lush physical and emotional detail that, once again, a Haley became part of your family. It was your grandmother dipping snuff, swatting and spitting at the lightning bugs, rocking in the pine chair and talking about old times.

[Haley] pulled us into the drawing rooms of living history and created characters that became part of the American lexicon.

—Jacqueline Trescott

And, as Haley listed his various projects—a miniseries on Queen, a series of interviews with black filmmakers, the long-awaited story of Henning—once again you knew something of magnitude was brewing. "Queen was born near Florence, Alabama, on a plantation called the Forks of Cypress," he said. "Her father was the master and her mother a mulatto weaver. She was raised as the servant of her half-sisters. She was what they called 'a child of the plantation.'" After the Civil War, Queen was freed and was chased into a forest. "There she joined three couples, and this was the first time she had ever confronted what being black was. I just can't wait to write that scene."

Haley, who died at age 70 . . . in Seattle, where he had

been scheduled to speak, pulled us into the drawing rooms of living history and created characters that became part of the American lexicon.

The Autobiography of Malcolm X in 1965 gave us the words and lessons of a complex leader, and a new generation hungry for Malcolm material has made the book a bestseller again. Even further back Haley had let us sit by his side as he talked to Miles Davis in the first structured *Playboy* interview, and then to Martin L. King Jr., Melvin Belli and Malcolm X. In reading his astonishing conversation with George Lincoln Rockwell, the leader of the American Nazi Party, you could feel the same chills down your spine that Haley felt and wasn't ashamed to reveal.

And then there was *Roots.* For 12 years Haley, stocky and freckled-bronze, traveled around to book club luncheons and church assemblies talking about his search for his ancestors. All of us who listened, and cared, could recite Haley's stories about earning his first money as a writer by composing love letters for his shipmates in the Coast Guard, the thrill he experienced as he churned the microfilm in the National Archives and saw his great-grandfather's name, and the time he met the griot in The Gambia.

The folklore became fact. The story of his family won a Pulitzer Prize and became a phenomenal bestseller and a miniseries in 1977 with one of the largest television audiences ever. Alexander Palmer Haley now belonged to everyone. We marveled as he read onstage at Lincoln Center. His Italian American chauffeur for his round of appearances during the week *Roots* was broadcast couldn't wait to tell everyone he was driving the author around. We were all running through the trees with Kunta Kinte.

The fame rested nicely on Haley. He joked about his high-rise office at Century Plaza in Los Angeles, about being invited to lunch at the Beverly Hills Tennis Club and then right afterward swinging by a barbecue joint in Central Los Angeles, about the bookcases of foreign editions of *Roots.* He shook his head over the tons of mail he received each week, much of it from people who had caught the genealogical fever he inspired, and the autograph gantlet that materialized whenever he walked through an airport.

"I don't let it get to me. I stay within the bounds of where Sister Scrap Green in Henning used to keep people. Once when my father was pontificating about his fraternity key, Sister Scrap said, 'Fine, 'fessor Haley, but what do it open?' All this is nice. . . . But I have to keep thinking what do it open?" he said as we drove around Los Angeles in his brand-new Mercedes.

He worried whether his natural tendency to accommodate people was colliding with the demands of celebrity. Once, when a store manager announced he was leaving after a five-hour autograph session, Haley stood up. "Right behind me the voice boomed out of a lady I didn't need to see to know that she was big, black and angry. 'He ain't goin' nowhere!'" Haley recalled hearing, as he told how he sat back down, having "known doubles of that woman all of my life. I knew that for hours she'd been inching along in that line, her feet hurting—and people cheered as I signed her five copies of *Roots* right there on the spot."

This post-***Roots*** period was not the easiest time for Haley. Lawsuits followed his new money. He settled one plagiarism suit out of court and was philosophical about the experience. "When I settled I did think about what it would look like. . . . I know the one person the lawsuits didn't mar my reputation with is me," he said. He didn't like controversy. Last year, when a verbal sparring match erupted between Spike Lee and Amiri Baraka over a Malcolm X film project, Haley said he had turned down a million-dollar deal to do another Malcolm book last spring because he just didn't want to get embroiled in everyone's interpretation of Malcolm's contribution.

The Haley family story continued with ***Roots: The Next Generation,*** another miniseries, broadcast in 1979. The two adaptations of ***Roots*** had provided a short-lived but enjoyable period of full employment for many black actors. It was this proper paternalism that he brought to his recent interviews, airing now on Black Entertainment Television, with the new generation of black filmmakers. "Spike is confrontative, tough," said Haley last week of the best-known of the group. Haley said he thought since he had known Malcolm he could ask Spike Lee what he would say to Malcolm to convince him he could do this film. "And Spike said he 'had worked very hard to develop his craft and I love the man.' Then he took me to see some of the roughs," says Haley. "It was pure power. What I saw was heavy, heavy stuff."

With Haley, you were comfortable that the material was in his sturdy hands and suspected that the publishing and entertainment muckety-mucks would have passed over similar stories from lesser phenomena. Our archives would have been sadly shortchanged without him.

But those of us who were fortunate enough to hear him know he also represented a unique oral tradition. He could talk. Once I saw him almost meet his match when I invited him to brunch and P. H. Polk, the late photographer of Tuskegee Institute, was another guest. The two laughed, cussed and pulled away the veneer of famous blacks. For years Haley reminded me of Polk's charm and the Southern fried tomatoes that day.

Haley has two brothers in Washington, George, a lawyer who is chairman of the U.S. Postal Rate Commission, and Julius, an architect. Their famous older brother always made time for their activities and always had a family story to tell about them. When Alex arrived at the Postal Rate Commission for coffee and a brief speech last Wednesday, he sat in the audience. Reminded that George expected him up front, he said, "Oh, I do this because it just drives him crazy. When I was here for his daughter's wedding, I went by the Florida Avenue Grill to get some pig feet because I knew he would be annoyed." It was the last time his brothers saw him.

He looked rested, the kind of penetrating glow that comes from being at sea, which is where Haley retreated to finish many writing projects—the kind of rest you don't expect from someone who keeps a grueling schedule. He didn't look 70.

He stood at the side of the podium, going far beyond his announced time, talking about the ironies of his family's life. A passenger on the train where Haley's father was working as a porter during the summers was so impressed by the father that he sent his tuition of $480.20 to a North Carolina agricultural college. Once he didn't have to work, Haley's father's grades improved and he won a scholarship from Cornell University. The man who had helped his father turned out to be an executive of Curtis publishing. "So when I had my first story published by the Saturday Evening Post, I went to New York for coffee with the editor. And I just started crying, put my hands up to my face because I realized if the man hadn't helped Dad I wouldn't have been there," said Haley last week.

It was a morning where he shared his gifts once again. He connected with people, displaying with and charm, giving all of us a family anecdote that could become our own. (pp. E1-E2)

> *Jacqueline Trescott, "Alex Haley, Taking Us Back Home," in* The Washington Post, *February 11, 1992, pp. E1-E2.*

Garry Abrams   (essay date 12 February 1992)

[*In the following essay, Abrams extols Haley for his contributions to American culture, particularly the interest in ancestry and pride in racial identity engendered by* Roots.]

Alex Haley told friends he was just a writer trying to make a living. But his death is a poignant reminder that the former Coast Guard cook tapped the hearts of Americans with two monumental books that transcended literature to become cultural icons.

Roots and ***The Autobiography of Malcolm X*** inspired millions to trace their family origins, take pride in racial identity and broaden their grasp of history. And the success that ***Roots*** bestowed on Haley, who died of a heart attack Monday at age 70, was the kind of fame usually reserved for world leaders, saints and rock stars.

Fellow writers and others familiar with Haley's work agree that his legacy is enduring and diverse.

"A friend once told me that [the impact of] ***Roots*** was the equivalent of putting a man on the moon," says novelist Charles Johnson, author of *Middle Passage,* a National Book Award-winning account of a 19th-Century voyage into slavery.

Although Haley was not the first to cover the territory, his success in print and television with the story of his family's African origin and enslavement breathed "dramatic life" into the American slave experience and made it "broadly acceptable" as a historical topic, Johnson says, adding: "In ***Roots,*** he found a way to present history in a very popular, commercial format—not just to black people, but to everyone."

Published in 1976, ***Roots: the Saga of an American Family*** established a genre, "the novel of memory," about black life in the United States, Johnson notes.

By sparking pride in black American roots, Johnson believes, Haley played a role in the growing preference for the term *African-American*. "Clearly, Haley is in some sense responsible for that, because **Roots** puts the hyphen there," he explains.

In person, Haley was impressive, he says, recalling a vivid memory of Haley lecturing to one of his college classes in the late 1960s: "It was one of the best classes I ever attended."

Beyond literature, Haley's impact is both sociological and historical, others say.

Myrlie Evers, widow of slain civil rights leader Medgar Evers, says Haley's contributions to interracial understanding "are almost immeasurable," adding that anyone reading his books "would be forever influenced in their thinking and their level of consciousness."

"I think that what Haley did was put the black family in the center of the history of this country," says E. Ethelbert Miller, director of the African-American Resource Center at Howard University in Washington.

And, Miller adds, "a considerable amount of credit" should go to Haley for raising the profile of Black History Month, observed in February. Indeed, Miller and others were struck by the fact that Haley died in the month that is part of his legacy.

Miller's comments on Haley and history are echoed by Eric Foner, a visiting professor at UCLA who has written extensively on slavery, the Civil War and the Reconstruction period, including the widely acclaimed *Reconstruction: America's Unfinished Revolution.*

In general, Foner says, historians tend to regard **Roots** as a work of fiction and doubt that Haley located his particular ancestor.

"Having said that," Foner stresses, "Haley is very well respected [among historians] for having stimulated interest [in academia] in black genealogy and history and the heritage of African-Americans.

"The whole idea of blacks having this family history was a very important cultural contribution," he adds. "Whatever the accuracy of the actual research, American historians owe a debt of gratitude to him for galvanizing interest in the academic world—and in the broader public, which we academics seldom manage to speak to effectively."

For Mazisi Kunene, who has been in exile from his native South Africa for 32 years, Haley made the grim historic connections between Africa and America palpable.

"He made the perspective of originating in that world very real," says Kunene, a UCLA professor of African literature and a member of the African National Congress. "He recaptured the journey from [African freedom to American slavery]. The journey became physical. . . . He reestablished the link in a very real way."

In fact, Haley's broadest impact may have been to impart a curiosity about the past to black and white Americans alike. Haley's delving into his family's history inspired many to explore their own family trees.

"We've lost a trailblazer," says Myra Vanderpool Gormley, who writes a syndicated genealogical column.

> He probably did more to popularize [genealogy] than anybody in the 20th Century. I think of Alex Haley as the one who took the snobbery out of genealogy. He made us all aware we have families, and we can find the evidence of them in the historical record. They don't have to have been rich and famous. Genealogy had been a bit snobby up until then. Most [who pursued their roots] were wealthy or looking for an illustrious ancestor.

Shortly after the broadcast of **Roots** in 1977, requests for information from the Mormon Church's vast genealogical archives in Salt Lake City doubled to about 1,600 inquiries a day, says Tom Daniels, spokesman for the church's Family History Library.

"We don't know that we can lay it all at Alex's feet . . . but certainly a great deal of it," Daniels says. "He was the most prominent [influence] in turning people to their ancestry, their heritage. We can't think of anyone else who has had an impact as great."

Haley's success with **Roots** was not all smooth sailing, however. He was sued three times for plagiarism over the book, a labor of 12 years. Two of the suits were dismissed; the other was settled out of court.

As for Haley's other towering work, *The Autobiography of Malcolm X,* much of its impact still lies in the future. A movie of Malcolm X's life by celebrated and controversial director Spike Lee is due out later this year. The film seems certain to multiply the audience for Haley's book, based on lengthy interviews with the ex-convict, Black Muslim leader and political activist, who was assassinated in 1965.

If it had not been overshadowed by the enormous popularity of **Roots,** the Malcolm X book alone would have given Haley a solid reputation. First published in 1965, it has sold 6 million copies and is said to be a staple in prisons, where it is cited as an example of "the transformation of the spirit." The book also is a centerpiece in the resurgence of interest in Malcolm X that began in the late 1980s.

The autobiography sprang from an interview with Malcolm X for *Playboy.* Haley was among the pioneers of extensive interviews in the men's magazine.

While Haley's works are likely to march on, his death brought an immediate sense of personal loss to many. Howard University's Miller recounts that his mother called him at 6:30 a.m. to give him the news, as if Haley were a family member.

And Myrlie Evers was moved when told of Haley's death: "It comes as a shock, a very painful shock." (pp. E1, E8)

Garry Abrams, "An Enduring Legacy," in Los Angeles Times, *February 12, 1992, pp. E1, E8.*

Howard Rosenberg (essay date 12 February 1992)

[*In the following excerpt, Rosenberg praises Haley's humility and storytelling ability.*]

> At this certain time, in this certain village, lived this certain person.
>
> —Grandma Yaisa,
> telling a story to enthralled
> Mandinka children in *Roots,*
> by Alex Haley.

Perhaps it was because enormous commercial success came to him relatively late in his life. Perhaps it was because of his upbringing in Henning, Tenn.

Whatever the reason, humility was among *Roots* author. Alex Haley's greatest assets and most endearing qualities.

No doubt he savored the fame and wealth he gained from writing a best-selling book about his ancestors that was dubbed an epic and was transformed into a miniseries that became one of the most popular and celebrated television programs of all time.

Yet Haley, who died Monday, was not a man who sought pretense or affectation. Because of who he was, he had access to the highest circles. When you met him, however, he seemed to be such a natural guy. He was just folks.

For me, Alex was the modern-day equivalent of the *griot,* the man in the African village charged with handing down history from generation to generation.

—*Stan Margulies*

Haley was an amazing storyteller not only in print but also in person. No wonder he was sought after as a lecturer and continually traveled on speaking engagements. Like the grandfather in "Avalon" detailing his youth for his grandchildren, and like his own grandmother in Henning, Haley could captivate listeners with stories not only about his ancestors in Africa but also with stories from his own childhood.

"For me, Alex was the modern-day equivalent of the *griot,* the man in the African village charged with handing down history from generation to generation," said *Roots* producer Stan Margulies.

Returning to Africa, Haley found *griots* still surviving, and heard one of them describe tribe members that an astonished Haley realized were the same ancestors his grandmother had spoken of. "I sat as if I were carved of stone," he wrote.

> My blood seemed to have congealed. This man whose life-time had been in this back-country African village had no way in the world to know that he had just echoed what I had heard all through my boyhood years on my grandma's front porch in Henning. . . .

The *griot* in Haley surfaced often. A story he once told me—an especially memorable one because it reflected Haley's own values—concerned a cousin from his hometown. The cousin was a stuffy, unbearably arrogant, vain and pedantic college graduate who never went anywhere without his Phi Beta Kappa key hanging like a medallion from a chain around his neck.

Well, it seemed that Haley also had an elderly aunt in Henning, a simple, guileless woman with no formal education, but someone who instinctively got to the heart of matters. One day, as Haley told it (putting on a thick, Southern black dialect for emphasis), his aunt took a close look at the cousin's Phi Beta Kappa key resting so prominently on his chest, and was genuinely puzzled.

"Very nice," she said, "But what do it open?"

The question exposed the man for the phony, ostentatious boob he was, and Haley, an enemy of pomposity himself, made it clear that he approved of his aunt's innocent skewering of his cousin. When he told the story, slowly and in dialect, he drew you into his history.

"His storytelling was his most memorable trait," Margulies recalled this week.

> David [*Roots* executive producer David Wolper] and I discovered it when we went to lunch with him for the first time. I don't think David or I got off the edge of our chairs. He could make these stories come alive. You could see everybody. You could see the town. You knew everything you needed to know.

Could Margulies recall one of those stories? He paused for a few seconds, and then responded with great enthusiasm.

"I'll tell you a great Alex Haley story! He told it at someplace where he was being honored, and he told it about himself. It was his way of deflecting or at least sharing the honor." The story was a parable.

"It seems," said Margulies,

> that all the animals from miles around gathered in Farmer Brown's yard one morning. Everyone from the animal community was there, because there was an absolute miracle to be seen. The miracle was that there was a pig atop a three-tiered fence. Right on top. And all the animals gaped and admired and gasped and said, 'We've never seen anything like that.' And finally someone said to the pig, 'Could you explain this?'
>
> And the pig said, 'The first thing is, I didn't get here by myself.'

It was that Haley humility again, showing just how well-grounded he was, despite being praised, revered and inflated into a national icon.

"Alex and I talked about that after the avalanche of *Roots,*" Margulies said.

> It [his temperament] came from all those years he worked and showed nothing for it except a mountain of rejection slips. So this overnight success, as always, had been preceded by hard work. He knew how ephemeral it was. So he

stayed the same in the good times as the hard times.

Margulies spent "hours, days, lots and lots of time" with Haley.

> And the only way you could discern he was a celebrity was that you could not go into a restaurant with him or go down the street without people coming up and wanting to shake his hand. But never, with anything he ever did, did stardom rear its head.

Nevertheless, **Roots** the miniseries conveyed on him a level of celebrity rarely bequeathed any author, for never before or since have a book and television movie been so tightly interwoven, both creatively and perceptually.

And perhaps never has a writer merged so completely with his creation, granting him a sort of immortality.

Words that Maya Angelou used to memorialize an angrier James Baldwin apply also to easy-speaking Alex Haley: "I hear his voice."

> Howard Rosenberg, "Alex Haley, a 'Griot' for Modern Times," in Los Angeles Times, February 12, 1992, p. F9.

Chalmers Hood   (essay date 16 February 1992)

[*In the following essay, Hood recalls his friendship with Haley and the ancestral link between their respective families.*]

This is about Alex Haley, but it is also about memory, those countless experiences that make us what we are.

I am the descendant of two Alabama families, as white as they come. Both emigrated from the Celtic fringe of Britain, some broke, some with prices on their heads—all trying to escape the endless problems of religious and political oppression. The halves met in our American Promised Land of cotton and slaves. In 1861, we had lots of both.

As with many Southern families, the tradition of oral history was as much a part of dinner as cornbread and black-eyed peas. We talked every evening about family and place and what these meant to us. In my case, growing up meant living in New York City, where Daddy had migrated after 1945, following his newspaper career. Fortunately, he preserved many of the family letters that told of our ups and downs over the past two centuries.

Included among these were the old slave lists, made up every decade as part of an agricultural census. Because slaves were property, they had to be reported to the tax man. When I touched these lists for the first time, I wondered what happened to all those people listed simply by first name, age and dollar value. Somehow, I wanted to use these papers in a book, but what kind? My experience had been with drier, footnoted stuff. After much thought, I plunged into my own family's saga.

One afternoon, just as I was completing a draft, a call came from my mother who had returned to live in her native Alabama. (How powerful those links between flesh and soil!) This was about four years ago, and she and some

cousins had gone out that day, snake sticks in hand, to visit one of the old family cemeteries. The excuse was to check up on the place, but the real motive, I think, was a chance to talk and reminisce in a secluded place about things long since vanished.

Lightning had burned the "big house" to the ground, leaving only a ring of columns to mark the site. Along an old dirt trail, the ladies met up with an elderly black man—evidently lost. He was looking for the same family cemetery, for a specific grave, in fact. My mother showed the way and personal introductions followed; the man, as you will have guessed by now, was Alex Haley.

He was going then on his first visit to the place where the other half of his family came from—the half not described in **Roots.** The grave was there and the family stood around wondering about the visitor's interest. He told a story about a slave girl who once bore a child named Queen by the white man buried beneath that granite slab.

The man in that grave had been a Confederate colonel, son of the Irish immigrant who had built the plantation. Alex Haley and the ladies met again that evening to share more memories. That evening marked the start of his next and final story. Once done, he could rest—his cycle fulfilled.

When my mother hung up, I wrote to Alex Haley and told him of my own work. He called me and we met first in Alabama and several other times at his retreat near Knoxville, Tenn. We threw ourselves into passing things back and forth—about where to find this and how to interpret that. We talked and talked and talked. The experience was exhilarating. Later, he read my manuscript and gave me some pointers.

To my surprise, he took a real liking to my daughter, then age 5, and she to him, and they chatted about everything under the sun. On their second encounter, she walked right over and hugged him gently, as though he were her grandfather, and then together they wandered off across his estate, churdling away. Her high squeaks and his deep bass responses echoed back and forth in the dark. Naturally, at the dinner table the subjects were Alabama and ancestors. Our last visit was done especially for the children. They got permission to take two days off from school just to be with "Mr. Alex Haley," as my daughter always called him.

He told my children and myself how thankful he was for his God-given talents and the success that had come his way. He was modest about his achievements. He recalled the sacrifices his parents had made for him and the joys of growing up in a small community—segregated though it was—where things seemed to work out.

This came back to me just moments ago, as I opened my first, battered copy of **Roots,** purchased 10 years before I asked him to sign it. His inscription reads: "To the Hoods—Chalmers, Lucy, Chalmers IV and Reed—WITH BROTHERLY LOVE!"

My most precious moments with Alex Haley came during our first meeting in Alabama when I took him to see another of our cemeteries—this one from my father's side. We drove in my old jalopy; he refusing to wear a seat belt,

I terrified because his life hung in my hands. When we got out, he stopped talking and just moved among the stones. The entire family is buried there, from first settlers to Daddy.

He read each inscription aloud, asking me about parts of the Alabama legend we had in common. Later, we dropped in on my mother, in whose house the portraits of these people hang, witnesses from an incredible past. He entered the front door and stood frozen for a moment looking my great-great-grandmother in the eye. Her image presided over my childhood dinner table and today greets newcomers at my mother's front door. Mary was her name, a Scottish girl who came to America as an orphan in 1815, marrying a Protestant Irishman who left earlier to avoid the hangman's noose.

The next day was Sunday and at the First Presbyterian Church, the sermon was given by "Mr. Alex Haley." There he sat in a gray suit, between two clergy in black robes, spiritual heirs to Knox and Calvin. One hundred thirty years earlier, William Lowndes Yancey stood in the same spot, urging Alabamians to vote for Breckinridge and secession. Back then, the balcony was for the slaves of the masters who sat below.

As Alex Haley looked up at the same balcony, he saw the choir, a number of whom were descendants of the very same masters. Subject of the day's sermon: the story of John Newton and his famous hymn, "Amazing Grace." The choir sang it magnificently, every word from the heart. When they finished, the congregation fell silent as Haley stepped forward to tell of John Newton, the man humbled by his years as captain of a slave ship.

On that day and in all the other extraordinary meetings I had with him, Alex Haley came back to one theme. In spite of all the hateful things we hear today about race and ethnicity and all the miseries that his family faced, he seemed to feel no bitterness.

"We have to accept the past for what it is," he told me, "learn as much as we can from it and move on." There is so much that is horrible in our human past that we can become overwhelmed by it all; instead, he said, let's focus on what's good, remembering who we are and where we've come from. Surely, he was the embodiment of Newton's words, " 'Tis grace has brought me safe thus far and grace will lead me home."

A few days later, as I sat in front of my computer, struggling with my own work, I glanced at the list of names scrawled out so long ago on a tattered piece of paper: "Judah, $700; Keeser, $600; Patsy and child, $700," etc., etc. Finally it dawned on me. After all these years, I had the great fortune to know that at least one of these families—part of my own tribe—turned out beautifully. Coincidence or predestination? I can't decide. No matter but thank you for your life, Mr. Alex Haley. My daughter says so.

Chalmers Hood, "Alex Haley and the Brotherhood of Memory," in The Washington Post, *February 16, 1992, p. C2.*

Juan Williams   (essay date 16 February 1992)

[*An American journalist and nonfiction writer, Williams is the author of* Eyes on the Prize: America's Civil Rights Years, 1954-1965 *(1987). In the following essay, he discusses Haley's ideas on race and describes the book Haley had planned to write about his white ancestors.*]

The week before he died, Alex Haley sent me a letter. He had just come off one of his writing trips, taken on an ocean freighter to insure the privacy and quiet that allowed him to focus on his writing. He had seen an article of mine and had some encouraging words to say about writing and, without explicitly saying so, the importance of writing about race in America.

The letter picked up on conversations we'd had on two airline flights we took together almost a year ago. Haley was seated in first class and I was in coach. As I got on board he said hello to me and we spoke briefly. Once the plane lifted off he came back and joined me.

He told me he was at work on a book about his hometown, Henning, Tenn., and all the characters and history that made the town so wonderfully evocative for storytelling. We talked a bit about *Roots* and its origins in the stories told by his grandmother and relatives about relatives long dead, including the mysterious man called the "African." He talked about sitting on that porch with the storytellers, in the summer heat, with fireflies flickering and syrupy lemonade on his tongue.

He talked, too, about sitting in a small apartment in Harlem, drinking cup after cup of black coffee with Malcolm X for two night-long interviews—interviews that became the basis of *The Autobiography of Malcolm X,* now required reading in high schools and colleges across America. Haley saw Malcolm X as a confused, emotionally tortured man whose life is very misunderstood by young people who see him as an advocate of violence.

> **Haley's idea was that this next book would take America beyond *Roots* by breaking down what he called the artificial lines of race, lines that too many conclude are walls.**
>
> **—*Juan Williams***

But what Haley really wanted to talk about was what he called his last book. He had started research on his white ancestors. I don't recall the exact details of which members of his family were white in past generations. But Haley's point sticks in my mind. He touched the coffee-with-milk brown skin on the back of his left hand and said there were few black Americans who didn't have whites in their family background. And there were many whites, he said, who not only had black ancestors, but who, if they took the time to dig in the local archives, would find that they had living black relatives. Some of them might be light-skinned blacks passing for white, he said. Others might be dark-skinned people never publicly associated with the white family but acknowledged in secret whispers between grandparents as the father, mother or sibling of relatives treated as whites in race-conscious America.

Haley's idea was that this next book would take America beyond **Roots,** by breaking down what he called the artificial lines of race, lines that too many conclude are walls. To Haley the walls were illusions that had somehow grown into fearsome reality in the American mind. He wanted to puncture the myth by writing about whites in his own family but also in the families of other people, people who consider themselves black, as well as blacks in the families of people considered white.

And it didn't stop there, Haley said with a wicked smile. Haley spoke about American Indian blood in black people and in white people; Hispanic mixtures and Asian mixtures. He talked about East Indians, Chinese, blacks and whites mixing in the Caribbean. Hispanics from Central America mixing with American Indians and whites from Texas. From his geneological research had come a vision of a common humanity, and especially of an American population that drew strength from the mixing of its gene pools.

Waving his arm in an arc, he told me to look at the people we passed in the airport. "How can you divide them as black and white?" he asked. There are, he said, all kinds of people with all kinds of facial features, skin colors, hair colors, hair texture. We laughed about a story involving a Louisiana woman in her thirties who found out that while she thought she was white, her birth certificate classified her as black. Haley found high amusement in the artificial barriers that Americans erect. The great heroes of America would be in his book, he said. He said researchers had documents showing famous people, ranging from Thomas Jefferson to Thurgood Marshall, have progeny with mixed racial background.

He never did tell me the name of his planned book, but he clearly saw it as the final message to emerge from his lifetime of listening to stories and collecting secrets. America is poorer for having missed that message.

Juan Williams, "White Roots in Black America," in The Washington Post, *February 16, 1992, p. C2.*

Additional coverage of Haley's life and career is contained in the following sources published by Gale Research: *Black Literature Criticism,* **Vol. 2;** *Black Writers;* *Contemporary Authors,* **Vols. 77-80, 136;** *Contemporary Literary Criticism,* **Vols. 8, 12;** *Dictionary of Literary Biography,* **Vol. 38; and** *Major 20th-Century Writers.*

Satyajit Ray

May 2, 1921—April 23, 1992

Indian filmmaker, screenwriter, cinematographer, novelist, short story writer, essayist, poet, illustrator, translator, and composer.

For further information about Ray's life and works, see *CLC,* Volume 16.

INTRODUCTION

One of the most respected and admired filmmakers of the post-war era, Ray is best known in the United States for the films *Pather Panchali, Aparajito,* and *Apur Sansar (The World of Apu),* collectively known as *The Apu Trilogy.* In these films, which are strongly influenced by the works of French filmmaker Jean Renoir and the early neo-realist films of Italian filmmaker Vittorio De Sica, Ray chronicled the life of a boy named Apu and introduced the central theme of his work: the clash between the old and the new, the traditional and the modern. A student of Indian Nobel Laureate Rabindranath Tagore, Ray was born to middle-class, artistic parents who encouraged him to study and appreciate Western culture. Consequently, Ray's films are highly literary, aesthetically sophisticated, and are generally described by Western critics as deeply humanistic and politically liberal; these same qualities, however, have irritated some critics in India who have attacked his work for being insufficiently Indian and ignorant of the country's pressing social and political problems. Despite these charges, many of his films deal with political themes and modern mores: *Simabaddha (Company Limited)* depicts a young businessman's abandonment of principle in pursuit of advancement; *Ashani Sanket (Distant Thunder)* examines the man-made famine of 1943 that killed five million Bengalis; and *Shatranj Ke Khilari (The Chess Players),* his only big-budget English language film, concerns British colonialism in nineteenth-century India. Ray, whose distinguished and varied career has led many admirers to call him "India's Renaissance man," was honored in 1992 with a special Academy Award for Lifetime Achievement in Film. His funeral ceremony, conducted with full state honors and declared an official holiday by the government of West Bengal, was attended by over one million mourners.

PRINCIPAL WORKS

*Pather Panchali (screenplay) 1955
*Aparajito (screenplay) 1956
Jalsaghar (screenplay) 1957
  [*The Music Room,* 1963]
*Apur Sansar (screenplay) 1959
  [*The World of Apu,* 1960]
Devi (screenplay) 1960
  [*The Goddess,* 1962]
Rabindranath Tagore (screenplay) 1961
Teen Kanya (screenplay) 1961
  [*Two Daughters,* 1963]
Kanchenjungha (screenplay) 1962
Mahanagar (screenplay) 1963
  [*The Big City,* 1964]
Charulata (screenplay) 1964
Kapurush-O-Mahapurush (screenplay) 1965
Nayak (screenplay) 1966
  [*Nayak—The Hero,* 1974]

Badaahi Amti (novel) 1969
Goupi Gyne Bagha (screenplay) 1969
†*Aranyer Din Ratri* (screenplay) 1970
 [*Days and Nights in the Forest,* 1970]
Prophesara Sankura Kandakarakhana (short stories)
 1970
†*Pratidwandi* (screenplay) 1971
 [*The Adversary,* 1972]
†*Simabaddha* (screenplay) 1971
 [*Company Limited,* 1974; also released as *The Target*]
Ashani Sanket (screenplay) 1973
 [*Distant Thunder,* 1973]
Sonar Kella (screenplay) 1974
 [*The Golden Fortress,* 1974]
Jana Aranya (screenplay) 1975
 [*The Middleman,* 1976]
Nonsense Rhymes (poetry) 1975
Rayela Bengala Rabasya (novel) 1975
Our Films, Their Films (essays) 1976
Shatranj Ke Khilari (screenplay) 1977
 [*The Chess Players,* 1977]
Joi Baba Felunath (screenplay) 1978
 [*The Elephant God,* 1978]
Heerak Rajar Deshe (screenplay) 1979
 [*The Kingdom of Diamonds,* 1980]
Ghare Bahire (screenplay) 1984
 [*The Home and the World,* 1984]
Ganashatru (screenplay) 1989
 [*An Enemy of the People,* 1989]
Shakha Proshakha (screenplay) 1990
 [*Branches of the Tree,* 1990]
Agantuk (screenplay) 1991
 [*The Stranger,* 1991]

*These works are collectively known as *The Apu Trilogy.*

†These films are commonly referred to as *The Calcutta Trilogy.*

OVERVIEW

Edward A. Gargan   (essay date 16 February 1992)

[*In the following essay, written a few months before Ray's death, Gargan discusses Ray's career and quotes the filmmaker on a variety of topics.*]

Slouched in his favorite leather armchair, a fine wool shawl pulled around his cloud-white cotton pajama-style kurta, Satyajit Ray peers around his familiar study, books and manuscripts stacked and crammed into sagging wooden shelves, a desk smothered with letters—many congratulatory epistles for winning an Oscar for his life's work—while an overhead lamp flickers momentarily as Calcutta's persnickety power supply seems to dither over what to do. As he often does, he lets his fingertips play along the edge of his lips, almost as if he wants to sculpt each word, each thought.

In the streets beneath his genteelly shabby and rambling apartment on the third floor of what Indians call a "mansion," horns blat and trucks grind their gears as they attempt to navigate a maelstrom of vehicles, people and ideas. At each sunrise, there seem to be more people, more slums, more garbage, more political rallies, all compressed into a metropolis of blackening buildings, moonscaped roadways and thick swaddlings of air pollution. Visitors shake their heads here, wondering what can become of this city, once so grand and now often politely referred to as a hellhole.

"Calcutta? Where is it going?" the 70-year-old Mr. Ray asks with mock weariness. "The same question has been asked for the last 50 years." He laughs loudly, a deep, euphonious rumble that almost jiggles his china teacup.

> It's heading. It's heading. Nobody knows where. But it's heading. Things are happening. People are buying tickets to see theater or cinema, going to concerts, buying books, going to the book fair—it takes place in all the big cities of India, but it is only in Calcutta that it is a total success.

It is always said that Calcutta is a place of poets and singers, novelists and dreamers. Taxi drivers and postmen, hotel maids and office workers all take up pens and compose and publish. Bengalis here think of themselves as better than other Indians, more intellectual, more thoughtful, less superstitious, less materialistic. Their intellectual saint, Rabindranath Tagore, won the Nobel Prize in Literature. Now, their patron of the screen, Satyajit Ray, has won Hollywood's highest accolade for his moving pictures.

The honorary Academy Award, announced prior to this week's revelation of the traditional nominees in various categories, will be presented March 30 during the annual ceremonies. The citation recognizes Mr. Ray's "rare mastery of the art of motion pictures, and of his profound humanitarian outlook, which has had an indelible influence on film makers and audiences throughout the world." Among directors who have been similarly honored are Akira Kurosawa, Hal Roach, Jean Renoir, Howard Hawks, King Vidor, Charles Chaplin and Orson Welles.

"I'm surprised," admitted Mr. Ray, a tall, lanky man who looks a bit like the silent, gaunt statues on Easter Island.

> I'm surprised particularly because my films are not that well known in the States. They are much better known in Britain, Paris certainly now, and even Japan. But obviously there is a certain section, in any case, who like my films. Anyway, it means a lot to me. It means a lot to me because I've learned my craft of making films by watching Hollywood films of the 30's, 40's and 50's. And I never went to a school. That was my school.

It is not only in the United States that Mr. Ray's work is scantily known. Here, few Indians will admit to having seen one of his films. No theater in India is currently showing a movie by him, and it is unlikely, despite the Oscar, that they will. Like that of Bunuel or Renoir or De Sica, or Federico Fellini or even Mr. Kurosawa, Mr. Ray's work is thoughtful, wrenching, uncomfortable, often distressingly quotidian in its explorations. Instead, India's theaters are filled with the commercial froth of Bombay's huge movie studios, what they call Bollywood, which churn out saccharine and predictable stories of love and violence, all liberally lathered with song and dance.

Even in his beloved Calcutta, it is virtually impossible to find a showing of a movie by Mr. Ray. Every few years, for a week or so, a theater will run his latest endeavor, but despite this city's intellectual pretensions, his films rarely run longer. Partly, Mr. Ray says, this is because of the changes sweeping across India, the pressures of work and, perhaps ultimately, television.

"There are still poets and novelists and film makers and whatnot, but not as many as there used to be," he said, his long fingers toying with his pipe.

> And the novelists and the poets all have very good jobs with good salaries, and the writing has fallen down. They have no new experience to write from. It's very disappointing. Films, of course, are not doing very well at all because of video partly, partly because the theaters are so badly maintained. In summer, there's no air conditioning. They won't run the air conditioning. They use the fans, the electric fans. The projection is bad. The sound is bad. The seats are bad. I mean, we had some of the finest cinemas in India. But no longer. I have stopped going to the cinema. I watch films on video.
>
> Video is not the same as films. . . . Certain films work all right, like a film like *Scenes From a Marriage* by Bergman. That sort of thing works all right because that's made with the television in mind, because it's two people talking most of the time in close-up, fighting and quarrelling and loving and whatnot. But, for instance, my first film, *Pather Panchali:* there's a lot of pictorial quality about it. All that is lost. You can hardly see them on the screen. There is such a thing as a special subject for the cinema. One of the reasons why I enjoy making films is that I enjoy also eventually watching the films with the audience. Otherwise, there's no feedback.
>
> (p. 13)

It was in 1955 that Mr. Ray filmed *Pather Panchali,* the first realistic look at life in the Bengal countryside and the problems individuals and families wrestle with, a picture far from the idealized notions of rural life portrayed in the commercial song-and-dance films beginning to take hold in India. He went on to complete two other films— *Aparajito* (1956) and *The World of Apu* (1959)— following the protagonist in *Pather Panchali* from adolescence to adulthood, through tragedy to a sort of spiritual renewal, from rural naivete to glossy urbanism. Together the three films became known as the *Apu Trilogy,* and they established Mr. Ray as one of the world's finest directors.

In 1955, the Museum of Modern Art in New York gave *Pather Panchali* its United States premiere, and in 1981, it gave Mr. Ray a retrospective. "We consider Satyajit Ray one of the great film makers of all time," said Mary Lea Bandy, the director of the museum's department of film.

"I think he ranks as one of the great humanists in cinema, and he has done a great deal to influence film making and to demystify India."

But film is not Mr. Ray's only pursuit. Like all Bengalis, he has been propelled into other realms by his catholic curiosities. Indeed, the reluctance of India movie houses to show his films means that many Indians know him better as an author of a detective series and several works of science fiction dealing with the derring-do of the mysterious Professor Shonku, inventor of the micromagnascope. He has also written a popular children's book, *The Golden Fortress,* which later was made into a thriller, and he edits *Sandesh,* a children's magazine. "Some of the stories I have written," he wrote in an introduction to one of his collections, "reflect my love of Verne and Wells and Conan Doyle, whose works I read as a schoolboy."

Despite his own health problems—two heart attacks and bypass surgery—Mr. Ray has plunged on. "I will tell you what happened," he said, his storytelling impulse bubbling to the surface.

> After my bypass surgery, for four years I did nothing. I was not allowed to do anything. Finally the doctor said, "You can make a film, but you have to make it entirely in the studio. I won't let you work on location." So for the first time in my life I adapted a play, Ibsen's *Enemy of the People.* I shot it entirely in the studio. But I Indianized it. Well, in his play, the spa water is polluted. But there is no such thing as a spa in India, so I converted it into a temple tank that people drank from. That was polluted. That caused all the drama.

This film, released under the title *Ganashatru* was received unkindly by many of India's critics, critics who have traditionally been admiring of his work despite its lack of commercial appeal.

Undeterred, Mr. Ray went back to his camera and returned with a film that has unsettled many of his Indian viewers. The film, *Shakha Proshakha* or *Branches and Trees* examines a father's awakening to his sons' moral corruption despite his own determined, almost Gandhran, rectitude. In Mr. Ray's characteristic fashion, the themes of family transition, betrayal and tragedy are superimposed upon India's changing face, the contrast between small-town life and the virtues inherent in family life there, and the veneer and sophisticated alienations of urban existence. His film portrays not only a father's disillusionment but hints at the fragility of Indian moral values as an invading modernity rearranges the priorities of the new generation. "You can see corruption in India, can't you," sighed Mr. Ray. "At every level. At every level. I don't know what it means for India."

The idea for his most recent film [*The Stranger*], unreleased yet, . . . came to him after delving into the work of the French anthropologist Claude Levi-Strauss. As in *Shakha Proshakha,* Mr. Ray again looks for the inner soul of man, this time asking whether truth and wisdom inhere in the simplicity of primitive peoples. "This film," Mr. Ray said "questions urban civilization. The idea came to me of civilization itself."

These films, like his others, are unlikely to find a wide audience in India, yet Mr. Ray continues to believe that his work is meant first and foremost for the eyes of his countrymen, for average Indians, if only they would take time to watch. This, he laments, is not true for the crop of new young directors in Calcutta who aspire to follow in his footsteps.

"In Calcutta," he said,

> what happens is that the young film makers make films which are shown privately to friends and small cinemas. They slap each others' backs and say, "How wonderful." Then the films are sent immediately to the festival, get some good reviews from English critics, maybe even win a prize. But they are never released in Calcutta.

> I think that's a horrible situation because I never made films without my own audience in mind. I never made films for England or America. I make films for Bengalis to watch.

India's critics puzzle over Hollywood's recognition of his work. "Belated," is an adjective that has seen prominence in newspapers in recent weeks. In fact, there is a touch of irony to Mr. Ray's Oscar, for it contrasts with his own rather difficult association with America's movie capital. Once, in 1968, he attempted to have a screenplay of his produced there. It was called "The Alien" and recounted the tale of a young Indian village boy who encounters an extra-terrestrial, a script illustrated with Mr. Ray's own drawings of space creatures with large heads and wispy bodies. Despite the widespread circulation of Mr. Ray's script, it was never produced.

Now, though, it does not seem to matter much to Mr. Ray. He has plans to return to his camera before traveling to Hollywood for the Oscar ceremony, a trip he will combine with a visit to his cardiologists in Texas. "I could kill two birds with one stone," he said.

In the meantime, Mr. Ray responds to his well-wishers' letters, frets over where to put the bounty of flowers that arrives daily and watches movies on his television.

> I started as a film fan, writing letters to Deanna Durbin and Ginger Rogers. I look at Ginger Rogers and Fred Astaire quite often. Astaire is incredible. There's no one like Fred Astaire, even the early comics like Buster Keaton and Chaplin and all the rest. I've been watching them again and they haven't faded, you see.

(pp. 13, 21)

Edward A. Gargan, "Satyajit Ray Honored, without Profit in His Land," in The New York Times, *Section 2, February 16, 1992, pp. 13, 21.*

INTERVIEW

Satyajit Ray with Gowri Ramnarayan   (interview date 1992)

[In the following posthumously published interview, Ray discusses his career, his filmmaking techniques, and some of his best-known films.]

Ray, a recipient of a special Oscar at this year's Academy Awards, was consistently true to his art. He combined detached observation with a sensitive understanding of the human predicament, starting with **Pather Panchali (Song of the Little Road,** 1955), the first installment in his great *Apu Trilogy,* through his films about women (**The Goddess,** 1960; **The Big City,** 1963; **The Lonely Wife,** 1964) and Calcutta life (**Company Limited,** 1971; **Distant Thunder,** 1973), to such variegated later works as **The Chess Players** (1977) and **The Stranger** (1991).

Ray harnessed cinema to refract Indian life in ways never seen before, and rarely equaled since. It was only in recent years that his preeminence had been questioned. Some Indian critics and filmmakers found Ray dated in his rigid value systems and naive about contemporary issues; he in turn questioned their integrity and accused them of pandering to Western taste. A few months before his death in April, under strict medical supervision for his heart ailment, the seventy-year-old director reluctantly agreed to a twenty-minute "audience," which, to my delight, stretched to two hours. The epitome of old-world courtesy, Ray was slow to open out, his formal correctness gradually melting to warmth and acceptance.

. . . . .

[*Ramnarayan*]: *Why, having established yourself as one of the most original advertising artists in India, did you give up that career to become a filmmaker?*

[Ray]: Cinema is a great compendium of the arts, requiring everything I am good at—storytelling, visual design, camera work, acting, ingredients theatrical and dramatic, and, finally, musical elements. Advertising techniques, illustration, and calligraphy are involved in planning the scenes, their composition, credit sequences, posters, decor, and costumes. Yes, I had been good at my job as the director of a British advertising agency, but soon realized that an advertising artist is never free. He has to contend with the winds of time. Cinema is the only medium where I could have total creative independence.

In India, where the film industry churns out escapist extravaganzas for mass consumption, you could not hope to get a large audience for the kind of low-budget films you wanted to make—serious, realistic, restrained, literary in tone. Whom are you making your films for?

Oh, for an ideal audience and for my own pleasure. I have to have an audience in mind, and I think for those who will appreciate the niceties and nuances. There *is* such a sophisticated audience, and it is quite large, when you come to think of it in terms of all of India.

You have not only made films for children but used them savvily in many of your other films, in main and supporting roles. How were you able to get them to act so naturally, with all their innocence and insouciance intact?

It is probably something hereditary, a genetic aptitude. My grandfather and father wrote and illustrated books for children and published a children's magazine. The moment I decided to revive that magazine I felt I had to contribute. I began to get more and more ideas for stories, poems, limericks, puzzles, nonsense verse, and before I knew it I had become a successful children's writer. I no longer had to depend on filmmaking to run my family. If I don't make a film a year I won't starve!

My first film, *Pather Panchali,* had two children: a girl of thirteen who was a natural actress and a boy of six who was extremely difficult to handle. I had to devise all sorts of methods, many little tricks to extract what I wanted out of him, which seem funny when I think back. For instance, I needed an expression of shock from the boy when he saw the mother drag his sister violently by the hair. I made him stand on a stool, and, at the crucial moment, had my art director strike the stool with a hammer. We captured the reactive shudder. Very mechanically contrived, but you could not tell the difference on the screen. Here I would like to say that I have no fetish of any sort in making my films. Anything that serves the purpose, whether spontaneous or consciously achieved, is acceptable to me. It is the end that matters.

In the early part of your career you focused on individuals. Later, your canvas widened, in terms of ideologies and issues like unemployment, alienation, corruption, changing values. Was this deliberate?

Yes. I was getting more and more conscious of issues that affect the people in the urban context. In the '70s, Calcutta, this city where I live, was swept by the currents of politics, including the Naxalite agitation [an extremist uprising against the government]. So when I made my films about the city dwellers, I could not ignore them. *The Adversary* [1970] was about a jobless young man, *Company Limited* about an ambitious man's attempts to become one of the directors of his company.

Whether you tie up all the threads neatly or leave a film open-ended, you have never deviated from the code of absolute values you have set for yourself. Isn't your stance of rigid moral rectitude somewhat dated?

You have to accept me as I am, and if you have drawn conclusions from my films, then obviously they are also about the person who made them. The conflict between the old and the new has been a persistent theme which I have played with from many angles. I am not a prude. If I were, I could not have made *The Middle Man* [1975]. I think my films do reflect my preferences for right conduct, an upright lifestyle, the psychological attitudes and the kinds of human relationships I consider admirable and those which I do not.

Your last four films evoke desolation. To the father of **The Branches of the Tree** [*1990*], *the brain-damaged son becomes the true inheritor of virtues, as he has been rendered incorruptible. The "normal" sons are contaminated by dishonesty. Is this your perception of life today?*

Well, almost. Looking around me I feel that the old values of personal integrity, loyalty, liberalism, rationalism, and fair play are all completely gone. People accept corruption as a way of life, as a method of getting along, as a necessary evil. In acquiring material comforts you grow numb with placid acceptance. Maybe you resist in the beginning. But the internal and external pressures crowd to a point where you learn to overlook the moral decline they spell. In *The Branches of the Tree,* the younger son's qualms are not quelled by a colleague's advice. He tries to escape the net to walk the straight line. But we do not know whether he can successfully insulate himself against the pervasive infection. The father says to the mentally deranged son, "You are the only one I have." Bleak, you say. Yes, but somehow uplifting, too, don't you think?

To see your films is to experience your sensitivity to human feelings. But how is it that you have built up such a reputation for standoffishness?

[*Nonplussed*] I haven't the faintest idea how this occurred. Some journalist had come during the shooting of *The Chess Players* and tried to interview me there and then. I had answered, perhaps somewhat rudely, "Later." Well, he wrote rather nastily about me. I am not denying that such things have happened once or twice. But I do let people come and watch me shoot. I answer their questions in the middle of takes. It is my wife who resents such demands on my time. I am generally very accessible. I always pick up my own telephone. I did with you, didn't I? You have noticed that I don't have a secretary. People knock on the door, I open it myself. This reputation for hauteur is something I cannot understand. I don't think I am that kind of person. I feel that I am far more normal, well-behaved, and naturally polite than I am given credit for.

You received an English education at school and college, developing a passion for Western art forms. Have you ever felt torn between the East and the West?

I have felt perfectly harmonious. I think that the Western background in education and my love for Western music, painting, and literature proved invaluable, because cinema is a Western medium. I was very much a Westernized young man when I went to study painting at Santiniketan [Bengali writer Rabindranath Tagore's alternative school]. My three years there helped me to find my roots in Indian culture, so that I began to feel at home in India while my mind wandered around in the West.

Was that when you started thinking in your mother tongue, Bengali?

[*Testily, in "Oxbridge" accent*] I have always thought in Bengali. I do my scripts and my stories in it, you know.

And do you also dream in Bengali?

[*Eyebrows go up*] Dream? Yes, of course.

Your approach to making films has always been oblique, restrained, objective. Is this an acquired Western trait?

I think it is a personal inclination toward subtlety, suggestive elements as opposed to open statements. In *The World of Apu* [1959] the intimacy between the newlywed couple is implied without a single embrace, let alone a kiss. This is my oblique method—of glances and looks—and it works. I am perfectly happy with censorship. Perhaps I have been unconsciously influenced by ancient Indian aesthetic traditions. I don't know. Certainly not Indian films. Consciously, I have admired the approach of certain Western directors like Jean Renoir.

You are a master of characterization, but you have chosen to depict only recognizably "normal" people. Why have you avoided the perverse, the psychotic, and the deviant?

I am more interested in the contrasts and inconsistencies of "normal" patterns of behavior. It is not that everybody is goody-goody—my characters do exhibit great variety. I think large-scale villains are obsolete in India. At least, I can't think of any. I find it interesting to note that seemingly decent people are capable of pettiness and evil. Take my *Branches of the Tree.* The elder sons are certainly villains—trading in black money as they do. Up to that point I permit villainy. Beyond that, the classical type of epic villain is no longer credible, not in my kind of realistic narrative, anyway.

What kind of woman interests you?

Intelligent, sophisticated, untrammeled, independent, with a mind of her own.

Would this include sexual freedom?

Why not?

I ask because you have scrupulously avoided explicit sex and permissive indulgence in your films.

Whenever I come across extreme permissiveness in a foreign film I wonder whether it was thematically obligatory or whether it was a thrust-in titillation. Permissiveness is not something I can accept without very good reasons. There is a suggestive scene in my *Chess Players,* where the wife wants to make love, she makes advances, she unbuttons the husband's jacket, tries to seduce him. He cannot reciprocate; he cannot perform because his mind is obsessed with the game. [*Chuckles*] That, I liked very much. It was my idea, not in the story.

You grew up in the midst of the national struggle for freedom from British rule, in a state that was, and is, perennially in ferment. Though you have at times professed some leftist sentiments, they have remained vague.

I ascribe it to my complete dedication to music and cinema. Young people in Bengal inevitably write poetry. I never did, because I was immersed in discovering the splendors of Western classical music. I don't know if I can convey to you the breathless passion I felt for Beethoven at that time. Those harmonies haunted me night and day. I had no energy left for anything else. Politics, well . . .

Haven't you felt concerned with the cataclysmic upheavals which have rocked the subcontinent continually in your lifetime?

I always felt that there were other people to take care of those national problems, political leaders to direct the action. As a bystander, I observed that there was much friction among the groups. The leaders themselves quite often openly disapproved of one another's methods. I felt this was not my domain. [*Pauses, then continues gently*] You see, there is also the question of money. As a Bengali filmmaker I had a very small market. I couldn't think deep. It would not have been economically viable to think big on such subjects. If you study the first twenty years of my filmmaking, you will find that I am always with intimate subjects. With *The Chess Players* I could be more venturesome, as it was made in Hindi and English—accessible, therefore, to larger audiences. These films only *look* expensive. I kept the costs very low.

What about your spiritual beliefs? At different times, you've described yourself as an atheist or an agnostic!

Did I ever describe myself as an atheist? One lives and learns. I was born into the Brahmo community, but I dislike such labels. Hinduism attracts me, with its coiled cultural layers, only as a rich source of contrastive situations and personalities. Well, I guess I am an agnostic.

Prayer, worship, rituals—do they mean anything to you?

No. They are part of the phenomena I cannot explain, those areas where human knowledge and understanding have not penetrated as yet. Rabindranath Tagore believed in contacts with the dead. Once, during a planchette-induced séance in 1930, he had an hour-long conversation with my dead father. When I made a documentary film on Tagore, I had access to the records of that event—I cannot simply brush it away as bunkum. I have a little grandson now. Watching him makes me realize how complex the evolution of human life has been. So intricate, with its organs for hearing, seeing, eating. There is a master plan, an order, in it. Whether it is the work of a bearded god or a thundering messiah, I don't know.

As you grow older, is it not comforting to believe in God?

[*Sitting up straight*] I don't need that comfort! I get all my fulfillment, my elation, from the work I do.

What does your family mean to you?

We are a very close-knit family. My wife, Bijoya, is really my best friend, as is my only son, Sandip.

Which film gave you the greatest satisfaction to work on?

The last two. *The Branches of the Tree* and *The Stranger.* Among my earlier films, unquestionably *The Lonely Wife.*

Are you content with what you have achieved?

[*Pauses, then, with a faraway look*] More than that . . . Oh, much more than that. (pp. 22, 24, 26)

Satyajit Ray and Gowri Ramnarayan, in an interview in Interview, *Vol. XXII, No. 6, June, 1992, pp. 22, 24, 26.*

OBITUARIES AND TRIBUTES

Peter B. Flint   (essay date 24 April 1992)

[*In the following obituary, Flint reviews Ray's life and career.*]

Satyajit Ray, the versatile and prolific Indian film maker whose *Apu Trilogy* of a childhood, youth and manhood in Bengal was one of the most luminous series in film history, died yesterday in Calcutta. He was 70 years old.

Mr. Ray (his name was pronounced satya-JIT RAY) received an honorary Academy Award last month for lifetime achievement in cinema. He had been suffering from a heart ailment compounded by breathing problems, and was admitted to Belle Vue Hospital in Calcutta on Jan. 29. A three-member delegation from the Oscar committee visited him there on March 16 to present him with the golden statuette. The occasion was filmed, and Mr. Ray's acceptance speech was shown as part of the Academy Awards broadcast on March 30.

Early this month, he also won two top Indian awards—best film and best director—for his 1991 movie, *Agantuk* (*The Visitor*). He was also the recipient of India's highest civilian award, the Bharat Ratna.

The first film in Mr. Ray's spare and sensitive triptych—*Pather Panchali* (*Song of the Road*)—won a special jury prize at the 1956 Cannes International Film Festival and 15 other international awards and is considered by many experts to be one of the best films ever made. The two later works, *Aparajito* (1956) and *The World of Apu* (1959), confirmed his status as a highly talented and at times magical film maker.

Writing in *The New York Times* in 1985, Vincent Canby hailed Mr. Ray as a great and extraordinary movie maker, concluding that "no matter what the particular story, no matter what the social-political circumstances of the characters," his cinema "is so exquisitely realized that an entire world is evoked from comparatively limited details."

To many Western filmgoers, Indian movies are Satyajit Ray, but to most poor, uneducated Indians, his austere delicacy is unsettling. "They usually show my films in Delhi at 8 o'clock on Sunday morning," he said in an interview in *The Times*. "Bengali films don't have a wide audience."

After receiving his Oscar last month, Mr. Ray said: "I have survived because of my foreign market. Without that I wouldn't have survived at all. I would have stopped making films and gone back to my old profession, advertising."

Mr. Ray described himself as "completely self-taught" and said he had learned his craft by watching American films. Even so, he said in an interview in February, there was much more to be learned.

> You had to find out yourself how to catch the hushed stillness of dusk in a Bengali village . . . when the wind drops and turns the ponds into sheets of glass dappled by the leaves of the trees, and the smoke from ovens settles in wispy trails over the landscape, and the plaintive blows on conch shells from homes far and wide are joined by the chorus of crickets, which rises as the light falls, until all one sees are the stars in the sky, and the stars blink and swirl in the thickets.

In 1984, Mr. Ray had two heart attacks and stopped making films for five years. He came back in 1989 with *An Enemy of the People,* an adaptation of the Ibsen play.

Mr. Ray fashioned understated, humanistic films on the various classes of Bengali society, the clash of old and new values and the effects of rapid political and economic change on individuals. His best films won many awards at international festivals.

The Music Room is a tragic 1958 study of an aristocrat in a crumbling mansion who squanders his dwindling resources on elegant musicales. *Two Daughters* combines two bittersweet 1961 vignettes, one about a lonely postmaster and his 10-year-old orphaned housekeeper, the other about an endangered marriage that unexpectedly works. *Charulata* (1964) is a subtle exploration of a marital triangle.

A second Ray series, the *Calcutta Trilogy,* consisted of *Days and Nights in the Forest* (1969), celebrating the joy of living; *The Adversary* (1971), dealing with the frustrations of joblessness, and *The Target* (1972), about a clever manipulator.

Other major works by India's leading director included *Distant Thunder* (1973), about a man-made 1943 famine that killed five million Bengalis, and *The Home and the World* (1984), about an approaching revolution as observed by an affluent woman from her drawing room windows.

Mr. Ray's *Branches of the Tree,* which sought to depict the loss of ethics in an increasingly money-hungry India, was shown at the Walter Reade Theater at Lincoln Center in Manhattan last weekend. In his review in *The New York Times,* Vincent Canby, generally an admirer of Mr. Ray's, lamented that "nothing gets in the way of the talk. . . ."

Mr. Ray produced memorable images in his films and created credible characters in an indirect, Chekhovian manner, remaining sympathetic to them despite their follies and faults.

Detractors accused Mr. Ray of muting the existence of evil and of being so exquisite that he came dangerously close to being precious. They said his movies were slow-paced and lacked continuity. The consensus was that Westerners had to be patient to follow his leisurely rhythm. "What some consider slow," he responded, "may seem eloquent to Indians."

His Bengali-language films were in sharp contrast to the escapist and formula confections of music, dance, romance and violence of the vast Hindi-language film industry in Bombay.

His comparatively small audience forced him to adhere to minuscule budgets (rising to $100,000 from $40,000 over the decades) and to do much of the work himself. In addition to directing, he wrote scripts and music, designed sets, operated cameras, was sometimes the producer and even supervised advertising copy.

In recent weeks, as his country read of Mr. Ray's struggle for life in the Calcutta hospital, the state-run television system broadcast a retrospective of his best-known films in a tribute.

Satyajit Ray was born in Calcutta on May 2, 1921, into a family involved with art and literature. His grandfather, Upendrakisore Ray, wrote juvenile books and founded the first Bengali children's magazine. His father, Sukamar Ray, a merchant, wrote and illustrated two books of nonsense prose and verse that are still popular in Bengal. His mother specialized in handicrafts. His father died when he was 3, and he was raised in the home of a maternal uncle, a devotee of both Eastern and Western music.

Mr. Ray graduated with honors from the University of Calcutta, where he majored in economics and minored in physics. He then studied painting for three years at Visva-Bharati University, which was headed by the Hindu poet Rabindranath Tagore. His major hobby was going to and reading about movies.

He gained notice as a layout artist in the Calcutta office of a British advertising agency he joined in 1943, and became the art director in 1949. During a six-month business trip to London in 1950, he conferred with many film theorists and critics, saw Vittorio de Sica's neo-realist classic *The Bicycle Thief* and resolved to make movies.

On a ship returning to India, he wrote the first draft of a screenplay adapted from *Pather Panchali,* a novel by Bhibuti Bashan Bannerjee, which Mr. Ray had fondly illustrated. He then gained his first taste of movie making by assisting Jean Renoir, who was directing *The River* in Bengal.

Mr. Ray tried repeatedly and unsuccessfully to raise money to film **Pather Panchali.** Undaunted, he began shooting the movie in authentic locales on weekends and holidays in 1952 with about $3,000 he had borrowed and scraped together and with a largely amateur and unpaid crew. He sold all his possessions and pawned his wife's jewelry to keep the faltering project going, but after 18 months it seemed hopeless, until the director John Huston, visiting Calcutta, saw the rough cut of the film in progress. He praised it so highly that the West Bengali government agreed to finance it without a viewing, providing more than $35,000 in return for its ownership. **Pather Panchali** was completed after three years and was said to have bewildered government officials. They thought they had been financing a travelogue.

Nonetheless, the poignant tale of a high-caste but poor village family was an immediate hit among educated Bengalis, and Mr. Ray became a full-time film maker.

The *Apu Trilogy* provided a microcosm of the changing society of modern India by progressing from a tightly knit family in a primitive village through migration to the cities and ending with the educated protagonist nearly isolated.

The movie maker was an amiable, introspective 6-foot-4 figure with a strong face and a commanding voice. He

spoke English with a British accent and had a passion for the cultural heritage of India. He and his wife, Bijoya Das, a former schoolteacher, lived for many years in a bright, airy, book-lined apartment overlooking a courtyard in downtown Calcutta. They had one son, Sandip, also a film maker.

"Calcutta is love and hate with me," Mr. Ray told *The New York Times.*

> I can't work anywhere else. I have my roots here. It can be a depressing place, but it's vital. I have no desire to work outside of India. I have had offers to go to California, but I'm not used to working in a studio setup. I fear I'll lose my freedom, my confidence, I don't know. I couldn't tolerate memos, front offices and temperamental stars.

The Communist-led coalition in his home state of West Bengal declared today a state holiday to honor Mr. Ray and said he would be cremated with full state honors.

He is survived by his wife and son.

> *Peter B. Flint, in an obituary in* The New York Times, *April 24, 1992, p. A25.*

The Times, London   (essay date 24 April 1992)

[*In the following obituary, the writer provides an overview of Ray's life and career.*]

A month ago Satyajit Ray was awarded an honorary Oscar for a lifetime's achievement in the cinema, the only Indian to receive such a prize. He was too ill to receive it and three members of the Academy of Motion Picture Arts and Sciences flew to Calcutta to present him with the award in the hospital where he had been since the beginning of the year.

That Oscar was fully deserved. Ray was one of the great humanists of world cinema, a man who towered above other Indian directors. He chose to work totally apart from India's vast, brash commercial film industry centred on Bombay, staying quietly in his native Bengal where, starting in 1954, he turned out a stream of more than 35 films, mostly low-budget, which encompassed the full range of local society from the rich to the achingly poor.

His warm compassion for people of all kinds, together with his rich sense of their comic and pathetic sides, led him to be compared to Jean Renoir; his wistful, poetic nostalgia, and his awareness of life's wasted opportunities, brought echoes of Chekhov; and his feeling for the social nuances and hidden tensions of a still puritanical and repressed society led to comparisons with Henry James.

Though deeply sensitive to Bengali culture and spirituality, Ray was a cosmopolitan, much more at ease with Western culture than, say, the great Japanese directors. He was thus able to interpret Indian life and values to Western audiences as vividly and sympathetically as any other artist has ever done. This did not stop local critics being censorious about Ray's more recent films which, they claimed, were insufficiently critical of the society around him. Non-Bengalis were ready to attack him for being too rarified and for presenting an India for overseas consumption.

Ray was fond of describing himself as middle class. He was born into an artistic family—his father was a writer and painter, his grandfather a friend of Rabindranath Tagore. He studied for three years in Tagore's shadow, in the college that the great man had founded at Santinekatan. Tagore was to be a life-long influence. Another early mentor was Renoir who encouraged Ray to start making films when he himself was in Bengal, shooting *The River*.

While earning his living as an illustrator in an advertising agency, Ray spent his Sundays over three years filming *Pather Panchali,* the first part of his celebrated *Apu Trilogy* about Bengal peasant life. The film's gentle simplicity and lyric vision excited the 1956 Cannes Festival where it came as a new voice from a little-known world. Around the globe it won ten prizes. The two later films followed the boy Apu into manhood and the inevitable Indian struggle for survival.

Another early film, *The Music Room* (1958), was the elegiac portrait of a decaying landowner, neglecting his business and burying himself in music and art: it showed that Ray, despite his Leftish views, could be as sensitive to the dying world of patrician grace as he was to the plight of the peasantry. In his middle period, two poetic masterpieces were *Charulata* (1963) and *Days and Nights in the Forest* (1970). The first, from a story by Tagore set in the 1880s, was a delicate study of an educated woman torn between her neglectful husband and a literary cousin. The languor of Indian upper-class life, the sounds and shadows of the household, the gentle regret of desire unfulfilled—all were beautifully conveyed. In *Days and Nights,* Ray took a seemingly trivial tale of four young men from Calcutta, fooling about on a holiday jaunt in the hills, and made of it a serene and perceptive study, both comic and tender, of the transience of happiness and the search for love. The delightful pastoral setting was counterpointed by the theme of the tensions of Indian city life.

Ray was by now being accused by some Indians of neglecting political and urban realities and escaping into rural and historical idylls. Partly in answer to this he next made a number of films about urban life in Calcutta. *Company Limited* (1970) was a study of India's new managerial ruling class—of an ambitious young man who sells his integrity to advance his career as a factory executive. *The Middleman* (1975), equally acute and ironical, was about a young upper-caste graduate who—like so many—fails to find a proper job and is reduced to the ignominy of touting and pimping for businessmen.

Other notable films of this period looked at some of the social and political problems of India's past. *Distant Thunder* charted the impact on a Bengal village of the great famine of 1943, and also examined the cruelties of the caste system. *The Chess Players* (1977) was Ray's only film to be made not in Bengali but in Hindi and English, and with a relatively large budget: starring Richard Attenborough, it was about the British annexation of Oudh in 1856. Ray carefully avoided passing judgment on the cultured but effete local rulers whose corruption had made

the take-over inevitable. But his clear implication was that Indians had only themselves to blame for British colonisations—and this did not endear him to his fellow countrymen. In 1982 came *Ghare Baire (Home and the World),* based on a Tagore novel about the Bengal bourgeoisie.

Ray was a majestic 6 ft. 4 in. with handsome patrician features—a kindly man, shy and modest, lacking in "side" or that species of mere bad temper that so often passes for artistic temperament.

Amazingly versatile (India's Renaissance Man, he was called), he wrote his own scripts, composed the music for his films, even operated the camera. Steeped in literature both of East and West, he was a man who bridged cultures. This often exposed him to the inevitable criticism that he had become too westernised. Indian radicals also disliked the ambivalence which appeared to result from his combining progressive views with a sympathy for traditional Indian values, spiritual and aristocratic. Though he did class himself as a radical, and felt concern for the poor and outcast, yet Ray grew increasingly impatient with doctrinaire Leftism.

He was certainly more highly regarded in the West than in his own country. The Indian film industry resented his refusal to compromise with it. Repeatedly, he refused offers to work in Bombay or Hollywood, believing that his strength lay in staying close to his Bengali roots, where in his early work he was a true neo-realist, much influenced by de Sica and, like him, often using non-professional actors.

His essential quality was his feeling for character, its quirks and oddities as well as its deeper emotions, and his subtle portrayal of loyalty, humiliation, love and yearning. His constant theme was the tension between change and tradition in modern India, and his method was a gently contemplative style of filmmaking, rich in understatement—"I try," he said, "to capture the half-shades, the hardly audible notes."

He thus appeared a rather old-fashioned and "literary" director. Typically, one of his last films *Ganashatru* masterminded from his apartment in a crumbling Victorian house, was based on Ibsen's *An Enemy of the People.* For this "bookishness" he was criticised, as he was for the slow pace of his films. But his admirers would reply that the latter reflected the true tempo of Indian life, leisurely, lethargic. The sum of his achievement was that he made the lives of Bengalis into something universal, and was able to project the joys and travails of his native land into the hearts and minds of the West. For this he will be permanently remembered.

One token of his culture-bridging, and of his skill, is that he succeeded in translating Edward Lear and Lewis Carroll into Bengali. He had, after all, in true middle class fashion been brought up on *The Boy's Own Paper* and Wodehouse.

Satyajit Ray is survived by his wife, Bijoya and his son, Sandip.

An obituary in The Times, *London, April 24, 1992, p. 13.*

Paul Levy   (essay date 29 April 1992)

[*In the following essay, Levy describes the scene at Ray's state funeral, the reputation his work has earned in India and abroad, and his importance to the people of his home state, West Bengal, India.*]

How big is a crowd of one million people? It's impossible to convey the sensation of being in such a throng of humanity, but that's how many of the citizens of the communist-ruled state of West Bengal gathered here for the funeral of Satyajit Ray on Friday. The Academy Award-winning film maker's body was lying in state at the West Bengal Film Institute in a section of the city called Nandan, and the sheer number of mourners made it impossible for some time to maneuver the flower-garlanded open coffin onto the gun carriage, a decoratively painted flatbed truck. The police were worried that the half-million or so who hadn't succeeded in entering Nandan might riot.

A state holiday had been declared, allowing many of Calcutta's working people to view the hastily embalmed body, with its distressingly evident cotton wool plugs in the nostrils, and his heavy-rimmed glasses perched awkwardly on his illness-ravaged face. Mr. Ray, who was 70 when he died Thursday, on Shakespeare's birthday, had been in a nursing home for three months.

Ministers of the state and central governments, members of the family and scores of film industry notables and stars (but only one from Bombay's tawdry "Bollywood," whose collective absence was remarked negatively by the press) placed tributes of jasmine and sickly perfumed tuberoses on the coffin. So did thousands of schoolchildren, women in their best saris and ordinary working men wearing the Bengali *dhoti,* the starched, finely pleated skirtlike traditional dress. The stifling atmosphere, as the temperature was in the high 90s, was scented even more strongly by the cooling rose water ladled onto the body by mourners.

But how did a maker of such highbrow films as ***Pather Panchali*** (Mr. Ray's first film, made in 1954, the first part of his *Apu Trilogy* so widely acclaimed in the West) and his only non-Bengali film, ***The Chess Players*** (1977), come to be the object of mass veneration? He was seriously underappreciated in India until his international celebrity was confirmed by an Oscar for lifetime achievement earlier this year. The Indian film industry then belatedly acknowledged his genius with two major awards. Moreover, as one of his associates on ***The Chess Players,*** the sole representative of "Bollywood" present for the rites here, remarked bitterly to me, there was no national mourning for Mr. Ray, though flags routinely fly at half-staff when ordinary politicians die.

The answer is that Mr. Ray meant much more to the fiercely cultured people of this extraordinarily literate region of the east coast of India than his films or his Oscar. In Bengal, he actually *was* a commercial success, not just a maker of art movies. But, more than that, he was the last man of the Bengal renaissance, a popular cultural hero, a writer, musician and composer, illustrator and designer of books and creator of three widely used typefaces that bear his name, even editor of a children's magazine founded by

his father, for which Mr. Ray personally drew the comic strip.

> ## To the people of West Bengal it is as though William Shakespeare and John Lennon died on the same day.
>
> —*Vir Sanghvi*

It is difficult for outsiders to understand the intensity with which he was loved by Bengalis, who are said to have poetry in their soul as well as their language. To Bengalis under 25, though, Mr. Ray is remembered not as a film maker but as a writer, especially of children's books. He was the best-selling author in the Bengali language, and the largest royalty earner in all India.

Vir Sanghvi, the Oxford-educated editor of *Sunday,* India's largest weekly news magazine, the editorial offices of which are in Calcutta, explained Mr. Ray to me: "To the people of West Bengal it is as though William Shakespeare and John Lennon died on the same day. He was not just a cultural icon, but for the past 40 years a popular hero whose following rivaled any Western pop star's."

India's largest circulation daily newspaper, the Bengali-language *Anandabazar Patrika,* printed half a million copies on Friday, and sold out minutes after the papers hit the streets. "This was 100,000 more than the usual print run," said the editor, Aveek Sarkar, "and as a mark of respect to Ray, that day's edition did not carry a single advertisement."

Satyajit Ray was the last representative of the city's liberal, humanist Hindu reform Brahmo movement, and its greatest figure after India's only Nobel Prize-winning writer (1913), Rabindranath Tagore, whose own funeral in 1941 was perhaps the last time crowds of this size massed here. The Ray last rites were Brahmo, a Jesuit-influenced religion founded by Tagore's father, and transformed into a cultural movement by Tagore and ultimately absorbed into the larger culture of India, becoming the "politics of Nehru," according to V. S. Naipaul. The ceremonies were identical with orthodox Hindu rites, except for the omission of ritual feedings of the pundits or Brahmans.

By tradition, cremations must take place by 9:40 p.m. Finally at 9:38—only one hour late—the body was consigned to the flames of the electric crematorium of Keoratala. There was a scuffle, as two hooligans had gotten through security and heckled and threw punches at officials. But the commotion was nothing compared with that at Tagore's funeral, where the crowds went berserk.

The mood was somber. Calcutta was mourning for itself. Mr. Ray had been the emblem of Bengal's self-esteem. The city's infrastructure is decaying, and though the dirt and the beggars are not as evident as I expected them to be, the press worries about lack of attention from the central government, economic decline and "the yokelisation of Calcutta."

A *Calcutta Telegraph* editorial said: "Satyajit Ray's death on Thursday was not merely a national tragedy, it was a Bengali disaster . . . Ray has been unkind to Bengal. By leaving it orphaned he has also taken away its only source of self-respect."

> *Paul Levy, "In the Huge Crowd at Ray's Last Rites," in* The Wall Street Journal, *April 29, 1992, p. A16.*

Stanley Kauffmann   (essay date 15 June 1992)

[*In the following essay, Kauffmann praises Ray's life and career and reviews his last film,* The Stranger.]

What is a hero? One definition: Satyajit Ray. His protracted death last month, news of which arrived just as his **Branches of the Tree** appeared here, concluded a courageous life. Like tens of thousands around the world, I felt through the years that, whatever the many ebbs and occasional flows of film integrity, Ray was off there in Calcutta working—succeeding, sometimes succeeding less, but living in art. For him, it wasn't at all a matter of not selling out. Although he had offers from Hollywood and elsewhere, his persistence at his own work was not noble resistance of temptation. It was the highest form of self-indulgence. He did what he wanted to do.

He was born in 1921 into a family active in several arts and finished his education at the "world university" founded by Rabindranath Tagore, who was a friend of his father and grandfather. During World War II Ray was constrained to take a job with a British-run advertising agency in Calcutta and became its art director. He stayed there for ten years, toward the end of which Jean Renoir arrived in Calcutta to make *The River.* Ray called on him, proposed himself as a location scout, and assisted Renoir as much and as often as he could.

Ray was fond of a novel by Bibhutibhusan Banerjee called *Pather Panchali* and stored it away in his mind as a possible project for the filmmaking he wanted to try. At this time his agency sent him to its London office for a six-month stay. Later he said:

> Within three days of arriving I saw *Bicycle Thieves.* I knew immediately that if I ever made **Pather Panchali** . . . I would make it in the same way, using natural locations and unknown actors.

As for method: "Simplicity of plot allows for intensive treatment. . . . De Sica, and not DeMille, should be [the Indian filmmaker's] ideal." In fact, although he later used well-known actors, he was more consistently faithful to that ideal than his exemplar.

When Ray returned to Calcutta, he took the plunge into a life of filmmaking, prepared a script of **Pather Panchali,** and tried to set to work. The details of the difficulties and discouragements and delays are too many to recount. I note only that much of the work had to be done on weekends and during vacations because many of the friends who helped him were holding down other jobs. In 1955, five years later, the film was finished.

I thought of this five-year struggle when I read in Ray's obituary that the state of West Bengal would give him high funeral honors and had declared a state holiday for the occasion. It's no longer ironic, it's simply a fact of existence that a society does much to impede an artist or scientist or intellectual, especially at the beginning, and then climbs on the bandwagon, or funeral train, at the end. True, Ray got some financial assistance from the government for **Pather Panchali,** but they kept every penny of foreign revenue from the picture and they tried to get him to give the film an upbeat ending. Ray withstood the pressure. Now the government declares a holiday in his honor, and India will probably put his face on a postage stamp.

Ray made more than thirty films; here is the last of them. **The Stranger** is representative Ray. It uses a simple, rather familiar plot—the mysterious visitor—and makes it fresh chiefly by paying little attention to it, by concentrating on the people as such. The first thing we see is an envelope addressed to a woman. She is a well-to-do Calcuttan woman with a husband and small son, and she learns from the letter that an uncle she hasn't seen or heard from in thirty years is coming to visit.

Her husband immediately suspects that the uncle is a phony; but phony or not, he must be after a share of a family inheritance that is being held in escrow and that they would otherwise get. The uncle appears sooner than expected, stays with them, and proceeds on a course of charm and domination. He has traveled widely, including America, he says, and has spent much of his life with primitive tribes. After various quizzes of him, subtle and less subtle, through all of which he is unfazed and poised, he suddenly disappears.

The family tracks him to the country home of the guardian of the legacy. The uncle has got his money but is pleased to see them and takes them to a dance festival in a nearby village—people descended from the earliest inhabitants of India. The dancing is so moving that the niece herself joins in.

Very soon the uncle is on his way again, wandering around the world. He leaves an envelope with his niece that, as he requests, she opens only after he leaves. It contains a check for his entire share of the legacy, made out to her. Thus the film ends as it begins, with a letter from this uncle.

Two themes are apparent. The first—Ray said that [anthropologist Claude] Lévi-Strauss had affected him—is the joining of modern people with the ancient essences of their culture. But much more fully developed is the theme of the uncle's identity. It is never conclusively proved that he is who he claims to be. When the film is finished, this ambiguity is less important than the fact that he appeared, had a beneficent effect, and moved on. If Ray is not implying a mystical visitant in hearty, vernacular guise, he is saying something about mundane guardedness and suspicion, about the maiming of openness in modern life.

Prominent in the cast is Utpal Dutt, who has worked with Ray before. Dutt, an influential leader in the radical theater movement of Bengal, plays the uncle with the chordal quality of a man who is simultaneously overbearing and winning.

Ray wrote the pleasant score as well as, of course, the screenplay, and directed at his best, which is to say his most confidently simple. The camera becomes just another occupant of the room. (Except for a few sequences near the end, the film takes place indoors.) Editing is never done for effect, only to assist natural flow. Occasionally Ray moves the camera slowly away from or toward a speaker, but always for an intrinsic reason, never merely for variety. He himself said that his later work consisted of chamber-music films. The term is apt.

The Stranger, like *Branches of the Tree,* was first presented at the Walter Reade Theater in New York for a limited engagement. Both films ought to be seen by the audience—it does exist in this country—that would be moved and heartened by them. (pp. 30-1)

> *Stanley Kauffmann, "Farewell and Hail," in* The New Republic, *Vol. 206, No. 24, June 15, 1992, pp. 30-1.*

REVIEWS OF RAY'S RECENT WORKS

Stanley Kauffmann   (review date 11 May 1992)

[*In the following review, written shortly before the film-maker's death, Kauffmann discusses Ray's* Branches of the Tree *and the "essentially cinematic" qualities that characterize Ray's work.*]

Satyajit Ray makes an assumption about his viewers. He assumes that they can be interested in a film that simply dwells with its characters, rather than one that imposes dramatic patterns on their lives. Part of his assumption rests on a common culture with his immediate public. ("All my films are made with my own Bengali audience in view," he has said.) But by now, after nearly forty years of filmmaking and more than thirty films, he knows that his work touches other viewers as well, that, by being faithfully Bengali, he can also reach other sorts of people. His films are one more example of the truism that the road to universality starts in a particularized place.

This is a far cry from saying that Ray's films are international smasheroos. (They aren't even national smasheroos: only 55 million of India's 840 million speak Bengali.) At home, in West Bengal, the films cut across several social strata; abroad they are epicurean. The critic Rustom Bharucha, himself Calcuttan but writing in America, said, "If one had to select an essentially cinematic quality that epitomizes Ray's films, it would be his acute awareness of the minuscule," which limits their occidental appeal.

Sometimes Ray can carry this minuscular quality so far that his films become not daintily precious but almost busily bland, as if the camera had been stuck through a win-

dow somewhat in Andy Warhol fashion to record undifferentiated dailiness. But at his best, as in the *Apu Trilogy* and *Charulata* and *The Chess Players,* Ray creates a tension between our general expectations of film and his refusal to fulfill those expectations, thus showing—proving—that film can be and do more.

One of his latest films to reach us, *Branches of the Tree,* restates that quiet proposition quietly. . . . The new film is above the middle level of Ray's work, not in the class of the titles above but a gratifying experience for Blakean world-in-a-grain-of-sand people. A much-respected Bengali man, prosperous and public-minded, is given a celebration for his 70th birthday at which he has a heart attack. One of his sons, whose mind was unsettled in an auto accident, lives with the father but is unable to comprehend what has happened. The man's three other sons hurry from their fairly distant homes, with their families, to be near him. In the week of his recuperation, we grow to know these sons and perceive the moral spectrum that they and their wives encompass. That is all.

The father has always said there is white money and black money; we find out which of the sons has opted for which. The presence in the house of the father's father, aged 93, and of a child helps to give us a sense of the line in which these ethical questions are set, and the mentally incompetent son supplies a kind of null amorality. (One of the sons has been so revolted by the peculations of his employer that he has quit his job to enter a purer world, the theater. Evidently purity, like beauty, is in the eye of the beholder.)

Almost all of the film takes place indoors, in the ill man's house. The camera opens on a huge flower arrangement in the middle of a drawing-room table, then concentrates on the paterfamilias and his afflicted son. A servant comes in to clear things and leaves, walking past the camera with seeming disregard of his place in focus. When Ray is operating at his most astute, as he is here, he is trying to controvert the Heisenberg principle: these people are observed without disturbing the order of their lives. This pleasant artifice of non-artifice continues throughout.

Ray, who writes his own screenplays though often from other material, is sometimes called Chekhovian. This seems to me superficial. Chekhov, incomparably subtle and implicative though he was, used those qualities to dramatize lives. Ray's intent is more like Yasujiro Ozu's. (In fact, *Branches of the Tree* has some resemblance to the last section of *Tokyo Story*.) The artist's vocation, according to this intent, is to find revealing currents of life, to respect them and let them flow. Ray lacks Ozu's complete technical mastery; there is some bumpy editing. And the performances sometimes stray into theatricality. But his ambition is the same as Ozu's.

Those who saw the last Oscar telecast saw Ray accepting a special award in his hospital bed in Calcutta. He has been gravely ill for some time. But there is at least one more completed film, *The Stranger,* coming. . . . (p. 30)

> *Stanley Kauffmann, "Assumptions," in* The New Republic, *Vol. 206, No. 19, May 11, 1992, pp. 30-1.*

Terrence Rafferty   (review date 18 May 1992)

[*In the following review, Rafferty examines Ray's last film,* The Stranger, *and assesses his body of work.*]

The hero of Satyajit Ray's *The Stranger* (*Agantuk*) is a mysterious visitor. In the opening scene, a middle-class Calcutta woman named Anila Bose receives a letter from someone claiming to be her long-lost uncle Manmohan Mitra, who left India for Europe in 1955 and has never returned; no one in the family has had so much as a postcard from him in over twenty years. He will, he says, be passing through Calcutta for a week, and hopes to stay with his niece. Anila, who was only two years old when she last saw her uncle, is confused and upset by the letter. Her husband, a businessman named Sudhindra, is openly skeptical; he isn't keen on extending hospitality to a man who might well be an impostor, even a criminal. But Anila, despite her own uncertainty, persuades her husband to take the alleged uncle in; they'll reserve judgment and lock up their valuables. Mitra proves to be a charming, erudite, and not particularly threatening middle-aged man—a lively raconteur who seems to have travelled all over the world, and who becomes especially animated when he muses on the differences between primitive and developed societies. He gave up his early artistic ambitions, he says, when he saw a prehistoric painting of a charging bison, and realized that he could never achieve the power of the primitive artist's simple, expressive strokes. The Boses are—warily—fascinated by their house guest, and they recognize rather quickly that there's no easy, conclusive way for them to resolve their doubts about his identity. Mitra acknowledges their suspicion right away: in his first conversation with Sudhindra, he says, "I know who you are, but you don't know who I am." What's more, he doesn't *want* his hosts to make up their minds too readily. "Only time," he says, can tell them if he is who he claims to be. A little later, without being asked, he shows Sudhindra his passport, and the younger man, eager for something definitive, looks entirely satisfied. To our surprise, and Sudhindra's, Mitra argues vehemently that the passport "proves nothing." He won't allow the Boses to decide the issue of his integrity on the basis of that sort of evidence.

This odd exchange, which takes place about half an hour into the picture, gives resonance to everything that happens after it. In a sense, Mitra's refusal to let the passport settle the case is the key to understanding not only *The Stranger* but all of Ray's work. This movie, like each of the twenty-seven other features that Ray wrote and directed, from 1955 on, doesn't announce itself immediately: both its style and its story are based on the principle that knowledge of people can be acquired only gradually and tentatively, by means of a patient accumulation of intimate experiences. His films require us to live with his characters for a while before we decide who they really are. For Ray, as for Mitra in *The Stranger,* Sudhindra's instantaneous reversal of judgment, from profound distrust to total acceptance, is inconceivable, absurd. After that scene, the nature of the movie's dramatic (and comic) tensions seems to shift. We're less concerned with the stark question of whether the visitor is or is not who he says he is, and more interested in the contradictory ways in which

the hosts deal with their uncertainty: at times, they appear to be letting down their guard, holding their suspicions in abeyance, as they share food and conversation with their likable guest; at other times, their desire for an unambiguous resolution gets the better of them, and they start scrambling around in search of a clue, a decisive piece of evidence for conviction or acquittal.

The Stranger . . . is a modest picture, a graceful domestic comedy made in a serene, leisurely classical style. Ray's manner here is unusually direct and plain-spoken: there are a handful of awkward moments in which he seems to be lecturing the audience on the shallowness of contemporary society. This is a lovely, flawed movie rather than a great one, but if we listen closely and wait until the end before making up our minds about it we can still hear in it the voice of a great artist. And it's the last movie we'll ever have from Satyajit Ray: he died on April 23rd in Calcutta, a few days short of his seventy-first birthday. Three weeks earlier, Ray was seen, on tape, on the Academy Awards show. Lying in a hospital bed and gripping the honorary Oscar that the Academy had given him, he looked and sounded shockingly frail. (In the last eight years of his life, he suffered from a serious heart condition, which prevented him from making films between 1984 and 1989.) Despite his weakened state, he delivered (in English) a lucid, touching, and elegantly phrased speech about his love of movies, in which he acknowledged, graciously, his debt to the Hollywood pictures he saw as a child and as a young man. His words followed a hectic, clumsily assembled two-minute montage of moments from his films, a jumble of striking "exotic" images that must have given viewers unfamiliar with his work the impression that he was some sort of primitive artist whose films were being honored for their anthropological value. And it must have been difficult for those viewers to connect the crude-looking images with the courtly, cultured man who appeared on the screen a few seconds later. With a filmmaker like Ray, film clips—moments ripped out of the slow-building, lifelike flow of experience that each of his movies seeks to re-create—are worthless. They tell us as little about him as a passport would.

Ray's first feature, *Pather Panchali,* which is the story of a boy, Apu, growing up in a poor Bengali village, is the only one of his movies that was widely seen in the United States. In two subsequent films, *Aparajito* (1956) and *The World of Apu* (1959), he continued the story of Apu through adolescence and young manhood: the hero goes to school, moves to Calcutta, and tries to become a writer. The *Apu Trilogy* isn't Ray's autobiography. He was born into a family of middle-class Calcutta artists and intellectuals: he began where Apu aspires to end up. Although most of Ray's movies are about people whose background is closer to his own than to that of the boy Apu, the De Sica-like depiction of rural poverty in *Pather Panchali* remains his best-known achievement. It's a wonderful movie, but the full Apu trilogy is more wonderful still, and the body of work that Ray built over three decades—much of which appeared only briefly in America, and only in big-city theatres, and very little of which is currently available on videocassette—is as rich and various as any in movie history. His best historical films—the grandly passionate *The Music Room* (1958) and the delicate, lyri-cal *Charulata* (1964)—are dense with felt detail and imaginative sympathy with the traditions of Bengali culture. The films with contemporary settings, like *Days and Nights in the Forest* (1969) and *The Middleman* (1975), are distinguished by an extraordinary sense of moral urgency—a search for values that are strong and yet not inhumanly rigorous. Like Jean Renoir, one of his early idols, Ray combined a complex, restless intelligence with a deep simplicity of spirit, and shared them with his audience.

In the final scenes of *The Stranger,* Ray takes us out of Calcutta and into the countryside, where the mysterious visitor watches an ecstatic tribal dance with the Boses and then—after a cut back to the city—says goodbye to them. He leaves with them an envelope that contains a polite thank-you note and something else: an unexpected legacy. The last shot of Satyajit Ray's last movie is of the Boses looking at each other in astonishment. They don't know what to make of the gift they've been given, don't quite understand the man who has given it to them. The movie, which has ostensibly solved its central mystery, thus ends with a moment of fresh wonderment, a sense of further human mysteries to be puzzled over. The visitor's parting gesture closes the narrative with a satisfying snap, and yet seems to open up something else, which is harder to define. He has left his hosts grateful and unsettled in just about equal measure: his gift is an answer that reframes the question. Satyajit Ray is gone now, and at the conclusion of his twenty-eighth movie we still feel as if he hadn't reached the end of his explorations, as if we hadn't really got to the bottom of who he was, as if the visit had been too short. (pp. 79-80)

> *Terrence Rafferty, "Legacy," in* The New *Yorker, Vol. LXVIII, No. 13, May 18, 1992, pp. 79-81.*

Vincent Canby   (review date 22 May 1992)

[*In the following review, Canby praises* The Stranger's *parable-like narrative and sense of "enchantment," calling the film "a fitting grace note" to a brilliant career.*]

Satyajit Ray's last film, *The Stranger,* is a fitting grace note to the career of the great Indian film maker, who died last month, just short of his 71st birthday. *The Stranger* is a small, gentle, exquisitely realized comedy about, among other things, family loyalties and trust in a world in which traditions have been devalued.

The film, written and directed by Ray, has the shapeliness and some of the mystery of a parable. One morning a letter arrives at the perfectly ordered upper-middle-class household of Sudhindra Bose. It is for his wife, Anila. "Ah," says Sudhindra in English, "a massive missive."

His good spirits disappear when he hears that the letter is from Anila's long-lost uncle, Manomohan, who left home

in 1955 and hasn't been heard from since 1968. Manomohan writes with a somewhat majestic air, "I have finished my travels in the West." He says he is returning to Calcutta and wants to spend a week with his niece.

Sudhindra, who doesn't otherwise appear to be unusually suspicious, immediately suggests that the letter could be from an imposter, someone out to borrow money or even to steal their valuable antique bronzes. Sudhindra's small son is ecstatic at the prospect of the visit: "A fake great uncle!" Anila says they have to take the man in. Traditional Indian hospitality demands that they receive him.

The Stranger is a kind of elegiac *Man Who Came to Dinner.* Manomohan arrives and settles in, to the delight of the little boy, the confusion of Anila and the increasing suspicions of her husband. One of the more disconcerting things about the aging uncle is that he is completely aware of their discomfort, which both amuses and saddens him.

He charms the boy with tales of his travels in Europe, the American West and Machu Picchu in South America. He explains the difference between solar and lunar eclipses. He seems to know the answers to the mysteries of the universe. For Sudhindra's benefit, he produces his passport with his name and picture. Anila is convinced of his identity but Sudhindra remains sceptical.

In a series of beautifully observed (and acted) encounters, including one in which Manomohan is rudely cross-examined by a journalist friend of the family, he slowly turns the tables on Anila's suspicious husband. When Manomohan finally leaves, this time to check out Australia, he has forever changed the lives of Sudhindra, Anila and the boy, Satyaki.

The name of the boy suggests that Ray may be recalling some incident from his own childhood. Maybe not. Yet *The Stranger* has about it an air of enchantment, of a story out of the past, repeatedly retold and embellished through time. Manomohan . . . is a boy's idealized great-uncle, someone who has been nearly everywhere, seen nearly everything and has the freedom to keep on going. As he passes through this household he transforms the boy's mother and father into better parents. More important, he teaches the boy to question life, to pursue his own independent course and finally to respect the past.

The Stranger doesn't necessarily change one's perception of Ray's career. It doesn't compete with the great films—the *Apu Trilogy,* *Charulata,* *Distant Thunder* and *The Chess Players*. Yet it couldn't have been made by any other film maker. *The Stranger* is a sweet and enriching dividend.

> *Vincent Canby, "Satyajit Ray: A Work of Closure," in* The New York Times, *May 22, 1992, p. C13.*

Additional coverage of Ray's life and career is contained in the following sources published by Gale Research: *Contemporary Authors,* Vols. 114, 137 (obituary); and *Contemporary Literary Criticism,* Vol. 16.

Obituaries

In addition to the authors represented in the In Memoriam section of the *Yearbook,* the following notable writers died during 1992:

William Christopher Barrett
December 30, 1913—September 8, 1992
American philosopher and nonfiction writer

Barrett is widely recognized for introducing the European theory of existentialism to the United States in his first book, *Irrational Man* (1958), which is regarded as the definitive text for the general reader. Although Barrett was a Marxist during his youth and an anti-communist liberal during the Cold War, he later promoted a mixture of liberal and conservative views that became known as neo-conservatism. Throughout his career Barrett published numerous works on philosophy and intellectual life, including *The Truants: Adventures among the Intellectuals* (1982) and *Death of the Soul: From Descartes to the Computer* (1986). [For further information on Barrett's life and works, see *CLC,* Volume 27.]

Allan David Bloom
September 14, 1930—October 7, 1992
American philosopher, essayist, and educator

A professor of political philosophy, Bloom became famous for his indictment of higher education in America, *The Closing of the American Mind: How Higher Education Has Failed Democracy and Impoverished the Souls of Today's Students* (1987). In this work, Bloom argued that American universities began to decline during the 1960s as a result of liberal approaches to education that neglected classic works of Western culture and traditional morality. While many critics lauded the work, Bloom's views on such issues as multiculturalism and political correctness have generated widespread controversy. Bloom was awarded the Jean Jacques Rousseau Prize in 1987 and the Charles Frankel Prize from the National Endowment for the Humanities in 1992.

Kay Boyle
February 19, 1902—December 27, 1992
American short story writer, novelist, poet, essayist,
translator, author of children's books, and editor

Often associated with the Lost Generation literary movement of the 1920s and 1930s, Boyle is best known for novels and short story collections in which she employs terse understatement, interior monologue, stream-of-consciousness narrative, and surrealist prose to reflect the alienation and disillusionment associated with the years surrounding World Wars I and II. Her works—which include the short story collections *Wedding Days, and Other Stories* (1930), *The White Horses of Vienna, and Other Stories* (1936), *Life Being the Best, and Other Stories* (1988), and the novels *Plagued by the Nightingale* (1931), *Death of a Man* (1936), *Avalanche* (1944), and *A Frenchman Must Die* (1946)—delineate her experiences in Europe and examine contemporary social issues. Boyle received the O. Henry Prize for the short stories "Defeat" and "The White Horses of Vienna," which are considered two of the finest short stories of the twentieth century. [For further information on Boyle's life and works, see *CLC,* Volumes 1, 5, 19, and 58.]

Laurie Colwin
1944—October 24, 1992
American novelist, short story writer, and essayist

Praised for the humor and distinctive style of her writing, Colwin is best known for novels and short stories that center on characters living in New York City. She is also noted for her examination of the psychological aspects of romantic relationships and use of happy endings. Colwin's works include the novels *Family Happiness* (1982) and *Shine On, Bright and Dangerous Object* (1975), and the short story collections *Another Marvelous Thing* (1986), *The Lone Pilgrim* (1981), and *Passion and Affect* (1974). Colwin was also a food columnist for *Gourmet* magazine and wrote two books on culinary arts. [For further information on Colwin's life and

369

career, see *CLC,* Volumes 5, 13, and 23.]

Henry Ephron
May 26, 1911—August 6, 1992
American screenwriter, playwright, and producer

Best known for the film *The Desk Set* (1957), Ephron, along with his wife Phoebe, wrote eighteen plays and screenplays in a career that spanned more than three decades. Generally characterized as optimistic, the Ephrons' films include *Daddy Long Legs* (1955), *Carousel* (1956), and *Captain Newman, MD* (1963); the latter received an Academy Award nomination for best screenplay adaptation in 1964. Following his wife's death in 1971, Ephron ceased writing screenplays. Two years later he published *We Thought We Could Do Anything* (1973), a memoir about their experiences in Hollywood.

Frederick Earl Exley
March 28, 1929—June 17, 1992
American novelist

Exley won a cult following in the United States with a trilogy comprised of the novels *A Fan's Notes* (1968), *Pages from a Cold Island* (1975), and *Last Notes from Home* (1988). Classified as "fictional memoirs" by Exley, the three novels are highly autobiographical accounts of Exley's struggles with such afflictions as alcoholism and mental illness. While *A Fan's Notes* won the 1968 William Faulkner Foundation Award for the year's most promising first novel and was nominated for a National Book Award, Exley's subsequent novels generated mixed critical reaction but remained extremely popular among devotees. [For further information on Exley's life and career, see *CLC,* Volumes 6 and 11.]

William M. Gaines
March 1, 1922—June 3, 1992
American publisher

Gaines was the publisher of *Mad* magazine, the irreverent journal of satirical humor known for its grinning, gap-toothed mascot Alfred E. ("What, Me Worry?") Neuman. Gaines took over his father's successful but somewhat staid comic book publishing company in 1947 and launched a series of horror titles, of which *Tales from the Crypt* was the most famous. In 1954, after these comics drew the attention of a Congressional committee investigating juvenile delinquency, Gaines focused his time and resources on *Mad,* which was originally entitled *Tales Calculated to Drive You Mad: Humor in a Jugular Vein.* Gaines neither wrote for *Mad* nor drew any of its cartoons. "My staff and contributors create the magazine," he said. "What I create is the atmosphere."

Jim C. Garrison
November 20, 1921—October 21, 1992
American nonfiction writer and novelist

A lawyer, district attorney, and judge, Garrison is best known for his nonfiction works about the assassination of President John F. Kennedy. Garrison first received national attention in 1967 when he charged a New Orleans businessman with plotting to kill the president. In his *An Almanac of Jim Garrison's Investigation into the Assassination of John F. Kennedy: The Crime of Silence* (1968), *A Heritage of Stone* (1970), and *On the Trail of the Assassins: My Investigation and Prosecution of the Murder of President Kennedy* (1989), Garrison linked Kennedy's murder to the CIA, the FBI, and the United States industrial-military complex; he also accused the Warren Commission of deliberately suppressing and altering evidence. These conspiracy theories became the basis for Oliver Stone's controversial film, *JFK* (1991). Garrison was also the author of the political novel *The Star Spangled Contract* (1976).

William Douglas Home
June 3, 1912—September 23, 1992
English playwright

Best known for his light-hearted situation comedies, Home wrote over forty plays during a career that spanned four decades. As a British officer during World War II, Home refused to bombard the French city Le Havre, believing the attack would unjustly endanger the civilian population. Home was later court-martialed and sentenced to a year in prison. There he wrote *Now Barabbas* (1947), a play about his experiences. He also achieved critical and popular success with witty plays about the British upper class, including *The Chiltern Hundreds* (1947), which depicts an aristocratic family trying to deal with social and political change, and *The Reluctant Debutante* (1956), a droll portrait of a young girl rebelling against social conventions.

Ivar Vidrik Ivask
December 17, 1927—September 23, 1992
Estonian-born American poet and critic

Founder of the Neustadt International Prize for Literature, Ivask served as editor of the journal *World Literature Today* from 1967 to 1991. After emigrating to the United States in 1949, Ivask earned a Ph.D. in German literature and art history from the University of Minnesota. He wrote book-length monographs on the German poets Gottfried Benn and Hugo von Hofmannsthal and edited critical anthologies on several writers, including Jorge Luis Borges and Octavio Paz. Ivask also published poetry collections in German, Estonian, and English, some of which include *Gespiegelte Erde* (1967), *Elukogu* (1978), *Snow Lessons* (1986), and *Baltic Elegies* (1990). Often including images of lakes and woodlands of Estonia and Finland, Ivask's poetry has been praised for its lyricism. [For further information on Ivask's life and works, see *CLC,* Volume 14.]

Fritz Reuter Leiber, Jr.
December 24, 1910—September 5, 1992
American novelist and short story writer

Six-time winner of the prestigious Hugo award, Leiber was a highly respected writer of the science fiction subgenre he called "sword and sorcery." Drawing on themes and images from the works of Shakespeare, Edgar Allan Poe, and H. P. Lovecraft, Leiber explored the horror lurking beneath the quotidian surfaces of modern urban life. He won his first Hugo award for *The Big Time* (1958), an anti-war novel based on the Law of the Conservation of Reality, a theory of time travel which holds that any changes made to the past by time travelers will have only minimal effect on the future. Among his most popular short stories are those that chronicle the adventures of two thieves, Fafhrd and the Grey Mouser. Leiber's other notable works include *Gather, Darkness* (1943), *Night's Black Agents* (1947), *Conjure Wife* (1953), and *The Wanderer* (1964). [For further information on Leiber's life and works, see *CLC,* Volume 25.]

Audre Geraldine Lorde
February 18, 1934—November 17, 1992
American poet, essayist, autobiographer, and nonfiction writer

Self-described as a "black lesbian feminist mother lover poet," Lorde is known for depicting racial, religious, and sexual prejudice as well as other problems faced by African-American women. In *The Black Unicorn* (1978), generally recognized as her most poetically mature work, Lorde incorporated elements of African mythology and emphasized the themes of motherhood, black pride, and spiritual rebirth. Other notable poetry collections include *From a Land Where Other People Live* (1973), which was nominated for a National Book Award, and *The New York Head Shop and Museum* (1974). Lorde is also known for her nonfiction works, particularly *The Cancer Journals* (1980) and *A Burst of Light* (1988), which document her experiences with cancer and chemotherapy as well as her attempts to accept her own mortality. A leader in social and political reform, Lorde helped found Sisterhood in Support of Sisters in South Africa (SISA) and was active on the editorial boards of the Feminist Press and Kitchen Table: Women of Color Press. [For further information on Lorde's life and works, see *CLC,* Volumes 18 and 71.]

William Shawn
August 31, 1907—December 8, 1992
American editor, essayist, and reporter

The editor of the *New Yorker* for over thirty-five years, Shawn was responsible for shifting the magazine's focus from literary and humorous topics to contemporary social issues. Known for demanding a high quality of writing from his staff and for supporting New York artists, Shawn is credited with shaping the American literary scene and influencing the works and careers of such popular figures as Woody Allen and Truman Capote. Shawn was also responsible for including in the *New Yorker* excerpts from such popular and controversial works as J. D. Salinger's *The Catcher in the Rye,* Rachel Carson's *Silent Spring,* and John Hersey's *Hiroshima.*

William Andrew Swanberg
November 23, 1907—September 17, 1992
American biographer

Best known for *Citizen Hearst: A Biography of William Randolph Hearst* (1961), Swanberg authored ten biographies including the Pulitzer Prize-winning portrait of Henry R. Luce, *Luce and His Empire* (1972). Praised for their factual accuracy, painstaking attention to detail, and lucid prose, Swanberg's biographies chronicle the lives of nineteenth- and twentieth-century entrepreneurs and personages who have received little attention in traditional accounts of American history. Swanberg's only literary biography, *Dreiser* (1965), received high praise from scholars and is generally considered the most accomplished full-scale study of the author. Swanberg's other biographies include *Sickles the Incredible* (1956), the story of Civil War general and New York politician Daniel Edgar Sickles, and *Pulitzer* (1967), a study of the New York publisher. *Norman Thomas: The Last Idealist* (1976), Swanberg's account of the life of the socialist politician and presidential candidate, won the National Book Award in 1977.

Glendon Swarthout
April 8, 1918—September 23, 1992
American novelist, short story writer, and playwright

Author of more than twenty novels, Swarthout wrote in a variety of genres including comedy, mystery, romance, and Western. Usually set in his native Michigan or the Western United States, Swarthout's novels address such diverse subjects as factory work in a World War II bomber plant, *Willow Run* (1943), and life in the contemporary American West, *The Cadillac Cowboys* (1964). Swarthout's best-known novel, *Bless the Beasts and the Children* (1970), concerns a group of boys at an Arizona summer camp who discover that they can think and act competently despite their reputation as misfits. As with three of his other novels—*They Came to Cordura* (1958), *Where the Boys Are* (1960), and *The Shootist* (1975)—*Bless the Beasts and the Children* was adapted for film. Swarthout received an O. Henry Prize in 1960 and a gold medal from the National Society of Arts and Letters in 1972. [For further information on Swarthout's life and career, see *CLC,* Volume 35.]

David Harry Walker
February 9, 1911—March 5, 1992
Scottish-born Canadian novelist and short story writer

The author of twenty adventure novels, Walker incorporated personal experiences into his work and addressed such subjects as survival in the wilderness and the conservation of natural resources. His most notable novels include *Geordie* (1950), *Harry Black* (1956), *Where the High Winds Blow* (1960), and *The Pillar* (1952), a story based on his experiences as a prisoner of war in Germany during World War II. A two-time recipient of the Governor General's Award for Literature, Walker published his autobiography *Lean, Wind, Lean* in 1984. [For further information on Walker's life and works, see *CLC,* Volume 14.]

Richard Yates
February 3, 1926—November 7, 1992
American novelist and short story writer

Yates is best known for works in which he repudiated the American dream and focused on unexceptional people trapped in frustrating, lonely lives. Praised for his realistic and compassionate writing, Yates revealed the inadequacies of his characters and the banality of their lives. His works include *Revolutionary Road* (1961), a novel about a suburban salesman whose marriage deteriorates, and the short fiction collections *Eleven Kinds of Loneliness* (1962) and *Liars in Love* (1981). At the time of his death, Yates was writing a novel about life in Washington during the early 1960s, "Uncertain Times," which was based on his experiences as a speech writer for Attorney General Robert F. Kennedy. [For further information on Yates's life and works, see *CLC,* Volumes 7, 8, and 23.]

Avot Yeshurun
September 1904—February 22, 1992
Polish-born Israeli poet

Characterized by distorted syntax, idiosyncratic rhyme, and the incorporation of Yiddish, Polish, and Arabic words, Yeshurun's poetry addresses such topics as the Holocaust and Jewish-Palestinian relations. Having emigrated to Palestine in 1925, Yeshurun, who was born Yehiel Perlmutter, published his first collection of verse, *Al Hahmot Derahim* (*The Wisdom of the Road*), in 1942. One of the first Israeli poets to discuss issues related to the establishment of a Palestinian homeland, Yeshurun was popular among younger poets but largely ignored by Israeli literati until the mid-1960s. He received the Brenner Prize in 1968 and the Israel Prize in 1992.

Topics in Literature: 1992

Feminism in the 1990s:
Commentary on Works by Naomi Wolf, Susan Faludi, and Camille Paglia

INTRODUCTION

The 1990s have marked a resurgence of interest in feminism and women's studies that has been reflected in the publishing industry. Three best-selling works have been at the forefront of critical discussion in 1992: Naomi Wolf's *The Beauty Myth: How Images of Beauty Are Used against Women* (1991), Susan Faludi's *Backlash: The Undeclared War against American Women* (1991), and Camille Paglia's *Sexual Personae: Art and Decadence from Nefertiti to Emily Dickinson* (1990). Each of these books has generated heated debate concerning the current social and economic status of women and the role of feminism in modern society and academia.

In *The Beauty Myth* Wolf argues that modern society's obsession with feminine beauty is evidence of a subtle conspiracy to undermine women's social and economic advances. To support her theory, Wolf associates the prominence of idealized images of women in advertising and pornography and the influence of a multibillion-dollar cosmetic industry with an increase in such problems suffered by women as eating disorders and sexual harassment. Although many critics praised Wolf's confrontation of the rise in antifeminist attitudes during the 1980s, some believed that it is overly simplistic and pessimistic to blame the beauty myth for a broad range of social problems.

Faludi's *Backlash* also postulates the existence of a reactionary conspiracy against feminism. In *Backlash* Faludi asserts that during the 1980s the American media promoted various antifeminist views, including the notions that women no longer perceive a need to fight for greater social and economic equality and that career-oriented women who delay marriage and childbearing incur problems ranging from depression to infertility. Faludi provides evidence that the media's reportage on women's issues was largely inaccurate and that problems suffered by American women are the result of continued oppression and discrimination rather than of feminism. While many reviewers have deemed *Backlash* the watershed book for a new wave of feminists, others have questioned the accuracy of Faludi's evidence and the validity of her theory.

Whereas Wolf and Faludi's books focus on gender politics and are intended for a general audience, Paglia's *Sexual Personae* is a scholarly work that has provoked much fervent discussion on the relevance and meaning of feminism in society and art. A critical history of Western art and culture from ancient Egypt to the nineteenth century, this study intends, in Paglia's words, "to demonstrate the unity and continuity of Western culture" as opposed to "the modernist idea that culture has collapsed into meaningless fragments." Liberal and feminist critics have expressed anger over Paglia's theory that revolutionary accomplishments in art and science belong exclusively to men. Males, according to Paglia, are compelled by the need to escape the feminine powers of sex and nature, which she refers to as "chthonic"—or earthbound—forces, and to overcome nature and social convention in the process of creating new forms of art. Correspondingly, Paglia believes that women "lack the violent agression to change, to revolutionize," and thus to create: "If civilization had been left in female hands we would still be living in grass huts." Arguing that rape and murder are historical constants, Paglia derides attempts to eradicate sexual stereotypes, stating that they simply offer women "a sanitized, censored view of human psychology and sexual relations." Identifying herself with such early feminists as Simone de Beauvoir and Jane Harrison, Paglia attacks a modern feminist tendency to blame men for the historical situation of women, and she professes her goal to "bring back the prewar feminism that stresses self-reliance—not blaming other people for your problems." Some reviewers have commended Paglia's unfettered examination of feminism, liberalism, and other totems of academia; others, however, have found her work ignorant of contemporary feminist scholarship.

REPRESENTATIVE WORKS ON WOMEN AND FEMINISM

Beauvoir, Simone de
  The Second Sex 1953
Brownmiller, Susan
  Against Our Will: Men, Women, and Rape 1975
Faludi, Susan
  Backlash: The Undeclared War against American Women 1991
French, Marilyn
  The War against Women 1991
Friedan, Betty
  The Feminine Mystique 1963
Gordon, Suzanne
  Prisoners of Men's Dreams: Striking Out for a New Feminine Future 1991
Greer, Germaine
  The Female Eunuch 1970
Hewlett, Sylvia Ann

REVIEWS OF NAOMI WOLF'S *THE BEAUTY MYTH: HOW IMAGES OF BEAUTY ARE USED AGAINST WOMEN*

Emily Mitchell   (review date 4 March 1991)

[*In the following review, Mitchell provides an overview of* The Beauty Myth *and discusses critical reactions to the work.*]

Beauty is a conspiracy of pain forced upon women. Anorexia, induced by the pursuit of attractiveness, turns girls into something resembling skeletons. In the boardroom and in the bedroom, women are entrapped by a cult that is the equivalent of the iron maiden, a medieval torture instrument that impaled its captives on iron spikes.

These are only some of the assertions of *The Beauty Myth*, a provocative work by San Francisco-born Naomi Wolf, 28. . . . Already, and as might be expected, reaction is divided. Fans of the work call it daring and disturbing, but when it appeared in Britain last fall, many critics dipped their pens in acid, variously describing it as lurid and dishonest, and slamming the author as a "clever child." Others have extolled it as a feminist handbook for the '90s.

Among other things, Wolf, a Yale graduate in literature, contends that today's women have been victimized in unprecedented ways by a "violent backlash against feminism that uses images of female beauty as a political weapon against women's advancement." This victimization produces deep inside women "a dark vein of self-hatred, physical obsession, terror of aging and dread of lost control."

The beauty myth of Wolf's title is reinforced, she argues, by a global industry worth billions that could be far better used for social purposes; for example, the money spent on cosmetics each year could finance 2,000 women's health

clinics or pay for three times the amount of day care offered by the U.S. government. In addition, cosmetic surgery has boomed by playing on questionable ideas of health and sickness. Wolf chronicles the multiple ways that mass-culture images of women in advertising and pornography undermine female sexual self-worth. As a result of this bombardment, women learn, even as young girls, that sexual attraction is the "desire to be desired."

As a Rhodes scholar at Oxford in 1986, Wolf had planned to write about the theme of beauty in literature. *The Beauty Myth* began taking shape when she heard someone remark that she had won the scholarship because of her looks. Says Wolf: "I had an image of the documents I had presented to the committee—my essay, a book of poems I had written, letters of recommendation—and the whole of it being swept away by that one sentence." Once she learned that other female Rhodes scholars had had similar tales told about them, she developed a new theme: that discussions of feminine beauty are actually about undermining women's achievements.

A number of other personal experiences went into the book. As a junior high school student, Wolf was anorexic, as were many of her peers. She has combined those painful memories with alarming statistics in a chapter about eating disorders titled "Hunger," which argues that those ailments can be traced to a "cult of thinness" inculcated into women at an early age. Girls will continue to starve, she warns, until they are made to feel valuable with or without the excuse of beauty.

Those personal touches have been the focus of much hostility. A reviewer for London's *Independent on Sunday* accused Wolf of steamrollering her experiences "into a theory which takes no account of what has been happening in the rest of the Western world." A. S. Byatt, author of the best-selling novel *Possession* and a former University of London lecturer, agrees that images of beauty oppress women, but she is dubious about Wolf's notion of a conscious conspiracy. Instead, she says, the beauty business is pandering to dreams.

Pioneer feminist Betty Friedan dismisses the book as an "obsolete rehash" and criticizes Wolf for dwelling on superficialities rather than coming to grips with the modern-day political challenges that confront females. While Friedan agrees that women often go to extremes in their pursuit of good looks, enduring repeated face-lifts and possibly risking their health by having silicone injected into their breasts, she thinks Wolf's book distorts the relationship between feminism and beauty. Women, she says, do not have to choose between the two, but can delight in a frivolous enjoyment of fashion without becoming a slave to it. In contrast, Joan Jacobs Brumberg, an associate professor of women's studies at Cornell University, who wrote a 1988 history of anorexia titled *Fasting Girls*, welcomes Wolf's book as another exposé of the kind of self-inflicted damage that women undergo as a matter of course. "At this moment," she says, "looking good is the only coherent philosophy of the self that women are offered."

Instead of surrendering to the myth, Wolf is calling, if

vaguely, for nothing less than its overthrow. The first step, she says, is to recognize the underlying issues of domination and female competition. Then she exhorts women to refuse to suffer any longer for the sake of an ideal beauty in which adornment and style are a source of pain rather than pleasure. That is both an old challenge and a tall order.

> Emily Mitchell, "The Bad Side of Looking Good," in Time, New York, Vol. 137, No. 9, March 4, 1991, p. 68.

Caryn James   (review date 7 May 1991)

[*In the following review of* The Beauty Myth, *James questions the validity of Wolf's evidence of a conspiracy to oppress women through unrealistic standards of beauty, but praises her forceful confrontation of anti-feminist attitudes.*]

One of the most astute and troubling feminist observations I can recall leaped out of the least likely place: a movie about an aircraft carrier caught in a time warp. When the ship went spiraling from the 1980's back to 1941, there was the film's token woman, Katharine Ross as a senator's beautiful, brilliant speech writer. "I've spent a lot of time trying to hide the way I look, hoping to be recognized for my abilities," she confessed to a man from the future, who asked, "How's it going so far?"

"Let me put it this way," she said, calmly acknowledging her beauty, her brains and her exasperation at living in a man's world. "If the way I look helps me get in the door, then God help 'em when I get through." It was an utterly modern and dangerously honest statement, something 1980's feminists might have thought but never said.

Naomi Wolf's slick, provocative book, *The Beauty Myth: How Images of Beauty Are Used Against Women* is very much like that fraught feminist scene embedded in the silly movie *The Final Countdown*. One of several current books that are staking out the next wave of feminist thought, this sloppily researched polemic against the tyranny of beauty may seem as dismissible as a hackneyed adventure film. Often it gets lost in a time-warp all its own, an age when Betty Friedan was more influential than Jane Fonda.

But Ms. Wolf's theory—that the pressure on women to look thin, young and gorgeous is the last bastion of male power, a reactionary way to undermine the feminist gains of the last 25 years—is valuable nonetheless. No other work has so forcefully confronted the anti-feminism that emerged during the conservative, yuppified 1980's, or so honestly depicted the confusion of accomplished women who feel emotionally and physically tortured by the need to look like movie stars. Even by the standards of pop-cultural feminist studies, *The Beauty Myth* is a mess, but that doesn't mean it's wrong.

Ms. Wolf, a 28-year-old American who began devising her theory while studying at Oxford, created a stir last fall [1990] when her book appeared in Britain, where it became a best seller. It has been praised by women with impeccable feminist credentials, like the novelist Fay Wel-

don, whose dust-jacket blurb calls the author an "early heroine of Women's World, 90's Style." But British reviewers also responded with a great, angry chorus of "So what's new?" as if *The Beauty Myth* was just so much publishers' hype.

In fact, the book's post-feminist 90's perspective is what's new and important. Ms. Wolf cites the growth of eating disorders like anorexia, the surge in cosmetic surgery and the prevalence of pornography as evidence that "we are in the midst of a violent backlash against feminism that uses female beauty" as a weapon to thwart women. In effect, the pressure to look beautiful undermines ordinary women's self-esteem and makes them weak just at the moment when the social advances of the past two decades ought to make them feel better and stronger.

Ms. Wolf sees this as a fearful response by men, whose power is threatened by feminist gains. Women internalize the myth because it "exploits female guilt and apprehension about our own liberation." These claims of an intensified anti-feminism are plausible, but Ms. Wolf doesn't begin to prove them because her logic is so lame, her evidence so easily knocked down.

She examines how women's magazines have substituted the impossible ideal of youthful beauty for the pre-feminist goal of a clean house and domestic bliss. But she writes as if women's magazines were as powerful today as they were in the 1950's. More damaging, she virtually ignores how television, film and videos have shaped women's self-images and their bodies. How can any credible analysis of the way beauty tyrannizes women afford to ignore Oprah Winfrey's liquid diet, Jane Fonda's mega-hit exercise tapes or Madonna's ever-changing sexual parade?

Her statistics are shamefully secondhand and outdated. When she makes the preposterous claim that in the United States only 48 percent of women use contraception regularly, her source is a 1984 pop-psychology book called *Swept Away: Why Women Confuse Love and Sex.* And who knows where those old numbers came from?

But if *The Beauty Myth* offers pathetic answers, at least it stirs up some essential questions for our times. The fact that Oprah and Jane come so easily to mind as omissions from the book may be the best evidence that it touches a nerve about the ever-changing mass-media images of strong, beautiful women. Is Oprah no longer beautiful now that she has put weight back on? What does Jane Fonda's widely reported breast-implant surgery say about women and aging? Do women still need looks to get them through the door so they can play hardball once they get in?

These are the kinds of questions that go to the heart of contemporary feminism, but because of their pop-cultural edge they are also issues that serious feminist writers seem reluctant to address.

It says something about images of women that *The Beauty Myth* is the most powerful among the spate of recent books about female identity, work as varied as Camille Paglia's crackpot anti-feminism and Louise J. Kaplan's well-informed feminist psychology.

Ms. Paglia's erudite and widely publicized *Sexual Personae: Art and Decadence from Neferfiti to Emily Dickinson* is angry and reactionary in its blithe, unsupported assumption that women are part of a chaotic, destructive natural world and that men, running from the clutches of the Great Mother, have compensated with logic and all the major achievements of Western civilization and art. This is the kind of approach, heavily loaded with Freud, that leads Ms. Paglia to assert that "if civilization had been left in female hands, we would still be living in grass huts," and to find "submerged lesbian incest" in the romance between Cathy and Heathcliff in *Wuthering Heights.* At the very least, *The Beauty Myth* makes more sense than that.

On the opposite side of the barricade from Ms. Paglia, Ms. Kaplan's *Female Perversions: The Temptations of Emma Bovary* is a solidly researched feminist corrective and complement to Freud. Fluently written for a general audience, it explores the female versions of the sexual fetishes and complexes that have ordinarily been associated only with men.

In a passing comment, Ms. Kaplan intersects *The Beauty Myth* by noting that after the most recent wave of feminist achievements there was a backsliding into a "myth" of femininity that is "manipulated by those hostile to feminist causes." Her observation that opponents of abortion are part of the new myth of old-fashioned femininity supports Ms. Wolf's conspiracy theory much better than Ms. Wolf does herself. It is more evidence that *The Beauty Myth* may be on target in spite of itself.

It wouldn't be the first time Ms. Wolf was right for the wrong reasons. In her book she recalls a college meeting of women who objected to soft-core pornography on campus. "I mentioned politics, symbolism, male cultural space," she writes, only to admit that the last word about the photos went to another student who told her: "I have no idea what you're talking about. All I know is that they make me feel incredibly bad about myself." Ms. Wolf still has trouble figuring out why, but *The Beauty Myth* is an important breakthrough in dragging that bad feeling into the public forum.

> *Caryn James, "Feminine Beauty as a Masculine Plot," in* The New York Times, *May 7, 1991, p. C18.*

Margo Jefferson   (review date 19 May 1991)

[*In the following review, Jefferson concurs with Wolf's indictment of oppressive standards for feminine beauty but faults the polemical nature of* The Beauty Myth.]

I am gazing at a glossy, full-color, seven-page advertisement for a new line of cosmetics produced by Ultima II, a division of Revlon sold mostly in department stores. They are called the Nakeds II. The Nakeds offer "HUNDREDS OF SHADES IN EVERY NUANCE OF NEUTRAL . . . FOR WHENEVER A WOMAN WANTS THE LOOK OF LESS FOR SATURDAY" (she's likely to be around trees, bushes and other naturalistic props), "THE LOOK OF MORE FOR WORK" (more money, more competence, hence more fa-

cial armature), "OR FOR EVENING, THE LOOK OF WOW!" ("Apply 2 coats of black mascara. Brush the blush in 'Bashful' on apples of cheeks. . . . Line lips with lipliner in 'Smooch.' ").

It's utterly ridiculous—still, I can't help liking the packaging, those cream-colored makeup containers with black piping that so resemble ladies' hatboxes in the photograph on the three-page foldout. But that's my weakness, and it's there to be played on. How could it be otherwise, Naomi Wolf asks in *The Beauty Myth,* a sweeping, messy, vigorous, callow but stouthearted book dedicated to the proposition that the icon of the educated, middle-class woman as wife, mother and tasteful sexual appliance has been replaced by the icon of the educated, middle-class, wage-earning woman as a flaw-free specimen of physical perfection. The operative principle here is that no society ever rights a wrong without finding a new one to put in its place: ours, having yielded ground on matters of social, political, economic and sexual freedom for women, dug in its heels when faced with the more psychologically nuanced issues of female beauty, desirability and self-esteem.

Ms. Wolf, a graduate of Yale who is now a Rhodes scholar at New College, Oxford, believes that from the Cult of Domesticity to the Feminine Mystique to the Beauty Myth and its backlash—that is, over the past 35 years—"inexhaustible but ephemeral beauty work took over from inexhaustible but ephemeral housework. As the economy, law, religion, sexual mores, education, and culture were forcibly opened up to include women more fairly, a private reality colonized female consciousness. By using ideas about 'beauty,' it reconstructed an alternative female world with its own laws, economy, religion, sexuality, education, and culture, each element as repressive as any that had gone before."

Ms. Wolf maps out this "alternative female world" by recording just about every form of obsession and exploitation a $20 billion-a-year cosmetics industry, a $33 billion diet industry, a $300 million cosmetic-surgery industry and a $7 billion pornography industry can nurture and supply.

There's the language of upwardly mobile beauty and fitness, austere one moment, sweetly lascivious the next: packed with technological intimidation (makeup containing mock-scientific ingredients such as "reticulin and mucopolysaccharides") and with born-again bullying ("Take the shades from your eyes and face the truth of the situation," says one ad. "Does your flesh wobble and seem dimpled?"). There are the women who take cosmetic surgery to she-devil lengths of pain and desperation, and the many more who empty their pocketbooks daily to look like any and everyone but themselves. There is anorexia and there is bulimia; anorexia alone is said to kill 150,000 American women each year; together with bulimia it afflicts one million a year.

Is this new information? No (as Ms. Wolf's plentiful footnotes verify), but it is information we keep refusing to process, and we must be reminded of it until we begin to do so. As a feminist muckraker and media critic, Naomi Wolf does her work well. But as a feminist cultural historian, she has two big problems. The first is the intellectual equivalent of beauty follies. She overdoes glittery, special-effect metaphors—beauty as the cult millenarianism; beauty as the Iron Maiden, a body-shaped casket painted with the limbs and face of a young woman that served as a medieval instrument of torture. She is also addicted to cosmetic touch-ups of her thesis in the form of brief quotations and one-liners from critics, scholars and poets through the ages.

I'll put the second problem in question form: Why does every generation frame its recognition of lies and injustice in the claim that no previous generation has ever suffered them so acutely? I believe Ms. Wolf when she writes that "today's children and young men and women have sexual identities that spiral around paper and celluloid phantoms: from *Playboy* to music videos to the blank female torsos in women's magazines, features obscured and eyes extinguished, they are being imprinted with a sexuality that is mass-produced, deliberately dehumanizing and inhuman."

But I don't believe this is taking place "for the first time in history": it's taking place at this moment in history through the particular methods that media and technology provide. After all, the conventions, excesses and grotesqueries of the beauty industry were securely in place by the 1920's, from the pseudoscientific jargon and *faux intime* exhortations to the carelessly regulated health and safety standards to the ties that bind advertisers to women's magazines.

As for beauty standards—from body shape to feature size—they were a lot more restrictive and bigoted just 25 years ago than they are now, and while Ms. Wolf is right to say that the muscled and worked body in fashion today has its alien and bionic side, the 1950's exaggeration of "natural" female flesh and curves was just as artificial and (if you lacked them) debilitating. One body canonized pseudowomanliness, the other appropriates pseudomanliness.

Beauty is such a strange thing—it's a fantasy, a pastime and a profession (like sports), and we bring a daunting range of emotions and associations to it. I like the fact that Ms. Wolf ends her book by saying we need more, not less of it, "The beauty myth is harmful and pompous and grave because so much, too much, depends upon it," she writes: we should treat it (and we do, sometimes) like theater and play.

The Beauty Myth shows us yet again how much we need new ways of seeing, I regret that it also shows how much we need new ways of writing—polemics and manifestoes that will make room amidst their facts and theories for the contradictory particulars of each reader's life.

> *Margo Jefferson, "Does Your Flesh Wobble and Seem Dimpled?" in* The New York Times Book Review, *May 19, 1991, p. 11.*

An excerpt from *The Beauty Myth: How Images of Beauty Are Used against Women*

Why does the social order feel the need to defend itself by evading the fact of real women, our faces and voices and bodies, and reducing the meaning of women to these formulaic and endlessly reproduced "beautiful" images? Though unconscious personal anxieties can be a powerful force in the creation of a vital lie, economic necessity practically guarantees it. An economy that depends on slavery needs to promote images of slaves that "justify" the institution of slavery. Western economies are absolutely dependent now on the continued underpayment of women. An ideology that makes women feel "worth less" was urgently needed to counteract the way feminism had begun to make us feel worth more. This does not require a conspiracy; merely an atmosphere. The contemporary economy depends right now on the representation of women within the beauty myth. Economist John Kenneth Galbraith offers an economic explanation for "the persistence of the view of homemaking as a 'higher calling' ": the concept of women as naturally trapped within the Feminine Mystique, he feels, "has been forced on us by popular sociology, by magazines, and by fiction to disguise the fact that woman in her role of consumer has been essential to the development of our industrial society. . . . Behavior that is essential for economic reasons is transformed into a social virtue." As soon as a woman's primary social value could no longer be defined as the attainment of virtuous domesticity, the beauty myth redefined it as the attainment of virtuous beauty. It did so to substitute both a new consumer imperative and a new justification for economic unfairness in the workplace where the old ones had lost their hold over newly liberated women.

> *Naomi Wolf, in her* The Beauty Myth: How Images of Beauty Are Used against Women, *Morrow, 1991.*

Maureen Dowd   (essay date 26 May 1991)

[*Below, Dowd focuses on Wolf's examination of the relationship between physical appearance and sex discrimination in* The Beauty Myth.]

Once upon a time, women assumed that when they became a force in the workplace, they would be judged on their merits rather than their appearance.

But three decades after the dawn of liberation, things have not exactly worked out that way. Indeed, the more successful women have become in infiltrating the male-dominated sphere, the more their looks, clothing and grooming have inspired discussion, litigation and even obsession.

There is a stormy debate right now among American women writers and academics about the connection between looks and economic progress, about whether it is all right for feminists to enjoy wearing lipstick and shopping for sensual clothes, about whether women have victimized themselves by inculcating an artificial MTV-Madison Avenue-*Vogue* standard of youth and beauty that sabotages their ascension in the marketplace. . . .

Historically, a woman's worth in society has been defined

by her youth and beauty. Now, Ms. Wolf and others argue, that standard has been applied to the work place, so that women must compete both romantically and professionally in terms of appearance.

Gloria Steinem, who took a job in the early 1960's as a Playboy Bunny to write an article, came to the conclusion that "All women are Bunnies." [In *The Beauty Myth*] Ms. Wolf says that greater success in the office has done nothing to change that equation.

"The working woman was told she had to think about 'beauty' in a way that undermined, step for step, the way she had begun to think as a result of the successes of the women's movement," Ms. Wolf writes. "The closer women come to power, the more physical self-consciousness and sacrifice are asked of them."

Ms. Wolf's premise, considered naïve and wrong-headed by some feminists and ground-breaking and brilliant by others, was underscored by a couple of events in the news recently.

In the first, Continental Airlines fired Teresa Fischette from her part-time job at the ticket counter at Boston's Logan International Airport after she refused to comply with the company directive on wearing makeup. After a furor ensued, Continental hired back Ms. Fischette and said that from now on, compliance with the 45-page appearance code would be suggested rather than mandatory.

And *The Wall Street Journal* reported last week that United States District Judge E. B. Haltom dismissed a suit by a woman who said she lost her job after spurning her boss. The judge sided with the defendant after considering the evidence, which included a picture of the boss's wife to contrast with the plaintiff. His opinion noted that the former employee "wore little or no makeup and her hair was not colored in any way" and therefore, she "was not attractive" to the boss.

In Judge Haltom's view, a woman does not merit sexual harassment if she has not devoted enough time and attention to adorning herself. Of course, if she has, she is vulnerable to the argument that she "asked for" indecent attention from the men in her office or men on the street.

If women are penalized for not looking feminine enough, they are also penalized for looking too feminine. In her book, Ms. Wolf cites several legal cases, including that of a San Francisco policewoman, Nancy Fahdl, who was dismissed because she looked "too much like a lady," and *Diaz v. Coleman,* in which a dress code of short skirts was set by an employer who allegedly sexually harassed his female employees.

It is, to say the least, a confusing time for professional women.

In the late 1970's, when women were beginning to be assimilated into corporations in large numbers, their bible was John T. Molloy's *Dress for Success.* Mr. Molloy believed that women should adopt a masculine uniform, like navy blue suits, little bow ties and oxford shirts, as a way of suppressing distracting sexuality and gaining an equal footing with respect to image.

But as women grew more confident, they stopped emulating men in dress.

Many professional women say that dressing with a hint of flirtatiousness, in softly cut silks and satins and cashmeres, has made them feel more powerful, because they can express themselves as individuals rather than camouflaging themselves to look like men. But it is a double-edged sword since studies find that most women who are harassed feel guilty and blame themselves for provoking the comments by dressing "inappropriately."

Ms. Wolf asserts that the fashion industry helped scuttle Mr. Molloy's movement, to the detriment of women. "The consequence of men wearing uniforms where women do not has simply meant that women take on the full penalties as well as the pleasures of physical charm in the workplace, and can legally be punished or promoted, insulted or even raped accordingly," she writes.

Camille Paglia, a professor of humanities at the University of the Arts in Philadelphia and the author of *Sexual Personae: Art and Decadence from Nefertiti to Emily Dickinson* calls Ms. Wolf's book "a shabby mess" that reinforces American puritanical tendencies.

"Women enjoy color and fabric and fashion and we should not have to apologize for that," Ms. Paglia said. "American feminism has gotten itself in a corner, because it is unable to explain the attraction of women to beauty and pleasure and sexuality."

Ms. Paglia said that it was an ironic surprise to feminists who felt that they were "going to make a perfect world where people would no longer be judged by beauty or talent" to find that "maybe the problems between the sexes can not be solved by passing more regulations."

In a recent issue of *Allure* magazine, Betty Friedan argues that it is not wrong for feminists to want to be beautiful. "Women could all stop wearing lipstick and blusher, eye shadow and moisturizing cream tomorrow, and I doubt it would help them break through the glass ceiling or get child care or parental leave within the structures of the workplace," she said, adding: "If feminism really meant a war against men—a repudiation of love and beauty and home and children—most women would not want it."

In an interview, Ms. Wolf said that her aim is not to tell women how to look; her aim is simply to get rid of the double standard and make sure that women are not demoted or harassed because of their appearance.

"Only women are told 'You've got a choice: you can either be sexual or serious,' " she said. "With men, their seriousness enhances their sexuality. When you tell a woman she must choose, you disempower her. Because it is human to be both sexual and serious."

> *Maureen Dowd, "Yes, but Can She Make Them Swoon?" in* The New York Times, *Section 4, May 26, 1991, p. 3.*

Mary G. Gotschall   (review date 8 July 1991)

[*In the following review, Gotschall faults the central*

premise of The Beauty Myth *as oversimplified, overly pessimistic, and extreme.*]

In *The Beauty Myth,* a provocative new feminist tract which should take its place alongside such polemics as Betty Friedan's *The Feminine Mystique,* Naomi Wolf argues that American women are enslaved by the cultural edict to be beautiful. They are victims of an impossible standard. The pressure, according to Miss Wolf, has become relentless during the past decade, as women have begun competing head-on with men in the professional sphere.

For Naomi Wolf, the beauty business isn't just a ploy by Madison Avenue to make a buck. What truly powers the $33-billion-a-year diet industry, the $20-billion cosmetics industry, the $300-million cosmetic-surgery industry, and the $7-billion pornography industry, she argues, is a far more insidious and destructive agenda. It is a political tool to keep women down: "The beauty myth is not about women at all. It is about men's institutions and institutional power."

According to Miss Wolf, the myth has a number of uses. It pits women against one another, thereby diluting their political influence; as she puts it, "What women look like is considered important because what we say is not." It stokes the consumerist engine of our economy, where women shoppers play a pivotal role; and it enables employers to get away with paying women less than men. Indeed, Miss Wolf charges that the success of Western economies is linked to the chronic underpayment of women.

The skepticism of the modern age evaporates when the subject is women's beauty. Indeed, it is described not as if it were determined by mortal men, shaped by politics, history, and the marketplace, but as if there were a divine authority who issues deathless scripture about what it is that makes a woman good to look at.

—Naomi Wolf, in her "Faith Healers & Holy Oil," Ms., May-June 1991.

The author notes the historical roots of this problem. The modern beauty myth can be traced to the social upheaval following industrialization, around 1830, when a new class of literate, idle women was suddenly in a position to challenge male dominance. The upshot, she concludes, is that "Women are mere 'beauties' in men's culture so that culture can be kept male."

The beauty myth—in Miss Wolf's view—transforms women into self-destructive, fearful, even paranoid creatures who have a love-hate addiction to food, a negative body image, poor self-esteem, and tenuous relationships with the men in their lives. They frequently become anorexic or undergo dangerous cosmetic surgery to achieve

the perfect body. They pursue this fruitless quest with the zealotry of religious fanatics, and yet they are doomed to fail because they are pursuing a chimera.

The author cites a raft of data to prove her point. She notes that cosmetic surgery is the fastest-growing medical specialty in America, and she claims 10 per cent of women are afflicted by eating disorders—a marked rise during the last decade. And many of these women are among the best educated in American society. Miss Wolf rails against the frauds perpetrated by the cosmetics industry, and roundly criticizes women's magazines for their docile collusion in this fraud.

Ultimately, Miss Wolf ascribes all of modern women's social ills to the beauty myth, including the rise in rape, mental illness, and sexual abuse of children during the last decade. In so doing, she falls into the trap of oversimplification.

Women's stature in modern society is the product of a confluence of factors, and the "beauty myth" is merely one of them. One must also weigh such factors as the force of tradition, our evolution from a "hunter-gatherer" society, the legal and political system, institutional pressures, religion, portrayals of beautiful women in Western art, biological and physiological functions, and innate sex differences. The list goes on and on.

Beyond that, I would argue that much of what Miss Wolf criticizes in our culture springs from basic animal drives. Among many species, one sex uses decoration to entice the other to mate. Male birds, for example, sport colorful plumage to attract females. There is a competition to attract the strongest, most desirable mates with the best genes. Women's pursuit of beauty serves a similar reproductive agenda. On the most fundamental level, it is a behavior that has evolved as part of a competitive courtship ritual to attract a powerful male and mate with him. Until recent times, this mating ritual was all-important to women, who relied upon it for their economic survival as well as that of their children. Thus, women beautify themselves to ensnare men. The beauty industry has correspondingly sprung up as a response to the way women conduct their half of the mating dance.

There is also scientific evidence indicating that there are cognitive differences between men and women, which in turn manifest themselves in different styles of communication and behavior. Deborah Tannen chronicles some of these communication differences in her current book, *You Just Don't Understand.* From an early age, boys are object-oriented and girls are person-oriented; from these different orientations flow correspondingly different behavior. And ornamentation may be one such difference. Women take pleasure in adornment.

Women have free will, contrary to Miss Wolf's assertion, and they are not forced to buy beauty products. They choose to do so. If this were not so, fashion and the beauty industry would not thrive. The capitalist system is driven by the bottom line and not by politics. If women stopped buying beauty products and services, the industry would die, as other industries have died in the past.

The central flaw of *The Beauty Myth* is its extremism. It

lacks moderation, balance, judiciousness. Miss Wolf goes overboard, hammering away at her central theme with the same fanaticism that she ascribes to women hooked on diet fads. *The Beauty Myth* shades into caricature—even paranoia—when she writes that, because of the pursuit of pulchritude, "life-fearing neuroses are everywhere."

Indeed, the book projects many of Miss Wolf's own psychological hang-ups onto all of womankind. In the section on eating disorders, for example, she admits that she was an anorexic when she was 13 years old, and one of her best friends died of anorexia. Presumably, her views on women's eating disorders have been shaped by these personal experiences.

Further, her solutions to the beauty myth seem less than compelling. They include making age discrimination, "beauty" harassment, and the double standard for appearance issues in labor negotiations; creating female rituals and rites of passage; encouraging all-female communal nakedness to overcome fears about body image; and encouraging inter-generational contact among women. Much of this already takes place in various settings without achieving the effect Miss Wolf desires.

Despite excellent writing and wonderful breadth of scholarship, *The Beauty Myth* suffers from a flawed central premise. It is suffused with pessimism and refuses to acknowledge the real gains that women have made professionally and politically in the last two decades—and no doubt will continue to make. (pp. 42-4)

> *Mary G. Gotschall, "Poisoned Apple," in* National Review, *New York, Vol. XLIII, July 8, 1991, pp. 42-4.*

Maurice Cranston   (review date August 1991)

[*Cranston is an English political scientist and critic. In the following review of* The Beauty Myth, *he disputes the accuracy of Wolf's evidence and the validity of her arguments, suggesting that the feminist movement is responsible for various social problems experienced by women.*]

The Beauty Myth has already caused something of a stir in England and, being English, I think I can understand why. The argument is outrageous, and it is written in a wild and witty way by a glamorous American graduate student, aged 28, who is at Oxford on a "Rhodes scholarship"—that is, with a fellowship endowed by the racist imperialist Cecil Rhodes, although her own views are those of the most radical-feminist left. Like Cecil Rhodes, however, Miss Wolf is rather a bully, and the people she is out to bully are the millions of American women who try to make themselves look pretty. She wants them to stop it.

Miss Wolf's argument is that the male tyrants who rule America are conspiring to frustrate the liberation of women by imposing standards of beauty as conditions of equal acceptance in professional and social life. American women, she maintains, have absorbed and internalized these standards so completely that vast numbers of them have taken to starving themselves in order to be thin, submitting their breasts and hips to the knives of cosmetic

surgeons, paying out fortunes for phony weight-loss formulae and sojourns at fat farms, and pumping iron daily, in obedience to such martinets as the exercise "guru" Jane Fonda, as Miss Wolf calls her—for even fellow female radicals get no mercy in these pages if they subscribe to the "beauty myth."

Miss Wolf goes on to argue that, since their superhuman efforts to attain the standard of beauty imposed by the male conspirators are seldom successful, American women today are depressed and displeased with themselves, and so bend humbly to the "anti-feminist backlash of the 1990s." The "beauty myth," she suggests, is perpetuated by women's magazines, the cinema, television, and advertising to such effect that women not only want to look the way men think they ought to look, but start to hate themselves if they don't.

In a sense, Miss Wolf is entirely justified in saying that beauty is overrated. Montesquieu married a very plain wife and urged others to do the same on the grounds that a beautiful wife is more likely to be unfaithful and is almost certain to have been spoiled by a doting father. Looking at photographs of upper-class weddings down through the years, one notices that, however pretty the bridesmaids, the bride is seldom a beauty. And ugliness need not be a handicap even in the higher walks of life. The greatest achievers I can claim to have met among American women—Eleanor Roosevelt, Gertrude Stein, and Hannah Arendt—were all rather ugly, although, of course, extremely charming as well.

On the other hand, it is absolutely natural for a woman to want not to be ugly. Only a woman who is herself very pretty—as Miss Wolf, on the evidence of her publicity photographs, clearly is—could write a book like this one, expressing scorn for the efforts of plain women to improve their looks. Vanity is imposed not by the male conspirators who rule the world, but by nature itself. A woman looking into her mirror every day must see an image that pleases her before she can think of pleasing others. If she observes a nose like Jimmy Durante's, she is bound to wish it looked instead like that of Mme. de Pompadour, and if she hears of a cosmetic surgeon who could bring about that transformation for her, it is only natural that she should seek his services. She would make herself happier by doing so, and make herself a more attractive item in the furniture of the world.

One of the pleasures for the foreign visitor to the United States has long been the company of well-groomed, well-dressed, attractive women, many of them looking ten years younger than their age. Recently this pleasing scene has been marred by a sizable minority with weight problems—not Miss Wolf's anorexic and bulimic women, but fat ones. Female obesity is obviously a national problem, which European doctors ascribe to the stress and bad eating habits that have resulted from the decline of traditional family life in America. Miss Wolf will hear none of this. She quotes a 1985 survey in which 90 percent of American women said they thought they weighed too much, but says this is evidence they had been brainwashed—not that they actually did weigh too much.

What is wrong in America, Miss Wolf protests, is not that so many women are fat, but that so many are on diets—25 percent are on one and 50 percent are either finishing, breaking, or starting one. Female fat, she asserts categorically, is not unhealthy: "Where poor health is correlated to fatness in women, it is due to chronic dieting and the emotional stress of self-hatred." The male tyranny wants to keep women hungry, since "hunger makes women feel poor and think poor," and so remain docile. "A cultural fixation with female thinness is not an obsession with female beauty but an obsession with female obedience."

One is not easily persuaded, however, that our Rhodes scholar is wholly reliable on scientific matters, and her statistics are sometimes bizarre. She would have us believe, for example, that up to 44 percent of women in San Francisco have "suffered rape or attempted rape," that "date rape" is "more common than left-handedness, alcoholism and heart attacks," and that "100 million young girls worldwide are being raped by adult men—usually their fathers—often day after day, week after week, year in, year out." It is hard to imagine how such figures could have been gathered, especially as Miss Wolf tells us that "women who are raped by men they know don't even identify their experience as rape."

No one can deny that American women today have a hard time of it, one way or another. Ironically, it is the radical feminists who express such solicitude for them who are responsible for much of the trouble. For example, Miss Wolf points out that women "work harder than men," and for once gives sound statistical evidence to show that the working week of American women is twenty-one hours longer than that of men. Why is this so? Plainly because feminist propaganda has propelled women out of the home to add a man's working week to the inescapable duties of a wife and mother. The situation is especially bad in America, because American men do not take their jobs easily, as British and Australian men do—they work hard, and keeping up with them clearly takes a grim toll on the energies of American women.

And it is true that women are among the victims of the violence that is so lamentably rampant in modern civilization, but Miss Wolf simply adds to the climate of fear. She raises "rape-awareness" to such a fevered pitch that young female readers will close the book terrified of dating their classmates. Miss Wolf cites surveys of undergraduate males in which 61.7 percent say it would be exciting to use force to subdue a woman, 91.3 say they like to dominate a woman, and 30 percent say they would commit rape if they could get away with it. In other words, male undergraduates are dangerous animals. No wonder so many all-American boys nowadays prefer to go out with Chinese, Korean, Filipina, and other foreign girls, who are still sweet and serene and not tensed up with fear of "date rape" from reading books like this one.

Although Miss Wolf's attack is on "the male gender" in general, she singles out cosmetic surgeons as being particularly sadistic and rapacious. She fails, however, to acknowledge that it is feminist reforms that have provided the opportunity and the market for plastic surgeons. For it was feminists, as Miss Wolf notes with satisfaction, who liberated the bodies of American women by persuading them to stop wearing girdles. Yet it was the wearing of just such corsetry which for generations had enabled a woman to mold her silhouette to the shape she chose, to present herself to the world in whatever slender or curvaceous form her fancy took. But, once compelled by her liberators to put on unisex underwear, bike shorts, and other unflattering garments, a woman could only achieve the shape she wanted by getting a cosmetic surgeon to work on the body itself.

Miss Wolf looks forward to what she calls a "pro-woman redefinition of beauty," but she does not tell us what that might be. She simply instructs her female readers to let themselves go, to be "greedy," to "eat, to be sexual, to age," to allow their bodies to "wax and wane," to "cover up or go practically naked, to do whatever we choose in following—or ignoring—our own aesthetic." All very well for the svelte and sensuous Miss Wolfs of the world, most women will reply. They are already following their own aesthetic, which is precisely that of the "beauty myth" Miss Wolf derides. Her alternative proposal will seem to them as alien as that of the late-nineteenth-century *Naturphilosophen*, who unlaced their flabby torsos to cavort on the shores of the Baltic, secure in the syllogism that, since they were part of nature and all nature was beautiful, they too must be beautiful—despite the evidence of the photographs. Unfortunately for Miss Wolf, the modern American woman does not have that old-fashioned German aptitude for metaphysics. (pp. 36-7)

Maurice Cranston, in a review of "The Beauty Myth: How Images of Beauty Are Used against Women," in The American Spectator, *Vol. 24, No. 8, August, 1991, pp. 36-7.*

Diane Johnson   (review date 16 January 1992)

[*Johnson is an American novelist, biographer, critic, scriptwriter, and short story writer. Below, she argues that Wolf's focus on power struggles between men and women in* The Beauty Myth *is too narrow and suggests other motivations for the importance of fashion and beauty in modern culture.*]

[In *The Beauty Myth,* Naomi Wolf] argues that the patriarchy, and its agents the film makers and magazine editors of both sexes, and the marketplace generally, imposes unattainable images of beauty as a way of keeping women in their places, and that women, lacking other forms of power, accede to this form of subjection. Wolf details a dismal catalog of anorexia, bulimia, and job discrimination against the plain or fat. She is witty on the "holy" oils sold them in ads, in which "unseen dangers assault an unprotected female victim" (she quotes a long passage of excerpts from Elizabeth Arden, Estée Lauder, and a dozen more, identifying the language of "defense" against "attack," "danger" to the skin "assaulted by age and ultraviolet exposure," and "external aggressions," language she suggests is used subliminally to frighten and control).

No doubt women are insecure about their bodies, too much preoccupied with appearance and easily alarmed by such rhetoric. Social change is slow, cyclical, and must be both outward and inward, both "equal opportunity" and "transformative." Beauty is a useful commodity, and one of the most powerful assets some women have had with which to secure material privileges and "success"; and it takes time to unlearn old ways or be willing to squander proven assets. At present one sees women trying, as a last gasp before taking the real plunge into the man's world, to compete in the old female way because for many it is easier to be pretty than to go to law school.

Whether the desire for beauty is innate, as Plato would have said, or a male plot is less knowable. If it is a plot, there is at least some evidence that it is not succeeding. In a few cases anyway, women are challenging legal issues relating to their appearance and are winning, like the Delta employee who won the right not to wear makeup. In any case, one could also say it is the profit motive, not men, who are at fault. "Going on appearances" is a way we all make judgments, and to take appearance into account is not necessarily evidence of deep social pathology.

Might it not be that women, pressed to give up some of the perquisites of the narcissistic, passive female role in their move toward "selfless agency," cling to fashion and "beauty" as evidence of a femininity they wish to conserve as anxiously as men wish to conserve masculinity? The resonant little phrase of [David D. Gilmore's in his *Manhood in the Making*] to the effect that manhood is marked by a transition from the self-directed mood of childhood to selfless action in the world seems meaningful here, for it could be argued that not only the beauty victims but also the "caregivers" are, like patriarchs, arrested in a state of passive narcissism—in the case of caregivers, the narcissism of powerless moral superiority. It has been noted that today's anorexic is yesterday's religious mystic. There have never been many avenues of adventure or opportunities for mastery for girls, and anorexia, like piety, may be at least a form of agency.

Wolf does not appear to have much sympathy for the project of self-perfection in any form; nor does she apparently think much of the pleasures of pursuing beauty—the fun of spas, back rubs, and facials—seeing only sadistic surgeons, bruises, scars, and pain. In fact, she ultimately attributes all social evils, including child abuse and the increase in violence against women, to the frenzied thrashings of threatened manhood, and here it is possible that she has not cast her net wide enough, ascribing to the beauty myth what Susan Faludi in *Backlash: The Undeclared War Against American Women* finds in many more places besides, and documents with an impressive array of examples taken from popular culture, and more alarmingly from politics, quoting various New Right figures on their unashamedly antifeminist political agenda—which until the Thomas hearings one would have thought was on the fringe, but which those hearings all too aptly confirmed. (p. 16)

Diane Johnson, "Something for the Boys," in The New York Review of Books, Vol. XXXIX, No. 192, January 16, 1992, pp. 13-17.

Gayle Greene   (review date 10 February 1992)

[*In the review excerpted below, Greene provides a positive assessment of* The Beauty Myth *and discusses the media's promotion of oppressive standards for feminine beauty.*]

Those who are living through change may be the last to know it, until something we read brings things together in a way that makes us see that yes, things really are different—it's not just us growing older. [Naomi Wolf's *The Beauty Myth* and Susan Faludi's *Backlash: The Undeclared War Against American Women*]—both written by young women, both bristling with indignation—demonstrate that something has changed profoundly in the culture's attitudes toward and representations of women, that we are undergoing a "cultural onslaught" that is the more "remarkable for how little it has been remarked upon at all." Both books contextualize this backlash in relation to earlier backlashes—in the late nineteenth century, the early twentieth century and the fifties—and both explain its ferocity in economic terms.

Just when women were making some progress toward equality, just when we were mobilizing against job discrimination and sexual harassment, the Reagan Administration began dismantling federal programs and blocking progressive legislation. Just when young women were supporting feminism in record numbers, the media declared the advent of a "post-feminist" generation and began publishing scare stories (the man shortage, the infertility epidemic, career-woman burnout) and promoting retrotrends (nesting, cocooning, the "New Traditionalism"). No, it's not a conspiracy, but neither is it innocent: Both these books show how legal setbacks, put-downs from mass media and Hollywood, denunciations from political and religious leaders, firebombings of women's clinics, rape, and a beauty ideal that eroticizes violence are all parts of the same picture—of "a counterassault on women's rights" that is intensifying in nastiness and volume.

Women earn 60 cents to a man's dollar; and, as Wolf points out, the economies of industrialized countries depend on this "pool of cheap female labor." Thus in addition to the lucrative industries preying on women—the $33-billion-a-year diet industry, the $20 billion cosmetics industry, the $300 million cosmetic surgery industry and the $7 billion pornography industry—there are powerful economic incentives for keeping women subordinate. By defining women's value in terms of appearance and making it depend on male approval, the Beauty Myth keeps us anxious, insecure and vulnerable, while also affirming a man's right to confer judgment—that last bastion of male privilege. An ideology that makes us feel "worth less" became even more necessary when feminism was beginning "to make us feel worth more."

Wolf analyzes the Beauty Myth as a form of social coercion that took over from where the Feminine Mystique left off, as "a direct consequence of, and a one-to-one check and balance upon" women's new rights and powers. Whereas the women's movement gave us some control of our minds, bodies and sexuality, the Beauty Myth wrested

> **The Beauty Myth not only sets women in competition with one another on a daily basis but sets younger women against older, which is part of the reason the struggle for women's rights has to begin anew with each generation.**
>
> *—Gayle Greene*

this control away, barraging us with "time-consuming and mind-consuming fictions" that drain our energies and absorb our attentions. Whereas feminism challenged the stereotype that we were defined by our appearance, the Beauty Myth insists that a woman *is* her body and that her body is unsatisfactory. Whereas the sexual revolution promoted women's discovery and experience of sexuality, suddenly the weight of fashion models plummeted to 23 percent below that of ordinary women in a new ideal that keeps us off-balance, food-obsessed, hungry; and a new "beauty pornography" linked self-worth to sexuality at the same time that it degraded female sexuality.

The more legal and material gains we made in the world, the more foolish and insecure we were made to feel in our bodies, and the more strictly and cruelly beauty images were forced upon us. The ideal of female beauty that has evolved in recent years—excessively thin, shockingly young and erotically degraded—is a direct response to our new powers. There is nothing arbitrary about any of these qualities: Each aspect—youth, thinness, erotic degradation—performs important work of social control. Dropping "the official weight one stone below women's natural level and redefining a woman's womanly shape" as "fat" plunges women into endless, time- and energy-consuming cycles of dieting and bingeing and produces self-hate such that the norm now is to be a sufferer of some form of eating disorder: More people die of anorexia in a year than died of AIDS from the beginning of the epidemic until the end of 1988.

Nor is it an accident—as Faludi points out—that this ideal flies in the face of demographics: that the ideal beauty is in her late teens or early 20s at the very time when the largest proportion of the female population is entering middle age. It was no misunderstanding that prompted the fashion industry to push baby-doll lines, bubble skirts, party-girl gowns, miniskirts and pouf dresses, at a time when the average American woman was 32, weighed 143 pounds and wore a size 10 or 12; infantile imagery promotes "a retreat from female adulthood" and "bears a vindictive subtext." As Wolf emphasizes, the devaluing of older women also eradicates female power. Whereas older men move into positions of prominence—and power is eroticized for men but not for women—older women have to be made to disappear. Making our aging appear unseemly, unsightly, unacceptable assures that we will. Moreover, it performs the crucial work of cutting the links between generations of women and assuring that power is not passed on. This is why the caricature of the Ugly Fem-

inist appears with every backlash—to scare young women away from identifying with older women and prevent the transmission of authority. The Beauty Myth not only sets women in competition with one another on a daily basis but sets younger women against older, which is part of the reason the struggle for women's rights has to begin anew with each generation.

Wolf points out that young people today are bombarded with more images of "impossibly 'beautiful' women engaged in 'sexual' posturing" than their grandmothers were in a lifetime, and that these images are different not only in quantity but in kind from anything women had to deal with in the past. They glamorize female degradation and masochism in a way that reasserts imaginatively the power inequities that the women's movement challenged. "In a crossover of imagery in the 1980s, the conventions of high-class pornographic photography, such as *Playboy*'s, began to be used generally to sell products," and "the furious pouting glare of the violated woman" and images of "chic violence" and "designer bondage" entered mainstream advertising. Rock videos, which "set the beauty index" for young women, showing them "how to move, strip, grimace, pout, breathe, and cry out during a 'sexual' encounter," define beauty as "that which never says no," as that which is abused. Young people are being imprinted with a sexuality that is mass-produced, inhuman and dehumanizing, and the changes are momentous: "Nothing comparable has ever happened in the history of our species; it dislodges Freud." It may also be producing a generation that confuses sexuality with violence—a generation for which date rape is "more common than left-handedness, alcoholism, and heart attacks."

Wolf's chapter "Violence" is not about rape or male violence, however. It is about cosmetic surgery—which makes the point that the violence done to us makes us more inclined to do violence to ourselves. Reading of the self-mutilation women inflict on themselves in breast implants, liposuction and face lifts, I was struck by how numbed we have become to our own pain. Smoking to stay thin, risking death for thinner thighs, killing the breast as a site of sexual pleasure to make it the object of another's pleasure (which is what silicone implants do) indicate new levels of alienation from our bodies. But such practices also make sense in terms of a culture that values a woman's appearance more than her mind, where a woman can still make more money selling her body than her skills (the average streetwalker earns more than a secretary).

The Beauty Myth claims to be about sexuality while actually being repressive of female sexuality, leaving women alienated from their bodies and desires. It purports to be about individuality while in fact reducing "the meaning of women to . . . formulaic and endlessly reproduced . . . images," which then become the "reality" against which women are measured and found wanting. It claims to be about freedom while actually being about control, and it disguises its coercions in the language of choice, the language of feminism: Now you can choose to have perfect breasts, higher cheekbones. But in fact it leaves us no choice—we will only have a choice when the loss of "beauty" does not mean the loss of esteem, self-esteem, identity, love.

Wolf urges that we exercise real choice and learn to see differently. Her book shows how we might rethink beauty, the body, and—in a powerful and moving passage—how we might re-envision age:

> You could see the signs of female aging as diseased. . . . Or you could see that if a woman is healthy she lives to grow old; as she thrives, she reacts and speaks and shows emotion, and grows into her face. Lines trace her thought and radiate from the corners of her eyes after decades of laughter. . . . You could call the lines a network of "serious lesions," or you could see that in a precise calligraphy, thought has etched marks of concentration between her brows, and drawn across her forehead the horizontal creases of surprise, delight, compassion, and good talk. . . . The darkening under her eyes, the weight of her lids, their minute crosshatching, reveal that what she has been part of has left in her its complexity and richness. She is darker, stronger, looser, tougher, sexier. The maturing of a woman who has continued to grow is a beautiful thing to behold.

Wolf suggests that we turn to women's films, novels and art to discover alternative images of beauty and unalienated female desire. Second-wave feminism produced many such works, and Wolf urges young women to draw on them and to forge intergenerational links that will strengthen them in coming together in a third wave. (pp. 166-68)

> Gayle Greene, "The Empire Strikes Back," in The Nation, *New York, Vol. 254, No. 5, February 10, 1992, pp. 166-70.*

REVIEWS OF SUSAN FALUDI'S *BACKLASH: THE UNDECLARED WAR AGAINST AMERICAN WOMEN*

Susan Faludi with Jane Ayres   (interview date 20 September 1991)

[*In the following interview, Faludi discusses what influenced her to write* Backlash *and the history of the women's movement as a cycle of gains followed by setbacks.*]

Early in 1986, a young reporter in San Jose read an article that was to become infamous. Single, college-educated women over 30, trumpeted a national news magazine, were more likely to be killed by terrorists than to marry. By that winter, the research that supported this marriage dirge was found to be seriously flawed, but the media that had seized on the original story showed no interest in debunking it.

What is more, the reporter began to conclude, just behind

the lip-service paid to the myth that women now "have it all" hissed the breath of malice: The message that women were losing out in the happiness stakes—as a direct result of their drive for independence—was being delivered relentlessly by the press and popular culture.

Backlash: The Undeclared War Against American Women, by Susan Faludi may well be the watershed feminist work of the '90s, much as Betty Friedan's *The Feminine Mystique* was for the '60s.

The author is a reporter for the San Francisco bureau of the *Wall Street Journal.* In April, Faludi won a Pulitzer Prize for explanatory journalism for her *Journal* story, "The Reckoning," which profiled the human costs of the leveraged buyout of Safeway Stores.

A summa cum laude graduate of Harvard University (1981), Faludi's work has appeared in *Ms.* and *Mother Jones* magazines and the *Miami Herald,* the *San Jose Mercury News* and the *Wall Street Journal. Backlash* is her first book.

Faludi is slight and looks younger than her 32 years. Speaking in an unhurried, low voice, she considers questions for a second, then answers in finely crafted paragraphs.

"I read this awful cover story in *Newsweek*—the one that said college-educated women at 30 had a 20 percent chance of getting married, and that at 35 the odds dropped to a 5 percent chance. I was 26 years old at the time—you have no idea how women in their 20s wonder about things! Actually, a former boyfriend had called and urged me to read it. Other women I knew told me that three different men had told each of them to read the story.

"It's amazing how no one bothered to check the method of arriving at that forecast."

Faludi meticulously documents her investigations into the backlash against women's rights, "an attempt to retract the handful of small and hard-won victories that the feminist movement did manage to win for women."

There is not a telephone conversation, personal observation or a wife's afterthoughts as she says farewell at the front door that is not supported in the text or footnotes.

Backlash argues that just when American women's rights seem closest to achievement—a recurring phenomenon in American history—they are struck down by the mass media that pander to the most recently disenfranchised men, and plays on women's anxieties about themselves.

The "man shortage" tale started with a Valentine's Day story for the *Stamford* [Conn.] *Advocate.* Looking for something substantive "for the third paragraph," reporter Lisa Marie Petersen told Faludi she contacted Neil Bennett, a 31-year-old sociologist at Yale University who had almost completed, with two colleagues, a study on women's marriage patterns.

Calling up the nearest prestigious university is nothing new in legitimizing a trend story. Printing sensational statistics on the front page (as the *Stamford Advocate* did) is par for the course, too. What struck Faludi during her investigation was the eagerness with which the bad news was blared from every newspaper, magazine and afternoon talk show.

"No one suggested that women were taking their time because there was no compelling reason to marry," Faludi says. "Women are not economically motivated to marry now, and that's why they don't marry quickly in desperation. But this deliberation is threatening to men. After the *Newsweek* article, I began to see the same theme of women who asked for equality being punished. It appeared in popular novels, movies."

Faludi was born in New York City, and grew up in New York Town Heights, a suburb about 50 miles north of New York. She dedicated *Backlash* to her mother "because, if she had been born 30 years later, she would have been a career woman. This is an era in which she would have flourished. She was trapped in the last backlash described in *The Feminine Mystique*. She did not have the opportunities I had."

Faludi has been blessed with opportunities. After Harvard, where she was managing editor of the *Harvard Crimson*, she took a job as a "copy kid" at the *New York Times*.

Faludi ran errands "half the night in exchange for getting freelance stories for the *Times* in the daytime," she recalls. "Mine were for the Metro section." A three-month internship for the *Times* business section followed, "I learned what a subordinated debenture was."

In a quick succession of moves she worked for the *Miami Herald*, the *Atlanta Constitution* and in 1986 joined the *San Jose Mercury News*, where she was a writer for its Sunday magazine, *West*.

"At first I wrote a story for *West* about the backlash I saw growing, then I proposed it as a book, got the contract and began working on the book and continuing to work for *West*."

In 1987, Faludi decided to take a leave of absence to work on the book exclusively, conducting research at the Stanford Institute on Women and Gender and traveling around the nation conducting in-person interviews.

"I know that this book is sitting on the shoulders of women who have gone before me," she says. "If it weren't for the last 15 or 20 years of feminist scholarship, the book couldn't have been written."

Faludi completed the book and in January 1990 took a reporting job at the *Wall Street Journal*'s San Francisco bureau, where she covers stories examining the intersection between business and social issues, particularly how high finance affects workers.

Her book attempts to explain a complex social issue Faludi has been observing for a decade.

Faludi says, "From 'the man shortage' to 'the infertility epidemic' to 'female burnout' to 'toxic day care,' these so-called female crises have had their origins not in the actual conditions of women's lives but rather in a closed system that starts and ends in the media, popular culture, and ad-

vertising—an endless feedback loop that perpetuates and exaggerates its own false images of womanhood."

What women are really unhappy about, Faludi says, citing poll after poll, is their inequality in the workplace, at home and in the streets. Rape worries women more than their biological clocks. And no wonder. Sex-related murders rose 160 percent between 1976 and 1984.

When the battle appears to be over is the most dangerous time, Faludi says, citing suffragists who believed in 1913 that the struggle was almost won. But, over and over, just as the eyes are on the prize, another backlash surfaces. In the words of women's historian Dale Spender, "While men proceed on their developmental way, building on inherited traditions, women are confined to cycles of lost and found."

Women forget their history during each backlash, Faludi maintains. She likens women's struggle for their rights to a spiral that has made four revolutions. The first began in 1848, when the first American women's rights convention took place at Seneca Falls, N.Y.

From this meeting, Elizabeth Cady Stanton and Susan B. Anthony led women to demand voting rights, education, jobs, marital and property rights, "voluntary motherhood" and health and dress reform.

The second women's rights movement began just after the turn of the century, when the suffragists began a campaign for the vote and an equal rights amendment, working women formed their own trade unions and struck for equal pay and Margaret Sanger led a national movement to educate women about birth control.

This time, according to Faludi, the backlash invoked the specter of communism when the U.S. War Department, the American Legion and the Daughters of the American Revolution banded together to hound feminist leaders such as Charlotte Perkins Gilman, label Jane Addams a communist and exile Emma Goldman.

Women's hopes of controlling their own destinies surged again in the 1940s, when the wartime economy offered them industrial jobs and even threw in a bit of day care and household assistance.

Rosie the Riveter and Wonder Woman emerged at this time, but the end of World War II was the end of this movement. Women factory workers lost their jobs to returning veterans, and an anti-ERA coalition sprang into being.

The feminism that most of us remember, the "women's lib" of the early 1970s, made its greatest strides in equal employment and reproduction rights. It helped legalize abortion. And, Faludi says, it is meeting its own backlash.

Faludi numbers the so-called New Right political movement as among the most flagrant enemies of modern feminism. She accuses it of waging a war on women that she has termed "The Politics of Resentment." She profiles Paul Weyrich, founder of the Washington, D.C.-based Heritage Foundation in 1973, the New Right's first think tank.

It is the New Right's ability to use media buzzwords—such as "postfeminism" and "baby hunger"—to get back at "women's libbers" that Faludi finds most devastating.

Faludi details how movies fell into step with the backlash march. The '70s films with independent women heroines—*Julia, An Unmarried Woman, Alice Doesn't Live Here Any More*—gave way to '80s victims such as Patty Hearst, bound and gagged in Paul Schrader's film; a career woman gone haywire for someone else's husband in *Fatal Attraction,* or the fantasy of a successful, single executive who finds joy in adoptive motherhood and a gourmet baby food business in *Baby Boom.*

The multi-billion dollar fashion and beauty businesses, Faludi shows, are part of the current backlash. Despite the resounding no-vote by women in 1987 to the miniskirt, the fashion business continues to try to push expensive, inane and uncomfortable clothing.

In the '70s, women opted for the natural look, but the '80s found a renewed emphasis on makeup. And covering the wrinkles was not enough. Plastic surgery was promoted in women's magazines, including *Ms.,* which called it a way of "reinventing yourself."

In the chapter, "Ms. Smith Leaves Washington: A Backlash in National Politics," Faludi recounts how, with Ronald Reagan's election, women began disappearing from federal office. New female judicial appointments fell from 15 percent in Jimmy Carter's administration to 8 percent. On the White House staff, the number of women appointed dropped from 123 in 1980 to 62 in 1981.

Women at work have not closed the pay gap that separates them from men, and the occupational desegregation of the sexes started in the '70s stagnated in the '80s. Faludi asserts that as much as 45 percent of the pay gap is caused by sex segregation in the work force.

Nowhere is the backlash against women's rights more visible than at the abortion clinics, Faludi says. Faludi looks at Randall Terry, the founder of Operation Rescue, an antiabortion organization that practices civil disobedience at abortion clinics. Terry, and most Operation Rescue men, she writes, are not grizzled elders but youthful and angry men who have lost out through the modest gains made by women in the last 20 years.

"As resentment over women's increasing levels of professional progress became mixed with anxiety over the sexual freedoms women had begun to exercise, they developed a rhetoric of puritanical outrage to castigate their opponents."

While writing *Backlash,* Faludi frequently showed it to a trusted male friend. "It was important to me that a man look at it fairly," she says. "Yet, people who haven't read it might call it a male-bashing book. Any time women speak up, it will be seen as anti-male. I wanted it to be accessible. No feminist jargon, bogged down in arcane arguments about deconstruction and semiotics . . . I wanted it to be entertaining.

"*Backlash* is not a 'trend du jour,'" Faludi says. "There has been a constant battery, starting in the early '80s. The scenario repeats again and again. Modest gains are followed by retaliation. Yet, this backlash is happening just as women got started learning to control their own lives.

"Women should recognize the power they already have . . . they are more than half the population. In the voting booth and on the university campus they are in the majority. Male policymakers are aware of this. Women are seen as such a threat, yet women have the tools for demanding change in our society. Women have to stop apologizing."

Jane Ayres, "Gains and Losses," in Chicago Tribune, *September 29, 1991, p. 3.*

An excerpt from *Backlash: The Undeclared War against American Women*

The most recent round of backlash first surfaces in the late seventies on the fringes, among the evangelical Right. By the early eighties, the fundamentalist ideology had shouldered its way into the White House. By the mid-eighties, as resistance to women's rights acquired political and social acceptability, it passed into the popular culture. And in every case, the timing coincided with signs that women were believed to be on the verge of a breakthrough.

Just when women's quest for equal rights seemed closest to achieving its objectives, the backlash struck it down. Just when a "gender gap" at the voting booth surfaced in 1980, and women in politics began to talk of capitalizing on it, the Republican party elevated Ronald Reagan and both political parties began to shunt women's rights off their platforms. Just when support for feminism and the Equal Rights Amendment reached a record high in 1981, the amendment was defeated the following year. Just when women were starting to mobilize against battering and sexual assaults, the federal government cut funding for battered-women's programs, defeated bills to fund shelters, and shut down its Office of Domestic Violence—only two years after opening it in 1979. Just when record numbers of younger women were supporting feminist goals in the mid-eighties (more of them, in fact, than older women) and a majority of all women were calling themselves feminists, the media declared the advent of a younger "postfeminist generation" that supposedly reviled the women's movement. Just when women racked up their largest percentage ever supporting the right to abortion, the U.S. Supreme Court moved toward reconsidering it.

In other words, the antifeminist backlash has been set off not by women's achievement of full equality but by the increased possibility that they might win it. It is a preemptive strike that stops women long before they reach the finish line.

Susan Faludi, in her Backlash: The Undeclared War against American Women, Crown, 1991.

Leslie Bennetts   (review date January-February 1992)

[*In the following review of* Backlash, *Bennetts discusses the role of the media in promoting negative perceptions of feminism and generating feelings of fear and insecurity among women.*]

I came away from *Backlash: The Undeclared War Against American Women* feeling not only that it should be required reading for all Americans, but that every representative of any media organization in the country should be locked in a room until he or she has finished the last page. The unrelenting series of revelations provided by Susan Faludi's explosive and exhaustively researched new book is galvanizing enough for any citizen, let alone female; but for a journalist, *Backlash* is one long epiphany.

Faludi's analysis of the unthinking and utterly irresponsible contributions of the mass media to the aforementioned war is enough to make any journalist's blood run cold. There are precious few among us who are not guilty of buying into at least some of the unquestioned and, as Faludi makes clear, almost entirely erroneous assumptions the sheep-like herd has been purveying for lo these many years. On subjects relating to women, the performance of the national media during this period has all too often been a disgrace.

If Faludi's book were merely a polemic, however eloquent, one might disagree with such conclusions. But *Backlash* is a stunning work of reportage, complete with eighty pages of footnotes (including, I regret to say, one citing a story by this reporter), and the sheer accumulation of facts makes many of its arguments virtually unassailable. Particularly shocking are the author's case studies of how the media played several important and emblematic stories about women and their lives. If she demonstrates in excruciating detail the extent to which lazy practitioners of the worst kind of trend journalism failed to do their own homework, no one can say Faludi didn't do hers.

The most famous case in point is the notorious Harvard-Yale study on women's marriage patterns, word of which hit the front pages, network news programs, and talk shows of America like a bombshell in 1986. The thrust of the study was that women who failed to marry young could basically kiss off their chance for marrying at all: the so-called "man shortage" was allegedly so severe that, as *Newsweek* so memorably put it, by the age of forty an unmarried woman was more likely to be killed by a terrorist than to find her way to the altar.

The numbers provided by the study, which was both unpublished and unfinished, were chilling indeed. The only problem was that they weren't true—something that virtually nobody managed to report, although a single telephone call to the U.S. Census Bureau might quickly have indicated that something was amiss. Even a cursory check of population charts reveals that there were substantially more bachelors than unwed women in the age groups in question. "If anyone faced a shortage of potential spouses, it was *men* in the prime marrying years," Faludi notes. When a Census Bureau demographer named Jeanne Moorman recalculated the study's figures, she found that at the age of thirty, a college-educated woman who hadn't yet married had three times the chance posited by the Harvard-Yale report; at the age of thirty-five, her odds of getting married were seven times higher than those predicted

in the study; and at forty, her shot at wedlock was twenty-three times higher than the study had indicated.

Unfortunately, no one seemed to want to hear that the study was wrong—and when Moorman started talking to the press, Reagan administration officials clamped down and ordered her not to discuss the marriage study because it was "too controversial." (She was told to work instead on a study "about how poor unwed mothers abuse the welfare system.") However, Moorman completed her own analysis of marriage patterns and released it—but, as Faludi notes, "The media relegated it to the inside pages, when they reported it at all."

Within the field of demography, the Harvard-Yale study received so much criticism about its methodology and conclusions that by the time it was finally published three years later its authors had decided to leave out the infamous statistics about the "marriage crunch." But by then, of course, the damage was done: the perception of a bleak and lonely future facing the millions of working women who had foolishly delayed marriage in favor of career was firmly established in the national consciousness. As Faludi demonstrates, the media had succeeded not in reporting the news but in making it. Before the Harvard-Yale study was publicized, most attitudinal surveys found a high level of contentment and little anxiety about marriage among single women. But within a year of that terrifying blast of publicity, the proportion of all single women who feared they would never marry had nearly doubled, according to one yearly indicator, the Annual Study of Women's Attitudes. The barrage of warnings had succeeded in inspiring a tremendous level of distress among women who—until they found themselves assailed at every turn by dire pronouncements that they had made a terrible mistake and might already have ruined their lives forever—had been quite happy with their choices.

Equally instructive is Faludi's comparison of the difference between the way the media played the work of two social scientists—one overtly hostile to women's independence, the other sympathetic. When Shere Hite published the results of her national survey on sexuality and relationships, *Women and Love: A Cultural Revolution in Progress,* she was immediately ripped to shreds by the press, which seemed more interested in "attacking Hite personally," as Faludi puts it, than in any evenhanded treatment of her findings. To be sure, the results of Hite's inquiry were guaranteed to make many men uncomfortable: she found that most women were upset about the refusal of the men in their lives to treat them as equals, and about the domestic friction that resulted as they sought some respect. "Hite's findings were largely held up for ridicule, not inspection," Faludi states.

The treatment was very different for a man with opposing views. "At the same time the press was pillorying Hite for suggesting that male resistance might be partly responsible for women's grief, it was applauding another social scientist whose theory—that women's equality was to blame for contemporary women's anguish—was more consonant with backlash thinking," Faludi continues. Dr. Srully Blotnick, a *Forbes* magazine columnist and self-appointed media "expert," concluded that success at work "poisons both the professional and personal lives of women." His survey was widely and favorably reported by the national media. No one questioned his methodology, in contrast to the ferocious attacks on Hite's approach. This was unfortunate because, although Blotnick claimed his was a groundbreaking twenty-five year longitudinal study, he would have been only seventeen years old when he purportedly began his data collection. The "Dr." title he had adopted "turned out to be the product of a mail-order degree from an unaccredited correspondence school," Faludi reports. When a *U.S. News & World* reporter finally investigated Blotnick's credentials, it was discovered that "almost nothing on his résumé checked out"—but *U.S. News* never published that story. It was only after New York State launched a criminal fraud investigation against Blotnick that *Forbes* finally discontinued his column. News of Blotnick's fall from grace, however, was almost completely ignored by the press. As with the Harvard-Yale marriage study, the flaws in Blotnick's argument were never publicized, his conclusions never exposed as propaganda rather than legitimate social science. Because his "findings" confirmed preexisting negative biases about working women during the backlash era, the media never bothered to check out their validity or his credibility.

An even more egregious example of media malfeasance was provided by the treatment accorded a French study on what seemed to be a sudden and dramatic epidemic of infertility among women over thirty. *The New York Times* played the story on page one, praising the report as "unusually large and rigorous" and "more reliable" than previous studies that had indicated a considerably later onset of fertility problems among most women. The alarmist new study spawned not only the familiar round of national media attention but also a subsequent onslaught of books about women's "biological clock," not to mention a steady escalation in the fearsome statistics. "A self-help book was soon reporting that women in their thirties now faced a 'shocking 68 percent' chance of infertility—and promptly faulted the feminists, who had failed to advise women of the biological drawbacks of a successful career," Faludi reports.

However, the scare stories conveniently omitted a few salient facts. The patients used in the French study were all married to completely sterile men—hardly a representative sampling of the population—and were trying to get pregnant through artificial insemination in a process using frozen sperm, which is far less potent than fresh sperm. The study also pronounced as infertile any woman who was not pregnant after only a year of trying—a ridiculous cut-off, since it takes even newlyweds a mean time of eight months to conceive (and another study found that fully 80 percent of couples who failed to conceive after one year eventually succeeded). Indeed, although the national media had given the French study their uncritical approval, experts in the field debunked it so thoroughly that its own authors finally announced apologetically that they "never meant their findings to apply to all women."

But as usual with such sagas, it was too late. As Faludi observes, "Neither their retreat nor their peers' disparaging

assessments attracted press attention." Nor did a nationwide fertility survey of 8,000 women later released by the U.S. National Center for Health Statistics, which found that infertility had actually *declined* slightly, not only among women in their thirties but even among women in their forties. Thanks to the shoddy performance of the press, American women had once again been needlessly terrorized by a grossly flawed report that, because it confirmed a reactionary stereotype that the punishment for uppity women who delay childbirth was the probability of forfeiting it entirely, received virtually no critical scrutiny whatsoever.

It would be comforting if examples like the ones cited above were the exception rather than the rule, but *Backlash* is full of them. And even in the sections dealing with the offenses committed against women by institutions other than media outlets, the press often played an important role in helping to promote those offenses. Susan Faludi has laid it all out in sickening detail. Now that she'd done the hard work of ferreting out the truths that battalions of her peers had failed even to look for, it will be instructive indeed to see whether the major media organizations repeatedly cited in her reporting actually do anything to improve their coverage on such politically charged subjects as women's rights. Judging by past performance, I wouldn't bet the ranch. (pp. 53-5)

Leslie Bennetts, "Myths That Men (and the Media) Live By," in Columbia Journalism Review, *Vol. XXX, No. 5, January-February, 1992, pp. 53-5.*

Charlotte Allen (review date February 1992)

[*In the following review, Allen finds Faludi's credibility marred by a lack of objective evidence and oversimplification of the complex and ambivalent values held by American men and women.*]

Only a few years ago feminism was reported to be dead, done in at least in part by the backsliding of some of its own pioneers. By the mid-80's, Betty Friedan was criticizing her more militant sisters for their masculine hairstyles, and Germaine Greer was championing the traditional, family-centered cultures of rural Italy and India. Even Gloria Steinem tried to catch a man. In the middle class, the young career women who were supposed to be feminism's chief beneficiaries were buying silk dresses, voting Republican, looking for husbands, talking about children.

Reports of the movement's demise turned out to be premature. Comes now Susan Faludi, who, along with Naomi Wolf, deconstructionist of the "beauty myth," is at the forefront of a young and energetic second wave of feminism that makes the first wave seem as insipid and dated as the old "feminine mystique" of frilly aprons and Tupperware parties Friedan used to mock.

Backlash, an exceedingly long book, is also representative of the prolix new genre of 80's-bashing, already a little tired though we are only two years into the 90's. Most 80's-bashing books fixate on junk bonds and undertenanted office towers, twin symbols of the debt-loaded culture of the Reagan era. To Faludi, the same decade also witnessed a "backlash" against feminism that "moved through the culture's secret chambers, traveling through passageways of flattery and fear." *That,* she says, is what accounts for the silk dresses and the husband-hunting.

The 80's for Faludi would seem to have been not the Greed Decade but the Kneed Decade, a period when women who dared to be liberated really took it in the groin, not just from religious fundamentalists and conservative politicians but from those putative allies of feminism, the popular media, and, of course, the old-line feminists themselves. In Faludi's book, Friedan and Greer lie down (figuratively) with such bogeypersons as George Gilder, Robert Bork, Allan Bloom, Gary Bauer (Reagan's straight-arrow family-policy czar), and Randall Terry, leader of the anti-abortion group Operation Rescue. This is a book in which not to be part of the solution is emphatically to be part of the problem.

Faludi, a *Wall Street Journal* reporter, writes with a journalist's easy flair and an occasional striking turn of phrase reminiscent of Barbara Ehrenreich, who works the same ideological turf in a much more original fashion. (Ehrenreich has her own 80's-basher out, tellingly titled *The Worst Years of Our Lives.*) And *Backlash* is nothing if not thoroughly researched: Faludi devotes a full 89 pages to agate-size footnotes documenting the scholarly and media sources of every factual assertion she has stuffed into her dense, wordy chapters.

For all that, *Backlash* is a thin book, its workaholic scholarship and competent writing masking stick-figure stereotypes of relations between men and women, and between cultures and their artifacts. It is a pamphlet with but one point to make, repeated again and again like the drumbeat that calls to order those trendy men's-movement hugathons (another symptom of the "backlash"). In fact, when one has finished this book, practically the only thing one sees are the file folders of newspaper clippings and stacks of index cards that were its raw materials, with, protruding awkwardly here and there like skin grafts that failed to take, a few profiles of leading backlash instigators, typically a little off-point. There is little real reporting in the book, and none of the sustained theorizing or distanced observation that we might expect from a work of cultural criticism.

Here is Faludi's entire thesis:

> The backlash is not a conspiracy, with a council dispatching agents from some central control room, nor are the people who serve its ends often aware of their role; some even consider themselves feminists. For the most part, its workings are encoded and internalized, diffuse and chameleonic. Not all of the manifestations of the backlash are of equal weight or significance, either; some are mere ephemera, generated by a culture machine that is always scrounging for a "fresh" angle. Taken as a whole, however, these codes and cajolings, these whispers and threats and myths, move overwhelmingly in one direction: they try to push women back into their "acceptable" roles—whether as Daddy's girl or flut-

tery romantic, active nester or passive love object.

Although the backlash is not a movement, that doesn't make it any less destructive. In fact, the lack of orchestration, the absence of a single string-puller, only makes it harder to see—and perhaps more effective. A backlash against women's rights succeeds to the degree that it appears not to be political, that it appears not to be a struggle at all. It is most powerful when it goes private, when it lodges in a woman's mind and turns her vision inward, until she imagines the pressure is all in her head, until she begins to enforce the backlash, too—on herself.

This is an argument impossible to gainsay. It requires no proof; indeed, the very lack of proof demonstrates the insidiousness of the phenomenon, a seamless and invisible spider web stretching into every corner of contemporary culture. By maintaining that the backlash is a "movement" yet not an "organized" movement, a "struggle" that appears "not to be a struggle at all," a chimera-like phenomenon that exists now as concrete "threats" from the militant Right, now as mere media-generated "ephemera," now as disembodied feelings "in a woman's mind" with no objective correlatives whatsoever, Faludi can have it all ways, can seize all sticks with which to beat her opponents.

Seize them she does. One stick is the brouhaha that ensued when several researchers at Harvard and Yale issued a report in 1986 demonstrating that the chances of a college-educated, never-married woman at finding a husband start falling rapidly at age thirty and plunge to almost zero after age forty. The Harvard-Yale findings turned into a *Newsweek* cover story and generated quite a bit of panic among successful single women who would never see thirty again.

According to Faludi, this was a typical manifestation of the backlash at its most duplicitous and demoralizing. Her own first move is to attack the researchers' methodology, implying that they made up the statistics for ideological reasons. She cites a rival study by a female Census Bureau demographer—the Harvard-Yale team was headed by a man—which concluded that a never-married woman with a college degree actually has about a one-in-five chance of finding a husband after age forty. What a relief.

Faludi then proceeds to tactic No. 2: who cares, anyway? She cites polls showing that the happiness of single women *rose* during the 1980's, while that of their married sisters declined. Finally, she devotes five pages to the travails of a still-single thirty-six-year-old woman (not one of the happy ones, evidently) who signed up for $20,000 worth of plastic surgery in the hopes of winning a bet that she could beat the odds and find a spouse before reaching her fifth decade.

This is the kind of reasoning that used to make men say, "She's so cute when she gets mad." Faludi faults Gary Bauer because his wife is a full-time homemaker. Then she turns around and faults Michael Levin, an anti-feminist professor of philosophy at the City University of New York, because his wife has a career as a mathematician. Heads, I win; tails, you lose. As might be expected, she puts great stock in the "gender gap," the belief that all women are closet ultra-liberals. Did George Bush happen to get 49 to 50 percent of the female vote in the 1988 election? That was "not a real majority," sniffs Faludi.

Her most scathing denunciations, though, are reserved not for the right-wingers but for the hapless female scholars who have entertained revisionist thoughts about the fruits of the past two decades' liberation: such figures as the sociologist Lenore Weitzman, who reported a drastic decline in an ex-wife's living standards after a typical no-fault divorce (bad numbers, Lenore!), and Rosalind Rosenberg, a historian at Barnard who testified at a Sears, Roebuck sex-discrimination trial that female sales employees gravitated toward lower-paying no-commission jobs out of a preference for less competitive work (how could you, Rosalind?). Faludi likes to slip personal barbs into her critiques, pointing out Rosenberg's close friendship with one of the Sears lawyers, or the *haut-bourgeois* existence enjoyed by Sylvia Ann Hewlett, whose book, *A Lesser Life,* claims solidarity with working-class women against hardline feminists.

For all that, *Backlash* might actually have been an interesting book had Susan Faludi explored some of the phenomena she writes about rather than simply listing them in her catalogue of outrages. For example, she cites *Good Housekeeping*'s "New Traditionalist" advertising campaign, which shows contented mothers and children in cozy domestic settings. Neotraditionalism is, in fact, exactly what Faludi implies that it is: a veneer of comforting make-believe covering the severe social and familial dislocation of the late 20th century. It is an image of traditionalism, not its reality, serving to satisfy intense longings for the structure and order supplied by traditional institutions, chiefly religion and the authoritarian family, without forcing people to give up the things that they would have to give up if they adopted those institutions in their substance. Women can tie hair-ribbons around their little girls' pigtails, put a handmade quilt on the bed, bake a pie (or at least read about baking one), and still get to do pretty much whatever they want. Weddings become more elaborate and expensive as marriages become shorter and more contingent.

In truth, feminism is merely a part of a larger and longer-range trend of universal liberation, not just from oppressive husbands and fathers but from all demands, erotic and otherwise, that have seemed burdensome, annoying, or irrational. People in general have become free to pursue their self-interest—careers, wealth accumulation, romantic passions, sexual desires—unhindered. One might find the source of this trend, as Tom Wolfe does, in the four-decade surge of post-World War II prosperity that gradually melted down the chains of necessity binding people together in inconvenient relationships, combined with what Wolfe calls "the fifth freedom—freedom *from* religion." Or, looking back further in time, one might see feminism's roots in the Enlightenment idea of the social contract: people would be better off if their ties to others and to institutions were strictly voluntary, a matter of rational choice directed by mutual self-interest. This has naturally wreaked havoc upon the family, for hardly anyone would freely choose the grab-bag of embarrassing and uncongenial characters who happen to be his relatives. Having first stripped the family of its tribal, multigenerational character, social-contract theory then went to work on marriage itself—hence, easy divorce, the sexual revolution, the women's movement. It is currently playing itself out in the desire of middle-class parents to have "autonomous" children. Young people have their own cars, cash, designer clothes, telephones, and television sets, while doing fewer household chores than ever before in history.

Many women have found universal liberation to be as disturbing as it is supposed to be exhilarating. The disruption of traditional courtship and marriage patterns that has accompanied liberation means that young middle-class women spend years wondering when and where they will ever find a husband, all the while feeling varying degrees of dissatisfaction, contempt, and rage at the men they do meet and sleep with, or fight off sleeping with. Women who marry discover that it is more exhausting than glamorous to pursue a career outside the home while being a wife, let alone a mother of small children, at the same time.

Perhaps, as Susan Faludi suggests, it is wrong and reactionary for women to want to be wives and mothers—status roles left over from the days before all human relationships became matters of the marketplace. Yet most women do so want, and if Susan Faludi means to "liberate" them from those desires, she is talking about liberating them from womanhood itself. No wonder American women feel so ambivalent about feminism. Today, they will read *Backlash;* tomorrow, it will be *Smart Women, Foolish Choices.* Today, they will fret about the "glass ceiling"; tomorrow, they will have their chins resculpted. They will feel faintly discontented or wildly desperate. They will blame it on feminism, or on men, or on the media, or on themselves. But it is not a backlash. It is more a case of wanting and not really wanting to go back. (pp. 62-4)

Charlotte Allen, "New Wave Feminism," in Commentary, *Vol. 93, No. 2, February, 1992, pp. 62-4.*

Gayle Greene   (review date 10 February 1992)

[*Greene is an American critic who has written extensively on women's studies. In the following review of* Backlash, *she discusses the social and economic factors contributing to the rise of antifeminist views in America and praises both* Backlash *and Naomi Wolf's* The Beauty Myth *for reviving popular interest in feminist concerns.*]

Whereas [Naomi] Wolf addresses one aspect of the backlash [in *The Beauty Myth*], Faludi takes in a broader picture [in *Backlash: The Undeclared War against American Women*], and her book offers a rich compendium of fascinating information and an indictment of a system losing its grip and reeling from changes it does not begin to understand.

By the end of the eighties women were familiar with these "statistical developments"—a "man shortage" endangering our opportunities for marriage; burnout attacking single and career women; an infertility epidemic striking women over 30. While none of these were real, they did succeed in deflecting attention from problems that were. For along with these "developments" we were being fed a mystifying hype: that the pay gap between the sexes was closing and that women were charging into traditional male occupations. The reality was that college-educated women were still making less, on average, than men with high school diplomas, just as they had in the fifties, and the work force was becoming more segregated, with nearly 80 percent of working women as secretaries, administrative support workers and sales clerks; and that women represent less than one-half of 1 percent of top corporate managers, less than 6 percent of law partners, less than 8 percent of federal and state judges and a mere 10 percent of tenured faculty at four-year institutions and 3 to 4 percent at Ivy League colleges. If we were hearing less about discrimination, this was partly because Reagan had gutted the Equal Employment Opportunity Commission, hatcheting its budget and firing or silencing equal-opportunity investigators.

The press unquestionably passed along misleading government and private reports—the E.E.O.C.'s claim that sexual harassment on the job is declining, the Justice Department's report that rape rates are static, the Labor Department's claim that the wage gap has narrowed. Taking its cues from the Reagan Administration, which was taking its cues from the New Right, its movements weren't premeditated but they were "grossly susceptible to the prevailing political currents." Rather than investigating and exposing the causes of backlash in the coalescence of the New Right with a misogynous White House and intransigent social and religious institutions and attitudes, the media chose to "peddle the backlash."

In place of factual reporting on the erosion of women's rights the media circulated make-believe data and fabricated trends. They showcased the infamous Harvard-Yale marriage study that proclaimed that a woman over 40 had more chance of being killed by a terrorist than getting married, while ignoring actual census data and evidence that suggest it is *men* who are eager to marry and women who choose not to. They promoted bogus statistics on infertility in women over 30 while showing no interest in the real drop in fertility in women under 30, due to chlamydia. They pushed the central argument of backlash—that it's women's new freedoms that account for our unhappiness—while ignoring the actual social and political pressures on us (harassment from the media among them) and obfuscating the simple truth that it's not liberation but the lack of it that's our problem. Like the advice manuals that proliferated during the decade (*Smart Women/Foolish Choices, Women Who Love Too Much*), the media depoliticized the issues and blamed the woman.

Television and Hollywood portrayed single women as lonely and forlorn, panicked by the man shortage and the ticking of their biological clocks, overcome by baby craving, desperate for marriage. Baby craze films (*Three Men and a Baby, Baby Boom*) marketed a return to motherhood. *Fatal Attraction* is but one instance of the way

"women's lives were framed as morality tales in which the 'good mother' wins and the independent woman gets punished"; and tough-guy films, which were legion in the eighties, reasserted male authority. In television, strong single women vanished, to be replaced by cold careerists and depressed spinsters; and here, too, the hard-boiled male made a comeback (contrary to audience demand, actually: Faludi links shrinking network audiences to the cancellation of shows about independent women).

The press, television, movies, pop psychology and advertising function as what Faludi terms "an endless feedback loop," "a closed system" that perpetuates its own reality. Faludi shows how this loop works—how the media pick up statistical developments that corroborate their preconceptions and then authorize such developments by repeating them. Again and again the people she interviewed cited the movies—"It's like in *Fatal Attraction*"—or referred to trend stories to corroborate their assumptions. Trend stories refer to other trend stories or to advice manuals, which base their claims on trend stories or the movies. What is clear is that rather than reporting movements, the media are *creating* them—that while purporting to describe, they actually prescribe.

And the effects have been devastating: The backlash has divided and confused women and turned our pain and frustration inward, diminishing our sense of self-worth, of future possibilities, and our view of the legacy of feminism. Whereas in 1986 a Gallup poll showed a majority of women calling themselves feminists and only 4 percent describing themselves as "antifeminists," by the end of the decade the number of women willing to identify themselves as feminists dropped to one in three. By 1989 almost half of the women in a *New York Times* poll said "they now feared they had sacrificed too much for their gains." The year after an infamous 1986 *Fortune* cover story, "Why Women Are Bailing Out," the proportion of women applying to business schools began to shrink for the first time in a decade. The backlash has not succeeded in returning women to the home, but—as in the fifties—it has helped many to accommodate to discrimination, harassment and menial jobs. Then as now, "the ranks of women working didn't shrink . . . but . . . occupational segregation increased," which produced a paradoxical situation wherein "rising economic participation" coexists with "an embattled and diminished cultural stature."

Backlash offers fascinating stories—of con men and opportunists and wackos and desperadoes—that illustrate how private neuroses can catch a wave of popular opinion and become enormously influential: as with the losers who manned Operation Rescue or the masterminds of antifeminist (and wildly successful) ad campaigns for Guess jeans and Victoria's Secret. Faludi must be a crackerjack interviewer, letting subjects babble on until they blurt out marvelously self-incriminating revelations, offering up the real reasons they hate and fear feminists—motives that are self-serving, silly, often sinister—which Faludi simply, deadpan, recounts.

But this book also tells stories of courage and determination on the part of many women who stood their ground

> **In place of factual reporting on the
> erosion of women's rights the media
> circulated make-believe data and
> fabricated trends.**
>
> —*Gayle Greene*

in the face of harassment and hostility from male co-workers and management. Diane Joyce, who took "nearly ten years of battles to become the first female skilled crafts worker ever in Santa Clara County . . . another seven years of court litigation, pursued all the way to the U.S. Supreme Court, before she could actually start work," and then "the real fight" began; Pat Lorance, who took on A.T.&T. over a seniority system designed to lock out women—and lost; Rita Flynn, who was fired for trying to fight discrimination at ABC; Betty Riggs, who underwent sterilization in the name of "fetal rights" to keep a job that was then pulled out from under her—these are among the many women whose stories deserve to be known. I don't see a lot of men sticking up for women in all this, but I do see why more women do not fight back, how difficult and dangerous it is to attempt collective bargaining in today's workplace.

From this *comédie humaine* there emerges a picture of an economy in trouble, a system failing fast and thrashing about in search of an enemy; a resorting to that most primitive mechanism for dealing with fear, scapegoating:

> When the enemy has no face, society will invent one. All that free-floating anxiety over declining wages, insecure employment, and overpriced housing needs a place to light, and in the '80s, much of it fixed itself on women.

Faludi's analysis accounts not only for antifeminism but for the resurgence of racism and explains why the most virulent expressions of both have tended to come from those hurting from social and economic dislocation—blue-collar workers, put out of work by the millions by plant closings and the shift to a service economy; young men condemned by the eighties economy to earn less than their fathers, unable to afford houses or to provide for their families, losing control at work and home and focusing their rage and frustration on women. It is men like these who firebomb women's clinics and fill "the lists of plaintiffs filing reverse-discrimination and 'men's rights' law suits, [and] the steadily mounting police rolls of rapists and sexual assailants." But backlash is not confined to one class or income. Its message was framed by more affluent and influential men in media, business and politics—and by women too, the women of the New Right, the authors, both female and male, of antifeminist books and advice manuals.

What we're seeing, then, is the targeting of women for social problems that are hurting women as much as, if not more than, most men. Given what little progress we've made, how to account for the strength of the reaction?

Maybe, as Faludi suggests, it's because women really do have enormous unrecognized power (unrecognized by women, that is, but not by men). Maybe what looks like an overreaction is an accurate assessment of the threat we represent. It is gratifying to learn that in "the High Femininity year of 1987" women's refusal to buy "nearly decimated the fashion industry" and by 1989 Lacroix was reporting a $9.3 million loss—that his pouf dresses went poof; that women's viewing habits caused losses for the networks; that in 1989, when NOW suggested the formation of a third party, a gender gap in voting was sufficiently threatening that the press responded with such anger and derision—this should have clued women into the fact that maybe they were on to something.

Both Faludi and Wolf try to get women to recognize their power. Both books do what feminist classics—Simone de Beauvoir's *The Second Sex,* Betty Friedan's *The Feminine Mystique*—did: They name and identify the problem and give us a new way of seeing. If they are at times prone to exaggeration and hyperbole, so too were de Beauvoir and Friedan. I do wish Faludi had more fully acknowledged Wendy Kaminer's *A Fearful Freedom: Women's Flight from Equality* and other analyses of the backlash that cover some of the same ground that she does—for example, Katha Pollitt's ["Being Wedded Is Not Always Bliss," September 20, 1986]. And I also wish she had found a way of discussing Carol Gilligan that did not blame her for what reactionary forces made of her. But what is enormously important is that both books move the discussion outside academic feminist discourse, which has tended to become turgid, inward-looking and politically ineffectual, and into a more public arena.

I'm delighted that these books were written by young women, that they are being marketed enthusiastically for large audiences, that they are available even in Southern California bookstore chains, that the authors are appearing widely on talk shows. I love their indignation—both books crackle with energy and anger. What they do not note—and so I will—is that it's the success of feminism (as much as its failures) that has fueled this energy: It's precisely because feminism has taught us to expect more—that things might be better—that these young women are so angry. So they give us a new way of viewing the legacy of feminism of which the authors may not be aware. I think there are a lot of women out there who will get the message—since these books appeared, Clarence Thomas happened along like Exhibit A—and I hope they will help re-ignite the women's movement to face the challenges that still confront us. (pp. 168-70)

> *Gayle Greene, "The Empire Strikes Back," in* The Nation, *New York, Vol. 254, No. 5, February 10, 1992, pp. 166-70.*

Gretchen Morgenson   (review date 16 March 1992)

[*In the following review, Morgenson criticizes* Backlash *for presenting what she perceives as a sensationalistic, inaccurate, and harmful depiction of women as victims.*]

In a triumph of political correctness over literary merit and common sense, Susan Faludi has a hot book on her hands. *Backlash: The Undeclared War Against American Women* has vaulted to near the top of the *New York Times* bestseller list. It has been on the list for over 14 weeks. It even won the National Book Critics Circle Award for non-fiction. Never mind that it is badly written, shoddily reported and insulting to intelligent women.

Backlash alleges that during the Eighties American women lost ground in their battles for equality and a significant role on the world stage. Today, Faludi argues, females are worse off than we were in the Seventies, when feminism was just taking off.

If you are naturally paranoid, you may like the book. It weaves an intriguing if improbable theory: Women today are the victims of a conspiracy perpetrated by the media, government, Hollywood, lawyers, fashion designers, and men of all stripes.

Women who pick up *Backlash* looking for a jaunty bit of male bashing will be disappointed. Faludi doesn't write, she pomposes. "The backlash has moved through the culture's secret chambers, travelling through passageways of flattery and fear," she writes, meaning heaven knows what. "If the American man can claim no ancestral coat of arms on which to elevate himself from the masses, perhaps he can fashion his sex into a sort of pedigree." Another musing: "Nothing seems to crush the masculine petals more than a bit of feminist rain—a few drops are perceived as a downpour." Yech!

Why has this claptrap made the bestseller list and won plaudits? It's a sign of the times. The book is politically correct in the worst sense. Therefore, all true believers—who infest the media—must rally round it. The persecution theme resonates in the vast and deep echo chamber that exists among women's pop culture magazines. Women's magazine editors, in constant search of something to slip in between stories on crash diets and new plastic surgery techniques, are happy to tout anyone talking up the women-as-victims theme. Faludi turned up in December in *Vanity Fair,* about the same time she scored three pages in *People* magazine.

Book reviewers—also part of the echo chamber—have been kind to *Backlash* as well. Reviews in the influential *New York Times Book Review,* the *New Yorker* and *Atlantic* were glowing. In all this praise there is a certain amount of logrolling: Author and columnist Barbara Ehrenreich called Faludi's book "a rich and juicy read, informed by powerful logic and moral clarity." Ehrenreich's own writings are cited no fewer than 12 times in Faludi's book.

Faludi tries to build her conspiracy theory by pelting the reader with factoid after factoid; she's also big on the supposedly telling anecdote. What results: a labyrinth of nonsense followed by 80 pages of footnotes.

Such footnoting may pass for "dazzling investigative powers," as reviewer Ehrenreich puts it. But a trip through Faludi's footnotes reveals that her case is largely built on a rehash of feminist works from the past two decades and a slew of dated magazine and newspaper articles. Lamentably few of Faludi's sources in *Backlash* are primary—

odd, for an investigative reporter. Of the thousands of citations in her footnotes, most are quotes from books and articles that appeared in *Vanity Fair, People,* the *National Enquirer,* the *New York Times,* the *American Journal of Public Health,* the *San Francisco Chronicle* and other periodicals. *Backlash* is basically a clip-and-paste job.

Here's how the backlash allegedly works. A 1986 Harvard-Yale study said college-educated, unwed women over the age of 35 had but a 5% chance of getting married. According to Faludi, this study had an enormous impact on American women. Following the release of the Harvard-Yale study, women everywhere went into a simultaneous depression. We did? Then she claims the study pushed women to marry earlier than they had been marrying before. Oh? What's the proof? Faludi: "In a *Los Angeles Times* story, therapists reported that after the study's promotion, single female patients became 'obsessed' with marriage, ready to marry men they didn't even love, just to beat the 'odds.' "

Want to see more of the backlash in action? Start with the wildly popular 1987 film *Fatal Attraction.* The villain, a maniacal single working gal, loses her man to a beneficent homemaker—evidence, Faludi claims, that working women are resented by men. Move on to the fashion world. You may have thought Christian Lacroix was a designer whose clients were wealthy, frivolous females; wrong again. Lacroix is a backlash co-conspirator, humiliating women by dressing them as "daddy's little girls."

The women Faludi describes react to backlash stimuli like so many marionettes on strings. To the millions of spirited, accomplished females in this country, this is deeply insulting.

—*Gretchen Morgenson*

Plastic surgeons are in the backlash gang, too. They don't operate on women because they're asked to; they put women under the knife to control them. After all, "women under anesthesia don't talk back," says Faludi.

Though the media has rallied around Faludi, she considers newspapers and magazines, including *Forbes,* major contributors to the backlash. For instance, Faludi argues that one 1986 story in *Fortune* discouraged oodles of women from applying to M.B.A. schools and pursuing a career in commerce. "The *Fortune* story left an especially deep and troubling impression on young women aspiring to business and management careers." Her conclusion: "The year after *Fortune* launched the 'bailing out' trend, the proportion of women applying to business schools suddenly began to shrink—for the first time in a decade."

Interesting. But wrong. There was no shrinkage following the *Fortune* story. According to the American Assembly of Collegiate Schools of Business, which reports on business school graduates, the proportion of women graduates increased every year from 1967 through 1989, the most recent figures available.

There is more such disinformation. As evidence of the backlash in the beauty business, Faludi states that in the recent past fewer and fewer plastic surgeons were operating on women "who might actually benefit from plastic surgery." Instead, most of these misogynist doctors were performing more frivolous but profitable face-lifts, breast enlargements and liposuction, thereby "improving their own control over their patients." As a result, according to *Backlash,* the number of reconstructive operations performed on burn victims and breast cancer patients declined in the late Eighties.

Not according to the American Society of Plastic & Reconstructive Surgeons in Illinois, the outfit Faludi claims as her source. The society says that reconstructive breast surgery increased 25% from 1988 to 1990; between 1981 and 1990, 114%. Total reconstructive surgery increased 4% in the last two years of the decade and 70% from 1981.

So women have made little progress in the executive suite? The U.S. Bureau of Labor Statistics reports the percentage of women executives, administrators and managers among all managers in the American work force has risen from 32.4% in 1983 to 41% in 1991. Faludi ignores such inconvenient facts. She writes: "Women were pouring into many low-paid female work ghettos."

To determine exactly how many women "poured" into these ghettos, turn to the notes for this documentation: "The secretarial pool, for example, went from 98.9% female in 1979 to 99.2% in 1986." Sound like a tidal wave? It's a three-tenths of 1% increase over seven years.

When asked about these discrepancies, Faludi dithers and has trouble recalling sources other than vaguely related magazine articles.

Faludi is a reporter for the *Wall Street Journal,* and reporters don't make big money; so you can't blame a reporter for wanting to supplement her income. The trouble is that this kind of book is damaging to women. In encouraging women to think of themselves as victims, Faludi discourages them from making the efforts required to succeed in a murderously competitive society; people who feel sorry for themselves don't usually put forth maximum effort.

The women Faludi describes react to backlash stimuli like so many marionettes on strings. To the millions of spirited, accomplished females in this country, this is deeply insulting. Only mindless bimbos can be maneuvered the way women in Faludi's world seem to be. How many women do you know who would retreat, sobbing, into the kitchen because of something they read in a magazine?

In the opinion of this career woman, *Backlash* is a last gasp of Seventies feminism, a final attempt to rally women to a shrill, anti-male cause that has been comatose for years. (pp. 152-53)

Gretchen Morgenson, "A Whiner's Bible," in

Forbes, *Vol. 149, No. 6, March 16, 1992, pp. 152-53.*

Karen Lehrman   (review date 16 March 1992)

[*In the following review, Lehrman discusses* Backlash *in relation to revisionist theories of feminism. She acknowledges the validity of the concept of backlash but faults Faludi's conspiracy theory as overly defensive and extreme.*]

"We intend simply to be ourselves," declared Marie Jenney Howe in the early part of this century. "Not just our little female selves, but our whole big human selves." Howe was the founder of Heterodoxy, a kind of primitive consciousness-raising group in Greenwich Village that demanded only that its members not have orthodox views. Above all, Heterodoxy urged an escape from the cramping classification of "woman," which was being imposed not only by male-dominated society, but also by the "woman movement" of the late nineteenth century. "Woman" was defined by her duties to men, society, God. A feminist's duty, these fiercely individualistic women believed, was primarily to herself.

Heterodoxy deserves to be rescued, especially these days, from the dustbin of history. For in its zeal to abolish women's "little" femaleness, our own women's movement has ended up trapping women in a big femaleness, in a grandiloquent collective identity. Women's ability "simply to be ourselves" has been undermined in the process. But we may again be at the kind of turning point that prompted the birth of Heterodoxy and won it discontented, independent members, eager to pursue the cause of women's equality—on their own terms.

Women (and men) today endorse many or most of the basic goals that belong under the broad banner of feminism: equal job and education opportunities, the same pay for the same work, shared domestic work, access to child care—the prerequisites to overall equality and justice for women. Yet most women (and men) are unlikely to call themselves feminists, to want to be part of any sort of radical, self-conscious movement whose primary purpose is to secure women's rights. The reigning explanation for this discrepancy is summed up in what has suddenly become the feminist buzzword for the 1990s: backlash.

In her best-selling book by that title, [*Backlash: The Undeclared War against American Women*], Susan Faludi, a reporter for *The Wall Street Journal,* argues that over the past decade women have confronted a concerted cultural and intellectual effort to turn back the progress of women's liberation. She chronicles the daunting extent of the phenomenon, which began with the New Right and now extends into our underwear drawers. The backlash, according to feminists, has succeeded in again turning "feminist" into a dirty word, in making all feminists out to be whiny, shrill, man-hating, ugly.

There is, however, another and contradictory explanation for women's rejection of the label: women believe that they are strong, independent, and can do it all on their own. Or at any rate they believe that the kind of help offered by the organized women's movement is at best beside the point. To some degree this skepticism is a measure of the feminist movement's success. Yet underlying it is a deep discomfort with the orthodoxy of the movement, with a mentality that conceives of only one kind of feminist.

There is equal discomfort with the fundamental tenet that launched the movement in the 1960s: that the "personal is political." In other words, the quest for women's individual advancement does not belong in the private sphere, because for women there is no private sphere: the entirety of our lives has been shaped by political oppression. According to this analysis, the solutions to our problems, from domestic violence to eating disorders, are to be found in society. Ironically, this feminist doctrine has promoted an adversarial stance that has all too often burdened women with precisely the status they have been struggling to escape: the status of victim.

It is also an approach that, in focusing so intently on the public sphere, has tended to ascribe to women goals that they don't necessarily have, and more important, to deny the domestic concerns that they most certainly do have. Concerned about those omissions, such high-profile feminist revisionists as Betty Friedan, Germaine Greer, and Susan Brownmiller, along with "relational" scholars in academia, have offered another explanation of feminism's fading appeal. "First-stage" feminism, they began arguing a decade ago, has run its course, and the time has come to shift to a "second stage," which would correct for the zealous oversimplifications that helped to launch the crusade for women's rights. Women are different from men, they have argued, and there is such a thing as a "woman's sphere," in and through which women can and should exert influence. Taking this line of thought to its extreme, Suzanne Gordon has recently argued in *Prisoners of Men's Dreams* that equal opportunity feminism must be replaced by "transformative feminism": women's goal should be to change capitalism into a system based on caring, not competition.

Now another grande dame of feminism has retreated to the personal realm, in a very different way. In *Revolution from Within: A Book of Self-Esteem,* Gloria Steinem attributes most of women's problems to external factors, but as her title suggests, her cure is internal. In place of the relational feminists' emphasis on distinctively female characteristics, Steinem, like the early feminists, focuses on self-completion, reclaiming women's strong, independent, assertive side. But she too has joined the growing chorus urging that the political be personalized.

Faludi would dismiss these revisionisms as the unwitting product of "backlash," as a sad sort of entrenchment that has emerged from the onslaught by the media, government, and industry on the whole idea of equality for women. And certainly "second-stage" thinking is guilty of treading too close to a pernicious, retrograde view of women (in addition to subscribing to a facile criticism of capitalism). But the mystique of the backlash, and the reception of Faludi's book, which is being hailed as "feminism's new manifesto," are perhaps the best evidence of the limitations of traditional, first-stage feminism. Although Faludi's credo ostensibly endorses individualism

and self-assertion—she invokes Nora's declaration in *A Doll's House,* "Before everything else I'm a human being"—the truth is that her book is a good indication of how far modern-day feminism has strayed from its classically liberal foundations. The ready embrace of an external enemy, and the insistence on an aggressively collective response to that enemy, may have served the movement well at its origins in the '60s; but the strategy seems to have exhausted its usefulness, not to mention its accuracy as a description of women's predicaments. It has hardened feminism into a rigid orthodoxy that will readily disparage women's free choice if it conflicts with the movement line. And, ironically, it has been destructive not only to women as individuals, but to the cause of true equality.

Faludi's indictment is sweeping: the method of the backlash has been to convince women that feminism has proved to be our own "worst enemy," that too much independence is making women miserable—that all of our problems are, in fact, personal. Her substantiation is equally exhaustive. Case by case, she sets out to show that the backlash has tried to persuade the public that the liberation of women is responsible for female burnout, "toxic" day care, an infertility epidemic, the man shortage, depression, stress-induced disorders (hair loss, bad nerves, alcoholism, heart attacks, anorexia/bulimia, adult acne), and loneliness. Yet "these so-called female crises," writes Faludi, "have had their origins not in the actual conditions of women's lives but rather in a closed system that starts and ends in the media, popular culture, and advertising—an endless feedback loop that perpetuates and exaggerates its own false images of womanhood."

It is not Faludi's evidence—a dizzying array of examples, anecdotes, and studies—that is dubious; it is her argument about the motives that have generated the evidence and the responses that have greeted it. Though her account is full of qualifiers, it is basically a conspiracy theory. Faludi essentially implies that a cabal of villains has been at work successfully intimidating a large class of victims: women.

The book's most solid and disconcerting section is on the media, in which she debunks the myths underlying each of the decade's big trend stories: the man shortage, the infertility epidemic, the mommy track, the day care crisis. Not only was feminism not responsible for the latest "female" problem, but there often was no problem at all. And when there was a problem, it was usually men who were the cause. For example, the "biological clock" crisis was spawned by a study—sponsored by a federation of artificial insemination centers—that looked only at French women who were married to completely sterile men and were trying to get pregnant through artificial insemination; the research scientists never meant the findings to apply to all women. According to sounder studies, Faludi writes, women in their early 30s face only a slightly greater risk of being infertile than women in their early 20s, and the infertility rate is actually lower among college-educated and higher-income women.

When she turns to the entertainment industries, Faludi offers some concrete evidence to support the charge that at least in some cases there has been an explicit agenda at work, and that the agenda is not simply the province of the backwater right. She has unearthed examples of shows being canceled or scripts being rewritten solely to reflect the more "traditional" values of a producer: single women or working women had to be portrayed as evil or miserable, mothers as both good and happy.

Yet it is quite a leap to the conclusion that the (putatively liberal) media as a whole were out to get women during the '80s, that all promotions in the media or on the screen of "family values" stemmed from a sinister sexism. Moreover, Faludi neglects to mention all of the articles inspired by debates over Eurocentrism, date rape, and pornography, which can just as facilely be ascribed to the rise of political correctness that supposedly infiltrated the media at the same time as the backlash.

In any case, an emphasis on "family values" in the second decade of feminism's ascendancy is not all that surprising; nor, for that matter, is the right wing's cynical manipulation of the term. The rise during the 1980s of single-parent families, drug use, violence, and divorce rates made the fate of the family a legitimate concern. And the focus on women's "lifestyle" predicaments doubtless reflects at least in part the rise of women to positions of formative authority in some of the media. To address the tensions that have been one result of women's changing aspirations is hardly an anti-feminist enterprise; to address them superficially, sensationally, misleadingly is hardly a new development in journalism or in Hollywood.

Clearly change has not come painlessly or pervasively, but it is Faludi's implicit expectation that somehow it should have that makes her book disappointingly schematic and off-puttingly defensive. She extends her backlash umbrella over practically every cultural event of the '80s, from Andrew Dice Clay to the relational feminists. Following the traditional feminist impulse, Faludi seems to have felt that she needed to exaggerate just how persecuted women are. If you look hard enough, of course, anything can be seen as a reaction to feminism, and Faludi is a good reporter.

Perhaps the best examples of this kind of reductionism lie in her chapters on the fashion and beauty industries—the standard targets of feminist ire. Faludi claims that the "High Femininity" design trend of the '80s was a literal response to the women's movement. Promoting "punitively restrictive clothing" (e.g., miniskirts), designers evidently thought, would not only hamper women's advancement, but force them to buy lots of clothes again: dress them like little girls and they will follow the dictates of fashion. The likelihood that merchandisers were simply responding to a major downturn in the market with a new gimmick apparently eludes her. Instead she herself seems to subscribe to the condescending logic underlying their supposed strategy. In one of her frantic, humorless anxiety attacks about the ominous impact of the trend, she writes: "But was Lacroix offering women 'fun'—or just making fun of them?"

Faludi then devotes six pages to a discussion of the "Intimate Apparel Explosion," as though it could end life in America as we know it. She doesn't like neo-Victorian lingerie (she prefers Jockeys for Her). In fact, she doesn't like neo-Victorian anything, seeing it as yet another way to turn women into brainless statuettes. She lambastes designers who propose that it is good that women feel secure enough to dress in more feminine clothes again.

Whether or not the designers are being sincere, the point is that they are right. Women no longer have to choose between femininity (or sexuality) and equality. But Faludi doesn't seem to get this. "Late-'80s lingerie celebrated the repression, not the flowering, of female sexuality. The ideal Victorian lady it had originally been designed for, after all, wasn't supposed to have any libido," she writes without irony. (She has plenty of company; remember the feminist outcry over Florence Griffith Joyner's lace running tights in the '88 Olympics.) Of course most haute couture is preposterous and unwearable; that's the point of it. Moreover, the miniskirt is not a modern form of foot binding. (In fact, it first made a splash in the '60s, in the heady early days of women's liberation.) Feminists are so intent on not having society judge women by the way we look that they end up challenging the right to allow one's looks to reflect one's individuality. And isn't there something slightly confused about feminists complaining in one breath that the new fashions call for more full-figured models (further evidence of the effort to promote a barefoot and pregnant mindset) and continuing to complain in another breath that our beauty standards encourage anorexia?

But Faludi's implicit model of women as victims is perhaps most distorting when it comes to her conclusions. The rhetoric, the tone, the drama, and the sheer weight of her book lead one to believe that the backlash was quite successful in determining women's fate during the '80s. But Faludi's own facts tell a far more complicated story. Women spurned nearly every effort that was made (according to Faludi) to push them back into the kitchen, from watching TV shows with "nesting goodwives" to buying garter belts and teddies. In fact, they continued to increase their participation in the work force each year in record numbers. As Faludi herself writes: "No matter how bruising and discouraging her collisions with the backlash wall, each woman in her own way persisted in pushing against it."

The problem is that Faludi doesn't fully acknowledge women's actual responses until her epilogue, where she adds that "this quiet female resistance was the uncelebrated counterpoint to the anti-feminist campaign of the '80s." But it is nowhere less celebrated than in her own book. Writing this in the introduction would have undermined her portrayal of women as helpless, passive victims of society's devious designs. And indeed, Faludi goes out of her way to disparage what women can do individually to improve their lot: "To remove the backlash wall rather than to thrash continually against it, women needed to be armed with more than their privately held grievances and goals. Indeed, to instruct each woman to struggle alone was to set each woman up, yet again, for defeat."

For the same reason, in order for Faludi to counter the backlash's premise that all women's problems are personal, the message of *Backlash* had to be: working women have no personal problems. After expertly demolishing the media's hyped-up myths, Faludi fails to acknowledge that in many cases when you peel away the layers of hype, you find kernels of truth. She might have devoted at least a few sentences, for example, to the fact that, infertility statistics aside, the physical experience of childbearing tends to be easier on a woman in her early 20s than on a woman in her late 30s. And in debunking the "toxic" day care myth (one of the most commonly quoted studies used monkeys as subjects), she implicitly makes extreme and dubious assertions of her own: that children don't get sick more often in day care; that day care doesn't diminish maternal bonds; that there is no harm whatsoever to infants.

The truth is that women do have personal problems, some of which are the direct result of changes in women's expectations and opportunities. But these problems no more make us the victims of feminism than our continuing inequality makes us the victims of backlash. Moreover, acknowledging the existence of these problems does not represent defeat. As if Faludi has never talked to a woman who works, the implication of her analysis is that working women do not suffer from burnout, stress-related ailments, depression, lack of self-esteem. It's no doubt true, as she shows through numerous studies, that single women and working women are in better mental health than mothers who work in the home. But that doesn't mean that balancing domestic and professional desires and duties is painless. As feminists and Faludi herself rightly argue, working women's lives would be considerably more manageable if housework and child care could be shared equally with men, and if women no longer felt they had to work twice as hard as their male colleagues to prove their worth.

Clearly there is no single path to such equitable arrangements. But the expectation that most of the solutions will come from an organized single-constituency group has been proving its inadequacy every day. Of course women internalize a lot of sexist stereotypes—parents who discourage independence, teachers who ignore us, employers who demean us, husbands who abuse us—and of course years of this will wear down our ability to assert our demands, our will to walk away from bad situations. But so will thinking of ourselves as victims. We need to recognize and to resist external evils, but we don't need to exaggerate them. Pornography, for example, has become a feminist metaphor for everything that besets women in the social sphere; attempts to censor it exclusively for the welfare of women are *real* manifestations of neo-Victorianism, though Faludi curiously never mentions them. Moreover, we don't need external evils to become our excuses. Just as we don't excuse men for hurting others by blaming their "socialization," we shouldn't excuse women for hurting themselves. (pp. 30-2)

> *Karen Lehrman, "The Feminist Mystique," in* The New Republic, *Vol. 206, No. 11, March 16, 1992, pp. 30-4.*

Maggie Gallagher (review date 30 March 1992)

[*In the following review, Gallagher argues that* Backlash *does not merit the level of critical and popular attention it has received and assails Faludi for dismissing evidence that contradicts her theory of a media conspiracy against feminism.*]

Pity poor Susan Faludi. Just when she thought she had everything—a high-status job as a *Wall Street Journal* reporter, the joys of single life, power breakfasts, the right to an abortion, even a Pulitzer Prize—suddenly, sometime in the Eighties, she began to feel unloved. Legions of women, instead of following—or at least envying—women like her, began to do unspeakable things: like vote for Reagan, or don miniskirts, or have babies. How to account for this inexplicable backsliding? Why was feminism losing its hold on women at the moment of its (and Miss Faludi's) greatest triumph? Suddenly an answer came to her: It must be a *media conspiracy.*

Backlash is her attempt to stretch that threadbare argument into a five-hundred-page manifesto on the glories of hard-core feminism, and for a surprising number of supposedly sophisticated women, it works. Seldom has a book received the kind of unalloyed worship heaped on *Backlash.* Ellen Goodman sounded a common note by praising Miss Faludi's careful handling of evidence "debunking the studies, experts, and trend stories." To top off the praisefest, *Backlash* was recently nominated for the National Book Award.

Listen carefully to the roar of applause for *Backlash:* it is the sound of feminism committing suicide.

For a decade feminist leaders have striven mightily to throw off the reputation they earned in the early Seventies, to convince American women of the existence of a kinder, gentler feminism. Feminism, they said, is ready to enter a Second Stage devoted to helping women balance the needs of family and work and improve relationships between the sexes. Real feminists, they told us, do not burn bras, hate men, or dislike babies.

Susan Faludi is having none of it. Betty Friedan's Second Stage is just "a call for a murkily defined new order that is heavy on old Victorian rhetorical flourishes." If women are losing faith in feminism, it is because we are being brainwashed (poor things) by a male-dominated media conspiracy into believing certain ridiculous myths. Thirty- and forty-something career women like her aren't having trouble finding mates, they just love long hours, lonely nights, and whipping up microwave dinners for one too much to even *think* of relinquishing their freedom. Divorce doesn't impoverish women or damage children, and the sudden emergence of silk bustiers and pouf skirts is proof that evil men are out to demean and control women.

Evidence is not Miss Faludi's strong point. In fact, while she prides herself on (and has been widely praised for) uncovering errors in other people's statistics, misreporting data appears to be something of a personal hobby with her. On numerous occasions, when she quotes a study or poll with which I happen to be familiar, she seriously distorts the results, and in ways so blatant as to suggest more than mere incompetence at work.

Sometimes she outright misquotes data. For example, to dispute the man shortage, she cites a 1986 government study to the effect that one-third of unmarried women are living with a man; the actual figure is 4 per cent—although the study did note that one-third of currently single women have cohabited at some point in their lives.

At other times, she more subtly misconstrues. She cites a 1986 *Newsweek* poll as "proof" that 75 per cent of working mothers want careers; in fact, according to the poll, only 13 per cent of full-time working mothers wanted to work full-time—a plurality (34 per cent) preferred part-time work, and the rest were divided between wanting more flexible hours or a home-based business, and wanting to be full-time housewives.

The reality that Miss Faludi, like most other feminists, willfully refuses to face is that mothers—even working mothers—overwhelmingly choose to make caring for children their first priority. According to Census Bureau data, almost two-thirds of married mothers either don't work or work part-time. And according to a 1990 poll, even a majority of working mothers now want to go home.

But by far her most common tactic is simply to ignore the voluminous evidence that contradicts her point of view. Her preferred strategy is to pick one study, find some (often trivial) error or methodological quibble, and airily dismiss the whole argument as a media invention. She is convinced, for example, that media revisionism is responsible for Americans' growing reservations about a 50 per cent divorce rate. Lenore Weitzman's famous figures—that women's incomes drop 73 per cent after divorce—are wrong, Miss Faludi maintains: women's income drops "only" 30 per cent after divorce. Anyway feminists can't be responsible because they didn't promote no-fault divorce reform, she says, conveniently ignoring that feminists certainly did heavily promote divorce.

And she remains one of divorce's biggest cheerleaders, despite the mounting evidence of its disastrous economic effects on women. Single mothers are six times more likely to be poor than married mothers, and one-third of all divorced women end up on welfare. None of which bothers Miss Faludi in the least. As for the pain divorce inflicts on children—well, she just isn't interested. Judith Wallerstein, whose *Second Chances* reported that five years after the divorce one-third of the children involved remain clinically depressed, "never bothered to test her theory on a control group" Miss Faludi says, and, having "disposed" of just one of the thousands of studies pointing to the traumatic effects of divorce on children, she quickly drops the subject.

Backlash is an ignorant, nasty, *little* book, for all its 552 pages and pseudo-scholarly footnotes—small-minded, crafty, conniving, a disgrace even to journalistic standards, and an insult to women. Feminism, Faludi style, ultimately fails because it cannot come to terms with women's unaccountable desire not only to have babies, but actually to spend time raising them, in intact families, with men. Hard experience has taught a growing number of women that the biggest danger facing us today comes not from discrimination in the workplace but from the collapse of the family—a disaster which feminism partly engineered, loudly applauded, and, as the reception of *Backlash* proves, does not know how to disown. (pp. 41-2)

Maggie Gallagher, "Exit, Stage Back," in Na-tional Review, New York, Vol. XLIV, March 30, 1992, pp. 41-2.

REVIEWS OF CAMILLE PAGLIA'S *SEXUAL PERSONAE: ART AND DECADENCE FROM NEFERTITI TO EMILY DICKINSON*

Martha Duffy   (review date 13 January 1992)

[*In the following review, Duffy discusses Paglia's neo-conservative philosophy of culture, the reactions of feminist authors to* Sexual Personae, *and significant events of Paglia's life and career.*]

"There is something in my book to offend absolutely everybody. I am proabortion, pro the legal use of drugs, propornography, child pornography, snuff films. And I am going after these things until Gloria Steinem screams."

The speaker—at nonstop, sewing-machine speed—is Camille Paglia, contrarian academic and feminist bête noire, and her 1990 book, *Sexual Personae: Art and Decadence from Nefertiti to Emily Dickinson,* is the most explosive tome to emerge from academe in quite some time. The book is about many things—paganism, pop culture, androgyny, sexual conflicts—but what has drawn the media with magnetic force is the author's contempt for modern feminists. Paglia writes with freshness and blithe arrogance, and she does not hesitate to hurl brazen insults. She accuses author Germaine Greer, for example, of becoming "a drone in three years," sated with early success. Susan Sontag is another victim of celebrity. Princeton feminist Diana Fuss's output is "just junk—appalling!"

Along with the zingers, Paglia articulates positions that many people of both genders seem to want to hear these days. To them feminism has gone quite far enough, and they like *Personae's* neoconservative cultural message: Men have done the work of civilization and can take credit for most of its glories. Women are powerful too, but as the inchoate forces of nature are powerful. Religion and marriage are historically the best defenses against chaos.

Such theories have aroused profound displeasure among feminist authors. For one thing, as Teresa L. Ebert at the State University of New York, Albany, points out, they were caught napping by Paglia. "She wasn't taken seriously, but her attacks are part of Ronald Reagan's and Margaret Thatcher's conservatism," says Ebert. "They mean a backlash against women. Paglia is reviving old stereotypes with new energy." Harvard's Helen Vendler says Paglia "lives in hyperbole. It is a level of discourse appropriate to politics, sermons, headlines. She should be on talk shows, talking to Geraldo." She probably will be.

In fairness it should be said that nothing about *Personae* was calculated to bring its author notoriety. The book was rejected by an honor roll of prestigious publishers. But when success finally came, nine years after the manuscript was completed, the star was ready and waiting to be born. *Personae* climbed to seventh place on the paperback best-seller list, a true rarity for a scholarly book.

Paglia is the new media princess, and acts the part. When she accepts a speaking engagement now, she generally shows up with two massive bodyguards togged out in black leather jackets. She has been featured in the *New Republic, Playboy, New York, NYQ* (for New York Queer), Russian, Japanese and French publications.

One reason for her high profile is that Paglia has bristling opinions on subjects other than feminism—particularly education. She advocates a core curriculum based mostly on the classics and rails against what she considers politicized frills, such as most African-American studies and the currently chic French theorists Michel Foucault and Jacques Lacan. Never one to let consistency get in her way, Paglia has a strong libertarian streak—on subjects like pornography—that go straight to her '60s coming-of-age.

Loquacious is too impoverished a word to describe Paglia's speaking style. She talks at triple speed, rarely even using contractions, hurtling along in a grating pitch that comes perilously close to a cackle. Her aural punctuation is hilarious. A recent SRO lecture at the Massachusetts Institute of Technology was typical. Yuh? Yuh? O.K.? O.K.? peppered her speech, and the audience answered right back.

Someone recently compared Paglia with Phyllis Schlafly, and she was appalled. Despite all the brickbats, Paglia considers herself a lifelong feminist; *Personae* took shape when she read Simone de Beauvoir's *The Second Sex* and resolved "to do something massive for women." But Paglia believes the current movement has declined into smug formulas and codes of political correctness. "What began as a movement of eccentric individualists has turned into an ideology that attracts weak personalities who are looking for something to believe in." Or, she adds, someone to blame: to her, rape is a dreadful crime, but women who make their accusations years later—not to mention those who complain of date rape and sexual harassment—are deluded. Anita Hill should have stepped forward at once when Clarence Thomas was offensive to her, she argues. "My feminism is, like, deal with it!" says Paglia. "Not ten years later."

Paglia's ideal women are independent, like Amelia Earhart or Katharine Hepburn. She became obsessed with Earhart as a teenager and even wrote a book-length manuscript about her. Little Camille's enthusiasms were something her Italian immigrant parents fostered. Her father, a French professor at Le Moyne College in Syracuse, taught her to pursue goals aggressively. Today the daughter says ruefully, "He created a monster he couldn't control."

She can't remember a time when she was not scuffling with boys to be first in line. When she devoured books on ancient Egypt, her father was gratified. But movies also held her in thrall. Paglia's love affair with popular culture, which forms the forthcoming second volume of *Personae,* was already blossoming when she was a child. "Egypt and

Hollywood were equivalent phenomena to me, equally rich and fabulous," she says. Her father demurred. "He lectured me on Voltaire's disapproval of actors," Camille recalls, "and this was the time when I was making my collection of 599 Elizabeth Taylor pictures."

In 10th grade Paglia got her first taste of social ostracism and its consequences. Some of the pretty blonds in her class suddenly turned into bland, cliquish sorority queens. She was left behind as a tomboy with a serious case of ambition. The lesson was not lost on her; to this day she sides fiercely with the outsider.

She was class valedictorian at the State University of New York, Binghamton, in 1968, "when it was full of radicals." The students were throwing off '50s shackles and looking to other cultures for solutions. The Doors' battle cry, "We want the world, We want it now," exhilarated Paglia. After four restless years at Yale getting her Ph.D. in English, she found herself teaching at Bennington.

Her seven-year stint there was a series of explosions. For one thing, she is, as she says in a rare understatement, "physical." Paglia throws punches. She kicks people twice her size. Once she even called the president of the college to inform her that she was about to kick an obnoxious male student. Fine, said the president, who was new on the job and probably thinking in metaphors. Paglia landed one that sent the fellow sprawling in the cafeteria. Says the woman warrior: "Committees were always convening over me." After leaving Bennington in 1979—one tiff too many—she struggled for a decade to support herself.

Paglia usually refers to her private life as a disaster. Through the years she has had relationships with both women and men and for a while considered herself a lesbian. "But lesbians don't like me," she notes, in part because she insists that most women are bisexual, that the role of hormones accounts for an inevitable attraction between the sexes. Lately Paglia has been going out with men. But, she asks, "what man is going to take me seriously? I'm not a nurturer. Men have flashes of ego and confidence followed by relapses. They have to be stroked, and I don't have that patience." There is also the age problem. Recently she dated men around her age, 44, but found them over the hill sexually. She would prefer younger men, but her pride restrains her. "Like there's something faintly ridiculous about Cher with that young guy: she looks like a dowager with a gigolo." Some dowager.

Paglia will take next fall off from her academic and speechifying schedule to get the second volume of *Personae* into shape. The book promises to be a whopper, the author's thoughts on a lifetime of blustery enthusiasm for popular culture. The sport section, for instance, will deal with baseball vs. football: Paglia is passionately in favor of the latter. Baseball she considers an academic pastime: "Wasp, cerebral, Protestant." Football, on the other hand, she wishes she could have played: "The rhythms of my writing are high impact. Colleagues have seen my ability to look downfield and see pockets of trouble. And I hit them."

What she will say about her beloved rock idols is less clear. Megasuccess may be poisoning them. She finds Michael

Jackson's current album "appalling," Prince a letdown, Madonna drifting. "She wants to cover all frontiers, but she has very little talent for acting," says one of the Material Girl's most vocal fans. "O.K.?"

O.K. But Paglia is determined to hit a few frontiers too. Kafka once said "a book must be the ax for the frozen sea inside us." Paglia wants to write that book—"not the Band-Aid, not the comforter, not the down quilt." The ax. (pp. 62-3)

> *Martha Duffy, "The Bête Noire of Feminism,"* in Time, *New York, Vol. 139, No. 2, January 13, 1992, pp. 62-3.*

Paglia's impatience with the sentimentality of feminism blinds her to her own sentimentality toward the masculine, Jack the Ripper and all.

—Helen Vendler, in her "Feminism and Literature," The New York Review of Books, *30 May 1990.*

Naomi Wolf (essay date 16 March 1992)

[*Wolf is author of* The Beauty Myth: How Images of Beauty Are Used against Women. *In the following essay, she characterizes Paglia as "a spokeswoman for the anti-feminist backlash" and refutes several of Paglia's criticisms of feminism.*]

When times are such that white male commentators—Patrick Buchanan excepted—can no longer express bigoted beliefs, but not yet such that those impulses don't arise, there is a high demand for court jesters ready to bash their own out-groups. Many of them use a smoke screen of progressive language, from lynching to lesbianism, to pass off their regressive ideas. Camille Paglia's distortion of the relationship between sex and feminism [in "The Joy of Presbyterian Sex," *The New Republic,* December 2, 1991] is a shining example of this pattern. The nipple-pierced person's Phyllis Schlafly, Paglia poses as a sexual renegade but is in fact the most dutiful of patriarchal daughters. By decorating a stale set of values with the baubles of pop culture and postmodernism, she reassures social conservatives—traditionally the dweebs of the intellectual schoolyard—that to hang out in the rearguard of social change is not uncool after all. The problem is that Paglia manages her task not through verve and style alone, but with the help of a howling intellectual dishonesty. Backlash sensibility has helped her do this in two ways: while it selects her as the only middle-aged female to appear on a magazine cover otherwise devoted to men or to female fashion models, it has also kept the public safely out of contact with actual feminist debate. So Paglia has been at remarkable liberty to misrepresent feminism—most recently in [*The New Republic*]. It is time for the record to be put straight.

Paglia's status as spokeswoman for the anti-feminist backlash is not unprecedented. The end of the nineteenth century saw a surge of feminist activism much like our own, and by the 1890s the "Woman Question" was a burning one. In the face of women agitating for votes, education, and sexual freedom, a growth industry burgeoned, producing highly rewarded—often female—anti-feminist commentators. Paglia's message recapitulates, without irony and sometimes almost word for word, the metaphors and pseudo-scientific sophistries of the last great period of anti-feminism, 1890-1920. Her anti-feminist themes are "new" only insofar as those bombarded with them the first time are conveniently dead.

Paglia's feminists, like the Victorians', are ill-dressed "drabs" and "hangdog dowdies." The late Victorian press bristled with caricatures of suffragettes' dress and appearance, branding them as "she-men," "monsters in bloomers," "hens that crow." Then there is the crisis of sexual failure attributed to women leaving the "separate sphere," the well-documented Edwardian scenario of voracious women and impotent men. Paglia writes: "Once there was the world of men and the world of women. Now the sexes, freely mingling, know each other too well"; they have "come too close" and have "lost their allure." Dr. Arabella Kenealy, an anti-feminist polemicist catapulted to fame at the turn of the century, wrote likewise: "Where before [woman's] beauty was suggestive and elusive, now it is defined . . . the haze, the elusiveness, the subtle suggestion of the face are gone. . . . Her voice is louder, her tones are assertive. She says everything—leaves nothing to the imagination."

Paglia's theory of cultural evolution comes straight out of the Edwardian popular press: men build civilization, asserts Paglia, while women—primitive, undifferentiated, essential—"water the ground." According to Winfield Scott Hall, who wrote "Sexual Knowledge" in 1925, "Males were made to 'vary,' that is, to fill a variety of functions in the social division of labor. Females, being more primitive, were non-varying and identical in evolutionary function, and that function was to reproduce." This is a play on Darwin's understanding of the relationship of biological evolution to social hierarchy: "Some of [women's] faculties," he wrote, "are characteristic of the lower races, and therefore of a past and lower state of civilization." This social Darwinism, discredited beyond repair when it applies to race, is reconjured and reanimated by Paglia to intimidate our thinking about gender.

In Paglia's . . . article ["The Joy of Presbyterian Sex"], she commits not merely to recycled Darwinism, but to goggling and shameless untruths. "Feminists," she states, want "men and women to be the same." My jaw dropped when I read this. Paglia has been in Philadelphia, not Oz. "Academic feminism" has centered on sexual *difference* for the entire past decade, at least. The landmark theories of "difference" range from the *Ecriture Feminine* of linguist Luce Irigaray to sociologist Carol Gilligan's study of the different moral reasoning of boys and girls to social critic Suzanne Gordon's *Prisoners of Men's Dreams,* which argues that women err by imitating men. A core

1985 anthology of feminist criticism is titled, characteristically enough for the decade, *Making a Difference.*

Paglia romps still further into the rockless pastures of intellectual deception: "There is," she writes, "a century of rich commentary on sex—including important work by such women as Melanie Klein and Karen Horney—that women's studies, mired in the shallow present, ignores." In fact, Klein and Horney are midcentury psychologists of femininity, central to the American feminist canon. I first read them—along with the rest of "a century's rich commentary on sex" that Paglia claims women's studies ignores—in a women's studies course at Yale. It would be difficult to find a women's studies program that does not teach them.

To refute the folly of feminism in struggling for an egalitarian society, Paglia snorts, "Go read *King Lear.*" To rebut critics of patriarchal law, she huffs, "Next read the Oresteia." But for every classical allusion that dismisses feminism's aims, another will endorse them. An early feminist critique of marriage? Milton's *Areopagitica.* An impassioned protest at the sexual double standard? *The Miller's Tale* by tenured woman of color Geoffrey Chaucer. A dissident analysis of the systematic oppression of women? *The Subjection of Women* by that third-rate lesbian writer John Stuart Mill. A cursory look at the Western tradition scores against Paglia more easily than for her: our greatest thinkers, it appears, are natural feminists.

Most slippery of all these arguments is the way Paglia has tried to steal the erotic high ground. She casts feminism as "prudish" and "puritanical," unable to deal with "sexuality outside its feminist frame of reference." She sneers at "feminism, with its solemn Carrie Nation repressiveness." "The feminist" is a mustachioed, loveless composite of Hustler cartoons and frat-boy catcalls, whose role is to peer under bedclothes with a flashlight and a bucket of ice water. This caricature lets Paglia side herself with Madonna, the Stones, and the maligned principle of "sweaty virility."

Now I'm as partial to the principle of sweaty virility as the next girl. But more important, feminism, like no other revolutionary movement except gay liberation, is sparked, driven, and fueled on the combustion of sexual desire. Ever since its first modern stirrings—since the Woman Question swept into the early nineteenth century on the impetus of the sexual anarchism of the Romantic movement—feminism has been a vanguard of sexual ex-stasis. Carrie Nation repression? In the 1890s feminism was the bedmate of the Free Love movement, and Olive Schreiner talked dirty with G. B. Shaw. In America the beautiful, scandalous suffragist Victoria Woodhull ran for president on a platform of erotic liberationism. The 1970s wave of feminism had its path smoothed by its affiliation with the sexual revolution—a "liberated woman" was liberated to swing.

The great feminists have been women of passionate impulses, sensuous beauty, and intense sexual magnetism. Think of Yeats's Maud Gonne, of the Princesse de Clèves; of Mary Wollstonecraft Shelley, Josephine Baker, Colette, and Simone de Beauvoir; of Frida Kahlo, George Eliot

with her younger man, George Sand with her transvestism and *scandales;* remember Emma Goldman's erotic correspondence and Germaine Greer's self-portrait of her vulva; think of Edna St. Vincent Millay's well-publicized heterosexual promiscuity ("What lips my lips have kissed, and where, and when / I have forgotten"). Think of Madonna.

Abstract principles can enlist our loyalties, but they can't fire the blood; political commitment often comes from intense physical experience. Many Jewish boys became Zionists not from reading Herzl's biography, but from getting beaten up. Many gay activists, while earnest students of *Bowers v. Hardiwck,* owe their political energy to an early revelation of sexual bliss. While the rights to vote, be educated, and get equal access to wages and health care all serve as gateways to feminism, the gleaming secret, the unspoken pulse, of feminist commitment is the orgasm. Orgasm is the body's natural call to feminist politics: if being a woman can feel this good, women must be worth something.

I became a feminist because when I was 15, I was given the essential feminist gift: a safe loss of virtue unmarked by social ostracism; an orgasm that was pure heat and light, unshadowed by the specter of death from septicemia on a basement gurney. I became a feminist because a kindly young intern in a white lab coat at Planned Parenthood handed me, with no lectures or questions, a rubber disk and a trial-size tube of gel. No one made me sign a release that it would be used for non-threatening, egalitarian, unphallocentric activity. It—and hence my body—were mine to do with what I pleased. That is feminism, and that's why it's sexy.

By casting "feminists" as "the new sexual commissars," hostile to all delicacies and excesses of the heart, eye, and loins, Paglia performs a useful service to the forces of the anti-feminist backlash. All women have recently gained tiny victories in renegotiating the sexual contract. Though these victories are mostly titular—as we saw from the treatment of Anita Hill and Patricia Bowman—society is shuddering and stamping nonetheless, like a mastodon that has seen a mouse.

The Wall Street Journal wails, "Is It the End of Love and Laughter?" A *New York Times* editorial accuses anti-rape activists of denying women's sexuality. *Esquire* plans a feature on how campus sex, in the wake of date-rape consciousness, just ain't the same. This mainstream uneasiness is not about the end of sex; it is about the beginning of female sexual entitlement.

For what has not been named in the debate over sexual violence is why, truly, we fight it: we do so in order to have sexual pleasure. The right to say no must exist for the right to say yes to have any meaning. Feminists agitate against rape not just because it is a form of violence—but because it is a form of violence that uniquely steals from the survivor her sexual spontaneity and delight. It is to the extent that many feminists love sex that we hate rape.

Paglia sets up her "ecstasy" versus feminist "repressiveness," but the truth goes the other way around. Paradoxically, it is because feminism is about female ecstasy and desire that Paglia's actual repressiveness is so marketable now. The basic principle of social organization is not just who gets power—but who gets pleasure. Paglia extols the Dionysian frenzy of sexual release. But look closer: Who is doing what to whom in that frenzy of hers? Nietzsche defines the Dionysian ecstasy as "complete self-forgetfulness." In blaming young women for date rape, Paglia cuts them out of those who are allowed Nietzsche's "blissful merging." Her version of ecstasy—in which "women are never safe"—collides with a fundamental tenet of Western liberalism. If women are human beings, we Westerners must admit, within our own value system, that your right to your Dionysian ecstasy stops at the point where you try to have it in someone else's orifice against her will.

What Paglia offers is a salve for the intellectually and sexually exhausted. She soothes the mental cowardice of those who cannot bear the rapid, gendered evolution of our time. Her central metaphor says it all: the Dionysian "pain-pleasure continuum" is just a restatement of the same old conventional sado-masochism. Dionysus, let us remember, was torn apart. Paglia's message to women, faced with a mass culture filled with images of bruising misogyny, is: relax and enjoy it.

Paglia paraphrases rock 'n' roll to give her old-time repressiveness some steam heat. But in our postmodern air there are many frequencies. My radio is picking up on new music: it is raunchy, witty, crashing, humming, flirting, roaring. These songs are about women, and nothing like them has ever been sung before. These songs make some people nervous. Salt n' Peppa are singing: "Give me that driving satisfaction. Give me that positive reaction." Michelle Shocked is murmuring: "If love were a train, I think I would ride me a slow one." And Billy Idol is belting out a mixture of admiration and fear: "Through the midnight hours—she wants more, more, more. With a rebel yell—more, more, more." It is those songs that provoke Paglia's reactionary white noise. But they're coming through anyway, through the static—urgent and scary and sweet. That's what my radio plays. (pp. 23-5)

Naomi Wolf, "Feminist Fatale," in The New Republic, *Vol. 206, No. 11, March 16, 1992, pp. 23-5.*

Todd Seavey   (review date June 1992)

[*In the following review, Seavey characterizes Paglia as a libertarian who embraces neither right- nor left-wing political views and who interprets society in terms of nature and biology rather than ideology.*]

So I pay a weekend visit to Brown University, and Camille Paglia is giving a lecture. (She's the "post-feminist" whose book *Sexual Personae* irked feminists by suggesting that gender and art are rooted in nature rather than mere patriarchal social codes.) It turns out Paglia's not only against the intervention of the state in matters of sex, drugs, and economics but is actively "pro-pornography and pro-prostitution." ("Post-porn" performer Annie Sprinkle defended pornography and prostitution a few days later at Brown—in keeping with the politics-and-bisexual-women

theme of my weekend—but for some reason she doesn't seem to anger the leftists.)

Naturally, I was delighted with Paglia, but I probably shouldn't have been surprised—and I don't just mean because Paglia praises capitalism within the first three pages of *Sexual Personae*. I should have expected great things from Paglia because she has so many enemies at Brown University. Brown has been functioning as a useful detector of greatness in this way at least since the anti-P. J. O'Rourke protest there in 1988.

Paglia's opposition included angry, sometimes hissing, feminists in the audience, whose jeers she in some sense deserved, tending as she did to shout at her opponents and call them brainwashed toadies. What she didn't deserve—and what was far stranger—were flyers from the International Socialist Organization and Teachers for a Democratic Culture that were distributed outside the lecture hall by students who called Paglia a token "voicebox for the right, like Dinesh D'Souza." One student suggested Paglia is simply one more tool of the Reagan-Bush establishment, bent on denying equal access to health care, education, and employment for women and people of color, which is interesting, since she spends all her time talking about art and literature.

What would the meeting where the conservative establishment plotted to unleash Paglia sound like? I wonder. Perhaps John Sununu was sitting at a White House staff meeting a year ago and said, "What we need is a bisexual literature professor who loves Nietzsche, Oscar Wilde, and the Marquis de Sade, who compares herself to Madonna and a gay man in a woman's body, calls herself a 'vampire resurrected from the dead to take revenge' on academic feminism, deplores semiotics and French literary theory, praises our society's latent paganism, and calls on us to examine the chthonian nature of gender construction. Send a memo to Quayle—I think someone on his staff might fit the bill."

Actually, I think Paglia embodies two trends, neither of them Republican plots: the tendency of people who can't take either the right or the left seriously (like humorist Dave Barry) to end up as libertarians and the growing tendency of people to look to nature and biology, instead of ideology, to explain society. Examples of the latter trend include not only the book *Bionomics* and several works on the idea that ethics have evolved from instincts but also the films of David Cronenberg and David Lynch, both of whom take heat from feminists for their attempts to depict the brutal organic matrix at work beneath the veil of society. (And you thought those scenes of exploding heads and deformed babies were strictly there to horrify—shows what *you* know.)

In any case, I think it's valuable to have a libertarian among us who has opinions on cultural matters instead of just economics. Paglia gives one hope that diverse cultural threads, from the psychedelic '60s to conservatism to avant-garde art can be claimed by libertarians, that political libertarians can appeal to a broad cultural spectrum the way F. A. Hayek's work appeals to a broad philosophical spectrum.

On the down side, Paglia can be as nuts as Nietzsche and has some unsympathetic things to say about date-rape victims. And even libertarians aren't necessarily going to embrace her—look at the review *Sexual Personae* got in the December *Reason,* or worse, at the letter in the April issue that says no libertarian should be interested in reading *Sexual Personae* anyway.

Well, I'll just point out that she's getting more press coverage than, say, California's pollution-trading program or privatization in Sweden. Could it be that the public is more interested in art and sex than in property rights?

Todd Seavey, "Bisexual Vampire Women," in Reason, *Vol. 24, No. 2, June, 1992, p. 22.*

I was expelled from the feminist movement. There is something very wrong with a movement that began by silencing women like me, who had been very pioneering. I have been in absolute rebellion against my sex role and the established order since I was a child.

—Camille Paglia, in an interview with Working Woman, March 1992.

Lesley White   (review date 7 June 1992)

[*In the following review, White discusses Paglia's criticism of feminism and "politically correct" ideologies.*]

The only silent thing about the American writer Camille Paglia is the third letter of her second name. This is a woman whose publicist calls to warn you to bring a tape-recorder to the interview because even the most accomplished shorthand writer could not hope to keep up. Preaching, screeching, scorching the air with yards of high-speed self-promotion, Paglia is not your average feminist academic. Most, let's face it, do not carry flick-knives, perpetrate physical violence on their intellectual adversaries and toss out personal insults like Joan Rivers on double time.

But then Camille Paglia, self-appointed scourge of Political Correctness, the woman the feminist establishment loves to hate, is as much a performer as a scholar. "I am so sick of feminists saying that they refuse to accept male standards of achievement," she screams. "Those wishy-washy fools won't even acknowledge that Michelangelo was a genius—because he was a man. Absurd! Insane! It is a recipe for mediocrity. All those women teaching 'women's studies' in America are pathetic mediocrities."

Show Professor Paglia a male standard and she will die before failing to eclipse it, railing as she goes against whiney women who blame men for their failures, feminists who take the balls out of sex, the anti-pornography activists and anyone who dares to stand in her way. In a climate of what she might consider moral vegetarianism, she takes

her steaks bloody, and preferably twice a day. She calls herself a pro-sex feminist, meaning not that she encourages the activity, but that she believes in nature's separate destinies for men and women. If running the world had been left to women, we would still be living in grass huts, she has famously commented, shouting down the wails of protest.

[In Summer 1992] she was in London to oversee the paperback publication of the book that started the fun, a flamboyant and highly subjective history of art and sex called *Sexual Personae: Art and Decadence from Nefertiti to Emily Dickinson.* This is the book feminists returned to bookshops asking for a refund on the basis of its offensive content; the book that took Paglia from the University of the Arts in Philadelphia and put her on the cover of *New York* magazine and the "Donahue" show. In 700 densely cerebral pages it says that this current generation of feminists has got it all wrong, that it is a madness to dismiss Shakespeare and Socrates from the academic curriculum because they are "Dwims" (Dead, White Males) and replace them with a harem of newly discovered female geniuses.

Paglia's message has won her glamorous friends. The actress and model Lauren Hutton has called her "the greatest living American philosopher" while Annette Benning and Nick Nolte possess heavily annotated copies of the thesis. "Yeah," says Paglia, "Lauren wants me to quit teaching and come to New York—but I gotta guard against all this fame. Germaine Greer stopped teaching when she got famous, started acting like a queen and now they tell me she's writing gardening columns, puh-lease!"

She reserves the same tone for the rest of the women's movement's first XI: "That little twit Naomi Wolf", the "utterly misled" Susan Faludi, the "messed-up Gloria Steinem". In a world that is deemed to run on sisterly co-operation, this heretical vitriol is both wildly shocking and strangely exciting. Why, after all, should the boys have all the best punch-ups? "I never read out lectures at the university," she says. "I'm just there shouting and the students are shouting back and hissing at me and I'm shaking my fist at them—it's, like, interacting, right?" Her students obviously adore her. The sacred feminist cows she derides can barely contain their bile.

Steinem said recently that for Paglia to call herself a feminist was akin to a Nazi calling himself pro-semitic; Marilyn French was pleased to report that Paglia clearly loathed the female body. "A pretty peculiar thing to say about someone who has spent half their life as a lesbian," she bellows. A group of previously rowdy young men in the restaurant of her Kensington hotel turn to stare in silent disbelief. She doesn't even notice.

"The way I have been treated," Paglia says,

> reveals the Kremlin-like insularity of the feminist establishment around the world. An intellectual's role is to challenge dogma and received ideas—but challenge the liberal establishment and they automatically call you a conservative. This is very bizarre for me because my record of Sixties activism is out there, proven.

Most people support equal opportunities, but, beyond that, you can't make legislation for people's personal lives. I absolutely abhor the intrusion of rules into dating, for example. On American campuses, if a girl goes on a date and something goes wrong she can haul the guy up before a grievance committee. This is Stalinism. These feminists are crazy. Women have got to learn to take full responsibility in a dating situation—they cannot have 10 tequilas, put on a Madonna outfit, go to a guy's room and expect everything to be okay.

Nor do Paglia's views on sexual harassment fit with the current thinking. Women's professional garb, she insists, is deeply and necessarily erotic: a silk shirt worn to the office, an exposed calf, an arousingly tailored business suit will all lead to explosions of uninhibited lust.

There is absolutely nothing we can do to desexualise the workplace, so women must be constantly signalling what their intentions are and how they want to be treated. When a man has crossed that line and said something vulgar, she must stop it immediately. It's up to her. The Anita Hill-Clarence Thomas thing was just a crock . . . you're telling me that this guy said he liked her breasts and this girl went home and cried. Oh, puh-lease, give me a break. The idea that women are victims of men and have to get help from committees is absurd . . . it's so easy to make men wilt, to crush and demean them, women have much tougher egos.

In Paglia's view the advancement of women cannot afford to be based on a need for male change: that is simply too much to ask for. As she warms to her central theme, her sentences lose their full stops and her eyes assume an almost demented gleam. Under no circumstances do you try to interrupt her.

Oh listen, men have not changed at all. Okay, a few middle-class white-collar guys may feel they can no longer go around the office saying, "Hey, babe, love your tits," but men must be permitted to have their masculinity. We are never going to get hot sex from them if we deny them that.

Paglia does not believe in male-bashing except in a strictly literal sense. "Wake up," is her war cry. "Men and women are different." She watched with despondent fatalism as her androgynous rock-and-roll heroine Patti Smith became a mother and got gooey about life. "The hormones of pregnancy change women, make them less determined to achieve success for themselves alone. I've seen it happen

---

> **[Paglia] calls herself a pro-sex feminist, meaning not that she encourages the activity, but that she believes in nature's separate destinies for men and women.**
>
> *—Leslie White*

---

over and over again, it's no good denying it, it's true." She clearly hopes that the same fate will not befall her current pop idol: "Madonna and I have a lot in common, both Italian Catholics, both self-disciplined and determined, both women who have projected their imaginations despite dictatorial father figures and without bitching about the patriarchy." They have yet to meet.

The 45-year-old daughter of an American-Italian academic, Paglia was encouraged by her father to break all taboos and defend herself with her fists.

At six I was wearing male Halloween costumes, by 10 I was rejecting everything my father said and he realised he had created a monster. I rebelled against everything, I had a violent outlaw quality . . . and I think it makes me a better role model for women today than all these sexphobic feminists. I've always lived a solitary life—okay, so my sex life has been a disaster—never allowed my inner voice to be swamped by men, always stayed on the dangerous edge. Just because I believe in the power of nature does not mean that I cannot fight against it. I have all my life.

At university, her future dissension from the women's movement was fuelled when she mentioned that she thought the Rolling Stones were the greatest rock group in the world. No, her friends corrected, the Rolling Stones were sexist. They may be horrible people, countered Paglia, but surely we could still allow them to be great musicians. No, came the reply, since they were sexist they could not be great musicians. "It seemed like crap at the time, and it still is."

It is difficult, Paglia says with a sympathetic tone, for a European to imagine the loony extremes of American Political Correctness. "They are giving people teaching jobs at the universities just because they are gay, black or women. I have never fitted in with that so they blackball me." Does it hurt? "No, I've been hurt for 20 years, those women have never let me in, I am used to it."

Men, she says, cannot be excluded from the study of art for without them there would be no art worth having. It is apparently a question of Oedipus.

There is no female Mozart because there was no female Jack the Ripper. Great art and great crime are similar deviations from the norm that require a megalomania, an utter obsession. Revolutionary art needs violence, a willingness to break the rules like Picasso did, to kill the father . . . most women have too much empathy to want to be involved in anything like that. They want things to be comfortable, they want to be compassionate.

Compassion is indeed a quality that Paglia prides herself on doing without. She is inspired not by acts of kindness but by military strategy, prefers to use her time not nursing the wounded but annihilating the enemy. Her detractors say she is merely bitter at not being offered a prestigious Ivy League platform from which to spin her theories. She laughs and says they are merely getting twitchy about her fame. "They call me a conservative—crap! How could I be sending women back to the kitchen when I my-self am a woman of ideas? All I am saying is that if women want to spend their time rearing children, why shouldn't they?"

Asked why she escaped the distractions of security and love and needing to belong, Camille Paglia laughs like a little demon and spits this at you. "I am an Aries woman like Joan Crawford and Bette Davis—we are aggressive, competitive, ready to murder the father. You know, they had to teach that tennis player Gabriella Sabatini how to develop the killer instinct. Me, I was born with it."

Lesley White, "CP, Feminist Firebrand Bent on Reversing the Evil of PC," in The Sunday Times, *London, June 7, 1992, p. 5.*

An excerpt from *Sexual Personae: Art and Decadence from Nefertiti to Emily Dickinson*

Sex is a far darker power than feminists have ever been will-ing to admit. Feminists grossly oversimplify the problem of sex when they reduce it to a matter of social convention; re-adjust society, they say, eliminate sexual inequality, purify sex roles, and happiness and harmony will reign. Here femi-nism, like all liberal movements of the past 200 years, is heir to Rousseau.

Rousseau's idea of man's innate goodness led to social en-vironmentalism, now the dominant ethic of American human services, penal codes, and behaviorist therapies. It assumes that aggression, violence, and crime come from so-cial deprivation—a poor neighborhood, a bad home.

Thus feminism blames rape on pornography and smugly in-terprets outbreaks of sadism as a backlash against itself. But rape and sadism have existed throughout history and in all cultures. Aggression is innate. Society is not the criminal but the force that keeps crime in check. Feminists, whose goal is to remove power relations from sex, have set them-selves against nature. For sex is a subset of nature. Sex is the natural in man.

From the beginning of time, woman has seemed an uncanny being. Man honored but feared her. She was the black maw that had spit him forth and would devour him anew. The identification of woman with nature is considered by many to be merely a myth. I think the identification is real, though most feminist readers will disagree. Nature's cycles are woman's cycles.

Male bonding and patriarchy were the recourse to which man was forced by his terrible sense of woman's power. Feminism has been simplistic in arguing that female arche-types were politically motivated falsehoods created by men. By its techniques of demystification, feminism has painted itself into a corner. Sexuality is a murky realm of contradic-tion and ambivalence. It cannot always be understood by the social models that feminism constantly relies on.

Camille Paglia, in her Sexual Personae: Art and Decadence from Nefertiti to Emily Dickinson, *Vintage, 1990.*

James Wolcott (essay date September 1992)

[*In the following essay, based on a conversation with Wolcott, Paglia discusses her views on sexuality, West-ern culture, and feminism.*]

"I always embarrass my friends in bookstores," Camille Paglia chirps as we climb the stairs of Tower Books. So I can't say I haven't been warned.

We have just wolfed down lunch across the street at Man-hattan's Time Cafe, where between bites of pizza Paglia expounded on the unsung prevalence of kiddie porn in popular culture. "People don't realize the eroticization of the infant body that's going on in Valentine's Day cards. You have a fat little innocent body with wings and a bare behind, O.K.? They don't want to acknowledge that subli-minally there is a kind of swishy, erotic, tactile attraction that you have to the buttocky softness of the infant body." As she speaks her arched eyebrows seem to wing her brain 'atcha, like Patrick McGoohan's scowling head making a beeline toward the camera at the beginning of *The Prison-er*. Surrounding us was a battery of cocked ears as nearby diners eavesdropped while pretending to pursue their own line of chat. "I can't command the full attention of an au-dience if I'm wearing pants," said Paglia as the couple at the next table exchanged flickers. After lunch I suggested we drop into a secondhand bookstore on adjoining Great Jones Street. "No, not secondhand! Old books—bad juju," she explained. As if the groaning sense of failure would grab at her from the walls—the ghosts of rejection past. It was time for Mighty Mouse to save the day.

"Well, we could go over to Tower," I suggested. "Some-times you see well-known writers browsing around, and there seem to be a lot of models in the area. I've seen Ra-chel Williams a couple of times. I wouldn't want to mess with her."

Tower it is. At the top step of Tower Books, Paglia flings up her arms in hallelujah. Plop on the wall is the poster for *Sexual Personae*, the powerhouse study of eros across the eons that made her a star. Weeks earlier I spotted Paglia's friend Lauren Hutton in the nonfiction section of Tower Books. Seeing her arms loaded with the latest biog-raphies, I thought, Ah, cramming for Camille. (When Paglia subsequently spoke at the New York Public Li-brary, she introduced Hutton, who was sitting in the audi-ence.) As we circle those same displays, Paglia provides a color commentary on anything that catches her eye. "Oh, here's the paperback for *The Beauty Myth*. Let's see how Naomi looks on the back. Not a good picture. Isn't she a little old to be wearing her hair that way? She's such a—" She picks up Dalma Heyn's *The Erotic Silence of the American Wife*. "Oh, here's a blurb from Gloria Steinem. 'Because patriarchy has restricted women's bodies as the means of reproduction—' I mean, really, *please*. No one's said sex equals reproduction for at least thirty years. Get with it, Gloria!" Ears perk up as we pass. It's like playing sidekick to a giant bee.

Then Paglia's eyes open up an f-stop as she spies Andrew Morton's sob story of the Princess of Wales. Everything else on the floor does a liquid shimmy. With hunger al-most, Paglia flips the book open to the pictures. "Tell me that this isn't child porn," she says, pointing to a snapshot of a pouting Di. She riffles ahead. "Look at those legs! Tell me those aren't the legs of a Botticelli! Tell me those aren't Botticelli legs." Now we're really drawing the neck craners. Paglia leaves, effervesced. When we hit the street, a bigger treat is in store.

Striding down the sidewalk in denim and neck bandanna is all six feet of streaked-blonde model Rachel Williams. The sunlight itself seems to blink. There in person is Amazonian proof of Paglia's core belief: Beauty is Power. Paglia pauses, a rarity for her, and says, "You were just mentioning her, and she *materialized.* Don't you think that's strange? Don't you think that's weird?" Her questions come so fast I realize she isn't waiting for answers.

The cartoon conception of the academic pundit is a placid pipe smoker who deflects difficult questions by tut-tutting with a tinge of regret, "I'm afraid that isn't my field." The pedant in his pigeonhole, playing tiddlywinks with footnotes. But there's also a tradition of the intellectual as gnomic know-it-all, an Anglo-American lineup that includes Isaiah Berlin, George Steiner, Leslie Fiedler, Harold Bloom, and the late John Gardner, who used a pipe as a prop but still mumbled at ninety miles an hour. Mere dawdlers!

When it comes to word count, no one can outclock Camille Paglia, who teaches humanities at Philadelphia's University of the Arts and is the author of two books, *Sexual Personae* and the brand-new *Sex, Art, and American Culture.* "I'm manic-depressive without the depressive," she has said. Once she starts talking, it's hard for her to foot the brakes. Seeing someone else's lips move, she has to *force* herself to stop, snapping herself shut like a purse. And yet for all her nonstop clack (listening to her at length is like having Woody Woodpecker repair your roof), she's no fly-by-night operation.

Born in 1947, Paglia was raised in the upstate New York of *The Twilight Zone's* Rod Serling, with whom she feels a stranger-in-a-strange-land affinity. "Surrealism is more powerful when it accepts the norm, as Serling did, then stretches it," says Paglia. She certainly stretched the norm. Her Italian-Catholic upbringing primed her for cruel pageantry. One of her first role models was the witch queen in *Snow White,* a dominatrix who dressed like a haute couture nun and talked to herself in the mirror, a practice Paglia found captivating. As a child she displayed mythic aspirations. Where other kids trick-or-treated as Casper the Friendly Ghost, she dressed as Napoleon and Hamlet—a tomboy androgyny that later found its fulfillment in her early hero worship of Amelia Earhart and Katharine Hepburn. She received her academic bent from her father, a professor of Romance languages. In the sixties she attended Harpur College, the State University of New York at Binghamton.

It was the height of hippiedom. Barefoot Pre-Raphaelites strummed guitars beneath the trees. Poetry readings drew S.R.O. crowds. *Peace, man.* The Jewish love of learning zapped her like lightning in the person of Milton Kessler, whose "Introduction to Poetry" was in the bearded, bardic tradition of Walt Whitman hugging the world whole.

"Harold Bloom and Milton Kessler are less professors than they are visionary rabbis." Paglia came under the gnomic spell of Bloom, a whirring mind quagmired in a pudding of flesh, while doing her dissertation at Yale. A Neo-Freudian, Bloom saw poetry as a series of Oedipal overthrows—the Romantics trying to topple the marble bust of the Miltonic sublime, etc. There was more sweat and sinew in this spectacle of poets struggling with their predecessors than in a Saturday-night slate of professional wrestling. The cataclysm in Bloom's work echoes in Paglia's, in which every chapter builds toward orgasm (followed by a fainting spell). Her grad-school dissertation served as the launchpad for *Sexual Personae,* published in 1990 by Yale University Press.

A surprise best-seller, *Sexual Personae* (the first of a two-book project—Paglia will begin updating part two this fall) took more than a decade to write. "In a sense *Sexual Personae* is my prison book. I felt like Cervantes, Genet. It took all the resources of being Catholic to cut myself off and sit in my cell." The *Golden Bough* of genital strife and dynamic synthesis, *Sexual Personae* is a literary-historical-archaeological-psychological-theological compendium of stature, scope, scholarship, and bravado. It flies in the face of all our modern complacencies, which is why it was brought out by a university press rather than a New York publisher. Such heresies! Where liberal commentators claim that sexual differences are merely a matter of conditioning (let little Johnny play with dolls), Paglia sees a chasm. Where tree-huggers view the planet as a cradle of innocence, Paglia's view of nature is as tooth-and-nail as any poem out of Ted Hughes's barnyard. At a time when Western Civ is considered a crumbling Colosseum, the carcass of late capitalism, she argues that Dead White Males (Shakespeare, Spenser, Sade) were the demigods of consciousness. They forged greatness out of the Dionysian fire for destruction and the Apollonian dictates of form. "Everything great in western culture has come from the quarrel with nature," Paglia contends—including our own inner nature.

Identity is conflict, declared Freud. Art is a zodiac of masked intent, elaborated Paglia. The famous cover of *Sexual Personae* splices Emily Dickinson and Nefertiti, showing the continuity of Western culture's all-encompassing cat eye. Perhaps the key sentence in *Sexual Personae* is "There is no such thing as 'mere' image." Images being the movie projections of our psyche, every picture tells a story. Decadence she diagnoses as a disease of the eye, an overdose of visual candy.

It was the lower organs that got Paglia into trouble with some critics. She stated that where female genitals are furtive, unsightly, the penis is bold, upright. It writes its name upon the future. "Male urination really is a kind of accomplishment, an arc of transcendence. A woman merely waters the ground she stands on." No wonder men are in awe of their wallies. First thing in the morning, a penis is a pretty magnificent sight. But make no mistake, buster, it crinkles compared to the power of Woman. The orgasm men pursue over hill and dale offers but a brief pop of pleasure. "Men enter in triumph but withdraw in decrepitude." Meanwhile, the little wigglies we launch have to fend for themselves: "Sperm are miniature assault troops, and the ovum is a solitary citadel that must be breached. Weak or passive sperm just sit there like dead ducks. Nature rewards energy and aggression." And should the seed bear fruit, man shrivels even more in the scheme of things. "Woman is the primeval fabricator, the real First Mover. She turns a gob of refuse into a spreading web of sentient being, floating on the snaky umbilical by which she leashes every man." Leashed, he lashes back. Hence Sade, with his voluminous violations, which eventually erupt through the shattered eye of Emily Dickinson. Harmony is an illusion. From birth we are at war with the body of the world. Beat me, Daddy, eight to the bar.

Barnburning as *Sexual Personae* is, it's Paglia's soapbox performances in op-ed pieces and interviews that have made her Public Enemy Number One on the politically correct hit list. Those sparks have been collected in *Sex, Art, and American Culture,* which could almost be called *Paglia Speaks!* because it has the effect of an oral onslaught. Her tiny cubbyhole at the University of the Arts is bedecked with bumper stickers that read, I HAVE AN ATTITUDE and I DON'T HAVE PMS—I'M JUST NATURALLY BITCHY. These are not idle boasts. "This is the number-one rebellion I've made as a woman—people in the fifties wanted women to be nice. And that's why I'm so nasty all the time, because I'm sick and tired of this forcing of niceness. Suddenly, niceness is no longer applied just to girls—it's expected now of everyone in academe or the media. You have to be nice—well, that's just so ridiculous."

Not since Mary McCarthy (another Paglia role model) have American letters housed such a killer instinct in the female of the species. But McCarthy, with her Cheshire-cat grin, prided herself on her cool incisions, on being ladylike in her diction as she dissected. Paglia is a throwback to seventies feminism, when (writes Norman Mailer in *The Prisoner of Sex*) women began to write like "tough faggots." Dainty diction be damned. She slings around slang. Equipped with a mouth like an outboard motor, Paglia talks in torrents, churning up blood with her blades—Susan Sontag, Naomi Wolf, Susan Faludi, Gloria Steinem, Jacques Lacan, Michel Foucault, Jacques Derrida, Paul de Man, Stanley Fish, Helen Vendler, the entire politically correct establishment, they're all meat for her ad-lib mind. She personalizes her attacks. Woe to those who cross her. THIS MEANS WAR. When the critic Robert Scholes had the *unmitigated gall* to twinkle in print about the "libidinal" energy of Foucault, Paglia could almost be heard snapping her bubble gum in disbelief: "The crabbed, pinched, scrunch-shouldered, refrigerated, antiseptic Foucault, Mr. Constipation, as 'libidinal'?" (Scholes himself she dubbed "a mighty small dollop of refried beans.") Her one-sided feud with Susan Sontag is rooted in an early snub.

"I [had] a very pivotal encounter with her in 1973. I was one year out of graduate school, much more flamboyant than I am now. And I was so disappointed, she had no interest in me as a mind." She now considers Sontag a dilettante who queens around town with her coterie. "She should have stayed in academe, where she could have grown as a writer. *On Photography,* for example, is lazy,

completely ignorant of visual history. She became a socialite—her career declined as New York declined. And there's a psychological component as well. She has said that she weeps at movies whenever a father who has been away a long time returns home. Her quest for the ultimate male European writer [Walter Benjamin, E. M. Cioran, Roland Barthes] is a search for a distant authoritative father. It's auto-medication for the Missing Father in her life." Another feminist suffering from the Missing Father syndrome is Germaine Greer, who a few years ago actually published a memoir about trying to mend the breach with Dad. Paglia:

"I was so excited when she appeared with *The Female Eunuch.* There was that great moment at Town Hall when she debated with Norman Mailer and said afterwards that she had expected this hard, nuggety man, but he was positively blowsy. She was witty and stylish. Three years later I saw her at SUNY, Albany, and she looked like a harridan, ranting about the economic problems of the Third World. Rage is fine, we need rage, but it's hopeless becoming addicted to rage. Anyway: I asked her if she planned to write any more about art or literature and she was totally dismissive, saying that there are other things in the world that are far too important. That's when the whole thing went downhill." For Paglia, art is paramount. As she told one audience, art is the history of human consciousness, compared with which politics is mere shifting of sand. Greer finked out on art in pursuit of orthodoxy. "*The Obstacle Race* [Greer's tome on women artists] shows an absolute lack of judgment, ideology run amok. In the very last paragraph she says that the reason there are no great women artists is because you can't get great art from mutilated egos. That's absurd. All great art has come from mutilated egos—Michelangelo, Beethoven."

Paglia holds Sontag and Greer responsible for not trying to rescue feminism from itself when it began to go off the rails into man-hating and victim-mongering. "Both these women attracted the attention of the world. Women would have listened to them. Sontag was born with one of the great brains of our time. Men didn't crush them. They weren't silenced. *They failed.* And so we ended up with all these third-rate minds running feminism, turning it into a closed shop."

When you're in sync with nature, you have a sense of identity. . . . Your identity is much bigger than the career identity. Women are miserable now because they are being taught that their entire identity is in a social realm.

—Camille Paglia

Custodian of the closed shop is Gloria Steinem, a founding editor of *Ms.* "She became the Stalin of our time, addicted to the highlife and choking off feminist dialogue. She became a party animal, the cliquishness of her life-style forming this circle around her. With Naomi Wolf and Susan Faludi now she's like a mother hen with her little chicks. They don't know how to handle me. I've come out of the cannon: boom! Steinem told *The Advocate,* 'Her calling herself a feminist is sort of like a Nazi saying they're not anti-Semitic.' Well! The historical record will show that I am one of the great feminists of the twentieth century." When a member of the National Organization for Women's national board accused Paglia of cashing in on the feminist backlash, she retorted, "I'm not in it for the money, you stupid bitches!"

Even those who attempt to side with her are mailed home in a cigar box. When literary critic Frederick Crews wrote Paglia a congratulatory note on her work, icing his praise with some advice about how she really *must* stop invoking Freud and Jung as paragons of science, she let fly with a reply that threatened to put a new crease in his hair. Crews: "She characterized my letter as 'insulting,' which is a strange thing for an intellectual to say about intellectual criticism. She was basically saying, 'I don't need any advice from you.' " A literary editor trying to ooze a contribution from her received a similar buzz-off. Etiquette is for eunuchs. She doesn't believe in playing fair. "I'm Italian," Paglia told the audience at the New York Public Library. "I don't believe in an eye for an eye. For me, it's two eyes for an eye. Ten eyes for an eye." She was photographed for *People* magazine wielding a shiv. To paraphrase the poet Ogden Nash, it's like finding yourself in a dark alley with Lucretia Borgia / And she's coming torgia.

Perhaps into your very town. For Paglia has taken her act on the road. Sowing sunshine wherever she goes, she delivers speeches that create a rock-concert rhubarb on college campuses and in lecture halls. Traveling "under the aegis of African-American culture," Paglia is flanked onstage by two black bodyguards named Rennard Snowden and Brian Roach, macho bookends in matching shades and black leather. "My centurions," she calls them. "I don't have to be butch—they do it for me." They read the crowd to protect Paglia from enemies and fans. She arouses both. Trying to repeal all repressions, she says ("My ability to suspend moral judgment is sublime, really"), she releases the energy of those repressions. Hysteria hawks the air. Her fans want a piece of her. Her enemies want her in pieces. At Brown University young feminists shrieked over her stand on date rape, which she pooh-poohs as a fancy fit of overreacting. At M.I.T. she found herself on the hostile turf of homosexual historian David M. Halperin, whom she had hung from the scaffold in an essay reprinted in *Sex, Art, and American Culture* on the flatulent influence of Foucault on the study of sex, about which Foucault (and by extension, Halperin) knew fuck-all nothing. "You could feel a pocket of hostility, right? Feel it, O.K.? I didn't know what was going to happen. I didn't know whether I was going to be attacked."

Paglia's ability to crank up the crazies bothers some bystanders. Susan Sontag's son, David Rieff, the author of books on Miami and Los Angeles, detects little-dictator tendencies in Paglia's stand-up act. "She's a useful counterirritant to a certain type of academic cant. But she's

substituting her own brand of unpleasantly self-promoting cant. When she calls herself 'the most fascinating woman in the world'—you can't pretend to be upholding standards and then do this Ali shuffle. She strikes me as a Ross Perot figure, a symptom of the mediocrity of others. I don't like crusaders, especially crusaders with an unlimited and particular access to truth. She is always attacking people for being 'soft'—'He's soft,' 'She's soft'—in this disdainful tone. It's neo-fascist talk." The attacks on Sontag he dismisses as no big deal. "My mother excites jealousy." But he does note that the two people who have made a meal out of attacking his mother are Paglia and Hilton Kramer, the neoconservative raja of *The New Criterion,* who also models himself on Moses the Lawgiver.

Being lumped in with the neocons doesn't make Paglia break out in monkey bites. "I am the one who put them on to the neoconservative agenda, made them for the first time ever in their lives take seriously issues of pornography, prostitution, homosexuality. If the neoconservatives are [co-opting] *Sexual Personae,* let them—it's a Trojan horse. A Trojan horse that contains pornographers, prostitutes, drag queens, sadomasochists, and so on. I am radicalizing the neoconservatives," rather than vice versa.

Another reason Paglia could never become a card-carrying neocon is that neoconservatism cannot, will not accommodate popular culture. One of the reasons Hilton Kramer got his bow tie in a twist over Sontag was that she said she dug the Supremes. Sontag soon abandoned silver lamé to humble herself proudly as a high-culture priestess. She used to pride herself on not owning a TV. Paglia, however, is a true pophead. She approaches new sensations like an R. Crumb hippie, wide-eyed and openmouthed. She calls it the three-*W* response: "Wow. Weird. Whoa." In literature, she believes the Beats have gotten a bum rap. She reviles poetry criticism's gatekeeper, Helen Vendler, for not admitting them into the canon (with the exception of Allen Ginsberg). In nonfiction prose, she praises Bloom, Fiedler, Mailer, Norman O. Brown, Pauline Kael, Robert Hughes. In cinema her enthusiasms span the art house (*Sexual Personae* was inspired by Ingmar Bergman's *Persona*) to Hollywood. Her movie goddess is Elizabeth Taylor, who wears white slips as if they were sewn onto her skin, with Sharon Stone making thoroughbred progress on the outside track. She shuns snobbery ("snob" is one of her pet put-downs of Sontag), scanning the bar code of every pop-cult archetype.

"It's amazing, the *Batman* promotion, the way that I go into a McDonald's and it's everywhere on the bags, on the cups. Have you seen the giant, more than life-size, beautiful stand-up of Batman, sexy and [bulging]. More and more bulges now, genital bulges, are occurring. I mean, it is very revolutionary, because it used to be Superman was always absolutely neuter down there. You're starting to see the balls. I mean, that's great. Now the look on his face under the mask is getting more and more macho. He's sort of like the Marquis de Sade or something." When not checking out Batman's unit, Paglia channel-surfs across the TV dial, breaking off one of our chats to catch the Daytime Emmy Awards. Her TV heroines include not only the cast of *The Young and the Restless* but such stalwarts as Suzanne Pleshette, Jessica Walter, Donna Mills. She often writes with the TV blasting. "I have a multitrack mind," a sensory mesh she attributes to being a child of the sixties.

She's also a rock freak, her chief hero that rag-and-bone shop of the heart, Rolling Stones guitarist Keith Richards. But her greatest glow-on is for Madonna, the subject of two chapters in *Sex, Art, and American Culture.* Paglia doesn't so much idolize Madonna as identify with her. She and Madonna are soul sisters. "Maybe strong fathers breed strong women. Madonna and me, our fathers were always home. Our fathers were dictatorial, but not unjustly so. In other words, you were struck with these authoritarian figures who are also very positive . . . and were forced to develop your strength next to this image of positive manhood. So the thing is, look at the results. Madonna and I are workaholics, O.K. We are drug-free, O.K. We are strong women who have projected our hallucinatory pornographic visions to the world, O.K."

Paglia's faith in the Material Girl has been sorely tested of late, however. When Madonna appeared on *Arsenio* to plug *A League of Their Own,* she giggled and smirked at her own inane innuendos, her scalp as stretched as Norma Desmond's in *Sunset Boulevard.* She has never been more excruciating. "Madonna lacks words, O.K. And so what she does is borrow language. All she did that night was two voices. She was being Sandra Bernhard and then she was doing Rosie [Rosie O'Donnell, one of her co-stars in *A League of Their Own*]. She knew she wasn't coming across. You could feel her physically thinking. She was hiding behind Rosie O'Donnell, sort of like a mother figure. It's like she needs me to open up her life, I'm telling you. She needs help. Because all she ever sees are people in the performing arts. You know, there's no substance. Sandra Bernhard is her best friend. And Sandra Bernhard is a very mouthy—and 'mouthy' is the word—woman. Sandra Bernhard is a walking, talking neurotic."

Catching herself, Paglia worries about me messing up her plans for mentoring Madonna. "If you quote something negative about Madonna, make sure you [quote something positive], so you don't get me in Dutch with Madonna, O.K.? Because then I'll never meet her, O.K.?" Don't worry, I couldn't Live with Myself if I came between you two spunky gals. I wouldn't want to wipe out the mind-boggling possibility of someday seeing Madonna shopping at Tower Books, cramming for Camille. "I mean it, don't blow it for me. O.K.?" *Awright, awready.*

Like Madonna, Camille Paglia wishes to be a glamorous gender bender, dishing with gay men, dallying with her own sex. BORN-AGAIN BISEXUAL, says a button on her desk. The problem is getting the other teams to play. Political correctness is in danger of making gay men a bunch of pills, complains Paglia. The anger of ACT UP is unleavened by any sense of joyful ministry. Gay men at their pagan-studliest celebrate play, physicality, pretense, not to mention Greco-Roman grappling. For all the flak she has gotten in the gay press (an item in *QW* accused her of skipping a gay friend's funeral because she feared her star presence would be a distraction, and took what Paglia interpreted as a sideswipe at Lauren Hutton), she affirms that

the two biggest influences on her are the Catholic Church and gay men. With gay men she could appreciate glamour unabashedly. Lesbians lack that aesthetic feel. They're frumps, sleeping bags with legs.

"I conclude that to my regret exclusive lesbianism is emotional retardation. . . . When lesbians cut themselves off from men, the end result [is] that the middle-aged lesbian personality is childish. It's infantile, O.K.? I'm not saying stop being lesbians. I'm not saying stop sleeping with women. You must. But you must accept your power over men—you cannot be constantly trapped in this ideology of male power, male tyranny, female victimization. If you are trapped in it, that is the projection of a child.

"I mean, I am amazed, I'm just amazed at the lack of actual strength of the lesbian personality. I thought that lesbianism was a way for women to be strong, O.K.? Strong vis-à-vis men. And now I have to conclude that women become lesbian out of weakness, not out of strength, and that is why I can't get along with them."

I wonder if Paglia may not be behind the beat when it comes to the work-shirt puritanism of butch lesbians. In my quiet, discreet East Village war zone, I've noticed this outbreak of *sexy lesbianism,* with young, lanky, tattooed boho babes looping their arms around each other and body-rubbing each other up in front of onlookers. Twice in one week I found myself facing a woman fondling her girlfriend while she made eye contact with me. (Both times I nearly dropped my Beatnik's sketch pad.) Others have reported similar flirty encounters, *so it isn't just me, O.K.?* Far from conforming to scowling stereotype, young lesbians seem to have given themselves permission to feel foxy. I chalk it up to the impact of *Basic Instinct,* the scene in which Sharon Stone and her sweetie make Michael Douglas grow a mustache of sweat beads with their snaky gyrations. When Paglia saw *Basic Instinct,* she said her response was, I've been looking for sexy lesbians like that all my life—where are they? My answer is, Look around. They're here. They've got nose rings, granted, but they're here.

Not that Paglia is any less estranged from most straight feminists. She holds highest esteem for such Dead White Females as Mary Wollstonecraft and Simone de Beauvoir. "Not since Simone de Beauvoir has there been a feminist with my frame of reference," she told London's *Late Show.* The current scene she finds *quel* drag, although she does compliment Wendy Lesser's *His Other Half.* Her greatest snort is reserved for "yuppie feminists" Naomi Wolf (*The Beauty Myth*) and Susan Faludi (*Backlash*), who represent what is being called the Third Wave of feminism. Such ideologues argue that life is a series of *choices.* Like Freud, whose value she has done much to revive, Paglia posits that we are only partly aware of the forces that move us, that conscious decision is but a small part of our makeup. Programmatic change only ripples the surface of our psyches. And so when programmatic change fails to make women happier, feminists play a blame game, scapegoating everything from politics to fashion.

Fashion is Naomi Wolf's whipping boy. Paglia in turn disparages Wolf as an ill-educated hustler peddling a

Swiss-cheese thesis. "She's the Dan Quayle of feminism—a pretty airhead." Since adornment pre-dates Christ ("The Egyptians were the first aesthetes"—*Sexual Personae*), it's absurd for Wolf to claim the Beauty Myth was something sprung on women unawares by the editors of slick monthlies, says Paglia. However distorted by commerce, the quest for beauty is an inner craving for emblematic selfhood (Rachel Williams stenciled against the sky), not a pernicious secret program to make women passive. Wolf and Paglia recently squared off about sexual politics in the pages of *The New Republic,* with Wolf describing her first orgasm in hues usually reserved for church frescoes. Right now the distance between them is a loud hum. Paglia refuses to appear in person with Wolf (too small-fry, she says), and Wolf declined to discuss Paglia with me.

(Although I subsequently did bump into Wolf at a party, where she informed me with her flashing gypsy eyes and a toss of her ebony mane that, despite what Paglia says, *The Beauty Myth* is *not* "puritanical"—"I say in the book that we should touch, sense, savor, and experience *everything.*")

Paglia *has* appeared on *Donahue* with Faludi, whom she considers sincere but essentially mush. "It's so easy to shift her. During a commercial break, I would say, 'There are no great women composers.' [Faludi:] 'It's because women have not had ample training.' I said, 'Susan, women have had access to the piano since 1790. Middle-class, upper-class women have been training on the keyboard for two hundred years.' And her eyes would open. 'Really?' "

Intellectually, Paglia may rout Wolf, Faludi, and all the yuppie feminists, but she occupies the burning fringe, despite her claim "*I* am the Third Wave." She's too individual, too irate, to be a consensus builder. Like Larry Kramer on the gay left, she has a voice that registers the hoarseness of someone who insists on being right all the time. It's a rigidity which leaves no room for doubt or compromise. ("Compromise" is almost a curse word.) For all their wide-eyed wonderment, Wolf and Faludi have won a constituency. The presence of their books on the best-seller list is proof of a deep-seated dissatisfaction among educated young women. A critic at *Entertainment Weekly* told me that every woman on the staff has *Backlash* in her cubicle, like a Gideon Bible. Everywhere, American women feel frazzled, frustrated—women who have opportunities their mother's and certainly grandmothers never had. Something is gnawing at them, something deeper than the standard litany of the Hill-Thomas hearings/*Roe v. Wade*/William Kennedy Smith. What gives? Why are they so angry?

"Because feminism is teaching them to be angry," Paglia answers. "There's something very wrong with how we're educating young women, O.K. They're being taught that they're the equal of men, they can do anything that men can. On the contrary. Their bodies are fantastically complex. Their emotions are fantastically complex. And what's going on inside of us, with the hormones and stuff, we know nothing about it. Science fails to know anything about it. There's not one single thing from menopause to menstruation to childbirth that science knows anything about hormonally. I know this to be true, because I think every doctor will say, 'Well, we're just at the beginning. We don't know anything.' [No one] is telling them this." So women are out of whack with nature.

"When you're in sync with nature, you have a sense of identity. You are oriented toward your own history as a sex. A mother who accepts the fact that she's a woman and loves the fact that she's a woman is honored for her motherhood as all the Mediterranean cultures honor the mother. You feel coming into yourself all of history and all of nature. It makes you what you are. Your identity is much bigger than the career identity. Women are miserable now because they are being taught that their entire identity is in a social realm. And what I'm saying—I say this constantly—is to me there are two spheres of life. There's a social sphere, O.K., and there's a sexual, emotional, or spiritual sphere, O.K. These two spheres overlap, each circle overlaps. That's the area where the personal is political, as the feminists might say. But feminism's error of the last twenty years is to say that we are nothing but our social self." And the social self can never quell the inner call.

But what of Paglia's own inner call? To that I must confess that I haven't a Freudian clue. She doesn't permit psychological access. Although Paglia jokes about her voluptuous Italian figure, her bosomy bosoms (for her *Vanity Fair* photo shoot, Lauren Hutton offered to bring her "an emergency bag of push-up bras"), her body seems locked-in, a gun emplacement for her sky-strafing mind. She barrages a listener with such cloudburst flak that the words seem to cluster of their own accord, with no person behind them. There's no letup, no sense of inclusion. I have phone messages from her which resemble uncut monologues from William Gaddis novels, a tape loop recorded in a tollbooth on an interstate to nowhere. If I were Camille Paglia's handler (next stop, the Foreign Legion), I would advise her to entertain the notion that OTHER PEOPLE EXIST. She's in danger of creating a closed system. But it's difficult to imagine her abandoning the obsessional mode. As she herself says, it's the art that matters, not the artist ("My attitude is that if Picasso took a machine gun and cut down a line of grandmothers, okay, it would not affect my opinion of his art," she told *New York* magazine)—the message, not the messenger. We mortals are but passing shadows. Her message is pitched to the stainless-steel future.

I recall that there was once an upscale porn movie called *Camille 2000.* Certainly, Camille Paglia has her pyramid eye on the next century. On London's *Late Show,* she sketched out a feminism for the twenty-first century, which would be more realistic and honor sexual differences rather than try to erase them. She would be for the next generation what Amelia Earhart was for her—a blinking light on the horizon. "I am a wonderful role model for young women," she told *The Late Show.* "I'm completely self-reliant. I don't look to approval from anyone. I've never lived with a man. My epitaph could be 'She served no man.' " There *is* a mental strut to her style which is thrilling. It reminds you of Ezra Pound, before he went totally crackers. It will be fascinating to see if the second part of *Sexual Personae* (which will span pop culture—rock, football, Hollywood, TV) coheres, or if it fractures into brilliant, bombastic fragments, like Pound's later cantos. Even in pieces, beauty has power.

Whatever the outcome, Camille Paglia feels her own position is rock-solid. Gold-plated. Unassailable. After reading a feebly argued essay by a woman academic in *The New Republic,* Paglia announced to me, "I have no rivals." Her only *true* challenger, Susan Sontag, has abdicated the race. Says Paglia with a gloat that could girdle the globe, "I've been chasing that bitch for twenty-five years, and at last I've passed her." (pp. 239-41, 300-03)

> *James Wolcott, "Paglia's Power Trip," in* Vanity Fair, *Vol. 55, No. 9, September, 1992, pp. 239-41, 300-03.*

FURTHER READING

Faludi, Susan, and Wolf, Naomi. "Have Men Really Changed?" *Glamour* (December 1992): 228-31.
> Presents a conversation between Faludi and Wolf in which they focus on relationships between the sexes and the status of feminism in the 1990s.

Fielding, Helen. "It's Much Too Late for the Blaming of the Shrew." *The Sunday Times* (29 March 1992): 2, Section 4.
> Discusses the resurgence of interest in feminism sparked by the notion of a backlash against the women's movement.

Ivins, Molly. "I Am the Cosmos." *Mother Jones* 16, No. 5 (September-October 1991): 8, 10-11.
> Dismisses several tenets of the philosophy of art and sexuality Paglia presents in *Sexual Personae.*

Pogash, Carol. "The Brains Behind *Backlash.*" *Working Woman* (April 1992): 64-7, 104.
> Discusses Faludi's life and career and the reactions of feminists to *Backlash: The Undeclared War against American Women.*

Shapiro, Laura. "Why Women Are Angry." *Newsweek* CXVIII, No. 17 (21 October 1991): 41, 43-4.
> Examines such issues as sex discrimination and the political and economic status of women that Faludi addresses in *Backlash.*

Shore, Paul. Review of *Backlash: The Undeclared War against American Women,* by Susan Faludi. *The Humanist* 52, No. 5 (September-October 1992): 47-8.
> Praises *Backlash* for doing "more than any other recent work . . . to compel us to see the forces controlling and crippling women for what they really are: forces working against the interests of *everyone.*"

Simson, Maria. "Cry Wolf: Morrow Explores the Burdens of Beauty." *Publishers Weekly* 238, No. 9 (15 February 1991): 64.
> Discusses the publishing history of and critical reception to Wolf's *The Beauty Myth.*

Wheelwright, Julie. "The New Avengers." *New Statesman & Society* 5, No. 196 (3 April 1992): 44-5.
> Compares Faludi's *Backlash* with Marilyn French's *The War against Women*, a nonfiction work that also addresses the concept of a backlash against feminism.

Additional coverage of Faludi and Paglia is contained in the following sources published by Gale Research: *Contemporary Authors,* **Vol. 138 [Faludi]; and** *Contemporary Literary Criticism,* **Vol. 68 [Paglia].**

Gay and Lesbian Literature

INTRODUCTION

Gay and lesbian literature has been identified as a rapidly emerging field in mainstream publishing. Although commentators have noted homosexual themes and subjects throughout literary history, it was not until the 1970s that publishing houses such as Naiad Press and Alyson Publications, which specialize in gay and lesbian literature, were founded. Recognizing the commercial potential of this market, mainstream publishing houses began to establish gay and lesbian imprints during the late 1970s. Other factors contributing to the rise of gay and lesbian literature include increasing political and social activism of the gay rights movement, establishment of gay and lesbian studies programs on college campuses, and growing awareness of the impact of AIDS. Authors who have achieved popular and critical success among both homosexual and heterosexual audiences include Lillian Faderman, David Leavitt, Audre Lorde, and Edmund White. Although some commentators contend that gay and lesbian fiction is rarely read by heterosexuals, George Stambolian, the editor of *Men on Men: Best New Gay Fiction,* has observed that "there is every indication that increasing numbers of nongay readers have begun to read books from small gay presses, which continue to serve the vital function of nurturing new talent by publishing works that, for whatever reason, have a more limited commercial appeal. Despite the reluctance of many mainstream critics to acknowledge the phenomenon, gay fiction is an exciting and undeniable reality."

PRINCIPAL WORKS DISCUSSED BELOW

Brown, Rita Mae
  Rubyfruit Jungle (novel) 1973
Duberman, Martin
  Cures: A Gay Man's Odyssey (nonfiction) 1991
Faderman, Lillian
  Odd Girls and Twilight Lovers: A History of Lesbian Life in Twentieth-Century America (nonfiction) 1991
Fierstein, Harvey
  Torch Song Trilogy (drama) [first publication] 1980
Gide, André
  Si le grain ne meurt (autobiography) 1920-21
    [*If It Die: An Autobiography,* 1935]
Hall, Radclyffe

  The Well of Loneliness (novel) 1928
Holleran, Andrew
  Dancer from the Dance (novel) 1978
  Nights in Aruba (novel) 1983
  Ground Zero (essays) 1988
Isherwood, Christopher
  A Single Man (novel) 1964
Kramer, Larry
  Faggots (novel) 1978
  The Normal Heart (drama) 1985
Leavitt, David
  The Lost Language of Cranes (novel) 1986
Marcus, Eric
  Making History: The Struggle for Gay and Lesbian Equal Rights, 1945-1980 (nonfiction) 1992
Maupin, Armistead
  Tales of the City (short stories) 1978
McCarthy, Mary
  The Group (novel) 1963
Morgan, Clare
  The Price of Salt (novel) 1952
Penelope, Julia
  Call Me Lesbian: Lesbian Lives, Lesbian Theory (nonfiction) 1992
Picano, Felice
  The Lure (novel) 1979
  Late in the Season (novel) 1981
Routsong, Alma
  A Place for Us [as Isabel Miller] (novel) 1969; also published as *Patience and Sarah,* 1972
Rule, Jane
  Desert of the Heart (novel) 1964
Stambolian, George
  Men on Men: Best New Gay Fiction [editor] (short stories) 1986
  Men on Men 2: Best New Gay Fiction [editor] (short stories) 1988
  Men on Men 3: Best New Gay Fiction [editor] (short stories) 1990
  Men on Men 4: Best New Gay Fiction [editor] (short stories) 1992
White, Edmund
  Nocturne for the King of Naples (novel) 1978
  A Boy's Own Story (novel) 1982
  The Faber Book of Gay Short Fiction [editor] (short stories) 1992
Willkie, Phil, and Baysan, Greg
  The Gay Nineties: An Anthology of Gay Fiction [editors] (short stories) 1991
Young, Ian
  The Male Muse [editor] (poetry) 1971

GAY AND LESBIAN PUBLISHING

Bob Summer   (essay date 29 June 1992)

[*In the following essay, Summer traces the recent growth of gay and lesbian publishing.*]

"I have seen more gay and lesbian books of excellence this past month from publishers large and small than I saw over the course of a year five or six years ago," says Mark Thompson, who covers books for the *Advocate,* a national gay and lesbian news magazine. "Even specialists in the field have a hard time keeping up with what's being published," adds Martin Duberman, the biographer of Paul Robeson and author of *Cures: A Gay Man's Odyssey,* one of BOMC's [Book of the Month Club's] top five alternate selections in the past year in hardcover (Dutton).

The quality and quantity of recent books by gay and lesbian authors is perhaps the most obvious measure of an emerging niche market, for mainstream publishers and specialty houses alike. And evidence from across the industry suggests that gay and lesbian publishing—once known chiefly through fiction writers like Edmund White and David Leavitt—is a healthy, diverse and growing sector of publishing. On June 28, Eric Marcus's *Making History: The Struggle for Gay and Lesbian Equal Rights 1945-1990* (Harper Collins) and Lillian Faderman's *Odd Girls and Twilight Lovers: A History of Lesbian Life in Twentieth-Century America* (Columbia Univ.) were prominently reviewed together on the front page of the *New York Times Book Review. Odd Girls,* which won the Editors' Choice Award at the fourth annual Lambda Literary Awards banquet during the ABA, as well as the ALA's 1992 Gay/Lesbian Award for nonfiction, has now made the transition from university press to trade, with Penguin USA paying a six-figure advance for paperback rights.

Something is surely happening here, enough so that Walter Kendrick, in a *New York Times Book Review* essay about "the new erotica," noted "an embarrassment of riches" available in homoerotica.

And when you hear that a promotion for the first annual National Lesbian and Gay Book month garnered "enthusiastic" inquiries from the chains, as publicist Michelle Karlsberg reports, it is clear that a groundswell of recognition is forming for what was once a small, niche market.

One can even go to Ingram and get a separate list of all the gay and lesbian titles available in its warehouses. Sherry Thomas, publisher of Spinsters Book Co. in San Francisco, may have captured the change best, at least among retailers. Commenting in Anaheim on the sharply increased traffic in the lesbian/feminist/gay row, she said that "booksellers who couldn't bring themselves to say 'lesbian' five years ago would still come by if they had a need for one of our books. Now we're seeing booksellers from the chains and everywhere stopping by and saying, 'We've got to have these books!' "

Tracking a 'Dream Market'

What is it that is prompting the growth and creative vitality of gay and lesbian publishing and bookselling at a time when the economy is not all that good? Does publishing success 23 years after the Stonewall Inn rebellion—an encounter between gays and New York City police that is now considered the founding incident of the gay-rights movement—indicate that the movement has finally won the acceptance of society at large? "No, it doesn't mean that at all," responds Barbara Grier, who founded Naiad Press, the nation's oldest ongoing lesbian publisher, with Donna McBride in 1972. "We're still a homophobic society, and there are lots of walls still to be broken down." But recent growth, nevertheless, means "several things are happening," not the least of which is a wider recognition of the numbers and "buying power" of gays and lesbians in the book market.

Last year the *Wall Street Journal* identified the gay and lesbian community as "a dream market," noting such U.S. Bureau of the Census demographics as homosexuals' average yearly household income ($55,430 versus the national average of $33,144) and percentage of college graduates (59.6% versus 18%). And in a survey of 35,000 gay men and lesbians, Overlooked Opinions, a Chicago market research firm, found that reading is a favorite hobby of 82% of them.

Early gay and lesbian publishers were compelled more by a personal commitment to helping further liberation, Grier says, than by "a dream of making money. Both Donna and I had other jobs when we started, and didn't take any salaries from Naiad until we could afford to leave them in 1982." Sasha Alyson began Alyson Publications in 1979 as the outgrowth of a small company, and he began to distribute books from feminist and progressive publishers as well as the few gay books he knew of. "There weren't many available then," he recalls, "so I decided to publish them myself."

Writer Felice Picano began the Gay Presses of New York group in 1979, and a year later published (under the Seal Press imprint) Harvey Fierstein's *Torch Song Trilogy,* which went on to win a Tony Award as the best play produced in New York during the 1982-1983 season. Picano also published books by Brad Gooch, Dennis Cooper, George Stambolian and Martin Duberman before these authors moved on to larger trade houses.

John Gill, co-publisher with Elaine Goldman-Gill of Crossing Press, published *The Male Muse,* an anthology of contemporary gay poetry, in 1971.

> That was one of our first books, and we sold 10,000 copies. We publish in other areas, such as spirituality, recovery and health, but books for gay men and lesbians/feminists—it's hard to separate those two—have always been important to us. We published *Shy,* which was nominated for a 1991 Lambda Book Award, and last year we brought out Phil Willkie and Greg Baysans's *The Gay Nineties: An Anthology of Gay Fiction.* One of our new books is Julia Penelope's *Call Me Lesbian: Lesbian Lives, Lesbian Theory.* Also, we were among the first to distribute books

from women's presses before Inland, Bookpeople, Bookslinger and other distributors began handling small presses.

The San Francisco branch of Harper & Row (now Harper San Francisco) published Letha Scanzoni and Virginia Ramey Mollenkott's *Is the Homosexual My Neighbor?* in 1980, and since then Harper has steadily developed a strong gay and lesbian line. Among its most recent titles are Diana Souhami's *Gertrude and Alice* (already selling well as a British import from the company's Pandora imprint) and Craig O'Neill and Kathleen Ritter's *Coming Out Within: Stages of Spiritual Awakening for Lesbians and Gay Men.* The house is also committed to publishing books about the AIDS crisis. Forthcoming this fall is *Wise Before Their Time: People Living with AIDS and HIV Tell Their Stories,* edited by Ann Richardson and Dietmar Rollo; royalties from this book will be donated to AIDS charities.

Mainstream Slow to Notice

Larger New York publishers were slower to develop lists for gay and lesbian readers, although Grove Press and some avant-garde imprints regularly offered books that appealed to gay readers. Still, as both Carol Seajay, editor of *Feminist Bookstore News,* and Michael Denneny, senior editor at St. Martin's, note, some commercial houses did try to publish books of gay and lesbian interest long before the gay-rights movement gathered momentum in the late '70s and early '80s.

In 1977, Denneny contends, St. Martin's became the first house to make a concerted effort to develop a strong list of books by gay authors. Edmund White's second book, *Nocturne for the King of Naples,* was published there in 1978. Meanwhile at Dutton, then an independent house, editor Bill Whitehead began working with White, Robert Ferro and other influential writers in the first wave of post-Stonewall gay fiction. "The renaissance in gay writing," Denneny comments, "didn't happen overnight. It was under way before the AIDS epidemic struck."

Now the St. Martin's gay and lesbian list (which includes the Stonewall Inn Editions trade paperback line) is rivaled only by the collective lists of NAL, Viking, Dutton and Plume, all imprints of Penguin USA. NAL's involvement with gay books began when it acquired paperback rights to Edmund White's *A Boy's Own Story,* recalls Arnold Dolin, senior vice-president, publisher and editor-in-chief of Plume. "Bill Whitehead had published it at the 'old' Dutton, and we had two gay editors at NAL who read it but, surprisingly, didn't like it." But Dolin and Elaine Koster, now executive vice-president and publisher of NAL/Dutton, read it also and had a much different reaction. "We thought it was a lovely novel, and went for it. We paid a large advance, and published it in Plume very successfully. It became apparent that there was a large audience hungry for gay literary fiction, and it was easily identifiable."

Strong sales of Plume's reprint of Robert Ferro's *The Family of Max Desir* confirmed that analysis, and prompted NAL to build a gay list by publishing Dutton originals and buying rights for other gay books in order to publish

them as Plume trade paperbacks. "This became a very important element in our publishing," Dolin notes, crediting the late George Stambolian's *Men on Men* anthologies of new gay fiction with playing a pivotal role. "George's anthologies have become quite popular, and they have introduced us to new writers whose books we later published." *Men on Men 4,* which Stambolian completed editing shortly before he died of AIDS last December, will be published simultaneously in Dutton hardcover and Plume paperback in October.

Men on Men 4 has been selected by BOMC and QPB, and both clubs will offer the book as part of a set that also includes the previous three anthologies. Dolin predicts that *Men on Men 4* will do quite well, since "BOMC has discovered it has a large audience among its members for gay books. Certainly BOMC has done well with books of ours it has offered during the past year—Martin Duberman's *Cures,* Neil Bartlett's *Ready to Catch Him Should He Fall,* and John Preston's *Big Gay Book* and *Hometowns* anthology. The buyers seem to come from all over the country."

But Dolin refrains from claiming that BOMC members' interest in gay books is evidence of a crossover market for gay books, and he thinks that in fact there are few gay or lesbian titles that cross over to a larger heterosexual audience. "Although it has grown tremendously, this is a finite world we're talking about." As a result, he predicts that sales of gay titles will level off, as will sales of books aimed at lesbian readers.

Ed Iwanicki, Penguin USA's director of group publishing, also doubts that there is a crossover market for gay and lesbian books (though he allows that there are exceptions), and sees confusion in how the term crossover is used. "A lot of people in publishing assume if a gay or lesbian book is sold in a non-gay bookstore, it is a crossover book. That is not so." Rather, he contends that virtually all titles with gay or lesbian themes sold at chain or general stores are bought by gay or lesbian readers. Nevertheless, Iwanicki, who also edits Viking Penguin authors David B. Feinberg, Joe Keenan and Richard Hall, acknowledges that occasionally a gay or lesbian author—such as Armistead Maupin or Rita Mae Brown—crosses over to a heterosexual readership. But that results from "how they are presented to the trade," he adds, noting that in many instances jacket copy for such books will disguise their homosexual themes.

The Key Role of Booksellers

Both Iwanicki and Denneny give the lion's share of the credit for the growth of gay and lesbian publishing to the specialty bookstores. When St. Martin's began developing its gay and lesbian list in 1977, there were eight gay and lesbian bookstores in the U.S. Now there are "about 35," according to Scott Fuchs, head of telephone sales at Penguin USA, and others think 50 is a more realistic number.

Whatever their numbers, Denneny notes, gay and lesbian stores are "among the nation's healthiest." Robert Riger, a consultant with Market Partners International in New York and formerly a BOMC managing editor and Doubleday Book Clubs president, backs this up by citing the sales per square foot at the nation's largest gay and lesbian booksellers, Lambda Rising and A Different Light, each of which has three stores. While the national average is just under $300 in sales per square foot, Lambda Rising's Washington store claims $1102, and A Different Light's New York store reports $1100. In its San Francisco store, managed by Richard Labonte, the figure is $650. Both Lambda Rising and A Different Light had sales exceeding $2 million in 1991, and last year Lambda Rising saw a sales growth of 11% in its stores, in D.C., Baltimore and Rehoboth Beach, Del.

Ron Hanby, general manager of Golden-Lee Book Distributors, which publishes catalogues of gay and lesbian books each year, adds another salient fact. "Gay and lesbian bookstores are very much backlist businesses," he says, and that helps account for their "unusually low" returns rate. The mail-order catalogues both Lambda Rising and A Different Light regularly send to their extensive customer lists, Hanby speculates, also help keep returns down.

But with the rise of gay and lesbian publishing has come a marketing imperative to expand on the sound base of those specialty stores. Golden-Lee has what Hanby describes as a "starter kit" for chain and general stores interested in enlarging their inventories of gay and lesbian titles.

Getting non-specialty stores interested in gay and lesbian books was one of the goals the Publishing Triangle had in mind in establishing June as National Lesbian and Gay Book Month. Financed by the <i>Advocate,</i> Alyson Publications, Bookpeople, Penguin USA, Firebrand, Harper San Francisco, HarperCollins, Inland Book Co., Masquerade, Naiad Press and St. Martin's Stonewall Editions, the theme month follows the precedents of Black History and Women's History months, says Riger. Although the response of booksellers and members of the media has been gratifying, he hopes that next year planning will begin early enough to involve libraries and gay and lesbian newspapers and magazines more than they were this year.

Michelle Karlsberg, who along with Denneny, Riger and Roz Parr of A Different Light in New York formed an ad hoc marketing committee for Lesbian and Gay Book Month, reports that responses from the chains indicate that their effort has caught their attention. The Little Professor Book Center, for example, alerted its 133 stores to NLGBM; and Ileene Kaufman, Barnes & Noble's author promotions coordinator, has lined up Martin Duberman, Lillian Faderman, Quentin Crisp, Ethan Mordden, Paul Russell, Essex Hemphill and Jaime Manrique for readings and signings during Gay Pride Week at B. Dalton.

NLGBM also gives publishers an effective marketing tool. "We are publishing Eric Marcus's new book this month, and it has gotten lots of attention from booksellers, reviewers, and the media," says HarperCollins editor Rick Kot of <i>Making History,</i> a project he developed after seeing <i>Eyes on the Prize,</i> the PBS documentary series and related book about the black civil rights movement. "We underbid on [that book], so it was published elsewhere, but it gave me the idea for a similar book on the gay rights movement. We have been in this area for some time and have

a good list, which does quite well. So I began looking for a writer." Kot had worked with Marcus on <i>The Male Couple's Guide,</i> and he seemed the appropriate choice to write the book Kot had in mind. And June, Stonewall's anniversary month, was the logical time to publish it.

Among the stops on Marcus's national tour for <i>Making History</i> is Lambda Rising in Washington. But his tour also includes chain stores and general independents. That's fine with L. Page "Deacon" Maccubbin, who established Lambda Rising in 1974.

> I'm glad to see any store anywhere sell gay and lesbian books. I'm glad that the Borders Bookshop stores and the Little Professors as well as the larger chains are doing that business, because they are able to reach customers we can't. Not everyone who is a potential customer for gay and lesbian books will go into a gay and lesbian store to buy them. Maybe [the larger stores] will get people interested in gay and lesbian books, and maybe those people will get a thirst for more books than those stores can carry. So eventually they will wind up as our customers, due to the depth we have.

Women's Movement and Publishing

A very crucial outlet for lesbian books over the years has been the feminist bookstore, and it is no less true today. In 1991 there were 106 feminist bookstores in America and Canada, with sales of $31 million, according to Carol Seajay, editor of the <i>Feminist Bookstore Newsletter.</i> Forty percent of those sales were of lesbian books, a figure that publishers have only begun to notice. The larger commercial publishers, that is. Feminist stores and smaller women's presses, "including lesbian presses," Seajay explains, are by now integral parts of a single cultural movement.

Sherry Thomas finds this "historical phenomenon" unparalleled. "This wave of the women's movement—the one that began in the early '70s—was organized in its earliest days around writing. There was a whole network of newspapers, magazines, small publishers, bookstores and printing presses who would print our books before we could afford larger commercial printers. I can't find any other movement for social or cultural change in the country that's been as print-based. I don't have an answer for why that is, but publishing is integral to how women began to see themselves. And in many ways women's bookstores have been our backbone."

Thomas, who is also director of development/special gifts of the Library Foundation of San Francisco and head of the Gay and Lesbian Center slated to open in 1995 in that city's new main library, praises Inland's David Wilk for recognizing the cultural force of women's publishing.

Founded in 1981, Inland has expanded its service to small publishers with InBook, a merged division that has exclusive distribution rights for the books of over 50 publishers. Spinsters, Firebrand Books, Cleis Press, The Women's Press, Lace Publications and Third House Publishers now have their inventories at InBook, as do such publishers of gay men's books as Alyson, Amethyst Press, Banned Books and Gay Men's Press. Wilk estimates that 20% of

Inland's sales are derived from lesbian and gay books. "But it's hard to say, since we don't break out our sales by subject. But I will say it's been a crucial part of our business, and as we've grown it's grown. Gay and lesbian presses have always been at the heart of progressive publishing, which is our orientation."

Barbara Smith of Kitchen Table: Women of Color Press in Latham, N.Y., candidly admits that she would like to sign on with InBook but feels she publishes too few books. But as a publisher with deep roots in social activism and as a shaping force in black women's studies, Smith has an impact that far outweighs the size of her list. Her *Home Girls: A Black Feminist Anthology,* which has sold 25,000 copies, and *But Some of Us Are Brave,* winner of the Outstanding Women of Color Award and edited with Gloria T. Hull and Patricia Bell Scott, continue to be influential. "Our books have an authentic focus on the real lives of women," says Smith.

Kitchen Table Press has added poet Audre Lorde's *Need: A Chorale of Black Woman Voices* to its Freedom Organizing Pamphlet series. Lorde has also published with Norton, but Smith agrees with Thomas that large trade publishers tend not to be on the cutting edge. John Preston, who writes a column on publishing for the bimonthly *Lambda Book Report,* has made the observation that lesbian writers who first published with women's presses are often ambivalent about publishing commercially.

Joan Nestle published *Women on Women: An Anthology of American Lesbian Short Fiction,* edited with Naomi Holoch, at Plume, because she hoped to find a wide audience for the "wonderful women" in the collection. But Nestle—who founded the Herstory Story archive in New York, and who will give the first endowed Kessler lecture at CUNY's Center for Lesbian and Gay Studies this fall—thinks she could not have gotten her start as a writer without the courage of Nancy Bereano, Firebrand's publisher. She was also saddened by Sasha Alyson's recent decision to seek buyers for his press and leave publishing altogether. He published her most recent book, *The Persistent Desire: A Femme-Butch Reader,* and she thinks small presses have played an essential role in nurturing gay and lesbian liberation.

Susie Bright, former editor of *On Our Backs* magazine (billed as for "the Adventurous Lesbian") furthered her renown with *Susie Sexpert's Lesbian Sex World* (Cleis), and has added to it with *Herotica 2* (Plume), which follows the original *Herotica,* from San Francisco's Down There Press.

UPs Deepen the Scholarship

University presses also are adding to their lists of books on gay and lesbian subjects. David Bartlett, Temple University Press's director and the president of AAUP, sees a parallel between this development and the growing awareness of gay and lesbian issues on university campuses. Courses in gay and lesbian studies, sometimes offered under the auspices of gender studies, are being established at many schools, and university presses not only reflect what is happening in their home institutions but the culture as well. Under Bartlett's guidance, Temple University

Press has started a list in the interdisciplinary area of gay and lesbian studies, the latest entry of which is editor Suzanne Sherman's *Lesbian and Gay Marriage: Private Commitments, Public Ceremonies.* [In fall 1992] Columbia University Press will publish Ellen Zweig's *The Homoerotic Photograph: Male Images From Durieu/Delacroix to Mapplethorpe* in its Between Men-Between Women series. The University of Minnesota Press is launching a gay and lesbian studies series with David Savran's *Communists, Cowboys, and Queers: The Politics of Masculinity in the Work of Arthur Miller and Tennessee Williams.* New York University Press recently published a 20th-anniversary edition of Karla Jay and Allen Young's *Out of the Closets: Voices of Gay Liberation,* with a foreword by John D'Emilio, and announced a new series devoted to lesbian life and literature, called Cutting Edge. Other university presses have sprinkled their lists with gender studies books, often ones that focus on gay and lesbian subjects. And many of these books are selling surprisingly well, according to editor Ann Miller of Columbia.

But historian George Chauncey thinks few if any of these books will have the impact of John Boswell's *Christianity, Social Tolerance, and Homosexuality,* now a landmark book of interdisciplinary history, which the University of Chicago Press published in 1980 after several other presses had rejected it. Chauncey emphasizes that Chicago senior editor Doug Mitchell made the effort to sign the book and contends that gay and lesbian scholars are in Mitchell's debt whether they know his name or not. Modestly taken aback by such praise, Mitchell insists that Boswell's scholarship was so outstanding that it simply *had* to be published. But in 1980, he admits, few people knew what gender studies were. Today, Chicago publishes a large series of gender studies books.

Author Martin Duberman, who is also director of the Center for Lesbian and Gay Studies at City University of New York, has noted a parallel between what is happening in academia and publishing. Just as Lambda Rising and A Different Light compile their catalogues, Duberman's Center is compiling a syllabus to all the gay and lesbian studies courses now being offered across the country. Savvy marketers have already identified the students in those classes, many of them in literature, as an expanding market.

But not everyone is energized by what's happening in gay and lesbian publishing and bookselling. There have been repeated reports of stores being pressured into removing gay and lesbian books from their shelves. Sales reps have found that in many parts of the country such books aren't welcome or are stocked only by alternative stores. And Beacon Press has had difficulty in finding a printer for *Gay Ideas: Outing and Other Controversies* by Richard D. Mohr, who teaches at the University of Illinois-Urbana. Mohr is the founding general editor of Columbia's Between Men-Between Women series, but his own book has been rejected by a number of university presses (in part because of its provocative illustrations), becoming a *cause célèbre* in the process. His experience shows that despite the growth of gay and lesbian studies courses, many in academia remain timorous.

The poet Adrienne Rich delivered this year's Bill Whitehead lecture at the Lambda Book Awards banquet in Anaheim. In her speech, which evoked a stirring ovation, she
challenged her audience to be vigilant:

> Writers matter in a society to the extent that we
> can help that society hear its unvoiced longings,
> encounter its erased and disregarded selves,
> break with complacency, numbness, despair.
> Lesbian and gay writers have developed fertile
> stratagems to critique social hypocrisy, unlock
> closets of self-hatred. We are now irrevocably
> facing, along with everyone else, deep social cre-
> vasses, in which human lives are being swal-
> lowed up as devastatingly as AIDS continues to
> swallow up so many. . . . What will we do now
> with our imaginations, our words, our access to
> print?

(pp. 36-40)

*Bob Summer, "A Niche Market Comes of
Age," in* Publishers Weekly, *Vol. 239, No. 29,
June 29, 1992, pp. 36-40.*

HOMOSEXUAL DISCOURSE

David Bergman   (essay date 1991)

[*In the following excerpt, taken from his* Gaiety Transfigured: Gay Self-Representation in American Literature, *Bergman examines the influence of predominant
heterosexual views on the structure of homosexual discourse.*]

Robert Gluck could have been speaking for virtually all
gay authors when he wrote, "Society wants its stories; I
want to return to society the story it has made." For gay
writers have not generally tried to create their own mythology independent of the heterosexual world; rather in
the last three hundred years, they have sought to modify
the sexual terms they have received, inscribing less a "reverse discourse" of homosexuality, than a subdominant
one, a transcription of the original into a distant, unrelated
key. As [Michel] Foucault acknowledged [in *The History
of Sexuality*], "There is not, on the one side, a discourse
of power, and opposite, another discourse that runs counter to it. Discourses are tactical elements or blocks operating in the field of force relations." Since homosexuals have
fashioned their sense of themselves out of and in response
to the heterosexual discourse about them, homosexuality—even as conceived by homosexuals—cannot be viewed
outside of the constructs of heterosexuality.

Jonathan Dollimore has identified the two major strategies homosexual men and women use to fashion their
sense of what homosexuality is and who homosexuals are.
The first strategy is fitting homosexuality within categories valorized by heterosexuality. For example, since heterosexuality approves of sex that is "natural," gay writers
showed that homosexuality is "natural," and, thus, wor-

thy of approval. Discussing *The Well of Loneliness,* Dollimore writes, "Radclyffe Hall not only appropriates the
'authority' of the medical discourse currently transferring
homosexuality from the realm of crime to that of nature;
she also brilliantly merges and so transforms the medical
model with other positive identifications usurped from the
dominant culture." Yet Dollimore finds this strategy ultimately unsatisfying because "it authenticates both the
dominant and the subordinate, unable to acknowledge
fully the extent to which the former negates the latter. . . . it seeks legitimacy for its deviant hero/ine in the
categories of the very order which denies her legitimacy."

Instead Dollimore prefers a more radical strategy, one
perfected by Oscar Wilde, who changed the categories of
approval while accepting the dominant assessment of homosexuality. Wilde's method, according to Dollimore "is
inversion and hierarchical reversal, especially the substitu-
tion of surface for depth and the superficial for the essential." Wilde finds unnaturalness as the chief virtue of homosexuality; for him "artificial" is a term of approbation.
Yet this second strategy also has its weakness: dependence
on the categories it attempts to invert and subvert. No
matter what means radically gay writers have used in their
attempts to break from the discourse of the heterosexual,
they have remained tied to it, according to Dollimore, in
a "violent dialectic."

Because homosexuality in Euro-American culture is so
tied to the dominant culture from which it emerges, and
because its terms and values are generated out of the "violent dialectic" with that discourse, it is mistaken to connect the structure of current, western homosexuality with
the male-male sexual activity of other times or cultures.
The modern Euro-American homosexual views him- or
herself in vastly different ways than the Greek pederast or
the Melanesian pubescent. Though both progay and anti-
gay forces have linked Euro-American homosexuality to
institutional male sex in other cultures—especially the
Greeks—such linkage only further distorts and obscures
the nature of homosexuality in Europe and North America.

One must, I believe, distinguish sexual relations between
men generally—what we may call "intramale sexuality"—from the sexual relations between men that has occurred in Euro-American society since the eighteenth century, what is generally termed "homosexuality." Homosexuality is the specific form of intramale sexuality that
has developed within the framework of institutionalized
heterosexuality, an antithesis, which gives heterosexuality
its particular force and focus and has acted to alter and
enrich—as Edward Carpenter and others have noted so
long ago—the structure of Euro-American culture.

Homosexuality and other forms of sex between males get
confused because they occur simultaneously in this society. According to the Kinsey Institute intramale sexual relations are a common (if undiscussed) part of American
life. In the original study, Kinsey and his colleagues found
that 60 percent of all males had had at least one sexual experience to orgasm with another male. Yet Kinsey indicated that only 10 percent of all males were "more or less exclusively homosexual" for three years or more, and a cer-

tain percentage of these numbers had engaged in such relations only during adolescence. Such individuals do not in the main regard themselves or their actions as homosexual nor does society regard them as such. Instead, the activity falls under the rubric of "experimentation" or "sexual release," perfectly acceptable heterosexual outlets of libido. The discourse of heterosexuality allows for a large number of contingencies in which the ostensibly heterosexual male may engage in sexual relations with other males. As James Baldwin has remarked, "Straight cats invented faggots so they can sleep with them without becoming faggots themselves." Prisoners engaged in intramale sexual acts, for example, may avoid the label of homosexual, provided that they are confined to single-sex institutions and that upon release they revert to heterosexual relations. Male prostitutes, especially "street hustlers," do not have to regard themselves as homosexuals—though many do—if they engage in such practices *only* for money.

The complexity of society's rules governing who must and who cannot be considered homosexual is epitomized in the population Bruce Jackson studies in "Deviance as Success: The Double Inversion of Stigmatized Roles." Male prisoners divide themselves sexually into three groups: queens, those who are homosexual outside of prison; studs, those who while in prison play the inserter role with other men; punks, those who while in prison play the receptor. If asked, studs and punks, in this system, say they played their roles because they are denied access to women. Jackson argues, however, that many of "those argot-role actors . . . would very much like to be homosexual outside, but they just *did not know how*" (Jackson's italics). According to Jackson, "prison was the only place they had a moral structure that permitted them to be acting-out homosexuals, a place where there was a grand body of folk culture that legitimized their behavior." Consequently, these men often commit crimes immediately after their release so that they can be returned to prison where they may reenter their desired sexual roles. "By adopting the convict stigma they were enabled to act out the homosexual roles without any of the attendant stigma they would have suffered (and self-applied) in the free world." Their male egos can better accept being criminal than being gay.

Sexual identity and sexual practice are frequently separate in the discourse of both homo- and heterosexuality. In both discourses, the way you feel about what you do is far more important than what you do, and your experience of the sexual act is more determinate of its nature than the identity of the person with whom it is performed. Under the code of heterosexuality, some sexual roles are taboo for those men who wish to retain their heterosexual identity. Often the conditions under which an act is performed determine its acceptability. But the most important factor in determining the nature of a particular act is the kind of emotional and psychological awareness involved in its performance. People recognize themselves as homosexual without ever having sexual relations; similarly the vast majority of males who have had sex with other males regard themselves as heterosexuals. Individuals seem to hold within themselves a subtle, graduated scale which determines the spectrum lying between hetero- and homo-

sexual experience. David Leavitt's novel *The Lost Language of Cranes* chronicles the evolution of awareness as a man moves from exclusive heterosexuality to intramale sexual activity, and ultimately, to homosexual consciousness. His is the classic progression found in "the coming-out story," the homosexual *Bildungsroman*.

David M. Halperin argues in *One Hundred Years of Homosexuality,* his study of "Greek love," what is more important to the Greeks in establishing sexuality is the style of one's desires. The Greeks, according to Halperin, "constructed male desire as wide-ranging, acquisitive, and object-directed, while constructing feminine desire . . . as objectless, passive, and entirely determined by the female body's need for regular phallic irrigation." Since boys and male slaves possessed a feminine desire, they could service male desire just as satisfactorily as women. Halperin believes this emphasis on the style of desire rather than on the sex of the object of desire is a central contrast between Greek sexuality and modern American sexuality, but it seems to me that stylistics of desire is exactly what distinguishes the homosexual from the heterosexual male who engages in periodic sex with other men, what distinguishes in James Baldwin's terms, the "faggot" from the "straight cats" who "sleep with them." The stylistics of desire remains a determining factor in sexual identity.

What then is the structure of the discourse of homosexual experience? How does it differ from the discourse of intramale sexuality? And how is it related to heterosexuality? There are, I believe, several axes around which one can distinguish the homosexual from other sexual discourses.

1. The most significant term and the one from which the other differences derive is otherness. Although a sense of otherness affects us all, the otherness that affects the homosexual—or effects his sense of homosexuality—is more profound. For while otherness is an unavoidable part of any self's awareness of its own subjectivity and its difference to other persons around it, the homosexual suffers a categorical, perhaps even ontological, otherness since he is made to feel his "unlikeness" to the heterosexual acts and persons who gave him being. The otherness of the homosexual is not merely a heightening of the separateness which is a central feature of the ego structure of the heterosexual male, a separateness created by the hard and fixed boundaries heterosexual males erect both to protect their egos from the dangers of castration and to further their identifications with their fathers. The homosexual's separateness occurs with neither firm boundaries nor with heightened identification with the father. He is distanced without definition. Herbert Blau has spoken eloquently of the "egolessness in the diplomacy of the anus" which characterizes the site of homosexual desire. The very object world of the homosexual differs from that of the heterosexual so that he is constantly inscribing himself in Blau's phrase, in the "heraldic sign . . . which presupposes no first person, no ego, no *face* of power." This negativity of self mirrors the sociological fact that no homosexual is raised as such; he finds no likeness in the family circle. Thus, the homosexual misses the bonding and identification which for the heterosexual bridges the gap between

himself and others. Indeed the family reminds the homosexual of his own "unlikeness."

2. Homosexuality, unlike other intramale sexual states, is a lifelong condition. It is not a "phase" that one goes through, as heterosexual males go through a "phase" of homoeroticism. Nor is it a ritualized period of behavior as it was in the culture of the ancient Greeks or as it is in the Melanesian society which Gilbert Herdt has so exhaustively studied in *Guardians of the Flute*. In these cultures specific sexual roles are determined by age. The male passes from one intrasexual role to another, at the end of which in Sambian society he becomes exclusively heterosexual. In contrast Euro-American homosexuality is for all ages.

3. A corollary of the lifelong condition of homosexuality is its genuineness of experience. Homosexuality is not a passing fancy or a substitute for heterosexual contact. The "heterosexual" male prisoner who has repeated sex with another man claims that his sexual activity is merely a substitute for his real desire which is for a woman. The homosexual, however, experiences his desire for men as genuine and often characterizes heterosexual activities in contrast as "shallow" or "false" or "pretended."

4. Finally, homosexuality differs from other intramale sexual relations and heterosexual relations by the equality of its relations. By equality I do not mean that in individual relationships the partners are equal—clearly, such is not the case—but rather that the institution of homosexuality does not assign specific roles to specific individuals. In Sambia, ancient Greece, or in parts of Africa, roles are rigidly polarized. Older, dominant, or ostensibly heterosexual males may—if they wish—play the inserter role in anal or oral intercourse. But they must *not* play the receptor role without being stigmatized. Younger, subordinate, and ostensibly homosexual males can *only* play the receptor roles. In Euro-American homosexuality these roles are not proscribed; indeed, homosexuality has developed a remarkable fluidity of roles and role-playing that cuts across racial, social, and cultural boundaries. No doubt, hierarchical forces come to play their part in homosexual relations—homosexuality exists only within the patriarchy—but homosexuality is more notable in the way it resists hierarchies than in the way it bends to them.

These may not be the only four terms that differentiate homosexual from either intramale sexual or heterosexual discourse, but they are significant terms and in combination give homosexuality and the homosexual their distinctive idiom of expression.

Otherness was not a homosexual invention; the term was applied to gay men by the discourse of heterosexuality. Indeed, heterosexual discourse calculated and labeled the homosexual with all the permutations of otherness. He was *not* Christian, *not* natural, *not* manly, *not* a woman, *not* of the heterosexual's country or region or continent, *not* human, *not* animal, *not* even to be named. An anonymous editor wrote in 1699 as preface to the proceeding of the trial against Lord Castlehaven for various sexual offenses, that the abomination

shocks our natures and puts our modesty to

blush so commonly perpetrated . . . the devilish and unnatural sin of buggery, a crime that sinks a man below the basest epithet, is so foul it admits of no aggravation and cannot be expressed in its horror, but by the doleful shrieks and groans of the damned. . . . The sin [is] now being translated from sodomitical original, or from the Turkish and Italian copies into English.

The editor would like to believe that no Englishman, by himself, could have sunk to buggery without foreign and demonic influence. The very term "buggery"—a corruption of "Bulgarian," a nationality in which heresy and perversion were thought to flourish—suggests the foreign nature of the vice. The editor has used virtually all the categories of negation to assert the otherness of sodomy, but the otherness of homosexuality is perhaps most dramatically presented by the failure of language to give it a name. It can be known, according to the editor, only by being "translated" or through "copies," which are less horrible than its native tongue.

Yet one must question whether the feeling of otherness proceeds from the recognition (even subconscious) of being homosexual, or whether it precedes and lays the groundwork for homosexuality. In their memoirs, gay men repeatedly speak of feeling "different" before they have any sense of their sexual orientation. Richard Isay, a psychoanalyst, claims that "almost all the gay men" he has treated "report that, starting from the age of four, they felt that they were 'different' from their peers." This sense of being "different" begins long before any conscious awareness of their sexual orientation. In *If It Die* [Andre] Gide recalls how at the age of ten and for no apparent reason he broke into uncontrollable sobs at the dining room table. Without understanding the cause of his enormous sorrow, he wailed to his mother, "I am not like other people. I am not like other people . . ." For Gide, "It was as though the special sluice-gate of some unknown, unbounded, mystic sea had suddenly been opened and an overwhelming flood poured into my heart."

But not just people like Gide, whose extraordinary sensibility might account for such perceptions of otherness, record such experiences; ordinary gay men have reported the same feelings. One of the most striking accounts appears in Claude Hartland's autobiography *The Story of a Life* published in St. Louis in 1901. Hartland "offers to the medical world the strange story of [his] own life, hoping that it may be a means by which other similar sufferers may be reached and relieved." At the age of nine, Hartland is sent with two or three brothers to school; "the first day," he recalls, "brought me to realize how different I was from other boys of my own age." Many children, affected by the fear and anxiety of leaving home and starting school, are made self-consciously aware of their differences. But Hartland's sense of difference is, compared with his brothers', beyond the normal discomfort and self-consciousness. It is a force that separates him. This was not the first time Hartland had felt different, but the first time he could *judge* the difference.

At four, which is "as far back as [his] memory extends," he comes to feel "I was not like other children," wording remarkably similar to Gide's formulation. His recognition comes after burning three of his fingers and having them bandaged in splints. One may wonder whether the burnt fingers represent some subconscious desire for castration or whether the "stalls" in which they are wrapped represent erections, yet such symbols are far beyond Hartland's conscious awareness, for what is particularly striking about his memoir is its innocence of any other published work on sexual inversion. Although by 1901, Havelock Ellis had published *Sexual Inversion* and Oscar Wilde had stood for his highly publicized trial, Hartland seems completely unaware of such events. His expressions of otherness have all the painful genuineness of the naive. His is no self-conscious trope, but the guileless—if lachrymose and pietistic—confessions of a sufferer.

The homosexual's otherness is particularly distinguished from the difference or alienation we might expect in all persons brought up in Euro-American culture in the last three or four hundred years, a separateness in which each in the cell of himself is aware of others in their cells. Under such conditions, one's particular sense of otherness is at least partially ameliorated by the awareness of one's likeness to others in a similar state of isolation. [Theodor] Adorno, for example [in his essay "Subject and Object"], writes of the necessary epistemological separation of subject and object, in which subjectivity must constitute itself as other in order to regard itself at all. Yet, according to Adorno, that split is almost immediately mediated by ideology, which—he states in language that already anticipates the triumph of heterosexism—"is indeed its normal form." In the "normal form," "the sense of identity of mind . . . repressively shapes its Other in its own image." The dominance of the social order operates to mediate through narcissistic reflexivity the breach between subject and object. But the homosexual is not open to the normal forms of mediation; since he does not identify with the dominant father, the ideology of dominance cannot perform the same assuagement of the epistemological rupture that it can perform for the heterosexual. At best he is left with the sublime onrush of the undifferentiated that Gide describes as the "overwhelming flood" of "some unknown, unbounded, mystic sea." Rather than bridge the epistemological split by narcissism, the homosexual fills the gap with his unlikeness. For the rigid boundedness of the heterosexual male's ego structure, he posits unbounded, undifferentiated otherness.

The homosexual is made to feel the weight of his otherness in yet another manner that distinguishes it from the general alienation of society, for the homosexual is made to bear the onus of the heterosexual's homophobic paranoia. "Freud's famous 'persecutory paranoia,'" Guy Hocquenghem reminds us, "is in actual fact a paranoia that *seeks to persecute*" (Hocquenghem's italics). The homosexual's sense of persecution is *not* a fantasy, but a social reality, and yet he is made to feel his anxiety as his own distortion. Indeed, for Hocquenghem, the official discourse of homosexuality is produced by the homosexual panic of ostensibly heterosexual institutions. "Society's discourse," he argues "is the fruit of the paranoia through which a dominant sexual mode [heterosexuality] . . .

manifests its anxiety at the suppressed but constantly recurring sexual modes [homosexuality]."

But not all homosexuals find their otherness to be the stigma heterosexual discourse has labeled it. As Mary McIntosh observed in the sixties, homosexuals "welcome and support the notion of their otherness because it appears to justify the deviant behavior as being appropriate for [them]." Indeed, many transform otherness from a mark of shame into the very sign of their superiority. As Dollimore has pointed out, no one has done more to invert the categories of heterosexual discourse than Oscar Wilde. In his *De Profundis,* a work inscribed by the abyss of otherness, Wilde seeks to overturn the language that has dominated him. Despite his imprisonment, he proudly declares: "I am far more of an individualist that I ever was. My nature is seeking a fresh mode of self-realization. That is all I am concerned with." And later he asserts, "I am one of those who are made for exceptions, not for laws."

Usually, however, gay writers have not attempted to overturn the category of otherness so directly or so personally. One of the forms that gay writers have particularly favored is the ethnographic account or essay. Melville in *Typee* and *Mardi,* Charles Warren Stoddard in *South-Sea Idylls* and *The Island of Tranquil Delights,* Gide in his *Travels in the Congo,* Edward Carpenter in his *Intermediate Types Among Primitive Folk* and *Iolaus: Anthology of Friendship,* Edward Karsch-Haack in *The Same-Sex Life of Primitive Peoples,* Edward Westermarck in "Homosexual Love," and Tobias Schneebaum in *Keep the River on Your Right,* all have sought to legitimize otherness by finding other cultures that have accepted intramale sex. Indeed no literary form was more congenial to gay writers of the nineteenth and early twentieth centuries than the ethnographic study, and it was in ethnographic discourse that homosexual writers often found the terms for their own attacks on heterosexuality. As I explore in the chapter on the conjunction of homosexuality and cannibalism, ethnography provides the gay writer with the opportunity to subvert several types of otherness. The foreign, attacked by xenophobic heterosexual discourse, is elevated, and the pagan (non-Christian) is extolled for its honesty, vision, and humanity. But the most important effect of gay ethnography is its assertion of the naturalness of homosexuality. Gay writers are at pains to show that exclusive heterosexuality is an artificial barrier erected against the polymorphous perversity of nature.

Though we cannot doubt the power of heterosexual discourses to affect consciousness and to make their own reality, nevertheless, they do not explain why the four-year-old Hartland—who has yet to be labeled by society, feel its stigmatization, or even be aware of his sexual orientation—should conceive of himself as other. Some other force must come into play that affects, not so much his sexual orientation, as his ego development at the early stages of object-relations. Though one can imagine a number of scenarios that might lead to a homosexual orientation, the evidence of gay writing suggests that one's identity as other precedes and prepares for the later development of a homosexual identity.

Though children who will become homosexual have

strong feelings toward their fathers—often warm, loving feelings toward them—they rarely identify with them. Nor do many identify with their mothers. Indeed, this early sense of otherness seems to reflect alienation from both parents, a vague, amorphous, and potentially empty selfhood. But though the child does not identify with his father, he is repeatedly encouraged to admire and emulate the father, and what the son cannot be he wishes to love and be loved by. His failed identification charges the father with additional desirableness.

The crisis for the gay child is in the tension between other people's views and expectations of him, and the views and expectations he has of himself. "The conscious feeling of having a personal identity is based on two simultaneous observations," according to Erik Erikson [in his *Identity: Youth and Crisis*], "the perception of selfsameness and continuity of one's existence in time and space and the perception of the fact that others recognize one's sameness and continuity." The son who will be gay learns early that how he is perceived differs sharply from how he perceives himself. But to the loss of "personal identity" is added the loss of what Erikson calls "ego identity" when the *"style of one's individuality"* does not coincide with "one's *meaning for significant others* in the immediate community" (Erikson's italics). Erikson's analysis permits us to view the modes of homosexual transformation of heterosexual otherness. The homosexual child experiences a sense of limitlessness, an otherness unbounded by the forms and shapes of his parents. But being free of any specific form, the child is free to put on any number of masks, or, . . . in some Whitmanesque expansion, absorb within himself the various styles around him. Insofar as the feelings of otherness stem from the structure of the bourgeois family, such feelings are part of a historical constellation and not a necessary part of intramale sexual relations.

These ways of dealing with otherness develop early in children and may, in fact, determine the success with which they deal with their sexual orientation later in life. John Addington Symonds's *Memoirs,* which was expressly written to provide a picture of the development and life of a homosexual, grants us the opportunity to examine the style of his individuality. "It is significant," he insists,

> that two tales made a deep impression. . . . One was Andersen's story of the ugly duckling. I sympathized passionately with the poor bird swimming round and round the duck-puddle. I cried convulsively when he flew away to join the beautiful wide-winged white brethren. . . . Thousands of children have undoubtedly done the same, for it is a note of childhood, in souls destined for expansion, to feel solitary and disbarred from privileges due to them. The other [was] called "The Story Without End." . . . The mystical, dreamy communion with nature in wild woods and leafy places took my fancy.

In his passionate sympathy for the duckling, Symonds identified with what was "solitary and disbarred from privileges," but such loss prepared him for the communion with all of nature. Later Symonds could throw himself into a state of "gradual but swiftly progressive obliteration of space, time and sensation" in which he achieved

"a pure, absolute, abstract self" and "the apprehension of coming dissolution."

In defending itself against homosexuality, patriarchal discourse has tried to deny both its permanence and its genuineness. All three of the ways in which patriarchy has conceived of homosexuality—as sin, crime, and disease—place it within frameworks that deny it permanence since sins may be overcome, crimes avoided, and diseases cured.

On the two occasions in western history when society has bothered to recognize intramale sexuality—as part of Greek culture and as a biblical abomination—the focus has been on those relations that were phaseal or fashionable. The Greek model of pederastia—which has largely been ignored but cannot be forgotten—assigns sexual and emotional roles by age. In the *Symposium* Socrates envisions a hierarchy of erotic states which culminates in a purely spiritual love. The Bible conceives of intramale sexual relations as a foreign import—a fashion adopted from outside of the tribe. In 1 Maccabees is an account of how Hebrew men "made themselves prepuces . . . and joined themselves to [Romans]" (1:15) whom they admired in the bathhouses and gymnasiums, and Paul is particularly upset by early Christians adopting the Roman sexual fashion of homosexuality. Heterosexual discourse has sought to limit homosexuality to the passing fad or a certain phase of development. As horrible as sodomy is in heterosexual discourse, it can have no permanent hold.

Patriarchal insistence on the impermanence of homosexual desire reappears in psychoanalytic theory which hypothesizes homosexuality as "arrested sexual development." For Freud every male (or female) goes through a period of bisexuality in which both mother and father are cathected objects. Homosexuality, thus, is "normally" a temporary and transitional stage; its prolongation in some people constitutes its abnormality. What the psychoanalyst attempts to do—though Freud *never* believes that it is possible—is to alleviate this infantile fixation and lead the homosexual toward a permanent heterosexual adjustment. In so doing, most psychoanalytic theory reinscribes even lifelong homosexuality within the transitional.

Popular gay literature, however, systematically distinguishes between phasic intramale sexual acts (which are accepted within the discourse of heterosexuality because they are empty of significance) and the "genuine" homosexual act. Aaron Fricke's *Reflections of a Rock Lobster,* written while Fricke was still a teenager, distinguishes the boundaries between accepted and unacceptable same-sex activities. Though once a participant in the sexual play that occurred in his grade school boys' bathroom, he drops out of such games in the fourth grade from fear of discovery. Explains Fricke: "At this point, I was already conscious that I was a homosexual." As a homosexual he can no longer freely and unselfconsciously join in the fun. What he discovered, and what he fears others will discover, is his genuine pleasure in these activities. Such pleasures can be enjoyed only if they are not desired. In Fricke's case, desire terminates pleasure.

Fricke reverses the entire category of permanence: for him heterosexuality seems vague, impermanent, unfixed, and unreal. His father's anxious explanation of "the raw truth about heterosexuality" did not elicit in the twelve-year-old Aaron the desired shock of recognition:

> The concept of heterosexuality did not immediately sink in. I didn't reject it, I just found it difficult to swallow. *This* was the alternative that had somehow eluded me through childhood years. *This* was the thing that separated me from the beasts. . . . Surely it didn't have anything to do with me; I had no desire to try any of these heterosexual techniques. It all seemed like just conjecture; I didn't believe it could ever affect *me.* (Fricke's italics).

The "genuine" is the homosexual, for Fricke; the heterosexual is mere illusion, the *Arabian Nights* tale of patriarchal authority.

If Fricke's uncertainty places in question the "naturalness" of heterosexuality, Oscar Wilde subverts the approved categories even more radically. As Dollimore has shown, Wilde questions the very categories of patriarchal approval, subverting Max Nordau and Cesare Lombroso's concept of degeneration in which certain moral habits disintegrate through overuse or interbreeding. Wilde begins with the seemingly humble confession that he is a victim of his own excess. "I let myself be lured into long spells of senseless and sensual ease. . . . I became the spendthrift of my own genius, and to waste an eternal youth gave me a curious joy. Tired of being on the heights, I deliberately went to the depths in search of new sensations" (*De Profundis*). He would have us believe that his homosexuality results from boredom with the common and "healthier" forms of sexuality. His pleasure in normal sexual acts exhausted, where else could he turn but to the arms of men? "People thought it dreadful," he wrote, "to have entertained at dinner the evil things of life." But Wilde is not to be ruled by what others think. "From the point of view through which I, as an artist in life, approach them they were delightfully suggestive and stimulating. It was like feasting with panthers" (*De Profundis*). Since desire, for Wilde, gains its allure from being transitory and from its ability to both construct and deconstruct the desirer and the object of his desire, heterosexuality is no more permanent to the artist than homosexuality. Desire and its objects—if worth the desiring—are valuable *because* they are mutable. Wilde believes that nothing worth having should last forever.

To argue that homosexuality is, on the one hand, historically contingent and, on the other hand, lifelong and permanent may appear contradictory. Permanence seems to place homosexuality into an essentialist frame of reference at odds with the historicism of the rest of the analysis. But though homosexuality is permanent for those reared at a certain historical moment, it is not transhistorical or universal. What makes it difficult to separate the permanence of homosexuality from essentialism is that the very discourse of sexuality is itself grounded in humanistic and essentialist terms. But like class awareness—which is a historical contingency, but an inescapable component of our psyches—so, too, does homosexuality insist upon its permanence even as it dreams of a time when people and acts are no longer differentiated into sexual categories.

The most radical innovation of modern homosexuality is the egalitarian ideal to which it aspires. The discourse of equality between sexual partners distinguished Euro-American homosexuality from many forms of intramale sexual activity. Alan Bray, who has studied the emergence of a distinctly homosexual lifestyle and its beginning in England at the end of the seventeenth century, links the construction of homosexuality to changes in heterosexuality. Homosexuality, according to Bray, is a product of what Lawrence Stone has called "affective individualism," the more private domestic and affectional relationships which replaced the kinship, client-oriented, community-based relationships as the cement of the family. Homosexuality could not develop until men began to look at their own affections as the reason for intimate relations.

Although hysterically stigmatized by clerical and judicial authority in the early seventeenth century, sodomy was punished only when the perpetrator violated patriarchal order. In general, according to Bray, homosexuality was invisible because it developed no subculture and, more important, it respected and imitated the hierarchical structures of patriarchy. "Despite the contrary impression given by legal theorists," writes Bray, "so long as homosexual activity did not disturb the peace or the social order, and in particular so long as it was consistent with patriarchal mores, it was largely in practice ignored." As evidence, Bray cites the noticeable absence of prosecutions between master and servant, teacher and student, guildman and apprentice.

With the advent of molly houses—places of homosexual assignation—come the first mass arrests of homosexuals in England. For Bray, the reason is clear: "The society of the molly houses did not follow class lines but rather tended to dissolve them. It did so because it was not mediated by existing social forms, of class, or otherwise: it was set alongside them, a social institution in its own right." Molly houses were symbolic of, indeed, seemed to be the only structure in the homosexual subculture. In the tendency to dissolve class lines—the hierarchy of the patriarchy—homosexuality challenged the basic categories of patriarchal discourse and found itself immediately oppressed.

I do not mean to say that homosexuality achieves the democratic vista to which it aspires. Michael Moon, for example, sees in the homoerotic world of Horatio Alger's novels "an encapsulation of corporate/capitalist America's long-cherished myth." Michael Pollak has argued that "of all the different types of masculine sexual behavior, homosexuality is undoubtedly the one whose functioning is most strongly suggestive of a market." Patriarchal structures often reestablish themselves in their most nakedly oppressive forms within the gay community, but we must remember that Alger represents homosexuality in what Moon calls its most "fiercely repressed" form and Pollack discusses a limited historical and urban condition. Since gay men are raised within the patriarchy, they understandably import its features into their construction of homosexuality. What is notable is the degree to which they have resisted patriarchal hierarchies.

Against the patriarchal reinscriptions Moon and Pollack

find in the fictions and mores of homosexuals, Joseph Allen Boone places the American quest romance whose "socially subversive content [is] . . . filtered first through the private realm of individual desire." Boone finds three countertraditional possibilities in the "questing hero's escape from a marriage-oriented culture." Among those "possibilities" is "the elevation of mutuality—rather than polarity—in the male bond [which] presents a conceptual alternative to the gender inequality institutionalized by marriage in heterosexual relations."

"Eros is a great leveler," declares Edward Carpenter, "perhaps the true Democracy rests, more firmly than anywhere else, on sentiment which easily passes the bounds of class and caste, and unites in the closest affection the most estranged ranks of society," those who fall into what Carpenter called "the intermediate sex" (*Intermediate Sex*). Like his hero Walt Whitman, Carpenter believed that homosexuals were in the vanguard of a new social order that would do away with class and sexual hierarchies and promote a true democracy. He was not alone. Goldsworthy Lowes Dickinson, C. R. Ashbee, John Addington Symonds, and Carpenter all tried to restructure their lives in ways which may not meet with our approval today, for as Jeffrey Weeks has commented, their encounters with working-class men could trail off into "avidly exploitive sexual colonialism." Nevertheless, they sought "the dream of class reconciliation." Homosexuality was one of the most important avenues by which generations of Englishmen broke through the barriers of class, privilege, and rank.

If this is true for the English, it is especially true for Americans. *Democratic Vistas* is based in large measure on the sexual politics of male adhesiveness. According to Robert K. Martin, Melville went even further than Whitman. "The homosexual relationship is invested by Melville with radical social potential," Martin argues; "it is through the affirmation of the values of nonaggressive male-bonded couples that the power of the patriarchy can be contested and even defeated" (*Hero*). The marriage of Queequeg and Ishmael constitutes a primal transgression against patriarchal rules; within the American racist and sexist ethos, no union could be more iconoclastic.

Despite formidable obstacles, the discourse of equality seems to have been translated widely into the lives of gay men. In *The Social Organization of Gay Males,* Joseph Harry and William B. DeVall have examined how gay men look at their relationships with their domestic partners. Their conclusion is that "rather than utilizing the conventional heterosexual marriage as a model for relationships, it seems that [gay] relationships are patterned after the nonexclusive conventional best friends model." When they examined the specific connection between income and decision-making roles, Harry and DeVall discovered that though "those who made more money reported that they made more decisions," such inequalities in gay relationships still did not "come near to approximating the inequalities of heterosexual marriages." In short, they conclude that "the marital relationships of gays tend to be modeled on the egalitarian friendship model." In fact, the egalitarianism of the relationship

translated into the bedroom where gay couples tended to exchange in reciprocal manner the various erotic positions.

However, lower-class gays tended to prefer less egalitarian relationships and more frequently used such inequalities to determine roles in sexual intercourse. Harry and DeVall infer that lower-class gays, just as their heterosexual counterparts, have much stronger tendencies to polarize roles. Inequalities seem to reflect social class, rather than sexual orientation.

Eve Kosofsky Sedgwick argues in *Between Men* that although the present society is both sexist and homophobic, "it has yet to be demonstrated that because most patriarchies structurally include homophobia, therefore patriarchy structurally *requires* homophobia." She continues: "the example of the Greeks demonstrates, I think, that while heterosexuality is necessary for the maintenance of a patriarchy, homophobia, against males at any rate, is not. In fact, for the Greeks, the continuum between 'men loving men' and 'men promoting the interests of men' appears to have been quite seamless." Sedgwick presents a telling argument for seeing all male behavior as existing on a continuum and viewing homosexuality as merely an extreme form of male bonding. Yet I believe a closer examination of the various structures of these same-sex relationships would reveal the distinction between intramale sexuality, which can be countenanced by the patriarchy, and homosexuality, which cannot be.

Sedgwick is mistaken when she says that the Greeks approved of "men loving men." Pederastia was approved only between men and boys, and the hierarchical relations were analogous—though not identical to—the relationship between men and women. To the Greeks a hairy bottom was a decided obstacle no masculine free-man would surmount. Alkaios writes:

> Nicander, ooh, your leg's got hairs!
> Watch they don't creep up into your arse.
> Because, darling, if they do, you'll soon know
> How the lovers flee you, and years go.

Strato is no less explicit about the relationship between age and sexual acceptability:

> I delight in the prime of a boy of twelve,
> but a thirteen-year-old's better yet.
> At fourteen he's Love's even sweeter flower,
> & one going on fifteen's even more delightful.
> Sixteen belongs to the gods, & seventeen . . .
> it's not for me, but Zeus to seek.
> If you want the older ones, you don't play
> any more, but seek & answer back.

Not only was there an acceptable limit to the boy's age, but as mentioned earlier, the sex roles were strictly apportioned. The older man had to be the inserter; the younger the receiver. Thus, Greek pederastia differed from Euro-American homosexuality by being phaseal and unequal, and by having pederasts experience no sense of otherness. It mirrored the patriarchal hierarchies of Athenian life and, therefore, did not threaten the structure of the patriarchy. Euro-American homosexuality, however, in its discourse of otherness, permanence, and equality, challenges the hierarchies of patriarchal structure.

Homosexuality has assumed a shape, a form, a language, which though borrowed from patriarchy, finds itself in a "violent dialectic" with it. It does not—by and large—comfortably rest in a continuum with other forms of male bonding or homosocial desire. Unlike other intramale sexual activities, it does not require the forcible exclusion of the feminine or triangulation through the feminine. By being based on terms of otherness, permanence, genuineness, and equality, homosexuality stands apart from the patriarchal terms that it has co-opted or inverted and will continue to remain structurally separate from the heterosexual discourse that gave it birth. (pp. 26-43)

> *David Bergman, "The Structure of Homosexual Discourse," in his* Gaiety Transfigured: Gay Self-Representation in American Literature, *The University of Wisconsin Press, 1991, pp. 26-43.*

GAY FICTION

Edmund White   (essay date 16 June 1991)

[*White is an acclaimed American novelist, short story writer, essayist, and critic, who has also edited* The Faber Book of Gay Short Fiction *(1992). In the following essay, he discusses the evolution of the gay male novel.*]

For me the revolution of the gay male novel has seemed breathlessly rapid and strangely personal. As a young teen-ager I looked desperately for things to read that might excite me or assure me I wasn't the only one, that might confirm an identity I was unhappily piecing together. In the early 1950's the only books I could find in the Evanston, Ill., Public Library were Thomas Mann's *Death in Venice* (which suggested that homosexuality was fetid, platonic and death-dealing) and the biography of Nijinsky by his wife (in which she obliquely deplored the demonic influence of the impresario Diaghilev on her saintly husband, the great dancer—an influence that in this instance had produced not death but madness).

In the 1960's I was lucky enough to discover *A Single Man* by Christopher Isherwood, a sane, unapologetic picture of George, a British professor living in Los Angeles whose lover has recently died. George muddles through a long, eventful day and confides his feelings to his straight friends, but these feelings are shown to be the same ones everyone knows—the suffering that arises from the death of loved ones, the numbing of routine, the fear of loneliness. The protagonist, neither more nor less witty or wise or courageous than his friends, is not presented as damned in ways supposedly peculiar to homosexuals.

I also came across André Gide's journals and his memoir *If It Die,* which showed a civilized adult mind given over

to far-ranging interests (classical piano music, Greek theater, Russian politics, travel in Africa) as well as to a veiled attraction to boys. William S. Burroughs's *Naked Lunch,* John Rechy's *City of Night* and Jean Genet's *Our Lady of the Flowers* moved in the opposite direction; they rendered gay life as exotic, marginal, even monstrous. Not incidentally, all of these books were original and genuine works of art. Burroughs's collage techniques, Rechy's ear for gay speech and sympathy for the gay underdog, Genet's way of turning ordinary values upside down—these were shock tactics for transforming our received notions of reality.

The beginning of gay liberation in 1969 did not produce a new crop of fiction right away, but by 1978 the new gay novel was beginning to emerge. That was the year Larry Kramer's controversial *Faggots* and Andrew Holleran's romantic *Dancer From the Dance* were published. Both books documented the new gay culture that had been spawned by liberation, prosperity and societal tolerance.

By 1979 seven New York gay writers, myself included; had formed a casual club named the Violet Quill. We'd meet once a month in one another's apartments. Four of us each time would read our latest pages, then settle down to high tea. The members were Felice Picano (who had written a gay psychological thriller, *The Lure,* and later on an elegiac love story, *Late in the Season*); Andrew Holleran (writing his second novel, *Nights in Aruba*); Robert Ferro (*The Family of Max Desir*); George Whitmore (*The Confessions of Danny Slocum* and *Nebraska*); Christopher Cox (*A Key West Companion*); Michael Grumley (then at work on *Life Drawing,* a lyrical autobiographical novel soon to be published posthumously). I was in the midst of my autobiographical novel *A Boy's Own Story.* Our occasional visitor was Vito Russo, who was writing the authoritative book about homosexuals in Hollywood, *The Celluloid Closet.*

I left the group in 1983, when I moved to Paris. When I came back to the States in 1990 this literary map had been erased. George Whitmore, Michael Grumley, Robert Ferro and Chris Cox were dead; Vito Russo was soon to die. Of our original group only Felice Picano, Andrew Holleran and I were still alive; better than anyone else, Holleran has captured the survivors' sense of living posthumously in his personal essays, *Ground Zero.* Many younger writers had also died; of those I knew I could count Tim Dlugos, Richard Umans, Gregory Kolovakos, the translator Matthew Word and the novelist John Fox (who'd been my student at Columbia). My two closest friends, the literary critic David Kalstone and my editor, Bill Whitehead, had also died.

For me these losses were definitive. The witnesses to my life, the people who had shared the same references and sense of humor, were gone. The loss of all the books they might have written remains incalculable.

The paradox is that AIDS which destroyed so many of these distinguished writers, has also, as a phenomenon, made homosexuality a much more familiar part of the American landscape. The grotesque irony is that at the very moment so many writers are threatened with extinction gay literature is healthy and flourishing as never before. Perhaps the two contradictory things are connected, since the tragedy of AIDS has made gay men more reflective on the great questions of love, death, morality and identity, the very preoccupations that have always animated serious fiction and poetry. Or perhaps AIDS has simply made gay life more visible. As a result even straight readers are curious to read books about this emerging, troubled world that throws into relief so many of the tensions of American culture.

Skeptics object that gay fiction is, after all, rather . . . specialized, ghettoized, limited. But those of us who write it are convinced that the potential audience for our work is no more circumscribed than it is for any other constituency. "It's no less universal than the writing of urban male Jews or black women," argues Michael Denneny of St. Martin's Press. "It's particularized—but so is all great fiction, as a second's consideration of Dostoyevsky, Synge or Flaubert should make clear. When reviewers say they're tired of reading about gay life, they're in the same position as Bill Moyers when he asked August Wilson if he ever got tired of talking about black life."

George Stambolian—the editor of three anthologies of gay fiction called *Men on Men*—is also convinced that gay lit has entered the mainstream. "We have to remember that America is a pluralistic society, and the pluralism also governs the evolution of its literature," he says. "In the past, our literature has been changed by writers from different ethnic and racial minorities, and that change has always involved struggle, a turf war for power. Now the time has come for gay fiction to renew American literature in the only way it can be renewed—by contesting its social and literary assumptions."

Not everyone, of course, looks at the matter in the same way. I recently attended the Out/Write writers' conference in San Francisco, along with some 1,800 lesbians and gay men; one of the keynote speakers, Edward Albee, was booed when he deplored the literary ghetto and suggested that writers who happened to be homosexual accomplished more when they were forced to disguise their feelings or infiltrate society from within—Proust, Mann, Forster. . . .

It seems to me I've heard every aspect of this question explored in the last decade. When the first European gay literary conference was held in London a few years back, not a single male writer from France accepted the invitation to attend; they all felt the sobriquet "gay writer" was insulting. I remember that when the French gay literary magazine *Masques* asked me if I was a gay writer, the editors told me I was the first writer they'd ever interviewed who answered yes.

The other extreme was expressed at the San Francisco Out/Write conference by a young short-story writer named Bo Huston, who said he thought the term "ghetto" was inappropriate; no one was forcing us to wear this label. Still, he was personally delighted to have an all-gay readership, he said, and wouldn't mind if in 50 years he was listed as a minor gay writer of the 90's.

What seems undeniable is that there *is* a gay literary move-

ment in America, even if no one can exactly define it. Gay short stories are appearing in such quality reviews as *Outlook, The James White Review, Christopher Street* and *Tribe*. Lesbian and gay studies are being introduced on many American campuses, and people who follow such things claim that these gender-related pursuits will soon enjoy the cachet that once belonged to semiotics and structuralism. Certainly an academic critic like Eve Kosofsky Sedgwick, whose *Epistemology of the Closet* was recently published (a study of Melville, Wilde, Nietzsche, James and Proust), is as highly esteemed as Yale's gay medieval historian John Boswell (*The Kindness of Strangers*) and the French feminist critic Luce Irigaray (*This Sex Which Is Not One*). Harvard recently sponsored a huge lesbian and gay conference, and Yale now has an extracurricular Center for Lesbian and Gay Studies. At Brown, where I teach, I'm currently offering a course in lesbian and gay literature that examines such classic authors as Virginia Woolf, Willa Cather, Djuna Barnes, Forster and Proust.

Arnold Dolin is a bit guarded about this renaissance. As the editor of the Plume imprint that includes gay paperback fiction at NAL/Dutton, whose 30 titles constitute perhaps the most successful gay male list in the States, he's well placed to express an opinion. "Even though there's a lot of talk about crossover books and the whole phenomenon of gay publishing," he told me, "my own impression is that the audience isn't growing. David Leavitt and Michael Cunningham"—two of the younger stars of gay fiction—"may be the only writers who've actually 'crossed over.'"

But enthusiasm within the publishing world itself belies this skepticism. The Publishing Triangle, a group of lesbian and gay editors and book people, now counts more than 250 members. Among other activities, it gives the annual Bill Whitehead Award to a gay writer for a lifetime of distinguished achievement. There are some 20 prosperous bookstores in the United States that specialize in lesbian and gay literature. While ordinary shops return unsold books after the shelf life of a mayfly, gay bookstores maintain year after year a strong backlist of gay titles—a durability that gives gay writers time to find their public. In addition, all of these stores have a large mail-order business. Glad Day in Boston, Giovanni's Room in Philadelphia, A Different Light in New York, San Francisco and Los Angeles are among leading stores, as is Lambda Rising, with outlets in Washington, Baltimore and Rehoboth Beach, Del.

Nor does Arnold Dolin's skepticism take into account Armistead Maupin, perhaps the biggest money-maker in gay publishing. His beloved *Tales of the City* has sold more than 600,000 copies in the States alone. These vignettes about eccentric straight and gay San Franciscans began as a regular column in *The San Francisco Chronicle*. Speculating about his success, Maupin says:

> My innovation was simply to incorporate gay characters naturally into a larger world, which is what David Leavitt does and Michael Cunningham does. I've never made any bones about being gay and I don't mind being called a gay

writer, but I know I reach a large heterosexual audience as well. I see myself as a bit like Bette Midler, who had a gay following who told their straight friends about her.

Has the "mainstream" accepted this literature? Many lesbian and gay critics argue that judgments of quality are inevitably politically motivated. Certain negative epithets—adjectives like "overstated," "uncontrolled," "precious," "trivial," "sentimental," "tendentious," "preachy," "underdramatized"—reveal as much about hostile heterosexual critics, in their view, as about the gay books they're supposed to be evaluating. Such acknowledged literary virtues as understatement and control may suit writers with conventional values and conventional lives: they can afford to "show not tell" since they can be sure their equally conventional reader will make the same safe assumptions that are axiomatic for the writer.

But it could be argued with equal plausibility that gay writers have been liberated by the extremity of their situation. What interests them is the exploration of their own most intimate feelings, the struggle to orient themselves in a world—the gay world—they're just beginning to map. The reticence that you find in, say, a Raymond Carver story about a troubled marriage just isn't meaningful to a gay writer, who finds himself faced with a whole constellation of relationships—between men and men, men and women, women and women—that have almost never been described before. I'm slightly nervous about discussing the "gay sensibility," since I think any discussion of a group's sensibility (the "black sensibility"? the "Jewish sensibility"?) is too general to be useful. But if such a sensibility does exist in gay fiction being written now, it's more lyric than dramatic, more psychological than oriented to action, more conscious than unconscious.

Perhaps unexpectedly, gay fiction is often open to the problems of other minorities. At the Out/Write conference I met gay Japanese-American writers, gay Pueblo Indians, gay black writers, and heard a whole panel devoted to gay Jews. There were panels conducted by writers recovering from addiction, by authors with disabilities, by Latin American authors, by Chicanos and Chicanas, and of course by those with AIDS. Few of these writers are interested in how mainstream America evaluates them, though quite a few would like to change public opinion. For most of them questions of artistic excellence cannot be separated from questions of political persuasion. One heard many heated references to "canon formation," the process by which powerful critics select a few books to become classics, to be taught in college curriculums and earmarked as the essential books of our civilization. Certainly as our society becomes more and more pluralistic and its minorities more vocal, the canon will be stretched wider and wider—perhaps to the bursting point.

I, for one, find much to admire in contemporary gay authors. One of my favorites is Robert Glück, who in his novel, *Jack the Modernist,* explores nuances of love never annotated before:

> How did he see me? I experimented. "I know I'm being a pest." My sentence fell like a pebble down a well. After waiting in vain for a splash,

"I must be boring you." I asked this in a higher voice—my fear annoyed me. Jack maintained that the opposite was true. "I really can't believe this, Jack, do you think I'm a fool?"

> Jack put a finger to his temple and deliberated a moment. "No, you're not a fool." I was startled. He took the question seriously, had to consider the answer. Finally, still smiling, I was humiliated. I couldn't have felt more suddenly chilled and excluded if I'd learned Jack was a ghost.

One of the best new novelists to emerge in recent years, straight or gay, is Allan Gurganus, whose *Oldest Living Confederate Widow Tells All* was a spectacular debut. In 1974, however, long before his novel appeared, Gurganus had published "Minor Heroism" in *The New Yorker*—the first story in the magazine to deal with homosexuality as a central theme. In his new collection of short stories, *White People* (which includes "Minor Heroism"), he has included several gay stories, although what seems to intrigue him most is homoerotic excitement between ostensibly heterosexual men—D. H. Lawrence's turf:

> He'd turn up at Little League games, sitting off to one side. Sensing my gratitude at having him high in the bleachers, he'd understand we couldn't speak. But whenever one of my sons did something at bat or out in center field (a pop-up, a body block of a line drive), I could feel Barker nodding approval as he perched there alone; I'd turn just long enough to see a young bachelor mumbling to himself, shaking his head Yes, glad for my boys.

While such gay writers as Michael Cunningham, David Leavitt and Armistead Maupin show gay men living in the larger context of straight friends and relatives, another group of writers insists on gay singularity. The strongest (and sometimes the most repellent) of these writers is Dennis Cooper, the author of *Closer, Safe* and the just-published *Frisk*. As obsessive as Sade and as far from ordinary morality as Georges Bataille, Cooper meditates ceaselessly on violence and perversion. This is the very stuff of Jesse Helms's worst nightmares. Cooper is the spokesman for the bored, sensitive, nearly inarticulate Blank Generation dedicated to drugs, kink and a fragile sense of beauty fashioned out of the detritus of American suburbs. He also has a terrifying gift for finding a death's head under every pretty face:

> The man grapples forward and locates a skull in Mark's haircut. He picks out the rims of caves for his eyeballs and ears. The lantern jaw fastens below them, studded with teeth. He comes to the long shapely bones of Mark's shoulders, toying with them until two blades resembling manta rays swim the surface. He clutches his way to both elbows. Ribs ride short breaths to the touch. He grasps Mark's hips and their structure floats up to him.

Perhaps no other body of literature is as subject to political pressures from within the community as gay fiction. Few writers in history have ever been "politically correct" (a notion that rapidly changes in any case), and there's no reason to imagine that gay writers will ever suit their readers, especially since that readership is splintered into ghettos within ghettos. ("What about the plight of the Jewish lesbian in Mexico?" one participant at the Out/Write conference called out.)

Even the question of whether to write about AIDS or not is strife-torn. Some gay writers think that it's unconscionable to deal with anything else; others believe that since gay culture is in imminent danger of being reduced to a single issue, one that once again equates homosexuality with a dire medical condition, the true duty of gay writers is to remind readers of the wealth of gay accomplishments. Only in that way, they argue, will a gay heritage be passed down to a post-plague generation.

This generation is imperiled. Every other writer at the Out/Write conference appeared to be ill. People who were HIV positive (like me) exchanged T-cell counts as though they were the latest Wall Street figures. Many who were robust a year ago were now dramatically thin or blind or covered with lesions. During the last session of the last day of the conference a member of the audience seized the microphone, ostensibly to denounce Edward Albee once again. But in an instant the pale, emotional man had segued into a cry from the heart: "I wanted everything to be perfect since obviously I won't be at the conference next year."

Gay fiction, written by anguished writers for readers in disarray, is under extraordinary pressures. Holocaust literature, exiles' literature, convicts' literature—these are the only possible parallels that spring to mind. Seldom has such an elusive and indirect artistic form as fiction been required to serve so many urgent needs at once. Some of our best imaginative writers, like Larry Kramer and Andrew Holleran, have turned away from fiction to essays, as though only direct address is adequate to the crisis. But many have remained true to their art. Will the world recognize those writers who have had the courage and energy and honesty and sympathy to raise a cenotaph to this era of blasted lives? (pp. 22, 24, 35)

> *Edmund White, "Out of the Closet, Onto the Bookshelf," in* The New York Times, *June 16, 1991, pp. 22, 24, 35.*

LESBIAN CULTURE AND LITERATURE

Bonnie Zimmerman (essay date 1990)

[*In the following excerpt, taken from her* The Safe Sea of Women: Lesbian Fiction, 1969-1989, *Zimmerman provides a history and definition of contemporary lesbian fiction.*]

During the past two decades, more than two hundred novels, memoirs, and short story collections have been written and published by women who align themselves with the lesbian movement. A few of these works have been published by mainstream publishers, but since the mid-

seventies the vast majority have been published by alternative, usually feminist or gay, presses. They are advertised through lesbian networks, sold in women's bookstores, and reviewed in lesbian, gay, and feminist newspapers. Like Isabel Miller's *A Place for Us,* they are passed around from friend to friend. Their politics, ideas, and literary quality are hotly debated both privately and publicly. Lesbian fiction, therefore, provides unparalleled source material with which to explore the ideas and beliefs of the lesbian community. If the lesbian novel merely mirrored the political and cultural concerns of lesbians, it still would serve an important historical function. But, I will argue, it has helped shape a lesbian consciousness, community, and culture from the movement's beginning.

Fiction is a particularly useful medium through which to shape a new lesbian consciousness, for fiction, of all literary forms, makes the most complex and detailed use of historical events and social discourse. By incorporating many interacting voices and points of view, novelists give the appearance of reality to a variety of imaginary worlds. Novels can show us as we were, as we are, and as we would like to be. This is a potent combination for a group whose very existence has been either suppressed or distorted. Lesbian novelists, then, have taken on the project of writing us into our own version of reality. To do this, they have revised the fragmented and distorted plots inherited from the past as new and "charming" lesbian stories that possess "a beginning and a middle and an ending." My purpose . . . is to show what these stories are and how the lesbian community endows them with meaning. (p. 2)

The Roots of Contemporary Lesbian Literature

In a 1976 essay on lesbian literature [in *Our Right to Love,* ed. Ginny Vida], novelist Bertha Harris argued that to "make a body of work that can be immediately perceived as a 'literature' . . . there must first exist cultural *identity:* a group or a nation must know that it exists *as a group* and that it shares sets of characteristics that make it distinct from other groups." To have a literature, she continued, lesbians must see themselves as a group with a history and sense of "realness." To understand lesbian literature as a specific genre, therefore, it is necessary to consider how lesbians developed an identity as lesbians.

Prior to the twentieth century, women certainly loved other women, chose them as companions, and expressed erotic longings for them. We can draw this conclusion from Greek myths of virgin goddesses and their female followers, from international tales of female transvestites and amazons, from the Old Testament story of Ruth and Naomi, and especially from the lyric poetry written by Sappho (ca. 612-558 B.C.) on the Mediterranean island of Lesbos. On occasion, woman-to-woman eroticism erupts in works by writers such as the medieval troubador Bieris de Romans, the British restoration playwright Aphra Behn, and the nineteenth-century Chinese poet Wu Tsao.

Moreover, between the seventeenth and twentieth centuries in western Europe and North America, some women experienced loving and supportive (although not necessarily sexual) relationships with other women that literary historian Lillian Faderman has named "romantic friendships." These passionate and spiritual relationships were recorded in letters and diaries, and recreated in numerous novels and poems, including Sarah Scott's *Millenium* [*sic*] *Hall* (1762), Mary Wollstonecraft's *Mary: A Fiction* (1787), Christina Rossetti's "Goblin Market" (1859), Louisa May Alcott's *Work* (1873), George Meredith's *Diana of the Crossroads* (1885), and Sarah Orne Jewett's "Martha's Lady" (1897).

Women in the past, however, lacked the "sense of historical continuity" that Bertha Harris claims is a requirement for an explicit lesbian literature. Few felt themselves to be different from other women of their time, or to have an identity defined by a particular sexuality. Although we can recognize lesbian *behavior* or *feelings* throughout the centuries and across all cultures and nationalities, lesbian *identity* was the creation of the late nineteenth century.

Historians identify a number of factors that account for the rise of modern-day lesbianism in the western world. Among these was the increased participation of women in the workforce that permitted some women sufficient economic independence to choose where to live and with whom. In female enclaves such as boarding schools, colleges, and settlement houses, some middle-class women chose lifelong companionship with other women over conventional marriages. The nineteenth-century women's rights movement, like its counterpart in the 1970s, further stimulated the emergence of lesbian identity by increasing women's self-esteem, criticizing heterosexual norms, and providing another female space in which political passions might be eroticized. Sex-segregated factories may have provided similar opportunities for working-class women, although low wages made independent living difficult. Perhaps because of these economic barriers some of these women chose to live, work, and marry as men, often exposed only at their deaths as women.

Not all the influences on emerging lesbian (and gay) culture and identity were salutary, however. In the late nineteenth century, medical experts, or sexologists, began to define same-sex love and sexuality. At first they proclaimed homosexuality to be a congenital condition, if not defect, characterized primarily by cross-gender identification. In other words, lesbians belonged to a "third sex"; they were male souls trapped in women's bodies. This theory was challenged and displaced by Freud and his followers, who described lesbians as women whose normal sexual development had been arrested at an immature, adolescent stage. Although strikingly different from each other, both congenital and psychoanalytic theories "morbidified," as Lillian Faderman puts it, the love between women that in earlier centuries had been tolerated or even sanctified.

In addition, the public presence and influence of the women's rights movement throughout the second half of the nineteenth century generated an anti-feminist reaction that we today would call lesbian-baiting. Women might write glowingly about living together in eternal bliss when they were economically, politically, and legally dependent upon men, but when suffragists and "new women" took advantage of their hard-won legal rights and economic opportunities to turn fantasy into reality, society drew the

line. Sylvia Stevenson's recently rediscovered novel *Surplus* (1924) illustrates how post—World War I literature shifted public attitudes by providing cautionary stereotypes of unnatural, "race suicidal" women who preferred female friendships to heterosexual love and childbearing.

Among these stereotypes was the figure of the sinister monster who preys upon innocent younger women. A lesbian version of the femme fatale, or dangerous woman, the man-hating spinster with her unnatural control over another woman took on mythic proportions in late-nineteenth and twentieth century literature. In Sheridan LeFanu's ghost story, "Carmilla" (1871), she becomes an actual blood-sucking vampire. This unnatural creature inhabits the pages of novels as different in historical era and literary significance as Henry James's *The Bostonians* (1885), Clemence Dane's *Regiment of Women* (1915), D. H. Lawrence's *The Fox* (1922), and Dorothy Baker's *Trio* (1943). Along with the immature child afraid of womanhood and the masculine woman, both inspired by sexology theories, the predatory monster became a common lesbian stereotype persisting to the present day. Hence, as the nineteenth century turned into the twentieth, lesbians began to have a label, an identity, for themselves, but that label was connected to notions of sickness and perversion.

Competing with these anti-feminist and medical discourses, however, was the distinctly lesbian literature and sensibility that arose at the beginning of the twentieth century in Paris. With the growth of urban centers during the nineteenth century, newly independent women could find meeting places, such as bars, social clubs, and salons, which were safely anonymous. For some, the "sexual undergrounds" of New York, Berlin, and Paris—the latter vividly portrayed by Toulouse-Lautrec—offered a welcome respite from the moralism of the dominant culture.

For others, the literary movement of modernism provided new forms through which to express the radical changes occurring in attitudes toward sexuality and gender.

Of particular importance to the development of a self-conscious lesbian literary tradition was the group of economically-privileged and artistically-inclined women centered in Paris around the expatriate authors Natalie Barney and Renée Vivien. From classical mythology, biblical stories, historical examples, and the feminist ideology of their era, Barney and Vivien fashioned an image of lesbians as extraordinary and superior creatures possessing a unique sensitivity to life and literature. In particular, they seized upon Sappho—who had recaptured public imagination in 1892 when archaeologists discovered fragments of previously unknown poems—as their inspiration and model. Barney and Vivien explicitly identified themselves as Sappho's heirs, and, in their lives and their texts, tried to re-establish her circle of women-loving poets. Many of Vivien's erotic poems, which initiated self-defined lesbian writing, are responses to and rewritings of her great precursor, Sappho.

But Renée Vivien (like Djuna Barnes, author of the modernist classic *Nightwood* [1936]), borrowed her image of Sappho and lesbians from the exotic "femme damnée," intoxicated with death and lust, of the Symbolist poets Baudelaire, Swinburne, and Pierre Louÿs. Vivien's version of lesbianism thus oscillates between exquisite damnation (the tone of Colette's depiction of Vivien in *The Pure and the Impure* [1932]) and astonishing feminism, the latter most notable in her philosophical novella, *A Woman Appeared to Me* (1904).

Nonetheless, Vivien was noteworthy for her unambiguous inscriptions of lesbian sexuality and identity. Many other serious writers of that era—such as Gertrude Stein, Virginia Woolf, Angelina Weld Grimké, Amy Lowell, and Willa Cather—relied instead upon codes and subterfuge to express lesbian desire, a strategy that protected them from censure. By suppressing pronouns, changing the gender of characters, inventing a cryptic language for sexuality, or hinting obliquely at relationships between women, these writers could tell, but not quite tell, lesbian stories. Through codes, Woolf could evoke lesbian love ecstatically in *Mrs. Dalloway* (1925) and whimsically in *Orlando* (1928), a fantasy portrait of her lover, author Vita Sackville-West. Stein, a significant role model for contemporary lesbian writers, wrote (but never published) *Q. E. D.* (1903), a realistic novella about a lesbian triangle, and *The Autobiography of Alice B. Toklas* (1933), which clearly portrays the domestic side of her relationship with Toklas. But to write about sexuality and passion, Stein created an elaborate private code in texts like "Lifting Belly" (1915-17) and "A Sonatina Followed By Another" (1921).

Natalie Barney, virtually unique in her era, declined both the damnation of Renée Vivien and the codes of Gertrude Stein. She survives today not through her writing—plays and epigrams which have yet to be translated and published in any significant number—but through the representations of her life by other writers. Her most significant manifestation is as Valerie Seymour in the classic lesbian novel, *The Well of Loneliness* (1928), by Radclyffe Hall. Valerie offers a welcome relief from the tortured self-hatred of the hero, Stephen Gordon, that wounded male soul trapped in a woman's body. It is ironic that Hall, a writer of modest talents compared to her illustrious contemporaries, should have created the novel and hero that have had the most profound and lasting influence on modern-day notions of lesbians. Yet, for all its old-fashioned rhetoric about "inversion" and its stylistic infelicities, *The Well of Loneliness* never obscures its central premise: that homosexuals deserve a place within nature and society. It is, moreover, an old-fashioned, readable novel with a strong plot, a noble and martyred hero, sharply-defined secondary characters, plentiful romance, and a tearjerker ending. It was shocking enough to be condemned by moralists, apologetic enough to be approved by sympathetic liberals, and explicit enough to be eagerly welcomed by lesbians. Hence, for over forty years, *The Well of Loneliness* and Stephen Gordon virtually defined lesbianism.

Shortly after its publication, *The Well of Loneliness* was condemned as obscene and officially banned in Britain until the 1960s. This was but the first sign of the periodic waves of repression that would attempt to wipe lesbians and gay men out of public consciousness and even existence. The Stalinist era in the Soviet Union effectively reversed the liberatory policies enacted during the early years of the Russian Revolution; for example, homosexuality was recriminalized in 1934. The contemporaneous Nazi movement went far further by destroying thriving gay communities throughout Europe, sending myriads of gay men and lesbians into exile or concentration camps.

On the cultural front, the situation was more mixed. Tightening moral standards throughout the 1930s rendered lesbianism so invisible in the mass media that the first film vresion of Lillian Hellman's famous 1934 play, *The Children's Hour,* eliminated the accusation of lesbianism around which the plot revolves. But lesbianism remained an acceptable, even popular, literary subject. Many novels published during the 1930s deserve a place in literary and lesbian history, among them the aforementioned *The Autobiography of Alice B. Toklas, Nightwood,* and *The Pure and the Impure,* Vita Sackville-West's *The Dark Island* (1934), Dorothy Richardson's *Dawn's Left Hand* (1931), Gale Wilhelm's *We Too Are Drifting* (1935) and *Torchlight to Valhalla* (1938), and Christa Winsloe's *The Child Manuela* (1933; a novel based on her play and film, *Mädchen in Uniform*). Jeannette Foster's 1956 classic, *Sex Variant Women in Literature,* surveys dozens of other novels, plays, and stories by male and heterosexual female writers that depict lesbians at length or in passing. Most of these, however, were strongly laced with the homophobic stereotypes of predatory, masculine, infantile, or hopelessly unhappy lesbians that were the legacy of early twentieth-century writing.

In the United States after World War II, Joseph McCarthy's House Committee on Un-American Activities identified homosexuals, along with communists and liberals, as subversives. The resulting purges of suspected homosexuals from government service inspired similar witch-hunts in virtually every sector of society throughout North America and Europe. Retaliation against known homosexuals was certain, swift, and brutal. Stories of those days record how gay people lost their jobs and homes, suffered incarceration in mental institutions and prisons, and endured violent attacks in the streets and bars. Lesbians and gay men lived double lives, always fearing exposure, except for the few political activists and overt "butches" and "queens" who, by their choice of lifestyle, were forced to the margins of society. Although the 1950s also saw the formation of gay and lesbian organizations, such as the Mattachine Society and The Daughters of Bilitis, the years between *The Well of Loneliness* (1928) and the rise of gay liberation (1969) were bleak ones indeed. Nonetheless, hidden, underground gay communities survived in large urban centers. Centered around bars and private friendship networks, they formed a subculture that, as the language of the time reminds us, existed "in the shadows" or "in the twilight world," but not in the bright, open light of day.

Perhaps because lesbian life was so hidden during those decades, the written word was crucial to sustaining and promoting lesbian identity. More lesbian novels were published in the United States during the 1950s and early 1960s than at any other time in history. Most, however, were pulp paperbacks that depicted lesbians as tragic, maimed creatures trapped in a world of alcohol, violence, and meaningless sex. The plots either doomed them to a cycle of unhappy love affairs or redeemed them through heterosexual marriage. Many of these novels were soft-core pornography written by men for men. Those written by women (whether lesbian or not) seldom challenged the insidious conventions and formulas, although occasionally an author revealed an affirmative and subversive subtext beneath the homophobic surface. Ann Bannon, in her Beebo Brinker series, created several strong lesbian characters, while Valerie Taylor gave her protagonist, Erika Frohmann, surprisingly feminist attitudes. Whatever their quality or perspective, however, the pulp novels were read avidly by lesbians and reviewed seriously in *The Ladder,* the one lesbian journal of that era.

These pulp paperbacks were crucial to the lesbian culture of the 1950s because they offered proof of lesbian existence. Any story that depicted a lesbian world, no matter how deeply submerged in the shadows, was valuable to a woman who otherwise felt herself to be alone. Moreover, the recurrent theme of suffering and sacrifice, as in *The Well of Loneliness,* invested a character with nobility, allowing the reader to feel, if not happy, at least purged and uplifted. The pulp novels also provided some women with welcome representations of lesbian sexuality and relationships. These women may have read against the grain, finding in the excesses and distortions of the text an ironic and amusing affirmation of their membership in a hidden and special subculture. Finally, the best of these stories portrayed lesbians as strong and independent women, and thus indicated the feminist direction that lesbian politics and literature were to take.

Serious and substantial fiction also emerged in the 1950s and 60s, bridging the gap between the great modernist writers of the 1920s and 1930s—Woolf, Barnes, and Stein—and the explicitly feminist literature of the late 1960s and early 1970s. Catharine Stimpson, in her essay on the twentieth-century lesbian novel [in *Critical Inquiry,* Vol. 8 (Winter 1981)], identifies Mary McCarthy's best-seller, *The Group* (1963), as a turning point in public consciousness because its appealing lesbian character, Lakey, breaks with the stereotypes of the past. I would point to two other, less mainstream, novels that have a central place in the development of a lesbian literary tradition. *The Price of Salt* (1952) by Clare Morgan and *Desert of the Heart* (1964) by Jane Rule, both sensitive and dignified novels in the tradition of the 1950s romance, demonstrated how lesbian fiction, freed from the stereotypes and narrative conventions of the past, might determine its own voice. Unlike the tragic or childish characters in most pulp paperbacks, the lesbian lovers in these novels are complex characters who make choices for themselves. Although they struggle with their identities and their place in society, they are permitted satisfying and authentic endings. These novels, and a handful of others, such as May Sarton's *Mrs. Stevens Hears the Mermaids Singing* (1965) and Maureen Duffy's *The Microcosm* (1966), signaled the beginning of an entirely different way of writing about lesbians.

In 1969, Alma Routsong's *A Place for Us,* or *Patience and*

Sarah was published. *A Place for Us* came into the world quietly and would not have had its current significance had it not been for the political and social events transforming western societies during the 1960s and 1970s. Lesbian life and literature was never the same after this time.

Lesbian Feminism and Lesbian Culture

In 1969, the hidden gay world exploded into the open when drag queens and dykes at a Greenwich Village bar, the Stonewall Inn, fought back against one police raid too many. Gay liberation was born that night into a political arena already established by the civil rights movement, the new left, the anti-war movement and the emerging women's liberation movement. Very quickly, lesbians within gay liberation and women's liberation coalesced into what came to be called lesbian liberation, and later lesbian feminism. Although not the first generation to openly proclaim their lesbianism, the women who came of age during the 1960s were able to establish the most dynamic and pervasive sense of lesbian cultural identity ever recorded. More than any group of lesbians in history, we (for I belong to this generation) insisted upon our right to say who we are, what we think and feel, how we live and love.

Many factors combined to make this transformation possible. The first was the sheer number and variety of women—bar dykes, college students, housewives, working women—who initially sought out lesbian organizations and social events. These numbers provided clear evidence that we were a distinct and potentially powerful group. Furthermore, the example of Black nationalism spurred many groups, lesbians being just one among them, to solidify their cultural identities. The process of separating from women's liberation or gay liberation groups also intensified our perception of ourselves as a group. Political activism, as well, bonded lesbians together. And, perhaps most important of all, feminist ideas, like ripples spreading out on water, eventually touched most lesbian communities and all lesbian creativity.

Those of us who began to identify as lesbian feminists asked anew the simple question, who or what is a lesbian? One answer is that lesbians are women who love and desire women rather than men. For some women that is definition and identity enough, but for lesbian feminists in the early 1970s, it was only a starting point. We argued that when women commit their passion and attention to other women, we defy society's most fundamental expectations and prohibitions for female behavior. Hence, lesbian feminists evolved a political or metaphoric sense of what it means to be a lesbian.

The theory or political position of lesbian feminism combined a commitment to female integrity, bonding, and sexual passion with an uncompromising rejection of male-centered ways of thinking and being. In place of these old ways, lesbian feminism presented a perspective from the margins of patriarchal society, a point of view rooted in women's forbidden love and desire for one another. Lesbian feminists proposed, therefore, that the word "lesbian" *stood for* a specific relationship to the dominant society rather than simply being a name for women who "happen" to make love to other women.

The first such use of "lesbian" can be found in a manifesto written in 1970 by the Radicalesbians collective, "The Woman Identified Woman," which defined the lesbian as "the rage of all women condensed to the point of explosion." To French theorist and writer Monique Wittig, "lesbian" signified that which disrupts western patriarchal and heterosexual dualism. The lesbian does so because she lives outside the rule of the fathers, because she is, as Bertha Harris put it, an outlaw and monster. Critic Mary Carruthers further argued that in lesbian poetry (and, as we shall see, in lesbian fiction as well):

> The word *lesbian* encapsulates a myth of women together and separate from men. . . . *Lesbian* is also the essential outsider, woman alone and integral, who is oppressed and despised by traditional society, yet thereby free to use her position to re-form and remember. . . . *Lesbian* is also erotic connection, the primary energy of the senses which is both physical and intellectual, connecting women, a woman with herself, and women through time. Finally, *lesbian* signifies a change of relationships, radical internal transformation; it is a myth of psychic rebirth, social redemption, and apocalypse. [*The Hudson Review,* Vol. 36 (Summer 1983)]

To all these writers, the word "lesbian" represented a point of view, or mode of interpretation, rather than a sexual behavior or innate identity. In the late 1980s, some lesbians, including a number of novelists, replaced this expansive political definition with the more specific sexual definition of lesbianism. But during the 1970s and early 1980s, the meaning of the word "lesbian" was profoundly influenced by feminist politics and ideology.

In the process of creating this feminist point of view, contemporary lesbians shaped a distinctive lesbian, or lesbian feminist, culture. The term "culture," as I use it, refers to more than literature, music, theater, and art, although the production of these creative forms has been one of the most notable activities of the lesbian community. Culture also encompasses the ideals and ethos of a group, all the intangibles that distinguish it from other groups. In the words of critics Billie Wahlstrom and Caren Deming, culture "limits and organizes human experiences. It does so by providing a version of reality that guarantees the shared meanings necessary for social existence."

Unlike many other social groups, lesbians, as we have seen, have had a difficult time establishing a "version of reality" that makes sense of our experiences *to us.* Lesbian existence has been so shrouded in "lies, secrets, and silence," to borrow Adrienne Rich's phrase, that we have struggled mightily to establish those "shared meanings." The events of 1969 broke the silence surrounding lesbian existence and thus stimulated the creation of the group identity that Bertha Harris, in 1976, named as a requirement for a distinctly lesbian literature. That identity was shaped in accordance with feminist beliefs and further refined by our artistic endeavors.

Feminism, in every historical era, emphasizes the right of

women to develop their own voice and speak (or write) about their own reality. Accordingly, the creation of a lesbian feminist identity has gone hand-in-hand with the creation of specific cultural artifacts, such as novels. Between 1969 and 1978 lesbian writers, invigorated by political radicalism and literary experimentation, set out the premises of a new genre. Many of them consciously hearkened back to lesbian writers of earlier decades: Bertha Harris to Djuna Barnes, Monique Wittig to Renée Vivien and Natalie Barney, Jill Johnston to Gertrude Stein, and June Arnold to Virginia Woolf. Elana Nachmann (who later renamed herself Elana Dykewomon) and Sharon Isabell wrestled with the legacy of Radclyffe Hall, while Jane Rule and Isabel Miller emerged from the lesbian romance genre of the 1950s. Some of them fashioned their stories directly out of the materials of their own lives; others created an imaginative and daring language unique to this period in contemporary lesbian literary history. Together, they created an audience for the coming out stories, romances, and utopias that have been the staple forms of lesbian fiction ever since.

These lesbian writers, along with artists, musicians, political theorists, and myriads of unnamed women, deliberately and self-consciously established a sense of continuity with lesbians of the past and community among lesbians in the present. This community—or Lesbian Nation—possesses, in the words of Monique Wittig, "its own literature, its own painting, music, codes of language, codes of social relations, codes of dress, its own mode of work." Wittig goes on to claim that this lesbian community and culture is diverse and international: "Just as they are unlimited by national frontiers (the lesbian nation is everywhere), so lesbians come from all social categories."

While Wittig's claim is theoretically compelling, in reality this lesbian culture has been embraced so far primarily by white western women. Lesbian culture is not delineated by actual geographical boundaries, which may explain why the territorial metaphor of Lesbian Nation is so widely used. We do not have a common language, although lesbian "wimmin" love to play with etymology, creating new words and original spellings. Nor is lesbian identity established through a shared birth heritage; lesbians "come out" rather than being born into a culture as African-Americans or Jews may be. No matter what your desires are at age two or twelve, you still must choose to act upon your feelings and identify with the community.

Lesbian culture is like a philosophical or religious system that provides its adherents with a way of viewing the world anew. A Jew, Christian, or Moslem, for example, finds a ready-made mythology, history, literature, and ethos waiting for her. For the past fifteen to twenty years, lesbians have been constructing a similar cultural identity from existing traditions, lifestyles, myths, and stories. We mix together Sappho, amazons, Gertrude Stein, and Natalie Barney (who herself manipulated and recreated myths and symbols); add bar culture from the fifties; season liberally with new left politics and new age consciousness; strain through traditional literary metaphors; and cover over completely with feminism to produce a lesbian culture. Today when a woman comes out as a lesbian, she has an identity and belief system waiting for her should she choose to embrace it.

Defining Lesbian Fiction

Among the products of lesbian culture is the flourishing genre of lesbian fiction. What defines this genre? What do we mean by "lesbian writing" and "lesbian writer"? Like the category "women's literature," "lesbian literature" is not defined by inherent, static characteristics that can be easily and uniformly identified and agreed upon, but by the perspective of a community of writers and readers. The boundaries of the genre are and always will be fluid, since writers may enter or leave and readers may disagree over its exact perimeters. "Lesbian" is not an ethnic or national designation, nor is it a stylistic or historical one, although it combines elements of each.

Instead, lesbian writing can best be defined through a *cluster* of factors; if a writer or text exhibits enough specific characteristics we can call her or it "lesbian." The factors vary according to historical era; what identifies a lesbian in 1980 may differ from what did so in 1880 or 1930. [Focusing on] the period from roughly 1969 to 1989, the following are the factors I use to identify lesbian writing.

The first is the writer herself, for the nature of lesbian fiction makes it impossible to separate the text from the imagination that engenders it. Lesbian writers, unlike those writers who incorporate a lesbian character or lesbian scene in a novel, are women who identify themselves in some way with the lesbian community. They may identify themselves as lesbians in their creative writing (by stressing autobiographical elements, for example) or in biographies or interviews. They may do so through their choice of publisher, since certain presses are exclusively or primarily lesbian or gay. They may publish their works in lesbian journals, give readings at lesbian bookstores and centers, or attend lesbian panels at conferences.

Since writers do not always leave obvious clues to their identity, we next turn to the literary text itself. A lesbian novel has a central, not marginal, lesbian character, one who understands herself to be a lesbian. In fact, it has many or mostly lesbian characters; it revolves primarily around lesbian histories. A lesbian novel also places love between women, including sexual passion, at the center of its story. Fiction that inscribes relationships between women through codes and allusions does not belong in the genre of self-defined lesbian literature. A contemporary lesbian novel very often exhibits lesbian intertextuality; that is, it refers to famous lesbians of the past and present, to lesbian events such as music festivals, and to other lesbian books. It also expresses a women-centered point of view. Unlike heterosexual feminist literature (which also may be very women-centered), a lesbian text places men firmly at the margins of the story.

Third, I include audience reception—who reads the books, and for what purpose—as part of this definition. Lesbian novels are read by lesbians in order to affirm lesbian existence. Conversely, the books a woman reads are what make her a lesbian feminist, or a member of "the lesbian community." Lesbian fictions function like the coming out stories that Julia Penelope Stanley and Susan

Wolfe describe [in their introduction to *The Coming Out Stories*]; they "are the foundation of our lives as Lesbians, as real to ourselves; as such, our sharing of them defines us as participants in Lesbian culture, as members of a community."

A number of critics have identified a possible fourth factor—lesbian style. Since lesbianism is a disruptive, experimental lifestyle, the argument runs, lesbian writing ought to be radically transformative. Adopting Virginia Woolf's attack on the patriarchal sentence, these critics argue that lesbian writers, like their early twentieth century foremothers, reject conventional language, plot, and structure. We might expect, therefore, to find contemporary writers employing postmodernist techniques (such as self-referentiality, unconventional plot structure, an unstable chronology and narrative voice) to disrupt the illusion that the goings-on in the text simply mirror "real life."

Although this aesthetic theory is intellectually compelling, I see little evidence that lesbians employ a unique style or form. Only a handful of writers—such as Bertha Harris, Monique Wittig, June Arnold, and Elana Nachmann, all of whom published important works between 1973 and 1976—use experimental techniques. June Arnold herself offered a provocative definition of the lesbian novel as a collective form "developing away from plot-time via autobiography, confession, oral tradition into what might finally be a spiral. Experience weaving in upon itself, commenting on itself, *in*clusive, not ending in final victory/defeat but ending with the sense that the community continues." In fact, neither the "disruptive" nor the "spiraling" form survived much beyond the 1970s. Instead, most lesbian novels have become so conservative in style and form that the representational mode reigns virtually unchallenged today.

But if there is no unique lesbian style, there are, finally, subjects and themes characteristic of lesbian fiction, particular ways in which lesbian writers express the visions and beliefs of the lesbian community. Through these, the writers of novels, short stories, and fictionalized memoirs attempt to establish the "real story," the "truth" about lesbian existence. However, truth is not exactly the same thing as objective reality; moreover, reality itself is an elusive concept. I shall argue, therefore, that lesbian writers create a *mythology* for the lesbian community, one that can be both inspirational and stifling. What we present as the truth about lesbians certainly includes representations of real life, but it also includes the myths and fantasies that provide us with a sense of ourselves as what Monique Wittig calls "lesbian peoples."

The Question of Quality

Although the genre I have defined has an avid following of addicted readers, ever-increasing numbers criticize the literature for being naive and unsatisfying in both form and content. This criticism, originating within the community itself, makes it necessary to address the question of whether or not lesbian fiction is "good" enough to merit serious attention from literary critics, or to satisfy the common reader. Julia Penelope, for example, asks, "Why do I usually feel 'ripped off' somehow, as though I expected something from a book that the writer didn't, and couldn't, give to me? What do I want that I'm not getting?" Joanna Russ responds by castigating the existing body of lesbian feminist fiction:

> Oppressed minorities experience a cultural and artistic deprivation which makes any art about our lives precious to us whether it's good, bad or mediocre.
>
> Nonetheless the literature that gives people a sense of identity and pride in one way can also be clumsy, stupid, anti-sexual, romantic in the bad sense, simple-minded, evasive about such gritty realities as money and power, contemptuous of the old or those who look "funny" or are the "wrong color," snobbish, thin, humanly empty and in all ways disrespectful of the beauty, horror, power and infinite variety of the universe. I find most Lesbian novels (like most other novels) unbearable for the above reasons.

Russ and Penelope join a long line of readers, both scholarly and common, who remain unsatisfied and in gastric distress after heavy meals of lesbian fiction. To an extent this distress arises from the narrow and static definitions some apply to lesbian fiction. If we refer only to those popular romances published by a handful of overtly lesbian presses, we may well characterize the genre as "unbearable." But we overlook many other texts that qualify such pessimism. We also fail to notice the changes that occur over time, such as a striking improvement in style and content. Moreover, to understand why contemporary lesbian fiction only sporadically fulfills our expectations, we must consider aspects of lesbian culture that affect literary quality.

The lesbian feminist culture that dominated the 1970s, and continues as one strong voice among many in the 1980s, was fiercely egalitarian. Unlike the dominant culture, or even mainstream feminist culture, both of which expect artists and writers to possess special talents, lesbian culture operates under the assumption that if any woman can be a lesbian, then any lesbian can (and should) be a writer. The breaking of the long silencing of lesbian speech has led to a flood of intense, immediate, intimate, and sometimes awkward written expression. Writers are more likely to be motivated by politics than by art, as the lesbians who named themselves C.L.I.T. (Collective Lesbian International Terrors) both mandated and predicted:

> We are also training ourselves to respond in writing, to make up for the present lack of Lesbian literature and media. This is a beginning step in demolishing the "creative artist" or "writer" mystique that separates and inhibits us, giving some the role of active "star" while the rest remain the passive audience.

Lesbians often write not because they feel compelled to create art or because they love language, but because lesbians need a literature that is honest and true (or at least true to the image we are creating about ourselves). They begin to write as amateurs (in the original sense of the word, as "lovers"), one reason for the preponderance of autobiographical novels, which may be assumed to be the easiest form for a neophyte to master.

When combined with a characteristic lesbian distrust of all standards perceived to be male, heterosexual, middle-class, and elitist, such ultra-egalitarianism can produce naive or poor writing. At the same time, it can be an asset. Women who have historically been shut out from the literary establishment are encouraged to tell their stories, thereby adding to the supply of plots, images, and fantasies that constitutes the language of lesbian literature. Lesbian literature, in principle at least, is unusually sensitive to varieties of experience, to the needs of a diverse community, and to the integration of politics and art.

But while the lesbian community has developed alternative standards of *content*—standards based upon honesty and fidelity to the range of lesbian lives—it has yet to redefine artistic quality. Instead, the community holds to a leveling imperative which can lead to "trashing," the lack of support for, or outright condemnation of, expertise (as we see in the quotation from C.L.I.T.). Reviewers may avoid serious criticism in favor of sisterly support, except when political values are in question. When Joanna Russ, for example, demolished the embarrassingly bad fantasy novel, *Retreat,* she herself was attacked by other writers for failing in sisterhood.

If, on the other hand, a writer steps over the line of acceptable political belief—if she is "politically incorrect"—she may be savaged by her more correct critics. Political correctness, a lesbian version of "socialist realism," can be a straightjacket for the lesbian writer. Even though the community began to joke about political correctness in the 1980s, most lesbian writers have internalized a rigid censor. We (for I fight this censor in myself) still write with fetters on, fearing to alienate any segment of the community. As a result, much lesbian fiction exhibits a subtle or not-so-sublte party line, avoids satire and irony, and is ambivalent about the imagination and experimentation.

The dominance of these community standards may account for the fact that novelists abandoned experimental style and form after the 1970s. Since no clearly-defined lesbian audience existed at first, writers wrote for themselves, or for other writers. They certainly felt political responsibility, but not to any established lesbian "truth." This situation has changed dramatically. Writers today write for a community that wants its fiction accessible, entertaining, and just "correct" enough to be a bit bland. Like most readers, this audience is unfamiliar with experimental techniques; hence, lesbian novels are, ironically, "straight" forward—that is, traditional and realistic—in form. We might ponder the question of what lesbian publisher in the 1990s would take a chance with Bertha Harris's complex and difficult novel, *Lover.*

In short, many novels are produced by inexperienced writers who, despite their best intentions, construct conventional plots and flat characters; who are unfamiliar with the varieties of narrative voice; who pay little attention to literary history and theory or to other writers; and who consider style to be the means to an end (the story) and not part of the end itself. Many lesbian writers, like the readers and writers of formula romances that Janice Radway studies in *Reading the Romance,* perceive language as nothing more than "a tool for accomplishing some purpose. In sum, it 'says' things." In lesbian narratives, the "thing" that language "says" is the experience of being a lesbian—and the quicker we get on with it, the better. Few individual writers use language as a complex signifying system, or present multiple and interacting layers of plot, character, or theme. Moreover, even the most skilled and sophisticated writers may be sufficiently receptive to the political and popular demands of the community to avoid experimentation, ambiguity, irony, philosophizing, or controversy. Although readers increasingly call for more complexity and subtlety, many lesbian novels remain disappointingly thin and transparent.

Because so many novels are written within the context of what has become a dominating and forceful lesbian mythos, in certain ways lesbian fiction resembles a popular genre. Like the historical romance or the mystery, it is molded by specific conventions and formulas. To give an obvious example, most lesbian novels require good lesbians, bad men, and happy endings. As a result, too many are a mere cut above potboilers. Even fiction that aims conscientiously at verisimilitude can be obvious and often forgettable. The most realistic texts can be so heavily laced with politically correct ideas and conventional images that their portrayal of reality is compromised by romanticism and sentimentality.

These inadequacies must be attributed in part to the reluctance of critics and publishers to sort out the good from the bad, the effective from the ineffective, the original from the clichéd, and thereby encourage a more complex approach to storytelling. But even were we to do so, junk novels might still prevail because, twenty years after its inception, lesbian fiction is as much a commodity as is its mainstream counterpart. The hungry audience that now exists demands sustenance from a commercially successful alternative publishing industry. Novels that need revising or even abandoning are instead rushed into print; some of our most popular authors publish one or more novels a year.

But to say that much lesbian fiction is conventional is not to say that it is bad. It is to say, rather, that the fiction is bound to the community that engenders and absorbs it. The significance of lesbian fiction lies not so much in the individual text abstracted from its political and social context, but in the genre taken *as a whole,* in its interplay of ideas, symbols, images, and myths. The purpose of this writing—self-aware or not—is to create lesbian identity and culture, to say, *this* is what it means to be a lesbian, *this* is how lesbians are, *this* is what lesbians believe. Whatever their aesthetic value, lesbian texts are "sacred objects" that bind the community together and help express—by which I mean both reflect and create—its ideas about itself. (pp. 3-21)

Bonnie Zimmerman, " 'It Makes a Great Story': Lesbian Culture and the Lesbian Novel," in her The Safe Sea of Women: Lesbian Fiction, 1969-1989, *Beacon Press, 1990, pp. 1-32.*

FURTHER READING

Bergman, David. *Gaiety Transfigured: Gay Self-Representation in American Literature.* Madison: University of Wisconsin Press, 1991, 237 p.

    Examines themes, techniques, structure, and rhetoric in gay literature.

Butters, Ronald R.; Clum, John M.; and Moon, Michael, eds. *Displacing Homophobia: Gay Male Perspectives in Literature and Culture.* Durham, N. C.: Duke University Press, 1989, 313 p.

    Reprints twelve essays originally published in a 1989 special issue of *South Atlantic Quarterly* on various aspects of homosexual literature and culture.

Clum, John M. *Acting Gay: Male Homosexuality in Modern Drama.* Between Men—Between Women: Lesbian and Gay Studies, edited by Lillian Faderman and Larry Gross. New York: Columbia University Press, 1992, 317 p.

    Examines the presentation of homosexual themes, characters, and subjects in twentieth-century British and American drama.

Foster, David William. *Gay and Lesbian Themes in Latin American Writing.* Austin: University of Texas Press, 1991, 178 p.

    Studies literary representations of the moral, social, and political difficulties of being homosexual in Latin America.

Harris, Simon. *Lesbian and Gay Issues in the English Classroom: The Importance of Being Honest.* English, Language, and Education Series, edited by Anthony Adams. Philadelphia: Open University Press, 1990, 146 p.

    Examines the legal and social aspects of teaching sexuality and gay and lesbian literature in British schools. Harris includes two case studies with lesson plans and an annotated bibliography of gay and lesbian fiction for young adults.

Levin, James. *The Gay Novel in America.* Garland Gay and Lesbian Studies, edited by Wayne R. Dynes, No. 4. New York: Garland Publishing, 1991, 363 p.

    Focuses on the depiction of male homosexuals in American fiction.

Lilly, Mark, ed. *Lesbian and Gay Writing: An Anthology of Critical Essays.* Philadelphia: Temple University Press, 1990, 218 p.

    Collects ten essays on gay and lesbian literature with an introduction by the editor.

Roof, Judith. *A Lure of Knowledge: Lesbian Sexuality and Theory.* Between Men—Between Women: Lesbian and Gay Studies, edited by Richard D. Mohr. New York: Columbia University Press, 1991, 285 p.

    Examines the portrayal of lesbian sexuality in films and literature from literary, political, and psychoanalytical perspectives.

Summers, Claude. *Gay Fictions—Wilde to Stonewall: Studies in a Male Homosexual Literary Tradition.* New York: Continuum, 1990, 245 p.

    Analyzes the fictional representation of male homosexu-

als in the works of English and American gay and lesbian writers.

Van Dyke, Annette. *The Search for a Woman-Centered Spirituality.* The Cutting Edge: Lesbian Life and Literature, edited by Karla Jay. New York: New York University Press,
1992, 227 p.

Studies the importance of female-centered spiritual traditions in the works of lesbian and feminist writers.

Woods, Gregory. *Articulate Flesh: Male Homo-Eroticism and
Modern Poetry.* New Haven: Yale University Press, 1987, 278
p.

Examines homoerotic themes in twentieth-century poetry, with chapters focusing on W. H. Auden, Hart Crane,
Allen Ginsberg, Thom Gunn, and D. H. Lawrence.

Native American Literature

INTRODUCTION

The 1992 celebration of the quincentennial of Christopher Columbus's arrival in the New World brought international attention to indigenous peoples throughout the Americas. Responding to a celebration they described as a glorification of an event that initiated centuries of exploitation, Native Americans called for increased awareness of Indian cultures and recognition of the contributions that indigenous peoples have made to Western civilization. While the media attention this received has resulted in a surge of interest in Native American literature, Indian writers note that readers and critics often fail to recognize the distinctiveness of individual works or the problems associated with defining what Native American literature is. Some, like Kiowa writer N. Scott Momaday, believe that Native American literature is merely an expression of self-identity, while others assert that it is a body of literature comprised of writing by Native writers for Native audiences. Still others maintain that Native American literature cannot exist as a genre because there is no single Indian language or culture and that the concept of "the Indian" is nothing but a stereotype and abstraction.

Although there were once over 500 separate Indian cultures with as many language variations, some general characteristics of contemporary Native American literature have been identified. These include the use of circular narrative structures, multiple voices, and ambiguous language to explore such concerns as environmentalism, spirituality, and mysticism. The cultural significance many Native Americans attach to language is also an important aspect of Indian literature. Many Indians believe that language is an incarnation of reality and that words themselves have the power to create. Momaday has stated: "[In] a certain sense we are all made of words; [our] most essential being consists in language. It is the element in which we think and dream and act, in which we live our daily lives. There is no way we can exist apart from the morality of a verbal dimension."

In addition to the difficulties involved in defining Native American literature, scholars have also identified several critical issues that have caused the works of Indian writers to be marginalized within the larger canon of American literature. Many commentators note that while white critics are primarily responsible for introducing Indian literature to non-Native audiences, they have at the same time polemicized the canon. For example, white critics often overlook the fact that Native oral traditions, a crucial part of Indian cultures and value systems for thousands of years, are an integral part of contemporary Native Ameri-

can literature. They also often question the authenticity of works by Indian writers, noting that because Native writers use such European forms as the novel and seldom write in their native languages, their works are not truly representative of Native culture. In response to such judgments, Acoma poet Simon Ortiz has argued: "[It] is entirely possible for a people to retain and maintain their lives through the use of any language. There is not a question of authenticity here, rather it is the way Indian people have creatively responded to forced colonization. And this response has been one of resistance; there is no clearer word for it than resistance." Critics also identify the increasing popularity of "white shamanism"—a trend associated with the New Age movement in which white writers imitate Native literary forms and romanticize Indian culture—as another reason why Native American literature is not always understood or taken seriously. However, Indian writers hope that with the increasing emphasis on multiculturalism, Native American literature will no longer be ignored or simplified and that the contributions of Native Americans to American culture and literature will be fully recognized. Rodney Simard has asserted: "American history, literature, and society must now all be revised in the light of their inconvenient but very real complexities; essential to such an effort is the acknowledgement of [America's] first citizens, their enduring roles, and their formidable contributions."

PRINCIPAL WORKS DISCUSSED BELOW

Alexie, Sherman
The Business of Fancydancing: Stories and Poems (poetry and prose) 1992

Apess, William
On Our Own Ground: The Complete Writings of William Apess, a Pequot [edited by Barry O'Connell] (autobiography) 1992

Chrystos
Dream On (poetry) 1991

Coldsmith, Don
Walks in the Sun (novel) 1992

Coltelli, Laura, ed.

Winged Words: American Indian Writers Speak
(interviews) 1990
Cook-Lynn, Elizabeth
The Power of Horses, and Other Stories (short
stories) 1990
From the River's Edge (novel) 1991
Dorris, Michael, and Erdrich, Louise
The Crown of Columbus (novel) 1991
Erdrich, Louise
Love Medicine (novel) 1984
Tracks (novel) 1988
Gould, Janice
Beneath My Heart (poetry) 1990
Mathews, John Joseph
Sundown (novel) 1988
McFadden, Steven, ed.
*Profiles in Wisdom: Native Elders Speak about the
Earth* (interviews) 1991
McNickle, D'Arcy
The Surrounded (novel) 1978
Medicine Eagle, Brooke
*Buffalo Woman Comes Singing: The Spirit Song of a
Rainbow Medicine Woman* (poetry and prose)
1991
Momaday, N. Scott
House Made of Dawn (novel) 1968
The Way to Rainy Mountain (autobiography) 1969
The Names (nonfiction) 1976
The Ancient Child (novel) 1989
Moss, Robert
Fire Along the Sky (novel) 1992
Owens, Louis
The Sharpest Sight (novel) 1992
Red Hawk
The Sioux Dog Dance: Shunk Ah Weh (poetry)
1991
Savageau, Cheryl
Home Country (poetry) 1992
Seals, David
The Powwow Highway (novel) 1990
Silko, Leslie Marmon
Ceremony (novel) 1977
Almanac of the Dead (novel) 1992
Swan-Abdullah, Madonna
Madonna Swan: A Lakota Woman's Story [edited by
Mark St. Pierre] (autobiography) 1991
Vizenor, Gerald
Landfill Meditation: Crossblood Stories (short
stories) 1991
Dead Voices: Natural Agonies in the New World
(novel) 1992
Waters, Frank
The Man Who Killed the Deer (novel) 1974
Welch, James
Winter in the Blood (novel) 1974
The Death of Jim Loney (novel) 1979
The Indian Lawyer (novel) 1990
Young Bear, Ray A.
Black Eagle Child: The Facepaint Narratives (poetry
and prose) 1992

HISTORICAL OVERVIEW

Arnold Krupat (essay date 1989)

[*Krupat is an American novelist, educator, critic, and essayist who specializes in Native American literature. Krupat has stated: "My aim has been to raise the theoretical sophistication of criticism of Native American literature, and to achieve a deeper understanding of the cultural contributions of Native Americans to American culture in general." In the excerpt below, taken from his* The Voice in the Margin: Native American Literature and the Canon, *he traces the history of Native American literature and asserts that works by Native Americans ought to be included in the American canon.*]

Although the rich and various literatures of Native American peoples, apart from their inherent interest and excellence, by virtue of their antiquity and indigenousness, have a strong claim to inclusion in the canon of American literature, this claim . . . has not yet been granted with any fullness.

From the very first period of invasion and settlement until the close of the "frontier," Americans tended to define their peculiar national distinctiveness . . . in relation to a perceived opposition between the Europeans they no longer were and the Indians they did not wish to become. The development of autobiography as a major genre of American writing is instructive in this regard, as in so many others. Eastern autobiographers like Jonathan Edwards in the colonial period, Benjamin Franklin in the Revolutionary period, and Henry Thoreau in the period preceding the Civil War, all wrote and thought about Indians, although finally choosing the European polarity as decisive for self- and literary definition. In contrast, western autobiographers like Daniel Boone, Davy Crockett, Kit Carson, and William F. Cody ("Buffalo Bill"), all ultimately loyal to white "civilization," nonetheless fashioned themselves and their books on models deriving in varying degrees from Indian "savagery." But this particular tension never operated in the definition of an American literature generally for the simple reason that Indians, who did not write, were not regarded as actually possessing a "littera-ture" that might be studied and imitated.

"Littera-ture," of course, meant precisely the culture of letters (as agri-culture meant the culture of the fields), and the man of letters, European or Euramerican, was the man of culture; Native Americans—Indians—were "children of nature" precisely because they were not men of letters. And oral literature, at least until near the nineteenth century, was simply a contradiction in terms. American literature, seeking to define itself as a body of national writing and as a selection of distinctively literary texts, considered only European models because no other models—no local or Native models, no "autochthonic" own—seemed to be present. Here is just that relation of avoidance justified by an imagined absence that I noted at the outset.

Yet even after Indian literature was "discovered," attempts to open the canon to it based themselves—mistakenly, to be sure, yet powerfully, nonetheless—on an appeal to the "naturalness" of this literature, as though it was not individuals and cultural practices but the very rocks and trees and rivers that had somehow produced the Native poem or story, and somehow spoke directly in them. This peculiar "naturalness" of Native American literature, currently linked . . . to a "biological" consciousness, continues to be its primary claim to attention. Thus I will not apologize for repeating yet again that for all the dramatic immediacy of Native American discourse; for all its rootedness in a consciousness very different from that of the West, it nonetheless remains the complex product of historical tradition and cultural convention as these are manipulated by individual performers who take technical problems—of pacing and pronunciation and pausing; the use of archaisms and neologisms; possibilities of condensation and expansion, and the like—altogether as seriously as the authors known to the Western tradition. In these regards, Native American literary expression is like literary expression everywhere. Nor does this contradict the point I insisted upon earlier, the cultural and technical difference of Native American literatures from the literatures of the West. To urge the inclusion of Indian literature in the canon of American literature, then, is not only to propose an addition but a reevaluation of what "American literature" means.

For all that sporadic attempts to read, teach, and use Native American literature as a model for written literature extend back well over a century, it is only in the past thirty years or so that the formal principles of many Indian languages have been established on anything like a sound scientific basis. Only in this time have dictionaries and grammars of some of these languages become available so that the scholar might come closer to an accurate understanding of what Indian performers actually said and meant. Ethnographic studies have also developed over these years to provide an enriched sense of the cultures that provide the matrix for specific performances. Still, as Dell Hymes has remarked, it would yet be premature to specify a canon of Native American literature area- or continentwide. There remain too many old recordings to listen to and retranscribe; too many older texts to retranslate and compare to contemporary variants; too much sorting and typing, comparing and evaluating yet to do for anyone to propose the "masterworks" of the Indian tradition. And so it is too soon to say exactly which Native American texts ought properly enter the canon of American literature. For all this, efforts have been made to urge some Native texts upon the broader national literary awareness. Thus I now turn to some literary history.

The first invader-settlers of America responded to the verbal productions of Native orality as a satanic or bestial gibberish that, unmarked in letters nor bound in books, could never be thought to constitute a littera-ture. John Eliot translated the Bible into an Algonquian language in the seventeenth century, but the Puritans did not inscribe the wicked or animal noise of Native song or story. The scientist-revolutionaries of the eighteenth century were more interested in Indian cultural activity than were their Puritan forebears and made efforts to describe, catalogue, and subdue its various manifestations—just as they did with other natural phenomena like lightning or steam pressure. Although the child of nature, in this period, was

as frequently deemed the noble as the murderous savage—a change prompted less by Rousseau than by the colonists' need to establish trade and military alliances with the powerful interior tribes—it was still difficult to conceive that without writing he could have a littera-ture. Washington, Franklin, and Jefferson, according to Roy Harvey Pearce, "encouraged the collection of Indian wordlists as part of an international project in comparative linguistics," and Jefferson quoted a well-known (perhaps apocryphal) speech of Chief Logan as an example of Native oratorical ability. But this was still far from recognizing an Indian capacity for literary production. Nonetheless, what may be the first translation of an Indian "poem" dates from the pre-Revolutionary period. This appears in the *Memoirs* of Henry Timberlake, a young Virginian, who, after serving under Washington, embarked upon a mission to the Cherokee. Timberlake apparently did not know Cherokee and so had to work from the rendition of an interpreter. In his "Translation of the WAR-SONG. *Caw waw noo dee,&c.*," we encounter Indian poetry in the form of heroic couplets. Here are the first few lines:

> Where'er the earth's enlighten'd by the sun,
> Moon shines by night, grass grows, or waters run,
> Be't known that we are going, like men, afar,
> In hostile fields to wage destructive war;
> Like men we go, to meet our country's foes,
> Who, woman-like, shall fly our dreaded blows.

Timberlake made no effort to transcribe the original Cherokee; only scholarly reconstruction might provide an approximation of what this song was like.

In the Romantic nineteenth century, littera-ture came to mean not simply the written culture generally but a selection from it of imaginative and expressive utterance—in writing, to be sure, but also in the speech and song of common men and the "folk" who might themselves be unable to write. "Nature" became the "keyword" of culture, and "oral literature," something other than a contradiction in terms. Once these ideas crossed the ocean to the American east, it was but a short step to hear Native expression as "naturally" poetic and as constituting a literature in need of no more than textualization and formal—"civilized"—supplementation.

English Romanticism had reached the east by the 1830s (Timberlake had reached England earlier: Robert Southey used the *Memoirs* for his 1805 epic, *Madoc*), but in those years the social and cultural dominance of the east was challenged by the Jackson presidency and the "rise of the west." So far as Indians were concerned, the 1830s were the years of President Jackson's Indian Removal policy, which made the forcible relocation of the eastern tribes to the west of the Mississippi a national priority. During that decade, easterners interested in Indians were primarily concerned to preserve Indian lives and lands before trying to preserve Indian literature. History writing rather than poetry writing appeared the more urgent task. For, as B. B. Thatcher put it in the preface to his *Indian Biography*, published in Boston in 1832, "We owe, and our Fathers owed, too much to the Indians . . . to deny them the poor restitution of historical justice at least."

In the 1840s and 1850s, it was American "civilization" that began to proclaim itself "Nature's nation," in Perry Miller's phrase, proclaiming all the louder as aggressive expansion threatened to destroy the forests, the grasslands, and, as always, their aboriginal inhabitants, nature's children, the Indians. In this period, the work of Henry Rowe Schoolcraft came to wide attention. Schoolcraft, an Indian agent interested in *la pensée sauvage*—"savage mentality," as he called it—had been publishing since 1839, but it was what Roy Harvey Pearce calls his "masterwork," a study undertaken, appropriately, at the instigation of the secretary of war—the *Historical and Statistical Information Respecting the History, Condition, and Prospects of the Indian Tribes of the United States* (1851-1857, and reissued under various titles)—that marks the increasingly important contribution of what we would call anthropological scholarship to our understanding of Indian literature. Indeed, according to A. Grove Day, "the beginning of wide interest in native poetry in translation properly dates from the year 1851, when a history of the Indians was published by Henry Rowe Schoolcraft which included samples of Chippewa poetry."

One example from Schoolcraft, quoted by Day, has repeatedly been anthologized; it has also occasioned some trenchant commentary by John Greenway and, particularly, by Dell Hymes. Schoolcraft's procedure—a transcription of the original, a literal translation, and a "literary" translation—continues often to be followed today. His Chippewa "Chant to the Fire-Fly" is literally translated:

> Flitting-white-fire-insect! waving-white-fire-bug! give me light before I go to bed! give me light before I go to sleep. Come, little dancing white-fire-bug! Come, little flitting white-fire-beast! Light me with your bright white-flame-instrument—your little candle.

The first few lines of his "literary" translation read:

> Fire-fly, fire-fly! bright little thing,
> Light me to bed, and my song I will sing.
> Give me your light, as you fly over my head,
> That I may merrily go to my bed.

This translation is as typical of its period's deliquescent Romanticism as Timberlake's couplets are of the high Drydenesque. Obviously, the translation of Indian poetry (like poetic translation generally) reveals as much about the translator's culture and literary predilections as it does about the Indian's. Schoolcraft also published, without literary elaboration, some brief Chippewa Midé—medicine society—songs such as the two following:

> All around the circle of the sky I hear the Spirit's voice.

> I walk upon half the sky.

His contemporaries, however, did not seem interested in these—which, today, probably appear both more attractive and more "Indian." In any case, although Schoolcraft's translations spurred interest in Native American poetry, they seem to have had no influence on American poetry in their time. Not Indian poetry but, rather, poetry

with an Indian subject did enter the American canon in the 1850s, however.

Composed by a Harvard professor of European literature, the first to teach *Faust* in an American College, Henry Wadsworth Longfellow's *Song of Hiawatha* (1855) sold out its first printing of four thousand copies on the day of its publication and completed its first year in print with sales of thirty-eight thousand. Longfellow derived his Indian materials from Schoolcraft's earlier work, the *Algic Researches* (1839); he derived his attitudes toward Indians from eastern progressiveist thought (Alas, the Noble but Vanishing Savage); and he derived his meter from the Finnish epic, *Kalevala*. Longfellow's Hiawatha comfortably counsels the people to abandon the old ways and adapt themselves to the coming of "civilization," and he does so in a meter that only "civilization" can provide. It is necessary, of course, to mention Longfellow in any consideration of possible Indian influence on American literature, but *The Song of Hiawatha,* in fact, shows no such influence at all. Longfellow did not make use of Schoolcraft's Chippewa translations (themselves mostly "civilized" in their formal conventions), nor did he have any sense of his own about what Native American literary composition might actually be like or whether it might somehow stand without Finnish support and supplementation. The admission of *Hiawatha* into the American canon had nothing to do with the possibility of expanding the canon; *Hiawatha* merely assimilates the Indian to the persisting Eurocentrism of the east.

Euramericans continued to move westward, appropriating Native American lands by force and by fraud. Once the west had been "won," as the "frontier" approached its "close" in 1890, American thought about Indians situated itself within a broader debate between Americanism and cultural pluralism. The "Indian problem" was related to the "immigrant problem"; the various "solutions" proposed rested upon particular visions of the social order. The "Americanizers" gained the ascendant in 1887 with the passage of the General Allotment Act, known as the Dawes Severalty Act. The Dawes Act was an attack on Indian culture ("for the Indians' own good") by way of an attack on the Indians' collectively held land base—a "mighty pulverizing engine to break up the tribal mass," as Theodore Roosevelt called the act in presciently cyclotronic imagery. The Dawes Act was also—and intended to be—an attack on all "communistic" systems. Opposed (for the most part) to Dawes and the Americanizers were the anthropologists of the newly founded Bureau of Ethnology (1879; after 1894, the Bureau of American Ethnology), whose studies of the rich, Native tribal heritage committed them to its preservation rather than destruction. An important exception, however, was Alice Fletcher. One of the first, in the 1880s, to study the forms of Native American music, Fletcher, nonetheless, was "one of the most vigorous opponents of tribalism and played an influential role in the agitation . . . to force the allotment of land in severalty upon the Indians without tribal consent," as Wilcomb Washburn has commented.

Fletcher was more interested in the music of Indian songs than in their texts; her influence on the study of Native

American poetry comes through Frances Densmore and, more particularly, Natalie Curtis Burlin, whose work she inspired. Densmore, trained in piano, organ, and harmony at the Oberlin Conservatory of Music and at Harvard, began in 1901 a lifetime of work with Indian music by transcribing a Sioux woman's song that she heard near her home in Red Wing, Minnesota. Densmore continued to publish on Indian music until her death in 1957. Of the vast body of material she transcribed and translated, it may be the Midé songs of the Chippewa—these attracted her as they had Schoolcraft—which she published for the Bureau of American Ethnology in 1910, that have most often appeared in the anthologies (although not in the earliest ones).

It was Burlin, the third of these early collectors of Native song, who had the greatest impact on the anthologies. In 1907, Burlin published *The Indians' Book,* a wide-ranging collection that presented not only the music of Native American songs (in special notation) but also poems and short narratives from the tribes. Burlin's particular appreciation of Native artistic production is entirely that of the antiquarian looking back upon what President Theodore Roosevelt called, in a prefatory letter to her book, "the simple beauty and strange charm—the charm of a vanished elder world—of Indian poetry." Like Fletcher, Burlin had no doubt that the "child races" of Indians must give way to the "adult races" of Anglo-Saxon peoples. She recommended the charming and simple songs of the Indians to her white audience for the wisdom they might—somehow, vaguely—teach, and, as well, as an act of—sentimental—justice to this soon-to-be-vanished race. Indeed, Burlin's Indians are so childlike and simple as to be entirely creatures of nature; their art, she says, is "spontaneous," the talent to produce it "inborn" in every member of the race. In these beliefs, Burlin completely ignores the major developments of scientific anthropology in her time, which insisted upon the cultural, not racial, explanation of cultural things. Some of her translations—they are, curiously, the ones chosen by Louis Untermeyer for his 1931 anthology of American poetry . . .—are full of exclamation points and archaic diction, but others, like this Winnebago "Holy Song," are somewhat less elaborated and point more nearly forward:

> Let it fly—the arrow,
> Let it fly—the arrow,
> Pierce with a spell the man, oh!
> Let it fly—the arrow.
>
> Let it fly—the arrow,
> Let it fly—the arrow,
> Pierce with a spell the woman!
> Let it fly—the arrow.

Burlin's work, for all its mistaken inspiration and its partly dubious execution, remains the locus of much that is available nowhere else.

The Dawes Act was a disaster for the Indians; yet it was not officially abandoned until the 1930s. By that time, American anthropology was no longer based in the government bureau, nor in the great urban museum, but, instead, in the university. Franz Boas, who had come to Columbia University just before the turn of the century to train a new generation of anthropologists, was the dominant force in ethnographic science. I will not attempt a full discussion of Boas's contribution to the preservation of Native American culture but, rather, quote Hymes at some length; his description of what happened on the northwest coast of America is largely true for the literatures of most Indian peoples.

> Often non-Indians did not wish to preserve the culture of the Indians. Conviction or guilt persuaded them that it was already gone, or best gone. It is a shameful fact that most of what can be known today about the cultures of the Indians of my state, Oregon, is due to the efforts of men who came across the continent. Franz Boas, a German Jew unable to aspire to scholarly advancement in his native country but versed in the German intellectual tradition that valued individual cultures and their works, recorded Shoalwater and Kathlamet Chinook. His student Sapir recorded Wishram and Takelma; another student, L. J. Frachtenberg, recorded Alsea, Siuslaw, Coos, and Kalapuya. Frachtenberg was followed by a later student with a better ear, Melville Jacobs, who provided superior texts from Coos and Kalapuya, all that has been published so far in Sahaptin, and all that is known, save for one scrap, of Clackamas. To repeat, most of what we can know of the first literature of Oregon is due to representatives of German and Jewish intellectual tradition, who crossed the continent to record it. With regard to that first literature, they are the pioneers. The pioneers of Western song and story and their descendants did little or nothing.

These German and Jewish intellectuals were entirely skeptical of the Americanizers' claims to WASP cultural superiority and asserted their sense of the importance to American culture not only of Continental philosophy and philology but of the aboriginal American culture of the Indians as well. Whereas early attempts at "ethnographic salvage" were made in the name of history, and the Americanizers' attempts at ethnographic destruction were made, generally, in the name of religion, what Boas and his students preserved was in the name of science. The work of Fletcher, Densmore, and Curtis began specifically from an interest in Indian music and coincided with imagism and a movement in poetry to privilege the genre of the brief lyric. But Boas and his students sought knowledge. Although they recorded songs, which would early be anthologized, they also recorded lengthy narratives that were performed but not sung. Hardly inimical to poetry, their commitment to science led them to prefer the most literal prose translations—which usually obscured completely the dynamics of Indian performances and made it very difficult for anyone to discover a genuine poetry among Native peoples. The full value of what Boas and his students recorded would only begin to be revealed in the 1950s and after, when developments in anthropological linguistics would permit their translations to be modified for accuracy and to yield new translations of more apparent poetic value.

It was just after World War I that the first concerted effort to present Native American poetry as a part of American literature occurred. This effort was associated with the American radicals' call for cultural pluralism, with the imagist challenge to a canon still dominated by Emerson, Longfellow, and James Russell Lowell, and, in particular, with the work of Mary Austin. If Schoolcraft's Chippewa translations may be said to have opened the way to interest in North American poetry, then it was George Cronyn's anthology of Indian poetry, *The Path on the Rainbow* (1918), that began to broaden that way. Cronyn's volume was hardly, as Austin called it in her introduction, "the first authoritative volume of aboriginal American verse," for Cronyn was often uncritical and/or misinformed. (It might be said that no "authoritative" collection appeared before Margot Astrov's in 1946; it might also be said that no "authoritative" collection has yet appeared.) Yet Cronyn had the acumen to take translations from the superb student of Navajo, Washington Matthews, from John Swanton, and from Boas himself. Whatever its quality, finally, Cronyn's volume—which attracted a good deal of attention—at least made it possible to imagine, as Austin predicted in her introduction, that a relationship was "about to develop between Indian verse and the ultimate literary destiny of America."

In Austin's view, to know the Native American heritage was not, as Curtis believed, for the "adult" American to honor some indigenous childlike past; rather, it was for the contemporary American poet to "put himself in touch with the resident genius of his own land" in the living present. There is an "extraordinary likeness," Austin remarked, "between much of this native product and the recent work of the Imagists, *vers librists,* and other literary fashionables." Thus, "the first free movement of poetic originality in America finds us just about where the last Medicine Man left off."

A year later, in 1919, Austin wrote in the *Dial* that "vers libre and Imagism are in truth primitive forms, and both of them generically [*sic*] American forms, forms instinctively selected by people living in America and freed from outside influence." Austin ascribed these "forms" to nature, most particularly to what D. H. Lawrence was soon to call "the spirit of place." In Indian poetry, Austin wrote, "the shape of the lines is influenced by the contours of the country." So determining was this geographical influence that "before 1900" she "could listen to aboriginal verses on the phonograph in unidentified Amerindian languages, and securely refer them by their dominant rhythms to the plains, the deserts and woodlands," as she explained in 1923, in the introduction to her own collection of versions of Indian poems, *The American Rhythm.* Austin wittily admitted that she took the anthropologists of her day more seriously than they took her; but if she did take them seriously, she understood them badly, for her sort of simplistic environmental determinism was unacceptable to them as an explanation of cultural variation.

Nonetheless, Austin's often-repeated conviction "that American poetry must inevitably take, at some period of its history, the mold of Amerind verse, which is the mold of the American experience shaped by the American environment" took a clear stand on the future of American poetry. This stand was not only in opposition to the Longfel-low—Emerson—Lowell eastern past but in opposition, as well, to the futures envisioned by Austin's contemporaries, T. S. Eliot and Ezra Pound, who looked not to the West but to the East and Far East, and to a past very different from that of "the last Medicine Man." Yet Austin shared with Eliot and Pound what F. H. Matthews has called the "revolt against Americanism."

"In the 1920's," in Matthews' cogent summary,

> the revulsion from Americanism and the search for a viable cultural community intensified into a major quest. Intellectuals in a position to assert their identity with some minority now fanned the embers of recently-declining traditions, or raised folk arts to self-conscious status. . . . Writers who lacked a vital region or ethnic minority with which to identify turned instead, like Sherwood Anderson and William Carlos William[s], to quarrying the national past in search of lost virtue.

This "revulsion from Americanism" serves to link Austin, Williams, Eliot, and Pound, although the solutions each proposed to the common problem they shared were incompatible with one another. The modernist internationalism of the "paleface" and the nativism of the "redskin" were united in the young Yvor Winters. As poet-critic, first, and, subsequently, as scholar-teacher, Winters urged the claims of Indian literatures as part of a broader challenge to the established canon.

In 1922, that *annus mirabilis* of *Ulysses* and *The Waste Land,* Winters published *The Magpie's Shadow;* the "Indians especially were an influence on *The Magpie's Shadow,*" Winters would later write. The linked poems of *The Magpie's Shadow* are introduced by an epigraph from Rimbaud, and Japanese poetry is also an influence, although it is impossible to tell what Winters may have taken from the Native American and what from the Japanese (the two non-Western traditions have often appeared as parallel influences on those poets looking beyond the European tradition—and William Stafford has published a "Sioux Haiku"). The brief, titled stanzas of the poem's three sections seem familiar enough from imagist practice. Thus, from part 2, "In Spring":

"May"

Oh, evening in my hair!

Or, from part 3, "In Summer and Autumn":

"The Walker"

In dream my feet are still.

"Blue Mountain"

A deer walks that mountain.

A year earlier, Winters had published in *Poetry* magazine a poem with an Indian subject, "Lament, beside an Acéquia, for the Wife of Awa-Tsireh." He later identified Awa-Tsireh as a painter from the pueblo of San Ildefonso. That was in 1928, in "The Indian in English," a review for *Transition* of two important Native American poetry anthologies, Cronyn's *Path on the Rainbow* and Nellie Barnes's *American Indian Love Lyrics and Other Verse.*

Winters quoted from the translators he admired and also offered, "finally," what he called an example of "nonreligious and purely dramatic material" in a "more modern group of Chinook songs" translated by Boas. I should also note Winters's 1926 "Open Letter to the Editors of *This Quarter*," in which he protested the exploitation of Indian materials. This "notion of interpreting the Indian," Winters wrote, "is too much for me. They are in no need of assistance whatsoever, as anyone is aware who has ever read the really great translations of Frances Densmore, Washington Matthews, Frank Russell, and Jeremiah Curtin—translations that can take their place with no embar[r]assment beside the best Greek or Chinese versions of H. D. or Ezra Pound and which some day will do so."

Winters's own poetic development would not follow Native American models; yet Winters continued to press the canon to open itself not only to Frederick Tuckerman, Thomas Sturge Moore, and Elizabeth Daryush but to Native American poetry as well. Winters directed A. Grove Day's doctoral dissertation, which became one of the important anthologies of Indian verse; another of his doctoral students was the Kiowa N. Scott Momaday, whose work I will discuss.

In Winters's *Transition* article, he approved of Cronyn's collection as, of the two reviewed, "by all odds the better and larger selection, despite its being saddled with a selection of 'interpretations'." In his approval of Cronyn, he placed himself at odds with Untermeyer, another great canon maker of the time. In 1919, Untermeyer had also reviewed Cronyn's volume, for the *Dial*, rather sniffily concluding that this Indian anthology was "as an ethnic document . . . of indubitable value; as a contribution to creative Americana [?] it may grow to have importance. But as a collection for the mere man of letters it is a rather forbidding pile—a crude and top-heavy monument with a few lovely and even lively decorations." Austin quickly responded in a piece from which I have already quoted. Characterizing Untermeyer as "one whose mind has so evidently never visited west of Broadway," Austin made the telling point that "if Mr. Untermeyer could get his mind off the Indian Anthology as a thing of type and paper, he might have got something more out of it."

By the 1930s, however, Untermeyer had apparently come nearer to Austin's estimate of Native American poetry. His *American Poetry: From the Beginning to Whitman* (1931)—according to H. Bruce Franklin the "most widely used anthology of poetry" in the schools—included a section on American Indian poetry along with sections on Negro spirituals and blues, cowboy songs, and city gutturals. Untermeyer quoted from Austin's introduction to *The Path on the Rainbow* and recommended Curtis's *Indians' Book*, Barnes's *American Indian Love Lyrics*, and Austin's *American Rhythm*. This last, he said, included "a penetrating essay in interpretation." Austin's essay, however, offers no more than the geographical determinism I have already remarked; Untermeyer tended to prefer "adaptations" rather than more literal translations, just the sort of "interpretations" Winters, quite wisely, warned against.

Translation versions of Native American poetry had earli-

er appeared in another anthology widely used in the schools. In 1928, Mark Van Doren, also an admirer of Curtis, had published his *Anthology of World Poetry*, consisting of poetic translations from literatures around the world. A section on "American" poetry comes last; this contains twenty poems from translators ranging from Schoolcraft to Austin and Curtis; there is nothing from Boas and his students.

These influential anthologies, for all their confusions about Indians and Indian literature—not to say their thoroughgoing ignorance of what anthropological scholarship of their time had made it possible to understand about Native Americans and their literature—nonetheless were clear gestures toward that pluralism intended to open the canon. In this regard, they were cultural equivalents of the political change from Herbert Hoover to FDR, from the Dawes Act's policy of cultural destruction and Indian assimilation to the Indian New Deal of Roosevelt's commissioner of Indian affairs, John Collier, who sought to preserve and protect traditional Native cultures.

Paula Gunn Allen on Native American literature:

[Native American literature] tells us who we are; it tells us what our history is; it tells us what we look like; and it tells us of the significance of our lives within the human community. It takes us out of the realm of oblivion, which is where we've been. If we live in the past, and by 1850 it's all over, you know what that tells a young Indian person? It tells a young Indian person you died in 1890, so what are you doing here? Now we can say, look what you're doing here, look at this literature, it's so fine, it's superb literature, and they can read it and they can say—I got some letters back from those students and they were saying—"it's so wonderful to listen to our own—it's like listening to ourselves. It's like hearing who we are and feeling comfortable and going 'oh, I recognize that.' " Now instead of having to strain and understand when you're reading a poem by an English poet—well, what do we know about England? it's an exotic place to me—instead I can read about Cubero, I can read about Laguna, I can read about Jemez. I know these places, I know the landscape, I know the people, I know the sounds. I know, I understand. It's giving us our sanity back, person by person, and tribe by tribe. In a way we all died, but we're still here. And the literature allows us to come to terms with both facts. Because both things are true.

Paula Gunn Allen, in Winged Words: American Indian Writers Speak, *1990.*

World War II brought Claude Lévi-Strauss to the New School for Social Research in New York, where, as legend has it, he learned structural linguistics from his colleague Roman Jakobson, another displaced European. Lévi-Strauss's essay "The Structural Study of Myth" appeared in the *Journal of American Folklore* in 1955. Whatever its influence on method in America, this text was an important encouragement to the study of Indian "myth," if not—and the two were distinct for Lévi-Strauss—Indian "poetry." It was just after the war, in 1946, that Astrov's anthology of Native prose and poetry, *The Winged Ser-*

pent, was published—still, in 1965, as Hymes judged, one of the "two major contemporary anthologies in English" and, according to William Bevis in 1974, "the best general anthology in paperback." Astrov's introduction and notes pay special attention to the scientific, anthropological contexts of Indian literatures, and the translations she chooses, as well as the commentary she provides, reflect the considerable advances ethnography had made in the Boasian period.

The second of the "two major contemporary anthologies" is Day's *The Sky Clears,* published in 1951. Unlike Astrov, Day pointed, as Austin had, specifically to the possibility of Indian influence on modern American poetry—although only, as Hymes has noted, in relation to existing translations. Day was, as I have said, Winters's doctoral student, and he dedicated the anthology, an outgrowth of his dissertation, to "Yvor Winters, Singer of Power."

Boas had died in 1942; but by that time his students occupied major positions of influence in American anthropology. It was one of Boas's later students, Melville Jacobs, who, in 1958, published the first of an important series of narratives from the Northwest. These appeared as numbers of the *International Journal of American Linguistics,* issued by the Indiana University Research Center in Anthropology, Folklore, and Linguistics. It was also in 1958 at Indiana that Thomas Sebeok convened the interdisciplinary conference on style that provided the occasion for Jakobson's well-known concluding paper, "Linguistics and Poetics." (Sebeok's earlier symposium on myth had provided a forum for Lévi-Strauss's "Structural Study of Myth.") Through the work of Hymes, a participant in that conference, the insights and method of Lévi-Strauss and Jakobson would be brought together to advance the study of Native American literatures as they might be encountered and/or restructured in their original languages.

As early as 1953, while working at Indiana University, Hymes began to conceive the possibility of what he has called a "living relation, through fresh translation and study of the [Native American] originals, to modern poetry." But in the 1950s—to take a single suggestive instance—it was Sputnik and the challenge to further conquest of nature, rather than nature itself, that most engaged Americans. The federal government renewed its efforts to Americanize the Indian under the policy known as "termination." Washburn has described it as "the forced dissolution of tribal organizations and the break-up of existing tribal assets." This was not a time in which the social order encouraged a cultural opening to Native American influences—although some would turn to it for alternatives.

But by 1960, neither presidential candidate supported the termination policy; and by 1970, Richard Nixon, as president, declared government policy toward the Indians to be self-determination without termination. One of Nixon's first official acts was to return the sacred Blue Lake of the Taos Pueblo people. The rights not only of Native peoples but of all those who had traditionally been excluded from full social and literary representation were asserted in the 1970s, arousing a broad increase of interest in traditional Native American culture and literature.

As early as 1951, Gary Snyder, then a senior at Reed College, had written his B.A. thesis on a Haida myth and, in 1960, Snyder's *Myths and Texts,* work done between 1952 and 1956, appeared; I shall return to this shortly. In 1961, Kenneth Rexroth's important essays "The Poet as Translator" and "American Indian Songs" were published, while, a year later, Jerome Rothenberg inaugurated what would be a major and ongoing poetic program with his performance- and event-oriented *From a Shaman's Notebook: Poems from the Floating World.* This was an early attempt, as Rothenberg wrote in 1969, "to get as far away as I could from *writing.*" By that time, Rothenberg had also published *Technicians of the Sacred: A Range of Poetries from Africa, America, Asia, and Oceania* (1968). Rothenberg's presumptuously global reach has been properly and abundantly criticized; yet this volume performed a service for non-Western poetries generally, and for Native American poetry in particular. Rothenberg was not only perspicacious in his selection from the older translators—he included Densmore, Washington Matthews, and Pliny Earle Goddard, while excluding Austin, for example—but also collected newer translations by William Carlos Williams, W. S. Merwin, and Rochelle Owens. Perhaps most important, Rothenberg went to great lengths to demonstrate the way in which some modern and contemporary poetry follows "primitive" (" 'primitive' means complex") directions.

In the section of his "Pre-Face" to *Technicians of the Sacred* called "Primitive and Modern: Intersections and Analogies," Rothenberg tried to show "some of the ways in which primitive poetry and thought are close to an impulse toward unity in our own time, of which the poets are forerunners." Rothenberg lists six "important intersections" in some detail, which I shall abbreviate. These are: (1) "the poem carried by the voice," (2) "a highly developed process of image-thinking," (3) "a 'minimal' art of maximal involvement," (4) "an 'intermedia' situation" in which "the poet's techniques aren't limited to verbal maneuvers but operate also through song, non-verbal sound, visual signs, and the varied activities of the ritual event," (5) "the animal-body-rootedness of 'primitive' poetry," and (6) "the poet as shaman." Some of the "important intersections (analogies)" Rothenberg lists are: jazz and rock poetry, "Blake's multi-images," surrealism, random poetry, concrete poetry, happenings, dada, "lautgedichte (sound poems)," projective verse, "Rimbaud's voyant, Rilke's angel, Lorca's duende," beat poetry and psychedelic "poetry."

Rothenberg then illustrated contemporary intersections with the "primitive" by quoting a number of contemporary poems in his extended commentaries. He drew from his own work, as well as from Owens, Robert Creeley, Denise Levertov, and Diane Wakoski, among others, and included a translation from Pablo Neruda done by Robert Bly. Rothenberg also quoted a poem from Snyder's *Myths and Texts.* This volume of poems, published, as I have noted, in 1960, takes its title, as Snyder later wrote, "from the happy collections Sapir, Boas, Swanton, and others made of American Indian folktales early in this century." It is no surprise, then, to find, as the poet and anthropologist Nathaniel Tarn puts it, "Indians everywhere."

In the 1960s, a considerable number of American poets turned from European models and sources to acquaint themselves with Native American models and sources—as they also turned to the cultural productions of Afro-Americans and women. To turn to Indians was to valorize the natural, the communal and the collective; it was to seek the dramatically immediate, and to reject the New Critical conception of the poem as object. Many poets in the 1960s wrote, in Louis Simpson's phrase, "Indian poems"; so many, that it seemed, in Simpson's 1972 recollection, that

> the Indian was being taken up again as a symbol. It was nostalgia, and something more: in their search for a way of life to identify with, poets were turning to an idea of the dark, suppressed American. . . . Poems about Indians were a fantasy of sophisticated twentieth-century people who were trying to find ways out of the materialism that was everywhere around them.

In 1975, in response to an interviewer's question, Simpson elaborated:

> We were trying to use the Indian as a means of expressing our feeling about the repressed side of America that should be released. However, if I or anyone were to continue to try to write Indian poems, we should know more about Indians than we did, than I did.

This is surely correct; and it may serve to point up the obvious fact that poems with Indian subjects do not necessarily have much to do with Indians or, even less, with Indian models. Poets like Rothenberg and Snyder have an informed awareness of Native cultures and their literary productions; others like Stafford and Richard Hugo have a deep feeling for the places so important to traditional Native cultures. Then there are poets like James Tate, whose "One Dream of Indians" proclaims:

> When I thought of Indians
> before, I thought of slender
> muscular men with feather
>
> heads wailing hallelujah,
> of blood spears on white flesh, their
> two-toned ponies insane.

But, the speaker tells us, " . . . There was one dream / of Indians I didn't / dream, however. That was you." Here is that determined reduction to the merely personal that marked a good deal of writing-school verse in the 1950s, that carried into the 1960s, and that persists today. The appearance of Indians in such poems is purely incidental and indicative of no particular relation whatever to Native Americans and their literature.

It was in the 1960s as well that a number of powerful Native American writers began to appear in print, among them Duane Niatum, Simon J. Ortiz, Roberta Hill, and James Welch. By the end of the decade, in 1969, the Pulitzer Prize for literature went to the Kiowa professor of English literature N. Scott Momaday for his novel *House Made of Dawn*. That same year, Momaday published his widely noticed, cross-cultural experiment in autobiography, *The Way to Rainy Mountain*. Momaday, as I have

noted, was a student of Winters and for his doctoral dissertation prepared an edition of the poems of Frederick Tuckerman, Winters's candidate for major American poet of the nineteenth century. Momaday, like Welch, writes both poetry and fiction; his verse, however, seems closer to the formal manner of later Winters than to anything discoverable in traditional Native literature. Here are the opening stanzas of Momaday's "Angle of Geese," which appeared in a volume of the same name:

> How shall we adorn
> Recognition with our speech?
> Now the dead firstborn
> Will lag in the wake of words.
>
> Custom intervenes;
> We are civil, something more:
> More than language means,
> The mute presence mulls and marks.

And here is Welch's "Snow Country Weavers":

> A time to tell you things are well.
> Birds flew south a year ago.
> One returned, a blue-wing teal
> wild with news of his mother's love.
>
> Mention me to friends. Say
> wolves are dying at my door,
> the winter drives them from their meat.
> Say this: say in my mind
>
> I saw your spiders weaving threads
> to bandage up the day. And more,
> those webs were filled with words
> that tumbled meaning into wind.

In Welch's poem, regular reference to animals is made, but formally the regular stanzas and irregular rhymes (in particular, the final "mind" / "wind" and the brooding-earnest tone) derive from the Euramerican rather than the Native American literary tradition. This is often the case as well with the work of Hill and Niatum, who, with Welch and Momaday, probably appear most frequently in general anthologies of American poetry. Their technical conservatism seems a recognition of the inevitable presence, in written verse in English, of the European poetic tradition.

I am far from implying, with these observations, a negative judgment upon the work of these writers; obviously, Native American poets are entitled to the same freedom accorded their non-Native counterparts in their choice of subject matter and formal manner. And, in any case, there are decided occasions on which these poets adopt a more open, more voice-oriented style. The relation of other contemporary Indian poets—I think of Ortiz, Ray A. Young Bear, and Joy Harjo—to European poetics is more tentative, more marginal. I will quote in full Ortiz's "This Preparation" as an example:

> these sticks i am holding
> i cut down at the creek.
> i have just come from there.
> i listened to the creek
> speaking to the world,
> i did my praying,
> and then I took my knife

and cut the sticks.
there is some sorrow in leaving
fresh wounds in growing things,
but my praying has relieved
some of my sorrow, prayers
make things possible, my uncle said.
before i left i listened again
for words the creek was telling,
and i smelled its smell which
are words also. and then
i tied my sticks into a bundle
and came home, each step a prayer
for this morning and a safe return.
my son is sleeping still
in this quietness, my wife
is stirring at her cooking,
and i am making this preparation.
i wish to make my praying
into these sticks like gods have taught.

On one hand, the reverential stance toward "ordinary" life, the sense of human responsibility to nature, the commitment to a relationship of "participant maintenance" (in Robert Redfield's phrase) toward the universe: these are all attitudes familiar to the Native tradition. The poem is presented as spoken-performed, with gestures implied, as an aspect of some larger (ritual) event. On the other hand, "This Preparation" is not radically different from poems by certain non-Native poets; it is by and large assimilable to the Euramerican tradition. It will take further work on traditional Native American literatures—new translations and new studies and greater general familiarity—to indicate to what degree its methods as well as its outlook can figure in written verse in English.

In any case, it should be obvious that just as the mere existence of poems with Indian subjects by non-Native poets does not in itself constitute evidence of a genuine opening to Native American influences, so, too, the mere existence of poems in print by Native American poets does not indicate any effective influence of traditional Native American literature on the canon. It does not seem possible or fruitful to attempt strictly to distinguish Native American from European influences in the work of Indian writers and non-Indians interested in Indian traditions, although the nature of the technical mix may well be worth attention. The errors to avoid, I believe, are to urge (as Leslie Marmon Silko has done) that Anglos simply stick to their own traditions, on the one hand, and, on the other, to insist (as Thomas Sanders and Walter Peek have done) that some "remembered Indianness" or "inherited and unconsciously sublimated urge to employ the polysynthetic structure of Native American languages" must somehow come through the English of poetry written by Native Americans.

Some other developments of the late 1960s also bear importantly on our subject. For it was in 1968—the year Dover reissued Burlin's *Indians' Book,* while fighting was reported in Vietnam and the streets of Chicago—that rebellion took place among the professoriate at the MLA convention in New York City: a concerted effort to naturalize the canon and to revise its traditional hierarchies of race and gender. Earlier that same year, students in France had rebelled against their professors and the gov-

ernment that employed them, calling for the burning of the libraries and a return to nature: "Sous les paviers, la plage!" ("Under the pavement, the beach!"). Earlier still, in 1966, French structuralism—*hors de Lévi-Strauss*—had arrived in force upon American shores to deliver the fourth blow, as it were, to Western humanistic narcissism (following the first three blows that Freud specified, those delivered by Galileo, Darwin, and Freud himself), with the symposium called "The Languages of Criticism and the Sciences of Man," held at the Johns Hopkins University. Michel Foucault was not present, but Barthes, Jacques Lacan, and the youthful Jacques Derrida were in attendance. At Johns Hopkins, Barthes announced that "to write" might be an intransitive verb; and Lacan dissolved the individual subject as "a fading thing that runs under the chain of signifiers. For the definition of a signifier is that it represents a subject not for another subject but for another signifier." Derrida, already displaying his characteristic total assurance, told his audience that "one can say in total assurance that there is nothing fortuitous about the fact that the critique of ethnocentrism—the very condition of ethnology—should be systematically and historically contemporaneous with the destruction of the history of metaphysics. Both belong to a single and same era." This denial of the privileged place of man—and modern anthropology's contribution to the conditions of possibility for such a denial (an early subject, as well, of Foucault's discourse)—projects exactly the sort of revision of the Western consciousness that would bring it nearer to appreciating the world view of Native American peoples and thus contribute to a more ready understanding of traditional Native American literatures and their claims upon the canon.

Throughout the 1970s and to the present moment, the developments I have been tracing have continued. In 1973, an excellent formal textbook, *Literature of the American Indian,* appeared; by 1975 there were at least five available anthologies of American Indian poets, many of whom had originally published in prestigious quarterlies. In 1981, Joseph Bruchac, himself part Abnaki and a poet, collected the work of more than thirty Indian poets in *American Indian Writings,* a special issue of the *Greenfield Review.* Duane Niatum's *Harper's Anthology of Twentieth-Century Native American Poetry* [came out in 1988]. The 1970s also saw the publication of John Bierhorst's valuable anthologies of Native American materials; Rothenberg's erratic but powerful volume of translation-versions, *Shaking the Pumpkin;* and Merwin's working of some of Robert Lowie's *Crow Texts.* Merwin's work appeared in *Alcheringa,* a journal of ethnopoetics, edited by Rothenberg and by the anthropologist Dennis Tedlock. *Alcheringa* not only published non-Western texts but occasionally included recordings with some of its issues. In 1979, Snyder's B.A. thesis was published as *He Who Hunted Birds in His Father's Village: The Dimensions of a Haida Myth,* with a preface by Tarn. *Myths and Texts,* which had been in and out of print since its original appearance in 1960, was finally reissued by Snyder's principal publisher, New Directions, in 1978.

Two important books of poetic translations from the 1970s deserve particular mention—one by Tedlock and one by Howard Norman. On the basis of recent work, I think it's reasonable to require that translations of Native American literature, if they are to be considered approximately accurate, meet two specific conditions. First, they must derive from an actual, taped, or re-creative audition of the Native performance. Second, they must be produced in accord with what Hymes has called "philological recognition of the original, not bilingual control," at least a rough working knowledge of the language in question. To produce his translations from the Zuni, *Finding the Center* (1972), Tedlock himself tape-recorded the narratives he would translate. Highly competent in Zuni, Tedlock sought to indicate the structural principles of Zuni narrative performance by attention to its metalinguistic features, its changes of pace and volume, the gestures of the narrator, and the audience responses; these he attempted to present by means of typographical variations. Although a shift from large to small type does not strictly represent a shift in volume from loud to soft, it does insist that something has changed; spaces on the page are not silences—but we are sufficiently accustomed to the analogy to respond to it.

Tedlock's translations are of Zuni *narrative;* yet they are arranged on the page in a manner that corresponds more closely to Euramerican poetry than to the more usual Euramerican medium for narrative, prose. Tedlock has argued long and well, however, that prose has "no existence outside the written page." In one way or another, he has been supported in this conclusion by the practices of Barre Toelken and Hymes, who have both advanced the artful science of what Toelken calls the "poetic retranslation" of Indian narrative that formerly had been transcribed in blocks of "prose."

Similarly, Norman's collection, *The Wishing Bone Cycle: Narrative Poems of the Swampy Cree* (1976), translates Indian stories into what appear, on the page, as poetry. Norman, a non-Native, grew up in proximity to Cree people and learned their language. A poet himself, he gathered these stories and presented them so effectively as to make a strong case for the power of Native American literary production—as well as to point out that traditional examples of that production are still discoverable. (Tedlock's collection performs the same service.)

The Wishing Bone Cycle, according to Norman, is a trickster cycle, but "the inventor and initiator of these particular poems was Jacob Nibenegenesabe, who lived for ninety-four years northeast of Lake Winnipeg, Canada." Nibenegenesabe says, "I go backward, look forward, as the porcupine does," and Norman explains: "The idea is that each time these stories about the past are told they will be learned for the future." These are, again, stories; they are narrated rather than sung or otherwise accompanied by music or dance; and they are both traditional and original, more or less in the same ways that traditional "authors" in Native cultures were always both originators and augmenters—as, indeed, the etymology of our word "author," from the Latin *augere,* indicates. An example:

> One time I wished myself in love.
> I was the little squirrel
> with dark stripes.

I climbed shaky limbs for fruit for her.
I even swam with the moon on the water
to reach her.
That was a time little troubled me.
I worked all day to gather food
and watched her sleep all night.
It is not the same way now
but my heart still sings
when I hear her
over the leaves.

Among other interesting texts in Norman's volume are a group of "short poems," which "may be spoken by anyone in a Cree community. Once told, even poems derived from the most personal experiences become community property." Here is one from John Rains:

> I am the poorest one.
> I cook bark.
> I have bad luck in hunting.
> A duck caught my arrow
> and used it
> for her nest.
>
> I am the poorest one.
> I sit in mud and weep.
> I have bad luck in hunting.
> A goose caught my arrow
> and broke it
> in two.
>
> I am old, old.
> Don't bring me pity,
> but food
> yes.

(pp. 96-131)

Arnold Krupat, in his The Voice in the Margin: Native American Literature and the Canon, *University of California Press, 1989, 259 p.*

DISCUSSION OF THE CANON

Rodney Simard   (essay date Spring 1992)

[*Simard is an American educator and critic. In the following essay, he emphasizes the complexity of Native American literature and asserts that the contributions Native American writers have made to American culture must be recognized.*]

Not long ago, former U.S. Secretary of Education William Bennett stood in the increasingly crowded doorway of the temple of American cultural integrity and wailed his prophetic lamentation: the recent curricular reconsiderations at such institutions as Stanford and the University of California at Berkeley are the beginning of the end of Western civilization as we know it; to bow to a revaluation of the canon of "great books" can only be culturally subversive, a sign of moral and intellectual bankruptcy in a professoriat that will all too easily cave in to popular fad and an ignorantly compelled call for greater "relevance" and "political correctness." To suggest that the canon implies that the locus of "greatness" lies in the white male experience is not, according to the former secretary's implications, culturally inaccurate: the masculine WASPishness of the canon is no more than a fact, however lamentable, of Western civilization. Perhaps the course of events will—even should—change, allowing greater participation by those in the disenfranchised minorities, but at this point to replace *Macbeth* with *The Color Purple* is to distort the history of esthetic achievement and intellectual contribution.

The bad news is that Bennett was essentially right: Walker's inclusion in the canon does indeed destroy the presumed integrity of the canon. Her presence compromises its very existence and marks the beginning of the end. Western culture and civilization as we have known them are in serious and immediate danger of disintegration, and I for one applaud this development, not because I am an anarchist, but because I am a traditionalist, if not the sort to sit back in the smug I-told-you-so vein; my conservatism in this matter is not in the former secretary's manner, nor in that of Allan Bloom, especially as represented in *The Closing of the American Mind;* neither do I wish to suggest that the canonical decay represented by its recent expansion is necessarily good in and of itself. Walker has been included for the wrong reasons, in the wrong manner, at least as regards the American canon of literature; the Western canon may well be another matter. Her inclusion is indeed the bellwether of the end, and this is to be welcomed only because the ideological foundation of the canon is itself fraudulent.

To pretend that the American (if not the Western) literary canon is a collection of the greatest texts written, those most inspiring and transcendent, is to argue from a religious, not a critical basis. Indeed, all questions of esthetics necessarily involve some subjective assessment—individually or culturally—that, like the religious, is a matter of both faith and indoctrination into esoteric matters revealed only to the cognoscenti. However, if we continue the metaphor into reality, the priestly class that guards the divine secrets, revealing their mystery to the uninitiated, is the professoriat, an American social class long dominated by white males. Criticism, as practiced in the American academy, does not deal in matters of faith but rather in something less privileged and individual, something more inherently social. Theory, as we currently understand it, is a social activity; therefore it *must* be political, and I believe that any theoretical consideration of American literature must acknowledge this dimension, whatever the theory in question, if it is modeled, as I think is correct, on some approximation of the scientific method rather than on leap-of-faith judgment—even though at this very moment the quantum physics of chaos continues seriously to challenge our inherent Newtonian biases, as the University of California at Santa Cruz mutates from an intellectual Bangkok into a postmodern Vienna.

What is "great" or "good" or "true" to a group of white male academics frequently is not so to another group differently composed, and greatness, goodness, and verity are not absolute qualities; yet the American literary canon is founded on just this assumption. Perhaps the Western tradition of letters, from which the American springs, is, however, so based. In some Aristotelian sense, worth is supposed to be inherent, emanating from the universals of the human condition: what is good rises (a sort of esthetic Darwinism). The fundamental questions are, of course, intimately linked to a predominantly Judeo-Christian sense of "goodness" and a misguided sense of who "we" are, as writers, as readers, as students, and as teachers. Our canon of instructive texts is not simply those that are the "best" in any absolute way, but those that are the best in conveying, sustaining, and confirming the dominant social order of the moment, something far more mutable than the rubric *American* might suggest. To attempt to transcend politics in favor of an arguably higher order, that of esthetics, is to deny fundamental realities. Literature not only does not transcend social issues; it is the *text* of society, the body of verbal artifacts offered up in support of the current sociopolitical "reality" or, perhaps more appropriately, "fiction."

So far, my primary concern here, American Indian literatures, has been referenced only in my title, and I have made claims to critical conservatism in the same breath with calls for canonical dissolution. These seemingly contradictory impulses find unity, however, in theory. Concerned as I am with Native American matters, both professionally and personally, particularly as they relate to the humanities and noncanonical literatures in general, I find that any examination and consideration of such matters compels me to employ the tools of both Marxism and feminism with increasing organic regularity. Any claim for American Indian literatures is necessarily allied with movements toward cultural pluralism and away from monocultural purism, with movements toward racial, ethnic, and sexual equality and away from the enduring linear Western hierarchies of race and gender. In both history and culture Native American does not equal Euramerican. Pluralism does not mean a diffusion of quality; it means a redefinition of quality.

Try though I might to be a semiotician, I find I am inherently—perhaps holistically—a feminist and Marxist, or, perhaps more properly as the term is coming to be defined, a neohistoricist. New Criticism, structuralism (to a lesser extent), and deconstructionism—all formalist theoretical schools—have all for too long emphasized literature as artifact or experience, a proposition that has decidedly political implications for the study of Indian literatures. Parallels to the current issue of the repatriation of Indian remains and artifacts spring to mind, as does a remark recently made by a colleague from California State University at Chico, who noted with horror that her campus has more Indians in boxes than in classrooms. I propose that our national literature, as a single entity, must be viewed as the text of the country in its multifaceted, multicultural, multiethnic, multiexperiential reality.

Esthetically, culturally, and historically, the American Indian voice, in its various expressive forms, "has been ignored, marginalized, or, more recently, reduced to a merely statistical potency as one of the 'multiethnic' literatures of the United States" [Arnold Krupat in his *The Voice in the Margin: Native American Literature and the Canon*]. To date, the only real blip on this graph has been the 1969 award of the Pulitzer Prize to N. Scott Momaday for his novel *House Made of Dawn,* an event slurred as ethnic pandering, as an anomaly, or as fraudulent, since Momaday isn't "really Indian," for, though he does have some mixed blood and does indeed look the part, he is, after all, a professor of comparative literature with a doctorate from Stanford who had to, at best, reinvent an Indian identity. Alarmingly, some of that criticism has come from within the Indian community, a suspicious eye cast toward Momaday's Anglo-Kiowa-Cherokee heritage, and even Arnold Krupat, among the most enlightened and sophisticated of commentators on Indian literatures, jabs at what he perceives to be Momaday's racism and sexism.

Such a discussion leads to another problem: the definition of "Indianness." The oft-cited contemporary definition comes from Momaday: "An Indian is an idea which a given man [*sic*] has of himself," a poetic designation, to be sure, but one Krupat calls hopelessly vague and sexist. To be more prosaic, more approximately scientific, do we turn to anthropology's three essential criteria: 1) genetic, 2) cultural, and 3) social? But how might these be applied? Are the key factors blood quantum, degree of tribal enculturation, and native-language facility? How are even these standards measured, and, what is most important, by whom?

The larger issues of authenticity impinge on literature in three different ways: authentic text, authentic translation, and authentic author. Leslie Marmon Silko has addressed one aspect of an ongoing debate, identifying two "racist assumptions": the first, "that the white man [*sic*], through some innate cultural or racial superiority, has the ability to perceive and master the essential beliefs, values, and emotions of persons from Native American communities"; and the second, "that the prayers, chants, and stories weaseled out by the early white ethnographers, which are now collected in ethnological journals, are public property." Silko's grouse, here most specifically against Gary Snyder, can be directed toward many significant American poets and is a complicated issue (discussed by Michael Castro in *Interpreting the Indian*); indeed, many writers have played at being neo- or pseudo-Indian, but much literature has also been enriched enormously by Indian influence, both in form and in subject. From Henry Wadsworth Longfellow to Oliver La Farge to Michael Blake, Anglo novelists have depicted Indian life and thought with varying degrees of success (just as Martin Cruz Smith selected the Russians in his *Gorky Park*); but to argue province is a moral, not an esthetic point, beyond the scope and intent of this discussion. Making a distinction between Indian and scholar, Dell Hymes posits: "Let those who are not Indian leave the continuing reworking of traditional materials to Indian People," perhaps overstating the positions and superb advances made in ethnopoetics in recent years by such sensitive and enlightened scholars (and writers) as Krupat, Swann, Dennis Tedlock, Jarold Ramsey, Andrew Wiget, Barre Toelken, Paula Gunn Allen, and Hymes himself, among several others. Susan Hegeman notes [in *American Quarterly* (June 1989)] that "the search for authoritative authenticity is a kind of longing for a guru or the perfect cultural informant," appealing "to textual authenticity" and representing "the longing for an 'ur-text,' a primary source," ultimately a Sisyphean task.

The issues of text and translation merge with authenticity of authorship in several additional ways. Paradigmatic is the "problem" of *Black Elk Speaks,* a textual knot charted by Raymond J. DeMallie and Julian Rice, among others. Who here is "author": Nick Black Elk, John Neihardt, Ben Black Elk, Enid Neihardt, all or a combination of these folks, or the oral/storytelling/coup tale tradition itself? Is the text "authentic," and, if so, by what criteria? And is not audience (another imponderable) a key issue in determining authenticity, of whatever flavor? From their beginnings, the history of written Indian literatures bristles with such thorny problems.

Less problematic but perhaps more disturbing are those authors who obscure or alter their Native heritages, or those who simply pose as Indians; the much-discussed cases of Jamake Highwater and Hyemeyohsts Storm come easily to mind. In such instances motive as well as authenticity becomes an issue, for, as Hegeman observes, "However one feels about the issue of 'authenticity' in relation to native American texts, there is a disconcerting tendency to ascribe a moral dimension to every possible position in the debate," and "Prescriptive notions from the academy about what is 'authentic,' valuable, or accurately presented only serve to limit the range of texts, opinions, and perspectives to which native Americans have access."

Problems of text and translation will always be complex and will continue; authorship would seem to be less so—that is, until someone resurrects a charge that a particular Indian author is not "Indian enough," as novelist David Seals recently did while reviewing James Welch's novel *The Indian Lawyer.* Various established authors, Momaday chief among them, have suffered this charge in the past, and indeed some consideration must be paid to the case of a mixed-blood writer with advanced academic training in the traditional American canon who might be, to some degree, reinventing his or her Native heritage. Few, however, would consider this bad faith, but attacks against their works persist. Seals's polemic is a very odd one, embracing malign perceptions of American universities and the contemporary publishing industry, as well as Louise Erdrich, while making some peculiar leaps of logic. Still, it does represent a persistent point of view.

Seals's closing question is, "Why do we have to write polished prose to make it in America?", building from his contention that Welch, like Erdrich, "is so grim and relentless that most Indians can't read" his novels, that both writers represent a "failure," having lost sight of "the sublime spirituality bursting like the new buffalo herds all over the Western prairies" as well as "the transcendent visions" and "secrets that have kept us alive despite 500 years of genocide." Welch's novel is "a little alien to Indians," and "polished prose is not inherently where 'Indian literature' comes from." Poetically implicit is the charge that the novel form is European, not Indian, and to write one is somehow to betray tradition and thus "authentic" Indianness.

Nonsense. Speaking of the ritual tradition ("defined as a procedure whose purpose is to transform someone or something from one condition or state to another"), Paula Gunn Allen says that "because it is an ongoing tradition, it is an adaptive tradition, and its adaptations are often strikingly dynamic." Seals charges that Welch "has written a very 'authentic' book, except . . . in the style of the storytelling itself," relieved that "the reader does not have to dwell in deep dissertations or complex stylistic extravaganzas such as we must endure at the hands of so-called [?] great writers like Joyce or Proust." Allen is far less myopic when she observes:

> Native Americans reared in the oral tradition of the tribes, however, are not ignoring or "experimenting" with accepted conventions when they do not follow Western structural conventions. Indeed, when they write within the conventions of the tradition from which James Joyce departs, they are being as experimental as he was when he wrote *Finnegans Wake*.

> American Indian novelists who write more or less chronological narratives that center on Indian themes and materials and adapt ritual narrative structures while maintaining the unities of location, time, and action, and the conflict-resolution structure of Western plots are very daring indeed.

Speaking specifically of Momaday, Michael Dorris says that "he may, in *House Made of Dawn,* be best understood as a Native American Henry James, Ralph Ellison, or James Joyce."

Any cursory familiarity with the majority of contemporary Indian novels uncovers a range of qualities and techniques embedded in the novelistic form that are characteristic of the Native oral tradition: circularity, polyvocalism, ambiguity, an ecosystemic view, tribalism, inherent mysticism and spirituality, strong place identification, and the like. Such generalizations abound, perhaps dangerously, signaling that the novel has been adapted to tradition and is not in opposition to older literary forms. Simon Ortiz takes this concept further, asserting that "because in every case where European culture was cast upon Indian people of this nation there was . . . creative response and development, it can be observed that this was the primary element of a nationalistic impulse to make use of foreign ritual, ideas, and material in their own—Indian—terms. Today's writing by Indian authors is a continuation of that elemental impulse." Tradition is an organic, evolving pattern, and growth does not necessarily mean assimilation or termination.

About language levels, Ortiz continues:

> The indigenous peoples of the Americas have taken the languages of the colonialists and used them for their own purposes. Some would argue that this means that Indian people have succumbed or become educated into a different linguistic system and have forgotten or have been forced to forsake their native selves. This is sim-

ply not true. . . . This is a crucial item that has to be understood, that it is entirely possible for a people to retain and maintain their lives through the use of any language. There is not a question of authenticity here, rather it is the way Indian people have creatively responded to forced colonization. And this response has been one of resistance; there is no clearer word for it than resistance.

Allen identifies "the novels most properly termed American Indian novels because they rely on native forms, themes, and symbols far more than on nonIndian ones and so are not colonial or exploitative. Rather, they carry on the oral tradition at many levels, furthering and nourishing it and being furthered and nourished by it." Dorris is even bolder, discussing Welch's *Winter in the Blood* with Silko's *Ceremony:* "It may well be among the first manifestations of a new era in Native American literary expression; at long last a pan-tribal tradition of true 'Native American literature' may be happening." The work of most contemporary Indian writers seems Indian enough for most—as does, ironically, Seals's own novel, *The Powwow Highway*.

Most "objective" criteria for authenticity, literarily or otherwise, are bad news for me; for although I identify myself as a Cherokee, that being my dominant blood line, I also have Choctaw, Osage, and Quapaw heritage, among other Indian as well as Anglo progenitors, including the Irish great-grandmother whose genes so pervasively make my physical appearance immediately suspect to Indians and whites alike. I represent the fourth generation of what has been a militantly assimilationist family, yet I am trying to study the Cherokee language; given my peculiar and evidently stunted language facility, however, I fear that I may never do any better with it than I have done with Latin, French, German, and Spanish, which is to say appallingly little. Besides, is not the Cherokee syllabary, developed by Sequoyah in 1821 and (perhaps) the first Native written linguistic system excepting petroglyphs and pottery markings, inherently suspect because of Sequoyah's own mixed blood and the Anglo influences it evinces? And further, is not Cherokee heritage in and of itself suspect, for, as Vine Deloria Jr. notes, everyone seems to claim a Cherokee grandmother—interestingly matrilineal—and, as a tribe, have not the Cherokees always been a little too readily assimilationist? After all, they were the primary of the so-called "Five Civilized Tribes," far too early developing a constitutionally based government and always insisting that they were a "Nation" rather than just a tribe. Everyone knows that they crossbred like bunnies, and they even owned slaves! Thus a lad can find himself marginalized and dismissed within the microcosm—if indeed it even is one.

Indian, 'Skin, 'Blood, 'Breed, or even ethnic slummer—the distinctions may be meaningful in context, but they do little to inform a serious inquiry into the nature of American Indian literatures. Perhaps, divested of its probably unintentional sexism, Momaday's definition remains the best: a matter of self-identification with some measure of genetic or cultural basis. Still, one contingent will insist on defining Indian literatures as those that are primarily for an Indian audience by Indian authors whose primary self-identification is Indian, working in forms historically evolved or most readily accessible to that primary audience. Krupat suggests that "oral performances, . . . spoken/sung rather than written in a Native language, and controlled by traditional forms 'internal to the culture,' . . . seem the best representatives of what might be meant by an Indian literature." Qualified and rather coy, such designations do much unnatural violence to the Native canon and would exclude, for example, even such an important work as *House Made of Dawn*.

Dorris contends that there is no such thing as Native American literature, because there has never been and is no such thing as a single Indian language or a single Indian culture. (Pan-Indianism was evidently a phenomenon of the 1960s and 1970s, however promising it might be as a political and perhaps cultural stance for the future.) On the other hand, the curriculum committee of my university initially objected to my proposal for English 314, "American Indian Literatures," on the grounds that its monoculturalism did not meet our new general-education requirements for multiculture and gender. Thus the distinctions embrace both amorphousness and tidiness, inclusive to the point of meaninglessness and exclusive to the point of obscurity.

A useful and familiar analogy can be made to an established term, of dubious validity, such as "European literature." As a curricular rubric, the term suggests similarity, even mutuality, between such disparate cultures, histories, and world views as those between the Norwegian and the Italian. Indeed, both are European, but the designation is also where the similarity ends; without resorting to Jungian archetypes, these two literatures, and the peoples who produced them, could hardly be more different. Nevertheless, the term persists, as does "Native American literature" (always in the singular).

Older North American literatures—for they are indeed profoundly plural—derive from the (mostly) oral traditions of at least twelve different racial sub-types and five hundred separate cultures with as many language variations (fifty different language groups having been identified) and thousands of years of development, altogether unrelated to written European languages, cultures, and histories; therefore my analogy begins to break down. Although the historical circumstances are still debated, Native Americans probably arrived from Asia in successive waves over several millennia via the land bridge (currently 160 feet under water) now known as Beringia, which was open for several periods, the first beginning around 60,000 B.C. and the last ending around 7000 B.C. However, recent research into cellular mitochondria at Southern Methodist University tends to suggest that all Native peoples may be descended from a group of as few as four women. Consensus suggests that 50,000 B.C. is a convenient date for the historical moment, so to speak, that shamanic religion and the core mythological literatures arrived or developed in North America. The following years are shrouded in mystery partly archeological and partly attributable to a continuing cultural chauvinism, but in the years immediately prior to contact with European settlers (or before the

Invasion) at least two thousand different tribes seem to have flourished, embracing four to eight million people.

The genericization of American Indians has proven something of a stumbling block as well. Margot Astrov, in her important 1946 anthology *The Winged Serpent* (retitled *American Indian Prose and Poetry* upon reissue in 1962), noted that the idea of "the" Indian is an abstraction, a reductive one, although it can be methodologically useful and helpful at times. An accuracy of diversity springs from at least the three formative influences she identifies: "individual disposition, group configuration, and natural environment." Most would agree that the matter is far more complex than even this refreshing catholicity would suggest. Nevertheless, there is no such clinically ideal person, in the past or present. The pervasive American mentality is awash with a limited selection of images, culled from a variety of unreliable sources, chief among them television and film.

Next in consideration are two intimately related matters: the oral tradition and the "appropriate" avenue for intellectual inquiry. To say that Native American studies are holistic is, on one level, only to summarize what I have already asserted; but, in the wider cultural net, the implications are more profound. The Euramerican tradition, like the European one upon which it was initially patterned, allows for categorization: literature, for example, can be separated from the cultural continuum and can be examined as a distinct entity, either as an artifact or as a microcosm of the culture at large. Not necessarily so in Indian matters, and part of this can be explained by Native attitudes toward language.

Kenneth Lincoln of UCLA speaks of a cultural/linguistic continuum with the tribal ear on one end and the existential eye on the other, emphasizing that literature is only an aspect of a larger whole, inseparable from it. Just as the academy is coming to understand that writing—as one medium of creative expression and self-definition—is more accurately (and profitably, in a pedagogic sense) thought of as a process rather than as a product, so too is language organic to Indian cultures rather than a separate manifestation. Lincoln cites the example of Ikinilik, an Inuit (or Eskimo), interviewed by Knud Rasmussen: "From what you say . . . it would seem that folk in that far country of yours *eat* talk marks just as we eat caribou meat." Delightful and seemingly naïve on the surface, Ikinilik's remark points to an essential and profound truth: language is not necessarily a symbolic representation of reality; it can be an incarnation of reality in itself. One view of language is of a human dimension (not just a human capacity) magically powerful and alive with spirit, whereas another is of an esthetically functioning semiotic system, existing primarily to transmit ideas. What emerges is the distinction between language that affects and creates reality and language that represents and approximates reality.

Lincoln notes that words are "beings in themselves, incantory, with spirits and bodies. Stories, songs, visions, and names lived empirically in the world." He speaks of the epistemological complex of the literal and metaphorical dimensions of the word, which *is* and which represents simultaneously. In most Indian cultures articulation is reality: to speak (and often simply to think) something brings it into being. The system is not semiotic, for words do not only represent a reality; they create it. Thus one of the characteristics that binds Indian literatures and begins to define a canon distinct from others is a belief in the primacy and potency of the word and utterance: "The empowering primacy of language weds people with their native environment: an experience or object or person exists interpenetrant with all other creation, inseparable from its name." Articulation is reality, which embraces both the natural and the supernatural, the physical and the metaphysical, and "A thought is a spiritual act; a word has the magical power to actualize spirits." To many and various Indians, the word is a tool designed not only to perpetuate but also to actuate.

To understand the words and thus the texts, one must at least recognize the cultural matrix of which they are organic elements. What emerges in many Indian linguistic systems and thus literatures is a concept of wholeness, balance, and integrity of form or being, closely related, as various critics have noted, to the Greek *harmonia* or the Hebrew *shalom,* as well as a marked inseparability of culture and cultural expression. Any oral literature is necessarily fragile, being always only one generation away from extinction; but it still is the basis for *all* literatures, and it is no less distinguished because of its orality. Written or printed literatures may represent a technological advance, but that is no esthetic accomplishment. As Walter Ong recently reminded us, Western civilization may be entering into its secondary orality in this electronic age, for a print culture is certainly receding.

The inseparability of language, and thus literature, from its larger cultural matrix points to the other holistic problem of American Indian literatures. Just whose province are they anyway? The linguist's, the anthropologist's, the historian's, the archeologist's? These academic disciplines all have made their claims, and all are legitimate; but each too frequently tends to assume that it is dealing with a discrete artifact of some sort, tending to ignore the messy persistence of contemporary—even modern—Indians, and particularly their literatures. Granting continuity, is the field of inquiry then the province of the sociologist, the political scientist, the psychologist? Certainly these disciplines can claim their pounds of flesh legitimately, but the humanist always seems sidelined in the division of the spoils—unless, of course, the philosopher, in her or his role as theologian, is allowed access.

I firmly believe that Indians as well as literary critics and scholars are weary of this compartmentalized academic process. Too much that is of exceedingly independent and authentic value has been sidelined, dismissed, or ignored for far too long. American history, literature, and society must now all be revised in the light of their inconvenient but very real complexities; essential to such an effort is the acknowledgment of her first citizens, their enduring roles, and their formidable contributions. Only then can we fully embrace those who came later—and continue to come—to our hemisphere, continent, and country, those who comprise our national texts. (pp. 243-48)

Rodney Simard, "American Indian Literatures, Authenticity, and the Canon," in World Literature Today, *Vol. 66, No. 2, Spring, 1992, pp. 243-48.*

[I] think that there is a real hesitation, and perhaps even an impossibility, a lack of willingness to accept the Native American people and all that we stand for in America. Because if they really looked at the Native American writer, and that means looking at the Native American people, and that writer's work, the critics would have to look at the underpinning, the structure of their own country, at their own conscience.

—*Simon Ortiz, in* Winged Words: American Indian Writers Speak, *1990.*

CRITICISM

Andrew Wiget   (essay date Spring 1992)

[*Wiget is an American educator and critic. In the following essay, he discusses the relationship between writer and reader in Native American literature, focusing particularly on Leslie Marmon Silko's novel* Ceremony *(1977).*]

The current interest in what has come to be called "multicultural" literature has focused critical attention on defining its most salient characteristic: authoring a text which appeals to at least two different cultural codes. Two recent and important discussions [James Ruppert in *Texas Studies in Literature and Language* 26 (1986) and Reed Way Dasenbrock in *PMLA* 102 (1987)] have focused on how an author manipulates the expectations of the reader by creating a discourse that requires the reader to negotiate between two cultural codes to establish conditions of signification and evaluation. Both essays, however, treat the cultural codes themselves as determinate realities, available whole as resources to the author, which the author then elects to use as he or she determines. This "code-switching" model does not seem to me to be a particularly useful way of describing the relationship of an author to the production of "multicultural" discourse. It should be clear that, far from being determinate realities, the cultural codes of which an author avails himself or herself are themselves mental constructs, and that multicultural discourse, like any discourse, is at the least a form of secondary representation. In this essay I want to examine how an author instantiates in that secondary discourse his or her primary act of representation, which establishes the author's self-conceived relationship to those cultural traditions, thus creating the "codes" which become esthetic resources. More simply, how does an author authorize himself to represent another culture's discourse to readers to whom it is alien?

Artistic authority is the focal term for a complex of issues having to do with the way in which an individual relates to tradition. In verbal art, whether oral or literary, authority has customarily been understood in two ways. Frequently authority is located in certain features of the discourse itself, whether matters of content or form, which counted as signs of continuity with previous instances of the same kind of discourse. Texts rich in such elements were considered "authoritative." Authority could also be located in the social role of the speaker as a sanctioned performer of the tradition. Speakers so sanctioned were considered "authoritative." This conventional view of things is unsatisfactory, precisely because it locates authority *either* in the text *or* in the speaker, when it seems to me that authority is more properly understood as naming the effect of narrative voice upon an audience. More precisely, artistic authority is an effect produced by the multivocality of some narrative, when the voice of the present narration (which is not, I will argue, the same as the voice of the person speaking) is located in and made intelligible by its relationship to another, earlier voice also represented in the narration. (This, I will further argue, is not the same as having "traditional" content.)

The problem of authority is inescapable in Native American literature. Although the comments I have just been making relate principally to oral tradition, contemporary Native American writers are also continually confronted with the issue. The prevailing popular assumption is that a Native American writer must in some isomorphic way "reflect" or "represent" the culture of her origin. But when asked how her Indian heritage entered into her art, Wendy Rose, a prominent contemporary Native American poet, responded tartly: "Indian is what I am. Writing is what I do." Indian writers today are often very ambivalent toward the cultures of their origin and wary, even defensive, about discussing the relationship between ethnicity and authorial function.

After reviewing briefly how the problem of artistic authority came to be articulated in its present terms, and discussing how American Indian fiction emerged in relationship to the Anglo-American discourse on Indianness, I will explore the ways in which Leslie Marmon Silko's *Ceremony* provides an original and powerful response to the dilemma of authority facing a bicultural writer. In the end I want to suggest that we cannot adequately appreciate Native American literature unless we understand the relationship of the writer to tradition as a rhetorical construction as well as a substantive ethnographic reality.

The history of the problem of artistic authority is familiar. *Authority,* like its cognate *author,* derives from the Latin verb *augere.* This root came into English with several meanings. One meaning—"to augment or add to"—was common in the Renaissance, when a person could refer to "the authorities" and an individual gained authority by participating in the tradition, as John Milton or Alexander Pope claimed to do. Even today a conservative position still views literary history as a complex of intertextual relationships anchored by the key "originating" texts of Homer, Vergil, Dante, Shakespeare, and Milton. The most prominent twentieth-century exponent of this view was T. S. Eliot, who suggested that each new creation necessarily establishes some relationship to that which came before, which relationship is the basis for esthetic evaluation, a position Harold Bloom's work on influence usefully complicates.

This is not the predominant meaning today, however. The current sense that "to author" does not mean "to augment" but rather "to originate" gained almost exclusive hold in the early nineteenth century as romanticism swayed Western Europe. This sense is related to another cognate, *augury,* i.e. "prophecy." To "augur well" was to discover the will of the gods, their original intention, which tradition had displaced into or hidden in signs. Work was valued as creative because it was original: that is, it shaped personal vision into an irreplicable texture of words and images that supposedly transcended historical and cultural constraints. A work had authority because it was characterized by a distinctive "voice," as if the spirit or "genius" of the author were transubstantiated and made present in his work. So thoroughly did this emphasis penetrate criticism and philosophies of art that one could credibly assert that an author was known best through her work rather than through nonliterary data—her family affiliations, politics, religion, socioeconomic status, sexual preferences, and so on.

This emphasis on uniqueness as the principal esthetic value also preoccupied folklore study during the age of romantic nationalism, though at the level of collective rather than individual expression. Folklore was collected and studied in order to identify the distinctive "genius" of different peoples. Both in folklore and in literature, then, authority derived from an appeal to absolute origins which, on the model of particular revelations from some "genius or spirit" on high, constituted the condition of a work's uniqueness and thus its value. The larger ideological struggles that dominated Europe in the nineteenth century, however, significantly altered this esthetic of creativity by powerfully transvaluing the category of the collective. Whereas on the one hand both a nation's folklore and the literary productions of its novelists and poets were viewed similarly as expressions of genius, on the other hand traditional lore was denigrated and literature elevated precisely because literature was an individual, not a collective production. Only literature—"high art"—could be genuinely "authored." This became the prevailing view: authority was opposed to tradition, as the original was opposed to the derivative.

For the most part, the claim of individual creativity and artistic autonomy has remained a pillar of conventional philosophies of art up to the present. It has also been presumed to distinguish effectively between folklore and literature, in ways to which most folklorists would object. The "folk" were assumed to be anonymous, without individual identity or artistic freedom. Folk artists were thought to be more authoritative, more authentic, more genuine, to the degree that their performances minimized variation. Elite artists, in precisely the opposite way, were considered more authoritative to the degree that they maximized variation to a condition approaching idiosyncrasy. This way of thinking about the two domains was established and is maintained by the academies and other institutions of elite culture which in some sense continue to require the appositional category of folklore as a way of validating their claims for what they count as fine literature.

The consequences of reifying tradition and isolating literature from folklore are very clear to such writers as Leslie Silko, Louise Erdrich, and Wendy Rose, and the principal reason they reject being labeled as "Indian" writers. They reject demands that self-expression must be articulated through some conventionalized "Indian" discourse, often sarcastically called "beads and feathers," not only (or even principally) because it is ethnographically inaccurate, but because such a position hypostasizes identity and so not only constrains the expectations of their audience but also deprives the writers of their artistic freedom. In this ill-conceived model, "ethnic" writers, like storytellers, become authoritative to the degree that they become quotative; criticism is reduced to the hunt for extra literary sources from which to create an ethnographic intertext that will mediate the work to the reader; and reading becomes a kind of shadow anthropology. This positivist model persists despite repeated demonstrations that the validity and force of its critical concepts and assumptions depend upon a positivist misunderstanding of realities which are in fact better understood in social-interactionist terms.

For example, in a very important 1984 article in the *Journal of American Folklore* entitled "Tradition, Genuine or Spurious," the folklorists Handler and Linnikin argue that "'traditional' is not an objective property of phenomena but an assigned meaning." They continue:

> Ongoing cultural representations refer to or take account of prior representations, and in this sense the present has continuity with the past. But this continuity of reference is constructed in the present. . . . To refer to the past, to take account of or interpret it, implies that one is located in the present, that one is distanced or apart from the object constructed. In sum, the relationship of prior to present representations is symbolically mediated, not naturally given; it encompasses both continuity and discontinuity.

This in not a new idea, of course—philosophers of history have been saying it for many years—but if allowed to work its way, it must necessarily change how creativity is understood.

For one thing, locating the motive for a claim on tradition in compelling interests of the present moment relocates the source of authority from the past to the present. When considered not from a philological or historical but from a social-interactionist perspective, authority—like the concept of "the traditional" on which it depends—must surely be understood not merely in terms of received content criteria but as a function of the exigencies of the per-

formance at hand. Authority, in interactionist terms, is rhetorical: the power to command the floor, compel attention, and manage interest. From the performer's point of view, authority means effective frame construction and management for the sake of what Goffman has called "engrossment." As Richard Bauman so concisely puts it, "The performer elicits the participative attention and energy of his audience, and to the extent that they value his performance, they will allow themselves to be caught up in it."

The phenomenon of engrossment underscores the social construction of identity. Because the experience of framing provides the conditions under which some identity features are highlighted, "being caught up" means, in affective terms, that audience members experience some of their identity features, formerly highlighted, become suppressed and others, formerly obscured, become highlighted. Performance theory in folklore articulates well with reader-response approaches to literature because both invoke the rhetorical as well as the formal dimensions of speaking. Consequently, the point about identity construction just made with regard to the audience of an oral performance has also been made by Wolfgang Iser with regard to reading.

> The manner in which the reader experiences the text will reflect his own disposition, and in this respect the literary text acts as a kind of mirror; but at the same time, the reality which this process helps to create is one that will be *different* from his own (since, normally, we tend to be bored by texts that present us with things we already know perfectly well ourselves). Thus we have the apparently paradoxical situation in which the reader is forced to reveal aspects of himself in order to experience a reality which is different from his own.

Creating engrossment, however, depends upon sustaining and deepening the frame which supports the performance. This requires role-switching not merely on the part of the audience, but on the part of the performer as well. In the case of a storyteller, for instance, a new voice must be created. By *Voice* I mean more than audible language. By *Voice* I mean a discourse characterized by a particular set of values and by a particular position relative to the characters and the audience, and it is this Voice which is the rhetorical focus of the writer's authority, not any biographical data. If a storyteller's authority were based on biographical indices alone, it would amount to little more than deference. This is also true of any writer, of course, but what might be called the autobiographical or ethnographic presumption rests especially heavily upon writers whose original language is not English or whose culture of origin is not Euro-American. This is not simply a matter of cross-cultural intelligibility; writers, including Native American writers, have employed a number of strategies to illuminate or obfuscate cultural differences as required by their esthetic purposes. And truly the work of criticism does include the illumination of what is often called "cultural background" for the sake of an informed reading. Still, the most important struggle is not for intelligibility, which is always a matter of accommodation, but for authority; and that struggle to liberate the narrative voice from a colonialist discourse is made more difficult, complicated by the usurpation by Euro-American writers of the space into which a Native American voice might emerge.

Native American writers, to oversimplify the matter greatly for the sake of brevity, necessarily participate in two worlds. One of these is Indian, often but not always characterized by specific ties to particular reservations, societies, and histories. By virtue of their advanced education, mixed blood, and inability to speak a native language, however, their Indian world is increasingly detribalized, marginalized, and pan-Indian. No wonder then that the key mythic subtext in *The Woman Who Owned the Shadows* by the Laguna Pueblo writer Paula Gunn Allen, and one of the principal symbols in Louise Erdrich's brilliant *Love Medicine,* is the automobile. The other world is Anglo-American, the world of their education, their literature, their publishers, and, if the truth be told, their principal audience. Indian people who read Silko and Momaday profitably can do so precisely because they, like the authors who satisfy them, are marginalized sufficiently from their own communities to read complex literary forms and comprehend an elaborate structure of allusion to those structures of knowledge (economics, psychology, physical science, literary criticism) that undergird contemporary Euro-American life.

However much Native American writers may wish to locate themselves in relationship to some sense of a Native tradition, insofar as they are writers, they can only do so with the consent of their Anglo audience and to some degree in Anglo terms. That means participating in the Anglo-authored discourse of "Indianness," though certainly without any presumption of affirming it. This discourse has evolved in several important stages. Initially, in the first half of the nineteenth century Indians were imagined as the nameable Others, whose otherness was constituted precisely as the projection of those characteristics which Euro-Americans repressed in themselves. By midcentury the ambivalence of Cooper, who bemoaned the passing of the frontier as a loss of possibility and a refuge for the unconscious, was being replaced by an arrogance fictionalized in Adolph Bandelier's book *The Delight Makers* and sustained by Lewis Henry Morgan's theorizing about the evolution of cultures. Far from being any kind of model or refuge, Indians and the frontier were a horror from which to flee, our desire to "go Indian" something to be violently suppressed. In this century Anglo writers admiring the Indian but persuaded of his absolute Otherness, no longer presumed to speak for Indians but found themselves reduced to silence. So Byers, the trader in Frank Waters's novel *The Man Who Killed the Deer,* seeks "a means, a tongue, a bridge to span the wordless chasm that separates us all; it is the cry of every human heart. And Byers looked at Martiniano but neither spoke." If, in the nineteenth century, the Indian as Cultural Icon had come to wear over his historical reality the projections of the shadow of the Euro-American unconscious, for better (Cooper) or for worse (Bandelier), in the twentieth century the Indian lost all concreteness and became the void into which we could indiscriminately pour our unnameable aspirations. The unqualified sum of our

infinite Unsayable, he was trapped in another people's dreams.

The evolution of an Anglo-American discourse on Indians had enormous consequences for Indian writers. A Native American writer who approaches the creation of literature in bicultural terms finds herself caught up in the literary dimension of a historical dilemma in which each of the voices rising within her cancels the authority of the other. How, thus, to speak? Quotation of tradition is not possible because form, language, and audience are principally Euro-American. Thus, tradition can only be misrepresented. Neither can she create something utterly Other from her historical and cultural entanglements, because that space is occupied by Euro-American voices. In short, whatever she creates will emerge or be inserted into the larger Anglo-American discourse. Realization of this reality is often rendered as silence and impotence, an important theme in Native American fiction beginning with the earliest Indian writers in this century. In John Joseph Mathews's novel *Sundown* the inability of the protagonist to communicate is paralleled by an inability to enact his desires. D'Arcy McNickle's novel *The Surrounded* concludes with the arrest of the protagonist and his girlfriend, who are trying to escape but, more ominously, discover that, in fleeing the reservation, they have brought their alienation with them and that it will divide them from each other forever. Finally, at a key moment in Momaday's *House Made of Dawn* the protagonist, Abel, hears experts discussing him and silently observes, "They were disposing of me in words. Their words." The silence of these novels—even the informed, "full" silence of Abel in *House Made of Dawn*—testifies to the inability of writers to create a voice that would effectively speak the vision he sees, one which is traditional yet contemporary, outside the Anglo-authored discourse of projected faith or fear.

It has been argued recently that, far from being an impediment, biculturalism is a resource for writers who are not really "caught in between two worlds." In *Beyond Ethnicity* Werner Sollers has recently argued that literary figures can choose to take up the marks of community identity, a position which would be especially welcomed, though with some important qualifications, by those contemporary Indian writers who reject the constraints of a crude kind of cultural determinism. The real question "beyond ethnicity," however, is whether it is possible to write as an Indian apart from the Anglo-authored discourse of Indianness. The only authentic solution would be a multivocal discourse, to write as a marginalized person whose ethnicity is negotiated in a plurality of voices on every page. This, it seems to me, is the particular achievement of Leslie Silko's *Ceremony*. Clearly a gifted writer, in *Ceremony* Silko has nevertheless adopted a posture of consciously denying a commanding narrative voice, in effect sublimating her attachment to an Anglo notion of authorship which, if anything, presumes the freedom to dictate the nature and conditions of storytelling. By such an act of sublimation, she distances herself from the conscious repression of native beliefs and interests in which the Anglo discourse of Indianness—with its stories *about* Indians— is historically implicated. Indeed, at several points in the novel she calls attention to the Anglo discourse by having one of her characters evaluate the course of the protagonist's life as a counterplot to the Anglo master plot. At one point, near the climax of the narrative, the woman who represents the voice of tradition to the protagonist tells him:

> The end of the story. They want to change it. They want it to end here, the way all their stories end, encircling slowly to choke the life away. The violence of the struggle excites them, and the killing soothes them. They have their stories about us—Indian people who are only marking time, waiting for the end. And they would end this story right here, with you fighting to your death alone in these hills. Doctors from the hospital and the BIA police come. . . . They'll call to you. Friendly voices. If you come quietly, they will take you and lock you in the white walls of the hospital. But if you don't go with them, they'll hunt you down and take you any way they can. Because this is the only ending they understand.

This sublimation of authority, which derives from the recognition that we live in a world made of stories, stories which compete with one another for our attention, also creates a space for an Indian voice, so that instead of "stories about Indians" we can create "an Indian's story." But what would "an Indian voice" be like? One might expect an Indian voice to be larded with ethnographic detail, committed to a "thick description" of the customs, language, and beliefs particular to a historically specifiable tribal community. However, such a voice, which one might call the "ethnographic" voice, would certainly signal a false attempt to authorize the speaker by locating her in relationship to a tradition she has never experienced. Indian communities today do not have the kind of static cultural integrity represented in the ethnographic record developed in the first decades of this century; indeed, they never did. In a world of VCR's and 4×4's the central reality is change. This too is the central theme of Silko's fiction. As the Navajo medicine man tells Tayo: "Accidents happen, and there's little we can do. But don't be so quick to call something good or bad. There are balances and harmonies always shifting, always necessary to maintain. . . . It is a matter of transitions, you see; the changing, the becoming must be cared for closely."

Change is more than the central thematic concern of *Ceremony;* the experience of change is its formal organizing principle. This is clear from the way Silko uses oral tradition. Like other Indian writers, she employs stories from tribal oral traditions, especially Navajo, as a resource for the novel. Unlike these others, however, Silko is less concerned with stories than with story*telling,* which she uses to create a decentered, multivocal text. The narrative voice in a novel by a lesser writer might compel a certain interpretation by highlighting just those actions of the protagonist which conform to a particular story from oral tradition being employed as a subtext. In such a situation the novel is essentially univocal, because the narrative voice controls not only the unfolding drama but also all the expository means, such as the use of oral tradition as subtext. In other words, simply supplying oral tradition as subtext does not pluralize a narrative. Silko realizes this. Her re-

sponse is to frame her narrative with the invocation of a traditional muse. This simple act has two consequences. First, because this traditional voice, which is the voice of Thought-Woman, a Laguna creator figure, preexists, it has an existence independent of the novel. This voice is telling a story of the history of the world, fragments of which are interspersed throughout the narrative of Tayo. As this larger story unfolds, it provides a frame of reference for interpreting Tayo's story without ever getting enmeshed in it. Rather than a *sub*text, in other words, it functions as a *side*text. Second, since all stories are part of this larger story, the perpetual storytelling of this traditional voice actually authorizes the particular narrating instance before us: i.e., the story of Tayo. Silko opens her novel with this framing poem:

> Ts'its'tsi'nako, Thought Woman,
>   is sitting in her room
> and whatever she thinks about
>   appears.
>   . . . . .
> She is sitting in her room
> thinking of a story now
>
> I'm telling you the story
>
> she is thinking.

Satisfaction in reading Silko's novel depends upon the reader's comprehending how the narrative of Tayo is informed by being embedded in the narrative of Ts'its'tsi'nako. The reading can be disconcerting, since the traditional voice erupts into Tayo's narrative without any kind of accommodation or transition except for a page break. The reader must give himself over to the task of creating a dialogic relationship between the two voices, an activity in which he is encouraged by continual references in the narrative of Tayo to self-conscious storytelling. The reader is thus required to recognize certain violations of narrative conventions. These violations have the effect of displacing artistic authority and decentering the text, because we have been trained to assume that we are being told the story by the voice of the writer.

The decentering of an Anglo authorial voice has double consequences, each deeply implicated in the other. On the one hand it liberates a genuine, previously suppressed voice, now recognized as legitimate—the "Indian voice" if you will—and so sublimation enables a form of self-realization: i.e., realization of what is recognizable and communicably Indian about the author's persona. On the other hand, however apparently benign its consequences, this decentering is accomplished only by assuming a precarious, almost Olympian position from which to manage both voices. This ultimate assumption of power satisfies all the expectations for control and demands for originality that constitute authority in Euro-American literary tradition. Silko, in other words, can both eat her cake and have it too, because she uses her biculturality not only as two distinct literary resources, supplying images, types, and so on, but as two distinct fields of action, of meaning-*making*. Like a figure between two mirrors, Silko's authorial stance presents us with two simultaneous images of herself, realized in the narrative through the two voices, each of which, like reflections of reflections, continually evokes the other.

Artistic authority describes how an artist locates himself in relation to tradition. Conventionally, this has been understood differently for folklore and for literature. Folk narrators were assumed to be authoritative in proportion to the degree to which they minimized variation and allied themselves with the substance of some putative tradition; literary artists were supposed to be authoritative in precisely the opposite way, by being "original" and distancing themselves from tradition. I have tried to demonstrate that such an understanding of the artist's relationship to tradition is inadequate, principally because it is based upon positivist assumptions which treat the Self, the Past, and the Text as entities, not as phenomena. Moreover, this model has been particularly oppressive to Native American writers, who are "recognized" as Native American only when they participate in the Anglo-authored discourse of Indianness, by locating their appeal to authority in quotations from ethnography. I have argued that when Self, Past, and Text are understood in interactionist terms, as emergent phenomena, the focus of critical attention must turn from Theme to Voice. By identifying Voice as the effect of artistic choices, I have tried to establish authority not as a function of content but as an index of performance: that is, as a uniquely produced relationship to a sense of the past which is both created by the artist and conceded by the audience, and realized in the experience of form as it emerges in the act of reading or hearing. Such a perspective, it seems to me, heightens our sense of the complexity of narrative, whether literary or folk. (pp. 258-63)

> *Andrew Wiget, "Identity, Voice, and Authority: Artist-Audience Relations in Native American Literature," in* World Literature Today, *Vol. 66, No. 2, Spring, 1992, pp. 258-63.*

Alan R. Velie   (essay date Spring 1992)

[*An American educator and critic, Velie has contributed to such books as* Man and Nature in Literature *(1974) and* American Indian Literature: An Anthology *(1979). In the following essay, he discusses the recent emergence of middle-class protagonists in the novels of James Welch, N. Scott Momaday, Louise Erdrich, and Michael Dorris.*]

The first generation of novels, the books that have become the classics of the American Indian Literary Renaissance—[N. Scott Momaday's] *House Made of Dawn,* [James Welch's] *Winter in the Blood,* [Leslie Silko's] *Ceremony,* [Louise Erdrich's] *Love Medicine*—generally present a bleak picture of life in Indian Country. Although the authors treat their subjects with humor and compassion, and the reader gets a full sense of the characters' essential humanity, for the most part the protagonists are poor, shiftless, heavy-drinking drifters who are usually out of work and often in jail. For instance, Abel in *House Made of Dawn* is lost and alcoholic after returning from World War II. He serves eight years for killing an albino Indian before finally adjusting to life in his tribe. Gerry Nanabush, if not the protagonist of *Love Medicine* then

certainly the most dramatic character, makes a specialty of escaping from prison. The nameless hero of *Winter in the Blood* avoids jail and is less poor than broke, but he has little aim in life; he drifts from one bar to another, picking up women, getting beaten up. Tayo, in *Ceremony,* is a lost bibulous soul who, with the help of a Navajo healer, eventually pulls his life together.

In the past five years, with what might be called the second generation of novels, Indian fiction features middle-class protagonists, Indians in the professions. Scott Momaday's *Ancient Child* is about a Kiowa painter who exhibits in galleries in New York and Paris. In James Welch's most recent book, *The Indian Lawyer,* the hero, a Blackfeet, is a successful corporation lawyer who runs for Congress. *The Crown of Columbus,* by Louise Erdrich and Michael Dorris, depicts the adventures of a mixed-blood professor at an Ivy League university. The change from lumpen to *haut-bourgeois* protagonist represents a shift in focus of the Indian novel from depicting ethnic experience of the tribal group to dealing with problems of personal identity of Indians who have lost or weakened their ties to their tribe because they live their lives primarily among whites.

In the earlier novels the authors were chiefly concerned with depicting the Indian ethnic experience, the texture of tribal life. Although certainly there are many middle-class Indians, statistically most Indians on and off the reservation are working-class. The U.S. Census Bureau reported that in 1980—the most pertinent date for the novels under discussion—31 percent of Indians had finished high school, 17 percent had attended college (8 percent graduated), and 28 percent were living below the poverty line. So, an author concerned with depicting the Indian experience is not likely to make his protagonist a yuppie. Furthermore, ethnic characteristics are more obvious at the lower end of the social scale. Poor Indians, especially rural ones who live with their tribes, are more likely to retain traditional patterns of ethnic behavior, whereas generally speaking, an Indian banker living in the suburbs is likely to live pretty much as his white neighbor does.

Also contributing to the depiction of the characters of the early novels is the archetype of the trickster, the most important culture hero to the Indians of North America. Trickster takes different forms in different tribes—Coyote, Raven, Hare, Old Man—but in all cases he plays tricks and is the victim of tricks, has prodigious appetites for food and sex and adventure, is always on the move, and is totally amoral, beyond good and evil. In contemporary Indian literature this means that Trickster is more likely to be a bum than a businessman. He is found far more often in a bar than in an office; he is traditionally a drifter who is usually out of work and often in jail. He may be lovable, but he is rarely respectable.

In general, the first generation of novels of the Indian Renaissance is about tribal identity. The structure of Momaday's *House Made of Dawn* is based on Abel's quest to find his place in the tribal community in which he was raised, Walatowa Pueblo. That place is in question because, although his mother is a member of the tribe, Abel, as an illegitimate child, is an outsider; he does not know who his father is, or even what tribe his father belonged to.

Throughout the book Abel is lost and disoriented. When he returns from World War II, he cannot adjust to tribal life. When an albino Indian named Fragua humiliates him at a tribal ceremony, Abel kills him and is sent to prison for eight years. When Abel finishes his term, the government relocates him in Los Angeles, where he attacks a policeman while drunk and suffers a terrible beating.

Having lost his job in Los Angeles, Abel returns home, and the novel ends on a positive note with his reintegration into his mother's tribe. When his maternal grandfather dies, Abel buries him in the prescribed Walatowan fashion, then runs in the ritual race for good hunting and harvests that his grandfather had won decades before. He has discovered that his father was Navajo, and so as he runs he sings "House Made of Dawn," a Navajo prayer song, acknowledging the paternal side of his cultural identity.

James Welch's *Winter in the Blood* also treats the theme of a lost soul finding his place in his family and tribe. The hero, whose name we never learn, suffers from emotional numbness brought on by the death of his father and brother. He drifts through life, cruising bars, picking up women, losing fights. At the climax of the novel the hero discovers the identity of his grandfather, the man who kept his grandmother alive during the great Blackfeet famine. Like *House Made of Dawn, Winter in the Blood* ends with the funeral of one of the hero's grandparents. In this case the funeral does not follow tribal traditions—there is a coffin and a grave—but following the Blackfeet custom of burying the deceased's possessions with him or her, the hero throws into the grave his grandmother's last possession, a tobacco pouch with an arrowhead in it, a relic of the days when she was the wife of a great chief.

Leslie Silko's *Ceremony* deals with similar themes. Like Abel in *House Made of Dawn,* Tayo is an outsider because he is illegitimate. His mother was a prostitute who raised Tayo in a shelter of rusted tin in an arroyo in Little Africa, a ghetto in Gallup, New Mexico, where poor blacks, Mexicans, and Indians lived in terrible squalor. When his mother died, Tayo went to live with his aunt and grandmother. Like Abel, Tayo serves in World War II and has a hard time adjusting afterward. Both characters are reminiscent of Ira Hayes, the Pima who was one of the Marines who raised the flag on Mount Suribachi, Iwo Jima. Hayes died of alcohol-related problems when he returned to New Mexico after the war. Tony Curtis's film *The Outsider* made Hayes into a literary stereotype: the Indian who can die for his country but not live in it.

Tayo suffers severe mental problems from the trauma of having seen the Japanese kill his cousin while on the Bataan Death March in the Philippines. Tayo's problems are compounded by the guilt he feels because he believes that his prayers to stop the rain on the march have caused the drought on his tribe's lands in New Mexico. When military and civilian psychiatrists are unable to help him, Tayo enlists the aid of the Navajo healer Betonie. Betonie knows that the proximate cause of Tayo's problems is his experience with the Japanese, but that the ultimate cause is the witchery, the supernatural evil set loose centuries ago by Indian witches. Betonie sets Tayo on a quest; when Tayo completes it, he not only cures himself but also ends

the drought that has plagued the tribe. Tayo is the modern avatar of Sun Man, the trickster hero of Laguna myth who defeats the Evil Gambler who had caused a drought by imprisoning the rain clouds.

Louise Erdrich's *Love Medicine* may seem at first reading to be more a set of related stories than a novel with a coherent structure, but there is a framework to the book: Lipsha Morrissey emerges as the central character, the protagonist whose adventures and discoveries give the novel its shape. The narrative begins with the death of Lipsha's mother June, climaxes with Lipsha's discovery that his father is Gerry Nanapush, the trickster escape artist (Nanapush is the Chippewa name for Trickster), and ends with Lipsha's helping Gerry escape to Canada.

Lipsha is an unprepossessing figure, a man who says of himself, "I never really done much with my life, I suppose. I never had a television." He inadvertently kills his adoptive grandfather Nector while trying to work a love-medicine spell that will make the old man fall in love with the wife he has cheated on for years. Lipsha is a figure of fun, a man given to hilarious malapropisms (he confuses the Philippines with the Philistines, for instance). He does not gain a great deal of stature even at the end, but when he helps his fugitive/trickster father escape, the novel concludes on an upbeat note.

All these novels close on a note of hope, the protagonists having increased their sense of self-respect by discovering who they are and how they belong to the tribal community. Still, although their degradation seems to be behind them, and they are personally better adjusted, they end socially as they began, marginally above the poverty line, uneducated, without much chance—or desire, for that matter—to be successful in middle-class white American terms.

The novels of the past five years, by the same authors, treat a very different class of protagonists: Indian professionals who have achieved a great deal of success and prestige in the white world. It seems that Momaday, Welch, and Erdrich turned from depicting life in the tribal community to a matter that touches them more closely: the question of the cultural identity of an Indian who leaves the tribe to live among whites and becomes so successful he can't go home again.

There had been middle-class Indian characters in minor roles before: Kate Loney in Welch's novel *The Death of Jim Loney* (1979), for instance, has a prestigious job with the federal government, and Myron Pretty Weasel, in the same book, is a successful rancher. Albertine Johnson in *Love Medicine,* who seems like a young Erdrich, is in medical school. In fact, one might argue that Gerald Vizenor's Griever de Hocus, who appears in several novels and short stories, starting with "Luminous Thighs," is the first middle-class protagonist. Griever, who functions as Vizenor's alter ego, is a filmmaker who receives a grant from Robert Redford's Sundance Institute in "Luminous Thighs" and teaches English at Zhou Enlai University in Tianjin in *Griever: A Monkey King in China.* Griever is primarily a trickster, however, a protean character who evades easy classification and seems to strain the limits of the term *middle-class.*

The first real, honest-to-God yuppie protagonist in Indian fiction is Locke Setman in Momaday's *Ancient Child.* "Set," as he calls himself, is a highly successful painter in San Francisco, counted "in the first rank of American artists." He exhibits in galleries in New York and Paris, and "it was fashionable—and expensive—to own one of his paintings." Although his father was Kiowa, Set has very little knowledge of his Indian cultural heritage. His parents died when he was a child, and after a few years in an orphanage he was adopted and raised in San Francisco by a white philosophy professor. He is in love with a beautiful and talented blonde woman, a pianist and archivist who graduated from Berkeley.

On one level Set represents one side of Scott Momaday. The author is also Kiowa on his father's side but not on his mother's. Like Set, Scott was not raised among the Kiowas; he spent most of his youth in New Mexico at Jemez Pueblo, where his parents taught in the reservation school. Although there are pan-Indian movements, Indians generally identify themselves as members of a tribe; and so although Scott was an Indian, as he relates in *The Names,* he was an outsider among the Jemez, not simply an Indian among Indians. From the time Scott went away to boarding school, he has lived mostly among whites. Much of the time, like Set, he lived in the Bay area. Although Scott is better known as a novelist and poet, like Set he is a painter of some renown.

Still, *The Ancient Child* is very complex, and there is more than one side to Scott Momaday. Another side, what we might call his traditional, tribal side, is represented by the wild young medicine woman known only as Grey, who calls herself the "mayor of Bote, Oklahoma." *Bote* is the Kiowa word for cow (originally buffalo) innards, a dish the Kiowa eat raw. A taste for bote is a test of ethnic authenticity. Grey is Kiowa on her father's side and Navajo on her mother's. In his youth in the Southwest Momaday spent some time in the *Dine* (Navajo country) and became familiar with Navajo culture and language. His first love as a young man was riding his horse, and Grey is a wonderful rider, able to perform a trick that Scott himself used to do: picking up a dollar from the ground while riding at a gallop.

Perhaps the strongest resemblance between Momaday and Grey lies in the fact that in *The Ancient Child* the latter is the author of a collection of essays and poems called "The Strange and True Story of My Life with Billy the Kid." Momaday had published some of the essays in the Santa Fe *New Mexican* in the early 1970s and had added the poems shortly afterward, though he never published the work as a whole. He now makes a few minor changes (e.g., when Scott rode with Billy, he saved a young woman from the Indians, whereas Grey saves a young man) and works the whole piece into the novel as Grey's dream vision.

The Ancient Child is more than a realistic novel; there is a strong mythical element to it. It may sound like belaboring the obvious to mention this, since the book begins with the Kiowa myth of the transformation of a boy into a bear and ends with the transformation of Locke into a bear. However, the way Momaday employs and blends myths is not at all obvious and can use some elucidation. For one thing, although the Kiowa myth is the most important, it is not the only one. Locke's childhood nickname is "Loki," the name of the Germanic god famous for his ability to change shapes. Locke calls himself "Set," which is not only the Kiowa word for "bear" but also the name of the Egyptian god of the desert often regarded as the embodiment of evil. Locke's transformation occurs in the desert near Lukachuki, New Mexico, and as Locke feels the power of the bear within him, he senses it as the power of evil.

The primary myth, however, is the Kiowa story of the boy who is playing with his sisters when he turns into a bear. He chases them to the base of Tsoai, the rock tree, which they clamber up and escape as the stars of the Big Dipper. This myth is particularly important to Momaday, since his tribal name is Tsoai-talee, "Rock Tree Boy." Tsoai is a granite monolith in Wyoming that is sacred in Kiowa mythology; Momaday exercises poetic license in moving it to New Mexico for the novel. It is at the base of Tsoai, outside Lukachuki, that Locke turns into the boy and then into the bear.

On one level it appears that Locke's transformation into a bear represents a form of wish fulfillment. Momaday, living in the tame, white world of academia—he has been a professor at Santa Barbara, Berkeley, Stanford, and now Arizona—perhaps feels cut off from his tribal culture and thus from a more feral sense of himself. To return to tribal culture is to move closer to nature, as the beautiful passages about the grasslands of western Oklahoma indicate; but to become a bear is to become part of nature, as revealed in the transformation passage, when Set as bear can hear the feathers of a hawk ruffling in the sky and smell rain in the mountains miles away.

Nothing so dramatic happens in Welch's *Indian Lawyer,* a novel that follows the conventions of traditional realism. There is a transformation, however: Sylvester Yellow Calf develops from a shy, lonely child, abandoned by alcoholic parents, living in poverty on the Blackfeet reservation, into a highly successful lawyer with the most prestigious law firm in Montana. Sylvester achieves this transformation in easy stages, one success after another. He is a basketball star in high school, leading his reservation team to the Montana state championship. He is all-conference in basketball at the University of Montana as well as a good prelaw student. He attends Stanford Law School.

As the novel opens, Sylvester has just won a major court case against the Anaconda Company, the most powerful corporation in Montana. The national Democratic Party has heard of Sylvester and wants him to run for Congress. Like Locke Setman, Sylvester is dating a beautiful blonde, a relationship which seems to be a symbol of an ethnic's integration into white society. The woman, Shelley Hatton, has degrees from Swarthmore and the University of Pennsylvania and is the daughter of a wealthy rancher and politician.

Despite his success, Sylvester is uneasy, partially because he has guilt feelings at succeeding where so many of his tribal members have failed. In Montana, Indians excel in basketball much the way that African Americans do in other states. A major difference is that although many African Americans have used basketball as a way out of the ghetto and into college, Indians by and large have not. Perhaps because of a tighter sense of tribal community, Indians in Montana have felt so lonely and alienated when they left home, even to attend state schools, that they rarely play sports in college.

Sylvester's success has made him an outsider in his tribe, and he feels uncomfortable. He knows that although he has made it, the rest of his high-school teammates, the rest of his people, are trapped in a life of poverty and failure on the reservation. Perhaps it is this feeling of guilt that causes Sylvester unconsciously to undermine his career. As a member of the Montana Parole Board, he meets the wife of a prisoner and has an affair with her. As a result, the prisoner's friends attempt to blackmail Sylvester. He is able to face them down, but he abandons the race for Congress. The book ends inconclusively; Sylvester defeats his enemies and avoids destroying his career, but that career, which has been one triumph after another, has temporarily stalled.

Welch paints a far bleaker picture of Indian life than does Momaday. It is not that Sylvester Yellow Calf endangers his career, but that his success is so uncharacteristic of Blackfeet. Like Momaday, Welch portrays an Indian who succeeds in white America, as Momaday and Welch themselves have (Welch teaches at Cornell), but he heavily emphasizes the point that an Indian who succeeds in white America is an anomaly who is likely to feel as much concern as satisfaction with that success.

The latest of the Indian novels with a middle-class protagonist is *The Crown of Columbus* by Louise Erdrich and Michael Dorris, her husband. The novel centers on the adventures of Vivian Twostar, a mixed-blood ("Coeur d'Alene-Navajo-Irish-Hispanic-Sioux-by-marriage" is the way she describes it) professor of anthropology at Dartmouth. Vivian is in a precarious position as the novel opens: she is ponderously pregnant with the child of a man she refuses to marry, and she is coming up for tenure but has only a slender publication record. She is not given to self-pity, however; she has a marvelously wry way of looking at herself ("a sort of backyard-barbecue Colette"), her field ("Native American Studies, my so-called discipline"), and the world in general. The father of her child is Roger Williams, a caricature of the repressed, upper-class, WASP professor of English. In the section narrated by Vivian she lampoons him: he "knew a lot about the world, and little about himself." In the section Roger narrates he lampoons himself: in thinking about his as yet unborn child, he wonders, "Would it expect me to play baseball?"

Erdrich and Dorris make Vivian so attractive and paint such a ludicrous picture of Professor Williams that it is hard for the reader to want Vivian to marry him, although that is clearly where the novel is headed. In a sense Roger represents white America in the way that the blonde

women did in *The Ancient Child* and *The Indian Lawyer:* having a relationship with a prototypical WASP is the sign that the protagonist has arrived in the white world. Vivian needs Roger, but she is full of soul and is appalled at his whitebread ways.

Through Vivian, Erdrich and Dorris give a humorous yet very complex and perceptive view into what it feels like to be a token ethnic surrounded by whites. The plot revolves around the Columbus quincentennial, an event about which the Indians are understandably ambivalent: "My primary urge, the same as every other sensible person of full or partial American Indian descent, was to duck it." The politically correct editor of a local journal won't let her duck it, however; he wants a "revisionist" account of Columbus from an outraged Indian, and although Vivian objects to the way he is using her, she agrees under pressure to do an article for him.

Vivian's research on Columbus takes her to the Caribbean, and with the change of setting we get a totally different novel. The half that takes place at Dartmouth is a subtle and hilarious comedy of manners about life in academe, a book reminiscent of David Lodge's Brummidge novels. The Caribbean portion of the book is more like a Peter Benchley novel: white beach, blue skies, and improbable violence at sea, as Vivian, though tied to an aluminum chair, manages to win a fight on board a boat, kicking her tormentor overboard. Roger tries to make it to shore with Vivian's baby but punctures his rubber raft and has to abandon the child in it. The raft is pursued by a shark. In the most improbable development of all, the crown of Columbus that Vivian is pursuing turns out not to be a Renaissance treasure but Jesus' crown of thorns. When Vivian discovers it, all the thorns fall off—a provocative image, possibly symbolic of the fact that things will no longer be thorny for the heroine.

Naturally there is a happy ending to this melodrama: Vivian is recognized as a world-renowned expert on Columbus. The villain who tried to kill her goes to jail. She and Roger build a house and live together, presumably happily ever after. She has achieved fame, fortune, love, and a happy family. The book needed to change from a satire to an adventure fantasy to accomplish this, and that is what happens.

Locke Setman, Sylvester Yellow Calf, and Vivian Twostar are three examples of the new breed of Indian protagonist, Native Americans who make it in the white world. Their fates are quite different: Locke not only eventually leaves the white world; he ceases to be human altogether. Sylvester takes a sabbatical from his law firm but seems poised to return to the world of corporate law, though perhaps with a heightened consciousness of ethnic and ethical considerations. And Vivian exits a winner; she keeps her ethnic integrity and conquers the white world. (pp. 264-68)

Alan R. Velie, "American Indian Literature in the Nineties: The Emergence of the Middle-Class Protagonist," in World Literature Today, *Vol. 66, No. 2, Spring, 1992, pp. 264-68.*

James R. Kincaid   (essay date 3 May 1992)

[*Kincaid is an American educator and critic who has written books on Charles Dickens, Alfred Tennyson, and Frances Trolope. In the essay below, he examines numerous recent works by Native American writers.*]

What can it mean to go one-on-one, white on red, with the large number of important recent works by and about American Indians? Putting the question in that snug way focuses once more on the heart-shredding (uplifting) dilemmas of sensitive (guilty) whites (me)—Kevin Costner among the noble savages—but it can also be a wedge into disruptive questions about literary and political power.

How do our stories of what is past, passing or to come get to be manufactured, circulated and understood? Whose stories are they? Who gets to make and tell them? Who is listening—and how well? American Indian writing and experience may offer much more to all of us than the excuse for one more bout of maudlin self-examination or an invitation to join Jane Fonda and Ted Turner for tomahawk chops.

But we have little to hope for, any of us, if those in the dominant culture cannot get past sympathizing so fully and understanding so readily. The poet, novelist and critic Paula Gunn Allen, who is of mixed Laguna and Sioux descent, says that some books on Indians are good precisely because "they make no sense"; they resist our attempts to sag back into the usual habits of sense-making, heaving melancholy sighs and thinking knowing thoughts. Ms. Allen's diagnosis is supported by virtually all 11 of the interviews with the writers collected in *Winged Words: American Indian Writers Speak.* They agree with her that

those other Americans who outnumber Indians by more than 200 to 1 can smother any threatening difference with empathetic awareness: "Everybody, or almost everybody, is well intentioned, sympathetic," and "everybody in this country thinks they know what Indian is." Some of these writers take on what the poet Wendy Rose, who is of Hopi and Miwok ancestry, calls, with sarcasm surprisingly gentle, "white shamans, people who say they have some special gift to really see how Indians think, how Indians feel." Many love deeply (or deeply need) all Indians—Indian ecology, Indian earthiness, Indian mysticism—"forgetting," the poet and novelist Linda Hogan says, "that enlightenment can't be found in a weekend workshop, forgetting that most Indian people are leading the crisis of American life."

Such amnesia, according to Ms. Hogan, who is of Chickasaw ancestry, gives us the "beautiful," "wonderful" Indian image we can gaze at and gush: "like looking at Jews in concentration camps." We see what our situation allows us to see. Even our scientists, our anthropologists, invent the idea of culture they need and then, lo and behold, "find" it. About Indians "they've never been right once," says Gerald Vizenor, a novelist and critic of Chippewa descent.

The first step, it appears, is not to blubber, or to see so easily: our sympathetic intelligence is always wanting to tell stories that belong to others. But none of the contributors to *Winged Words* are separatists, arguing that Indian writings should be hidden from view. Despite all our focusing difficulties, they know it is crucial that more people start looking. "Somebody," Wendy Rose says, "is benefiting by having Americans ignorant about what non-European Americans are doing and what they have done; what European Americans have done to them." This ignorance, several writers in the collection agree, is instrumental. The poet and novelist James Welch, of Blackfeet and Gros Ventre descent, says "it's really advantageous for . . . power people not to know anything about the culture," for if they know "they're going to have to do something about the Indian situation." The poet Simon Ortiz, who was born at the Pueblo of Acoma in New Mexico, says that if people read this material, they "would have to say, yes, and agree and press the Supreme Court and U.S. Congress to give the Black Hills back to the Lakota people. . . . to say, yes, the Native American people do own Arizona."

If we read differently, we do differently—reading better, we do better. This optimism fires through the well-earned skepticism and anger of almost all the interviews in *Winged Words.* The poet and memoirist N. Scott Momaday, of Cherokee and Kiowa descent, says we are already doing a little better, having "dislodged" the frozen image of the devil pursued by John Wayne for something "more vital and infinitely more adaptable." And Leslie Marmon Silko, of Laguna and Mexican ancestry, has often expressed her belief that language will work, will make us do, will create community.

Lest we lapse back into "understanding," though, or sign up with our local travel agent for a weekend GetaWay Vision Quest (the visit to the sweat lodge is extra), Ms. Silko, the author, most recently, of the novel *The Almanac of the*

Dead, contends that the distance remains great and that our insidious colonial-genocidal power endures: "I'm still a believer in subversion. I don't think we're numerous enough . . . to take them by storm." The challenge is to honor the integrity and generosity of this subversion by reading more widely and warily, I suppose, trying harder to understand less.

Having said that, I'll violate it at once by ordering the works I'll be discussing into conventional categories: memoirs and autobiographies, novels and poems, anthropological studies, mysticism and New Age materials, biographies and histories. There's nothing very wary (or interesting) about that systematizing, you'll be saying; but just grant me this initial move and we'll have ice cream later.

No one would suppose that memoirs and autobiographies could give us direct contact with the essence of Indian, but the best recent books in one of the oldest genres of Indian writing are unusually artful and slippery. Barry O'Connell's *On Our Own Ground: The Complete Writings of William Apess, a Pequot,* makes available in a superb scholarly edition not only the first published autobiography by a native American (1829 originally), but also a range of historical, political and personal writings. The anger in Apess's work, though often Swiftian—"I could not find [the word "Indian"] in the Bible and therefore concluded that it was a word imported for the special purpose of degrading us"—and always eloquent, serves a depth of analysis and a layered irony that make pressing claims on any catalogue of what is finest and most significant in American literary history.

Apess, of mixed Pequot and white parentage, was born in Massachusetts in 1798 and became a minister and an early campaigner for Indian rights. He is also a powerful and demanding writer, who habitually anticipates and deflects the expectations (sentimental, condescending or degrading) of white readers so astutely that Mr. O'Connell (a professor of English at Amherst College) can mount a convincing comparison of his methods to those of black "signifying": "doubling and redoubling the assumed meaning of words and concepts in a dominant discourse."

Even the title of Apess's autobiography, *A Son of the Forest,* throws our romantic racism back in our faces by pretending to offer up one more noble savage for easy consumption and delivering a shrewd ironist instead. I suppose we could find a way to adjust to what Mr. O'Connell calls Apess's "refusals," were they exercised consistently, but they aren't: often he seems gentle enough, even mainline (white-line) platitudinous, as when he is talking about his Christianity. There is enough humdrum sanctimony here to throw us off balance, make us uncertain how to read, though even what Huck Finn would call a heavy smear of soul-butter is sharply peppered: Apess is careful to distinguish his own religion from the white deployment of Christianity to savage and barbarous ends.

Apess effectively nudges us out of the positions we customarily occupy when viewing the Indian. He is neither primitive nor simple nor one with the earth nor otherworldly. He leaves those slots for us.

Madonna Swan: A Lakota Woman's Story presents a voice, though it is our own contemporary's, every bit as compelling and hard to place. We may even be willing to look past a problem endemic to this genre: the presence of an intermediary who either translates or, as here, edits and arranges.

Mark St. Pierre, Madonna Swan's friend and editor, employs a set of practices that are tooth-rattling in their placid intrusiveness. He arranges what he calls "the best aspects" from versions of the stories Madonna Swan tells so as to get a set of "unified vignette[s]," all, when provided with "the proper mood and feeling," acting together to give us something much more than "a mere remembrance of a tribal past." Instead of the merely tribal we have "a story of life, dreams and human yearnings," the "human" and the "tribal" being not so much differentiated as mixed together into what Mr. St. Pierre sees as a transcendent effluvium: "the universality of the human condition."

Luckily, Mr. St. Pierre's actual skills as a medium and Madonna Swan's extraordinary voice and story leave this insulting idealizing buncombe far behind. Madonna Swan, who was born in 1928 on the Cheyenne River Sioux Reservation in South Dakota, speaks matter-of-factly of a life of horrors—long-term battles with tuberculosis, sanitariums that were mere holding pens for the dying, bigots and cheats stationed at every desk and bureau. As a child in the Sioux sanitarium in Rapid City, S.D., she and a friend passed the boring and terrifying hours by keeping a log of the daily activities enlivening the place, death mainly, more than 500 that she encountered personally in her years there.

We would expect her to attribute her survival to her early training or to luck, God, medical miracles or something; but it is characteristic of Madonna Swan that she allows her emergence from the nightmare, her later great success as a Head Start teacher, and her election in 1983 as North American Indian Woman of the Year by the women of the Cheyenne River Sioux Reservation to go unattributed. They simply happened.

Readers will certainly want to characterize this woman and her life, but one gets the feeling that Madonna Swan would resist the terms we would like to apply: courage, generosity, strength. The terms seem apt enough, but they do not do much for us either to explain or to encapsulate the experience we have with this figure. For one thing, she will not wear the traditional saintly costume we'd like to deck her out in, the one we've grown so fond of. We love to see those who triumph over our cruelties as wonderfully (but somehow predictably) unresentful, but Madonna Swan has attended to the words of her grandfather—"Never trust a white man behind your back! They will stab you, in one way or another!"—and her father—"God damn you white sons of bitches."

She is always canny, quick to sense danger and to protect herself from the white savages hiding behind the trees: she fights off an employer who tries to molest her by kicking him "where it hurts men the most," and another white who pats her bottom is knocked cold by an uppercut from her purse, receiving also some choice words as he crashes to the cold and sodden barroom floor: "No white man is ever going to touch this 'squaw.' . . . Get up and I'll knock hell out of you again."

Later she and her husband laugh uproariously when they discover that the KO was delivered by a bottle of hand cream concealed like brass knuckles in her purse: the wannabe macho man was "done in by Jergens lotion."

More slyly, Madonna Swan deflects all the sentimental clichés tying Indians to the cutesy in our vocabulary. She repeats, for instance, a story of her mother's about how mice answered the prayers of her grandmother, trapped in a cabin in winter without food or fuel, by inspiring Madonna's mother to go and check on the cabin, how the grateful family prepared an offering of thanks for the mice people, and how we can see from this how "everything on this earth has a purpose," exactly the sentimental conclusion we find so satisfactory from stories of people who are, after all, so very ecological, now aren't they!

But her mother goes on: "Everything on this earth has a purpose, the ants, badger, deer, even the flies! Everything but zuzeca [snakes]!" Madonna Swan is not going to have her story sentimentalized or otherwise easily "understood."

The finest of the new novelists and poets emerging from among Native American writers are equally elusive, none more than Ray A. Young Bear, the brilliant and widely recognized post-modernist trickster. His *Black Eagle Child: The Facepaint Narratives,* a dizzying re-creation in prose and poetry of the author's life (he is of Mesquakie ancestry) and his "own laborious Journey of Words," mixes voices, landscapes and tones in such a way as to move us deeply without letting us settle into any sense of tragic participation.

Partly this is a matter of Mr. Young Bear's relentless instancing of our "cosmic insignificance"; his bullying, Hardyesque deflation of any grandeur, even any consistent patterning of events. Mostly, though, we are unsettled by the merging of points of view, of naturalistic detail with the visionary (a combination of spiritual journeys, chemical inducements and U.F.O. sightings), and by the mastery of all the registers and modes he is moving through—pathos, for instance. Describing his grandmother doing ribbon appliqué on dress panels or peeling potatoes at the table, he offers this image of how he is suddenly hit by the reality of their poverty:

> The distant oceans I only read about came over
> the top of the wooded hill, and the waves raced
> down, topping what was otherwise a sem-
> blance
> of a strong household.

Even Mr. Young Bear's grotesque comedy refuses to release us into simplicity, not only because it reaches toward pain but because its distortions also dignify, as in the following passage where the narrator, the Mexican-American girl attracted to his "blood," and their dance-floor nuzzlings are ridiculed so thoroughly that somehow the bizarre poultry-bodies are redeemed:

> It was at best an uneven trade-off:
> a glimpse of ancient Woodlands wisdom

> for a precious face and body. Physically,
> we fit like a puzzle: my gut on her trim,
> muscular stomach, her famous breasts
> on my flat, bony chest; culturally
> we were separated by galaxies. All that
> could be seen when we slow-danced were my
> chicken legs, leading, shuffling about,
> and scratching the floor for support.

More formally traditional than Mr. Young Bear but equally startling and perhaps just as talented is Louis Owens, of Choctaw and Cherokee descent, whose novel, *The Sharpest Sight,* constitutes a spectacular inaugural for a series on American Indian literature from the University of Oklahoma Press.

The tendency to start these series—and there are a rush of them—is encouraging, but it also marks our rage to get all this material under control: to arrange series, give prizes, employ scholars and university presses as sorters, establish Indian sections at B. Dalton. But the abilities of Mr. Owens, who is a professor of literature at the University of California, Santa Cruz, and the author of several scholarly studies, are strong enough to prevail over any series or awards ceremonies.

In *The Sharpest Sight* he sets up what seems at first to be an intriguing but rather easily handled whodunit. At least that's what I thought before, some 50 pages in, I realized with some chagrin how thoroughly I'd been bamboozled. The mystery story doesn't go away, and it's great fun; but it's entwined with an artfully interfolded story of how knowledge is reached, constructed, approximated, or just plain faked. How do we arrive at what we are finally willing to take as "knowing"?

But that makes the work sound abstract and pretentious, when it is, in fact, invitingly loose-jointed, mixing in jokes, barbs, deep-cutting mockery of sympathetic whites ("I've always been fascinated by Indians. . . . Collected arrowheads and stuff. It was like I was trying to find out who I was. . . . I always thought Indians had names like Afraid-of-His-Horses. . . . You speak Indian?"), topical joys ranging from the idiocy of Christian "worship" ("because God told them they'd better") to the names of baseball teams (why not, he ponders, the "Wasco Wetbacks, or the Guadalupe Gringos," the "Pismo Palefaces" or the "San Francisco Whitemen"?).

Alternating between the central California coast and the Mississippi swamps, *The Sharpest Sight* makes both seem equally dangerous and uncontrollable. One especially profound current in this extraordinary novel traces the ways in which whites make genocide erotic, mixing their tingling desire for death with their lust for Indians, murdering them in a frenzy of love.

Don Coldsmith's *Walks in the Sun* sets itself up as a potboiler: it's the *20th* novel in his immensely successful and apparently endless Spanish Bit Saga, which, crows the publisher, now has "more than three million copies . . . in print," many of which have been sold. The book features very short chapters, lots of illustrations, and a sharply focused plot with few enough characters and a brisk enough narrative that it would fit comfortably into a harried traveler's mind buckled in from, say, Omaha to Atlanta.

Beyond that, *Walks in the Sun* masquerades as an H. Rider Haggard rip-off, a colonial adventure story of an exploring party of Indians from the Great Plains who "went too far south" in the 1720's, wandering among the exotics in Central America and encountering comic-book terrors in every mudhole and under every tent flap. There are deadly alligators ("thunder-lizards"), snarling pythons dropping out of trees to strangle and swallow even big people whole, monstrous "tooth-fish" (sharks, I think), jaguars who feed mainly on humans, cannibals wielding blowguns (double-dip savagery), mutiny and jungle fever.

But this simple, plain-spoken story actually carries the enormous charge of subversive fable, giving us mythmaking of the most alarming variety. As it comes to resemble more and more the form of the legend, it offers to us a seditious wisdom: the knowledge that we cannot understand.

This deceptively subtle work quietly refutes virtually every point of received wisdom about Indians and Indian culture, suggesting, for instance, that "tribes" were far less separate and distinct than we have liked to think and that Indian "beliefs" were far more sophisticated, provisional and metaphoric than we have understood. More pointedly, the story concerns a venture into a new culture, a new mode of experience, a venture that is a disaster not only physically but also conceptually.

The title character, possessed of powerful medicine and magic, finds that the farther he moves out of his habitual climate, economy, religion and hunting territory, the less is he able to cast and read his bones, the less is he able to understand or to be understood: "Some of our stories, like that of how Bobcat lost his tail, were useless. It is not the same when the listeners have never seen a bobcat."

Indeed, things are so much "not the same" that this wise man is finally left with a host of revealed mysteries, "but not enough to know of their ways." Mr. Coldsmith, who is not of Indian ancestry, makes this point nicely by way of the monkeys encountered by Walks in the Sun at the southernmost point of this dystopia, monkeys he cannot ever quite see as animal or as human. These things, mocking his keen intelligence and flexible imagination, shriek at him, *"It is more than you can understand!"*

It seems clear that such devastatingly assured writing as Ray Young Bear's, Louis Owens's and Don Coldsmith's represents not so much formidable entrants into traditional fields but the formation of new modes and generic possibilities before our eyes.

In this process, perhaps the most commanding voice will belong to Sherman Alexie, a Spokane/Coeur d'Alene Indian, whose first publication, *The Business of Fancydancing,* is so wide-ranging, dexterous and consistently capable of raising your neck hair that it enters at once into our ideas of who we are and how we might be, makes us speak and hear his words over and over, call others into the room or over the phone to repeat them. Mr. Alexie's is one

of the major lyric voices of our time. He is also one of the most forgiving of those who see farthest.

His work in this volume, which ranges formally from short verses to elliptical short stories, vignettes and epigrams, set largely in the small towns and Indian reservations of the Northwest, is wonderfully grounded, often comically and usually poignantly. He writes not so much *of* but *out of* basketball and convenience stores, old cars and new loves, bad food and good jokes.

Here are some shots from a poem called "Distances": "I do not speak my native tongue. Except that is, for the dirty words. I can tell you what I think of you in two languages." "There is nothing as white as the white girl an Indian boy loves." "A photograph: Trina Andrews, reservation girl, 9 years old, in a wheelchair, legs useless because of cancer, wearing a wig because of the baldness induced by chemotherapy, holding a bag of Christmas goodies, Santa Claus hovering over her; a dozen kids surrounding her, all staring into the lens, back at me and you. In that bag: an orange, a handful of peanuts, a few hard candies, and miles and miles of air."

Another, from "Powwow": "This isn't love exactly / it's love approximately."

Finally, a poem, entitled "Penance":

> I remember sun-
> days when the man I
> call my father made
>
> me shoot free throws, one
> for every day of my life
> so far. I remember
> the sin of imperfect
>
> spin, the ball falling in-
> to that moment between
> a father and forgive-
>
> ness, between the hands reach-
> ing up and everything
> they can possibly hold.

It is a long and thudding fall from the levels achieved by these writers to the flatlands where many anthropologists, folklorists and purveyors of Indian "mysticism" slog along. The worthy research into and collecting of traditional stories and oral tales continue, adding both to our store of fascinating and useful primary material and to our much larger collection of useless commentary.

That may sound harsh, but I invite anyone not enrolled in structuralist or Jungian orthodoxies to swim for a while in the indexes of motifs or the classification systems designed to order and register these wild tales and then emerge, towel off and feel refreshed.

It was one thing for Joseph Campbell in the 1940's to be cocky about his ability to spot in different cultures and their stories, no matter how apparently diverse, the never-changing sameness, the overarching oneness, "the divine images that have sprung out of the depths of the soul since the beginnings of human existence," as Campbell describes it in his introduction to *Where the Two Came to Their Father: A Navaho War Ceremonial Given by Jeff*

King. But it is depressing to encounter the same dreary universalizing animating the naïve arithmetic empiricism of so many of today's collectors and scholars, apparently living in backwaters where news of the strangulation of structuralism has never reached.

Almost as common as burdensome commentaries on Indian ceremonies and dubious "interpretations" of native life seem to be impressionistic versions of what Indians may have actually said, tailored to provide us with lessons in life. A book that was on *The New York Times* nonfiction best-seller list until this week, *Brother Eagle, Sister Sky: A Message From Chief Seattle,* offers a startling recent example of this tendency. The book purports to quote from a letter or speech delivered by Chief Seattle in the mid-19th century, warning (in noble terms) of the dangers of environmental catastrophe brought about by the white man's abuse of the earth. Chief Seattle did exist, was a great orator and did give a speech in 1854, on the occasion of the arrival of the Federal Government's Indian superintendent in the Northwest. But the original translation of the speech includes no such lamentations. The material on the environment first appeared in a version of the speech offered in a 1971 film on ecology, was apparently added by the screenwriter, and has repeatedly been credited to Chief Seattle since. *Brother Eagle, Sister Sky,* has been recategorized under Advice, How-to and Miscellaneous on *The Times* best-seller list this week. (It was not among the top five titles.)

Just as spirit-sagging is the popularity of many forms of over-the-counter mysticism, the most vulgar of which is represented by *Buffalo Woman Comes Singing: The Spirit Song of a Rainbow Medicine Woman,* by Brooke Medicine Eagle (who is described by her publisher as "earthkeeper, visionary, teacher, poet and psychologist," raised "on a Crow reservation in Montana"). It offers Kmart spiritualism in variety paks: "Go within and begin to visualize that Golden Seed Atom within your heart"; then explore the "golden line" leading from that Seed Atom to the "Great Spirit"; then "take another 15 minutes to establish this golden line of communion," adding another five minutes to connect that line to the "All That Is."

I don't know the schedules in your area, but out here I can do all that between Donahue and Oprah. I can also, after dinner, change the name I have now, which won't do, to the true name for my current being, checking my choices for "their vibration through numerology" and, I suppose, asking for advice from the Seed Atom and the All That Is, as well. Once found, I can confirm both name and being by way of a ceremony (optional but very nice). It asks for "red ocher/earth pigment," but if I don't have that (I don't think I do), "an old lipstick will do" (I have that).

Several miles above such dank tarns are works like *Profiles in Wisdom: Native Elders Speak About the Earth,* a collection of interviews conducted by Steven McFadden, that perhaps could be used for a quick fix on mysticism but that does a fine job not only of presenting the dignity, complexity and wit of important Indian philosophers and religious leaders but also of issuing cautions against easy uplift and wisdom injections: according to the Mohawk teacher Tom Porter, "There is no big garage sale on native ceremonies. . . . We don't have a great mystique. And we don't have gurus. We're just human beings."

All the same, I do believe that there are some stirring and unexpected powers unleashed in this book. I think anyone reading a remarkable celebration of change by Twylah Nitsch, a Seneca elder, will emerge a little different. And then there's her story about the pigeon feathers: walking to the store one day, while living in California, she was stepping off a curb and spotted four pigeon feathers; "I said, 'Woo,' and I picked them up. 'Oh, you're beautiful.' " Realizing she's talking out loud, she looks up and sees four people sitting on a porch watching her. Instead of collapsing into embarrassment, she walks over to them and explains how Seneca Indians honor all feathers as messengers of peace.

"I thought you might be interested," she says. They say, "Well, thank you." And now when she walks by, wheeling her granddaughter in a carriage, these people smile at her: "I thought, well, seeing me each time must remind them of that lady who picked up the feathers and thought it was so great."

That's it. Picking up such a Joycean story, we might also remark on its inexplicable beauty and say "Woo" out loud.

We won't be saying "Woo" to what remains the largest and most stolid genre in the Indian writing field, histories written by white scholars, romancers and buttinskys. We still find even regressive modes like the swashbuckling historical yarn where the white fellow learns a thing or two about himself and about the earth by spending some time (not too much) with the Indians and their special, special ways, Robert Moss's *Fire Along the Sky* being an especially witless and stupefying example. Mr. Moss (the author of such thrillers as *Death Beam* and *Moscow Rules*) offers us a narrative of the adventures of Shane Hardacre, half-Irish, late of London, who tumbles into a series of adventures during the French and Indian War in the mid-18th century, repeatedly menaced and saved by various Indian bands.

Perhaps as bad are standard histories that are so loudly sympathetic to the tragedy of American Indian life that they make this sympathy the actual subject of the book, like David Lavender's egregious and horribly written *Let Me Be Free: The Nez Percé Tragedy,* for instance. Mr. Lavender, the author of a number of works of Western history, including *Bent's Fort* and *The Way to the Western Sea,* retells the story of the remarkable 1,700-mile flight of the Nez Percé tribe in 1877 from the Northwest toward Canada, pursued by Army troops. The Nez Percés' extraordinary leader, Chief Joseph, has in modern times become an increasingly unreal figure, turned by many writers into a one-dimensional hero. The real (and noticeably complex) Chief Joseph was never pursued by meaner foes.

There are also, in the conventional line, the big hero warrior biographies like Allan W. Eckert's crushingly lively epic *A Sorrow in Our Heart: The Life of Tecumseh,* a hybrid kind of "narrative biography" about the charismatic Indian leader, born in 1768, who forged a coalition of tribes to oppose the white settlers and soldiers pouring into the upper Midwest. Mr. Eckert's work enlivens history by using "all the better elements of the novel form," dialogue especially, not invented dialogue but *"reconstituted dialogue"* that Mr. Eckert (the author of a number of works about the history of white and Indian clashes, including *The Frontiersmen* and *Twilight of Empire*) cooks up from historical records.

This vastly sentimental effort to relive the past through a Carlylean hero-worshiping of noble warriors wouldn't be so bad, given Mr. Eckert's enormous skills as a researcher, were those "better elements of the novel form" not so obtrusive. But they are, and they overlay with fields of waving corn a celebratory biographical history.

Against all this we have, first of all, revisionary histories, some of which, like *A Spirited Resistance: The North American Indian Struggle for Unity, 1745-1815,* by Gregory Evans Dowd, angrily reject the Eurocentric assumptions of works that center on big-chief-hero or on isolated tribes.

Mr. Dowd departs from such atomized approaches to describe the attempt to combat colonialism through a religiously charged, pan-Indian militant movement, a wide-scale operation that certainly was not invented by Pontiac and Tecumseh, who were merely its "adherents." This enduring and vigorous movement arose to counter with sacred power Anglo-American strategies to divide Indians into distinct, isolated tribes and control tribal leadership. Mr. Dowd is sophisticated and exceptionally self-aware, recognizing how indebted even his counter-history is to European assumptions, and he tells an important and persuasive story, though in a manner that will strike many as unnecessarily tendentious and repetitive.

But it does mark a difference, as do the increasing number of biographies of Indians whom Carlyle would have ignored, Indians who led no war parties, like the subject of Daniel F. Littlefield Jr.'s straightforward biography, *Alex Posey: Creek Poet, Journalist and Humorist.* Posey is an especially interesting subject, since he will not read the usual script for tragic victims. A talented and very funny editor and journalist (he owned and edited the popular weekly newspaper *Indian Journal*), one of the most influential Indians in Oklahoma, Posey (1873-1908) also worked enthusiastically for the Dawes Commission, created by Congress with the intention of breaking up traditional Indian tribal and national arrangements (even obliterating their names and identities), and he went so far as to suggest that those who resisted be shipped off to Mexico.

He called himself a "progressive," adapting to the times, making the best of a bad situation, fitting into white society with some skill: he became successful at real-estate grubbing and learned a virulent racist language he could direct at blacks. He represents an image far harder for whites to cozy up to than the framed portraits of Sitting Bull or Pocahontas.

Finally, and at long last, we have Indian histories done by Indian historians, in this case Joe S. Sando, who provides, in *Pueblo Nations,* the first insider's story of the 800-year history of the 19 distinct but coordinated pueblos in New Mexico. This is an excellent and patient book, not always organized along traditional lines but still accessible—or so we will think.

Mr. Sando, the director of archives at the Pueblo Indian Study and Research Center in Albuquerque, N.M., is very generous to his readers and very moderate, allowing himself only a few expressions of anger. One of these, however, suggests the importance not only of his own endeavor at undertaking this intimate history but also of our own tenuous position as regards all this material: "The American educational system is successful only in teaching dominant society values, methods, and superiority. We read only of *their* successes and *their* heroes. Perhaps this is because non-Indians write the books."

If whites have written all the books, it follows that they have directed all the reading too. It is not enough, then, to have different writers. If we read them in the same way, we'll read the same things as always. We need to go back to school, find some primers. Leslie Marmon Silko is one of those offering to help with this Peace Corps project, bringing light into the darkness. She opens one of her charitable events, an essay ("Language and Literature From a Pueblo Indian Perspective," included in *Critical Fictions: The Politics of Imaginative Writing,* edited by Philomena Mariani), by issuing a bemused shrug of an invitation: "I ask you to set aside a number of basic approaches that you have been using, and probably will continue to use, and instead, to approach language from the Pueblo perspective, one that embraces the whole of creation and the whole of history and time."

To get to that new language, that new vision and way of being that might (maybe, who knows?) heal us and our world, we need to set aside what we will not be able to set aside, we need to give up habits of mind so deep and prolonged they very nearly constitute what we *are.* To see differently, we must be and do differently; and to be and do better we must see better.

It's all one circle, and we are outside it. We'll "probably" stay outside it—but maybe not. I cannot imagine myself ever being thankful for pigeon feathers or saying "Woo!" when I found some. But possibly the imagination can itself be reforged, hammered into new forms. If so, writers like Leslie Marmon Silko, William Apess, Madonna Swan, Joe S. Sando, Ray A. Young Bear, Louis Owens and Sherman Alexie are the smiths to go at it. (pp. 1, 24-9)

James R. Kincaid, "Who Gets to Tell Their Stories?" in The New York Times Book Review, *May 3, 1992, pp. 1, 24-9.*

Sam Cornish   (review date September-October 1992)

[*Cornish is an American poet and author of children's books. In the following review, he discusses two poetry collections by Native American writers, Red Hawk's* The Sioux Dog Dance: Shunk Ah Weh *(1991) and Cheryl Savageau's* Home Country *(1992).*]

Two new books of poetry, [Red Hawk's *The Sioux Dog Dance: Shunk Ah Weh* and Cheryl Savageau's *Home Country*], explore themes of Native American heritage and history. The poems range in setting from the French Canadian and New England worlds of Cheryl Savageau, who is part Abenaki and French Canadian, to the mythic, western world of Red Hawk. As biographical information on Red Hawk is unavailable, I will not guess as to his specific ethnic or tribal background—though of the two writers, he has the firmer grasp of history. In the poem "What The Old Cheyenne Woman At Sand Creek Knew," he examines a familiar historical atrocity from a fresh point of view and relates it through an account of how nightmares and dreams give us knowledge and foreshadow events: "the old women knew how to move / from one dream to another / and take the children safely through; / the old women knew / what men in a bad dream could do." The poems reach also into the darker side of male life, that of the stern disciplinarian: "He beat his wife, he beat / his daughter, he beat me."

This honest book is more truthful than confessional and is told in a bold, realistic voice that focuses on past and present. This reviewer wishes only that there was space to quote more extensively from it, but Red Hawk's observations of women and men and American history are filled with the irony of a subject the author knows well. Other poems in this vein are "The Old Men Go To Church," and "The Wheat Farmer Says Goodbye To His Only Daughter."

Sioux Dog Dance: Shunk Ah Weh is a collection of poems so carefully selected that it reads like a book of related observations or stories. It is a book which could have leaned heavily on a crutch of multiculturalism, but with its thematic range and tense, its lean poetic language offers much to the reader on a number of levels: racial, poetic, multicultural and, if you will, men's studies.

Home Country by Cheryl Savageau also deals with the often-conflicting issues of identity and gender, but the poems seem less interrelated and the result is an occasional unevenness of tone and style. This is not, however, a comment on the quality of *Home Country,* which is certainly a noteworthy first collection by a woman who writes of poverty, mixed ancestry, nature, and family with a crafted maturity.

Although both books are divided into sections, the difference in tone and subject is more apparent in Savageau's book. The two sections are "The Dirt Road Home" and "The Water Flowing Through Me." "Dirt Road" is lyric and readable, and Savageau is able to create a softness that makes the most realistic social statements seem slick and workmanlike, but the sense of detail is so acute that the reader is grateful that the material is presented this way. "The Sound of My Mother Singing" is about a marriage of difficulty, seen from a child's point of view. While conveying the horror of the scene, it is told with a child's sense of guilt and naïveté. Because the child cannot understand what is going on, her voice and observations convey the information to us, "She pours coffee / slouched over his plate / he has forgotten his rage / forgotten the butcher knife."

Red Hawk and Cheryl Savageau deal with similar materials, although their viewpoints differ. They lack sentimen-

tality and do not belittle their subject, although it is apparent that the observations are painful for both poets. Savageau's "Hanging Clothes in the Sun" is another example of the family poem about poverty. The father works thankless jobs despite his aspirations: "he squeezes water / Out of shirts and towels / He knows he drinks too much. / He dreams of moving to New Hampshire, / where his people walked / for 10,000 years." This could have been written by a social realist but for its economy of line and the remarkable ability to choose a moment to reflect on a person's life. Savageau's poems of home are insightful portraits of a real working family living out troubled lives in a racially and economically troubled society.

The section "The Water Flowing Through Me" contains poems about nature; others about Native America have less bite and are sometimes confusing. These are from a more distant adult point of view which seems to understand what the child in the early poems did not. Both sections have strong poems and showcase Savageau's ability to understand her characters on their own terms.

Both *Home Country* and *Sioux Dog Dance* are promising first books. They contain memorable poems that should affect anyone interested in Native American or white American perspectives on ethnic heritage as it impacts American life. (pp. 37-8)

Sam Cornish, in a review of "The Sioux Dog Dance: Shunk Ah Weh" and "Home Country," in Boston Review, *Vol. XVII, No. 5, September-October, 1992, pp. 37-8.*

N. Scott Momaday on the sense of place in Native American literature:

[I] think that the sense of place is very important in American Indian oral tradition. And the question is how does one acquire such a sense and I think it is a long process of appropriation. The American Indian has a very long experience of the North American continent, say, going back thousands of years, maybe thirty thousand. So I think of that as being a very great investment, a kind of spiritual investment in the landscape, and because he has that experience he is able to think of himself in a particular way, think of himself in relation to the land, and he is able to define for himself a sense of place, belonging, and to me that is very important and characterizes much of the American Indian oral tradition. Probably writing too, more recently, because the writing, I think, springs in a natural way from the oral tradition and the sense of place is crucial to both.

N. Scott Momaday, in Winged Words: American Indian Writers Speak, *1990.*

John Purdy (review date December 1992-January 1993)

[*An American critic and editor, Purdy has written several essays on such Native American writers as James Welch, Leslie Marmon Silko, and Louise Erdrich. In the following review, he assesses Elizabeth Cook-Lynn's*

The Power of Horses, and Other Stories *(1990) and From the River's Edge (1991).*]

Elizabeth Cook-Lynn (Crow Creek Sioux) has figured prominently in Native American circles and issues for quite some time. Born and raised on the Crow Creek Reservation in South Dakota, she is a professor emerita of English and Native American studies from Eastern Washington University and also has taught elsewhere, most recently at the University of California-Davis. She is the editor of *The Wicazo Sa Review,* a biannual journal of Native American Studies that publishes poetry and fiction as well as scholarly articles. Her own poetry and fiction have appeared in several national journals, as well as in the major anthologies of Native American literatures. *The Power of Horses* is her first book-length collection of short fiction, but its publication was followed within a year by her first novel, *From the River's Edge.*

The Power of Horses includes some of the best stories from the anthologies, and they share the powerful voice of the more recent ones in the volume. Moreover, taken together, they reflect a very clear vision of the life of Crow Creek, as seen by Cook-Lynn. Her stories over the years have been wonderful in their sparse brevity, but now they are given a context that makes them even more compelling. Like Sherwood Anderson's *Winesburg, Ohio* or Faulkner's *Go Down, Moses, The Power of Horses* is a collage of individual characters' experiences that draws one into a specific landscape over a long period of time. We come very close to this place and the people who inhabit it.

Cook-Lynn's fiction is as stark, rolling, and sometimes startling as the northern prairie she describes. Set on the reservation, these thirteen stories share a set of central historical events: the last battles against European incursion and therefore the establishment of the reservation itself; the equally damaging onslaught of Christian missionaries; the Reorganization years of the John Collier administration in the Bureau of Indian Affairs; and the damming of the Missouri River for a hydroelectric project. They are, of course, all related and they mark the ebb and flow of the Dakotah sense of self-determination, an identity based upon the people's ability to direct their own future. When the battle is lost, the ceremonial practices outlawed, the ancient, crucial places submerged under a blanket of muddy water, what is left? To her credit, Cook-Lynn shows us the effects clearly, but does not let us misconstrue her lesson. *The Power of Horses* is not a book that perpetuates the stereotypical "doomed Indian" myth; it is a tribute to survival.

The opening story, "Mahpiyato," is a good example and an apt introduction to what follows. In it, an old woman and her granddaughter walk to the river to pick berries, "as they had done all their lives," and find a moment of sudden beauty as a cloud passes over the water. The woman emphasizes with "the sound of her voice that a sober and interesting phenomenon was taking place right before their very eyes." And the child, "a steadfast and modest companion of the old woman, knew from long experience about the moments when the stories came on. . . ." The woman quizzes the child and we learn that this sudden vision is called *Mahpiyato,* and it can be en-

compassed only in terms of Dakotah language and literature: "To say just 'blue' or 'sky' or 'cloud' in English, you see, doesn't mean much." Instead, there must be a comprehension accompanying the description: "You see, she is blue. And she is gray. *Mahpiyato* is, you see, one of the Creators. Look! Look! *Look at Mahpiyato!*" The next line, the final one of the story, is equally telling: "Her voice was low and soft and very convincing."

The story is only one-and-a-half pages long, and it says everything. Cook-Lynn faces the dilemma of every Native writer who wishes to convey a tribal point of view through the English language and euramerican written literary conventions. Her characters must speak English so that her non-Native audience can understand. Like the woman in her story, she must educate by demarcating the differences in perspective, but also by taking us inside her cultural milieu. We learn that Mahpiyato is a Creator, that the Creator is feminine, that she exists in a variety of ways simultaneously (that she may be a being of apparent oppositions and contradictions), that we can learn about her from stories, and that one can find joy and identity by witnessing her manifestations. (We also witness a fundamental linking of generations, and therefore an implied continuity of identity over time.) Finally, we are called to look at her through the stories that follow in the collection, stories told in a voice that is "low and soft and very convincing." We have been given the aesthetic of *The Power of Horses.*

But Cook-Lynn does not paint a romantic human landscape. Life in this place over the last century has been hard, traumatic, and always tenuous. Characters face threats and challenges not only to their individual survival, but to the survival of their cosmos: Young Nephew returns from Vietnam to the place where explosive violence is easily justifiable and always self-destructive; Gracie faces the self-limitation—the memories and emotional scars—created by an abusive, Anglo father whose "rights," even in death, supersede hers and her siblings'; Anita loses her children in a custody battle and is powerless to recapture their love; and Magpie is gunned down in jail at a time when his future is at its brightest. Throughout the book, one cannot help but feel the pervasive sense of frustration and hopelessness that continuously threatens the fundamental unity of the Dakotah and therefore their identity as a people, yet this sense is mitigated by an equally powerful message of endurance and survival.

It is sadly ironic that *The Power of Horses* was published in a year that also gave us the immensely popular movie *Dances with Wolves.* It is ironic because both deal with tribal groups of the Sioux nation, but from very different points of view, sad because the wrong one was enjoyed by so many. *Dances* uses an Anglo hero to idealize and romanticize Native Americans (although novelist David Seals has pointed out its inadequacies, including the humor of male Sioux using the feminine form of the language); *The Power of Horses,* on the other hand, paints a compelling, realistic, detailed water color of life on the Crow Creek Reservation in this century, with all its bleak and beautiful moments, its history written in terms of human endurance. There are no Lieutenant John Dunbars

471

or Natty Bumppos in this collection, only characters who struggle and then go on.

From the River's Edge, set against an ever-present history of appropriation, exploitation, and colonial genocidal purges, likewise records the endurance of traditional lifeways, viewpoints, and values, and affirms their veracity in modern times. In the preface to the novel, for example, we witness (from the river's edge) the initial flooding of the Missouri River by the Oahe Dam, a hydroelectric project the federal government has imposed upon the Dakota landscape and Dakotah people, but even in the face of such a radical and onerous change "it is easy to believe that this vast region continues to share its destiny with a people who have survived hard winters, invasions, migrations, and transformations unthought of and unpredicted." It is a destiny, however, that is—as all futures are, inherently—tentative.

Cook-Lynn's years of experience—on the reservation, and as a writer, historian and activist—enliven the novel. At once, it is the story of John Tatekeya (pronounced Tah-TAY-kee-yah), of a hundred years of history, of the changing landscape, and of a potentially fundamental shift in the interactions of a people. As she tells us very early on, "it takes only a small event in the life of an ordinary man to illuminate the ambiguities of an entire century." A court trial over the theft of Tatekeya's cattle provides the small event that illuminates the century for us, and at the physical and thematic center of the novel we are given the fundamental question of the work, and of the century for the Sioux: is a life of honor and community still possible in a modern, changing world?

One wonders, for as the trial progresses attention shifts from the thief and the missing cattle to John himself, and then something terrible happens: a fellow tribesman testifies against him, for personal reasons. The foundations of Sioux identity quake as John acknowledges "in his heart the uncompromising pride and courage inherent in the Dakotah way of life, and the loss of it, momentarily at least, in the behavior of everyone connected with this miserable trial." The unquestionable has been questioned, and this is "the price of the entrenchment of white civilization in his life and the lives of others." Of course, questions require answers, and Cook-Lynn provides them, but they are at once similar to, and subtly different from those of her contemporaries.

The story is set in the mid-1960s, at a time when the first vestiges of the activism that was to become the American Indian Movement appeared in cities around the country. Within a few years, the reclamation/occupation of Wounded Knee, southwest of Crow Creek Reservation, would dramatize both an outspoken idealization of "Indian," pantribal identity and the debate within and between tribes about the future of traditional lifeways and sociopolitical structures. In other words, Cook-Lynn takes us to an historical crux, a moment at which individuals assessed their situations and reacted.

John Tatekeya is the embodiment of the debate. Much of the narrative is devoted to exploring his internal dilemma as he faces the "ambiguities" inherent in his situation.

(The internal monologues of his lover, Aurelia, late in the novel are equally revealing and perhaps as central to the novel.) While most of this exploration is well handled, there are moments, however, when the narrator becomes too intrusive, and this is the one weak point in an otherwise useful narrative device. We are lectured, at times, on the history of Anglo/Native American relations, and while this may be new territory for some, the number of readers not sufficiently versed in that history will be minimal. These historical facts are indeed significant and noteworthy, but intrusions and redundant nonetheless. Tatekeya's personal reflections are wholly adequate to carry the history of who he is and how he came to be at this moment that may spell a distinct change in his people's lifeways, and therefore result in a very different people in the future.

Cook-Lynn's strengths are amply apparent in the novel. She composes short chapters that, like her short stories, are powerful in themselves. There are moments of truly wonderful insight shared with a voice clear and resonant. We follow Tatekeya on his associative wanderings through time as he wrestles with what is happening to him and to his community. In order to resolve his problems and answer the central question of what will happen to his people in the future, he must measure his own life in terms of Dakotah values, as Cook-Lynn explicates them and the ways that they are passed from generation to generation. Appropriately, at moments when he surveys his own experience (his internal landscape), he also surveys the physical landscape of Crow Creek, which is inseparable from his identity, and this is where we find the nondramatic revelation.

> He lifted his eyes toward the hills which spread out and away from the river, like earthen monuments of the past, forever, ophidian, resolute. . . . John Tatekeya of the Dakota prairielands and his people had forever possessed great confidence in their collective presence in their homelands. More than he thought about it, John felt it and simply held it in his heart.

Cook-Lynn offers answers and resolutions to his dilemma; as elsewhere, they are muted, understated and poignant. Unfortunately, literary critics are fond of the big splash, the loud, ponderous event. For this reason, when one reads about contemporary Native American literatures, one date is prominent: 1969. In that year N. Scott Momaday won the Pulitzer Prize for his first novel, *House Made of Dawn,* the first time a Native American won such a prestigious literary award. The publication of Cook-Lynn's first novel has not made as big a noise in literary circles, but it deserves to. It is compelling and relevant and wonderfully engaging. (pp. 1, 3)

John Purdy, "Bleak and Beautiful Moments," in The American Book Review, *Vol. 14, No. 5, December, 1992 & January, 1993, pp. 1, 3.*

Kimberly Blaeser (review date December 1992-January 1993)

[*Blaeser is an American educator and critic of Ojibway*

descent. *In the following excerpt, she praises Gerald Vizenor's* Landfill Meditation: Crossblood Stories *(1991) and* Dead Voices: Natural Agonies in the New World *(1992).*]

[Vizenor's] recent works of fiction take up the theme of survival in a crossblood world. Through exaggerated caricatures of contemporary society, *Landfill Meditation: Crossblood Stories* and *Dead Voices: Natural Agonies in the New World* provide a comic reappraisal of twentieth-century American culture. Between them, the two books address nearly all of Vizenor's most characteristic themes: the dangerous plague of cosmetic culture and consumer mentality, the power of story and imagination and the threat of their loss in "dead" literature, the invented India phenomenon, the distortions of history and the social sciences, the survival of tribal culture in an urban world, and the simultaneous and noncontradictory needs for liberation and responsibility: liberation from convention and the realization of a new kind of responsibility to the world.

This is not to say that these works seem stale. In many ways they offer some of the most clear and compelling statements Vizenor has made to date on his favorite subjects. And he applies his basic principles to much previously uncharted ground.

Both works also exhibit Vizenor's distinctively playful, if sometimes puzzling, prose. Zany plots link historical, literary, mythic, and imaginative figures who often deliver opaque or nearly opaque lines, casually alluding to all manner of sophisticated cultural and literary theories. A reader who follows the dialogue only on the most basic level misses much of Vizenor's play and brilliance. Form in the books is generally complex as Vizenor constructs layers of stories within stories. Ultimately the roughly drawn plots give sway to ideology: idea, not plot, is the *raison d' être* of these works. Vizenor presents his ideas in a variety of forms, from dialogue to commentary to fictionalized critiques of the actual, but seldom in a straightforward manner. He makes us work for them. We may find ourselves lamenting, as does the narrator in *Dead Voices,* "I was never sure how to hear the stories," or confessing, "I pretended to understand, but some of her stories were obscure and she never responded to my constant doubts." But just as Laundry, the narrator, finds ultimate liberation in the tales of Bagese in *Dead Voices,* so too do Vizenor's readers find a certain kind of reward in meeting the challenge of his writing. It promises, at the very least, to break open our tightly constructed ideas, to raise questions, to raise our consciousness, to raise Cain with common ideas. To those most diligent readers, it offers new ways to think about reading, writing, speaking, and being.

Indeed, language, culture, and being are the very themes of Vizenor's *Dead Voices.* Constructed around a wanaki game involving tarot-like cards, bizarre transformations, and a cycle of seven stories, this novel is a tale of imaginative trickster liberation in urban America. The stories present our world through the eyes of crows, beavers, and praying mantises, and are interwoven with satirical comments on sexuality, environmental ethics, our education system, and the predator nature of politics. This novel operates like a gyroscope, wildly spinning in all directions

while the center remains stable. That center, the most important theme of *Dead Voices,* is the legacy or the liability of our written culture.

Here, more clearly than in any of his earlier works, Vizenor calls us to consider the place of the oral and the written in our culture, and to reconsider both the representations of Native Americans in written documents and the effects of those written works. Indians, Vizenor holds, have been effectively deadened by the printed word, captured and dehumanized in stereotypes: "The tribes are dead, our voices are traced, published, and buried, our voices are dead in the eye of the missionaries." But *Dead Voices* asks us not to continue debating those written accounts of "the tragedies of a vanishing race," but to abandon the "dead voices" to their creators and to "go on" as mixedblood creators of our own cultural reality. Indianness, Vizenor claims in passages throughout this book, should not be measured by dance scars, reservation status, or plastic beads. Indians and mixedbloods survive in the cities, they survive by chance, they survive by overturning cultural expectations. *Dead Voices* calls for our liberation from all invented Indian stereotypes.

The stories in Vizenor's *Landfill Meditation* also concern themselves with the collection of our cultural inheritance as mixedbloods and the canceling of our social debts as invented Indians. Many of the stories in this collection tell of unusual crossbloods who survive as entrepreneurs and eccentrics, with the best humor and in clear violation of invented Indian images. Cedarbird supports his graduate career as "an informer and a novelist, connected in mythic time with two independent computer editors." Almost Browne appears as the publisher of blank books, the creator of postmodern laser light shows, and the cocreator of an ice trickster in a sculptor contest. Almost, like many of Vizenor's other characters in these stories, inhabits "the almost world" of imaginative liberation, "a better world, a sweeter dream than the world we are taught to understand in school."

Despite its thirty years of transformations, Vizenor's work continues to challenge, to surprise, to elude easy definition. Another of his descriptions of the tribal trickster

---

An excerpt from Sherman Alexie's *The Business of Fancydancing: Stories and Poems*

I walk into the bar, after being gone for a while, and it's empty. The Bartender tells me all the Indians are gone, do I know where they went? I tell him I don't know, and I don't know, so he gives me a beer just for being Indian, small favors, and I wonder where all the Skins disappeared to, and after a while, I leave, searching the streets, searching storefronts, until I walk into a pawn shop, find a single heart beating under glass, and I know who it used to belong to, I know all of them.

Sherman Alexie, in "Pawn Shop," in his The Business of Fancydancing: Stories and Poems, *Hanging Loose Press, 1992.*

could as easily apply to his writing: it "wavers on the rim, a warrior on a coin that never lands twice on the same side" (*Trickster of Liberty*).

Readers who liked Vizenor's earlier fiction will probably like *Dead Voices* and *Landfill Meditation* even more. To those who appreciate his candid and witty evaluations of contemporary issues, *Crossbloods* will become an important collection. (pp. 6-7)

> Kimberly Blaeser, "Trickster Signatures," in
> The American Book Review, *Vol. 14, No. 5,*
> *December, 1992 & January, 1993, pp. 6-7.*

Patricia Clark Smith   (review date December 1992-January 1993)

[*Smith is an American poet, critic, and educator. In the review below, she assesses three volumes of Native American poetry.*]

Sherman Alexie (Spokane/Coeur D'Alene), Janice Gould (Maidu), and Chrystos (Menominee) are three American Indian poets very different from one another, yet because of their very strengths all three may have trouble finding as wide a readership as should be theirs. In part, it's the old story: "ethnic" writers, two of them lesbian, all publishing with small presses. Moreover, when it comes to what gets called American Indian writing, a majority of readers prefer Anglo writer Tony Hillerman's weary but hopeful Navajo cops who pretty well solve things by the end of each book, or feel-good "shamans" who'll tell you how to set up your own medicine wheel in the back yard. Alexie, Chrystos, and Gould may deliver more real news than many readers wish to hear. But here is true magic and memory, true wonder and terror and laughter. This writing is rooted hard not only in the tribal cultures, but in urban, mixed-blood, and contemporary reservation experience. The people who inhabit these poems and narratives are not always pretty. But I promise you, they are beautiful.

Sherman Alexie [in his *The Business of Fancydancing: Stories and Poems*] explores lives lived on and off the Spokane Indian reservation of eastern Washington State. He evokes the centrality of sports—and of aging athletes—to reservation life, recalling to us that games have always been ceremonially central to native peoples. Basketball and football are the main games here. In "Love Hard," Alexie elegiacally summons up his father, surrounded by friends equipped with memories "like news clippings," all celebrating the hard-loving loser who could once

> . . . drink all night long and wake up
> in the morning hitting jumpshots from thirty
>   feet
> until forever.

This myth-sized father is impelled by his own memories to awesome feats of violence in later life, as in "Sudden Death":

> . . . my father dreams of 1956
>
> and the field goal he missed in the snow,
> ball bouncing off the upright, falling

back to the tattered couch, where my father
  throws
a spiral across the room, suspended

between the sound of a glass thrown
and a glass shattering against the corner . . .

That heart-stopping shape-shift between one line and the next is only one of Alexie's own smooth moves.

In an evening evoked throughout the book, the father burns down the family house, using furniture for kindling, and is found later in the ruins on his hands and knees, as if he were trying to find lost dice or the mislaid sticks from a stick game,

> . . . gathering ash
> in his hands, planning to bury it all
> in the graves we had chosen for each other.

The laughter that bursts out amid this violence rings true: the father remarking bitterly of the daughter who's disappeared off into the powwow circuit, "Should have named her Roadkill"; the 7-11 disseminating milk cartons with *Have you seen . . . ?* pictures of Crazy Horse (of whom no photos actually exist); the challenge of sneaking whiskey into a powwow, each man walking past guards with a mouthful and carefully spitting into a waiting fifth, then selling shots, "and I guess / you could say / we won again but it's only Indians versus Indians and no one / is developing a movie script."

Games—basketball or stick games, fancydance competitions or res politics—are never *just* games. They're about cockiness, trickster strategies, ceremonial recurrences, the gamble of liking everyday life, the hope of winning this time, whether the stakes are gas money or some larger replenishment. The high spirit of Crazy Horse, who went down amid some fine fancy daring in his nineteenth-century incarnation, is alive in this book and dances powerfully throughout.

Alexie tells mostly about men's wars. Chrystos [in her *Dream On*] writes from the mixed-blood lesbian woman's front, the off-res front, the poverty front; she writes out of her own life about incest, prostitution, hard-drug addiction, homelessness. I do not know another American poet in 1992 able to present terrible common experience with so much fierce heart, understanding, and gentleness. She can also be very funny and meltingly erotic. Chrystos's work is hard to fit into book review format because she's got a generous Whitmanesque line and takes her own time to tell a story. But here is a thirteen-year-old caught trying to cut her wrist by the male relative who's just incested her:

> What did I want to do that to myself for? I
> didn't have the sense mon dieu gave me More
>   hitting
>   Threw
> my clothes at me so I must have been naked by
>   then
>   He liked to
> look at my breasts *Get dressed you can do that*
>   *right*
>   *can't you?* This is the man who really loves
> me,

look at all he goes through for
me, I believe him Not that different from my
    mother
        when she
screams at me hits me & says she loves me

And one of those racist spots-of-time few render better:

Those tears
of a white woman who came to the group for
    Women
        of Color
only
her grief cuts us into guilt while we clutched the
    straw
of this tiny square inch we have which we need
so desperately when we need so much more
We talked her into leaving
which took 10 minutes of our precious 60

I've heard Chrystos read for a full house at 11:00 on a Sunday morning to cheers, tears, belly laughter; when I assigned this book to my graduate students, they were astonished, indignant they had not met with her work earlier.

Janice Gould's work concerns itself most centrally with healing, though [*Beneath My Heart*] has plenty to say about the wars and the wounds. At a Yom Kippur service last fall in the Bay Area, Ronnie Gilbert read to the congregation "History Lesson," Gould's spare and terrifying account of postinvasion Maidu history, climaxing in 1984 with the speaker, a Maidu student in white academia:

There are some things I don't want to think
    about.
That chapter, for example, on California Indians
    that read
California Indians were a naturally shiftless and
    lazy people.
The mission padres had no trouble bringing them
    into the Mission
for these Indians were more submissive than the
    Plains warriors.

The poem ends with the speaker dreaming of herself weeping in rage before an indifferent class to whom she is giving a report on Columbus; the teacher tells her. "You can finish your talk . . . / when you pull yourself together."

This book doesn't miss a step. The excitement of it begins right with the opening poem, "Coyotismo," an exuberant lesbian-trickster account:

. . . the night began a rumor
that I'd hump anything that moved.
What did she know? When she opened her
    mouth to laugh
I pulled her tongue real hard.
She vomited a trail of stars no one can clean up.

The final section begins with poems that tell *family* stories of illness and cures in the early years of this century. In "She Comes Homes," Gould's maternal grandmother, dying of cancer, employs a medicine man who gently tells the family, "no Indian medicine could change / the day of her last breath"; later, she undergoes a botched operation, hemorrhaging on the train back home:

At Belden Station
the men strapped her to a chair

and carried her into town.
Already she was moaning
in a voice so changed and low
it belonged to no woman.

In that sound she drifted
unaware it was death who sang.

The section segues into the poet watching over her own mother's death, an experience that stirs all the "Questions of Healing" these three books variously raise:

When I watched my mother die
with no recourse to laurel,
sweet birch or pine, no baskets
to burn on the pyre in October (ourselves
the sticks of charcoal, shaved heads,
black face, purified by smoke),
I found only half-questions:
What in our world? How close to death?
What can change? What have I lost?

Patricia Clark Smith, "True Magic and Memory," in The American Book Review, *Vol. 14, No. 5, December, 1992 & January, 1993, p. 8.*

FURTHER READING

The American Book Review, Special Issue: Living to Tell the Tale 14, No. 5 (December 1992-January 1993): 1-12.
  Contains numerous reviews of recent works by or about Native American writers, including Leslie Marmon Silko's *Almanac of the Dead,* Peter Matthiessen's *In the Spirit of Crazy Horse,* and Ray A. Young Bear's *Black Eagle Child: The Facepaint Narratives.*

Charyn, Jerome. Review of *The Man Who Fell in Love with the Moon,* by Tom Spanbauer. *The New York Times Book Review* (22 September 1991): 20.
  Discusses Tom Spanbauer's novel *The Man Who Fell in Love with the Moon* as a "revisionist tale of the Wild West."

Fiction International, Special Issue: American Indian Writers 20 (Fall 1991): 1-219.
  Collection of short stories, poems, and essays by such Native American writers as Joseph Bruchac, LeAnne Howe, and Ray Maracle. Also includes a review of two works cowritten by Brian Swann and Arnold Krupat: *I Tell You Now: Autobiographical Essays by Native American Writers* and *Recovering the Word: Essays on Native American Literature.*

Jongeward, David. "A Feast of Native American Stories." *Christian Science Monitor* 84, No. 24 (30 December 1991): 13.
  Offers a favorable assessment of *Talking Leaves: Contemporary Native American Short Stories,* edited by Craig Leslie. Jongeward states: "There's good, polished writing in this anthology, with only occasional awkwardness or predictability. Taken as a whole, this is an important collection, replete with memorable characters and situations."

Kirsch, Jonathan. "A Road Beckons, the Mind Wanders." *Los Angeles Times* (30 October 1991): E5.

Reviews Jerry Ellis's *Walking the Trail: One Man's Journey along the Cherokee Trail of Tears.*

World Literature Today, Special Issue: From This World—Contemporary American Indian Literature 66, No. 2 (Spring 1992): 223-300.

Contains essays on Native American literature by such writers and critics as Gerald Vizenor, Kimberly M. Blaeser, and Robert Allen Warrior.

Rap Music

INTRODUCTION

Described by many reviewers as a loud, aggressive, and realistic portrayal of inner-city life, rap music has been subjected to intense criticism for the explicit violence and sexuality described in its lyrics. Also known as hip-hop, rap combines rhythmically spoken lyrics with sounds from drum machines and synthesizers and is often interspersed with excerpts from other artists' records. Despite the controversy surrounding rap, it continues to elicit praise from musicians and critics. The composer Quincy Jones, for instance, has described rap as "the jazz of the 90s," and Jon Pareles has called it "the most startlingly original and fastest-growing genre in popular music."

As part of an African-American subculture that included break dancing and graffiti art, rap first became popular in New York City during the mid-1970s. Its origins, however, can be traced to "the dozens" and "toasting." "The dozens," a competitive game of rhyming sexual insults, developed in American urban ghettos between the world wars; "toasting," a form of reggae music in which one speaks over records, originated in Jamaica during the 1960s. Intended as dance music, early hip-hop emphasized the rhythms disk jockeys created by scratching records and mixing cuts from different songs. The goal of the rapper was simply to match the words to the rhythm, with the lyrics often being irrelevant and incomprehensible. As hip-hop evolved, the rapper's importance increased, with many songs featuring a rapper boasting about his verbal skills and sexual prowess. From New York, rap quickly spread to Philadelphia, Boston, and other cities. The first hip-hop recording to achieve widespread success was "Rapper's Delight," a song about Lois Lane and Superman. Recorded in 1979 by the Sugar Hill Gang, the song reached the top five on the rhythm and blues charts. Social commentary became an issue in rap during the early 1980s with Kurtis Blow's single "The Breaks" and Grandmaster Flash's "The Message," songs about inner-city life. Rap achieved popularity among a mass white audience in 1984 when Run-DMC's album *Run-DMC* went gold. Since the mid-1980s, rap has undergone a rapid surge in popularity with such rap musicians as the Beastie Boys, Tone-Lōc, M.C. Hammer, Vanilla Ice, and N.W.A. recording albums that reached the number one spot on *Billboard*'s album chart.

Critical reaction to rap has centered on the content of its lyrics, with many reviewers questioning its artistic merits and value to society. Detractors have noted the extreme sexism, bigotry, and violence often depicted in many songs. For instance, Slick Rick's single "Treat Her Like a Prostitute" and the raps on 2 Live Crew's album *As Nasty as They Wanna Be* graphically depict women as sexual objects. Public Enemy has attracted criticism for the anti-Semitic content of songs like "Welcome to the Terrordome," which, according to some commentators, accuses Jews of deicide. Critics have also censured Ice-T and Ice Cube for such songs as "Cop Killer" and "Amerikkka's Most Wanted" which respectively describe the murder of a police officer and random violence committed by blacks against whites. Some contend that these images of violence have no basis in reality and are simply fantasies and stereotypes marketed to white, suburban youths who believe they are gaining access to the realities of African-American life. Others argue that rap, as simple entertainment, should not be taken seriously and attribute its popularity, like the rock and roll of the 1950s, to its rebelliousness.

Proponents of rap have lauded it as the creative expression of an alienated underclass, emphasizing its positive themes and literary qualities. Commentators have observed that the raps of Ice Cube, Ice-T, and Public Enemy are often critical, negative depictions of inner-city crime and that such songs as "You Must Learn" by KRS-One emphasize the value of education. Other critics have commended rap for focusing on the issues of race and class. Citing Public Enemy's *Fear of a Black Planet*, John Leland has argued that "rap is locating white insecurity about race—and black insecurity about class." Professor Henry Louis Gates, Jr., has commented on rap's literary value and metaphorical qualities, arguing that the lyrics are difficult to produce and that the songs are sophisticated parodies of black, male stereotypes.

Rap is also at the center of an ongoing debate about music censorship. In 1990 three members of 2 Live Crew were tried and acquitted of breaking Florida's obscenity laws after they performed songs from their album *As Nasty as They Wanna Be,* which a federal judge had declared obscene. Ice-T's song "Cop Killer" drew criticism in 1992 from various police organizations which threatened to lead a boycott against Time Warner, the parent company of Sire/Warner Brothers Records. Ice-T eventually deleted the song from his album *Body Count.* Critics of 2 Live Crew and Ice-T have argued that such obscene and violent material, intended only to tantalize its audience, should not be recorded. Noting rap's emphasis on controversial issues, David Toop has responded: "[The] lyrics of popular music offer a comparatively harmless escape valve for pent-up feelings. . . . If they are to stay relevant, lyrics must reflect all the news, whether fit to print or not."

PRINCIPAL WORKS DISCUSSED BELOW

2 Live Crew
  Move Somethin' 1988
  As Nasty as They Wanna Be 1990
  Banned in the U.S.A.: The Luke LP Featuring the 2 Live Crew 1990
Arrested Development
  3 Years, 5 Months and 2 Days in the Life of . . . 1992
Beastie Boys
  Licensed to Ill 1987
Big Daddy Kane
  Taste of Chocolate 1991
  Check Your Head 1992
Boogie Down Productions
  By Any Means Necessary 1988
  Ghetto Music: The Blueprint of Hip Hop 1989
  Edutainment 1990
D. J. Jazzy Jeff and the Fresh Prince
  He's the D. J., I'm the Rapper 1988
De la Soul
  De la Soul Is Dead 1991
Geto Boys
  Geto Boys 1990
  We Can't Be Stopped 1991
Grandmaster Flash
  "The Message" 1982
House of Pain
  House of Pain 1992
Ice Cube
  AmeriKKKa's Most Wanted 1990
  Death Certificate 1991
Ice-T
  Power 1988
  O. G. Original Gangster 1991
  Body Count 1992
Kurtis Blow
  "The Breaks" 1980
L. L. Cool J
  Radio 1986
  Bigger and Deffer 1987
  Mama Said Knock You Out 1991
M. C. Hammer
  Please Hammer Don't Hurt 'Em 1990
  Too Legit to Quit 1991
N.W.A.
  Straight Outta Compton 1988
  Efil4zaggin 1991
Public Enemy
  Yo! Bum Rush the Show 1987
  It Takes a Nation of Millions to Hold Us Back 1988
  Fear of a Black Planet 1990
  Apocalypse 91 . . . The Enemy Strikes Back 1991
Queen Latifah
  Nature of a Sista' 1991
Run-DMC
  Run-DMC 1984
  King of Rock 1985
  Raising Hell 1986
  Back from Hell 1991
Sir Mix-A-Lot
  Mack Daddy 1992

Sugar Hill Gang
  "Rapper's Delight" 1979
Tone-Lōc
  Lōc-ed after Dark 1989
  Cool Hand Lōc 1991
Vanilla Ice
  To the Extreme 1990
Young M. C.
  Stone Cold Rhymin' 1990

HISTORY, THEMES, AND SOCIAL RELEVANCE

Terry Teachout (essay date March 1990)

[*Teachout is an American editor, musician, and music critic. In the following essay, he remarks on the major themes expressed in rap music, particularly racism, anti-Semitism, and "self-help."*]

For the average middle-class listener, whether black or white, rap music is a landscape too alien for anything but discomfort. That rap is loud, aggressive, and often obscene is the least of it. Every New Yorker who reads the papers knows that the teenagers who allegedly raped and brutalized a woman jogger in Central Park [in 1989] entertained themselves after their arrest by collectively chanting the lyrics to "Wild Thing," a popular record by the Los Angeles rapper Tone-Loc. Many well-informed Americans know, too, that a member of the rap group Public Enemy gave an interview to the Washington *Times* in which he delivered an anti-Semitic tirade of shocking virulence. And yet rap now fills the most popular daily program on MTV. It has been called by the composer Quincy Jones "the jazz of the 90's." And it has been described by Jon Pareles of the *New York Times* as "the most startlingly original and fastest-growing genre in popular music."

Rap, also known as "hip-hop," is typically performed by a three-man group. The "DJ" (which of course stands for disk jockey) operates a pair of turntables on which he plays bits and pieces of phonograph records, turning them by hand in short, sharply accented rhythmic patterns called scratches. A second man, variously known as the "producer" or "programmer," operates a beat box, an electronic device that simulates the sound of a drum set, and a sampler, a synthesizer that holds various sounds in its computerized memory and reproduces them when triggered by the operator. Working together, these two people lay down a collage-like background of beats, scratches, and electronic sound effects over which the "rapper" recites lyrics (true rappers never sing) generally consisting of semi-improvised couplets in rough-and-ready tetrameter.

From its beginnings in the mid-70's, rap has chiefly been performed by young black males, and their subject matter is as uniform as their age, color, and gender. Though women rappers do exist, and though their work is regularly singled out for special attention by critics, to date none has contributed significantly to the development of rap. (Neneh Cherry, recently profiled in the *New York Times Magazine,* is not a true rapper but a popular singer who makes highly effective use of rap devices in her work.) White rappers also exist, but their work is derivative and of no musical interest.

In most raps, the rapper "disses" (attacks) other rappers and asserts his own superior verbal skills. Many raps consist solely of this kind of boasting. Beyond that, the content of rap can be summarized in terms of two commonly leveled criticisms, that it is obscene and that it is "sexist." Indeed, most rappers do make elaborate use of profanity, and also equate verbal with sexual prowess. Rapping is itself an outgrowth of "the dozens," a highly competitive verbal game of rhyming sexual insults developed between the world wars in the ghettos of urban America. Just as victory in this game is understood as a token of sexual superiority, so the verbally proficient rapper is assumed to be sexually proficient in like degree. When L. L. Cool J (short for "Ladies Love Cool James") proclaims "No rapper can rap quite like I can / I'll take a muscle-bound man and put his face in the sand," the implication is clear.

Not surprisingly, women in the world of rap are largely, if not exclusively, objects of transient sexual gratification. Many raps consist of a graphic description of a night's trolling. ("Evil 'E' was out coolin' with a freak one night / Fucked the bitch with a flashlight / Pulled it out and left the batteries in / So he could get a charge when he begin.") In the world of rap it is the destiny of women to be picked up, casually fornicated with, and left behind by their men.

Some rappers, to be sure, are quite far removed from the life evoked by lyrics like these. Run-D. M. C., for instance, is an extremely popular ensemble of thoroughly middle-class black teens who have endorsed Adidas sneakers and Coca-Cola; DJ Jazzy Jeff and the Fresh Prince, a clean-cut rap team that has successfully "crossed over" to a fully integrated mainstream teenage audience, specialize in sanitized raps like "Parents Just Don't Understand" ("She said, 'What's wrong? This shirt cost twenty dollars!' / I said, 'Mom! This shirt is plaid with a butterfly collar!' "). But such sentiments are comparatively rare. More typical is Ice-T, a former member of a Los Angeles gang, whose raps are mosaics of sex and violence in which the brutality of street life in a culture where drugs are sold around the clock is taken for granted. His 1988 album *Power* features on its jacket a photograph of a nearly nude woman holding a sawed-off shotgun, and the songs within are stark, obscenity-ridden narratives of gang life. ("Copped an alias, bailed out in an hour or less / I keep a bank for that don't know about the rest / Copped another piece, hit the dark streets / Rollin' once again, fuck the damn police!")

Ice-T is frequently accused of glorifying violence. He claims in his own defense that his music is a realistic portrait of a violent world desperately in need of change. Similar arguments can be heard from the rapidly growing number of rappers who espouse "socially-conscious" rap. Many albums now contain at least one track extolling the virtues of self-help and attacking the evils of drugs and black-on-black violence, and several groups put a consistent emphasis on self-help as a means of enhancing racial pride and breaking the cycle of poverty. Boogie Down Productions' *Ghetto Music: The Blueprint of Hip Hop* is devoted almost entirely to songs like "You Must Learn," a paean to the importance of teaching black history in the public schools:

> Pump my mind with "See Jane run."
> See John walk in a hard-core New York?
> Come on, now, that's like a chocolate cow,
> It doesn't exist, no way, no how.
> It seems to me that in a school that's ebony,
> African history should be pumped up steadily.
> But it's not—and this has got to stop.
> "See Spot run? Run, get Spot!"
> Insulting to a black mentality,
> A black way of life or a jet-black family.

Unfortunately there is sometimes more to "self-help" than meets the eye. Boogie Down Productions' first album, *By Any Means Necessary,* took its title from a speech by Malcolm X, a figure greatly esteemed by rappers, and another figure held in high regard in certain rap quarters is Malcolm's successor as chief spokesman for the Black Muslim community, Louis Farrakhan.

Among rappers, to speak of Louis Farrakhan is to speak of Public Enemy, winner of the 1988 *Village Voice* critics' poll and the most celebrated and controversial of all rap groups. Spike Lee brought Public Enemy to the attention of the general public when he featured its recording "Fight the Power" in his movie *Do the Right Thing.* The members of Public Enemy all belong to the Nation of Islam, the Black Muslim sect led by Farrakhan; members of the Fruit of Islam, the paramilitary wing of the Nation of Islam, provide on-stage security at Public Enemy concerts. "Bring the Noise," one of Public Enemy's popular numbers, contains the lines "Farrakhan's a prophet and I think you ought to listen to / What he can say to you, what you ought to do." Other tracks on the group's latest album, *It Takes a Nation of Millions to Hold Us Back,* contain explicit references to "black nationalism" and to the Black Muslim demonology familiar to readers of *The Autobiography of Malcolm X:*

> To those that disagree, it causes static
> For the original Black Asiatic man
> Cream of the earth
> And was here first
> And some devils prevent this from being known
> But you check out the books they own
> Even Masons they know it
> But refuse to show it—yo
> But it's proven and fact . . .

The pro-Farrakhan sentiments of Public Enemy were not widely noticed until the *Washington Times* ran its interview with the group's "minister of information," one Professor Griff, [in May 1989]. The *Village Voice* later published extended excerpts from this interview, and other newspapers too began to report that Professor Griff had called Jews "wicked" and had blamed them for "the majority of wickedness that goes on across the globe." In fact, he had much more to say on the subject:

How come we don't talk about how the Jews finance these experiments on AIDS with black people in South Africa? How come we don't talk about those things? . . .

[The Jews] *have* to keep black people in check in America. That's wicked. They have to say Qaddafi is a hater; they have to say Farrakhan is a hater; they have to say the Ayatollah Khomeini is just a religious fanatic; they have to say Idi Amin kills his own people. . . . Personally speaking, these men I admire. . . .

Is it a coincidence that the Jews run the jewelry business, and it's named *jew*-elry? No coincidence. Is it a coincidence to you that probably the gold from this ring was brought up out of South Africa, and that the Jews have a tight grip on our brothers in South Africa? . . .

[The Jews] have a history of killing black men. What am I supposed to fear? I fear no one but Allah. I fear God alone. So the Jews can come against me. They can send the IRS after me. They can send their faggot little hit men.

Asked by David Mills of the *Times* for evidence of these accusations, Professor Griff cited Henry Ford's anti-Semitic tract, *The International Jew,* plus a book circulated by the Nation of Islam called *The Secret Relationship Between Blacks and Jews,* and "a series of tapes" by "a brother by the name of Steve Cokely." Cokely, then an adviser to the mayor of Chicago, claimed in 1988 that 300 Jewish doctors were inoculating blacks with the AIDS virus. [See Joseph Epstein, "Racial Pervisity in Chicago," *Commentary* (December 1988).]

The *Village Voice* story was published on June 20, [1989]. The next day, Professor Griff was "fired" from Public Enemy by Chuck D, the group's leader and chief rapper, who called a press conference to apologize to "anyone who might have been offended by Griff's remarks." A week later, Def Jam Recordings, the rap division of CBS Records and Public Enemy's record label, announced that the group was "disbanding for an indefinite period of time."

By August 10, however, Public Enemy had already announced its "reorganization," with Professor Griff rehired under the title of "supreme allied chief of community relations." A number of Jewish groups reacted heatedly to the news. Said Rabbi Abraham Cooper of the Simon Wiesenthal Foundation: "Imagine if there was a country-music group in which one of the members was an open member of the Ku Klux Klan, repeating all the slanders against blacks, Jews, and Vietnamese boat people. How long would he last in the music community?" In fact, reaction within the music community was tepid at best; Russell Simmons, president of Def Jam Recordings, told David Mills that the members of Public Enemy were "ideological idiots" but added irrelevantly that "I listen to Frank Sinatra, too, but I don't listen to him for ideology."

[In December 1989], Def Jam released a new Public Enemy single, "Welcome to the Terrordome," which includes a reference by Chuck D to the controversy over Professor Griff's *Washington Times* interview: "Crucifix-ion ain't no fiction / So-called chosen, frozen / Apologies made to whoever pleases / Still, they got me like Jesus." On December 28, a letter was sent by the Anti-Defamation League of B'nai Brith to CBS Records protesting "Welcome to the Terrordome" on the grounds that it "contains blatantly anti-Semitic lyrics, including the repulsive and historically discredited charge of deicide on the part of the Jews. . . ." In response, Chuck D told the *Washington Post* that the passage in question was not anti-Semitic, and dismissed criticism of "Welcome to the Terrordome" as "paranoiac."

As for CBS, Walter Yetnikoff, head of CBS Records, issued a memorandum on January 11, [1990] calling upon CBS employees to ensure that "none of our recordings promote bigotry." Public Enemy was not mentioned. Earlier, Def Jam had announced that Public Enemy's next album, *Fear of a Black Planet,* would be released on February 21, the 25th anniversary of Malcolm X's assassination, and would include "Welcome to the Terrordome." And when the Grammy Award nominees for 1990 were announced on January 14, one of the songs nominated in the rap category was Public Enemy's "Fight the Power."

Many people who know Chuck D, including Rabbi Cooper, maintain that he is not personally anti-Semitic. I should note, too, that I have failed to encounter any examples of directly anti-Semitic lyrics or public statements by rappers other than the ones made by Professor Griff in the *Washington Times* and by Chuck D in "Welcome to the Terrordome." But the anti-Semitism in those two instances is blatant and unmistakable; and it is not the only pernicious doctrine circulating in the world of rap. Russell Simmons says that "Chuck D is very, very important to a lot of black kids in America—he's contributed so much to black youth, to the growth of black awareness and black pride." The question naturally arises: what kind of awareness? What kind of pride?

One example can be found in a statement Chuck D made [in August 1989] during an interview with David Hinckley of the *New York Daily News:*

> You have to tell people why, for example, you see so many drug dealers in the black community and not in the white. You explain who's *behind* the drug thing, why it's the brothers who are dying. You point out that Jesse Jackson had twice the qualities of any other candidate, but because we have this system where people are judged by their characteristics, he couldn't win. And then you tell kids to stop wanting a gold chain and a fly [stylish] car and get educated—because black people have to take care of themselves and the only way to do it is as a community.

The last sentence of this statement could have come from any one of a dozen rappers advocating black self-help. The preceding sentences are another matter entirely. They allude to the theory, increasingly popular among urban blacks, that there is a conspiracy by powerful whites to commit "genocide" against the black community. In fact, more or less explicit talk of genocide is not uncommon among "socially conscious" rappers. In their songs, policemen kill blacks casually and deliberately, and the federal government, usually personified by Ronald Reagan or, more recently, George Bush, is the mortal enemy of all blacks. White racism, one and indivisible, is the principle of American social organization; all blacks are its perpetual objects; white and black America are in a state of de-facto war.

What the black response should be to these "facts" is the subject of a recent recording by Ice-T, "This One's for Me":

> Griff is my man, I don't care what he said
> You know what I'm saying?
> And I ain't gonna let them go out like that. . . .
> Anybody out there got problems with Public
>   Enemy,
> Come talk to me. . . .
> I gotta speak my mind, it's time to unload
> On this so-called government we got
> I lied like them, I think I'd get shot
> They sell drugs to kids and say it's us
> And when the cops are crooks, who can you
>   trust? . . .
> Selling drugs is straight-up genocide
> They're gonna laugh while we all die.

Critics of rap are fairly quick to decry "sexism" in recordings like Slick Rick's "Treat Her Like a Prostitute." But when it comes to such raps as "This One's for Me" or "Welcome to the Terrordome," many of these critics are even quicker to mount the nearest fence. Peter Watrous, who reviewed a concert by Public Enemy for the *New York Times*, noted that it opened with a lecture by Professor Griff claiming that the U.S. and Soviet governments were jointly responsible for the AIDS epidemic (admittedly, a slight improvement on blaming the Jews). To this and comparable statements, Watrous's response was that "while the group's political discourse is undigested at best and secondary to the urgency of their overall sound, it at least opens the always necessary debate about racism." So it does—although not the kind of racism Watrous seems to have in mind. (pp. 60-2)

> Terry Teachout, "Rap and Racism," in Commentary, *Vol. 89, No. 3, March, 1990, pp. 60-2.*

Jerry Adler (essay date 19 March 1990)

[*In the following excerpt, Adler relates rap to a new musical culture that emphasizes anger, bigotry, and self-assertion.*]

Let's talk about "attitude."

And I don't mean a good attitude, either. I mean "attitude" by itself, which is always bad, as in, you'd better not be bringing any attitude around here, boy, and, when that bitch gave me some attitude, I cut her good. I mean attitude as a cultural style, marrying the arrogance of Donald Trump to the vulgarity of Roseanne Barr. Comedians have attitude, rock bands have attitude, in America today even *birthday cards* have attitude. In the rap-music group N.W.A, which stands for Niggas With Attitude, you don't have to guess what kind of attitude they mean: jaunty and sullen by turns; showy but somehow furtive, in glasses as

opaque as a limousine window and sneakers as white as a banker's shirt. Their music is a rhythmic chant, a rhyme set to a drum solo, a rant from the streets about gunning down cops. Now *that's* attitude.

OK, here it is: the first important cultural development in America in 25 years that the baby-boom generation didn't pioneer: The Culture of Attitude. It is heard in the thundering cacophony of heavy metal and the thumping, clattering, scratching assault of rap—music so postindustrial it's mostly not even *played,* but pieced together out of pre-recorded sound bites. It is the culture of American males frozen in various stages of adolescence: their streetwise music, their ugly macho boasting and joking about anyone who hangs out on a different block—cops, other races, women and homosexuals. Its most visible contribution has been the disinterment of the word nigger, a generation after a national effort to banish it and its ugly connotations from the American language. Now it is back, employed with savage irony by black rappers, and dumb literal hostility by their white heavy-metal counterparts. *Nigger! Faggot!* What ever happened to the idea that rock and roll would make us free?

Although most Americans may never have heard of them, these are not obscure bands playing in garages and afterhours clubs. In the '70s, urban rappers performed in parks, plugging loudspeakers into lampposts. Now they fill major arenas—although more and more arenas won't have rap concerts any longer, because of fear that the violence can spill over from the stage to the crowd. Public Enemy, a rap group caught up in a protracted anti-Semitic controversy, and N.W.A, have had platinum albums, with more than a million in sales. . . . Major companies are behind them: Public Enemy's releases for the Def Jam label are distributed by CBS/Columbia Records. (p. 56)

Attitude! Civilized society abhors attitude, and perpetuates itself by keeping it under control. There are entire organizations devoted to this job, most notably the Parents' Music Resource Center in Arlington, Va. The center has an extensive file of lyrics in rap and heavy-metal music, describing every imaginable perversity from unsafe sex to Devil worship. . . . But executive director Jennifer Norwood is careful to point out that the center takes "no position on any specific type of music." There are rap ballads whose sentiments would not have brought a blush to the cheek of Bing Crosby, and rap acts that promote an anti-drug message. The center does support printing song lyrics on album jackets for the information of parents—although such a step might also make it easier for kids to learn them—and a warning label, which some record companies already apply voluntarily, about "explicit lyrics."

Others who stand against attitude include Florida Gov. Bob Martinez, who asked the statewide prosecutor to investigate the Miami rap group The 2 Live Crew for alleged violations of obscenity laws in the album *As Nasty as They Want to Be.* "If you answer the phone one night and the voice on the other end begins to read the lyrics of one of those songs, you'd say you received an obscene phone call," reasoned Martinez. This proved to be outside the governor's jurisdiction. But [in March 1990] a Broward County judge . . . cleared the way for prosecutors to charge record-shop owners who *sell* the album; courts would then rule on whether the material was obscene. And the Kentucky-based chain that operates 121 Disc Jockey record stores announced that it would no longer carry records with warning stickers. In part, says company executive Harold Guilfoil, this is a move to pre-empt mandatory-labeling and sales-restriction laws under consideration in at least 10 states. A Pennsylvania bill that has already passed in one House would require labels for lyrics describing or advocating suicide, incest, sodomy, morbid violence or several other things. "That about takes care of every opera in the world," observes Guilfoil.

Particularly concerned is the Anti-Defamation League, whose civil-rights director, Jeffrey Sinensky, sees evidence in popular music that "hatred is becoming hip." The rap group Public Enemy was the most notorious offender, not even for anything in their music, but for remarks by a non-singing member of the group, Professor Griff, a hanger-on and backup dancer with the grandiloquent but meaningless title of Minister of Information. Griff, a follower of Louis Farrakhan's Nation of Islam, gave an interview [in Spring 1989] in which he parroted some Farrakhanesque nonsense about Jews being behind "the majority of wickedness that goes on across the globe." After the predictable outcry Griff was fired and the group disbanded; but soon it re-formed, and Griff came back as "Supreme Allied Chief of Community Relations," a position in which he is not allowed to talk to the press. And Public Enemy proceeded to discuss the episode in ominous, if somewhat obscure, terms in "Welcome to the Terrordome," a single prereleased from its forthcoming album, *Fear of a Black Planet*:

> Crucifixion ain't no fiction
>   So-called chosen, frozen
> Apology made to whoever pleases
>   Still they got me like Jesus.

That's *attitude* for you: bombastic, self-aggrandizing and yet as scary as suden footsteps in the dark. "I mean, I made the apology, but people are still trying to give me hell," elaborates Public Enemy's lead rapper, Chuck D. "The media crucified me, comparable to another brother who caught hell." If you add up all the Jewish blood that has been spilled over the slander of deicide, it makes Chuck D's sufferings at the hands of his critics seem mild by comparison. The ADL [Anti-Defamation League] reacted swiftly to what appeared to be a gratuitous incitement to anti-Semitism, and took its protest to where it would do the most good, CBS Records. CBS Records Inc. president Walter Yetnikoff responded with a commitment to police future releases for "bigotry and intolerance." While "it goes without saying that artists have the right of freedom of expression," Yetnikoff wrote in a memo to the rest of the company, "when the issue is bigotry, there is a fine line of acceptable standards which no piece of music should cross." And once again, Chuck D is saying that Professor Griff will leave the group. . . .

N.W.A's attitude even got it into trouble with the FBI. In a letter last summer to N.W.A's distributor, FBI Assistant Director Milt Ahlerich observed that the group's album *Straight Outta Compton* "encourages violence against and disrespect for the law-enforcement officer." But Ahlerich couldn't do much more than make the company "aware of the FBI's position" on lyrics in a song ("F--- tha Police") he couldn't bring himself to name:

> Pullin' out a silly club so you stand
>   With a fake-ass badge and a gun in your
>   hand
> Take off the gun so you can see what's up
>   And we'll go at it, punk, and I'm 'a f--- you
>   up . . .
> I'm a sniper with a hell of a 'scope . . .
>   Takin' out a cop or two . . .

Are even such appalling expressions of attitude protected by the First Amendment? Yes, according to an American Civil Liberties Union official, who told *The Village Voice* that "the song does not constitute advocacy of violence as that has been interpreted by the courts." (Although in plain English, it's hard to imagine what else it might be advocating.) Asked whether his music doesn't give the impression that the gang culture in the sorry Los Angeles slum of Compton is fun, Eazy-E, the group's coleader, replied, "It *is* fun." " 'F--- tha police' was something people be wanting to say for years but they were too scared to say it," he says. "The next album might be 'F--- tha FBI'."

Yes, having an attitude means it's always someone else's fault: cops who disrespect (or "dis") you when you walk through a housing project with a gold chain that could lock up a motorcycle, immigrants so dumb they can't speak the language, women who are just asking for it anyway. The outrageous implication is that to *not* sing about this stuff would be to do violence to an artistic vision as pure and compelling as Bach's. The viler the message, the more fervent the assertion of honesty that underlies it. Eazy sometimes calls himself a "street historian" to deflect the charge that he is a rabble-rouser. "We're like underground reporters," he says; "We just telling it like it is, we don't hold back." The fact is, rap grows out of a violent culture in which getting shot by a cop is a real fear. But music isn't reportage, and the way to deal with police brutality is not to glorify "taking out a cop or two." By way of self-exculpation, Eazy denies any aspirations toward being a role model. As he puts it, "I don't like anybody want to look at me and stop being theyself." (pp. 57-8)

Attitude primarily is a working-class and underclass phenomenon, a response to the diminishing expectations of the millions of American youths who forgot to go to business school in the 1980s. *If* they had ever listened to anything except the homeboys talking trash, *if* they had ever studied anything but the strings of a guitar, they might have some more interesting justifications to offer. They could quote the sainted Woody Guthrie about "Pretty Boy Floyd," who "laid [a] deputy down" (for disrespecting his wife, as it happened in the song). Apropos of their penchant for exaggerated sexual braggadocio, they could point out that the great jazz pianist Jelly Roll Morton didn't get his nickname because he liked pastry. They could point out that as recently as a generation ago, racial epithets that today would make Morton Downey Jr. swoon with embarrassment came tripping innocently off the tongues of educated, decent people. *Then* we might have a sensible discussion with them; but they haven't, so we can't.

But of course attitude resists any such attempt at intellectualizing. To call it visceral is to give it the benefit of the doubt. It has its origins in parts of the body even less mentionable, as the pioneering California rapper Ice-T puts it: "Women have some eerie connection with gangsters. They always want the rebel more than the brain. Girls want somebody who can beat everybody up."

OK, girls, if that's what you want, here's Ice-T at his most revoltingly passionate:

> Girls, Let's get butt naked and f---
> I mean real stupid and nasty
> . . .my crew got to have it
> And after they dog it, I autograph it

This is the height of gallantry for Ice-T: no one gets killed. More often, when attitude meets woman, woman is by far the worse for it. If she's lucky, she gets made love to with a flashlight ("Shut Up, Be Happy" by Ice-T). Otherwise, she finds herself in the even less healthy company of Eazy E:

> Now back on the street and my records are clean
> I creeped on my bitch with my Uzi machine
> Went to the house and kicked down the door
> Unloaded like hell, cold smoked the ho'.

It is not just that romance has gone out of music—attitude has done the seemingly impossible and taken sex out of teenage culture, substituting brutal fantasies of penetration and destruction. Girls who want to have fun this way need to have their heads examined.

But that's the point. The end of attitude is nihilism, which by definition leads nowhere. The culture of attitude is repulsive, but it's mostly empty of political content. [As Todd Gitlin, director of the mass-communications program at the University of California, Berkeley] puts it, "There's always a population of kids looking to be bad. As soon as the establishment tells them what's bad this season, some of them are going to go off and do it." And that's not good, but it's probably not a case for the FBI, either. If we learned one thing from the '60s, it's how *little* power rock and roll has to change the world. (p. 59)

> Jerry Adler, *"The Rap Attitude,"* in Newsweek, *Vol. CXV, No. 12, March 19, 1990, pp. 56-9.*

David Gates   (essay date 19 March 1990)

[*In the following excerpt, Gates outlines the principal themes and characteristics of rap and discusses hip-hop's increasing emphasis on social topics.*]

Sooner or later you're just going to have to deal with it. The guys with the names you don't understand—what is a Tone-Lōc, anyway?—chanting over gut-whomping drumbeats and those noises like somebody scratching a needle across the damn record. You know that American popular music is unimaginable without such black contributions as blues, jazz, and rock and roll. Maybe you even agree that rap is the next evolutionary step. And you recognize its social significance as a communiqué from the "underclass"—or, less euphemistically, poor blacks. An ongoing history of the streets in doggerel couplets, chanted by self-taught poets armed with rhyming dictionaries and microphones. It *still* drives you up a wall.

Since Tone-Lōc's 1988-89 hit "Wild Thing"—the bestselling single since "We Are the World"—you can't get away from the stuff anywhere. TV ads. "Boom cars" with the bass up loud enough to shatter windshields. Your kid's bedroom. And don't think it's only white-bread throwbacks to the Age of Mantovani reaching for the aspirin. Black radio-station owners fear rap will drive off the thirtysomethings and louse up the demographics. (MTV programs more rap than many black outlets.) And black and white parents alike fret over what rap is telling their kids. The popularity of wholesome rappers like Young M. C. and the Fresh Prince has also brought rap's hard core—the sub-Chaucerian 2 Live Crew, the gun-happy N.W.A, the fiercely political Public Enemy—under heavy scrutiny. Not just from outraged parents and the media, but (in N.W.A's case) from the FBI. The notoriety sells still more records.

And rappers today are doing some scrutinizing of their own. For over a decade, the music had remained largely unassimilated; crossover hits like "Wild Thing" now seem to threaten its integrity. "I'm glad as hell," says Tone-Lōc, when taxed with selling out. "Anybody saying something would love to be played on the pop charts." But, if anything, most rap has come to sound *less* like "normal" music. "Fresh" is rap's quintessential compliment; in creating ever new beats and textures, going easy on the ears isn't the first consideration. As Chuck D of Public Enemy once said, "I wanted some s--- where, when a car passed my house, I'd know that's my song."

Yet rap is more than just a manifesto from the esthetic cutting edge: it's a series of bulletins from the front in a battle for survival. Despite a growing minority of women (Salt-N-Pepa, MC Lyte) and whites (the Beastie Boys, 3rd Bass), rap is mostly produced by young black men—and one quarter of their homeboys end up in serious trouble with the law. Rappers and athletes are about the only credible role models for inner-city kids. Does that mean rap stars have a responsibility beyond flaunting gold chains and purveying def jams (*def jams:* enjoyable music)? Are they artists, answerable only to themselves? Or are they the high-tech *griots* of the inner city, whose job is to educate and mobilize? Ask a different rapper, get a different answer. Tone-Lōc is about fun. (*Do the wild thing:* do the hanky-panky.) Chuck D of Public Enemy disses (*dis:* to evince disrespect for) frivolous materialism, and his group's original goal was "to take the gold chains off of kids' necks." But whatever the answer, within the rap community, these questions are Topic A.

Rap's coded language, mystic monikers and Martian-sounding background noises *keep* outsiders outside—and create a sense of community among those in the know. No rapper in his right mind would explicitly warn off white record buyers—indeed, at least half of the audience for Public Enemy's stern black nationalism is white. But the liner notes for the latest LP by Boogie Down Productions, a group staunchly on the political tip (*on the political tip:* political), discourage slumming: "Only Ghetto consciousness will understand it and only Ghetto consciousness will enjoy it."

For whites the music is a window. For homeboys, it's a lifeline—a way for Too Short of Oakland, Calif., say, to communicate with Chuck D of Long Island. From Too Short's records, says Chuck, "I know what kind of car he drives, I know the police give him a hard time, I know that there's *trees* in the area, you know what I'm sayin'? It's like a CNN that black kids never had." The language may be harsh, but rap reflects the wit, energy and hope of a generation who've contrived to make art out of what they were given. It also neatly refutes the canard that the black "underclass" is inarticulate.

Even at its scariest, rap is a positive development in a miserable environment. What? Even N.W.A, threatening to "smoke any motherf----- that sweats me"? (*Smoke:* shoot dead. *Sweat:* hassle.) Well, rapping about smoking people is still *rapping,* not smoking people. Whether such theatrics vent your rage or aggravate it, they keep you on the mike and off the streets. (One of rap's oft-repeated themes is that rap itself is the safe and legal road to riches.) And the ubiquitous nicknames suggest folks like Carlton Ridenhour (Chuck D) and Tony Smith (Tone-Lōc—"loc" from "loco") are playing roles much as actors do; the official bio for Too Short (né Todd Shaw) notes that part of his daily routine is riding around "projecting the Too Short image."

But even colleagues wonder if N.W.A isn't throwing itself into the role of gangbangers (*gangbangers:* gang members) with too much relish. No one denies their verbal and musical skills; Daddy-O of the group Stetsasonic plays N.W.A for aspiring rappers because their records tell stories with cinematic clarity. But KRS-One of Boogie Down Productions—a rapper so politically correct he's called "The Teacher"—talks in circumspect circles when asked about N.W.A. "In a broader sense," he says, "I can see where they are doing some good because I can then come out on my own spectrum and downplay an N.W.A." Rough translation: *They represent what I'm fighting against.*

As their name (Niggas With Attitude) suggests, N.W.A caricatures ghetto misbehavior partly to rub white America's nose in its own racism. But what about those 12-year-old boys out there unused to disentangling ironies? "There's a lot of impressionable people listening to the music," says Young M. C., the straight-arrow college economics major who won this year's rap Grammy. "If I wasn't to take notice of that I would be shirking responsibility." Rap's recent wild popularity gives the question of responsibility a new urgency. But the question is nearly as old as rap itself.

Hip-hop (*hip-hop:* the music that has *rapping*) began in New York basement clubs in the 1970s, when disc jockeys like the Bronx's DJ Kool Herc kept dance rhythms going by seamlessly cutting back and forth between snatches of the same record on two separate turntables. (One well-kept secret: a few hot seconds by the Monkees.) As they cut rhythms—sometimes just a few seconds of drums, cued and recued, played and replayed—they also functioned as masters of ceremonies, chanting rhymed catch phrases to celebrate their own wonderfulness and to egg on the dancers. The term hip-hop comes from the early master DJ Hollywood: "Hippity hip hop / don't stop . . ."

Technical difficulty demanded the roles of deejay and rapping MC be split; as front men, rappers naturally took precedence. Since the 1979 "Rapper's Delight," hip-hop's first hit, MCs have mostly worked variations on the theme of how def I am and how wack you are (*def:* good; *wack:* bad). This isn't as insane as it sounds. There's a continuity from the African-American insult game of "the dozens" to saxophone cutting contests to the self-mythologizing rhymes of Muhammad Ali to rap braggadocio. "Maybe boasting," writes critic Nelson George, "is just in the bones of brothers."

But as early as 1982, MCs content to be merely engaging were challenged to become politically engaged by New York's Grandmaster Flash, a hip-hop Horowitz on the wheels of steel (*wheels of steel:* turntables), whose hit "The Message" warned of a generation getting "close to the edge." And that was *before* the full impact of Reagan-era cuts on social spending, assaults on affirmative action, the Howard Beach racial attack, the crack epidemic. Now, more and more rappers speak of getting down with the Program (*get down with:* embrace). The Program isn't a specific plan, but a range of attitudes. Crack, racism and black-on-black crime are impermissible; education (especially in African-American history) and a determination to stop getting stepped on are imperative.

No new act is more "Afrocentric" and "positive"—favorite words among those on the political tip—than the Jungle Brothers. As Edenic as Public Enemy is apocalyptic, they juxtapose Tarzan-movie imagery with a real-life urban jungle. The JBs eat veggies, drink nothing stronger than orange juice, revere the motherland and exalt black womanhood. (Truly a radical stance in a market dominated by the likes of The 2 Live Crew.) "I'll be glad when you ladies just take over the world," sighs one Brother. "We men have messed it up so bad." Even apolitical MCs like Tone-Lōc now trade sweats for quasi-African tunics: if you're not down with the Program, fans may not be down with you.

Consider the case of LL Cool J. One of rap's biggest stars, Hollywood handsome, witty, wickedly adept at rapid-fire tongue twisters. At the age of 22, he's passé. His record sales are down (*down:* down), and last summer he was booed at a Harlem rally following the murder of a black teenager by whites in Brooklyn. Why? Insufficient political consciousness. "I'm conscious," says LL. "Of *course* I am. I see it every day on the news. I walk *past* it every day. I wanted to take people's minds *away* from it. Unfortunately, when the majority of rappers are serious, the minority who *aren't* seem silly instead of lighthearted."

LL's archrival, Kool Moe Dee, was smarter. Their pro-wrestling-style feud began in fun: LL's trademark Kangol (*Kangol:* a small-brim hat) flattened by a jeep on Moe's album cover. It turned ugly over LL's lack of high seriousness. These days you won't find them on the same bill. Even Chuck D thinks that's nuts. "They've forgotten they're both entertainers," he says. "They should have said, 'Let's go out and make some money'." But Moe, a veteran of rap's first generation, does fine on his own, combining social concern with showbiz shtik. "How many pretty ladies are there in the house tonight?" he'll ask. Big cheer. "How many of you pretty ladies have jobs?" Biggish cheer. "How many of you pretty ladies with jobs talk to drug dealers?" Smaller cheer. Stony glare through wrap-around shades. "You stupid bitches."

Harsh language lends Kool Moe Dee credibility with the tough customers he hopes to educate. But he's nowhere near as graphic as N.W.A, whose "Dopeman," about a crack dealer's "bitch" ("'Ho, if you want a hit you gotta get your knees dirty"), may be the strongest anti-drug rap ever recorded. "To get across to the hardheads," says Chuck D, "they've got to *be* hard." The need to establish that you're tough enough to be listened to helps explain rap music's cult of the Uzi. Public Enemy's paramilitary dancers brandish plastic ones onstage; even the mild-mannered M. C. Hammer fancies himself "shot with an Uzi by old Cupid." And KRS-One, active in rap's Stop the Violence Movement—which has raised more than $200,000 for the National Urban League—holds a fake Uzi on an album cover. "I'm not here to heal the *healed,*" he explains. "I'm here to talk to the sick."

This makes sense—sort of. But rappers are hardly systematic political theorists, and their messages can get confusing. Critic Nelson George says rap "reflects both the best and the worst of young black thought"; it often happens on the same album. The raps on the latest LP by Philadelphia's tough-talking Schoolly D, for instance, range from "Education of a Black Man" to "Pussy Ain't Nothin'." And, speaking of mixed messages, check the liner notes to the N.W.A album, in which rap's scariest act gives "extra special thankz" to God and "our mothers and fathers." Say *what?*

Even KRS-One himself, one of rap's inspirational figures, goes off on some disquieting tangents. As teenage Kris Parker, he lived in New York's subways, parks and homeless shelters. As KRS-One—the nom de mike stands for "Knowledge Reigns Supreme Over Nearly Everyone"—he once lectured at Harvard and has published a *New York Times* op-ed piece. So respectable has he become that during last year's controversy over N.W.A's "F--- tha Police," nobody noted KRS-One's own police revenge fantasy, "Bo! Bo! Bo!" The story begins when a cop, on scant provocation, whacks the *New York Times* essayist in the face with his shotgun:

> On the ground was a bottle of Snapple I broke
>   the bottle in his f------ Adam's apple
> As he fell, his partner called for backup Well, I
>   had the shotgun and began to act up
> With that "bo bo bo bo bo, kak kak kak kak
>   kak"
> . . . The only way to deal with racism if you're
>   black

The *only* way? We'd all better hope not.

And yet, just when you're thinking these characters could

really do some damage if they don't get a grip on themselves, along comes a sharp, funny detail like that bottle of Snapple. Then you wonder if, even at its scariest, rap isn't a safety valve rather than an opened floodgate. N.W.A may have been the first to say "f--- the police" on a platinum album, but the sentiment is hardly novel in the black community. Is it a good idea to make it a catchy anthem for 12-year-olds to chant? No, though back in the Dead-End-Kids days, policemen survived taunts about what pennies were made outta. (Dirty copper.) To insist that all rappers confine themselves to shaking a solemn, responsible finger at violence and racism—where they live, these are more than editorial-page abstractions—is like telling blues singers to lighten up. While "F--- Tha Police" and its ilk are nothing the kiddies should hear, they're not the end of civilization either. That comes when the rhyming dictionaries and microphones are gone. (pp. 60-1, 63)

> *David Gates, "Decoding Rap Music," in* Newsweek, *Vol. CXV, No. 12, March 19, 1990, pp. 60-1, 63.*

Tricia Rose on hip-hop and black women:

[Hip-hop] has had a double-edged effect, creating a powerful self-constructed language and cultural perspective, but at the same time it has seriously encouraged notions of black women as money diggers, as bitches, as sexual objects to be owned, contained, discarded, and that has been taking place right alongside some of the most powerful female voices in popular culture. It's a strange, contradictory space. On the one hand it seems to have encouraged the very things we're calling for the dissolution of, but at the same time, it holds the most promise for other dialogues.

Elizabeth Alexander and Tricia Rose, in their "Call and Response," Voice Literary Supplement, October, 1992.

Jon Pareles   (essay date 17 June 1990)

[*In the following excerpt, Pareles notes the similarities between rap and other forms of black literature and praises rap as a creative and positive means of self-expression.*]

Rap music now has a criminal record. On June 6, [1990] United States District Court Judge Jose Gonzalez of Fort Lauderdale, Fla., declared that *As Nasty as They Wanna Be,* an album by the 2 Live Crew, a rap group that is based in Miami, was obscene in the three counties under his jurisdiction, making it the first recording to be declared obscene by a Federal court. In the next few days, a record-store owner who had continued to sell the album was arrested; two members of the group were also arrested for performing one of the album's songs before an adults-only audience.

It was only the latest, if potentially the most far-reaching, of rap's skirmishes with mainstream culture. As the voice of the young black male, rap has become a vivid, contentious cultural symbol. From its beginnings in the mid-1970's—when rap was part of New York's emerging hip-hop subculture, which also included break dancing and graffiti art—rap has been met by condescension, rejection and outright fear from those outside its domain.

Although rappers have made a point of denouncing black-on-black crime, many promoters refuse to book rap concerts fearing the audience would include violent members of a troubled community already plagued by crime. Some radio stations chose not to play rap music because their research shows that the music alienates many listeners. People who monitor rock lyrics—from pop critics to the Parents' Music Resource Center (a group that advocates voluntary warning stickers on potentially offensive albums) to the Gay and Lesbian Alliance Against Defamation—worry about some rappers' overt homophobia, sexism and other bigotry along with their descriptions of violence.

To many listeners, white and black, rap is the sound of a threatening underclass—although, increasingly, suburbanites as well as urban teen-agers are embracing rap, which includes tall tales, jokes, ethical advice, political statements and baroquely exuberant metaphorical flights. Like the punk rock that appeared almost simultaneously in the 1970's, rap has as much to do with attitude as with conventionally defined musical skills. Rappers live by their wit—their ability to rhyme, the speed of their articulation—and by their ability to create outsized personas through words alone.

"The skills you need to be a good rapper are the same skills you need to get ahead in mainstream society," said Philippe Bourgois, an assistant professor of anthropology at San Francisco State University who is writing a book, *Scrambling,* about street culture. "You have to write well and speak well in a creative manner, which are exactly the skills you need in an information-processing city like New York. And rap is about making something of yourself—it's the American dream."

Put simply, rap is an affirmation of self. It might define that self as successful, well paid, flaunting status symbols like jewelry and cars. And often, it defines that self as a sexually insatiable guy with a touch of the outlaw—an exaggerated version of the demeaning stereotypes young black men have grown up with.

"When you're faced with a stereotype, you can disavow it or you can embrace it and exaggerate it to the nth degree," said Henry Louis Gates, the John Spencer Bassett professor of English at Duke University. "The rappers take the white Western culture's worst fear of black men and make a game out of it."

With the furor over the 2 Live Crew, rap machismo has undergone ever closer scrutiny. The 2 Live Crew has been accused of misogyny and glorifying abuse of women. Yet while their rhymes on *As Nasty as They Wanna Be* are openly, loutishly sexist, treating women entirely as objects, the lyrics are so single-mindedly concerned with self-gratification that the consequences for women don't seem to enter their minds.

Taken literally, the bulk of rap songs (like much heavy-metal rock) reveal adolescent attitudes toward women, who are often presented as either materialistic and cold or easy sexual conquests. But not all rap machismo should be taken entirely at face value. Like other black literary and oral traditions, rap lyrics also involve double entendre, allegory, and parody. Some rap machismo can be a metaphor for pride or political empowerment, it can be a shared joke, as it often is in 2 Live Crew's wildly hyperbolic rhymes. And while machismo has been a convention during rap's first decade, it is now under fire from female rappers like Queen Latifah and Roxanne Shanté.

By bringing the fractured rhythms and unlikely juxtapositions of the television age to the dance floor, rap revolutionized popular music and became the commercial success story of the 1980's. The recent No. 1 album on the Billboard pop charts was *Please Hammer Don't Hurt 'Em* by the Oakland rapper M.C. Hammer.

Over the last decade, while major record companies waited for the supposed fad to run its course, street-level independent labels made fortunes from rap hits. Now all the major companies have signed rap groups, and rap has its own daily show on MTV, where "Yo! MTV Raps" garners some of the cable channel's highest ratings. Rap is out of the ghetto.

While there are a few female rappers, and a handful of white rappers, rap is still an overwhelmingly black male style. Rap emerged when disk jockeys at clubs and parties in the South Bronx began improvising rhymes over the instrumentals of dance records, perhaps inspired by Jamaican disk jockeys or "toasters" who had been doing the same thing. It spread and diversified. Soon there were specialists in rhyming, or M.C.'s, and virtuosic disk jockeys, who created a musical backdrop by intercutting shorter and shorter pieces of more and more records, often "scratching" the records—twitching them backward and forward under the needle—to create percussive sounds.

Early rap mixed party chants with the braggadocio of the blues, jailhouse chants and the dozens, a primarily male game of escalating insults. But soon after the first rap recordings appeared, at the end of the 1970's, some songs took on deeper content. With "The Breaks" by Kurtis Blow in 1980 and "The Message" by Grandmaster Flash and the Furious Five featuring Melle Mel in 1982, rap began to talk about ghetto life, often with humorous or belligerent candor.

In its constantly changing slang and shifting concerns . . . , rap's flood of words presents a fictionalized oral history of a brutalized generation.

—Jon Pareles

Rap evolved fast. Using turntables and drum machines,

rap groups could cut a single in a basement, and rap entre-preneurs could press records quickly and sell them from the trunks of their cars. As the music changed, stars and styles rose and fell within months. In its constantly chang-ing slang and shifting concerns—no other pop has so many antidrug songs—rap's flood of words presents a fic-tionalized oral history of a brutalized generation.

"The difference between public culture and private culture has disappeared," Mr. Gates said. "There was material that was exclusively the province of the black oral tradi-tion and race-record tradition, but now people have decid-ed to cross the line. People like Keenan Ivory Wayans and Spike Lee and Eddie Murphy, along with the rappers, they're saying all the things that we couldn't say even in the 1960's about our own excesses, things we could only whisper in dark rooms. They're saying we're going to ex-plode all these sacred cows. It's fascinating, and it's upset-ting everybody—not just white people but black people. But it's a liberating moment."

Where the old style was mostly bragging—and went with a fashion statement of fat gold chains and other showy possessions—current rap embraces jokers, nice guys, bawdy fantasists, storytellers, romantics, and political ac-tivists. Public Enemy brings black nationalist and Black Muslim ideas of self-determination to rap's most advanced sonic collages, sometimes with divisive effect. Public Enemy was branded anti-Semitic because of statements by a member who has since left the group.

The controversy was revived when Public Enemy's "Wel-come to the Terrordome" alluded to the incident with these cryptic lines: "Crucifixion ain't no fiction / So called chosen frozen / Apology made to whoever pleases / Still they got me like Jesus." Some listeners interpreted the lyr-ics as blaming the Jews for crucifying Christ.

N.W.A and Ice-T chant stylized, calmly observed tales of ghetto violence, including N.W.A's infamous (and widely misread) "— Tha Police," which starts with a scene of po-lice brutality and ends with what a band member has called a "revenge fantasy" about shooting policemen. In an unusual response to an artistic work, the Federal Bu-reau of Investigation wrote a letter to the band's record company complaining that the song advocated violence against police officers.

"I see rap as reflective," Mr. Bourgois said, "and what people should be scared about is the extent to which the songs reflect reality. That there is such unbelievable vio-lence in these communities is a national tragedy. While the fact that people express themselves in terms of violence is a part of American culture, a way of thinking that goes back to the Wild West. I wouldn't worry about rap music leading to violence. On the contrary, rap music leads to a productive expression of alienation and oppression, and it's good that it gets channeled into creative outlets rather than drug addiction or physical violence. I see people, high-school dropouts, who carry around notebooks in their back pockets so they can compare their latest rhymes."

Of all the complaints against rap, the one that seems most unequivocal is about homophobia. Too few rappers can re-sist making some sort of swipe at gays, often taking a de-tour in a song to do so and rarely suggesting any double meaning. It seems an unexamined prejudice.

Rap's remarkable rate of change may make some com-plaints quickly obsolete. In a short time, simple boasts have given way to multileveled storytelling and political comment; when some rappers made a connection between gold chains and the South African gold industry, many rappers' neckwear of choice became leather Africa medal-lions instead of gold "dooky ropes." It's conceivable that a newer generation will not take sexism and homophobia so lightly. Rap will no doubt continue to reveal the ten-sions of the communities it speaks to. But with its humor, intelligence and fast-talking grace, it may also represent a way to transcend those tensions. (pp. 1, 5)

> *Jon Pareles, "Rap: Slick, Violent, Nasty and, Maybe, Hopeful," in* The New York Times, *June 17, 1990, pp. 1, 5.*

Laura Parker   (essay date 20 October 1990)

[*In the following excerpt, Parker presents excerpts from Professor Henry Louis Gates, Jr.'s testimony at the ob-scenity trial of three 2 Live Crew members. Gates, an American educator and critic who has written extensive-ly on African-American culture and fiction, maintains that rap is a form of literature.*]

The witness for the defense, a soft-spoken English profes-sor from Duke University, was on the stand today to clear up a few misconceptions about rap music. Rap, he assert-ed, is indeed a genre of literature.

Even Shakespeare, he noted, used four-letter words "a lot."

The defense lawyer smiled. "Is rap music serious art?" he asked.

"Absolutely," the witness said. "To be able to produce those stanzas is very, very difficult."

"Is there precedence in Western literature for use of these lewd words?" the defense lawyer asked.

"Absolutely," the witness said. "From Geoffrey Chaucer to James Joyce's *Ulysses,* published in 1922. Many of the greatest classics of Western literature contain quote-unquote lewd words."

Professor Henry Louis Gates, of Duke's English depart-ment, was Witness No. 3 in the obscenity trial of three members of the 2 Live Crew. Although the prosecution had not completed its presentation, Gates was allowed to testify early because of a scheduling conflict. He ap-proached his task as any college professor would on the first day of class. Peering through his spectacles, he lec-tured about the relationship among art, literature, black culture and the 2 Live Crew, whose members Luther Campbell, Mark Ross and Christopher Wongwon are charged with staging an obscene performance at a Florida nightclub in June. If convicted, they face up to one year in jail and a $1,000 fine.

"These songs have taken the worst stereotypes of black

men and blown them up," Gates said. "And that is that we are oversexed or hypersexed individuals.

"It evolved in the 16th century when the Europeans were discovering Africa and stealing Africans. They had to find a way to justify their enslavement of other human beings. Most often it was said that the blacks have overly large sexual organs."

From there, it was back to the Crew. "One of the brilliant things about these four songs is they embrace that stereotype," Gates continued. "They name it and they explode it. You can have no reaction but to burst out laughing. The fact that they're being sung by four virile young black men is inescapable to the audience. Everyone understands what's going on. Their response is to burst out laughing. To realize it's a joke. A parody."

Gates hesitated briefly. "That's p-a-r-o-d-y."

For those disinclined to buy the position that the 2 Live Crew's lowbrow lyrics should be compared to highbrow literature, Gates had his Archie Bunker analogy.

It goes like this: Archie Bunker was put on television so people could laugh at an ignorant racist.

"Archie Bunker is a metaphor in the same way the lyrics of these four songs are metaphors. They are not to be taken on their literal level."

Metaphor for what?

"It's like Shakespeare's 'My love is like a red, red rose.' That doesn't mean your love is red and has petals," Gates said. "No, it means your love is beautiful."

The prosecutor, Pedro Dijols, strode to the lectern.

The prosecution has not been having a good go of it. It has been bogged down in its attempt to overwhelm the jury with foul language uttered at Club Futura by the rappers the night of their arrest. (pp. D1, D3)

After Gates was called to testify, the prosecution resumed the agonizing effort of extracting the necessary expletives from Detective Debbie Werder. It was not easy. Werder could not hear the tape without earphones. Provided with them, she translated some words, mostly words the jury could already hear. She looked uncomfortable when she said them and rolled her eyes at the ceiling. So it went for two excruciating hours.

But Werder was a later frustration for the prosecution. First Dijols needed to discredit Gates.

Dijols read a few lines of what none of the reporters have been able to print.

"Point out the great literary value there, sir," he said.

"For a critic, you have to take a work of art as a whole," Gates replied.

The prosecutor read another unprintable phrase, then snapped: "That's great literary classic poetry."

"I never said it was Shakespeare," Gates answered.

"You obviously compared him . . . " Dijols began.

"I did not compare the rhyme scheme to any sonnet of Shakespeare," Gates said. "No, I did not do that." (p. D3)

Laura Parker, "Rap Lyrics Likened to Literature," in The Washington Post, *October 20, 1990, pp. D1, D3.*

David Samuels   (essay date 11 November 1991)

[*In the following essay, Samuels characterizes rap as a manipulation and inversion of racial stereotypes by both blacks and whites. He also examines the marketing strategies record companies use to sell the music to white suburban youths.*]

[In the summer of 1990] Soundscan, a computerized scanning system, changed *Billboard* magazine's method of counting record sales in the United States. Replacing a haphazard system that relied on big-city record stores, Soundscan measured the number of records sold nationally by scanning the bar codes at chain store cash registers. Within weeks the number of computed record sales leapt, as demographics shifted from minority-focused urban centers to white, suburban, middle-class malls. So it was that America awoke on June 22, 1991, to find that its favorite record was not *Out of Time*, by aging college-boy rockers R.E.M., but *Niggaz4life*, a musical celebration of gang rape and other violence by N.W.A., or Niggers With Attitude, a rap group from the Los Angeles ghetto of Compton whose records had never before risen above No. 27 on the Billboard charts.

From *Niggaz4life* to *Boyz N the Hood*, young black men committing acts of violence were available this summer in a wide variety of entertainment formats. Of these none is more popular than rap. And none has received quite the level of critical attention and concern. Writers on the left have long viewed rap as the heartbeat of urban America, its authors, in Arthur Kempton's words, "the pre-eminent young dramaturgists in the clamorous theater of the street." On the right, this assumption has been shared, but greeted with predictable disdain.

Neither side of the debate has been prepared, however, to confront what the entertainment industry's receipts from this summer prove beyond doubt: although rap is still proportionally more popular among blacks, its primary audience is white and lives in the suburbs. And the history of rap's degeneration from insurgent black street music to mainstream pop points to another dispiriting conclusion: the more rappers were packaged as violent black criminals, the bigger their white audiences became.

If the racial makeup of rap's audience has been largely misunderstood, so have the origins of its authors. Since the early 1980s a tightly knit group of mostly young, middle-class, black New Yorkers, in close concert with white record producers, executives, and publicists, has been making rap music for an audience that industry executives concede is primarily composed of white suburban males. Building upon a form pioneered by lower-class black artists in New York between 1975 and 1983, despite an effective boycott of the music by both black and white radio that continues to this day, they created the most influential pop music of the 1980s. Rap's appeal to whites rested in its evocation of an age-old image of blackness: a foreign, sexually charged, and criminal underworld against which the norms of white society are defined, and, by extension, through which they may be defied. It was the truth of this latter proposition that rap would test in its journey into the mainstream.

Since the early 1980s a tightly knit group of mostly young, middle-class, black New Yorkers, in close concert with white record producers, executives, and publicists, has been making rap music for an audience that industry executives concede is primarily composed of white suburban males.

—David Samuels

"Hip-hop," the music behind the lyrics, which are "rapped," is a form of sonic bricolage with roots in "toasting," a style of making music by speaking over records. (For simplicity, I'll use the term "rap" interchangeably with "hip-hop" throughout this article.) Toasting first took hold in Jamaica in the mid-1960s, a response, legend has it, to the limited availability of expensive Western instruments and the concurrent proliferation of cheap R&B instrumental singles on Memphis-based labels such as Stax-Volt. Cool DJ Herc, a Jamaican who settled in the South Bronx, is widely credited with having brought toasting to New York City. Rap spread quickly through New York's poor black neighborhoods in the mid- and late 1970s. Jams were held in local playgrounds, parks, and community centers, in the South and North Bronx, Brooklyn, and Harlem.

Although much is made of rap as a kind of urban streetgeist, early rap had a more basic function: dance music. Bill Stephney, considered by many to be the smartest man in the rap business, recalls the first time he heard hip-hop: "The point wasn't rapping, it was rhythm, DJs cutting records left and right, taking the big drum break from Led Zeppelin's 'When the Levee Breaks,' mixing it together with 'Ring My Bell,' then with a Bob James Mardi Gras jazz record and some James Brown. You'd have 2,000 kids in any community center in New York, moving back and forth, back and forth, like some kind of tribal war dance, you might say. It was the rapper's role to match this intensity rhythmically. No one knew what he was saying. He was just rocking the mike."

Rap quickly spread from New York to Philadelphia, Chicago, Boston, and other cities with substantial black populations. Its popularity was sustained by the ease with which it could be made. The music on early rap records sounded like the black music of the day: funk or, more often, disco. Performers were unsophisticated about image and presentation, tending toward gold lamé jumpsuits and

Jericurls, a second-rate appropriation of the stylings of funk musicians like George Clinton and Bootsy Collins.

The first rap record to make it big was *Rapper's Delight,* released in 1979 by the Sugar Hill Gang, an ad hoc all-star team drawn from three New York groups on Sylvia and Joey Robinson's Sugar Hill label. Thanks to Sylvia Robinson's soul music and background, the first thirty seconds of *Rapper's Delight* were indistinguishable from the disco records of the day: light guitars, high-hat drumming, and hand-claps over a deep funk bass line. What followed will be immediately familiar to anyone who was young in New York City that summer:

> I said, hip-hop, de-hibby, de-hibby-dibby,
> Hip-hip-hop you don't stop.
> Rock it out, Baby Bubba to the boogie de-bang-bang,
> Boogie to the boogie to be.
> Now what you hear is not a test,
> I'm rapping to the beat . . .
> I said, "By the way, baby, what's your name?"
> She said, "I go by the name Lois Lane
> And you can be my boyfriend, you surely can
> Just let me quit my boyfriend, he's called Super-man."
> I said, "he's a fairy, I do suppose
> Flying through the air in pantyhose . . .
> You need a man who's got finesse
> And his whole name across his chest" . . .

Like disco music and jumpsuits, the social commentaries of early rappers like Grandmaster Flash and Mellie Mel were for the most part transparent attempts to sell records to whites by any means necessary. Songs like "White Lines" (with its anti-drug theme) and "The Message" (about ghetto life) had the desired effect, drawing fulsome praise from white rock critics, raised on the protest ballads of Bob Dylan and Phil Ochs. The reaction on the street was somewhat less favorable. "The Message" is a case in point. "People hated that record," recalls Russell Simmons, president of Def Jam Records. "I remember the Junebug, a famous DJ of the time, was playing it up at the Fever, and Ronnie DJ put a pistol to his head and said, 'Take that record off and break it or I'll blow your fucking head off.' The whole club stopped until he broke that record and put it in the garbage."

It was not until 1984 that rap broke through to a mass white audience. The first group to do so was Run-DMC, with the release of its debut album, *Run-DMC,* and with *King of Rock* one year later. These albums blazed the trail that rap would travel into the musical mainstream. Bill Adler, a former rock critic and rap's best-known publicist, explains: "They were the first group that came on stage as if they had just come off the street corner. But unlike the first generation of rappers, they were solidly middle class. Both of Run's parents were college-educated, DMC was a good Catholic schoolkid, a mama's boy. Neither of them was deprived and neither of them ever ran with a gang, but on stage they became the biggest, baddest, streetest guys in the world." When Run-DMC covered the Aerosmith classic "Walk This Way," the resulting video made it onto MTV, and the record went gold.

Rap's new mass audience was in large part the brainchild

of Rick Rubin, a Jewish punk rocker from suburban Long Island who produced the music behind many of rap's biggest acts. Like many New Yorkers his age, Rick grew up listening to Mr. Magic's Rap Attack, a rap radio show on WHBI. In 1983, at the age of 19, Rubin founded Def Jam Records in his NYU dorm room. (Simmons bought part of Def Jam in 1984 and took full control of the company in 1989.) Rubin's next group, the Beastie Boys, was a white punk rock band whose transformation into a rap group pointed rap's way into the future. The Beasties' first album, *Licensed to Ill,* backed by airplay of its anthemic frat-party single "You've Got to Fight for Your Right to Party," became the first rap record to sell a million copies.

The appearance of white groups in a black musical form has historically prefigured the mainstreaming of the form, the growth of the white audience, and the resulting dominance of white performers. With rap, however, this process took an unexpected turn: white demand indeed began to determine the direction of the genre, but what it wanted was music more defiantly black. The result was Public Enemy, produced and marketed by Rubin, the next group significantly to broaden rap's appeal to young whites.

Public Enemy's now familiar mélange of polemic and dance music was formed not on inner-city streets but in the suburban Long Island towns in which the group's members grew up. The children of successful black middle-class professionals, they gave voice to the feeling that, despite progress toward equality, blacks still did not quite belong in white America. They complained of unequal treatment by the police, of never quite overcoming the color of their skin: "We were suburban college kids doing what we were supposed to do, but we were always made to feel like something else," explains Stephney, the group's executive producer.

Public Enemy's abrasive and highly politicized style made it a fast favorite of the white avant-garde, much like the English punk rock band The Clash ten years before. Public Enemy's music, produced by the Shocklee brothers Hank and Keith, was faster, harder, and more abrasive than the rap of the day, music that moved behind the vocals like a full-scale band. But the root of Public Enemy's success was a highly charged theater of race in which white listeners became guilty eavesdroppers on the putative private conversation of the inner city. Chuck D denounced his enemies (the media, some radio stations), proclaimed himself "Public Enemy #1," and praised Louis Farrakhan in stentorian tones, flanked onstage by black-clad security guards from the Nation of Islam, the SIWs, led by Chuck's political mentor, Professor Griff. Flavor Flav, Chuck's homeboy sidekick, parodied street style: oversize sunglasses, baseball cap cocked to one side, a clock the size of a silver plate draped around his neck, going off on wild verbal riffs that often meant nothing at all.

The closer rap moved to the white mainstream, the more it became like rock 'n' roll, a celebration of posturing over rhythm. The back catalogs of artists like James Brown and George Clinton were relentlessly plundered for catchy hooks, then overlaid with dance beats and social commen-

tary. Public Enemy's single "Fight the Power" was the biggest college hit of 1989:

> Elvis was a hero to most
> But he never meant shit to me, you see
> Straight-up racist that sucker was simple and
>   plain
> Motherfuck him and John Wayne
> 'Cause I'm black and I'm proud
> I'm ready and hyped, plus I'm amped
> Most of my heroes don't appear on no stamps
> Sample a look back, you look and find
> Nothing but rednecks for 400 years if you check.

After the release of "Fight the Power," Professor Griff made a series of anti-Semitic remarks in an interview with *The Washington Times.* Griff was subsequently asked to leave the group, for what Chuck D termed errors in judgment. Although these errors were lambasted in editorials across the country, they do not seem to have affected Public Enemy's credibility with its young white fans.

Public Enemy's theatrical black nationalism and sophisticated noise ushered in what is fast coming to be seen as rap's golden age, a heady mix of art, music, and politics. Between 1988 and 1989 a host of innovative acts broke into the mainstream. KRS-One, now a regular on the Ivy League lecture circuit, grew up poor, living on the streets of the South Bronx until he met a New York City social worker, Scott La Rock, later murdered in a driveby shooting. Together they formed BDP, Boogie Down Productions, recording for the Jive lable on RCA. Although songs like "My Philosophy" and "Love's Gonna Get 'Cha (Material Love)" were clever and self-critical, BDP's roots remained firmly planted in the guns-and-posturing of the mainstream rap ghetto.

The ease with which rap can create such aural cartoons, says Hank Shocklee, lies at the very heart of its appeal as entertainment: "Whites have always liked black music," he explains. "That part is hardly new. The difference with rap was that the imagery of black artists, for the first time, reached the level of black music. The sheer number of words in a rap song allows for the creation of full characters impossible in R&B. Rappers become like superheroes. Captain America or the Fantastic Four."

By 1988 the conscious manipulation of racial stereotypes had become rap's leading edge, a trend best exemplified by the rise to stardom of Schoolly D, a Philadelphia rapper on the Jive lable who sold more than half a million records with little mainstream notice. It was not that the media had never heard of Schoolly D: white critics and fans, for the first time, were simply at a loss for words. His voice, fierce and deeply textured, could alone frighten listeners. He used it as a rhythmic device that made no concessions to pop-song form, talking evenly about smoking crack and using women for sex, proclaiming his blackness, accusing other rappers of not being black enough. What Schoolly D meant by blackness was abundantly clear. Schoolly D was a misogynist and a thug. If listening to Public Enemy was like eavesdropping on a conversation, Schoolly D was like getting mugged. This, aficionados agreed, was what they had been waiting for: a rapper from whom you would

Public Enemy.

flee in abject terror if you saw him walking toward you late at night.

It remained for N.W.A., a more conventional group of rappers from Los Angeles, to adapt Schoolly D's stylistic advance for the mass white market with its first album-length release, *Straight Out of Compton,* in 1989. The much-quoted rap from that album, "Fuck the Police," was the target of an FBI warning to police departments across the country, and a constant presence at certain college parties, white and black:

> "Fuck the Police" coming straight out the underground
> A young nigger got it bad 'cause I'm brown
> And not the other color. Some police think
> They have the authority to kill the minority . . .
> A young nigger on the warpath
> And when I'm finished, it's gonna be a bloodbath
> Of cops, dying in L. A.
> Yo, Dre I've got something to say: Fuck the Police.

Other songs spoke of trading oral sex for crack and shooting strangers for fun. After the release of *Straight Out of Compton,* N.W.A.'s lead rapper and chief lyricist, Ice

Cube, left the group. Billing himself as "the nigger you love to hate," Ice Cube released a solo album, *Amerikkka's Most Wanted,* which gleefully pushed the limits of rap's ability to give offense. One verse ran:

> I'm thinking to myself, "why did I bang her?"
> Now I'm in the closet, looking for the hanger.

But what made *Amerikkka's Most Wanted* so shocking to so many record buyers was the title track's violation of rap's most iron-clad taboo—black on white violence:

> Word, yo, but who the fuck is heard:
> It's time you take a trip to the suburbs.
> Let 'em see a nigger invasion
> Point blank, on a Caucasian.
> Cock the hammer and crack a smile:
> "Take me to your house, pal . . ."

Ice Cube took his act to the big screen this summer in *Boyz N the Hood,* drawing rave reviews for his portrayal of a young black drug dealer whose life of crime leads him to an untimely end. The crime-doesn't-pay message, an inheritance from the grade-B gangster film, is the stock-in-trade of another L. A. rapper-turned-actor, Ice-T of *New Jack City* fame, a favorite of socially conscious rock critics. Tacking unhappy endings onto glorifications of drug dealing and gang warfare, Ice-T offers all the thrills of the form while alleviating any guilt listeners may have felt about consuming drive-by shootings along with their popcorn.

It was in this spirit that "Yo! MTV Raps" debuted in 1989 as the first national broadcast forum for rap music. The videos were often poorly produced, but the music and visual presence of stars like KRS-One, LL Cool J, and Chuck D proved enormously compelling, rocketing "Yo!" to the top of the MTV ratings. On weekends bands were interviewed and videos introduced by Fab Five Freddie; hip young white professionals watched his shows to keep up with urban black slang and fashion. Younger viewers rushed home from school on weekdays to catch ex-Beastie Boys DJ Dr. Dre, a sweatsuit-clad mountain of a man, well over 300 pounds, and Ed Lover, who evolved a unique brand of homeboy Laurel and Hardy mixed with occasional social comment.

With "Yo! MTV Raps," rap became for the first time the music of choice in the white suburbs of middle America. From the beginning, says Doug Herzog, MTV's vice president for programming, the show's audience was primarily white, male, suburban, and between the ages of 16 and 24, a demographic profile that "Yo!" 's success helped set in stone. For its daytime audience, MTV spawned an ethnic rainbow of well-scrubbed pop rappers from MC Hammer to Vanilla Ice to Gerardo, a Hispanic actor turned rap star. For "Yo" itself rap became more overtly politicized as it expanded its audience. Sound bites from the speeches of Malcolm X and Martin Luther King became de rigueur introductions to formulaic assaults on white America mixed with hymns to gang violence and crude sexual caricature.

Holding such polyglot records together is what *Village Voice* critic Nelson George has labeled "ghettocentrism," a style-driven cult of blackness defined by crude stereotypes. P.R. releases, like a recent one for Los Angeles rapper DJ Quik, take special care to mention artists' police records, often enhanced to provide extra street credibility. When Def Jam star Slick Rick was arrested for attempted homicide, Def Jam incorporated the arrest into its publicity campaign for Rick's new album, bartering exclusive rights to the story to *Vanity Fair* in exchange for the promise of a lengthy profile. Muslim groups such as Brand Nubian proclaim their hatred for white devils, especially those who plot to poison black babies. That Brand Nubian believes the things said on its records is unlikely: the group seems to get along quite well with its white Jewish publicist, Beth Jacobson of Electra Records. Anti-white, and, in this case, anti-Semitic, rhymes are a shorthand way of defining one's opposition to the mainstream. Racism is reduced to fashion, by the rappers who use it and by the white audiences to whom such images appeal. What's significant here are not so much the intentions of artist and audience as a dynamic in which anti-Semitic slurs and black criminality correspond to "authenticity," and "authenticity" sells records.

The selling of this kind of authenticity to a young white audience is the stock-in-trade of *The Source,* a full-color monthly magazine devoted exclusively to rap music,

founded by Jon Shecter while still an undergraduate at Harvard. Shecter is what is known in the rap business as a Young Black Teenager. He wears a Brooklyn Dodgers baseball cap, like Spike Lee, and a Source T-shirt. As editor of *The Source,* Shecter has become a necessary quote for stories about rap in *Time* and other national magazines.

An upper-middle-class white, Shecter has come in for his share of criticism, the most recent of which appeared as a diatribe by the sometime critic and tinpot racist Harry Allen in a black community newspaper, *The City Sun,* which pointed out that Shecter is Jewish. "There's no place for me to say anything," Shecter responds. "Given what I'm doing, my viewpoint has to be that whatever comes of the black community, the hip-hop community which is the black community, is the right thing. I know my place. The only way in which criticism can be raised is on a personal level, because the way that things are set up, with the white-controlled media, prevents sincere back-and-forth discussion from taking place." The latest venture in hip-hop marketing, a magazine planned by Time Warner, will also be edited by a young white, Jonathan van Meter, a former *Condé Nast* editor.

In part because of young whites like Shecter and van Meter, rap's influence on the street continues to decline. "You put out a record by Big Daddy Kane," Rubin says, "and then put out the same record by a pop performer like Janet Jackson. Not only will the Janet Jackson record sell ten times more copies, it will also be the cool record to play in clubs." Stephney agrees: "Kids in my neighborhood pump dance hall reggae on their systems all night long, because that's where the rhythm is. . . . People complain about how white kids stole black culture. The truth of the matter is that no one can steal a culture." Whatever its continuing significance in the realm of racial politics, rap's hour as innovative popular music has come and gone. Rap forfeited whatever claim it may have had to particularity by acquiring a mainstream white audience whose tastes increasingly determined the nature of the form. What whites wanted was not music, but black music, which as a result stopped really being either.

White fascination with rap sprang from a particular kind of cultural tourism pioneered by the Jazz Age novelist Carl Van Vechten. Van Vechten's 1926 best seller *Nigger Heaven* imagined a masculine, criminal, yet friendly black ghetto world that functioned, for Van Vechten and for his readers, as a refuge from white middle-class boredom. In *Really the Blues,* the white jazzman Mezz Mezzrow went one step further, claiming that his own life among black people in Harlem had physically transformed him into a member of the Negro race, whose unique sensibility he had now come to share. By inverting the moral values attached to contemporary racial stereotypes, Van Vechten and Mezzrow at once appealed to and sought to undermine the prevailing racial order. Both men, it should be stressed, conducted their tours in person.

The moral inversion of racist stereotypes as entertainment has lost whatever transformative power it may arguably have had fifty years ago. MC Serch of 3rd Bass, a white rap traditionalist, with short-cropped hair and thick-rimmed

Buddy Holly glasses, formed his style in the uptown hip-hop clubs like the L.Q. in the early 1980s. "Ten or eleven years ago," he remarks, "when I was wearing my perma-nent-press Lee's with a beige campus shirt and matching Adidas sneakers, kids I went to school with were calling me a 'wigger,' 'black wanna-be,' all kinds of racist names. Now those same kids are driving jeeps with MCM leather interiors and pumping Public Enemy."

The ways in which rap has been consumed and popular-ized speak not of cross-cultural understanding, musical or otherwise, but of a voyeurism and tolerance of racism in which black and white are both complicit. "Both the rap-pers and their white fans affect and commodify their own visions of street culture," argues Henry Louis Gates Jr. of Harvard University, "like buying Navajo blankets at a res-ervation road-stop. A lot of what you see in rap is the guilt of the black middle class about its economic success, its inability to put forth a culture of its own. Instead they do the worst possible thing, falling back on fantasies of street life. In turn, white college students with impeccable gen-der credentials buy nasty sex lyrics under the cover of get-ting at some kind of authentic black experience."

Gates goes on to make the more worrying point: "What is potentially very dangerous about this is the feeling that by buying records they have made some kind of valid so-cial commitment." Where the assimilation of black street culture by whites once required a degree of human contact between the races, the street is now available at the flick of a cable channel—to black and white middle class alike. "People want to consume and they want to consume easy," Hank Shocklee says. "If you're a suburban white kid and you want to find out what life is like for a black city teenager, you buy a record by N.W.A. It's like going to an amusement park and getting on a roller coaster ride—records are safe, they're controlled fear, and you al-ways have the choice of turning it off. That's why nobody ever takes a train up to 125th Street and gets out and starts walking around. Because then you're not in control any-more: it's a whole other ball game." This kind of consump-tion—of racist stereotypes, of brutality toward women, or even of uplifting tributes to Dr. Martin Luther King—is of a particularly corrupting kind. The values it instills find their ultimate expression in the ease with which we watch young black men killing each other: in movies, on records, and on the streets of cities and towns across the country. (pp. 24-6, 28-9)

> *David Samuels, "The Rap on Rap," in* The New Republic, *Vol. 205, No. 20, November 11, 1991, pp. 24-6, 28-9.*

David Toop   (essay date 24 November 1991)

[*In the following excerpt, Toop comments on the music of N.W.A. and speculates on the reasons for its populari-ty among white, suburban youths.*]

Not since the shock-horror scandal of video nasties has popular culture caused such offence and outrage. But does rap music deserve a similar reaction? Rage, wit, despair, mysticism, militancy, integrationism, wisdom, idiocy, in-sight and numb (even dumb) brutality: all of these can be found in rap lyrics. If this broad spectrum simply confirms the fact that black inner city life is not all shootings and drug wars, the media spotlight is still magnetically attract-ed to rap's sleazy side.

The most notorious representatives of calculated sleaze are NWA, a group from the Los Angeles suburb of Comp-ton. Sharp entrepreneurs, adroit media manipulators and inventive and professional music producers, they have cornered the market in offensiveness with an album enti-tled *Efil4Zaggin*. Reverse the title and it becomes Niggaz For Life. This encryption, along with the abbreviation of the group's full name—Niggers With Attitude—suggests that NWA have a shrewd grasp of the value of packaging, but an inconsistent grasp of public relations: they are cur-rently in the news for the alleged assault on Dee Barnes, a television presenter, by NWA member Dr Dre.

As films and books like *Terminator 2* and Bret Easton Ellis's *American Psycho* have demonstrated, slick pack-ages of brutality exert an allure for current mass market tastes. NWA also proved the appeal of the formula in June this year when *Efil4Zaggin* shot to the top of *Billboard* magazine's US album charts within two weeks of release. In Britain, similar possibilities were curtailed by an unusu-al police action which involved a June raid on the Poly-gram Records distribution plant, seizure of all copies of *Efil4Zaggin* and a complete ban on all air-play. (Ironical-ly, this is 20 years from the June 1971 obscenity trial of the Schoolkids issue of *Oz* magazine.) NWA, the obscene publications squad decided, were prime candidates for joining *Lady Chatterley's Lover* and *Oz* as potential de-pravers and corruptors of the nation. The album, freely available in the US and across Europe, was banned under section 3 of the 1959 Obscene Publications Act. Five months later, on November 7, after a lame case by the prosecuting counsel, the confiscated copies of the album were released: a clear victory for NWA and freedom of speech.

Behind its title, *Efil4Zaggin* threw up a confused mess of sexual violence, self-consciously rationalised misogyny and crime fiction style portrayals of shootings. Squeezed between the obscenities and blasting shotguns was a dash of moralising, a gleeful spirit of amorality, a thread of high seriousness. NWA's theme is interesting and valid. Black-ness is instantly identifiable and inescapable, they say. Thus, everybody who has black skin, no matter what their income, environment or beliefs, is subject to lifelong stereotyping. If you are young, male and live in Compton, or the bleaker, highrise projects of Detroit, Chicago and New York, then the stereotyping will blanket you in a web of peer pressure, lurid media images and police harass-ment. The effect is akin to a wall, erected at the boundaries of mainstream society. "They fear me but never wanna hear me," NWA's Eazy-E raps on *Real Niggaz Don't Die.*

A recent book about Los Angeles gangs, *Do Or Die* by Leon Bing, makes a similar point. Despite the relentless analysis and glamorisation of Los Angeles street gangs, few outsiders have taken the trouble to listen to the voices of the gang members themselves. Paradoxically, the same rigid racial divisions that have led many American inner cities to the brink of ruin, have also performed a conjuring trick on the grinding hopelessness of black residential areas like Compton. Out in the upscale suburbs, safe from harm, white teenagers compare the stability and good fortune of their daily lives to the gun battles and dramatic arrests, the crack dealer paraphernalia of automatic weapons, fast cars and beepers, that they see on their television sets. Black life, they surmise, is exotically packed with knife-edge drama. The intoxicating lure of this instability has led many of them to rap and, in particular, to NWA. According to Timothy White, editor of *Billboard* magazine: "Our demographics show that the record [*Efil4Zaggin*] has been bought almost entirely by middle-class white boys in their early teens." According to Jon Shecter, editor of the US hip hop magazine *The Source,* "Among a peer group of white males, it's a cool status symbol to like NWA."

This is perhaps the first real breakdown of racially demarcated music consumption in America since disc jockey Alan Freed began playing black rhythm and blues to a 70 per cent white audience on his radio shows in the mid-Fifties. In the era of racial segregation, the worst act a young white American could perpetrate on their parents was to buy records made by black people, stemming from black experience, disseminating black culture. Now that one of America's biggest concerns is inner city strife, the same syndrome holds true once more.

Rap is far more dangerous than rock 'n' roll ever was. It's a form of music, vernacular poetry, attitude and style which grew out of the project housing slums of New York City, decaying urban districts predominantly occupied by black and Hispanic families. Despite rap's growth into a global medium—perhaps the most vital and creative in current popular music—it has always reflected the conflicting moods, strategies and experiences of young African-Americans. The music is a means to an end and, for these young people, it is only the beginning . . . (pp. 68-9, 71)

> *David Toop, "America's Most Wanted," in The Sunday Times, London, November 24, 1991, pp. 68-9, 71.*

John Leland   (essay date 29 June 1992)

> [*In the following excerpt, Leland maintains that racial distinctiveness has replaced racial ambiguity as a theme in popular music and that the surge in rap's popularity epitomizes this change.*]

With Bill Clinton attacking Sister Souljah, and Dan Quayle joining the police of America in condemning Ice-T, pop music careened into national politics last week. And it did so as a stand-in for an inconvenient topic that had been looming over the campaign all along: race. If the politicians weren't ready to get dirty on the subject, the music sure was. While plain talk about race and our real racial divisions has been absent from the campaign, it has become the rhetorical center of pop music. After nearly three decades of reflecting the promises of integration, pop music—from country to hard-core rap—has become our most pointed metaphor for volatile racial polarization.

Whether the candidates get it or not, we've moved past the warm and fuzzy age of "We Are the World."

Clinton tagged the previously little-known Sister Souljah (Lisa Williamson) at the Rev. Jesse Jackson's Rainbow Coalition Leadership Summit. Chiding the coalition for inviting her to speak, Clinton said, "She told *The Washington Post* . . . 'If black people kill black people every day, why not take a week and kill white people?' . . . If you took the words 'white' and 'black' and reversed them, you might think David Duke was giving that speech." Angry black leaders attacked him for, in Jackson's words, exploiting her "purely to appeal to conservative whites." Clinton defended his remarks: "I called for an end to division, which I've been calling for since I first began this race." Sister Souljah last week explained that her inflammatory nonsense hadn't been a call to violence: "I was just telling the writer that . . . if a person would kill their own brother, or a baby in a drive-by, or a grandmother, what would make white people think that [he] wouldn't kill them too?" But her reasoning didn't much matter. She and Clinton, the sax player in shades, were singing different songs. While pols cling to nice talk about a harmonious society that's just a social program away, musicians and fans, black and white, are declaring the massive schism between the races—consuming the rift as entertainment, a world view and a beat you can dance to.

[June 1992 was] a rough month for rap. Police organizations around the country called for a boycott of Time Warner over a song called "Cop Killer," by the Warner Records rapper Ice-T and his heavy-metal band, Body Count. The song includes the lyrics "I'm 'bout to bust some shots off / I'm 'bout to dust some cops off " and a chant, "Die, Die, Die Pig, Die!" On June 5 a Macomb County, Mich., prosecutor warned local record stores about selling albums by Houston rappers the Geto Boys, which "satisfy the [criminal] obscenity definition." Bill Adler, a rap publicist and longtime defender of the music, last week published an 83-page booklet denouncing anti-Semitism in the rap community. He singled out Ice Cube for touting the Nation of Islam's inflammatory text "The Secret Relationship Between Blacks and Jews," which blames the slave trade on Jews. And a commentary in *Billboard,* written by punky white folk singer Michelle Shocked and her fiancé, writer Bart Bull, dismissed hard-edged rap as a new species of blackface minstrelsy: "The chicken-thieving, razor-toting 'coon' of the 1890s is the drug-dealing, Uzi-toting 'nigga' of today . . . [The mostly white] audience will eventually feel justified in all manner of acts of racism, predicated on Zip Coon stereotypes sold with the enthusiastic support of the entertainment industry."

For anyone with a sense of recent history, all this hand-wringing ought to look familiar. The volatility of rap, both in its creative brio and its ability to alienate, feels like rock and roll all over again. Popular music is now reflecting deep changes in American society better than any other form of public discussion—just as it did 30 years ago. When Los Angeles boiled over in response to the Rodney King verdict in April, the last people surprised were the fans of rap music, black and white.

F--- the police, coming straight from the under-
ground
A young nigger got it bad 'cause I'm brown
And not the other color. Some police think
They have the authority to kill the
minority . . .

These words, from the notorious "— tha Police," by the
equally notorious Compton, Calif., rap crew N.W.A (it
stands for Niggers With Attitude), are already almost four
years old, from an album that sold close to 2 million copies. As Ice-T, whose music covers similar turf, says, "People ask me, 'What about the riot?' Well, refer to album
three, track one. Or, 'What about the cops?' Refer to
album four, track 15 . . . I've already explained it."

If the heart of the culture in the '60s was a fascination with
youth, the heart now is a fascination with race. Race has
replaced the generation gap as the determining force not
just in what music says and sounds like but in how it is
promoted, and what it means to different listeners. Just a
decade ago, when Michael Jackson began veering toward
racial ambiguity with the aid of plastic surgery, he became
the most popular singer the world had ever known. This
year, when he argued on his latest album, "It don't matter
if you're black or white," he became a national joke. A
new orthodoxy has set in, racially charged and financially
very profitable. The key strands of pop-music culture—
questions of identity, community, authenticity, language,
fashion—all now filter through notions of race.

Rappers are the musicians leading the change. "It took
white groups to take rock and roll to the max," says com-
poser-producer Quincy Jones, 59. In the early days of
rock, Jones wrote arrangements for songs that were recorded by black singers for the black or "race" market,
then by white singers—"diluted a little bit"—for the white
market. "This time the creators are staying in control of
their culture for the first time," says Jones. "Young black
males are speaking the truth at the most dramatic and theatrical level. It's a swagger that from young black males
has always threatened America." But rap acts and entrepreneurs are finding that it doesn't just threaten. It attracts.

"We're marketing black culture to white people," says
André Brown, a. k. a. Doctor Dré. Brown, 28, is the jocu-
lar cohost of the daily video program "Yo! MTV Raps,"
one of the most popular programs on the cable music
channel. For a half hour each weeknight and one hour on
Saturdays, MTV's largely white viewership can tune in to
what Saturday host Fab 5 Freddy has called "the cutting
edge of black culture." In rap, MTV has found a music
equal to its visual jump-cutting rhythms; and in MTV,
rap—which has long been shunned by black radio—has
finally found a home.

Because of its emphasis on visual style, MTV has intensified pop music's fascination with race. When the channel
first went on the air, 11 years ago, it was almost closed to
black performers. Of the first 750 clips shown, fewer than
two dozen were by black acts. The black jazz musician
Herbie Hancock, who scored a pop hit in 1983 with the
song "Rockit," kept his face out of his own video in order
to get airplay. When Michael Jackson's album "Thriller"

and single "Billie Jean" topped the charts in 1983, MTV
still rejected his video. It was only after Jackson's next single, "Beat It," went No. 1 that the network relented.

Once MTV became integrated, the medium's promise was
clear: pop stars were free to invent themselves. Identity
was not bound by sexuality or ethnicity. The new stars created by the network—Boy George, Prince, George Michael, Madonna and the light-skinned, post-op Michael
Jackson—all made a virtue of ambiguity. They weren't authentic; they were brilliantly made up. While Jackson
lightened his skin and George Michael learned to rap,
Prince, in the loosely autobiographical 1984 film "Purple
Rain," made his roots ambiguous, inventing for himself a
white mother. The next year, 45 of America's biggest pop
stars, black and white, joined in the triumphant anthem
"We Are the World" to benefit Ethiopian-famine relief.
"We Are the World," which was the best-selling single of
all time, was a massive symbolic victory over racial difference: our identities lay not in our genes but in our big, loving arms.

Rap hit this celebration of racial melding broadside. Typically, when any genre music wants to "cross over" to a
broader audience, it becomes softened in the process. Motown creator Berry Gordy, for example, set up a charm
school for his acts, to make them more palatable to white
America. Rap was different. "Forget about watering
down," says Bill Stephney, a rap entrepreneur and co-
founder of the group Public Enemy. "I think there's dehy-
dration. Not only are we not going to add water, we're
going to take water out. In many respects, that was done
on purpose . . . to curry favor with a white audience by
showing rebellion." The plan worked. The harder the
music got, the more white audiences bought in.

Public Enemy, a mostly middle-class rap group from suburban Long Island, N.Y., carried this strategy the farthest. In its imagery, sound and lyrics, the band was pure
confrontation. Tapping the potential of video, Public
Enemy created and marketed an entire band around the
concept of racial warriors. The group's logo showed a
black youth in the cross hairs of a rifle sight; each song
dramatized racial conflict.

Embraced from the start by white audiences as well as
black, Public Enemy replaced the racial indeterminacy of
Michael Jackson and Prince with hard-core determinism—the "blacker" the better. The group's 1987 single,
"Bring the Noise," began with a recording of Malcolm X's
voice saying, "Too black, too strong." This snippet—half
self-promotion, half challenge—defined the new direction
of rap boasting. "Blackness," suddenly, was what distinguished the real from the fake, the significant from the in-
consequential.

This "realness," or authenticity, was a conceit, like any
other on MTV. From Bruce Springsteen's faded blue jeans
to Public Enemy's pose of "pure blackness," pop's gifts—
even at their most heartfelt and moving—are images and
stances, not flesh and blood. But, like the past conceit of
racial ambiguity, this racial purism was a conceit that
caught on. Says Stephney, production supervisor on
"Bring the Noise," "From this [song], an orthodoxy de-

veloped of certain politics you can have, a certain look, a certain way that you refer to women, to whites, to homosexuals, a certain way that you comport yourself"—all based on macho aggression. "There's definitely a religion that has developed out of this."

The religion is racial authenticity. You gotta have it. The white rapper Vanilla Ice, whose 1990 "Ice Ice Baby" made him the first rap act ever to top the pop singles charts, felt compelled to invent fraudulent "black" roots for himself, such as having grown up in a black neighborhood and having attended a black high school, to seem closely connected to "authentic" black experience. It didn't matter if a rapper's roots were real or not: N.W.A, from the ghetto of Compton, sells the same pop conceit of authenticity. Peppering their raps with tales of gang brutality and misogyny, N.W.A members pitch themselves—to a largely white audience—as "Real Niggaz." Anything less brutal, the thinking goes, is racially adulterated, and therefore inauthentic. The conceit has worked. N.W.A's *NIG-GAZ4LIFE* became the top album in the country within two weeks of its release last summer, eventually selling nearly 2 million copies.

The adorable Atlanta rap duo Kris Kross, currently the No. 2 act in the country, best illustrates how the conceit of authenticity shapes pop identities. Both just 13 years old, the rappers get more identity from rap than they give to it. As schoolboys they are Chris Kelly and Chris Smith. As rappers, they are Mack Daddy and Daddy Mack. A mack daddy, from the French *maquereau,* is a pimp. As ludicrous poses of authenticity go, this is topped only by that of Seattle rapper Sir Mix-A-Lot, whose salacious top-10 pop single "Baby Got Back" argues for black supremacy on the basis of rear-end size. (pp. 47-9)

Like any story of race in America, rap's trip to the white mainstream comes with contradictions and anxieties. As Ice-T puts it, "People always ask me, 'How do you feel about dancing for the white people? You dance for them and they cheer. And then they walk out of here and they just talk about niggers' . . . At this point, man, I can't really care. Thirty years ago we were still in the back of the bus, so what makes me think it's going to end in my lifetime?" There is nothing new about white people embracing African-American styles. Since the blackface minstrel shows of the 19th century, race has been the great conundrum at the core of American music. It is both our music's original sin and its creative juice, an ever-changing formula of fascination and fear.

What is new is the conceit—sometimes borne out, sometimes pure marketing—that rap isn't just entertainment, it's reportage. Chuck D has called rap Black America's CNN, the documentary news service the inner cities have never had. The curiosity rap sparks outside the inner cities, he believes, is not just natural but part of the music's huge appeal. "You tell me how a white kid in Indiana is going to pick up a slice of black life if not from a video or a rap record," he asks. "Not from the school system. Not on the news. Not in his household. And he's not going to go into the neighborhood himself to get a face-to-face confrontation with some s–t that could be termed dangerous."

For more than 30 years, one of the promises of pop music has been to bring white and black *people* together, at least on the dance floor. Rap cuts into this equation, offering interaction with music and videos in place of interaction with actual people. Ed Eckstine, president of Mercury Records and son of the great jazz singer Billy Eckstine, calls this simply "minstrelism of a different order. You can hear [ghetto violence], see it, feel it, blast it in your car. But when it comes to doing something about it, [white fans] don't want to come near it."

During periods of integration, when the focus of racial insecurities was miscegenation—sex—the common ground shared by white and black listeners was rock and roll, a euphemism for the sex act. Now, as we pull apart, and our insecurities focus more and more on violence, the shared ground is the often violent frontier of rap. The music that once drew people together now mediates between them, providing a metaphor for the separation. This explains the white fetish for the most extreme rap: it's the most extreme measure of the division between the races. It also explains the overreactions to rap and its lyrics: when art stands in for life, it's easy to confuse the two.

> **One of the contradictions most often overlooked in rap is that it is a radical voice with an often conservative agenda.**
>
> *—John Leland*

Rap taps racial insecurities, soothing them with the promise that one can experience "real" black life vicariously through records—but it stokes the insecurities, too. Look at the titles: Public Enemy's *Fear of a Black Planet,* Ice Cube's *The Nigga You Love to Hate.* Both were enormously popular with white audiences. Rap is locating white insecurity about race—and black insecurity about class—and selling it back as entertainment. As a tidy projection of the messy fears people live under, rap gives its white audience a chance to explore—or ignore—them.

For black audiences, even violent rap can send a different set of messages. One of the contradictions most often overlooked in rap is that it is a radical voice with an often conservative agenda. Public Enemy's last album is largely a rant against black vice. Ice Cube's *Death Certificate* builds, through a series of images of white devils and black gangbangers, to the self-critical song "Us": "And all you dope dealers / You're as bad as the police 'cause you kill us . . . Sometimes I believe the hype, man / We mess it up ourselves and blame the white man." This has always been a secret undercurrent of rap: beneath the sometimes harsh imagery, it embraces very old-fashioned social norms (even, in its take on gender roles and homosexuality, primitive norms). "[Rap] represents the self-determining practices some of these black conservatives always talk about," says Stephney. "Here were people who couldn't get their music on the radio, so they said,

'Screw it, we'll create our own mini radio stations in parks, our own lingo, our own code of behavior and dress.' The schools had all dropped their music programs, so they invented a music played on turntables. Isn't that the self-sufficiency that Thomas Sowell and Clarence Thomas and Bush prescribe?"

As Cornel West, director of Princeton's Afro-American Studies program, notes, "Rap is an attempt to socialize black children by young black artists. When KRS-One talks about 'edutainment,' and Public Enemy speak of themselves as a cable channel for the black community, they are saying that we will socialize, acculturize ourselves, given the breakdown in the black family, community and nurturing system . . . It sounds bad, but look at the job the mamas and the daddies have done." For more than four years before the Los Angeles riots, rap had anticipated the rage that ultimately boiled over on April 29. And it had done so in the most graphic images of gang-bangers, dead police and civil war. But all along, the music also held to other values: nurturing, education, self-sufficiency. These are some of the forces that must come together to rebuild Los Angeles and the country. However modestly, rap has hinted at a way to that regeneration, too. (pp. 51-2)

John Leland, "Rap and Race," in Newsweek, *Vol. CXIX, No. 26, June 29, 1992, pp. 46-52.*

James Bowman   (essay date 20 July 1992)

[*In the following essay, Bowman argues that the imagery and themes in the songs of such rappers as Ice-T and Sister Souljah bear little relation to reality and that rap is therefore harmful to society.*]

> I meant what I said
> And I said what I meant:
> An elephant's faithful
> One hundred per cent!
> —From *Horton Hatches the Egg*
>   by Dr. Seuss

Although he is not exactly renowned for his faithfulness, Bill Clinton may be said to resemble the elephant in more than just its appetite as he eats his way through the grueling (more like porridging, actually) presidential campaign. At least his attack on the rap chanteuse, Sister Souljah, was a welcome attempt to penetrate the rhetorical fog in which Jesse Jackson lurks by calling his protégée to account for her words.

This is apparently not something one is supposed to do to a rapper. With the weary contempt of the sophisticate for the literal-minded, both Sister Souljah and another rap artiste, Mr. Ice T, have denied that their advocacy of killing white people meant what it said. "The song is fiction, not fact," says Ice T about "Cop Killer," which goes "Die, die, die, pig, die! / F--- the police!" and depicts the poet preparing to kill a policeman. "At no point do I go out and say, 'Let's do it.' I'm singing in the first person as a character who is fed up with police brutality. I ain't never killed no cop. I felt like it a lot of times. But I never did it."

Likewise, Sister Souljah denies that she meant what she

said in an interview with the *Washington Post* about the Los Angeles riots: "If black people kill black people every day, why not have a week and kill white people?" Like Ice T she claims that this was dramatic license, designed only to represent the "mindset" of a typical rioter. "I was in no way advocating that people go out and kill anybody, whether white or black."

It is easy to dismiss such excuses as disingenuous. On her rap tape, called *360 Degrees of Power* and issued earlier this year by Sony Music Entertainment, Sister Souljah claims that black people are "in a state of war" with whites, that George Bush is a terrorist, and that "America's no damn good." No doubt she would say that it is only in the same spirit of dramatic empathy that she seems to advocate the killing of a black CIA agent and a policeman and imagines an official announcement by a white American President in 1995 that black slavery is to be re-introduced, but her persistent claims that "White people and the American government / Want to destroy Black African people wherever they are in the world" are pretty explicit to the naïve listener.

Yet to say that may be in a way as much beside the point as to insist that statements like "We are at war" or "Slavery's back in effect" are meant to be all in good fun. It is always hard to tell when a liar is telling the truth, but I am inclined to believe Ice T and Sister Souljah when they say they don't really mean it.

That is not to say that I accept the loathsome assurances of the spokesmen for Time Warner who are trying to fend off a spreading police boycott of "Cop Killer," which that corporation produced. In an attempt to claim the noblest of motives for selling thousands of copies of this hateful recording, Gerald Levin, the president of the company, wrote in the *Wall Street Journal* of his "willingness not just to tolerate creative freedom but to encourage it, even when the viewpoints expressed run counter to the norms of our mainstream culture." Murder is to him evidently just an alternative "viewpoint" or "norm" to that of the "mainstream." Thus he rejects calls to withdraw the album: "Given the natural instinct of corporations to avoid controversy, that's undoubtedly the easiest course. But to follow it would be to dishonor the truth."

Gag! Who invited truth and honor in here? Next to such hypocrisy the rappers themselves are models of almost elephantine integrity. Yet there does seem to be independent evidence that Levin and others with a pecuniary interest in believing so may be right to say that even such explicit words as those of "Cop Killer" are not intended "to advocate an assault by black street kids on the police"—that, in short, rap does not mean what it says to those for whom it is intended.

In a vox-pop piece in the *Washington Post,* for example, more than one of the black interviewees piped up, apparently unprompted, that "Souljah used exaggeration to make a point" and that she was not to be taken literally. When she says, "I'll shoot that motherf----," does she really mean that she only intends to beat him up? Perhaps it is true after all that, in the words of Mr. Antwan Parker,

18, of Southeast Washington, "You got to be black to understand it."

That is itself an exaggeration, but the truth of it is that what we are dealing with here is a peculiarly black version of the rhetoric of oppression. It is not that Sister Souljah or Ice T or even the Los Angeles ghetto dwellers for whom both of them have at various times purported to speak are actually oppressed; rather, they have inherited from their ancestors, who were, a form of speech and imagery characterized by a kind of fantastical moral chiaroscuro. So far from being a discussion of what Mr. Levin comically calls "the reality of the streets," it depends precisely upon its unreality—an unreality that takes the form of Mittyesque fantasies. Think of the ones you sometimes see in movies where a poor worm of a man imagines himself throttling some authority figure who is harassing him. It wouldn't be entertaining if there were any chance of his really doing it.

And entertaining, primarily, it is meant to be. The artistic effect of such poetry is comic, in the broadest sense. And sometimes in a more narrow sense too. Comic as in funny. Take, for example, another selection from Ice T's *Body Count,* the album which contains "Cop Killer." It is called "Momma's Gotta Die Tonight."

> She taught me things that simply were not true.
> She taught me hate for race—
> That's why I hate you!
> There's only one way I can make it right:
> Momma's gotta die tonight.

So he gets some lighter fluid from the corner store, douses her bed in it, and sets her on fire. When she gets up, he clubs her with the Louisville Slugger she got him for his 12th birthday, then cuts her up in little pieces with a handy carving knife ("that we only use on special occasions like bulls--- Thanksgiving"), puts her into some "little green Hefty bags," and distributes her parts all over the country:

> Yo, you wanna go to Connecticut, bitch?
> Ohio, Detroit, Texas, L. A.?
> Who's laughin' now, momma?
> Who's laughin' now, bitch?

We are, clearly. What is interesting here is not only that the authority figure who becomes the object of Ice T's violent fantasies can just as easily be his own mother as a policeman, but also that she deserves to die for having taught him racial hatred:

> So if you got a mother or a grandmother or a father
> Who wants to carry on the same racist bulls---
> that's
> F--- this world up from day one

you can go and do likewise. Poetically speaking, of course.

Ugly as this imagery is, it occurs in a highly moral context. It is like Richard Wright's *Native Son* chanted by an evangelical black preacher. Sister Souljah, too, is at times a moralist of a surprisingly old-fashioned kind:

> If you're going with a brother
> And all you have is his beeper number,

That's not your man.
If you never met his momma,
That's not your man.
If you never been to his house
That's not your man.
And like my great-grandmother used to say:
Who buys the goddam cow when you can get all
    the milk for free?

Imagine what the feminists would say about that traditional image! But Sister Souljah is as scathing about feminists as she is about the police:

> White feminists say that they are the sisters of
>   Black women,
> Ask you to join their women's movement,
> And then they want to give you five hundred
>   reasons why
> You should leave your Black man
> And let them eat your . . .

Well, that's a little below the belt. But Sister Souljah is no liberal:

> White people give you welfare with a set of rules
>   and restrictions
> Designed to keep you on welfare, ignorant and
>   lazy,
> And then talk about you on TV.

In such a context, the rap about the police is at least understandable, and the talk of killing whites has about it a rough and ready sort of morality. That was the point of Sister Souljah's bringing up the Code of Hammurabi and the lex talionis with the *Washington Post* interviewer, and of these lines in "The Hate That Hate Produced":

> They say two wrongs don't make it right
> But it damn sure makes it even.

Both the morality and the violence in these songs are ninetenths disconnected from reality. That is why they try to make up in lurid rhetorical energy what they lack in plausibility. It is also why the rappers seem genuinely surprised when you take them at their word, and vehemently insist that they don't want to kill anyone.

So is rap quite harmless then? No. Disconnection from reality on such a scale is a form of cultural madness. Violent fantasy, more even than other kinds of fantasy, encourages the persistence of the inveterate victim's delusion that the world is plotting against him. In a recent survey of New Yorkers by the *New York Times,* clear majorities of blacks believed that it was at least plausible that the government was singling out black officials for investigation so that they would be discredited and that it was making sure drugs were available in poor neighborhoods. And 29 per cent were even prepared to believe that AIDS was developed by the government to kill black people. Such paranoia can only be exacerbated by the persecution mania and the delusions of grandeur of rap music.

It is obviously unhealthy for the polity to have attached to it a canker of such madness—especially one which seems to grow by feeding off the larger unreality of the general culture. Time Warner can afford to pay Mr. Levin so much money not just because of Ice T but also because of blockbuster films like *Lethal Weapon 3* and *Batman Re-*

turns, which have even less to do with the realities of crime and law enforcement than the crude police caricatures of the black rappers. I know, I know: the First Amendment says that we have to allow these "artists" to have their fun. But once in a while it ought to be OK for a critic to say that honest art, art that says what it means and means what it says, is better. (pp. 36-8, 53)

James Bowman, "Plain Brown Rappers," in
National Review, *New York, Vol. XLIV, July
20, 1992, pp. 36-8, 53.*

Elizabeth Wurtzel (essay date 28 September 1992)

[*In the following essay, Wurtzel compares rap and rock
n' roll, maintaining that the popularity of rap stems
from its extreme rebelliousness.*]

A man in his forties, a former S.D.S. [Students for a Democratic Society] member who was once teargassed by the National Guard during an antiwar rally, recently told me that because of rap music he was no longer afraid to die. "At last, a kind of music has come along that completely baffles me and everyone else in my generation," he explained. "I just—I don't understand why *anyone* likes it.'

This man is far from alone in his feelings. But at least he's just bewildered. More often, rap seems to inspire responses from its detractors which are as incendiary and hyperbolic as the genre itself tends to be. What began in the seventies as a small dance-hall phenomenon in Harlem and the South Bronx, with disk jockeys making up rhymes and scratching disco records in order to break up the monotony and isolate the strong beats, has now become the most significant musical happening of the last decade—and, without doubt, rock's most revolutionary movement since its own invention. In the early sixties, Mitch Miller, the head of A. & R. at Columbia Records, said of rock and roll, "It's not music, it's a disease"—a statement not so very different from what people are saying about rap today. This past summer, in response to "Cop Killer," a song by Ice-T and his heavy-metal band, Body Count, in which the singer assumes the persona of a man who guns down a police officer as an act of revenge against trigger-happy cops, George Bush declared Ice-T's work "sick," Dan Quayle called it "obscene," and sixty members of Congress (fifty-seven Republicans and three Democrats) asked Time Warner, the album's distributor, to pull the eponymously titled *Body Count* disk off the shelves, on the ground that it was "despicable" and "vile." Oliver North wants Time Warner brought up on sedition charges. The Combined Law Enforcement Associations of Texas (CLEAT) threatened to organize an across-the-board boycott of all Time Warner products. (That would have meant, if you were going to be strict about it, no *Batman Returns,* no CNN, no *People,* no HBO, no Cinemax, no *Mad,* no DC Comics, and no joining the Book-of-the-Month Club, even if you do get three books for three bucks.) Other police groups planned to divest their pension funds of the company's stock, and still others picketed its annual shareholders' meeting.

Throughout this controversy, references were made to the "rapper" Ice-T and the "rap" song "Cop Killer," even

though, with its screechy pile of guitars and mass of thrash, the song in question is pure metal, and is about as close to hip-hop in sound and spirit as Paul McCartney's "Liverpool Oratorio" is to a Beatles album. But somehow just adding the word "rap" to the equation gave the debate a racially divisive slant and helped inflame the terms of the argument even further.

Eventually, Ice-T himself, with both a motion-picture and a recording career hanging in the balance, decided to take the offending cut off the album. The net result was that the economics of controversy prevailed: *Body Count* catapulted from No. 73 on *Billboard's* chart to No. 26 the week before the bowdlerized version was to replace it. The following week, it fell back down to No. 77. And police groups are still not satisfied: because Ice-T is supposed to become the host of an HBO talk show, they are trying to organize a boycott of Time Warner's cable system, which is the second largest in the country.

Every year or so, there's yet another controversy surrounding the lyrics of some rap song—whether it's 2 Live Crew's adolescent pillow talk or Public Enemy's suggestion that we go kill politicians in Arizona—and these problems usually assume soap-operatic proportions and push a career that might have been tinny at best into the realm of multi-platinum. The routine response to such cultural uproars is well established: free-speech advocates make their requisite appearances on "Nightline" and "Good Morning America"; there are words of dismay

Ice-T.

from PTA groups and Tipper Gore; there is much invoking of First Amendment rights, sometimes by people whose only previous relationship to any law was breaking it; often a lawyer or two from the American Civil Liberties Union is involved; and then the whole thing blows over and nothing has really changed.

While it's something of a relief that the focus of these controversies has shifted from subliminal messages to actual, discernible lyrics, whenever a "Cop Killer"-type brouhaha erupts I worry not so much about serious issues like free speech as about the eerie diminishing of some of the more lighthearted aspects of our culture, such as the ability to process messages with due humor, irony, and perspective. I mean, it's *only* rock and roll. What's so strikingly absurd about these public debates is that they take the lyrics to rock songs with such gravity at a point in American history when the words and promises of our political leaders, whom we *should* be taking seriously, are usually greeted with cynicism and incredulity.

If you want an index of how seriously rap is taken in some quarters, consider this: At a press conference about a year ago, Ice Cube, the former leader of N.W.A. (Niggas With Attitude), endorsed *The Secret Relationship Between Blacks and Jews,* a book compiled by some researchers at Louis Farrakhan's Nation of Islam which "chronicles" the Jewish people's involvement in hundreds of years of black subjugation and claims that Jews ran the African slave trade. The book has been compared to *The Protocols of the Elders of Zion,* and should it be widely read it would no doubt exacerbate the already ugly relations between blacks and Jews in the urban areas where Farrakhan finds the bulk of his following. According to Ice Cube's spokesperson, the rapper had never read the book and was handed it for the first time only moments before he brandished it in front of the press and gave it his praise, but he advocated it because "he really believes in reading as many books as you can and educating yourself." Whatever.

At any rate, Bill Adler, a rap publicist and the biographer of Run-D.M.C., stapled together an eighty-three-mimeographed-page booklet called *Jew on the Brain: A Public Refutation of the Nation of Islam's "The Secret Relationship Between Blacks and Jews."* The bulk of the text was written by Harold Brackman, a scholar affiliated with the Simon Wiesenthal Center who is an expert on black-Jewish relations, and it includes point-by-point arguments against the Nation of Islam's allegations. It has an afterword written by a Princeton professor, Cornel West, and the book's epigraphs include a quotation from the historian Richard Hofstadter's *The Paranoid Style in American Politics.*

All this for a book Ice Cube never even opened.

Rap artists are determined to keep the issue of race front and center, and many rappers—among them KRS-One, of Boogie Down Productions; Chuck D, of Public Enemy; and Queen Latifah—have done quite well for themselves on the lecture circuit by talking about race at colleges and prisons or by appearing on panels such as the one held at Harvard a couple of years ago as part of a course on rap

and hip-hop as "African-American street epic." But since rappers have begun fashioning themselves as community spokespeople with political agendas that are at least as important as their music, many have undermined their own good intentions with what appears to be hypocrisy, or, at the very least, inconsistency. Ice Cube frequently complains that there are no role models for young black males, but he serves as a spokesman for St. Ides Malt Liquor, which, like other brands of malt liquor, is cheap and is sold in large bottles, and has often been blamed for helping to destroy the inner city; Public Enemy condemns criminal behavior, but the group is friendly with Mike Tyson, and one of its members, Flavor Flav, recently complained on MTV News that the boxer is being incarcerated for a crime that can't be proved; Sister Souljah is given to lyrics like "Honkies join the peace corps so they can spy on other people's culture / And make money off of the things they learn." Chuck D has said that rap serves as a CNN for the black community, but when you consider how much incoherent harangue and blather it contains it often seems much more like a late-night public-access cable station.

Still, despite such inconsistencies, many of these socially conscious rappers have for years given us songs that spoke about police brutality, the enormous social costs of institutionalized racism, and the life of the ghetto, and have done so with a candor we had never known before—and this was long before the Rodney King videotape and court case brought these problems to national attention and turned Los Angeles into a bonfire. Priority Records, an L.A.-based rap label that earned fifty-three million dollars last year, has just released *Street Soldiers,* a compilation of raps that anticipated the riots, and the proceeds from the album's sales are to go to help rebuild South Central Los Angeles. Included in this collection, which is an excellent primer for people wondering what hard-core "gangsta" rap is all about, are N.W.A.'s breakthrough cop-bashing jam "Fuck tha Police," Public Enemy's exhilarating "Fight the Power," Sir Mix-A-Lot's proud and forthright "One Time's Got No Case," and Ice-T's funny tale of being awakened by a drug raid, "Six 'n the Mornin'."

If *Street Soldiers* showcases political rap at its best, the intelligence of these particular songs helps to underscore the reasons that so many people—right-minded, liberal people—find rap so objectionable. The problem is that most rap, like most rock music, is really stupid stuff, full of wrongheaded, sexist, indefensible viewpoints that become shabby excuses for invoking the First Amendment: if N.W.A. founded a political party, its platform would basically be pro-AK-47 and anti-foreplay. But in the era of political correctness—and in the hands of music critics, who tend to be white and nervous—rap has been granted a kind of diplomatic immunity, either on the ground that free speech is all that matters or because too many people shrug and say, "It's a black thing." Even when critics are willing to condemn rap's misogyny, very few are comfortable pointing out that Ice-T might do one song complaining that the L.A. police are brutal and oppressive but talk in another about keeping ten semi-automatic weapons hidden in his house. If this is, as rappers insist, an accurate depiction of life in South Central, where the Bloods and the Crips have been carrying on a war of attrition for years now, then shouldn't somebody be pointing out what a difficult situation the L.A.P.D. is up against? But in the light of the Rodney King incident, and because organizations like the Parents' Music Resource Center spend so much time beating up on rap, people who think of themselves as hip and fair-minded are often too busy defending the music to notice its weaknesses.

The simple truth is that if you're going to like Public Enemy and N.W.A.—as I have to admit I do—you have to park the rational part of your brain somewhere else before you turn on the stereo. The terms that political rap sets up for its listeners—the idea that the boast and bravado that make up the bulk of the lyrical content are really about "self-esteem" and "community activism"—must be accepted without question or the music won't make any sense. In fact, the lawlessness becomes part of rap's appeal: its perceived value as an experience of "how the other half lives" tends to cancel any guilt one might experience from enjoying its obnoxiousness. (Guns N' Roses, on the other hand, may be equally obnoxious but has no redeeming social merit.) It's now finally being acknowledged out loud that as rap has become more "bad" and "street," its authenticity—combined with the fact that it seems to allow white kids a view of inner-city life without asking them to actually go north of 125th Street—has enhanced and broadened its appeal. People listen to N.W.A. because it feels so *real,* and if Eazy-E and M.C. Ren revel in sexually abusing their women—well, heck, they're just being honest. David Samuels pointed out in *The New Republic,* in a controversial article that is surely the sanest and smartest thing ever written about hip-hop, "Rap's appeal to whites rested in its evocation of an age-old image of blackness: a foreign, sexually charged, and criminal underworld against which the norms of white society are defined, and, by extension, through which they may be defied." (A teen magazine recently revealed that the most popular album at Beverly Hills High School is Ice Cube's *Death Certificate.*) When white kids listen to rap—and even Ice-T has acknowledged that eighty per cent of his audience is white and collegiate—they're experiencing the great high on rebellion which has been mostly sanitized out of music since the sixties.

And I think that's why hard-core rap scares people so much. It has an intractable quality to it, something that rock and roll has not been touched with in a long time. Rap didn't start out this way. In the beginning, in 1979, there was "Rapper's Delight," a catchy song by the Sugar Hill Gang with a giddy, giggly, cartoonish spirit (the song was about Superman and Lois Lane) that fitted in perfectly with the dance music it was spawned from. This innocent ditty might have represented what rap was to become, but then, in 1980, Kurtis Blow created social-commentary rap with "The Breaks," and in 1982 Grand Master Flash & The Furious Five scored a hit with "The Message," a topical rap about urban blight and the downs of ghetto life which included the infectious refrain "Don't push me 'cause I'm close to the edge / I'm tryin' not to lose my head / It's like a jungle sometimes it makes me wonder how I keep from going under." During the mid-eighties, there were rap groups here and there, like the Fat Boys, whose gimmicky size made them appear to be a nov-

elty act, but the movement lost momentum, mainly because the songs' abrasiveness and lyrical density made rap seem more like a singles medium that would never be able to graduate to the album format. At that point, rap might well have gone the way of British punk rock—a brief gathering of Angry Young Men that is extremely influential to this day but long ago dissolved as a coherent entity.

It wasn't until Run-D.M.C.—a bunch of gangly guys from Hollis, Queens, who wore thick gold rope chains and brass-knuckle I.D. rings, which gave them a thuggish appearance that belied their middle-class origins—crossed over that rap achieved true mainstream success. While the group's previous records had been hip-hop hits, its third album, *Raising Hell,* went platinum, the single "Walk This Way" (an Aerosmith cover) went gold, and the band set a new standard for fellow-rappers to aspire to. At the same time, the all-white Beastie Boys were bringing a party-hearty, frat-boy hedonism to rap with their No. 1 hit "Fight for Your Right to Party." (In the summer of 1987, in a rare display of hip-hop racial harmony, the Beasties and Run-D.M.C. toured together.) While Run-D.M.C. seem laughably tame by 1992 standards, when they first broke they were considered terribly tough, and every rap group with any credibility had a mission to one-up them. The smash-your-idols philosophy on which the rap scene was built led to Public Enemy's displacing Run-D.M.C. With its white-bashing vitriol, P.E. became the subject of much controversy and negative press, which ultimately inspired the group's rap "Don't Believe the Hype." (Bad publicity is a frequent topic of rap songs.) Public Enemy might have held sway forever, but in 1988 N.W.A. delivered its first full-length album, *Straight Outta Compton* (Ruthless/Priority), elicited a nasty letter from the F.B.I., and introduced us to the L.A. rap scene, which, bred in the sphere of gang warfare, made anything coming from the East Coast seem mild by comparison. Once N.W.A. hit the scene, it set a standard of street credibility that was so hard to surpass that publicists occasionally enhanced rappers' résumés by mentioning their police records or time spent in prison. Ice-T claimed in his rap "Power," "So you say that I'm a fake think, you really must be a fool / I been to jail more times than you have probably been in school." It seemed likely that record-company talent scouts might be searching for the next big rap thing on death row.

While just as many rappers are law-abiding as are products of the depravity and deprivation of the streets, the idea of rap as some form of salvation for black youth has become so entrenched that a record-company president recently told me that he feels a moral obligation to give contracts to a certain number of rappers, simply because "it's one way to stop the violence and get these kids off the streets." By this logic, rap is actually a kind of social sublimation, like boxing. Ice-T called one of his albums *Rhyme Pays,* and in it he boasts, "My mind's a riot gun."

Anyone who doesn't "get" rap and would like to should take a moment to listen to Public Enemy's "Fight the Power," which originally appeared on the soundtrack of Spike Lee's film *Do the Right Thing.* The song opens with a hooting, sirenlike sound that seems intended to alert us to the urgent message to come. Throughout the rap, Chuck D gives his usual angry rant, while Flavor Flav, who sometimes wears his pajamas onstage and accessorizes them with big hats and bright sunglasses (he's the court jester of rap), chimes in now and again for effect. As hot and bothered as the pair sound throughout the song, nothing could have prepared me for the climactic moment when they shout, "Elvis was a hero to most / But he never meant shit to me, you see / Straight-up racist that sucker was simple and plain / Motherfuck him and John Wayne / 'Cause I'm black and I'm proud / I'm ready and hyped, plus I'm amped / Most of my heroes don't appear on no stamps." With these lines, Public Enemy dismisses these two white pop icons as if they were just a couple of flies that needed to be swatted. I remember how the first time I heard "Fight the Power" I thought, Ring out the old, ring in the new. I remember feeling exhilarated. If anyone ever wanted to know what rock and roll was supposed to be about—never mind rap—I'd tell them that all they needed to do was listen to "Fight the Power."

As for Ice-T, who knows what's next? He seems to be taking it all in good humor, posing for the cover of *Rolling Stone* in a police uniform and promising an audience at the New Music Seminar, last June, that this controversy will just fuel his next effort. The irony of Ice-T's situation is that, as the gangsta rappers go, it couldn't have happened to a more amiable and unlikely guy. Ice-T even played a cop in *New Jack City*. With striking hazel eyes and lined pale skin, which give him a look that suggests he knows whereof he speaks, Ice-T is a natural for the sort of multimedia career that Time Warner must have envisioned for him: he's sexy and articulate, and it's easy to imagine him charming the corporate brass at meetings to decide what to do about "Cop Killer." Ice-T is so good at straddling the line between hip-hop culture and white America that he occasionally flew out to wherever the Lollapalooza '92 Tour happened to be playing to coach his friend Ice Cube, who was on the bill and was having a lot of trouble dealing with the white alternative-music scene. And Ice-T isn't entirely a bad role model: several of his songs have been strongly anti-drug ("I'm Your Pusher," "The Winner Loses"), and his albums tend to be filled with bits of information like "A statistic: At this moment there are more black males in prison that there are in college."

But even if Ice-T were an awful, despicable guy, it would be beside the point. *Body Count* is so often so over the top and nutty in its excess that it's crazy to take any of it seriously. And Ice-T has pointed out in several interviews that he chose to make a heavy metal album because that type of music lends itself to creating a crazed, psychopathic howl. "When I invented Body Count, I said that this group is just gonna be an angry voice," he told *Spin.* "This is the anger, this is the scream from the bottom. Body Count, in a way, should be slightly ignorant—meaning it can't be too intelligent. . . . You'll hear lyrics on the Body Count album, and you'll say, 'Ice-T knows better than that.' But I'm not singing as *me.* I'm singing as somebody who don't know, somebody who's just mad about shit." (pp. 110-13)

Elizabeth Wurtzel, "Fight the Power," in The

New Yorker, *Vol. LXVIII, No. 32, September 28, 1992, pp. 110-13.*

Alexs Pate   (essay date 5-7 February 1993)

[*Pate, who teaches poetry and fiction at the University of Minnesota and Macalester College, is writing a book on rap. In the following essay, he defines rap as a distinct genre of postmodern African-American poetry.*]

Every culture needs its poets. And yet, with notable exceptions—Lucille Clifton, Alice Walker, Maya Angelou, Rita Dove—there are virtually no prominent black poets with books published by major presses.

Still, there are scores of young black poets, and more developing every day. They just don't publish books. They press their art into the grooves of slamming beats stolen from wherever they can get them.

It's called rap. Music you can dance or nod your head to. It's a chaotic mixture that challenges the listener to suffer the poetic.

Yes, rap has at least two faces. One is superficial, defined by its reputation for being racist and sexist, and for promoting violence. And in certain instances this reputation is deserved. But the other face, which begins with recognizing each rap song as a poetic expression, leads to a deeper recognition of rap's cultural and artistic significance.

I know there is a fair amount of rap that gives us virtually nothing except the beat that carries it to our ears. But you don't have to listen very long before you discover the literary genius just below the beat.

To be a legitimate poet of the people, a writer must speak the language. And, at least since the Black Arts Movement of the 1960s, black poets have largely been a collection of honest and angry voices.

Chuck D of Public Enemy has called rap "black America's CNN." He proves his point with the words to "Hazy Shade of Criminal," from the latest Public Enemy disc:

> Never understood why the 'hood
> half of who's in da joint

Perhaps he read the recent statistics showing that 56 percent of black men in Baltimore between 18 and 35 are behind bars, on parole, being pursued by the police or in some other way in the criminal justice system. And for Washington, D.C., the number was 42 percent.

In the same poem, to demonstrate his ability to communicate irony, Chuck D writes:

> Jeffrey Dahmer enter the room without cuffs
> how the hell do we get stuffed
> in da back of a cell
> on an isle
> ain't it wild
> what's a criminal?

Or we can go back to Ice-T, much under siege for his song "Cop Killer," which is more rock than rap. But Ice-T drops deft social commentary into "The House":

You know the house down the street
where the kids are
and every day they seem to have a new scar
something strange is going on
and everybody knows
doors always shut
windows always closed
the little girl had a burn
the boy was black and blue
they said it came from play
you know that s--- ain't true
the boy's arm's broke
girl's scared to speak
their parents drink all day
couple of deadbeats . . .
act like you give a damn
won't someone save these kids
do something, call a cop
the other night I heard gunshots!

This is the voice of a socially responsible poet, not a cop killer. Therein lies one of the complexities of rap poetry: It offers the flesh, the blood, the ideas, the shame, the beauty of the inner city. The struggling, angry, glorious world of besieged African Americans. A world that was waiting for hip-hop—a broader term for rap culture—to arrive. Hip-hop is the messenger that carries the poetry.

As in the Beat poetry of the late '50s and early '60s, slang and word-play are everything. Rap poets create language. And while it may come to the uninitiated listener as alien, it actually is a hyperactive, mutating version of the slang that I grew up with. "Cool" is now "def" or "hype." We used to "scream on" people to put them down. Now we "dis" them. It's the same urban language system; we just didn't have a multimillion-dollar industry pumping it up.

And within the body of a rap poem we have all the elements of poetry. We can find rap poems in iambic pentameter with an almost classical construction. And newer rap poets are engaged in a range of structural experiments, playing with line length, mixing rhyming patterns for frenetic rhythms.

In 1992 there was an explosion of diversity in the rap community. Of course, there always has been diversity among rappers. The poetry of the gifted and prophetic Ice Cube always has been different from Big Daddy Kane's. There always has been a division between what is popularly considered "hard-core"—poetry that is totally uncompromising in language and story selection—and "soft"—poetry that is more accessible and more acceptable to the middle class.

In the past year, the growth in poetic styles has been pronounced. Added to the voices of the continuing poets are more recent ones like Kris Kross, TLC, Arrested Development, X-Clan, the Disposable Heroes of Hiphoprisy, Pete Rock & CL Smooth, P.M. Dawn, Das EFX, Naughty by Nature, House of Pain, Cypress Hill and many more.

While it's true that rap groups come and go with the speed of sound bites, the best tend to survive. This is true in all good art. And the beauty in this diversity is what we do not have in the traditional literary arts: It's always one "flavor of the year" for black authors, but there is a rich variety of rap poets.

Unfortunately, within the context of this pressure, the history of black storytelling and their relative youth, rap poets often indulge their sexual insecurities and their proclivities for aggression in their poems. Their characterization of women is particularly troubling. Women are routinely referred to as "ho's," bitches or "skinz." What is new is that increasingly they are answered by female rappers like TLC, Salt-N-Pepa, Queen Latifah, Yo-Yo and MC Lyte who are rising in power and popularity.

From Queen Latifah's "Fly Girl":

Tell me why is it when I walk past the guys
I always hear "Yo, baby,"
I mean like what's the big idea
I'm a queen, nuff respect
treat me like a lady,
and no, my name ain't yo, and I ain't got your
     baby
I'm looking for a guy who's sincere
one with class and savoir faire
I'm looking for someone who has to be
perfect for the queen
Latifah, me

Effective rap poets are engaged in a three-way dialogue among themselves, their communities and white America. In this poetic dialogue lie all kinds of dangers. The main danger is that, in the process of telling the truth about their environment, they also reveal the failures of social and economic policies. They reveal the attraction of gangs and sexism, and the roots of homophobia and anger toward the police. It is society's lack of effective attention to these issues and an inadequate education that scream back from rap poems. The poets only tell the stories of their people.

When I heard Pete Rock & CL Smooth's "They Reminisce Over You," I knew that rap was growing. Here was a poem about the silent, invisible black men of the inner city who work hard all of their lives but go unremembered, uncelebrated.

When I think back
I recall a man
off the family tree
my right hand
Papa Doc I see
took me from a boy to a man
so I always had a father
when my biological didn't bother

Then, later in the poem:

but only you saw
what took many times to see
I dedicate this to you
for believin in me

One of 1992's best collections of rap comes from Arrested Development. From "Raining Revolution," "Tennessee" and "People Everyday" to the astoundingly moral "Mr. Wendal," Arrested Development proves rap poets are taking seriously their role in the education of young people.

Here have a dollar, in fact, naw, brotherman
  here, have two.
Two dollars is a snack for me,
but it means a big deal to you.
Be strong, serve God only that if you do
beautiful heaven awaits.
That's the poem I wrote for the first time.
I saw a man with no clothes, no money, no plate.
Mr. Wendal, that's his name
no one ever knew his name
cuz he's a know one
never thought twice about spending on an ole
  bum
until I had a chance to really get to know one!
Now that I know 'em
to give him money isn't charity,
he gives me some knowledge
I buy him some food.
And to think blacks spend all that money on big
  colleges still
most of y'awll come out confused

Rap continues to thrive. This is because, in spite of its reputation and the white noise of controversy that swirls around it, rap is art. In fact, rap poetry is the emergent African-American literary form of the postmodern age. It is all the more sweet that the Grammys have been forced, to a degree, to reckon with rap music. Black poets making money and winning awards—who would've thunk it? (pp. 18, 20)

Alexs Pate, "Rap: The Poetry of the Streets,"
in USA Weekend, February 5-7, 1993, pp. 18,
20.

CENSORSHIP AND FREEDOM OF SPEECH

Rolling Stone (essay date 9 August 1990)

[*In the following excerpt, the commentator argues that the June 1990 obscenity ruling against 2 Live Crew set a precedent for restricting obscene material and that such actions constitute a direct threat to the right of free speech.*]

It would be easy to minimize the significance of the . . . obscenity ruling leveled at the 2 Live Crew. The album in question, *As Nasty As They Wanna Be,* is a monotonous litany of crude sex talk, straight out of a boys' high-school locker room. The publicity that resulted from the decision and from the subsequent arrest of three band members has driven the album back up the charts. The ruling—based on "contemporary community standards," as all obscenity charges must be—is a localized decision, applying only to three counties in Florida.

But the 2 Live Crew decision is a direct assault on one of our most precious rights as American citizens. Judge Jose Gonzalez's ruling marked the first time in history that a record album has been deemed obscene, and the arrest of the Crew members at a Miami concert a few days later was the first instance in years in which a performer was charged with obscenity strictly on the basis of speech.

The Supreme Court has held, in 1973's *Miller v. California,* that "obscenity" is determined by three specific criteria. The product must be patently offensive—which, arguably, *Nasty* is—but it also must appeal to prurient interests and lack serious artistic merit. Hard as it is to imagine anyone getting turned on by the Crew's raunchy rhymes, it is even harder to believe that an album that almost 2 million people have bought, laughed with and danced to has no value as a creative work.

The 2 Live Crew and its leader, Luther Campbell, have acknowledged from the beginning that their material is not for everyone. They put out two versions of this album, modifying the words for *As Clean As They Wanna Be,* and voluntarily placed prominent warnings on the *Nasty* record. The explicitness of the group's stage shows is determined by the concert promoters. If the show is advertised to the general public, the Crew puts on an expurgated performance; if it is billed as an "adults only" show—as it was in Miami—the audience has to show proof of age at the door.

Clearly, the real issue here isn't obscenity. Nor is it about "protecting the children." It's about fear. It's about one culture, predominantly older and white, that controls the structures of power and about another, younger, blacker world that has created a medium called rap through which individuals can communicate with one another. Public Enemy's Chuck D has called rap "black America's CNN." The 2 Live Crew's graphic language is also an extension of a comic tradition that has passed from Redd Foxx to Eddie Murphy. And as rap's popularity continues to grow with a young white audience, it is provoking the same angry, confused response from parents that rock & roll did a generation ago. But as America has gotten more chaotic, more violent, more desperate, so has its racism, and what once got parents up in arms now goes directly to our already overloaded courts.

Now that this country's cold-war terror has subsided, we are left to confront the fears we face on the street every day—crack, AIDS, crime, poverty. Overwhelmed by the enormity of these crises, people are looking for something to blame. In Florida, they seem to have found something. Something loud and dirty and frankly sexual. Something expressing the voice of a minority.

Meanwhile, the record industry has once again proven its spinelessness with its unforgivable silence during this crucial time. The major labels look on as a young black entrepreneur recording on his own label far away from the media centers fights for a cause that, as the recent record-stickering agreement demonstrates, the industry would rather not draw attention to. The leaders of this industry are afraid—afraid that people protesting recordings will cut into their all-important sales. One rare and admirable exception to the industry's shameful behavior is Bruce Springsteen's decision to authorize Luther Campbell's use of the "Born in the U.S.A." melody for a new song ["Banned In the U.S.A."]—and to take the heat that has come with that decision.

There is no reason to believe that if we sacrifice the 2 Live Crew, this harassment of recording artists will stop. Performers from N.W.A. to Madonna to Andrew Dice Clay have already been threatened or investigated. Once the slippery precedent of obscene recorded material is established, what will stop the far right from continuing to redefine the unacceptable "fringe" of pop music until its power exceeds that of record producers or consumers?

"The signs are evident and very ominous and a chill wind blows." Thus did Justice Harry Blackmun conclude his dissenting opinion in the *Webster v. Reproductive Health Services* abortion-funding decision [in 1989]. This chill wind has continued to gather force, spreading to our fundamental right of free speech. And until we start fighting back, it will keep blowing.

> *"The Issue Is Fear,"* in Rolling Stone, *No. 584, August 9, 1990, p. 24.*

Los Angeles Times   (essay date 29 August 1990)

[*In the following excerpt, the commentator discusses the decision of Geffen Records not to distribute an album by the Geto Boys.*]

Geffen Records has rocked the music industry with its decision not to distribute an album by the rap music group Geto Boys. We hope the move helps focus debate on the *content* of rap lyrics, about which, it seems to us, reasonable people can raise reasonable questions.

The Geto Boys is one of those angry-young-men rap groups that has made its mark with a jaunty, street-smart, anti-Establishment irreverence. A lot of people like the irreverence; it's the lyrics that some people don't like.

Geffen says some Geto Boy lyrics endorse "violence, racism and misogyny," and concludes it wants out of distributing the group. The decision comes at an auspicious moment in American cultural history: In a controversial Florida case, local authorities prosecuted the rap group 2 Live Crew for obscenity. So people are sure to worry that Geffen's decision is a kind of new corporate censorship (with the target once again a black rap group). Added to the increasing government intervention, from Florida to the National Endowment for the Arts flap, the development would seem to bode ill for artistic creativity and individual choice.

The truth is that the group should have little problem finding a new distributor; its previous album, which was marketed independently, was a big seller. So the consumer will not likely be denied choice. But neither should a distributor. The appropriate place for the exercise of judgment is in the marketplace, and as a player in that market a firm like Geffen has the right to exercise judgment about the kind of product it wishes to produce.

What's wrong is when government steps in and dictates to business what it cannot produce or what the consumer cannot purchase. That's a different matter from a business deciding to forgo a certain product or the consumer deciding not to buy.

The best art, to be sure, can provoke and upset. It would be a national creative disaster if the parameters of conventional aesthetics were the sole permissible playing field for artists. But some music is a turn-off, and perhaps deserves to be turned off. This should happen through legitimate market decisions and not through governmental edict.

> *"The Rap on Some Rock Music,"* in Los Angeles Times, *August 29, 1990, p. B6.*

Michael Kinsley   (essay date 20 July 1992)

[*In the following excerpt, Kinsley describes Ice-T's "Cop Killer" as cynical and commercial and criticizes Time Warner for recording and selling it.*]

How did the company that publishes [*Time*] come to produce a record glorifying the murder of police?

> I got my 12-gauge sawed off
> I got my headlights turned off
> I'm 'bout to bust some shots off
> I'm 'bout to dust some cops off . . .
> Die, Die, Die Pig, Die!

So go the lyrics to "Cop Killer" by the rapper Ice-T on the album *Body Count*. The album is released by Warner Bros. Records, part of the Time Warner media and entertainment conglomerate.

In a *Wall Street Journal* op-ed piece laying out the company's position, Time Warner CO-CEO Gerald Levin makes two defenses. First, Ice-T's "Cop Killer" is misunderstood. "It doesn't incite or glorify violence . . . It's his fictionalized attempt to get inside a character's head . . . "Cop Killer" is no more a call for gunning down the police than "Frankie and Johnny" is a summons for jilted lovers to shoot one another." Instead of "finding ways to silence the messenger," we should be "heeding the anguished cry contained in his message."

This defense is self-contradictory. "Frankie and Johnny" does not pretend to have a political "message" that must be "heeded." If "Cop Killer" has a message, it is that the murder of policemen is a justified response to police brutality. And not in self-defense, but in premeditated acts of revenge against random cops. ("I know your family's grievin'—f--- 'em.")

Killing policemen is a good thing—that is the plain meaning of the words, and no "larger understanding" of black culture, the rage of the streets or anything else can explain it away. This is not Ella Fitzgerald telling a story in song. As in much of today's popular music, the line between performer and performance is purposely blurred. These are political sermonettes clearly intended to endorse the sentiments being expressed. Tracy Marrow (Ice-T) himself has said, "I scared the police, and they need to be scared." That seems clear.

The company's second defense of "Cop Killer" is the classic one of free expression: "We stand for creative freedom. We believe that the worth of what an artist or journalist has to say does not depend on preapproval from a government official or a corporate censor."

Of course Ice-T has the right to say whatever he wants.

But that doesn't require any company to provide him an outlet. And it doesn't relieve a company of responsibility for the messages it chooses to promote. Judgment is not "censorship." Many an "anguished cry" goes unrecorded. This one was recorded, and promoted, because a successful artist under contract wanted to record it. Nothing wrong with making money, but a company cannot take the money and run from the responsibility.

The founder of *Time,* Henry Luce, would snort at the notion that his company should provide a value-free forum for the exchange of ideas. In Luce's system, editors were supposed to make value judgments and promote the truth as they saw it. *Time* has moved far from its old Lucean rigidity—far enough to allow for dissenting essays like this one. That evolution is a good thing, as long as it's not a handy excuse for abandoning all standards.

No commercial enterprise need agree with every word that appears under its corporate imprimatur. If Time Warner now intends to be "a global force for encouraging the confrontation of ideas," that's swell. But a policy of allowing diverse viewpoints is not a moral free pass. Pro and con on national health care is one thing; pro and con on killing policemen is another.

A bit of sympathy is in order for Time Warner. It is indeed a "global force" with media tentacles around the world. If it imposes rigorous standards and values from the top, it gets accused of corporate censorship. If it doesn't, it gets accused of moral irresponsibility. A dilemma. But someone should have thought of that before deciding to become a global force.

And another genuine dilemma. Whatever the actual merits of "Cop Killer," if Time Warner withdraws the album now the company will be perceived as giving in to outside pressure. That is a disastrous precedent for a global conglomerate.

The Time-Warner merger of 1989 was supposed to produce corporate "synergy": the whole was supposed to be more than the sum of the parts. The "Cop Killer" controversy is an example of negative synergy. People get mad at "Cop Killer" and start boycotting the movie *Batman Returns.* A reviewer praises "Cop Killer" ("Tracy Marrow's poetry takes a switchblade and deftly slices life's jugular," etc.), and TIME is accused of corruption instead of mere foolishness. Senior Time Warner executives find themselves under attack for—and defending—products of their company they neither honestly care for nor really understand, and doubtless weren't even aware of before controversy hit.

Anyway, it's absurd to discuss "Cop Killer" as part of the "confrontation of ideas"—or even as an authentic anguished cry of rage from the ghetto. "Cop Killer" is a cynical commercial concoction, designed to titillate its audience with imagery of violence. It merely exploits the authentic anguish of the inner city for further titillation. Tracy Marrow is in business for a buck, just like Time Warner. "Cop Killer" is an excellent joke on the white establishment, of which the company's anguished apologia ("Why can't we hear what rap is trying to tell us?") is the punch line.

Michael Kinsley, "Ice-T: Is the Issue Social Responsibility . . . ," in Time, *New York, Vol. 140, No. 3, July 20, 1992, p. 88.*

Ice-T on freedom of speech:

There's freedom of speech, but you can't speak out against the government. I listen to all the people's gripes and their complaints, they're like "Well, I'm down with freedom of speech, but he shouldn't have said that." That's all bullshit. I have the right to say how I feel. I have many days of my life that I wanted to just get dressed up and go out there and kill the fucking pigs. They are totally out of control. There's no jail terms for them, there's nothing.

Why aren't there any cops on death row? Why aren't there any cops doing any severe prison terms? They're above the law. We saw Daryl Gates tell the mayor to kiss his ass, the city council to kiss his ass, and say, "I'm not going out of this office." I think people should have looked at that and realized how much power he's got.

If you really want to know what the record's whole angle was, it was just a check on them. It *is* a threat record, and they need to be threatened.

Ice-T, in "Ice-T: The Rolling Stone Interview,"
in Rolling Stone, *1992.*

Barbara Ehrenreich   (essay date 20 July 1992)

[*Ehrenreich is an American nonfiction writer, educator, and prominent feminist. In the following essay, she argues that Ice-T's "Cop Killer" is little more than a statement of macho defiance and therefore does not deserve the reaction it has received.*]

Ice-T's song "Cop Killer" is as bad as they come. This is black anger—raw, rude and cruel—and one reason the song's so shocking is that in postliberal America, black anger is virtually taboo. You won't find it on TV, not on the *McLaughlin Group* or *Crossfire,* and certainly not in the placid features of Arsenio Hall or Bernard Shaw. It's been beaten back into the outlaw subcultures of rap and rock, where, precisely because it is taboo, it sells. And the nastier it is, the faster it moves off the shelves. As Ice-T asks in another song on the same album, "Goddamn what a brotha gotta do / To get a message through / To the red, white and blue?"

But there's a gross overreaction going on, building to a veritable paroxysm of white denial. A national boycott has been called, not just of the song or Ice-T, but of all Time Warner products. The President himself has denounced Time Warner as "wrong" and Ice-T as "sick." Ollie North's Freedom Alliance has started a petition drive aimed at bringing Time Warner executives to trial for "sedition and anarchy."

Much of this is posturing and requires no more courage than it takes to stand up in a VFW hall and condemn communism or crack. Yes, "Cop Killer" is irresponsible and vile. But Ice-T is as right about some things as he is righteous about the rest. And ultimately, he's not even dangerous—least of all to the white power structure his songs condemn.

The "danger" implicit in all the uproar is of empty-headed, suggestible black kids, crouching by their boom boxes, waiting for the word. But what Ice-T's fans know and his detractors obviously don't is that "Cop Killer" is just one more entry in pop music's long history of macho hyperbole and violent boast. Flip to the classic-rock station, and you might catch the Rolling Stones announcing "the time is right for violent revoloo-shun!" from their 1968 hit "Street Fighting Man." And where were the defenders of our law-enforcement officers when a white British group, the Clash, taunted its fans with the lyrics "When they kick open your front door / How you gonna come / With your hands on your head / Or on the trigger of your gun?"

"Die, Die, Die Pig" is strong speech, but the Constitution protects strong speech, and it's doing so this year more aggressively than ever. The Supreme Court has just downgraded cross burnings to the level of bonfires and ruled that it's no crime to throw around verbal grenades like "nigger" and "kike." Where are the defenders of decorum and social stability when prime-time demagogues like Howard Stern deride African Americans as "spear chuckers"?

More to the point, young African Americans are not so naive and suggestible that they have to depend on a compact disc for their sociology lessons. To paraphrase another song from another era, you don't need a rap song to tell which way the wind is blowing. Black youths know that the police are likely to see them through a filter of stereotypes as miscreants and potential "cop killers." They are aware that a black youth is seven times as likely to be charged with a felony as a white youth who has committed the same offense, and is much more likely to be imprisoned.

They know, too, that in a shameful number of cases, it is the police themselves who indulge in "anarchy" and violence. The U.S. Justice Department has received 47,000 complaints of police brutality in the past six years, and Amnesty International has just issued a report on police brutality in Los Angeles, documenting 40 cases of "torture or cruel, inhuman or degrading treatment."

Menacing as it sounds, the fantasy in "Cop Killer" is the fantasy of the powerless and beaten down—the black man who's been hassled once too often ("A pig stopped me for nothin'!"), spread-eagled against a police car, pushed around. It's not a "responsible" fantasy (fantasies seldom are). It's not even a very creative one. In fact, the sad thing about "Cop Killer" is that it falls for the cheapest, most conventional image of rebellion that our culture offers: the lone gunman spraying fire from his AK-47. This is not "sedition"; it's the familiar, all-American, Hollywood-style pornography of violence.

Which is why Ice-T is right to say he's no more dangerous than George Bush's pal Arnold Schwarzenegger, who wasted an army of cops in *Terminator 2*. Images of extraordinary cruelty and violence are marketed every day, many of far less artistic merit than "Cop Killer." This is our free market of ideas and images, and it shouldn't be any less free for a black man than for other purveyors of "irresponsible" sentiments, from David Duke to Andrew Dice Clay.

Just, please, don't dignify Ice-T's contribution with the word sedition. The past masters of sedition—men like George Washington, Toussaint-Louverture, Fidel Castro or Mao Zedong, all of whom led and won armed insurrections—would be unimpressed by "Cop Killer" and probably saddened. They would shake their heads and mutter words like "infantile" and "adventurism." They might point out that the cops are hardly a noble target, being, for the most part, honest working stiffs who've got stuck with the job of patrolling ghettos ravaged by economic decline and official neglect.

There is a difference, the true seditionist would argue, between a revolution and a gesture of macho defiance. Gestures are cheap. They feel good, they blow off some rage. But revolutions, violent or otherwise, are made by people who have learned how to count very slowly to 10.

> Barbara Ehrenreich, ". . . Or Is It Creative Freedom?" in Time, New York, Vol. 140, No. 3, July 20, 1992, p. 89.

Anthony DeCurtis   (essay date 17 September 1992)

[*In the following excerpt, DeCurtis contends that efforts to control rap lyrics are likely to increase in the wake of Ice-T's removal of "Cop Killer" from his album* Body Count.]

Ice-T fought the law, and the law won. Unfortunately, that's the only assessment that can be made in the wake of Ice-T's decision to pull the track "Cop Killer" from his album *Body Count.*

By all accounts, Ice-T rescinded the song voluntarily, but you can be sure that Time Warner, the parent company of Ice-T's label, Warner Bros., was relieved. The boycotts and stock divestments organized by law-enforcement groups were beginning to generate real heat—the kind of heat that melts corporate resolve. Along with those pressures came threats against Time Warner employees. Ice-T understands the distinction between putting your own life on the line and risking the lives of people who lack both your economic resources and your security guards, and that no doubt contributed to his decision. The larger issue facing Ice-T and every other artist at this point, however, is, what happens now?

In the short term, the heat is off. Time Warner will not impose the code of standards that was rumored to be in the offing if the company could find no other way to pacify its stockholders. The company and, ironically, those stockholders can now also enjoy the profits that are rolling in as *Body Count*—an album that was stone dead commercially before police groups decided it was a moral threat—storms up the charts and becomes a collectors' item.

But yielding to censors is a strategy that never works in

the long run. Agreeing to parental-advisory labels on records seven years ago, for example, was supposed to put an end to more extreme demands. It's obvious where that has led: The situation has only worsened. And code of standards or no, when one of the world's largest media conglomerates backs down on an indisputable First Amendment issue, what filmmaker, songwriter, author or journalist can feel safe? Every pressure group in the country now knows that as long as it chooses its targets carefully, even the most powerful companies and the most outspoken artists can be forced to yield.

The key, of course, is choosing the right target. As Ice-T has repeatedly pointed out, this country was founded in a revolution, and at least one thread in the national weave is the urge to support outlaws and underdogs against the authorities. In song, this is one of our country's oldest and most consistent themes: Woody Guthrie's "Pretty Boy Floyd" and Johnny Cash's "Folsom Prison Blues" are only two relatively recent examples, and Eric Clapton had a Number One hit covering Bob Marley's "I Shot the Sheriff." No one sought to ban those songs. So what's the problem with "Cop Killer"?

The problem is that Ice-T is black and, although "Cop Killer" is a rock song, a rapper. That's also why he's an effective target. Gangsta rap—Ice-T's beat—is the voice of black insurgency and the primary art form through which the tense relations between the police and the black community have been dramatized. From "The Message," by Grandmaster Flash and the Furious Five, which ends in a police assault, to Boogie Down Productions' "Who Protects Us From You?" and N.W.A.'s "Fuck tha Police," rap has presented the street-side view of police corruption, harassment and racism.

Though they do occasionally sensationalize them, rappers do not make these problems up. Can anyone deny the shameful record of the LAPD—the focus of Ice-T's rage—in serving the minority populations of Los Angeles? Significantly, black police organizations have supported Ice-T to the point of expressing disappointment with his withdrawal of "Cop Killer."

Rappers will continue to write songs about violent confrontations with the police because conditions have not changed. According to a sampler put out by their label, Tommy Boy, both Paris and Live Squad have such songs scheduled for their forthcoming albums. Tommy Boy is owned by Time Warner. Whether those tracks appear—and how police groups and Time Warner react if they do—will likely provide the first test of what one police spokesperson has defined as a "cease-fire" in the censorship wars.

One thing is certain: That cease-fire will never last. Police groups and other would-be censors, charged up by their victory in the "Cop Killer" case, are not going to be in any mood to back off. Rappers, rockers and everybody else interested in freedom of speech will want to reclaim lost ground. That's not a cease-fire at all: It's the calm before the firestorm.

Anthony DeCurtis, in an excerpt from Rolling Stone, *No. 639, September 17, 1992, p. 32.*

FURTHER READING

Bowman, James. "Prisoner Exchange." *Reason* 22, No. 8 (January 1991): 45-6.
Suggests that the poet Jenny Holzer should be jailed instead of Luther Campbell of 2 Live Crew and asserts that censorship can have positive effects on the quality of art and literature.

Douglas, Susan. "Race, Rap, and White Blindness." *The Progressive* 56, No. 8 (August 1992): 16.
Comments on the controversy caused by Bill Clinton's negative remarks about Sister Souljah.

Gates, Henry Louis, Jr. "Taking the Rap." *The New Republic* 203, No. 23 (23 December 1990): 4.
Letter to the editor in which Gates comments on freedom of expression and his testimony at 2 Live Crew's obscenity trial.

Jennings, Nicholas. "The Big Rap Attack: A Black Form Conquers the Mainstream." *Maclean's* 103, No. 46 (12 November 1990): 74-5.
Notes the rising popularity of rap music and its acceptance as part of mainstream culture.

"Raunchy Rap Lyrics Stir National Uproar." *Jet* 78, No. 12 (2 July 1990): 36-8.
Contends that attempts to censor such rap bands as 2 Live Crew are racially motivated.

Light, Alan. "Rappers Sounded Warning: The Violence in Los Angeles Didn't Surprise Those Who Were Paying Attention." *Rolling Stone, Special Double Issue,* Nos. 634-635 (9-23 July 1992): 15-17.
Argues that rap music presents a realistic and thought-provoking portrait of inner-city life.

———. "Rap." *Rolling Stone: 1992 Yearbook, Special Double Issue,* Nos. 645-646 (10-24 December 1992): 79.
Provides an overview of news and events related to rap during 1992 with particular emphasis on the controversy over Ice-T's "Cop Killer" and the emergence of new bands such as Arrested Development.

Rockwell, John. "Hammer and Ice, Rappers Who Rule Pop." *The New York Times* (18 November 1990): 30, 32.
Maintains that although M. C. Hammer and Vanilla Ice have produced top-selling albums by creating rap music that is acceptable to a broad audience, their success does not threaten the integrity of rap music.

Simpson, Janice C. "Yo! Rap Gets on the Map." *Time* 135, No. 6 (5 February 1990): 60-2.
Discusses the increasing popularity and acceptance of rap music outside the African-American community.

Toop, David. "Taking the Rap for Their Rhymes." *The Times,* London (17 December 1991): 12.
Commends such rap musicians as Queen Latifah and Ice Cube for addressing such controversial issues as racial tension in New York City and date rape in their work.

Zimmerman, Kevin. "Hip-hop Hub Hewn by Recent Racial Uproar." *Variety* 347, No. 10 (22 June 1992): 48, 54.

Remarks on the controversies surrounding Ice-T's song "Cop Killer" and Bill Clinton's negative remarks about Sister Souljah.

☐ Contemporary Literary Criticism

Indexes

Literary Criticism Series
Cumulative Author Index
Cumulative Topic Index
Cumulative Nationality Index
Title Index, Volume 76

How to Use This Index

The main references

list all author entries in the following Gale Literary Criticism series:

CLC = *Contemporary Literary Criticism*
CLR = *Children's Literature Review*
CMLC = *Classical and Medieval Literature Criticism*
DC = *Drama Criticism*
LC = *Literature Criticism from 1400 to 1800*
NCLC = *Nineteenth-Century Literature Criticism*
PC = *Poetry Criticism*
SSC = *Short Story Criticism*
TCLC = *Twentieth-Century Literary Criticism*

The cross-references

list all author entries in the following Gale biographical and literary sources:

AAYA = *Authors & Artists for Young Adults*
AITN = *Authors in the News*
BLC = *Black Literature Criticism*
BW = *Black Writers*
CA = *Contemporary Authors*
CAAS = *Contemporary Authors Autobiography Series*
CABS = *Contemporary Authors Bibliographical Series*
CANR = *Contemporary Authors New Revision Series*
CAP = *Contemporary Authors Permanent Series*
CDALB = *Concise Dictionary of American Literary Biography*
CDBLB = *Concise Dictionary of British Literary Biography*
DLB = *Dictionary of Literary Biography*
DLBD = *Dictionary of Literary Biography Documentary Series*
DLBY = *Dictionary of Literary Biography Yearbook*
HW = *Hispanic Writers*
MAICYA = *Major Authors and Illustrators for Children and Young Adults*
MTCW = *Major 20th-Century Writers*
SAAS = *Something about the Author Autobiography Series*
SATA = *Something about the Author*
WLC = *World Literature Criticism, 1500 to the Present*
YABC = *Yesterday's Authors of Books for Children*

Literary Criticism Series
Cumulative Author Index

Appleton, Lawrence
See Lovecraft, H(oward) P(hillips)

Apuleius, (Lucius Madaurensis)
125(?)-175(?) . . . . CMLC 1

Aquin, Hubert 1929-1977. . . . . CLC 15
See also CA 105; DLB 53

Aragon, Louis 1897-1982. . . . . CLC 3, 22
See also CA 69-72; 108; CANR 28;
DLB 72; MTCW

Arany, Janos 1817-1882. . . . . NCLC 34

Arbuthnot, John 1667-1735 . . . . LC 1
See also DLB 101

Archer, Herbert Winslow
See Mencken, H(enry) L(ouis)

Archer, Jeffrey (Howard) 1940- . . . . CLC 28
See also BEST 89:3; CA 77-80; CANR 22

Archer, Jules 1915- . . . . CLC 12
See also CA 9-12R; CANR 6; SAAS 5;
SATA 4

Archer, Lee
See Ellison, Harlan

Arden, John 1930- . . . . CLC 6, 13, 15
See also CA 13-16R; CAAS 4; CANR 31;
DLB 13; MTCW

Arenas, Reinaldo 1943-1990 . . . . CLC 41
See also CA 124; 128; 133; HW

Arendt, Hannah 1906-1975 . . . . CLC 66
See also CA 17-20R; 61-64; CANR 26;
MTCW

Aretino, Pietro 1492-1556 . . . . LC 12

Arguedas, Jose Maria
1911-1969 . . . . CLC 10, 18
See also CA 89-92; DLB 113; HW

Argueta, Manlio 1936- . . . . CLC 31
See also CA 131; HW

Ariosto, Ludovico 1474-1533. . . . . LC 6

Aristides
See Epstein, Joseph

Aristophanes
450B.C.-385B.C. . . . . CMLC 4; DC 2

Arlt, Roberto (Godofredo Christophersen)
1900-1942 . . . . TCLC 29
See also CA 123; 131; HW

Armah, Ayi Kwei 1939- . . . . CLC 5, 33
See also BLC 1; BW; CA 61-64; CANR 21;
DLB 117; MTCW

Armatrading, Joan 1950- . . . . CLC 17
See also CA 114

Arnette, Robert
See Silverberg, Robert

**Arnim, Achim von (Ludwig Joachim von
Arnim)** 1781-1831 . . . . NCLC 5
See also DLB 90

Arnim, Bettina von 1785-1859. . . . NCLC 38
See also DLB 90

Arnold, Matthew
1822-1888 . . . . NCLC 6, 29; PC 5
See also CDBLB 1832-1890; DLB 32, 57;
WLC

Arnold, Thomas 1795-1842 . . . . . . NCLC 18
See also DLB 55

Arnow, Harriette (Louisa) Simpson
1908-1986 . . . . CLC 2, 7, 18
See also CA 9-12R; 118; CANR 14; DLB 6;
MTCW; SATA 42, 47

Arp, Hans
See Arp, Jean

Arp, Jean 1887-1966. . . . . CLC 5
See also CA 81-84; 25-28R

Arrabal
See Arrabal, Fernando

Arrabal, Fernando 1932- . . . CLC 2, 9, 18, 58
See also CA 9-12R; CANR 15

Arrick, Fran. . . . . CLC 30

Artaud, Antonin 1896-1948 . . . . . TCLC 3, 36
See also CA 104

Arthur, Ruth M(abel) 1905-1979. . . . CLC 12
See also CA 9-12R; 85-88; CANR 4;
SATA 7, 26

Artsybashev, Mikhail (Petrovich)
1878-1927 . . . . TCLC 31

Arundel, Honor (Morfydd)
1919-1973 . . . . CLC 17
See also CA 21-22; 41-44R; CAP 2;
SATA 4, 24

Asch, Sholem 1880-1957 . . . . TCLC 3
See also CA 105

Ash, Shalom
See Asch, Sholem

Ashbery, John (Lawrence)
1927- . . . CLC 2, 3, 4, 6, 9, 13, 15, 25, 41
See also CA 5-8R; CANR 9, 37; DLB 5;
DLBY 81; MTCW

Ashdown, Clifford
See Freeman, R(ichard) Austin

Ashe, Gordon
See Creasey, John

Ashton-Warner, Sylvia (Constance)
1908-1984 . . . . CLC 19
See also CA 69-72; 112; CANR 29; MTCW

Asimov, Isaac
1920-1992 . . . . . . CLC 1, 3, 9, 19, 26, 76
See also BEST 90:2; CA 1-4R; 137;
CANR 2, 19, 36; CLR 12; DLB 8;
DLBY 92; MAICYA; MTCW; SATA 1,
26

Astley, Thea (Beatrice May)
1925- . . . . CLC 41
See also CA 65-68; CANR 11

Aston, James
See White, T(erence) H(anbury)

Asturias, Miguel Angel
1899-1974 . . . . CLC 3, 8, 13
See also CA 25-28; 49-52; CANR 32;
CAP 2; DLB 113; HW; MTCW

Atares, Carlos Saura
See Saura (Atares), Carlos

Atheling, William
See Pound, Ezra (Weston Loomis)

Atheling, William Jr.
See Blish, James (Benjamin)

Atherton, Gertrude (Franklin Horn)
1857-1948 . . . . TCLC 2
See also CA 104; DLB 9, 78

Atherton, Lucius
See Masters, Edgar Lee

Atkins, Jack
See Harris, Mark

Atticus
See Fleming, Ian (Lancaster)

Atwood, Margaret (Eleanor)
1939- . . . . CLC 2, 3, 4, 8, 13, 15, 25, 44;
SSC 2
See also BEST 89:2; CA 49-52; CANR 3,
24, 33; DLB 53; MTCW; SATA 50; WLC

Aubigny, Pierre d'
See Mencken, H(enry) L(ouis)

Aubin, Penelope 1685-1731(?) . . . . LC 9
See also DLB 39

Auchincloss, Louis (Stanton)
1917- . . . . CLC 4, 6, 9, 18, 45
See also CA 1-4R; CANR 6, 29; DLB 2;
DLBY 80; MTCW

Auden, W(ystan) H(ugh)
1907-1973 . . . . . CLC 1, 2, 3, 4, 6, 9, 11,
14, 43; PC 1
See also CA 9-12R; 45-48; CANR 5;
CDBLB 1914-1945; DLB 10, 20; MTCW;
WLC

Audiberti, Jacques 1900-1965 . . . . . . CLC 38
See also CA 25-28R

Auel, Jean M(arie) 1936-. . . . . CLC 31
See also AAYA 7; BEST 90:4; CA 103;
CANR 21

Auerbach, Erich 1892-1957 . . . . TCLC 43
See also CA 118

Augier, Emile 1820-1889 . . . . NCLC 31

August, John
See De Voto, Bernard (Augustine)

Augustine, St. 354-430. . . . . CMLC 6

Aurelius
See Bourne, Randolph S(illiman)

Austen, Jane
1775-1817 . . . . NCLC 1, 13, 19, 33
See also CDBLB 1789-1832; DLB 116;
WLC

Auster, Paul 1947- . . . . CLC 47
See also CA 69-72; CANR 23

Austin, Frank
See Faust, Frederick (Schiller)

Austin, Mary (Hunter)
1868-1934 . . . . TCLC 25
See also CA 109; DLB 9, 78

Autran Dourado, Waldomiro
See Dourado, (Waldomiro Freitas) Autran

Averroes 1126-1198 . . . . CMLC 7
See also DLB 115

Avison, Margaret 1918-. . . . . CLC 2, 4
See also CA 17-20R; DLB 53; MTCW

Ayckbourn, Alan
1939- . . . . CLC 5, 8, 18, 33, 74
See also CA 21-24R; CANR 31; DLB 13;
MTCW

Aydy, Catherine
See Tennant, Emma (Christina)

Ayme, Marcel (Andre) 1902-1967. . . CLC 11
See also CA 89-92; CLR 25; DLB 72

Bitov, Andrei (Georgievich) 1937-... **CLC 57**

Biyidi, Alexandre 1932-
    See Beti, Mongo
    See also BW; CA 114; 124; MTCW

Bjarme, Brynjolf
    See Ibsen, Henrik (Johan)

Bjornson, Bjornstjerne (Martinius)
    1832-1910 .... **TCLC 7, 37**
    See also CA 104

Black, Robert
    See Holdstock, Robert P.

Blackburn, Paul 1926-1971 ...... **CLC 9, 43**
    See also CA 81-84; 33-36R; CANR 34;
    DLB 16; DLBY 81

Black Elk 1863-1950 .... **TCLC 33**

Black Hobart
    See Sanders, (James) Ed(ward)

Blacklin, Malcolm
    See Chambers, Aidan

Blackmore, R(ichard) D(oddridge)
    1825-1900 .... **TCLC 27**
    See also CA 120; DLB 18

Blackmur, R(ichard) P(almer)
    1904-1965 .... **CLC 2, 24**
    See also CA 11-12; 25-28R; CAP 1; DLB 63

Black Tarantula, The
    See Acker, Kathy

Blackwood, Algernon (Henry)
    1869-1951 .... **TCLC 5**
    See also CA 105

Blackwood, Caroline 1931- .... **CLC 6, 9**
    See also CA 85-88; CANR 32; DLB 14;
    MTCW

Blade, Alexander
    See Hamilton, Edmond; Silverberg, Robert

Blaga, Lucian 1895-1961 .... **CLC 75**

Blair, Eric (Arthur) 1903-1950
    See Orwell, George
    See also CA 104; 132; MTCW; SATA 29

Blais, Marie-Claire
    1939- .... **CLC 2, 4, 6, 13, 22**
    See also CA 21-24R; CAAS 4; CANR 38;
    DLB 53; MTCW

Blaise, Clark 1940- .... **CLC 29**
    See also AITN 2; CA 53-56; CAAS 3;
    CANR 5; DLB 53

Blake, Nicholas
    See Day Lewis, C(ecil)
    See also DLB 77

Blake, William 1757-1827 .... **NCLC 13**
    See also CDBLB 1789-1832; DLB 93;
    MAICYA; SATA 30; WLC

Blasco Ibanez, Vicente
    1867-1928 .... **TCLC 12**
    See also CA 110; 131; HW; MTCW

Blatty, William Peter 1928-........ **CLC 2**
    See also CA 5-8R; CANR 9

Bleeck, Oliver
    See Thomas, Ross (Elmore)

Blessing, Lee 1949-.............. **CLC 54**

Blish, James (Benjamin)
    1921-1975 .... **CLC 14**
    See also CA 1-4R; 57-60; CANR 3; DLB 8;
    MTCW; SATA 66

Bliss, Reginald
    See Wells, H(erbert) G(eorge)

Blixen, Karen (Christentze Dinesen)
    1885-1962
    See Dinesen, Isak
    See also CA 25-28; CANR 22; CAP 2;
    MTCW; SATA 44

Bloch, Robert (Albert) 1917-....... **CLC 33**
    See also CA 5-8R; CANR 5; DLB 44;
    SATA 12

Blok, Alexander (Alexandrovich)
    1880-1921 .... **TCLC 5**
    See also CA 104

Blom, Jan
    See Breytenbach, Breyten

Bloom, Harold 1930- .... **CLC 24**
    See also CA 13-16R; CANR 39; DLB 67

Bloomfield, Aurelius
    See Bourne, Randolph S(illiman)

Blount, Roy (Alton) Jr. 1941-...... **CLC 38**
    See also CA 53-56; CANR 10, 28; MTCW

Bloy, Leon 1846-1917............ **TCLC 22**
    See also CA 121; DLB 123

Blume, Judy (Sussman) 1938-... **CLC 12, 30**
    See also AAYA 3; CA 29-32R; CANR 13,
    37; CLR 2, 15; DLB 52; MAICYA;
    MTCW; SATA 2, 31

Blunden, Edmund (Charles)
    1896-1974 .... **CLC 2, 56**
    See also CA 17-18; 45-48; CAP 2; DLB 20,
    100; MTCW

Bly, Robert (Elwood)
    1926- .... **CLC 1, 2, 5, 10, 15, 38**
    See also CA 5-8R; DLB 5; MTCW

Bobette
    See Simenon, Georges (Jacques Christian)

Boccaccio, Giovanni 1313-1375
    See also SSC 10

Bochco, Steven 1943-............ **CLC 35**
    See also CA 124; 138

Bodenheim, Maxwell 1892-1954 ... **TCLC 44**
    See also CA 110; DLB 9, 45

Bodker, Cecil 1927- .... **CLC 21**
    See also CA 73-76; CANR 13; CLR 23;
    MAICYA; SATA 14

Boell, Heinrich (Theodor) 1917-1985
    See Boll, Heinrich (Theodor)
    See also CA 21-24R; 116; CANR 24;
    DLB 69; DLBY 85; MTCW

Bogan, Louise 1897-1970..... **CLC 4, 39, 46**
    See also CA 73-76; 25-28R; CANR 33;
    DLB 45; MTCW

Bogarde, Dirk .... **CLC 19**
    See also Van Den Bogarde, Derek Jules
        Gaspard Ulric Niven
    See also DLB 14

Bogosian, Eric 1953- .... **CLC 45**
    See also CA 138

Bograd, Larry 1953-.............. **CLC 35**
    See also CA 93-96; SATA 33

Boiardo, Matteo Maria 1441-1494 .... **LC 6**

Boileau-Despreaux, Nicolas
    1636-1711 .... **LC 3**

Boland, Eavan 1944-.......... **CLC 40, 67**
    See also DLB 40

Boll, Heinrich (Theodor)
    1917-1985 ... **CLC 2, 3, 6, 9, 11, 15, 27,
                              39, 72**
    See also Boell, Heinrich (Theodor)
    See also DLB 69; DLBY 85; WLC

Bolt, Lee
    See Faust, Frederick (Schiller)

Bolt, Robert (Oxton) 1924-........ **CLC 14**
    See also CA 17-20R; CANR 35; DLB 13;
    MTCW

Bomkauf
    See Kaufman, Bob (Garnell)

Bonaventura..................... **NCLC 35**
    See also DLB 90

Bond, Edward 1934-....... **CLC 4, 6, 13, 23**
    See also CA 25-28R; CANR 38; DLB 13;
    MTCW

Bonham, Frank 1914-1989......... **CLC 12**
    See also AAYA 1; CA 9-12R; CANR 4, 36;
    MAICYA; SAAS 3; SATA 1, 49, 62

Bonnefoy, Yves 1923-........ **CLC 9, 15, 58**
    See also CA 85-88; CANR 33; MTCW

Bontemps, Arna(ud Wendell)
    1902-1973 .... **CLC 1, 18**
    See also BLC 1; BW; CA 1-4R; 41-44R;
    CANR 4, 35; CLR 6; DLB 48, 51;
    MAICYA; MTCW; SATA 2, 24, 44

Booth, Martin 1944-.............. **CLC 13**
    See also CA 93-96; CAAS 2

Booth, Philip 1925-............... **CLC 23**
    See also CA 5-8R; CANR 5; DLBY 82

Booth, Wayne C(layson) 1921- ..... **CLC 24**
    See also CA 1-4R; CAAS 5; CANR 3;
    DLB 67

Borchert, Wolfgang 1921-1947 ..... **TCLC 5**
    See also CA 104; DLB 69, 124

Borges, Jorge Luis
    1899-1986 ... **CLC 1, 2, 3, 4, 6, 8, 9, 10,
                      13, 19, 44, 48; SSC 4**
    See also CA 21-24R; CANR 19, 33;
    DLB 113; DLBY 86; HW; MTCW; WLC

Borowski, Tadeusz 1922-1951...... **TCLC 9**
    See also CA 106

Borrow, George (Henry)
    1803-1881 .... **NCLC 9**
    See also DLB 21, 55

Bosman, Herman Charles
    1905-1951 .... **TCLC 49**

Bosschere, Jean de 1878(?)-1953... **TCLC 19**
    See also CA 115

Boswell, James 1740-1795.......... **LC 4**
    See also CDBLB 1660-1789; DLB 104;
    WLC

Bottoms, David 1949-............. **CLC 53**
    See also CA 105; CANR 22; DLB 120;
    DLBY 83

Boucolon, Maryse 1937-
    See Conde, Maryse
    See also CA 110; CANR 30

Bourget, Paul (Charles Joseph)
    1852-1935 .... **TCLC 12**
    See also CA 107; DLB 123

Bronte, Anne 1820-1849......... **NCLC 4**
See also DLB 21

Bronte, Charlotte
    1816-1855 .... **NCLC 3, 8, 33**
See also CDBLB 1832-1890; DLB 21; WLC

Bronte, (Jane) Emily
    1818-1848 .... **NCLC 16, 35**
See also CDBLB 1832-1890; DLB 21, 32;
    WLC

Brooke, Frances 1724-1789 .... **LC 6**
See also DLB 39, 99

Brooke, Henry 1703(?)-1783 .... **LC 1**
See also DLB 39

Brooke, Rupert (Chawner)
    1887-1915 .... **TCLC 2, 7**
See also CA 104; 132; CDBLB 1914-1945;
    DLB 19; MTCW; WLC

Brooke-Haven, P.
See Wodehouse, P(elham) G(renville)

Brooke-Rose, Christine 1926-...... **CLC 40**
See also CA 13-16R; DLB 14

Brookner, Anita 1928-...... **CLC 32, 34, 51**
See also CA 114; 120; CANR 37; DLBY 87;
    MTCW

Brooks, Cleanth 1906-........... **CLC 24**
See also CA 17-20R; CANR 33, 35;
    DLB 63; MTCW

Brooks, George
See Baum, L(yman) Frank

Brooks, Gwendolyn
    1917-.......... **CLC 1, 2, 4, 5, 15, 49**
See also AITN 1; BLC 1; BW; CA 1-4R;
    CANR 1, 27; CDALB 1941-1968;
    CLR 27; DLB 5, 76; MTCW; SATA 6;
    WLC

Brooks, Mel.................... **CLC 12**
See also Kaminsky, Melvin
See also DLB 26

Brooks, Peter 1938-.............. **CLC 34**
See also CA 45-48; CANR 1

Brooks, Van Wyck 1886-1963...... **CLC 29**
See also CA 1-4R; CANR 6; DLB 45, 63,
    103

Brophy, Brigid (Antonia)
    1929-................. **CLC 6, 11, 29**
See also CA 5-8R; CAAS 4; CANR 25;
    DLB 14; MTCW

Brosman, Catharine Savage 1934-.... **CLC 9**
See also CA 61-64; CANR 21

Brother Antoninus
See Everson, William (Oliver)

Broughton, T(homas) Alan 1936- ... **CLC 19**
See also CA 45-48; CANR 2, 23

Broumas, Olga 1949-.......... **CLC 10, 73**
See also CA 85-88; CANR 20

Brown, Charles Brockden
    1771-1810 .... **NCLC 22**
See also CDALB 1640-1865; DLB 37, 59,
    73

Brown, Christy 1932-1981........ **CLC 63**
See also CA 105; 104; DLB 14

Brown, Claude 1937-............ **CLC 30**
See also AAYA 7; BLC 1; BW; CA 73-76

Brown, Dee (Alexander) 1908- .. **CLC 18, 47**
See also CA 13-16R; CAAS 6; CANR 11;
    DLBY 80; MTCW; SATA 5

Brown, George
See Wertmueller, Lina

Brown, George Douglas
    1869-1902 .... **TCLC 28**

Brown, George Mackay 1921-.... **CLC 5, 48**
See also CA 21-24R; CAAS 6; CANR 12,
    37; DLB 14, 27; MTCW; SATA 35

Brown, (William) Larry 1951-...... **CLC 73**
See also CA 130; 134

Brown, Moses
See Barrett, William (Christopher)

Brown, Rita Mae 1944-........ **CLC 18, 43**
See also CA 45-48; CANR 2, 11, 35;
    MTCW

Brown, Roderick (Langmere) Haig-
See Haig-Brown, Roderick (Langmere)

Brown, Rosellen 1939-............ **CLC 32**
See also CA 77-80; CAAS 10; CANR 14

Brown, Sterling Allen
    1901-1989 .... **CLC 1, 23, 59**
See also BLC 1; BW; CA 85-88; 127;
    CANR 26; DLB 48, 51, 63; MTCW

Brown, Will
See Ainsworth, William Harrison

Brown, William Wells
    1813-1884 .... **NCLC 2; DC 1**
See also BLC 1; DLB 3, 50

Browne, (Clyde) Jackson 1948(?)-... **CLC 21**
See also CA 120

Browning, Elizabeth Barrett
    1806-1861 .... **NCLC 1, 16; PC 6**
See also CDBLB 1832-1890; DLB 32; WLC

Browning, Robert
    1812-1889 .... **NCLC 19; PC 2**
See also CDBLB 1832-1890; DLB 32;
    YABC 1

Browning, Tod 1882-1962 .... **CLC 16**
See also CA 117

Bruccoli, Matthew J(oseph) 1931- .. **CLC 34**
See also CA 9-12R; CANR 7; DLB 103

Bruce, Lenny.................... **CLC 21**
See also Schneider, Leonard Alfred

Bruin, John
See Brutus, Dennis

Brulls, Christian
See Simenon, Georges (Jacques Christian)

Brunner, John (Kilian Houston)
    1934-..................... **CLC 8, 10**
See also CA 1-4R; CAAS 8; CANR 2, 37;
    MTCW

Brutus, Dennis 1924-............. **CLC 43**
See also BLC 1; BW; CA 49-52; CAAS 14;
    CANR 2, 27; DLB 117

Bryan, C(ourtlandt) D(ixon) B(arnes)
    1936-..................... **CLC 29**
See also CA 73-76; CANR 13

Bryan, Michael
See Moore, Brian

Bryant, William Cullen
    1794-1878 .... **NCLC 6**
See also CDALB 1640-1865; DLB 3, 43, 59

Bryusov, Valery Yakovlevich
    1873-1924 .... **TCLC 10**
See also CA 107

Buchan, John 1875-1940 .... **TCLC 41**
See also CA 108; DLB 34, 70; YABC 2

Buchanan, George 1506-1582 .... **LC 4**

Buchheim, Lothar-Guenther 1918- ... **CLC 6**
See also CA 85-88

Buchner, (Karl) Georg
    1813-1837 .... **NCLC 26**

Buchwald, Art(hur) 1925-.......... **CLC 33**
See also AITN 1; CA 5-8R; CANR 21;
    MTCW; SATA 10

Buck, Pearl S(ydenstricker)
    1892-1973 .... **CLC 7, 11, 18**
See also AITN 1; CA 1-4R; 41-44R;
    CANR 1, 34; DLB 9, 102; MTCW;
    SATA 1, 25

Buckler, Ernest 1908-1984......... **CLC 13**
See also CA 11-12; 114; CAP 1; DLB 68;
    SATA 47

Buckley, Vincent (Thomas)
    1925-1988 .... **CLC 57**
See also CA 101

Buckley, William F(rank) Jr.
    1925-.................. **CLC 7, 18, 37**
See also AITN 1; CA 1-4R; CANR 1, 24;
    DLBY 80; MTCW

Buechner, (Carl) Frederick
    1926-................. **CLC 2, 4, 6, 9**
See also CA 13-16R; CANR 11, 39;
    DLBY 80; MTCW

Buell, John (Edward) 1927-........ **CLC 10**
See also CA 1-4R; DLB 53

Buero Vallejo, Antonio 1916- ... **CLC 15, 46**
See also CA 106; CANR 24; HW; MTCW

Bufalino, Gesualdo 1920(?)-........ **CLC 74**

Bugayev, Boris Nikolayevich 1880-1934
See Bely, Andrey
See also CA 104

Bukowski, Charles 1920-.... **CLC 2, 5, 9, 41**
See also CA 17-20R; CANR 40; DLB 5,
    130; MTCW

Bulgakov, Mikhail (Afanas'evich)
    1891-1940 .... **TCLC 2, 16**
See also CA 105

Bullins, Ed 1935-.............. **CLC 1, 5, 7**
See also BLC 1; BW; CA 49-52; CAAS 16;
    CANR 24; DLB 7, 38; MTCW

Bulwer-Lytton, Edward (George Earle Lytton)
    1803-1873 .... **NCLC 1**
See also DLB 21

Bunin, Ivan Alexeyevich
    1870-1953 .... **TCLC 6; SSC 5**
See also CA 104

Bunting, Basil 1900-1985.... **CLC 10, 39, 47**
See also CA 53-56; 115; CANR 7; DLB 20

Bunuel, Luis 1900-1983 .... **CLC 16**
See also CA 101; 110; CANR 32; HW

Bunyan, John 1628-1688 .... **LC 4**
See also CDBLB 1660-1789; DLB 39; WLC

Burford, Eleanor
See Hibbert, Eleanor Burford

Burgess, Anthony
  1917- . . . . . **CLC 1, 2, 4, 5, 8, 10, 13, 15,**
                      22, 40, 62
  See also Wilson, John (Anthony) Burgess
  See also AITN 1; CDBLB 1960 to Present;
  DLB 14

Burke, Edmund 1729(?)-1797. . . . . **LC 7**
  See also DLB 104; WLC

Burke, Kenneth (Duva) 1897- . . . . **CLC 2, 24**
  See also CA 5-8R; CANR 39; DLB 45, 63;
  MTCW

Burke, Leda
  See Garnett, David

Burke, Ralph
  See Silverberg, Robert

Burney, Fanny 1752-1840 . . . . **NCLC 12**
  See also DLB 39

Burns, Robert 1759-1796. . . . . . **LC 3; PC 6**
  See also CDBLB 1789-1832; DLB 109;
  WLC

Burns, Tex
  See L'Amour, Louis (Dearborn)

Burnshaw, Stanley 1906- . . . . . **CLC 3, 13, 44**
  See also CA 9-12R; DLB 48

Burr, Anne 1937- . . . . **CLC 6**
  See also CA 25-28R

Burroughs, Edgar Rice
  1875-1950 . . . . **TCLC 2, 32**
  See also CA 104; 132; DLB 8; MTCW;
  SATA 41

Burroughs, William S(eward)
  1914- . . . . **CLC 1, 2, 5, 15, 22, 42, 75**
  See also AITN 2; CA 9-12R; CANR 20;
  DLB 2, 8, 16; DLBY 81; MTCW; WLC

Busch, Frederick 1941- . . . **CLC 7, 10, 18, 47**
  See also CA 33-36R; CAAS 1; DLB 6

Bush, Ronald 1946- . . . . **CLC 34**
  See also CA 136

Bustos, F(rancisco)
  See Borges, Jorge Luis

Bustos Domecq, H(onorio)
  See Bioy Casares, Adolfo; Borges, Jorge
  Luis

Butler, Octavia E(stelle) 1947- . . . . . **CLC 38**
  See also BW; CA 73-76; CANR 12, 24, 38;
  DLB 33; MTCW

Butler, Samuel 1612-1680 . . . . **LC 16**
  See also DLB 101, 126

Butler, Samuel 1835-1902 . . . . . . **TCLC 1, 33**
  See also CA 104; CDBLB 1890-1914;
  DLB 18, 57; WLC

Butler, Walter C.
  See Faust, Frederick (Schiller)

Butor, Michel (Marie Francois)
  1926- . . . . **CLC 1, 3, 8, 11, 15**
  See also CA 9-12R; CANR 33; DLB 83;
  MTCW

Buzo, Alexander (John) 1944- . . . . . . **CLC 61**
  See also CA 97-100; CANR 17, 39

Buzzati, Dino 1906-1972 . . . . **CLC 36**
  See also CA 33-36R

Byars, Betsy (Cromer) 1928- . . . . **CLC 35**
  See also CA 33-36R; CANR 18, 36; CLR 1,
  16; DLB 52; MAICYA; MTCW; SAAS 1;
  SATA 4, 46

Byatt, A(ntonia) S(usan Drabble)
  1936- . . . . **CLC 19, 65**
  See also CA 13-16R; CANR 13, 33;
  DLB 14; MTCW

Byrne, David 1952-. . . . . **CLC 26**
  See also CA 127

Byrne, John Keyes 1926-. . . . . **CLC 19**
  See also Leonard, Hugh
  See also CA 102

Byron, George Gordon (Noel)
  1788-1824 . . . . **NCLC 2, 12**
  See also CDBLB 1789-1832; DLB 96, 110;
  WLC

C.3.3.
  See Wilde, Oscar (Fingal O'Flahertie Wills)

Caballero, Fernan 1796-1877. . . . . **NCLC 10**

Cabell, James Branch 1879-1958 . . . **TCLC 6**
  See also CA 105; DLB 9, 78

Cable, George Washington
  1844-1925 . . . . **TCLC 4; SSC 4**
  See also CA 104; DLB 12, 74

Cabral de Melo Neto, Joao 1920-. . . **CLC 76**

Cabrera Infante, G(uillermo)
  1929- . . . . **CLC 5, 25, 45**
  See also CA 85-88; CANR 29; DLB 113;
  HW; MTCW

Cade, Toni
  See Bambara, Toni Cade

Cadmus
  See Buchan, John

Caedmon fl. 658-680. . . . . **CMLC 7**

Caeiro, Alberto
  See Pessoa, Fernando (Antonio Nogueira)

Cage, John (Milton Jr.) 1912-. . . . . . **CLC 41**
  See also CA 13-16R; CANR 9

Cain, G.
  See Cabrera Infante, G(uillermo)

Cain, Guillermo
  See Cabrera Infante, G(uillermo)

Cain, James M(allahan)
  1892-1977 . . . . **CLC 3, 11, 28**
  See also AITN 1; CA 17-20R; 73-76;
  CANR 8, 34; MTCW

Caine, Mark
  See Raphael, Frederic (Michael)

Calderon de la Barca, Pedro
  1600-1681 . . . . **DC 3**

Caldwell, Erskine (Preston)
  1903-1987 . . . . **CLC 1, 8, 14, 50, 60**
  See also AITN 1; CA 1-4R; 121; CAAS 1;
  CANR 2, 33; DLB 9, 86; MTCW

Caldwell, (Janet Miriam) Taylor (Holland)
  1900-1985 . . . . **CLC 2, 28, 39**
  See also CA 5-8R; 116; CANR 5

Calhoun, John Caldwell
  1782-1850 . . . . **NCLC 15**
  See also DLB 3

Calisher, Hortense 1911-. . . . **CLC 2, 4, 8, 38**
  See also CA 1-4R; CANR 1, 22; DLB 2;
  MTCW

Callaghan, Morley Edward
  1903-1990 . . . . **CLC 3, 14, 41, 65**
  See also CA 9-12R; 132; CANR 33;
  DLB 68; MTCW

Calvino, Italo
  1923-1985 . . . . **CLC 5, 8, 11, 22, 33, 39,**
                      73; SSC 3
  See also CA 85-88; 116; CANR 23; MTCW

Cameron, Carey 1952-. . . . . **CLC 59**
  See also CA 135

Cameron, Peter 1959-. . . . . **CLC 44**
  See also CA 125

Campana, Dino 1885-1932. . . . . . . **TCLC 20**
  See also CA 117; DLB 114

Campbell, John W(ood Jr.)
  1910-1971 . . . . **CLC 32**
  See also CA 21-22; 29-32R; CANR 34;
  CAP 2; DLB 8; MTCW

Campbell, Joseph 1904-1987 . . . . **CLC 69**
  See also AAYA 3; BEST 89:2; CA 1-4R;
  124; CANR 3, 28; MTCW

Campbell, (John) Ramsey 1946- . . . . **CLC 42**
  See also CA 57-60; CANR 7

Campbell, (Ignatius) Roy (Dunnachie)
  1901-1957 . . . . **TCLC 5**
  See also CA 104; DLB 20

Campbell, Thomas 1777-1844 . . . . **NCLC 19**
  See also DLB 93

Campbell, Wilfred . . . . **TCLC 9**
  See also Campbell, William

Campbell, William 1858(?)-1918
  See Campbell, Wilfred
  See also CA 106; DLB 92

Campos, Alvaro de
  See Pessoa, Fernando (Antonio Nogueira)

Camus, Albert
  1913-1960 . . . **CLC 1, 2, 4, 9, 11, 14, 32,**
                      63, 69; DC 2; SSC 9
  See also CA 89-92; DLB 72; MTCW; WLC

Canby, Vincent 1924-. . . . . **CLC 13**
  See also CA 81-84

Cancale
  See Desnos, Robert

Canetti, Elias 1905- . . . . . . **CLC 3, 14, 25, 75**
  See also CA 21-24R; CANR 23; DLB 85,
  124; MTCW

Canin, Ethan 1960-. . . . . **CLC 55**
  See also CA 131; 135

Cannon, Curt
  See Hunter, Evan

Cape, Judith
  See Page, P(atricia) K(athleen)

Capek, Karel
  1890-1938 . . . . **TCLC 6, 37; DC 1**
  See also CA 104; WLC

Capote, Truman
  1924-1984 . . . . . **CLC 1, 3, 8, 13, 19, 34,**
                      38, 58; SSC 2
  See also CA 5-8R; 113; CANR 18;
  CDALB 1941-1968; DLB 2; DLBY 80,
  84; MTCW; WLC

Capra, Frank 1897-1991. . . . . **CLC 16**
  See also CA 61-64; 135

Caputo, Philip 1941-. . . . . **CLC 32**
  See also CA 73-76; CANR 40

Card, Orson Scott 1951- . . . . **CLC 44, 47, 50**
  See also CA 102; CANR 27; MTCW

Cardenal (Martinez), Ernesto
1925- . . . . **CLC 31**
See also CA 49-52; CANR 2, 32; HW;
MTCW

Carducci, Giosue 1835-1907. . . . . . **TCLC 32**

Carew, Thomas 1595(?)-1640. . . . . . . **LC 13**
See also DLB 126

Carey, Ernestine Gilbreth 1908- . . . . **CLC 17**
See also CA 5-8R; SATA 2

Carey, Peter 1943- . . . . **CLC 40, 55**
See also CA 123; 127; MTCW

Carleton, William 1794-1869. . . . . . **NCLC 3**

Carlisle, Henry (Coffin) 1926- . . . . . . **CLC 33**
See also CA 13-16R; CANR 15

Carlsen, Chris
See Holdstock, Robert P.

Carlson, Ron(ald F.) 1947- . . . . **CLC 54**
See also CA 105; CANR 27

Carlyle, Thomas 1795-1881 . . . . . . **NCLC 22**
See also CDBLB 1789-1832; DLB 55

Carman, (William) Bliss
1861-1929 . . . . **TCLC 7**
See also CA 104; DLB 92

Carossa, Hans 1878-1956. . . . . **TCLC 48**
See also DLB 66

Carpenter, Don(ald Richard)
1931- . . . . **CLC 41**
See also CA 45-48; CANR 1

Carpentier (y Valmont), Alejo
1904-1980 . . . . **CLC 8, 11, 38**
See also CA 65-68; 97-100; CANR 11;
DLB 113; HW

Carr, Emily 1871-1945. . . . . **TCLC 32**
See also DLB 68

Carr, John Dickson 1906-1977 . . . . . . **CLC 3**
See also CA 49-52; 69-72; CANR 3, 33;
MTCW

Carr, Philippa
See Hibbert, Eleanor Burford

Carr, Virginia Spencer 1929- . . . . **CLC 34**
See also CA 61-64; DLB 111

Carrier, Roch 1937- . . . . **CLC 13**
See also CA 130; DLB 53

Carroll, James P. 1943(?)- . . . . **CLC 38**
See also CA 81-84

Carroll, Jim 1951- . . . . **CLC 35**
See also CA 45-48

Carroll, Lewis . . . . **NCLC 2**
See also Dodgson, Charles Lutwidge
See also CDBLB 1832-1890; CLR 2, 18;
DLB 18; WLC

Carroll, Paul Vincent 1900-1968. . . . **CLC 10**
See also CA 9-12R; 25-28R; DLB 10

Carruth, Hayden 1921- . . . . **CLC 4, 7, 10, 18**
See also CA 9-12R; CANR 4, 38; DLB 5;
MTCW; SATA 47

Carson, Rachel Louise 1907-1964 . . . **CLC 71**
See also CA 77-80; CANR 35; MTCW;
SATA 23

Carter, Angela (Olive)
1940-1992 . . . . **CLC 5, 41, 76**
See also CA 53-56; 136; CANR 12, 36;
DLB 14; MTCW; SATA 66; SATO 70

Carter, Nick
See Smith, Martin Cruz

Carver, Raymond
1938-1988 . . . **CLC 22, 36, 53, 55; SSC 8**
See also CA 33-36R; 126; CANR 17, 34;
DLB 130; DLBY 84, 88; MTCW

Cary, (Arthur) Joyce (Lunel)
1888-1957 . . . . **TCLC 1, 29**
See also CA 104; CDBLB 1914-1945;
DLB 15, 100

Casanova de Seingalt, Giovanni Jacopo
1725-1798 . . . . **LC 13**

Casares, Adolfo Bioy
See Bioy Casares, Adolfo

Casely-Hayford, J(oseph) E(phraim)
1866-1930 . . . . **TCLC 24**
See also BLC 1; CA 123

Casey, John (Dudley) 1939- . . . . **CLC 59**
See also BEST 90:2; CA 69-72; CANR 23

Casey, Michael 1947- . . . . **CLC 2**
See also CA 65-68; DLB 5

Casey, Patrick
See Thurman, Wallace (Henry)

Casey, Warren (Peter) 1935-1988 . . . **CLC 12**
See also CA 101; 127

Casona, Alejandro . . . . **CLC 49**
See also Alvarez, Alejandro Rodriguez

Cassavetes, John 1929-1989. . . . . . . **CLC 20**
See also CA 85-88; 127

Cassill, R(onald) V(erlin) 1919- . . . **CLC 4, 23**
See also CA 9-12R; CAAS 1; CANR 7;
DLB 6

Cassity, (Allen) Turner 1929- . . . . **CLC 6, 42**
See also CA 17-20R; CAAS 8; CANR 11;
DLB 105

Castaneda, Carlos 1931(?)- . . . . **CLC 12**
See also CA 25-28R; CANR 32; HW;
MTCW

Castedo, Elena 1937- . . . . **CLC 65**
See also CA 132

Castedo-Ellerman, Elena
See Castedo, Elena

Castellanos, Rosario 1925-1974. . . . . **CLC 66**
See also CA 131; 53-56; DLB 113; HW

Castelvetro, Lodovico 1505-1571. . . . . **LC 12**

Castiglione, Baldassare 1478-1529 . . . **LC 12**

Castle, Robert
See Hamilton, Edmond

Castro, Guillen de 1569-1631. . . . . . . **LC 19**

Castro, Rosalia de 1837-1885 . . . . . **NCLC 3**

Cather, Willa
See Cather, Willa Sibert

Cather, Willa Sibert
1873-1947 . . . . . . **TCLC 1, 11, 31; SSC 2**
See also CA 104; 128; CDALB 1865-1917;
DLB 9, 54, 78; DLBD 1; MTCW;
SATA 30; WLC

Catton, (Charles) Bruce
1899-1978 . . . . **CLC 35**
See also AITN 1; CA 5-8R; 81-84;
CANR 7; DLB 17; SATA 2, 24

Cauldwell, Frank
See King, Francis (Henry)

Caunitz, William J. 1933- . . . . **CLC 34**
See also BEST 89:3; CA 125; 130

Causley, Charles (Stanley) 1917- . . . . . **CLC 7**
See also CA 9-12R; CANR 5, 35; CLR 30;
DLB 27; MTCW; SATA 3, 66

Caute, David 1936- . . . . **CLC 29**
See also CA 1-4R; CAAS 4; CANR 1, 33;
DLB 14

Cavafy, C(onstantine) P(eter) . . . . . . **TCLC 2, 7**
See also Kavafis, Konstantinos Petrou

Cavallo, Evelyn
See Spark, Muriel (Sarah)

Cavanna, Betty . . . . **CLC 12**
See also Harrison, Elizabeth Cavanna
See also MAICYA; SAAS 4; SATA 1, 30

Caxton, William 1421(?)-1491(?). . . . . **LC 17**

Cayrol, Jean 1911- . . . . **CLC 11**
See also CA 89-92; DLB 83

Cela, Camilo Jose 1916- . . . . . **CLC 4, 13, 59**
See also BEST 90:2; CA 21-24R; CAAS 10;
CANR 21, 32; DLBY 89; HW; MTCW

Celan, Paul . . . . **CLC 53**
See also Antschel, Paul
See also DLB 69

Celine, Louis-Ferdinand
. . . . **CLC 1, 3, 4, 7, 9, 15, 47**
See also Destouches, Louis-Ferdinand
See also DLB 72

Cellini, Benvenuto 1500-1571 . . . . **LC 7**

Cendrars, Blaise
See Sauser-Hall, Frederic

Cernuda (y Bidon), Luis
1902-1963 . . . . **CLC 54**
See also CA 131; 89-92; HW

Cervantes (Saavedra), Miguel de
1547-1616 . . . . **LC 6**
See also WLC

Cesaire, Aime (Fernand) 1913- . . **CLC 19, 32**
See also BLC 1; BW; CA 65-68; CANR 24;
MTCW

Chabon, Michael 1965(?)- . . . . **CLC 55**
See also CA 139

Chabrol, Claude 1930- . . . . **CLC 16**
See also CA 110

Challans, Mary 1905-1983
See Renault, Mary
See also CA 81-84; 111; SATA 23, 36

Challis, George
See Faust, Frederick (Schiller)

Chambers, Aidan 1934- . . . . **CLC 35**
See also CA 25-28R; CANR 12, 31;
MAICYA; SAAS 12; SATA 1, 69

Chambers, James 1948-
See Cliff, Jimmy
See also CA 124

Chambers, Jessie
See Lawrence, D(avid) H(erbert Richards)

Chambers, Robert W. 1865-1933. . . **TCLC 41**

Chandler, Raymond (Thornton)
1888-1959 . . . . **TCLC 1, 7**
See also CA 104; 129; CDALB 1929-1941;
DLBD 6; MTCW

Chang, Jung 1952- . . . . **CLC 71**

Channing, William Ellery
    1780-1842 .... **NCLC 17**
    See also DLB 1, 59

Chaplin, Charles Spencer
    1889-1977 .... **CLC 16**
    See also Chaplin, Charlie
    See also CA 81-84; 73-76

Chaplin, Charlie
    See Chaplin, Charles Spencer
    See also DLB 44

Chapman, George 1559(?)-1634...... **LC 22**
    See also DLB 62, 121

Chapman, Graham 1941-1989 ...... **CLC 21**
    See also Monty Python
    See also CA 116; 129; CANR 35

Chapman, John Jay 1862-1933 ..... **TCLC 7**
    See also CA 104

Chapman, Walker
    See Silverberg, Robert

Chappell, Fred (Davis) 1936-....... **CLC 40**
    See also CA 5-8R; CAAS 4; CANR 8, 33;
    DLB 6, 105

Char, Rene(-Emile)
    1907-1988 .... **CLC 9, 11, 14, 55**
    See also CA 13-16R; 124; CANR 32;
    MTCW

Charby, Jay
    See Ellison, Harlan

Chardin, Pierre Teilhard de
    See Teilhard de Chardin, (Marie Joseph)
    Pierre

Charles I 1600-1649 .... **LC 13**

Charyn, Jerome 1937- .... **CLC 5, 8, 18**
    See also CA 5-8R; CAAS 1; CANR 7;
    DLBY 83; MTCW

Chase, Mary (Coyle) 1907-1981 ...... **DC 1**
    See also CA 77-80; 105; SATA 17, 29

Chase, Mary Ellen 1887-1973....... **CLC 2**
    See also CA 13-16; 41-44R; CAP 1;
    SATA 10

Chase, Nicholas
    See Hyde, Anthony

Chateaubriand, Francois Rene de
    1768-1848 .... **NCLC 3**
    See also DLB 119

Chatterje, Sarat Chandra 1876-1936(?)
    See Chatterji, Saratchandra
    See also CA 109

Chatterji, Bankim Chandra
    1838-1894 .... **NCLC 19**

Chatterji, Saratchandra .... **TCLC 13**
    See also Chatterje, Sarat Chandra

Chatterton, Thomas 1752-1770 .... **LC 3**
    See also DLB 109

Chatwin, (Charles) Bruce
    1940-1989 .... **CLC 28, 57, 59**
    See also AAYA 4; BEST 90:1; CA 85-88;
    127

Chaucer, Daniel
    See Ford, Ford Madox

Chaucer, Geoffrey 1340(?)-1400 ..... **LC 17**
    See also CDBLB Before 1660

Chaviaras, Strates 1935-
    See Haviaras, Stratis
    See also CA 105

Chayefsky, Paddy .... **CLC 23**
    See also Chayefsky, Sidney
    See also DLB 7, 44; DLBY 81

Chayefsky, Sidney 1923-1981
    See Chayefsky, Paddy
    See also CA 9-12R; 104; CANR 18

Chedid, Andree 1920-............ **CLC 47**

Cheever, John
    1912-1982 ..... **CLC 3, 7, 8, 11, 15, 25,
        64; SSC 1**
    See also CA 5-8R; 106; CABS 1; CANR 5,
    27; CDALB 1941-1968; DLB 2, 102;
    DLBY 80, 82; MTCW; WLC

Cheever, Susan 1943-.......... **CLC 18, 48**
    See also CA 103; CANR 27; DLBY 82

Chekhonte, Antosha
    See Chekhov, Anton (Pavlovich)

Chekhov, Anton (Pavlovich)
    1860-1904 ...... **TCLC 3, 10, 31; SSC 2**
    See also CA 104; 124; WLC

Chernyshevsky, Nikolay Gavrilovich
    1828-1889 .... **NCLC 1**

Cherry, Carolyn Janice 1942-
    See Cherryh, C. J.
    See also CA 65-68; CANR 10

Cherryh, C. J. .... **CLC 35**
    See also Cherry, Carolyn Janice
    See also DLBY 80

Chesnutt, Charles W(addell)
    1858-1932 .... **TCLC 5, 39; SSC 7**
    See also BLC 1; BW; CA 106; 125; DLB 12,
    50, 78; MTCW

Chester, Alfred 1929(?)-1971....... **CLC 49**
    See also CA 33-36R; DLB 130

Chesterton, G(ilbert) K(eith)
    1874-1936 .... **TCLC 1, 6; SSC 1**
    See also CA 104; 132; CDBLB 1914-1945;
    DLB 10, 19, 34, 70, 98; MTCW;
    SATA 27

Chiang Pin-chin 1904-1986
    See Ding Ling
    See also CA 118

Ch'ien Chung-shu 1910-........... **CLC 22**
    See also CA 130; MTCW

Child, L. Maria
    See Child, Lydia Maria

Child, Lydia Maria 1802-1880 .... **NCLC 6**
    See also DLB 1, 74; SATA 67

Child, Mrs.
    See Child, Lydia Maria

Child, Philip 1898-1978 .... **CLC 19, 68**
    See also CA 13-14; CAP 1; SATA 47

Childress, Alice 1920-.......... **CLC 12, 15**
    See also AAYA 8; BLC 1; BW; CA 45-48;
    CANR 3, 27; CLR 14; DLB 7, 38;
    MAICYA; MTCW; SATA 7, 48

Chislett, (Margaret) Anne 1943-.... **CLC 34**

Chitty, Thomas Willes 1926-....... **CLC 11**
    See also Hinde, Thomas
    See also CA 5-8R

Chomette, Rene Lucien 1898-1981 .. **CLC 20**
    See also Clair, Rene
    See also CA 103

Chopin, Kate .... **TCLC 5, 14; SSC 8**
    See also Chopin, Katherine
    See also CDALB 1865-1917; DLB 12, 78

Chopin, Katherine 1851-1904
    See Chopin, Kate
    See also CA 104; 122

Chretien de Troyes
    c. 12th cent. - .... **CMLC 10**

Christie
    See Ichikawa, Kon

Christie, Agatha (Mary Clarissa)
    1890-1976 ...... **CLC 1, 6, 8, 12, 39, 48**
    See also AAYA 9; AITN 1, 2; CA 17-20R;
    61-64; CANR 10, 37; CDBLB 1914-1945;
    DLB 13, 77; MTCW; SATA 36

Christie, (Ann) Philippa
    See Pearce, Philippa
    See also CA 5-8R; CANR 4

Christine de Pizan 1365(?)-1431(?) .... **LC 9**

Chubb, Elmer
    See Masters, Edgar Lee

Chulkov, Mikhail Dmitrievich
    1743-1792 .... **LC 2**

Churchill, Caryl 1938- .... **CLC 31, 55**
    See also CA 102; CANR 22; DLB 13;
    MTCW

Churchill, Charles 1731-1764........ **LC 3**
    See also DLB 109

Chute, Carolyn 1947-............ **CLC 39**
    See also CA 123

Ciardi, John (Anthony)
    1916-1986 .... **CLC 10, 40, 44**
    See also CA 5-8R; 118; CAAS 2; CANR 5,
    33; CLR 19; DLB 5; DLBY 86;
    MAICYA; MTCW; SATA 1, 46, 65

Cicero, Marcus Tullius
    106B.C.-43B.C. .... **CMLC 3**

Cimino, Michael 1943-........... **CLC 16**
    See also CA 105

Cioran, E(mil) M. 1911-........... **CLC 64**
    See also CA 25-28R

Cisneros, Sandra 1954-............ **CLC 69**
    See also AAYA 9; CA 131; DLB 122; HW

Clair, Rene .... **CLC 20**
    See also Chomette, Rene Lucien

Clampitt, Amy 1920- .... **CLC 32**
    See also CA 110; CANR 29; DLB 105

Clancy, Thomas L. Jr. 1947-
    See Clancy, Tom
    See also CA 125; 131; MTCW

Clancy, Tom .... **CLC 45**
    See also Clancy, Thomas L. Jr.
    See also AAYA 9; BEST 89:1, 90:1

Clare, John 1793-1864 .... **NCLC 9**
    See also DLB 55, 96

Clarin
    See Alas (y Urena), Leopoldo (Enrique
    Garcia)

Clark, (Robert) Brian 1932-........ **CLC 29**
    See also CA 41-44R

Clark, Eleanor 1913- .... **CLC 5, 19**
See also CA 9-12R; DLB 6

Clark, J. P.
See Clark, John Pepper
See also DLB 117

Clark, John Pepper 1935- .... **CLC 38**
See also Clark, J. P.
See also BLC 1; BW; CA 65-68; CANR 16

Clark, M. R.
See Clark, Mavis Thorpe

Clark, Mavis Thorpe 1909- .... **CLC 12**
See also CA 57-60; CANR 8, 37; CLR 30;
MAICYA; SAAS 5; SATA 8

Clark, Walter Van Tilburg
1909-1971 .... **CLC 28**
See also CA 9-12R; 33-36R; DLB 9;
SATA 8

Clarke, Arthur C(harles)
1917- ...... **CLC 1, 4, 13, 18, 35; SSC 3**
See also AAYA 4; CA 1-4R; CANR 2, 28;
MAICYA; MTCW; SATA 13, 70

Clarke, Austin C(hesterfield)
1934- .... **CLC 8, 53**
See also BLC 1; BW; CA 25-28R;
CAAS 16; CANR 14, 32; DLB 53, 125

Clarke, Austin 1896-1974........ **CLC 6, 9**
See also CA 29-32; 49-52; CAP 2; DLB 10,
20

Clarke, Gillian 1937- .... **CLC 61**
See also CA 106; DLB 40

Clarke, Marcus (Andrew Hislop)
1846-1881 .... **NCLC 19**

Clarke, Shirley 1925- .... **CLC 16**

Clash, The .... **CLC 30**
See also Headon, (Nicky) Topper; Jones,
Mick; Simonon, Paul; Strummer, Joe

Claudel, Paul (Louis Charles Marie)
1868-1955 .... **TCLC 2, 10**
See also CA 104

Clavell, James (duMaresq)
1925- .... **CLC 6, 25**
See also CA 25-28R; CANR 26; MTCW

Cleaver, (Leroy) Eldridge 1935- .... **CLC 30**
See also BLC 1; BW; CA 21-24R;
CANR 16

Cleese, John (Marwood) 1939- ..... **CLC 21**
See also Monty Python
See also CA 112; 116; CANR 35; MTCW

Cleishbotham, Jebediah
See Scott, Walter

Cleland, John 1710-1789 .... **LC 2**
See also DLB 39

Clemens, Samuel Langhorne 1835-1910
See Twain, Mark
See also CA 104; 135; CDALB 1865-1917;
DLB 11, 12, 23, 64, 74; MAICYA;
YABC 2

Clerihew, E.
See Bentley, E(dmund) C(lerihew)

Clerk, N. W.
See Lewis, C(live) S(taples)

Cliff, Jimmy..................... **CLC 21**
See also Chambers, James

Clifton, (Thelma) Lucille
1936- .... **CLC 19, 66**
See also BLC 1; BW; CA 49-52; CANR 2,
24; CLR 5; DLB 5, 41; MAICYA;
MTCW; SATA 20, 69

Clinton, Dirk
See Silverberg, Robert

Clough, Arthur Hugh 1819-1861 .. **NCLC 27**
See also DLB 32

Clutha, Janet Paterson Frame 1924-
See Frame, Janet
See also CA 1-4R; CANR 2, 36; MTCW

Clyne, Terence
See Blatty, William Peter

Cobalt, Martin
See Mayne, William (James Carter)

Coburn, D(onald) L(ee) 1938- ...... **CLC 10**
See also CA 89-92

Cocteau, Jean (Maurice Eugene Clement)
1889-1963 .... **CLC 1, 8, 15, 16, 43**
See also CA 25-28; CANR 40; CAP 2;
DLB 65; MTCW; WLC

Codrescu, Andrei 1946- .... **CLC 46**
See also CA 33-36R; CANR 13, 34

Coe, Max
See Bourne, Randolph S(illiman)

Coe, Tucker
See Westlake, Donald E(dwin)

Coetzee, J(ohn) M(ichael)
1940- .... **CLC 23, 33, 66**
See also CA 77-80; MTCW

Cohen, Arthur A(llen)
1928-1986 .... **CLC 7, 31**
See also CA 1-4R; 120; CANR 1, 17;
DLB 28

Cohen, Leonard (Norman)
1934- .... **CLC 3, 38**
See also CA 21-24R; CANR 14; DLB 53;
MTCW

Cohen, Matt 1942- .... **CLC 19**
See also CA 61-64; CANR 40; DLB 53

Cohen-Solal, Annie 19(?)- .... **CLC 50**

Colegate, Isabel 1931- .... **CLC 36**
See also CA 17-20R; CANR 8, 22; DLB 14;
MTCW

Coleman, Emmett
See Reed, Ishmael

Coleridge, Samuel Taylor
1772-1834 .... **NCLC 9**
See also CDBLB 1789-1832; DLB 93, 107;
WLC

Coleridge, Sara 1802-1852 ...... **NCLC 31**

Coles, Don 1928- .... **CLC 46**
See also CA 115; CANR 38

Colette, (Sidonie-Gabrielle)
1873-1954 ...... **TCLC 1, 5, 16; SSC 10**
See also CA 104; 131; DLB 65; MTCW

Collett, (Jacobine) Camilla (Wergeland)
1813-1895 .... **NCLC 22**

Collier, Christopher 1930- .... **CLC 30**
See also CA 33-36R; CANR 13, 33;
MAICYA; SATA 16, 70

Collier, James L(incoln) 1928- ..... **CLC 30**
See also CA 9-12R; CANR 4, 33;
MAICYA; SATA 8, 70

Collier, Jeremy 1650-1726.......... **LC 6**

Collins, Hunt
See Hunter, Evan

Collins, Linda 1931- .... **CLC 44**
See also CA 125

Collins, (William) Wilkie
1824-1889 .... **NCLC 1, 18**
See also CDBLB 1832-1890; DLB 18, 70

Collins, William 1721-1759 .... **LC 4**
See also DLB 109

Colman, George
See Glassco, John

Colt, Winchester Remington
See Hubbard, L(afayette) Ron(ald)

Colter, Cyrus 1910- .... **CLC 58**
See also BW; CA 65-68; CANR 10; DLB 33

Colton, James
See Hansen, Joseph

Colum, Padraic 1881-1972........ **CLC 28**
See also CA 73-76; 33-36R; CANR 35;
MAICYA; MTCW; SATA 15

Colvin, James
See Moorcock, Michael (John)

Colwin, Laurie (E.)
1944-1992 .... **CLC 5, 13, 23**
See also CA 89-92; 139; CANR 20;
DLBY 80; MTCW

Comfort, Alex(ander) 1920-........ **CLC 7**
See also CA 1-4R; CANR 1

Comfort, Montgomery
See Campbell, (John) Ramsey

Compton-Burnett, I(vy)
1884(?)-1969 ...... **CLC 1, 3, 10, 15, 34**
See also CA 1-4R; 25-28R; CANR 4;
DLB 36; MTCW

Comstock, Anthony 1844-1915 .... **TCLC 13**
See also CA 110

Conan Doyle, Arthur
See Doyle, Arthur Conan

Conde, Maryse .... **CLC 52**
See also Boucolon, Maryse

Condon, Richard (Thomas)
1915- .... **CLC 4, 6, 8, 10, 45**
See also BEST 90:3; CA 1-4R; CAAS 1;
CANR 2, 23; MTCW

Congreve, William
1670-1729 .... **LC 5, 21; DC 2**
See also CDBLB 1660-1789; DLB 39, 84;
WLC

Connell, Evan S(helby) Jr.
1924- .... **CLC 4, 6, 45**
See also AAYA 7; CA 1-4R; CAAS 2;
CANR 2, 39; DLB 2; DLBY 81; MTCW

Connelly, Marc(us Cook)
1890-1980 .... **CLC 7**
See also CA 85-88; 102; CANR 30; DLB 7;
DLBY 80; SATA 25

Connor, Ralph .... **TCLC 31**
See also Gordon, Charles William
See also DLB 92

Crockett, Davy
See Crockett, David

Croker, John Wilson 1780-1857 . . **NCLC 10**
See also DLB 110

Crommelynck, Fernand 1885-1970 . . **CLC 75**
See also CA 89-92

Cronin, A(rchibald) J(oseph)
1896-1981 . . . . **CLC 32**
See also CA 1-4R; 102; CANR 5; SATA 25,
47

Cross, Amanda
See Heilbrun, Carolyn G(old)

Crothers, Rachel 1878(?)-1958 . . . . . **TCLC 19**
See also CA 113; DLB 7

Croves, Hal
See Traven, B.

Crowfield, Christopher
See Stowe, Harriet (Elizabeth) Beecher

Crowley, Aleister . . . . **TCLC 7**
See also Crowley, Edward Alexander

Crowley, Edward Alexander 1875-1947
See Crowley, Aleister
See also CA 104

Crowley, John 1942- . . . . **CLC 57**
See also CA 61-64; DLBY 82; SATA 65

Crud
See Crumb, R(obert)

Crumarums
See Crumb, R(obert)

Crumb, R(obert) 1943- . . . . **CLC 17**
See also CA 106

Crumbum
See Crumb, R(obert)

Crumski
See Crumb, R(obert)

Crum the Bum
See Crumb, R(obert)

Crunk
See Crumb, R(obert)

Crustt
See Crumb, R(obert)

Cryer, Gretchen (Kiger) 1935- . . . . . . **CLC 21**
See also CA 114; 123

Csath, Geza 1887-1919 . . . . **TCLC 13**
See also CA 111

Cudlip, David 1933- . . . . **CLC 34**

Cullen, Countee 1903-1946 . . . . . **TCLC 4, 37**
See also BLC 1; BW; CA 108; 124;
CDALB 1917-1929; DLB 4, 48, 51;
MTCW; SATA 18

Cum, R.
See Crumb, R(obert)

Cummings, Bruce F(rederick) 1889-1919
See Barbellion, W. N. P.
See also CA 123

Cummings, E(dward) E(stlin)
1894-1962 . . . . . **CLC 1, 3, 8, 12, 15, 68;**
PC 5
See also CA 73-76; CANR 31;
CDALB 1929-1941; DLB 4, 48; MTCW;
WLC 2

Cunha, Euclides (Rodrigues Pimenta) da
1866-1909 . . . . **TCLC 24**
See also CA 123

Cunningham, E. V.
See Fast, Howard (Melvin)

Cunningham, J(ames) V(incent)
1911-1985 . . . . **CLC 3, 31**
See also CA 1-4R; 115; CANR 1; DLB 5

Cunningham, Julia (Woolfolk)
1916- . . . . **CLC 12**
See also CA 9-12R; CANR 4, 19, 36;
MAICYA; SAAS 2; SATA 1, 26

Cunningham, Michael 1952- . . . . **CLC 34**
See also CA 136

Cunninghame Graham, R(obert) B(ontine)
1852-1936 . . . . **TCLC 19**
See also Graham, R(obert) B(ontine)
Cunninghame
See also CA 119; DLB 98

Currie, Ellen 19(?)- . . . . **CLC 44**

Curtin, Philip
See Lowndes, Marie Adelaide (Belloc)

Curtis, Price
See Ellison, Harlan

Cutrate, Joe
See Spiegelman, Art

Czaczkes, Shmuel Yosef
See Agnon, S(hmuel) Y(osef Halevi)

D. P.
See Wells, H(erbert) G(eorge)

Dabrowska, Maria (Szumska)
1889-1965 . . . . **CLC 15**
See also CA 106

Dabydeen, David 1955- . . . . **CLC 34**
See also BW; CA 125

Dacey, Philip 1939- . . . . **CLC 51**
See also CA 37-40R; CAAS 17; CANR 14,
32; DLB 105

Dagerman, Stig (Halvard)
1923-1954 . . . . **TCLC 17**
See also CA 117

Dahl, Roald 1916-1990 . . . . **CLC 1, 6, 18**
See also CA 1-4R; 133; CANR 6, 32, 37;
CLR 1, 7; MAICYA; MTCW; SATA 1,
26, 73; SATO 65

Dahlberg, Edward 1900-1977 . . . **CLC 1, 7, 14**
See also CA 9-12R; 69-72; CANR 31;
DLB 48; MTCW

Dale, Colin . . . . **TCLC 18**
See also Lawrence, T(homas) E(dward)

Dale, George E.
See Asimov, Isaac

Daly, Elizabeth 1878-1967 . . . . **CLC 52**
See also CA 23-24; 25-28R; CAP 2

Daly, Maureen 1921- . . . . **CLC 17**
See also AAYA 5; CANR 37; MAICYA;
SAAS 1; SATA 2

Daniels, Brett
See Adler, Renata

Dannay, Frederic 1905-1982 . . . . **CLC 11**
See also Queen, Ellery
See also CA 1-4R; 107; CANR 1, 39;
MTCW

D'Annunzio, Gabriele
1863-1938 . . . . **TCLC 6, 40**
See also CA 104

d'Antibes, Germain
See Simenon, Georges (Jacques Christian)

Danvers, Dennis 1947- . . . . **CLC 70**

Danziger, Paula 1944- . . . . **CLC 21**
See also AAYA 4; CA 112; 115; CANR 37;
CLR 20; MAICYA; SATA 30, 36, 63

Dario, Ruben . . . . **TCLC 4**
See also Sarmiento, Felix Ruben Garcia

Darley, George 1795-1846 . . . . **NCLC 2**
See also DLB 96

Daryush, Elizabeth 1887-1977 . . . . **CLC 6, 19**
See also CA 49-52; CANR 3; DLB 20

Daudet, (Louis Marie) Alphonse
1840-1897 . . . . **NCLC 1**
See also DLB 123

Daumal, Rene 1908-1944 . . . . **TCLC 14**
See also CA 114

Davenport, Guy (Mattison Jr.)
1927- . . . . **CLC 6, 14, 38**
See also CA 33-36R; CANR 23; DLB 130

Davidson, Avram 1923-
See Queen, Ellery
See also CA 101; CANR 26; DLB 8

Davidson, Donald (Grady)
1893-1968 . . . . **CLC 2, 13, 19**
See also CA 5-8R; 25-28R; CANR 4;
DLB 45

Davidson, Hugh
See Hamilton, Edmond

Davidson, John 1857-1909 . . . . **TCLC 24**
See also CA 118; DLB 19

Davidson, Sara 1943- . . . . **CLC 9**
See also CA 81-84

Davie, Donald (Alfred)
1922- . . . . **CLC 5, 8, 10, 31**
See also CA 1-4R; CAAS 3; CANR 1;
DLB 27; MTCW

Davies, Ray(mond Douglas) 1944- . . **CLC 21**
See also CA 116

Davies, Rhys 1903-1978 . . . . **CLC 23**
See also CA 9-12R; 81-84; CANR 4

Davies, (William) Robertson
1913- . . . . **CLC 2, 7, 13, 25, 42, 75**
See also BEST 89:2; CA 33-36R; CANR 17;
DLB 68; MTCW; WLC

Davies, W(illiam) H(enry)
1871-1940 . . . . **TCLC 5**
See also CA 104; DLB 19

Davies, Walter C.
See Kornbluth, C(yril) M.

Davis, B. Lynch
See Bioy Casares, Adolfo; Borges, Jorge
Luis

Davis, Gordon
See Hunt, E(verette) Howard Jr.

Davis, Harold Lenoir 1896-1960 . . . . **CLC 49**
See also CA 89-92; DLB 9

Davis, Rebecca (Blaine) Harding
1831-1910 . . . . **TCLC 6**
See also CA 104; DLB 74

Davis, Richard Harding
1864-1916 . . . . **TCLC 24**
See also CA 114; DLB 12, 23, 78, 79

Davison, Frank Dalby 1893-1970 . . . **CLC 15**
See also CA 116

Davison, Lawrence H.
See Lawrence, D(avid) H(erbert Richards)

Davison, Peter 1928- . . . . **CLC 28**
See also CA 9-12R; CAAS 4; CANR 3;
DLB 5

Davys, Mary 1674-1732 . . . . **LC 1**
See also DLB 39

Dawson, Fielding 1930- . . . . **CLC 6**
See also CA 85-88; DLB 130

Dawson, Peter
See Faust, Frederick (Schiller)

Day, Clarence (Shepard Jr.)
1874-1935 . . . . **TCLC 25**
See also CA 108; DLB 11

Day, Thomas 1748-1789 . . . . **LC 1**
See also DLB 39; YABC 1

Day Lewis, C(ecil)
1904-1972 . . . . **CLC 1, 6, 10**
See also Blake, Nicholas
See also CA 13-16; 33-36R; CANR 34;
CAP 1; DLB 15, 20; MTCW

Dazai, Osamu . . . . **TCLC 11**
See also Tsushima, Shuji

de Andrade, Carlos Drummond
See Drummond de Andrade, Carlos

Deane, Norman
See Creasey, John

de Beauvoir, Simone (Lucie Ernestine Marie
Bertrand)
See Beauvoir, Simone (Lucie Ernestine
Marie Bertrand) de

de Brissac, Malcolm
See Dickinson, Peter (Malcolm)

de Chardin, Pierre Teilhard
See Teilhard de Chardin, (Marie Joseph)
Pierre

Dee, John 1527-1608 . . . . **LC 20**

Deer, Sandra 1940- . . . . **CLC 45**

De Ferrari, Gabriella . . . . **CLC 65**

Defoe, Daniel 1660(?)-1731 . . . . **LC 1**
See also CDBLB 1660-1789; DLB 39, 95,
101; MAICYA; SATA 22; WLC

de Gourmont, Remy
See Gourmont, Remy de

de Hartog, Jan 1914- . . . . **CLC 19**
See also CA 1-4R; CANR 1

de Hostos, E. M.
See Hostos (y Bonilla), Eugenio Maria de

de Hostos, Eugenio M.
See Hostos (y Bonilla), Eugenio Maria de

Deighton, Len . . . . **CLC 4, 7, 22, 46**
See also Deighton, Leonard Cyril
See also AAYA 6; BEST 89:2;
CDBLB 1960 to Present; DLB 87

Deighton, Leonard Cyril 1929-
See Deighton, Len
See also CA 9-12R; CANR 19, 33; MTCW

Dekker, Thomas 1572(?)-1632 . . . . **LC 22**
See also CDBLB Before 1660; DLB 62

de la Mare, Walter (John)
1873-1956 . . . . **TCLC 4**
See also CA 110; 137; CDBLB 1914-1945;
CLR 23; DLB 19; MAICYA; SATA 16;
WLC

Delaney, Franey
See O'Hara, John (Henry)

Delaney, Shelagh 1939- . . . . **CLC 29**
See also CA 17-20R; CANR 30;
CDBLB 1960 to Present; DLB 13;
MTCW

Delany, Mary (Granville Pendarves)
1700-1788 . . . . **LC 12**

Delany, Samuel R(ay Jr.)
1942- . . . . **CLC 8, 14, 38**
See also BLC 1; BW; CA 81-84; CANR 27;
DLB 8, 33; MTCW

Delaporte, Theophile
See Green, Julian (Hartridge)

De La Ramee, (Marie) Louise 1839-1908
See Ouida
See also SATA 20

de la Roche, Mazo 1879-1961 . . . . . . **CLC 14**
See also CA 85-88; CANR 30; DLB 68;
SATA 64

Delbanco, Nicholas (Franklin)
1942- . . . . **CLC 6, 13**
See also CA 17-20R; CAAS 2; CANR 29;
DLB 6

del Castillo, Michel 1933- . . . . **CLC 38**
See also CA 109

Deledda, Grazia (Cosima)
1875(?)-1936 . . . . **TCLC 23**
See also CA 123

Delibes, Miguel . . . . **CLC 8, 18**
See also Delibes Setien, Miguel

Delibes Setien, Miguel 1920-
See Delibes, Miguel
See also CA 45-48; CANR 1, 32; HW;
MTCW

DeLillo, Don
1936- . . . . . **CLC 8, 10, 13, 27, 39, 54, 76**
See also BEST 89:1; CA 81-84; CANR 21;
DLB 6; MTCW

de Lisser, H. G.
See De Lisser, Herbert George
See also DLB 117

De Lisser, Herbert George
1878-1944 . . . . **TCLC 12**
See also de Lisser, H. G.
See also CA 109

Deloria, Vine (Victor) Jr. 1933- . . . . **CLC 21**
See also CA 53-56; CANR 5, 20; MTCW;
SATA 21

Del Vecchio, John M(ichael)
1947- . . . . **CLC 29**
See also CA 110; DLBD 9

de Man, Paul (Adolph Michel)
1919-1983 . . . . **CLC 55**
See also CA 128; 111; DLB 67; MTCW

De Marinis, Rick 1934- . . . . **CLC 54**
See also CA 57-60; CANR 9, 25

Demby, William 1922- . . . . **CLC 53**
See also BLC 1; BW; CA 81-84; DLB 33

Demijohn, Thom
See Disch, Thomas M(ichael)

de Montherlant, Henry (Milon)
See Montherlant, Henry (Milon) de

de Natale, Francine
See Malzberg, Barry N(athaniel)

Denby, Edwin (Orr) 1903-1983 . . . . . **CLC 48**
See also CA 138; 110

Denis, Julio
See Cortazar, Julio

Denmark, Harrison
See Zelazny, Roger (Joseph)

Dennis, John 1658-1734 . . . . **LC 11**
See also DLB 101

Dennis, Nigel (Forbes) 1912-1989 . . . . **CLC 8**
See also CA 25-28R; 129; DLB 13, 15;
MTCW

De Palma, Brian (Russell) 1940- . . . . **CLC 20**
See also CA 109

De Quincey, Thomas 1785-1859 . . . **NCLC 4**
See also CDBLB 1789-1832; DLB 110

Deren, Eleanora 1908(?)-1961
See Deren, Maya
See also CA 111

Deren, Maya . . . . **CLC 16**
See also Deren, Eleanora

Derleth, August (William)
1909-1971 . . . . **CLC 31**
See also CA 1-4R; 29-32R; CANR 4;
DLB 9; SATA 5

de Routisie, Albert
See Aragon, Louis

Derrida, Jacques 1930- . . . . **CLC 24**
See also CA 124; 127

Derry Down Derry
See Lear, Edward

Dersonnes, Jacques
See Simenon, Georges (Jacques Christian)

Desai, Anita 1937- . . . . **CLC 19, 37**
See also CA 81-84; CANR 33; MTCW;
SATA 63

de Saint-Luc, Jean
See Glassco, John

de Saint Roman, Arnaud
See Aragon, Louis

Descartes, Rene 1596-1650 . . . . **LC 20**

De Sica, Vittorio 1901(?)-1974 . . . . . **CLC 20**
See also CA 117

Desnos, Robert 1900-1945 . . . . **TCLC 22**
See also CA 121

Destouches, Louis-Ferdinand
1894-1961 . . . . **CLC 9, 15**
See also Celine, Louis-Ferdinand
See also CA 85-88; CANR 28; MTCW

Deutsch, Babette 1895-1982 . . . . **CLC 18**
See also CA 1-4R; 108; CANR 4; DLB 45;
SATA 1, 33

Devenant, William 1606-1649 . . . . **LC 13**

Devkota, Laxmiprasad
1909-1959 . . . . **TCLC 23**
See also CA 123

Epsilon
  See Betjeman, John

Epstein, Daniel Mark 1948- .... **CLC 7**
  See also CA 49-52; CANR 2

Epstein, Jacob 1956- .... **CLC 19**
  See also CA 114

Epstein, Joseph 1937-............. **CLC 39**
  See also CA 112; 119

Epstein, Leslie 1938- .... **CLC 27**
  See also CA 73-76; CAAS 12; CANR 23

Equiano, Olaudah 1745(?)-1797...... **LC 16**
  See also BLC 2; DLB 37, 50

Erasmus, Desiderius 1469(?)-1536.... **LC 16**

Erdman, Paul E(mil) 1932- .... **CLC 25**
  See also AITN 1; CA 61-64; CANR 13

Erdrich, Louise 1954-.......... **CLC 39, 54**
  See also AAYA 10; BEST 89:1; CA 114;
  MTCW

Erenburg, Ilya (Grigoryevich)
  See Ehrenburg, Ilya (Grigoryevich)

Erickson, Stephen Michael 1950-
  See Erickson, Steve
  See also CA 129

Erickson, Steve .... **CLC 64**
  See also Erickson, Stephen Michael

Ericson, Walter
  See Fast, Howard (Melvin)

Eriksson, Buntel
  See Bergman, (Ernst) Ingmar

Eschenbach, Wolfram von
  See Wolfram von Eschenbach

Eseki, Bruno
  See Mphahlele, Ezekiel

Esenin, Sergei (Alexandrovich)
  1895-1925 .... **TCLC 4**
  See also CA 104

Eshleman, Clayton 1935-.......... **CLC 7**
  See also CA 33-36R; CAAS 6; DLB 5

Espriella, Don Manuel Alvarez
  See Southey, Robert

Espriu, Salvador 1913-1985......... **CLC 9**
  See also CA 115

Espronceda, Jose de 1808-1842... **NCLC 39**

Esse, James
  See Stephens, James

Esterbrook, Tom
  See Hubbard, L(afayette) Ron(ald)

Estleman, Loren D. 1952- .... **CLC 48**
  See also CA 85-88; CANR 27; MTCW

Evan, Evin
  See Faust, Frederick (Schiller)

Evans, Evan
  See Faust, Frederick (Schiller)

Evans, Mary Ann
  See Eliot, George

Evarts, Esther
  See Benson, Sally

Everett, Percival
  See Everett, Percival L.

Everett, Percival L. 1956- .... **CLC 57**
  See also CA 129

Everson, R(onald) G(ilmour)
  1903- .... **CLC 27**
  See also CA 17-20R; DLB 88

Everson, William (Oliver)
  1912-.................. **CLC 1, 5, 14**
  See also CA 9-12R; CANR 20; DLB 5, 16;
  MTCW

Evtushenko, Evgenii Aleksandrovich
  See Yevtushenko, Yevgeny (Alexandrovich)

Ewart, Gavin (Buchanan)
  1916-................. **CLC 13, 46**
  See also CA 89-92; CANR 17; DLB 40;
  MTCW

Ewers, Hanns Heinz 1871-1943 ... **TCLC 12**
  See also CA 109

Ewing, Frederick R.
  See Sturgeon, Theodore (Hamilton)

Exley, Frederick (Earl) 1929-.... **CLC 6, 11**
  See also AITN 2; CA 81-84; 138; DLBY 81

Eynhardt, Guillermo
  See Quiroga, Horacio (Sylvestre)

Ezekiel, Nissim 1924-............. **CLC 61**
  See also CA 61-64

Ezekiel, Tish O'Dowd 1943-....... **CLC 34**
  See also CA 129

Fagen, Donald 1948-............. **CLC 26**

Fainzilberg, Ilya Arnoldovich 1897-1937
  See Ilf, Ilya
  See also CA 120

Fair, Ronald L. 1932-............. **CLC 18**
  See also BW; CA 69-72; CANR 25; DLB 33

Fairbairns, Zoe (Ann) 1948- .... **CLC 32**
  See also CA 103; CANR 21

Falco, Gian
  See Papini, Giovanni

Falconer, James
  See Kirkup, James

Falconer, Kenneth
  See Kornbluth, C(yril) M.

Falkland, Samuel
  See Heijermans, Herman

Fallaci, Oriana 1930-............. **CLC 11**
  See also CA 77-80; CANR 15; MTCW

Faludy, George 1913-............. **CLC 42**
  See also CA 21-24R

Faludy, Gyoergy
  See Faludy, George

Fanon, Frantz 1925-1961.......... **CLC 74**
  See also BLC 2; BW; CA 116; 89-92

Fanshawe, Ann .... **LC 11**

Fante, John (Thomas) 1911-1983 ... **CLC 60**
  See also CA 69-72; 109; CANR 23;
  DLB 130; DLBY 83

Farah, Nuruddin 1945-............ **CLC 53**
  See also BLC 2; CA 106; DLB 125

Fargue, Leon-Paul 1876(?)-1947 ... **TCLC 11**
  See also CA 109

Farigoule, Louis
  See Romains, Jules

Farina, Richard 1936(?)-1966 .... **CLC 9**
  See also CA 81-84; 25-28R

Farley, Walter (Lorimer)
  1915-1989 .... **CLC 17**
  See also CA 17-20R; CANR 8, 29; DLB 22;
  MAICYA; SATA 2, 43

Farmer, Philip Jose 1918-....... **CLC 1, 19**
  See also CA 1-4R; CANR 4, 35; DLB 8;
  MTCW

Farquhar, George 1677-1707........ **LC 21**
  See also DLB 84

Farrell, J(ames) G(ordon)
  1935-1979 .... **CLC 6**
  See also CA 73-76; 89-92; CANR 36;
  DLB 14; MTCW

Farrell, James T(homas)
  1904-1979 .... **CLC 1, 4, 8, 11, 66**
  See also CA 5-8R; 89-92; CANR 9; DLB 4,
  9, 86; DLBD 2; MTCW

Farren, Richard J.
  See Betjeman, John

Farren, Richard M.
  See Betjeman, John

Fassbinder, Rainer Werner
  1946-1982 .... **CLC 20**
  See also CA 93-96; 106; CANR 31

Fast, Howard (Melvin) 1914- ...... **CLC 23**
  See also CA 1-4R; CANR 1, 33; DLB 9;
  SATA 7

Faulcon, Robert
  See Holdstock, Robert P.

Faulkner, William (Cuthbert)
  1897-1962 .... **CLC 1, 3, 6, 8, 9, 11, 14,
  18, 28, 52, 68; SSC 1**
  See also AAYA 7; CA 81-84; CANR 33;
  CDALB 1929-1941; DLB 9, 11, 44, 102;
  DLBD 2; DLBY 86; MTCW; WLC

Fauset, Jessie Redmon
  1884(?)-1961 .... **CLC 19, 54**
  See also BLC 2; BW; CA 109; DLB 51

Faust, Frederick (Schiller)
  1892-1944(?) .... **TCLC 49**
  See also CA 108

Faust, Irvin 1924-................. **CLC 8**
  See also CA 33-36R; CANR 28; DLB 2, 28;
  DLBY 80

Fawkes, Guy
  See Benchley, Robert (Charles)

Fearing, Kenneth (Flexner)
  1902-1961 .... **CLC 51**
  See also CA 93-96; DLB 9

Fecamps, Elise
  See Creasey, John

Federman, Raymond 1928- ...... **CLC 6, 47**
  See also CA 17-20R; CAAS 8; CANR 10;
  DLBY 80

Federspiel, J(uerg) F. 1931-........ **CLC 42**

Feiffer, Jules (Ralph) 1929-.... **CLC 2, 8, 64**
  See also AAYA 3; CA 17-20R; CANR 30;
  DLB 7, 44; MTCW; SATA 8, 61

Feige, Hermann Albert Otto Maximilian
  See Traven, B.

Fei-Kan, Li
  See Li Fei-kan

Feinberg, David B. 1956-.......... **CLC 59**
  See also CA 135

Feinstein, Elaine 1930-........... **CLC 36**
See also CA 69-72; CAAS 1; CANR 31;
DLB 14, 40; MTCW

Feldman, Irving (Mordecai) 1928-.... **CLC 7**
See also CA 1-4R; CANR 1

Fellini, Federico 1920-........... **CLC 16**
See also CA 65-68; CANR 33

Felsen, Henry Gregor 1916-....... **CLC 17**
See also CA 1-4R; CANR 1; SAAS 2;
SATA 1

Fenton, James Martin 1949-....... **CLC 32**
See also CA 102; DLB 40

Ferber, Edna 1887-1968.......... **CLC 18**
See also AITN 1; CA 5-8R; 25-28R; DLB 9,
28, 86; MTCW; SATA 7

Ferguson, Helen
See Kavan, Anna

Ferguson, Samuel 1810-1886..... **NCLC 33**
See also DLB 32

Ferling, Lawrence
See Ferlinghetti, Lawrence (Monsanto)

Ferlinghetti, Lawrence (Monsanto)
1919(?)-........ **CLC 2, 6, 10, 27; PC 1**
See also CA 5-8R; CANR 3;
CDALB 1941-1968; DLB 5, 16; MTCW

Fernandez, Vicente Garcia Huidobro
See Huidobro Fernandez, Vicente Garcia

Ferrer, Gabriel (Francisco Victor) Miro
See Miro (Ferrer), Gabriel (Francisco
Victor)

Ferrier, Susan (Edmonstone)
1782-1854 .... **NCLC 8**
See also DLB 116

Ferrigno, Robert .... **CLC 65**

Feuchtwanger, Lion 1884-1958..... **TCLC 3**
See also CA 104; DLB 66

Feydeau, Georges (Leon Jules Marie)
1862-1921 .... **TCLC 22**
See also CA 113

Ficino, Marsilio 1433-1499 .... **LC 12**

Fiedler, Leslie A(aron)
1917- .... **CLC 4, 13, 24**
See also CA 9-12R; CANR 7; DLB 28, 67;
MTCW

Field, Andrew 1938-.............. **CLC 44**
See also CA 97-100; CANR 25

Field, Eugene 1850-1895 .... **NCLC 3**
See also DLB 23, 42; MAICYA; SATA 16

Field, Gans T.
See Wellman, Manly Wade

Field, Michael .... **TCLC 43**

Field, Peter
See Hobson, Laura Z(ametkin)

Fielding, Henry 1707-1754 .... **LC 1**
See also CDBLB 1660-1789; DLB 39, 84,
101; WLC

Fielding, Sarah 1710-1768 .... **LC 1**
See also DLB 39

Fierstein, Harvey (Forbes) 1954-... **CLC 33**
See also CA 123; 129

Figes, Eva 1932-................. **CLC 31**
See also CA 53-56; CANR 4; DLB 14

Finch, Robert (Duer Claydon)
1900- .... **CLC 18**
See also CA 57-60; CANR 9, 24; DLB 88

Findley, Timothy 1930- .... **CLC 27**
See also CA 25-28R; CANR 12; DLB 53

Fink, William
See Mencken, H(enry) L(ouis)

Firbank, Louis 1942-
See Reed, Lou
See also CA 117

Firbank, (Arthur Annesley) Ronald
1886-1926 .... **TCLC 1**
See also CA 104; DLB 36

Fisher, M(ary) F(rances) K(ennedy)
1908-1992 .... **CLC 76**
See also CA 77-80; 138

Fisher, Roy 1930-................ **CLC 25**
See also CA 81-84; CAAS 10; CANR 16;
DLB 40

Fisher, Rudolph 1897-1934 .... **TCLC 11**
See also BLC 2; BW; CA 107; 124; DLB 51,
102

Fisher, Vardis (Alvero) 1895-1968.... **CLC 7**
See also CA 5-8R; 25-28R; DLB 9

Fiske, Tarleton
See Bloch, Robert (Albert)

Fitch, Clarke
See Sinclair, Upton (Beall)

Fitch, John IV
See Cormier, Robert (Edmund)

Fitgerald, Penelope 1916- .... **CLC 61**

Fitzgerald, Captain Hugh
See Baum, L(yman) Frank

FitzGerald, Edward 1809-1883 .... **NCLC 9**
See also DLB 32

Fitzgerald, F(rancis) Scott (Key)
1896-1940 .... **TCLC 1, 6, 14, 28; SSC 6**
See also AITN 1; CA 110; 123;
CDALB 1917-1929; DLB 4, 9, 86;
DLBD 1; DLBY 81; MTCW; WLC

Fitzgerald, Penelope 1916-...... **CLC 19, 51**
See also CA 85-88; CAAS 10; DLB 14

FitzGerald, Robert D(avid)
1902-1987 .... **CLC 19**
See also CA 17-20R

Fitzgerald, Robert (Stuart)
1910-1985 .... **CLC 39**
See also CA 1-4R; 114; CANR 1; DLBY 80

Flanagan, Thomas (James Bonner)
1923- .... **CLC 25, 52**
See also CA 108; DLBY 80; MTCW

Flaubert, Gustave
1821-1880 ..... **NCLC 2, 10, 19; SSC 11**
See also DLB 119; WLC

Flecker, (Herman) James Elroy
1884-1915 .... **TCLC 43**
See also CA 109; DLB 10, 19

Fleming, Ian (Lancaster)
1908-1964 .... **CLC 3, 30**
See also CA 5-8R; CDBLB 1945-1960;
DLB 87; MTCW; SATA 9

Fleming, Thomas (James) 1927- .... **CLC 37**
See also CA 5-8R; CANR 10; SATA 8

Fletcher, John Gould 1886-1950... **TCLC 35**
See also CA 107; DLB 4, 45

Fleur, Paul
See Pohl, Frederik

Flooglebuckle, Al
See Spiegelman, Art

Flying Officer X
See Bates, H(erbert) E(rnest)

Fo, Dario 1926-.................. **CLC 32**
See also CA 116; 128; MTCW

Fogarty, Jonathan Titulescu Esq.
See Farrell, James T(homas)

Folke, Will
See Bloch, Robert (Albert)

Follett, Ken(neth Martin) 1949- .... **CLC 18**
See also AAYA 6; BEST 89:4; CA 81-84;
CANR 13, 33; DLB 87; DLBY 81;
MTCW

Fontane, Theodor 1819-1898..... **NCLC 26**
See also DLB 129

Foote, Horton 1916-............. **CLC 51**
See also CA 73-76; CANR 34; DLB 26

Foote, Shelby 1916- .... **CLC 75**
See also CA 5-8R; CANR 3; DLB 2, 17

Forbes, Esther 1891-1967.......... **CLC 12**
See also CA 13-14; 25-28R; CAP 1;
CLR 27; DLB 22; MAICYA; SATA 2

Forche, Carolyn (Louise) 1950-..... **CLC 25**
See also CA 109; 117; DLB 5

Ford, Elbur
See Hibbert, Eleanor Burford

Ford, Ford Madox
1873-1939 .... **TCLC 1, 15, 39**
See also CA 104; 132; CDBLB 1914-1945;
DLB 34, 98; MTCW

Ford, John 1895-1973............. **CLC 16**
See also CA 45-48

Ford, Richard 1944-............. **CLC 46**
See also CA 69-72; CANR 11

Ford, Webster
See Masters, Edgar Lee

Foreman, Richard 1937-.......... **CLC 50**
See also CA 65-68; CANR 32

Forester, C(ecil) S(cott)
1899-1966 .... **CLC 35**
See also CA 73-76; 25-28R; SATA 13

Forez
See Mauriac, Francois (Charles)

Forman, James Douglas 1932-...... **CLC 21**
See also CA 9-12R; CANR 4, 19;
MAICYA; SATA 8, 70

Fornes, Maria Irene 1930-...... **CLC 39, 61**
See also CA 25-28R; CANR 28; DLB 7;
HW; MTCW

Forrest, Leon 1937- .... **CLC 4**
See also BW; CA 89-92; CAAS 7;
CANR 25; DLB 33

Forster, E(dward) M(organ)
1879-1970 .... **CLC 1, 2, 3, 4, 9, 10, 13,
15, 22, 45**
See also AAYA 2; CA 13-14; 25-28R;
CAP 1; CDBLB 1914-1945; DLB 34, 98;
DLBD 10; MTCW; SATA 57; WLC

Forster, John 1812-1876 .... **NCLC 11**

Gaines, Ernest J(ames)
    1933- .... **CLC 3, 11, 18**
    See also AITN 1; BLC 2; BW; CA 9-12R;
    CANR 6, 24; CDALB 1968-1988; DLB 2,
    33; DLBY 80; MTCW

Gaitskill, Mary 1954-............ **CLC 69**
    See also CA 128

Galdos, Benito Perez
    See Perez Galdos, Benito

Gale, Zona 1874-1938 .... **TCLC 7**
    See also CA 105; DLB 9, 78

Galeano, Eduardo (Hughes) 1940-... **CLC 72**
    See also CA 29-32R; CANR 13, 32; HW

Galiano, Juan Valera y Alcala
    See Valera y Alcala-Galiano, Juan

Gallagher, Tess 1943-......... **CLC 18, 63**
    See also CA 106; DLB 120

Gallant, Mavis
    1922- .... **CLC 7, 18, 38; SSC 5**
    See also CA 69-72; CANR 29; DLB 53;
    MTCW

Gallant, Roy A(rthur) 1924- .... **CLC 17**
    See also CA 5-8R; CANR 4, 29; CLR 30;
    MAICYA; SATA 4, 68

Gallico, Paul (William) 1897-1976 ... **CLC 2**
    See also AITN 1; CA 5-8R; 69-72;
    CANR 23; DLB 9; MAICYA; SATA 13

Gallup, Ralph
    See Whitemore, Hugh (John)

Galsworthy, John 1867-1933 .... **TCLC 1, 45**
    See also CA 104; CDBLB 1890-1914;
    DLB 10, 34, 98; WLC 2

Galt, John 1779-1839 .... **NCLC 1**
    See also DLB 99, 116

Galvin, James 1951-............ **CLC 38**
    See also CA 108; CANR 26

Gamboa, Federico 1864-1939...... **TCLC 36**

Gann, Ernest Kellogg 1910-1991.... **CLC 23**
    See also AITN 1; CA 1-4R; 136; CANR 1

Garcia, Christina 1959- .... **CLC 76**

Garcia Lorca, Federico
    1898-1936 .. **TCLC 1, 7, 49; DC 2; PC 3**
    See also CA 104; 131; DLB 108; HW;
    MTCW; WLC

Garcia Marquez, Gabriel (Jose)
    1928- ... **CLC 2, 3, 8, 10, 15, 27, 47, 55;**
                                          SSC 8
    See also Marquez, Gabriel (Jose) Garcia
    See also AAYA 3; BEST 89:1, 90:4;
    CA 33-36R; CANR 10, 28; DLB 113;
    HW; MTCW; WLC

Gard, Janice
    See Latham, Jean Lee

Gard, Roger Martin du
    See Martin du Gard, Roger

Gardam, Jane 1928-.............. **CLC 43**
    See also CA 49-52; CANR 2, 18, 33;
    CLR 12; DLB 14; MAICYA; MTCW;
    SAAS 9; SATA 28, 39

Gardner, Herb................ **CLC 44**

Gardner, John (Champlin) Jr.
    1933-1982 .... **CLC 2, 3, 5, 7, 8, 10, 18,**
                              28, 34; SSC 7
    See also AITN 1; CA 65-68; 107;
    CANR 33; DLB 2; DLBY 82; MTCW;
    SATA 31, 40

Gardner, John (Edmund) 1926-..... **CLC 30**
    See also CA 103; CANR 15; MTCW

Gardner, Noel
    See Kuttner, Henry

Gardons, S. S.
    See Snodgrass, William D(e Witt)

Garfield, Leon 1921-.............. **CLC 12**
    See also AAYA 8; CA 17-20R; CANR 38;
    CLR 21; MAICYA; SATA 1, 32

Garland, (Hannibal) Hamlin
    1860-1940 .... **TCLC 3**
    See also CA 104; DLB 12, 71, 78

Garneau, (Hector de) Saint-Denys
    1912-1943 .... **TCLC 13**
    See also CA 111; DLB 88

Garner, Alan 1934-.............. **CLC 17**
    See also CA 73-76; CANR 15; CLR 20;
    MAICYA; MTCW; SATA 18, 69

Garner, Hugh 1913-1979 .... **CLC 13**
    See also CA 69-72; CANR 31; DLB 68

Garnett, David 1892-1981 .... **CLC 3**
    See also CA 5-8R; 103; CANR 17; DLB 34

Garos, Stephanie
    See Katz, Steve

Garrett, George (Palmer)
    1929- .... **CLC 3, 11, 51**
    See also CA 1-4R; CAAS 5; CANR 1;
    DLB 2, 5, 130; DLBY 83

Garrick, David 1717-1779 .... **LC 15**
    See also DLB 84

Garrigue, Jean 1914-1972 .... **CLC 2, 8**
    See also CA 5-8R; 37-40R; CANR 20

Garrison, Frederick
    See Sinclair, Upton (Beall)

Garth, Will
    See Hamilton, Edmond; Kuttner, Henry

Garvey, Marcus (Moziah Jr.)
    1887-1940 .... **TCLC 41**
    See also BLC 2; BW; CA 120; 124

Gary, Romain .... **CLC 25**
    See also Kacew, Romain
    See also DLB 83

Gascar, Pierre .... **CLC 11**
    See also Fournier, Pierre

Gascoyne, David (Emery) 1916-.... **CLC 45**
    See also CA 65-68; CANR 10, 28; DLB 20;
    MTCW

Gaskell, Elizabeth Cleghorn
    1810-1865 .... **NCLC 5**
    See also CDBLB 1832-1890; DLB 21

Gass, William H(oward)
    1924- .... **CLC 1, 2, 8, 11, 15, 39**
    See also CA 17-20R; CANR 30; DLB 2;
    MTCW

Gasset, Jose Ortega y
    See Ortega y Gasset, Jose

Gautier, Theophile 1811-1872 ..... **NCLC 1**
    See also DLB 119

Gawsworth, John
    See Bates, H(erbert) E(rnest)

Gaye, Marvin (Penze) 1939-1984 ... **CLC 26**
    See also CA 112

Gebler, Carlo (Ernest) 1954-....... **CLC 39**
    See also CA 119; 133

Gee, Maggie (Mary) 1948-........ **CLC 57**
    See also CA 130

Gee, Maurice (Gough) 1931-....... **CLC 29**
    See also CA 97-100; SATA 46

Gelbart, Larry (Simon) 1923- ... **CLC 21, 61**
    See also CA 73-76

Gelber, Jack 1932-........... **CLC 1, 6, 14**
    See also CA 1-4R; CANR 2; DLB 7

Gellhorn, Martha Ellis 1908- ... **CLC 14, 60**
    See also CA 77-80; DLBY 82

Genet, Jean
    1910-1986 ... **CLC 1, 2, 5, 10, 14, 44, 46**
    See also CA 13-16R; CANR 18; DLB 72;
    DLBY 86; MTCW

Gent, Peter 1942-................ **CLC 29**
    See also AITN 1; CA 89-92; DLBY 82

George, Jean Craighead 1919-...... **CLC 35**
    See also AAYA 8; CA 5-8R; CANR 25;
    CLR 1; DLB 52; MAICYA; SATA 2, 68

George, Stefan (Anton)
    1868-1933 .... **TCLC 2, 14**
    See also CA 104

Georges, Georges Martin
    See Simenon, Georges (Jacques Christian)

Gerhardi, William Alexander
    See Gerhardie, William Alexander

Gerhardie, William Alexander
    1895-1977 .... **CLC 5**
    See also CA 25-28R; 73-76; CANR 18;
    DLB 36

Gerstler, Amy 1956-............. **CLC 70**

Gertler, T. .... **CLC 34**
    See also CA 116; 121

Ghalib 1797-1869 .... **NCLC 39**

Ghelderode, Michel de
    1898-1962 .... **CLC 6, 11**
    See also CA 85-88; CANR 40

Ghiselin, Brewster 1903- .... **CLC 23**
    See also CA 13-16R; CAAS 10; CANR 13

Ghose, Zulfikar 1935-............. **CLC 42**
    See also CA 65-68

Ghosh, Amitav 1956- .... **CLC 44**

Giacosa, Giuseppe 1847-1906 ...... **TCLC 7**
    See also CA 104

Gibb, Lee
    See Waterhouse, Keith (Spencer)

Gibbon, Lewis Grassic .... **TCLC 4**
    See also Mitchell, James Leslie

Gibbons, Kaye 1960- .... **CLC 50**

Gibran, Kahlil 1883-1931........ **TCLC 1, 9**
    See also CA 104

Gibson, William (Ford) 1948-... **CLC 39, 63**
    See also CA 126; 133

Gibson, William 1914-........... **CLC 23**
    See also CA 9-12R; CANR 9; DLB 7;
    SATA 66

Gide, Andre (Paul Guillaume)
1869-1951 .... **TCLC 5, 12, 36**
See also CA 104; 124; DLB 65; MTCW;
WLC

Gifford, Barry (Colby) 1946-....... **CLC 34**
See also CA 65-68; CANR 9, 30, 40

Gilbert, W(illiam) S(chwenck)
1836-1911 .... **TCLC 3**
See also CA 104; SATA 36

Gilbreth, Frank B. Jr. 1911-....... **CLC 17**
See also CA 9-12R; SATA 2

Gilchrist, Ellen 1935-.......... **CLC 34, 48**
See also CA 113; 116; DLB 130; MTCW

Giles, Molly 1942-............... **CLC 39**
See also CA 126

Gill, Patrick
See Creasey, John

Gilliam, Terry (Vance) 1940-....... **CLC 21**
See also Monty Python
See also CA 108; 113; CANR 35

Gillian, Jerry
See Gilliam, Terry (Vance)

Gilliatt, Penelope (Ann Douglass)
1932-.............. **CLC 2, 10, 13, 53**
See also AITN 2; CA 13-16R; DLB 14

Gilman, Charlotte (Anna) Perkins (Stetson)
1860-1935 .... **TCLC 9, 37**
See also CA 106

Gilmour, David 1944-............ **CLC 35**
See also Pink Floyd
See also CA 138

Gilpin, William 1724-1804 .... **NCLC 30**

Gilray, J. D.
See Mencken, H(enry) L(ouis)

Gilroy, Frank D(aniel) 1925-........ **CLC 2**
See also CA 81-84; CANR 32; DLB 7

Ginsberg, Allen
1926- ..... **CLC 1, 2, 3, 4, 6, 13, 36, 69;**
PC 4
See also AITN 1; CA 1-4R; CANR 2;
CDALB 1941-1968; DLB 5, 16; MTCW;
WLC 3

Ginzburg, Natalia
1916-1991 .... **CLC 5, 11, 54, 70**
See also CA 85-88; 135; CANR 33; MTCW

Giono, Jean 1895-1970......... **CLC 4, 11**
See also CA 45-48; 29-32R; CANR 2, 35;
DLB 72; MTCW

Giovanni, Nikki 1943- ..... **CLC 2, 4, 19, 64**
See also AITN 1; BLC 2; BW; CA 29-32R;
CAAS 6; CANR 18; CLR 6; DLB 5, 41;
MAICYA; MTCW; SATA 24

Giovene, Andrea 1904-............ **CLC 7**
See also CA 85-88

Gippius, Zinaida (Nikolayevna) 1869-1945
See Hippius, Zinaida
See also CA 106

Giraudoux, (Hippolyte) Jean
1882-1944 .... **TCLC 2, 7**
See also CA 104; DLB 65

Gironella, Jose Maria 1917-....... **CLC 11**
See also CA 101

Gissing, George (Robert)
1857-1903 .... **TCLC 3, 24, 47**
See also CA 105; DLB 18

Giurlani, Aldo
See Palazzeschi, Aldo

Gladkov, Fyodor (Vasilyevich)
1883-1958 .... **TCLC 27**

Glanville, Brian (Lester) 1931-...... **CLC 6**
See also CA 5-8R; CAAS 9; CANR 3;
DLB 15; SATA 42

Glasgow, Ellen (Anderson Gholson)
1873(?)-1945 .... **TCLC 2, 7**
See also CA 104; DLB 9, 12

Glassco, John 1909-1981 .... **CLC 9**
See also CA 13-16R; 102; CANR 15;
DLB 68

Glasscock, Amnesia
See Steinbeck, John (Ernst)

Glasser, Ronald J. 1940(?)-........ **CLC 37**

Glassman, Joyce
See Johnson, Joyce

Glendinning, Victoria 1937-........ **CLC 50**
See also CA 120; 127

Glissant, Edouard 1928-........ **CLC 10, 68**

Gloag, Julian 1930-............... **CLC 40**
See also AITN 1; CA 65-68; CANR 10

Gluck, Louise (Elisabeth)
1943-................. **CLC 7, 22, 44**
See also Glueck, Louise
See also CA 33-36R; CANR 40; DLB 5

Glueck, Louise................. CLC 7, 22
See also Gluck, Louise (Elisabeth)
See also DLB 5

Gobineau, Joseph Arthur (Comte) de
1816-1882 .... **NCLC 17**
See also DLB 123

Godard, Jean-Luc 1930-........... **CLC 20**
See also CA 93-96

Godden, (Margaret) Rumer 1907-... **CLC 53**
See also AAYA 6; CA 5-8R; CANR 4, 27,
36; CLR 20; MAICYA; SAAS 12;
SATA 3, 36

Godoy Alcayaga, Lucila 1889-1957
See Mistral, Gabriela
See also CA 104; 131; HW; MTCW

Godwin, Gail (Kathleen)
1937- .... **CLC 5, 8, 22, 31, 69**
See also CA 29-32R; CANR 15; DLB 6;
MTCW

Godwin, William 1756-1836...... **NCLC 14**
See also CDBLB 1789-1832; DLB 39, 104

Goethe, Johann Wolfgang von
1749-1832 ..... **NCLC 4, 22, 34; PC 5**
See also DLB 94; WLC 3

Gogarty, Oliver St. John
1878-1957 .... **TCLC 15**
See also CA 109; DLB 15, 19

Gogol, Nikolai (Vasilyevich)
1809-1852 ..... **NCLC 5, 15, 31; DC 1;**
SSC 4
See also WLC

Gold, Herbert 1924-....... **CLC 4, 7, 14, 42**
See also CA 9-12R; CANR 17; DLB 2;
DLBY 81

Goldbarth, Albert 1948-........ **CLC 5, 38**
See also CA 53-56; CANR 6, 40; DLB 120

Goldberg, Anatol 1910-1982 .... **CLC 34**
See also CA 131; 117

Goldemberg, Isaac 1945-.......... **CLC 52**
See also CA 69-72; CAAS 12; CANR 11,
32; HW

Golden Silver
See Storm, Hyemeyohsts

Golding, William (Gerald)
1911- ..... **CLC 1, 2, 3, 8, 10, 17, 27, 58**
See also AAYA 5; CA 5-8R; CANR 13, 33;
CDBLB 1945-1960; DLB 15, 100;
MTCW; WLC

Goldman, Emma 1869-1940...... **TCLC 13**
See also CA 110

Goldman, Francisco 1955-......... **CLC 76**

Goldman, William (W.) 1931-.... **CLC 1, 48**
See also CA 9-12R; CANR 29; DLB 44

Goldmann, Lucien 1913-1970 ...... **CLC 24**
See also CA 25-28; CAP 2

Goldoni, Carlo 1707-1793 .... **LC 4**

Goldsberry, Steven 1949-......... **CLC 34**
See also CA 131

Goldsmith, Oliver 1728-1774........ **LC 2**
See also CDBLB 1660-1789; DLB 39, 89,
104, 109; SATA 26; WLC

Goldsmith, Peter
See Priestley, J(ohn) B(oynton)

Gombrowicz, Witold
1904-1969 .... **CLC 4, 7, 11, 49**
See also CA 19-20; 25-28R; CAP 2

Gomez de la Serna, Ramon
1888-1963 .... **CLC 9**
See also CA 116; HW

Goncharov, Ivan Alexandrovich
1812-1891 .... **NCLC 1**

Goncourt, Edmond (Louis Antoine Huot) de
1822-1896 .... **NCLC 7**
See also DLB 123

Goncourt, Jules (Alfred Huot) de
1830-1870 .... **NCLC 7**
See also DLB 123

Gontier, Fernande 19(?)-.......... **CLC 50**

Goodman, Paul 1911-1972.... **CLC 1, 2, 4, 7**
See also CA 19-20; 37-40R; CANR 34;
CAP 2; DLB 130; MTCW

Gordimer, Nadine
1923- .... **CLC 3, 5, 7, 10, 18, 33, 51, 70**
See also CA 5-8R; CANR 3, 28; MTCW

Gordon, Adam Lindsay
1833-1870 .... **NCLC 21**

Gordon, Caroline
1895-1981 .... **CLC 6, 13, 29**
See also CA 11-12; 103; CANR 36; CAP 1;
DLB 4, 9, 102; DLBY 81; MTCW

Gordon, Charles William 1860-1937
See Connor, Ralph
See also CA 109

Gordon, Mary (Catherine)
1949-................. **CLC 13, 22**
See also CA 102; DLB 6; DLBY 81;
MTCW

Gordon, Sol 1923-................ **CLC 26**
See also CA 53-56; CANR 4; SATA 11

Gordone, Charles 1925- .... CLC 1, 4
See also BW; CA 93-96; DLB 7; MTCW

Gorenko, Anna Andreevna
See Akhmatova, Anna

Gorky, Maxim.................... TCLC 8
See also Peshkov, Alexei Maximovich
See also WLC

Goryan, Sirak
See Saroyan, William

Gosse, Edmund (William)
1849-1928 .... TCLC 28
See also CA 117; DLB 57

Gotlieb, Phyllis Fay (Bloom)
1926- .... CLC 18
See also CA 13-16R; CANR 7; DLB 88

Gottesman, S. D.
See Kornbluth, C(yril) M.; Pohl, Frederik

Gottfried von Strassburg
fl. c. 1210- .... CMLC 10

Gottschalk, Laura Riding
See Jackson, Laura (Riding)

Gould, Lois .... CLC 4, 10
See also CA 77-80; CANR 29; MTCW

Gourmont, Remy de 1858-1915.... TCLC 17
See also CA 109

Govier, Katherine 1948-.......... CLC 51
See also CA 101; CANR 18, 40

Goyen, (Charles) William
1915-1983 .... CLC 5, 8, 14, 40
See also AITN 2; CA 5-8R; 110; CANR 6;
DLB 2; DLBY 83

Goytisolo, Juan 1931- ...... CLC 5, 10, 23
See also CA 85-88; CANR 32; HW; MTCW

Gozzi, (Conte) Carlo 1720-1806 .. NCLC 23

Grabbe, Christian Dietrich
1801-1836 .... NCLC 2

Grace, Patricia 1937-............ CLC 56

Gracian y Morales, Baltasar
1601-1658 .... LC 15

Gracq, Julien................. CLC 11, 48
See also Poirier, Louis
See also DLB 83

Grade, Chaim 1910-1982 .... CLC 10
See also CA 93-96; 107

Graduate of Oxford, A
See Ruskin, John

Graham, John
See Phillips, David Graham

Graham, Jorie 1951-............. CLC 48
See also CA 111; DLB 120

Graham, R(obert) B(ontine) Cunninghame
See Cunninghame Graham, R(obert)
B(ontine)
See also DLB 98

Graham, Robert
See Haldeman, Joe (William)

Graham, Tom
See Lewis, (Harry) Sinclair

Graham, W(illiam) S(ydney)
1918-1986 .... CLC 29
See also CA 73-76; 118; DLB 20

Graham, Winston (Mawdsley)
1910- .... CLC 23
See also CA 49-52; CANR 2, 22; DLB 77

Grant, Skeeter
See Spiegelman, Art

Granville-Barker, Harley
1877-1946 .... TCLC 2
See also Barker, Harley Granville
See also CA 104

Grass, Guenter (Wilhelm)
1927- .. CLC 1, 2, 4, 6, 11, 15, 22, 32, 49
See also CA 13-16R; CANR 20; DLB 75,
124; MTCW; WLC

Gratton, Thomas
See Hulme, T(homas) E(rnest)

Grau, Shirley Ann 1929-......... CLC 4, 9
See also CA 89-92; CANR 22; DLB 2;
MTCW

Gravel, Fern
See Hall, James Norman

Graver, Elizabeth 1964-.......... CLC 70
See also CA 135

Graves, Richard Perceval 1945- .... CLC 44
See also CA 65-68; CANR 9, 26

Graves, Robert (von Ranke)
1895-1985 ..... CLC 1, 2, 6, 11, 39, 44,
45; PC 6
See also CA 5-8R; 117; CANR 5, 36;
CDBLB 1914-1945; DLB 20, 100;
DLBY 85; MTCW; SATA 45

Gray, Alasdair (James) 1934- ...... CLC 41
See also CA 126; MTCW

Gray, Amlin 1946- .... CLC 29
See also CA 138

Gray, Francine du Plessix 1930-.... CLC 22
See also BEST 90:3; CA 61-64; CAAS 2;
CANR 11, 33; MTCW

Gray, John (Henry) 1866-1934 .... TCLC 19
See also CA 119

Gray, Simon (James Holliday)
1936- .... CLC 9, 14, 36
See also AITN 1; CA 21-24R; CAAS 3;
CANR 32; DLB 13; MTCW

Gray, Spalding 1941-............ CLC 49
See also CA 128

Gray, Thomas 1716-1771....... LC 4; PC 2
See also CDBLB 1660-1789; DLB 109;
WLC

Grayson, David
See Baker, Ray Stannard

Grayson, Richard (A.) 1951-....... CLC 38
See also CA 85-88; CANR 14, 31

Greeley, Andrew M(oran) 1928-.... CLC 28
See also CA 5-8R; CAAS 7; CANR 7;
MTCW

Green, Brian
See Card, Orson Scott

Green, Hannah .... CLC 3
See also CA 73-76

Green, Hannah
See Greenberg, Joanne (Goldenberg)

Green, Henry................... CLC 2, 13
See also Yorke, Henry Vincent
See also DLB 15

Green, Julian (Hartridge)
1900- .... CLC 3, 11
See also CA 21-24R; CANR 33; DLB 4, 72;
MTCW

Green, Julien 1900-
See Green, Julian (Hartridge)

Green, Paul (Eliot) 1894-1981...... CLC 25
See also AITN 1; CA 5-8R; 103; CANR 3;
DLB 7, 9; DLBY 81

Greenberg, Ivan 1908-1973
See Rahv, Philip
See also CA 85-88

Greenberg, Joanne (Goldenberg)
1932-..................... CLC 7, 30
See also CA 5-8R; CANR 14, 32; SATA 25

Greenberg, Richard 1959(?)-....... CLC 57
See also CA 138

Greene, Bette 1934-............. CLC 30
See also AAYA 7; CA 53-56; CANR 4;
CLR 2; MAICYA; SAAS 16; SATA 8

Greene, Gael .... CLC 8
See also CA 13-16R; CANR 10

Greene, Graham (Henry)
1904-1991 ... CLC 1, 3, 6, 9, 14, 18, 27,
37, 70, 72
See also AITN 2; CA 13-16R; 133;
CANR 35; CDBLB 1945-1960; DLB 13,
15, 77, 100; DLBY 91; MTCW;
SATA 20; WLC

Greer, Richard
See Silverberg, Robert

Greer, Richard
See Silverberg, Robert

Gregor, Arthur 1923-............. CLC 9
See also CA 25-28R; CAAS 10; CANR 11;
SATA 36

Gregor, Lee
See Pohl, Frederik

Gregory, Isabella Augusta (Persse)
1852-1932 .... TCLC 1
See also CA 104; DLB 10

Gregory, J. Dennis
See Williams, John A(lfred)

Grendon, Stephen
See Derleth, August (William)

Grenville, Kate 1950-............. CLC 61
See also CA 118

Grenville, Pelham
See Wodehouse, P(elham) G(renville)

Greve, Felix Paul (Berthold Friedrich)
1879-1948
See Grove, Frederick Philip
See also CA 104

Grey, Zane 1872-1939 .... TCLC 6
See also CA 104; 132; DLB 9; MTCW

Grieg, (Johan) Nordahl (Brun)
1902-1943 .... TCLC 10
See also CA 107

Grieve, C(hristopher) M(urray)
1892-1978 .... CLC 11, 19
See also MacDiarmid, Hugh
See also CA 5-8R; 85-88; CANR 33;
MTCW

Griffin, Gerald 1803-1840 .... NCLC 7

Griffin, John Howard 1920-1980.... **CLC 68**
See also AITN 1; CA 1-4R; 101; CANR 2

Griffin, Peter .... **CLC 39**

Griffiths, Trevor 1935-........ **CLC 13, 52**
See also CA 97-100; DLB 13

Grigson, Geoffrey (Edward Harvey)
1905-1985 .... **CLC 7, 39**
See also CA 25-28R; 118; CANR 20, 33;
DLB 27; MTCW

Grillparzer, Franz 1791-1872...... **NCLC 1**

Grimble, Reverend Charles James
See Eliot, T(homas) S(tearns)

Grimke, Charlotte L(ottie) Forten
1837(?)-1914
See Forten, Charlotte L.
See also BW; CA 117; 124

Grimm, Jacob Ludwig Karl
1785-1863 .... **NCLC 3**
See also DLB 90; MAICYA; SATA 22

Grimm, Wilhelm Karl 1786-1859 .. **NCLC 3**
See also DLB 90; MAICYA; SATA 22

Grimmelshausen, Johann Jakob Christoffel
von 1621-1676 .... **LC 6**

Grindel, Eugene 1895-1952
See Eluard, Paul
See also CA 104

Grossman, David .... **CLC 67**
See also CA 138

Grossman, Vasily (Semenovich)
1905-1964 .... **CLC 41**
See also CA 124; 130; MTCW

Grove, Frederick Philip .... **TCLC 4**
See also Greve, Felix Paul (Berthold
Friedrich)
See also DLB 92

Grubb
See Crumb, R(obert)

Grumbach, Doris (Isaac)
1918- .... **CLC 13, 22, 64**
See also CA 5-8R; CAAS 2; CANR 9

Grundtvig, Nicolai Frederik Severin
1783-1872 .... **NCLC 1**

Grunge
See Crumb, R(obert)

Grunwald, Lisa 1959-............ **CLC 44**
See also CA 120

Guare, John 1938- .... **CLC 8, 14, 29, 67**
See also CA 73-76; CANR 21; DLB 7;
MTCW

Gudjonsson, Halldor Kiljan 1902-
See Laxness, Halldor
See also CA 103

Guenter, Erich
See Eich, Guenter

Guest, Barbara 1920-............ **CLC 34**
See also CA 25-28R; CANR 11; DLB 5

Guest, Judith (Ann) 1936-....... **CLC 8, 30**
See also AAYA 7; CA 77-80; CANR 15;
MTCW

Guild, Nicholas M. 1944-......... **CLC 33**
See also CA 93-96

Guillemin, Jacques
See Sartre, Jean-Paul

Guillen, Jorge 1893-1984......... **CLC 11**
See also CA 89-92; 112; DLB 108; HW

Guillen (y Batista), Nicolas (Cristobal)
1902-1989 .... **CLC 48**
See also BLC 2; BW; CA 116; 125; 129;
HW

Guillevic, (Eugene) 1907-......... **CLC 33**
See also CA 93-96

Guillois
See Desnos, Robert

Guiney, Louise Imogen
1861-1920 .... **TCLC 41**
See also DLB 54

Guiraldes, Ricardo (Guillermo)
1886-1927 .... **TCLC 39**
See also CA 131; HW; MTCW

Gunn, Bill .... **CLC 5**
See also Gunn, William Harrison
See also DLB 38

Gunn, Thom(son William)
1929- .... **CLC 3, 6, 18, 32**
See also CA 17-20R; CANR 9, 33;
CDBLB 1960 to Present; DLB 27;
MTCW

Gunn, William Harrison 1934(?)-1989
See Gunn, Bill
See also AITN 1; BW; CA 13-16R; 128;
CANR 12, 25

Gunnars, Kristjana 1948-......... **CLC 69**
See also CA 113; DLB 60

Gurganus, Allan 1947-........... **CLC 70**
See also BEST 90:1; CA 135

Gurney, A(lbert) R(amsdell) Jr.
1930- .... **CLC 32, 50, 54**
See also CA 77-80; CANR 32

Gurney, Ivor (Bertie) 1890-1937... **TCLC 33**

Gurney, Peter
See Gurney, A(lbert) R(amsdell) Jr.

Gustafson, Ralph (Barker) 1909-.... **CLC 36**
See also CA 21-24R; CANR 8; DLB 88

Gut, Gom
See Simenon, Georges (Jacques Christian)

Guthrie, A(lfred) B(ertram) Jr.
1901-1991 .... **CLC 23**
See also CA 57-60; 134; CANR 24; DLB 6;
SATA 62; SATO 67

Guthrie, Isobel
See Grieve, C(hristopher) M(urray)

Guthrie, Woodrow Wilson 1912-1967
See Guthrie, Woody
See also CA 113; 93-96

Guthrie, Woody.................. **CLC 35**
See also Guthrie, Woodrow Wilson

Guy, Rosa (Cuthbert) 1928-........ **CLC 26**
See also AAYA 4; BW; CA 17-20R;
CANR 14, 34; CLR 13; DLB 33;
MAICYA; SATA 14, 62

Gwendolyn
See Bennett, (Enoch) Arnold

H. D. .... **CLC 3, 8, 14, 31, 34, 73; PC 5**
See also Doolittle, Hilda

Haavikko, Paavo Juhani
1931- .... **CLC 18, 34**
See also CA 106

Habbema, Koos
See Heijermans, Herman

Hacker, Marilyn 1942-....**CLC 5, 9, 23, 72**
See also CA 77-80; DLB 120

Haggard, H(enry) Rider
1856-1925 .... **TCLC 11**
See also CA 108; DLB 70; SATA 16

Haig, Fenil
See Ford, Ford Madox

Haig-Brown, Roderick (Langmere)
1908-1976 .... **CLC 21**
See also CA 5-8R; 69-72; CANR 4, 38;
DLB 88; MAICYA; SATA 12

Hailey, Arthur 1920-............. **CLC 5**
See also AITN 2; BEST 90:3; CA 1-4R;
CANR 2, 36; DLB 88; DLBY 82; MTCW

Hailey, Elizabeth Forsythe 1938-... **CLC 40**
See also CA 93-96; CAAS 1; CANR 15

Haines, John (Meade) 1924-...... **CLC 58**
See also CA 17-20R; CANR 13, 34; DLB 5

Haldeman, Joe (William) 1943-..... **CLC 61**
See also CA 53-56; CANR 6; DLB 8

Haley, Alex(ander Murray Palmer)
1921-1992 .... **CLC 8, 12, 76**
See also BLC 2; BW; CA 77-80; 136;
DLB 38; MTCW

Haliburton, Thomas Chandler
1796-1865 .... **NCLC 15**
See also DLB 11, 99

Hall, Donald (Andrew Jr.)
1928- .... **CLC 1, 13, 37, 59**
See also CA 5-8R; CAAS 7; CANR 2;
DLB 5; SATA 23

Hall, Frederic Sauser
See Sauser-Hall, Frederic

Hall, James
See Kuttner, Henry

Hall, James Norman 1887-1951 ... **TCLC 23**
See also CA 123; SATA 21

Hall, (Marguerite) Radclyffe
1886(?)-1943 .... **TCLC 12**
See also CA 110

Hall, Rodney 1935- .... **CLC 51**
See also CA 109

Halliday, Michael
See Creasey, John

Halpern, Daniel 1945-........... **CLC 14**
See also CA 33-36R

Hamburger, Michael (Peter Leopold)
1924-................... **CLC 5, 14**
See also CA 5-8R; CAAS 4; CANR 2;
DLB 27

Hamill, Pete 1935-.............. **CLC 10**
See also CA 25-28R; CANR 18

Hamilton, Clive
See Lewis, C(live) S(taples)

Hamilton, Edmond 1904-1977....... **CLC 1**
See also CA 1-4R; CANR 3; DLB 8

Hamilton, Eugene (Jacob) Lee
See Lee-Hamilton, Eugene (Jacob)

Hamilton, Franklin
See Silverberg, Robert

Hamilton, Gail
See Corcoran, Barbara

Hamilton, Mollie
   See Kaye, M(ary) M(argaret)

Hamilton, (Anthony Walter) Patrick
   1904-1962 .... **CLC 51**
   See also CA 113; DLB 10

Hamilton, Virginia   1936- .... **CLC 26**
   See also AAYA 2; BW; CA 25-28R;
   CANR 20, 37; CLR 1, 11; DLB 33, 52;
   MAICYA; MTCW; SATA 4, 56

Hammett, (Samuel) Dashiell
   1894-1961 .... **CLC 3, 5, 10, 19, 47**
   See also AITN 1; CA 81-84;
   CDALB 1929-1941; DLBD 6; MTCW

Hammon, Jupiter   1711(?)-1800(?).. **NCLC 5**
   See also BLC 2; DLB 31, 50

Hammond, Keith
   See Kuttner, Henry

Hamner, Earl (Henry) Jr.   1923- .... **CLC 12**
   See also AITN 2; CA 73-76; DLB 6

Hampton, Christopher (James)
   1946- .... **CLC 4**
   See also CA 25-28R; DLB 13; MTCW

Hamsun, Knut   1859-1952... **TCLC 2, 14, 49**
   See also Pedersen, Knut

Handke, Peter   1942- .. **CLC 5, 8, 10, 15, 38**
   See also CA 77-80; CANR 33; DLB 85,
   124; MTCW

Hanley, James   1901-1985 ... **CLC 3, 5, 8, 13**
   See also CA 73-76; 117; CANR 36; MTCW

Hannah, Barry   1942- .... **CLC 23, 38**
   See also CA 108; 110; DLB 6; MTCW

Hannon, Ezra
   See Hunter, Evan

Hansberry, Lorraine (Vivian)
   1930-1965 .... **CLC 17, 62; DC 2**
   See also BLC 2; BW; CA 109; 25-28R;
   CABS 3; CDALB 1941-1968; DLB 7, 38;
   MTCW

Hansen, Joseph   1923- .... **CLC 38**
   See also CA 29-32R; CAAS 17; CANR 16

Hansen, Martin A.   1909-1955 ..... **TCLC 32**

Hanson, Kenneth O(stlin)   1922- .... **CLC 13**
   See also CA 53-56; CANR 7

Hardwick, Elizabeth   1916- .... **CLC 13**
   See also CA 5-8R; CANR 3, 32; DLB 6;
   MTCW

Hardy, Thomas
   1840-1928 ..... **TCLC 4, 10, 18, 32, 48;**
                                 SSC 2
   See also CA 104; 123; CDBLB 1890-1914;
   DLB 18, 19; MTCW; WLC

Hare, David   1947- .... **CLC 29, 58**
   See also CA 97-100; CANR 39; DLB 13;
   MTCW

Harford, Henry
   See Hudson, W(illiam) H(enry)

Hargrave, Leonie
   See Disch, Thomas M(ichael)

Harlan, Louis R(udolph)   1922- ..... **CLC 34**
   See also CA 21-24R; CANR 25

Harling, Robert   1951(?)- .... **CLC 53**

Harmon, William (Ruth)   1938- ..... **CLC 38**
   See also CA 33-36R; CANR 14, 32, 35;
   SATA 65

Harper, F. E. W.
   See Harper, Frances Ellen Watkins

Harper, Frances E. W.
   See Harper, Frances Ellen Watkins

Harper, Frances E. Watkins
   See Harper, Frances Ellen Watkins

Harper, Frances Ellen
   See Harper, Frances Ellen Watkins

Harper, Frances Ellen Watkins
   1825-1911 .... **TCLC 14**
   See also BLC 2; BW; CA 111; 125; DLB 50

Harper, Michael S(teven)   1938- .. **CLC 7, 22**
   See also BW; CA 33-36R; CANR 24;
   DLB 41

Harper, Mrs. F. E. W.
   See Harper, Frances Ellen Watkins

Harris, Christie (Lucy) Irwin
   1907- .... **CLC 12**
   See also CA 5-8R; CANR 6; DLB 88;
   MAICYA; SAAS 10; SATA 6

Harris, Frank   1856(?)-1931 .... **TCLC 24**
   See also CA 109

Harris, George Washington
   1814-1869 .... **NCLC 23**
   See also DLB 3, 11

Harris, Joel Chandler   1848-1908 ... **TCLC 2**
   See also CA 104; 137; DLB 11, 23, 42, 78,
   91; MAICYA; YABC 1

Harris, John (Wyndham Parkes Lucas)
   Beynon 1903-1969 .... **CLC 19**
   See also CA 102; 89-92

Harris, MacDonald
   See Heiney, Donald (William)

Harris, Mark   1922- .... **CLC 19**
   See also CA 5-8R; CAAS 3; CANR 2;
   DLB 2; DLBY 80

Harris, (Theodore) Wilson   1921- .... **CLC 25**
   See also BW; CA 65-68; CAAS 16;
   CANR 11, 27; DLB 117; MTCW

Harrison, Elizabeth Cavanna   1909-
   See Cavanna, Betty
   See also CA 9-12R; CANR 6, 27

Harrison, Harry (Max)   1925- ...... **CLC 42**
   See also CA 1-4R; CANR 5, 21; DLB 8;
   SATA 4

Harrison, James (Thomas)   1937-
   See Harrison, Jim
   See also CA 13-16R; CANR 8

Harrison, Jim .... **CLC 6, 14, 33, 66**
   See also Harrison, James (Thomas)
   See also DLBY 82

Harrison, Kathryn   1961- .... **CLC 70**

Harrison, Tony   1937- .... **CLC 43**
   See also CA 65-68; DLB 40; MTCW

Harriss, Will(ard Irvin)   1922- ...... **CLC 34**
   See also CA 111

Harson, Sley
   See Ellison, Harlan

Hart, Ellis
   See Ellison, Harlan

Hart, Josephine   1942(?)- .... **CLC 70**
   See also CA 138

Hart, Moss   1904-1961 .... **CLC 66**
   See also CA 109; 89-92; DLB 7

Harte, (Francis) Bret(t)
   1836(?)-1902 .... **TCLC 1, 25; SSC 8**
   See also CA 104; CDALB 1865-1917;
   DLB 12, 64, 74, 79; SATA 26; WLC

Hartley, L(eslie) P(oles)
   1895-1972 .... **CLC 2, 22**
   See also CA 45-48; 37-40R; CANR 33;
   DLB 15; MTCW

Hartman, Geoffrey H.   1929- ...... **CLC 27**
   See also CA 117; 125; DLB 67

Haruf, Kent   19(?)- .... **CLC 34**

Harwood, Ronald   1934- .... **CLC 32**
   See also CA 1-4R; CANR 4; DLB 13

Hasek, Jaroslav (Matej Frantisek)
   1883-1923 .... **TCLC 4**
   See also CA 104; 129; MTCW

Hass, Robert   1941- .... **CLC 18, 39**
   See also CA 111; CANR 30; DLB 105

Hastings, Hudson
   See Kuttner, Henry

Hastings, Selina .... **CLC 44**

Hatteras, Amelia
   See Mencken, H(enry) L(ouis)

Hatteras, Owen .... **TCLC 18**
   See also Mencken, H(enry) L(ouis); Nathan,
   George Jean

Hauptmann, Gerhart (Johann Robert)
   1862-1946 .... **TCLC 4**
   See also CA 104; DLB 66, 118

Havel, Vaclav   1936- .... **CLC 25, 58, 65**
   See also CA 104; CANR 36; MTCW

Haviaras, Stratis .... **CLC 33**
   See also Chaviaras, Strates

Hawes, Stephen   1475(?)-1523(?) ..... **LC 17**

Hawkes, John (Clendennin Burne Jr.)
   1925- ...... **CLC 1, 2, 3, 4, 7, 9, 14, 15,**
                                 27, 49
   See also CA 1-4R; CANR 2; DLB 2, 7;
   DLBY 80; MTCW

Hawking, S. W.
   See Hawking, Stephen W(illiam)

Hawking, Stephen W(illiam)
   1942- .... **CLC 63**
   See also BEST 89:1; CA 126; 129

Hawthorne, Julian   1846-1934 ..... **TCLC 25**

Hawthorne, Nathaniel
   1804-1864 .... **NCLC 39; SSC 3**
   See also CDALB 1640-1865; DLB 1, 74;
   WLC; YABC 2

Haxton, Josephine Ayres   1921- .... **CLC 73**
   See also CA 115

Hayaseca y Eizaguirre, Jorge
   See Echegaray (y Eizaguirre), Jose (Maria
   Waldo)

Hayashi Fumiko   1904-1951 .... **TCLC 27**

Haycraft, Anna
   See Ellis, Alice Thomas
   See also CA 122

Hayden, Robert E(arl)
   1913-1980 ...... **CLC 5, 9, 14, 37; PC 6**
   See also BLC 2; BW; CA 69-72; 97-100;
   CABS 2; CANR 24; CDALB 1941-1968;
   DLB 5, 76; MTCW; SATA 19, 26

Hayford, J(oseph) E(phraim) Casely
  See Casely-Hayford, J(oseph) E(phraim)

Hayman, Ronald 1932-.............. **CLC 44**
  See also CA 25-28R; CANR 18

Haywood, Eliza (Fowler)
  1693(?)-1756 .... **LC 1**

Hazlitt, William 1778-1830 ...... **NCLC 29**
  See also DLB 110

Hazzard, Shirley 1931- .... **CLC 18**
  See also CA 9-12R; CANR 4; DLBY 82;
  MTCW

Head, Bessie 1937-1986 .... **CLC 25, 67**
  See also BLC 2; BW; CA 29-32R; 119;
  CANR 25; DLB 117; MTCW

Headon, (Nicky) Topper 1956(?)- ... **CLC 30**
  See also Clash, The

Heaney, Seamus (Justin)
  1939- .... **CLC 5, 7, 14, 25, 37, 74**
  See also CA 85-88; CANR 25;
  CDBLB 1960 to Present; DLB 40;
  MTCW

Hearn, (Patricio) Lafcadio (Tessima Carlos)
  1850-1904 .... **TCLC 9**
  See also CA 105; DLB 12, 78

Hearne, Vicki 1946-.............. **CLC 56**
  See also CA 139

Hearon, Shelby 1931-............. **CLC 63**
  See also AITN 2; CA 25-28R; CANR 18

Heat-Moon, William Least......... **CLC 29**
  See also Trogdon, William (Lewis)
  See also AAYA 9

Hebert, Anne 1916- .... **CLC 4, 13, 29**
  See also CA 85-88; DLB 68; MTCW

Hecht, Anthony (Evan)
  1923- .... **CLC 8, 13, 19**
  See also CA 9-12R; CANR 6; DLB 5

Hecht, Ben 1894-1964 .... **CLC 8**
  See also CA 85-88; DLB 7, 9, 25, 26, 28, 86

Hedayat, Sadeq 1903-1951....... **TCLC 21**
  See also CA 120

Heidegger, Martin 1889-1976 ...... **CLC 24**
  See also CA 81-84; 65-68; CANR 34;
  MTCW

Heidenstam, (Carl Gustaf) Verner von
  1859-1940 .... **TCLC 5**
  See also CA 104

Heifner, Jack 1946-.............. **CLC 11**
  See also CA 105

Heijermans, Herman 1864-1924 ... **TCLC 24**
  See also CA 123

Heilbrun, Carolyn G(old) 1926-..... **CLC 25**
  See also CA 45-48; CANR 1, 28

Heine, Heinrich 1797-1856 .... **NCLC 4**
  See also DLB 90

Heinemann, Larry (Curtiss) 1944- .. **CLC 50**
  See also CA 110; CANR 31; DLBD 9

Heiney, Donald (William) 1921-..... **CLC 9**
  See also CA 1-4R; CANR 3

Heinlein, Robert A(nson)
  1907-1988 ...... **CLC 1, 3, 8, 14, 26, 55**
  See also CA 1-4R; 125; CANR 1, 20;
  DLB 8; MAICYA; MTCW; SATA 9, 56,
  69

Helforth, John
  See Doolittle, Hilda

Hellenhofferu, Vojtech Kapristian z
  See Hasek, Jaroslav (Matej Frantisek)

Heller, Joseph
  1923- .... **CLC 1, 3, 5, 8, 11, 36, 63**
  See also AITN 1; CA 5-8R; CABS 1;
  CANR 8; DLB 2, 28; DLBY 80; MTCW;
  WLC

Hellman, Lillian (Florence)
  1906-1984 ..... **CLC 2, 4, 8, 14, 18, 34,**
                        44, 52; DC 1
  See also AITN 1, 2; CA 13-16R; 112;
  CANR 33; DLB 7; DLBY 84; MTCW

Helprin, Mark 1947- ..... **CLC 7, 10, 22, 32**
  See also CA 81-84; DLBY 85; MTCW

Helyar, Jane Penelope Josephine 1933-
  See Poole, Josephine
  See also CA 21-24R; CANR 10, 26

Hemans, Felicia 1793-1835 ...... **NCLC 29**
  See also DLB 96

Hemingway, Ernest (Miller)
  1899-1961 ... **CLC 1, 3, 6, 8, 10, 13, 19,**
        30, 34, 39, 41, 44, 50, 61; SSC 1
  See also CA 77-80; CANR 34;
  CDALB 1917-1929; DLB 4, 9, 102;
  DLBD 1; DLBY 81, 87; MTCW; WLC

Hempel, Amy 1951-.............. **CLC 39**
  See also CA 118; 137

Henderson, F. C.
  See Mencken, H(enry) L(ouis)

Henderson, Sylvia
  See Ashton-Warner, Sylvia (Constance)

Henley, Beth .... **CLC 23**
  See also Henley, Elizabeth Becker
  See also CABS 3; DLBY 86

Henley, Elizabeth Becker 1952-
  See Henley, Beth
  See also CA 107; CANR 32; MTCW

Henley, William Ernest
  1849-1903 .... **TCLC 8**
  See also CA 105; DLB 19

Hennissart, Martha
  See Lathen, Emma
  See also CA 85-88

Henry, O. .... **TCLC 1, 19; SSC 5**
  See also Porter, William Sydney
  See also WLC

Henryson, Robert 1430(?)-1506(?).... **LC 20**

Henry VIII 1491-1547............. **LC 10**

Henschke, Alfred
  See Klabund

Hentoff, Nat(han Irving) 1925-..... **CLC 26**
  See also AAYA 4; CA 1-4R; CAAS 6;
  CANR 5, 25; CLR 1; MAICYA;
  SATA 27, 42, 69

Heppenstall, (John) Rayner
  1911-1981 .... **CLC 10**
  See also CA 1-4R; 103; CANR 29

Herbert, Frank (Patrick)
  1920-1986 .... **CLC 12, 23, 35, 44**
  See also CA 53-56; 118; CANR 5; DLB 8;
  MTCW; SATA 9, 37, 47

Herbert, George 1593-1633 .... **PC 4**
  See also CDBLB Before 1660; DLB 126

Herbert, Zbigniew 1924- .... **CLC 9, 43**
  See also CA 89-92; CANR 36; MTCW

Herbst, Josephine (Frey)
  1897-1969 .... **CLC 34**
  See also CA 5-8R; 25-28R; DLB 9

Hergesheimer, Joseph
  1880-1954 .... **TCLC 11**
  See also CA 109; DLB 102, 9

Herlihy, James Leo 1927-.......... **CLC 6**
  See also CA 1-4R; CANR 2

Hermogenes fl. c. 175- .... **CMLC 6**

Hernandez, Jose 1834-1886 ...... **NCLC 17**

Herrick, Robert 1591-1674 .... **LC 13**
  See also DLB 126

Herriot, James .... **CLC 12**
  See also Wight, James Alfred
  See also AAYA 1; CANR 40

Herrmann, Dorothy 1941-......... **CLC 44**
  See also CA 107

Herrmann, Taffy
  See Herrmann, Dorothy

Hersey, John (Richard)
  1914- .... **CLC 1, 2, 7, 9, 40**
  See also CA 17-20R; CANR 33; DLB 6;
  MTCW; SATA 25

Herzen, Aleksandr Ivanovich
  1812-1870 .... **NCLC 10**

Herzl, Theodor 1860-1904........ **TCLC 36**

Herzog, Werner 1942-............. **CLC 16**
  See also CA 89-92

Hesiod c. 8th cent. B.C.-.......... **CMLC 5**

Hesse, Hermann
  1877-1962 ... **CLC 1, 2, 3, 6, 11, 17, 25,**
                        69; SSC 9
  See also CA 17-18; CAP 2; DLB 66;
  MTCW; SATA 50; WLC

Hewes, Cady
  See De Voto, Bernard (Augustine)

Heyen, William 1940- .... **CLC 13, 18**
  See also CA 33-36R; CAAS 9; DLB 5

Heyerdahl, Thor 1914-............. **CLC 26**
  See also CA 5-8R; CANR 5, 22; MTCW;
  SATA 2, 52

Heym, Georg (Theodor Franz Arthur)
  1887-1912 .... **TCLC 9**
  See also CA 106

Heym, Stefan 1913-.............. **CLC 41**
  See also CA 9-12R; CANR 4; DLB 69

Heyse, Paul (Johann Ludwig von)
  1830-1914 .... **TCLC 8**
  See also CA 104; DLB 129

Hibbert, Eleanor Burford 1906-..... **CLC 7**
  See also BEST 90:4; CA 17-20R; CANR 9,
  28; SATA 2

Higgins, George V(incent)
  1939-................. **CLC 4, 7, 10, 18**
  See also CA 77-80; CAAS 5; CANR 17;
  DLB 2; DLBY 81; MTCW

Higginson, Thomas Wentworth
  1823-1911 .... **TCLC 36**
  See also DLB 1, 64

Highet, Helen
  See MacInnes, Helen (Clark)

Horn, Peter
  See Kuttner, Henry

Horovitz, Israel 1939- .... **CLC 56**
  See also CA 33-36R; DLB 7

Horvath, Odon von
  See Horvath, Oedoen von
  See also DLB 85, 124

Horvath, Oedoen von 1901-1938... **TCLC 45**
  See also Horvath, Odon von
  See also CA 118

Horwitz, Julius 1920-1986........ **CLC 14**
  See also CA 9-12R; 119; CANR 12

Hospital, Janette Turner 1942- ..... **CLC 42**
  See also CA 108

Hostos, E. M. de
  See Hostos (y Bonilla), Eugenio Maria de

Hostos, Eugenio M. de
  See Hostos (y Bonilla), Eugenio Maria de

Hostos, Eugenio Maria
  See Hostos (y Bonilla), Eugenio Maria de

Hostos (y Bonilla), Eugenio Maria de
  1839-1903 .... **TCLC 24**
  See also CA 123; 131; HW

Houdini
  See Lovecraft, H(oward) P(hillips)

Hougan, Carolyn 19(?)- .... **CLC 34**
  See also CA 139

Household, Geoffrey (Edward West)
  1900-1988 .... **CLC 11**
  See also CA 77-80; 126; DLB 87; SATA 14,
  59

Housman, A(lfred) E(dward)
  1859-1936 .... **TCLC 1, 10; PC 2**
  See also CA 104; 125; DLB 19; MTCW

Housman, Laurence 1865-1959 ..... **TCLC 7**
  See also CA 106; DLB 10; SATA 25

Howard, Elizabeth Jane 1923- ... **CLC 7, 29**
  See also CA 5-8R; CANR 8

Howard, Maureen 1930- ..... **CLC 5, 14, 46**
  See also CA 53-56; CANR 31; DLBY 83;
  MTCW

Howard, Richard 1929- ...... **CLC 7, 10, 47**
  See also AITN 1; CA 85-88; CANR 25;
  DLB 5

Howard, Robert Ervin 1906-1936... **TCLC 8**
  See also CA 105

Howard, Warren F.
  See Pohl, Frederik

Howe, Fanny 1940- .... **CLC 47**
  See also CA 117; SATA 52

Howe, Julia Ward 1819-1910 ..... **TCLC 21**
  See also CA 117; DLB 1

Howe, Susan 1937- .... **CLC 72**
  See also DLB 120

Howe, Tina 1937- .... **CLC 48**
  See also CA 109

Howell, James 1594(?)-1666 .... **LC 13**

Howells, W. D.
  See Howells, William Dean

Howells, William D.
  See Howells, William Dean

Howells, William Dean
  1837-1920 .... **TCLC 41, 7, 17**
  See also CA 104; 134; CDALB 1865-1917;
  DLB 12, 64, 74, 79

Howes, Barbara 1914- .... **CLC 15**
  See also CA 9-12R; CAAS 3; SATA 5

Hrabal, Bohumil 1914-........ **CLC 13, 67**
  See also CA 106; CAAS 12

Hsun, Lu .... **TCLC 3**
  See Shu-Jen, Chou

Hubbard, L(afayette) Ron(ald)
  1911-1986 .... **CLC 43**
  See also CA 77-80; 118; CANR 22

Huch, Ricarda (Octavia)
  1864-1947 .... **TCLC 13**
  See also CA 111; DLB 66

Huddle, David 1942- .... **CLC 49**
  See also CA 57-60; DLB 130

Hudson, Jeffrey
  See Crichton, (John) Michael

Hudson, W(illiam) H(enry)
  1841-1922 .... **TCLC 29**
  See also CA 115; DLB 98; SATA 35

Hueffer, Ford Madox
  See Ford, Ford Madox

Hughart, Barry .... **CLC 39**
  See also CA 137

Hughes, Colin
  See Creasey, John

Hughes, David (John) 1930- .... **CLC 48**
  See also CA 116; 129; DLB 14

Hughes, (James) Langston
  1902-1967 .... **CLC 1, 5, 10, 15, 35, 44;**
                  DC 3; PC 1; SSC 6
  See also BLC 2; BW; CA 1-4R; 25-28R;
  CANR 1, 34; CDALB 1929-1941;
  CLR 17; DLB 4, 7, 48, 51, 86; MAICYA;
  MTCW; SATA 4, 33; WLC

Hughes, Richard (Arthur Warren)
  1900-1976 .... **CLC 1, 11**
  See also CA 5-8R; 65-68; CANR 4;
  DLB 15; MTCW; SATA 8, 25

Hughes, Ted 1930- ..... **CLC 2, 4, 9, 14, 37**
  See also CA 1-4R; CANR 1, 33; CLR 3;
  DLB 40; MAICYA; MTCW; SATA 27,
  49

Hugo, Richard F(ranklin)
  1923-1982 .... **CLC 6, 18, 32**
  See also CA 49-52; 108; CANR 3; DLB 5

Hugo, Victor (Marie)
  1802-1885 .... **NCLC 3, 10, 21**
  See also DLB 119; SATA 47; WLC

Huidobro, Vicente
  See Huidobro Fernandez, Vicente Garcia

Huidobro Fernandez, Vicente Garcia
  1893-1948 .... **TCLC 31**
  See also CA 131; HW

Hulme, Keri 1947- .... **CLC 39**
  See also CA 125

Hulme, T(homas) E(rnest)
  1883-1917 .... **TCLC 21**
  See also CA 117; DLB 19

Hume, David 1711-1776............. **LC 7**
  See also DLB 104

Humphrey, William 1924-........ **CLC 45**
  See also CA 77-80; DLB 6

Humphreys, Emyr Owen 1919-..... **CLC 47**
  See also CA 5-8R; CANR 3, 24; DLB 15

Humphreys, Josephine 1945-.... **CLC 34, 57**
  See also CA 121; 127

Hungerford, Pixie
  See Brinsmead, H(esba) F(ay)

Hunt, E(verette) Howard Jr. 1918-... **CLC 3**
  See also AITN 1; CA 45-48; CANR 2

Hunt, Kyle
  See Creasey, John

Hunt, (James Henry) Leigh
  1784-1859 .... **NCLC 1**

Hunt, Marsha 1946-............. **CLC 70**

Hunter, E. Waldo
  See Sturgeon, Theodore (Hamilton)

Hunter, Evan 1926- .... **CLC 11, 31**
  See also CA 5-8R; CANR 5, 38; DLBY 82;
  MTCW; SATA 25

Hunter, Kristin (Eggleston) 1931-... **CLC 35**
  See also AITN 1; BW; CA 13-16R;
  CANR 13; CLR 3; DLB 33; MAICYA;
  SAAS 10; SATA 12

Hunter, Mollie 1922-............. **CLC 21**
  See also McIlwraith, Maureen Mollie
  Hunter
  See also CANR 37; CLR 25; MAICYA;
  SAAS 7; SATA 54

Hunter, Robert (?)-1734............. **LC 7**

Hurston, Zora Neale
  1903-1960 .... **CLC 7, 30, 61; SSC 4**
  See also BLC 2; BW; CA 85-88; DLB 51,
  86; MTCW

Huston, John (Marcellus)
  1906-1987 .... **CLC 20**
  See also CA 73-76; 123; CANR 34; DLB 26

Hustvedt, Siri 1955-.............. **CLC 76**
  See also CA 137

Hutten, Ulrich von 1488-1523....... **LC 16**

Huxley, Aldous (Leonard)
  1894-1963 .. **CLC 1, 3, 4, 5, 8, 11, 18, 35**
  See also CA 85-88; CDBLB 1914-1945;
  DLB 36, 100; MTCW; SATA 63; WLC

Huysmans, Charles Marie Georges
  1848-1907
  See Huysmans, Joris-Karl
  See also CA 104

Huysmans, Joris-Karl.............. **TCLC 7**
  See also Huysmans, Charles Marie Georges
  See also DLB 123

Hwang, David Henry 1957-........ **CLC 55**
  See also CA 127; 132

Hyde, Anthony 1946-............. **CLC 42**
  See also CA 136

Hyde, Margaret O(ldroyd) 1917-... **CLC 21**
  See also CA 1-4R; CANR 1, 36; CLR 23;
  MAICYA; SAAS 8; SATA 1, 42

Hynes, James 1956(?)-.............. **CLC 65**

Ian, Janis 1951-.................. **CLC 21**
  See also CA 105

Ibanez, Vicente Blasco
  See Blasco Ibanez, Vicente

Ibarguengoitia, Jorge 1928-1983 . . . . **CLC 37**
See also CA 124; 113; HW

Ibsen, Henrik (Johan)
1828-1906 . . . . . **TCLC 2, 8, 16, 37; DC 2**
See also CA 104; WLC

Ibuse Masuji 1898- . . . . **CLC 22**
See also CA 127

Ichikawa, Kon 1915- . . . . **CLC 20**
See also CA 121

Idle, Eric 1943- . . . . **CLC 21**
See also Monty Python
See also CA 116; CANR 35

Ignatow, David 1914- . . . . . . **CLC 4, 7, 14, 40**
See also CA 9-12R; CAAS 3; CANR 31;
DLB 5

Ihimaera, Witi 1944- . . . . **CLC 46**
See also CA 77-80

Ilf, Ilya . . . . **TCLC 21**
See also Fainzilberg, Ilya Arnoldovich

Immermann, Karl (Lebrecht)
1796-1840 . . . . **NCLC 4**

Inclan, Ramon (Maria) del Valle
See Valle-Inclan, Ramon (Maria) del

Infante, G(uillermo) Cabrera
See Cabrera Infante, G(uillermo)

Ingalls, Rachel (Holmes) 1940- . . . . . **CLC 42**
See also CA 123; 127

Ingamells, Rex 1913-1955 . . . . **TCLC 35**

Inge, William Motter
1913-1973 . . . . **CLC 1, 8, 19**
See also CA 9-12R; CDALB 1941-1968;
DLB 7; MTCW

Ingelow, Jean 1820-1897 . . . . **NCLC 39**
See also DLB 35; SATA 33

Ingram, Willis J.
See Harris, Mark

Innaurato, Albert (F.) 1948(?)- . . **CLC 21, 60**
See also CA 115; 122

Innes, Michael
See Stewart, J(ohn) I(nnes) M(ackintosh)

Ionesco, Eugene
1912- . . . . **CLC 1, 4, 6, 9, 11, 15, 41**
See also CA 9-12R; MTCW; SATA 7; WLC

Iqbal, Muhammad 1873-1938 . . . . . **TCLC 28**

Ireland, Patrick
See O'Doherty, Brian

Irland, David
See Green, Julian (Hartridge)

Iron, Ralph
See Schreiner, Olive (Emilie Albertina)

Irving, John (Winslow)
1942- . . . . **CLC 13, 23, 38**
See also AAYA 8; BEST 89:3; CA 25-28R;
CANR 28; DLB 6; DLBY 82; MTCW

Irving, Washington
1783-1859 . . . . **NCLC 2, 19; SSC 2**
See also CDALB 1640-1865; DLB 3, 11, 30,
59, 73, 74; WLC; YABC 2

Irwin, P. K.
See Page, P(atricia) K(athleen)

Isaacs, Susan 1943- . . . . **CLC 32**
See also BEST 89:1; CA 89-92; CANR 20;
MTCW

Isherwood, Christopher (William Bradshaw)
1904-1986 . . . . **CLC 1, 9, 11, 14, 44**
See also CA 13-16R; 117; CANR 35;
DLB 15; DLBY 86; MTCW

Ishiguro, Kazuo 1954- . . . . . . **CLC 27, 56, 59**
See also BEST 90:2; CA 120; MTCW

Ishikawa Takuboku
1886(?)-1912 . . . . **TCLC 15**
See also CA 113

Iskander, Fazil 1929- . . . . **CLC 47**
See also CA 102

Ivan IV 1530-1584 . . . . **LC 17**

Ivanov, Vyacheslav Ivanovich
1866-1949 . . . . **TCLC 33**
See also CA 122

Ivask, Ivar Vidrik 1927-1992 . . . . . . **CLC 14**
See also CA 37-40R; 139; CANR 24

Jackson, Daniel
See Wingrove, David (John)

Jackson, Jesse 1908-1983 . . . . **CLC 12**
See also BW; CA 25-28R; 109; CANR 27;
CLR 28; MAICYA; SATA 2, 29, 48

Jackson, Laura (Riding) 1901-1991 . . **CLC 7**
See also Riding, Laura
See also CA 65-68; 135; CANR 28; DLB 48

Jackson, Sam
See Trumbo, Dalton

Jackson, Sara
See Wingrove, David (John)

Jackson, Shirley
1919-1965 . . . . **CLC 11, 60; SSC 9**
See also AAYA 9; CA 1-4R; 25-28R;
CANR 4; CDALB 1941-1968; DLB 6;
SATA 2; WLC

Jacob, (Cyprien-)Max 1876-1944 . . . **TCLC 6**
See also CA 104

Jacobs, Jim 1942- . . . . **CLC 12**
See also CA 97-100

Jacobs, W(illiam) W(ymark)
1863-1943 . . . . **TCLC 22**
See also CA 121

Jacobsen, Jens Peter 1847-1885 . . **NCLC 34**

Jacobsen, Josephine 1908- . . . . **CLC 48**
See also CA 33-36R; CANR 23

Jacobson, Dan 1929- . . . . **CLC 4, 14**
See also CA 1-4R; CANR 2, 25; DLB 14;
MTCW

Jacqueline
See Carpentier (y Valmont), Alejo

Jagger, Mick 1944- . . . . **CLC 17**

Jakes, John (William) 1932- . . . . **CLC 29**
See also BEST 89:4; CA 57-60; CANR 10;
DLBY 83; MTCW; SATA 62

James, Andrew
See Kirkup, James

James, C(yril) L(ionel) R(obert)
1901-1989 . . . . **CLC 33**
See also BW; CA 117; 125; 128; DLB 125;
MTCW

James, Daniel (Lewis) 1911-1988
See Santiago, Danny
See also CA 125

James, Dynely
See Mayne, William (James Carter)

James, Henry
1843-1916 . . . . . **TCLC 2, 11, 24, 40, 47;
SSC 8**
See also CA 104; 132; CDALB 1865-1917;
DLB 12, 71, 74; MTCW; WLC

James, Montague (Rhodes)
1862-1936 . . . . **TCLC 6**
See also CA 104

James, P. D. . . . . **CLC 18, 46**
See also White, Phyllis Dorothy James
See also BEST 90:2; CDBLB 1960 to
Present; DLB 87

James, Philip
See Moorcock, Michael (John)

James, William 1842-1910 . . . . . **TCLC 15, 32**
See also CA 109

James I 1394-1437 . . . . **LC 20**

Jami, Nur al-Din 'Abd al-Rahman
1414-1492 . . . . **LC 9**

Jandl, Ernst 1925- . . . . **CLC 34**

Janowitz, Tama 1957- . . . . **CLC 43**
See also CA 106

Jarrell, Randall
1914-1965 . . . . **CLC 1, 2, 6, 9, 13, 49**
See also CA 5-8R; 25-28R; CABS 2;
CANR 6, 34; CDALB 1941-1968; CLR 6;
DLB 48, 52; MAICYA; MTCW; SATA 7

Jarry, Alfred 1873-1907 . . . . **TCLC 2, 14**
See also CA 104

Jarvis, E. K.
See Bloch, Robert (Albert); Ellison, Harlan;
Silverberg, Robert

Jeake, Samuel Jr.
See Aiken, Conrad (Potter)

Jean Paul 1763-1825 . . . . **NCLC 7**

Jeffers, (John) Robinson
1887-1962 . . . . **CLC 2, 3, 11, 15, 54**
See also CA 85-88; CANR 35;
CDALB 1917-1929; DLB 45; MTCW;
WLC

Jefferson, Janet
See Mencken, H(enry) L(ouis)

Jefferson, Thomas 1743-1826 . . . . **NCLC 11**
See also CDALB 1640-1865; DLB 31

Jeffrey, Francis 1773-1850 . . . . **NCLC 33**
See also DLB 107

Jelakowitch, Ivan
See Heijermans, Herman

Jellicoe, (Patricia) Ann 1927- . . . . . . **CLC 27**
See also CA 85-88; DLB 13

Jen, Gish . . . . **CLC 70**
See also Jen, Lillian

Jen, Lillian 1956(?)-
See Jen, Gish
See also CA 135

Jenkins, (John) Robin 1912- . . . . **CLC 52**
See also CA 1-4R; CANR 1; DLB 14

Jennings, Elizabeth (Joan)
1926- . . . . **CLC 5, 14**
See also CA 61-64; CAAS 5; CANR 8, 39;
DLB 27; MTCW; SATA 66

Jennings, Waylon 1937- . . . . **CLC 21**

Jensen, Johannes V. 1873-1950 . . . . **TCLC 41**

Jensen, Laura (Linnea) 1948- ...... **CLC 37**
See also CA 103

Jerome, Jerome K(lapka)
1859-1927 .... **TCLC 23**
See also CA 119; DLB 10, 34

Jerrold, Douglas William
1803-1857 .... **NCLC 2**

Jewett, (Theodora) Sarah Orne
1849-1909 .... **TCLC 1, 22; SSC 6**
See also CA 108; 127; DLB 12, 74;
SATA 15

Jewsbury, Geraldine (Endsor)
1812-1880 .... **NCLC 22**
See also DLB 21

Jhabvala, Ruth Prawer
1927- .... **CLC 4, 8, 29**
See also CA 1-4R; CANR 2, 29; MTCW

Jiles, Paulette 1943- .... **CLC 13, 58**
See also CA 101

Jimenez (Mantecon), Juan Ramon
1881-1958 .... **TCLC 4**
See also CA 104; 131; HW; MTCW

Jimenez, Ramon
See Jimenez (Mantecon), Juan Ramon

Jimenez Mantecon, Juan
See Jimenez (Mantecon), Juan Ramon

Joel, Billy .... **CLC 26**
See also Joel, William Martin

Joel, William Martin 1949-
See Joel, Billy
See also CA 108

John of the Cross, St. 1542-1591 .... **LC 18**

Johnson, B(ryan) S(tanley William)
1933-1973 .... **CLC 6, 9**
See also CA 9-12R; 53-56; CANR 9;
DLB 14, 40

Johnson, Charles (Richard)
1948- .... **CLC 7, 51, 65**
See also BLC 2; BW; CA 116; DLB 33

Johnson, Denis 1949- .... **CLC 52**
See also CA 117; 121; DLB 120

Johnson, Diane (Lain)
1934- .... **CLC 5, 13, 48**
See also CA 41-44R; CANR 17, 40;
DLBY 80; MTCW

Johnson, Eyvind (Olof Verner)
1900-1976 .... **CLC 14**
See also CA 73-76; 69-72; CANR 34

Johnson, J. R.
See James, C(yril) L(ionel) R(obert)

Johnson, James Weldon
1871-1938 .... **TCLC 3, 19**
See also BLC 2; BW; CA 104; 125;
CDALB 1917-1929; DLB 51; MTCW;
SATA 31

Johnson, Joyce 1935- .... **CLC 58**
See also CA 125; 129

Johnson, Lionel (Pigot)
1867-1902 .... **TCLC 19**
See also CA 117; DLB 19

Johnson, Mel
See Malzberg, Barry N(athaniel)

Johnson, Pamela Hansford
1912-1981 .... **CLC 1, 7, 27**
See also CA 1-4R; 104; CANR 2, 28;
DLB 15; MTCW

Johnson, Samuel 1709-1784........ **LC 15**
See also CDBLB 1660-1789; DLB 39, 95,
104; WLC

Johnson, Uwe
1934-1984 .... **CLC 5, 10, 15, 40**
See also CA 1-4R; 112; CANR 1, 39;
DLB 75; MTCW

Johnston, George (Benson) 1913- ... **CLC 51**
See also CA 1-4R; CANR 5, 20; DLB 88

Johnston, Jennifer 1930- .... **CLC 7**
See also CA 85-88; DLB 14

Jolley, (Monica) Elizabeth 1923- ... **CLC 46**
See also CA 127; CAAS 13

Jones, Arthur Llewellyn 1863-1947
See Machen, Arthur
See also CA 104

Jones, D(ouglas) G(ordon) 1929-.... **CLC 10**
See also CA 29-32R; CANR 13; DLB 53

Jones, David (Michael)
1895-1974 .... **CLC 2, 4, 7, 13, 42**
See also CA 9-12R; 53-56; CANR 28;
CDBLB 1945-1960; DLB 20, 100; MTCW

Jones, David Robert 1947-
See Bowie, David
See also CA 103

Jones, Diana Wynne 1934- .... **CLC 26**
See also CA 49-52; CANR 4, 26; CLR 23;
MAICYA; SAAS 7; SATA 9, 70

Jones, Edward P. 1951- .... **CLC 76**

Jones, Gayl 1949- .... **CLC 6, 9**
See also BLC 2; BW; CA 77-80; CANR 27;
DLB 33; MTCW

Jones, James 1921-1977.... **CLC 1, 3, 10, 39**
See also AITN 1, 2; CA 1-4R; 69-72;
CANR 6; DLB 2; MTCW

Jones, John J.
See Lovecraft, H(oward) P(hillips)

Jones, LeRoi .... **CLC 1, 2, 3, 5, 10, 14**
See also Baraka, Amiri

Jones, Louis B. .... **CLC 65**

Jones, Madison (Percy Jr.) 1925-.... **CLC 4**
See also CA 13-16R; CAAS 11; CANR 7

Jones, Mervyn 1922- .... **CLC 10, 52**
See also CA 45-48; CAAS 5; CANR 1;
MTCW

Jones, Mick 1956(?)- .... **CLC 30**
See also Clash, The

Jones, Nettie (Pearl) 1941- .... **CLC 34**
See also CA 137

Jones, Preston 1936-1979 .... **CLC 10**
See also CA 73-76; 89-92; DLB 7

Jones, Robert F(rancis) 1934-...... **CLC 7**
See also CA 49-52; CANR 2

Jones, Rod 1953- .... **CLC 50**
See also CA 128

Jones, Terence Graham Parry
1942- .... **CLC 21**
See also Jones, Terry; Monty Python
See also CA 112; 116; CANR 35; SATA 51

Jones, Terry
See Jones, Terence Graham Parry
See also SATA 67

Jong, Erica 1942- .... **CLC 4, 6, 8, 18**
See also AITN 1; BEST 90:2; CA 73-76;
CANR 26; DLB 2, 5, 28; MTCW

Jonson, Ben(jamin) 1572(?)-1637..... **LC 6**
See also CDBLB Before 1660; DLB 62, 121;
WLC

Jordan, June 1936-.......... **CLC 5, 11, 23**
See also AAYA 2; BW; CA 33-36R;
CANR 25; CLR 10; DLB 38; MAICYA;
MTCW; SATA 4

Jordan, Pat(rick M.) 1941- .... **CLC 37**
See also CA 33-36R

Jorgensen, Ivar
See Ellison, Harlan

Jorgenson, Ivar
See Silverberg, Robert

Josipovici, Gabriel 1940-........ **CLC 6, 43**
See also CA 37-40R; CAAS 8; DLB 14

Joubert, Joseph 1754-1824 .... **NCLC 9**

Jouve, Pierre Jean 1887-1976...... **CLC 47**
See also CA 65-68

Joyce, James (Augustine Aloysius)
1882-1941 .... **TCLC 3, 8, 16, 35; SSC 3**
See also CA 104; 126; CDBLB 1914-1945;
DLB 10, 19, 36; MTCW; WLC

Jozsef, Attila 1905-1937......... **TCLC 22**
See also CA 116

Juana Ines de la Cruz 1651(?)-1695 ... **LC 5**

Judd, Cyril
See Kornbluth, C(yril) M.; Pohl, Frederik

Julian of Norwich 1342(?)-1416(?) .... **LC 6**

Just, Ward (Swift) 1935- .... **CLC 4, 27**
See also CA 25-28R; CANR 32

Justice, Donald (Rodney) 1925- .. **CLC 6, 19**
See also CA 5-8R; CANR 26; DLBY 83

Juvenal c. 55-c. 127 .... **CMLC 8**

Juvenis
See Bourne, Randolph S(illiman)

Kacew, Romain 1914-1980
See Gary, Romain
See also CA 108; 102

Kadare, Ismail 1936- .... **CLC 52**

Kadohata, Cynthia................. **CLC 59**

Kafka, Franz
1883-1924 ...... **TCLC 2, 6, 13, 29, 47;
SSC 5**
See also CA 105; 126; DLB 81; MTCW;
WLC

Kahn, Roger 1927-............... **CLC 30**
See also CA 25-28R; SATA 37

Kain, Saul
See Sassoon, Siegfried (Lorraine)

Kaiser, Georg 1878-1945 .... **TCLC 9**
See also CA 106; DLB 124

Kaletski, Alexander 1946-........ **CLC 39**
See also CA 118

Kalidasa fl. c. 400- .... **CMLC 9**

Kallman, Chester (Simon)
1921-1975 .... **CLC 2**
See also CA 45-48; 53-56; CANR 3

Kaminsky, Melvin 1926-
See Brooks, Mel
See also CA 65-68; CANR 16

Kaminsky, Stuart M(elvin) 1934- ... **CLC 59**
See also CA 73-76; CANR 29

Kane, Paul
See Simon, Paul

Kane, Wilson
See Bloch, Robert (Albert)

Kanin, Garson 1912-............. **CLC 22**
See also AITN 1; CA 5-8R; CANR 7;
  DLB 7

Kaniuk, Yoram 1930-............. **CLC 19**
See also CA 134

Kant, Immanuel 1724-1804 ...... **NCLC 27**
See also DLB 94

Kantor, MacKinlay 1904-1977 ...... **CLC 7**
See also CA 61-64; 73-76; DLB 9, 102

Kaplan, David Michael 1946- ...... **CLC 50**

Kaplan, James 1951- .... **CLC 59**
See also CA 135

Karageorge, Michael
See Anderson, Poul (William)

Karamzin, Nikolai Mikhailovich
  1766-1826 .... **NCLC 3**

Karapanou, Margarita 1946-....... **CLC 13**
See also CA 101

Karinthy, Frigyes 1887-1938 ...... **TCLC 47**

Karl, Frederick R(obert) 1927-..... **CLC 34**
See also CA 5-8R; CANR 3

Kastel, Warren
See Silverberg, Robert

Kataev, Evgeny Petrovich 1903-1942
See Petrov, Evgeny
See also CA 120

Kataphusin
See Ruskin, John

Katz, Steve 1935-................ **CLC 47**
See also CA 25-28R; CAAS 14; CANR 12;
  DLBY 83

Kauffman, Janet 1945-............ **CLC 42**
See also CA 117; DLBY 86

Kaufman, Bob (Garnell)
  1925-1986 .... **CLC 49**
See also BW; CA 41-44R; 118; CANR 22;
  DLB 16, 41

Kaufman, George S. 1889-1961..... **CLC 38**
See also CA 108; 93-96; DLB 7

Kaufman, Sue .... **CLC 3, 8**
See also Barondess, Sue K(aufman)

Kavafis, Konstantinos Petrou 1863-1933
See Cavafy, C(onstantine) P(eter)
See also CA 104

Kavan, Anna 1901-1968........ **CLC 5, 13**
See also CA 5-8R; CANR 6; MTCW

Kavanagh, Dan
See Barnes, Julian

Kavanagh, Patrick (Joseph)
  1904-1967 .... **CLC 22**
See also CA 123; 25-28R; DLB 15, 20;
  MTCW

Kawabata, Yasunari
  1899-1972 .... **CLC 2, 5, 9, 18**
See also CA 93-96; 33-36R

Kaye, M(ary) M(argaret) 1909-..... **CLC 28**
See also CA 89-92; CANR 24; MTCW;
  SATA 62

Kaye, Mollie
See Kaye, M(ary) M(argaret)

Kaye-Smith, Sheila 1887-1956..... **TCLC 20**
See also CA 118; DLB 36

Kaymor, Patrice Maguilene
See Senghor, Leopold Sedar

Kazan, Elia 1909-........... **CLC 6, 16, 63**
See also CA 21-24R; CANR 32

Kazantzakis, Nikos
  1883(?)-1957 .... **TCLC 2, 5, 33**
See also CA 105; 132; MTCW

Kazin, Alfred 1915- .... **CLC 34, 38**
See also CA 1-4R; CAAS 7; CANR 1;
  DLB 67

Keane, Mary Nesta (Skrine) 1904-
See Keane, Molly
See also CA 108; 114

Keane, Molly..................... **CLC 31**
See also Keane, Mary Nesta (Skrine)

Keates, Jonathan 19(?)-........... **CLC 34**

Keaton, Buster 1895-1966 .... **CLC 20**

Keats, John 1795-1821..... **NCLC 8; PC 1**
See also CDBLB 1789-1832; DLB 96, 110;
  WLC

Keene, Donald 1922- .... **CLC 34**
See also CA 1-4R; CANR 5

Keillor, Garrison................. **CLC 40**
See also Keillor, Gary (Edward)
See also AAYA 2; BEST 89:3; DLBY 87;
  SATA 58

Keillor, Gary (Edward) 1942-
See Keillor, Garrison
See also CA 111; 117; CANR 36; MTCW

Keith, Michael
See Hubbard, L(afayette) Ron(ald)

Kell, Joseph
See Wilson, John (Anthony) Burgess

Keller, Gottfried 1819-1890....... **NCLC 2**
See also DLB 129

Kellerman, Jonathan 1949- .... **CLC 44**
See also BEST 90:1; CA 106; CANR 29

Kelley, William Melvin 1937-...... **CLC 22**
See also BW; CA 77-80; CANR 27; DLB 33

Kellogg, Marjorie 1922-........... **CLC 2**
See also CA 81-84

Kellow, Kathleen
See Hibbert, Eleanor Burford

Kelly, M(ilton) T(erry) 1947-....... **CLC 55**
See also CA 97-100; CANR 19

Kelman, James 1946-............. **CLC 58**

Kemal, Yashar 1923- .... **CLC 14, 29**
See also CA 89-92

Kemble, Fanny 1809-1893 .... **NCLC 18**
See also DLB 32

Kemelman, Harry 1908-........... **CLC 2**
See also AITN 1; CA 9-12R; CANR 6;
  DLB 28

Kempe, Margery 1373(?)-1440(?) ..... **LC 6**

Kempis, Thomas a 1380-1471 .... **LC 11**

Kendall, Henry 1839-1882....... **NCLC 12**

Keneally, Thomas (Michael)
  1935-...... **CLC 5, 8, 10, 14, 19, 27, 43**
See also CA 85-88; CANR 10; MTCW

Kennedy, Adrienne (Lita) 1931- .... **CLC 66**
See also BLC 2; BW; CA 103; CABS 3;
  CANR 26; DLB 38

Kennedy, John Pendleton
  1795-1870 .... **NCLC 2**
See also DLB 3 .

Kennedy, Joseph Charles 1929-...... **CLC 8**
See also Kennedy, X. J.
See also CA 1-4R; CANR 4, 30, 40;
  SATA 14

Kennedy, William 1928-... **CLC 6, 28, 34, 53**
See also AAYA 1; CA 85-88; CANR 14,
  31; DLBY 85; MTCW; SATA 57

Kennedy, X. J...................... **CLC 42**
See also Kennedy, Joseph Charles
See also CAAS 9; CLR 27; DLB 5

Kent, Kelvin
See Kuttner, Henry

Kenton, Maxwell
See Southern, Terry

Kenyon, Robert O.
See Kuttner, Henry

Kerouac, Jack ..... **CLC 1, 2, 3, 5, 14, 29, 61**
See also Kerouac, Jean-Louis Lebris de
See also CDALB 1941-1968; DLB 2, 16;
  DLBD 3

Kerouac, Jean-Louis Lebris de 1922-1969
See Kerouac, Jack
See also AITN 1; CA 5-8R; 25-28R;
  CANR 26; MTCW; WLC

Kerr, Jean 1923-................ **CLC 22**
See also CA 5-8R; CANR 7

Kerr, M. E. .... **CLC 12, 35**
See also Meaker, Marijane (Agnes)
See also AAYA 2; SAAS 1

Kerr, Robert .... **CLC 55**

Kerrigan, (Thomas) Anthony
  1918-..................... **CLC 4, 6**
See also CA 49-52; CAAS 11; CANR 4

Kerry, Lois
See Duncan, Lois

Kesey, Ken (Elton)
  1935-........... **CLC 1, 3, 6, 11, 46, 64**
See also CA 1-4R; CANR 22, 38;
  CDALB 1968-1988; DLB 2, 16; MTCW;
  SATA 66; WLC

Kesselring, Joseph (Otto)
  1902-1967 .... **CLC 45**

Kessler, Jascha (Frederick) 1929-.... **CLC 4**
See also CA 17-20R; CANR 8

Kettelkamp, Larry (Dale) 1933- .... **CLC 12**
See also CA 29-32R; CANR 16; SAAS 3;
  SATA 2

Kherdian, David 1931-........... **CLC 6, 9**
See also CA 21-24R; CAAS 2; CANR 39;
  CLR 24; MAICYA; SATA 16

Khlebnikov, Velimir .... **TCLC 20**
See also Khlebnikov, Viktor Vladimirovich

Khlebnikov, Viktor Vladimirovich 1885-1922
See Khlebnikov, Velimir
See also CA 117

Khodasevich, Vladislav (Felitsianovich)
1886-1939 . . . . **TCLC 15**
See also CA 115

Kielland, Alexander Lange
1849-1906 . . . . **TCLC 5**
See also CA 104

Kiely, Benedict 1919- . . . . **CLC 23, 43**
See also CA 1-4R; CANR 2; DLB 15

Kienzle, William X(avier) 1928- . . . . **CLC 25**
See also CA 93-96; CAAS 1; CANR 9, 31;
MTCW

Kierkegaard, Soeren 1813-1855 . . . **NCLC 34**

Kierkegaard, Soren 1813-1855 . . . . **NCLC 34**

Killens, John Oliver 1916-1987 . . . . . **CLC 10**
See also BW; CA 77-80; 123; CAAS 2;
CANR 26; DLB 33

Killigrew, Anne 1660-1685 . . . . **LC 4**

Kim
See Simenon, Georges (Jacques Christian)

Kincaid, Jamaica 1949- . . . . **CLC 43, 68**
See also BLC 2; BW; CA 125

King, Francis (Henry) 1923- . . . . . **CLC 8, 53**
See also CA 1-4R; CANR 1, 33; DLB 15;
MTCW

King, Stephen (Edwin)
1947- . . . . **CLC 12, 26, 37, 61**
See also AAYA 1; BEST 90:1; CA 61-64;
CANR 1, 30; DLBY 80; MTCW;
SATA 9, 55

King, Steve
See King, Stephen (Edwin)

Kingman, Lee . . . . **CLC 17**
See also Natti, (Mary) Lee
See also SAAS 3; SATA 1, 67

Kingsley, Charles 1819-1875 . . . . . **NCLC 35**
See also DLB 21, 32; YABC 2

Kingsley, Sidney 1906- . . . . **CLC 44**
See also CA 85-88; DLB 7

Kingsolver, Barbara 1955- . . . . **CLC 55**
See also CA 129; 134

Kingston, Maxine (Ting Ting) Hong
1940- . . . . **CLC 12, 19, 58**
See also AAYA 8; CA 69-72; CANR 13,
38; DLBY 80; MTCW; SATA 53

Kinnell, Galway
1927- . . . . **CLC 1, 2, 3, 5, 13, 29**
See also CA 9-12R; CANR 10, 34; DLB 5;
DLBY 87; MTCW

Kinsella, Thomas 1928- . . . . **CLC 4, 19**
See also CA 17-20R; CANR 15; DLB 27;
MTCW

Kinsella, W(illiam) P(atrick)
1935- . . . . **CLC 27, 43**
See also AAYA 7; CA 97-100; CAAS 7;
CANR 21, 35; MTCW

Kipling, (Joseph) Rudyard
1865-1936 . . . . **TCLC 8, 17; PC 3; SSC 5**
See also CA 105; 120; CANR 33;
CDBLB 1890-1914; DLB 19, 34;
MAICYA; MTCW; WLC; YABC 2

Kirkup, James 1918- . . . . **CLC 1**
See also CA 1-4R; CAAS 4; CANR 2;
DLB 27; SATA 12

Kirkwood, James 1930(?)-1989 . . . . . . **CLC 9**
See also AITN 2; CA 1-4R; 128; CANR 6,
40

Kis, Danilo 1935-1989 . . . . **CLC 57**
See also CA 109; 118; 129; MTCW

Kivi, Aleksis 1834-1872 . . . . **NCLC 30**

Kizer, Carolyn (Ashley) 1925- . . . **CLC 15, 39**
See also CA 65-68; CAAS 5; CANR 24;
DLB 5

Klabund 1890-1928 . . . . **TCLC 44**
See also DLB 66

Klappert, Peter 1942- . . . . **CLC 57**
See also CA 33-36R; DLB 5

Klein, A(braham) M(oses)
1909-1972 . . . . **CLC 19**
See also CA 101; 37-40R; DLB 68

Klein, Norma 1938-1989 . . . . **CLC 30**
See also AAYA 2; CA 41-44R; 128;
CANR 15, 37; CLR 2, 19; MAICYA;
SAAS 1; SATA 7, 57

Klein, T(heodore) E(ibon) D(onald)
1947- . . . . **CLC 34**
See also CA 119

Kleist, Heinrich von 1777-1811 . . . . **NCLC 2**
See also DLB 90

Klima, Ivan 1931- . . . . **CLC 56**
See also CA 25-28R; CANR 17

Klimentov, Andrei Platonovich 1899-1951
See Platonov, Andrei
See also CA 108

Klinger, Friedrich Maximilian von
1752-1831 . . . . **NCLC 1**
See also DLB 94

Klopstock, Friedrich Gottlieb
1724-1803 . . . . **NCLC 11**
See also DLB 97

Knebel, Fletcher 1911- . . . . **CLC 14**
See also AITN 1; CA 1-4R; CAAS 3;
CANR 1, 36; SATA 36

Knickerbocker, Diedrich
See Irving, Washington

Knight, Etheridge 1931-1991 . . . . . . **CLC 40**
See also BLC 2; BW; CA 21-24R; 133;
CANR 23; DLB 41

Knight, Sarah Kemble 1666-1727 . . . . . **LC 7**
See also DLB 24

Knowles, John 1926- . . . . . . **CLC 1, 4, 10, 26**
See also AAYA 10; CA 17-20R; CANR 40;
CDALB 1968-1988; DLB 6; MTCW;
SATA 8

Knox, Calvin M.
See Silverberg, Robert

Knye, Cassandra
See Disch, Thomas M(ichael)

Koch, C(hristopher) J(ohn) 1932- . . . **CLC 42**
See also CA 127

Koch, Christopher
See Koch, C(hristopher) J(ohn)

Koch, Kenneth 1925- . . . . **CLC 5, 8, 44**
See also CA 1-4R; CANR 6, 36; DLB 5;
SATA 65

Kochanowski, Jan 1530-1584 . . . . **LC 10**

Kock, Charles Paul de
1794-1871 . . . . **NCLC 16**

Koda Shigeyuki 1867-1947
See Rohan, Koda
See also CA 121

Koestler, Arthur
1905-1983 . . . . **CLC 1, 3, 6, 8, 15, 33**
See also CA 1-4R; 109; CANR 1, 33;
CDBLB 1945-1960; DLBY 83; MTCW

Kohout, Pavel 1928- . . . . **CLC 13**
See also CA 45-48; CANR 3

Koizumi, Yakumo
See Hearn, (Patricio) Lafcadio (Tessima
Carlos)

Kolmar, Gertrud 1894-1943 . . . . **TCLC 40**

Konrad, George
See Konrad, Gyoergy

Konrad, Gyoergy 1933- . . . . . . **CLC 4, 10, 73**
See also CA 85-88

Konwicki, Tadeusz 1926- . . . . . **CLC 8, 28, 54**
See also CA 101; CAAS 9; CANR 39;
MTCW

Kopit, Arthur (Lee) 1937- . . . . **CLC 1, 18, 33**
See also AITN 1; CA 81-84; CABS 3;
DLB 7; MTCW

Kops, Bernard 1926- . . . . **CLC 4**
See also CA 5-8R; DLB 13

Kornbluth, C(yril) M. 1923-1958 . . . . **TCLC 8**
See also CA 105; DLB 8

Korolenko, V. G.
See Korolenko, Vladimir Galaktionovich

Korolenko, Vladimir
See Korolenko, Vladimir Galaktionovich

Korolenko, Vladimir G.
See Korolenko, Vladimir Galaktionovich

Korolenko, Vladimir Galaktionovich
1853-1921 . . . . **TCLC 22**
See also CA 121

Kosinski, Jerzy (Nikodem)
1933-1991 . . . **CLC 1, 2, 3, 6, 10, 15, 53,
70**
See also CA 17-20R; 134; CANR 9; DLB 2;
DLBY 82; MTCW

Kostelanetz, Richard (Cory) 1940- . . **CLC 28**
See also CA 13-16R; CAAS 8; CANR 38

Kostrowitzki, Wilhelm Apollinaris de
1880-1918
See Apollinaire, Guillaume
See also CA 104

Kotlowitz, Robert 1924- . . . . **CLC 4**
See also CA 33-36R; CANR 36

Kotzebue, August (Friedrich Ferdinand) von
1761-1819 . . . . **NCLC 25**
See also DLB 94

Kotzwinkle, William 1938- . . . **CLC 5, 14, 35**
See also CA 45-48; CANR 3; CLR 6;
MAICYA; SATA 24, 70

Kozol, Jonathan 1936- . . . . **CLC 17**
See also CA 61-64; CANR 16

Kozoll, Michael 1940(?)- . . . . **CLC 35**

Kramer, Kathryn 19(?)- . . . . **CLC 34**

Kramer, Larry 1935- . . . . **CLC 42**
See also CA 124; 126

Author Index

Larkin, Philip (Arthur)
    1922-1985 ...   **CLC 3, 5, 8, 9, 13, 18, 33,
                                                39, 64**
    See also CA 5-8R; 117; CANR 24;
    CDBLB 1960 to Present; DLB 27;
    MTCW

Larra (y Sanchez de Castro), Mariano Jose de
    1809-1837 .... **NCLC 17**

Larsen, Eric   1941- .... **CLC 55**
    See also CA 132

Larsen, Nella   1891-1964 .... **CLC 37**
    See also BLC 2; BW; CA 125; DLB 51

Larson, Charles R(aymond)   1938-... **CLC 31**
    See also CA 53-56; CANR 4

Latham, Jean Lee   1902-........... **CLC 12**
    See also AITN 1; CA 5-8R; CANR 7;
    MAICYA; SATA 2, 68

Latham, Mavis
    See Clark, Mavis Thorpe

Lathen, Emma .... **CLC 2**
    See also Hennissart, Martha; Latsis, Mary
    J(ane)

Lathrop, Francis
    See Leiber, Fritz (Reuter Jr.)

Latsis, Mary J(ane)
    See Lathen, Emma
    See also CA 85-88

Lattimore, Richmond (Alexander)
    1906-1984 .... **CLC 3**
    See also CA 1-4R; 112; CANR 1

Laughlin, James   1914-........... **CLC 49**
    See also CA 21-24R; CANR 9; DLB 48

Laurence, (Jean) Margaret (Wemyss)
    1926-1987 .. **CLC 3, 6, 13, 50, 62; SSC 7**
    See also CA 5-8R; 121; CANR 33; DLB 53;
    MTCW; SATA 50

Laurent, Antoine   1952- .... **CLC 50**

Lauscher, Hermann
    See Hesse, Hermann

Lautreamont, Comte de
    1846-1870 .... **NCLC 12**

Laverty, Donald
    See Blish, James (Benjamin)

Lavin, Mary   1912-...... **CLC 4, 18; SSC 4**
    See also CA 9-12R; CANR 33; DLB 15;
    MTCW

Lavond, Paul Dennis
    See Kornbluth, C(yril) M.; Pohl, Frederik

Lawler, Raymond Evenor   1922- .... **CLC 58**
    See also CA 103

Lawrence, D(avid) H(erbert Richards)
    1885-1930 ...... **TCLC 2, 9, 16, 33, 48;
                                                SSC 4**
    See also CA 104; 121; CDBLB 1914-1945;
    DLB 10, 19, 36, 98; MTCW; WLC

Lawrence, T(homas) E(dward)
    1888-1935 .... **TCLC 18**
    See also Dale, Colin
    See also CA 115

Lawrence Of Arabia
    See Lawrence, T(homas) E(dward)

Lawson, Henry (Archibald Hertzberg)
    1867-1922 .... **TCLC 27**
    See also CA 120

Lawton, Dennis
    See Faust, Frederick (Schiller)

Laxness, Halldor .... **CLC 25**
    See also Gudjonsson, Halldor Kiljan

Layamon   fl. c. 1200-........... **CMLC 10**

Laye, Camara   1928-1980 .... **CLC 4, 38**
    See also BLC 2; BW; CA 85-88; 97-100;
    CANR 25; MTCW

Layton, Irving (Peter)   1912- ..... **CLC 2, 15**
    See also CA 1-4R; CANR 2, 33; DLB 88;
    MTCW

Lazarus, Emma   1849-1887....... **NCLC 8**

Lazarus, Felix
    See Cable, George Washington

Lea, Joan
    See Neufeld, John (Arthur)

Leacock, Stephen (Butler)
    1869-1944 .... **TCLC 2**
    See also CA 104; DLB 92

Lear, Edward   1812-1888 .... **NCLC 3**
    See also CLR 1; DLB 32; MAICYA;
    SATA 18

Lear, Norman (Milton)   1922- ...... **CLC 12**
    See also CA 73-76

Leavis, F(rank) R(aymond)
    1895-1978 .... **CLC 24**
    See also CA 21-24R; 77-80; MTCW

Leavitt, David   1961-.............. **CLC 34**
    See also CA 116; 122; DLB 130

Leblanc, Maurice (Marie Emile)
    1864-1941 .... **TCLC 49**
    See also CA 110

Lebowitz, Fran(ces Ann)
    1951(?)-................... **CLC 11, 36**
    See also CA 81-84; CANR 14; MTCW

le Carre, John .... **CLC 3, 5, 9, 15, 28**
    See also Cornwell, David (John Moore)
    See also BEST 89:4; CDBLB 1960 to
    Present; DLB 87

Le Clezio, J(ean) M(arie) G(ustave)
    1940-.................... **CLC 31**
    See also CA 116; 128; DLB 83

Leconte de Lisle, Charles-Marie-Rene
    1818-1894 .... **NCLC 29**

Le Coq, Monsieur
    See Simenon, Georges (Jacques Christian)

Leduc, Violette   1907-1972........ **CLC 22**
    See also CA 13-14; 33-36R; CAP 1

Ledwidge, Francis   1887(?)-1917 ... **TCLC 23**
    See also CA 123; DLB 20

Lee, Andrea   1953- .... **CLC 36**
    See also BLC 2; BW; CA 125

Lee, Andrew
    See Auchincloss, Louis (Stanton)

Lee, Don L. .... **CLC 2**
    See also Madhubuti, Haki R.

Lee, George W(ashington)
    1894-1976 .... **CLC 52**
    See also BLC 2; BW; CA 125; DLB 51

Lee, (Nelle) Harper   1926- ...... **CLC 12, 60**
    See also CA 13-16R; CDALB 1941-1968;
    DLB 6; MTCW; SATA 11; WLC

Lee, Julian
    See Latham, Jean Lee

Lee, Lawrence   1903- .... **CLC 34**
    See also CA 25-28R

Lee, Manfred B(ennington)
    1905-1971 .... **CLC 11**
    See also Queen, Ellery
    See also CA 1-4R; 29-32R; CANR 2

Lee, Stan   1922-................. **CLC 17**
    See also AAYA 5; CA 108; 111

Lee, Tanith   1947-................ **CLC 46**
    See also CA 37-40R; SATA 8

Lee, Vernon .... **TCLC 5**
    See also Paget, Violet
    See also DLB 57

Lee, William
    See Burroughs, William S(eward)

Lee, Willy
    See Burroughs, William S(eward)

Lee-Hamilton, Eugene (Jacob)
    1845-1907 .... **TCLC 22**
    See also CA 117

Leet, Judith   1935- .... **CLC 11**

Le Fanu, Joseph Sheridan
    1814-1873 .... **NCLC 9**
    See also DLB 21, 70

Leffland, Ella   1931- .... **CLC 19**
    See also CA 29-32R; CANR 35; DLBY 84;
    SATA 65

Leger, (Marie-Rene) Alexis Saint-Leger
    1887-1975 .... **CLC 11**
    See also Perse, St.-John
    See also CA 13-16R; 61-64; MTCW

Leger, Saintleger
    See Leger, (Marie-Rene) Alexis Saint-Leger

Le Guin, Ursula K(roeber)
    1929-.......... **CLC 8, 13, 22, 45, 71**
    See also AAYA 9; AITN 1; CA 21-24R;
    CANR 9, 32; CDALB 1968-1988; CLR 3,
    28; DLB 8, 52; MAICYA; MTCW;
    SATA 4, 52

Lehmann, Rosamond (Nina)
    1901-1990 .... **CLC 5**
    See also CA 77-80; 131; CANR 8; DLB 15

Leiber, Fritz (Reuter Jr.)
    1910-1992 .... **CLC 25**
    See also CA 45-48; 139; CANR 2, 40;
    DLB 8; MTCW; SATA 45; SATO 73

Leimbach, Martha   1963-
    See Leimbach, Marti
    See also CA 130

Leimbach, Marti .... **CLC 65**
    See also Leimbach, Martha

Leino, Eino .... **TCLC 24**
    See also Loennbohm, Armas Eino Leopold

Leiris, Michel (Julien)   1901-1990... **CLC 61**
    See also CA 119; 128; 132

Leithauser, Brad   1953-............ **CLC 27**
    See also CA 107; CANR 27; DLB 120

Lelchuk, Alan   1938-.............. **CLC 5**
    See also CA 45-48; CANR 1

Lem, Stanislaw   1921-........ **CLC 8, 15, 40**
    See also CA 105; CAAS 1; CANR 32;
    MTCW

Lemann, Nancy   1956-............ **CLC 39**
    See also CA 118; 136

Lynx
See West, Rebecca

Lyons, Marcus
See Blish, James (Benjamin)

Lyre, Pinchbeck
See Sassoon, Siegfried (Lorraine)

Lytle, Andrew (Nelson) 1902- ...... CLC 22
See also CA 9-12R; DLB 6

Lyttelton, George 1709-1773 .... LC 10

Maas, Peter 1929- .... CLC 29
See also CA 93-96

Macaulay, Rose 1881-1958 ..... TCLC 7, 44
See also CA 104; DLB 36

MacBeth, George (Mann)
1932-1992 .... CLC 2, 5, 9
See also CA 25-28R; 136; DLB 40; MTCW;
SATA 4; SATO 70

MacCaig, Norman (Alexander)
1910- .... CLC 36
See also CA 9-12R; CANR 3, 34; DLB 27

MacCarthy, (Sir Charles Otto) Desmond
1877-1952 .... TCLC 36

MacDiarmid, Hugh ..... CLC 2, 4, 11, 19, 63
See also Grieve, C(hristopher) M(urray)
See also CDBLB 1945-1960; DLB 20

MacDonald, Anson
See Heinlein, Robert A(nson)

Macdonald, Cynthia 1928- ...... CLC 13, 19
See also CA 49-52; CANR 4; DLB 105

MacDonald, George 1824-1905 ..... TCLC 9
See also CA 106; 137; DLB 18; MAICYA;
SATA 33

Macdonald, John
See Millar, Kenneth

MacDonald, John D(ann)
1916-1986 .... CLC 3, 27, 44
See also CA 1-4R; 121; CANR 1, 19;
DLB 8; DLBY 86; MTCW

Macdonald, John Ross
See Millar, Kenneth

Macdonald, Ross ..... CLC 1, 2, 3, 14, 34, 41
See also Millar, Kenneth
See also DLBD 6

MacDougal, John
See Blish, James (Benjamin)

MacEwen, Gwendolyn (Margaret)
1941-1987 .... CLC 13, 55
See also CA 9-12R; 124; CANR 7, 22;
DLB 53; SATA 50, 55

Machado (y Ruiz), Antonio
1875-1939 .... TCLC 3
See also CA 104; DLB 108

Machado de Assis, Joaquim Maria
1839-1908 .... TCLC 10
See also BLC 2; CA 107

Machen, Arthur .... TCLC 4
See also Jones, Arthur Llewellyn
See also DLB 36

Machiavelli, Niccolo 1469-1527 ...... LC 8

MacInnes, Colin 1914-1976 ...... CLC 4, 23
See also CA 69-72; 65-68; CANR 21;
DLB 14; MTCW

MacInnes, Helen (Clark)
1907-1985 .... CLC 27, 39
See also CA 1-4R; 117; CANR 1, 28;
DLB 87; MTCW; SATA 22, 44

Mackenzie, Compton (Edward Montague)
1883-1972 .... CLC 18
See also CA 21-22; 37-40R; CAP 2;
DLB 34, 100

Mackintosh, Elizabeth 1896(?)-1952
See Tey, Josephine
See also CA 110

MacLaren, James
See Grieve, C(hristopher) M(urray)

Mac Laverty, Bernard 1942- .... CLC 31
See also CA 116; 118

MacLean, Alistair (Stuart)
1922-1987 .... CLC 3, 13, 50, 63
See also CA 57-60; 121; CANR 28; MTCW;
SATA 23, 50

MacLeish, Archibald
1892-1982 .... CLC 3, 8, 14, 68
See also CA 9-12R; 106; CANR 33; DLB 4,
7, 45; DLBY 82; MTCW

MacLennan, (John) Hugh
1907- .... CLC 2, 14
See also CA 5-8R; CANR 33; DLB 68;
MTCW

MacLeod, Alistair 1936- .... CLC 56
See also CA 123; DLB 60

MacNeice, (Frederick) Louis
1907-1963 .... CLC 1, 4, 10, 53
See also CA 85-88; DLB 10, 20; MTCW

MacNeill, Dand
See Fraser, George MacDonald

Macpherson, (Jean) Jay 1931- ...... CLC 14
See also CA 5-8R; DLB 53

MacShane, Frank 1927- .... CLC 39
See also CA 9-12R; CANR 3, 33; DLB 111

Macumber, Mari
See Sandoz, Mari(e Susette)

Madach, Imre 1823-1864 .... NCLC 19

Madden, (Jerry) David 1933- .... CLC 5, 15
See also CA 1-4R; CAAS 3; CANR 4;
DLB 6; MTCW

Maddern, Al(an)
See Ellison, Harlan

Madhubuti, Haki R.
1942- .... CLC 6, 73; PC 5
See also Lee, Don L.
See also BLC 2; BW; CA 73-76; CANR 24;
DLB 5, 41; DLBD 8

Madow, Pauline (Reichberg) .... CLC 1
See also CA 9-12R

Maepenn, Hugh
See Kuttner, Henry

Maepenn, K. H.
See Kuttner, Henry

Maeterlinck, Maurice 1862-1949 ... TCLC 3
See also CA 104; 136; SATA 66

Maginn, William 1794-1842 .... NCLC 8
See also DLB 110

Mahapatra, Jayanta 1928- .... CLC 33
See also CA 73-76; CAAS 9; CANR 15, 33

Mahfouz, Naguib (Abdel Aziz Al-Sabilgi)
1911(?)-
See Mahfuz, Najib
See also BEST 89:2; CA 128; MTCW

Mahfuz, Najib .... CLC 52, 55
See also Mahfouz, Naguib (Abdel Aziz
Al-Sabilgi)
See also DLBY 88

Mahon, Derek 1941- .... CLC 27
See also CA 113; 128; DLB 40

Mailer, Norman
1923- ...... CLC 1, 2, 3, 4, 5, 8, 11, 14,
28, 39, 74
See also AITN 2; CA 9-12R; CABS 1;
CANR 28; CDALB 1968-1988; DLB 2,
16, 28; DLBD 3; DLBY 80, 83; MTCW

Maillet, Antonine 1929- .... CLC 54
See also CA 115; 120; DLB 60

Mais, Roger 1905-1955 .... TCLC 8
See also BW; CA 105; 124; DLB 125;
MTCW

Maitland, Sara (Louise) 1950- ...... CLC 49
See also CA 69-72; CANR 13

Major, Clarence 1936- .... CLC 3, 19, 48
See also BLC 2; BW; CA 21-24R; CAAS 6;
CANR 13, 25; DLB 33

Major, Kevin (Gerald) 1949- .... CLC 26
See also CA 97-100; CANR 21, 38;
CLR 11; DLB 60; MAICYA; SATA 32

Maki, James
See Ozu, Yasujiro

Malabaila, Damiano
See Levi, Primo

Malamud, Bernard
1914-1986 ..... CLC 1, 2, 3, 5, 8, 9, 11,
18, 27, 44
See also CA 5-8R; 118; CABS 1; CANR 28;
CDALB 1941-1968; DLB 2, 28;
DLBY 80, 86; MTCW; WLC

Malcolm, Dan
See Silverberg, Robert

Malherbe, Francois de 1555-1628 ..... LC 5

Mallarme, Stephane
1842-1898 .... NCLC 4; PC 4

Mallet-Joris, Francoise 1930- ...... CLC 11
See also CA 65-68; CANR 17; DLB 83

Malley, Ern
See McAuley, James Phillip

Mallowan, Agatha Christie
See Christie, Agatha (Mary Clarissa)

Maloff, Saul 1922- .... CLC 5
See also CA 33-36R

Malone, Louis
See MacNeice, (Frederick) Louis

Malone, Michael (Christopher)
1942- .... CLC 43
See also CA 77-80; CANR 14, 32

Malory, (Sir) Thomas
1410(?)-1471(?) .... LC 11
See also CDBLB Before 1660; SATA 33, 59

Malouf, (George Joseph) David
1934- .... CLC 28
See also CA 124

Malraux, (Georges-)Andre
1901-1976 ...... **CLC 1, 4, 9, 13, 15, 57**
See also CA 21-22; 69-72; CANR 34;
CAP 2; DLB 72; MTCW

Malzberg, Barry N(athaniel) 1939-... **CLC 7**
See also CA 61-64; CAAS 4; CANR 16;
DLB 8

Mamet, David (Alan)
1947- .... **CLC 9, 15, 34, 46**
See also AAYA 3; CA 81-84; CABS 3;
CANR 15; DLB 7; MTCW

Mamoulian, Rouben (Zachary)
1897-1987 .... **CLC 16**
See also CA 25-28R; 124

Mandelstam, Osip (Emilievich)
1891(?)-1938(?) .... **TCLC 2, 6**
See also CA 104

Mander, (Mary) Jane 1877-1949... **TCLC 31**

Mandiargues, Andre Pieyre de....... **CLC 41**
See also Pieyre de Mandiargues, Andre
See also DLB 83

Mandrake, Ethel Belle
See Thurman, Wallace (Henry)

Mangan, James Clarence
1803-1849 .... **NCLC 27**

Maniere, J.-E.
See Giraudoux, (Hippolyte) Jean

Manley, (Mary) Delariviere
1672(?)-1724 .... **LC 1**
See also DLB 39, 80

Mann, Abel
See Creasey, John

Mann, (Luiz) Heinrich 1871-1950... **TCLC 9**
See also CA 106; DLB 66

Mann, (Paul) Thomas
1875-1955 ... **TCLC 2, 8, 14, 21, 35, 44;**
SSC 5
See also CA 104; 128; DLB 66; MTCW;
WLC

Manning, David
See Faust, Frederick (Schiller)

Manning, Frederic 1887(?)-1935 ... **TCLC 25**
See also CA 124

Manning, Olivia 1915-1980 ...... **CLC 5, 19**
See also CA 5-8R; 101; CANR 29; MTCW

Mano, D. Keith 1942- .... **CLC 2, 10**
See also CA 25-28R; CAAS 6; CANR 26;
DLB 6

Mansfield, Katherine... **TCLC 2, 8, 39; SSC 9**
See also Beauchamp, Kathleen Mansfield
See also WLC

Manso, Peter 1940- .... **CLC 39**
See also CA 29-32R

Mantecon, Juan Jimenez
See Jimenez (Mantecon), Juan Ramon

Manton, Peter
See Creasey, John

Man Without a Spleen, A
See Chekhov, Anton (Pavlovich)

Manzoni, Alessandro 1785-1873 .. **NCLC 29**

Mapu, Abraham (ben Jekutiel)
1808-1867 .... **NCLC 18**

Mara, Sally
See Queneau, Raymond

Marat, Jean Paul 1743-1793 .... **LC 10**

Marcel, Gabriel Honore
1889-1973 .... **CLC 15**
See also CA 102; 45-48; MTCW

Marchbanks, Samuel
See Davies, (William) Robertson

Marchi, Giacomo
See Bassani, Giorgio

Margulies, Donald................. **CLC 76**

Marie de France c. 12th cent. -.... **CMLC 8**

Marie de l'Incarnation 1599-1672.... **LC 10**

Mariner, Scott
See Pohl, Frederik

Marinetti, Filippo Tommaso
1876-1944 .... **TCLC 10**
See also CA 107; DLB 114

Marivaux, Pierre Carlet de Chamblain de
1688-1763 .... **LC 4**

Markandaya, Kamala .... **CLC 8, 38**
See also Taylor, Kamala (Purnaiya)

Markfield, Wallace 1926-........... **CLC 8**
See also CA 69-72; CAAS 3; DLB 2, 28

Markham, Edwin 1852-1940 ..... **TCLC 47**
See also DLB 54

Markham, Robert
See Amis, Kingsley (William)

Marks, J
See Highwater, Jamake (Mamake)

Marks-Highwater, J
See Highwater, Jamake (Mamake)

Markson, David M(errill) 1927-.... **CLC 67**
See also CA 49-52; CANR 1

Marley, Bob..................... **CLC 17**
See also Marley, Robert Nesta

Marley, Robert Nesta 1945-1981
See Marley, Bob
See also CA 107; 103

Marlowe, Christopher
1564-1593 .... **LC 22; DC 1**
See also CDBLB Before 1660; DLB 62;
WLC

Marmontel, Jean-Francois
1723-1799 .... **LC 2**

Marquand, John P(hillips)
1893-1960 .... **CLC 2, 10**
See also CA 85-88; DLB 9, 102

Marquez, Gabriel (Jose) Garcia...... **CLC 68**
See also Garcia Marquez, Gabriel (Jose)

Marquis, Don(ald Robert Perry)
1878-1937 .... **TCLC 7**
See also CA 104; DLB 11, 25

Marric, J. J.
See Creasey, John

Marrow, Bernard
See Moore, Brian

Marryat, Frederick 1792-1848 .... **NCLC 3**
See also DLB 21

Marsden, James
See Creasey, John

Marsh, (Edith) Ngaio
1899-1982 .... **CLC 7, 53**
See also CA 9-12R; CANR 6; DLB 77;
MTCW

Marshall, Garry 1934-............ **CLC 17**
See also AAYA 3; CA 111; SATA 60

Marshall, Paule 1929-.. **CLC 27, 72; SSC 3**
See also BLC 3; BW; CA 77-80; CANR 25;
DLB 33; MTCW

Marsten, Richard
See Hunter, Evan

Martha, Henry
See Harris, Mark

Martin, Ken
See Hubbard, L(afayette) Ron(ald)

Martin, Richard
See Creasey, John

Martin, Steve 1945-.............. **CLC 30**
See also CA 97-100; CANR 30; MTCW

Martin, Webber
See Silverberg, Robert

Martin du Gard, Roger
1881-1958 .... **TCLC 24**
See also CA 118; DLB 65

Martineau, Harriet 1802-1876.... **NCLC 26**
See also DLB 21, 55; YABC 2

Martines, Julia
See O'Faolain, Julia

Martinez, Jacinto Benavente y
See Benavente (y Martinez), Jacinto

Martinez Ruiz, Jose 1873-1967
See Azorin; Ruiz, Jose Martinez
See also CA 93-96; HW

Martinez Sierra, Gregorio
1881-1947 .... **TCLC 6**
See also CA 115

Martinez Sierra, Maria (de la O'LeJarraga)
1874-1974 .... **TCLC 6**
See also CA 115

Martinsen, Martin
See Follett, Ken(neth Martin)

Martinson, Harry (Edmund)
1904-1978 .... **CLC 14**
See also CA 77-80; CANR 34

Marut, Ret
See Traven, B.

Marut, Robert
See Traven, B.

Marvell, Andrew 1621-1678......... **LC 4**
See also CDBLB 1660-1789; WLC

Marx, Karl (Heinrich)
1818-1883 .... **NCLC 17**
See also DLB 129

Masaoka Shiki................... **TCLC 18**
See also Masaoka Tsunenori

Masaoka Tsunenori 1867-1902
See Masaoka Shiki
See also CA 117

Masefield, John (Edward)
1878-1967 .... **CLC 11, 47**
See also CA 19-20; 25-28R; CANR 33;
CAP 2; CDBLB 1890-1914; DLB 10;
MTCW; SATA 19

Maso, Carole 19(?)- .... **CLC 44**

Mason, Bobbie Ann
1940- .... **CLC 28, 43; SSC 4**
See also AAYA 5; CA 53-56; CANR 11,
31; DLBY 87; MTCW

Mason, Ernst
See Pohl, Frederik

Mason, Lee W.
See Malzberg, Barry N(athaniel)

Mason, Nick 1945-.............. **CLC 35**
See also Pink Floyd

Mason, Tally
See Derleth, August (William)

Mass, William
See Gibson, William

Masters, Edgar Lee
1868-1950 .... **TCLC 2, 25; PC 1**
See also CA 104; 133; CDALB 1865-1917;
DLB 54; MTCW

Masters, Hilary 1928-............ **CLC 48**
See also CA 25-28R; CANR 13

Mastrosimone, William 19(?)-...... **CLC 36**

Mathe, Albert
See Camus, Albert

Matheson, Richard Burton 1926-... **CLC 37**
See also CA 97-100; DLB 8, 44

Mathews, Harry 1930-.......... **CLC 6, 52**
See also CA 21-24R; CAAS 6; CANR 18,
40

Mathias, Roland (Glyn) 1915-...... **CLC 45**
See also CA 97-100; CANR 19; DLB 27

Matsuo Basho 1644-1694........... **PC 3**

Mattheson, Rodney
See Creasey, John

Matthews, Greg 1949-............ **CLC 45**
See also CA 135

Matthews, William 1942-.......... **CLC 40**
See also CA 29-32R; CANR 12; DLB 5

Matthias, John (Edward) 1941-...... **CLC 9**
See also CA 33-36R

Matthiessen, Peter
1927- .... **CLC 5, 7, 11, 32, 64**
See also AAYA 6; BEST 90:4; CA 9-12R;
CANR 21; DLB 6; MTCW; SATA 27

Maturin, Charles Robert
1780(?)-1824 .... **NCLC 6**

Matute (Ausejo), Ana Maria
1925- .... **CLC 11**
See also CA 89-92; MTCW

Maugham, W. S.
See Maugham, W(illiam) Somerset

Maugham, W(illiam) Somerset
1874-1965 .... **CLC 1, 11, 15, 67; SSC 8**
See also CA 5-8R; 25-28R; CANR 40;
CDBLB 1914-1945; DLB 10, 36, 77, 100;
MTCW; SATA 54; WLC

Maugham, William Somerset
See Maugham, W(illiam) Somerset

Maupassant, (Henri Rene Albert) Guy de
1850-1893 .... **NCLC 1; SSC 1**
See also DLB 123; WLC

Maurhut, Richard
See Traven, B.

Mauriac, Claude 1914-............. **CLC 9**
See also CA 89-92; DLB 83

Mauriac, Francois (Charles)
1885-1970 .... **CLC 4, 9, 56**
See also CA 25-28; CAP 2; DLB 65;
MTCW

Mavor, Osborne Henry 1888-1951
See Bridie, James
See also CA 104

Maxwell, William (Keepers Jr.)
1908- .... **CLC 19**
See also CA 93-96; DLBY 80

May, Elaine 1932- .... **CLC 16**
See also CA 124; DLB 44

Mayakovski, Vladimir (Vladimirovich)
1893-1930 .... **TCLC 4, 18**
See also CA 104

Mayhew, Henry 1812-1887 ...... **NCLC 31**
See also DLB 18, 55

Maynard, Joyce 1953-............ **CLC 23**
See also CA 111; 129

Mayne, William (James Carter)
1928- .... **CLC 12**
See also CA 9-12R; CANR 37; CLR 25;
MAICYA; SAAS 11; SATA 6, 68

Mayo, Jim
See L'Amour, Louis (Dearborn)

Maysles, Albert 1926- .... **CLC 16**
See also CA 29-32R

Maysles, David 1932-............. **CLC 16**

Mazer, Norma Fox 1931- .... **CLC 26**
See also AAYA 5; CA 69-72; CANR 12,
32; CLR 23; MAICYA; SAAS 1;
SATA 24, 67

Mazzini, Guiseppe 1805-1872 .... **NCLC 34**

McAuley, James Phillip
1917-1976 .... **CLC 45**
See also CA 97-100

McBain, Ed
See Hunter, Evan

McBrien, William Augustine
1930- .... **CLC 44**
See also CA 107

McCaffrey, Anne (Inez) 1926-...... **CLC 17**
See also AAYA 6; AITN 2; BEST 89:2;
CA 25-28R; CANR 15, 35; DLB 8;
MAICYA; MTCW; SAAS 11; SATA 8,
70

McCann, Arthur
See Campbell, John W(ood Jr.)

McCann, Edson
See Pohl, Frederik

McCarthy, Cormac 1933-........ **CLC 4, 57**
See also CA 13-16R; CANR 10; DLB 6

McCarthy, Mary (Therese)
1912-1989 ... **CLC 1, 3, 5, 14, 24, 39, 59**
See also CA 5-8R; 129; CANR 16; DLB 2;
DLBY 81; MTCW

McCartney, (James) Paul
1942- .... **CLC 12, 35**

McCauley, Stephen 19(?)- .... **CLC 50**

McClure, Michael (Thomas)
1932- .... **CLC 6, 10**
See also CA 21-24R; CANR 17; DLB 16

McCorkle, Jill (Collins) 1958-...... **CLC 51**
See also CA 121; DLBY 87

McCourt, James 1941-............. **CLC 5**
See also CA 57-60

McCoy, Horace (Stanley)
1897-1955 .... **TCLC 28**
See also CA 108; DLB 9

McCrae, John 1872-1918........ **TCLC 12**
See also CA 109; DLB 92

McCreigh, James
See Pohl, Frederik

McCullers, (Lula) Carson (Smith)
1917-1967 .. **CLC 1, 4, 10, 12, 48; SSC 9**
See also CA 5-8R; 25-28R; CABS 1, 3;
CANR 18; CDALB 1941-1968; DLB 2, 7;
MTCW; SATA 27; WLC

McCulloch, John Tyler
See Burroughs, Edgar Rice

McCullough, Colleen 1938(?)-...... **CLC 27**
See also CA 81-84; CANR 17; MTCW

McElroy, Joseph 1930- .... **CLC 5, 47**
See also CA 17-20R

McEwan, Ian (Russell) 1948- ... **CLC 13, 66**
See also BEST 90:4; CA 61-64; CANR 14;
DLB 14; MTCW

McFadden, David 1940-........... **CLC 48**
See also CA 104; DLB 60

McFarland, Dennis 1950- .... **CLC 65**

McGahern, John 1934-...... **CLC 5, 9, 48**
See also CA 17-20R; CANR 29; DLB 14;
MTCW

McGinley, Patrick (Anthony)
1937- .... **CLC 41**
See also CA 120; 127

McGinley, Phyllis 1905-1978 ...... **CLC 14**
See also CA 9-12R; 77-80; CANR 19;
DLB 11, 48; SATA 2, 24, 44

McGinniss, Joe 1942-............ **CLC 32**
See also AITN 2; BEST 89:2; CA 25-28R;
CANR 26

McGivern, Maureen Daly
See Daly, Maureen

McGrath, Patrick 1950-........... **CLC 55**
See also CA 136

McGrath, Thomas (Matthew)
1916-1990 .... **CLC 28, 59**
See also CA 9-12R; 132; CANR 6, 33;
MTCW; SATA 41; SATO 66

McGuane, Thomas (Francis III)
1939- .... **CLC 3, 7, 18, 45**
See also AITN 2; CA 49-52; CANR 5, 24;
DLB 2; DLBY 80; MTCW

McGuckian, Medbh 1950-......... **CLC 48**
See also DLB 40

McHale, Tom 1942(?)-1982....... **CLC 3, 5**
See also AITN 1; CA 77-80; 106

McIlvanney, William 1936-........ **CLC 42**
See also CA 25-28R; DLB 14

McIlwraith, Maureen Mollie Hunter
See Hunter, Mollie
See also SATA 2

McInerney, Jay 1955- .... **CLC 34**
See also CA 116; 123

McIntyre, Vonda N(eel) 1948- ..... **CLC 18**
See also CA 81-84; CANR 17, 34; MTCW

McKay, Claude .... **TCLC 7, 41; PC 2**
See also McKay, Festus Claudius
See also BLC 3; DLB 4, 45, 51, 117

McKay, Festus Claudius 1889-1948
See McKay, Claude
See also BW; CA 104; 124; MTCW; WLC

McKuen, Rod 1933- . . . . **CLC 1, 3**
See also AITN 1; CA 41-44R; CANR 40

McLoughlin, R. B.
See Mencken, H(enry) L(ouis)

McLuhan, (Herbert) Marshall
1911-1980 . . . . **CLC 37**
See also CA 9-12R; 102; CANR 12, 34;
DLB 88; MTCW

McMillan, Terry 1951- . . . . **CLC 50, 61**

McMurtry, Larry (Jeff)
1936- . . . . **CLC 2, 3, 7, 11, 27, 44**
See also AITN 2; BEST 89:2; CA 5-8R;
CANR 19; CDALB 1968-1988; DLB 2;
DLBY 80, 87; MTCW

McNally, Terrence 1939- . . . . . . **CLC 4, 7, 41**
See also CA 45-48; CANR 2; DLB 7

McNamer, Deirdre 1950- . . . . **CLC 70**

McNeile, Herman Cyril 1888-1937
See Sapper
See also DLB 77

McPhee, John (Angus) 1931- . . . . . . **CLC 36**
See also BEST 90:1; CA 65-68; CANR 20;
MTCW

McPherson, James Alan 1943- . . . . . **CLC 19**
See also BW; CA 25-28R; CAAS 17;
CANR 24; DLB 38; MTCW

McPherson, William (Alexander)
1933- . . . . **CLC 34**
See also CA 69-72; CANR 28

McSweeney, Kerry . . . . **CLC 34**

Mead, Margaret 1901-1978 . . . . **CLC 37**
See also AITN 1; CA 1-4R; 81-84;
CANR 4; MTCW; SATA 20

Meaker, Marijane (Agnes) 1927-
See Kerr, M. E.
See also CA 107; CANR 37; MAICYA;
MTCW; SATA 20, 61

Medoff, Mark (Howard) 1940- . . . **CLC 6, 23**
See also AITN 1; CA 53-56; CANR 5;
DLB 7

Meged, Aharon
See Megged, Aharon

Meged, Aron
See Megged, Aharon

Megged, Aharon 1920- . . . . **CLC 9**
See also CA 49-52; CAAS 13; CANR 1

Mehta, Ved (Parkash) 1934- . . . . **CLC 37**
See also CA 1-4R; CANR 2, 23; MTCW

Melanter
See Blackmore, R(ichard) D(oddridge)

Melikow, Loris
See Hofmannsthal, Hugo von

Melmoth, Sebastian
See Wilde, Oscar (Fingal O'Flahertie Wills)

Meltzer, Milton 1915- . . . . **CLC 26**
See also AAYA 8; CA 13-16R; CANR 38;
CLR 13; DLB 61; MAICYA; SAAS 1;
SATA 1, 50

Melville, Herman
1819-1891 . . . . . . **NCLC 3, 12, 29; SSC 1**
See also CDALB 1640-1865; DLB 3, 74;
SATA 59; WLC

Menander
c. 342B.C.-c. 292B.C. . . . . **CMLC 9; DC 3**

Mencken, H(enry) L(ouis)
1880-1956 . . . . **TCLC 13**
See also CA 105; 125; CDALB 1917-1929;
DLB 11, 29, 63; MTCW

Mercer, David 1928-1980 . . . . **CLC 5**
See also CA 9-12R; 102; CANR 23;
DLB 13; MTCW

Merchant, Paul
See Ellison, Harlan

Meredith, George 1828-1909 . . . **TCLC 17, 43**
See also CA 117; CDBLB 1832-1890;
DLB 18, 35, 57

Meredith, William (Morris)
1919- . . . . **CLC 4, 13, 22, 55**
See also CA 9-12R; CAAS 14; CANR 6, 40;
DLB 5

Merezhkovsky, Dmitry Sergeyevich
1865-1941 . . . . **TCLC 29**

Merimee, Prosper
1803-1870 . . . . **NCLC 6; SSC 7**
See also DLB 119

Merkin, Daphne 1954- . . . . **CLC 44**
See also CA 123

Merlin, Arthur
See Blish, James (Benjamin)

Merrill, James (Ingram)
1926- . . . . **CLC 2, 3, 6, 8, 13, 18, 34**
See also CA 13-16R; CANR 10; DLB 5;
DLBY 85; MTCW

Merriman, Alex
See Silverberg, Robert

Merritt, E. B.
See Waddington, Miriam

Merton, Thomas
1915-1968 . . . . **CLC 1, 3, 11, 34**
See also CA 5-8R; 25-28R; CANR 22;
DLB 48; DLBY 81; MTCW

Merwin, W(illiam) S(tanley)
1927- . . . . . . **CLC 1, 2, 3, 5, 8, 13, 18, 45**
See also CA 13-16R; CANR 15; DLB 5;
MTCW

Metcalf, John 1938- . . . . **CLC 37**
See also CA 113; DLB 60

Metcalf, Suzanne
See Baum, L(yman) Frank

Mew, Charlotte (Mary)
1870-1928 . . . . **TCLC 8**
See also CA 105; DLB 19

Mewshaw, Michael 1943- . . . . **CLC 9**
See also CA 53-56; CANR 7; DLBY 80

Meyer, June
See Jordan, June

Meyer-Meyrink, Gustav 1868-1932
See Meyrink, Gustav
See also CA 117

Meyers, Jeffrey 1939- . . . . **CLC 39**
See also CA 73-76; DLB 111

Meynell, Alice (Christina Gertrude Thompson)
1847-1922 . . . . **TCLC 6**
See also CA 104; DLB 19, 98

Meyrink, Gustav . . . . **TCLC 21**
See also Meyer-Meyrink, Gustav
See also DLB 81

Michaels, Leonard 1933- . . . . **CLC 6, 25**
See also CA 61-64; CANR 21; DLB 130;
MTCW

Michaux, Henri 1899-1984 . . . . . . **CLC 8, 19**
See also CA 85-88; 114

Michelangelo 1475-1564 . . . . **LC 12**

Michelet, Jules 1798-1874 . . . . **NCLC 31**

Michener, James A(lbert)
1907(?)- . . . . **CLC 1, 5, 11, 29, 60**
See also AITN 1; BEST 90:1; CA 5-8R;
CANR 21; DLB 6; MTCW

Mickiewicz, Adam 1798-1855 . . . . . **NCLC 3**

Middleton, Christopher 1926- . . . . . . **CLC 13**
See also CA 13-16R; CANR 29; DLB 40

Middleton, Stanley 1919- . . . . **CLC 7, 38**
See also CA 25-28R; CANR 21; DLB 14

Migueis, Jose Rodrigues 1901- . . . . . **CLC 10**

Mikszath, Kalman 1847-1910 . . . . . **TCLC 31**

Miles, Josephine
1911-1985 . . . . **CLC 1, 2, 14, 34, 39**
See also CA 1-4R; 116; CANR 2; DLB 48

Militant
See Sandburg, Carl (August)

Mill, John Stuart 1806-1873 . . . . . **NCLC 11**
See also CDBLB 1832-1890; DLB 55

Millar, Kenneth 1915-1983 . . . . **CLC 14**
See also Macdonald, Ross
See also CA 9-12R; 110; CANR 16; DLB 2;
DLBD 6; DLBY 83; MTCW

Millay, E. Vincent
See Millay, Edna St. Vincent

Millay, Edna St. Vincent
1892-1950 . . . . **TCLC 4, 49; PC 6**
See also CA 104; 130; CDALB 1917-1929;
DLB 45; MTCW

Miller, Arthur
1915- . . . . . . **CLC 1, 2, 6, 10, 15, 26, 47;
DC 1**
See also AITN 1; CA 1-4R; CABS 3;
CANR 2, 30; CDALB 1941-1968; DLB 7;
MTCW; WLC

Miller, Henry (Valentine)
1891-1980 . . . . **CLC 1, 2, 4, 9, 14, 43**
See also CA 9-12R; 97-100; CANR 33;
CDALB 1929-1941; DLB 4, 9; DLBY 80;
MTCW; WLC

Miller, Jason 1939(?)- . . . . **CLC 2**
See also AITN 1; CA 73-76; DLB 7

Miller, Sue 19(?)- . . . . **CLC 44**
See also BEST 90:3; CA 139

Miller, Walter M(ichael Jr.)
1923- . . . . **CLC 4, 30**
See also CA 85-88; DLB 8

Millett, Kate 1934- . . . . **CLC 67**
See also AITN 1; CA 73-76; CANR 32;
MTCW

Millhauser, Steven 1943- . . . . **CLC 21, 54**
See also CA 110; 111; DLB 2

Millin, Sarah Gertrude 1889-1968 .. **CLC 49**
See also CA 102; 93-96

Milne, A(lan) A(lexander)
1882-1956 .... **TCLC 6**
See also CA 104; 133; CLR 1, 26; DLB 10,
77, 100; MAICYA; MTCW; YABC 1

Milner, Ron(ald) 1938- .... **CLC 56**
See also AITN 1; BLC 3; BW; CA 73-76;
CANR 24; DLB 38; MTCW

Milosz, Czeslaw
1911- .... **CLC 5, 11, 22, 31, 56**
See also CA 81-84; CANR 23; MTCW

Milton, John 1608-1674 .... **LC 9**
See also CDBLB 1660-1789; WLC

Minehaha, Cornelius
See Wedekind, (Benjamin) Frank(lin)

Miner, Valerie 1947- .... **CLC 40**
See also CA 97-100

Minimo, Duca
See D'Annunzio, Gabriele

Minot, Susan 1956- .... **CLC 44**
See also CA 134

Minus, Ed 1938- .... **CLC 39**

Miranda, Javier
See Bioy Casares, Adolfo

Miro (Ferrer), Gabriel (Francisco Victor)
1879-1930 .... **TCLC 5**
See also CA 104

Mishima, Yukio
...... **CLC 2, 4, 6, 9, 27; DC 1; SSC 4**
See also Hiraoka, Kimitake

Mistral, Gabriela .... **TCLC 2**
See also Godoy Alcayaga, Lucila

Mistry, Rohinton 1952- .... **CLC 71**

Mitchell, Clyde
See Ellison, Harlan; Silverberg, Robert

Mitchell, James Leslie 1901-1935
See Gibbon, Lewis Grassic
See also CA 104; DLB 15

Mitchell, Joni 1943- .... **CLC 12**
See also CA 112

Mitchell, Margaret (Munnerlyn)
1900-1949 .... **TCLC 11**
See also CA 109; 125; DLB 9; MTCW

Mitchell, Peggy
See Mitchell, Margaret (Munnerlyn)

Mitchell, S(ilas) Weir 1829-1914 .. **TCLC 36**

Mitchell, W(illiam) O(rmond)
1914- .... **CLC 25**
See also CA 77-80; CANR 15; DLB 88

Mitford, Mary Russell 1787-1855.. **NCLC 4**
See also DLB 110, 116

Mitford, Nancy 1904-1973 .... **CLC 44**
See also CA 9-12R

Miyamoto, Yuriko 1899-1951 ..... **TCLC 37**

Mo, Timothy (Peter) 1950(?)- ...... **CLC 46**
See also CA 117; MTCW

Modarressi, Taghi (M.) 1931- ...... **CLC 44**
See also CA 121; 134

Modiano, Patrick (Jean) 1945- ..... **CLC 18**
See also CA 85-88; CANR 17, 40; DLB 83

Moerck, Paal
See Roelvaag, O(le) E(dvart)

Mofolo, Thomas (Mokopu)
1875(?)-1948 .... **TCLC 22**
See also BLC 3; CA 121

Mohr, Nicholasa 1935- .... **CLC 12**
See also AAYA 8; CA 49-52; CANR 1, 32;
CLR 22; HW; SAAS 8; SATA 8

Mojtabai, A(nn) G(race)
1938- .... **CLC 5, 9, 15, 29**
See also CA 85-88

Moliere 1622-1673 .... **LC 10**
See also WLC

Molin, Charles
See Mayne, William (James Carter)

Molnar, Ferenc 1878-1952 .... **TCLC 20**
See also CA 109

Momaday, N(avarre) Scott
1934- .... **CLC 2, 19**
See also CA 25-28R; CANR 14, 34;
MTCW; SATA 30, 48

Monroe, Harriet 1860-1936 ...... **TCLC 12**
See also CA 109; DLB 54, 91

Monroe, Lyle
See Heinlein, Robert A(nson)

Montagu, Elizabeth 1917- .... **NCLC 7**
See also CA 9-12R

Montagu, Mary (Pierrepont) Wortley
1689-1762 .... **LC 9**
See also DLB 95, 101

Montague, John (Patrick)
1929- .... **CLC 13, 46**
See also CA 9-12R; CANR 9; DLB 40;
MTCW

Montaigne, Michel (Eyquem) de
1533-1592 .... **LC 8**
See also WLC

Montale, Eugenio 1896-1981 ... **CLC 7, 9, 18**
See also CA 17-20R; 104; CANR 30;
DLB 114; MTCW

Montesquieu, Charles-Louis de Secondat
1689-1755 .... **LC 7**

Montgomery, (Robert) Bruce 1921-1978
See Crispin, Edmund
See also CA 104

Montgomery, Marion H. Jr. 1925- ... **CLC 7**
See also AITN 1; CA 1-4R; CANR 3;
DLB 6

Montgomery, Max
See Davenport, Guy (Mattison Jr.)

Montherlant, Henry (Milon) de
1896-1972 .... **CLC 8, 19**
See also CA 85-88; 37-40R; DLB 72;
MTCW

Monty Python .... **CLC 21**
See also Chapman, Graham; Cleese, John
(Marwood); Gilliam, Terry (Vance); Idle,
Eric; Jones, Terence Graham Parry; Palin,
Michael (Edward)
See also AAYA 7

Moodie, Susanna (Strickland)
1803-1885 .... **NCLC 14**
See also DLB 99

Mooney, Edward 1951- .... **CLC 25**
See also CA 130

Mooney, Ted
See Mooney, Edward

Moorcock, Michael (John)
1939- .... **CLC 5, 27, 58**
See also CA 45-48; CAAS 5; CANR 2, 17,
38; DLB 14; MTCW

Moore, Brian
1921- .... **CLC 1, 3, 5, 7, 8, 19, 32**
See also CA 1-4R; CANR 1, 25; MTCW

Moore, Edward
See Muir, Edwin

Moore, George Augustus
1852-1933 .... **TCLC 7**
See also CA 104; DLB 10, 18, 57

Moore, Lorrie .... **CLC 39, 45, 68**
See also Moore, Marie Lorena

Moore, Marianne (Craig)
1887-1972 ... **CLC 1, 2, 4, 8, 10, 13, 19,
47; PC 4**
See also CA 1-4R; 33-36R; CANR 3;
CDALB 1929-1941; DLB 45; DLBD 7;
MTCW; SATA 20

Moore, Marie Lorena 1957-
See Moore, Lorrie
See also CA 116; CANR 39

Moore, Thomas 1779-1852 .... **NCLC 6**
See also DLB 96

Morand, Paul 1888-1976 .... **CLC 41**
See also CA 69-72; DLB 65

Morante, Elsa 1918-1985 .... **CLC 8, 47**
See also CA 85-88; 117; CANR 35; MTCW

Moravia, Alberto .... **CLC 2, 7, 11, 27, 46**
See also Pincherle, Alberto

More, Hannah 1745-1833 .... **NCLC 27**
See also DLB 107, 109, 116

More, Henry 1614-1687 .... **LC 9**
See also DLB 126

More, Sir Thomas 1478-1535 .... **LC 10**

Moreas, Jean .... **TCLC 18**
See also Papadiamantopoulos, Johannes

Morgan, Berry 1919- .... **CLC 6**
See also CA 49-52; DLB 6

Morgan, Claire
See Highsmith, (Mary) Patricia

Morgan, Edwin (George) 1920- ..... **CLC 31**
See also CA 5-8R; CANR 3; DLB 27

Morgan, (George) Frederick
1922- .... **CLC 23**
See also CA 17-20R; CANR 21

Morgan, Harriet
See Mencken, H(enry) L(ouis)

Morgan, Jane
See Cooper, James Fenimore

Morgan, Janet 1945- .... **CLC 39**
See also CA 65-68

Morgan, Lady 1776(?)-1859 ...... **NCLC 29**
See also DLB 116

Morgan, Robin 1941- .... **CLC 2**
See also CA 69-72; CANR 29; MTCW

Morgan, Scott
See Kuttner, Henry

Morgan, Seth 1949(?)-1990 .... **CLC 65**
See also CA 132

Morgenstern, Christian
1871-1914 .... **TCLC 8**
See also CA 105

Morgenstern, S.
See Goldman, William (W.)

Moricz, Zsigmond   1879-1942 . . . . . **TCLC 33**

Morike, Eduard (Friedrich)
1804-1875 . . . . **NCLC 10**

Mori Ogai . . . . **TCLC 14**
See also Mori Rintaro

Mori Rintaro   1862-1922
See Mori Ogai
See also CA 110

Moritz, Karl Philipp   1756-1793 . . . . . . **LC 2**
See also DLB 94

Morland, Peter Henry
See Faust, Frederick (Schiller)

Morren, Theophil
See Hofmannsthal, Hugo von

Morris, Bill   1952- . . . . **CLC 76**

Morris, Julian
See West, Morris L(anglo)

Morris, Steveland Judkins   1950(?)-
See Wonder, Stevie
See also CA 111

Morris, William   1834-1896 . . . . **NCLC 4**
See also CDBLB 1832-1890; DLB 18, 35, 57

Morris, Wright   1910- . . . **CLC 1, 3, 7, 18, 37**
See also CA 9-12R; CANR 21; DLB 2;
DLBY 81; MTCW

Morrison, Chloe Anthony Wofford
See Morrison, Toni

Morrison, James Douglas   1943-1971
See Morrison, Jim
See also CA 73-76; CANR 40

Morrison, Jim . . . . **CLC 17**
See also Morrison, James Douglas

Morrison, Toni   1931- . . . . . **CLC 4, 10, 22, 55**
See also AAYA 1; BLC 3; BW; CA 29-32R;
CANR 27; CDALB 1968-1988; DLB 6,
33; DLBY 81; MTCW; SATA 57

Morrison, Van   1945- . . . . **CLC 21**
See also CA 116

Mortimer, John (Clifford)
1923- . . . . **CLC 28, 43**
See also CA 13-16R; CANR 21;
CDBLB 1960 to Present; DLB 13;
MTCW

Mortimer, Penelope (Ruth)   1918- . . . . **CLC 5**
See also CA 57-60

Morton, Anthony
See Creasey, John

Mosher, Howard Frank . . . . **CLC 62**
See also CA 139

Mosley, Nicholas   1923- . . . . **CLC 43, 70**
See also CA 69-72; DLB 14

Moss, Howard
1922-1987 . . . . **CLC 7, 14, 45, 50**
See also CA 1-4R; 123; CANR 1; DLB 5

Motion, Andrew   1952- . . . . **CLC 47**
See also DLB 40

Motley, Willard (Francis)
1912-1965 . . . . **CLC 18**
See also BW; CA 117; 106; DLB 76

Mott, Michael (Charles Alston)
1930- . . . . **CLC 15, 34**
See also CA 5-8R; CAAS 7; CANR 7, 29

Mowat, Farley (McGill)   1921- . . . . . **CLC 26**
See also AAYA 1; CA 1-4R; CANR 4, 24;
CLR 20; DLB 68; MAICYA; MTCW;
SATA 3, 55

Moyers, Bill   1934- . . . . **CLC 74**
See also AITN 2; CA 61-64; CANR 31

Mphahlele, Es'kia
See Mphahlele, Ezekiel
See also DLB 125

Mphahlele, Ezekiel   1919- . . . . **CLC 25**
See also Mphahlele, Es'kia
See also BLC 3; BW; CA 81-84; CANR 26

Mqhayi, S(amuel) E(dward) K(rune Loliwe)
1875-1945 . . . . **TCLC 25**
See also BLC 3

Mr. Martin
See Burroughs, William S(eward)

Mrozek, Slawomir   1930- . . . . **CLC 3, 13**
See also CA 13-16R; CAAS 10; CANR 29;
MTCW

Mrs. Belloc-Lowndes
See Lowndes, Marie Adelaide (Belloc)

Mtwa, Percy   (?)- . . . . **CLC 47**

Mueller, Lisel   1924- . . . . **CLC 13, 51**
See also CA 93-96; DLB 105

Muir, Edwin   1887-1959 . . . . **TCLC 2**
See also CA 104; DLB 20, 100

Muir, John   1838-1914 . . . . **TCLC 28**

Mujica Lainez, Manuel
1910-1984 . . . . **CLC 31**
See also Lainez, Manuel Mujica
See also CA 81-84; 112; CANR 32; HW

Mukherjee, Bharati   1940- . . . . **CLC 53**
See also BEST 89:2; CA 107; DLB 60;
MTCW

Muldoon, Paul   1951- . . . . **CLC 32, 72**
See also CA 113; 129; DLB 40

Mulisch, Harry   1927- . . . . **CLC 42**
See also CA 9-12R; CANR 6, 26

Mull, Martin   1943- . . . . **CLC 17**
See also CA 105

Mulock, Dinah Maria
See Craik, Dinah Maria (Mulock)

Munford, Robert   1737(?)-1783 . . . . **LC 5**
See also DLB 31

Mungo, Raymond   1946- . . . . **CLC 72**
See also CA 49-52; CANR 2

Munro, Alice
1931- . . . . **CLC 6, 10, 19, 50; SSC 3**
See also AITN 2; CA 33-36R; CANR 33;
DLB 53; MTCW; SATA 29

Munro, H(ector) H(ugh)   1870-1916
See Saki
See also CA 104; 130; CDBLB 1890-1914;
DLB 34; MTCW; WLC

Murasaki, Lady . . . . **CMLC 1**

Murdoch, (Jean) Iris
1919- . . . . . . **CLC 1, 2, 3, 4, 6, 8, 11, 15,**
22, 31, 51
See also CA 13-16R; CANR 8;
CDBLB 1960 to Present; DLB 14;
MTCW

Murphy, Richard   1927- . . . . **CLC 41**
See also CA 29-32R; DLB 40

Murphy, Sylvia   1937- . . . . **CLC 34**
See also CA 121

Murphy, Thomas (Bernard)   1935- . . . **CLC 51**
See also CA 101

Murray, Albert L.   1916- . . . . **CLC 73**
See also BW; CA 49-52; CANR 26; DLB 38

Murray, Les(lie) A(llan)   1938- . . . . . **CLC 40**
See also CA 21-24R; CANR 11, 27

Murry, J. Middleton
See Murry, John Middleton

Murry, John Middleton
1889-1957 . . . . **TCLC 16**
See also CA 118

Musgrave, Susan   1951- . . . . **CLC 13, 54**
See also CA 69-72

Musil, Robert (Edler von)
1880-1942 . . . . **TCLC 12**
See also CA 109; DLB 81, 124

Musset, (Louis Charles) Alfred de
1810-1857 . . . . **NCLC 7**

My Brother's Brother
See Chekhov, Anton (Pavlovich)

Myers, Walter Dean   1937- . . . . **CLC 35**
See also AAYA 4; BLC 3; BW; CA 33-36R;
CANR 20; CLR 4, 16; DLB 33;
MAICYA; SAAS 2; SATA 27, 41, 70, 71

Myers, Walter M.
See Myers, Walter Dean

Myles, Symon
See Follett, Ken(neth Martin)

Nabokov, Vladimir (Vladimirovich)
1899-1977 . . . . **CLC 1, 2, 3, 6, 8, 11, 15,**
23, 44, 46, 64; SSC 11
See also CA 5-8R; 69-72; CANR 20;
CDALB 1941-1968; DLB 2; DLBD 3;
DLBY 80, 91; MTCW; WLC

Nagy, Laszlo   1925-1978 . . . . **CLC 7**
See also CA 129; 112

Naipaul, Shiva(dhar Srinivasa)
1945-1985 . . . . **CLC 32, 39**
See also CA 110; 112; 116; CANR 33;
DLBY 85; MTCW

Naipaul, V(idiadhar) S(urajprasad)
1932- . . . . **CLC 4, 7, 9, 13, 18, 37**
See also CA 1-4R; CANR 1, 33;
CDBLB 1960 to Present; DLB 125;
DLBY 85; MTCW

Nakos, Lilika   1899(?)- . . . . **CLC 29**

Narayan, R(asipuram) K(rishnaswami)
1906- . . . . **CLC 7, 28, 47**
See also CA 81-84; CANR 33; MTCW;
SATA 62

Nash, (Frediric) Ogden   1902-1971 . . **CLC 23**
See also CA 13-14; 29-32R; CANR 34;
CAP 1; DLB 11; MAICYA; MTCW;
SATA 2, 46

Nathan, Daniel
See Dannay, Frederic

Nathan, George Jean   1882-1958 . . . **TCLC 18**
See also Hatteras, Owen
See also CA 114

Natsume, Kinnosuke   1867-1916
See Natsume, Soseki
See also CA 104

Natsume, Soseki . . . . TCLC **2, 10**
See also Natsume, Kinnosuke

Natti, (Mary) Lee 1919-
See Kingman, Lee
See also CA 5-8R; CANR 2

Naylor, Gloria 1950- . . . . CLC **28, 52**
See also AAYA 6; BLC 3; BW; CA 107;
CANR 27; MTCW

Neihardt, John Gneisenau
1881-1973 . . . . CLC **32**
See also CA 13-14; CAP 1; DLB 9, 54

Nekrasov, Nikolai Alekseevich
1821-1878 . . . . NCLC **11**

Nelligan, Emile 1879-1941 . . . . TCLC **14**
See also CA 114; DLB 92

Nelson, Willie 1933- . . . . CLC **17**
See also CA 107

Nemerov, Howard (Stanley)
1920-1991 . . . . CLC **2, 6, 9, 36**
See also CA 1-4R; 134; CABS 2; CANR 1,
27; DLB 6; DLBY 83; MTCW

Neruda, Pablo
1904-1973 . . . . CLC **1, 2, 5, 7, 9, 28, 62;**
PC 4
See also CA 19-20; 45-48; CAP 2; HW;
MTCW; WLC

Nerval, Gerard de 1808-1855 . . . . . . NCLC **1**

Nervo, (Jose) Amado (Ruiz de)
1870-1919 . . . . TCLC **11**
See also CA 109; 131; HW

Nessi, Pio Baroja y
See Baroja (y Nessi), Pio

Neufeld, John (Arthur) 1938- . . . . . . CLC **17**
See also CA 25-28R; CANR 11, 37;
MAICYA; SAAS 3; SATA 6

Neville, Emily Cheney 1919- . . . . CLC **12**
See also CA 5-8R; CANR 3, 37; MAICYA;
SAAS 2; SATA 1

Newbound, Bernard Slade 1930-
See Slade, Bernard
See also CA 81-84

Newby, P(ercy) H(oward)
1918- . . . . CLC **2, 13**
See also CA 5-8R; CANR 32; DLB 15;
MTCW

Newlove, Donald 1928- . . . . CLC **6**
See also CA 29-32R; CANR 25

Newlove, John (Herbert) 1938- . . . . . CLC **14**
See also CA 21-24R; CANR 9, 25

Newman, Charles 1938- . . . . CLC **2, 8**
See also CA 21-24R

Newman, Edwin (Harold) 1919- . . . . CLC **14**
See also AITN 1; CA 69-72; CANR 5

Newman, John Henry
1801-1890 . . . . NCLC **38**
See also DLB 18, 32, 55

Newton, Suzanne 1936- . . . . CLC **35**
See also CA 41-44R; CANR 14; SATA 5

Nexo, Martin Andersen
1869-1954 . . . . TCLC **43**

Nezval, Vitezslav 1900-1958 . . . . . TCLC **44**
See also CA 123

Ngema, Mbongeni 1955- . . . . CLC **57**

Ngugi, James T(hiong'o) . . . . CLC **3, 7, 13**
See also Ngugi wa Thiong'o

Ngugi wa Thiong'o 1938- . . . . CLC **36**
See also Ngugi, James T(hiong'o)
See also BLC 3; BW; CA 81-84; CANR 27;
MTCW

Nichol, B(arrie) P(hillip)
1944-1988 . . . . CLC **18**
See also CA 53-56; DLB 53; SATA 66

Nichols, John (Treadwell) 1940- . . . . CLC **38**
See also CA 9-12R; CAAS 2; CANR 6;
DLBY 82

Nichols, Peter (Richard)
1927- . . . . CLC **5, 36, 65**
See also CA 104; CANR 33; DLB 13;
MTCW

Nicolas, F. R. E.
See Freeling, Nicolas

Niedecker, Lorine 1903-1970 . . . . CLC **10, 42**
See also CA 25-28; CAP 2; DLB 48

Nietzsche, Friedrich (Wilhelm)
1844-1900 . . . . TCLC **10, 18**
See also CA 107; 121; DLB 129

Nievo, Ippolito 1831-1861 . . . . NCLC **22**

Nightingale, Anne Redmon 1943-
See Redmon, Anne
See also CA 103

Nik.T.O.
See Annensky, Innokenty Fyodorovich

Nin, Anais
1903-1977 . . . . . CLC **1, 4, 8, 11, 14, 60;**
SSC 10
See also AITN 2; CA 13-16R; 69-72;
CANR 22; DLB 2, 4; MTCW

Nissenson, Hugh 1933- . . . . CLC **4, 9**
See also CA 17-20R; CANR 27; DLB 28

Niven, Larry . . . . CLC **8**
See also Niven, Laurence Van Cott
See also DLB 8

Niven, Laurence Van Cott 1938-
See Niven, Larry
See also CA 21-24R; CAAS 12; CANR 14;
MTCW

Nixon, Agnes Eckhardt 1927- . . . . . . CLC **21**
See also CA 110

Nizan, Paul 1905-1940 . . . . TCLC **40**
See also DLB 72

Nkosi, Lewis 1936- . . . . CLC **45**
See also BLC 3; BW; CA 65-68; CANR 27

Nodier, (Jean) Charles (Emmanuel)
1780-1844 . . . . NCLC **19**
See also DLB 119

Nolan, Christopher 1965- . . . . CLC **58**
See also CA 111

Norden, Charles
See Durrell, Lawrence (George)

Nordhoff, Charles (Bernard)
1887-1947 . . . . TCLC **23**
See also CA 108; DLB 9; SATA 23

Norfolk, Lawrence 1963- . . . . CLC **76**

Norman, Marsha 1947- . . . . CLC **28**
See also CA 105; CABS 3; DLBY 84

Norris, Benjamin Franklin Jr.
1870-1902 . . . . TCLC **24**
See also Norris, Frank
See also CA 110

Norris, Frank
See Norris, Benjamin Franklin Jr.
See also CDALB 1865-1917; DLB 12, 71

Norris, Leslie 1921- . . . . CLC **14**
See also CA 11-12; CANR 14; CAP 1;
DLB 27

North, Andrew
See Norton, Andre

North, Captain George
See Stevenson, Robert Louis (Balfour)

North, Milou
See Erdrich, Louise

Northrup, B. A.
See Hubbard, L(afayette) Ron(ald)

North Staffs
See Hulme, T(homas) E(rnest)

Norton, Alice Mary
See Norton, Andre
See also MAICYA; SATA 1, 43

Norton, Andre 1912- . . . . CLC **12**
See also Norton, Alice Mary
See also CA 1-4R; CANR 2, 31; DLB 8, 52;
MTCW

Norway, Nevil Shute 1899-1960
See Shute, Nevil
See also CA 102; 93-96

Norwid, Cyprian Kamil
1821-1883 . . . . NCLC **17**

Nosille, Nabrah
See Ellison, Harlan

Nossack, Hans Erich 1901-1978 . . . . . CLC **6**
See also CA 93-96; 85-88; DLB 69

Nosu, Chuji
See Ozu, Yasujiro

Nova, Craig 1945- . . . . CLC **7, 31**
See also CA 45-48; CANR 2

Novak, Joseph
See Kosinski, Jerzy (Nikodem)

Novalis 1772-1801 . . . . NCLC **13**
See also DLB 90

Nowlan, Alden (Albert) 1933-1983 . . CLC **15**
See also CA 9-12R; CANR 5; DLB 53

Noyes, Alfred 1880-1958 . . . . TCLC **7**
See also CA 104; DLB 20

Nunn, Kem 19(?)- . . . . CLC **34**

Nye, Robert 1939- . . . . CLC **13, 42**
See also CA 33-36R; CANR 29; DLB 14;
MTCW; SATA 6

Nyro, Laura 1947- . . . . CLC **17**

Oates, Joyce Carol
1938- . . . . . CLC **1, 2, 3, 6, 9, 11, 15, 19,**
33, 52; SSC 6
See also AITN 1; BEST 89:2; CA 5-8R;
CANR 25; CDALB 1968-1988; DLB 2, 5,
130; DLBY 81; MTCW; WLC

O'Brien, E. G.
See Clarke, Arthur C(harles)

Author Index

Ozick, Cynthia 1928- ...... **CLC 3, 7, 28, 62**
See also BEST 90:1; CA 17-20R; CANR 23;
DLB 28; DLBY 82; MTCW

Ozu, Yasujiro 1903-1963 .... **CLC 16**
See also CA 112

Pacheco, C.
See Pessoa, Fernando (Antonio Nogueira)

Pa Chin
See Li Fei-kan

Pack, Robert 1929- .... **CLC 13**
See also CA 1-4R; CANR 3; DLB 5

Padgett, Lewis
See Kuttner, Henry

Padilla (Lorenzo), Heberto 1932- ... **CLC 38**
See also AITN 1; CA 123; 131; HW

Page, Jimmy 1944- .... **CLC 12**

Page, Louise 1955- .... **CLC 40**

Page, P(atricia) K(athleen)
1916- .... **CLC 7, 18**
See also CA 53-56; CANR 4, 22; DLB 68;
MTCW

Paget, Violet 1856-1935
See Lee, Vernon
See also CA 104

Paget-Lowe, Henry
See Lovecraft, H(oward) P(hillips)

Paglia, Camille 1947- .... **CLC 68**

Pakenham, Antonia
See Fraser, Antonia (Pakenham)

Palamas, Kostes 1859-1943 .... **TCLC 5**
See also CA 105

Palazzeschi, Aldo 1885-1974 ...... **CLC 11**
See also CA 89-92; 53-56; DLB 114

Paley, Grace 1922- ... **CLC 4, 6, 37; SSC 8**
See also CA 25-28R; CANR 13; DLB 28;
MTCW

Palin, Michael (Edward) 1943- ..... **CLC 21**
See also Monty Python
See also CA 107; CANR 35; SATA 67

Palliser, Charles 1947- .... **CLC 65**
See also CA 136

Palma, Ricardo 1833-1919 .... **TCLC 29**

Pancake, Breece Dexter 1952-1979
See Pancake, Breece D'J
See also CA 123; 109

Pancake, Breece D'J .... **CLC 29**
See also Pancake, Breece Dexter
See also DLB 130

Papadiamantis, Alexandros
1851-1911 .... **TCLC 29**

Papadiamantopoulos, Johannes 1856-1910
See Moreas, Jean
See also CA 117

Papini, Giovanni 1881-1956 .... **TCLC 22**
See also CA 121

Paracelsus 1493-1541 .... **LC 14**

Parasol, Peter
See Stevens, Wallace

Parfenie, Maria
See Codrescu, Andrei

Parini, Jay (Lee) 1948- .... **CLC 54**
See also CA 97-100; CAAS 16; CANR 32

Park, Jordan
See Kornbluth, C(yril) M.; Pohl, Frederik

Parker, Bert
See Ellison, Harlan

Parker, Dorothy (Rothschild)
1893-1967 .... **CLC 15, 68; SSC 2**
See also CA 19-20; 25-28R; CAP 2;
DLB 11, 45, 86; MTCW

Parker, Robert B(rown) 1932- ...... **CLC 27**
See also BEST 89:4; CA 49-52; CANR 1,
26; MTCW

Parkes, Lucas
See Harris, John (Wyndham Parkes Lucas)
Beynon

Parkin, Frank 1940- .... **CLC 43**

Parkman, Francis Jr. 1823-1893 .. **NCLC 12**
See also DLB 1, 30

Parks, Gordon (Alexander Buchanan)
1912- .... **CLC 1, 16**
See also AITN 2; BLC 3; BW; CA 41-44R;
CANR 26; DLB 33; SATA 8

Parnell, Thomas 1679-1718 .... **LC 3**
See also DLB 94

Parra, Nicanor 1914- .... **CLC 2**
See also CA 85-88; CANR 32; HW; MTCW

Parrish, Mary Frances
See Fisher, M(ary) F(rances) K(ennedy)

Parson Lot
See Kingsley, Charles

Partridge, Anthony
See Oppenheim, E(dward) Phillips

Pascoli, Giovanni 1855-1912 ...... **TCLC 45**

Pasolini, Pier Paolo
1922-1975 .... **CLC 20, 37**
See also CA 93-96; 61-64; DLB 128;
MTCW

Pasquini
See Silone, Ignazio

Pastan, Linda (Olenik) 1932- ...... **CLC 27**
See also CA 61-64; CANR 18, 40; DLB 5

Pasternak, Boris (Leonidovich)
1890-1960 ..... **CLC 7, 10, 18, 63; PC 6**
See also CA 127; 116; MTCW; WLC

Patchen, Kenneth 1911-1972 ... **CLC 1, 2, 18**
See also CA 1-4R; 33-36R; CANR 3, 35;
DLB 16, 48; MTCW

Pater, Walter (Horatio)
1839-1894 .... **NCLC 7**
See also CDBLB 1832-1890; DLB 57

Paterson, A(ndrew) B(arton)
1864-1941 .... **TCLC 32**

Paterson, Katherine (Womeldorf)
1932- .... **CLC 12, 30**
See also AAYA 1; CA 21-24R; CANR 28;
CLR 7; DLB 52; MAICYA; MTCW;
SATA 13, 53

Patmore, Coventry Kersey Dighton
1823-1896 .... **NCLC 9**
See also DLB 35, 98

Paton, Alan (Stewart)
1903-1988 .... **CLC 4, 10, 25, 55**
See also CA 13-16; 125; CANR 22; CAP 1;
MTCW; SATA 11, 56; WLC

Paton Walsh, Gillian 1939-
See Walsh, Jill Paton
See also CANR 38; MAICYA; SAAS 3;
SATA 4, 72

Paulding, James Kirke 1778-1860 .. **NCLC 2**
See also DLB 3, 59, 74

Paulin, Thomas Neilson 1949-
See Paulin, Tom
See also CA 123; 128

Paulin, Tom .... **CLC 37**
See also Paulin, Thomas Neilson
See also DLB 40

Paustovsky, Konstantin (Georgievich)
1892-1968 .... **CLC 40**
See also CA 93-96; 25-28R

Pavese, Cesare 1908-1950 .... **TCLC 3**
See also CA 104; DLB 128

Pavic, Milorad 1929- .... **CLC 60**
See also CA 136

Payne, Alan
See Jakes, John (William)

Paz, Gil
See Lugones, Leopoldo

Paz, Octavio
1914- ...... **CLC 3, 4, 6, 10, 19, 51, 65;
PC 1**
See also CA 73-76; CANR 32; DLBY 90;
HW; MTCW; WLC

Peacock, Molly 1947- .... **CLC 60**
See also CA 103; DLB 120

Peacock, Thomas Love
1785-1866 .... **NCLC 22**
See also DLB 96, 116

Peake, Mervyn 1911-1968 .... **CLC 7, 54**
See also CA 5-8R; 25-28R; CANR 3;
DLB 15; MTCW; SATA 23

Pearce, Philippa .... **CLC 21**
See also Christie, (Ann) Philippa
See also CLR 9; MAICYA; SATA 1, 67

Pearl, Eric
See Elman, Richard

Pearson, T(homas) R(eid) 1956- .... **CLC 39**
See also CA 120; 130

Peck, John 1941- .... **CLC 3**
See also CA 49-52; CANR 3

Peck, Richard (Wayne) 1934- ...... **CLC 21**
See also AAYA 1; CA 85-88; CANR 19,
38; MAICYA; SAAS 2; SATA 18, 55

Peck, Robert Newton 1928- .... **CLC 17**
See also AAYA 3; CA 81-84; CANR 31;
MAICYA; SAAS 1; SATA 21, 62

Peckinpah, (David) Sam(uel)
1925-1984 .... **CLC 20**
See also CA 109; 114

Pedersen, Knut 1859-1952
See Hamsun, Knut
See also CA 104; 119; MTCW

Peeslake, Gaffer
See Durrell, Lawrence (George)

Peguy, Charles Pierre
1873-1914 .... **TCLC 10**
See also CA 107

Pena, Ramon del Valle y
See Valle-Inclan, Ramon (Maria) del

Puzo, Mario 1920- .... CLC 1, 2, 6, 36
See also CA 65-68; CANR 4; DLB 6;
MTCW

Pym, Barbara (Mary Crampton)
1913-1980 .... CLC 13, 19, 37
See also CA 13-14; 97-100; CANR 13, 34;
CAP 1; DLB 14; DLBY 87; MTCW

Pynchon, Thomas (Ruggles Jr.)
1937- .. CLC 2, 3, 6, 9, 11, 18, 33, 62, 72
See also BEST 90:2; CA 17-20R; CANR 22;
DLB 2; MTCW; WLC

Qian Zhongshu
See Ch'ien Chung-shu

Qroll
See Dagerman, Stig (Halvard)

Quarrington, Paul (Lewis) 1953-.... CLC 65
See also CA 129

Quasimodo, Salvatore 1901-1968 ... CLC 10
See also CA 13-16; 25-28R; CAP 1;
DLB 114; MTCW

Queen, Ellery.................... CLC 3, 11
See also Dannay, Frederic; Davidson,
Avram; Lee, Manfred B(ennington);
Sturgeon, Theodore (Hamilton); Vance,
John Holbrook

Queen, Ellery Jr.
See Dannay, Frederic; Lee, Manfred
B(ennington)

Queneau, Raymond
1903-1976 .... CLC 2, 5, 10, 42
See also CA 77-80; 69-72; CANR 32;
DLB 72; MTCW

Quin, Ann (Marie) 1936-1973 .... CLC 6
See also CA 9-12R; 45-48; DLB 14

Quinn, Martin
See Smith, Martin Cruz

Quinn, Simon
See Smith, Martin Cruz

Quiroga, Horacio (Sylvestre)
1878-1937 .... TCLC 20
See also CA 117; 131; HW; MTCW

Quoirez, Francoise 1935-............ CLC 9
See also Sagan, Francoise
See also CA 49-52; CANR 6, 39; MTCW

Raabe, Wilhelm 1831-1910 .... TCLC 45
See also DLB 129

Rabe, David (William) 1940-... CLC 4, 8, 33
See also CA 85-88; CABS 3; DLB 7

Rabelais, Francois 1483-1553 .... LC 5
See also WLC

Rabinovitch, Sholem 1859-1916
See Aleichem, Sholom
See also CA 104

Radcliffe, Ann (Ward) 1764-1823 .. NCLC 6
See also DLB 39

Radiguet, Raymond 1903-1923 .... TCLC 29
See also DLB 65

Radnoti, Miklos 1909-1944 .... TCLC 16
See also CA 118

Rado, James 1939-................ CLC 17
See also CA 105

Radvanyi, Netty 1900-1983
See Seghers, Anna
See also CA 85-88; 110

Raeburn, John (Hay) 1941-........ CLC 34
See also CA 57-60

Ragni, Gerome 1942-1991 .... CLC 17
See also CA 105; 134

Rahv, Philip..................... CLC 24
See also Greenberg, Ivan

Raine, Craig 1944-............... CLC 32
See also CA 108; CANR 29; DLB 40

Raine, Kathleen (Jessie) 1908- ... CLC 7, 45
See also CA 85-88; DLB 20; MTCW

Rainis, Janis 1865-1929 .... TCLC 29

Rakosi, Carl..................... CLC 47
See also Rawley, Callman
See also CAAS 5

Raleigh, Richard
See Lovecraft, H(oward) P(hillips)

Rallentando, H. P.
See Sayers, Dorothy L(eigh)

Ramal, Walter
See de la Mare, Walter (John)

Ramon, Juan
See Jimenez (Mantecon), Juan Ramon

Ramos, Graciliano 1892-1953 ..... TCLC 32

Rampersad, Arnold 1941-.......... CLC 44
See also CA 127; 133; DLB 111

Rampling, Anne
See Rice, Anne

Ramuz, Charles-Ferdinand
1878-1947 .... TCLC 33

Rand, Ayn 1905-1982....... CLC 3, 30, 44
See also AAYA 10; CA 13-16R; 105;
CANR 27; MTCW; WLC

Randall, Dudley (Felker) 1914-...... CLC 1
See also BLC 3; BW; CA 25-28R;
CANR 23; DLB 41

Randall, Robert
See Silverberg, Robert

Ranger, Ken
See Creasey, John

Ransom, John Crowe
1888-1974 .... CLC 2, 4, 5, 11, 24
See also CA 5-8R; 49-52; CANR 6, 34;
DLB 45, 63; MTCW

Rao, Raja 1909-............... CLC 25, 56
See also CA 73-76; MTCW

Raphael, Frederic (Michael)
1931-.................... CLC 2, 14
See also CA 1-4R; CANR 1; DLB 14

Ratcliffe, James P.
See Mencken, H(enry) L(ouis)

Rathbone, Julian 1935-........... CLC 41
See also CA 101; CANR 34

Rattigan, Terence (Mervyn)
1911-1977 .... CLC 7
See also CA 85-88; 73-76;
CDBLB 1945-1960; DLB 13; MTCW

Ratushinskaya, Irina 1954-........ CLC 54
See also CA 129

Raven, Simon (Arthur Noel)
1927-.................... CLC 14
See also CA 81-84

Rawley, Callman 1903-
See Rakosi, Carl
See also CA 21-24R; CANR 12, 32

Rawlings, Marjorie Kinnan
1896-1953 .... TCLC 4
See also CA 104; 137; DLB 9, 22, 102;
MAICYA; YABC 1

Ray, Satyajit 1921-1992....... CLC 16, 76
See also CA 114; 137

Read, Herbert Edward 1893-1968.... CLC 4
See also CA 85-88; 25-28R; DLB 20

Read, Piers Paul 1941- ...... CLC 4, 10, 25
See also CA 21-24R; CANR 38; DLB 14;
SATA 21

Reade, Charles 1814-1884 .... NCLC 2
See also DLB 21

Reade, Hamish
See Gray, Simon (James Holliday)

Reading, Peter 1946-............. CLC 47
See also CA 103; DLB 40

Reaney, James 1926-............. CLC 13
See also CA 41-44R; CAAS 15; DLB 68;
SATA 43

Rebreanu, Liviu 1885-1944 .... TCLC 28

Rechy, John (Francisco)
1934-................. CLC 1, 7, 14, 18
See also CA 5-8R; CAAS 4; CANR 6, 32;
DLB 122; DLBY 82; HW

Redcam, Tom 1870-1933 .... TCLC 25

Reddin, Keith................... CLC 67

Redgrove, Peter (William)
1932-.................... CLC 6, 41
See also CA 1-4R; CANR 3, 39; DLB 40

Redmon, Anne................... CLC 22
See also Nightingale, Anne Redmon
See also DLBY 86

Reed, Eliot
See Ambler, Eric

Reed, Ishmael
1938-........ CLC 2, 3, 5, 6, 13, 32, 60
See also BLC 3; BW; CA 21-24R;
CANR 25; DLB 2, 5, 33; DLBD 8;
MTCW

Reed, John (Silas) 1887-1920 ...... TCLC 9
See also CA 106

Reed, Lou..................... CLC 21
See also Firbank, Louis

Reeve, Clara 1729-1807......... NCLC 19
See also DLB 39

Reid, Christopher 1949-........... CLC 33
See also DLB 40

Reid, Desmond
See Moorcock, Michael (John)

Reid Banks, Lynne 1929-
See Banks, Lynne Reid
See also CA 1-4R; CANR 6, 22, 38;
CLR 24; MAICYA; SATA 22

Reilly, William K.
See Creasey, John

Reiner, Max
See Caldwell, (Janet Miriam) Taylor
(Holland)

Reis, Ricardo
See Pessoa, Fernando (Antonio Nogueira)

Remarque, Erich Maria
1898-1970 . . . . **CLC 21**
See also CA 77-80; 29-32R; DLB 56;
MTCW

Remizov, A.
See Remizov, Aleksei (Mikhailovich)

Remizov, A. M.
See Remizov, Aleksei (Mikhailovich)

Remizov, Aleksei (Mikhailovich)
1877-1957 . . . . **TCLC 27**
See also CA 125; 133

Renan, Joseph Ernest
1823-1892 . . . . **NCLC 26**

Renard, Jules 1864-1910 . . . . **TCLC 17**
See also CA 117

Renault, Mary . . . . **CLC 3, 11, 17**
See also Challans, Mary
See also DLBY 83

Rendell, Ruth (Barbara) 1930- . . **CLC 28, 48**
See also Vine, Barbara
See also CA 109; CANR 32; DLB 87;
MTCW

Renoir, Jean 1894-1979 . . . . **CLC 20**
See also CA 129; 85-88

Resnais, Alain 1922- . . . . **CLC 16**

Reverdy, Pierre 1889-1960 . . . . **CLC 53**
See also CA 97-100; 89-92

Rexroth, Kenneth
1905-1982 . . . . . . **CLC 1, 2, 6, 11, 22, 49**
See also CA 5-8R; 107; CANR 14, 34;
CDALB 1941-1968; DLB 16, 48;
DLBY 82; MTCW

Reyes, Alfonso 1889-1959 . . . . **TCLC 33**
See also CA 131; HW

Reyes y Basoalto, Ricardo Eliecer Neftali
See Neruda, Pablo

Reymont, Wladyslaw (Stanislaw)
1868(?)-1925 . . . . **TCLC 5**
See also CA 104

Reynolds, Jonathan 1942- . . . . **CLC 6, 38**
See also CA 65-68; CANR 28

Reynolds, Joshua 1723-1792 . . . . **LC 15**
See also DLB 104

Reynolds, Michael Shane 1937- . . . . **CLC 44**
See also CA 65-68; CANR 9

Reznikoff, Charles 1894-1976 . . . . **CLC 9**
See also CA 33-36; 61-64; CAP 2; DLB 28,
45

Rezzori (d'Arezzo), Gregor von
1914- . . . . **CLC 25**
See also CA 122; 136

Rhine, Richard
See Silverstein, Alvin

Rhys, Jean
1890(?)-1979 . . . . **CLC 2, 4, 6, 14, 19, 51**
See also CA 25-28R; 85-88; CANR 35;
CDBLB 1945-1960; DLB 36, 117; MTCW

Ribeiro, Darcy 1922- . . . . **CLC 34**
See also CA 33-36R

Ribeiro, Joao Ubaldo (Osorio Pimentel)
1941- . . . . **CLC 10, 67**
See also CA 81-84

Ribman, Ronald (Burt) 1932- . . . . **CLC 7**
See also CA 21-24R

Ricci, Nino 1959- . . . . **CLC 70**
See also CA 137

Rice, Anne 1941- . . . . **CLC 41**
See also AAYA 9; BEST 89:2; CA 65-68;
CANR 12, 36

Rice, Elmer (Leopold)
1892-1967 . . . . **CLC 7, 49**
See also CA 21-22; 25-28R; CAP 2; DLB 4,
7; MTCW

Rice, Tim 1944- . . . . **CLC 21**
See also CA 103

Rich, Adrienne (Cecile)
1929- . . . **CLC 3, 6, 7, 11, 18, 36, 73, 76;
PC 5**
See also CA 9-12R; CANR 20; DLB 5, 67;
MTCW

Rich, Barbara
See Graves, Robert (von Ranke)

Rich, Robert
See Trumbo, Dalton

Richards, David Adams 1950- . . . . . . **CLC 59**
See also CA 93-96; DLB 53

Richards, I(vor) A(rmstrong)
1893-1979 . . . . **CLC 14, 24**
See also CA 41-44R; 89-92; CANR 34;
DLB 27

Richardson, Anne
See Roiphe, Anne Richardson

Richardson, Dorothy Miller
1873-1957 . . . . **TCLC 3**
See also CA 104; DLB 36

Richardson, Ethel Florence (Lindesay)
1870-1946
See Richardson, Henry Handel
See also CA 105

Richardson, Henry Handel . . . . **TCLC 4**
See also Richardson, Ethel Florence
(Lindesay)

Richardson, Samuel 1689-1761 . . . . **LC 1**
See also CDBLB 1660-1789; DLB 39; WLC

Richler, Mordecai
1931- . . . . **CLC 3, 5, 9, 13, 18, 46, 70**
See also AITN 1; CA 65-68; CANR 31;
CLR 17; DLB 53; MAICYA; MTCW;
SATA 27, 44

Richter, Conrad (Michael)
1890-1968 . . . . **CLC 30**
See also CA 5-8R; 25-28R; CANR 23;
DLB 9; MTCW; SATA 3

Riddell, J. H. 1832-1906 . . . . **TCLC 40**

Riding, Laura . . . . **CLC 3, 7**
See also Jackson, Laura (Riding)

Riefenstahl, Berta Helene Amalia 1902-
See Riefenstahl, Leni
See also CA 108

Riefenstahl, Leni . . . . **CLC 16**
See also Riefenstahl, Berta Helene Amalia

Riffe, Ernest
See Bergman, (Ernst) Ingmar

Riley, Tex
See Creasey, John

Rilke, Rainer Maria
1875-1926 . . . . **TCLC 1, 6, 19; PC 2**
See also CA 104; 132; DLB 81; MTCW

Rimbaud, (Jean Nicolas) Arthur
1854-1891 . . . . **NCLC 4, 35; PC 3**
See also WLC

Ringmaster, The
See Mencken, H(enry) L(ouis)

Ringwood, Gwen(dolyn Margaret) Pharis
1910-1984 . . . . **CLC 48**
See also CA 112; DLB 88

Rio, Michel 19(?)- . . . . **CLC 43**

Ritsos, Giannes
See Ritsos, Yannis

Ritsos, Yannis 1909-1990 . . . . . **CLC 6, 13, 31**
See also CA 77-80; 133; CANR 39; MTCW

Ritter, Erika 1948(?)- . . . . **CLC 52**

Rivera, Jose Eustasio 1889-1928 . . . **TCLC 35**
See also HW

Rivers, Conrad Kent 1933-1968 . . . . . . **CLC 1**
See also BW; CA 85-88; DLB 41

Rivers, Elfrida
See Bradley, Marion Zimmer

Riverside, John
See Heinlein, Robert A(nson)

Rizal, Jose 1861-1896 . . . . **NCLC 27**

Roa Bastos, Augusto (Antonio)
1917- . . . . **CLC 45**
See also CA 131; DLB 113; HW

Robbe-Grillet, Alain
1922- . . . . . . **CLC 1, 2, 4, 6, 8, 10, 14, 43**
See also CA 9-12R; CANR 33; DLB 83;
MTCW

Robbins, Harold 1916- . . . . **CLC 5**
See also CA 73-76; CANR 26; MTCW

Robbins, Thomas Eugene 1936-
See Robbins, Tom
See also CA 81-84; CANR 29; MTCW

Robbins, Tom . . . . **CLC 9, 32, 64**
See also Robbins, Thomas Eugene
See also BEST 90:3; DLBY 80

Robbins, Trina 1938- . . . . **CLC 21**
See also CA 128

Roberts, Charles G(eorge) D(ouglas)
1860-1943 . . . . **TCLC 8**
See also CA 105; DLB 92; SATA 29

Roberts, Kate 1891-1985 . . . . **CLC 15**
See also CA 107; 116

Roberts, Keith (John Kingston)
1935- . . . . **CLC 14**
See also CA 25-28R

Roberts, Kenneth (Lewis)
1885-1957 . . . . **TCLC 23**
See also CA 109; DLB 9

Roberts, Michele (B.) 1949- . . . . **CLC 48**
See also CA 115

Robertson, Ellis
See Ellison, Harlan; Silverberg, Robert

Robertson, Thomas William
1829-1871 . . . . **NCLC 35**

Robinson, Edwin Arlington
1869-1935 . . . . **TCLC 5; PC 1**
See also CA 104; 133; CDALB 1865-1917;
DLB 54; MTCW

Robinson, Henry Crabb
1775-1867 . . . . **NCLC 15**
See also DLB 107

Russ, Joanna 1937-.............. **CLC 15**
See also CA 25-28R; CANR 11, 31; DLB 8;
MTCW

Russell, George William 1867-1935
See A. E.
See also CA 104; CDBLB 1890-1914

Russell, (Henry) Ken(neth Alfred)
1927-...................... **CLC 16**
See also CA 105

Russell, Willy 1947-............. **CLC 60**

Rutherford, Mark .... **TCLC 25**
See also White, William Hale
See also DLB 18

Ruyslinck, Ward
See Belser, Reimond Karel Maria de

Ryan, Cornelius (John) 1920-1974 ... **CLC 7**
See also CA 69-72; 53-56; CANR 38

Ryan, Michael 1946-............. **CLC 65**
See also CA 49-52; DLBY 82

Rybakov, Anatoli (Naumovich)
1911-.................... **CLC 23, 53**
See also CA 126; 135

Ryder, Jonathan
See Ludlum, Robert

Ryga, George 1932-1987 .... **CLC 14**
See also CA 101; 124; DLB 60

S. S.
See Sassoon, Siegfried (Lorraine)

Saba, Umberto 1883-1957 .... **TCLC 33**
See also DLB 114

Sabatini, Rafael 1875-1950 ...... **TCLC 47**

Sabato, Ernesto (R.) 1911-..... **CLC 10, 23**
See also CA 97-100; CANR 32; HW;
MTCW

Sacastru, Martin
See Bioy Casares, Adolfo

Sacher-Masoch, Leopold von
1836(?)-1895 .... **NCLC 31**

Sachs, Marilyn (Stickle) 1927- ..... **CLC 35**
See also AAYA 2; CA 17-20R; CANR 13;
CLR 2; MAICYA; SAAS 2; SATA 3, 68

Sachs, Nelly 1891-1970 .... **CLC 14**
See also CA 17-18; 25-28R; CAP 2

Sackler, Howard (Oliver)
1929-1982 .... **CLC 14**
See also CA 61-64; 108; CANR 30; DLB 7

Sacks, Oliver (Wolf) 1933- .... **CLC 67**
See also CA 53-56; CANR 28; MTCW

Sade, Donatien Alphonse Francois Comte
1740-1814 .... **NCLC 3**

Sadoff, Ira 1945-................. **CLC 9**
See also CA 53-56; CANR 5, 21; DLB 120

Saetone
See Camus, Albert

Safire, William 1929-............. **CLC 10**
See also CA 17-20R; CANR 31

Sagan, Carl (Edward) 1934-........ **CLC 30**
See also AAYA 2; CA 25-28R; CANR 11,
36; MTCW; SATA 58

Sagan, Francoise .... **CLC 3, 6, 9, 17, 36**
See also Quoirez, Francoise
See also DLB 83

Sahgal, Nayantara (Pandit) 1927-... **CLC 41**
See also CA 9-12R; CANR 11

Saint, H(arry) F. 1941- .... **CLC 50**
See also CA 127

St. Aubin de Teran, Lisa 1953-
See Teran, Lisa St. Aubin de
See also CA 118; 126

Sainte-Beuve, Charles Augustin
1804-1869 .... **NCLC 5**

**Saint-Exupery, Antoine (Jean Baptiste Marie
Roger) de** 1900-1944 .... **TCLC 2**
See also CA 108; 132; CLR 10; DLB 72;
MAICYA; MTCW; SATA 20; WLC

St. John, David
See Hunt, E(verette) Howard Jr.

Saint-John Perse
See Leger, (Marie-Rene) Alexis Saint-Leger

Saintsbury, George (Edward Bateman)
1845-1933 .... **TCLC 31**
See also DLB 57

Sait Faik .... **TCLC 23**
See also Abasiyanik, Sait Faik

Saki .... **TCLC 3**
See also Munro, H(ector) H(ugh)

Salama, Hannu 1936-............. **CLC 18**

Salamanca, J(ack) R(ichard)
1922-.................... **CLC 4, 15**
See also CA 25-28R

Sale, J. Kirkpatrick
See Sale, Kirkpatrick

Sale, Kirkpatrick 1937-.......... **CLC 68**
See also CA 13-16R; CANR 10

Salinas (y Serrano), Pedro
1891(?)-1951 .... **TCLC 17**
See also CA 117

Salinger, J(erome) D(avid)
1919-.... **CLC 1, 3, 8, 12, 55, 56; SSC 2**
See also AAYA 2; CA 5-8R; CANR 39;
CDALB 1941-1968; CLR 18; DLB 2, 102;
MAICYA; MTCW; SATA 67; WLC

Salisbury, John
See Caute, David

Salter, James 1925- .... **CLC 7, 52, 59**
See also CA 73-76; DLB 130

Saltus, Edgar (Everton)
1855-1921 .... **TCLC 8**
See also CA 105

Saltykov, Mikhail Evgrafovich
1826-1889 .... **NCLC 16**

Samarakis, Antonis 1919-.......... **CLC 5**
See also CA 25-28R; CAAS 16; CANR 36

Sanchez, Florencio 1875-1910..... **TCLC 37**
See also HW

Sanchez, Luis Rafael 1936-........ **CLC 23**
See also CA 128; HW

Sanchez, Sonia 1934-............. **CLC 5**
See also BLC 3; BW; CA 33-36R;
CANR 24; CLR 18; DLB 41; DLBD 8;
MAICYA; MTCW; SATA 22

Sand, George 1804-1876......... **NCLC 2**
See also DLB 119; WLC

Sandburg, Carl (August)
1878-1967 ... **CLC 1, 4, 10, 15, 35; PC 2**
See also CA 5-8R; 25-28R; CANR 35;
CDALB 1865-1917; DLB 17, 54;
MAICYA; MTCW; SATA 8; WLC

Sandburg, Charles
See Sandburg, Carl (August)

Sandburg, Charles A.
See Sandburg, Carl (August)

Sanders, (James) Ed(ward) 1939- ... **CLC 53**
See also CA 13-16R; CANR 13; DLB 16

Sanders, Lawrence 1920-.......... **CLC 41**
See also BEST 89:4; CA 81-84; CANR 33;
MTCW

Sanders, Noah
See Blount, Roy (Alton) Jr.

Sanders, Winston P.
See Anderson, Poul (William)

Sandoz, Mari(e Susette)
1896-1966 .... **CLC 28**
See also CA 1-4R; 25-28R; CANR 17;
DLB 9; MTCW; SATA 5

Saner, Reg(inald Anthony) 1931- .... **CLC 9**
See also CA 65-68

Sannazaro, Jacopo 1456(?)-1530...... **LC 8**

Sansom, William 1912-1976....... **CLC 2, 6**
See also CA 5-8R; 65-68; MTCW

Santayana, George 1863-1952 ..... **TCLC 40**
See also CA 115; DLB 54, 71

Santiago, Danny .... **CLC 33**
See also James, Daniel (Lewis); James,
Daniel (Lewis)
See also DLB 122

Santmyer, Helen Hooven
1895-1986 .... **CLC 33**
See also CA 1-4R; 118; CANR 15, 33;
DLBY 84; MTCW

Santos, Bienvenido N(uqui) 1911-... **CLC 22**
See also CA 101; CANR 19

Sapper .... **TCLC 44**
See also McNeile, Herman Cyril

Sappho fl. 6th cent. B.C.-.... **CMLC 3; PC 5**

Sarduy, Severo 1937-.............. **CLC 6**
See also CA 89-92; DLB 113; HW

Sargeson, Frank 1903-1982 .... **CLC 31**
See also CA 25-28R; 106; CANR 38

Sarmiento, Felix Ruben Garcia 1867-1916
See Dario, Ruben
See also CA 104

Saroyan, William
1908-1981 ..... **CLC 1, 8, 10, 29, 34, 56**
See also CA 5-8R; 103; CANR 30; DLB 7,
9, 86; DLBY 81; MTCW; SATA 23, 24;
WLC

Sarraute, Nathalie
1900- .... **CLC 1, 2, 4, 8, 10, 31**
See also CA 9-12R; CANR 23; DLB 83;
MTCW

Sarton, (Eleanor) May
1912-................. **CLC 4, 14, 49**
See also CA 1-4R; CANR 1, 34; DLB 48;
DLBY 81; MTCW; SATA 36

Sartre, Jean-Paul
1905-1980 ... **CLC 1, 4, 7, 9, 13, 18, 24,
44, 50, 52; DC 3**
See also CA 9-12R; 97-100; CANR 21;
DLB 72; MTCW; WLC

Sassoon, Siegfried (Lorraine)
1886-1967 .... **CLC 36**
See also CA 104; 25-28R; CANR 36;
DLB 20; MTCW

Satterfield, Charles
See Pohl, Frederik

Saul, John (W. III) 1942- .... **CLC 46**
See also AAYA 10; BEST 90:4; CA 81-84;
CANR 16, 40

Saunders, Caleb
See Heinlein, Robert A(nson)

Saura (Atares), Carlos 1932-....... **CLC 20**
See also CA 114; 131; HW

Sauser-Hall, Frederic 1887-1961.... **CLC 18**
See also CA 102; 93-96; CANR 36; MTCW

Saussure, Ferdinand de
1857-1913 .... **TCLC 49**

Savage, Catharine
See Brosman, Catharine Savage

Savage, Thomas 1915- .... **CLC 40**
See also CA 126; 132; CAAS 15

Savan, Glenn .... **CLC 50**

Saven, Glenn 19(?)- .... **CLC 50**

Sayers, Dorothy L(eigh)
1893-1957 .... **TCLC 2, 15**
See also CA 104; 119; CDBLB 1914-1945;
DLB 10, 36, 77, 100; MTCW

Sayers, Valerie 1952-............. **CLC 50**
See also CA 134

Sayles, John Thomas 1950-... **CLC 7, 10, 14**
See also CA 57-60; DLB 44

Scammell, Michael .... **CLC 34**

Scannell, Vernon 1922- .... **CLC 49**
See also CA 5-8R; CANR 8, 24; DLB 27;
SATA 59

Scarlett, Susan
See Streatfeild, (Mary) Noel

Schaeffer, Susan Fromberg
1941-.................. **CLC 6, 11, 22**
See also CA 49-52; CANR 18; DLB 28;
MTCW; SATA 22

Schary, Jill
See Robinson, Jill

Schell, Jonathan 1943-............ **CLC 35**
See also CA 73-76; CANR 12

Schelling, Friedrich Wilhelm Joseph von
1775-1854 .... **NCLC 30**
See also DLB 90

Scherer, Jean-Marie Maurice 1920-
See Rohmer, Eric
See also CA 110

Schevill, James (Erwin) 1920-....... **CLC 7**
See also CA 5-8R; CAAS 12

Schiller, Friedrich 1759-1805 ... **NCLC 39**
See also DLB 94

Schisgal, Murray (Joseph) 1926-..... **CLC 6**
See also CA 21-24R

Schlee, Ann 1934-................ **CLC 35**
See also CA 101; CANR 29; SATA 36, 44

Schlegel, August Wilhelm von
1767-1845 .... **NCLC 15**
See also DLB 94

Schlegel, Johann Elias (von)
1719(?)-1749 .... **LC 5**

Schmidt, Arno (Otto) 1914-1979.... **CLC 56**
See also CA 128; 109; DLB 69

Schmitz, Aron Hector 1861-1928
See Svevo, Italo
See also CA 104; 122; MTCW

Schnackenberg, Gjertrud 1953-..... **CLC 40**
See also CA 116; DLB 120

Schneider, Leonard Alfred 1925-1966
See Bruce, Lenny
See also CA 89-92

Schnitzler, Arthur 1862-1931 ...... **TCLC 4**
See also CA 104; DLB 81, 118

Schor, Sandra (M.) 1932(?)-1990 ... **CLC 65**
See also CA 132

Schorer, Mark 1908-1977 .... **CLC 9**
See also CA 5-8R; 73-76; CANR 7;
DLB 103

Schrader, Paul Joseph 1946-....... **CLC 26**
See also CA 37-40R; DLB 44

Schreiner, Olive (Emilie Albertina)
1855-1920 .... **TCLC 9**
See also CA 105; DLB 18

Schulberg, Budd (Wilson)
1914-.................... **CLC 7, 48**
See also CA 25-28R; CANR 19; DLB 6, 26,
28; DLBY 81

Schulz, Bruno 1892-1942......... **TCLC 5**
See also CA 115; 123

Schulz, Charles M(onroe) 1922- .... **CLC 12**
See also CA 9-12R; CANR 6; SATA 10

Schuyler, James Marcus
1923-1991 .... **CLC 5, 23**
See also CA 101; 134; DLB 5

Schwartz, Delmore (David)
1913-1966.......... **CLC 2, 4, 10, 45**
See also CA 17-18; 25-28R; CANR 35;
CAP 2; DLB 28, 48; MTCW

Schwartz, Ernst
See Ozu, Yasujiro

Schwartz, John Burnham 1965- .... **CLC 59**
See also CA 132

Schwartz, Lynne Sharon 1939-..... **CLC 31**
See also CA 103

Schwartz, Muriel A.
See Eliot, T(homas) S(tearns)

Schwarz-Bart, Andre 1928-....... **CLC 2, 4**
See also CA 89-92

Schwarz-Bart, Simone 1938-....... **CLC 7**
See also CA 97-100

Schwob, (Mayer Andre) Marcel
1867-1905 .... **TCLC 20**
See also CA 117; DLB 123

Sciascia, Leonardo
1921-1989 .... **CLC 8, 9, 41**
See also CA 85-88; 130; CANR 35; MTCW

Scoppettone, Sandra 1936-......... **CLC 26**
See also CA 5-8R; SATA 9

Scorsese, Martin 1942- .... **CLC 20**
See also CA 110; 114

Scotland, Jay
See Jakes, John (William)

Scott, Duncan Campbell
1862-1947 .... **TCLC 6**
See also CA 104; DLB 92

Scott, Evelyn 1893-1963.......... **CLC 43**
See also CA 104; 112; DLB 9, 48

Scott, F(rancis) R(eginald)
1899-1985 .... **CLC 22**
See also CA 101; 114; DLB 88

Scott, Frank
See Scott, F(rancis) R(eginald)

Scott, Joanna 1960- .... **CLC 50**
See also CA 126

Scott, Paul (Mark) 1920-1978.... **CLC 9, 60**
See also CA 81-84; 77-80; CANR 33;
DLB 14; MTCW

Scott, Walter 1771-1832......... **NCLC 15**
See also CDBLB 1789-1832; DLB 93, 107,
116; WLC; YABC 2

Scribe, (Augustin) Eugene
1791-1861 .... **NCLC 16**

Scrum, R.
See Crumb, R(obert)

Scudery, Madeleine de 1607-1701..... **LC 2**

Scum
See Crumb, R(obert)

Scumbag, Little Bobby
See Crumb, R(obert)

Seabrook, John
See Hubbard, L(afayette) Ron(ald)

Sealy, I. Allan 1951- .... **CLC 55**

Search, Alexander
See Pessoa, Fernando (Antonio Nogueira)

Sebastian, Lee
See Silverberg, Robert

Sebastian Owl
See Thompson, Hunter S(tockton)

Sebestyen, Ouida 1924-........... **CLC 30**
See also AAYA 8; CA 107; CANR 40;
CLR 17; MAICYA; SAAS 10; SATA 39

Sedges, John
See Buck, Pearl S(ydenstricker)

Sedgwick, Catharine Maria
1789-1867 .... **NCLC 19**
See also DLB 1, 74

Seelye, John 1931-................ **CLC 7**

Seferiades, Giorgos Stylianou 1900-1971
See Seferis, George
See also CA 5-8R; 33-36R; CANR 5, 36;
MTCW

Seferis, George .... **CLC 5, 11**
See also Seferiades, Giorgos Stylianou

Segal, Erich (Wolf) 1937- .... **CLC 3, 10**
See also BEST 89:1; CA 25-28R; CANR 20,
36; DLBY 86; MTCW

Seger, Bob 1945-................. **CLC 35**

Seghers, Anna .... **CLC 7**
See also Radvanyi, Netty
See also DLB 69

Seidel, Frederick (Lewis) 1936-..... **CLC 18**
See also CA 13-16R; CANR 8; DLBY 84

Seifert, Jaroslav 1901-1986 . . . . . **CLC 34, 44**
See also CA 127; MTCW

Sei Shonagon c. 966-1017(?) . . . . . . **CMLC 6**

Selby, Hubert Jr. 1928- . . . . . . **CLC 1, 2, 4, 8**
See also CA 13-16R; CANR 33; DLB 2

Selzer, Richard 1928- . . . . **CLC 74**
See also CA 65-68; CANR 14

Sembene, Ousmane
See Ousmane, Sembene

Senancour, Etienne Pivert de
1770-1846 . . . . **NCLC 16**
See also DLB 119

Sender, Ramon (Jose) 1902-1982 . . . . **CLC 8**
See also CA 5-8R; 105; CANR 8; HW;
MTCW

Seneca, Lucius Annaeus
4B.C.-65. . . . . **CMLC 6**

Senghor, Leopold Sedar 1906- . . . . . **CLC 54**
See also BLC 3; BW; CA 116; 125; MTCW

Serling, (Edward) Rod(man)
1924-1975 . . . . **CLC 30**
See also AITN 1; CA 65-68; 57-60; DLB 26

Serna, Ramon Gomez de la
See Gomez de la Serna, Ramon

Serpieres
See Guillevic, (Eugene)

Service, Robert
See Service, Robert W(illiam)
See also DLB 92

Service, Robert W(illiam)
1874(?)-1958 . . . . **TCLC 15**
See also Service, Robert
See also CA 115; SATA 20; WLC

Seth, Vikram 1952- . . . . **CLC 43**
See also CA 121; 127; DLB 120

Seton, Cynthia Propper
1926-1982 . . . . **CLC 27**
See also CA 5-8R; 108; CANR 7

Seton, Ernest (Evan) Thompson
1860-1946 . . . . **TCLC 31**
See also CA 109; DLB 92; SATA 18

Seton-Thompson, Ernest
See Seton, Ernest (Evan) Thompson

Settle, Mary Lee 1918- . . . . **CLC 19, 61**
See also CA 89-92; CAAS 1; DLB 6

Seuphor, Michel
See Arp, Jean

**Sevigne, Marie (de Rabutin-Chantal) Marquise
de** 1626-1696 . . . . **LC 11**

Sexton, Anne (Harvey)
1928-1974 . . . **CLC 2, 4, 6, 8, 10, 15, 53;
PC 2**
See also CA 1-4R; 53-56; CABS 2;
CANR 3, 36; CDALB 1941-1968; DLB 5;
MTCW; SATA 10; WLC

Shaara, Michael (Joseph Jr.)
1929-1988 . . . . **CLC 15**
See also AITN 1; CA 102; DLBY 83

Shackleton, C. C.
See Aldiss, Brian W(ilson)

Shacochis, Bob . . . . **CLC 39**
See also Shacochis, Robert G.

Shacochis, Robert G. 1951-
See Shacochis, Bob
See also CA 119; 124

Shaffer, Anthony (Joshua) 1926- . . . . **CLC 19**
See also CA 110; 116; DLB 13

Shaffer, Peter (Levin)
1926- . . . . **CLC 5, 14, 18, 37, 60**
See also CA 25-28R; CANR 25;
CDBLB 1960 to Present; DLB 13;
MTCW

Shakey, Bernard
See Young, Neil

Shalamov, Varlam (Tikhonovich)
1907(?)-1982 . . . . **CLC 18**
See also CA 129; 105

Shamlu, Ahmad 1925- . . . . **CLC 10**

Shammas, Anton 1951- . . . . **CLC 55**

Shange, Ntozake
1948- . . . . **CLC 8, 25, 38, 74; DC 3**
See also AAYA 9; BLC 3; BW; CA 85-88;
CABS 3; CANR 27; DLB 38; MTCW

Shanley, John Patrick 1950- . . . . **CLC 75**
See also CA 128; 133

Shapcott, Thomas William 1935- . . . **CLC 38**
See also CA 69-72

Shapiro, Jane . . . . **CLC 76**

Shapiro, Karl (Jay) 1913- . . **CLC 4, 8, 15, 53**
See also CA 1-4R; CAAS 6; CANR 1, 36;
DLB 48; MTCW

Sharp, William 1855-1905 . . . . **TCLC 39**

Sharpe, Thomas Ridley 1928-
See Sharpe, Tom
See also CA 114; 122

Sharpe, Tom . . . . **CLC 36**
See also Sharpe, Thomas Ridley
See also DLB 14

Shaw, Bernard . . . . **TCLC 45**
See also Shaw, George Bernard

Shaw, G. Bernard
See Shaw, George Bernard

Shaw, George Bernard
1856-1950 . . . . **TCLC 3, 9, 21**
See also Shaw, Bernard
See also CA 104; 128; CDBLB 1914-1945;
DLB 10, 57; MTCW; WLC

Shaw, Henry Wheeler
1818-1885 . . . . **NCLC 15**
See also DLB 11

Shaw, Irwin 1913-1984 . . . . . . **CLC 7, 23, 34**
See also AITN 1; CA 13-16R; 112;
CANR 21; CDALB 1941-1968; DLB 6,
102; DLBY 84; MTCW

Shaw, Robert 1927-1978 . . . . **CLC 5**
See also AITN 1; CA 1-4R; 81-84;
CANR 4; DLB 13, 14

Shaw, T. E.
See Lawrence, T(homas) E(dward)

Shawn, Wallace 1943- . . . . **CLC 41**
See also CA 112

Sheed, Wilfrid (John Joseph)
1930- . . . . **CLC 2, 4, 10, 53**
See also CA 65-68; CANR 30; DLB 6;
MTCW

Sheldon, Alice Hastings Bradley
1915(?)-1987
See Tiptree, James Jr.
See also CA 108; 122; CANR 34; MTCW

Sheldon, John
See Bloch, Robert (Albert)

Shelley, Mary Wollstonecraft (Godwin)
1797-1851 . . . . **NCLC 14**
See also CDBLB 1789-1832; DLB 110, 116;
SATA 29; WLC

Shelley, Percy Bysshe
1792-1822 . . . . **NCLC 18**
See also CDBLB 1789-1832; DLB 96, 110;
WLC

Shepard, Jim 1956- . . . . **CLC 36**
See also CA 137

Shepard, Lucius 19(?)- . . . . **CLC 34**
See also CA 128

Shepard, Sam
1943- . . . . **CLC 4, 6, 17, 34, 41, 44**
See also AAYA 1; CA 69-72; CABS 3;
CANR 22; DLB 7; MTCW

Shepherd, Michael
See Ludlum, Robert

Sherburne, Zoa (Morin) 1912- . . . . . . **CLC 30**
See also CA 1-4R; CANR 3, 37; MAICYA;
SATA 3

Sheridan, Frances 1724-1766 . . . . **LC 7**
See also DLB 39, 84

Sheridan, Richard Brinsley
1751-1816 . . . . **NCLC 5; DC 1**
See also CDBLB 1660-1789; DLB 89; WLC

Sherman, Jonathan Marc . . . . **CLC 55**

Sherman, Martin 1941(?)- . . . . **CLC 19**
See also CA 116; 123

Sherwin, Judith Johnson 1936- . . . **CLC 7, 15**
See also CA 25-28R; CANR 34

Sherwood, Robert E(mmet)
1896-1955 . . . . **TCLC 3**
See also CA 104; DLB 7, 26

Shiel, M(atthew) P(hipps)
1865-1947 . . . . **TCLC 8**
See also CA 106

Shiga, Naoya 1883-1971. . . . . **CLC 33**
See also CA 101; 33-36R

Shimazaki Haruki 1872-1943
See Shimazaki Toson
See also CA 105; 134

Shimazaki Toson . . . . **TCLC 5**
See also Shimazaki Haruki

Sholokhov, Mikhail (Aleksandrovich)
1905-1984 . . . . **CLC 7, 15**
See also CA 101; 112; MTCW; SATA 36

Shone, Patric
See Hanley, James

Shreve, Susan Richards 1939- . . . . . . **CLC 23**
See also CA 49-52; CAAS 5; CANR 5, 38;
MAICYA; SATA 41, 46

Shue, Larry 1946-1985 . . . . **CLC 52**
See also CA 117

Shu-Jen, Chou 1881-1936
See Hsun, Lu
See also CA 104

Smart, Christopher 1722-1771....... **LC 3**
See also DLB 109

Smart, Elizabeth 1913-1986....... **CLC 54**
See also CA 81-84; 118; DLB 88

Smiley, Jane (Graves) 1949- .... **CLC 53, 76**
See also CA 104; CANR 30

Smith, A(rthur) J(ames) M(arshall)
1902-1980 .... **CLC 15**
See also CA 1-4R; 102; CANR 4; DLB 88

Smith, Betty (Wehner) 1896-1972... **CLC 19**
See also CA 5-8R; 33-36R; DLBY 82;
SATA 6

Smith, Charlotte (Turner)
1749-1806 .... **NCLC 23**
See also DLB 39, 109

Smith, Clark Ashton 1893-1961 .... **CLC 43**

Smith, Dave.................. **CLC 22, 42**
See also Smith, David (Jeddie)
See also CAAS 7; DLB 5

Smith, David (Jeddie) 1942-
See Smith, Dave
See also CA 49-52; CANR 1

Smith, Florence Margaret
1902-1971 .... **CLC 8**
See also Smith, Stevie
See also CA 17-18; 29-32R; CANR 35;
CAP 2; MTCW

Smith, Iain Crichton 1928- .... **CLC 64**
See also CA 21-24R; DLB 40

Smith, John 1580(?)-1631 .... **LC 9**

Smith, Johnston
See Crane, Stephen (Townley)

Smith, Lee 1944-............. **CLC 25, 73**
See also CA 114; 119; DLBY 83

Smith, Martin
See Smith, Martin Cruz

Smith, Martin Cruz 1942-........ **CLC 25**
See also BEST 89:4; CA 85-88; CANR 6, 23

Smith, Mary-Ann Tirone 1944-..... **CLC 39**
See also CA 118; 136

Smith, Patti 1946- .... **CLC 12**
See also CA 93-96

Smith, Pauline (Urmson)
1882-1959 .... **TCLC 25**

Smith, Rosamond
See Oates, Joyce Carol

Smith, Sheila Kaye
See Kaye-Smith, Sheila

Smith, Stevie .... **CLC 3, 8, 25, 44**
See also Smith, Florence Margaret
See also DLB 20

Smith, Wilbur A(ddison) 1933-..... **CLC 33**
See also CA 13-16R; CANR 7; MTCW

Smith, William Jay 1918- .... **CLC 6**
See also CA 5-8R; DLB 5; MAICYA;
SATA 2, 68

Smith, Woodrow Wilson
See Kuttner, Henry

Smolenskin, Peretz 1842-1885.... **NCLC 30**

Smollett, Tobias (George) 1721-1771 .. **LC 2**
See also CDBLB 1660-1789; DLB 39, 104

Snodgrass, William D(e Witt)
1926- .... **CLC 2, 6, 10, 18, 68**
See also CA 1-4R; CANR 6, 36; DLB 5;
MTCW

Snow, C(harles) P(ercy)
1905-1980 .... **CLC 1, 4, 6, 9, 13, 19**
See also CA 5-8R; 101; CANR 28;
CDBLB 1945-1960; DLB 15, 77; MTCW

Snow, Frances Compton
See Adams, Henry (Brooks)

Snyder, Gary (Sherman)
1930- .... **CLC 1, 2, 5, 9, 32**
See also CA 17-20R; CANR 30; DLB 5, 16

Snyder, Zilpha Keatley 1927-...... **CLC 17**
See also CA 9-12R; CANR 38; MAICYA;
SAAS 2; SATA 1, 28

Soares, Bernardo
See Pessoa, Fernando (Antonio Nogueira)

Sobh, A.
See Shamlu, Ahmad

Sobol, Joshua.................... **CLC 60**

Soderberg, Hjalmar 1869-1941 .... **TCLC 39**

Sodergran, Edith (Irene)
See Soedergran, Edith (Irene)

Soedergran, Edith (Irene)
1892-1923 .... **TCLC 31**

Softly, Edgar
See Lovecraft, H(oward) P(hillips)

Softly, Edward
See Lovecraft, H(oward) P(hillips)

Sokolov, Raymond 1941-.......... **CLC 7**
See also CA 85-88

Solo, Jay
See Ellison, Harlan

Sologub, Fyodor .... **TCLC 9**
See also Teternikov, Fyodor Kuzmich

Solomons, Ikey Esquir
See Thackeray, William Makepeace

Solomos, Dionysios 1798-1857 ... **NCLC 15**

Solwoska, Mara
See French, Marilyn

Solzhenitsyn, Aleksandr I(sayevich)
1918- ... **CLC 1, 2, 4, 7, 9, 10, 18, 26, 34**
See also AITN 1; CA 69-72; CANR 40;
MTCW; WLC

Somers, Jane
See Lessing, Doris (May)

Sommer, Scott 1951- .... **CLC 25**
See also CA 106

Sondheim, Stephen (Joshua)
1930- .... **CLC 30, 39**
See also CA 103

Sontag, Susan 1933-... **CLC 1, 2, 10, 13, 31**
See also CA 17-20R; CANR 25; DLB 2, 67;
MTCW

Sophocles
496(?)B.C.-406(?)B.C.... **CMLC 2; DC 1**

Sorel, Julia
See Drexler, Rosalyn

Sorrentino, Gilbert
1929- .... **CLC 3, 7, 14, 22, 40**
See also CA 77-80; CANR 14, 33; DLB 5;
DLBY 80

Soto, Gary 1952-................. **CLC 32**
See also AAYA 10; CA 119; 125; DLB 82;
HW

Soupault, Philippe 1897-1990 ...... **CLC 68**
See also CA 116; 131

Souster, (Holmes) Raymond
1921- .... **CLC 5, 14**
See also CA 13-16R; CAAS 14; CANR 13,
29; DLB 88; SATA 63

Southern, Terry 1926- .... **CLC 7**
See also CA 1-4R; CANR 1; DLB 2

Southey, Robert 1774-1843 .... **NCLC 8**
See also DLB 93, 107; SATA 54

Southworth, Emma Dorothy Eliza Nevitte
1819-1899 .... **NCLC 26**

Souza, Ernest
See Scott, Evelyn

Soyinka, Wole
1934- .... **CLC 3, 5, 14, 36, 44; DC 2**
See also BLC 3; BW; CA 13-16R;
CANR 27, 39; DLB 125; MTCW; WLC

Spackman, W(illiam) M(ode)
1905-1990 .... **CLC 46**
See also CA 81-84; 132

Spacks, Barry 1931-.............. **CLC 14**
See also CA 29-32R; CANR 33; DLB 105

Spanidou, Irini 1946-............. **CLC 44**

Spark, Muriel (Sarah)
1918- .... **CLC 2, 3, 5, 8, 13, 18, 40;
SSC 10**
See also CA 5-8R; CANR 12, 36;
CDBLB 1945-1960; DLB 15; MTCW

Spaulding, Douglas
See Bradbury, Ray (Douglas)

Spaulding, Leonard
See Bradbury, Ray (Douglas)

Spence, J. A. D.
See Eliot, T(homas) S(tearns)

Spencer, Elizabeth 1921-.......... **CLC 22**
See also CA 13-16R; CANR 32; DLB 6;
MTCW; SATA 14

Spencer, Leonard G.
See Silverberg, Robert

Spencer, Scott 1945-.............. **CLC 30**
See also CA 113; DLBY 86

Spender, Stephen (Harold)
1909- .... **CLC 1, 2, 5, 10, 41**
See also CA 9-12R; CANR 31;
CDBLB 1945-1960; DLB 20; MTCW

Spengler, Oswald (Arnold Gottfried)
1880-1936 .... **TCLC 25**
See also CA 118

Spenser, Edmund 1552(?)-1599 .... **LC 5**
See also CDBLB Before 1660; WLC

Spicer, Jack 1925-1965 ...... **CLC 8, 18, 72**
See also CA 85-88; DLB 5, 16

Spiegelman, Art 1948-............ **CLC 76**
See also AAYA 10; CA 125

Spielberg, Peter 1929-............. **CLC 6**
See also CA 5-8R; CANR 4; DLBY 81

Spielberg, Steven 1947-........... **CLC 20**
See also AAYA 8; CA 77-80; CANR 32;
SATA 32

Spillane, Frank Morrison 1918-
See Spillane, Mickey
See also CA 25-28R; CANR 28; MTCW;
SATA 66

Spillane, Mickey . . . . CLC 3, 13
See also Spillane, Frank Morrison

Spinoza, Benedictus de 1632-1677 . . . . LC 9

Spinrad, Norman (Richard) 1940-. . . CLC 46
See also CA 37-40R; CANR 20; DLB 8

Spitteler, Carl (Friedrich Georg)
1845-1924 . . . . TCLC 12
See also CA 109; DLB 129

Spivack, Kathleen (Romola Drucker)
1938- . . . . CLC 6
See also CA 49-52

Spoto, Donald 1941-. . . . . CLC 39
See also CA 65-68; CANR 11

Springsteen, Bruce (F.) 1949- . . . . . . CLC 17
See also CA 111

Spurling, Hilary 1940-. . . . . CLC 34
See also CA 104; CANR 25

Squires, Radcliffe 1917-. . . . . CLC 51
See also CA 1-4R; CANR 6, 21

Srivastava, Dhanpat Rai 1880(?)-1936
See Premchand
See also CA 118

Stacy, Donald
See Pohl, Frederik

Stael, Germaine de
See Stael-Holstein, Anne Louise Germaine
Necker Baronn
See also DLB 119

Stael-Holstein, Anne Louise Germaine Necker
Baronn 1766-1817 . . . . NCLC 3
See also Stael, Germaine de

Stafford, Jean 1915-1979. . . CLC 4, 7, 19, 68
See also CA 1-4R; 85-88; CANR 3; DLB 2;
MTCW; SATA 22

Stafford, William (Edgar)
1914- . . . . CLC 4, 7, 29
See also CA 5-8R; CAAS 3; CANR 5, 22;
DLB 5

Staines, Trevor
See Brunner, John (Kilian Houston)

Stairs, Gordon
See Austin, Mary (Hunter)

Stannard, Martin. . . . . CLC 44

Stanton, Maura 1946- . . . . CLC 9
See also CA 89-92; CANR 15; DLB 120

Stanton, Schuyler
See Baum, L(yman) Frank

Stapledon, (William) Olaf
1886-1950 . . . . TCLC 22
See also CA 111; DLB 15

Starbuck, George (Edwin) 1931-. . . . CLC 53
See also CA 21-24R; CANR 23

Stark, Richard
See Westlake, Donald E(dwin)

Staunton, Schuyler
See Baum, L(yman) Frank

Stead, Christina (Ellen)
1902-1983 . . . . CLC 2, 5, 8, 32
See also CA 13-16R; 109; CANR 33, 40;
MTCW

Stead, William Thomas
1849-1912 . . . . TCLC 48

Steele, Richard 1672-1729. . . . . LC 18
See also CDBLB 1660-1789; DLB 84, 101

Steele, Timothy (Reid) 1948-. . . . . . CLC 45
See also CA 93-96; CANR 16; DLB 120

Steffens, (Joseph) Lincoln
1866-1936 . . . . TCLC 20
See also CA 117

Stegner, Wallace (Earle) 1909-. . . CLC 9, 49
See also AITN 1; BEST 90:3; CA 1-4R;
CAAS 9; CANR 1, 21; DLB 9; MTCW

Stein, Gertrude
1874-1946 . . . . TCLC 1, 6, 28, 48
See also CA 104; 132; CDALB 1917-1929;
DLB 4, 54, 86; MTCW; WLC

Steinbeck, John (Ernst)
1902-1968 . . . . . CLC 1, 5, 9, 13, 21, 34,
45, 75; SSC 11
See also CA 1-4R; 25-28R; CANR 1, 35;
CDALB 1929-1941; DLB 7, 9; DLBD 2;
MTCW; SATA 9; WLC

Steinem, Gloria 1934-. . . . . CLC 63
See also CA 53-56; CANR 28; MTCW

Steiner, George 1929-. . . . . CLC 24
See also CA 73-76; CANR 31; DLB 67;
MTCW; SATA 62

Steiner, Rudolf 1861-1925. . . . . . . TCLC 13
See also CA 107

Stendhal 1783-1842. . . . . NCLC 23
See also DLB 119; WLC

Stephen, Leslie 1832-1904 . . . . TCLC 23
See also CA 123; DLB 57

Stephen, Sir Leslie
See Stephen, Leslie

Stephen, Virginia
See Woolf, (Adeline) Virginia

Stephens, James 1882(?)-1950. . . . . . TCLC 4
See also CA 104; DLB 19

Stephens, Reed
See Donaldson, Stephen R.

Steptoe, Lydia
See Barnes, Djuna

Sterchi, Beat 1949-. . . . . CLC 65

Sterling, Brett
See Bradbury, Ray (Douglas); Hamilton,
Edmond

Sterling, Bruce 1954-. . . . . CLC 72
See also CA 119

Sterling, George 1869-1926 . . . . . . TCLC 20
See also CA 117; DLB 54

Stern, Gerald 1925- . . . . CLC 40
See also CA 81-84; CANR 28; DLB 105

Stern, Richard (Gustave) 1928-. . . CLC 4, 39
See also CA 1-4R; CANR 1, 25; DLBY 87

Sternberg, Josef von 1894-1969. . . . . CLC 20
See also CA 81-84

Sterne, Laurence 1713-1768. . . . . LC 2
See also CDBLB 1660-1789; DLB 39; WLC

Sternheim, (William Adolf) Carl
1878-1942 . . . . TCLC 8
See also CA 105; DLB 56, 118

Stevens, Mark 1951- . . . . CLC 34
See also CA 122

Stevens, Wallace
1879-1955 . . . . TCLC 3, 12, 45; PC 6
See also CA 104; 124; CDALB 1929-1941;
DLB 54; MTCW; WLC

Stevenson, Anne (Katharine)
1933- . . . . CLC 7, 33
See also CA 17-20R; CAAS 9; CANR 9, 33;
DLB 40; MTCW

Stevenson, Robert Louis (Balfour)
1850-1894 . . . . NCLC 5, 14; SSC 11
See also CDBLB 1890-1914; CLR 10, 11;
DLB 18, 57; MAICYA; WLC; YABC 2

Stewart, J(ohn) I(nnes) M(ackintosh)
1906- . . . . CLC 7, 14, 32
See also CA 85-88; CAAS 3; MTCW

Stewart, Mary (Florence Elinor)
1916- . . . . CLC 7, 35
See also CA 1-4R; CANR 1; SATA 12

Stewart, Mary Rainbow
See Stewart, Mary (Florence Elinor)

Still, James 1906-. . . . . CLC 49
See also CA 65-68; CAAS 17; CANR 10,
26; DLB 9; SATA 29

Sting
See Sumner, Gordon Matthew

Stirling, Arthur
See Sinclair, Upton (Beall)

Stitt, Milan 1941-. . . . . CLC 29
See also CA 69-72

Stockton, Francis Richard 1834-1902
See Stockton, Frank R.
See also CA 108; 137; MAICYA; SATA 44

Stockton, Frank R.. . . . . TCLC 47
See also Stockton, Francis Richard
See also DLB 42, 74; SATA 32

Stoddard, Charles
See Kuttner, Henry

Stoker, Abraham 1847-1912
See Stoker, Bram
See also CA 105; SATA 29

Stoker, Bram. . . . . TCLC 8
See also Stoker, Abraham
See also CDBLB 1890-1914; DLB 36, 70;
WLC

Stolz, Mary (Slattery) 1920-. . . . . . . CLC 12
See also AAYA 8; AITN 1; CA 5-8R;
CANR 13; MAICYA; SAAS 3;
SATA 10, 70, 71

Stone, Irving 1903-1989. . . . . CLC 7
See also AITN 1; CA 1-4R; 129; CAAS 3;
CANR 1, 23; MTCW; SATA 3; SATO 64

Stone, Oliver 1946-. . . . . CLC 73
See also CA 110

Stone, Robert (Anthony)
1937- . . . . CLC 5, 23, 42
See also CA 85-88; CANR 23; MTCW

Stone, Zachary
See Follett, Ken(neth Martin)

Stoppard, Tom
1937- . . . CLC 1, 3, 4, 5, 8, 15, 29, 34, 63
See also CA 81-84; CANR 39;
CDBLB 1960 to Present; DLB 13;
DLBY 85; MTCW; WLC

Author Index

Tsushima, Shuji 1909-1948
See Dazai, Osamu
See also CA 107

Tsvetaeva (Efron), Marina (Ivanovna)
1892-1941 .... **TCLC 7, 35**
See also CA 104; 128; MTCW

Tuck, Lily 1938-................ **CLC 70**
See also CA 139

Tunis, John R(oberts) 1889-1975 ... **CLC 12**
See also CA 61-64; DLB 22; MAICYA;
SATA 30, 37

Tuohy, Frank.................... **CLC 37**
See also Tuohy, John Francis
See also DLB 14

Tuohy, John Francis 1925-
See Tuohy, Frank
See also CA 5-8R; CANR 3

Turco, Lewis (Putnam) 1934- ... **CLC 11, 63**
See also CA 13-16R; CANR 24; DLBY 84

Turgenev, Ivan
1818-1883 .... **NCLC 21; SSC 7**
See also WLC

Turner, Frederick 1943-.......... **CLC 48**
See also CA 73-76; CAAS 10; CANR 12,
30; DLB 40

Tusan, Stan 1936-................ **CLC 22**
See also CA 105

Tutuola, Amos 1920- .... **CLC 5, 14, 29**
See also BLC 3; BW; CA 9-12R; CANR 27;
DLB 125; MTCW

Twain, Mark
.... **TCLC 6, 12, 19, 36, 48; SSC 6**
See also Clemens, Samuel Langhorne
See also DLB 11, 12, 23, 64, 74; WLC

Tyler, Anne
1941- .... **CLC 7, 11, 18, 28, 44, 59**
See also BEST 89:1; CA 9-12R; CANR 11,
33; DLB 6; DLBY 82; MTCW; SATA 7

Tyler, Royall 1757-1826......... **NCLC 3**
See also DLB 37

Tynan, Katharine 1861-1931 .... **TCLC 3**
See also CA 104

Tytell, John 1939- .... **CLC 50**
See also CA 29-32R

Tyutchev, Fyodor 1803-1873..... **NCLC 34**

Tzara, Tristan .... **CLC 47**
See also Rosenfeld, Samuel

Uhry, Alfred 1936-.............. **CLC 55**
See also CA 127; 133

Ulf, Haerved
See Strindberg, (Johan) August

Ulf, Harved
See Strindberg, (Johan) August

Unamuno (y Jugo), Miguel de
1864-1936 .... **TCLC 2, 9; SSC 11**
See also CA 104; 131; DLB 108; HW;
MTCW

Undercliffe, Errol
See Campbell, (John) Ramsey

Underwood, Miles
See Glassco, John

Undset, Sigrid 1882-1949......... **TCLC 3**
See also CA 104; 129; MTCW; WLC

Ungaretti, Giuseppe
1888-1970 .... **CLC 7, 11, 15**
See also CA 19-20; 25-28R; CAP 2;
DLB 114

Unger, Douglas 1952-............ **CLC 34**
See also CA 130

Unsworth, Barry (Forster) 1930-.... **CLC 76**
See also CA 25-28R; CANR 30

Updike, John (Hoyer)
1932- ...... **CLC 1, 2, 3, 5, 7, 9, 13, 15,**
23, 34, 43, 70
See also CA 1-4R; CABS 1; CANR 4, 33;
CDALB 1968-1988; DLB 2, 5; DLBD 3;
DLBY 80, 82; MTCW; WLC

Upshaw, Margaret Mitchell
See Mitchell, Margaret (Munnerlyn)

Upton, Mark
See Sanders, Lawrence

Urdang, Constance (Henriette)
1922-..................... **CLC 47**
See also CA 21-24R; CANR 9, 24

Uriel, Henry
See Faust, Frederick (Schiller)

Uris, Leon (Marcus) 1924-...... **CLC 7, 32**
See also AITN 1, 2; BEST 89:2; CA 1-4R;
CANR 1, 40; MTCW; SATA 49

Urmuz
See Codrescu, Andrei

Ustinov, Peter (Alexander) 1921-.... **CLC 1**
See also AITN 1; CA 13-16R; CANR 25;
DLB 13

V
See Chekhov, Anton (Pavlovich)

Vaculik, Ludvik 1926-............ **CLC 7**
See also CA 53-56

Valenzuela, Luisa 1938-.......... **CLC 31**
See also CA 101; CANR 32; DLB 113; HW

Valera y Alcala-Galiano, Juan
1824-1905 .... **TCLC 10**
See also CA 106

Valery, (Ambroise) Paul (Toussaint Jules)
1871-1945 .... **TCLC 4, 15**
See also CA 104; 122; MTCW

Valle-Inclan, Ramon (Maria) del
1866-1936 .... **TCLC 5**
See also CA 106

Vallejo, Antonio Buero
See Buero Vallejo, Antonio

Vallejo, Cesar (Abraham)
1892-1938 .... **TCLC 3**
See also CA 105; HW

Valle Y Pena, Ramon del
See Valle-Inclan, Ramon (Maria) del

Van Ash, Cay 1918-.............. **CLC 34**

Vanbrugh, Sir John 1664-1726 ...... **LC 21**
See also DLB 80

Van Campen, Karl
See Campbell, John W(ood Jr.)

Vance, Gerald
See Silverberg, Robert

Vance, Jack .... **CLC 35**
See also Vance, John Holbrook
See also DLB 8

Vance, John Holbrook 1916-
See Queen, Ellery; Vance, Jack
See also CA 29-32R; CANR 17; MTCW

Van Den Bogarde, Derek Jules Gaspard Ulric
Niven 1921-
See Bogarde, Dirk
See also CA 77-80

Vandenburgh, Jane .... **CLC 59**

Vanderhaeghe, Guy 1951- .... **CLC 41**
See also CA 113

van der Post, Laurens (Jan) 1906- ... **CLC 5**
See also CA 5-8R; CANR 35

van de Wetering, Janwillem 1931- .. **CLC 47**
See also CA 49-52; CANR 4

Van Dine, S. S. .... **TCLC 23**
See also Wright, Willard Huntington

Van Doren, Carl (Clinton)
1885-1950 .... **TCLC 18**
See also CA 111

Van Doren, Mark 1894-1972..... **CLC 6, 10**
See also CA 1-4R; 37-40R; CANR 3;
DLB 45; MTCW

Van Druten, John (William)
1901-1957 .... **TCLC 2**
See also CA 104; DLB 10

Van Duyn, Mona (Jane)
1921-.................. **CLC 3, 7, 63**
See also CA 9-12R; CANR 7, 38; DLB 5

Van Dyne, Edith
See Baum, L(yman) Frank

van Itallie, Jean-Claude 1936-....... **CLC 3**
See also CA 45-48; CAAS 2; CANR 1;
DLB 7

van Ostaijen, Paul 1896-1928 ..... **TCLC 33**

Van Peebles, Melvin 1932- ...... **CLC 2, 20**
See also BW; CA 85-88; CANR 27

Vansittart, Peter 1920-............ **CLC 42**
See also CA 1-4R; CANR 3

Van Vechten, Carl 1880-1964 ...... **CLC 33**
See also CA 89-92; DLB 4, 9, 51

Van Vogt, A(lfred) E(lton) 1912-..... **CLC 1**
See also CA 21-24R; CANR 28; DLB 8;
SATA 14

Vara, Madeleine
See Jackson, Laura (Riding)

Varda, Agnes 1928- .... **CLC 16**
See also CA 116; 122

Vargas Llosa, (Jorge) Mario (Pedro)
1936- .... **CLC 3, 6, 9, 10, 15, 31, 42**
See also CA 73-76; CANR 18, 32; HW;
MTCW

Vasiliu, Gheorghe 1881-1957
See Bacovia, George
See also CA 123

Vassa, Gustavus
See Equiano, Olaudah

Vassilikos, Vassilis 1933-......... **CLC 4, 8**
See also CA 81-84

Vaughn, Stephanie................ **CLC 62**

Vazov, Ivan (Minchov)
1850-1921 .... **TCLC 25**
See also CA 121

Veblen, Thorstein (Bunde)
1857-1929 .... **TCLC 31**
See also CA 115

Venison, Alfred
See Pound, Ezra (Weston Loomis)

Verdi, Marie de
See Mencken, H(enry) L(ouis)

Verdu, Matilde
See Cela, Camilo Jose

Verga, Giovanni (Carmelo)
1840-1922 .... **TCLC 3**
See also CA 104; 123

Vergil   70B.C.-19B.C. .... **CMLC 9**

Verhaeren, Emile (Adolphe Gustave)
1855-1916 .... **TCLC 12**
See also CA 109

Verlaine, Paul (Marie)
1844-1896 .... **NCLC 2; PC 2**

Verne, Jules (Gabriel) 1828-1905 ... **TCLC 6**
See also CA 110; 131; DLB 123; MAICYA;
SATA 21

Very, Jones 1813-1880 .... **NCLC 9**
See also DLB 1

Vesaas, Tarjei 1897-1970 .... **CLC 48**
See also CA 29-32R

Vialis, Gaston
See Simenon, Georges (Jacques Christian)

Vian, Boris 1920-1959 .... **TCLC 9**
See also CA 106; DLB 72

Viaud, (Louis Marie) Julien 1850-1923
See Loti, Pierre
See also CA 107

Vicar, Henry
See Felsen, Henry Gregor

Vicker, Angus
See Felsen, Henry Gregor

Vidal, Gore
1925- ..... **CLC 2, 4, 6, 8, 10, 22, 33, 72**
See also AITN 1; BEST 90:2; CA 5-8R;
CANR 13; DLB 6; MTCW

Viereck, Peter (Robert Edwin)
1916- .... **CLC 4**
See also CA 1-4R; CANR 1; DLB 5

Vigny, Alfred (Victor) de
1797-1863 .... **NCLC 7**
See also DLB 119

Vilakazi, Benedict Wallet
1906-1947 .... **TCLC 37**

Villiers de l'Isle Adam, Jean Marie Mathias
Philippe Auguste Comte
1838-1889 .... **NCLC 3**
See also DLB 123

Vincent, Gabrielle .... **CLC 13**
See also CA 126; CLR 13; MAICYA;
SATA 61

Vinci, Leonardo da 1452-1519 ...... **LC 12**

Vine, Barbara .... **CLC 50**
See also Rendell, Ruth (Barbara)
See also BEST 90:4

Vinge, Joan D(ennison) 1948- ...... **CLC 30**
See also CA 93-96; SATA 36

Violis, G.
See Simenon, Georges (Jacques Christian)

Visconti, Luchino 1906-1976 .... **CLC 16**
See also CA 81-84; 65-68; CANR 39

Vittorini, Elio 1908-1966 ...... **CLC 6, 9, 14**
See also CA 133; 25-28R

Vizinczey, Stephen 1933- .... **CLC 40**
See also CA 128

Vliet, R(ussell) G(ordon)
1929-1984 .... **CLC 22**
See also CA 37-40R; 112; CANR 18

Vogau, Boris Andreyevich 1894-1937(?)
See Pilnyak, Boris
See also CA 123

Vogel, Paula A(nne) 1951- .... **CLC 76**
See also CA 108

Voigt, Cynthia 1942- .... **CLC 30**
See also AAYA 3; CA 106; CANR 18, 37,
40; CLR 13; MAICYA; SATA 33, 48

Voigt, Ellen Bryant 1943- .... **CLC 54**
See also CA 69-72; CANR 11, 29; DLB 120

Voinovich, Vladimir (Nikolaevich)
1932- .... **CLC 10, 49**
See also CA 81-84; CAAS 12; CANR 33;
MTCW

Voltaire 1694-1778 .... **LC 14**
See also WLC

von Daeniken, Erich 1935- .... **CLC 30**
See also von Daniken, Erich
See also AITN 1; CA 37-40R; CANR 17

von Daniken, Erich .... **CLC 30**
See also von Daeniken, Erich

von Heidenstam, (Carl Gustaf) Verner
See Heidenstam, (Carl Gustaf) Verner von

von Heyse, Paul (Johann Ludwig)
See Heyse, Paul (Johann Ludwig von)

von Hofmannsthal, Hugo
See Hofmannsthal, Hugo von

von Horvath, Odon
See Horvath, Oedoen von

von Horvath, Oedoen
See Horvath, Oedoen von

von Liliencron, (Friedrich Adolf Axel) Detlev
See Liliencron, (Friedrich Adolf Axel)
Detlev von

Vonnegut, Kurt Jr.
1922- ...... **CLC 1, 2, 3, 4, 5, 8, 12, 22,**
40, 60; SSC 8
See also AAYA 6; AITN 1; BEST 90:4;
CA 1-4R; CANR 1, 25;
CDALB 1968-1988; DLB 2, 8; DLBD 3;
DLBY 80; MTCW; WLC

Von Rachen, Kurt
See Hubbard, L(afayette) Ron(ald)

von Rezzori (d'Arezzo), Gregor
See Rezzori (d'Arezzo), Gregor von

von Sternberg, Josef
See Sternberg, Josef von

Vorster, Gordon 1924- .... **CLC 34**
See also CA 133

Vosce, Trudie
See Ozick, Cynthia

Voznesensky, Andrei (Andreievich)
1933- .... **CLC 1, 15, 57**
See also CA 89-92; CANR 37; MTCW

Waddington, Miriam 1917- .... **CLC 28**
See also CA 21-24R; CANR 12, 30;
DLB 68

Wagman, Fredrica 1937- .... **CLC 7**
See also CA 97-100

Wagner, Richard 1813-1883 ...... **NCLC 9**
See also DLB 129

Wagner-Martin, Linda 1936- .... **CLC 50**

Wagoner, David (Russell)
1926- .... **CLC 3, 5, 15**
See also CA 1-4R; CAAS 3; CANR 2;
DLB 5; SATA 14

Wah, Fred(erick James) 1939- ...... **CLC 44**
See also CA 107; DLB 60

Wahloo, Per 1926-1975 .... **CLC 7**
See also CA 61-64

Wahloo, Peter
See Wahloo, Per

Wain, John (Barrington)
1925- .... **CLC 2, 11, 15, 46**
See also CA 5-8R; CAAS 4; CANR 23;
CDBLB 1960 to Present; DLB 15, 27;
MTCW

Wajda, Andrzej 1926- .... **CLC 16**
See also CA 102

Wakefield, Dan 1932- .... **CLC 7**
See also CA 21-24R; CAAS 7

Wakoski, Diane
1937- .... **CLC 2, 4, 7, 9, 11, 40**
See also CA 13-16R; CAAS 1; CANR 9;
DLB 5

Wakoski-Sherbell, Diane
See Wakoski, Diane

Walcott, Derek (Alton)
1930- .... **CLC 2, 4, 9, 14, 25, 42, 67, 76**
See also BLC 3; BW; CA 89-92; CANR 26;
DLB 117; DLBY 81; MTCW

Waldman, Anne 1945- .... **CLC 7**
See also CA 37-40R; CAAS 17; CANR 34;
DLB 16

Waldo, E. Hunter
See Sturgeon, Theodore (Hamilton)

Waldo, Edward Hamilton
See Sturgeon, Theodore (Hamilton)

Walker, Alice (Malsenior)
1944- ...... **CLC 5, 6, 9, 19, 27, 46, 58;**
SSC 5
See also AAYA 3; BEST 89:4; BLC 3; BW;
CA 37-40R; CANR 9, 27;
CDALB 1968-1988; DLB 6, 33; MTCW;
SATA 31

Walker, David Harry 1911-1992 .... **CLC 14**
See also CA 1-4R; 137; CANR 1; SATA 8;
SATO 71

Walker, Edward Joseph 1934-
See Walker, Ted
See also CA 21-24R; CANR 12, 28

Walker, George F. 1947- .... **CLC 44, 61**
See also CA 103; CANR 21; DLB 60

Walker, Joseph A. 1935- .... **CLC 19**
See also BW; CA 89-92; CANR 26; DLB 38

Walker, Margaret (Abigail)
1915- .... **CLC 1, 6**
See also BLC 3; BW; CA 73-76; CANR 26;
DLB 76; MTCW

Walker, Ted . . . . **CLC 13**
See also Walker, Edward Joseph
See also DLB 40

Wallace, David Foster 1962- . . . . . . **CLC 50**
See also CA 132

Wallace, Dexter
See Masters, Edgar Lee

Wallace, Irving 1916-1990 . . . . **CLC 7, 13**
See also AITN 1; CA 1-4R; 132; CAAS 1;
CANR 1, 27; MTCW

Wallant, Edward Lewis
1926-1962 . . . . **CLC 5, 10**
See also CA 1-4R; CANR 22; DLB 2, 28;
MTCW

Walpole, Horace 1717-1797 . . . . **LC 2**
See also DLB 39, 104

Walpole, Hugh (Seymour)
1884-1941 . . . . **TCLC 5**
See also CA 104; DLB 34

Walser, Martin 1927- . . . . **CLC 27**
See also CA 57-60; CANR 8; DLB 75, 124

Walser, Robert 1878-1956 . . . . **TCLC 18**
See also CA 118; DLB 66

Walsh, Jill Paton . . . . **CLC 35**
See also Paton Walsh, Gillian
See also CLR 2; SAAS 3

Walter, William Christian
See Andersen, Hans Christian

Wambaugh, Joseph (Aloysius Jr.)
1937- . . . . **CLC 3, 18**
See also AITN 1; BEST 89:3; CA 33-36R;
DLB 6; DLBY 83; MTCW

Ward, Arthur Henry Sarsfield 1883-1959
See Rohmer, Sax
See also CA 108

Ward, Douglas Turner 1930- . . . . **CLC 19**
See also BW; CA 81-84; CANR 27; DLB 7,
38

Ward, Peter
See Faust, Frederick (Schiller)

Warhol, Andy 1928(?)-1987 . . . . **CLC 20**
See also BEST 89:4; CA 89-92; 121;
CANR 34

Warner, Francis (Robert le Plastrier)
1937- . . . . **CLC 14**
See also CA 53-56; CANR 11

Warner, Marina 1946- . . . . **CLC 59**
See also CA 65-68; CANR 21

Warner, Rex (Ernest) 1905-1986 . . . . **CLC 45**
See also CA 89-92; 119; DLB 15

Warner, Susan (Bogert)
1819-1885 . . . . **NCLC 31**
See also DLB 3, 42

Warner, Sylvia (Constance) Ashton
See Ashton-Warner, Sylvia (Constance)

Warner, Sylvia Townsend
1893-1978 . . . . **CLC 7, 19**
See also CA 61-64; 77-80; CANR 16;
DLB 34; MTCW

Warren, Mercy Otis 1728-1814 . . . **NCLC 13**
See also DLB 31

Warren, Robert Penn
1905-1989 . . . **CLC 1, 4, 6, 8, 10, 13, 18,
39, 53, 59; SSC 4**
See also AITN 1; CA 13-16R; 129;
CANR 10; CDALB 1968-1988; DLB 2,
48; DLBY 80, 89; MTCW; SATA 46, 63;
WLC

Warshofsky, Isaac
See Singer, Isaac Bashevis

Warton, Thomas 1728-1790 . . . . **LC 15**
See also DLB 104, 109

Waruk, Kona
See Harris, (Theodore) Wilson

Warung, Price 1855-1911 . . . . **TCLC 45**

Warwick, Jarvis
See Garner, Hugh

Washington, Alex
See Harris, Mark

Washington, Booker T(aliaferro)
1856-1915 . . . . **TCLC 10**
See also BLC 3; BW; CA 114; 125;
SATA 28

Wassermann, (Karl) Jakob
1873-1934 . . . . **TCLC 6**
See also CA 104; DLB 66

Wasserstein, Wendy 1950- . . . . . . **CLC 32, 59**
See also CA 121; 129; CABS 3

Waterhouse, Keith (Spencer)
1929- . . . . **CLC 47**
See also CA 5-8R; CANR 38; DLB 13, 15;
MTCW

Waters, Roger 1944- . . . . **CLC 35**
See also Pink Floyd

Watkins, Frances Ellen
See Harper, Frances Ellen Watkins

Watkins, Gerrold
See Malzberg, Barry N(athaniel)

Watkins, Paul 1964- . . . . **CLC 55**
See also CA 132

Watkins, Vernon Phillips
1906-1967 . . . . **CLC 43**
See also CA 9-10; 25-28R; CAP 1; DLB 20

Watson, Irving S.
See Mencken, H(enry) L(ouis)

Watson, John H.
See Farmer, Philip Jose

Watson, Richard F.
See Silverberg, Robert

Waugh, Auberon (Alexander) 1939- . . **CLC 7**
See also CA 45-48; CANR 6, 22; DLB 14

Waugh, Evelyn (Arthur St. John)
1903-1966 . . . **CLC 1, 3, 8, 13, 19, 27, 44**
See also CA 85-88; 25-28R; CANR 22;
CDBLB 1914-1945; DLB 15; MTCW;
WLC

Waugh, Harriet 1944- . . . . **CLC 6**
See also CA 85-88; CANR 22

Ways, C. R.
See Blount, Roy (Alton) Jr.

Waystaff, Simon
See Swift, Jonathan

Webb, (Martha) Beatrice (Potter)
1858-1943 . . . . **TCLC 22**
See also Potter, Beatrice
See also CA 117

Webb, Charles (Richard) 1939- . . . . . . **CLC 7**
See also CA 25-28R

Webb, James H(enry) Jr. 1946- . . . . **CLC 22**
See also CA 81-84

Webb, Mary (Gladys Meredith)
1881-1927 . . . . **TCLC 24**
See also CA 123; DLB 34

Webb, Mrs. Sidney
See Webb, (Martha) Beatrice (Potter)

Webb, Phyllis 1927- . . . . **CLC 18**
See also CA 104; CANR 23; DLB 53

Webb, Sidney (James)
1859-1947 . . . . **TCLC 22**
See also CA 117

Webber, Andrew Lloyd . . . . **CLC 21**
See also Lloyd Webber, Andrew

Weber, Lenora Mattingly
1895-1971 . . . . **CLC 12**
See also CA 19-20; 29-32R; CAP 1;
SATA 2, 26

Webster, John 1579(?)-1634(?) . . . . **DC 2**
See also CDBLB Before 1660; DLB 58;
WLC

Webster, Noah 1758-1843 . . . . **NCLC 30**

Wedekind, (Benjamin) Frank(lin)
1864-1918 . . . . **TCLC 7**
See also CA 104; DLB 118

Weidman, Jerome 1913- . . . . **CLC 7**
See also AITN 2; CA 1-4R; CANR 1;
DLB 28

Weil, Simone (Adolphine)
1909-1943 . . . . **TCLC 23**
See also CA 117

Weinstein, Nathan
See West, Nathanael

Weinstein, Nathan von Wallenstein
See West, Nathanael

Weir, Peter (Lindsay) 1944- . . . . **CLC 20**
See also CA 113; 123

Weiss, Peter (Ulrich)
1916-1982 . . . . **CLC 3, 15, 51**
See also CA 45-48; 106; CANR 3; DLB 69,
124

Weiss, Theodore (Russell)
1916- . . . . **CLC 3, 8, 14**
See also CA 9-12R; CAAS 2; DLB 5

Welch, (Maurice) Denton
1915-1948 . . . . **TCLC 22**
See also CA 121

Welch, James 1940- . . . . **CLC 6, 14, 52**
See also CA 85-88

Weldon, Fay
1933(?)- . . . . **CLC 6, 9, 11, 19, 36, 59**
See also CA 21-24R; CANR 16;
CDBLB 1960 to Present; DLB 14;
MTCW

Wellek, Rene 1903- . . . . **CLC 28**
See also CA 5-8R; CAAS 7; CANR 8;
DLB 63

Weller, Michael 1942- . . . . **CLC 10, 53**
See also CA 85-88

Weller, Paul 1958- . . . . CLC 26

Wellershoff, Dieter 1925-. . . . . CLC 46
　See also CA 89-92; CANR 16, 37

Welles, (George) Orson
　1915-1985 . . . . CLC 20
　See also CA 93-96; 117

Wellman, Mac 1945- . . . . CLC 65

Wellman, Manly Wade 1903-1986 . . CLC 49
　See also CA 1-4R; 118; CANR 6, 16;
　SATA 6, 47

Wells, Carolyn 1869(?)-1942 . . . . . . TCLC 35
　See also CA 113; DLB 11

Wells, H(erbert) G(eorge)
　1866-1946 . . . . . . TCLC 6, 12, 19; SSC 6
　See also CA 110; 121; CDBLB 1914-1945;
　DLB 34, 70; MTCW; SATA 20; WLC

Wells, Rosemary 1943-. . . . . CLC 12
　See also CA 85-88; CLR 16; MAICYA;
　SAAS 1; SATA 18, 69

Welty, Eudora
　1909- . . . . CLC 1, 2, 5, 14, 22, 33; SSC 1
　See also CA 9-12R; CABS 1; CANR 32;
　CDALB 1941-1968; DLB 2, 102;
　DLBY 87; MTCW; WLC

Wen I-to 1899-1946 . . . . TCLC 28

Wentworth, Robert
　See Hamilton, Edmond

Werfel, Franz (V.) 1890-1945 . . . . . . TCLC 8
　See also CA 104; DLB 81, 124

Wergeland, Henrik Arnold
　1808-1845 . . . . NCLC 5

Wersba, Barbara 1932-. . . . . CLC 30
　See also AAYA 2; CA 29-32R; CANR 16,
　38; CLR 3; DLB 52; MAICYA; SAAS 2;
　SATA 1, 58

Wertmueller, Lina 1928- . . . . CLC 16
　See also CA 97-100; CANR 39

Wescott, Glenway 1901-1987. . . . . . . CLC 13
　See also CA 13-16R; 121; CANR 23;
　DLB 4, 9, 102

Wesker, Arnold 1932- . . . . CLC 3, 5, 42
　See also CA 1-4R; CAAS 7; CANR 1, 33;
　CDBLB 1960 to Present; DLB 13;
　MTCW

Wesley, Richard (Errol) 1945-. . . . . . CLC 7
　See also BW; CA 57-60; DLB 38

Wessel, Johan Herman 1742-1785 . . . . LC 7

West, Anthony (Panther)
　1914-1987 . . . . CLC 50
　See also CA 45-48; 124; CANR 3, 19;
　DLB 15

West, C. P.
　See Wodehouse, P(elham) G(renville)

West, (Mary) Jessamyn
　1902-1984 . . . . CLC 7, 17
　See also CA 9-12R; 112; CANR 27; DLB 6;
　DLBY 84; MTCW; SATA 37

West, Morris L(anglo) 1916-. . . . . CLC 6, 33
　See also CA 5-8R; CANR 24; MTCW

West, Nathanael
　1903-1940 . . . . TCLC 1, 14, 44
　See also CA 104; 125; CDALB 1929-1941;
　DLB 4, 9, 28; MTCW

West, Paul 1930- . . . . CLC 7, 14
　See also CA 13-16R; CAAS 7; CANR 22;
　DLB 14

West, Rebecca 1892-1983 . . CLC 7, 9, 31, 50
　See also CA 5-8R; 109; CANR 19; DLB 36;
　DLBY 83; MTCW

Westall, Robert (Atkinson) 1929-. . . CLC 17
　See also CA 69-72; CANR 18; CLR 13;
　MAICYA; SAAS 2; SATA 23, 69

Westlake, Donald E(dwin)
　1933- . . . . CLC 7, 33
　See also CA 17-20R; CAAS 13; CANR 16

Westmacott, Mary
　See Christie, Agatha (Mary Clarissa)

Weston, Allen
　See Norton, Andre

Wetcheek, J. L.
　See Feuchtwanger, Lion

Wetering, Janwillem van de
　See van de Wetering, Janwillem

Wetherell, Elizabeth
　See Warner, Susan (Bogert)

Whalen, Philip 1923- . . . . CLC 6, 29
　See also CA 9-12R; CANR 5, 39; DLB 16

Wharton, Edith (Newbold Jones)
　1862-1937 . . . . TCLC 3, 9, 27; SSC 6
　See also CA 104; 132; CDALB 1865-1917;
　DLB 4, 9, 12, 78; MTCW; WLC

Wharton, James
　See Mencken, H(enry) L(ouis)

Wharton, William (a pseudonym)
　. . . . . CLC 18, 37
　See also CA 93-96; DLBY 80

Wheatley (Peters), Phillis
　1754(?)-1784 . . . . LC 3; PC 3
　See also BLC 3; CDALB 1640-1865;
　DLB 31, 50; WLC

Wheelock, John Hall 1886-1978 . . . . CLC 14
　See also CA 13-16R; 77-80; CANR 14;
　DLB 45

White, E(lwyn) B(rooks)
　1899-1985 . . . . CLC 10, 34, 39
　See also AITN 2; CA 13-16R; 116;
　CANR 16, 37; CLR 1, 21; DLB 11, 22;
　MAICYA; MTCW; SATA 2, 29, 44

White, Edmund (Valentine III)
　1940- . . . . CLC 27
　See also AAYA 7; CA 45-48; CANR 3, 19,
　36; MTCW

White, Patrick (Victor Martindale)
　1912-1990 . . CLC 3, 4, 5, 7, 9, 18, 65, 69
　See also CA 81-84; 132; MTCW

White, Phyllis Dorothy James 1920-
　See James, P. D.
　See also CA 21-24R; CANR 17; MTCW

White, T(erence) H(anbury)
　1906-1964 . . . . CLC 30
　See also CA 73-76; CANR 37; MAICYA;
　SATA 12

White, Terence de Vere 1912-. . . . . . CLC 49
　See also CA 49-52; CANR 3

White, Walter
　See White, Walter F(rancis)
　See also BLC 3

White, Walter F(rancis)
　1893-1955 . . . . TCLC 15
　See also White, Walter
　See also CA 115; 124; DLB 51

White, William Hale 1831-1913
　See Rutherford, Mark
　See also CA 121

Whitehead, E(dward) A(nthony)
　1933- . . . . CLC 5
　See also CA 65-68

Whitemore, Hugh (John) 1936-. . . . . CLC 37
　See also CA 132

Whitman, Sarah Helen (Power)
　1803-1878 . . . . NCLC 19
　See also DLB 1

Whitman, Walt(er)
　1819-1892 . . . . NCLC 4, 31; PC 3
　See also CDALB 1640-1865; DLB 3, 64;
　SATA 20; WLC

Whitney, Phyllis A(yame) 1903-. . . . CLC 42
　See also AITN 2; BEST 90:3; CA 1-4R;
　CANR 3, 25, 38; MAICYA; SATA 1, 30

Whittemore, (Edward) Reed (Jr.)
　1919- . . . . CLC 4
　See also CA 9-12R; CAAS 8; CANR 4;
　DLB 5

Whittier, John Greenleaf
　1807-1892 . . . . NCLC 8
　See also CDALB 1640-1865; DLB 1

Whittlebot, Hernia
　See Coward, Noel (Peirce)

Wicker, Thomas Grey 1926-
　See Wicker, Tom
　See also CA 65-68; CANR 21

Wicker, Tom . . . . CLC 7
　See also Wicker, Thomas Grey

Wideman, John Edgar
　1941- . . . . CLC 5, 34, 36, 67
　See also BLC 3; BW; CA 85-88; CANR 14;
　DLB 33

Wiebe, Rudy (H.) 1934-. . . . . . CLC 6, 11, 14
　See also CA 37-40R; DLB 60

Wieland, Christoph Martin
　1733-1813 . . . . NCLC 17
　See also DLB 97

Wieners, John 1934-. . . . . CLC 7
　See also CA 13-16R; DLB 16

Wiesel, Elie(zer) 1928-. . . . . CLC 3, 5, 11, 37
　See also AAYA 7; AITN 1; CA 5-8R;
　CAAS 4; CANR 8, 40; DLB 83;
　DLBY 87; MTCW; SATA 56

Wiggins, Marianne 1947-. . . . . CLC 57
　See also BEST 89:3; CA 130

Wight, James Alfred 1916-
　See Herriot, James
　See also CA 77-80; SATA 44, 55

Wilbur, Richard (Purdy)
　1921- . . . . CLC 3, 6, 9, 14, 53
　See also CA 1-4R; CABS 2; CANR 2, 29;
　DLB 5; MTCW; SATA 9

Wild, Peter 1940-. . . . . CLC 14
　See also CA 37-40R; DLB 5

Wilde, Oscar (Fingal O'Flahertie Wills)
1854(?)-1900 . . . . **TCLC 1, 8, 23, 41;**
SSC 11
See also CA 104; 119; CDBLB 1890-1914;
DLB 10, 19, 34, 57; SATA 24; WLC

Wilder, Billy . . . . **CLC 20**
See also Wilder, Samuel
See also DLB 26

Wilder, Samuel 1906-
See Wilder, Billy
See also CA 89-92

Wilder, Thornton (Niven)
1897-1975 . . . . . **CLC 1, 5, 6, 10, 15, 35;**
DC 1
See also AITN 2; CA 13-16R; 61-64;
CANR 40; DLB 4, 7, 9; MTCW; WLC

Wilding, Michael 1942- . . . . **CLC 73**
See also CA 104; CANR 24

Wiley, Richard 1944- . . . . **CLC 44**
See also CA 121; 129

Wilhelm, Kate . . . . **CLC 7**
See also Wilhelm, Katie Gertrude
See also CAAS 5; DLB 8

Wilhelm, Katie Gertrude 1928-
See Wilhelm, Kate
See also CA 37-40R; CANR 17, 36; MTCW

Wilkins, Mary
See Freeman, Mary Eleanor Wilkins

Willard, Nancy 1936- . . . . **CLC 7, 37**
See also CA 89-92; CANR 10, 39; CLR 5;
DLB 5, 52; MAICYA; MTCW;
SATA 30, 37, 71

Williams, C(harles) K(enneth)
1936- . . . . **CLC 33, 56**
See also CA 37-40R; DLB 5

Williams, Charles
See Collier, James L(incoln)

Williams, Charles (Walter Stansby)
1886-1945 . . . . **TCLC 1, 11**
See also CA 104; DLB 100

Williams, (George) Emlyn
1905-1987 . . . . **CLC 15**
See also CA 104; 123; CANR 36; DLB 10,
77; MTCW

Williams, Hugo 1942- . . . . **CLC 42**
See also CA 17-20R; DLB 40

Williams, J. Walker
See Wodehouse, P(elham) G(renville)

Williams, John A(lfred) 1925- . . . . **CLC 5, 13**
See also BLC 3; BW; CA 53-56; CAAS 3;
CANR 6, 26; DLB 2, 33

Williams, Jonathan (Chamberlain)
1929- . . . . **CLC 13**
See also CA 9-12R; CAAS 12; CANR 8;
DLB 5

Williams, Joy 1944- . . . . **CLC 31**
See also CA 41-44R; CANR 22

Williams, Norman 1952- . . . . **CLC 39**
See also CA 118

Williams, Tennessee
1911-1983 . . . . **CLC 1, 2, 5, 7, 8, 11, 15,**
19, 30, 39, 45, 71
See also AITN 1, 2; CA 5-8R; 108;
CABS 3; CANR 31; CDALB 1941-1968;
DLB 7; DLBD 4; DLBY 83; MTCW;
WLC

Williams, Thomas (Alonzo)
1926-1990 . . . . **CLC 14**
See also CA 1-4R; 132; CANR 2

Williams, William C.
See Williams, William Carlos

Williams, William Carlos
1883-1963 . . . **CLC 1, 2, 5, 9, 13, 22, 42,**
67
See also CA 89-92; CANR 34;
CDALB 1917-1929; DLB 4, 16, 54, 86;
MTCW

Williamson, David Keith 1942- . . . . . **CLC 56**
See also CA 103

Williamson, Jack . . . . **CLC 29**
See also Williamson, John Stewart
See also CAAS 8; DLB 8

Williamson, John Stewart 1908-
See Williamson, Jack
See also CA 17-20R; CANR 23

Willie, Frederick
See Lovecraft, H(oward) P(hillips)

Willingham, Calder (Baynard Jr.)
1922- . . . . **CLC 5, 51**
See also CA 5-8R; CANR 3; DLB 2, 44;
MTCW

Willis, Charles
See Clarke, Arthur C(harles)

Willy
See Colette, (Sidonie-Gabrielle)

Willy, Colette
See Colette, (Sidonie-Gabrielle)

Wilson, A(ndrew) N(orman) 1950- . . **CLC 33**
See also CA 112; 122; DLB 14

Wilson, Angus (Frank Johnstone)
1913-1991 . . . . **CLC 2, 3, 5, 25, 34**
See also CA 5-8R; 134; CANR 21; DLB 15;
MTCW

Wilson, August
1945- . . . . **CLC 39, 50, 63; DC 2**
See also BLC 3; BW; CA 115; 122; MTCW

Wilson, Brian 1942- . . . . **CLC 12**

Wilson, Colin 1931- . . . . **CLC 3, 14**
See also CA 1-4R; CAAS 5; CANR 1, 22,
33; DLB 14; MTCW

Wilson, Dirk
See Pohl, Frederik

Wilson, Edmund
1895-1972 . . . . **CLC 1, 2, 3, 8, 24**
See also CA 1-4R; 37-40R; CANR 1;
DLB 63; MTCW

Wilson, Ethel Davis (Bryant)
1888(?)-1980 . . . . **CLC 13**
See also CA 102; DLB 68; MTCW

Wilson, John (Anthony) Burgess
1917- . . . . **CLC 8, 10, 13**
See also Burgess, Anthony
See also CA 1-4R; CANR 2; MTCW

Wilson, John 1785-1854 . . . . **NCLC 5**

Wilson, Lanford 1937- . . . . **CLC 7, 14, 36**
See also CA 17-20R; CABS 3; DLB 7

Wilson, Robert M. 1944- . . . . **CLC 7, 9**
See also CA 49-52; CANR 2; MTCW

Wilson, Robert McLiam 1964- . . . . . **CLC 59**
See also CA 132

Wilson, Sloan 1920- . . . . **CLC 32**
See also CA 1-4R; CANR 1

Wilson, Snoo 1948- . . . . **CLC 33**
See also CA 69-72

Wilson, William S(mith) 1932- . . . . . **CLC 49**
See also CA 81-84

Winchilsea, Anne (Kingsmill) Finch Counte
1661-1720 . . . . **LC 3**

Windham, Basil
See Wodehouse, P(elham) G(renville)

Wingrove, David (John) 1954- . . . . . . **CLC 68**
See also CA 133

Winters, Janet Lewis . . . . **CLC 41**
See also Lewis, Janet
See also DLBY 87

Winters, (Arthur) Yvor
1900-1968 . . . . **CLC 4, 8, 32**
See also CA 11-12; 25-28R; CAP 1;
DLB 48; MTCW

Winterson, Jeanette 1959- . . . . **CLC 64**
See also CA 136

Wiseman, Frederick 1930- . . . . **CLC 20**

Wister, Owen 1860-1938 . . . . **TCLC 21**
See also CA 108; DLB 9, 78; SATA 62

Witkacy
See Witkiewicz, Stanislaw Ignacy

Witkiewicz, Stanislaw Ignacy
1885-1939 . . . . **TCLC 8**
See also CA 105

Wittig, Monique 1935(?)- . . . . **CLC 22**
See also CA 116; 135; DLB 83

Wittlin, Jozef 1896-1976 . . . . **CLC 25**
See also CA 49-52; 65-68; CANR 3

Wodehouse, P(elham) G(renville)
1881-1975 . . . **CLC 1, 2, 5, 10, 22; SSC 2**
See also AITN 2; CA 45-48; 57-60;
CANR 3, 33; CDBLB 1914-1945;
DLB 34; MTCW; SATA 22

Woiwode, L.
See Woiwode, Larry (Alfred)

Woiwode, Larry (Alfred) 1941- . . . **CLC 6, 10**
See also CA 73-76; CANR 16; DLB 6

Wojciechowska, Maia (Teresa)
1927- . . . . **CLC 26**
See also AAYA 8; CA 9-12R; CANR 4;
CLR 1; MAICYA; SAAS 1; SATA 1, 28

Wolf, Christa 1929- . . . . **CLC 14, 29, 58**
See also CA 85-88; DLB 75; MTCW

Wolfe, Gene (Rodman) 1931- . . . . . . **CLC 25**
See also CA 57-60; CAAS 9; CANR 6, 32;
DLB 8

Wolfe, George C. 1954- . . . . **CLC 49**

Wolfe, Thomas (Clayton)
1900-1938 . . . . **TCLC 4, 13, 29**
See also CA 104; 132; CDALB 1929-1941;
DLB 9, 102; DLBD 2; DLBY 85;
MTCW; WLC

Wolfe, Thomas Kennerly Jr. 1930-
See Wolfe, Tom
See also CA 13-16R; CANR 9, 33; MTCW

Wolfe, Tom . . . . **CLC 1, 2, 9, 15, 35, 51**
See also Wolfe, Thomas Kennerly Jr.
See also AAYA 8; AITN 2; BEST 89:1

Zinoviev, Alexander (Aleksandrovich)
  1922- . . . . **CLC 19**
  See also CA 116; 133; CAAS 10

Zoilus
  See Lovecraft, H(oward) P(hillips)

Zola, Emile (Edouard Charles Antoine)
  1840-1902 . . . . **TCLC 1, 6, 21, 41**
  See also CA 104; 138; DLB 123; WLC

Zoline, Pamela 1941- . . . . **CLC 62**

Zorrilla y Moral, Jose 1817-1893 . . **NCLC 6**

Zoshchenko, Mikhail (Mikhailovich)
  1895-1958 . . . . **TCLC 15**
  See also CA 115

Zuckmayer, Carl 1896-1977 . . . . **CLC 18**
  See also CA 69-72; DLB 56, 124

Zuk, Georges
  See Skelton, Robin

Zukofsky, Louis
  1904-1978 . . . . **CLC 1, 2, 4, 7, 11, 18**
  See also CA 9-12R; 77-80; CANR 39;
  DLB 5; MTCW

Zweig, Paul 1935-1984 . . . . **CLC 34, 42**
  See also CA 85-88; 113

Zweig, Stefan 1881-1942 . . . . **TCLC 17**
  See also CA 112; DLB 81, 118

Literary Criticism Series
Cumulative Topic Index

This index lists all topic entries in the Gale Literary Criticism Series *Contemporary Literary Criticism, Literature Criticism from 1400 to 1800, Nineteenth-Century Literature Criticism,* and *Twentieth-Century Literary Criticism.*

Cumulative Topic Index

Cumulative Topic Index

CLC Cumulative Nationality Index

Nationality Index

Nationality Index

Nationality Index

Nationality Index

CLC-76 Title Index

ISBN 0-8103-4982-5